By Andrew Meier

Morgenthau: Power, Privilege, and the Rise of an American Dynasty

The Lost Spy: An American in Stalin's Secret Service

Black Earth: A Journey Through Russia After the Fall

MORGENTHAU

MORGENTHAU

POWER, PRIVILEGE, AND THE RISE OF AN AMERICAN DYNASTY

ANDREW MEIER

RANDOM HOUSE | NEW YORK

Published in the United States by Random House, an imprint and division of Penguin Random House LLC, New York.

RANDOM HOUSE and the HOUSE colophon are registered trademarks of Penguin Random House LLC.

Illustration credits appear on pages 997–999.

LIBRARY OF CONGRESS CATALOGING-IN-PUBLICATION DATA
Names: Meier, Andrew, author.
Title: Morgenthau : power, privilege, and the rise of an American dynasty / Andrew Meier.
Other titles: Power, privilege, and the rise of an American dynasty
Description: New York : Random House, an imprint and division of Penguin Random House LLC, [2022] | Includes bibliographical references and index.
Identifiers: LCCN 2021037373 | ISBN 9781400068852 (hardcover) | ISBN 9781588369499 (ebook)
Subjects: LCSH: Morgenthau family. | Morgenthau, Lazarus, 1815–1897. | Morgenthau, Henry, 1856–1946. | Morgenthau, Henry, 1891–1967. | Morgenthau, Robert M. | Capitalists and financiers—United States—Biography. | Jews—United States—Biography. | Jews in public life—United States. | United States—Politics and government—20th century. | United States—Foreign relations—20th century.
Classification: LCC CT274.M673 M45 2022 |
DDC 973/.04924022—dc23/eng/20220107
LC record available at https://lccn.loc.gov/2021037373

Printed in Canada on acid-free paper

randomhousebooks.com

9 8 7 6 5 4 3 2 1

FIRST EDITION

Book design by Simon M. Sullivan

for Sasha and Oona

*"I had to wait until I was fifty-five to enter public service,
but you don't have to—and you shouldn't. It's a privilege."*

—Henry Morgenthau, Sr., to his grandson Robert M. Morgenthau

Contents

PART III | **WAR**

PART IV | THE SOVEREIGN DISTRICT

PART V | THE BOSS

PROLOGUE **One Hogan Place**

" I never look back."

In a career unlike any other in the annals of American law, he pros-ecuted every order of crime and every species of criminal: bribe-takers and bribe-givers, serial killers and drug dealers, Mobbed-up families and Mobbed-up industries, molesters and rapists, stalkers and terrorists, gun-runners and gamblers, prostitutes and vigilantes, loan sharks and digital pirates, bookmakers and boiler-room operators, arms dealers and insider traders. He had seen the good go bad: crooked politicians, crooked cops, crooked bakers, crooked truckers, crooked union bosses, crooked bankers, crooked accountants, crooked ambassadors, crooked priests, crooked rabbis, crooked doctors, crooked coroners, crooked en-gineers, crooked PTA officers, crooked CIA agents, crooked philanthro-pists, crooked turnpike authority executives, crooked traders, crooked defense attorneys, crooked prosecutors, crooked judges, and crooked inspectors of everything made in New York City, from its steaks to its skyscrapers to the cement of Yankee Stadium. There were crimes of pas-sion, too, but few by comparison. The urge always seemed to start, and end, with money. Money was oxygen. "Stop the flow," he would say, "and you'll stop the crime."

Now, after thirty-five years as the district attorney of New York County, Robert Morris Morgenthau, at ninety years old, was leaving the job.

A quartet of reporters flanked the DA, one on either side, two across the long table. The last of the farewell press conferences had come weeks earlier; now as he spoke, photographers ducked in and out, edging the half-packed boxes that formed islands in the cavernous room to record the final hours. It was nearly eight o'clock on a cold Friday evening, New Year's Eve, in the last year of the first decade of the new century, and the district attorney, called "the Boss" by three generations of prosecutors, was holding court one last time.

Since 1937, when Thomas Dewey became district attorney, only three men in New York had won election to the office. Frank Hogan, the dapper Irishman who succeeded Dewey, served thirty-two years. Morgenthau assumed the post in 1975, and stayed in it until 2009. Previously, he had served nine years as the chief federal prosecutor in New York, the United States attorney for the Southern District of New York—from 1961, when John F. Kennedy appointed him, until 1970, when Richard Nixon could suffer him no more. In all, he had been a fixture in the firmament of law and order for six decades—and not only in New York City.

Bob Morgenthau, as only the few he let in close could call him, had no cause to rush his last press conference. Little had he loved more, all these years, than to hold a conclave in his thrall—and he knew he would miss it. Two inches shy of his former six feet, as lean as he was at twenty-one—156¼ pounds then, 157 now—he retained a lanky agility. His gait had slowed to a shuffle, and he had long since given up cigars—Bordeaux remained his lone indulgence—but for years he had practiced tai chi and yoga, switching between the two on alternate mornings.

The face was distinctive, long and angular. He was fine-boned and clean-shaven, his hair a cottony white. His forehead was broad and high, but it was the nose, bent like a hawk's and angled right, that was most prominent. His blue-gray eyes hinted at unseen strength. He seemed to use them as props now, squinting to forecast disbelief and shuttering them with one hand as if to conjure thought. They could be watery, but the eyes were keen, and when opened wide, they revealed a startling depth.

"What will you do?" a reporter asked.

"No plans to quit working," he said.

In the winter of 2009, Morgenthau was not only the retiring district attorney; he was a city institution. At one of the many dinners honoring him that year, he was introduced as the "DA for life—and maybe after." No prosecutor in U.S. history had served longer, and none had had a more profound influence on law enforcement. None of the contenders—Dewey, Hogan, Rudy Giuliani—came close. Even the new man in the

White House hailed the legacy. Introducing his first nominee to the Supreme Court—Sonia Sotomayor, one of the DA's celebrated protégées—Barack Obama affixed the adjective "legendary" to the Morgenthau name.

Morgenthau had long since outlived ambition or ideology. In his final months in office, asked to explain his endurance, he gave the credit to "luck and longevity." "You've got to have Lady Luck sitting on your shoulder," he would say. The line—a souvenir of the war, when he faced German bombers in the Mediterranean and Japanese kamikazes in the Pacific—had proven its worth; on the banquet circuit it cut short the questioning, but to his wife, children, and closest friends, the words rang untrue. He was a man, they knew, who drew his resolve and stamina from another source.

| | | |

Robert Morgenthau was a scion of one of the great American families. His great-grandparents, Lazarus and Babette Morgenthau, arrived in New York from Germany in 1866, the year after Appomattox. Once wealthy, Lazarus had lost everything; he would live to see his children grow rich again. In America, the Morgenthaus fulfilled a dream, becoming "one-hundred-percent American." They had helped elect presidents, expose a genocide, and wage war. They had formed a dynasty.

Henry Morgenthau, Robert's grandfather, born in the Grand Duchy of Baden in 1856, was among the first in the Democratic Party to back Woodrow Wilson for president. Henry Jr., Robert's father, born on the Upper West Side of Manhattan in 1891, was Franklin D. Roosevelt's longest-serving aide, a confidant of three decades—one of the first to see FDR unable to walk, and among the last to see him alive. And the DA, who raced sailboats with the Kennedys as a boy on Cape Cod, was at Bobby Kennedy's side on November 22, 1963.

The Morgenthaus belonged to that tribe of would-be patricians, the German Jews: "Our Crowd." The words could make the DA wince, but his Aunt Hattie, a Lehman, coined the phrase, and his family was one of the aristocracy's exemplars: New Yorkers who for centuries somehow managed to rise above every barrier—neither German nor Jew. Robert Morgenthau was a lifelong member of Our Crowd and, since his first term as DA, a trustee of Temple Emanu-El, the granite cathedral on Fifth Avenue built to rival St. Patrick's, fourteen blocks to the south. His "blood," as his future wife would reassure her Protestant grandmother, ran "as blue as yours." The Morgenthaus were called the Jewish Kennedys, and remained, as the former mayor Ed Koch remarked, "the closest we've got to royalty in New York City."

The DA relished the lineage. At six, he met Calvin Coolidge in the White House—and had met every president since. The family history also traced many of the century's decisive turns: the sea-swell of immigration to America, the Armenian genocide, the New Deal, the Holocaust, and the rise, and fall, of organized crime in New York City. Even before the advent of world war, the rise of dictators in Europe, and the appearance of the word "genocide," Morgenthaus had lent their power and privilege to lonely causes. They did not always succeed. But whether out of a foolhardy belief in their own authority, or merely to avoid the guilt of inaction, they seldom recoiled from a fight. Even more rarely did they give ground.

As a boy, Robert Morgenthau rode in his grandfather's Lincoln limousine, the old man pointing out the buildings along Broadway he had bought and sold. By 1920, Henry Morgenthau could claim world renown. Armenians revered his name. He had exposed their massacre at the hands of the Turks. At home, the powerbrokers of the Democratic Party, which he joked he had once "bought" for $30,000, called him Uncle Henry, their faithful financier. But he had risen as a real estate man. Others in New York—Astors, Vanderbilts, and Whitneys—gained greater fame, but Henry Morgenthau was one of the first to build a corporate trust. Great swaths of the city passed through his hands: dozens of square blocks of Harlem and Washington Heights, as well as many of its landmarks—the Flatiron, the old B. Altman flagship on Sixth Avenue, the sites of the Belmont and Plaza hotels, even Longacre (now Times) Square. In the decade before the Great War, few men owned more acreage in New York—and fewer still yearned for greater heights. Real estate was never to be Henry Morgenthau's sole pursuit.

The DA's father had faced the opposite danger. Henry Morgenthau, Jr., failed out of prep school, flunked out of college—twice—and never graduated either. To critics and rivals, he was Roosevelt's bagman, the entitled fool FDR entrusted to do his bidding, whether fetching bootleg liquor or selling the New Deal. Henry Jr. had done all that, and fulfilled untold other wishes. But with the rewards had come trials, none more taxing than when he was moved to question—never in distrust, but often in discontent—his greatest friend. Henry Jr. ruled the Treasury for a dozen years, loyal to Roosevelt but also the only member of the cabinet—

as Eleanor Roosevelt would say—able to prod FDR into action. It was too late, and too little, though Henry had forced Roosevelt not only to confront the Holocaust but to save the surviving Jews of Europe.

The district attorney had been raised on West Eighty-first Street off Central Park, and educated at the finest private schools. Yet Robert Morgenthau had "really grown up," he would say, on the land, on a thousand acres of apple orchards and dairy cows in Dutchess County, where his father sought escape. The farm, with its sweet-smelling dirt and gentle hills, would always draw him. As a toddler, Morgenthau could tell a McIntosh from a Macoun. On the farm, he also became a sportsman—a hunter, an athlete, a steeplechase champion. As their country neighbors, the old Dutch and English clans who had settled the rolling farmland more than a century earlier, learned, the Morgenthaus loved horses. Dutchess County had never seen so many Jews on horseback.

In his ninetieth year, the district attorney accepted it: Time had collapsed around him. In 1919, the year that he was born, the Treaty of Versailles, ending World War I, was signed, Prohibition became law, and a U.S. Navy airplane completed the first transatlantic flight. Days before his birthday, the U.S. Army had dispatched a survey team to learn whether an automobile could cross the country. The DA littered conversations with names from half a century ago, names of friends, family, and colleagues now inscribed on bridges and hospitals, colleges and high schools across the city. He spoke, too, a lost language, the tongue of Old New York: a talking-to was "unshirted hell," working stiffs were "dees-and-dems guys," a well-heeled family was "first line all the way."

Morgenthau could survey not only successes but irrevocable losses. He had seen his first wife, his college sweetheart, die young. At fifty-two, Martha had left five children, the youngest a nine-year-old girl. He had remarried, fathered another child, and adopted a seventh. One, his third daughter, was born severely mentally disabled. When she turned four, they had at last heeded the doctor's advice—"I was chicken," he would say—and moved her to a school upstate. By fourteen, she had the IQ of an infant. At sixty, she remained in a home. She had never spoken an intelligible word, her father would say.

|||||

The district attorney spent his final day at work cleaning out his desk. Treasures kept emerging. In one drawer, at the back, he discovered Tom Dewey's St. Christopher medallion. Another yielded letters from FDR.

("Dear Bobby," read one, "the president is delighted to send you these stamps for your collection.") Everywhere, it seemed, mementos resurfaced: his mother's diary; a Navy epaulet from the war; an album that his grandfather had commissioned. Its leather cover—stamped with gilded letters MORGENTHAU FAMILY—was giving way at the edges, but the miniature portraits inside, stretching back to 1773, remained intact, an assemblage that bridged two worlds. It was a family museum, briefly reassembled before disappearing again into boxes, relics that the DA would never see again.

Outside, the streetlights had come on. The windows were shut but the thrum of Foley Square, the no-man's-land of the city's legal battleground, came through. The armies of workers, every rank of the city and state, spilled out from the granite walls along the courthouses, as the holiday carousel spun. Lawyers, clerks, and cops crowded the sidewalks, joining stray tourists in the rush to mark the year's end.

Morgenthau had won nine terms, enduring five mayors and nine police commissioners. He'd suffered failure, even reigned over judicial miscarriages. Some, like the Central Park Jogger case, would be etched into his obituary. He hated the failures; they burned anew at each mentioning. Yet on his watch America almost forgot the crime epidemic that had once brought New York low. The drop in homicides—the result, he often acknowledged, of forces not wholly within his control—told the story: from 648 in Manhattan in 1975, the year he took office, to 48 in his last.

The DA shuffled past his private bathroom, a dark cubbyhole, its walls coated with downtown soot. A can of shaving cream, its red and white stripes rusted, sat on the chipped enamel. The DA descended to the street, as he always did, by private elevator—"the Judge's Elevator"—and exited a side door. The car at the curb was enormous and black, its windows darkened—the carriage of officialdom. Beside it, Robert Morgenthau, citizen, looked small.

| | | |

This is the story of four generations of an American family and of the America they served and built. The Morgenthaus span one hundred fifty years of American history. They were New Yorkers through and through, yet they looked to the national political horizon. There were Morgenthaus among the progressives in Woodrow Wilson's Washington, the New Dealers in FDR's, and the New Frontiersmen in JFK's. Abroad, this American saga touches down in the Rhine River valley in the nineteenth century, in the Ottoman Empire and Palestine on the eve of World War I, in the cold waters of the Mediterranean during World War II and the deadly seas of the Japanese home islands. At home, each Morgenthau generation broke the bounds of the permissible and the accepted, forging history amid a cast of the celebrated (Mrs. Astor, Eleanor Roosevelt, Bobby Kennedy) and the infamous (Joe Bonanno, Roy Cohn, Donald Trump). Hundreds of books have traced the historical turns of the last century—the mass murder of the Armenians, the recovery from the Depression, the fight to ready America for World War II, the struggle to save the Jews of Europe, and the campaign to curb organized crime in America—but the history looks different through the prism of the House of Morgenthau, whose sons played key roles in all of them. It poses new questions: How does one Morgenthau, the patriarch Lazarus, come to America having lost one fortune, manage to lose another—and to cheat prison only in death? How does another, Henry Sr., forced to quit college, rise to become one of New York City's first real estate barons? How does his son, Henry Jr., stand beside FDR, his closest friend, in anguish as millions of his fellow Jews are murdered in Europe, and then, straining his friendship, act to rescue them? Finally, how does the last of the line of America's most-storied Jewish family come to preside over the most important prosecutorial district in the country for five decades (first as U.S. attorney, then as DA)—overseeing, by a conservative tally, three million cases, from the advent of "white-collar crime" to the judicial miscarriage of the Central Park Five, and turn the Manhattan DA's office into a law-enforcement bureau for international financial crime?

The saga of the Morgenthau family has lain half-hidden in the American shadows for too long. At heart a family history, it is also a far-flung epic, as big and improbable as the country itself.

PART I

ARRIVAL

1. "Between Profit and Disaster"

1815–1866

America in the first days of June 1866 was still rent by blood. On the morning that the iron ship edged into New York Harbor, the Civil War lived on. In Virginia, Jefferson Davis awaited trial for treason. Elsewhere in the South, the warnings mounted: In Alabama, the cotton forecasts turned apocalyptic and they spoke of famine; in Arkansas, the Freedmen's Bureau reported ramifying destitution and a resurgent violence. Yet in the island-city that lay at the voyage's end, the ebbing of the war had brought an uncertain limbo: Everyone, it seemed, both those who had witnessed the horror and those who had not, wished only to forget the fields of dead.

The SS *Hermann*, the 318-foot steamship, twin masts shimmering and black hull streaked salt-white, had left the port of Bremen in May. Not all of its 734 passengers would complete the crossing. Eleven children perished en route, the youngest an infant girl who died hours before landfall. For the 64 people in first class, though, the crossing had been most pleasant. A distinguished crowd had filled the heated suites of luxury. Most were German gentlemen, men of trade and industry, who had come to America in search of commerce and brought their families in hopes of starting anew.

On the final day at sea they rose early, huddling at the great glass windows to catch sight of a city cloaked in gray. Amid the predawn murk, an unlikely traveler who had sported a white silk tie on each day of the crossing, no matter the weather, stood apart. At fifty, he had already revealed a gift for self-invention—turning from tailor to tradesman to entrepreneur. Married for more than two decades, he had fathered thirteen children. He had left Mannheim with his family, but forfeited all else: a string of factories, a thousand employees, a mansion on the town square.

In short, he had left behind all that he had ever built, owned, or known.

IIII

Lazarus Morgenthau was not an imposing man. He was of average height and slight of build. Yet whenever he entered a room, no matter how crowded, people took note. It was a talent that he had discovered as a boy: He commanded attention. Although the bright blond hair and beard of his youth had turned a silvery gray, it remained rakishly long, and his eyes, set deep beneath a broad forehead, still flashed electric blue. He took pains to lavish care on his appearance. The daily toilette was an orchestration: a concerto of minerals and elixirs, lotions and oils. Each morning, he trimmed his walrus mustache with precision. He wore the stiff wool suits of a Baden aristocrat (his Prince Albert, a knee-length, double-breasted frock coat, was his signature) and, no matter the season, a cravat. The necktie, always silk and pearl white, served as a talisman of his preposterous ascent.

Lazarus Morgenthau was a child of the narrow world of Bavaria's Jews, an unyielding realm of walls and boundaries, rules and ritual. It, too, was a world apart. In his father's native Gleusdorf, a hamlet of some three hundred residents, only a few dozen were Jews. Their arrival dated to 1660: six families who settled in a remote corner of Europe. In the two centuries since, their number had scarcely grown. The Jews of Gleusdorf lived crammed together, along a dead-end street on the edge of the village. Lazarus, though, was a born gambler, and intent on escape. He came of age in a world where change was a threat and games of chance a sacrilege, and he had risen by dint of a rare combination of ego, defiance, and ingenuity.

Lazarus's wife of twenty-three years, Babette, had made the voyage as well. Neither particularly pretty nor, as even the family chroniclers recorded, charming, Babette possessed a singular virtue noted by her descendants: an essential "stoic" bearing. At forty-one, she had not only suffered the mercurial ways of her husband, but borne children for nearly two decades. Eight were onboard: four boys, aged six to thirteen (Mengo, Julius, Heinrich, and Gustave), and four girls, aged eleven to twenty-one (Regine, Ida, Pauline, and Bertha).

Months earlier, Lazarus had dispatched the three he deemed most able, the two eldest sons, Max and Siegfried, aged eighteen and fourteen, and a daughter, Minna, fifteen. He sent them off in midwinter, a teenaged advance party instructed to secure a foothold across the sea. On November 29, 1865, Lazarus bid farewell to Max with characteristic flourish. "My dear son!" he wrote in a poetic farewell,

You are parting from us today, just for a short time
May you be the first to bring us hope and joy.
Through diligence and righteousness you will succeed
To bring your parents and siblings a bright future.
Travel now with God and my blessings and arrive
In health in New York—this is the wish of your loving father.

Now, as the *Hermann* neared land, Lazarus and Babette waited among the arrivals, eager for a glimpse of the city. The clouds were dark and low, threatening to draw a curtain across the sky. Lazarus kept his leather cases close. They were filled with ornate scrolls, the promise of elaborate schemes: patents from Germany and England for hygienic devices and household remedies. Since his youth, Lazarus had been a tinkerer. In recent months, though, even before he had been forced, as he saw things, to quit the very business that had made him rich and abandon Germany, the drive to invent had overtaken his life.

Behind every scheme lay two forces: a love of modernity and a fixation on health. The first in Mannheim to install a bathroom in his house, Lazarus pursued one hygienic invention after another. Just months before leaving Bremen, he'd launched the latest venture: In London, Lazarus and his son Max opened a "branch office" at No. 10 Basinghall Street, securing an English patent for a favorite invention: *Fichtennadel-Cigarren* ("Pine-Balsam Cigars"), as well as *Fichtennadel-Brustzucker* ("Pine-Balsam Pectoral Sugar")—bonbons, wrapped in foil and "containing a very little opium," to alleviate "irritable cough, hoarseness, tightness of the chest, asthma, stubborn lung affections, chronic catarrh, etc." To market the "wholesome cigars" among the Americans, he published a booklet filled with testimonials. Inside the embossed cover (crowded with the seals of fourteen European states), doctors and clergymen, opera singers and actresses, extolled Lazarus's wonders. "These cigars are not only enjoyable to smoke," a priest wrote, "they have truly earned their name, *Gesundheits-Cigarren*—Cigars for your Health."

And yet a third force now ruled Lazarus: He was desperate to start over. Years later, his grandchildren would excuse what his own children could not. The patriarch could never have imagined, they understood, all that he did not live long enough to see. Lazarus would never revisit the world he had left, nor regain the fortune that he had lost. And he would never adapt to his new land. Yet the feats of his descendants would surpass even the gambler's most fantastic dreams. His American-born heirs could afford to forgive him. As Castle Garden came into view, its stone walls looming above the Battery, it would have been as hard to forecast the turns of the century to come as to envision the birth of a dynasty.

| | | |

The journey had begun in tobacco and gold. From unremarkable roots, Lazarus Morgenthau had risen to become one of the biggest cigar manufacturers in Germany. He had received the Grand Duke of Baden at home and visited Napoleon III in the Tuileries. Decades later, after the change of worlds and fortunes, the royal visits would remain his brightest memory—and a reminder of how far he had fallen.

Lazarus was born on August 17, 1815, in Kleinwallstadt, a small market town on Bavaria's northern border. His father, Moses, born in 1773, was the first to take the name "Morgenthau." As the nineteenth century opened and Napoleon's influence spread, German Jews were permitted, like French Jews before them, to adopt surnames. For generations, Moses's heirs retold the story: As he stood in line awaiting his turn before the town clerk, Moses looked at the bare earth beneath his feet and saw the morning dew—the *Morgen-Thau*. Moses and his brothers lived by the trades of their faith: They were *schochets, melamdem,* and *khazonem* (butchers, teachers, and singers). But not Lazarus—as the boy studied the sacred texts, his eye strayed. Lazarus had joined his brothers as a singer in synagogue, but soon signaled that his intentions lay elsewhere, beyond the bounds of the permissible.

In 1842, at the age of twenty-seven, and having achieved little more than becoming a struggling tailor, Lazarus boldly wrote a *Lebensgeschichte,* an autobiography. The "diary," as it was known among successive generations, was written in an ornate script and runs more than a hundred pages. It tells the unlikely story of an escape from Orthodoxy. As if sensing that he would prosper one day, Lazarus set out to record his struggle, rendering in lapidary detail a childhood of poverty and upheaval.

In 1825, Moses, destitute and unable to feed his seven children, had sent his sons away. The boys would sing for their supper in the private homes of Frankfurt. The enterprise was humiliating, yet profitable. Too small to be seen by all those gathered, the Morgenthau boys would stand on chairs to sing, and be, as Lazarus recalled, "much complimented." Tours followed. Moses's sons—Lazarus was the third eldest—traveled the Jewish communities of the southern Palatinate and, in their spells at home, learned to beg provisions from local farmers.

By the time the brothers arrived in Hürben, in 1832, Lazarus had turned his back on his forefathers. "I realized that no object would be gained even if I achieved the position of cantor in ten years," he wrote. "I went home and told my parents I wanted to learn a trade." He settled on tailoring, and soon found an apprenticeship. Defying family and faith, Lazarus went to work with Christian tailors. He learned to make cravats, neckties that in cut and color marked an assault on the black-and-white uniforms of the Jews. After he made his first cravat, Lazarus dared to wear it to synagogue, standing on the bimah, the small stage at the center of the temple, where he had once sung as a cantor.

Lazarus had a canny sense for public relations, and he soon found another gift: He could pass for a Gentile. In 1838, after suffering a trading drought at a Munich fair, Lazarus sought a permit for a stall in Landshut, a town to the northeast. Officials there could not determine if he was a Jew, so "they held two booths in reserve"—one in the market street where the Jews were obliged to trade, and the other in the Hauptstrasse, the main street, where the Christians sold their wares. After arriving in town, Lazarus was given a permit to join the Christians. As he had brought "goods chiefly for the gentry," the chance to sell on the Hauptstrasse was a boon. In Landshut that day, Lazarus enjoyed his best trading ever. From then on, he took to traveling bareheaded, letting his blond locks grow unruly.

No matter how many conventions he had broken, Lazarus remained loyal to his long-suffering mother. Brunhilda had given birth to her first surviving child in 1809, and her last in 1831. As a young mother, she had contracted consumption, and each year she had grown steadily weaker. The sicker his mother became, the more money Lazarus devoted to her care. In 1834, on the final day of January, her lungs gave out. The day after Brunhilda's death, her husband, Moses, suffered a fatal stroke.

Lazarus's mother had died at fifty-one, and his father at fifty-three. Eight children were left as orphans, the youngest a boy not yet three. The death, and long decline, of his mother would never leave Lazarus. Years later, on the cusp of marriage, he vowed his own wife would never endure such misery.

||||

Babette Guggenheim was eleven years younger than Lazarus, a girl he had known since her childhood in the southern Bavarian town of Hürben. On their wedding day in 1843, Babette was not yet eighteen. Of the two, she could claim a deeper sense of faith and a greater appreciation of German culture. A member, on her mother's side, of one of the town's prominent families, Babette spent afternoons at the piano and evenings reading Heinrich Heine and Gotthold Ephraim Lessing. Her father, Joachim Guggenheim of the Guggenheims of Lengnau, Switzerland, was a rabbi whose authority reached beyond Hürben. In line with the traditions of her faith and strictures of her time, Babette was loyal, even devout, in yielding to her husband's every demand. In all, she would bear Lazarus fourteen children. But Babette was also a woman of capacity. When pushed, she, too, could make her desires known.

They had begun their life together in new surroundings. In their first year of marriage, Lazarus learned of Ludwig I's plans to build a Bavarian city to rival Mannheim, the town across the Rhine—a trading destination for centuries. For Lazarus, the allure of the new harbor town—Ludwigshafen, it was christened—was strong. Their first child, Bertha, was born there in 1844, and their first son, Max, arrived three years later. Before long, though, Lazarus "found that the growth of the new town was rather slow," Max recalled. "And having made friends in the larger and much older place"—Mannheim—"he moved across the Rhine." The city yielded stability, encouraging an accelerated expansion: In thirteen years there, Babette bore eleven children. For Lazarus, the move spelled the end of his career as a tailor.

A younger brother, Max, had been the pioneer, sailing for America in 1849, eventually settling in San Francisco in the years of the Gold Rush. He opened a small shop to cater to miners flush with cash, and in letters home, Max regaled Lazarus with tales of wild California, its natural riches, libertines, and fortune hunters. He also sent home uncommon gifts, among them a cane for the Grand Duke of Baden, its head a fist of gold inlaid with quartz.

Max not only mesmerized his brother with his stories; he offered a novel suggestion. The prospectors' cigars, he wrote, were in high demand and cost as much as fifty cents each. Max shipped home samples, some of American tobacco, some Cuban. He wrote his brother of the fields of Die Pfalz, the Morgenthaus' home region, where the Rhine floodplains filled the village markets with greens, wine, and tobacco. In his letters home, Max cast a lure to Lazarus: Why not try to compete? Why not make good cigars cheaply at home and sell them to the gold miners in California?

| | | |

It proved a shrewd idea. The partnership straddled two of the day's strongest markets for supply and demand, and by the early 1850s, *Gebrüder Morgenthau*—Morgenthau Brothers—was producing cigars in Mannheim that measured well against the miners' favored brands in California. The transatlantic trade, though, was not without challenges. Southern Germany was known for tobacco, not cigars. The cases, hand-made boxes of cedarwood, proved difficult to perfect. After a series of false starts, Lazarus finally fashioned a box that was both elegant and durable. Soon, the cigars were selling in San Francisco. Duties were low and profits high. Business boomed.

At home, Lazarus's stature grew rapidly. In the winter of 1856, he stunned local society, buying one of Mannheim's largest residences, a mansion formerly owned by a Catholic nobleman, Baron Heinrich Überbruck von Rodenstein. At 24,000 guilders (more than $1 million today), the price was beyond any merchant's means. But the house was a landmark: three stories tall, with eighteen rooms, and twenty-three windows overlooking a main square, across from the National Theater. Lazarus moved his office and warehouse from the outskirts of town to the mansion's first floor. The second floor he kept as living quarters. And on the third, he gathered a skilled workforce, a hundred young laborers, to roll, sort, and package the cigars.

By then, a single cigar factory had grown to four, and Lazarus now employed nearly a thousand men and women. In short order, he had built one of the largest industrial concerns along the Rhine and fashioned an operation as streamlined as any in Germany.

| | | |

It could have been a life of storied leisure, yet Lazarus could not sit idle. If his imagination had always been fired by new schemes, he now possessed the means to pursue them. He seemed bent, too, on reaching beyond his station. He had long made a practice, for example, of giving to other faiths. The spark, he would later say, had come during a performance in Munich of *Nathan der Weise*, the Lessing classic. With its lessons of religious tolerance, the play proved an awakening. Lazarus made a radical exchange, abandoning the Orthodoxy of his youth in favor of an ecumenical vision of religious freedom. The turn came in ever bolder breaches. In 1857, he donated a portal for the Catholic church in Ludwigshafen, its stone carrying the inscription "*Porta Fundata a L. Morgenthau.*" In 1860, he donated the first bell—christening it "Babette"—for the town's Protestant church. And in Mannheim, two years later, he gave money to the Free Religious Society, a group of freethinkers urging radical reform, and even set up their first bank.

The largesse paid dividends. At forty, Lazarus had not only amassed a fortune but won uncommon social status. In 1857, his devotion to modernity and the state found reward with the attentions of the grand duke. Friedrich of Baden came to inspect Lazarus's factory. He arrived with the Grand Duchess Luise, sole daughter of Wilhelm I, the future kaiser. After touring the cigar-making operation, the grand duke and duchess visited the family apartments. Lazarus had mastered the art of courting the nobility: Daughter Bertha, the eldest, played the royal hymn on the piano, while her eight siblings sat to the side, arranged by age, with little Henry cradled in the plump arms of Franziska, the family nanny. The tableau stunned the royals. As the grand duke and duchess entered, the children rose one by one to curtsy. "Your children," the grand duke told Babette, "remind me of organ pipes."

The year 1857 was one of hardship for many exporters in Baden. The panic in the United States, as the nation drifted toward civil war, caused prices to collapse across Europe. Yet Lazarus sailed on. At forty-two, he was producing the best, and most expensive, cigars in southern Germany. He had gained, as well, the privilege—rarely accorded Jews—of becoming "a free citizen" of Mannheim. The title endowed him with new legal standing, the full rights of citizenship in the city. Lazarus was verging on, as his son Max later wrote, "the zenith of his success."

And soon he won what he wanted the most: public affirmation of his social standing. On November 10, 1859, the Germans would celebrate the centenary of the poet Friedrich Schiller's birth. Across the German states, this holiday would prove the greatest display of German political aspirations since the 1848 Revolution. In Mannheim, where Schiller had premiered his first drama, *Die Räuber,* the preparations were a matter of grave consequence. City officials renamed the square by the National Theater "Schillerplatz" and commissioned a monument. In 1862, for the statue's unveiling, the elders announced the *Schillerfest,* a citywide party to feature a mass procession and an evening "illumination."

Lazarus, whose mansion faced the square, leapt at the chance to run the entertainments. He ordered expensive decorations, and brought in five hundred of his workers, outfitted in white costumes. The monument's unveiling was a rare pageant of national pride. Banners festooned the streets, as the tricolor of the 1848 Revolution wafted overhead. At five o'clock in the evening, trumpets blared and fireworks lit the town *Schloss,* its baroque palace. Two thousand torchbearers paraded through the streets, across the bridge over the Neckar, ending at the theater square, by a giant tree known as the Schiller Linden. The grand event would long be recalled as one of the town's most glorious celebrations. But it nearly did not take place. On the eve of the event, as Lazarus's men tested the illumination apparatus—a coiled complex of candles—a fire broke out. Lazarus sent for help, urgently summoning recruits from his closest factory. The corps worked through the night, finishing the repairs on the morning of the big day.

For weeks, the story filled the Mannheim papers. Lazarus Morgenthau, a Jew and an outsider, had become a local hero. Until his final days, he would summon the tale: how he had saved the *Schillerfest.* Over the years, with each telling, the glory burned more brightly, until the encounter with royalty ripened into a lasting friendship, and his rescue of the poet's celebration into a miracle. It would become a habit: the gilding of the past. Lazarus's achievements, though, were undeniable, and in the sixth decade of his life, he had gathered his family and followed his cigars to the New World.

Yet he had left Germany harboring a grim secret, a calamity he revealed to few beyond the family. When asked, he would say that the move to America was to give his sons "a chance to escape military service," and to test "the truth of the attractive stories of the United States." At home, though, the elders of Mannheim knew the truth: Lazarus was nearly broke.

| | | |

The trouble had begun with a one-term congressman from Illinois. In 1860, as Abraham Lincoln set his sights on the White House, the warning signs emerged. Lincoln argued that American farmers and manufacturers deserved a leg up: tariffs on foreign goods. At the Republican convention that spring, protectionism formed a central plank of the party platform. Soon Lincoln was stumping beneath banners that promised "Protection for Home Industry." None welcomed a tariff more than the tobacco growers of the Connecticut River Valley, eager to fend off competition from the old country.

As Lincoln campaigned, Lazarus watched from across the Atlantic with unease. He and his brother Max in San Francisco could foretell the danger. A Lincoln victory would surely yield a wall of duties. In August, Lazarus dispatched one of his nephews on a scouting mission. Twenty-three-year-old Carl Schnaittacher would open the New York office of Morgenthau Brothers, selling "segars" at 8 William Street, down near the seaport. Lazarus asked that his nephew follow the campaign, and relay the election results at once.

On the morning of November 7, 1860, Lazarus and his son Max, thirteen at the time, were strolling across Mannheim's Schlosspark when a messenger from the wire bureau brought the bad news: Lincoln had won. Telegrams from San Francisco soon followed. His brother urged Lazarus not to fire any workers, to keep operations "at full force," so that he would have "a large stock of goods on hand" when the tariffs came.

In 1862, Congress lived up to predictions, passing another tariff to curb imports. In desperation, Lazarus sent a final shipment, his largest ever, to New York. The freighter arrived a day late: The United States had instituted the tariff. "The day's delay meant the difference between profit and disaster to my father," Lazarus's son Henry recalled years later. "The cigars, which, when duty free, would have yielded a good return, were a dead loss." The duties climbed ever higher. Few Americans, whether gold miners or Wall Street barons, could afford cigars from Europe anymore. Lazarus had no choice: He shuttered his factories.

| | | |

The *Hermann* had been at sea nearly two weeks. The crossing in May 1866 had been quiet: the weather unusually fine, the waters calm.

The city that lay ahead was set to mark a renewal. On the first weekend in June, New York would celebrate the annual opening day of Central Park, a carriage parade filling the Mall. Even amid a morning downpour, they rolled in, "in good taste and bad," noted the *Times,* both those who had "known good fortune and carriages from their cradles" and those who "earned them bravely and filled them with honor." By midafternoon, as the tide of fancy dresses, mousseline, poult-de-soie, and grenadine flowed to the music pavilion, the rain would let up. And as the skies cleared, it would seem for a moment as if the war's shadow had lifted from the city.

Yet the spectacle in Central Park was fleeting. Fear gripped New York. A cholera quarantine loomed. The board of health, the newspapers warned, would have to annex Sandy Hook, Staten Island, or even the whole of Coney Island—"the barren islands and useless sandbars" could shelter the sick, the *Times* opined, and save "New-York harbor from becoming a floating lazarette of pestilence." On the *Hermann,* the mass of passengers—533 crowded into steerage—could not see above the waterline, but they, too, sailed past the horror. Those peering out of the upper saloons could catch a glimpse of the city elders' solution: "cholera ships," vessels loaded with the ill. Far across the bay, the ships formed an island of their own, hulks blackening the horizon. Seven hundred crowded the half-dismantled ships. German and Danish emigrants—no one would take them. Each day, the doctors extended their rosters. And as the headlines fanned fears, the specter of death grew. What would happen, New Yorkers asked, if the sick broke free?

As dawn had neared on that first Sunday in June, the city had been uncommonly quiet, an early-morning storm and the police conspiring to keep the vagrants and beggars off the streets. And in the chill murk, the German ship had at last reached the broad pier. Lazarus and Babette gathered their children and readied themselves to enter the New World, ten figures at the head of a sodden throng beside a half-hidden city.

2. At the Edge

1866–1870

Ninety-two Congress Street, the boardinghouse where Lazarus's eldest children had rented rooms that first winter, was a narrow brownstone in Brooklyn. It stood on Cobble Hill, near the river, steps from the wharf. For the Morgenthaus, it was a landing that betrayed their circumstances. Their arrival had been announced in the passenger listings in the *Times:* the first family to decamp first class from the *Hermann.* But the choice of Brooklyn, rather than a fine address in Manhattan, revealed their financial descent. Lazarus had come to America with money: $30,000 in cash, the proceeds of the sell-off in Mannheim— the mansion and the factories, even the furniture, auctioned in rapid succession. Yet to live at the water's edge in Brooklyn in 1866 was to mingle with the working classes. Congress Street was thick with Irish and Italian laborers, men who had abandoned their homelands not as a last resort, but as a first.

Lazarus had come late. Nearly all the founders of Our Crowd, the small circle of German Jews who presided over New York's banking and finance—the Lehmans and Wertheims, Seligmans and Loebs, Goldmans and Sachses—had made their fortunes before the Civil War. Lazarus was arriving years later, but his timing was lucky. New York, too, was being born anew, seized by a burst of industry, money, and greed. The city in the wake of the war was fast becoming the nation's manufacturing capital, a place of factories, plants, and shops. The harbor was clogged with lighters, steamers, and packers. The immigrant flood, too, had begun, and with it a boom in housing. The buildings went up quickly, and cheaply. Walt Whitman, writing in *The Brooklyn Times,* foretold the dangers. "Mingle a little philanthropy," the poet begged of the builders, with "money-making." It was not to be. In Manhattan, on the Lower East Side, more people lived in closer proximity and in greater squalor than nearly anywhere else on earth.

Brooklyn marked the open frontier. Once a patchwork of Dutch farms and orchards, it had become America's first suburb. Thirteen ferries now carried passengers to Manhattan each day, and the wharves stretched almost without interruption from Red Hook to Greenpoint. Construction, too, had hit fever pitch. Churches, storefronts, brownstones—the landscape shifted by the day. Six hundred nineteen buildings had gone up in the previous year, and on June 11, 1866, days after Lazarus and his family stepped ashore, the last of the old Brooklyn farms, the Theodore Bergen estate, was chopped up and sold off in five hundred lots.

| | | |

Ninety-two Congress stood out on one of Brooklyn's fastest-growing corners, near the water, where the gas lamps ended at the cobblestoned corner and the stones gave way to dirt. It was a derelict block: In the narrow low-slung brick tenements, two or three families, and often more, would squeeze into a single floor. For rents of $30 a month, they were thankful for hot and cold running water. At night, the sounds of the piers filled the boardinghouse. The dock at the block's end, a loading point for the barges and steamboats, had become a makeshift depot, and the police routinely nabbed thieves in flight: men staggering under sacks of sugar and coal lifted off the boats. It was less a neighborhood than a collection of longshoremen, stevedores, and lightermen, who carried cholera victims to the quarantine ships.

Congress Street, wrote Henry Reed Stiles, the local physician who would publish an epic history of the borough, was "in a very filthy condition." The winds carried off the waters, lifting the black coal-plumes off the roofs. The deep cellars were damp, and, wrote Stiles, "filled with refuse garbage, ashes and all kinds of dirt." Disease had long stalked the Sixth Ward, but the Morgenthaus' block gained special notice. Of the forty-six cases of yellow fever recorded several summers earlier, thirty-four victims lived on the stretch of Congress closest to the water.

"Cholera" became one of the first English words that the Morgenthau children learned. Arriving in midsummer, the family moved into their rented rooms just as the panic hit. Cholera, Lazarus and Babette discovered, surrounded them. It invaded the weakest first, settling into the rooming houses, attacking "the unwashed," as the newsmen called the immigrants. It struck the soldiers, too, at Governors Island, and the paupers on desolate Wards Island. Cholera, wrote the diarist George Templeton Strong, "has taken root at last and grows rankly." As the epidemic spread, New Yorkers searched for sulfate of iron, "diffusing it"—as a disinfectant—"in water-closets and wash-hand basins," and hoarding it by the pound.

If Cobble Hill was a mélange, it mirrored the shifting contours of the city. A few blocks away, a preserve of would-be gentry was emerging. Amid rows of prim brownstones, the cobblestoned streets were anchored by corner churches and their charities: the Sisters of the Poor of St. Francis, the Catholic Orphan Asylum, the Long Island College Hospital. Here, too, were the landmarks of new wealth: Italianate houses with cast-ironwork, outsized residences with brick stables, and, nearby, the brownstone where Jennie Jerome, daughter of Leonard Jerome, one of New York's wealthiest financiers, and future mother of Winston Churchill, was born.

A neighborhood with rectitude and aspirations, only a few blocks from the wharf, but a world apart. And for the newly arrived family from Germany, it offered an enviable image of the future.

I I I I

Babette had lost two children in Mannheim, both in their infancy. Caesar, born in 1857, had not survived a year, and Adele Louise had not lived to her second birthday, dying at winter's end in 1863. And yet, despite the threat of disease, Lazarus was eager that his children dive into the life of the city. Bertha, Max, and Pauline, the eldest three, were beyond school age. Bertha, at twenty, was already engaged to a darkly handsome German émigré, Gustave Zittel, son of a well-known paleontologist at the university in Munich. Gustave was notable in another regard: He was not a Jew. Max, at nineteen, was keen to enter the mercantile world. In Mannheim, he had graduated from the lyceum and apprenticed with his father. His eldest son, Lazarus could be sure, would help him find his way in New York.

Pauline, thirteen months Max's junior, had also finished her schooling in Mannheim. In New York, she faced a single challenge: marriage. Minna, the third daughter, born Wilhelmina, had turned sixteen before the rest of the family arrived. Without any English, though, she was deemed unworthy of formal schooling. An early illness, too, kept her back. What it was, and when it began, the records do not reveal, but Henry recorded a premonition in his diary: "Minna," he wrote, "says she will die v young," at "30–40 yrs." Her younger sisters, Ida and Recha (as Regine was now called), twelve and eleven, were of school age, but both would also take lessons at home, under the tutelage of the twenty-six-year-old *Fräulein,* Maurine Maurer, who had also made the journey from Germany. Only the youngest boys, the five shortest "organ pipes," would enroll at the local public school.

The DeGraw Street School, as P.S. 13 was known, stood a few blocks from Congress Street. In the first week of September, Lazarus put on his finest suit and presented to the principal five of his sons—Siegfried, recently turned fifteen; Gustave, younger by two years; Henry, born Heinrich, ten; Julius Caesar, whose middle name honored the brother lost in Mannheim, eight; and little Mengo, six.

Though the language of instruction and the customs of his classmates were daunting, ten-year-old Henry took to his new world with ease. He was undersized, but seemed to thrive on tall odds. Henry did not share Lazarus's fair skin or blond hair (his was a dark chestnut), yet he had inherited his father's marine-blue eyes. He shared, too, Lazarus's insatiable urge to stand out. The drive would overshadow all else and guide an accelerated rise, first in law, then in real estate and finance, finally in politics.

For Henry Morgenthau, the twin forces of ego and ambition would never leave him, but they were never stronger than when his journey began. In his first years in New York, like an explorer charting his way, he recorded his thoughts, actions, and feelings compulsively. He kept a chronicle nearly each day, at times almost to the hour, of his trials and errors. He filled diaries, copybooks, journals, ledgers, and notebooks. No detail was too small, no event irrelevant. Henry would preserve this meticulous accounting of his adolescence, labeled and boxed, until his last days. Perhaps it was a record born of prescience, a sense of the eminence to come. Or maybe it arose from an abundance of pride: To himself, he reasoned that his peers mistook "confidence" for "conceit." But Henry could be forgiven for his fastidious notation of his every waking moment: A private narrative could serve as a refuge from the disorder already circling the house on Congress Street, an encroaching threat that in time would engulf the family and divide it forever.

| | | |

Lazarus would call it a blessing. Babette may have sensed it straight-away, or maybe she had no notion until many months later—such were the standards of care in 1866—but within days of their arrival, she was pregnant.

Richard Nathan Paul Maximilian Morgenthau—named with a nod to the Bavarian monarch and Lessing's hero—was born on March 13, 1867, Babette's fourteenth child. To Lazarus, the arrival of an American son, robust and brown-eyed, foretold a bounty—and sped a departure from Brooklyn. Spring would bring a return of the "blue death." As Babette nursed the baby, cholera advanced up their block: Mary Mack, an Irish neighbor, succumbed at fifty, followed soon by Margaret Roach, a fifteen-year-old girl, sixteen hours after the doctor's visit. Lazarus, as always, had a plan. Brooklyn had never been more than an accommodation. Now he had to make the leap into Manhattan.

At a time when many German-Jewish immigrants went into dry goods, hawking their wares along the Bowery or in Yorkville far to the north, Lazarus entered the wine business. He had dabbled in spirits before—for a time running a wine shop in Ludwigshafen. In New York, it seemed a trade with promise. Germans were flooding in, fast becoming one of the city's largest, and wealthiest, immigrant communities. German wines, moreover, were scarce. But Lazarus had a family source: Gustave Zittel, his daughter Bertha's husband, knew winemakers at home. His first attempt, a wine shop on Cedar Street downtown, proved too small. Lazarus desired a grander stage to gain entrée into German New York: a restaurant.

The Bremer Rathskeller, named after one of the oldest wine cellars in Germany, took up the basement and sub-basement of two adjoining buildings on lower Broadway. One half held a dining room catering to Germanic tastes, the other a shop selling imported "wines, liquors, brandies, etc." The restaurant stood across from City Hall, close to St. Paul's, and within steps of the Astor House, the most famous hotel in America. Lazarus had set up shop at the heart of the city's financial and political power.

On May 1, 1867, after nearly a year at the edge of the Brooklyn wharves, he moved Babette and the children to Manhattan, renting a stately house on the East Side, not far from the southeastern corner of Central Park. Fifty-ninth Street, to New Yorkers who rarely ventured north of Madison Square, was the edge of civilization. The red-brick house on the corner of Second Avenue made a bold statement, but it spoke less to Lazarus's future than to his past. The horsecars rumbled by, dead-ending at Sixty-fourth Street, where the truck gardens—the small farms that fed the uptown neighborhoods—began. It was a far remove from the boardinghouses of Brooklyn. Lazarus had chosen a neighborhood with prospects, an outpost settled by German Jews who had escaped the Lower East Side.

It soon became clear, though, that Lazarus leapt too far. The house, a three-story, high-stooped brownstone, was a luxury he could not afford. He had nearly exhausted his savings when disaster struck. One night in the summer of 1867, a fire broke out in the Rathskeller. The kitchen burned, and whatever could be salvaged—"splendid counters, shelves, iron bedsteads, a large quantity of firewood"—was sold for pennies. Within days, the Irish auctioneer G. McKnight gaveled away the remnants—down to the empty wine casks—of Lazarus's first American dream.

His son Henry did not enjoy an easy start in Manhattan either. Short, slight, and new to the neighborhood, he was a natural target. Henry entered a new school—No. 18, on Fifty-first Street near Lexington Avenue—and learned that the boys in his class held a "general belief that all 'Dutchmen'"—as Germans were known—"were cowards." But one day, when a husky boy taunted him, Henry delivered a thrashing, "the result of sheer unscientific force." "Nothing evokes the admiration of the gallant Irish so much as a good fight," Henry would boast. In short order, his taunters became comrades.

At eleven, Henry was no longer Heinrich, but at home he still spoke German. He wrote, too, in his native tongue with far greater confidence than in English. (In his diary he proudly marked the day that he learned his thousandth word in the new language.) By his second summer in New York, Henry was mesmerized by the city. As he roamed its streets, he did not see the barriers that older immigrants faced, the chasms between rich and poor, Jew and Gentile. By the fall of 1867, Henry had started Sunday school at a new temple on Thirty-ninth Street, home of Dr. David Einhorn, a reforming rabbi scorned by some as too radical. On weekends, as he made his way to the rabbi's classes, Henry was dazzled. At school, he and his friends played tag on the foundation of St. Patrick's Cathedral, frozen in construction since the war. Now as he crossed town, he saw the city rising around him. Everywhere, the energy of the city stirred the young boy's imagination.

In Manhattan, Henry was free to roam, but at school he struggled to fit in. The unwieldy diphthongs of his native tongue plagued his pronunciation. The memories of Mannheim, too, the city where Jew and Gentile had mingled and his family had enjoyed luxury, proved hard to shake. Often, he would daydream of the *Heimat*—confiding in his diary a "longing" for the "Homeland." It was not only the wealth and status that he missed, but the stability of the past. Germany remained the lost world, a dream never to be regained.

| | | |

After a year of school in Manhattan, Henry had risen to the "first class"—the top rank in his grade. At eleven, he made up his mind: He would aim for a place at the new College of the City of New York. City College, as it would become known, had opened in the old Free Academy building, a turreted cathedral of learning (and masterwork of the architect James Renwick) that rose above Lexington Avenue at Twenty-third Street. The college had already become a landmark of opportunity, welcoming any child of immigrants who could pass its demanding entrance examinations. Students could start as young as twelve, and the courses were free.

With his sights set on college, Henry cast about for a stronger school to prepare him for the entrance exams. In March 1868, Henry was admitted into the "fourth class" at P.S. 14, on Twenty-seventh Street at Third Avenue. The school was a long walk from Fifty-ninth Street, and his new "class" of a lower level, but before turning twelve he finished the fourth and third classes, marking a rapid ascent.

Too young to graduate, Henry remained at P.S. 14 until the summer of 1869. His class of twenty-five was dominated by English and Irish boys, but there was at least one boy of Dutch ancestry. A class roster, compiled in Henry's best cursive, includes the name "George Wash. Rosevelt." George Washington Roosevelt, Jr., son of a hero of Bull Run, was a cousin of Teddy Roosevelt. Henry remained an outsider, but he had gained confidence. Whenever a trustee came to the school, his teacher would showcase Henry's gifts. At a school assembly, he asked Henry to display his "mental arithmetic"—to solve in his head complex problems, "such as computing the interest on $350 for three years, six months, and twelve days at 6 per cent." He made friends, but learning English remained a struggle. At night, Henry would diligently write out new words, one at a time, in row after row, until he'd filled dozens of pages. No matter how hard he worked at it, his pronunciation and spelling marked him as an immigrant, instilling a lifelong fear that his English was deficient.

Henry's first years in America were as great a testament to the strength of the New York school system as to the hunger of a new immigrant. In his second year at the school on Twenty-seventh Street, he earned perfect marks. In June 1870, Lafayette Olney, principal of P.S. 14, offered a recommendation for City College. Olney's letter—Henry would preserve it among his most treasured papers—carried a significance greater than its contents. It was the first in a lifetime of commendations, but in the years to come it represented a dream that had come true, only to be abruptly foreclosed. Henry had "passed through four higher classes," Olney wrote, and demonstrated a conduct "most gentlemanly." He sailed on through the exams, and that fall, on a crisp September morning, he added his name to the register at City College.

Henry Morgenthau was fourteen.

3. "A Declaration of Independence"

1870–1879

Lazarus would not give up. The patriarch of the Morgenthaus, even after the spectacular failure of his debut in the wine and restaurant businesses, placed a riskier bet: He would return to the hygienic schemes he had begun to craft in Mannheim. But what had been an avocation in Germany in New York became an obsession, as Lazarus turned into a dervish of homeopathic invention.

Once again, he claimed his pine-needle syrup was a universal elixir. He added it to cigars, cough drops, and toilet articles, and took out advertisements: "Cures: Colds, Sore Throats & c.," promised the notice in the *Times*. (The address listed—"L. Morgenthau's wholesale depot"— was in fact his son Max's insurance office.) But Lazarus now carried half a dozen calling cards. One day he was "Special Physician to Cure Rheumatism," the next, a "Director of Bathing Establishment." He labored on his contraptions, too: first a tongue-scraper, then a gum-labeling machine—enticing *Scientific American* to publish the patents. But as his finances worsened, Lazarus returned to his strong suit: courting the elite.

New York had no royalty, but even a man unfamiliar with the intricacies of the New World could discern a new aristocracy: a nobility bred of money, not blood. To enter its closed circles, Lazarus would try yet another device. To debut it, he chose the occasion with characteristic bravado. On the evening of November 30, 1870, in the grand armory of the Twenty-second Regiment on Fourteenth Street, six hundred of the city's wealthiest German Jews held the first "Hebrew Fair." A model of ecumenical entrepreneurship (to raise funds for the Mount Sinai Hospital and Hebrew Orphan Asylum Society), the evening came at the close of the season, on the heels of the German, Foundling, and French fairs. The Jews, though, were not to be outdone. Jesse Seligman, junior brother of Joseph, uncrowned leader of the community, had hired a top decorator, "Maxamilion," and as a popular ensemble entertained the guests, a thousand gas jets blazed on two dozen chandeliers, flooding the hall with light.

Charity, given the newfound wealth of the immigrant communities and the rising tide of the dispossessed, was a growth industry. As the asylums for the aged, infirm, and abandoned appeared, each ethnic constituency sought its own fair. But the events also fed an unspoken hunger. They offered a way to measure, and attain, social status. Guest lists were printed in the newspapers and tracked like sports scores. To some, it was a harmless by-product of noblesse oblige; to others, the arrogance of the arrivistes. To Lazarus, charity spelled opportunity.

At the Hebrew Fair, he unveiled a new product: The Golden Book of Life. A hybrid of commerce and religion, the "book" was an elegant register, bound in red morocco and standing nearly two feet tall. An ornate inscription marked the frontispiece, but inside its gilded pages were blank. The Golden Books, Lazarus vowed, would set down in print, for generations to come, the name of each donor. The first page was reserved for "subscriptions of not less than $100 each"; the middle pages "for subscriptions of any amount however small"; and the last pages for "family trees."

It was an ingenious fundraising tool. Jews knew well the annual ritual after the Day of Atonement, when the names of believers are "written into the Book of Life." Lazarus only refined the concept, exploiting the desire to advertise munificence. Few had seen leather books so large, or so extravagantly crafted. With his props on display, Lazarus stood at center stage, as he had as a boy, the cantor showcasing his cravats in synagogues. It was an instant success. He had the books patented, and soon presented them wherever he could—in Baltimore, at the Hebrew Waifs' Home; in Chicago, at a hospital for poor immigrants. In Philadelphia, at the consecration of the new Jewish Hospital, he nearly stole the show. It was an enormous turnout: two thousand Jews, including, *The Philadelphia Inquirer* noted, "the most influential and well-known of the Israelitish residents." He also maintained his nonsectarian embrace, bringing the Golden Books to the Masonic Fair, offering them in the service of the Mount Neboh Lodge, No. 257.

As institution after institution bought the books, Lazarus saw his reputation grow. The German papers, the Jewish press, and even the *Michigan Freemason* extolled this "devoted friend of charity." The Golden Books also yielded a large haul: $18,000 at the Hebrew Fair in New York, $11,000 at the hospital opening in Philadelphia. In time, Lazarus added the Silver Book, a less expensive product to broaden the subscription pool. In all, his books would raise as much as $250,000 for the charities—an enormous sum for the day. The scheme had appeal, but given the novelty, the sums involved, and a lack of transparency, it also bred suspicion—fears of an ulterior motive that, as all in the family knew, were sure to grow.

| | | |

Lazarus's ventures in New York might have brought him public notice, but they did not deliver profits. The lavish books were expensive to produce, and he charged a paltry fee. Lazarus insisted that his Golden Books would open doors in the New World and one day yield a handsome return, but in the meantime his financial straits only deepened. And the family suffered the fallout, none more so than Henry. Finishing college, his father insisted, was a luxury. "Father had the intention of letting me go all through," Henry wrote in a note to himself in the spring of 1871, but his "circumstances were worse and worse all the time." Henry may have been seeking reassurance, but he knew how fast, and far, Lazarus had fallen. With ten children at home, Lazarus could not support the household. Henry, at fourteen, would have to become a breadwinner. After only one term, Lazarus forced him to quit City College.

Henry did not quit his studies out of obedience to his father. It was a sacrifice made for the sake of his mother. Babette, unlike her husband, never had a choice. In Mannheim, she presided over a grand house and a corps of servants. She had not only a privileged vantage in the Jewish community but entrée to the Catholic and Lutheran elite. She took pleasure, as Henry wrote, in "good friends, good books, good dramas, and good music." But this agreeable life had increasingly faded from view. In New York, she was a stranger among strangers. Babette faced "an ever-constant and ever-pressing strain" to help her husband to make "both ends meet." Henry and his siblings feared that Babette would have to do "menial work." Deprived of his own dream, Henry vowed to keep his mother from stooping so low. He had suffered a setback, a wound too profound ever to heal, but he refused to cast aside his ambition.

For much of his first year out of school, Henry worked as an errand boy for $6 a week. Soon he got a better job: as a bookkeeper at $10 a week for Lyman and Joseph Bloomingdale in their small department store on Third Avenue. But he did not care for the goods—"hoop skirts, corsets and fancy goods"—and chafed to move on. As Lazarus still struggled to find his footing, Henry had no choice but to stay at work.

Ironically, the family's descent led to a new world. Henry would find mentors. He went to work (as a "general-utility lad") for Ferdinand Kurzman, a lawyer downtown and an acquaintance of his father's, determined to learn from his every word. Rabbi Einhorn, too, became a strong influence. His services—on Sundays, and not the Sabbath—extended the boundaries of the Reform movement. Organ music mingled with choral voices, husbands and wives sat in the same hall, as the rabbi charted the common ground between his congregants and their Protestant peers. But it was an accidental instructor who influenced Henry most. Dr. Samuel S. Whitall, not yet thirty, had earned a medical degree at Columbia, and now sought to rent rooms near work. He would become the Morgenthaus' boarder.

By 1871, Lazarus had moved the family again, this time to a brownstone on East Sixty-first Street, off Lexington Avenue. It was a fashionable address, but Lazarus could scarcely afford the coal to heat the house. He let out the rear parlor to a succession of young men, though it was Whitall who made the lasting impression. The doctor, a hunchback, was a Quaker who ran the nearby Colored Home and Hospital. Dr. Whitall was "a beautiful character," Henry remembered, "softened instead of embittered by his affliction."

Under the Quaker's tutelage, William Penn's *No Cross, No Crown* became a guiding text, opening Henry's mind, much as *Nathan der Weise* had for his father. Penn's ode to devotion, with its insistence on self-denial, temperance, and piety, appeared at odds with Judaism. To Henry, though, it confirmed that he was on the right path. Henry adopted a strict regime. He worked his muscles, alternating mornings between dumbbells and Indian clubs, and he kept watch on his appetite, too, chastising himself for each sweet eaten. In his diary, he celebrated his triumphs of self-denial. ("Avoided onanism," one entry declared.) He also discovered books, joining the Mercantile Library on Astor Place. Whitall sent him reading lists, twenty books in 1871 alone—and Henry plowed through them all, moving from Homer to Hume to Dickens.

At sixteen, Henry discovered Ben Franklin. His *Autobiography* became a compass. He read Franklin's "Thirteen Virtues"—from Temperance to Chastity to Order—and took them as commandments. Any hardship, Henry concluded, was "positively undoubtedly necessary in order that I should succeed in this world & I therefore made the following list." If Franklin had thirteen virtues, Henry would have two dozen maxims to live by—among them:

> Do not use any profane words.
> Do not eat much sweet or carbonic food as it darkens the mind and
>   dwarfs the soul.
> Spending nothing unnecessarily, for if you save when young, you can
>   spend when old.
> Never be idle as it will cause you to think of wrong things.
> Keep your own secrets, for if you do not keep them, no one will keep
>   them for you.
> Make few promises, but if you make any, fulfill them.
> Work for your employer as though it was for yourself.
> Deal fairly and honestly with your fellow clerks, but be not too inti-
>   mate.
> Trust none too much, but be not distrustful.
> Drink no kind of intoxicating liquors, nor smoke any weed.
> Never play at any game of chance.
> Conquer temptation though it is ever so powerful.
> Wonder not at the construction of man, but use your time in improv-
>   ing yourself.

Henry charted his progress in self-denial: lists of books to read, and those read; tallies of sins to avoid, and those committed; accounts of coins spent unwisely, and dollars tucked away in the German Uptown Savings Bank. Soon, he won a promotion at Kurzman's two-man firm downtown, becoming a law clerk—and quickly learned the tools of the trade. Henry began to write indictments of himself, even meting out penalties:

> Whereas during the last past week I had spent 5 cts more than al-
> lowed instead of saving about 50 cts or more, Whereas the above fact
> show that I am still very weak minded and my will has not yet gained
> control of all my habits & vices, Therefore be it RESOLVED that I
> shall be punished by saving at least 75 cts each & every week for the
> next four and that I am not allowed to eat any cakes, candies, pies or

sweets during the same period, as I hope after that period I shall be able to restrain myself without having to use such measures and means as these. It is further RESOLVED that I shall go up to my room every evening directly after supper for the same period.

A signature followed, and a hand-drawn seal: two interlocking initials, H. and M.

That spring, Henry embarked on a spiritual walkabout. If Rabbi Einhorn preached an "avant-garde Judaism" that sought to ease his congregation into the Protestant world, Henry took him at his word. Across New York the fiery sermons of its celebrated pulpit orators—Henry Ward Beecher, T. De Witt Talmage, Henry W. Bellows—lured thousands. On weekends, Henry joined the crowds in a whirlwind of progressive churchgoing. In his diaries of the time, Henry rarely wrote of Judaism. He recorded, instead, the lessons of the preachers. He was not searching for a new faith; he was assembling a code. At sixteen, Henry marshaled his strength. He no longer fretted about quitting college. He hoped to stave off a far worse fate.

||||

Lazarus and Babette were fighting a receding tide. After six years in America, the clan was breaking apart, and Henry, the middle of seven sons, was trapped at the center of the struggle. Three younger brothers—Julius, Mengo, and Richard—remained at home. The three eldest—Max, Siegfried, and Gus—had moved on. Siegfried left first, heading for San Francisco in 1871, the first leg of what would become a wayward odyssey. But even those who stayed behind yearned to escape.

As often happens in large families, the Morgenthau siblings divided along age lines. They paired up in alliances, squared off in rivalries. Max had taken Henry in when he went to work, inviting him to apprentice in the insurance office, but Julius—the brother closest in age—was the one Henry envied. Two years younger, Julius had taken Henry's place as the family intellectual. Allowed to stay on at City College, he excelled at philosophy, Latin, and Greek. With a strong jaw, open face, and pomaded hair combed straight back, Julius may have been the most handsome of the Morgenthau boys. He was certainly the one who paid least heed to their father's vicissitudes. Taking the measure of his brother's progress, Henry found confirmation of his fear: If any Morgenthau were to gain a foothold in the new world, it would be in spite of, and not thanks to, their father's desires.

If in Mannheim Lazarus's oddities had inspired parlor talk, in New York his name now raised eyebrows. For a time, his children gave him a wide berth. Lazarus had always managed a revival. If the wines did not support the family, the restaurant would. If fire took the business, he would peddle insurance. And for a time, he seemed to settle into the trade—proving adept at exploiting the immigrants' fears to sell policies. By the winter of 1871, though, among his children new fears mounted. In the surviving correspondence, diaries, and family accounts, the alarm is clear: Lazarus was no longer mercurial but unstable. In Germany there had always been demands, but now the moods swung wildly—and the lows were dangerously low. His sons and daughters worried Lazarus could turn violent; Babette, they insisted, could not stay by his side.

Their mother would hear none of it. Babette knew another Lazarus. Even in Germany, he could be headstrong, and flamboyant to a fault, but at his core, she would say, Lazarus was a sentimentalist. He could be endearing, even doting. On November 2, 1868, they had renewed their wedding vows, and again exchanged rings. Lazarus's was a hefty 14-karat band made with plaited hair, a fashion of the time. A goldsmith braided the strands of hair—by tradition the ring-giver's own—in a tight weave around the metal. The initials "L.M." shone on the band's outside, and inside, the words *Silberne Hochzeit,* Silver Anniversary, were inscribed. The rings marking their twenty-fifth anniversary were a grand gesture and, given the family's circumstances, an extravagance. But for Lazarus it was more than a desire to preserve appearances. He and Babette loved each other.

Evidence abounds of their affection. In the summer of 1873, Lazarus left, alone, for the seashore. The excuse was to escape the swelter of the city, yet a darker force pervades the family correspondence. The patriarch was unwell, suffering a spell of erratic behavior—and Babette's children insisted that she keep her distance. Babette refused. On August 7, 1873, she sent Lazarus a painful letter, refusing to abandon him. "My dearest good Lazarus!" Babette writes,

> *Yesterday I received your dear letter and am so very happy that you are enjoying yourself so much at the sea spas, and I hope your stay will do you well.*

> *Dear Lazarus! I agree with you entirely that it is best for me to go with you, for only in your company do I enjoy myself most completely. . . . I kiss you warmly and am, as always, your ever-loving*
>
> *Babette Morgenthau*

For Lazarus, the woes—money, and now mental health—would deepen. The New World did not agree with him, but no matter how far her husband fell, Babette could not find the will to leave him.

| | | |

If the Morgenthaus mourned the loss of a fortune, they were hardly alone. The trouble had begun four years earlier, on September 24, 1869—Black Friday. Two railroad investors, Jay Gould and Jim Fisk, had sought to corner the gold market in a scheme that would entangle President Ulysses S. Grant's brother-in-law. At the time speculation reigned on Wall Street, but Gould and Fisk were crooks: They had embezzled their investment "capital" from the Erie Railroad. The crash came when, out of suspicion or spite, President Grant ordered the U.S. Treasury to dump $4 million in gold and flood the market. Gould and Fisk survived, but the great majority of Americans who had speculated on gold were ruined overnight.

Henry had a front-row seat at the bloodletting. At Kurzman's firm, he saw the victims firsthand: No one with a stake in a bank, a building, or precious metals was safe. For Henry, it was a priceless schooling. When Kurzman foreclosed on a row of houses on West Thirty-ninth Street, Henry got an early lesson in real estate: Evictions were inevitable. He witnessed a line of women being carried out from the buildings. "Many of the tenants owned only a mattress and a few chairs," he would recall, "and no kitchen utensils of any kind." Often, they had paid their rents "in installments of less than one dollar."

Soon, he got a second lesson—in rent collection. At 218 Chrystie Street, another of Kurzman's properties, one rough block east of the Bowery, the tenants were Irish and German, newly arrived and, more often than not, reluctant to part with what little money they had. It was a narrow building with a storefront occupied by a saloon. For Kurzman, the investment had become an albatross and the saloonkeeper, Mr. Ryan, a volatile adversary. The bar was always crowded, no matter the hour.

Henry was not yet seventeen, and remained a slight, undersized boy. But for an extra five dollars a week, he agreed to brave Mr. Ryan, knock on every door, and gather in the monies.

Henry had become a debt collector—a service he would soon perform for his father as well. Ever the gambler, Lazarus carried a new set of calling cards. "Purveyor to Their R.H. the Grand Dukes of Baden and Hessen" he called himself, a "General Agent" registered to sell German and Austrian "*Staatspapieren und Obligationen,*" securities and bonds. He printed elegant handbills and placed advertisements in the German newspapers, offering "*Anlehens-Loose*"—bonds that doubled as lottery tickets. The securities were dubious, but familiar to his clients. For years, the European states had exploited such bonds, low denominations with lower interest rates, to shore up depleted government coffers.

Lazarus's scheme was simple. Any bondholder was entitled, as his circulars announced, "to a chance in the drawing of prizes every three months." One bond, he would claim, had yielded a win of 25,000 florins (guilders). Lazarus sold his *Loose* as "New Year's gifts" and staged the drawings as spectacles, fashionable evenings in the Terrace Garden, the East Side gathering place for Germans that was part concert pavilion, part beer hall. In other hands, the *Loose* might have brought quick riches. For Lazarus, they brought only trouble. He could sell the bonds with ease. But he left collecting the monies owed him to Henry.

|||||

By 1871, Boss Tweed, grand sachem of Tammany Hall, was at last headed for a downfall. Tweed had reigned as the unassailable ruler of the Manhattan political machine for years. In *Harper's Weekly,* the cartoonist Thomas Nast almost single-handedly indicted Tweed, caricaturing the boss as an ogre gorging on the unwitting populace. Within months, Tweed was jailed, locked away in the Ludlow Street prison that he had built.

As the tales of graft and greed filled the newspapers, Henry's anxiety reached a new height: He feared that his own father had also gone too far. In August, Henry had escorted Lazarus on his annual retreat, traveling by steamer to Sharon Springs, a village upstate known for its mineral waters. As father and son went up the Hudson, Lazarus revealed his dire straits: His debts were rising and the lottery schemes were beyond his control. He promised his son it would come right—"He told me all that was owing him for the '*Loose,*'" Henry wrote in his diary—but the son added another of his father's bleak confessions: "Nobody knows what may happen."

In the fall of 1872, Lazarus tried a desperate ploy. Seeing in the papers that President Grant would be coming to New York, Lazarus delivered a note to the Fifth Avenue Hotel. He sought an audience with the president, offering to exhibit his Golden Books. To his sons' astonishment, Horace Porter, Grant's secretary since the war, replied at once. The president welcomed a meeting.

Henry and his brother Max were right to be taken aback: Grant was not known as a philanthropist. Many of Lazarus's associates, moreover, considered him an anti-Semite. Ever since Vicksburg, when Grant signed Order No. 11, expelling Jews from the military district under his command, he had been scorned by Jews across the country. But the president had offered a mea culpa, and in New York made a friend of a prominent Jewish leader: Joseph Seligman, the banker whose brother ran the Hebrew Fair. Grant, running for reelection, was also hoping to recapture the Jewish vote that he had won in 1868. Whether it was mere curiosity or politics, the president decided to give the unknown German a hearing.

Shortly before noon on September 24, 1872, Lazarus, Max, and Henry took a carriage downtown. They wore their finest outfits. In the lobby, "Max sent up his card and we were admitted immediately," Henry would record in his diary that night. After Grant asked them to be seated, Max spoke "about the institutions and objective of the books." The conversation did not last long but ended with Grant "subscribing" to the Golden Books. A presidential audience could not rival a royal visit, but Lazarus turned giddy.

"I hope you will be president again," he said, as Max translated. "And live a hundred years more."

Henry left unimpressed. Grant more closely resembled "one who cannot count three, or one of those salt sailors," and "very little like a person who is the representative of such a large & intelligent and world famed republic." At sixteen, Henry thought he saw through the president. "The man is a mere tool, in the hands of the party," he wrote. "And I am sure Horace Porter does more of the presidential duties than Grant does."

Though Grant won reelection, and Lazarus worked hard to reap the dividends of his meeting, the afterglow did not last long.

Henry Morgenthau was seventeen when the Panic of '73 hit, but it would shape much of his life to come. "No man who lived through the

Panic," Henry would write, "can ever forget it." When word spread that Cooke & Co.—"in many respects the greatest house of the time"—was tottering, Henry was at work two blocks away in Kurzman's office. For years, Jay Cooke, financier of Grant's army, had tried to complete the Northern Pacific Railroad, which would run from the Great Lakes to Puget Sound. Kurzman was deep in "N.P." bonds, lured like so many by 8.5% returns. On the morning that Cooke shuttered his office, Kurzman fell into shock. Chaos descended as stocks plummeted.

Henry rushed to German Uptown Savings, where his savings totaled $80. As he stood in line to make a deposit, Henry looked into the teller's cage and saw "the president of the bank in very earnest conversation with three other men." He could not make out the words, but he sensed the fear. As he reached the teller, Henry did an about-face. On impulse, he emptied his account. Three days later, the bank collapsed.

The crash yielded the first depression of the industrial age. In the city, laborers were paid in scrip, the poor sought shelter in railway stations, and court cases—even murder trials—were postponed. In rural America, grain prices sank so low that farmers burned corn to stave off the cold. It was an inauspicious time to be starting out, but Henry had a plan: He had been reading law books in his spare hours. At the time, anyone who passed the entrance exams could attend law school. It would not come easily; he would have to earn his way through, while skirting the distractions of an increasingly erratic father. But Henry now set his mind on becoming a lawyer.

No sooner had he decided than he hit a setback. The long hours at Kurzman's had taken a toll. In the dark, smoke-filled office, Henry developed eyestrain. He suffered headaches, had trouble focusing his eyes, and feared a loss of sight. The doctor prescribed a "sea voyage."

There could be only one destination. In the summer of 1874, Henry returned to Germany. There were no savings for luxuries, but Henry spotted an ad in a German-language newspaper for a bargain freighter voyage: "thirty days for thirty-five dollars." His host would be Carl Simon, the younger brother of his sister Pauline's husband. Henry sailed to Hamburg, then traveled north to Kiel, the Prussian seaport.

The Franco-Prussian War had recently ended in a Prussian victory, and Kiel was awash in an exultant martial spirit. Everywhere he heard a new phrase: "the doctrine of world power." When the kaiser arrived to christen the *Friedrich der Große,* the first ship of the new German empire, Henry joined the crowds—the spectacle, he wrote years later, that marked "the very beginning of that colossal preparation for war."

At eighteen, Henry found himself an American stranger in his old *Heimat*. In Kiel that summer he witnessed not only the Prussian revival but a world far beyond the law offices of New York. For the first time, urged on by his adventuresome host, he went out on the town. A diary entry on August 18, 1874, even records a visit to a brothel:

> went walking out on the northern part of Kiel along the Knooper-weg. Saw the drum corps practice. . . . In the evening went to No. 60 Dammenstrasse, a house of ill repute which was very finely fitted up. We took some Brause lemonade and I felt very bashful and awkward.

The evening among the prostitutes appears to have remained no more than a sightseeing adventure, yet it was only one of a series of events that left a rift between guest and host. Still, the trip to Germany did have its desired effect: After four months, Henry's eyes improved. Equally important, the return to the homeland also yielded an unexpected turn: His gauzy memories of Mannheim receded. The Germans he met, Henry would write, "were not the easygoing people that I remembered from my earlier boyhood." His diary records how he had "some difficulty in becoming friendly with a pensioned wounded army captain," who saw Henry as a young American and held him "personally responsible" for the matériel that America had sold the French during the war. Such hostility to America, the first Henry had ever heard from a German, was hard to fathom. And it would linger.

| | | |

Henry came home by summer's end with renewed energy. In the fall, he won a job with Chauncey Shaffer, one of the city's top criminal lawyers. Shaffer was a master in court. The lead defense counsel in thirty-four murder cases, he could claim a record streak—successfully avoiding a first-degree conviction in each. An advance on clerkships, the job afforded Henry an entrée to a grander stage. Shaffer had recently settled into the new Bennett Building, a landmark of modernity in the city. James Gordon Bennett, Jr., who had taken over *The New York Herald* from his father, hoped that the building—seven stories tall with large windows to let in the light—would lure New York's top financiers and lawyers. To Henry's delight, Shaffer's office doubled as a kind of club-house; there he met many of the men who years later eased his climb. If Jewish merchants dominated Kurzman's orbit, Shaffer's circle ran from old-line New York Protestants to Irish Catholic immigrants. Colonel Henry A. Gildersleeve, born on a Dutchess County farm, was a regular, as was Henry Purroy, the young Irish lawyer who would soon become a Tammany boss. In time, Purroy would undergo a rare evolution: As president of the Board of Aldermen, he would take on Tammany and install his nephew, John Purroy Mitchel, as the "boy mayor" of New York.

In Shaffer's office, Henry also came to know a bright law student from Dublin: Bourke Cockran was a natural politician who would hold forth on Saturdays when the clerks did little but trade courthouse gossip. Henry never saw Cockran "poring over Blackstone or Kent," the classic legal texts, but he, too, learned from Shaffer's adroit oratory. Within a decade, Cockran would rise in Democratic circles, serving in Congress before becoming a national power broker. All the avenues for Henry's rise ran through Shaffer's office.

His plan was now in motion. By fall, Henry would attend law school at Columbia and pay for it himself. Thanks to lobbying by those he met at Shaffer's, he won an instructor's slot at an evening school. By September 1875, Henry was teaching English—$15 a week—in the *Abendschule* of the Nineteenth Ward. Founded for Germans, the school was now overrun with names such as O'Toole, Mooney, Fitzgerald, Quinn, Coughlin, and Mullin. They were laborers—carpenters and brakemen, stonecutters and butchers, coachmen and blacksmiths. Henry would teach there throughout his first year of law school. Watching the men turn up in his classroom each night, eyes washed out and clothes threadbare, made him work all the harder during the day. Forty-third Street on the East Side had yet to be cut through. Much of the neighborhood remained rock, one of the roughest corners of the city, where squatters had set up a shantytown. Many among his students, Henry noted in admiration, were "denizens of the rocks."

Perhaps it was the hours spent among the rough-hewn immigrants. Or maybe it was his entry into the halls of Columbia, or the flood of corruption and cries for reform arising from the bitter presidential contest between Samuel Tilden and Rutherford Hayes. But by 1876 something had changed. Henry always possessed drive. Now he found direction—and his voice. In July, as America celebrated its first century, he drafted a long essay entitled "A Centennial Reminiscence." Across eight pages in tightly wound cursive, he let loose a scathing critique of his own family. The document, which would remain private, served a second purpose: It was the twenty-year-old's own declaration of independence.

"The Family as now said by some of the folks, was never so low & its prospects so poor," Henry writes. A single cause, as he saw it, lay behind their woes: "They have lived beyond their means for the last few years." They were like the "animals" who foolishly luxuriate in "the autumn air," instead of storing food for winter—"& when winter comes they have to starve."

From his eldest brother, Max ("I do not think he has $500 of his own & yet he lives at the rate of $2500" a year), to the Chicago clothier Gustave ("He goes and plays billiards, whores and makes love to the store girls"), down to nine-year-old Richard (who had a "bad habit of lying and stealing which ought to be broken")—no Morgenthau escaped Henry's lash. His anger encompassed all, spouses included. (Within a decade of arriving in New York, Lazarus and Babette had presided over five weddings.) Henry had yet to give his opinion of Ida or her husband, William, when he quit. "There is no use of writing as I am sick to go further."

| | | |

The following spring, after four years of clerking, teaching, and studying, Henry graduated from Columbia. In June 1877, at twenty-one, he gained admission to the bar.

When Kurzman went to Europe on business, he asked Henry to return to the firm, if only temporarily. It proved a stroke of luck. Henry Behning, a German piano manufacturer and one of Kurzman's main clients, fell out with his partner. When the top lawyer in Kurzman's office could not decode Behning's broken English, he asked Henry to tell him that a German-speaking attorney would better serve him. Behning looked at Henry and said, "All right, I'll take you."

In the spring of 1878, when Behning's fight with his former partner threatened to destroy the company, Henry threw the company into bankruptcy. He checkmated the former partner, salvaging a handsome settlement.

Behning was overjoyed, but had no money for legal fees. Instead, he offered Henry shares in a company he was just incorporating. At the time, Steinway and the best piano makers depended on ivory. But ivory was scarce, and therefore expensive. Behning had hit on an idea to cover piano keys with celluloid, the world's first synthetic plastic, developed nearly a decade earlier in Albany. Behning offered Henry a single share in the new enterprise, the Celluloid Piano Key Company. Before long, when a New York trader cornered the market in ivory, the price of a set of ivory keys spiked to $30, and Henry realized his good fortune. Suddenly, celluloid keys were in demand. Behning needed keen young men. Henry had so impressed the piano maker that he took him on as secretary of the company, at the fat salary of $25 a week.

Even in those first months after law school, Henry checked out potential partners. Behning had given him a head start, but he knew he had to be careful. One afternoon, out on a boat on the Harlem River, Henry had learned a lesson. Alfred McIntyre, a native New Englander and one of the best conveyancers in the city, ran the title department at Kurzman's. He had been fond of Henry since Henry's days as an errand boy. A towering man, over six feet and nearly 250 pounds, McIntyre liked to row the Harlem River on weekends. One Sunday, he asked Henry to join him. "I was to do the rowing," Henry recalled. Their skiff had scarcely moved fifty yards before he realized he "could not pull such a load and get anywhere." The imbalance was "an omen." On the spot, he resolved to choose a partner "of my own age and weight," someone who could "do some of the pulling."

That winter, Henry received a visit from a Columbia classmate. Abraham Goldsmith confided that he and another old classmate, Samson Lachman, were setting up a firm. Henry and Goldsmith had been friends since City College. Lachman was not a close classmate, but Henry had heard him speak at graduation and envied his eleven Columbia prizes. The three lawyers, none older than twenty-three, soon struck a deal. On New Year's Day 1879, they opened their doors at 243 Broadway, a half block from where Lazarus had entertained his first customers in the Rathskeller twelve years earlier.

4. "True Happiness"

1880-1883

Whatever doubts he still had disappeared almost as soon as Henry opened his doors. New York City, he was certain—and not a lost *Heimat,* or a narrow patch of ancient desert half a world away—would be his promised land.

New York presented itself, Henry wrote, as a place where "every single man in the leity [*sic*] can rise to as high a position as he chooses, if he . . . actually does put his shoulder to the wheel." Anyone, no matter his station, could rise to untold heights. The city seemed a utopia— a world built on the distinctly American virtues, as he had first encountered them at the grammar school in Brooklyn, of competition and hard work. No other city—not "San Francisco, Chicago or St. Louis"— offered such a "substantial & positive future for gaining Empires."

Lachman, Morgenthau & Goldsmith started out like many firms of its day. Henry, Sam, and Abe took whatever business they could, scarcely earning enough to meet expenses. In court, Henry found he enjoyed trying cases, and by year's end, he had scored his first victory. It was a humbling triumph. So taken was he with the sound of his own voice, Henry had carried on arguing, stopping only after the judge admonished him, "I've already ruled in your favor."

Henry, though, unbeknownst to his partners, was marshaling his time, and his savings. By early 1880, he had stored away enough to buy his first investment property: No. 32 West Thirty-fifth Street, "a twenty-two-foot, white marble, high-stoop" brownstone, steps away from Fifth Avenue. He called the $15,000 price "modest," and within months resold it at "an advance of $500." He had not only turned a good profit but found a new pursuit. That spring, he spent every spare hour scouring the city for his next target. Within a year, he had discovered it: Harlem, in particular 125th and 126th streets, the broad prospects lined with shops and row houses. "Nearly all of Harlem was for sale," Henry remembered. Block after block of the stone and brick houses built a decade earlier had passed to mortgagees, while those who owned the houses were "thoroughly discouraged and could see little hope in the future." Henry moved slowly, only after exhaustive deliberation. And he set himself a simple formula: He would buy only adjoining houses, plots of three to five houses at a time, and quickly resell them at small profits. It was a bold start. Seeking independence, Henry had found his own ladder, started on the bottom rung—and begun to climb.

||||

The drive for self-improvement and self-denial soon merged in a new quest: At twenty-six, Henry resolved to find a wife. He surveyed the pool of candidates, the girls who frequented the Harmonie Club and Freundshaft Verein, social domains of the Jews barred from the Protestant clubs of the city. The Harmonie on Forty-second Street was the oldest and most exclusive of the "Hebrew clubs," while the Freundschaft, or Friendship Society, founded three years earlier, boasted an elegant clubhouse on Seventy-second Street at Park Avenue. Henry took to spending his hours after work in the clubs' gaming rooms—and in the ladies' parlors.

With characteristic precision, he drew up a list—406 girls—and tallied their merits. The candidates had one commonality: They were daughters of elite German-Jewish families, all members of Our Crowd. Henry kept the ledger meticulously. He noted as engagements narrowed the pool, and as always, he sought to leave as little room as possible for risk.

Still, Henry knew the hurdles on the path to marriage, and none were higher than those put up by his father. At sixty-seven, Lazarus had abandoned the insurance business, but he refused to retire. He insisted on plying his Golden Books and hosting the bond lotteries. His children no longer worried solely about his finances. They feared for his sanity. In the surviving diaries, there is no explicit report of violence, nor in the news accounts that would appear in the years to come. Yet throughout the family letters, the alarm rings clear: Lazarus had turned belligerent, his relations with Babette reaching a breaking point. Their father was in danger, Henry warned his siblings, of losing all restraint. His brothers and sisters were split on what to do, but Henry forced his father's hand: Lazarus and Babette, after nearly four decades of marriage, would be separated—physically, if not legally.

It was a dire measure. Divorce among German Jews was out of the question at the time, and even separations were rare. Babette remained loyal, unwavering in her love, but she consented. Henry had made the separation possible, buying his mother a small brownstone on 126th Street. For Babette, it was yet a further step down, but she found a consolation: In the backyard she could make a small garden, the plot of green that she had yearned for since leaving Germany.

Henry, at the same time, forged ahead. With his law practice taking root, and Babette out from under Lazarus's roof, he quickened his pace. A year after earning his "first real estate profit," Henry made his "first *good* real estate profits." Only one challenge, as he saw it, remained: to find a life partner for the climb to come.

Of the candidate-brides on his roster, Henry made a checkmark beside a number of names—a sign that he deemed them worthy. Several he awarded two marks. Only one did he give three. Josephine Sykes caught his eye the moment that they met. On January 11, 1882, a Wednesday evening in the depths of a long winter, he and his brother Julius went to a friend's on Fifty-second Street. "Was introduced to Miss Jo. Sykes," Henry wrote in his diary that night, adding that he "had a very nice time." Within days, he was back at the house, eager for another glimpse. Josie, as Henry soon took to calling her, did not seem a perfect match. Seven years younger, barely nineteen, she could not flaunt any academic laurels, and though not unattractive, she was hardly a beauty. She was shorter than many of her friends, with stern deep-set eyes and a pronounced hawk nose—the striking feature that future generations would, in error, call "the Morgenthau nose." Her social standing, moreover, was suspect: Her father had died two years earlier, leaving Mrs. Helen Sykes, a formidable woman whose considerable wealth was paired with a suspicious nature, alone with nine children.

In those first gatherings, Josie did not set the room aglow. She possessed neither winning repartee nor an incandescent smile. But Josie wielded a power that no other girl on his list could claim. She seemed capable, almost from the first, of seeing inside Henry Morgenthau. Josie saw the outsized ambition, understood the drive for self-perfection—and embraced it as her own.

It had not been a chance meeting. Henry had recruited a "reading circle"—a small group of young men and women, who would discuss the popular philosophical and literary works of the day. They gathered first at the home of Carrie Rosenfeldt, a twenty-year-old daughter of Bavarian Jews, at 65 West Fifty-second Street, just off Sixth Avenue. Josie lived in the middle of the block, at No. 36. Henry earnestly wished to study the texts, but the "circle" also offered a rare opportunity. Text in hand, he could gain an intimate vantage point on his most desirable candidate-brides.

Within a week, on January 19, 1882, the group reconvened. Emerson was on the menu (his essay on "Social Aims"), and Josie Sykes was again in attendance. This time, though, a star of their social set joined the five men and women in the room: Settie Lehman. A year younger than Josie, Settie had been raised in Selma, Alabama, a daughter of Mayer Lehman, youngest of the three brothers who ran a cotton trading company there before the Civil War. In 1867, Mayer Lehman had come to New York, and by 1882, the family firm—Lehman Brothers—had gained prominence. Settie's name was among those on Henry's roster, and decades later, she would reappear in his life, playing a decisive role in the Morgenthau family saga. But on that evening in the winter of 1882, as he and his friends settled into their Emerson, Henry had already set his sights elsewhere.

Josie was heavily defended. Samuel Sykes, her father, had died young, at fifty-six. The family remained shaken, and Mrs. Sykes was keenly aware of her vulnerability. She had been born Helen Himmelreich (or Heavenrich, as the family's English branch translated the surname) in Bavaria, and married a clothier born to Jewish immigrants, who were said to have come from the north of Germany. By 1853, Samuel and Helen had moved to Detroit. On the eve of the Civil War, Samuel hit on a windfall: a contract to outfit the Michigan state militia. After the war, still in his thirties, he'd cashed out, selling the business and taking his family abroad. Josie had been born in Stuttgart, before they returned to America. Settling in New York, Samuel had again taken up clothing manufacturing, opening a workshop downtown. But in 1880, on a return visit to England, he'd suffered a fatal heart attack.

Mrs. Sykes had long since grown wary of suitors. Henry was no exception. By all accounts, she took a strong and instant dislike to the brash young lawyer. She had good cause to be protective. Her household had servants—a Bavarian governess and two young Irish maids—but she ruled a family even "more expansive" than the Morgenthaus, as Henry wrote to his sister Ida. Of her nine children, six were girls—all but the eldest at home. Samuel had saved a small fortune, but Mrs. Sykes faced the delivery of five dowries.

Nothing, though, could dissuade Henry. Almost from his first days in Brooklyn, he had seen the need to marry up, to skip several rungs on the ladder—much as Lazarus and his grandfather Moses had done in the old country. In Josie Sykes, Henry found not only a woman who accepted his ambitions as her own, but one whose family presented him with a chance to rise by every imaginable measure.

| | | |

It was an accelerated courtship—nights out at the theater, the opera, the "Emerson evenings," as they called the evening salons—and one, given the Victorian mores of the time, that risked running aground. It was a question not only of the speed, but of the bridegroom's father. Throughout the summer, with Babette abroad visiting a German health spa, Henry steered clear of Lazarus. Night after night, he took refuge elsewhere. Often, as his notes record, he "slept Harlem"—at the house he had purchased for his mother. Or he ended his day at "334 W 46"—home of his brother-in-law's family, the Ehrichs. For Henry, the large house on Forty-sixth Street, occupied now only by Mrs. Ehrich, matriarch of the merchant family, and one of her four sons, had become his primary shelter. It was a tiring merry-go-round, but Henry refused to allow Lazarus to intervene in his life.

As fall approached, two events signaled a new beginning—one for the world, the other for the Morgenthaus. On September 4, 1882, at precisely three o'clock in the afternoon, an electrician threw a switch in lower Manhattan and a current surged underground across fourteen miles of cable. As three thousand incandescent lamps flickered on across the southern end of the city, the thirty-five-year-old inventor, Thomas Alva Edison, with J. P. Morgan his sponsor, inaugurated the world's first permanent electric power plant. Edison's beacons spelled the end of gas lamps, and the years of depression as well. The market would see a revival, and Morgan—his headquarters at 23 Wall Street were in the first building lit by the bulbs—would lead the resurgence.

The second event came two days later. On September 6, 1882, after more than nine months away, Babette Morgenthau came home from Europe. She had stayed abroad as long as she could, but two weddings awaited her arrival. Her daughter Minna, as long feared, had died young—at age twenty-eight, four years earlier. On the day after Babette's return, Recha, her youngest daughter, married Minna's widower, and within weeks, another union was set. Gus Morgenthau had followed Max, the eldest son, to Chicago. Max had done well there, bringing the New York emporium craze west and emulating his in-laws, the Ehrichs. Morgenthau Bros. & Co. had opened that spring on a downtown corner, and almost immediately found, as one Chicago chronicler noted, "phenomenal success." Once derided as the family ne'er-do-well, Gus had gained a stable footing. He was now engaged to Julia Mayer, one of the most-sought-after girls in the Chicago branch of Our Crowd. Julia was not only a beauty, but the eldest daughter of Nathan Mayer, one of the city's wealthiest clothiers.

On November 2, 1882, when Gus Morgenthau and Julia Mayer were wed, it was a small affair, but the Morgenthaus rejoiced: The Chicago expansion foretold a new stability. Henry served as best man, the champagne flowed, and the dancing lasted until late. Nathan Mayer had hosted a lavish feast, but no one could forget the absence of Lazarus, who remained in New York. For Babette, though, it was a rare night of joy. And for Henry, too, the celebration was a welcome respite, and a chance to consider his next move.

| | | |

In Chicago, Henry had discussed his courtship with his brothers and tried to chart a way forward. But for the first time in his life, he confessed that reason escaped him. Henry was in love.

On November 22, 1882, at two in the morning, he scrawled a note to himself. "To look things plainly in the face," he wrote, weighing his chances of winning Josie's hand, "I have no right to think of it." He then ranked his shortcomings: "I am still a wavering unsettled character"; "I am neither lawyer nor a man possessed of a business"; "My character is such that it leads with extravagant expenses at first and then the feelings of regret and uneasiness will follow." He worried, too, that he might be mistaken about Josie. "We know each other not ten months," he wrote. "These feelings have been too greatly encouraged by well-meaning friends, all of whom are insanely inclined towards match-making."

As his fears raced on, Henry began to see the decision more clearly. It was not a choice of the right bride, but between a life of "great good" or "failure." "I must first work out and develop my character," he chastised himself. "Am I going to complete its simplicity and the reliance upon myself, books, thoughts and small number of friends for happiness or will I allow myself to drift on amidst society & the distracting uncertainty of what my aim is & thus lead a meaningless aimless life." He was desperate to calm his nerves, but vowed not to rush. "The very process of doubting and waiting will be purifying," he wrote. "True happiness will follow." Sitting in darkness, Henry gave himself an order: "Shake off this baneful influence, and be your own engineer—if she is for me our happiness will be tenfold if well deserved."

By the following Sunday, Henry could take no more. In the evening, he called at the Sykes residence. As he dined with Josie and his sister Ida's brother-in-law, Julius Ehrich, Henry gave nothing away. But after supper, once they were alone, Henry proposed—and won Josie's acceptance. He could not rest: Josie posed one challenge, her mother another. In the whirlwind that followed, Henry scarcely slept, worried much, and tried in vain to soften up Mrs. Sykes.

A note sent from Josie's brother Willie, eldest of the three Sykes boys, a day later was blunt: "Mrs. Sykes opposes." Josie's mother fumed that Henry had dared to carry on a courtship without her knowledge. Henry turned to Julius Ehrich for help. At Delmonico's, they talked over the ominous turn, and that night Julius invited Henry to sleep at the Ehrich home. They stayed up late, searching for a solution. That night, he "did not sleep at all."

| | | |

Days passed in a blur. Henry wrote Josie a feverish letter, pleading for an audience to make his case, but her mother refused. Not only did his brashness offend her, his lack of wealth and standing worried her. Worse, Henry's greatest fear had come to pass: Mrs. Sykes knew the truth about Lazarus. Her daughter would never fall prey to the whims of a man prone to madness. Josie's mother forbade the two to see each other.

In shock, Henry scrawled another note. "My own dear Josie," he wrote. "It seems a very strange engagement between us. Here I am bubbling over with the most sincere, unselfish love for you & have no chance to tell you so." Henry resorted to intermediaries, relatives who slipped letters beneath closed doors. "I am willing to forego all other ambitions," he wrote Josie, "for the one to make you happy."

By December 10, one week after proposing, Henry seized on a new plan. If Josie's mother refused to listen, he would launch a counterattack. "I propose to carry the fortress by assault," he wrote, "& my methods of warfare do not permit waiting to be attacked." He cast aside Josie's brother—"a child compared to me"—and elected instead to use her brother-in-law, Charles Weil, a successful businessman, as a secret mediator.

On Monday, Henry and Weil met at the Celluloid office downtown. His diary omits the details, but the events that followed make clear that Josie's brother-in-law was won over: The two lunched, visited Henry's law office, and stopped by the Safety Deposit Company, confirming the finances were in place. "Everything," Henry wrote in a note to himself, was arranged "satisfactorily." At 8:10 that evening—he recorded the time—he returned to the Sykes residence. This time, Mrs. Sykes received him. He chose his words with care and overcame her remaining doubts—chiefly about his father. For the rest of the evening, Henry was left alone with his beloved. The skies had cleared. That night Henry and Josie—as he recorded in his diary—enjoyed their first kiss.

On the following morning, a cold Wednesday in December, he steeled himself and went to see Lazarus at the brownstone on the East Side. As expected, his father raised one objection after another: The girl lacked a father, her mother would be overbearing, the pair hardly knew each other. But Henry refused to listen. He returned to his mother, taking Babette to see Mrs. Sykes. The meeting of the mothers went well enough: Within a day, a notice appeared in the *Staatszeitung,* the broadsheet known as *die Staats* that served as the paper of record for the Germans of Manhattan. The engagement was official and, by the strictures of Josie and Henry's world, irreversible.

| | | |

The new year opened with stirrings of love and hope. Henry had wrested control of his future, yet remained fearful of Lazarus's mercurial ways. A wedding, given the fractured state of the family, was bound to bring trouble. For weeks, he agonized, searching for a way to ensure the day would not be ruined. Yet again, Henry devised a plan—and he set about to enlist the support of as many of his brothers and sisters as he could.

On Saturday, March 3, 1883, the day Henry and Josie celebrated their engagement's "¼ year anniversary," as he put it, he took the first step. That morning Henry took Lazarus to an asylum. "Bloomingdale's," as the clinic amid the trees of White Plains was known, was where the mentally ill of New York were dispatched for treatment. Lazarus, by all accounts, did not resist. He was not being packed off indefinitely, only for a few months, and few outside the family would know. The plan entailed a second step: to get Babette out of the city as well. If Lazarus were to miss the ceremony, Henry had decided, Babette must also. It would not be right for her to attend without her husband. So on March 22, Henry put his mother on a train to Chicago. Babette acquiesced: She would be away just long enough for Josie and Henry to be wed in peace.

Things, though, took an unexpected turn. After four weeks, the doctors let Lazarus out. Whether they deemed him healthy or he had once again plied his charm, Lazarus won a release. Henry, perhaps acting on doctors' orders, did not bring his father home, but took him instead to a hotel off Washington Square—and left him there.

In Chicago, Babette was shaken. "It is hard for me to know that Papa is in New York by himself," she wrote, "and I can do nothing for him."

For a week, Lazarus rested. Then, with renewed strength, he decided to make his own demands known. On a Saturday night, April 7, 1883, he appeared at the Sykes doorstep on Fifty-second Street. To Henry's surprise, Mrs. Sykes received him. Lazarus held court for hours, unspooling glorious tales of his Mannheim days. Henry and Josie were in the house as well, but the scene was too much to bear. They spent the evening upstairs "reading and talking," and managing to "amuse" themselves. Lazarus did not leave until near midnight, trying the limits of Mrs. Sykes's forbearance. Determined to forestall the marriage, he had produced his long-predicted spectacle.

In the days that followed, Henry continued to see Josie. But Lazarus's reappearance unnerved him. On April 9, Henry offered a compromise: He would ask his father to meet with an intermediary. Mr. H. C. Gordon, the insurance man who years earlier had given Lazarus a desk in his office, would hear out both sides—and bear witness to Henry's final warning. For two hours in Gordon's presence, Henry ridiculed his father, and warned Lazarus that "he ran the risk of being arrested for lottery business."

And "if any lawsuits were begun," Henry vowed, he would disown the Morgenthau name.

| | | |

Once again, civil war threatened to rend the family. Bertha, the eldest sister, now a widow in Paterson, came to Lazarus's aid. After Bloomingdale's, she had taken him in and written to her siblings in her father's defense. To Henry, such sympathy made his sister an enemy. "Not a single line of Bertha's letter is true," he warned his brother Max in a letter on April 12, 1883. "Bertha will write whatever LM"—Lazarus—"tells her. . . . She does her utmost to incite father against all. LM is not at all angry at you, but in his insanity he does not know what he says."

Lazarus, for his part, saw Henry's engagement as the last straw. His other sons may have been rash in moving out from his house. Chicago, Ohio, San Francisco—none of their destinations won his blessings. But Henry's impending marriage was a betrayal. No one had consulted him, and it was his obligation to defend his family. Lazarus had gone to see Mrs. Sykes and her son Willie to turn them against Henry. He had demanded, as Henry learned, a boycott of the wedding. He'd pleaded that they "not invite any of the family . . . or he"—Lazarus—"would have nothing to do" with the Sykeses. Lazarus, in fact, recognized what had happened during his time at Bloomingdale's: In his absence, he had lost control of the family. Henry and Josie's union would mark the final division.

Josie's mother could ignore the ravings, but Henry fumed. "If he is sane & makes that demand," he wrote to Max of their father, "he is too contemptible to be spat upon."

Henry was not only worried about his wedding day. He feared for his mother. Babette was agitating to return to New York—and to Lazarus. They had weathered storms in the past, she told her children, and she had always resumed her place by his side. But Henry was convinced it was no longer merely a matter of emotional torment. Their father, he wrote Max, "hates" Babette "most bitterly and is fit to do her all sorts of harm were he to come into contact with her." "Mama," he insisted, "must stay away for the present."

For days Henry wrestled with his conscience. "I myself again thought I could appeal to his better nature and bring him around," he wrote, "but to my sorrow I find he has no better nature." As he searched for a way to protect his mother, Henry worried not only about ethics—but also about the family's standing. "I have made it my business to ask about 5 of my acquaintances what the community say about the matter," he told Max, "& all of them tell me . . . it is all in our favor & that he is universally considered insane. You can therefore rest perfectly easy on that score." Henry arrived at the only solution: a total separation. Babette should stay in Chicago, and Lazarus be sent back to Bloomingdale's and, if need be, confined there against his will.

| | | |

In the second week of April, Henry wrote Babette. "Let us have a serious talk now," he began. The letter, written in German, was painful. "It would not be advisable," Henry wrote, to come home. "Papa makes various threats which he wants to carry out if you would come here." It was "terrible" that Lazarus was "spoiling everything," but "as long as I know you are not in danger," he assured Babette, "I will be content." "How much my heart cries at the prospect of having to marry without you being present, you can scarcely imagine. But . . . at all costs there must be peace."

On the bright morning of May 8, Henry at last won a reprieve.

"Papa," he told Josie, "has concluded not to come" to the wedding.

In Chicago on the same day, Babette drafted a long letter to the engaged couple. She had been blessed with many children, but Henry, she now confessed, was the favorite. "If the saying comes true, that 'a good son will be a good husband,'" she wrote Josie, "you can look the future in the eye with confidence." "Because," she went on, "without offending anyone, there is no better son than Henry."

> I can claim with pride that my children are all very good and have always fulfilled their duties towards me to a high degree, but am also entirely convinced that they will all agree with me that Henry was as loving a brother as a son. This praise dictates itself into my quill from my overflowing heart and because I know that you, dear Josie, know and value Henry, I hope that you concur with me and not think me immodest. Just this, that you two understand each other so well and fit together, is for me a guarantee for your future.

Henry and Josie had yet to receive Babette's letter when they sent a telegram to Chicago. "Sincerely regretting your forced absence," they wrote. "We offer you our deepest sympathy and assurances of greatest devotion and affection—and hope to make up the mutual deprivation."

| | | |

On the eve of his wedding, Henry scarcely slept. Lazarus again threatened to ruin the day. Even on the morning of the ceremony, he promised to "create a scandal" at the Sykes house on Fifty-second Street. But

Henry had taken an unusual precaution. He hired Pinkerton men, from the famed detective agency, to shadow his father and, if necessary, prevent him from crashing the wedding.

The operation began on the morning of the wedding day. The surveillance report bore the signatures of Allan Pinkerton, the agency's founder, and his son Robert, head of its New York office. Julius Ehrich, Henry's brother-in-law, had provided a photograph of Lazarus. "At 11 am. Morgenthal," as the detectives called him, "left his residence"—214 East Seventeenth Street, the rooming house where Lazarus was staying. He was in the company of a man in his late thirties, with black hair and a black mustache, and wearing a black derby and suit. They parted ways at Thirty-seventh Street, the unknown man taking the Elevated railroad. Lazarus walked on, the Pinkertons noted, "through 67th Street to Madison Avenue, where he entered the residence of Dr. W. S. Gottheil, 681 Madison." Dr. William Gottheil was the German-born eldest son of Gustav Gottheil, the rabbi who had succeeded Dr. Adler at Temple Emanu-El. At Henry's request, he had taken over Lazarus's care.

All afternoon, they "saw nothing of Morgenthal." At 4:30 P.M., one detective walked to the Sykes house to report Lazarus's whereabouts. One of Josie's brothers instructed him that both detectives should come to the house at five P.M., the start of the ceremony. A uniformed officer would also be at the door, he said, but the detectives should "procure a carriage and have it in readiness in case Mr. Morgenthal might create a disturbance."

At precisely five o'clock in the evening, as the guests were taking their seats ten blocks to the south, Lazarus emerged from Dr. Gottheil's. He was accompanied by a lady and a gentleman whom the Pinkertons took to be the doctor. The three walked to Sixty-second Street and Fourth Avenue, where the doctor left them. "Morgenthal and the lady," detectives recorded, returned to the building on East Seventeenth where he was staying. The Pinkertons proceeded to the Sykes house, arriving at 5:20 P.M. They engaged a coach, and took up positions nearby.

Inside, the celebration was under way. Not all of Henry's sisters and brothers were present: Siegfried was in Philadelphia (a rift over debts widening between the brothers), Julius had joined Ida and her husband, William, in Europe—William, having gone to the Alps on doctor's orders the previous fall, had extended their stay. But six siblings attended, including the youngest, Brooklyn-born Richard, now sixteen. The menu, printed in French, featured eleven courses, none of them kosher: It opened with clams, followed by *Timbales à la Rothschild, Truite de rivière vert pré, filet de Boeuf, Supremes de volaille à la Perigord, Sorbet,* and *Squabs farcis Bécassines,* and ended with sweets, ice cream, and cakes. By eleven o'clock, the Pinkertons had dismissed the coach, but they maintained their vigil. At one in the morning, the guests began to depart, and by two o'clock the house was closed up, and "the watch," wrote Robert Pinkerton, "was then discontinued."

The detectives had "closely observed all parties" arriving at the house, "but Morgenthal did not put in an appearance."

Henry and Josie took a carriage downtown to the Grand Hotel on Broadway. The next day, Josie rested and Henry spent much of the afternoon in the bridal suite writing letters, relating the joys of the day to all who had missed it. "We are now married!" he announced to his brother Julius. "We have had a hard fight & were compelled to submit to a great deal but now we are being amply repaid . . .

"How happy and *blissful* I feel," Henry wrote. "Yes my boy, we understand each other thoroughly & are well matched. I can't realize the fact that I could ever have been happy with any one else—how I would like to write you some of the little reasons why I am daily & hourly becoming more & more infatuated with her but I can't, the pen is not capable of picturing them. They are too delicate & tender."

| | | |

On May 24, two weeks after Henry and Josie were wed, President Chester Arthur arrived in New York to preside over the greatest public party the city had ever seen. After fourteen years and at least three dozen deaths, more than five thousand laborers, who had earned as little as two dollars a day, had finished the job. "The Great Bridge," as the Brooklyn Bridge was known, was open—a soaring cathedral of stone and steel. It had taken three times longer than expected, and cost nearly twice as much as estimated, but on the day of its opening, the bridge held all those who crowded its shores in awe.

For so many in the city, the new bridge marked a time not only of renewal, but of heightened possibility. Henry and Josie were no exception. For days after their wedding, they remained in "higher spheres," as Babette put it in her first letter to the newlyweds. She had heard the news of the wedding day, its melodrama and joy, but focused on the couple's happiness. "It is only important," Babette wrote, "that the two persons most involved are content with each other—and remain so." Forgoing a planned European honeymoon, Josie and Henry traveled instead to the South. They went to Baltimore by train, and then took a steamer to Old Point Comfort in Virginia, the seaside resort at the harbor of Hampton Roads. The Hygeia Hotel, named after the Greek goddess of health, had stood as a stately landmark near Fortress Monroe, in one incarnation or another, since 1820. With room for a thousand, it was hailed as "the largest caravansary of its kind south of New York." With its quarter-mile-long promenade above the Chesapeake Bay, seawater baths, and dancing pavilion where the U.S. Artillery Band played each evening, the hotel lured wealthy Northerners in winter, and Southern aristocrats in summer.

For Josie and Henry, the days passed in delight. "We talk earnestly," Henry wrote his brother Julius, "play childishly, kiss fondly and often, read Gibbon's *Decline and Fall of the Roman Empire* (abridged edition by Smith) and Rau's *Life of Mozart* alternately, play pool, walk along the beach, or into the Fortress & smilingly observe the mimic soldier life they lead here." Henry relished the unexpected pleasures, and recorded them with care: the long strolls on the promenade, the "lullaby" of the waves, and the alacrity with which the barkeeper proffered a Havana cigar. "Altogether it often astonishes us," he wrote, "how quickly the time passes."

They also enjoyed, for the first time in their lives, sex. "Let me state right here," Henry wrote his brother, "that all the self-denial I have practiced for so many years has been more than amply repaid during the past 12 days." Henry was overjoyed, but felt compelled to justify abstaining from intimacy for so long. "The thrill of pleasure, the ecstatic delight at beholding the beautiful, chiseled like form of Josie I can't describe," he wrote. "I never expected to find such a Venus in my wife. But it is as much of a treat to me to look at her as at the finest statue—could this have been so had I been impure?"

Josie, too, was elated. "It has been twelve days since we have been made One," she wrote Julius, the Morgenthau sibling she had come to know best, "and never during my life time have I ever been as thoroughly a child in spirit and in thought, and as such, I should like to say, 'O, I am so happy, and am having such lots of fun'!" She and Henry "never seem to grow tired playing with each other," she reported. "People say that you never understand each other until you have been in each other's company for years, but if there is such a thing as to know one another thoroughly we have accomplished that feat."

Making up for the months of anxiety, Henry and Josie went to bed early, rose late, and ate sumptuously. Yet even as the sea air calmed Henry's nerves, the turbulence at home troubled him. "The six months of my engagement," he wrote Julius, "I passed in a sort of dreamy state—half fearing all the time to be rudely awakened by volcanic eruption from sources but too well known to you." As they toured the Virginia countryside, Henry searched for the lesson in his trials. Fear, he told himself, was a thing of the past. "The afternoon of my wedding day was the closing scene of the old life," he wrote. "I will hereforth never allude to it again."

Henry had found his escape: Josie would save him from scandals, madness, and worry. "No doubt," he wrote Julius, "will ever enter again into my mind as to the Ideal Life we so often hoped to lead—for Josie is as anxious for it as I am." As he headed north again, Henry was buoyant. Come what may, he was certain that Josie would complete him. "With her to urge me on," he wrote of his bride, "there is scarcely anything beyond my capacities."

5. "43, 42, 41"

1884-1892

The sins of the father, Henry had always sensed, would haunt him. Of Lazarus's seven sons, Henry, the middle son, seemed destined to suffer most from his father's capricious ways. In their first year of marriage, Henry and Josie enjoyed respites from the madness, periods when Lazarus seemed to right himself and the doctors would deem him "healthy." During such interludes, Bertha and Pauline, Henry's sisters, would trade turns sheltering their father, but Henry remained vigilant. No matter how often the doctors counseled patience—Lazarus only needed rest and quiet, they said—Henry sought to preserve Babette's health and safety, and keep her at a distance from her husband.

On March 4, 1884, nearly a year after the wedding, as Babette again pined for Lazarus, Henry repeated his concerns. "Dear Mama!" he wrote to his mother, who was still in Chicago, "I don't think that you have missed something by your being not present" in New York. Lazarus, he added, "would have accepted your care, but what would have resulted after he had become healthy again?" His father's "miserliness" had only worsened; he was unable ever to make her happy again. Henry pushed for a last resort: a final, total break. He now hoped, he wrote, "that this will come to pass."

With Josie at his side, Henry had moved forward. He poured himself into his law practice, saw his stake in Behning's piano-key company rise, and received momentous news: Josie was expecting. Henry could not contain his joy. "I am so pleased by the anticipation," he wrote Babette, "that the reality will find it hard to satisfy me."

The prediction proved true: Henry had been desperate for a boy.

Helen Sykes Morgenthau, a baby born with outsized round eyes and auburn curls, arrived on May 27, 1884, days after Henry and Josie's first anniversary—and as, at least in the eyes of her father, a consolation prize. Letters of congratulations arrived, but the expansion of the Morgenthau brood was hardly news. In two decades in America, Lazarus and Babette had seen the arrival of twenty grandchildren—of whom two had died, one as an infant, another at age five. Yet baby Helen's birth was met by a departure from tradition: Babette and Lazarus were separated now; there would be no party to welcome her. For Josie, the final months had brought worry and discomfort. Now as a nurse took charge, she could rest. But Henry's elation, as he'd predicted, soon dimmed. From the day Josie told him of the pregnancy, he had made no secret of it: A girl was a gift, but a son remained his dream.

| | | |

Even as the Morgenthaus set down roots in New York and Chicago, the threat of disaster hovered close. It was not only Lazarus and his decline: In Philadelphia in the fall of 1885, weeks after his thirty-fourth birthday, Siegfried Morgenthau, Lazarus and Babette's second son, died suddenly. The death shocked all, even those in the family who had known Siegfried's worst secrets. Worse still, the news was announced in the most public of places: the front page of *The New York Times*. "A Victim of Opium—Siegfried Morgenthau Takes His Own Life in Philadelphia." The report—given prominence more for its salacious details than the family's status—was riddled with errors, yet contained enough particulars to suggest an intimate source. Someone close to the deceased, if not in his family, had confided in the reporter.

Although the signs had long been coming, Siegfried's death roiled the family. And yet, Henry—the fastidious chronicler—left no mention of his brother's demise, in his diary or elsewhere. From the start Siegfried had led an itinerant life, bouncing from New York to San Francisco to San Antonio, and back. It was a trail without a map, filled with failure and debt. For a time, Siegfried seemed to steady himself, and wrote home of a new start. "I've finally found employment," he wrote from Texas, "and even in a very noble house"—Theodore Schleuning, a German dealer in provisions and wine. Even then, though, Siegfried asked for a loan, vowing to make good on it. For years, his brothers—first Max, then Henry—bailed him out. Yet by the time Siegfried moved to Philadelphia, after a decade of unkept promises, Henry had drawn the line.

No matter how Babette pleaded on Siegfried's behalf, Henry refused to give him any more money.

A day after the scandalous front-page story, a sequel appeared. In two sentences, the *Times* reversed course: Siegfried's "friends," the paper now declared, denied "all intention of suicide on his part." The coroner had held an inquest, and the jury, according to local law, had rendered a verdict. "The deceased gentleman," its members held, had come "to his death from an overdose of opium, taken accidentally." Whether Henry managed to orchestrate the abrupt about-face or not, he, and all the Morgenthaus, could only have been relieved by its appearance. Opium use was scandal enough, but suicide the greater sin. And yet, the *Times* had kindled a fire that the whisperers would fan; the dishonor to the family, Henry knew, would not soon fade.

In the wake of his brother's death, Henry's vision for his own future gained only greater clarity. The years since the Civil War had seen a real estate boom—upper Manhattan was no longer a patchwork of farms and squatters' camps but an evolving grid. Still, even now real estate carried a tinge, a trade beneath the genteel men of Wall Street. It was one thing to draw rents from inherited lands, a Knickerbocker tradition, but to many, to be a "real estate man" was to join the corps of speculators and profiteers. Henry was undeterred: If until then he had been an attorney who dabbled in real estate, now he would dive in more deeply. As the city rose around him, and many sank their money into the "trusted" districts, the commercial blocks of lower Manhattan, Henry again looked north: first to Harlem, then the Bronx. In law he had opted for caution, but now he raced ahead. With each property deal, Henry raised the stakes. And as the risks grew, he found to his delight that the rewards followed in kind.

Henry had good timing, and an ear attuned to the rhythms of the market. In the early 1880s, the city's real estate trade had stalled. "The market rested," he later recalled, "and I did too." By 1885, Henry was worth only $27,000. With the bulk of his holdings in Celluloid Piano Key stock, he had little working capital. So when the markets began to revive, Henry saw only one choice. He turned to William J. Ehrich, his sister Ida's husband, eldest of the Ehrich brothers, convincing his brother-in-law to invest $40,000. William proved an ideal partner: He would leave it to Henry to find the best lots on the market, and stay out of the way.

By 1885, Babette had returned to New York. With Lazarus as unsettled as ever (he'd moved again, now to an apartment house down near Union Square), she returned to the house on 126th Street. As Henry took to visiting the uptown neighborhood, an idea hit. The street one block south was still little known to New Yorkers. Henry walked 125th Street, following its length from river to river, and saw value: It was the first broad street north of Fifty-ninth that ran the breadth of Manhattan. With immigrants flooding the city, he foresaw not only a center of commerce, but the city's northward expansion. "It seemed to me," Henry would write, "like the neck of a funnel into which the whole of the neighboring population was daily poured to reach the Elevated station at 125th Street and Eighth Avenue."

For weeks, he scouted the neighborhood, and consulted the public records. He filled notebooks with detailed tables, charting the city's geometric rise in immigrants and the growth of its factories and plants. Then he made his first big move.

The land was on the northern tip of Manhattan, overlooking Mount Morris Park in the Harlem heights and, until a decade earlier, still farmland. In early 1887, seven years after Henry and his partners opened their law practice, he set his sights on a square block of the city. For as long as anyone could remember, the land had belonged to Anna Ottendorfer, the formidable woman once at the helm of the *Staats-Zeitung*, the German paper, who had also been, until her death three years earlier, a leading philanthropist. Mrs. Ottendorfer's widower, Oswald, the *Staats* reporter who rose to become the paper's editor, handled the deal. For $375,000, Henry won the deeds to thirty-two lots, all facing Mount Morris Park, bounded east and west by Lenox and Mount Morris avenues, and north and south by 120th and 121st streets.

The Ottendorfers were no strangers to the Morgenthaus. Lazarus had long sought to turn Anna into a patroness. She and Lazarus had been born in Bavaria in the same year, but Anna had come to New York three decades ahead of the Morgenthaus. She had married Jacob Uhl, a printer who purchased the *Staats* and oversaw its rise. When Uhl died, Anna refused to sell, and took charge herself. Before long she had married the star reporter, Ottendorfer. Buoyed by the paper's profits, Mrs. Ottendorfer rose to a position of rare power and prominence. More people had attended her funeral, the newsmen claimed, than any other woman's in the history of New York.

While Lazarus tried to curry favor with Anna, Henry studied her holdings. After her death, he reasoned, the family would sell off the land.

Oswald, long retired from the *Staats,* had tried politics—serving as an alderman before failing in a long-shot run for mayor. He and his wife's heirs would demand a fat profit, but Henry struck a novel deal. "I induced the Ottendorfers to split the transaction," he later wrote in triumph. Henry had managed to sever the choicest holdings and keep them for himself: He and his partners bought "the Lenox Avenue front outright" and won "an option on the Mount Morris front"—an option that Henry, in turn, sold at a $10,000 profit to the Kilpatrick brothers, Irish builders who ran a huge lumberyard on the West Side. "Our total profits," Henry tallied, "were $43,424.10." It was a number he would oft enjoy reciting: "43" followed by "42" and "41." (And more than a million dollars in today's money.)

||||

Three weeks later, Henry struck again. As soon as he sold the Ottendorfers' square block, he bought an adjoining one. This time, the Kilpatricks joined in a purchasing group—"the Syndicate," the newsmen termed it. The second deal also yielded thirty-two lots, one block north, also bounded by Lenox and Mount Morris avenues. It was another coup. The old men of the city's real estate trade were shocked—not by the location, but by the identity of the sellers.

John Jacob Astor III owned the land. The deal may have marked the first time, as Henry boasted, "the Astors broke away from their policy of not selling any of their holdings." When it came to the contracts, though, trouble arose. In the first Harlem deal, Henry had had little friction with the Ottendorfers, their ties to the German-Jewish community easing the negotiations. But Henry and the Astors had no such common ground. He had never met the elder baron, nor his sole son, William Waldorf Astor. Thirty-nine at the time, Waldorf, as the young Astor was known, would soon inherit more than $100 million and become the richest man in America. The Astors, moreover, had directed their attorney, Charles Southmayd, to execute the sale—and Southmayd proved a stumbling block. Henry deemed it appropriate that the Astors adopt the terms of the Ottendorfer deal: The Ottendorfers had agreed to a series of separate mortgages, one "on every four lots"—making them easier to sell. The Astors' lawyer, though, refused to accept even "four mortgages on eight lots each, saying that he could not tell which was the most valuable." He demanded that Henry "give him one mortgage," for the balance of the sale price, $240,000.

Henry decided to negotiate with Mr. Astor himself. It would become a lifelong habit: going straight to the top man. He had, on occasion, glimpsed the Astors, father and son, walking on Fifth Avenue, "from their home to their office in 25th Street." The elder Astor, now sixty-four, was hard to miss: A stout figure, six feet tall, he boasted long white whiskers that jutted out over prodigious jowls. One morning, Henry waited and caught sight of the Astors on the sidewalk. He trailed them to their office and wrangled an audience. As Henry related the "plain statement of facts," the old man at first did not budge. But soon his guest coaxed "a smile," at least in Henry's telling, that "broke the severity of the elder's face." In due course, Astor relented. He allowed Henry to draw up separate mortgages, each with a relative value—and all, as Henry later gloated, that "were paid long before they were due."

||||

Henry had only begun his climb, but he had already gained a view from the heights of New York real estate. At the same time, though, for William Ehrich, the brother-in-law who had been more patron than partner, the ascent ended early.

On July 27, 1889, William was found "sunk to the floor" of his stable at Pinehurst, his summerhouse on Lower Saranac Lake in the Adirondacks. Saranac was home to the country's first tuberculosis sanatorium, and all the available evidence indicates that William suffered from the disease. He died at forty-five, leaving Ida and five children. Had he lived, he would have soon seen a dream come true. In September 1889, Ehrich Brothers opened a store on Sixth Avenue. Five stories tall, its granite façade stretching ninety-one feet, it became a landmark on the Ladies' Mile, the city's shopping district. With 100,000 square feet, an interior finished in quartered oak, and five passenger elevators, the new Ehrich Brothers, the *Times* proclaimed, was "a model of its kind."

Henry had lost his benefactor, but he would not quit. After the decade's sluggish opening, the city was alive again with possibility. "Success," Henry would recall of these early days in property speculation, "breeds enterprise." Soon, he again forged ahead—helping to break a logjam that had long stalled the development of the field. For fifteen years, ever since the first Rapid Transit Commission of 1875, the Tammany aldermen and Wall Street bankers had clashed over the route of the first subway lines. The great subway battles consumed wave after wave of political victims but remained unresolved. Until the winter of 1890.

On March 18, 1890, Henry helped to cobble together a new force, fifty-six leaders of the Real Estate Exchange, who petitioned the new man in City Hall to act. Mayor Hugh J. Grant, a Tammany acolyte, thirty years old when inaugurated the previous year, moved so swiftly, and "in obedience to the request of the property owners," that many considered it a prearranged deal. The mayor duly announced a new Rapid Transit Commission, and pronounced himself keen to start construction.

For Henry, the transit commission became an obsession. He sought to learn every detail of the proposed routes, probing its five members and in particular the German émigrés, August Belmont and William Steinway. He also began "to prospect the district" most likely to become the new subway's northern spur. By July 16, 1890, Belmont, the banker who chaired the commission, informed Mayor Grant of its recommendation: to build a four-track subway from lower Manhattan to the Bronx. As Henry canvassed for property, he looked north to the district above 181st Street, known as Washington Heights. For months, he collected maps and circled the potential lots. Money was no longer a problem. His first deals had brought eager investors. But he obsessed about making the right choice. Toward the end of the winter of 1891, he got his chance.

That March, he brought together a group of buyers and in one swoop captured a giant swath of Washington Heights. In the new "Morgenthau Syndicate," Henry expanded his partners—including not only Moses Goldsmith, his law partner's wealthy father, but also John Whalen, a district leader of northern Manhattan, as well as a host of Irish and Scottish bankers and lawyers from the northern neighborhoods. In all, the deal covered 411 lots across four blocks. Henry's fourth large purchase of land carried a purchase price that astonished: $1,000,000.

The Morton-Bliss estate, as the vast property on Washington Hill was called, was formerly owned by General Daniel Butterfield, a Civil War hero who had been caught up in the gold scandal of the Grant administration. Butterfield had sold it to a former governor of New York, Edwin D. Morgan. Governor Morgan died before the deal could be completed, but his executors carried out the contract, paying $450,000 for the land in 1885. Within months, Levi P. Morton and George Bliss had acquired it on the cheap, paying "about $500,000."

On March 27, 1891, for a down payment of only $50,000, the estate became the property of Henry Morgenthau and his partners. As the reporters swarmed, a beaming Henry signed the contracts. He had won, Henry told the man from the *Times,* "the largest tract on Manhattan Island owned by private parties." The news accounts made no mention of one key fact concerning the sale, because everyone knew it: Morton was now the vice president of the United States. If the seller sat at the right hand of President Benjamin Harrison, there could be little doubt that the deal would go through. More important, if Morton attested to the value of the land—as he did, publicly and repeatedly—Henry knew the buyers would need no prodding.

||||

Henry and his partners rushed to capitalize on the attention. In May, all 411 lots would be auctioned off in a single day. A long, dazzling write-up appeared in *The Real Estate Record and Buyers' Guide*. Henry could not have dreamed of better ad copy. "If Washington and his military contemporaries could return to Mother Earth and witness the transformation that has taken place on the Heights," the *Record* gushed, "where they had many a brush with the British soldiery more than a century ago, they would be amazed."

At noon, on May 26, 1891, the auction room of the Real Estate Exchange downtown could hold no more bidders. Henry had prepared for the day with characteristic focus on detail. He visited the bankers, escorted the speculators, and wooed the newsmen. He also convinced the directors of the exchange to display an enormous banner, "60 feet wide by 20 feet high," announcing the sale—for a month. James Gordon Bennett, editor of the *Herald,* who had his own substantial holdings on the Heights, also directed his paper to trumpet the Morgenthau auction. A *Times* advertisement helped, too: The property, it announced, lay just opposite "the new Washington Bridge," and it boldly predicted that "the proposed new rapid-transit line will probably pass the property on the westerly boundary," endowing the lots with a "prospective value" greater than "any other section in the city of New York."

For nearly seven hours on a warm day in late May, the auctioneer called out lot after lot. The bidding, almost from the start, moved quickly. One woman "lost her head early," when a lot on the corner of Audubon Avenue and 180th fell under the hammer. She had bid $5,000 when she meant to offer $3,000. The auctioneer obliged, putting the lot up a second time, and when the corner lots came up, western parcels at Eleventh Avenue and 181st, the bidding hit fever pitch. John Reilly—by no coincidence the former register of deeds and a Tammany veteran—paid the highest price of the day, $12,250, for the southwestern corner lot.

By day's end, the 411 lots had yielded a total of $1,493,975. The prices were steep, but even the savviest real estate men took the view, as one account recorded, "that the bidders were pretty well convinced that one of the new transit routes was going to make the lots easily accessible and to send values up in the neighborhood." Once the bidding closed, Henry announced a radical departure from standard practice: No member of his syndicate, he insisted to the reporters, had bought even one lot. Success had come on popular demand alone. Yet Henry neglected to say that "the Morgenthau Syndicate" had cleared, as the *Times* noted, "a neat little profit of half a million dollars."

| | | |

And yet, the money in fact had only enhanced Henry's private elation. His associates in business had little notion of his most treasured, and undisclosed, dream. To them, Henry seemed poised to claim a singular role in New York real estate—who among the German Jews now outranked him? Only his closest confidants, those few he let in, knew the hunger he rarely spoke of: how much he desired a son. Yet two weeks earlier, as he rushed to finish the last preparations for the auction, the secret was out: The dream had at last come true.

On May 11, 1891, after eight years of marriage and the birth of a second daughter (Alma had been born in 1887), a son arrived. Henry Morgenthau, Jr., would be the last of Josie's children born at home. Henry and Josie lived now in the Beresford Apartments, the original Beresford building that anchored the corner of Eighty-first Street and Central Park West. On the evening before, they had celebrated their wedding anniversary. Henry presented Josie with a bracelet. In the morning he sat on a bench outside, waiting out the hours, while Josie, upstairs, surrounded by nurses and the doctor, gave birth.

By the end of May, Henry Morgenthau, at thirty-five, stood over the baby's silk-lined cradle, and savored the joy. News of his triumph at the Real Estate Exchange had spread far, and would not soon be forgotten. Almost single-handedly, Henry had given a "spurt," the *Chicago Tribune* announced, to the most vital real estate market in the country. The fame of the Washington Heights deal would grow, entering the annals of real estate as one of the largest sales in the years between the end of the Civil War and the arrival of consolidation in 1898, when Greater New York was born as a single city. Decades on, property men remembered it as "the great Morgenthau sale."

| | | |

Still, there remained his parents' turmoil. As Henry climbed, his father fell. Ever since Lazarus's stay at the Bloomingdale asylum nearly a decade earlier, he and Babette had not shared a roof. If they met, it was only briefly, and with family present. Babette, now sixty-six, suffered the years of separation in steady decline. The ailments were various, and never clearly diagnosed, but persistent. Hoping that his mother might recuperate, Henry arranged a European sojourn. Babette toured spas from Italy to Switzerland, sometimes on her own, but found no cure.

A final insult came in May, as Henry savored the arrival of Henry Jr. On May 30, Babette's youngest son, Richard, died, at age twenty-four, in a rural town in the Midwest. At the time, Tiro, Ohio, was little more than a crossroads among cornfields. The paper trail—diaries, newspapers, archives—do not detail the journey, but family records claim a burial in Chicago, and no official notice of the death (neither its cause nor the event itself) exists. Babette fell into grief. In Germany, she'd lost the two children in infancy. In America, she had lost three in adulthood. And her husband, now seventy-six, constant only in the miseries he wrought, remained a relentless ache. Still, Babette would not yield to Henry's demands to break the last ties. Try as she might to explain it to her children, she could not bring them to understand: Without Lazarus, her life was without meaning.

By the spring of 1892, Lazarus was living alone, moving from rented room to rented room on the East Side. Henry was determined that Babette spend the summer out of the city. If her health did not permit a return to Europe, she should at least enjoy a holiday upstate. In July he sent her off with his sister Bertha to the Catskill Mountain House, a grand inn, once visited by presidents and generals. But Babette's health did not improve. She wrote seldom now, even to her beloved son.

Weeks passed before Henry received a letter. "It was such a joy," he wrote Babette, "to see your handwriting again!" He had given four checks, enough to cover a month's stay, and now sent two more. A granddaughter, Bianca, Pauline's girl, now nineteen, would come soon to keep her company. A few more weeks in the country, he wrote, would do her well.

The letter was Henry's last to his mother. On August 14, 1892, at sixty-six, in the company of only one daughter, Babette died. "Mrs. L. M. Morgenthau," the death notice would claim, had died "suddenly."

But her sons and daughters knew the truth. The end had not come suddenly, but by degree, a death march over the years that she had been
made to endure alone. Babette had enjoyed her small garden at the house
in Harlem, loved watching the flowers bloom each spring. But she had
never won the chance to establish a home of her own in a new land, and
she never regained the love that she treasured the most.

6. "The Temple of Humanity"

1892–1898

The loss stung, but to Henry's surprise the death of his mother served to liberate him. Lazarus had thrown every obstacle in his path, and his father's malign attentions were not yet spent, but even in grief, Henry found new focus. With the arrival of Ruth, their fourth (and last) child, he was determined to redouble his efforts in real estate. He would not only expand his holdings, but attempt to change the trade itself.

Henry looked now not to Harlem, but downtown. On January 8, 1895, a banner headline in the *Herald* announced the turn: "The Largest Deal in History." At $7 million, the price tag was the highest the city had ever seen. At the helm of a new syndicate, Henry had bought two and a half blocks on Sixth Avenue in the Ladies' Mile, and land nearby, on Eighteenth and Nineteenth streets. To many, the price seemed wildly high and the risks prohibitive. But Henry had a plan, and after months of negotiating, he was convinced it would succeed.

If Henry had no expertise in the retail trade, his brothers-in-law, the Ehrichs, did, as did his own brothers in Chicago. He had seen firsthand the boom in shopping and had painstakingly kept up his charts— tabulating the city's burgeoning population. As the city grew, it was plain to see, the Sixth Avenue shopping mecca was sure to boom. Yet for months, a dozen real estate men were mysteriously fighting over a single block on the avenue's eastern side. At last, Henry learned why: The Siegel-Cooper Company, the Chicago retail giant, was coming to New York. Once the emporium opened its doors, the Ladies' Mile would never be the same. The war, Henry reasoned, would be not only for space, but for proximity to the new landmark.

| | | |

Henry's crowning success came in Lazarus's eightieth year. Old age and the onset of disease had neither softened nor slowed his father. Lazarus still possessed the drive that had once bred a fortune. "Unique Idea of a New-York Philanthropist" proclaimed the headline on the *Times* front page, above the report of a new kind of charity, the Greater New-York German Orphan Dowry Society, brainchild of one Lazarus Morgenthau, "known to many beneficiaries as a great philanthropist." The announcement stirred a sensation among the city's German-Jewish society, and the news was relayed—along with a handsome drawing of the dowry society's founder in his trademark Prince Albert, but now trading the cravat for a bow tie—to cities across the country. It even appeared on the front page of the *San Francisco Chronicle*. Lazarus, it seemed, had at last built a stage to match his ego.

He had seized on a tradition of the day, the custom among those well enough off to give to charitable causes, and refashioned it—in characteristic outlandish measure—to suit his own purposes. Lazarus envisioned a fund for "orphan dowries" to afford even the lowest of society, young girls without parents, the chance to wed. The "fund," though, was just getting under way. He foresaw a stream of weddings, he patiently explained to the press: sixteen in the first year, four at a time. The charity, Lazarus said, would enhance his tradition of ecumenical giving. Each wedding would feature four brides: "one a Catholic, one a Protestant, one a Jewess and one the daughter of a Mason." The ceremonies, too, would unite Old World and New, falling on Washington's Birthday and the birthdays of several notables among the German Jews of the city, and even Ernst von Possart, director of the Royal Court Theatre in Munich. Maestro Possart would be honored, Lazarus said, as it was his rendition of *Nathan der Weise* that had inspired "the idea of the Society." The Metropolitan Opera House had been "engaged," and Mayor William Strong would perform the first ceremony. The venue (in the announcements) would soon shift, to Madison Square Garden, before Lazarus announced a final change: The unions, he said, would in fact be consecrated in a private sanctuary, a place he called the Temple of Humanity.

In February 1897, on the eve of St. Valentine's Day, a small crowd of

New York notables witnessed a ceremony that was, as the newsmen would record, without precedent in the city's history. An illuminated sign above the threshold marked the entrance to "The Temple of Humanity." The Temple comprised the rear parlor of Lazarus's latest residence, a brownstone on East Seventy-second off Park Avenue—newly rented to lend an air of solidity. Inside, the decorations were rich with symbolism: Life-size busts of Washington and Lincoln, each draped with American flags and crowned with laurels, stood on one side table; a bust of Schiller, encircled by a German flag, crowded a mantel nearby. On a raised platform at the rear, an altar held two miniature pine trees, and at its center, a crimson velvet square glittered with an array of gold coins. The velvet box held ten golden eagles—each, a reporter noted, facing the orphan bride "reassuredly." Every bride, Lazarus had promised, would claim one hundred dollars in gold.

"A hale German, who looks like Bismarck and talks like Marcus Aurelius," as one witness described the host, rang a small bell. An orchestra struck up "Ein feste Burg," Martin Luther's battle hymn of the Reformation. Footsteps sounded on the oilcloth floor. Bertha Horowitz, "a working girl," entered nervously to greet her bridegroom, Isaac Hoffman, an out-of-work carpenter. Red-haired Isaac stood waiting, "not so tall as the partner of his joy."

Lazarus, the master of ceremonies, spoke in mellifluous German, "with great emphasis and vigorous gestures," while a grandson, struggling to keep pace, translated. As John J. Jeroloman, president of the Board of Aldermen, sat by his side, Lazarus explained that the Temple was the culmination of a lifelong pursuit. He had always sought to forge bonds, to help his fellow man heedless of race, religion, or nation. His Temple, he said, would have "four brothers": Moses, Jesus Christ, Martin Luther, and himself. "They are the three founders of all religion," he said, pointing to the portraits on the walls, "and although not so great as these, I hope to bring all their followers together in the work of aiding such poor girls as have no earthly father."

"Moses was the lawgiver," Lazarus went on, but he had been "too rigorous and cruel." "Broadmindedness" had entered the world only "through the others." His would be the second Temple, after the Temple of Solomon. Solomon had needed strict rules to tame "a wild, self-willed people." The Hebrews, he said, had been "worse than the modern Russians." It was a joke that fell flat. "*Nun soll man lachen,*" he said to the translator at his side. "Now you can laugh." Only in America, Lazarus declared, could the new Temple, free from the blood of sacrifices, take hold.

Lazarus spoke for more than an hour, until at last Jeroloman rose. The couple clasped hands, moving closer to the golden eagles. After Jeroloman recited the vows, Lazarus produced three glasses of Rhine wine from beneath the table. All drank to the health of Mr. and Mrs. Hoffman.

Lazarus mingled with his guests until late. He insisted, as the reporters gathered, that he had no interest in publicity, but he regaled the crowd with remarkable tales of his rise. His factories in Germany had not employed a thousand men, but "six thousand." He had owned "tobacco factories" in America, too, and enjoyed triumphs in "what he described as a bond business" and the "railroad speculation" that had "made him a millionaire." He displayed, as well, a letter from Pope Pius IX, commending his tolerance. "You are the first Jew," the letter read, "that I ever heard of giving to a Catholic institution. You are like the dove returning to the ark with the olive branch." There was more: acclamations from Bismarck and royals at home, and a claim that his munificence had reaped "over $1,500,000" for his favored charities. The guests devoured their host's tales: "Since his 70th year," wrote a reporter, "he has lived on the fruits of his labors, occupying his time by certain scientific researches, the nature of which, owing to his aforetold desire for privacy, will not be divulged here."

Not all were taken in. Emanuel Lehman, who ran the Hebrew Benevolent and Orphan Asylum, called the scheme "superfluous," inasmuch as the men of his institution "always, privately and unostentatiously" presented "their wards with ample dowry." The façade was thin. Lazarus alone, one reporter concluded, made up "the German Orphan Dowry Society"—"for the institution is not yet chartered, and he is the sole member, president and patron."

After a celebratory meal upstairs, Lazarus reconvened his guests. He wished to "impress upon" them a final opportunity: They could see their "names and donations immortalized" before they departed the Temple. Any donor, he announced, could inscribe his name in a unique subscription book, a gilded ledger bound in red morocco that Herr Morgenthau held aloft—the Golden Book of Life.

| | | |

As his father's latest venture captured the headlines, Henry did all he could to keep his distance. Only something untoward, he was sure, would come of this latest harebrained scheme, and whatever it was—moral outrage, bankruptcy, charges of fraud—he knew it would end in infamy. And as Lazarus's most successful son, Henry desired to steer clear of the fallout.

He was, moreover, otherwise preoccupied. At forty-one, Henry oversaw a swelling property portfolio, and a growing reputation. In all the ink devoted to Lazarus and his dowry venture, Henry's name appeared only once, but that summer for the first time it appeared in the society pages. As the Fourth of July neared, *The Philadelphia Inquirer* announced that the Henry Morgenthaus would be staying at Lake Placid, in "the Clifford cottage." For Henry, if not Josie, the notice was a point of pride. Each time that his name appeared in print, and each time he received a gilt-edged dinner invitation, he filed away the paper. They were reminders of his progress.

By the end of the month, the rumblings of scandal reached the summer retreat. His father, once again, had disrupted his best-laid plans. Papa, came the cry from the family, needed help. Henry returned to the city to try and sort out the mess. In the second week of August, he wrote Josie that any attempt at a rescue would be in vain: "LM's affairs have reached a crisis, and the end of his Society & business enterprises have [*sic*] been reached."

Lazarus faced troubles on every front. That summer, he had been dragged into court: His housekeeper charged that he had "pinched her" on the arm and "tickled her under the chin." (Lazarus's doctors, she quoted her employer as saying, had told him "it would do him a great deal of good to engage in a little flirtation.") Another lawsuit concerned money. Lazarus had returned to Terrace Garden, hosting a gala for his dowry society. The "benefit" was a bust: The seventy-five-piece orchestra he hired went unpaid. Lazarus had moved out of the brownstone on Seventy-second Street and into a boardinghouse around the corner, half-furnished rooms rented by the week.

Henry sought out those who had known Lazarus the longest. Then he tallied the debts, studied his own ledgers, and went to see his father. No matter how hard Lazarus tried to explain, Henry saw only a dead end. He offered a bare minimum: "a weekly or monthly allowance to support him." Lazarus had no choice. The dogs at his back—his landlord, the bankers and donors, even the Third Avenue furniture man who had outfitted the Temple—had cornered him. At eighty-two, his health was giving way. He accepted Henry's offer, consented to his conditions. He would quit his "entire enterprises" and retire "dis-gracefully."

On the third Friday in August, the Temple of Humanity collapsed. The end, long rumored among the Morgenthaus, came in suitably dramatic fashion. A dozen policemen raided the abandoned house on Seventy-second Street, sealed its doors, and seized the furniture. The creditors had won.

Ten days later, Lazarus was dead. For a week at Mount Sinai Hospital, as the old man slipped away, the house surgeon did little but make spare notes. Lazarus had been beset by an array of unremitting maladies, but death, the doctor wrote, had come by way of "senility."

In his thirty-one years in America, Lazarus lived less as an immigrant than as an exile. Till the end, he nurtured a nostalgia for the Old World, and not merely for his fortune and factories. At home, he knew what the silences meant, but never in America. In New York, even among the Germans, he remained an outsider, a shape-shifter seeking the keys to acceptance.

Lazarus was interred in Salem Fields on the far edge of Brooklyn, the favored resting place of Our Crowd, beside Babette. They shared a single headstone, a simple slab of granite. There was plenty of room. Years earlier, he had bought a family plot, the only property Lazarus ever owned in his adopted land.

PART II

ASCENT

7. Among the Plutocrats

1898-1900

I t was as if all Europe wanted to come to New York.

By 1900, with a thousand immigrants arriving every week, the population had swelled to 3.4 million residents. Soon, there would be more Irish in New York than in Dublin, more Germans than in Hamburg, and more Italians than in Naples. From the lands of the czar came Jews fleeing pogroms, but also Poles, Armenians, and Balts. The Lower East Side became one of the most densely populated corners in the world.

In 1898, with the annexation of a reluctant Brooklyn, "Greater New York City" was born. The city grew from 44 square miles to almost 300, and New York City was gripped by an historic building boom. Manhattan raced northward, at a pace of two blocks a year. On an island two miles wide, ten miles of new street frontage appeared each year. As New York became the nation's main stage, its chief intersection of politics, society, and trade, a new class arose: men so preposterously rich they even took on a nickname, a term of derision adopted with pride—"the plutocrats."

| | | |

But Henry Morgenthau was a plutocrat before the plutocracy. If the papers had noted the biggest of his deals, few outside the trade knew the tally of Henry's successes. In the span of a few years, as the sandhogs dug the first subway tunnels in the bedrock, the price of land along the city's edges was soaring. Lots that fetched $200 in 1899 sold for $10,000 five years later. Measuring his pace, Henry had made a killing.

As a new vision of the city emerged, the old titans of Wall Street discovered real estate through the eyes of Henry Morgenthau. For all his conservative instincts, Henry assumed a radical role: He embodied a new species of businessman, a new kind of New Yorker. There were others, prominent Jews in business, the arts, and politics, who changed the landscape—men like Jacob Schiff, Otto Kahn, and Louis Brandeis. But as the twentieth century approached, Henry's career in real estate took on consequence. Perhaps more than anyone, he served as the bridge—between Jew and Gentile, sons of immigrants and heirs of pilgrims—uniting divergent worlds of money.

|||| |

The year 1898 marked the twentieth anniversary of Lachman, Morgenthau & Goldsmith. In spring, as Henry prepared to leave for a holiday with Josie in the Adirondacks, his partners asked him to help plan a celebration. As he fished the St. Lawrence, Henry looked back on his years at the firm and reached a conclusion that surprised him. "Instead of a celebration," he later wrote, "it would be a separation."

He had tried to set out on his own before. Each time, he'd been coaxed back. Mathematics now sealed the decision. At forty-three, Henry had embarked on his most voracious succession of deals. In late 1897, he bought two blocks of northern Manhattan from Collis Huntington, the railroad baron, for $400,000—and soon flipped the property for a fat profit. He also turned again to the Astors, wrangling a swath of the Lower East Side—forty-four parcels between Fifth and Eighth Streets—for $676,137. The land—the heart of the old Sampler Farm—had been in Astor hands since 1803, and Henry's negotiations stirred a great public debate. The leases on the properties were soon due to expire, and William Waldorf Astor—by then, after a family feud, living in self-exile in England—had threatened to double rents. The tenants were in an uproar. When news leaked that Henry would buy the land and raze the tenements to build "modern apartment houses"—an "improvement plan," the papers called it—the protests gained force. Ward politicians cried foul, and the tenants sent fiery cables to England. At last, Astor's agent came running. "Now, Morgenthau," he pleaded, "will you try to help us out?" Henry resold the lots for a fast profit of $284,632.

The deal also marked an evolution in New York real estate: Nearly all of the former tenement dwellers managed to buy their own houses. "The Immigrant as Landlord," declared the *Tribune* headline in praise. "How Frugal Foreigners Succeed to the Estates of the Astors and Other Old

Families." The "tenants who became buyers," the paper noted, "were mostly Germans."

As he fished the streams of the Adirondacks, away from the city, Henry tallied his profits so far: more than a million dollars. Few men in New York real estate, let alone German Jews, could claim such success. Another realization hit: He had never invested more than $500,000 in any deal, either his own money or his friends'. As he mulled over the two figures, his own assets and the holdings of his growing circle of associates, Henry sensed a new way forward. He would quit the law firm and, for one of the few times in his life, take a leap of faith. He would "do for real estate what the banking institutions had done for the railroads and industrials." He would create a "trust."

A "trust company" had to be greater than the sum of its parts. To build his own trust, Henry had to do what he had never done before: bring in the competition.

Southack & Ball, headquartered at 25 Broad Street, had pioneered the real estate development of the city. Frederick Southack and Alwyn Ball, Jr., heads of the firm, were fixtures of the world that Henry now sought to join. They were Protestant family men, prominent in the city's leading clubs and societies. For years, they had run one of the city's top brokerage houses. When Henry sought them out, Southack and Ball confided to thinking along similar lines, even securing a charter in Albany. Almost at once, the three agreed to join forces.

Recruiting a board for the new trust, Henry, as always, aimed high. For chief director, he proposed three candidates: J. P. Morgan, the most famous banker in America; James Stillman, the leading bank president; and Frederic P. Olcott, the leading trust president. Morgan was beyond reach. But Stillman, head of the National City Bank ("Rockefeller's bank," as it was popularly known), could be approached. He balked. Whether it was the association with German Jews or lingering fear of the Panic of '73, Stillman, like many on Wall Street, viewed real estate with suspicion. The third candidate, though, heard Henry out with interest.

Frederic Pepoon Olcott, descendant of Puritans, controlled the Central Trust Company. For a quarter of a century, nearly since the time Henry left Columbia Law, Olcott had cut a swath on Wall Street. One of the first to foresee the prospects of the Southern railroads after the Civil War, he had revived more than a dozen rail companies from Galveston to Brooklyn—restoring order, it was said, to "properties representing half a billion dollars and nearly 10,000 miles of railway." Though he scarcely knew Olcott, Henry knew how to reel him in.

A decade earlier, Hugh J. Grant, the former mayor, had appointed Olcott to the first Rapid Transit Commission. To win over Olcott, Henry had only to win over Grant, who was close to the financier. "Hughey" Grant, forty-two in 1899, was a child of Tammany. An orphan who had won a fat inheritance and attracted the favors of Dick Croker, Boss Tweed's notorious heir, Grant had served two terms in City Hall but seen his political star fall in scandal: altogether an unlikely ally for Henry Morgenthau. Yet Grant, too, represented a new New York. He had been among the first Roman Catholics to win office in the city. There was further common ground: Grant was a lawyer, a Columbia graduate who could also manage a conversation in German. But Henry was most attracted to his singular gift: "Hughey Grant," Henry wrote, could "sniff" success, "and through his tremendous amiability . . . was able to appeal to successful men, who heartily welcomed his cooperation on equal terms."

Grant needed little convincing: "We fell into each other's arms."

| | | |

Henry would always remember the first audience with Olcott. The "king of the trusts," as he was known, ruled from a granite fortress on Wall Street that had been built for a million dollars a decade earlier. Fifteen years Henry's senior, and as large and gruff as a bear, Olcott opened with a lecture. A trust president, he bellowed, can have "no yellow" in him. The man at the top had one job: to bring in business.

Henry steeled himself and offered a lesson of his own—on New York real estate. He told of the rise of neighborhoods, the push northward, and the rocketing demand for housing. Opening a window on a new world for Olcott, he knew he had piqued the old man's interest. Nearly every corner of the city, Henry went on, was undervalued—grossly. Years later Henry would come to regard Olcott as a genius, a financier of "rugged honesty," "utter fearlessness," and a "profane disregard of any man's importance." But on that first afternoon he realized that to men like Olcott, real estate was a "closed book" and one they would never open on their own. He belonged to the old guard, who had been bred on a disdain of property speculation as a ladies' game—or worse, a gamble without rules.

Henry was of course a "novice" in finance, he told Olcott, but he saw something the bankers missed: a way to leverage private monies through real estate. The city was fast maturing into neighborhoods and districts. Look at Wall Street and the financial world, he said, or Maiden Lane and the jewelry district. The trend was set: The neighborhoods would fill in across Manhattan Island, as the population spiraled ever higher. Real estate men could see it clearly. Only the financiers in their granite castles, Henry dared to say, remained blind. Property had once been deemed something inert, stable at best—now, Henry insisted, its value would skyrocket.

Olcott wanted in. Within days, even Stillman changed his mind, brought around by the swelling tide. In the spring of 1899, Henry paused to savor the moment. The Central Realty, Bond & Trust Company, his new trust, was set to enter the market with $2,000,000 in capital, and the backing of Wall Street giants. Within three months, the stock of Central Realty was selling at double its issue price.

| | | |

Backed by Olcott, Henry fielded a board of top-tier directors—some recruited, some who refused to be shut out. "They bought me," Henry boasted, "on my past performances."

Stillman and Olcott dominated, but Henry also brought in the leading, and opposing, figures of the insurance world: Augustus D. Juilliard and James Hazen Hyde. Juilliard, the dry goods baron and music patron, "personified" the Mutual Life Insurance Company, while young Hyde, a scion gaining notice for his outlandish dress and even more outlandish spending, represented the Equitable Life Assurance Society, the biggest insurance company in the world. Henry also recruited the sugar barons: Henry O. Havemeyer, "big, florid, and blustering," represented the sugar trust and James N. Jarvie, the independent refiners. Scarcely on speaking terms, the two insisted on facing one another, staring each other down across the table.

As a lawyer in a three-man firm, Henry had scored property coups. Now with a team of heavyweights at his back, he upped the ante. In the fall of 1900, as work on the subway tunnels intensified, Henry returned to Washington Heights. Central Realty scooped up 150 lots between 160th and 175th Streets, for "nearly $1 million." This time, Henry headed a closed club of "well-known capitalists." Among the bankers and newsmen, many knew who stood in the shadows, but Henry, for now, remained the hero.

8. "A Modest Man"

1896–1903

Henry had a habit—a sixth sense, his children would say—of sorting out the right men and women in any sphere. It was how he built relationships and forged alliances. None was more important than his friendship with the man atop *The New York Times*.

Adolph Ochs had come to New York in 1896, a thirty-eight-year-old publisher from Chattanooga, Tennessee, lost in the big city. A German Jew born in Cincinnati, Ochs had quit school at eleven and gone to work as a "printer's devil," sweeping the composing room floor. By nineteen, he had won a job at *The Chattanooga Times*, and within a year, he had borrowed $250 and bought the paper. Soon, he had fixed his sights on the biggest stage in American journalism. More than once he had tried to buy a New York daily and failed. It was not his first time in the city, but Ochs knew few locals. He asked a friend for a favor: Suggest "three men of fine judgment" who could give a newcomer sound advice. All others, Ochs said, would be candidates to invest in his paper, but not these first counselors: With these three men, he vowed, he "would never have business dealings of any kind." One was Henry Morgenthau.

No document records when Henry and Adolph Ochs first met, nor the name of the mutual friend who brought them together. The most likely candidate is Leopold Wallach, a lawyer who moved in the same circles as Henry. Wallach had known Ochs since 1890 and in 1896 had sent the telegram alerting him that the *Times*, laden with debt and its circulation slumping, was ripe for the taking. "The opportunity of your life lies before you," Wallach cabled.

Henry and Adolph hit it off. Henry found Ochs's sole stipulation—no money shall ever pass between them—an alluring challenge. They were never "partners," yet almost from the start, the two formed a lasting bond—an alliance in business, society, and politics that would serve both well. Political exigencies, in the years to come, might on occasion threaten a breach, but the friendship endured. Even after Ochs's death in 1935, their families—and in successive generations the Sulzbergers, heirs to the *Times*—would remain closely connected to the Morgenthaus.

That Ochs managed to buy the *Times*, he would always consider a miracle. Ochs had earned a national reputation as a good newsman but in Chattanooga, his newspaper's circulation was failing and the bills mounting. In New York, he opened a bank account, filling it with borrowed money. For weeks in the summer of 1896, relying on Wallach's counsel, Ochs desperately tried to wrest control of the *Times*.

His timing, in fact, was good. The *Times*'s circulation had sunk to 9,000—fewer readers than it had in 1851, in its first days. Armed with a letter of support from President Cleveland, Ochs sought out the financiers who owned the largest stakes in the newspaper: Morgan, Belmont, Schiff, and Hyde, founder of the Equitable Insurance giant. Each held $25,000 notes, collectively one-sixth of the newspaper's debt. Morgan, master of refinancing, saw in the young man from Chattanooga a chance to salvage a bad investment. The bondholders agreed to a rare concession, swapping their notes for lower-yielding bonds. Ochs turned next to the shareholders, buying back their stock at one-quarter of its face value. His daredevil wrangling worked: Ochs retired the debt and took control of the paper. He had come a long way, his wife, Effie, reminded him, from "the little boy who used to tramp the streets of Knoxville selling papers."

From his headquarters on Park Row in the twelve-story *Times* building overlooking City Hall, Ochs set out to create something unheard of in the highly partisan American press: a broadsheet without bias. On August 19, 1896, the first issue of the *Times* to bear his name, he promised "a high-standard newspaper, clean, dignified, and trustworthy." The *Times*, he pledged, would "give the news impartially, without fear or favor, regardless of party, sect, or interests involved."

Readership exploded, but trouble loomed. Ochs had taken only a year's lease on the headquarters, and its landlord, the Park Company, demanded a steep increase in rent. Ochs offered to renew at $25,000 a year, but the landlord dug in. "The premises now occupied by you," the property manager wrote, "are in our judgment worth $40,000 per annum for rent alone." Arbitration was the only path forward.

Desperate, Ochs turned, as he would time and again, to Henry Morgenthau. Less than a year into his reign, Ochs could ill afford to forfeit the *Times* headquarters. The building, as he wrote Henry, was the paper's best advertisement, "known to nearly every intelligent resident of New York and Brooklyn."

Henry argued for a neutral third party, a man to ensure a fair resolution. Richard Delafield, a respected man of Wall Street, met approval on all sides. As umpire, Delafield struck a quick deal. "The sum of $26,913.80," he wrote Henry and the landlord, seemed "a fair and conservative figure for the annual rental." It was a compromise that all could agree to.

By April 1898, Henry had won a new, favorable lease, and Ochs's fears subsided. The publisher would long remember how Henry had ended the tense weeks of uncertainty when the reborn *Times* had nearly lost its home. No money changed hands, but the two friends had already begun to bend the rules of their relationship.

| | | |

Central Realty was not yet three years old when, in the final days of July 1902, Henry announced the formation of a second trust, the United States Realty and Construction Company. It would be a behemoth, uniting nearly a dozen companies—in real estate, banking, insurance, and building, led by U.S. Steel, Charles Schwab's own newly created "Billion Dollar Trust." A contagion known as the "consolidation movement" was sweeping Wall Street, and Henry was caught up in it.

The *Times* unfurled the details on its front page under the headline "What Mr. Morgenthau Says." "The formation of the company, its plan of operation, and its success," the newspaper reported, were all "attributed" to Henry. In truth, the merger was not all his idea. It originated in the mind of the man who would chair its board: Harry St. Francis Black, the force behind a powerful Chicago construction company. A Canadian raised in a rural town on Lake Ontario, Black was a born salesman who owed his position atop the George A. Fuller Construction Company to a fortunate turn of events: In 1895, he married the boss's daughter. Black was thirty-two, Allon Mae Fuller nineteen. Five years later, when her father died at forty-nine, he left the company in his son-in-law's hands.

Black was a dynamo, a compact man of coiled energy. Driven by "a Napoleon complex," as Paul Starrett, a longtime protégé, recalled, Black "loved to amalgamate and expand." "Bigger and bigger" was his "watchword." In less than a decade, he had built a string of the world's most noteworthy buildings. "Skyscrapers," the newsmen called them: in Chicago, the Marquette Building; in Pittsburgh, the Frick; in New York, the Broad Exchange Building. And his latest, the Flatiron (christened the Fuller Building at birth), was fast rising. The Fuller Company raked in nearly two and a half million dollars a year.

Henry Morgenthau and Harry Black had little in common. Henry was a pragmatist and Harry a dreamer. But both saw how the new century would be born on the bedrock of New York. Down at the southern tip of Manhattan, where three centuries earlier the Dutch cut the first roads, the greatest revolution in construction since the advent of the Gothic cathedrals in Europe was under way. Buildings were no longer cakes of brick and wood, vulnerable to fire and the elements. With electricity pulsing through the streets and the arrival of the steam drill and the hydraulic elevator, builders could raise massive steel-frame skeletons.

"Not only has the outward appearance of the lower part of the old city been changed completely within a decade," declared *Harper's Weekly* in 1902, "but day by day some magic process startles the eye and dazzles the brain with a new manifestation of the conquering American spirit." "The city," *Harper's* added, "is simply busting its bonds. It is as if some mighty force were astir beneath the ground, hour by hour pushing up structures that a dozen years ago would have been inconceivable." It was a "transformation . . . for all time," and it was only beginning.

| | | |

To Henry and Harry, theirs was a partnership without limits. Each had his private designs, but coming together they were convinced of the mutual benefits of the new mega-trust. Neither imagined how quickly their dream would collapse.

The spotlight may have blinded Henry. When U.S. Realty published its first reports, Harry was listed as chairman and Henry as president. Yet Henry was the voice of the trust. "A Case in Point," declared the headline over a *Times* column promoting the merger. "Mr. HENRY MORGENTHAU, a prominent—it may fairly be said the chief—party" to the new "extensive corporation for dealing in realty," was cast as a visionary and a model of capitalism's limitless prospects:

Here is a man still young, possessing the educational advantages only which this progressive community offers to those who care to avail themselves of them—he is a graduate of the College of the City of New York—enjoying no special favors of fortune or connection, who has attained to a position of large influence and great possibilities to the future solely by his ability and character.

The gushing profile not only enhanced Henry's achievements (the City College degree), it offered protection: Henry's role in the merger served to rebut any worries about "the tendency of combinations of capital to diminish the opportunities for individual ability and character to secure the rewards of which they are deserving." Henry's "large returns" were earned. "In the result there had been nothing of 'luck,' still less of 'pull,' nothing adventitious." Henry's empire-building was "logical and intelligible"; the *Times* saw "no reason why it cannot be repeated by any one able to devote to it the same qualities." In a coda, Ochs's men paid a final compliment:

Mr. MORGENTHAU is a modest man, and we feel we ought to apologize to him for this reference to his noteworthy career, but it is at the moment so clearly in evidence, and it is so apposite and so instructive, that we could not forebear reference to it.

On October 30, 1902, the New York Stock Exchange listed U.S. Realty, and first quoted its stock: $75.50 a share for the preferred, and $32 for the common. Wall Street and the press, nearly unanimously, applauded. Walter Page's *The World's Work* noted that the new giant would "probably enjoy a peculiar advantage in the construction of steel buildings from the fact that the Steel Trust president is to be a director." The shares, though, never climbed higher.

Henry's handpicked board proved inept. In large part, Stillman was to blame. The banker had arranged an underwriting syndicate, run by Hallgarten & Co., an Our Crowd banking house founded in 1867, to raise $11 million in subscriptions. Before long, though, trouble loomed: By July 23, 1903, less than a year after its birth, U.S. Realty's preferred had sunk to $46 a share, and the common to $9. Even the mighty Stillman could do little by way of a rescue. The Hallgarten syndicate had invested in speculative syndicates (among them the new Underground railway of London and railways on the West Coast) and suffered huge losses. By

September 11, the syndicate was dissolved, and U.S. Realty was in financial quicksand.

It seemed the end was near. Word spread that Black and his cronies, taking advantage of the plunging share price, had bought large blocks of stock. Henry quit the board, and his partner Hughey Grant, as always, followed. Soon, ten more directors, including Cornelius Vanderbilt, great-grandson of the commodore, joined the exodus; by the second week of January 1904, seventeen of the thirty men on the board had jumped ship. Harry Black took over as president. U.S. Realty, chastened and reconstituted, would go on to build many of the grandest landmarks in the country. But the Canadian at its helm would in the coming years turn to drink and die—a suicide in Florida.

||||

Not even the demise of his mega-trust could slow Henry's rise. He was now a fixture in New York finance, a member of a half-dozen corporate boards. Thanks to his blanketing the Bronx with elevator apartment houses that relied on "Edison Service," Henry sat on Thomas Edison's Electric Illuminated Company board. Henry also delved into the realm where his father had infamously failed. Mount Sinai, the Jewish hospital that had accepted Lazarus's "novel" fundraising efforts, welcomed Henry onto its board.

Suddenly, too, Henry appeared everywhere in society. In March 1902, when Prince Henry of Prussia was feted at a Waldorf Astoria banquet, Henry sat amid the Seligmans and Schiffs. In September, he stood beside Grant, ardent fan of the races, to found the Empire City Trotting Club in Yonkers. Henry not only would break one of his oldest vows—never to give in to gambling—but would become the sole Jew among the club's dozen officers. Even his finances made news. When the *Times* published a roster of the city's biggest taxpayers, Henry ranked near the top.

On April 22, 1903, when the new Stock Exchange building opened, after an exile of two years in hired quarters, the celebration reminded New Yorkers of the opening of the Brooklyn Bridge twenty years earlier. Eighteen Broad Street was hailed a masterpiece. Giant Corinthian columns guarded its façade, and once inside the guests found themselves in a hall larger and grander than any they had ever seen. The "boardroom," as the trading floor was known, gleamed. Nearly one block square, its walls rose seventy-two feet to a gilt ceiling. On the Broad Street side, those assembled looked out a wall of glass, while a vast skylight washed the floor with a sea of sunlight. It was an arena for the new times. The new headquarters would be one of the first buildings in the world to enjoy air-conditioning. Giant annunciator boards—a feat of electric magic demanding twenty-four miles of wiring—would page the members, who would enjoy not only dining rooms but a medical clinic.

The guests filled dozens of rows before a stage at the rear, decked in palms and American flags, reserved for the most honored guests. At just after eleven o'clock, Mayor Seth Low entered to a swell of applause. As the Reverend Morgan Dix of Trinity Church offered a benediction— "The silver is Thine and the gold is Thine, O Lord of Hosts . . ."—the thousands on the floor studied the faces of the famous men seated on the platform. Throughout the proceedings, one man held all in his thrall. He had not spoken, but when he appeared on the platform they stood to applaud. When he joined in the cheering, they cheered louder. J. Pierpont Morgan, five days after celebrating his sixty-sixth birthday, had arrived fashionably late.

Henry Morgenthau, the German immigrant whose father had grown from an itinerant cantor to a cigar baron, and who died a ruined gambler in a bewildering world, sat in the same row, ten seats to Morgan's right.

At forty-seven, he had yet to reach his destination. Many in the great hall had attained so much, but few had come so far, so fast.

9. "Let Me Have the Boy"

1903-1911

I n the wake of the Harry Black debacle, Henry Morgenthau found himself, for the first time since quitting college, taking a step back. He retreated to his own trust, Central Realty. But even though chastened, he refused to sit idle. Culture, and primarily the allure of established patrons, had long loomed as another ladder to climb. And even as he smarted from financial defeat, Henry was determined to live up to his idea of himself.

Opera, a realm that he had loved since childhood, offered an open avenue into the city's highest society. As a young man, Henry had seen the pecking order. The Metropolitan on Broadway held 3,625 seats. But it was the Golden Horseshoe, a half circle of gilded boxes in the parterre, that stole attention—at its center, the "social throne," Box No. 7, the domain of Mrs. Astor. Opera in New York was ruled by the Four Hundred—a list of men and women, no more than four hundred, who could fill a ballroom. Among them could be no Jews. "Our good Jews might wish to put out a little book of their own," offered Ward McAllister, arbiter of the social roster. "Called something else, of course." They did: The *Hebrew Visiting List* had had a short run, disappearing quickly. The German Jews, though, knew who belonged, and who did not. While many of the Our Crowd Jews had long since abandoned aspirations to the "social throne," Henry Morgenthau was not among them.

He would set out to take over the Metropolitan Opera. In a near coup, he helped catapult Heinrich Conried, a young director who'd gained renown in German theater downtown, to the Met. In 1903, Conried was offered the lease of the opera company for $150,000. Henry came to the rescue. He turned to the rakish scion James Hazen Hyde, who leapt at the opportunity. Hyde and Henry would each give $75,000, but Hyde would also recruit to the board his friends and drinking partners, junior members of the city's elite clans: the Vanderbilt, Whitney, Winthrop, and Goelet (Astor kin) families. Henry in turn recruited others—George J. Gould, son of Jay Gould of Black Friday infamy, and Jacob Schiff's new partner, Otto Kahn, an upstart banker who'd emigrated from Mannheim a decade earlier. Henry had struck the right balance—limiting the number of German Jews on the board—and the opera house overlords approved: On February 14, 1903, by a vote of 7–6, Conried won the lease. He was elected president, and Hyde and Henry, vice presidents.

Josie was overjoyed: The Morgenthaus were now patrons themselves. In summer, the Conrieds would stay at the Morgenthau "cottage" on the New Jersey shore—from Deal to Elberon, the shoreline had become "a sort of ghetto," as Peggy Guggenheim called it. Once Conried had unpacked his phonograph, the whole Morgenthau family—Helen was nineteen, Alma fifteen, Henry twelve, and Ruth nearly seven—would listen in silence, mesmerized. Conried promised a magical first season. He would bring Caruso, the Italian tenor, and dare to stage *Parsifal*—flouting the ban, imposed first by Wagner, on performing the opera anywhere outside of Bayreuth.

Hurdles multiplied. The conductor threatened a boycott, singers refused to rehearse, the Society for the Prevention of Cruelty to Children vowed to keep young boys out of the chorus, and clergymen denounced it all as blasphemy. Still, Conried and Henry did not relent. And when Wagner's widow and son sued, seeking an injunction, Henry led the counterattack. The reporters feasted on the legal fight while Conried's nerves frayed, and Henry and Josie traveled to Vienna to oversee the selection of costumes. In the fall, when *Wagner v. Conried* went to court, Henry testified that Conried merely intended to serve "the best interests of art by enabling the lovers of Wagner's music to witness the performance of his last opera in New York." The opera, Henry promised, would be "in every respect fully equal, if not superior" to the productions at Bayreuth. Throughout the testimony, Conried kept rehearsing.

On November 23, 1903, the Conried Opera House opened its doors. *Rigoletto* marked Caruso's debut at the Metropolitan. On Broadway, counts and countesses, ambassadors and generals arrived, police herding the carriages. Henry and Josie were seated in the Golden Horseshoe with the Vanderbilts and Whitneys and Goelets, in flattering propinquity to J. P. Morgan and Mrs. Astor. For the maestro and the Morgenthaus, it was a stunning success. The next day brought more good news: In the *Wagner* case, the judge sided with Conried.

Parsifal opened on Christmas Eve. The first performance of the opera outside of Bayreuth was "without question," wrote the *Herald*, "the most important opera event that ever occurred in America." So great was the demand, Conried himself could not get tickets. Newsmen worried about "the Dinner Question": how, during intermission, "4,000 hungry people will besiege nearby restaurants." Even as he basked in acclaim, Conried thanked one man: Henry Morgenthau.

| | | |

In 1902, when his friend Adolph Ochs, owner of the *Times,* turned to him again, Henry sensed a second opportunity—another chance to burnish his name and reach social heights no Jew had scaled before.

The *Times* had outgrown its Park Row building. Ochs needed a new home—one, he told Henry, that reflected a grand vision for the paper's future. It would have to be "monumental," "dignified," and uptown. Park Row was dying, and the city was moving north. (The *Herald* had already migrated to Thirty-fifth Street.) Ochs wanted a location that stood out amid the checkerboard of streets. Only Broadway slashed across the avenues—Fifth, Sixth, and Seventh—allowing for a building to be seen from blocks away. Ochs had fixed on a lot where Broadway intersected Twenty-third Street at Fifth Avenue, beside the Flatiron Building. He had no idea who owned it, but Henry did. He was in fact the owner's broker—but he refused to sell it to Ochs, reminding him of their vow never to have "business dealings." Even with a fat commission at stake, he assured his friend it was "the wrong site." The city's energies were fast shifting. "You don't want to move to a passing neighborhood," Henry remembered telling Ochs. "You want to move to a coming neighborhood."

The ideal site, Henry said, was at Forty-second Street, where Broadway crossed Seventh Avenue, the expanse of open space and street frontage then known as Long Acre Square. Long Acre was a dingy corner, once home to a horse exchange, now a no-man's-land of lodging houses and second-rate restaurants. Ochs saw the logic: The theaters and hotels attracted people, and more hotels and playhouses would surely follow. To Henry, though, the Forty-second Street site offered more than visibility—it would also straddle the new subway. The Broadway line of August Belmont, Jr.'s IRT—the Interborough Rapid Transit Company—would soon open. If the *Times* headquarters stood on Long Acre Square, Henry said, the trains would run below—just beneath the presses. Ochs would have direct access to the fastest distribution system in the world.

"I think you are right," Ochs said, and commissioned his friend to buy the site.

Henry cobbled together a misshapen lot, on Broadway between Forty-second and Forty-third streets. With as much political muscle as money, he helped to combine four brownstones (purchased by Belmont's Subway Realty Company, set up to buy easements for the underground) with the Pabst Hotel next door—and pulled off the deal. Within months, Ochs sat in a hotel room overlooking Broadway and Forty-third Street, surveying the construction, and by fall, his dream—a modern version of Giotto's Florentine Tower—was rising. City Hall had complied as well, rechristening Long Acre Square as Times Square.

On January 18, 1904, Iphigene, Adolph and Effie's eleven-year-old daughter, laid the cornerstone of the Times Tower, twenty-five stories tall. Adolph Ochs, and generations of his heirs, would say that it could never have been done without their family friend: Henry Morgenthau had led the publisher to the site, secured the lot, and wrangled the financing. To commemorate the coup, the friends exchanged gifts. Ochs presented Henry with a George III two-handled silver loving cup. Henry gave Ochs an ornate reading lamp. "My dear friend," Ochs wrote Henry with gratitude, "the beautiful lamp gives a bright, and pleasing light, and symbolizes your many kind services when I was groping in the dark and needed light."

"I hope," Ochs told his friend, "that for many years we may have the pleasure of each other's success." Yet once again, as he had with the Park Row lease extension, Henry charged his friend no lawyering fee. Embarrassed, Ochs marched into Morgenthau's offices with a $25,000 check. Henry tore it up—reminding him once again that "no money was to pass between them." Henry, of course, knew he now possessed something of far greater value: a debt.

|||||

As the Wall Street trusts swelled, public distrust only grew. To many, "consolidation" meant one thing: unbridled greed. The city's wealthiest men, critics cried, would grasp as much as they could, and keep it in as few hands as possible. Across the city, labor bosses, muckrakers, and religious leaders clamored for reform. And in 1905, it came.

The Armstrong Commission, as it would become known for its chair, an upstate Republican, was a joint Senate and Assembly committee launched in Albany, and the first investigatory body charged with unearthing fraud on Wall Street. In a series of public hearings—seventy-seven in four months—led by the legal giant Charles Evans Hughes, the commission exposed the ugly truths of the insurance "industry"—an unseemly pageant of double-dealing, insider trading, greed, and nepotism. In a stunning about-face, Henry would become a star witness against the plutocrats. He would testify against former partners and stake out bold reformist turf, all while enhancing his own reputation. As the hearings transfixed the city, and much of the nation, Henry would be given his biggest stage yet.

James Hazen Hyde stood at the heart of the scandal. Not yet thirty, Hyde, who remained a director of Henry's realty trust and the opera, had inherited the Equitable Life Assurance Society, a giant that controlled "the futures," as one paper put it, of "2.5 or 3 million ultimate beneficiaries" of its policies. Hyde was notorious for his *bal masqué*, the party that transformed Sherry's restaurant for a single night into a replica of a Versailles hall—at a cost of $200,000. But as Hughes investigated, New Yorkers were shocked to learn that young Hyde, with only 501 shares (valued at $50,100), ruled over the life savings of more than 600,000 policyholders, as well as several banks and trust companies. Hyde defended himself with his usual insouciance. "My father," he said, "willed me this company just as he willed me his horses."

Caught in the middle was Henry Morgenthau. To New Yorkers, Hyde had become the symbol of the plutocrats' worst sins. But to Henry, it was also personal. Young Hyde had tried, more than once, to force him from the opera board that Henry had helped to build—and finally, a year earlier, he had won. For Henry, the indignity lingered. The Equitable board, meanwhile, had split amid the fallout of Hyde's shenanigans: James W. Alexander, its president, led one faction, and E. H. Harriman the other. Alexander, with the proxies of 90,000 shareholders, won out. He had persuaded Henry to join a committee of "prominent and trusted men" and force the outside investigation. Henry's impulse was to make a stand in defense of shareholders' rights, but first he had to overcome the protests of the insurance giants on his own Central Realty Board, and then rally the press to his side. He sought out Harriman's lawyer, Elihu

Root, recently returned to the city after serving as President Teddy Roosevelt's secretary of war, and threatened to "arouse public opinion." As the headlines blared, the scandal grew, and Albany had ordered Hughes to begin digging.

Henry quickly took to the Republican counsel, Hughes, the forty-three-year-old son of an upstate preacher. Hughes was precise, dispassionate, and, despite the risk, unsparing: He tallied the insurance giants' offenses—"campaign contributions, fabulous salaries, wasteful extravagance, gross favoritism, financial jugglery." As Hughes's marathon neared its end, Henry took the stand. He denounced the men on his own board, telling of how McCurdy, overlord of the Mutual, profited at the expense of his own policyholders, having pressured Henry to sell him a thousand shares in the Lawyers Title Insurance Company at $174, shares that McCurdy resold for double the price to the Mutual. If Charles Hughes had pried open the "barred doors of the insurance corporation's secret closets," as one reporter put it, Henry had laid out their contents.

The corruption hearings marked a watershed. In the slate of reforms that followed, policyholders—those whose life savings buffeted the luxuries of the insurance barons—gained greater control. The insurance giants could no longer own stock, control banks, or underwrite securities. McCurdy quit the Mutual, and Hyde—forced to sell his Equitable shares—fled to Paris. Henry took quiet pleasure in "being the instrument," as he wrote, of the "headlong fall." Seeing Hyde stripped of his golden goose brought a "certain element of poetic justice." Yet beyond the score-settling, the Hughes hearings had afforded Henry what he wanted most: a chance to showcase his ideals. An enterprise, gradual but intentional, was coming to the fore. Henry's vision of the city and the fault lines of its progress—whether corruption on Wall Street, overcrowding on the Lower East Side, or the unsafe labor conditions everywhere—would embrace the emergent reformist movement. In the city's news pages, pulpits, and political salons, "the progressives" were on the ascent—and Henry, a believer since boyhood in the power of enlightened reason, was determined to join the vanguard.

| | | |

Still, the drive to acquire did not stop. Henry had suffered misalliances—first with Black, then with Hyde—and yet by 1905, he still ranked high among the real estate titans who'd developed many of the grand buildings of Wall Street and Midtown. Henry had tied together the plots across the street from the Stock Exchange to build the twenty-story Broad Exchange Building. He'd purchased the Knox Hat Building, the Beaux-Arts landmark at Fortieth Street and Fifth Avenue. And in 1902 he had joined—"by means of a brief telephone conversation"—in the city's biggest purchase on record: the Plaza Hotel for $3,000,000, bought from the New York Life Insurance Co. But as Wall Street remained hell-bent on trust building, Henry turned in a different direction. He returned to his roots, and looked, again, to the north—to the upper reaches of Manhattan and the Bronx.

As Belmont's subway neared completion, Henry "was astonished to find," he recalled, "no activity in real estate in anticipation" of the new lines. He scoured the northern lots, enlisting a twenty-eight-year-old nephew, Robert Simon, son of his sister Pauline. Simon reminded Henry of himself: Forced to work at fourteen, he had left school, apprenticing at the real estate firm L. J. Phillips. By twenty-one, Simon had made partner.

Starting in 1905, Henry went on a blitz, buying swaths of northern Manhattan. In ninety days, he acquired nearly 2,500 lots, including "all the big plots" along the new subway lines—properties that, in time, were sold, at a great profit, for $9,000,000. Still, even as he rode "the Subway Boom," Henry sensed an "imminent" downturn and, fearing another panic, opted for caution. Just as he had done when quitting his old law firm, Henry deliberated for days before making a decisive move, merging Central Realty with the Lawyers Title Insurance Company—a deal that allowed him, as he wrote, "to pay our stockholders $550 in cash and one half share of Lawyers Title Stock for every share they owned in our company." He'd hedged his bets, but not quit. In March, after completing the merger, he repurchased all of Central Realty's property holdings, and by April, as his forty-ninth birthday neared, he'd set up an entirely new company. He would return to his roots, to real estate—"only," as he later recalled, "on a much larger scale than I had ever operated before." The new firm would have a grand vision, and $1,000,000 in stock, but it was, in essence, a one-man outfit—the Henry Morgenthau Company.

| | | |

Josie had made a warm home of their first house, 33 West Seventy-fourth Street. She filled it with French furniture and red damask, and in the evenings, piano music wafted through the rooms. She oversaw the staff—driver, cook, cleaners—with tact, and hosted a carousel of dinner parties.

Henry and Josie delighted in their children—Helen, the firstborn; Alma, her younger sister; Ruth, their youngest, born in 1894; and Henry Jr., the lone son.

Henry Morgenthau had not only wanted a lineage, he yearned for a junior partner, someone at his side—someone he could trust. "He was crazy to have me in business with him," Henry Jr. would recall decades later. "He would say to my poor mother, 'Josie, you can have the girls, let me have the boy.'"

From a very young age, the boy feared not meeting his father's standards. The demands were high, and the failure to live up to them would inform Henry Jr.'s earliest memories. When Henry Jr. was four years old, his father hired a young teacher to set up a kindergarten class at home. For two years, a half-dozen children from the neighborhood joined Henry and his sister Alma for instruction from Miss Lily Heyman, daughter of a German-Jewish family and a recent college graduate. Soon, it was clear to all that Henry Jr. was a slow learner.

His father wasted no time enrolling him at age seven in the Sachs School, a boys-only institution run by Dr. Julius Sachs on Central Park South. The school and its upper branch, the Sachs Collegiate Institute, were home to the children of the German-Jewish elite. Among Henry Jr.'s classmates were Warburgs, Loebs, Schiffs, and the future journalist Walter Lippmann. The Sachs School, though, proved too demanding. As Henry Jr. struggled, his father again interceded. He hired a tutor. "A sober young lady," as Henry Jr. would remember her, Martha Ornstein came to the house several mornings a week for drills in writing, spelling, and arithmetic. A Barnard alumna who had been born in Vienna, and would go on to earn a doctorate in mathematics, Ornstein had done wonders for young men seeking to enter Harvard or Yale. But Henry Jr., by his own estimation, was "inattentive" at best.

In the fall of 1904, Henry Sr., against the boy's wishes and his mother's protests, packed his son off to Exeter, the New Hampshire prep school, to which young Henry took an immediate and strong dislike. In his first year, as he later recalled, he studied "English, History, Mathematics, Latin, Latin, and more Latin." Classes ran from eight o'clock in the morning until six in the evening, six days a week. His voluminous correspondence from Exeter—some weeks he wrote home nearly every day—records his struggle.

His life was made worse by successive bouts of sickness—colds, fevers, rashes, and, in his own recollection, "a tendency toward rickets" that sent him time and again to the infirmary. He loved sports, and had become a good athlete, but his fragile health kept him off the teams and interrupted his studies. Often, he felt listless and sleepy in class. "Father was as worried about the lag in my scholarship," he later recalled, "as mother was about my physical strength." In New York, Henry Jr. had begun to suffer poor eyesight, but now he was forced to consult a doctor. Worse still, in one year he grew nearly nine inches. At fourteen, Henry Jr. stood six feet, one and a half inches. He ate poorly, was severely near-sighted, towered over his peers, and was painfully shy. Years later, class-mates would recall him standing apart, a gawky, awkward presence. His reticence deepened over time, a distance that few strangers could cross.

No influence, though, did Henry Jr. greater harm than that of his own father. If children are fated to struggle for parental approval, in Henry Jr's case, he faced an impossible goal: His father's standards seemed to grow with his own increasingly exalted idea of himself. Decades on, after he had risen on outrageous good fortune, Henry Jr. would take time to look over his shoulder, and speak, as he never did in public, of his fa-ther's dark shadow. "All for Tomorrow," a would-be autobiography, exists in manuscript only: 374 typewritten pages buried amid the moun-tain of Morgenthau papers at the Franklin D. Roosevelt Presidential Li-brary. Joseph Gaer, an aide who started to draft the manuscript after Henry Jr. had become the Treasury secretary, never made it beyond 1920 in his subject's life, and the book was never published. "All for Tomor-row" casts Henry Jr.'s life in the rosiest light, at times diverging from verifiable fact. But the typescript contains Gaer's notes to his subject; Henry Jr. had vetted every word.

Looking back on his first years at Exeter, he recalled his father as a "most severe taskmaster," who was "comparing me all the time, un-doubtedly, with his own record at the same age." Henry Sr. "devoted himself to me, and tied me to his will with a thousand ties," he wrote. "Like most parents he had great hopes for me; but unlike most parents he undertook to channel my ambitions, using me both as instrument and recipient."

In each of his first three terms at Exeter, Henry Jr. did miserably. His performance—even in German, his father's native tongue—became a matter of grave concern.

In his first weeks away, Henry Jr. began to keep notes in a simple, nar-row datebook. It was less a diary than a record of events and non-events, the start of a habit of obsessive recordkeeping that, over the decades, became legendary. On September 19, 1904, he noted that "the first check I ever drew from a bank" was to the order of "cash" for $2. And on February, 9, 1905: "It snowed all day . . . we had an English Exam and I received B"—a rare highlight—"as a mark." In his notes and letters, Henry Jr. also recorded a struggle to assimilate. Exeter remained a domain of Protestant privilege, thick with boys from old-line New England families. The chaplain, Henry Jr. complained to his father in a letter, could start his sermon benignly but soon "goes to work and tells all the bad points of the Jews."

Solitude pervades his letters. "No one realizes," Henry Jr. wrote in the unpublished autobiography, "how lonely a child can be away from home, attending a school or in a camp he dislikes yet must pretend to like."

At every chance, he escaped. On weekends in Boston, his aunt and uncle, Carrie and Charlie Weil, hosted him, and he would go out on the town with his elder cousin, Charlie Jr. At times, other relatives, the Filenes and Trounsteins, joined the Weils. When the weather allowed, Henry Jr. and Charlie would take the trolley out to the Nantasket Beach. But Henry Jr.'s most beloved weekends were spent with his father. "Last night I was so homesick, I have not got over it yet," he wrote his father on January 12, 1905, on returning to Exeter after Christmas. The snow had turned to rain. "I tell you what," he added, "there is no place like home. . . . Being with you so long its [sic] hard to leave you."

Henry Jr. had inherited the austere moral code that dominated his father's childhood. Whether he suffered homesickness, poor grades, or a failure on the sports fields, he chastised himself. He feared, above all, not the disapproval but the disappointment of his father.

Henry Sr. visited often, yet time and again it was the son who asked more of the father—not vice versa. After one rendezvous in Boston, Henry Jr. lamented that the time had passed too quickly. Next time, he pleaded, perhaps they could "not do so much family calling," so that he and his father could "be more together."

"Now don't forget," Henry Jr. wrote his father a few months later, "any time you get lonely, why just telegraph me and I will come at once." "PPS:" he added, "Please become lonely."

Henry's struggles only deepened, and by December, he pleaded for a reprieve. "I am sorry that I am so poor in my studies," he wrote his father, "and sometimes I despair about myself, whether I will ever amount to anything or not." In a postscript he added, "I am going to talk with you about my not going back to Exeter. . . . I have been thinking that perhaps I would be able to study better if I was near the family, and then I would not feel so home-sick." All the while, his eyes only worsened. He had gone to see a specialist in Boston who prescribed glasses and offered stern advice. The doctor, Henry duly informed his father, said that if he were his son, "he would have me leave school." But Henry did not want to fail his father. "If my eyes last out," he wrote, "I will stay here till the school closes, as I think it would be cowardly to stop now."

Before New Year's, the decision was made for him. Henry Jr., his father and the headmaster agreed, would leave Exeter. At sixteen, he came home, returning to the Sachs Collegiate Institute. His father also hired Otto Koenig, the Prussian martinet who had succeeded Dr. Sachs as head of the institute, as a tutor. Josie and Henry, along with his sisters Alma and Ruth, who were still at home, had moved to 30 West Seventy-second Street, a brownstone with a limestone façade and elevator. The new house, several notches above the old one two blocks north, was a sanctuary, and Henry's room beneath its roof a refuge—"a place," he told Gaer, his ghostwriter, "frequented by father who was eager to discuss my future with me."

Henry Sr., mindful of his own forced withdrawal from college, was determined to steer his son forward. He saw only one future for Henry Jr.: He would join him in real estate. The two had few secrets. "Ever since I was 10 years old," Henry Jr. said, "Father spoke to me as to an adult. He discussed with me his own plans and consulted me as if I were his partner. Even before I entered Exeter, father would take me for long walks and outline his various plans for business or social activities and solicit my reactions." His father laid bare the maneuvering behind his deals. "It was like watching a great chess player and hearing him explain each of his moves."

Father and son, Henry Sr. imagined, would work side by side in a family firm. But first he would have to ease Henry Jr. into it, and devise yet another plan: If his son did not take to the books, law or finance would be out of the question. What skills, other than a vision of the profit line and a knowledge of the legal guardrails, did the future of real estate demand? Architecture, the father reasoned, could prove an easier, and equally essential, avenue. Henry Sr. would continue to scout the best lots to buy, and Jr. would build the houses that "Henry Morgenthau & Son" offered to a grateful public.

| | | |

At age fifty, Henry Morgenthau had little time for regret. For decades, he had been "deeply absorbed," as he wrote in his memoirs, "in the chase for wealth." In that race, he won. He'd managed to skirt the Panic of 1907, when disaster again hit Wall Street, cutting short the building boom. Henry would look back and claim foresight: He had seen it coming. But whether it was prescience, the sting of the old defeats, or blind luck, he began to withdraw from finance. At midlife, he returned, instead, to a youthful passion: soul-searching.

"I had neglected," Henry would write, "the nobler path of duty." He resolved to retire "wholly from active business," to make good "the better resolutions of my boyhood." The yearnings of the young boy—the hunger for moral self-betterment—had fallen to the side amid the climb of the lawyer-turned-developer.

An emptiness loomed. He had yet to find a faith, a spiritual home of his own. The Quaker wisdom of Dr. Whitall, the guide of his youth, still inspired him, as did Emerson. The Morgenthaus had long been searching, even lured by a new wave, Christian Science. Several relatives— among them, Henry's sister Pauline and her family—had turned to the faith. Henry was intrigued. Once, when diagnosed with mumps, he'd summoned a Christian Scientist healer. Henry, though, was less interested in a new religion than in an ethical code: a civic spirituality, as he called it, a congregation that could serve as the conscience of a community, and a stage to expand his belief in individual self-betterment to social and political reform.

In the fall of 1906, when Henry met a spirited clergyman, a Hungarian émigré, he at last found his faith.

Stephen Samuel Wise more closely resembled a prizefighter than a rabbi. He was barrel-chested and handsome, with a face—Roman nose, square jaw, piercing eyes—that suggested resolute will. Born in Budapest in 1874, the seventh rabbi in his family, he'd grown up listening to his father's sermons in Brooklyn. By nineteen, Wise was helping at the pulpit of the Madison Avenue Synagogue; after the death of the head rabbi, he took over.

Wise was a born reformer: He attacked first in the pulpit, then in the streets, and, before long, in the halls of power. He said what he thought, with rare eloquence—whether the subject was Zionism, child labor, or women's suffrage. By age thirty-two, when Wise met Henry, he could fill any synagogue or church daring enough to host him. For a time he had abandoned New York and taken refuge on the West Coast. In six years in Portland, Oregon, Wise had aroused the liberal congregation, railing against social and political wrongs, and gaining the enmity of the local gamblers, liquor dealers, politicians, and even the sheriff, who floated a plan to sell five-dollar seats at a public hanging. Wise did not just preach reform. In Oregon, he drafted a law banning child workers in factories and served four years as the state's commissioner of child labor. For a priest, such a successful campaign would have been extraordinary. For a rabbi, it was revolutionary.

Wise had earned a national audience, but it was not enough. New York was now home to more than 700,000 Jews, and yet the congregations had not kept pace. Wise wanted to become the "People's Rabbi," emulating the leaders of the Social Gospel: Henry Codman Potter, the "People's Bishop," and Edward McGlynn, the Catholic "People's Priest." In 1905, Wise returned from Portland at the invitation of Temple Emanu-El, the cathedral synagogue on Fifth Avenue that remained home to the German-Jewish aristocracy. Officially, the trustees solicited Wise to give a guest sermon. In truth, it was a tryout for the main job.

Wise had studied under Gottheil, Emanu-El's famed former rabbi, and lectured there in the past. He took to the pulpit on November 26, 1905, preaching on "The New Conscience," a call to reform. Wise knew the power of Emanu-El, but he also knew that any sermon there was subject to preapproval. At a meeting with the trustees days later, he warned that he would not mince words. Turning to Daniel Guggenheim, the metals magnate, he said he'd preach against child labor in copper mines. Shifting his gaze, Wise vowed, as well, to denounce the relative of another board member, a young man running for office on a Tammany slate. Wise, in short, demanded a written guarantee of the freedom of speech he'd enjoyed in Portland. The trustees were aghast.

Wise returned to Portland and, with characteristic melodrama, rejected the top job at Emanu-El. He stood before his congregation and read an open letter to the trustees in New York. It was a manifesto, and he made sure it soon appeared, alongside the trustees' original letter of invitation, in the *Times*. Wise would accept the call to Emanu-El only on one condition: "That my pulpit not be muzzled." In New York, the trustees insisted that no job had been offered. The rabbi, though, had won the joust.

Wise came home to New York nine months later with an idea. He would establish a new kind of synagogue, one "on a higher ethical and spiritual plane." "The Free Synagogue" would not be confined within granite walls, and it would be liberal, open to Jews and non-Jews, rich and poor. The name was an attempt to salve a bitter memory. As a child, Wise had once entered Emanu-El and, finding it empty, walked toward a front pew. "You mustn't go in there," an usher scolded. "That's Mr. Guggenheim's pew." The Free Synagogue, Wise said, would not sell pews, nor bow to political or financial pressure.

The battle was on. Henry and a number of Our Crowd elders—Jacob Schiff, Adolph Lewisohn, and James Speyer among them—would break ranks with Emanu-El and back Wise. On April 15, a crowd of more than a hundred convened at the Hotel Savoy to elect Henry chair of the new congregation. By day's end, he announced that 192 men and women had joined the fold. The new congregation, Henry promised, would be "free and democratic," "pewless and dueless."

Wise had begun a movement. A year later, celebrating its first anniversary, Henry reminded the growing congregation that the Free Synagogue was "not organized simply to provide another place where some of us could come on New Year's Day and Yom Kippur and quiet our consciences." It had a mission: to fight for "liberty of thought and freedom of expressions thereof," and "to correct the indifference to our spiritual welfare displayed by most of us." As the men gathered before him enjoyed their dessert, Henry railed against the ills of the modern city: child labor, religious and racial prejudices, the rising "great wave of Commercialism."

It was intended, as received, as a slap in the face of Emanu-El. The new congregation held services in Carnegie Hall, and soon opened a branch on the Lower East Side, followed by a school. Not only did Wise have a following, but his roster of lecturers included the heroes of civic reform: from Jacob Riis, the muckraking journalist, to Florence Kelley, activist enemy of the sweatshops, to Lillian Wald, leader of the settlement reform movement. He also had rivals: "To start a free synagogue," one rabbi gibed, you had only to "cultivate a voice, place a pitcher of ice water on a stand, and marry an heiress." Wise did, in fact, have a wealthy wife, but he could also claim a chief patron: Henry Morgenthau.

For the rabbi, the Free Synagogue offered a soapbox to stir an exodus from the old rituals; for Henry, his benefactor, it opened a door to the political arena in New York. Jews, even the wealthiest German Jews, faced unwritten quotas: For years, the Strauses, Lehmans, and Seligmans had jockeyed for the few seats of civic power open to Jews. For Henry Morgenthau it was not the chief aim, but he could see it clearly: Long before the advent of ethnic politics in New York, the new congregation might serve as a bridge, a stage where Christian politicians eager to court Jews—reform-minded Jews and Jews with money—could find a constituency.

||||

After a year at the Sachs Collegiate Institute, Henry Jr. was packed off to a cram school in Ithaca, a school to prep boys for the Cornell entrance exams. He would be watched closely by one Mr. Kraemer, a tutor hired by his father, who would also room with him.

At the Cascadilla school, Henry Jr. at last gained focus. The diffident, forlorn child at Exeter was gone. "He was tall, handsome, very personable," a classmate, Edward Bernays, the public relations pioneer, would recall. "No table pounder or 'go-to-hell' kind of person, affable and gentle." Still, Henry longed for his father. "I am getting a double bed," he wrote Henry Sr. that first fall in Ithaca, "one over the other as you saw when you were up at Ithaca, so that when you come to visit me, which I hope you will, you can stay right with me." Father and son had entered a new dialogue. It was a one-sided disquisition on life, the nature of men, and, above all, how one should live in modern times. His father tried to instill "the thirst," as he called it, "for the better things." "Any old lunkhead can drift," he warned. "You must always strive to lift yourself upward and onward. Or else you will be carried down with the tide."

April brought a break from prepping for the Cornell exams. Henry Jr. came home for his sister Alma's wedding. Earlier his eldest sister, Helen, had married Mortimer Fox, a banker's son who had avoided his father's footsteps and become an architect. Maurice Wertheim, Alma's husband, was cultured, intelligent, and rich, another son of the German-Jewish establishment. His two older daughters well married, Henry could devote even more time to his son's education.

Henry Jr. had surprised himself—unexpected glee pervades his letters home—by passing the Cornell entrance exams. In September 1909, he enrolled in its College of Architecture. His first grades were poor, and he failed to get into a fraternity, but the letters home reflected a newfound fortitude. He joined the Drama Club, even acting in Ibsen's *An Enemy of the People*. In those first months at Cornell, something shifted. At Exeter his father had browbeat him; now he urged his son to have faith in his abilities, to swim against the stream, to stand up for himself. "I do not want you to yield to me without being convinced you are wrong," he wrote. "I shall respect you all the more if you argue your side as strongly as you can and I may and shall yield if you can convince me."

Another shift was emerging: The deeper Henry Morgenthau delved into reform issues, the more he included his son in his thinking and affairs. "I was over in Washington," he wrote in one letter, "and had an interview with the President, I shall tell you all about it when I see you." The openness sparked an enthusiasm. "Keep me in touch with the general situations," Henry Jr. wrote his father in the fall of 1909, "financial and political, etc., because you know it interests me." The distance had only strengthened their closeness: "You know, Papa," he wrote after just a month at Cornell, "that the twenty-four [hours] we spent together were one of the most pleasant times I ever had. When I awoke, in the following morning, I had to rub my eyes & think just where I was. It seemed like a dream."

The plan for the son's future, though, remained the father's. And the son, no matter how hard he tried, could not live up to it. Decades later, Henry Morgenthau, Jr., would blame his failings on his father's demands and his own poor health. But the underlying trouble went undetected and untreated. Dyslexia in the first decade of the twentieth century was not yet a diagnosis, yet Henry Jr. almost certainly suffered a severe learning disability. Time and again, whether at Exeter or Cornell, he described a fight against an invisible demon. "I want you to understand clearly my case," he pleaded with his father. "Now, Papa, if I write to you about my studies, please do not worry about them," he asked, "for it makes it only harder for me to write it to you." "I have not done well in two historie [*sic*] exams which I took a week ago. I have had a certain spell which comes over me at certain times and I am going to break away from it, let's hope, for good."

Henry Jr.'s striving for moral perfection remained. Yet as he matured, forever being measured, and measuring himself, against his father's success—an immigrant boy forced to quit college but who had risen fast with far less—the yearning took on greater meaning. At Cornell he came to see his struggles in the classroom as an existential battle. "I have not mastered myself yet," he wrote his father, "but it is going to come, for it has to—enough said. You can not tell me what to do, or anyone else, for I know only too well what I ought to do, and I am going to fight to the finish. I look at it as another part of myself which must be killed once & for all, and then I will be free to apply myself."

It was no use. After two semesters at Cornell, his marks dragged along near failure. In the fall of 1910, he faced the reality and dropped out.

|| ||

Over the coming year, Henry Jr. tried a succession of apprenticeships, each tethered to his father's affairs. He did stints as a machinist at the Underwood Typewriter plant in Hartford, a timekeeper at a construction site in New York, a settlement house worker, and a bank clerk. In each job, his father's long arm protected him. At Underwood—his father was now the second-largest stockholder—the foreman made sure the laborers did him no harm, even after Henry Jr. had slugged one worker over an initiation taunt. At the construction site, Henry Jr. turned up each morning in overalls but did no manual labor. His father had secured an easy spot for him: logging the workers as they came and left the site.

In summer, Lillian Wald, a friend of the Morgenthaus for years, offered a stint at her Henry Street Settlement. Each day Henry Jr. presided over a boys' club, sharing the supper table with a group of nurses and, on hot summer nights, dragging his mattress out on the fire escape. By fall, the son was through with the training stints, but not the father. "I thought Henry ought to study a little of the banking business," Henry Sr. would later recount to a reporter. "So I put him in a private banking house. He came to me after a few days and said, 'Pa, I feel as though I were confined. I feel as though I were in a cage.' Well, he was in a cage, the cashier's cage."

The year out of college tested Henry Jr. in ways that no teacher had. Outside the classroom, even on his father's short leash, he had been slowly gaining confidence—before he got sick. Henry Jr. had been at the typewriter plant only a few days before he was struck with typhoid. His father at once arranged a trip. After New Year's 1911, Henry Jr. boarded a train and headed to West Texas to recuperate. As always, his father relied on his contacts among the German-Jewish aristocracy. The C Ranch, ten miles north of Midland, was owned by Nelson Morris, a German Jew who had become one of Chicago's leading packers (the "C" stood for Chicago). Henry Jr. spent six weeks there, but he needed only a day amid the open sky and dry cattle fields to fall in love.

"Although I have only been here two days, I begin to feel at home," he wrote to his parents. His first letter home was long, filled with a rush of impressions. "This country and the life is wonderful to me, who has always lived in the city," he wrote. "It is just six, and we have finished our supper and the sun has set. I stood at the gate and watched the sun go down slowly. It is wonderful."

You could ride the C Ranch's 226,000 acres for hours and not come to an edge. It was one of the largest expanses of private land in the West, home to one of the world's largest herds of Black Angus. Henry lived in a small, one-story house, with Leonard Pence, the twenty-two-year-old son of the manager. For Henry Jr. the long days on the ranch opened a new world. He was treated as a tourist, an ailing New Yorker who had come for the dry air of the West. But the ranch life cast a spell.

"If I am not a different boy," the twenty-year-old pluckily vowed to his parents, "when I get back with this fresh air, frugal food and exercise, there will be something wrong."

10. Wilson's Call

SPRING–WINTER·1911

On April 24, 1911, the senior Henry Morgenthau's life changed forever. That evening more than two hundred men of consequence in business and finance, religion and social welfare, convened in the ballroom of the Astor Hotel on Broadway. Almost all were Jews, and they had come to celebrate the fourth anniversary of Rabbi Wise's improbable experiment, the Free Synagogue. Henry, who presided at the affair, and Wise had invited a stirring speaker.

The fifty-four-year-old governor of New Jersey, Woodrow Wilson, found himself in demand. His election scarcely six months earlier had given the Democrats hope. The party was in the midst of an epic drought: Fourteen years had passed since the last Democratic president, Grover Cleveland, left the White House. Governor Wilson almost immediately saw his name floated as a national candidate. The attention, though, was long in coming. Years earlier, when Wilson had served as president of Princeton, he'd attracted the notice of George Harvey, the editor of *Harper's Weekly,* who launched a boomlet. At the time, Wilson, the mild-mannered son of a Presbyterian minister, played coy, yet did little to quell the talk.

Wilson had set out to bring Princeton up with the times. He railed against the elite eating clubs, lobbied for a quad system (a nod to Oxford and Cambridge), and dared suggest new graduate schools. The reforms, to the conservative trustees, spelled a degradation. Wilson would wage a quixotic fight—and lose. But in defeat, he gained what his Scotch-Irish reticence had long checked: publicity.

The Democrats took notice. Before becoming governor, Wilson had never stepped foot in the state capitol, yet after a few months in office he had assumed a new role: avenger of the party bosses. By the time Henry Morgenthau's invitation came, the governor had heard the call to run. The Democratic bosses would never permit so radical a reformer to lead the ticket, but a new generation of progressives was urging him on. Wilson could prove a unifier, they said, the leader who could bring the party together and overtake, at last, the Great Commoner—William Jennings Bryan, who could carry every liberal in the party, but never enough conservatives. Bryan had run for president three times, and lost each time. Wilson, it was true, was little known. (He had scarcely traveled beyond New Jersey, his native Virginia, and New England.) But the rumblings stirred the arena: Theodore Roosevelt derided the governor as a "professor," too weak-kneed for Washington, let alone the battlefield.

Wilson felt a sense of destiny. "I am *not* a conservative," he wrote a confidant, "I am a radical." The governor had always seen himself as an agent of change. Now, as he spoke out with greater openness, critics and supporters alike discovered a rare eloquence.

||||

Years later, Henry Sr. would say it was a leap of faith—that his turn to politics was like a jump from a precipice. In fact, it was an evolution, a shift that happened over decades.

Henry had stumped the Lower East Side before he could vote. In 1876, at twenty, he knocked on tenement doors for Samuel Tilden, the Democratic candidate for the White House. The "younger generation's hero," Henry wrote of Tilden, "had rescued New York from corruption." His diary records his fear, and elation, of walking the streets. Campaigning had opened a new world, but business forced him to set it aside. By the turn of the century, he felt the pull more strongly than ever.

Tales from the lower depths of society filled newspapers. Nowhere in the world, not in "heathen Canton, nor Bombay," it was said, could one find "such conditions as prevail in modern, enlightened twentieth century Christian New York." Still, City Hall did little to ameliorate the blight, and Albany did less. In 1908, it fell to the settlement workers, among them Lillian Wald and Florence Kelley, to fight. The activists, nearly all women, forged the first public organization of its kind, part investigation, part soapbox, which came to be known as "the Congestion Committee." Benjamin C. Marsh, self-described "lobbyist for the people," a son of missionaries and devotee of Fabian socialism, would lead it. In need of a high-profile chairman, someone at home among both the activists and the landlords, Marsh brought in Henry Morgenthau.

Henry turned an honorary position into a bully pulpit. He railed against the tenement horrors, chastised the civic leaders, even lashed out at his fellow real estate men. In Washington, in May 1909, Henry debuted a new role: civic leader. Overcoming nerves—at first he could scarcely speak—he opened America's first conference on city planning. "There is an evil . . . gnawing at the vitals of the country," he declared. "An evil that breeds physical disease, moral depravity, discontent, and socialism—and all these must be cured and eradicated." He worried about the future, of allowing cities "to drift into a disease infected, Socialistically inclined mass, and then spending millions of dollars on hospitals to cure them, provisions to punish them, and police to repress them."

The forecast was prescient. Tensions in the factories soon boiled over. In late 1909, the shirtwaist workers' "uprising" seized New York, rousing hopes among the labor agitators across the country. As Clara Lemlich, a young seamstress, roused her fellow workers, the suffrage movement—once the preserve of wealthy women—gained a working-class battalion. College girls, settlement activists, patrician reformers, and labor leaders locked arms. Josie Morgenthau even joined in. She and half a dozen wives of Jewish bankers and lawyers—among them Mrs. O.H.P. Belmont, widow of Oliver, who was a son of August Sr.—formed "a bail brigade," helping to spring striking workers from jail.

As chair of the Congestion Committee, Henry stood in the vanguard. The city had a duty, he railed, to separate industrial and residential districts, build more parks and playgrounds, and develop transport lines that grew the city outward, not upward. Before long, though, Henry and Marsh fell out. Marsh advocated a "land tax" aimed at speculators, like Henry, who had held large tracts of suburban land for years without developing them. Henry quit the committee. He also kicked Marsh and his coterie out of the building where he had lent them free offices. But the Congestion Committee had opened an avenue for politics. Henry now had his cause; he only needed a candidate.

| | | |

At the Hotel Astor, the governor had sat in silence for hours. Wilson revealed patience, as ten men preceded him to the podium.

The horror of a recent catastrophe hung close. The Triangle Shirtwaist factory fire on March 25, 1911, had been the worst industrial tragedy in the nation's history. It came on a warm Saturday evening, with twenty minutes remaining in the workweek, behind locked doors on the eighth floor of the Asch Building, just east of Washington Square Park. The bodies, witnesses said, fell like bales of clothes. "I learned a new sound," William Shepherd, a young reporter, recalled, ". . . the thud of a speeding, living body on a stone sidewalk. Thud-dead, thud-dead, thud-dead, thud-dead. 62 thud-deads." One hundred forty-six workers had died, all but twenty-three of them young women, nearly all Italian or Jewish. Overnight, the hell of American factories had become the most urgent issue of the day, and the fight for social welfare no longer a lonely crusade. Workers and their families, more than a hundred thousand, had marched up Fifth Avenue. Even "Silent Charlie" Murphy, the Tammany boss, felt the shift. Immigrants had become a political force, and "progressive" a word that conjured a new future.

The Democratic race for the White House was fast taking shape. If tradition held, the nomination would be Champ Clark's to lose. The Speaker of the House, a warhorse from Missouri, had been in Congress since 1890. If Clark should fail, two others waited in the wings, Governor-elect John A. Dix of New York and Judson Harmon of Ohio. Their allure was plain: New York and Ohio had the most electoral votes of any state. New Yorkers had run as the nominee of one of the major parties in five of the last ten presidential elections, and the man who won the White House in all but three of those ten races had been an Ohio native. The New Jersey governor remained largely unknown. Still, the curiosity surrounding his presumed candidacy was rising.

The evening at the Astor had gone long. Through the five courses, cigars and cognac, Henry had anchored the head table, balancing Wilson on his right and William Borah, the populist senator from Idaho, on his left. As midnight neared, he introduced the governor. With his stern gaze, taut lips, and stiff back, Wilson seemed less a politician than a Presbyterian minister, like his father.

The governor opened his address with a taunt. Should there be any businessman among those gathered who conducted his affairs unjustly, he said, that man should leave. The room fell silent, but all could appreciate the rhetorical flourish. Wilson had already sounded the first salvo of a war on the plutocrats. It was an "old doctrine," he had said in Washington weeks earlier, that the public had no right to determine how "private business is conducted." But he had added a progressive left

hook: "Almost none of our private business," he said, "can now properly be described as private business at all."

At the podium, Wilson paused. "I feel as if I had come into an air of
serenity," he said at last. "I have gone through six months of ceaseless
vigilance at our state Capitol in fear that something might be done which
ought not to be done, and that some of the things which ought to be
done would go undone." He held no text in his hands. As would become
his custom, Wilson had jotted notes in shorthand. A speech must flow
freely, he would tell aides, from mind to tongue. On the night of the Free
Synagogue celebration, Wilson spoke on "Politics and Morals," excori-
ating the bosses and the businessmen, warning of graft and greed. But he
went further, to remedies:

"I hate that old maxim," he said,

> "Business is business." For I understand by it that business is not
> moral. The man who says, "I am not in business for my health,"
> means that he is not in business for his moral health, and I am the
> enemy of every business of this kind. . . . America simply demands
> that wealth which is made shall be made by distinct business service,
> giving honest weight, honest measure, and without deception. If your
> business is detrimental to the community it has stopped being ser-
> viceable, and then we must put you out of business.

"The corporations must be regulated," Wilson insisted. Fines would not
suffice—they "do not constitute a pressure but a relief from pressure."
Only prison—"jailing the gentlemen who misguide the corporations"—
would bring reform. "The reflections of confinement," he said, "are
soul-inspiring."

"I don't know," Stephen Wise wrote, "that I have heard a public address which made upon all uniformly the deep and convincing impression which his address did." Wilson "was simple, quiet, and precise in
his mode of utterance," added Wise. "But the man, real, genuine, single-
minded, shines through every luminous word."

"We are in the presence of a great body of changing opinions," Wilson had said. "And with this will come a change of atmospheric conditions, a general readjustment of our economic and political relations
with each other." As the governor spoke, Henry listened a few feet away.
"Influences are at work," Wilson said, "to re-create out of the debris of
debauchery and misuse a nation with a higher tone of individuality, with

a greater moral certitude, and with greater emphasis on its uplifting supremacy."

"It will be," the governor vowed, "a reconstructed age."

When Wilson returned to his side, Henry posed the question of the night.

"Governor," he leaned in to ask, "are you seriously a contender for the nomination for president?"

Wilson replied without pause. "I can only say this in answer, Mr. Morgenthau: I know a great deal more about the United States than I know about the state of New Jersey."

| | | |

The odds, all accepted, were long. Yet as Clark and Oscar Underwood, the House majority leader from Alabama, gathered their forces, Wilson went on the stump. If in New Jersey he had railed against the party bosses, he now reached out to the ethnic communities most candidates opted to ignore: He spoke to Germans, Italians, and Irish, and in the first week of December 1911, he came back to the Jews.

On December 6, Wilson stood in Carnegie Hall to speak on "The Rights of the Jews." All 3,300 seats were filled, the tiers packed, and hundreds more stood along the walls. Wilson's words were electric and entirely unexpected.

For decades, it had been a burning question: Should the United States abrogate the Treaty of 1832, the sole treaty governing trade with czarist Russia? Russia's mistreatment of American Jews—and Catholics—traveling and doing trade in Russia had caused American Jews to mount a campaign to force Washington to quit the treaty. Now after years of failure, they hoped to force a congressional vote. So as not to be dismissed "as a narrow racial Jewish protest," as one advocate wrote, Christian proxies were needed. The support of the New Jersey governor, it was hoped, could tip the balance.

As Wilson stepped toward the lectern, the crowd jumped to its feet, waving handkerchiefs and cheering wildly. "Our next president!" came the shouts from the rafters.

If at the Hotel Astor Wilson offered lofty idealism, at Carnegie Hall he drew a line. Forty years of Jewish protest had yielded little benefit. All Americans, he said, must defend the rights of a few. The treaty with Russia did "not merely affect the rights and essential privileges of our Jewish fellow-citizens as free men and Americans," he went on, but "the dignity of our government." America's Jews, Wilson declared, "have suddenly become representatives of us all."

The address was vintage Wilson: Each word seemed to soar and carry conviction. "Here is a great body of our Jewish fellow citizens," he said, "from whom have sprung men of genius in every walk of our varied life; men who have become part of the very stuff of America." The Jews, he went on, are "playing a particularly conspicuous part in building up the very prosperity" of the country.

"They are not Jews in America," Wilson said, staring out at a crowd ready to rise to its feet. "They are American citizens."

No one, certainly not a Presbyterian running for the White House, had ever said such things in public. "We are not here to express our sympathy with our Jewish fellow citizens," Wilson concluded, "but to make evident our sense of identity with them. This is not their cause; it is America's."

If Henry Morgenthau had any doubts, they were now gone.

11. Money Harvest

1912–1913

For Henry, Wilson had come along at just the right time. At fifty-five, Henry had made his fortune. He remained several ranks below the richest titans of New York, but he had ascended to a new class: the "multimillionaires." Henry could assure himself, and his family, of a future of considerable comfort, and at last begin a pursuit he'd long promised himself: to turn his fortune to the public good. In part, it was a search for a greater purpose—"social service," he called it—and in part, the ever-present hunger for greater notice. Yet there was something else: Having established himself, he felt an obligation to lend his wealth to his adopted land and prove a point. Henry had taken to proselytizing among the city's immigrants with a guiding belief—that they, too, could be "one-hundred-percent American"—and he was determined to demonstrate it in action.

Without hesitation—and against the advice of friends and partners who warned him—Henry threw himself headlong into Wilson's campaign. The candidate was the least-known man in a rare "three-cornered campaign." Taft was entrenched, and Teddy Roosevelt was sure to gather his loyal forces, but Henry would back Wilson the only way he knew how: He would raise money. He would cobble together another "syndicate"—only this time it was to sell a candidate. In the spring of 1912, he astonished Wilson with an unprecedented offer: He would give the campaign $4,000 a month, even as he encouraged others to join in.

William McCombs, an Arkansas lawyer who had only recently begun to dabble in New York City politics, led the campaign team. McCombs, a generation younger and deferential to the point of fawning, would be the one to bestow on Henry Morgenthau the honorific that he would carry, first in the party, then everywhere, for the rest of his life: "Uncle Henry." The nickname evoked Henry's avuncular good nature—his easy rapport and ever-ready optimism. But it had more to do with his financial largesse: Henry was the rich uncle, standing by to bail out the campaign whenever coffers ran dry.

On June 15, Woodrow Wilson moved his family—three daughters, Margaret, Jessie, and Eleanor, and wife, Ellen—to the governor's summer residence at Sea Girt, a wealthy hamlet on the Jersey seashore. It was intended as an end-of-campaign respite, but Wilson's attentions were fixed on the Republican convention in Chicago. Teddy Roosevelt was convinced that the party bosses would rob him of his rightful prize. In the first year that the party allowed direct primaries, T.R. had won nine of twelve states. President Taft managed to lose even his native Ohio, while Senator Robert La Follette, the progressive reformer from Wisconsin, won two states. Tradition dictated that candidates refrain from appearing at the nominating gatherings, but T.R. opted for a dramatic ploy: In an impassioned address on the convention's eve, he asked his delegates to remain faithful. "Some sixty to eighty lawfully elected delegates," T.R. said, belonged to him; he claimed to have won them in the primaries and caucuses. If the bosses did not award him the disputed delegates, he said, his backers should not vote. Before leaving the stage, T.R. let loose a battle cry that would become the first salvo of the Bull Moose Party. "Fearless of the future," he thundered, "unheeding of our individual fates; with unflinching hearts and undimmed eyes; we stand at Armageddon, and we battle for the Lord!"

The T.R. insurgency, however, fell short. On June 22, Taft won renomination by a majority of twenty-one votes. Recognizing that he could not unseat the president, T.R. left the party.

As the Republicans departed Chicago, the Democrats arrived in Baltimore for their convention. The race had narrowed to Clark and Wilson: Each had won several primaries, but Clark led in delegates—and remained heavily favored to win the nomination. On June 23, as Wilson remained in Sea Girt, under siege by the reporters, Henry Morgenthau boarded a train with a dozen other Wilson men headed for the convention. The most vivacious among them was a first-term state senator, a young lawyer so handsome and charming that women blushed in his presence and politicians bet on his future. He was an old-line Knicker-bocker, a man with a last name that conjured political magic: Franklin D. Roosevelt.

"We went to Baltimore," Henry later wrote, "with less than half enough pledged delegates to secure the nomination." Speaker Champ Clark remained in Washington. "Our hopes," added Henry, "lay in the splendid impression Wilson made upon the country, and in the general-ship we should exercise upon the floor of the convention." On the third day of the convention, with the tenth ballot at hand, their generalship was tested. Charlie Murphy, boss of Tammany Hall, delivered all ninety of New York's votes to Clark, giving him a majority of the delegates. Two-thirds were required to win the nomination, but the Clark troops erupted in euphoria. History was on their side: Only once previously had a Democratic candidate who had won a majority of the delegate vote not gone on to win the nomination.

The celebration would prove premature. Clark's floor managers, Henry argued years later, let victory slip. Had they forced a succession of quick ballots, the groundswell would have "carried him over the line to victory." Instead, the delegates were captivated by a sideshow: the Mis-souri delegation snake-dancing across the floor. The Clark supporters cheered themselves hoarse, even leading the candidate's young daughter, draped in the Stars and Stripes, to the dais to sit beside the convention chairman. It was a "pretty picture," Henry conceded, one that "pro-voked yet another round of triumphant cheering." But the Clark camp had wasted fifty-five minutes, frittering away the momentum. To Henry, they had committed an unforgivable error: They dared to celebrate "an assumed victory."

| | | |

But back at Sea Girt, Wilson was ready to give in. The governor tele-graphed McCombs to release all his delegates, but William McAdoo, the other manager of Wilson's campaign, declined to reply by telegram: McAdoo ran to a phone to convince the governor to hold firm. In a frenzy, Henry and other Wilson operatives worked the floor, cutting a deal with Congressman Underwood's supporters to hold fast and not switch to Clark. Unbeknownst to Wilson, McCombs promised the Indi-ana delegation that in exchange for the state's delegates, Wilson would offer the vice presidential nomination to the Indiana governor, Thomas R. Marshall.

"In three quarters of an hour," recalled Henry, "we had corralled our delegates safely out of the path of the Clark stampede." When the snake dance ended, and the next ballot was taken, "the Clark managers had a rude awakening: the result was practically unchanged." Congressman A. Mitchell Palmer, a young force in the Pennsylvania delegation, rose and, on behalf of Wilson, was granted an adjournment until the following morning. The break gave Clark's enemies time to regroup. In each of the thirty-five ballots that followed, the Missourians saw their candidate's lead fall ever shorter.

"The tide had turned," wrote Henry, when he set down his record of the convention. "Wilson's strength grew steadily, because as soon as a delegate realized that his own candidate's cause was hopeless, his thoughts turned from his personal preference to the welfare of the party, and, in almost every case, he realized that Wilson was the one man to lead it on to victory."

| | | |

On July 2, after four days of voting, on the forty-sixth ballot, with 990 votes, Wilson won out.

Within hours, a mile-long line of buggies and autos, aflutter with flags, had formed at the edge of the beach road in Sea Girt. A brass band arrived from Manasquan and played "Old Nassau" on the front porch, as the crowds brought the governor to the veranda. Wilson was overwhelmed. "I cannot express the heartfelt emotions that I feel," he said. A small girl with a blue ribbon tied in her hair took his hand. As all assembled on the lawn fell into a line to shake the governor's hand, a black motorcar approached, surprising the reporters. Henry Morgenthau had raced north from Baltimore, eager to be the first from the victory party to congratulate the candidate himself.

| | | |

The Wilson camp introduced the new chair of the national finance committee to the public as a novelty, an immigrant who embodied the progress of American capitalism and the evolution of the Democratic Party. "Mr. Morgenthau," reported *The Dallas Morning News*, "is the first real estate man to be selected for conspicuous party service." The *Times*, meanwhile, heaped lavish praise. "Henry Morgenthau is, in fact, the real estate corporation," one reporter wrote in a profile. "For it was largely his conception of the possibilities of scientific development of real estate that placed operations in land and building on the same plane as other big corporations. . . . There are few sections of New York in the improvement of which he has not had a hand at one time or another."

Wilson gave Henry only one instruction: The campaign must be built on small contributions, not the self-interest of Wall Street. To the envy of underfunded progressives nationwide, Henry devised a scheme for a "popular subscription." (Most would give $100 or less, he explained, with a maximum of $10,000.) He would shun all funds from the banks and corporate titans, vowing instead to build a network of individuals to fill the coffers. It was a bold promise, but hard to keep.

Henry could foresee a struggle. In the months before the convention, he had sold his candidate as aggressively as he had fought for any real estate deal, and only raised $193,000. Of that total, $20,000 was his own money. Now Henry would have to redouble his efforts, and still hew to Wilson's progressive principles. To make matters worse, two men were soon foisted on him—more as minders than as assistants. Wilson named as Henry's deputy Charles R. Crane, heir to a Chicago plumbing fortune. A world traveler known for his wealth and a fascination with Russia, Crane came with no fundraising expertise. The candidate also brought in Rolla Wells, the popular former mayor of St. Louis, and a fellow Princeton alum, to serve as treasurer. Crane and Wells showed little interest in the battle ahead. Wells, who had been hunting in the Michigan woods when Wilson first sought him out, conceded his surprise: The offer, he said, had come as "a kind of shock." Some saw the men as adding balance to the team—Wells had backed Clark, and Crane, La Follette—but among the press and party leaders, the unspoken reason was clear: Wilson needed to calm anti-Semitic fears. Henry Morgenthau, as one writer noted, would "raise the funds that Rolla Wells will take care of." A German Jew from New York could collect money, but a Princeton man, Episcopalian and American-born, would hold the purse strings.

Henry would continue to consult Wilson, often having his chauffeur drive him out to Sea Girt for updates, but each day now he went to work at headquarters. It was not only the first campaign where men of Irish, Scottish, English, and German-Jewish descent worked side by side, but the first modern presidential campaign. Running the finance effort as a corporation, Henry developed a new national strategy. He would team up with Josephus Daniels, the North Carolina publisher who'd come north to run the campaign's publicity bureau. Working closely with Daniels, whose virulent racism did not prevent him from finding common cause with a New York Jew, Henry charted an innovative blueprint: They would use state and local Democratic newspapers across the country to raise funds. Henry opened finance offices in Philadelphia, Boston, and Baltimore, recruiting nearly all his relatives and friends to the cause. Jacob Wertheim (his son-in-law's father) gave $2,500, Herbert Lehman $1,000, and his former law partners, Lachman and Goldsmith, $500. Henry even canvassed his sons-in-law, Maurice Wertheim and Mortimer Fox. The gifts, he boasted in September, as he made public the list of contributors, ranged from "ten cents to $10,000," and had come from across the nation. It was an unprecedented drive for small contributions. Wilson pronounced himself pleased, but Henry knew challenges remained.

By fall, the campaign had on hand a mere $175,000. The costs over the final stretch were sure to rise, reaching as high as $120,000 a week. "Our needs are imperative," Henry warned party leaders in October. "We require for necessary legitimate expenses another $750,000—and it must come from the people." He pushed on, hoping the "common folk" would buoy the campaign. It was not to be. In the end, political history repeated itself. A handful of the country's richest men sustained the fundraising drive: Crane led the way, giving $40,000; Cleveland Dodge, Wilson's old classmate and loyal friend, added $35,000; and Henry gave $30,000—officially. Unofficially, he may well have given more.

On the last day of October, Wilson held a final rally at Madison Square Garden. Teddy Roosevelt had survived an assassin's bullet two weeks earlier—a deranged saloonkeeper had shot the former president in Milwaukee, but a fifty-page speech, folded inside his breast pocket, slowed the bullet. T.R. had charged ahead, the slug lodged in a rib, holding his own Bull Moose spectacle at the Garden the night before Wilson appeared. But the governor outdid him: 16,000 packed the arena. Amid the heat and noise, Wilson—once dismissed as "a cold and bookish professor"—turned "a regular old-fashioned political meeting of thousands," wrote one reporter, into "a wild, waving, cheering, yelling, roaring, stamping mob of enthusiasts that needed no songs and no hymns and no encouragement to keep it at a high pitch."

"Uncle Henry" sat among the box holders that night and had cause to feel proud. Looking around the Garden, he could see many of the city's most prominent Jews, men he had helped to bring into the highest ranks of the party. But Henry took greatest pride in his operation. Early on, in one of the first meetings with Wilson, long before the campaign had become a cause, an aide in Wilson's circle had suggested that a war chest of $3 million "should suffice." The governor had blanched. Wilson had hoped, he said in reply, the campaign would not cost "anything like that."

Henry had reset the target. One million dollars, he had promised, could win the White House. By election day, he would surpass that goal, just slightly. The final tally—$1,159,446—was modest, later deemed "the smallest for a winner." (McKinley had raised $3.75 million in 1896, and T.R., in 1904, had won reelection with $2 million.) In the end, even with the support of some of the richest titans in the country, the Wilson men set a record: 89,854 individuals gave money, the largest number that had ever contributed to a presidential candidate—and all but 1,625 in amounts under $100.

| | | |

Wilson, a virtual political neophyte, knew he could never match the Roosevelt charm, but T.R.'s third-party run would come up short. Roosevelt far outdistanced Taft, who gained only 8 electoral votes, but finished second in the popular and electoral polls. Eugene Debs, standard-bearer for a generation of Socialists, won 901,551 votes—more than any Socialist in a presidential election. It had begun as a wide open race, and in what had been a rarity until then, all three of the main contenders (Taft had all but conceded defeat by fall) stumped widely across the country. But with the Republicans divided and the reform vote split, Wilson had beat the odds.

The first order of business for the president-elect would be to choose his cabinet. Throughout the deliberations, the president kept close counsel. He discussed names with almost no one but one man, who despite an absence of an official title and a preference to remain in the shadows, had emerged as the governor's chief confidant: Colonel Edward M. House, a wily Texan in self-imposed New York exile. The Colonel—the title was honorary, a vestige of his clout in Texas—possessed a large inheritance, genteel manners, and a lilting voice capable of resolving bitter disputes. He and Wilson had met only in late 1911, but enjoyed an accelerated friendship, and one that, to Wilson at least, seemed predestined. Weeks after their first meeting, House had asked Wilson "if he realized that we had only known one another for so short a time." "My dear friend," Wilson shot back, "we have known one another always."

House had spent the campaign, as Henry Morgenthau would write, "in the process of attracting Wilson's confidence in him, as a man above the wish for personal advancement." He did help Wilson carry the Texas primaries in May, but when the campaign stumbled, he'd slipped away, departing on a European tour. Only once the election neared did the Colonel return, and he soon claimed an outsized influence over the president-elect.

An early concern was what to do with the campaign's finance chairman. To include a Jew in the "family," as House called the cabinet in his correspondence with Wilson during the first days after his victory, would be a radical move. It had happened only once before. Grant had offered the Treasury post to Joseph Seligman, who politely declined, but Roosevelt in 1906 had appointed Oscar Straus as his secretary of commerce and labor.

Henry felt certain he would be rewarded with a seat in the cabinet—ideally, as secretary of the Treasury. Days after the election, he wrote his son Henry Jr. with pride that "Ochs told me last evening at the opera that he thought W. Wilson could not do better than take me in his Cabinet." The *Times*, too, was agitating for a high-level job: Henry, the paper declared, continuing an uninterrupted record of overstatement, had run "one of the most aggressive and businesslike national campaigns in the political history of this country." In public, Henry tried to keep quiet. Yet in the days before the inauguration, reports that he would get the Treasury job, whether wishful thinking or leaks from the Wilson camp, cropped up in the press.

The Colonel, though, advised caution. And by the time Wilson entered the White House, the Texan held unparalleled sway over the new president.

||||

On May 2, 1913, Colonel House hosted President Wilson for a tête-à-tête at his apartment. By the inauguration in early March, he and House had decided on the two biggest jobs: McAdoo, the railway entrepreneur who'd dug the first tunnel under the Hudson, would get the Treasury, and the three-time party standard-bearer William Jennings Bryan—whom the president had taken to calling "Primus"—would get the State Department. But weeks later, many of the important posts remained open.

"We talked of a multitude of matters at dinner," House recalled.

Again, Henry's future was discussed. "I told him that something should be done for Morganthau [*sic*]," wrote House. Wilson replied that "he would offer Morganthau [*sic*] the Turkish mission." Yet the idea of appointing Henry as ambassador to the Sublime Porte, as the government of the Ottoman Empire was known at the time, did not originate with Wilson. House had proposed it within weeks of Wilson's victory, and often repeated the suggestion. Though his detractors would later judge Colonel House's views on Jews harshly, his letters and voluminous diaries do not reveal an overt anti-Semitism. Rather, he had had only limited contact with "the Hebrews," as he called the Jews in his correspondence with the president. They were a distinct race, and a constituency, as he instructed Wilson, in need of placating. Others—Bryan, chiefly—might embrace the idea of a Jew in the cabinet, but House deemed the Turkish post more than enough. Still, he tried to warn Wilson. "I had heard that Morgenthau did not want it," he recalls telling the president, "and would not be complemented [*sic*] by the offer."

| | | |

When Henry arrived at the White House on Monday, June 2, 1913, he was already outraged. Smarting from losing out on the Treasury job, Henry had caught wind that he would be offered a far lesser prize. The post in Constantinople, capital of the Ottoman Empire, moreover, was known as "the Jewish seat." Oscar Straus had held it three times (before and after his tenure as T.R.'s secretary of commerce). For the State Department, a Jewish envoy in Constantinople was not a diplomatic necessity, but for decades the logic had held: Free of the antagonisms between Muslims and Christians, American Jews could maneuver among the Turks with greater ease, and more aptly arbitrate disputes. Wilson, assaying the domestic and foreign advantages, had become convinced. In Constantinople, a man like Henry Morgenthau would wield great influence.

At fifteen minutes past noon, Henry entered the Oval Office. His meeting with the president would be brief. As Henry began to explain that he had no desire to go to Turkey, Wilson cut him short.

It was an opportunity to do so much for "the American Jews," the president said.

Henry was taken aback.

Wilson was "aggressive in manner," he later recalled, "and almost angry in tone."

"I am an American," Henry told Wilson. That the president could see him only as a Jew infuriated him. "I wouldn't be going as a Jew. I would be going as an American."

The president tried to reason. The Turkish capital had become the focal point of Zionist politics. For nearly four hundred years, with only a brief interruption, the Turks had ruled Palestine.

"Constantinople is the point at which the interest of the American Jews in the welfare of the Jews of Palestine is focused," Wilson told Henry. "And it is almost indispensable that I have a Jew at that post."

Henry told the president he would have to decline the offer.

| | | |

Henry had promised Josie a long-overdue holiday in Europe. Before leaving, he sent Wilson a blunt letter, an attempt to explain his decision. "Why," Henry asked, "should Jews be treated any differently than anyone else?" The offer, he added, ran counter to Wilson's own policy of "selecting men solely on their merits." Religion, he argued, should have no place in the decision. "Would prominent Methodists or Baptists be told, here is a 'Position,' find one of your faith to fill it?"

Colonel House enlisted members of the new cabinet to persuade Henry to take the ambassadorship. Yet even when his friend Josephus Daniels, now secretary of the Navy, tried, Henry did not budge. All the while, among American Jewish leaders, resentment was building. Men like Rabbi Wise worried that Wilson would let them down. "As far as I have seen," the rabbi wrote Henry, "no Jew has been appointed to a single place of importance. It seems almost a deliberate slight."

Wilson did, in fact, hope to appoint at least one Jew. Louis Brandeis, the Boston legal reformer who'd gained fame as "the People's Lawyer," stood at the top of the list, as a candidate for attorney general or secretary of commerce. Wall Street and Colonel House, though, could not countenance the progressive Brandeis as attorney general. And for weeks, even after Henry told him he could not take the Turkish post, the president refused to accept his answer. As the lobbying continued, Henry resisted, hoping for a better offer. At fifty-seven, he had attained wealth and played a pivotal role in the election. He believed that he deserved greater recognition. If McAdoo had won the Treasury, Henry deserved, at least, the governorship of the new Federal Board of Control, a body Wilson vowed to create, and which would evolve into a precursor of the Federal Reserve system. He enlisted Senator James O'Gorman of New

York to lobby Wilson, and tried to ingratiate himself with McAdoo. He promised Daniels that he only wished to "devote the rest of my life for the public good." And he pleaded with Colonel House that his motives were "absolutely patriotic." The job would not be "a stepping-stone," Henry vowed, "as I am finished with money-making." And still, Wilson held firm. There would be only one job on offer.

As Henry and Josie had settled in for an extended sojourn in the south of France, Henry wrote Stephen Wise, then in Paris and on his way home from Palestine, to request a meeting. He was seized with indecision. In Dijon, Wise urged his friend to swallow his pride and accept Wilson's offer. Wise knew the Ottoman Empire's significance: As the U.S. envoy to the empire, Henry could help shape the future of Palestine. Henry listened intently, but told Wise that he would put off a final decision until he returned home in early September. Should the Turkish job still be open, he would reconsider it. Three days later, Henry received a telegram from the White House. The Turkish job, Wilson wrote, remained his.

In Europe, Henry came to see the posting as a mission worthy of his stature. Still, Josie had her own objections: She had no interest in living among the Turks. Henry Jr., too, saw the job as a slight—"Take something better or nothing," he telegraphed his father. Henry Sr. wanted to wait until they had returned to New York, to consult with his children and win over his wife, but in the end, Wilson won out. In the first week of August, the hand-wringing ended. In a rare reversal, Henry telegraphed the White House from Venice: "Have reconsidered," he wrote, "will accept." The president was relieved. "Sincerely glad you are willing," Wilson telegraphed in reply. "Will begin arrangements for appointment at once."

The next two years in Constantinople would become the fulcrum of Henry's life.

12. "I Want to Be a Farmer"

1912–1914

As word of the Turkish job spread, Henry's doubts disappeared. Across New York, friends and associates saw the appointment as a coup. Henry Jr. was Henry Sr.'s main worry now. Just as the father was poised for a triumphant move from private to public life, his son was in danger of bottoming out.

Henry adored his only son. But Henry Jr.'s serial failures taxed his father's indulgence. He had returned from Texas in restored health and with a new energy born of a widening imagination. Throughout the stints his father arranged, at the construction site, the settlement house, and the bank, Henry Jr. could not shake the ranch. On the West Texas plains, he had found what all his father's scheming could not instill: a calling. He came home from the bank one day and announced his new goal to his father: "Farming," he said. "I want to be a farmer."

Farming had always been considered a worthy pursuit among the family. Babette fondly remembered the farmlands of Bavaria and, in New York, dreamed of moving to a farm. But Henry balked at the idea of *his son* as a farmer. They struck a bargain: Henry Jr. could explore the idea, but only if he returned to university—this time to study agriculture.

Re-enrolling at Cornell in summer of 1912, Henry Jr., now twenty-one, felt far more assured of his path. Still, he again had trouble concentrating on his studies. After two years away, he struggled to keep up. He endured the coursework—"Farm Crops," "Soils," "Pomology"—through the fall, but by Christmas he feared he would have to quit again—for good this time.

Not only would Henry Jr. never graduate from Cornell, he would never earn a high school diploma. He learned by doing, not studying. He had a vision now—and thanks to his father he also had the means to achieve it. As a boy, his father gave him title to a single lot in the Bronx—bought for $500 in an early shopping spree—plus a share in a set of commercial buildings in the Bronx. One, the Hunts Point Palace, a ball-room Henry had recently built, was already a cash cow. Henry Jr. had enough for a down payment for a farm. But where?

Before he could begin a search, his father intervened once again. As always, when it came to questions beyond his expertise, Henry Sr. returned to a simple rule: "Ask the top man." In the second week of March 1913, days after the inauguration, Henry Jr. took the train to Washington. His father had arranged for him to see Wilson's secretary of agriculture, David F. Houston. Houston, the former president of Texas Agricultural and Mechanical College, was well aware of Henry Morgenthau's role in the campaign. He welcomed Henry Jr. warmly, and introduced him to an assistant, Carl Schurz Scofield.

A soft-spoken Minnesotan in his early thirties, Scofield was a veteran of the department. As Henry Jr. spoke nervously of his dream, Scofield just peered at him over his glasses. It was clear the young man knew nothing about farming. Scofield offered a suggestion: a transcontinental expedition. He would escort young Morgenthau from coast to coast, visiting farms and ranches to study the "latest innovations." Scofield's secretary, J. A. Taylor, would record the myriad data they would collect. Catching his son's enthusiasm, Henry Morgenthau announced he'd cover all expenses.

In planning sessions with Scofield, Henry Jr. scoured the farmers' bulletins, the Department of Agriculture's lists of warnings and recommendations, covering everything from poultry and cattle diseases to insects and fertilizers. He spent days charting his itinerary on a base map of the country, meticulously drawing in red ink. Henry Jr. kept the map for decades. It was the starting point, he later wrote, "of what proved to be more than an agricultural expedition."

On April 15, 1913, the party set out. In all, Henry and Scofield would visit 18 states in 126 days—traveling more than 10,000 miles by train, car, and horse—and Henry would assemble a 225-page record of the journey. They went first to St. Louis, then Michigan and Minnesota, on to the Great Plains, south to New Orleans and Texas, and finally, to the country's westernmost farmlands in the valleys of Northern California. In his letters home, Henry Jr. chronicled his on-the-road education for his father. In the Midwest, he studied purebred Holstein cattle, in the Northwest apple orchards, and in the South the canning clubs. Everywhere Henry Jr. tried to find the "ways and means of improving farming," and at night he dictated his discoveries to Taylor. The resulting account, he wrote, was to be devoid of opinion, a "strictly factual presentation of conditions carefully observed and objectively presented."

Under Scofield's tutelage, Henry Jr. gained the education he had abandoned at Cornell. He saw how American farmers raised cattle, ran dairies, and grew wheat, rice, potatoes, corn, alfalfa, sugar cane, and citrus. He studied, too, the latest trends: the experiments in scientific farming and canning for home consumption. "I am learning a great deal," Henry Jr. wrote his father. "I am again my normal self."

Along the way, something else stirred. The grim state of rural life in America left the young man in shock. As he saw firsthand how the land was worked—where the country's natural bounty was cultivated, and where it lay fallow—Henry Jr. noted, with new understanding, the human cost of the imbalance. He encountered "bad roads," flooded fields, and, all too often, farmers "who are not making any money."

Henry Jr. was learning not only about farming, but about economics. "As you go west in North Dakota," he wrote, "money gradually goes up to 10%"—the interest rates—"as the country is newer and less developed, the risks being proportionately greater." His letter from Fargo ran ten pages. "I believe this is the longest letter I have ever written to you," he told his father. "But I am bubbling over with enthusiasm, new ideas and energy."

| | | |

Hopewell Junction: For as long as Henry Jr. could remember, the name of this crossroads amid a bucolic stretch of the Hudson River valley resonated with romance and promise. As a young law clerk, Henry Sr. had spent spring weekends there. To escape Kurzman's dark, stuffy offices, he would take the train sixty miles up to Dutchess County to relax with his friend George Harpel at Hopewell. When his son was old enough, he resumed the practice, taking Henry Jr. along.

In the early autumn of 1913, as the U.S. Senate confirmed his father as Wilson's ambassador to the Ottomans, Henry Jr. looked at a thousand acres of farmland in East Fishkill, the village abutting Hopewell at the edge of the Fishkill Mountains. In "All for Tomorrow," his unpublished autobiography, the story is one of blind discovery—almost destiny.

Henry Jr. remembered experiencing "the strange feeling of one returning home after a long absence." The setting was certainly beautiful: A cluster of barns graced the flat top of a broad, gently sloping hill, while below, an apple orchard spread out in tidy rows, the trees laden with fruit.

It was an old farm, but in good shape and likely soon to be for sale. No one knew much about the owner, only that he was something of a recluse: Dr. Fritz Regeniter, a German-born doctor who never married, had practiced for a time in the city before retiring to the country. He had been only in his early thirties, and likely already ill, when he came to Fishkill. Now, still not forty, he was dying.

Henry Jr. had found his goal, and for the first time in his life, he was determined not to let it slip his grasp. Just how the relationship evolved, how Henry grew close enough to the ailing doctor, he did not record. In his unpublished memoirs, Henry Jr. claimed only that he had ministered to the man and been rewarded: "For a time, I attended him when he was on his deathbed, alone and without friends." Dr. Regeniter died on March 29, 1914. Two days earlier, the local paper had announced a "real estate transfer": Henry had bought the farm, for $55,000. He would also serve as the deceased's executor, placing a notice in the *Evening Enterprise,* a local paper, that the doctor's relatives in Germany had one month to lay claim to any inheritance.

At twenty-two, Henry Jr. had acquired a home, and a dream. Half of the money his father had put up, the other half was his own. Part came from the sale of his Underwood stock, the rest from the small Bronx lot his father had given him long ago. (Years earlier, Henry Jr. had sold the $500 lot for $10,000.) Henry would move to the farm, rechristening it Fishkill Farms. In time, it would grow. He would buy an adjacent farm, introduce nearly three dozen steers—something the old-timers hadn't seen for decades—and before long buy yet more farmland—700 acres—to add a dairy. But on the day he bought the old Regeniter place, Henry Morgenthau, Jr., became a farmer. It was the only occupation he ever declared on his passport, no matter how high in government he rose.

The soil was rich, and land cheap, but the location was providential. Twenty-six miles away, in a large house where the country roads ended at the steep bank of the Hudson, lived Franklin Roosevelt.

||||

As his departure to Turkey loomed, Henry Sr. was gripped by a rare unease. It was not just that Washington offered little guidance, with Secretary of State William Jennings Bryan knowing "no more about our relations with Turkey than I did." At the White House, the president had no advice to impart, other than to reassure Henry that watching out for the welfare of the Ottoman Empire's Jewish minority—and the Jews of Palestine, then under Ottoman control—was not only within bounds, but to be encouraged. "Remember," Wilson told him, "anything you can do to improve the lot of your co-religionists is an act that will reflect credit upon America, and you may count on the full power of the Administration to back you up."

Nor was it that Josie had no desire to go and insisted on staying behind; or that Ruth, their youngest, would also remain at home. At nineteen, their last unmarried daughter had become Josie's constant worry; someone would have to usher Ruth into society.

No—it was that Henry was seized by a fear that had shadowed him since he had accepted his "mission." It had even intruded on his farewell banquet in New York, in late October 1913, when hundreds packed the Hotel Astor for an elegant sendoff. All of Henry's worlds had gathered under one roof. It was a rare crowd: tenement activists mingling with Wall Street titans, clergymen with impresarios in the arts. At the head table, Henry sat beside Henry Stimson, Jacob Schiff, and Colonel House, and within reach of Ralph Pulitzer and John D. Rockefeller, Jr.

Still, a sense of dread hovered. As Oscar Straus, who had preceded him in the post and had long been a leader of Our Crowd and the Republican Party, spoke, Henry's fear achieved focus. Straus was six years older than Henry. Ever since Columbia Law, where Straus had blazed a trail ahead of him, Henry had been compared to Straus—unfavorably. "Turkey from a diplomatic standpoint has been the most interesting center of European diplomacy," Straus said, opening the evening. T.R.'s secretary of commerce, and three times Washington's envoy to Constantinople, Straus had reached the pinnacle. In matters Turkish, no American could claim greater expertise.

"We always could look upon the troubles that are seething and boiling there as any neutrals and peace-makers," Straus said, "and we should always take that position and no other." In Turkey, Henry should listen to its people, and not American companies. "Let your diplomacy be human diplomacy," Straus warned, "not dollar diplomacy."

When Henry at last took the podium, he startled his audience. "Do you know who I am?" he asked. "We have heard much about the 'Melting Pot' of America. . . . I am the amalgam of what's been produced by putting a little boy in that pot and mixing him with a part of yourselves." Henry had piqued their attention, and he knew it. "Whatever good is in me and whatever good I may do," he said, "is simply the result of my association with you."

And then the guests heard something rare: a confession from Henry Morgenthau. For years, he said, "I have felt somewhat in doubt. I've always had Oscar Straus held up to me—'If you will only be as good as Oscar.'" The line could have played to laughter, but Henry was serious. In his "mission to Turkey," Henry Morgenthau would at last get his chance.

| | | |

If Washington would not give lessons in diplomacy, Henry would consult the top men in the field. At the time, just ten envoys served the American president around the world. Henry sounded them all out, taking a circuitous route to Turkey, via London and Paris, Vienna and Budapest. At each stop, he heard the same warnings: Europe was nearing the abyss. War had recently scarred the Balkans: On a luxurious overnight train ride through Bulgaria, the final leg of his journey, wreckage filled the window. "Saw quite some remnants of war," Henry noted in his diary. "Burned down villages and neglected fields."

Henry, the diplomats had warned, was headed for the fault line. Turkey straddled the Bosphorus on the Black Sea, and the Dardanelles on the Aegean—whoever controlled the Turkish straits controlled the sea trade between England and Russia. Should the Balkans buckle anew in conflict, the fighting could spread to Constantinople. Henry had to prepare himself to be in the hot seat of Europe.

On Thanksgiving morning 1913, after a month-long journey, Henry arrived in Constantinople without his wife, Josie, but accompanied by his eldest daughter, Helen; her husband, Mortie; and their sons, Henry and Tim, five and three. As Henry stepped from the train, out into "a moving sea of silk hats" on the platform, his heart swelled. "At last," he wrote that first night, "I am on duty."

Anyone residing in Constantinople during the first years of the twentieth century, whether American, European, Slavic, or Turkish, had good cause to fear the future. Since the era of Abraham Lincoln, the remnants of the Ottoman Empire, once the world's largest, had become popularly known as "the Sick Man of Europe." It had been in terminal decline for decades. The Turks had endured the jealousy of two empires, the Russian and the Habsburg, while nationalist revolutions had torn away their Greek, Bulgarian, Slav, and Serb provinces. Stripped of its European lands, a humiliated Turkey was eager for revenge.

By late 1913, the armed forces were a shadow of the once-fearsome Ottomans', the central bank verged on bankruptcy, and the Young Turks, the country's untested new rulers, clung to the vestiges of empire by bravado. In 1908, the revolutionists had risen under the banner of "Union and Progress," deposing Abdul Hamid II, the monarch whom Gladstone had dubbed "the Great Assassin." The former sultan now sat a virtual prisoner in a palace, his younger brother enthroned as Mehmed V, a nominal successor shorn of any real power. Claiming to be reformers, the Young Turks had unveiled a new constitution and vowed a reign of "democracy and tolerance." At first, they won the support of the capital's elite, but doubts had set in. Many feared the new regime intended neither a Union nor Progress, and sought to govern by fomenting new conflicts along the empire's ethnic and religious fault lines.

Constantinople was itself divided in two. The capital sat astride the Bosphorus—the meeting point, according to the cartographers, of Europe and Asia. On the western side was the Pera quarter, once the Venetian, and now the European, district, and on the eastern, the ancient city of Stamboul, a labyrinth of minarets and cupolas, the glory of past empires, now monuments to decay. The Pera was a fabled maze of foreign embassies and legations, many of them housed in elegant mansions, a quarter where Germans, Russians, Bulgarians, Serbs, Austrians, Hungarians, Greeks, and Armenians had long lived among the Turks. At the heart of the jumble, near the Grand Rue de Pera, and beside the Pera Palace, Constantinople's finest hotel, stood the U.S. Embassy—Henry's new residence—three stories of marble towering over a broad set of stone stairs. The embassy boasted an ornate formal garden set off by a high wall and, across the Golden Horn, a spectacular view of Stamboul.

It was known as the Palazzo Corpi, after a Genoese shipowner, Ignazio Corpi, who had built it in the 1830s, importing marble and fresco painters from Italy. In 1882 the Americans had moved in, and in 1907 they bought the palazzo, the first American-owned diplomatic building in the world. With its ornate rooms and frescoes—Diana, Neptune, and an array of Muses and Graces floated above the grand stairway and Great Hall upstairs—the palazzo came with a large staff: a dozen diplomatic secretaries and a corps of twenty-three servants. The embassy even had its own gunboat, the *Scorpion*, a 775-ton former yacht converted for use in the Spanish-American War. Since 1908, it had been moored in the Bosphorus, manned by three officers and a crew of fifty-six.

Nearly everyone from the embassy was at the station to greet the new ambassador. Balthazar, his personal *kavass,* or guard, stood stiffly by the family, as Hofman Philip, the *conseiller,* made the introductions. At the head of the queue to shake hands were representatives of Washington's twin interests in the Ottoman Empire: Dr. William M. Peet, a leader of the American missionaries in Turkey, and Oscar Gunkel, director of the Standard Oil office in the capital. God and oil would vie for Henry's attentions.

No greeter, though, was more important than Arshag H. Schmavonian. His official title was "dragoman"—interpreter to the ambassador—but the courtly and erudite Armenian, as Henry quickly learned, was the key man at the embassy, having worked there for sixteen years, coming to know not only "every American interest in Turkey," but the Young Turks who had led the recent revolution.

| | | |

It was not a word often deployed in relation to Henry Morgenthau. But in those first days in Turkey, as he explored Constantinople—touring the spice markets, riding horseback in the chill mornings along the Bosphorus, and by calibrated small degrees testing himself on the diplomatic stage in "a continual succession of luncheons, teas, dinners and formal state functions"—Henry Morgenthau was "giddy."

His European counterparts left him dazzled with their noble bloodlines, resplendent uniforms, and mastery of diplomatic protocol. Before long, though, he learned that the Europeans were the anxious ones. If the Ottoman Empire was in its death throes, the European powers had lined up in an unseemly vigil. "They were acting the part of expectant legatees of a friendless dying man," Henry wrote, "sitting at tea in his parlour, and waiting for his last gasp as a signal for a scramble to divide his property among themselves." The diplomats—French, English, Italian, Hungarian, and Russian—were caught up in a high-stakes gamble, but the United States remained on the sidelines. It was one thing to pronounce your neutrality amid restive powers, and another to exercise it. The American ambassador would need to serve as ad hoc umpire, an envoy among envoys.

For Henry, it was a challenge to savor. On December 11, he enjoyed a first audience with the sultan. Mehmed V may have been the Young

Turks' puppet, but he still flaunted the trappings of power. A parade of five gilded carriages arrived at the embassy to pick the ambassador up— "me in the first carriage," Henry recorded, "driven by 4 horses, 3 out riders and 2 servants hanging on behind." At the sultan's palace, he was treated to rounds of wine and cigars. Although he attempted "the best French I could, which was bad enough," he and the sultan could hardly understand each other. Henry enjoyed the pomp, but he feared entering the diplomatic set. In part, it was protocol. He would have to wait for Josie, who'd agreed to come over in the New Year, to host an official event. Meanwhile his twenty-nine-year-old daughter, Helen, eagerly subbed in, playing the role of the ambassador's wife. With superb French and German, and a natural social ease, she accompanied her father on his diplomatic rounds and soon was hosting her own teas.

Washington had commercial interests in the Ottoman lands: In addition to Standard Oil's concessions, there were American-run copper mines, and the Singer Manufacturing Company operated a string of stores. The embassy, too, had to look after the purchasing agents: the Americans who came for Turkish tobacco, figs, and licorice root. But the embassy's "true mission" in Turkey, Henry would write, was to aid the "permanent civilizing work of the Christian missionaries," who'd been at work in the Near East for decades.

Henry would later say that he had come to Turkey with a distrust of the clergymen as "overzealous advance agents of sectarian religions." Yet on the voyage from New York, he made sure to travel with the "Boarders," as the leaders of the American Board of Commissioners for Foreign Missions of the Presbyterian, Congregational, United Presbyterian, Methodist, and Episcopal churches were called. At sea, the missionaries had turned an upper-deck parlor into a makeshift chapel. Henry had joined them in their "splendid service," Helen playing the hymns on a piano. For a man eager to prove himself a "hundred-percent American," and to prove himself to a president who was the son and grandson of Presbyterian ministers, the missionaries offered an ideal constituency.

The Americans ran two colleges in Constantinople, as well as schools, orphanages, and hospitals throughout the old empire. They could not proselytize among the Muslims, but they could convert the Armenians, who traditionally belonged to the Armenian Catholic Church. The missionaries saw an affinity in the Armenians: They, too, were industrious and resourceful Christians of the West, and outsiders in the Muslim world. Many saw it as their duty to rescue them. These men were Christian, but they aimed to spread a faith that Henry, too, had long preached: "the gospel of Americanism."

| | | |

Henry had heard of the reputation that preceded his arrival: The Turks, and much of the diplomatic corps, had formed an opinion of the new ambassador as an American tycoon sent to Turkey on an amateur's adventure. From the first, Henry set out to counter the image: He asked that he be driven about town in a simple carriage drawn by ponies, and whenever possible, he kept to himself within the embassy grounds. He asked for the recent embassy correspondence and spent days studying it. His hosts and the diplomats, he reasoned, would have to wait to discover his earnest interest in the job. Hosting a formal dinner without his wife by his side was out of the question. Josie's absence, he later wrote, "relieved me, for the moment, of social duties, and gave me time for a considered survey of the society." It was "an opportunity," he wrote, "to learn by indirection."

By Christmas week, Henry could no longer remain offstage. Sir Louis Mallet, the British ambassador who had arrived only a few months earlier, invited him, Helen, and his son-in-law Mortie to an embassy dinner. It would be Henry's entrée to diplomatic society—and they nearly missed it. Helen had hosted two teas on that afternoon, and in her urgency to dress—"busy trying to make myself gorgeous," as she wrote her mother—she forgot to wake her napping father. They had to hurry— "whistling for coats, servants, etc.," before tearing "up to the English Embassy at twenty minutes to nine."

The British Embassy was even larger and more elegant than the American. Uniformed *kavasses* framed the entrance, and powdered footmen in knee breeches, nearly two dozen in all, lined the foyer inside. The Morgenthaus were the last to arrive, and found a dining room filled with ambassadors and attachés and their wives. "You can't imagine my feelings as I was ushered in that room," Henry wrote Josie in a breathless letter the next day. As a voice announced "the American ambassador," and all eyes set on him, Henry froze. He had heard the title, he would confess to Josie, but wondered "Is that me?" For the first time in decades, Henry felt sorely out of place.

Sir Louis, an affable bachelor, who wore a monocle and seemed "very shy" to Helen, took the American around. It was a night of introductions: Markgraf von Pallavicini, a marquis from Vienna, was dean of the corps; Franz Joseph had sent Pallavicini, reputed to be one of the Dual Monarchy's savviest diplomats, to the Sublime Porte in 1906; the czar's envoy, Michel de Giers, was a son of the Russian foreign minister, a seasoned diplomat who had recently come to Constantinople after a decade in Romania. Bompard of France, Garroni of Italy, d'Anckarsvärd of Sweden—they all lined up to meet the American.

After Henry escorted Madame d'Anckarsvärd, the Swedish minister's American wife, to her seat, he took his own next to Baroness Wangenheim, "a fine, good-looking, typically aristocratic German—and a charming conversationalist." He spent most of the evening, though, conversing with her husband, Baron Hans Freiherr von Wangenheim, "a great personal friend of the Emperor," as Henry wrote Josie, who had come "all be-decorated." A hulking figure with a bull neck and piercing eyes, Wangenheim seemed to embody Prussian pride and German imperial hunger. He spoke English, French, and German with equal facility. Such was his stature in Berlin, he confided to Henry, the kaiser had taken him along on holidays to Corfu. Wangenheim, Henry concluded that evening, was one of the most imposing, and impressive, men he had ever encountered.

The Europeans, for all their splendor, were a sideshow. The evening's stars, as they would be on each such occasion throughout Henry's years in Turkey, were the Young Turks—Enver Pasha, Talaat Pasha, and Djemal Pasha—the triumvirate behind the Committee of Union and Progress, whose mercurial rule would reduce the foreign aristocrats to ingratiating supplicants. Talaat Pasha, minister of the interior, was the "big boss." A bear of a man with rough-hewn features, little about Talaat was delicate. At first blush, he struck Henry as a modest bureaucrat who remained proud of the menial jobs of his youth. A former letter carrier and telegraph operator, Talaat still lived, it was said, in a small, wooden house. He revealed nothing of his dark and lethal ambition.

Of the three, however, Enver Pasha may have wielded the greatest power. At twenty-six, he had helped spur the revolution. By thirty-two, he was the minister of war. Unlike Talaat, Enver lived lavishly: He kept a palatial home, and cared little about the rumors of his harem. He spoke fluent German, a vestige of his military training, and had a fondness for the Prussian martial spirit. With his clipped mustache and inky-black, immaculately groomed hair, Enver reminded Henry more of a movie star than a minister of war. Djemal Pasha, least known of the Young Turks, was bearded and barrel-chested, dressed in a uniform lined with medals.

In the shadow of Talaat and Enver, Djemal was still on the ascent, only recently appointed the prefect of Constantinople, its chief of police.

That evening, as Henry began to discern the forces at play, he also saw the grand vizier for the first time. A forty-eight-year-old Egyptian prince who had wed an Egyptian princess, Said Halim Pasha had been named by the Young Turks to the government's highest position. Serving as grand vizier had become a dubious honor. He had been in office only six months, but the Young Turks had radically revised the job: The trappings of the office remained, but none of its power.

For Henry Morgenthau, the evening was a revelation. Still, Henry felt like a trespasser. "And to think," he wrote, "we are a part of it—Young Princes, Barons, Sirs, and Americans from the Embassies, etc. and lots of Turks and Egyptians, etc. I shall never forget it."

Helen danced late and, exhausted, left at midnight. But Henry could not be pried loose. After dinner, Baron Wangenheim had asked him to join him in bridge, and the German and the German Jew sat in a half-lit corner, playing with "a Turk and a Greek banker" until one-thirty in the morning, when the dance floor cleared, and the young people sat down again for a second meal, only to return and dance for another hour.

When he finally left the embassy, his carriage echoing with the clatter of hooves on stone, Henry breathed with a new confidence. "I thoroughly enjoyed it," he wrote Josie. "I am not overstating when I repeat what I said. . . . I am *very glad* I came."

13. "Something Is Brewing"

WINTER–SPRING 1914

For months, the American colony, eager to begin the social season, had been awaiting the arrival of the ambassador's wife, whose presence was dictated by protocol. Henry, joined by Henry Jr., who'd arrived in January 1914, devised a plan to make an event of the welcoming. They would travel to meet the train in Adrianople, the old Ottoman capital in the west, near the Greek border.

Talaat was shocked by the ambassador's plans. "Going to all that trouble to meet one's wife!" he told Henry. "In Turkey we let our wives come to us. We do not go to them." In reply, Henry imparted a lesson in the cultural divide. "I cannot imagine an American failing to do it," he told Talaat. "In my country, our wives share all their husbands' interest, and I should certainly consider myself lacking in both respect and affection if I failed to show my wife this attention."

Henry had further reason to be solicitous. Josie, who would be making the crossing with their daughter Ruth, had dreaded coming, and he wanted to soften her arrival. To her, Turkey had loomed as "a dreary exile from home and friends," an unnecessary sojourn "in a dull and uncivilized community," as Henry later recalled. From the start, though, Josie found herself enjoying the attentions of the Turkish officials. In Adrianople, she was greeted in "an almost Royal setting." Talaat had telegraphed ahead, instructing the governor to spare no expense—the local governor, mayor, and chief of police all came to the station. When the train arrived, Josie was moved by the extent of the formalities. The Turks had urgently transformed one half of the town's City Hall into a makeshift hotel for the Americans. On the governor's orders, they installed a kitchen, dining room, and beds, even providing pajamas, slippers, and toothbrushes. Life among the Turks, Josie realized, would not be entirely uncomfortable.

Once back at the embassy, Henry promptly forgot his promise to allow Josie time to rest. On the following afternoon, he hosted a reception in her honor, a *"votre jour."* "There were over 70 callers," Henry recorded in his diary, and Josie received them all. She chatted with Marquis Pallavicini, Sir Louis, the Swedish minister d'Anckarsvärd and his American wife, and even, as the ambassador noted, a beautiful English aristocrat, a twenty-one-year-old poet on her honeymoon. She was introduced as Mrs. Nicholson (the newlywed bride of a third secretary in the British Embassy), but would later become known as Vita Sackville-West. Josie may have been exhausted, but her entrance into the diplomatic world was roundly deemed a success. "Ma, Helen and Ruth," wrote Henry, "enjoyed it immensely."

Josie and Ruth, hurting from being jilted by a suitor in New York, had scarcely settled in when Henry Jr. announced his departure. He feared abandoning his father to "the girls," but he was eager to return to his project at home. Within hours of stepping foot on the Westside pier in Manhattan, he made straight for the farm in Dutchess County.

In Constantinople Josie found her own way with an ease that surprised even herself. She knew how to discover causes, to find ways to do good and enter the community. In New York, she'd worked with the tenement activists and led the founding of the Bronx House, the settlement house and music school. In Constantinople, she quickly acquainted herself with the work of the Girls College, and a number of the city's schools and orphanages—Greek, Armenian, and Jewish. As Talaat and Turkish officialdom looked on in bemusement, Josie returned time and again, often with Ruth in tow, to meet with the local youth. Josie was most taken with the eager students at the Girls College. Soon she was standing at the helm of her own class there, teaching English to twenty-eight students.

| | | |

"There is a feeling here," Henry wrote in his diary, "that something is brewing and it is likely to cause trouble in the spring. The Young Turks are likely to be forced into action to maintain their hold on the government. I fear a *coup d'état* with Enver at its head."

In those final months of winter, Henry had only to tally the signs. The first was the money question. The subject had arisen on the afternoon of the British ambassador's dinner, when Talaat summoned Henry to his office for the first time and wasted no time laying out the grim picture: The regime was nearly broke, he said, before asking if the Turks might secure "a small loan from America," perhaps even a personal one from the new ambassador? The Turks needed the money, Talaat said, in order to pay off loans from French bankers. The government, he assured Henry, would make the money count. A loan of 500,000 Turkish pounds—$5,000,000 at the time—"could last 2 months."

It was not an isolated conversation. Time and again, the Young Turks took the American ambassador into their confidence, insisting that the state had "no money at all." They were reluctant, the Turks hinted, to turn to the Germans for assistance. Henry was sympathetic. "Their struggle for financial help," he wrote, was an opportunity to strengthen America's hand in a game long dominated by the European powers.

Henry promised the Young Turks nothing, but soon after Talaat broached the subject, the ambassador set out to make a loan happen. He went to see the Standard Oil men to secure their participation, and he cabled the secretary of state, asking for "consent to assist Turkey." He then asked Rob Simon, the nephew he put in charge of his business affairs in New York, to test the waters among the real estate men and bankers—but to be discreet. The news traveled too fast. Before Henry heard from New York, his fellow ambassadors were quizzing him: Was it true, they wondered, that the Americans were bailing out the Turks? Henry let the rumors swirl until March, when, answering the ambassador's call, a white knight sailed into Constantinople harbor.

C.K.G. Billings was one of the richest men in Virginia. An eccentric best known in New York for an obsession with horses, and the castle he had built above the Hudson on the site of the old Fort Tryon, Billings had made his fortune early in life, in gas and coke fuel in Chicago. In 1901, at forty, he had retired, buying a large swath of Washington Heights—at the time when Henry Morgenthau was the district's chief broker. In the United States, Billings had heard the plea for help from Henry's nephew and leapt at the chance to play savior, coming across the Atlantic on his yacht, the *Vanadis*. On Billings's second night in Constantinople, Henry hosted a dinner for the tycoon and his entourage—and Talaat was there. At the table, the ambassador was in a mood to celebrate; that afternoon, he had cabled Wilson congratulations on completing his first year in office. Everything went well, until coffee was served—and Talaat delivered an about-face. Billings's assistance was no longer needed, he announced, "as France was giving money." In fact, the French had signed a deal for a new loan tranche that very day. Talaat was willing, though, to grant the Americans a prized foreign concession: to run a lucrative state lottery in Turkey. Henry recoiled. He and Billings were "Haute Financiers," he said, "and my administration would not stand for my backing up a lottery."

The reversal was an affront that Henry would not forget, even long after Billings had set sail for home. The Turks had used the Americans to bait the Germans and seal a new deal with the French. Yet, ever the optimist, Henry allowed himself to imagine that in the Billings debacle he had bought a measure of goodwill with the Turks. In his diary and dispatches, too, a dominant thread now emerged: sympathy.

The Turkish leaders sensed it. They had become convinced, against their better judgment, that "America alone of the larger foreign nations had no private axe to grind as regards her relations with Turkey." The Turks not only turned to Henry for counsel—they invited him to join the government. Henry scoffed at the offer—Talaat had spoken of the post of finance minister—but privately he took pride in the suggestion; he was making progress.

||||

Henry had long hoped to see the Holy Land, even before Colonel House had raised the idea of the Turkish ambassadorship. At the White House, Wilson had spoken to Henry of Palestine and its importance. And Rabbi Wise had taken the liberty to turn Henry's dream into a plan, brokering introductions to the most prominent Zionists in Europe—Claude Montefiore in London, and Baron Rothschild in Paris—and lobbying for a fact-finding expedition. "Everyone," the ambassador would write, "urged me to go."

Henry Morgenthau remained a humanist, the founding president of the Free Synagogue and a believer in the Ethical Culture movement led by the reformist educator Felix Adler. In the eyes of so many of his "co-religionists," as Wilson called them, he was a non-practicing Jew. Yet Henry was captivated by the Ottoman Jewish world. The grand rabbi, Hayim Nahoum, a scholar in his forties, had become a frequent dinner companion. ("His Eminence," wrote Helen, "is an awfully nice soul, garbed in a flowing black *gouri* and a fez . . . something like a combination of a Greek priest and a Hadja.") To his family, and in his diary, Henry spoke of a returning tide: a religious renewal.

On a Sunday morning in late March, two days after Josie's fifty-first birthday, the Morgenthaus rose early and were driven down along the Bosphorus to Therapia, to board the *Peter the Great,* an elegant little Russian steamer that plied the sea-lanes between Odessa on the Black Sea and Alexandria on the Mediterranean. If Henry had envisioned a family excursion, he was soon at the helm of an impressive delegation. Even before reaching Palestine, the group of six had grown to twenty-six: including American missionaries, Arabic scholars, and the Reverend John Nevin Sayre, brother-in-law of President Wilson's daughter Jessie. The party would add the philanthropist Cleveland Dodge, a Wilson friend since Princeton and an early backer, and Dodge's son, Bayard, and his wife and father-in-law.

The *Peter the Great,* its mast flying the Stars and Stripes, stopped first in Smyrna, then in Piraeus. Henry had ordered the captain of the embassy's naval yacht, the *Scorpion,* to sail ahead to greet them in Alexandria. Leaving Smyrna, the ambassador recorded the day's events in his diary: saw "King George driving his automobile," "talked with the Turkish minister and saw Schlieman [*sic*]," son of the famous archeologist, now a Greek politician. A day later, as the steamer left Athens, and "the sun was setting most gorgeously," Josie announced that she felt "homesick after Alma." "She wanted to go home," her husband wrote. But Henry had rarely been in better spirits.

Egypt brought a series of discoveries: the twenty-eight-year-old acting governor of Alexandria, who stood at the quay with a bouquet for Josie and a box of *marrons glacés* for Ruth; the immensity of the pyramids; and most surprising, the Egyptians' distrust of the Young Turks. Henry was struck, too, by the unshakable sense of British superiority. Egypt nominally remained in the Turkish empire, but Lord Kitchener, the former field marshal, ruled as de facto viceroy. After hosting a luncheon for the Morgenthaus, Kitchener took Henry aside for a closed-door talk. Few Westerners could claim greater knowledge of the Near East: As a young man in the 1870s, Kitchener had spent three years in the Palestine Exploration Fund helping to survey the Holy Land, and in the decades since he had led the retaking of the Sudan and the command of the Second Boer War. After seven years atop the British Army in India, Kitchener had returned to Egypt as proconsul, the chief British official in the region. Kitchener was "anti-Turkish," Henry would conclude, after enduring a "very thorough cross-examination." The proconsul had been keen to hear Henry's take on the Young Turks, but was reluctant to share his own opinions. Kitchener, wrote Henry in his diary, delivered a private lecture on how the British remained "the best equipped for administration," and "Orientals" were "unable to accept Western methods as yet."

No matter where the delegation traveled, or whom Henry encountered, one question hung over the journey: the future of Palestine. For years, Henry had let it be known to all who would listen: He was no Zionist. He would tour Palestine, he had assured the Young Turks, not as a Jew, but as the envoy of "all Americans." In private, though, he saw the trip as a debate with Stephen Wise. Rabbi Wise had become ever more insistent, and vocal, in his Zionism. Henry fumed at the way Wise had raced ahead in his absence, pursuing his own agenda with the men whose acceptance Henry had been so careful to win: Wilson, Colonel House, and the Jewish leaders in New York.

Henry was no longer Wise's junior partner, and he refused to be bullied. "Has it ever occurred to you," he wrote Wise before setting out on the trip, "that if the Jews again become a nation either in Palestine or elsewhere, while they are developing and before they reach (even if they ever could) such importance that they would have their own army and navy, they would in case of prosperity become a prey to the cupidity of some great power who is so equipped that it should easily destroy them?" Rather than collecting the Jews of the world into one homeland, Henry argued, wouldn't they stand a better chance of success if they "continued to be spread amongst other nations," where they could "take advantage of their great results that they attained in the last fifty years in England, America, France, Italy and elsewhere?"

By April 2, Henry's party had arrived in Jaffa. He had set out to conduct a firsthand investigation of the Holy Land, and his first days did not disappoint. Palestine was still a region without borders, home to more than half a million Arabs and fewer than 100,000 Jewish settlers, by the best estimates. The "Yishuv," as the Jewish settlement was known, had seen two waves of Jewish immigration: the first "Aliyah" starting in 1882, and a second, beginning in 1904 and then coming to an end. The majority of the Jewish immigrants had come from the borderlands of czarist Russia. In the second wave, many had followed Theodor Herzl's messianic dream; others fled anti-Semitism—the pogroms igniting eastern Europe. By 1914, Americans still called it "the Holy Land," but to the Jewish settlers it was Eretz Yisrael—the Land of Israel.

Henry was keen to see the Zionists, the newest arrivals, many of them more interested in political institutions than in religion, and among them a hardy corps of farmers intent on building agrarian communities. The pioneers were after the most arable land, fertile and flat. Using their greatest weapon, money, they would buy it from Arab landowners, living at a remove in neighboring lands, by the *dunam* (one-fourth of an acre) or in large swaths. By 1914, the Jews could claim several dozen settlements, including the sparse contours, beyond the dunes north of Jaffa, of a town the settlers called Tel Aviv.

Henry discovered a "splendid example of what can be done in five years" in Tel Aviv. On a tour with Arthur Ruppin, the German-born head of the local Zionist office who for years had crisscrossed Palestine, scouting for fertile land, Henry pronounced it "a clean nice little town," with "an air of prosperity and comfort that would do credit anywhere in America." The farms of the Russian Jews impressed him, as well. They had overcome so many hurdles—the dry, sandy land, the Turks, the Arabs, and even the rigid administrators of Baron de Rothschild, who had donated the land—to grow "oranges, almonds, wines etc." To Henry, it was as if he had discovered a new kind of Jew, men and women of rare strength. "The condition of the people is far superior to any city Jews that I have seen," he wrote. "They showed the result of honest toil and open air, and the way they danced, the decency thereof, puts to shame the gilded youth of America."

Henry abandoned his usual restraint—"I am feeling as though I had been transplanted into the pre-Christian world"—while at night he turned to the Bible and Baedeker's to read up on the day's sights. He also felt a new pull: He was beginning to see the Zionist movement anew. "One feels impressed," he wrote in his diary, "that it would be a great thing for the Jews to have a real haven of Tolerance."

| | | |

It was not the easiest tour. As the delegation made their way from Jerusalem to Beirut, Henry found himself struggling to be seen as neutral among the local faiths. He hated being greeted, and honored, as "the Jewish Ambassador." Crowds appeared at every stop. "The Jews," wrote Ruth, "absolutely leave Pa no peace." And over the protests of the Jerusalem vice consul, Samuel Edelman, a Pennsylvanian in his late twenties, Henry insisted on meeting with Christians and Muslims. In Jerusalem, he joined the missionaries at Palm Sunday services, and in Bethlehem, he visited the Church of the Nativity. Edelman feared that the ambassador, a novice on his first trip to the region, would offend one of the contending sides. But Henry would not give in; "I insist on seeing all," he wrote, "and just judging and listening."

And yet, as the delegation moved on, the undertow was unmistakable. One night as Henry sat among a circle of settlers, Jews told of working the experimental farms of Aaron Aaronsohn, and they offered a blunt prediction: They would have no choice but "to drive out the Arabs."

Henry was determined to hear from the Arabs themselves. He went by horseback to Nablus, first spending the night in a tent to witness a midnight sacrifice of lambs, before the governor extended a rare offer: an audience with local Arab leaders. The American missionaries in his party were keen to go, as was another prominent British official, James Bryce, a latecomer to the group. Bryce was best known to Americans as the former ambassador to the United States, but he had long served as the Armenians' leading advocate in England—and Henry was eager to sound him out on Turkish matters.

They set out on foot, escorted by the Nablus chief of police and three constables, each carrying a table lamp. "We walked through the dark streets, weird and Arabian night like," Henry wrote. "Here and there was a shoemaker at work and a fruit store open, through one street, turning corners, and twisting, breathing in a fine aroma, until we landed suddenly in a square with a fountain and two well illuminated rooms." In the largest room, its walls lined with divans and covered with rugs, two dozen Arab men sat cross-legged. They seemed, to Henry, "bred of good stock." Their hospitality "was exactly like we read of." "They served us cigarettes, sweet syrup water, tea, coffee, and they were continually looking out for our comfort."

Walking home that night, Henry savored the encounter. "Nothing could have been more gracious or hospitable," he wrote, "than their manner toward us."

The party also visited the ancient Caves of Machpelah, home to the tombs of Abraham, Isaac, Sarah, Rebecca, Jacob, and Leah. For seven hundred years, the Muslims had held the site, barring Christians and Jews from entering. Rare exceptions were made for royalty, and ambassadors. The tombs—"the first assignment of property to the Hebrew people in the Holy Land"—were a landmark to the world's first known legal contract. Genesis 23, Henry knew, tells how Abraham bought the land for four hundred silver shekels to bury his wife, Sarah. The caves lay in Hebron, twenty miles north of Jerusalem. The Morgenthaus and the missionaries drove out in open carriages, arriving at the noonday prayer. As the local Arabs waited outside, inside the caves Henry asked all in his party to devote five minutes to silent prayer.

"There we stood," he would later write, "Moslems, Christians and Jews—all of us conscious of the fact that we were in the presence of the tombs of our joint forefathers—that no matter in what details we differed, we traced our religion back to the same source."

Palestine was a land not only in dispute, but desperately poor. He had looked out a hotel window and seen an alley filled with camels and donkeys carrying wood. "This is a large 'poor house,'" Henry wrote to himself, "supported by Europe and America." He had seen, too, the seductive promise of the Jewish settlers, but would long remember the candor of the governor in Damascus. Seeing "little hopes for adjustment between Turks and Arabs, Kourds and Jews," he had proposed a solution: "they should destroy all mosques, churches and synagogues and begin again."

Henry would leave the Holy Land invigorated, but confirmed in his faith. America, not Palestine, remained his Promised Land. Once back in Constantinople, he renewed his suspicion of Zionism. And yet, the Holy Land had changed him. The euphoric moments in the ancient tombs, sacred to three faiths, marked a return across a generation to Schiller's romantic universalism, to *Nathan der Weise* and Lazarus Morgenthau's belief in those first years in America, when his vision was still clear, in the power of ecumenicism. Henry would always remember the Caves of Machpelah and those minutes of quietude—"the most sacred," he would write, "I have ever spent in my life."

14. "Guns of August"

Europe stood on the precipice, set to erupt again in war—and Turkey, gateway to the all-important trade avenue between Russia and the West, was besieged by all sides. In Constantinople, no one spoke anymore of a way to skirt the turmoil—"*seferberlik*," the Turkish word for "mobilization," was on everyone's lips. All men twenty to forty-five years old were to be conscripted. On August 6, Henry sent an urgent cable to Washington: "Entire empire under martial law."

Four days later, the ambassador stepped aboard a wooden launch to sail down the Bosphorus to meet the *Sicilia,* an Italian steamer arriving from Venice. Onboard were the Wertheims—Henry and Josie's second-eldest daughter, Alma; her husband, Maurice; and their girls: Josephine, four years old, Barbara, two, and baby Anne, three months. A day earlier, on the Ionian Sea, they had stood on the deck to witness an extraordinary naval engagement—the first salvos, as little Barbara would call it decades later (when she'd become the historian Barbara Tuchman), of "the guns of August."

Once the Wertheims had made it to the American Embassy, Wangenheim and Pallavicini, the German and Austro-Hungarian ambassadors, respectively, raced over to hear them describe the drama. Alma and Maurice had been at lunch when "two strange-looking vessels" appeared on the horizon. "I ran for the glasses," Alma told the envoys, "and made out two large battleships, the first one with two queer, exotic-looking towers and the other one quite an ordinary-looking battleship." Transfixed, they saw another ship, going fast, come up behind the large ships.

"She came nearer and nearer," Alma said, "and then we heard guns booming." Pillars of water rose out of the sea, Henry's daughter said, and puffs of white smoke filled the air. The exchange "went on and on."

War had come so quickly. Amid "the secrecy of the diplomats and the swiftness of events," wrote Walter Lippmann, in London at the time, "it all seemed like a terrific plunge, let loose by a few men who consulted nobody." No one could have predicted when the first shots would sound, but the chain of alliances had been set for years. When, after the Serbian-abetted assassination of Archduke Ferdinand in Sarajevo on June 28, Austria-Hungary declared war on Serbia, Russia sided with Serbia, and Germany with Austria. Still, few foresaw that Turkey would leave the sidelines and ally with Germany and Austria-Hungary—the Central Powers—against Russia, France, and England—the "Triple Entente."

The ships that Henry's daughter and her family had seen, a battle cruiser and a light cruiser, were German, and the smaller ship was a British cruiser, the *Gloucester*. As Alma and Maurice finished the tale, Pallavicini thanked them politely. Wangenheim, though, could not suppress his glee. After months of secret deliberations among the Germans and the allies to force the Turks' hand, the turn had come. For days, the British had chased the *Goeben* and the *Breslau* across the Mediterranean. Eager to take refuge at Constantinople, part of a strategy to drag the Turks into the war on Berlin's side, the German ships had escaped, and remained, it now seemed, in the Dardanelles.

All summer, Henry had sensed the unwinding approaching. A week after the murder of the archduke, the diplomatic corps had gathered for a memorial in church. The service on July 4 marked a "strange day," Henry wrote—afterwards, he'd hosted the American colony and the diplomatic corps at a garden party, but the pall hung close. The next day, Bompard, the French ambassador, made it plain: War was imminent. By August 1, Germany had declared war on Russia. As France, England, and Russia closed ranks, Constantinople was seized with rumors that the Russians would declare war on Turkey. The French ambassador fumed that the *Goeben* and the *Breslau* were still flying the German flag. The Germans, he told Henry, were "acting as though they were the masters," bullying the Turks. Within two days it was over: Admiral Souchon, the German at the helm of the *Goeben*, arrived in Constantinople, and the Germans and the Turks announced a deal: The German battleships would be sold to Turkey, and Souchon was named to command the Ottoman fleet.

| | |

The streets of Constantinople had filled with jubilant Turks. As they greeted the German sailors—more than a thousand in all—as saviors, Henry watched with understanding. Many Turks still fumed at the British, outraged that the First Lord of the Admiralty, Winston Churchill, had weeks earlier "requisitioned" two Turkish battleships, the *Sultan Osman I* and the *Reshadieh,* from English shipyards. For years, the Turks had been desperate for new ships. They had paid a high price, too, through a public subscription drive. Churchill had snatched the ships, without compensation, just as they neared completion.

At the American Embassy, the reports and rumors now came almost by the hour. Sir Louis Mallet, the British ambassador, warned that if the Turks should use the *Goeben* and *Breslau* seamen, "there will be trouble." London would have no choice but to "treat the ships as German"— and would "fight to the finish."

Henry enjoyed a panoramic view of the Ottoman Empire, and his network of consuls and missionaries was flashing red. "All our telegrams show great agitation and fear," he wrote in his diary on August 20. "The Turks are absolutely reckless in their mode of requisition. . . . They are looting people under the flag of mobilization." Enver was leading Turkey down a fateful path: He would "plunge the country" into either "internal trouble or war with Russia."

Envoys of the Great Powers had already sounded the alarm. For weeks, the Europeans had been transfixed by a single fear: that the Young Turks would cast aside the Capitulations, the set of rules that dated to a 1536 treaty with France, granting legal and commercial privileges to European traders and pilgrims in the Ottoman Empire. By virtue of the Capitulations, Christians in the empire faced fewer taxes, were exempt from military service, and, above all, enjoyed virtual legal immunity. To describe the privileges, the diplomats used words like "order," "balance," and "custom." But to the Turks, the rules were sorely outdated, little more than camouflage for the foreigners' greed. Now the rumors carried the Europeans' worst fear: The end of the Capitulations was near.

Henry turned to Secretary of State Bryan for guidance. But Washington was in mourning: Ellen Wilson, the president's wife, long suffering from Bright's disease, had died on August 6, at fifty-four. The ambassador cabled condolences to Wilson, and then sent a long communiqué to

Bryan, laying out Germany's intentions, as relayed by the German ambassador. Henry and Baron Wangenheim had formed a warm, if cautious, relationship. They dined together, went on long horseback rides, and shared frank exchanges. For weeks, Wangenheim had sought to convince Henry that the kaiser had one goal: to keep the "Russians from entering Constantinople." "Germany has her foot on Russia's corn," Wangenheim told him, referring to the Germans' control of the Dardanelles, the sole shipping route for Russian crops to Europe, and would keep "it there until the end of the war." Constantinople, Berlin was convinced, would be "the prize that Russia, if victorious, will demand." It was as much a prediction as a threat. "The Dardanelles will not be closed for commerce," Wangenheim vowed, unless Britain—seeking to aid Russia—attacked the straits. In that contingency, the straits would be sealed "in less than half an hour." The Germans would do "their utmost to assist Turkey."

At the end of August, Secretary Bryan answered Henry at last. America must at all costs stay out of the fight. And the ambassador, Bryan instructed, must do all he could to see that Turkey, too, "remain[ed] neutral for the sake of humanity."

| | | |

In his first fall in Constantinople, Henry got the chance to take executive action. It came in response to an urgent plea from Palestine. The Jewish settlers were facing dire threats: Their breadwinners had been conscripted, and their lifeline—remittances from the Diaspora—was in jeopardy. Morgenthau could foresee the next step: If the Turks should join the Central Powers, the settlers would be cut off entirely. "Palestinian Jews facing terrible crisis," he cabled Jacob Schiff.

> *Belligerent countries stopping their assistance. Serious destruction*
> *threatens thriving colonies. Fifty thousand dollars needed by*
> *responsible committee. . . . Conditions certainly justify American*
> *help. Will you undertake matter? —Morgenthau*

Three days later, he cabled Schiff again, asking for "immediate assistance" to feed and clothe the Jewish colony. Schiff called an emergency meeting of the American Jewish Committee, the first group of its kind—founded to defend Jews "in any part of the world"—and promised Morgenthau $50,000, a substantial sum at the time, would be forthcoming. Schiff then extended himself further: "Should this not be possible," he wrote of gathering the funds, "I shall do it personally."

In the third week of September, the USS *North Carolina,* an armored cruiser, entered Jaffa harbor. Onboard, Maurice Wertheim, Henry Morgenthau's son-in-law, carried a suitcase filled with $43,000 in gold bullion, purchased with 8,600 Turkish pounds—5,500 from the Standard Oil safe in Constantinople, and the balance advanced from the American ambassador himself (all that Henry could raise). Henry had coaxed the Standard Oil men into fronting the gold, and requested that his friend from the campaign, Josephus Daniels, secretary of the Navy, order the *North Carolina* to transport it. Daniels had conceived of a mission "to fly the flag," a reminder to the Germans of the strength of the neutral United States. With Wilson's blessing, he dispatched the USS *Tennessee* from New York and the *North Carolina* from Boston. Both ships would be available for relief duty, with the *North Carolina* cruising off the coast of Palestine. Henry had recruited his son-in-law to escort the gold and deliver it into the hands of Dr. Ruppin, the Zionist leader the ambassador had met only months earlier.

At the landing station, a large crowd had gathered. At its head stood an old friend of President Wilson's, the Reverend Otis A. Glazebrook. The clergyman had long yearned to live in the Holy Land, and that spring Wilson had indulged his wish. At sixty-nine, after three decades of pastoring in New Jersey, Glazebrook was sent to Jerusalem as U.S. consul.

Days earlier, Glazebrook had cabled Henry Morgenthau with his own urgent plea. "Forty thousand Jerusalem Jews," he wrote, were "in desperate condition." The Turks had announced the "abolition of Capitulations for October 1st." The Jerusalem markets had flour for sale, but the Jews had "no means to purchase." Wertheim painted the picture even more darkly: "No money entering Palestine," he cabled his father-in-law, "shipping interrupted. Poor on verge starvation." He sketched out a relief plan: "First, soup kitchens for very poor. Second, food stores selling staples at cost. Third, loan institutions lending on security and also on labor."

The shipment of gold marked the first time that private Americans delivered aid to the Jews of Palestine. The crisis eased, and the bridge between the wealthy German Jews of New York and the Jews of Palestine was born. Wertheim had been careful to note that "the poor" of

Jerusalem would bear the brunt of the shortages, and not "the colonists." Still, years later, Henry's granddaughter, Barbara Tuchman, would claim that the ambassador had saved the Jewish settlers "from starvation and probable extinction."

||||

Throughout the fall, the Triple Entente desperately tried to keep Turkey neutral—but all entreaties were doomed to fail. By October, the envoys from Britain, France, Russia, and Belgium remained, but so many envoys from Entente-friendly countries had fled that Henry Morgenthau now oversaw the diplomatic concerns of nine other countries. On October 12, he dictated a long letter to Henry Jr., describing how the embassy had turned to a wartime footing. Before closing, he added a paragraph by hand:

> *Now have my 10th country—San Marino. It is wondrous strange really, in a fashion [I] enjoy my quasi-imprisonment here. You may call it isolation or what you like. I construe it into [sic] a visit to another world or planet—cut off from the earth—associating exclusively with people of whose existence I did not dream 2 years ago. It is passing strange, is it not? Now good bye, good boy,* auf baldiges wiedersehen.
>
> *Yours lovingly,*
> *Papa*

Thursday, October 29, would prove a momentous day. In the afternoon the ambassador was granted an overdue audience with Talaat. Henry could not even begin a plea for neutrality before Talaat suddenly admitted "that they had decided to side with the Germans, and sink or swim with them." The Turks, he explained, "had to have a strong country to lean on, and if they had not agreed to depend on Germans, they, when defeated, would have been the first to suggest cutting up Turkey."

That afternoon, Henry was still reeling, and struggling to reassure his own embassy staff, who'd grown increasingly anxious, when Ambassador Bompard came to ask him to take over France's affairs. Within hours, Moncher, the Belgian envoy, followed. Even as Talaat assured Henry that "there would be no war with England now," Sir Louis Mallet, London's ambassador, was also preparing to depart. So, too, was Giers, the

Russian ambassador. (The Russian's wife even asked a favor of Henry: Could he store her jewels in his safe?) And then by evening, the fateful news hit.

The *Scorpion* captain brought the word. "At about 7:40 McCauley came," Henry wrote in his diary, "and told me of Mallet's receiving a dispatch that the Turkish fleet had bombarded Odessa, a sugar factory, destroyed the *Donetz* (old cruiser), three Russian ships, and one French." The Young Turks had not bothered with a declaration of war. Enver had ordered Admiral Souchon to lead the *Breslau* and *Goeben* on a raid across the Black Sea. There would be no turning back. "The Germans having made slow progress were determined to take extreme steps to do some harm to Russians," Henry wrote feverishly that night. "And now they have succeeded and Wangenheim has won out. He . . . controls the Black Sea."

Standing in the shadow of the kaiser, the Turks had taken on the United Kingdom as well. Visiting the British Embassy that night, Henry noticed lights in every window of the grand building. The fireplaces were ablaze, the counselors and secretaries furiously burning documents.

Turkey was in the war.

15. "You Can See and Feel the Hatred"

n the fall of 1914, nearly three million ethnic Armenians lived in Asia Minor. As many as half resided to the east of Turkey, in the Caucasus Mountains at the foot of Mount Ararat, in Russian Armenia. A million others inhabited the six vilayets—provinces of Turkey—on the high plateaus of eastern Anatolia. Hundreds of thousands more filled the vilayet of Adana (known as the Kingdom of Little Armenia during the Crusades) along Turkey's southeast coast, the region stretching from the Taurus Mountains to the Mediterranean. There were Armenians, too, in the capital: a sizeable community, the most prominent of the non-Muslim ethnicities who had settled in Constantinople centuries earlier. Though famed as traders, Armenians also numbered among the empire's professional class—doctors, lawyers, writers, and artisans. They were also Christian—the first nation to adopt the new faith, in A.D. 301—in a Muslim world.

Religion was only one of several reasons the Armenians had been treated so badly across the empire. Ambassador Morgenthau knew the bloody history. In 1894, as many as 200,000 Armenians were slaughtered by the sultan's troops in a two-year rampage. "Another Armenian Holocaust" read a headline in *The New York Times* in 1895. Returning from the Holy Land, the ambassador learned firsthand of a more recent massacre in Adana, where in April 1909, less than a year after the Young Turks' coup, more than two thousand Armenians had been killed. After a day spent among the survivors, Henry wrote: "You can see and feel the hatred."

In the recent Balkan wars, when the Greeks, Serbs, and Bulgarians had fought to throw over Turkish rule, Armenians had served in the Turkish army with distinction. But many had escaped military duty, paying a tax to gain exemption. Under the war mobilization now under way, there would be no way out: All Armenian men aged twenty to forty-five were required to serve. Throughout the autumn, as Enver's army raced to amass supplies and move troops, the Turks had to rely on mule trains to carry goods long distances over rough terrain. At the American Embassy, the reports from across the network of consuls and missionaries began to trickle in: Instead of mules, the army was using Armenians, and many, overcome from exposure and exhaustion, were dying along the way.

By December, from the remote eastern vilayets bordering Russia, word came of renewed bloodshed. In Bitlis, rioters had attacked hundreds of Armenians, and marauding bands had raided the plateau villages of Erzerum. The German ambassador heard the news, too. *Der alter Hass,* the old hatred, was rising again, his consul reported from Erzerum. On the first of December, he recounted, three Turkish irregulars had visited a priest in the village of Osni, sharing a meal and spending the night in his home. In the morning, they forced the priest, a revered figure among the locals, "to accompany them to the edge of the village, where he was shot to death." Riots, pogroms, murder—it was the work, the villagers said, of a shadowy force. The "Special Organization," Teşkilât-i Mahsusa, as it was known in Turkish, was a militia of bandits and former convicts that Talaat had created to launch a terror campaign.

As his diary reveals, at first Henry Morgenthau did not believe the reports. He had doubts, but was intent on clarifying his questions. He turned to his aides, above all his confidant Schmavonian. He consulted the European envoys, and was surprised to hear Baron Wangenheim's concern. The German ambassador, unbeknownst to Henry, had already warned his own chancellor of the bandit militia's *Übergriffen und Ausschreitungen,* its abuses and outrages. Henry turned to Enver and Talaat, who dismissed the reports of raping and killing as hysteria. Yet as the American ambassador sifted through the Turks' repeated assurances, he feared the worst.

| | | |

The ambassador wrote his son often, at times nearly every day. So, after a week in mid-August without a letter, Henry Jr. worried that something was amiss in Constantinople. "Your silence to me is a bad omen," he wrote. As the news from Turkey grew darker, he decided his father needed him. In late December, Henry Jr. sailed again, the second trip within a year to be at his father's side.

Months earlier, Henry Jr. had witnessed embassy life in its elegant luxury; now the staff was on a war footing. Almost at once, he was put to work "as secretary-companion for Father." The ambassador took his son to see the European envoys, and to private conclaves with the Young Turks. "Partly, I suspect, because he wanted me to admire his technique," Henry Jr. would later recall. "And partly because my presence gave him strength."

The father also enlisted his son in an unofficial mission. For months the ambassador had been at work on a secret plan for "a separate peace." The Turks, he believed, could be persuaded to return to neutrality. Later, many would term the idea naïve; some would even call it insubordinate. Since the fall, Talaat and Enver had never been explicit, but Henry had heard a distinct desire for an umpire. The United States, he had come to believe, could pry the Turks away from the Germans and cut short the war.

In Washington, Henry knew, any peace plan, no matter how far-fetched, was sure to find a welcome. President Wilson had staked his presidency on preserving American neutrality. Secretary Bryan, more-over, not only insisted on keeping the United States on the sidelines, he was pushing hard for peace negotiations. "We owe it to other neutral nations," Bryan wrote Wilson in December, "to do everything in our power to bring the war to a close."

On January 15, Henry Morgenthau drafted a long letter to the president, making the case for his proposed peace deal. The German ambassador, he wrote, had never played coy about the kaiser's intentions. At the outset of war, Baron Wangenheim had told Henry that "unless Germany succeeded in its 'Rush Campaign' and reached Paris early in September, it would probably be unable to defeat France." In the months since, Wangenheim, Henry went on, could not hide "his great disappointment": Italy had refused to join the Germans, the Belgians had mounted a stubborn defense, and the British held firm. Wangenheim had only repeated that "Germany will fight to the end"; any German who proposed ending the war would be deemed "a coward and almost a traitor." "All suggestions of peace," the German had told him, "must come from a neutral Power."

Henry was certain of it: Only Wilson could broker the peace, and the window of opportunity was nearing. The French and Russians, Henry wrote Wilson, took "it for granted that you would be asked to arbitrate the matter." And the Turks, with their stores of coal, oil, and food running low, would "hail with delight *immediate* peace." When should the president issue his "*pronunciamento*"? "Of course you are the best judge," Henry offered, before answering his own question: "To me it looks as though the proper time is near at hand."

Rather than send his secret proposal by cable, the ambassador asked his son to hand-deliver it to Wilson. He also instructed Henry Jr. to scout the front lines and sound out the British. Henry Jr. traveled home via Germany and England. He tried out the "secret plan" on Sir Edward Grey, the British foreign secretary, and his father's old friend Walter Page, now the American ambassador. He also won an audience with Colonel House, who since the outbreak of war had taken to spending long stints in London and Paris. Serving as Wilson's eyes and ears abroad, House had all but sidelined Bryan, sending the president updates on the fighting and vivid portraits of the combatants.

The statesmen each listened as Henry Jr. presented his father's plan for peace. For a twenty-three-year-old amateur farmer with no college degree, it was a nervy performance. But Henry Jr. spoke with confidence, arguing that Wilson had a genuine chance to play peacemaker. The Turks, he relayed, had grown frustrated with their patrons in Berlin. They had not risked all merely "to obtain a protectorate under the Germans." The Turks, he insisted, could be won over.

The stopover in London was notable for a second debut: Henry Jr.'s first audience with a newsman. Adopting a ploy from his father (who doubtless suggested the idea), the son invited the local *New York Times* man to his hotel. The resulting interview, when published in New York days later, produced the desired effect. Henry Jr. praised the Young Turks and made no mention of any Turkish attacks on minorities or Christians. Constantinople, he reported, was an island of stability. "I can emphatically say," he told the reporter, "that the Turkish capital when I left it wore as normal an appearance as any of the cities I have been through." The English were unmolested, he added, insisting "neither in Constantinople, nor in other places in Turkey, have there occurred any anti-Christian riots, and such things as internment camps are non-existent." The performance hit its intended audience. The Turks were pleased. So, too, was the American ambassador. His son had helped prepare the ground, and his plan for "a separate peace," however fanciful, remained in the realm of the possible.

After three months abroad, Henry Jr. returned to New York. This time, the newsmen were waiting on the pier. He had come home for good and would not be returning to help his father, Henry Jr. told the reporters. "I assisted him as private secretary only temporarily," he said. "By profession I am a farmer."

| | | |

In Constantinople, spring had turned the parks in Pera green, but the strain on the ambassador only increased. By April 1915 the rumors had become unavoidable: The Armenians, Henry heard almost daily, were in danger. For months, Schmavonian, his dragoman, and Andonian, his secretary, had warned of the coming persecutions. His Armenian aides spoke with a feverish concern: Their people, once again, faced a wave of attacks. Yet whether fearing a confrontation or holding out for unimpeachable evidence, Henry was reluctant to put it to the most powerful man in the country: What are you doing to the Armenians?

On the evening of Saturday, April 24, Talaat was the guest of honor at the American Embassy. Over coffee Henry turned to him, and asked—for the first time—about the Armenians. Talaat admitted the police had "arrested a great many of them," but added that the government merely wanted "them to leave the city," to ensure that they would stir up no protests. The police had acted only to preserve the public order, and would resettle the Armenians, he said, "among Turks in the interior, where they can do no harm." Henry took Talaat at his word. In part, it was naïveté; it was also willful blindness.

On that same evening, as the two sat enjoying a last cigar, the streets of the capital betrayed the lie. Many Armenians were asleep, exhausted from the Easter celebrations; before the night ended, more than two hundred and fifty of them were taken away. Roused from bed, they were told they would be home soon; there was no need to pack any clothes. They were men of varied professions—clerics and shopkeepers, writers and teachers, journalists and lawyers, politicians and newspaper editors. Together, they were the elite of Armenian culture in Turkey. "Our nation," a survivor wrote, "was being decapitated."

Talaat had told the truth of the dark design—in part. The Armenians would be sent out of the city: two hundred miles east, to prisons in

Ayash, northwest of Ankara, and Chankiri, a hundred miles farther on. But Talaat, in the first of countless conversations with the American ambassador about the fate of the Armenians, had committed the first of countless sins of omission. He had not revealed their final destination. Most of the men arrested would never be released; most would be murdered. For the Armenians of the empire, April 24, 1915, was the day when their world ended.

The sweep came, as Talaat later assured the American ambassador, as a last resort. Fearing an Armenian revolt because of the upheaval among the Armenians in Russia, whose armies were advancing in the Caucasus toward the Turkish border, the regime felt the need to silence any subversive movement. Talaat, Henry wrote in his diary on the night of April 24, was "evidently as much afraid of internal trouble as the war." "And they"—the Turks—"have made up their mind to crush all possible attempts at revolution."

There were, as well, gathering threats from outside the empire. As Henry dined with Talaat, three hundred miles to the southwest the British were preparing a gamble "to force the Dardanelles"—to send an armada into the Turkish straits, restoring Russia's lifeline and opening the straits to European traffic. Nearly two hundred ships—"battleships, cruisers, destroyers, trawlers, supply ships, transports," Churchill wrote later—turned the sea dark beside the headlands of the narrow peninsula. The first Allied troops came ashore in near blackness. Fifteen hundred men from the Australian Third Brigade faced a bleak terrain, rugged cliffs and steep gullies that rose almost at once from the sand.

"Gallipoli" would become shorthand for Western military hubris: The Allied invasion of the peninsula would last nine months, claiming more than 40,000 British lives and 87,000 Turkish. But in its first hours, the assault sent the Turkish leaders into a panic. With the British forces clawing at their underbelly and the Russians coming fast across the mountains in the east, fears of enemies within and without gripped Constantinople.

By week's end, Henry sent a portentous dispatch to Washington, one of hundreds he would draft in the coming months. The urgency of his consuls' communiqués was growing: The embassy, he wrote Secretary of State Bryan, had received "reports from certain parts of the Empire of massacres, plunders, and persecutions of Armenians." On April 26, Caleb F. Gates and William W. Peet, leaders of the American missionary community, told of "massacres in the interior." "Very disquieting news,"

Henry recorded in his diary. "Gates gave me a long account prepared by the community which showed terrible condition." On April 27, the German ambassador told Henry "he would help Zionists but not Armenians. He told me that . . . 400 of them [Armenians] were killed there."

The next day, Henry went to see Enver to complain about Turkish troops that had taken over a missionary school in Harpout, a remote town in the interior: "He promised to again communicate with them and see that they quit the schools as soon as possible." Enver assured Henry that "very shortly all the soldiers would be placed in tents," but that the state had to act. Armenians had been "in control of Van"—a town deep within Asian Turkey at the edge of the eastern mountains, home to more than 20,000 Armenians—"for 12 days." They had bombed state buildings and, "lest they would do similar things in Constantinople," been packed off "where they would be prevented from doing any harm." Not to worry, Enver had told the ambassador, the offenders had been "routed out and a number of them killed" and "the situation in other Armenian districts was under control."

Henry relayed the news to Washington: "In justification of movement against Armenians," he wrote Secretary Bryan on April 30, "Enver told me that the Post-Office and Public Debt buildings were destroyed by Russian Armenians." The arrests in the capital, Enver insisted, had merely been a preventive act. But Henry noted another explanation for the bloodshed: It was reported, he wrote Bryan, that "while the Armenians were in possession of Van," they had killed the local governor, Enver's brother-in-law.

Henry Morgenthau had done his duty. After months of listening idly to the fears of his Armenian aides, his dragoman and secretary, he had warned Washington. Henry had dared, as well, to raise the question of the Armenians' fate with the Turkish leaders. "Talaat and Grand-Vizier have promised that no excesses or general massacres will take place," he reported to Bryan. The American ambassador could sleep better, but he would soon come to regret his calm. For in that first spring, even as the terror mounted, he had blindly taken the Turks at their word.

16. "A Campaign of Race Extermination"

SPRING–FALL 1915

They redirected cables, improvised codes, even stitched messages into the lining of clothes; but the consuls and missionaries in Henry's network in the remote corners of the empire—in Van, Harput, Moush, Aleppo, Beirut, Baghdad—managed to get messages through to the American Embassy in Constantinople. The ambassador's desk was soon piled high with macabre accounts—a paper trail of what history would condemn as the Armenian genocide.

On May 12, Jesse B. Jackson, the consul in Aleppo, reported that "about 28,000 persons" had been led away from the towns of Zeitoun and Marash, "driven in herds to the four points of the compass to a fate of which none can predict." The Turks had forced the Armenians out on foot. The old and infirm had not made it far. Fathers had been taken from their wives, children ripped from their mothers. The miseries were too great to contemplate.

Decades later, historians would decry the silence of the West. But in the spring of 1915, within two weeks of Jackson's cable, and only a month after the mass arrests in Constantinople, England, France, and Russia charged—in an official diplomatic note—the Turks with "crimes against humanity." Henry Morgenthau delivered the scalding document to the Sublime Porte. The grand vizier was taken aback. He "expressed regret," Henry cabled the State Department, "at being held personally responsible." He resented, too, the "attempted interference" by foreign states with "the sovereign rights of the Turkish government over their Armenian subjects." Yet even as he reported the rebuff, Henry closed with a warning: "Persecution against Armenians increasing in severity."

Before June was out, Leslie Davis, the consul at Harput, the most remote of the thirteen American consulates in the empire, sent the first of a series of anxious telegrams to the ambassador. Davis did not waste words. The Turks had deported the entire local population of Armenians, he wrote, herding them off "about five hours' distance from here"—where they could be killed unseen by foreign witnesses. The Turks, he added, sought "to destroy the Armenian race."

I I I I

In Washington, the Wilson administration was still reeling from the sinking of the *Lusitania,* torpedoed by a German submarine on May 7, and the loss of 128 American lives. Since the outbreak of war in Europe, the president had maintained the insistence on neutrality, but now the groundswell was too great. Wilson dispatched a threatening diplomatic note to Berlin, causing William Jennings Bryan, who warned of a slide into war, to resign. ("Colonel House," he told Wilson, "has been Secretary of State, not I, and I never had your full confidence.") To replace Bryan, the president promoted Robert Lansing, a stolid State Department attorney from upstate New York who was an expert in an emerging field: international law. With his pomaded silver hair, trim mustache, and bespoke suits, he looked the picture of a secretary of state. Although few men in Washington knew Lansing well, Wilson was assured the new secretary of state possessed one merit: He would live by the letter of the law. The president would seek to be "practically his own Secretary of State," as Colonel House wrote, with Lansing entrusted with finding legal justifications for American neutrality.

Henry Morgenthau was losing faith in American neutrality. Consuls, missionaries, and survivors had stood before his desk and told stories. One of the first, the Reverend Henry Riggs, a third-generation American missionary, risked his life to bear witness at the embassy. The disappearances, he said, had come over several weeks: Harput's "finest citizens," "all Armenians of prominence and influence," had been hauled off. There were reports from prison of "beating[s] and starvation," of "extraction of teeth, branding with hot irons, stabbing in the face of sharp irons, and burning of hair and beard." A boy who brought food to the prisoners had smuggled out a request scrawled on a scrap of cigarette paper—an Armenian professor begging for poison to escape "the unbearable ordeal."

From Urfa, a town in southeastern Turkey near the Syrian border, the

Reverend Francis H. Leslie described a "reign of terror." For four years, Leslie had been the sole American among the locals, running the missionaries' school for the blind and a factory where young men learned cabinetry and shoemaking and more than a thousand girls made lace. Urfa boasted a strong Christian presence: as many as 25,000 Armenians and several thousand Assyrian Christians. The Turks had seized on the threat of unrest as an excuse, ransacking the Armenian quarter, and disappearing the town's "most honorable men." For weeks, Leslie had also seen a stream of deportees from the north, Armenians forced south from Zeitoun and now on the long road to the desert. Women, children, and old men—"clubbed and beaten and lashed along as though they had been wild animals." The same fate, Leslie warned in a dispatch to Consul Jackson in Aleppo, awaited the Armenians of Urfa. The Turks accused the local Armenians of caching weapons, warning the local Armenian bishop that if they did not hand over their putative arsenal, all would be "destroyed."

| | | |

On July 10, a Saturday, Henry Morgenthau rose early and was at his desk dictating when the first light illuminated the Golden Horn. "Persecutions of Armenians," Henry wrote to Secretary Lansing, "assuming unprecedented proportions." The Turks, he said, were subjecting the Armenians to "arbitrary arrests, terrible tortures, whole-sale expulsions and deportations from one end of the Empire to the other." Accompanying the misery were "frequent instances of rape, pillage, and murder turning into massacre."

While Lansing was settling in, Henry had moved forward on his own, pleading with Wangenheim and Pallavicini to help end the onslaught. But Pallavicini proved reluctant to confront the Turks, and Wangenheim had lost much of his force; unbeknownst to Henry, the German ambassador was sick—secretly ailing for months with "neurasthenia." The Prussian bear would soon return to Berlin.

"These measures," Henry wrote Lansing, "are not in response to popular or fanatical demand but are purely arbitrary and directed from Constantinople in the name of military necessity, often in districts where no military operations are likely to take place." The official rationales had worn thin. Henry abandoned any ambiguity. "There seems," he concluded, "to be a systematic plan to crush the Armenian race." The reports had once come to the embassy by the week. By midsummer, they were arriving by the day. On July 11, Consul Leslie Davis again sent word from Harput. "Many thousands" had already been deported, and now the "public crier" had announced the next stage: "on Tuesday, July 13, every Armenian *without exception,* must go." "Everyone knows it is a case of going to one's death."

"From harrowing reports of eye witnesses," Henry wrote Lansing, "it appears that a campaign of race extermination is in progress under a pretext of reprisal against rebellion." Lansing was unmoved. In the absence of any American victims, he could offer no consolation. "The Department of State can make no other suggestion in connection with this most difficult situation," Lansing replied on July 20, "other than that the Ambassador continue to act as he has done." Henry's frustration only mounted. As Washington remained unmoved, and the flood of horrific reports continued unabated, he felt an encroaching sense of helplessness—and began to fear how long he could endure it.

At Gallipoli, at the same time, the Allied invasion had turned desperate. General Otto Liman von Sanders, the kaiser's man at the helm of the military mission in Constantinople, had taken over the Turkish defense. In the eastern mountains the Russians were fast giving ground. And yet the death marches only grew—spreading to the central plateau of Anatolia, a region far from any front. As the sea of deportees swelled, the Turks could hardly justify the campaign in the name of military security.

In late August, Francis Leslie wrote that the Armenians of Urfa had agreed to surrender any hidden arms, but "a mob of Turks and Kurds" staged a pogrom in the market, killing at least two hundred. Days earlier, Henry had sent the vice consul from Aleppo, Samuel Edelman, to shore up Leslie, whom Henry had designated an "emergency consul." The two Americans had pleaded with the *mutasarrif*—deputy to the *vali,* or provincial governor—to end the rampage. Only the diplomat's arrival, Leslie was certain, had staved off "a general massacre." But fear had seized the town, and the missionary worried that "a stampede" of refugees would storm the mission residence. "Since Aug 19th," he wrote, "we have had a guard constantly before our door and squads of police and gendarmes day and night patrol the streets."

Talaat demanded that the American ambassador order Edelman and Leslie to leave Urfa, but Henry refused. The Turks were holding nearly three hundred prisoners of war in the town—British, French, and Russian soldiers—who survived on relief allowances from the American Embassy in Constantinople, and Henry had tasked Leslie with ensuring that the funds be delivered. The missionary feared he could not manage: His work in Urfa, he wrote, was "too much of a load for one man to carry." "Pray for us," he begged the ambassador, "and suggest some way of getting help if possible." He saw the end nearing. Within weeks, after repeated failures to drive out the Armenians, Count Eberhard Wolffskeel von Reichenberg, a Bavarian officer assigned to the Fourth Ottoman Army in Syria, ordered his artillery to level the town's Armenian Quarter. Fleeing for their lives, Armenians forced their way into the orphanage of the American mission and took Reverend Leslie hostage, desperate to prevent the Turks from shelling the building.

Henry Morgenthau could take no more. "I earnestly beg," he cabled Lansing in August, "the Department to give this matter urgent and exhaustive consideration." He pleaded with Lansing to find some way "of checking this Government." If America could not stop the massacres, it could at least tend to the sick and starving. But Henry heard only the same reply: no.

"Technically, I had no right to interfere," he wrote in his memoirs. "According to the cold-blooded legalities of the situation, the treatment of Turkish subjects by the Turkish Government was purely a domestic affair; unless it affected American lives and American interests, it was outside the concern of the American Government." But in the fall of 1915, his frustration with the Turks, and his own government, burst the patient niceties of diplomacy. "Destruction of Armenian race in Turkey," he cabled Lansing on September 3, "is progressing rapidly."

| | | |

The American Embassy had become known, as a visitor would say, as "a Mecca for sufferers"—and, if anguish counted as suffering, its chief occupant numbered among them.

The American ambassador now stood as the most important foreign envoy in a city once flush with accomplished diplomats. Henry had charge of the affairs of Italy, Russia, and Montenegro—in addition to the countries, now more than a half dozen, whose envoys had already fled. The expanded portfolio had captured the Turks' attention.

"You represent all our enemies," quipped Talaat.

"Except that the U.S.," countered the ambassador, "my main principal, is your friend."

Since his arrival Henry had tried to win over the Young Turks, hoping to spread "the Gospel of Americanism," to convince the Turkish leaders of the value in hard work, honest profit, and equitable justice. Diplomacy, he had learned, demanded more delicate skills than real estate. Yet even in the face of the mounting evidence of the persecutions, he only stepped up his efforts. "It is a most trying task to continue doing business with the authorities," Henry wrote his son, "but I have to and therefore must." He had no choice: The front line had come to Constantinople. "I fear," Henry confessed, "that shortly they will begin their attacks on and deportations of Armenians in this city." Each day the terror came closer to the men at his side: Schmavonian and Andonian, his dragoman and secretary. "Our Embassy is far from cheerful," he confided, "but I have determined to stand it all as best I can—do my very utmost to alleviate things and rest on that."

||||

For months, Henry had been urging Josie to go, but she held out to the last. The woman who had never wished to play a diplomat's wife, who had delayed coming to Turkey, now did not want to leave. Josie gamely hosted the weekly receptions at the embassy, which soon became the only venue where the diplomats, belligerents or neutrals, could gather. Josie won friends not only across the American colony but among the foreign schools, colleges, hospitals, and orphanages. Even Wangenheim, when he sent his wife out to Berlin for her safety, had invited Mrs. Morgenthau to join her. But Josie refused.

She could not abandon her work. When Bompard and his wife fled, she had taken charge of the French Hospital, almost single-handedly keeping its doors open. She had helped to protect, as well, the Sion Sœurs, a French sisterhood that for years had run a girls' school in the city. She had even smuggled the sisters' savings out of the school for safekeeping. Twice she had hidden the gold coins beneath her clothes, marching past the gendarmes waiting by the doors to raid the school, to stash the money in the embassy safe.

The suffering of the Armenians consumed Josie. The wounded, the widows, the orphans—it became too much to bear. Josie decided to return home. The Girls College hosted a formal farewell, where its head, Dr. Mary Patrick, extolled Josie's generosity and good works in a hall filled with the American colony, and the remnants of the English. As Dr. Patrick spoke, though, a disheartening worry gathered in her voice: the question of how they would manage without the ambassador's wife.

Josie boarded the train alone, her purse filled with *laisser-passers* for a dozen countries across Europe. Bound first for Sofia, she took tea with Queen Eleanore and seized the chance to plead the Armenians' case. The Bulgarians had joined the Turkish side, but Josie's entreaty caused a stir. The queen sent a dispatch to the Bulgarian minister to rein in the Turks. The Bulgarians' rebuke, Henry reported, caused Talaat to fall into "an absolutely ugly humor."

In the days after Josie left, Henry rose early, before dawn. He tried to draft a Sunday sermon for one of the missionaries' local schools. Dr. Gates had asked him to expound on the "Power of Personal Influence." But Henry's mind roamed. "I could not concentrate on any one part of what I should say," he confided to his diary. He and Josie had parted often, but never had he felt the uncoupling "as keenly as this time." For the first time since coming to Turkey, Henry Morgenthau was on his own.

| | | |

In New York City on September 16, 1915, seventeen men gathered in the boardroom of Cleveland Dodge, the philanthropist and old friend of the president. The Committee on Armenian Atrocities brought together a distinguished crew, among them the Reverend Dr. James L. Barton, Stephen Wise, Charles Crane, and John Mott, the long-serving head of the YMCA. They had come on short notice, convinced of the urgency of the situation at hand. They had been summoned by a man half a world away: Henry Morgenthau.

The ambassador had devised a wild scheme to save the Armenians: He had approached Enver and Talaat and called their bluff. If the Turks were packing the Armenian people off merely out of military security, Henry said, then perhaps they would not object to their deportation to America? The western states, he reasoned, were sparsely populated, rich in minerals, and the Armenians would make an able labor force. Henry offered to organize the exodus himself. A young American reporter named John Reed who was traveling through Constantinople had picked up talk of the idea, and asked Henry if the rumors were true. Yes, the ambassador said; the Turks had even given their blessing.

"The United States might be the Moses to lead the Armenian people out of bondage," Henry told Reed. "They could be put in the unsettled region" of the country, the western states. The Armenians were "a clean, industrious, intelligent race, the best class for immigrants, farmers, and labourers, eager for education." Henry had done a quick calculation. He needed only "a hundred dollars a head" to equip, feed, and transport every surviving Armenian. He would put up $1 million of his own money and, recalling the money drives of the Wilson campaign, raise $4 million more by subscription. Whatever the cost, he told Reed, the United States would stand to gain. "It is a magnificent opportunity for America to save an entire race," he said, "and get a fine element of citizenship."

Henry had already tried to entice the secretary of state. "Minister of War has promised to permit departure of Armenians to the United States whose emigration I vouch for as *bona fide*," he cabled Lansing, even as he reported new massacres. The secretary of state should suggest, he wrote, that Dodge, Mott, Wise, and the others form a "committee to raise funds and provide means to save some of the Armenians." It was a rare request—an ambassador asking the State Department to urge private citizens to undertake a mass-scale relief effort—but Lansing consented. Within two weeks, Dodge had agreed to host the meeting.

America would not organize any exodus, large or small. Henry had overpromised. The Turks would never allow the Armenians to leave, and few in Washington would welcome more than half a million Armenians. But the formation of the committee marked a turning point. Before they left Dodge's office, the men set a goal of raising $100,000. The outpouring of support that followed was without precedent: Within a matter of weeks, the committee wired the money to the American ambassador. Of the total, $70,000 had come from John D. Rockefeller's foundation, newly established to disperse a slice of his Standard Oil fortune. By the summer of 1918, the committee would collect more than $10 million.

| | | |

On October 4, the committee went public, leaking a series of chilling highlights from the secret consular reports. "A Policy of Extermination Put in Effect Against a Helpless People" declared the banner headline on the front page of *The New York Times*. The story filled nearly an entire page. "In cruelty and in horror," the *Times* reported, "nothing in the past thousand years has equaled the present persecutions." According to the committee's "investigation," the article went on, "the use of the bastinado has been revived, high dignitaries of the Church have been hanged, families scattered to the four winds, and thousands upon thousands of defenseless, miserable persons herded together like cattle and driven into the desert lands of the empire, there to starve and die."

In England, Lord Bryce—who had accompanied Henry on the trip to

the Holy Land—stood before the House of Lords and declared that the
time was "past when any harm can be done by publicity." Railing against
Turkish abuses, he presented "unimpeachable testimonies" from the
Turkish lands. Bryce estimated that 800,000 had been killed, and commissioned a young Oxford historian named Arnold Toynbee to publish a
quick book, *Armenian Atrocities: The Murder of a Nation*. Toynbee,
then moonlighting as a clerk in the new Department of Information,
soon followed with a Parliamentary Blue Book—filled with 149 documents, the bulk of which had been lifted from the State Department files
Henry had compiled.

Two weeks later, the American committee staged a mass meeting at
the Century Theatre, the Central Park West venue that Henry Morgenthau had helped to build. Rabbi Wise was the last to speak. He was present, Wise said, to protest inhumanity, whether committed by Germans
against Belgians, Russians against Jews, or Turks against Armenians. If
Germany and Austria did not do more toward ending the Armenian
atrocities, they may find that "certain victories are more disastrous than
any defeats." The seats of the theater were blanketed with petitions addressed to the kaiser and the German people, imploring them to end the
atrocities. If the Germans wished to "alienate the good will of those who
still remain neutral," Wise said, they would "let these outrages go on
unchecked." But if they wished "to rehabilitate themselves," they would
tell the Turks, "Not one more drop of blood must be shed."

The months to come would see dozens of rallies and hundreds of headlines. In America and Britain, the Armenians had become synonymous
with a persecuted people. They were endangered, but not forgotten. The
propaganda war was on, and so was the fight for relief. It was an irony
not lost on Henry Morgenthau: In New York, it seemed, he could do
more to aid the Armenians than he could in Turkey. He had created the
committee. He had helped raise the Rockefeller money. He had worked
the *Times* and the reporters in Constantinople to bring the plight of the
Armenians to the public. Above all, he had overseen the appropriation of
the terrifying consular dispatches, reports that all involved—clergymen,
reporters, politicians—preferred to forget, and which remained the secret property of the United States government. Henry had taken a risk as
great as any financial gamble of his real estate career. This time, though,
he could foresee the consequences, both moral and political.

17. "We Are Through with Them"

1915

The red-brick steeple of the Fifth Avenue Presbyterian church towered over Fifty-fifth Street, hailed as the tallest structure in Manhattan when it was built four decades earlier. One Sunday in October 1915, the pews were packed to hear Dr. John Henry Jowett speak on the plight of the Armenians. Pastor Jowett told of the suffering of the Christians among the Turks, and praised the work of the nuns so far from home. But he went further: He asked his congregants to pray for the American ambassador—that the Lord might protect Mr. Morgenthau, maintain his health and safety, and ensure his work bore fruit.

That a congregation of Presbyterians in Manhattan would pray for a German-Jewish American ambassador in Constantinople was testament to an unprecedented publicity campaign. In newspapers and magazines across America, the Committee on Armenian Atrocities had successfully retailed a stark story: the clash between Muslim despots and a Christian nation, "the Terrible Turk" and his helpless Armenian victims. As the committee turned from propaganda to emergency relief, money poured in—from philanthropists, but also from schoolchildren and laborers. Yet for all the rallies, sermons, and marches, the defenders of the Armenians did not cross an unspoken boundary: No one dared call for the United States to send troops.

No one, that is, except Teddy Roosevelt. "The butchery of Armenia" was an affront to the world's conscience, T.R. wrote in a letter leaked to the *Times*. He castigated the American missionaries for waging a futile campaign. "Mass meetings on behalf of the Armenians amount to nothing whatever," he wrote, "if they are mere methods of giving a sentimental but ineffective and safe outlet to the emotion of those engaged in them."

Roosevelt demanded a military response. "Until we put honor and duty first," he soon added, "and are willing to risk something in order to achieve righteousness both for ourselves and for others, we shall accomplish nothing; and we shall earn and deserve the contempt of the strong nations of mankind."

| | | |

Since the summer, Henry Morgenthau had become convinced that among the Young Turk leaders it was Talaat who was most eager "to crush the poor Armenians." Talaat had boasted, Dr. Gates told Henry, that he had "accomplished more in three months about crushing the Armenians than Abdul Hamid"—the Bloody Sultan—"could do in 37 years." If the Germans would no longer listen, and Washington offered no relief, Henry would try to stop the slaughter on his own.

For months, Talaat had received the ambassador with obvious impatience. He no longer attempted to feign ignorance of the attacks. Once Talaat had even waved Henry's intercepted cables in his face—letting him know *he* knew that Henry was documenting the Armenian persecution in his correspondence with the State Department. Gone, too, were the diplomatic niceties.

"Why are you so interested in the Armenians, anyway?" Talaat asked Henry. "You are a Jew. These people are Christians."

"You don't seem to realize," Henry replied, "I am not here as a Jew but as the American Ambassador. My country contains something more than 97,000,000 Christians and something less than 3,000,000 Jews. So, at least in my ambassadorial capacity, I am 97 per-cent Christian. I do not appeal to you in the name of any race or religion, but merely as a human being."

On Saturday, January 15, Talaat came to the American Embassy for an elegant luncheon. Once again, Henry heard a stream of assurances— "Armenians in Constantinople could leave," Talaat said—but the declarations had worn thin. Talaat, too, had heard enough. It was pointless, he told Henry, to worry about the Armenians. "We are through with them. That's all over."

| | | |

Although news of the massacres had reached the White House with little delay, Morgenthau was determined that the president see and feel the brutal enormity of the slaughter. As an enclosure to one of his longest and most heartfelt reports, the ambassador included the chilling testimony that he received firsthand from Alma Johansson, a Swedish nun who for thirteen years had run the German orphanage in Moush, a town deep in eastern Anatolia and home to nearly 25,000 Armenians.

In the first week of November 1915, the snows had come to the European town in Pera, whitening the black ridge of Pera Hill. Alma had journeyed to the American Embassy exhausted and drained, to tell what she had seen. The American ambassador, she had heard, would not only listen: He was one of the few in a position to carry the news to the West and, if not stop the carnage, at least record it for posterity.

The ambassador sat across from Alma. The portrait of Josie and the family, framed in silver, stood before him on the desk. On a far wall hung old German etchings, town landmarks of Mannheim. As the nun recounted her ordeal, she told how she and a fellow missionary had endured the siege of Moush—ten weeks of shelling, surrounded by 20,000 Turkish troops. The local *mutasarrif*, considered an intimate of Enver Pasha, had urged them to flee: "Nothing will happen to you," he said, "they only cut off the heads of the Armenians." The sisters refused to go. They slept on the floor at night, leaving the orphans to fend on their own, as "the walls of the orphanage were broken through by cannon shots."

When Alma had finished, the ambassador asked her to sit with Miss Carp, his secretary, and retell her account from the beginning, this time dictating it in as much detail as possible. It was no use: Alma could not bring herself to speak of the horror again. Instead, she slowly composed by hand an affidavit for the American ambassador: "Feet, hands, chests were nailed with a piece of wood," she wrote. "Nails of fingers and toes were torn out; beards and eyebrows pulled out; feet were hammered with nails, same as they do with horses." The worst, though, was what the nuns heard from "a few millers and bakers" left unharmed as their "services were needed by the Government." They had seen the mass murder: men "tied together and shot outside of the town," and women and children "taken to the neighboring villages, placed in houses by [the] hundred, and either burned alive or thrown into the river."

The women and the orphans haunted Alma. They had passed by her house, their "blood streaming down, weeping." She could still see the "burning houses" and smell the "burning corpses," but who, she asked, could ever "describe such pictures?" After a week, the Armenian quarter lay in ruin. "The officers," Alma wrote, "boasted now of their bravery— that they had succeeded in exterminating the whole Armenian race."

The nun's statement arrived on President Wilson's desk on January 13— two months after she had written it. Secretary Lansing had forwarded the ambassador's report with a note. "I think you should read" the Morgenthau dispatch, Lansing told Wilson, "as it is very comprehensive." As for Alma's report—one of the most detailed and unflinching testimonies to emerge from the killings—it was "interesting," the secretary told the president, but "not necessary to read, unless you see fit to glance through it."

| | | |

Reading his father's letters in New York, Henry Jr. sensed a turn: The ambassador had become "unusually pessimistic," and "a note of loneliness" had emerged. In late November 1915, a month after his mother came home, the son would return to Turkey on his third and last journey. This time, Henry Jr. traveled on a diplomatic passport: He'd received "instructions" at the White House and stopped en route in London to meet with the U.S. ambassador and Colonel House (again in residence there), and consulted, as well, the Foreign Office officials struggling to come to terms with the catastrophic war effort in Turkey. Henry Jr. felt a new sense of purpose and exhilaration. He went on by rail, crossing thirteen borders, and as the train entered the Balkans, he saw the blur of devastation beyond the glass. "This traveling in wartime," he wrote home, "is some nerve wracking."

Back in Constantinople, Henry Jr. was eager to test himself: "I am restless and not very happy," he wrote home soon after his arrival. But he needed no reminding why he had returned to Turkey. "Pa is in a very difficult frame of mind," he wrote, "and I am glad to say that I can & am being helpful to him, in one of the most crucial moments of his life."

"My failure to stop the destruction of the Armenians had made Turkey for me a place of horror," Henry Morgenthau, Sr., would later write. "I had reached the end of my resources." He had stood witness to mass murder on a scale the world had never seen. For years, they would try to count the bodies and tally the cost. But the officers, politicians, and historians could never agree. The most authoritative accounts only offered estimates, by inexact subtraction, that between 800,000 and 1.5 million Armenians had been killed.

By the winter of 1916, Henry had reached an impasse—not with the Turkish state, but with his own government. Since the summer he had foreseen the limits of his power. He wrote Lansing, "I believe nothing short of actual force . . . would adequately meet the situation"— something "obviously the United States are not in a position to exert." He had asked the State Department, in turn, for permission to denounce the horrific crimes. No, he was told. The wages of nonintervention were silence.

Within weeks, Lansing would concede the obvious: The State Department was "withholding from the American people the facts now in its possession." It was a stunning acknowledgment of an official silence, but it appeared in a coded diplomatic cable. By the year's end, hoping to assure Wilson of the correctness of the U.S. policy on Turkey, Lansing would express sympathy for Constantinople's security concerns. The Armenians suffered "horrible brutality," he allowed, terrors that would remain "one of the blackest pages in the history of this war." But the deportations were "more or less justifiable," given the Armenians' "well-known disloyalty to the Ottoman Government and the fact that the territory which they inhabited was within the zone of military operations."

At the American Embassy in Constantinople, a discomfiting realization set in. The ambassador would have to look beyond the State Department for his next endeavor. He worried about the return to New York—and any future official post with Wilson. "My modesty," he confided to Henry Jr., "though often hidden, whispers to me that the country will progress just as well if I don't share in its protection." An escape plan, though, was forming. Father and son had turned over the possibilities, debating how to take advantage of the ambassador's new moral—and, at least in New York, popular—authority. It was the son's turn to shore up the father, insisting that the future held endless opportunities. "We will all live to see the day when he will have accomplished even greater and bigger things than he has here," Henry Jr. wrote in a letter home. Just as in the era after the Civil War, he went on, when the generals "held all the political positions for twenty years, now the successful War ambassadors will be the ones sought after in fields of political endeavor."

The ambassador was eager to sound out the president. In December, Henry had written Wilson to congratulate him on his engagement. Fifteen months after his wife Ellen's death, the president had announced that he would wed again. Edith Bolling Galt was a stylish Washington widow, whom Wilson had met only in March. The ambassador's note had moved the president. On December 9, nine days before the wedding, he thanked Henry for his warm words, adding that he was "very much complimented indeed that your thought should have found time to frame this personal message in the midst of all the absorbing and distressing duties you have been (so admirably) performing." "I hope you all keep well," Wilson wrote, "notwithstanding the strain upon you." And in closing, he added a wish: "It would be great if we could have a talk, wouldn't it, and exchange impressions directly?"

In the president's question, Henry heard an invitation. "I enthusiastically assent," he replied, asking for a leave of absence. The reelection campaign was fast approaching, Henry warned, and "we must not have a planless one." In 1912, there had been no need for a head start. "Owing to the split in the Republican Party," he reminded Wilson, "your election was an absolute, foregone conclusion." But 1916 would be different.

Henry had read the news accounts: The Democratic National Committee was at war with itself, fighting over who would lead the reelection campaign and how best to raise funds. The ambassador offered himself as savior. He would have "no trouble," he assured Wilson, "to raise double the amount" that he had the last time around. It was essential, though, to head off any dissension. "Without mentioning names or going into details," Henry wrote Wilson, "I greatly fear that the relations of the various members of the National Committee towards each other and towards some members of the administration are such that there will not be any systematic, thorough and hearty preparation unless it is undertaken by an independent outsider."

"If you have anyone else that will take this job," Henry wrote the president, "please do not think for one moment that I am craving for it."

| | | |

Six weeks later, on February 22, at half past seven in the morning, the Danish liner SS *Frederick VIII* eased into New York Harbor. The Morgenthaus, father and son, stood on the bridge, dark figures in mink-lined overcoats and black bowlers, searching in the mist for the honor corps. They had been awake for hours, the ship reaching quarantine by five o'clock. "We got up very early," Henry Sr. wrote in his diary, "had our breakfast, and were on the lookout for the boat which was to call for me." As the U.S. Coast Guard cutter *Manhattan* pulled close, through the fog Henry could make out his friend Cleveland Dodge and raised his arms in a windmill salute. Dodge echoed the greeting, waving in return. Josie, their daughters Ruth and Alma, and their sons-in-law, Mort and Maurice, were also aboard.

As the cutter drew near, and the shouts grew louder, the crew of the liner threw down a gangplank. From the icy deck, father and son climbed down and were engulfed by the commotion. Henry Morgenthau, Sr., pushed through the crowd—"belying his sixty years," a reporter would note—to embrace Josie and the girls. Henry wore a formal morning suit, his silver goatee trimmed to a mustache, his face thin but ruddy. A clutch of reporters and city leaders crowded the cutter deck. Mayor John Purroy Mitchel had assembled a large welcoming committee, sixty-nine men and one woman. Many had seen the ambassador off twenty-eight months earlier. Now, in the depth of winter, they had risen at dawn to give him a hero's welcome. They were all there: Ochs, Pulitzer, and their fellow publishers, Reid of the *Tribune* and Villard of *The Nation;* Seth Low, the former mayor; the lords of academia, Nicholas Murray Butler, president of Columbia, and Dr. John Finley, former head of City College; the financiers, Schiff, Lewisohn, and Vanderlip of the National City Bank; the Jewish leaders, from Rabbi Wise to Adler; Henry's former law partners, Lachman and Goldsmith; and the lone woman, Lillian Wald of Henry Street.

Coming up the bay, the ambassador stood in the frigid wind to address the reporters. "When I first went to Turkey," he said, "I had only the American interests to look after, principally missionaries." A dozen cameras and two moving picture machines got to work. "Later I took the Jews under my wing, and when war broke out I spread out the American flag like a huge umbrella. As one nation after another came under its folds, it was my duty to see that no one nation pulled too much of the flag down over its head." The Americans had come first, he said, then the Jews, followed by the English, French, Belgians, Serbians, and Swiss. The Armenians had sought shelter, as well, but he could not offer them "official protection."

At the end of the pier, Helen, eldest of the four Morgenthau children, joined the reunion. Before the party was ushered upstairs to the dock commissioner's offices for a greeting ceremony, a man from the State Department approached, thrusting a letter into Henry's hands. Robert Lansing had written in haste, asking that the ambassador be guarded in his public appearances. "While I realize that a large number of our fellow citizens will wish to offer you testimonials as a recognition of the splendid work which you are doing," he wrote, "it would seem to me that, in view of the international situation, a public meeting, however carefully arranged, might have unhappy results."

Henry returned the letter to its envelope, and slipped it into his coat pocket. Turning to the reporters, though, he made certain to announce that Lansing had instructed him to choose his words with care— "evidently fearful lest I should talk too much."

The reporters hungered for a scoop. Any truth, one yelled, to the rumor that Henry would be named secretary of war? "Nothing at all in it," he shouted back. But the talk of higher office—governor of New York, U.S. senator, congressman, even mayor—would only continue. Henry assured all that he had come home on a sixty-day vacation, his first in years. "My work is cut out for me," he said, "and I shall stick to my post." He offered the words as a promise, but they were only half true.

Soon he would tender his resignation. In time, there would be future assignments. Henry would be named a presidential envoy, a precursor to the roving ambassador without portfolio of modern times. Some of the missions would end in triumph, others in failure. But standing there at the pier, surrounded by the adoring lords of the city's financial, religious, and civic worlds, with Josie and his family gathered close, and the newsmen clicking and scribbling, Henry Morgenthau raised his chin against the wind and savored the moment.

The celebration would go on at the house on Seventy-fourth Street for all who wished to join. Henry escorted Josie and the family to the limousine at the curb, and climbed in. Once home, he walked past a heap of telegrams, letters, cards, and flowers. He took a seat center stage in the oak-paneled dining room overflowing with guests, and held court until darkness fell.

Amid the commotion Henry Jr. had slipped away to keep a rendezvous with a young woman in Central Park. By evening he would call home and shout above the din of the homecoming party, trying to tell his father the good news. Henry Sr. could not hear every word, but he caught the essence: Henry Jr. was engaged.

18. "A Tremendous Asset"

1915

The families had known each other for years. Ellie Fatman, at twenty-three, was bright, cultured, and well educated—a recent Vassar graduate. Ellie had a captivating presence, a warm intelligence, and, as a reporter would later write, "snapping black eyes." Her features were equally distinctive: sharp jaw, pearl-white skin, and a blunt profile dominated by a hawk nose—"Roman," she called it. Generations of relatives on her maternal line, male and female, had shared a certain look: the oval face and half-globe cheeks. It was the brows, though, that people remembered: bushy and black, swiftly converging in a glare of disdain. A gregarious girl, Ellie could turn stern in a moment, but she far preferred a different means of persuasion. Ellie had a gift, the power of which she was only just discovering: All too aware of the social constraints of her world, she could attempt to rise above them and, with her natural warmth and intelligence, attract people, drawing them close with an impassioned, and outsized, sense of the possible.

Henry Jr., like his father and grandfather, would marry up. The Fatmans and the Morgenthaus belonged to the same world, each a clan in the tribe of German Jews that populated a half-dozen square blocks of upper Manhattan. The Morgenthaus were wealthy, but Elinor Fatman had grown up amid the Lehmans, in a world of patrician drawing rooms, well-staffed weekend homes, and a celebrated family fortune. Her mother was Lisette "Settie" Lehman, one of the three daughters of Mayer Lehman. Born in Selma, Alabama, Settie had come north with her family after the Civil War, when Mayer Lehman and his older brother Emanuel transformed the family cotton brokerage into a New York banking house. By the turn of the century, Lehman Brothers was a pillar of Wall Street.

Settie Lehman had met Henry Morgenthau decades earlier, when he was only starting out in the law. Eight years younger, Settie had attended those long ago "Emerson Evenings," and even been among the prospective brides on Henry's roster. She had married Morris Fatman, a Cincinnati native who would become chairman of the Raritan Woolen Mills in New Jersey. The Fatmans were a formidable family, benefactors to a half-dozen civic and cultural institutions in New York. But Settie was, as she would never allow her Morgenthau grandchildren to forget, "a born Lehman." It was her sister Hattie who would give Stephen Birmingham the title of his best-selling history of the German Jews in America. "It was never an elite club," she told Birmingham, "just '*our crowd.*'"

Ellie, Settie's younger daughter, was proudest of her "Lehman Uncles," Herbert and Irving, the two sons of Mayer Lehman who would add the political luster to the financial dynasty. Uncle Irving, who had married "Sissie" Straus, a daughter of Nathan Straus (owner, with his brothers, of Macy's), had won a seat on the New York State Supreme Court in 1908. Uncle Herbert was only fourteen years older than Ellie, and they were close, like brother and sister. Herbert had married Edith Altschul, heiress to another German-Jewish banking fortune, and after a stint in the family firm, he had gone into public service, becoming a patron of the Henry Street Settlement House, among other worthy endeavors. In time, Herbert Lehman would have a long political career: Elected lieutenant governor at age fifty in 1928, then governor, and finally United States senator, he served as a leading liberal in New York State for four decades.

The Lehman brothers would come to embody the arrival of the German Jews in the American establishment. Yet no matter how high they rose, Ellie's "Lehman Uncles" would remain her guardians, protectors of her own path—be it in tenement work, state politics, or the life of her family to come.

| | | |

Henry Jr. and Ellie had been born on the same block of West Eighty-first Street—and delivered by the same doctor. She arrived on February 19, 1892, nine months after him, and lived in one of three brownstone houses that Mayer Lehman built for his daughters. Settie's house, No. 23, abutted her sister Hattie Goodhart's, No. 21, on the block between Central Park West and Columbus Avenue.

As infants, Henry Jr. and Ellie were strolled by German nannies along the same paths in the park, and played as children on the same stretches of green. They had not been close but had once shared a tutor; trying "to instill the love of learning" in young Henry, she would cite Ellie as a model of diligence, an example to emulate. Still, they had ample common ground: Like the Morgenthaus, the Fatmans and the Lehmans thought of themselves as more German than Jewish. Ellie and her sister Margaret, four years older, learned German before English. There were summer voyages to Europe, always in the company of a German governess, Fräulein Lena. For years Ellie would retain the hint of an accent.

Ellie had graduated from Miss Jacobi's, the school for Our Crowd girls that was housed in a brownstone on West Eightieth Street, two blocks from the Fatman home. Laura Jacobi had come from Germany at age twenty and first taught at the Ethical Culture School. Her school was "progressive," with strong political undercurrents: Jacobi girls were expected to work for those less fortunate, join the ranks of the suffragettes, and, above all, go to college—a milestone none of Ellie's family had reached. Her choice, Vassar, stunned her parents. If a wealthy New York City girl had to go to college, she was expected to attend Barnard and remain at home. Ellie's mother considered Vassar a "swell finishing school," as Gabrielle Elliot Forbush, a fellow student who would become a lifelong friend, would later recall. Settie sent her off with a roomful of steamer trunks filled with "all these lovely clothes," but little understanding of the Vassar traditions.

The campus, set in the bucolic Hudson Valley, presented a new world: Protestant girls with proud birthrights—and few Jews. Ellie made friends easily, but she had entered a foreign realm. Most of her friends were WASPs from professional families, girls whose parents considered a modern education essential. The Lehman aura helped to bridge the distance. If in the city, where all in her circles were wealthy, Ellie had never been made to feel a rich outsider, her college friends considered her to be "rolling in money." As her circle widened, Ellie would invite friends home. The Vassar girls enjoyed lunches in restaurants, evenings on the town, and elaborate teas in Settie's drawing room. Forbush would long remember Ellie taking her—in her aunt's horse and carriage—to see Wagner at the Metropolitan Opera. The family resources had eased the way. "Ellie's being Jewish," Forbush would say, "was completely ignored."

At Vassar, Ellie quickly found her place: the stage. In her sophomore year, the drama society, Philaletheis, staged Clyde Fitch's *Beau Brummel*. Ellie won the part of the Prince of Wales. (In keeping with tradition, women played the male roles.) It was a lead, and with it she gained a measure of renown on campus. The following year, Ellie was elected president of the society—and announced a first-ever "platform": "Our motto, which we shall doubtlessly fall short of frequently, must . . . be perfection of detail, and each performance must be a work of art itself." Ellie continued to do well in her studies, but the theater had become her passion. After a cosseted city childhood, she had found a chance to assert herself, and she seized it.

In college, Ellie had honed her gifts on the stage. Neither tall nor striking, she learned to command a room. It was a skill she shared with her mother, but in so many other ways, the two had diverged years earlier. Unlike Settie, for whom shopping was a vocation, Ellie cared little for adornments—jewelry or *objets*. Above all, Ellie and her mother differed on the role of women in society. Her mother had one abiding regulation by which she judged all women: A wife should never hold a job. To Settie's mind, the world could never yield a reason to abandon home and hearth. Her daughter was no radical, but if there was one Lehman rule that Ellie was resolved to break, it was the woman's role in the household.

||||

Henry Jr. had known that Ellie would be awaiting his arrival. Having graduated two years earlier, she had been back in the city, trying to break into a theatrical career, when he first invited her to join him on an outing. They were neighbors, and friends of friends, but for years had seen each other only on rare occasions. At Alma Morgenthau's wedding in 1909, Ellie's sister Margaret had been a bridesmaid and Henry Jr., not yet eighteen, an usher. They had crossed paths, too, at the Henry Street Settlement House downtown, where both volunteered for a time. But in the spring of 1915, when Henry Jr. and Ellie met again, they scarcely knew each other.

Henry Jr. had written his parents with news of his first social engagement since returning from Turkey, a theater party hosted by "Elly F." He had omitted any emotional stirrings that arose during the evening, but his parents could sense a relationship budding. Over the Fourth of July, they were again together, at a Guggenheim wedding on the Jersey shore.

In the months since, "Elly" would appear often in Henry Jr.'s letters to Turkey, and his parents would take note. By then, Ellie had thrown herself into the theatrical world, acting in an amateur company and directing children's plays at the Neighborhood Playhouse, a new addition to Henry Street. By fall, the two had grown serious.

Henry Jr. had had his dalliances. Frances Sullivan was the tall daughter of a Philadelphia street-railway baron. She and her sister were fixtures at the balls, horse shows, and ballet benefits in New York and Bar Harbor, Maine—where Henry Jr. had stayed with her the previous summer. He had considered, too, Beatrice Brinkerhoff, a Hudson Valley girl of Knickerbocker stock—"a gorgeous creature," he wrote his father, "beautiful in every way to the eye, but the fine spirit is lacking." Frances and Beatrice could be companions, even friends, but a marriage to a descendant of Dutch Protestants or Irish Catholics was out of the question.

By the winter of 1915, Henry Jr. was certain: Ellie was the one. She had none of Henry Jr.'s worry, suspicion, or reticence. She moved effortlessly in the limelight. She was bold and passionate, and unspoiled by wealth. She was a political animal, too—no revolutionary, but moved by instinct to reject the status quo. She devoured the newspaper, especially the "men's news," the pages filled with the affairs of the city and the capital. Henry Jr. apologized for sending home "political forecasts" from Turkey but knew that she reveled "in such topics." Ellie had no interest in competition, but long before Vassar, under her mother's sway, she had learned to overcome a challenge, to negotiate and win.

Henry Jr. had few close friends, and fewer intimates. The gawky youth had grown into a glowerer—his long face pinched into a grimace by the pince-nez. He was still too tall, too thin, untested in his endeavors, and unformed in his thought and desires. He spoke in fits and false starts. But there was much that bound him to Ellie: a love of long walks and horses, a fondness for pranks, and the silly skits that would long mark the holiday fests among family and political intimates. If at times he stumbled—twisted a sentence in knots, let slip a gaffe, blushed or bristled too easily—and if he still suffered bouts of insecurity, and looked to others for confidence, Ellie could forgive him. To her, Henry Jr. was "the essence of handsome": His eyes were sincere, and his face ever honest. He rarely revealed it, but Ellie—in that same way she insisted on seeing the promise in everything, even in challenges—saw his true self. She helped him see it, as well.

"I am a different man," Henry Jr. had written Ellie when he took his first leave of her, making his way to Turkey, "than I have ever been before."

||||

On May 6, 1914, Henry Jr. had written his father from Fishkill, the land he now called "our farm," and admitted a few mistakes: He'd bought the wrong plows, and was "a little slow in having my fertilizer mixed and potato seed cut." Nonetheless, he had managed "to put the spring work through." In true Morgenthau fashion, he had begun with a grand first step: planting 1,400 apple trees on 48 acres. "It was a big job," he conceded, "bigger than I had idea of." He'd employed every man in the neighborhood who would work, even going up to Poughkeepsie and down to New York to get as many hands as possible. It was a daunting undertaking, and one that would set the stage for a new life.

Domestic worries abounded, too. Henry Jr. hired a cook, Eva, and her husband, Stephan, was already painting and fixing up the house. He had a bookkeeper now, too: Mr. Picard, an accounts man on loan from his father's nephew, Rob Simon. At the same time, as he wrote his father, he was pulling away from the city. "I am cutting off more and more of my N.Y. connections," Henry Jr. wrote, "but just at present my place is on the farm."

To his father, the message was clear: His son, at last, had found a plan he might be able to see through. Days later, another update arrived. "I am writing this letter under the trees on our farm," Henry Jr. wrote. "The country is beautiful early in the morning (6:30–7:30)." After a wet spring, the laborers had pushed ahead on the planting. "I have practically all my potatoes in," Henry Jr. reported, "and about half my corn." The days were dry now, and the forecast bore promise. "I think we are going to have a very good season."

||||

To his embarrassment, headlines had accompanied Henry Jr.'s first summer on the farm. On June 14, 1914, the *Poughkeepsie Sunday Courier*— a broadsheet known to do the bidding of Ed Perkins, the Democratic county chair who had steered him to the property—profiled the "only son of Hon. Henry Morgenthau, Ambassador to Turkey," and his Fishkill Farms. "People will again have Dutchess County beef," the *Courier* proclaimed, in an article that hailed Henry Jr.'s purchase of thirty-two steers. "The success of the venture is assured and Mr. Morgenthau has the credit of again starting what may become one of the chief factors in giving our people better meat at cheaper prices."

The praise was lavish, and intentional—a gift from his father's friends, hoping to ease the entry of the interloper into the narrow world of dairy farmers and rural Republicans. "Mr. Morgenthau is a most entertaining young man," the *Courier* wrote, "and is fast acquiring a large host of friends in southern Dutchess. He is alive to the situation as he finds it. He is not in the country for a good time or stylish show." The article almost read like an advertisement. "He has no newfangled ideas," it went on. "He keeps no livery, no high priced chauffeur, or landscape gardeners, or unnecessary help but is devoting his time to plain, simple, practical farming." Within days, the *Herald,* still run by James Gordon Bennett, Jr., the editor his father had cultivated decades earlier in the big Washington Heights sale, heaped more praise: Young Morgenthau was "conducting experiments," it reported, in the belief "that scientific farming . . . will be one of the most important steps toward lowering the cost of living."

Henry Jr. would suffer, the ambassador had warned, for looking like a millionaire scion in the countryside. His son, though, overcame his discomfort as the publicity opened doors. Henry Jr. also took care to make his own inroads—joining the Wiccopee Grange and the Poughkeepsie Automobile Association, and soon accepting an offer to serve as a deputy sheriff. If in Turkey he had doubts about his choice, by that first summer they had faded. "I was kept so close to the farm and its problems," Henry Jr. would later recall, "that I often forgot the existence of the world."

| | | |

Father and son, despite the ocean between them, had only grown closer during the ambassador's tenure in Turkey. From Constantinople, Henry wrote Henry Jr., enclosing "something I wrote in March 1877—when I was 21." "How much of it applies to you at the present time?" he wondered.

We both hate Charlatans as I called them then, and bluffs as we call them now. I wonder how you will like to read my innermost thoughts at that time. It is sort of strange to be confronted with one's ghosts of the past. Unfortunately it proves how little we progress. My thoughts then were certainly as good as now after all these years of trying and learning. Perhaps I have not worked hard

*enough to develop my thinking qualities and devoted too much
time to chasing the almighty $.*

Since the visit to Palestine, the tone of his father's letters had shifted.
Writing from Nablus, Henry Sr. had renewed his call to "the higher
plane." By now, in the family "The Higher Plane" was known as the
father's favored theme. Whether with his daughters, the young men who
courted them, or his grandchildren, Henry Morgenthau had long sung
the virtues of sacrificing the physical for the metaphysical. "It is more
and more apparent to me," Henry instructed his son, "that the real joy-
ful thrills that result from truly moral intellectual exertions are the finest
that the human being can have." "Mere brutal and physical delights," he
added, "don't begin to compare."

From Beirut, he had sent his son a birthday check for $230—"Happy
23!"—adding that as much as he missed him, he supported his son's new
pursuit. "Land," he wrote, was "for centuries . . . the *real* estate of the
world and is the safest in which to put your funds." His return to the
land, he told Henry Jr., was a virtue; farming would develop "true manhood," and a "conscience." A plan was already taking shape in the father's mind: The ambassadorship would be the end of his climb, and he
would turn all his energies, and resources, to guiding his son's career.
Farming was a welcome vocation, and the rural life was a moral life.
"Don't let anyone who has his nose to the grindstone and whose horizon
is limited by his office window," Henry wrote, "try and check you in
your daring youthful flight upward to the hills and away from conventional roads." But even as his son was planting his orchards, Henry Morgenthau was plotting a future that extended beyond the dirt and trees—to
politics.

"I have no political ambition of any kind," Henry wrote his son that
July. "The sooner that I can transfer to you the influence that I possessed,
the better." In addition to the farm, he wrote, "you can, by a political
career, come in touch with and thoroughly learn the real people and not
fool away your life by communing with that artificial, superficial and
insincere crowd that you meet in rich society."

The father had already conjured his own grand idea. "Don't think
that I am satisfied with simply having a farm," he wrote his son. "I
should like to have you, if possible during my lifetime, start something
that would have a world-influence for good": a "model village." His son
should aim, he wrote, to grow his farm into "one of the Meccaic points

of the world." "I should like you," Henry suggested, "to start a coloniza-
tion scheme for Christians and Jews, and demonstrate to America and
the world that they can live in absolute harmony and peace together."
The scheme breathed not only with the spiritualism of the Caves of
Machpelah and his father's folly, but with the quixotic spirit of Lazarus:
It was romantic, nonsectarian, and preposterous.

His son elected not to hear his father's lofty instructions, worrying
instead that something was amiss in Constantinople. Henry Jr. had kept
abreast of events in Europe, but his concern centered on his father's own
future. "My only hope," he wrote, "is that you will be really satisfied
with life here in America after your sojourn abroad, your contact with
nobility & your taste of political success." The ambassador had not yet
been in his post a year, and his son was planning his return: He feared
lest his father spend the rest of his life "in constant, unsatiated ambition." "As soon as you come home," he wrote, "you must become connected with some large enterprise, either financial or philanthropic." His
father could rise further in politics, but he asked, "is the game worth the
candle?" "Are the hurts, the cuts, filled up and healed by final success?"

Although Henry Jr. had little interest in building a utopian "model
village," he did foresee a future that united father and son. "Henry Morgenthau & Son" had been his father's dream, as far back as the troubles
at Cornell. Now, finally, the son was envisioning the same horizon, and
almost pleading for its arrival. "My one hope and desire," he wrote, "is
that our paths of work & play & endeavor may soon come together &
that we may run a double-track railroad side by side through life." Henry
Jr. did not know if it would be "a large farm or a model city," but he was
sure that "the future will work itself out for us." The shift was subtle,
but unmistakable—the son was now reassuring the father. "In any case,"
he promised, "I am *with you*."

| | | |

By fall, the rolling hills of Dutchess County had turned amber, and Henry
Jr. could claim to have made headway on the farm. The harvest had proceeded apace, and Ruth was refurbishing the farmhouse—his father's
junior partner, Rob Simon, forwarding him a $500 advance to help cover
the costs. And yet, Henry Jr. found himself suffering a bout of loneliness,
a longing that may have masked a deeper quandary.

"God knows," he wrote his father, "there is nothing I would rather do
than be with you and Ma if only for a few days." It was a confession not

heard in his letters since Exeter. "My flesh hungers for your affection," Henry Jr. wrote, "which I have so long been used [to] and never have been without so long."

The farm would not come as easily as he imagined, he realized now. But he was determined, this time, not to quit. He would redouble his efforts. He studied seed catalogues and tractor manuals, canvassed growers and mapped the planting. He also took a trip to Washington to consult Carl Scofield, his guide and escort from the Agricultural Department on their cross-country expedition, about the farm. In the capital, he had a second motive: Henry Jr. sought news for his father, something he could not find in the State Department cables: a political forecast from the White House. He asked to meet with President Wilson, but settled for a talk with Joseph Tumulty, the Irishman from Trenton who had joined Wilson as his secretary. Leaving the White House, Henry Jr. headed directly down Pennsylvania Avenue to the Navy Department—as a letter to Constantinople records—to "drop in and see F. Roosevelt."

The visit on an early winter day in 1914 is the earliest known meeting between Henry Morgenthau, Jr., and Franklin D. Roosevelt. It may not, though, have been their first. Henry Jr. and his neighbor seemed destined to meet: The two men, as they would later joke, may have been the sole Democrats in Dutchess County. Henry Jr. had not been in East Fishkill "more than four months," as he would recall, before his name "came up for an elective office." As he delved deeper in local politics, it would not be long before the neighbors would start working together.

Two years earlier, Roosevelt had won a second term in the state senate by a wider margin than in his first victory. Returning to Albany with his wife, Eleanor, he had been made chair of the Agriculture Committee. But in the spring of 1913, Roosevelt had moved to Washington, and, following his uncle-in-law's climb, into the Naval Department as an assistant secretary. The next year, at summer's end, as the New York Democrats gathered in Saratoga for a pre-primary conference, Henry Jr. would have been sure to see Roosevelt. Increasingly, the son was stepping out into party affairs, led by the county broker Perkins, first in Dutchess, now in the state. The son was welcomed as a proxy for his absent father, and yet the diffidence remained: Henry Jr., an awkward presence among the party bosses, found comfort on the sidelines.

Roosevelt was then preparing, at William McAdoo's urging, a late primary run for the U.S. Senate. The progressives sought to take advantage of a hopeful turn: New York's two Senate seats for the first time would be filled by popular vote—the passage of the Seventeenth Amendment, taking the election of U.S. senators out of the hands of the state legislature, had been a triumph over the old ways of Boss Murphy and Tammany Hall. But the candidate had not been at the party conference in Saratoga: Roosevelt had joined Eleanor on Campobello, where she was resting after giving birth to a fifth child, Franklin Jr.

The island had become Roosevelt's escape. Campobello, just off the Maine coast, was wilderness—woods, rock, and no electricity. His parents had summered there since the 1880s, and he had been going there since he was a baby. Roosevelt relished his time on the small island; he was happy to let others work the Saratoga conference for him. Whether his attention was diverted, or he simply was not yet ready, Roosevelt would be crushed. By November, when Henry Jr. walked into his office on the third floor of the Naval Department, FDR had lost the primary, trounced by the Tammany candidate, James Watson Gerard, then still serving as Wilson's ambassador to Germany.

Henry Jr. and Roosevelt may have been neighbors, but the tie between them was Henry Morgenthau. Young Roosevelt had long known the elder Morgenthau as "Uncle Henry," the eager party financier. At the Navy Department, Henry Jr. did not raise agricultural questions or political concerns in Dutchess. He asked about his father. Naval Secretary Josephus Daniels, Roosevelt's boss, had become Henry Morgenthau's closest friend in the cabinet. What did they think of his father in Washington? Henry Jr. wondered. So thrilled was he with Roosevelt's reply, he delivered it directly to his father: "He said Billy Phillips (3rd Ass. Sec.) says that your father's dispatches are always cool and business-like, and that is a great deal more than you can say about some of the rest." Roosevelt, he added, had reported the compliment "in such a nice, full hearted manner, that it carried a great deal more conviction than I can put into mere words."

At thirty-two, Franklin D. Roosevelt had yet to perfect the commanding force, whether in the rhythmic cadence of his voice or the uplifting current of his words, that would win the adoration of millions. But he was a born charmer, and he would soon begin a drive to enlist Uncle Henry's son. Within weeks, a letter arrived at Fishkill Farms, marked "Confidential": Roosevelt wrote to ask "My dear Morgenthau" for his counsel "about filling the post office at Fishkill"—an important local position. Even from his office at the Navy Department, Roosevelt tried to keep one hand on the tiller of county politics at home. He may have railed against the evils of Tammany, but if patronage remained the currency of state politics, he was keen to use it to his advantage. In Washington, Roosevelt had curried favor with Daniel Roper, the South Carolinian in charge of doling out postal appointments—and he had won a request to offer names for the New York slots.

John Dugan, the town blacksmith, Roosevelt explained to Henry Jr., had stood for the job for two years, and of late had been backed by the Democratic powers, including John Mack, the former district attorney. "Judge" Mack, as he was known, was the reigning power broker in Democratic politics in Dutchess. It was the judge who had first urged Roosevelt into political office, encouraging him to run for the state assembly in 1910. But Roosevelt feared "friction": He had heard that some in Fishkill did not think the blacksmith "the right man." Roosevelt was solicitous ("We are all proud of your Father's work") and coy (he was merely asking for Henry Jr.'s "personal and confidential judgment"), but the Roosevelt method was already at work: The letter was less a request for advice than an invitation to join the team. Postmaster of Fishkill, a town of fewer than 15,000 souls, was no grand job. But Roosevelt was planning for the future. "If possible," he added to Henry Jr. in closing, "I should like to have everybody united in the township of Fishkill."

Over a long Sunday lunch at Hyde Park in June 1915, Roosevelt stepped up the recruitment drive, now making his intentions clear. The two sat alone and enjoyed, as Roosevelt would put it, "an interesting talk." Roosevelt had become the reigning attraction of the local Democratic set and now tried his best to entice the younger Morgenthau to run for county sheriff. Henry Jr., having already caught wind of the idea, did not hesitate to share his own plans. He was anxious to "take part in things in the county," as Roosevelt recounted days later. In the coming political season, he wanted "to get around the county and meet everybody possible and do all the work he can to help." But as for running himself, he begged off. He was just twenty-four, he said, and "really in the midst of starting his farm work on a big scale," Roosevelt reported.

If Roosevelt had targeted Henry Jr., Judge Mack and the other county Democrats did not mind if the newcomer gave it a pass: The Poughkeepsie boys were eager to fill the slate with their own cronies. "I can quite understand his position," Roosevelt wrote Mack, once Henry Jr. had declined to run, "and think on the whole I should have made the same decision." But Roosevelt reiterated his desire—he wanted the ambassador's son on his team. "He is an awfully nice fellow," Roosevelt added, "and one who will be a tremendous asset to us in the county." Perhaps, he suggested, come fall, the Democrats could put Morgenthau on the county committee. "Certainly we ought to do everything possible," he wrote Mack, "to keep him interested."

Within weeks, Henry Jr. was back at Springwood, the family estate in Hyde Park, this time for a formal luncheon on a stifling afternoon in mid-July. Springwood was fast becoming the expanding base of Roosevelt's political operations. Franklin had been born in the house and seen his family outgrow its fifteen rooms. That summer, construction was under way: Springwood would be more than doubled in size, the clapboard farmhouse becoming a thirty-five-room mansion, with two new fieldstone wings—Franklin's design—and a third floor. There would be plenty of room for the children—"the chicks" as he called them. But he and his mother, Sara, had another reason for the expansion: As Franklin's political circles widened, the house would need to host an ever-growing coterie of cohorts and friends.

The drawing room was crowded with local notables, but Henry Jr. was given a prime seat. Roosevelt stood at the center of the gathering, the country squire home from the halls of power, and had little trouble finding an apt balance between stroking the egos of the county men and retailing the latest rumors from Washington. On this July afternoon, Roosevelt shared a startling story. He had been bantering with two of the highest-ranking men in the Army and Navy, asking if they had to place a $1,000-bet on the outcome of the war, which would they choose: The Allies would win; there would be a draw; or Germany would win? Each man, Roosevelt said, depended "on his salary and balked at the sum." But when pinned down, both bet on Germany.

As Roosevelt held court, the guests gathered close. And once again, Henry Jr. felt the draw. It was more than wit or charm; it was nearly a gravitational pull. Henry Jr. had stayed late at Hyde Park, nearly into the evening. He could sense what the others had long known: Roosevelt was on the ascent, and he enjoyed the notice. Henry Jr. had even been "very much tempted," he would write, to run for sheriff, but was uncertain of the timing. Weeks earlier, he'd written his father that he would wait. The ambassador, in turn, praised his son's patience. "You will realize later on," he wrote, "how much better it is to have the office seek you than to have you seek it."

But Roosevelt was not easily deterred. Before summer was out he tried again, urging Henry Jr. to take his seat on the board of the First National

Bank of Poughkeepsie, the largest in the county. When Roosevelt moved to Washington, he had had to resign as chairman of the bank's board. Roosevelt was looking for a trusted proxy and in Henry Jr. believed he had found one. Yet again Henry Jr. declined the offer. Roosevelt would soon extend a third offer. As assistant secretary of the Navy, he was allowed two assistants. Roosevelt invited Henry Jr. to come to Washington as his purchasing agent, but again he refused. He cited inexperience as the reason, but Henry Jr. had no idea how Washington worked. As he would say years later, he was young, and still "politically innocent enough" to feel he hadn't the "right to accept."

PART III

WAR

19. Franklin and Henry

1916–1933

On Saturday morning, March 4, 1933, the skies were steel gray and the wind raw, but more than 100,000 people had swarmed the Capitol. Arms folded tight against the cold, they stood for hours in coats and hats hoping for a glimpse. Four months had passed since Franklin D. Roosevelt defeated Herbert Hoover, who had presided over an historic economic free fall. Officially, one out of four workers was unemployed. In truth, the toll was higher. And then, for a month on the eve of the inauguration, a new specter loomed: Americans had started a run on the banks. As the banking system teetered, the country seemed to have lost its way, and many feared it could not be righted.

The Roosevelts emerged from the East Portico of the Capitol, the new president gripping the arm of his eldest son, James. As the crowds cheered, they made their way slowly down the carpeted wooden ramp to the rostrum. Few could see the metal braces, and fewer still the look of unyielding determination in his eyes. To the left, right, and behind in the stands, stood family and friends: three generations of Roosevelts—nearly all Republicans, straining the limits of forbearance—beside the "New Dealers," as the press had nicknamed the professors and their former pupils who had joined the new administration. Economists and labor activists, lawyers and agricultural experts, they had come with grand ideas to save the country but few concrete plans.

Henry Morgenthau, Jr., watched from a few feet away, as his friend and neighbor was sworn in as the thirty-second president of the United States. Nearly twenty years had passed since that 1914 meeting at the Navy Department—the beginning of a cloudless friendship. The new president, Henry would say decades later, was his "best friend." From vastly different worlds, and possessing vastly different demeanors ("Henry the Morgue," FDR would nickname Morgenthau), there was yet much that bound them: a proud inheritance, a famous surname, and the wealth and property that made up great privilege. Both had been lucky enough to lead a life of "independence," as not having to work for a living was then called, to pursue a career in public service, to "do good, not well."

Yet there was a deeper affinity. Franklin and Henry were both loners, as any who knew them well could attest. Each was isolated in his own orbit, and both were at home only in "the county," as they called their shared remote corner of the countryside an hour or so north of New York City, amid the rolling hills along the eastern banks of the Hudson.

| | | |

Henry and Ellie had been married in the spring of 1916, less than two months after his return from visiting his father in Turkey.

Elinor Morgenthau had seen the farm in Fishkill just once before their engagement, but she, too, had fallen for the land. Ellie and Henry made their first home there, settling into a small white-frame farmhouse. The house had no electricity—the kerosene heater kept the rooms reeking of gas—and a chicken coop outside beside a narrow creek. It was simple, but more than enough. To Henry Sr.'s joy, their firstborn was a son, duly named Henry III, once again breaking the Jewish tradition of not giving a child the name of a living parent. Seventeen years old at the time of the Roosevelt inauguration, the next in "the dynasty," as the former ambassador called it, Henry III was born in the winter of 1917, not quite nine months after the wedding. He had been the last Morgenthau delivered at home, in a spacious apartment on West Seventy-third Street. Robert, now fourteen, had arrived in 1919, and Joan, ten, in 1922.

The children had enjoyed the freedom of the farm, running amok in the orchards, playing hockey on the frozen pond, and swimming in the granite-edged pool—a gift from Grandpa. They had also become expert horseback riders. One year, they even beat the Roosevelt children in the Dutchess County horse show, placing second in the "family class." When they reached school age, and they started to spend more time in the city, Henry and Ellie rented an apartment on West Eighty-sixth Street. All three children entered the Lincoln School, near Morningside Park, a "progressive experiment" run by Columbia and sponsored by the Rockefeller family that attracted the Our Crowd families.

Weekends were nearly always spent on the farm. Henry had diligently worked the land, spending long hours inspecting each corner, whether on horseback or in an old Model-T. He had begun by experimenting, trying his hand at almost every possible fruit, vegetable, and livestock: from apples, potatoes, and strawberries, to hogs, chickens, and cattle. Henry had hired a "boss farmer," a local who spoke little but was a veteran dirt farmer. Henry gave Jim Bailey a small house on the farm, and allowed him the illusion of independence, yet throughout the decades that "Mr. Bailey" ran things at Fishkill Farms, even in the darkest months of the war, not a week passed without Henry checking in to deliver a list of directions to be followed.

| | | |

Henry and Franklin could never be equals, but neither were they rivals. Eight years older, Roosevelt treated his neighbor like a little brother. The arrangement suited Henry Morgenthau. At an early stage in their friendship, Henry made clear his intentions. Burdened by an indecisive nature and weak self-esteem, he desperately wanted to prove himself. His chosen avenue, as Henry called it, was "service"—and serving FDR would become his life.

At thirty-eight, Franklin Roosevelt was eager to continue his climb, again following in his distant cousin's footsteps. (Two decades earlier, T.R. had been nominated for vice president at the age of forty-two.) On August 9, 1920, Roosevelt accepted the Democratic nomination as the running mate of Ohio governor James M. Cox, at a notification ceremony—long a party tradition—in Hyde Park. As FDR spoke from the front porch of the family home, Henry Morgenthau, Jr., stood beside him, chairman of the committee of local party men who organized the day. Henry had brought them all to Hyde Park: the mayors of nearly every town within a day's drive and Ed Perkins of Poughkeepsie. He also printed the pamphlets that advertised "A Vote for Cox and Roosevelt is a Vote for the League of Nations." The war had ended, but Wilson's legacy, and the memory of the American lives lost after the U.S. entry in April 1917, would form a central promise of the campaign. "Your 81,000 sons and brothers and husbands," the flyer read, "fought and died in France and Flanders to make an end of war. We must not break faith with those who died." The Republicans were calling for "a return to normalcy," but Roosevelt countered, "We can never go back." "The 'good old days' are gone past forever," he said. "We must go forward or flounder." But the election swept "normalcy," in the shape of that reassuring mediocrity, Warren Harding, into the White House, and Roosevelt, for the first time in ten years, back to private life.

Van Lear Black, the tycoon behind *The Baltimore Sun,* whom FDR had met at the 1912 convention, offered a convenient sinecure: a $25,000-a-year job with his Fidelity and Trust Company, one of the country's largest bond surety firms. Black welcomed Roosevelt to the firm—he would become a vice president and head of the New York office—at a banquet at Delmonico's. Adolph Ochs, the *Times* publisher, and nearly fifty bankers were there to mark FDR's "return to New York business life." Roosevelt knew little of the business, but was sure to become a rainmaker.

Henry Sr. remained a force in Democratic politics, and ever since the first Wilson campaign, he had taken care to keep in touch with Roosevelt. In the months before FDR was stricken with polio at Campobello in the summer of 1921, Henry Sr. and he had seen each other regularly: Henry Sr. was not alone in viewing him as the best hope to revive Wilson's reform movement—and in the spring of 1921, the elder Morgenthau had set up a Wilson Foundation—an "eternal memorial" to the former president—and recruited FDR as its chairman.

After Turkey, Henry Sr. had gone on to serve Wilson as a kind of ambassador at-large, a liaison to the Jewish community—and an opponent of Zionism. In June 1917, he had again pursued his belief that he could coax the Turks into a "separate peace." He proposed a secret plan to Wilson: He would rendezvous on Gibraltar—under the guise of providing relief for the Jews in Palestine—with Chaim Weizmann, the Russian-born chemist then leading the Zionist cause in London. Weizmann would represent the British, the French would send an envoy, and Henry Sr. would also invite Schmavonian, his former dragoman, as a go-between to the Turks.

Wilson consented. But the meeting in early July, in the British fortress on Gibraltar, did not go well. The secretary of war asked that Felix Frankfurter, a Harvard law professor attached to the War Department, join Henry Sr. as an assistant. But Frankfurter, an ardent Zionist and protégé of Justice Louis Brandeis, had a second purpose: to undermine the mission. The Zionists could not brook a peace deal that would allow the Turks to keep control over the Holy Land. Only a British victory in Palestine, the Zionists believed, would yield a Jewish homeland. Weizmann, who had formed an alliance with the British foreign secretary, Arthur Balfour, rebuffed Henry. In one of the meetings on Gibraltar, Weizmann denounced the Morgenthau plan as foolhardy. Later, he attacked Henry himself, as possessing "great ambition, not commensurate with his abilities and knowledge."

Years later, Frankfurter remembered Henry's mission as a "wild goose chase," and Morgenthau Sr. as a blowhard "incapable of continuity of thought, or effort." Even Schmavonian had disappointed his old boss, reporting that Morgenthau was no longer welcome in Constantinople. The Turks were fuming over public remarks he had made, claiming that they had offered to sell Palestine—"We'd even got down to figures," Henry Sr. had said in a speech that made headlines across the West. The secret mission not only failed, it was—as Colonel House was soon told by a protégé at State—a "fiasco."

Morgenthau regained his stature—in large part, thanks to his bestselling memoirs on his years in Turkey. *Ambassador Morgenthau's Story,* first published in April 1918 as a series of articles in Walter Page's *The World's Work,* was deemed essential reading in Washington. The author made sure a long list of notables received a copy, and as the congratulations flooded in—from President Wilson and his wife, the Roosevelts, Ochs—he kept them all in well-ordered files. But Uncle Henry could not sit idle. He felt himself the victim of the Zionists' cabal, and soon made a final break. In March 1919, after a dozen years Henry Morgenthau quit as president of the Free Synagogue. He made the announcement in dramatic fashion: by means of a public letter to his friend and mentor, Rabbi Stephen Wise. For Henry, Wise had crossed the line. The rabbi had made a secret weekend visit to the White House to lobby Wilson. Knowing Henry would oppose the idea, Wise went behind Henry's back—and only after asking Henry to fill in for him in his pulpit. In Washington, Wise and other Zionists had pressured Wilson to champion their cause at the upcoming peace conference in Paris. To Henry, it was a double-cross beyond forgiveness.

Among America's Jewish leaders, an unsubtle battle ensued for proximity to the president. By June, though, Henry had regained his place in the circle around Wilson, and he sailed for France in the company of Herbert Hoover, then head of Near East Relief. Henry was bound ostensibly for Cannes, to lead the American delegation at the conference to rebuild the Red Cross. But in true Uncle Henry fashion, he coaxed his way into the peace conference, where, from a seat beside General Pershing, he witnessed the peace signing. "We walked up and saw the treaty," Henry wrote in his diary, "like mourners reviewing a corpse."

In Paris, Wilson consented to two more Morgenthau missions—one concerning the Jews of Poland, the other the Armenians. Both ended inauspiciously.

Stories of the persecution of Jews in the newly formed Republic of Poland had brought outrage in the United States. In Paris, Henry had urged Wilson to send a delegation to investigate, but he never intended, or so he would later claim, to head it himself. The president had insisted: Henry, an anti-Zionist and Wilson loyalist, would be acceptable to the Polish leaders. The mission, though, would prove a failure. His friend Jacob Schiff had warned Henry, on the eve of his departure for Warsaw, not to be "misled by [the] Poles, for the eyes of Jewry are upon you." "The Morgenthau Commission" traveled across Poland throughout the summer of 1919, crowds of Jews, eager for American support, filling the streets at each stop. But the commission's findings, which minimized the blame of the Polish government, would be roundly criticized—and Henry accused of orchestrating a whitewashing.

At the same time, he would not abandon the Armenians. To help the Armenian remnant, Henry enlisted Hoover to lobby Wilson for an American mandate over the lands from Constantinople to Mount Ararat, where hundreds of thousands of Armenian refugees remained. Together, they convinced General James Harbord, Pershing's chief of staff in France, to lead a military expedition to investigate the chances for success. In October, Harbord took fifty officers to the region, but returned with a report detailing thirteen reasons in favor of a mandate, and as many against. The Harbord report was duly shelved, and any hopes for a U.S. mandate lost in the postwar battle for the League of Nations.

Uncle Henry moved on—never out of work, or the headlines, for long. In spring 1920, for a few heady weeks, he was headed for Mexico as Wilson's ambassador, before Republicans in the Senate, loath to extend the tenures of "Wilson men," forestalled the appointment. In New York, there was talk, as well, of a run for Congress. Then in 1923 came a final turn in the limelight: The League of Nations sent Henry to lead a commission to resettle the hundreds of thousands of Greeks who had fled the burning of Smyrna, the slaughter in the wake of the Turkish victory in 1922 under Mustafa Kemal Pasha.

At sixty-nine, Henry dove into the work: marshaling $50 million to move the refugees en masse, from Asia Minor and Eastern Thrace to their ancestral land. As he had with the Armenians, Henry earned the gratitude of a nation, gaining an honorary degree from the University of Athens and the Order of the Holy Saviour of Greece. Back in New York, he hired another ghostwriter for a new installment in his autobiographical series, the continuing chronicle of professional triumph: *I Was Sent to Athens.* This time, the book sat on the shelves, and Uncle Henry was left to look for a new preoccupation.

| | | |

Henry Sr. was determined that his son reach the political heights he had been denied. Uncle Henry had never found a sure footing with the man he wished to be his political patron. Wilson, he feared, could never get beyond his religion, or worse, his wealth. In the fall of 1919, the president had suffered a massive stroke, leaving him largely paralyzed on his left side. Within days of Harding's victory, Dr. Grayson, Wilson's physician and aide, came looking for funds to support the former president in his life after the White House. "Wilson was sick when he came" to Washington, Grayson said, and had previously lost vision in one eye. Now enfeebled, Wilson sought "10 to 12 retainers of $1,000 a year from people so as to keep well." Henry gave as readily as ever—"I became Number 1," he would recall. It was not only a matter of loyalty: Henry saw a new era beginning, and he was determined that Henry Jr. not miss his chance.

The great "relay race," as the son called it, was on.

Farming, Henry Jr. had begun to sense, would never be enough. By 1921, he had made up his mind. "There is nothing I would rather do than own an agricultural paper," he told his father. In the spring of 1922, Henry Jr. purchased the *American Agriculturist,* a weekly that claimed to be the oldest farm paper in the East (founded in 1842), and boasted a circulation of 120,000—mostly dirt farmers in upstate New York, New Jersey, and across New England. The *Agriculturalist* was flagging, though, and losing ground to a larger rival, the *Rural New Yorker.* Henry brought in a new editor—Ed Eastman, an upstate native who'd helped found the Dairymen's League Cooperative—and urged him to curb the paper's scientific bent and instead print articles that farmers could actually read and enjoy. Eastman added columns on finance, crops, and Washington politics, and features to attract "farm women," on breadmaking, dressmaking, and home management. Henry Jr. also organized, at his father's urging, a publicity blitz. In July, when the Morgenthaus hosted David Houston, Wilson's former secretary of agriculture, at a clambake to shill for the revamped paper before fifty of New York's top advertisers, Henry Sr. made sure all the city reporters were there to cover it—and that a photograph of his son, wearing white khakis, white shirt, and bow tie while holding a horseshoe, ran in the papers. The headline: "Publisher Pitches."

Henry Jr. had no experience in publishing, and leaned heavily on his wife for editorial judgment: Ellie became the journal's vice president. Subscriptions were $1 a year. By February 1924, his father had sunk $201,000, an enormous sum at the time, into the paper. Henry Sr. was investing in a stepping-stone to the political stage, but his son revealed no interest in a political career. As publisher, Henry Jr. was driven solely by a desire to stand up for the common farmer. He drafted editorials and ordered Eastman to push ahead on an investigative series, digging into the rampant exaggerations of the national farm product advertisers who preyed on credulous farmers. Lawsuits ensued. "Go the limit," Henry Jr. told his editor, "otherwise we might as well shut up the magazine." The campaigns continued.

For the first time, Henry Jr. had not only his own constituency—the farmers—but also access, his *own* access, to politicians. In Washington, he found himself consulting venerable senators like Carter Glass of Virginia and Royal S. Copeland of New York, and he began, too, to travel to Albany. In early 1924, the *Agriculturalist* published a petition on tax relief, and asked readers to send it to the governor. The ploy worked: Al Smith, the Irish son of the Lower East Side who had risen as a Tammany man, and who in his third term as governor was preparing a run for president, invited him to come and talk.

"Do you see," Henry wrote his father, "I am making a position for myself thru the paper."

20. Henry & Franklin, Elinor & Eleanor

1922–1928

Throughout the 1920s, Franklin and Eleanor Roosevelt developed twin courts as courtiers and rivals vied for their attentions. Each cultivated ever-growing circles of friends and intimates, allies and counselors, separate from the other. The Morgenthaus would become the singular exception.

Polio had a good deal to do with the closeness. In the summer of 1921, FDR had been on Campobello Island, seeking respite from Washington, when he was hit by a wave of exhaustion. "I'd never felt quite that way before," he would say. Whether he'd picked it up somewhere along the journey, or in mingling with the Boy Scouts at the Jamboree near Hyde Park a week earlier, Roosevelt, then thirty-nine, had caught a virus. He'd dressed for dinner, but by morning he was running a fever and his body ached. "By the end of the third day," Roosevelt would write a few years later, in a rare recollection of how the illness had struck, "practically all muscles from the chest down were involved." First he lost control of the right leg, and then the left.

In those trying first years of polio, as he retreated to Springwood and learned to cope with his disability, the relationship between the Morgenthaus and the Roosevelts turned quadrilateral. Henry and Elinor were the one couple, their family, friends, and even servants would all attest, whose company, politics, and family life Franklin and Eleanor enjoyed together. The foursome saw one another often, sharing meals and holidays, even birthdays and vacations.

The closeness came, too, from the land that surrounded them, the rolling hills and forests that, as FDR liked to claim, had stood untouched since before Henry Hudson's arrival. They had established a camaraderie that owed much to the local soil: When Henry bought saplings, he included an order for FDR, who would impress visitors with his knowledge of every stand of trees on the family estate. The two also nursed a rivalry, teasing each other as to which gentleman farmer had the greener thumb. They would long rehearse private jokes, begun in these trying months, arising from a competition for growing squash. "Please write me any further directions as to how the common stock should be planted," Roosevelt would write from Warm Springs, Georgia, while taking polio treatments, "whether it should be watered, whether the distribution should be wide or closely harrowed, whether it carries any bonus (beside bugs)."

At the same time, in the cosseted world of the "river families," Henry and Ellie found a cold welcome. Always, a pall hung close. "Young Mr. Morgenthau & his wife called this P.M.," Sara Roosevelt wrote her son in the summer of 1918 from Hyde Park. "And while they were here Mrs. F.W.V."—Frederick W. Vanderbilt's wife—"came bringing 5 people, & we had a pleasant tea." "Young Morgenthau," Sara reported, "was easy & yet modest & so nice & intelligent." Her consideration of Elinor, though, revealed the genteel anti-Semitism of the Hudson Valley: "The wife is very Jewish, but appeared very well."

Eleanor shared with her mother-in-law, at least until the early 1920s, the sense that Jews were a different sort, a race to avoid. In a letter to Franklin, written after they were married and he had chosen to enroll at Columbia Law over Harvard, Eleanor had worried about his classmates. "I am anxious to hear about the first day," she wrote, "and whether you found any old acquaintances or had only Jew Gentlemen to work with!" In Washington, when Franklin was in the Navy Department, Eleanor had dreaded going to a party for Bernard Baruch. "I'd rather be hung than seen at" the affair, she wrote to her mother-in-law, as the crowd would be "mostly Jews." "The Jew party was appalling," she later reported to Sara. "I never wish to hear money, jewels and sables mentioned again."

Perhaps the Morgenthaus avoided those topics. At any rate, as FDR and Mrs. Roosevelt carved out parallel lives, Henry and Elinor served as a bridge—the only couple with whom the Roosevelts could relax. In their company, Franklin and Eleanor could be unfettered by convention: They could float half-formed strategies and contrarian ideas, knowing the Morgenthaus, so valuing their proximity, would never betray the trust.

The friendships blossomed across the husbands and wives as well. Henry Jr. spoke more forthrightly with Eleanor Roosevelt than with nearly anyone else. Franklin, too, grew fond of Elinor Morgenthau. He enjoyed her intelligence and wit—and relied on Ellie to shake Henry from his doldrums. If her husband lapsed easily into self-doubt, FDR found Ellie a co-conspirator, a wife eager to help him prod, tease, and rejuvenate a friend. One year, on a formal invitation to his birthday dinner, Roosevelt scrawled a few lines of his beloved doggerel to Ellie:

ELINOR I WANT TO KNOW
WHAT MAKES HENRY ARGUE SO
DON'T HE GET A CHANCE AT HOME
TO MAKE HIS OPINIONS KNOWN?

In the years of Franklin's convalescence, the Roosevelts often came to Fishkill Farms for dinner. The evenings began with several rounds of cocktails, and Gretchen, the family cook (a German immigrant who'd arrived at Grandma Fatman's as a wet nurse), would require extra hands. At Fishkill, the table was always laden with food—smoked turkey and ham in the winter, lobster and clams in summer—and Franklin took the bait with glee.

"We are looking forward to the pool and supper with you on Saturday," he wrote Elinor in July 1925. "I will telephone you from Hyde Park on Friday (to confirm how many of us are coming) so you can kill the fatted calf for us! PS: Missy reminds me that I shall have to bring Roy"—LeRoy Jones, his valet at the time—"with me to get me in and out of the pool and dress me—that means you will have to provide 15 or 16 newly caught fish for him."

The entrance to the Morgenthau house had a set of rickety stairs. Roosevelt had not yet relearned how to "walk." Even attempting a single step was a laborious process: His braces ran up to his waist, and locked at the knee. He'd been given two canes, but he found them of little use. He would rely, instead, on other ways to get about: The wheelchair, lightweight and specially fashioned, was always nearby, and Roy was usually there to help. Yet at times, rare times, Roosevelt would allow, or be forced to allow, another man to help carry him. It was a scene that revealed his enfeebled state: a grown man cradled in the arms of another. Often, when he visited the Morgenthaus, he would turn his head aside as Henry helped to hoist him over the four front stairs. To those watching, the tension was dreadful, but Roosevelt attempted to lessen it. "All the while," Henry Morgenthau III, a young boy at the time, would recall, "FDR would make jokes, throwing back that great big head, and laughing to put my father at ease."

| | | |

In the country, as Franklin struggled to adapt to a new life, Eleanor Roosevelt and Elinor Morgenthau grew even closer than their husbands.

"The two Eleanors," as FDR liked to call them, were alike in indelible ways. Both disdained fashion, preferring clothes of simple design and material, as well as conventional notions of femininity and beauty. Theirs was a friendship founded in respect for each other's strengths, but there was more than a touch of envy, as well. When Elinor Morgenthau spoke of her years at Vassar, Eleanor Roosevelt listened with admiration. Elinor possessed an erudition that Eleanor, who endured a miserable childhood and never attended college, had been denied. Her friend was fluent, Mrs. Roosevelt would say, in the arts, theater, and literature—all gifts that could be put to good use in politics. They became horseback riding partners and, even more quickly than their husbands, political soul mates.

Eleanor Roosevelt had begun to take her own first uncertain steps into politics. In an arena dominated almost exclusively by men, Eleanor kept her husband's presence alive. In 1917, New York State had granted women the right to vote, and not long after the Nineteenth Amendment passed three years later, Eleanor had joined the local chapter of the newly formed League of Women Voters. But she had never stood on her own before an audience. That changed in the spring of 1922, when Nancy Cook, a prime force in the state Democratic committee, executive director of the new Women's Division, asked her to speak at a ladies' fund-raising luncheon. Though nervous, Eleanor accepted. Louis Howe, the gnome-like former reporter who had gone to work for FDR in Albany, sat at the back of the room. He'd coached her to lower her voice, not giggle, and keep her remarks short. "Have something to say," Howe told her, "say it, and sit down!"

With prodding and time, Eleanor gained skill, taking over as head of the Women's Division of the state party. Eleanor would lead a corps of five activists: In addition to Cook, the circle included Caroline O'Day, a wealthy widow who had turned to activism after her husband's death, and Marion Dickerman, who lived with Cook. Together, "the two Eleanors," Cook, and Dickerman founded a monthly bulletin, the *Women's Democratic News.* "Mrs. Franklin D. Roosevelt" would be the editor and treasurer, and "Mrs. Henry Morgenthau, Jr." the vice president. By May 1925, they had published their first issue, and Elinor and Eleanor had found a lasting, common pursuit. Eleanor Roosevelt later wrote, "Had Elinor Morgenthau and I not been thrown together . . . the miles that separated us in Dutchess County might have remained a barrier for a long time. However, through working closely together, as we did throughout all the years I was on the Committee, we became warm friends."

Politics came easily to Ellie. She readily adapted the skills gained on the Vassar stage—poise, timing, and a clear voice—to politics. As Elinor traveled the rural districts, she became known in the Women's Division as a rousing speaker. She not only loved to go out on the stump but led the way in creating the Junior Clubs—an experiment to bring young people, and young women in particular, into the party. By the summer of 1926, when Elinor stood before a gathering in Greene County, at the northern edge of the Catskills, she had helped form more than three dozen such clubs.

The speech was remarkable for its passion and prescience. "Say what you will of the Republican Party," Elinor told the group, "normalcy"—the old slogan of the Harding campaign of 1920—"has no soul, expediency has no soul, economy has no soul." She reminded her listeners of their party's ideals. "In our time," Ellie said, "Wilson again gave to the Democratic Party in the nation a soul. And Smith gave it to the party in our state." She went on to make a pitch for the League of Nations—less a partisan plea than a call to honor the vision of the most recent Democrat in the White House. She and her husband, Ellie said, had just returned from an extended holiday in Europe, where they had visited Geneva as the disarmament conference was still under way. "Okay, my friends," Ellie said, adopting what would become one of FDR's favored phrases, "your hearts would have throbbed as mine did had you talked to the people there in Geneva and heard how they revere Wilson."

She closed that day with a call to the future, a lesson from the past on how to build a Democratic road to the White House. "When we go about merely as a machine," Ellie warned, "we can't compete with the more highly organized, richly endowed, well greased Republican machine. *But* when our party follows a leader imbued with the principles of our glorious tradition, a leader who touches the heart of America, we cease to be a minority party and take our place as worthy descendants of Jefferson and Jackson and Cleveland and Wilson."

| | | |

As Eleanor and Elinor worked side by side, Henry supervised the work of the farm and the revival of the *Agriculturalist*. The paper proved a struggle: The advertisers kept balking, and he was forced to borrow time and again from the bank account he still shared with his father. Henry needed to convince the city men, he pleaded to his father, that it was "really a new paper with new blood and new readers." He also attempted to take more of an interest in financial affairs, tracking the stocks he shared with his father and their few joint rental properties. He was plagued again, as he had been in his youth, by bouts of poor health— migraines could bring him low for days. It was only when Henry spent time with Franklin, whether in the thermal pools of Warm Springs, on a houseboat in the Florida Keys, or on the farm in Fishkill, that the world seemed to gain a new purpose.

In those lonely years, as Roosevelt endured a political exile, he brought Henry closer. An inevitable shift ensued: His friend's weakness lent Henry strength. He was only grateful to have, to be privileged by, an intimate view of the transformation happening in his midst. To Henry, it was a turn that seemed nothing short of miraculous—"the resurrection," as he would call it, "of Roosevelt."

Many others felt the same way. Frances Perkins, the social worker who had led the campaign for the safety reforms after the Triangle fire, called it "a spiritual transformation." Perkins recalled Roosevelt's first years as a state senator: He "didn't really like people very much," she would say. Some saw him as sharp-elbowed, even self-righteous—and they were right. "You know," Roosevelt would confide years later, "I was an awfully mean cuss when I first went into politics." But "the years of pain and suffering," Perkins would write, "had purged the slightly arrogant attitude. . . . The man emerged completely warmhearted, with humility of spirit and with a deeper philosophy." Billy Phillips, his friend who had remained at the State Department, was stunned when he saw Roosevelt for the first time after the illness. To Phillips, he seemed "a different person from the charming and at times irresponsible young man of the Wilson days."

Eleanor Roosevelt, of course, measured the change better than anyone. "A blessing in disguise," the disease had given her husband, she would write, the "strength and courage he had not had before." There was much within FDR that the polio would draw out, but now, she wrote, "he had to think out the fundamentals of living and learn the greatest of all lessons—infinite patience and never-ending persistence."

Henry would always return to it, the period of convalescence. Witnessing Roosevelt's struggle to regain his life, he had seen how his friend suffered, endured, and grew. The great bluster and boundless appetite for life remained, but the young man's facile gift for evasion had shifted, turned into a heightened sense of strategy. Above all, the will had become tempered. Politics were no longer a mere challenge; they were the best means available to improve lives. "He had become conscious of other people," Perkins recalled, "of weak people, of human frailty."

"I am convinced," Henry would say years later, "that the Roosevelt that came out of the illness . . . was a completely new person."

| | | |

In New York City, the men who deemed themselves the party kingmakers lamented the loss of a blazing career. The mourning, though, came to an abrupt end in the summer of 1924. At the Democratic National Convention in Madison Square Garden, after thirty-five months of isolation, Roosevelt made a dramatic appearance onstage to nominate "the Happy Warrior," Al Smith, for president. To those who remembered the radiant Roosevelt of the 1920 campaign, this pale and thin version was a shock. He struggled forward on crutches, his son Jimmy, then seventeen, at his side. But when Roosevelt began to speak, he smiled, and his face shone with a warmth that seemed to envelop the hall. "He seemed," Perkins remembered, "to be sharing his personal victory."

Even as a young politician, FDR had been a gifted speaker, but he flirted with audiences, appearing to savor the entertaining as much as the message. Now his voice had gravity, and passion. When he finished his nominating speech, the crowd roared. Among those beaming widest, sitting in the front row of his box, was Henry Morgenthau, Sr. Just back from seven months abroad—the mission, on behalf of the League of Nations, to resettle the Greek refugees—it was Henry Sr. who had suggested FDR to Smith.

"My dear Al!" Henry Sr. had written two weeks earlier,

I forgot to tell you . . . that I think you ought to consider Franklin D. Roosevelt when you decide upon who is to nominate you. FDR

*is very well known and really popular and the fact that he has to be
carried or wheeled up to the platform will be most dramatic—Let
him make a 10 minute speech and then state that he has agreed to
divide his time with the lady you had in mind—or let him do it all.
The sympathy he would evoke from the delegates, and alternates,
the audience and the press would be enormous—and a great deal of
enthusiastic cheering would greet him—he would make a great and
beautiful picture.*

Uncle Henry had suggested the move to Smith with a clear eye, to play
on the passion of the party delegates and the sympathy of the press. Yet
he had gone further, even floating the idea of FDR running for president
that year—as he wrote FDR in a long letter:

My dear Franklin,
*Henry Jr. and I were discussing the situation last night and I think
you can be nominated as President and do your campaign over the
Radio. Everybody has thought of the possibility of a Crown of
Thorn speech—you can deliver it! Bryan's was more or less
bombastic—yours can be real . . .*
    *You take the floor today and speak against the KuKluxism and
end your speech—after describing what Wilson stood for on this
and other issues—end it by saying—a paraphrase on John Brown—
"Wilson's body lies mouldering in the Church—but his soul goes
marching on—and is in the convention and will not permit
KuKluxism or narrow isolation to prevail"—If you desire I can
come over to see you and talk further about it. Here is your
chance—seize it.*

Uncle Henry had been right: Roosevelt had won the spotlight, but Smith
lost the nomination to John W. Davis, Wilson's former solicitor general.
    Roosevelt had learned to feign walking, aided by his new braces and
two canes. By 1928, he could travel to the national convention in Houston, where once again he nominated Smith. The Morgenthaus went with
him, the only husband and wife among the New York delegates, and
giddy to be included—"like children in their joy," Mrs. R. would report
to FDR. The power brokers were desperate to find a Democrat who
could win the governorship in New York and ensure the state would go
for Smith. Robert F. Wagner ranked high on the list, and for lieutenant
governor, several Jewish leaders were under consideration. "There is

quite a little talk about running Senator Wagner," Henry wrote to his father abroad, adding news sure to please him: "There is also some talk of putting me on the state ticket with Wagner." Please do not tell a soul, he cautioned: "We are not discussing the matter with anybody as I do not want my friends to think that I was seeking this position and then be turned down."

FDR had only just arrived in Warm Springs when the state Democrats gathered in Rochester in September 1928. He steadfastly insisted that he would not run for office again, not until he could walk. But Ed Flynn, the party boss of the Bronx, worked the telephone from upstate relentlessly. His argument was simple: Al Smith could not carry New York—and its forty-five electoral votes—unless Roosevelt ran for governor. Settled into his cottage amid the Georgia mountains, FDR pretended not to hear and refused all calls. He was not healthy yet—he continued to insist that he would regain the use of his legs—and he was rebuilding the resort as a national treatment center for polio. The Warm Springs Foundation, he told the party men, had taken most of his money and demanded all of his time. Soon Smith himself called Roosevelt, but as FDR only grew more resistant, he put John J. Raskob, the millionaire who had quit General Motors to run the Smith campaign, on the line. They'd taken care of everything, he promised: Roosevelt could have all the money and time away that he needed. Raskob would fund the polio center, and Herbert Lehman, whom they'd recruited to run for lieutenant governor, would "spell him" in Albany. Roosevelt dug deeper, trying to fend off the barrage, and by all accounts he never said "yes," but when the state convention nominated him, there was no way he could refuse.

| | | |

The four-week campaign began in October. Howe presided over the headquarters in the city, while Henry Morgenthau, Jr., would carry the brunt of the upstate campaign. Roosevelt would attempt a feat almost unheard of: to become the first Democrat to sell himself to the solidly Republican rural villages and towns of upstate New York. For Henry, the work was taxing—his stamina flagged, and his anxiety, and migraines, only intensified. But with ten to twelve stumping stops a day, there was little time to worry. With Ellie sometimes by his side, Henry did it all: corralling the local worthies, leasing the speaking venues, hustling up the publicity, hiring the brass bands, even stringing the bunting. Henry and FDR covered nearly 7,500 miles in an old Buick, in a carousel of Grange halls, churches, farmers' cooperatives, and county fairs—an ordeal, Henry would say, not unlike those camping trips or sea voyages that break even the strongest friendships.

At each stop, Roosevelt honed his stump speech. He spoke of the dangers of religious intolerance—an effort to ease antipathy toward the Catholic Smith. In the smallest villages that lacked a hall, Roosevelt would sit in the rear of the Buick, arch his back, and let his voice boom. The crowds grew. FDR had an uncanny knack, as many noted even then, of making people feel close to him. When he bellowed "My friends," they imagined they truly were. The locals, whether party leaders or dirt farmers, pulled chairs close and confided their worries. Whenever possible, Roosevelt liked to enter a town hall by a side entrance, so as to avoid being seen laboring awkwardly down a center aisle—"stumping along," he would call it. Henry would do his best to forestall such a spectacle, even once, at a rural Grange hall, ensuring that FDR entered by way of the fire escape.

FDR had been told to run in order to strengthen Smith's hand, but once out on the campaign trail, he would not forfeit any opportunity. For as long as anyone could remember, Smith—who rose from "the sidewalks of New York"—had fought for better factory, health, and living conditions for city-dwellers. But Roosevelt made the problems of rural New York his central theme. In speech after speech, he worried openly about the future of the dirt farmer. In 1928, New York was not only the country's most populous state, it was an agricultural power. New York had 190,000 farms—25,000 fewer than Iowa, but 25,000 more than Kansas. Farmland in the Midwest and Great Plains, though, was worth a good deal more, and New York crops yielded far less profit. Apples and milk, the chief farm products, were costly to produce and transport. Above all, vast swaths of the land upstate were tough to farm. Millions of acres, lost to overfarming or disuse, faced abandonment. In the rural communities, farm relief was an urgent demand.

To those watching the early returns at the Biltmore Hotel on the night of November 6, the future looked dismal; Hoover claimed victory before midnight. Roosevelt's mother and Eleanor went home, but the candidate stayed on. Worried about the "cemetery vote" (the old practice of stuffing ballots with the names of voters who had died but remained on the rolls), Roosevelt made calls to a number of sheriffs upstate, threatening to send in state troopers to assist the local officials in ensuring a fair vote. It was well into the night, after Roosevelt had left the Biltmore, when the upstate returns came in. FDR had never imagined that Smith could lose the state while he won the governorship. He had gone home thinking the worst, but he awoke to a shock: Of more than four million votes cast, he had won by 25,564 votes.

"I am the one-half of one per-cent governor," FDR would soon joke with friends.

Eleanor was less than ecstatic. "I felt Gov. Smith's election meant something," she confided to Elinor Morgenthau days later. "But whether Franklin spends two years in Albany or not matters as you know comparatively little. It will have pleasant and unpleasant sides for him and the good to the State is problematical."

Henry and Ellie, though, could not have been more overjoyed. Years later, after six campaigns upstate, Roosevelt would hand his old friend a framed photograph of the two of them, riding side by side in an open car on the trail. "To Henry," FDR had written across it, "from one of two of a kind." It was not true, of course. But both men, for opposite reasons, wished it were.

21. Albany

1928–1932

" The Years in Albany," Eleanor Roosevelt would write, "cast their shadow before them." As governor, Roosevelt nurtured a close circle of aides who would go on to staff the New Deal in Washington. Sam Rosenman, despite Louis Howe's resentment, had become a trusted counselor and ghostwriter. Harry Hopkins, an Iowan who had spent years in settlement work on the Lower East Side, would soon arrive to work in the Temporary Emergency Relief Administration (TERA), a precursor of the federal relief agencies to come. Frances Perkins served as Roosevelt's industrial commissioner. From academia, too, Howe culled the first members of the crew that would become known as the "brains trust": Ray Moley and Rex Tugwell from Columbia.

Days after the election, Roosevelt summoned Henry to Warm Springs to discuss policy—and people. (It was Henry who urged that Roosevelt take on Rosenman.) Roosevelt soon announced the formation of an Advisory Agricultural Commission—twenty-one farmers, politicians, and professors. Henry chaired it, and the commission met in the offices of the *American Agriculturalist*.

In Albany, Henry set up an office just outside the governor's, and he and Elinor took a suite in the city's best hotel, the De Witt Clinton, across from the capitol. On November 28, 1928, before the Roosevelts had moved into the executive mansion, Henry's commission issued its first recommendations. Even as it did, the governor-elect reminded reporters that the body would take no state funds. When the Republicans announced their own conference on agriculture, Roosevelt orchestrated an end around, reconstituting Henry's "unofficial" commission as an official one. The message was clear: The farmers of New York State had a friend in Albany. In rapid fire, Henry's group sent the governor a series of proposals to improve the lives of the upstate farmers, from easing taxes to building farm-to-market roads. The reforms came so fast, Henry recalled, that few in Albany, Republican or Democrat, could foresee how far-reaching the shift in policies would be.

The Advisory Commission, as Henry's group was rechristened, aimed to correct the skewed relationship between taxation and state aid whereby the richer the town, the more aid it received—a punitive imbalance Henry was determined to end. Pushing such a radical plan through the Republican-controlled legislature would be no easy feat, but Roosevelt warmed to the fight. In his first address to the legislature, he put agriculture front and center. Within days, he took the pitch to the farmers, first on the radio, then on the road. On February 22, 1929, with Henry at his side, Roosevelt spoke at the Cornell Agricultural College, which Henry had left sixteen years earlier without a degree. His speech on that frigid day brought out more than three thousand farmers.

"I am new in this governorship game," FDR said. He joked that he felt like "I have started school all over again." Yet the governor could claim to be something of an expert on farming, and as he spoke of "a neighbor of mine . . . who knows a lot about rural conditions," Henry beamed beside him. Roosevelt told of the new commission and its proposals facing the legislature. The bills, FDR said, would fund new rural schools, lower the cost of "hard roads," and bring justice to the tax system. Upstate counties, he said, should not have to pay the same taxes as their urban counterparts. Relief was on the way, he vowed, and Henry had provided him with a list of examples. Twenty-one miles of highway would be built in Tompkins County—the cost under the existing law would have been $412,000, but under his commission's proposal, $147,000. It was only a beginning, Roosevelt cautioned: "I have never believed that it pays either in business or politics to try to fool the people that one remedy would be a panacea, or cure-all for every ill that may exist." The state needed "a long-time program," he insisted, a vision to recast the entire landscape.

Roosevelt and Morgenthau won their first battle. The Republicans might manage to substitute provisions, but they could not stop the reforms: Farm relief was long overdue. Tax relief, with near-universal approval, would be paid for by a two-cent gasoline tax, a tax previously adopted by every other state in the country. On April 8, the governor signed a series of new laws on farm relief, improving rural schools and roads, and relieving counties of some $9 million in costs—the most dramatic victory in memory for the upstate farmers, and a triumph for the novice governor, who allowed even those Republicans who'd tried to whittle down the bills a share in the credit.

Henry Morgenthau stood by FDR's side at the signing but sought no praise. The body he had headed—"and funded," as he later conceded privately—never became known as the "Morgenthau Commission." That had been his father's way: Lobby for a public position, then broadcast his achievements. For the son, the result of his quiet work was more than enough. Roosevelt, the man in the sunshine, was pleased.

| | | |

Albany had only brought the Morgenthaus and Roosevelts closer, and Henry and Elinor now had new, elegant surroundings in which to play host. Their new house on East Hook Road in Fishkill, nearly a hundred miles south of Albany, had long stood as a local landmark, a three-story Victorian crowning a hill across the road from the old farm. The grand house, though, was in disrepair. Ellie hired Aymar Embury II, an architect much in demand, to rebuild it almost from the ground up. To pay for the reconstruction project, she turned to her parents. If her husband's father was wealthy, her own was far richer: The following summer, Morris Fatman, the wool manufacturer, would die of a heart attack in Atlantic City, leaving an estate of more than $3 million—an enormous sum in 1930. Construction continued throughout the winter of the stock market crash, and a stately Georgian mansion emerged. The "Old Homestead" now boasted a white colonnade and overlooked a private pond, a tennis court, a rose garden, a stable for six horses, and the large swimming pool. Elms and maples lined the drive; out back, the vast lawn extended a thousand yards to the woods.

During Roosevelt's governorship, the couples found a new way to travel together. FDR had learned of a small yacht that the state maintained for canal trips, the *Inspector*. It had been used sparingly, ferrying officials to remote institutions in rural corners. Roosevelt, though, sensing an adventure, turned the canal trips into a seasonal habit. In the mid-1920s, the Morgenthaus had sailed aboard FDR's houseboat, the *Larooco,* through the Florida Keys. Now they would join Franklin and Eleanor on their travels along the narrow waterways as far west as Buffalo. The trips were an escape from Albany's skirmishes, a chance to play cards, grow sleepy watching the shoreline, and, each evening, enjoy rounds of still-prohibited cocktails.

On the excursions, Eleanor took on a new role: She learned to evaluate the state institutions: hospitals for the deaf, blind, insane, and aged. She soon learned the tricks: to lift the cooking pots and look inside to make sure the menus did not lie, and to check the beds to see if they were too close together (a sign they'd been moved, and otherwise filled the corridors). "Before the end of our years in Albany," Eleanor would recall, "I had become a fairly expert reporter." The boat trips became a staple of FDR's tenure, and his wife a personal inspector general. Elinor Morgenthau, in turn, became her partner—a practice that the two women repeated often in the years to come.

| | | |

No one really doubted that FDR would win reelection in 1930. His landslide was the surprise. Once again, Henry ran the campaign upstate. In the third week of October 1930, he took Roosevelt on a long stumping swing. They left Albany in two cars and after a picnic lunch, when they almost "froze to death," drove on to Binghamton. The party—Roosevelt, Morgenthau, Rosenman, and Basil O'Connor, the governor's old law partner—"had a lot of fun," Henry recollected, "joking and teasing one another." On the second day, it was on to Elmira, where Eleanor Roosevelt joined them for dinner and a long walk alone with Henry. In the evening, Henry pulled matchsticks with Rosenman "to see who would sleep with the Governor," and won. Sharing a room, the two acted like little boys at a sleepover: "Before retiring," Henry would say, "we had a grand rough house." Unlike in 1928, FDR was buoyant, and when he was in "an excellent mood," he made up "silly songs." The second campaign became a caravan of grown men on their own, having fun.

In a week they covered a thousand miles, to the counties along the Pennsylvania border and back. On the last day, as they parted at the Poughkeepsie Bridge, the governor turned to Henry and said, "This is the only day that you did not arrange and it is the only one we were late at every meeting." The work had taxed his stamina, but for Henry, as always, the single moment of gratitude was more than ample reward.

| | | |

FDR had done something even Al Smith could never have imagined: He had swept upstate New York. The election made clear what many had sensed: As a vote-getter—the margin of his plurality, 725,000 votes, had no precedent—Roosevelt could attract a far wider spectrum than his predecessor had ever managed.

After the election, the governor rewarded Henry with the job he coveted most: commissioner of conservation. With this title, Henry entered the cabinet and presided over the state's lands and forests, water power, fish and game. The agency also comprised a small administrative empire, and for the first time, Henry had patronage to award. He refused, though, to go along with the old game. "We had," the former Bronx boss Flynn would say, "some difficulty with Morgenthau." Instead of accepting names from the party bosses, Henry cleaned house.

He brought in new men, turning again to Cornell, recruiting two of his former professors, Dr. George F. Warren and Carl E. Ladd, now dean of the College of Agriculture. He also hired a chief deputy, Herbert Gaston, a former newspaperman and a soft-spoken, reserved Minnesotan who would join him in Washington. Most recently a night editor at the *New York World,* Gaston had made a long political journey: After the war he'd flirted with the fringe, overseeing propaganda for the radical farmers' Nonpartisan League, before moving on, first to T.R., then to the Socialists and La Follette, before coming to Smith in 1928.

Henry soon launched an ambitious program of reforestation, the largest ever attempted in the country. To put idled young men back to work, he pushed through an amendment to the state constitution, mandating $20 million over twenty years to plant trees. The scheme was visionary: a grand plan to turn the state's vast empty, uncared-for tracts, "the waste spaces of today," into green lands, a "natural playground" for humans.

FDR loved it. Conservation had long been one of the governor's chief concerns, stemming in part from T.R.'s campaign to save America's natural resources, but also from a love of the natural world in Hyde Park. As a young man, he had overseen the planting of thousands of poplar and pine seedlings on the estate, and as early as 1922, he decried the ruinous lumber companies and mused that private syndicates might buy up empty tracts for parkland, as he had seen in Europe. FDR had a gift for such dreams; now with Henry as his conservation chief, he could turn them into plans.

Henry began with an experiment. He brought in a crew of unemployed men to thin out a hundred acres, distributing the wood for free to the poor of a nearby village. He then calculated: How many men would be needed per acre to replicate the process across the state? He proceeded methodically, hiring unemployed men only in the counties where the reforestation would be done. He collected thousands of names from local officials—and when he needed still more men, he turned to Harry Hopkins.

Henry had come to admire Hopkins as the secretary of the TERA, the relief organization. When the agency's first head retired, he'd urged Roosevelt to make Hopkins chairman. The two shared ideals and social worker friends from the settlement world, but beyond politics, they were near opposites. Hopkins could be flamboyant, wanton even; fond of luxuries and parties, he loved to go out on the town. Yet in the reforestation campaign, Hopkins and Morgenthau meshed, uniting to bring thousands of jobless men from the city to the woods upstate. "We took the Gas House Gang," Henry would recall, "the bad boys . . . loafing the streets and getting into trouble."

Each day, the boys rode a four A.M. train to Bear Mountain, worked all day building roads and planting trees, and at night returned to the city. It was small-scale, but the operation may have been, as Henry would claim, the country's first public works program for the unemployed. The seed of the New Deal's most popular programs, the Civilian Conservation Corps and the National Youth Administration, it would also be adapted by the Tennessee Valley Authority.

Hoover's former secretary of agriculture, Arthur Hyde, snorted that the planting program was "chimerical," "little less than absurd." But Roosevelt saw it as a triumph: The governor was wont to recite the record of his conservation czar, and Henry kept him fed with the statistics: 10,000 men, FDR boasted without exaggeration, had planted more than 90 million trees during his years in Albany.

Henry seemed to come up with so many newfangled schemes, Missy LeHand, FDR's secretary, made a joke of it. What rabbits, she would ask, are you going to pull from your hat this morning? Henry knew Roosevelt loved nothing more than a good stunt. One morning, as he showed up at the governor's office, he reached into his black fedora, and pulled out a pair of squirming white rabbits.

| | | |

On June 4, 1930, Elinor and Henry arrived in Boston for the wedding of James Roosevelt, Eleanor and Franklin's oldest son. "I went up to Franklin's room at nine o'clock," he would record in his diary, "and spent one and a half hours with him. . . . He told me in the strictest confidence that . . . he was beginning to be suspicious of the fact that Alfred E. Smith was working for the nomination for President in 1932."

In Roosevelt's mind the target date had long been fixed. For Louis Howe and Jim Farley, the drive started the day after the 1928 election, when they drafted a statement that confirmed everyone's suspicions: With Smith defeated, the path was clear. FDR was the Democrats' leading candidate for the White House.

Even before the landslide of 1930, Roosevelt saw the road ahead. Other than Louis and Eleanor, he did not tell many people, but Henry Morgenthau, Jr., was in on the plan. When his father suggested, early that autumn, that the governor take on the publicity man from the national committee, Henry Jr. quashed the idea. "It would be a great mistake for Franklin," he replied, and added, "As everybody would say, 'Ah, ha, Roosevelt is getting ready for '32!' And we know that that is the one thing that Franklin does not want to be spread around more than is absolutely necessary."

Yet within months, in early 1931, Roosevelt's hunger led to an exploratory meeting. It began with Howe, of course, and the search for money. Uncle Henry got the ball rolling, summoning four men to his home on Fifth Avenue: William "Bill" Woodin, head of American Car and Foundry, one of the country's largest railcar makers; Colonel House, at seventy-seven, living a retirement out of the headlines; Frank Walker, a wealthy Montana lawyer who'd first met FDR in the 1920 campaign; and Louis Howe. "Uncle Henry rather casually invited me to join him for cocktails," Walker would recall. A month earlier, Henry Sr. had sat Walker and his wife, as his guests, at FDR's side at the Wilson Foundation's annual banquet at the Hotel Astor. But each of Henry's guests knew why they had been summoned.

At the session in Uncle Henry's apartment, Howe soon took charge. In circuitous fashion—"Louis always had an air of mystery about him," Walker would recall—he spoke of a groundswell in the country, a "demand" that Roosevelt run. If all agreed, Howe coyly offered, he would ask the governor's "approval" to start the wheels in motion. Within days, a finance committee was launched, with Henry Sr. as treasurer. "Uncle Henry, Colonel House, Bill Woodin, and I pledged ourselves to raise, get, or give, or in any event to have on call $10,000 apiece when needed," Walker later wrote. By April, Walker, Woodin, and Henry Sr. had each given $5,000.

Soon they scored a first recruit: a forty-two-year-old named Joseph P.

Kennedy. Roosevelt and Kennedy had met during the war, when Kennedy, who ran Charles Schwab's shipyards near Boston, had tried to sell ships to the Navy. The relationship had been frosty, at best, but Kennedy, after a recent sell-off of his Hollywood holdings, had become a rising power in New York City. Even amid the Depression, Kennedy had managed to amass more than $15 million. Henry Morgenthau, Jr., at his father's bidding, invited Kennedy to Albany for lunch with the governor—bringing "them together again," Rose Kennedy would recall, "for mutual reappraisal and exchange of ideas." Kennedy knew a good thing when he saw it. "Joe returned with his mind made up that Roosevelt was the man who could save the country."

Once the campaign got under way, Henry Jr. took on a greater role: He organized rallies, cajoled others to give money, and drafted speeches on agriculture. Under Hoover, the stock market continued to fall—it would not hit rock bottom until July, its lowest point during the Depression. Across the country, the farmers, too, had found scant relief. In May 1932, Henry decided to go to the Midwest and South to see the grim conditions for himself. Traveling mostly by plane—which always worried FDR, who feared flying—Henry visited Oklahoma City, St. Paul, and Birmingham. At each stop, he heard the same story: Hoover's attempt at price stabilization, the Federal Farm Board, was an utter failure. Foreclosures loomed, commodity prices were still sinking, and farmers were agitating for boycotts, with some calling for violence.

In Iowa, he met with Henry Wallace, the economist and editor who ran *Wallace's Farmer*, long one of the country's leading agricultural publications. Wallace insisted that if prices did not rise, the country faced "revolution or state socialism in the near future." The midwestern farmer was "numb," Morgenthau told reporters once he reached Warm Springs. He quoted Wallace's prediction that if prices stayed depressed, Roosevelt would win 65 percent of the Iowa farm vote. Wanting "a change," farmers would "leave the Republican fold."

After seeing off Smith's challenge at the Chicago convention, Roosevelt opened the fall campaign with a scathing indictment of Hooverism. His first big economic speech was a farm address in Topeka. Henry, with Herb Gaston at his side, drafted the passages on land use and debt. The message was simple: Roosevelt would bring the success of his New York experiments to the rest of the nation, launching mass-scale programs in reforestation and soil surveys, and cutting all marginal lands from production.

As he campaigned across the country, a resolve emerged. When he spoke of the mood of the people now, his voice was solemn. "No man can cross the continent in these times and return the same," Roosevelt told Anne O'Hare McCormick, a friendly *Times* reporter.

I find conditions different and worse than I expected. I have looked into the faces of thousands of Americans and they are the faces of people in want. I don't mean the unemployed alone. Of course, they would take anything. I mean those who still have jobs and don't know how long they'll last. They have the frightened look of lost children. And I don't mean physical want alone. There is something more.

He spoke of the end of the war, and the French faces he had seen when Wilson went to Paris in 1919. "I watched the crowds in the streets," FDR said, "and I noticed there, particularly in the faces of women, the same expression I see here today. A kind of yearning." In 1919, they were thinking the war, yet the hunger, he said, was the same. "Perhaps this man, their eyes were saying, can save our children from the horror and terror we have known. Now they are saying: We're caught in something we don't understand; perhaps this fellow can help us out."

"Franklin came home from the 1932 campaign," Eleanor would write, "with a conviction that the depression could be licked."

On the last day, as he had in each campaign for more than two decades, FDR returned to Poughkeepsie. At 10:45 in the evening on the night before the election, before friends, neighbors, and a radio audience nationwide, he gave one last speech. "Out of this unity," Roosevelt said, "this unity that I have seen, we may build the strongest strand to lift ourselves out of this depression."

Roosevelt awaited the returns in New York, in the headquarters on the Biltmore Hotel's first floor, surrounded by family and a few friends: Ed Flynn, Ray Moley, the O'Connors, Rosenmans, and Morgenthaus. Henry and Elinor had joined FDR's motorcade on the drive in from Hyde Park, and had been at the Biltmore since early evening. It had grown dark outside on the avenue jammed with exuberant young people when a short, gray-haired, fastidiously dressed man caused a stir as he tried to enter the hotel.

"Come on, Uncle Henry!" a policeman cried out, recognizing the former ambassador, "I'll get you in." Once inside, Henry Sr. marched straight to FDR, who was sitting at a long table lined with aides, eighteen telephones, and two teletype machines. The first returns put Roosevelt ahead, and there he remained: It was earlier than expected when FDR appeared in the ballroom, on the arm of his son James, to tell the crowd, "It looks, my friends, like a real landslide this time!"

By 1:40 A.M., with the West Coast returns in, Hoover sent a wire conceding defeat. FDR had left for the townhouse on East Sixty-fifth Street, where his mother awaited, but Eleanor stayed behind, amid the swirl of campaign workers in the ballroom. Yet as much as she tried to join in the celebration, something held her back. As she sat in a corner of a hectic room, fielding questions from a dozen reporters, some sensed a darkening mood.

"Of course, I'm pleased," Eleanor insisted, when asked about the triumph. "You're always pleased to have someone you're very devoted to have what he wants."

The Morgenthaus were jubilant. It was, Henry Jr. said, the closest he had ever come to tears in public.

22. "The Smell of Revolution Was in the Air"

WINTER–SPRING 1933

For the first time in three hard years, Americans felt a sensation they had nearly forgotten: hope.

Franklin D. Roosevelt's inaugural speech remains unmatched in presidential history. In fewer than two thousand eloquent, idealistic, and candid words, Roosevelt rallied the spirit of the nation. It was a battle cry to the "great army of our people" to join in "a disciplined attack upon our common problems." Roosevelt's voice was grave, and his face so grim that even old friends said he looked unfamiliar. As FDR spoke, Henry and Elinor Morgenthau, standing on the packed platform behind him, looked out on the sea of faces below. To Eleanor Roosevelt, the tableau—men holding aloft toddlers, women openly crying—was "a little terrifying." "You felt that they would do anything," she said later that day, her first in the White House, "if only someone would tell them what to do."

Roosevelt declared war on the lords of American capitalism, the "money changers," who had "fled from their high seats in the temple of our civilization," and must never be allowed to speculate with "other people's money" again. Extraordinary times, FDR declared, required extraordinary measures. He would abide by the Constitution, but demanded that Congress grant him "broad Executive power"—"as great as the power that would be given to me, if we were in fact invaded by a foreign foe."

"This nation calls for action, and action now," he said from the podium. Within hours, he had sworn in the cabinet: nine men and one woman, many who had begun to work before their official status was confirmed. On Sunday, he summoned the House and Senate leaders to the White House, laying out his urgent banking relief plan that called for an "extra" session of Congress, and a bank holiday. After dinner, he gathered his political family, including Henry Morgenthau, Jr., to read the proclamation aloud. Relying on a clause in the Trading with the Enemy Act of 1917, FDR would close the banks for a week and put a "temporary" ban on all gold exports. In truth, hundreds of banks had already shuttered. For Roosevelt, though, the bank holiday was the opening salvo of a war presidency.

Four days later, Congress convened and stayed in session until June 16— the storied "one hundred days." Congress proved uncommonly pliant; the politicians, too, sought a savior. On the first day of the extraordinary session, the Emergency Banking Act, the first of many bills Roosevelt would sign in his thirteen years in the White House, gave him greater control of the nation's finances than any president had ever enjoyed. Not only could FDR close insolvent banks, he could order them to remain closed until the Treasury determined their odds of survival. Six hours after FDR sent the bill to Capitol Hill, he signed it into law.

On the hundredth day came a flurry: a railroad regulatory act, the Farm Credit Act, and Glass-Steagall, the banking act that severed commercial from investment banking, and introduced federal insurance for deposits (FDIC).

"Seldom in any parliamentary history," the journalist John Gunther judged, "has so much been done so quickly."

| | | |

Henry Morgenthau, Jr., had one ambition. In the days after the election he had scolded himself for it, but Ellie tried to ease his worries. She understood her husband's sole desire: to stay by Roosevelt's side. To do so would mean doing something that he had never had to do in the two decades of their friendship: He would have to fight.

His father may have wanted him to get the job he'd missed under Wilson, Treasury secretary, but Henry coveted only one position: secretary of agriculture. In the days after the election, he received a raft of endorsements for the job from the big associations across the country: the cotton growers of North Carolina, wheat growers of Texas, poultry producers of California, and of course, dairymen of New York. On the last day of 1932, the rumors reached Harry Flood Byrd of Virginia, the former governor who was soon to become a power in the Senate. "I cannot imagine any better thing for the country," Byrd wrote Henry, "than for you to extend to the nation what you have already done for the farmers of New York State."

Yet as Roosevelt left Albany, Henry struggled to decode his intentions. "I cannot make this a formal letter," FDR had written him, "but before I go out I want you to know how very grateful I am to you for all the splendid work you have done for the people of this State . . . also for the splendid loyalty you have given me." The words, however warm, signaled nothing as to Henry's future in Washington. On the eve of the inauguration, Roosevelt again offered only vague assurance—he wanted to keep Henry "very close." Henry Sr. took it as a foregone conclusion. "If FDR wants you 'very close,'" he replied, "the only way he can do so is to put you *in*."

| | | |

Roosevelt made history with his appointments. Frances Perkins, the secretary of labor, was the first woman to hold cabinet rank. He also sought balance. Three cabinet members were, or had been, Republicans: Bill Woodin, the new secretary of the Treasury, the soft-spoken executive who had amply funded the campaign, garnered the most attention, and concern. FDR had tried to coax Carter Glass, the powerful senator from Virginia, into taking over the Treasury—and failed. Woodin, despite his uncertain health, had dutifully stepped in, and now both Republicans and Democrats feared that Woodin, already frail at sixty-four, was not up to the job of taming Wall Street. In the months since the election, the slump had only worsened. More than 17 million Americans remained without jobs, capital flight continued unchecked, and gold was being hoarded. To Henry Morgenthau, Jr., though, the fate of the nation's farms was the most urgent order of business.

FDR soon extended an offer, telling Henry he would name him to be "head of an agency for the unemployed." "He said it would be the most powerful agency in Washington," Morgenthau would recall. "He said I would have the Army and Navy working for me. He had thought this through almost to the last detail. But I could not grasp the possibilities and refused it. Later . . . I had the pleasure of telephoning Hopkins that he would get this job"—head of FERA, the government's top federal relief administrator.

Agriculture, though, remained open. It would be, Henry was sure, one of the "three most difficult posts," and FDR's success as president would depend in large part on how it was handled. As the jockeying intensified, Henry drafted a long list of reasons why he deserved the job. Among the mountains of paper he gave to the FDR Library in Hyde Park—millions of documents in all—this personal summary, three pages of typewritten, single-spaced text, may be the most revealing. With no formal heading—no date, title, or typist's initials—it records one of the few times in his life when Henry asked for what he felt he deserved.

He set down all the ways he had served Roosevelt, going back to 1919—all he had done to lay the foundation for Roosevelt's "reputation all over the United States as a 'friend of the farmer.' " As he tallied up the political capital, Henry noted, with an honesty that stung, his own modesty: "I have also kept myself in the background and have always given Roosevelt all of the credit for any ideas that I have had."

Morgenthau viewed the agriculture post with a kind of messianic zeal and thought he had a lock on the job. But Roosevelt turned to Henry Wallace, the son and grandson of famous farmers. "Between a Protestant from Iowa and a Jew from New York," Henry's son, Robert, later quipped, "it wasn't a tough call." To Morgenthau, though, Wallace represented the worst choice: a true believer in the latest panacea that promised to save the American farmer. Henry had been to Wallace's farm in Iowa and heard him preach the gospel of "domestic allotment," shorthand for the fiercely debated notion that to spur demand for farm products the government should curtail production—in short: Pay farmers to burn their crops. To Morgenthau, nothing could be more misguided. "We could never produce too much so long as there were hungry people at home and abroad," he wrote. "Above all, something instinctive within me revolted at the destruction of existing crops."

Underlying the fight was an irony: Morgenthau had brought Wallace into the inner circle. They had met in Iowa in the spring of 1932, and by August, when Morgenthau learned that Wallace was visiting Cornell, he decided to drive him down to Hyde Park. By December, when Roosevelt invited Wallace to Warm Springs, Morgenthau again served as chauffeur, meeting him at the station and delivering him to the president-elect's cottage in the woods. For hours, the two had sat beside Roosevelt, debating the virtues of domestic allotment. Wallace remembered the evening as productive, but a split had opened. Before dinner that night, cocktails were served—as always, FDR's favorite hour. "Henry Morgenthau's duty was to scurry around to see that the President got safe-liquor," Wallace recalled. "Details were given as to the particular local tycoons"

Henry would have to visit "in order to get the liquor." Wallace and Morgenthau shared a devout concern for the farmers, but their mutual antipathy would only grow.

Henry stewed as the frustration ruined his days and haunted his nights. He had to be by Roosevelt's side. It was "extremely important," he had written in his memo to himself, that FDR "have at least one member of the Cabinet who is an intimate friend and not be like Wilson who didn't have a real friend in his Cabinet. Time and again I have been able to tell Roosevelt of unfriendly actions by members of his present cabinet and I have told in time for him to 'check.'"

No evidence exists that Morgenthau ever showed his confidential "tally sheet" to Roosevelt—or anyone else. He did not raise his voice in public against Wallace's appointment; he played, as ever, the good soldier. The boss was pleased: Before 1932 was out, FDR called with a new offer.

IIII

Two days before the inauguration, Roosevelt named Henry the administrator of Hoover's Farm Board, with orders "to dissolve it."

Hoover had created the Farm Board before the stock market crash, in the summer of 1929, to stop commodity prices from crashing. But burdened by bureaucracy and sorely underfunded, it had proved a dismal failure. In its place, Roosevelt asked Henry to build a single, independent credit agency, consolidating the current hodgepodge of six federal agencies. It was a vital undertaking, as farm recovery depended on credit.

Annual agricultural income had fallen from $6 billion in 1929, a lean year, to $2 billion in 1933. Wheat prices had plummeted 63 percent, and the price of cotton had sunk even lower. Nature had also taken her toll—hailstorms, drought, and grasshopper plagues had hit the farmlands—but farmers blamed the bankers, insurance men, and politicians. Galvanized by the fiery speeches of Milo Reno and his National Farmer's Holiday Association, midwestern farmers were organizing. Reno's "holidays" meant strikes: the simplest way to keep farm products off the market and raise prices. As the Midwest seethed, dairymen dumped milk, ranchers tried to keep cattle from being shipped, and farmers increasingly faced off with police. To Reno, all the talk of "overproduction" was a lie: The real problem, he told his feverish audiences, was the "monopolization" of supply lines.

Lawlessness loomed. Roosevelt had been in office only a few weeks when hundreds of farmers in Le Mars, Iowa, their faces covered by bandanas, kidnapped a judge who had refused to halt foreclosures. Judge Charles C. Bradley was hauled from his courtroom, blindfolded, thrown in a truck, and driven to the edge of town, where a mob threatened to lynch him. Spared the noose, the judge was stripped, beaten, and left in a ditch. As the headlines spread across the country, the governor of Iowa put seven counties under martial law. As Morgenthau wrote, "The smell of revolution was in the air."

On May 16, after ten days in the job, Henry received his first reporters—a weekly appointment he would keep throughout his Washington years. His nerves were running high, as the newsreel men gathered in his office. Herb Gaston, the former reporter who had won Henry's confidence in Albany, looked on beside him, and in a corner of the room, taking down every word, sat a trim woman with cropped curls. Henrietta Klotz (née Stein) was a Jewish girl from the Bronx whose confidence was surpassed only by her secretarial skills. Mrs. Klotz, as Henry always called her, was blond, blue-eyed, and so striking that soon Morgenthau's rivals were commenting on her appearance. So did the press: "Despite the seemingly contradictory evidence," wrote one reporter, "of her appealing blondness, curly hair, misty blue eyes and heart-shaped face, this young woman is above all things an executive."

Klotz had come by way of a Vassar classmate of Ellie's, who'd suggested her for a job at the *American Agriculturalist*. She had forgone college to earn money for a younger brother's education. During the war she placed an ad in the newspaper; Gabrielle Elliot Forbush, Ellie's friend from Vassar, answered it. Forbush hired Henrietta for the small office she ran, managing musicians and Broadway stars. After a time, when Forbush had to close up the business, she passed along Klotz's name to her old friend from Vassar. The friend, she explained, had just married a would-be farmer who'd recently bought a newspaper and sorely needed secretarial help.

The interview had not lasted long. Henry looked at the twenty-one-year-old Henrietta and said, "Yes, I'll hire you." Taken aback, she asked if he didn't wish her to take a stenography test? No need, Henry said. There were other tests. Days later, when Henry asked her to bring him a file, as she pulled out the folder, a five-dollar bill fell to the floor. Mrs. Klotz picked it up, walked in with it, and said, "This is a funny place to file money." She handed her new boss the money, "and that was it." She had passed the test, and the $30-a-week job was hers.

At the paper, Mrs. Klotz had worked diligently, but her efficiency soon extended far beyond. From her office in the city, she took on the affairs of the farm, and her boss's finances—even collecting rents at the Hunts Point Palace ballroom he co-owned with his father. When FDR named him to Farm Credit, Henry had called Mrs. Klotz at once. Over the next twelve years, on each working day of his tenure in Washington, Mrs. Klotz was at Henry's side.

Farm Credit, Morgenthau assured the reporters, was central to the Roosevelt agenda. The president had ordered him to open credit offices in every state: "The idea he has in mind," he explained, "is that if a farmer wants to get credit from the government he can go to one place and get it without having to travel a thousand miles." The farmer, Henry vowed, would soon "get his money and get it faster, and if possible, at a lower rate of interest." The coffers, though, were low. Hoover's Farm Board had started with $500 million; in March 1933, only $36 million remained. "I might want to go in," Henry told the reporters, "with my hand out."

Henry had done political work only in Dutchess County, and with seven out of ten farmers unable to pay their mortgages there would be no time to learn. There were days when he doubted if he were up to the job. But as long as he could keep Wallace at arm's length—maintaining the independence of Farm Credit and keeping his own fief—Henry relished the challenge. He and Ellie had moved into a three-room suite at the Wardman Park Hotel above Rock Creek, and each day he walked the forty-five minutes to work. He took to the new routine, and with no team to speak of—Gaston and Mrs. Klotz were his sole lieutenants—he won an early battle: FDR saw to it that the Agriculture Department did not swallow Farm Credit, and that Henry got all the money he needed: "We had about two billion dollars in our kitty with which to stall off the sheriff."

Giving out so much money so fast would not be easy. Bureaucratic roadblocks abounded, but Henry had a privileged status, an understanding that preceded him wherever he went in Washington. By dint of his closeness with the Roosevelts, doors would open, and soon he would learn to rely on shortcuts that others, even those ostensibly higher placed, were denied. Within months, Henry created a streamlined bureaucracy: He cut duplication, brought five disparate divisions into a single agency, and opened loan offices across the country. He hoped to build a farmer-owned and farmer-operated enterprise that could borrow from the public at low rates in order to lend to farmers at low rates, but it was not to be.

In Henry's first seven months on the job, Farm Credit loaned more than $580 million to farmers. Henry may not have recognized it, but he had also achieved an old dream, one he first mused about on his cross-country expedition as a young man: a single rate of interest for farmers, no matter their distance from Wall Street. To the surprise of nearly all in Washington, he had built "the biggest agricultural credit agency in the world," as one reporter hailed it. Henry Morgenthau, Jr., now found himself with more money at his disposal than almost any banker anywhere.

| | | |

On the evening of April 18, after a long dinner, FDR wheeled himself into the Red Room of the White House to greet a circle of advisors: Treasury Secretary Woodin; Secretary of State Cordell Hull, a venerable Wilson man and former senator from Tennessee; Herbert Feis, State's keen young scholar on economic policy; Lewis Douglas, the young budget director from Arizona; and James P. Warburg, at the time the New Deal's only confirmed Wall Street man. At thirty-seven, Jimmy Warburg cut a figure that impressed Roosevelt: Son of the famous New York banker, he had run a financial house, published poetry, and written the lyrics for his songwriter wife's Broadway hit. Ray Moley, the brains trust economist who sat nearby, had tried to install him at the Treasury to shore up Woodin as his number two, but Warburg resisted. He opted instead to serve, without salary, as a liaison to Wall Street. Henry Morgenthau was not among the assembly, but he bore a peculiar responsibility for the thunderbolt FDR was about to let loose.

Roosevelt had called the men together to plan for upcoming meetings with the British in advance of an all-important international monetary conference scheduled for London in June. They never got to the Brits. Early in the banter, Roosevelt casually remarked that the country had "gone off gold." He held in his hands an amendment to the Agricultural Adjustment Act, giving him authority to devalue the dollar against gold by as much as 50 percent, and to print $3 billion in "greenbacks," currency lacking any gold backing.

"Here, Ray," said Roosevelt, handing the amendment to Moley. "You act like a clearing house to take care of this. Have it thoroughly amended, and then give them the word to pass it." Turning to the others, white with shock, FDR added, "Congratulate me."

When the men left the White House, it was nearly midnight. An hour later, they were still fuming: Moley had gone back to his suite at the Carlton Hotel two blocks away, found Warburg and Douglas, and the debate burned another two hours. Roosevelt, they were certain, had just made the most fateful move since the war, and as night gave way to morning, Douglas offered a prediction: "This means the end of Western civilization."

Henry was at home on the night that FDR took the country off the gold standard, but the decision, and the reasons behind it, set in motion a chain reaction that would fix his fate in Washington.

23. "He Could Trust Me Absolutely"

SPRING-FALL 1933

From the first, FDR had offered Henry a set appointment, a weekly lunch, every Monday—a routine that would continue, with rare interruptions, throughout their years in Washington. No other cabinet member, not even Hopkins, enjoyed such a privilege. Each week, FDR and Henry would meet to chart strategy, trade jibes, share gossip, and commiserate. It was during one early tête-à-tête that FDR offhandedly made the first entreaty that would form an unwritten law of their friendship and the crux, at least in those first years, of Henry's service to FDR: The president time and again would ask his friend to serve as a back-channel proxy. Henry could confound Roosevelt—the fragile ego and anxiousness drove him mad. But when FDR "wanted something personal and original to be done," Henry would say, "he would often turn to me to work out the ways and means." For Roosevelt, the risks were minimal: He could count on Morgenthau implicitly, and entirely. "If things went wrong," Henry recalled, "I kept my mouth shut. I had no kept columnist"—no Arthur Krock, no Drew Pearson—"and I never carried my fights to the press."

The unseen role threatened to overshadow Henry's main job, often infuriating his seniors in the cabinet. Some, like Harold Ickes, the interior secretary, would come to consider Morgenthau a kind of court servant, a none-too-bright vassal to be dispatched on uncertain missions. Henry took his role as a point of pride. He saw himself as a loyal stand-in: Whenever the president wished to launch risky trial balloons, widen a loophole, or even conceal a rekindled relationship with an old love—

for instance, with the woman formerly known as Lucy Mercer—Henry leapt to the call.

The secret role began, oddly enough for the head of Farm Credit, in foreign affairs. Seven years at the Navy Department during the Wilson administration had heightened FDR's instinctive sense for geopolitics. Even in those first months of domestic crises, Roosevelt had one eye on the darkening horizon in Europe, where, the day after the inauguration, the Nazis took charge of the Reichstag. The president was as concerned with the Soviet Union, which the United States had refused to recognize since the Bolshevik Revolution in 1917. "Non-recognition" meant no diplomatic ties, and no trade. To FDR, it was a costly mistake. Isolating Soviet Russia, he believed, kept one of the world's biggest markets shut off to American manufacturers and farmers. It also excluded Russian participation in the Wilsonian cause Roosevelt hoped to make his own: preventing a new war in Europe. FDR understood the latent power of a resurgent Germany, and he sensed that Russia, even under Communism, could become a vital ally.

In May he confided to Henry Morgenthau over lunch that he was thinking of sending a trade envoy to Moscow to "break the ice," but the bureaucracy, as always, had to be overcome. "Gosh," FDR said, in Morgenthau's record of the conversation, dictated that afternoon, "if I could only, myself, talk to some one man representing the Russians, I could straighten out the whole question." Roosevelt went on to sketch, as he would so often in the years to come, a seat-of-the-pants plan. Morgenthau was to find a back channel to the Soviets. "If you get the opportunity, Henry," FDR said, "you could say that you believe, but have no authority to say so, that the President would like to send some person to Moscow."

Henry's first reaction was fear, then doubt. He had no Soviet contacts; he could only reach out cautiously, at arm's length, to Amtorg, Moscow's trade office in New York. But above all, he was certain that any move toward recognition carried a high probability of failure. One leak and the talks would collapse, undermining an administration still finding its feet. The Republicans, and many in FDR's own party, would call for scalps. As Roosevelt set out the plan, Morgenthau joked nervously: If he went through the backdoor, and came up with a deal, he'd be a hero, "but if it flopped, I would have to leave Washington."

"Well, of course, you know that I stand back of you in these negotiations," FDR assured Henry. "And if you have to leave Washington, I will leave with you."

The State Department in 1933 was staunchly against any opening to the USSR. Cordell Hull, the patrician Southerner, abhorred Bolshevik atheism. FDR had chosen Hull not only for his Wilsonian idealism, but for a well-established lack of enterprise: The president wanted to run his own foreign policy. In front of intimates, Roosevelt would even mock Hull, mimicking his lisp—"Jesus Chwist!" FDR, aides feared, would rely on Sumner Welles, the assistant secretary, a friend since childhood, and a wealthy fellow Groton and Harvard man who'd amply backed his campaign, to run things at State. But Hull had found a strong old guard in the department, Foreign Service veterans who could not brook Lenin and company's persecution of their own Christian faith. To members of Congress, the Soviets posed another threat: a powerful propaganda machine that preyed on America's beleaguered and disillusioned workers. If Roosevelt turned his back on his own diplomats and much of the Congress, he would take an enormous risk. The first overture had to be made in strictest confidence.

"I think he chose me," Henry reflected, "primarily because he could trust me absolutely."

||||

Two weeks after the inauguration, Henry Sr. and Josie were back at the White House. At their first dinner with the Roosevelts, the elder Morgenthaus were joined by four reporters. The president seemed preoccupied with two topics: Russia and wheat. He probed the reporters, veteran wire-service men, on Moscow and Stalin. Turning to Uncle Henry, FDR spoke of the financial talks soon to open in Europe. The previous year Hoover had finally acquiesced to international demands for economic talks on the mounting global depression. FDR explained there would be two conclaves: In Geneva, the League of Nations would host the world's four largest wheat growers in an effort to halt the catastrophic fall in wheat prices, and then, in London, finance ministers from east and west would attempt a currency stabilization deal to revive the world economy.

Henry Sr. at once marked the date in his diary. The London Economic Conference was sure to be the biggest international congress since Versailles; he had to be there. For months he and Josie had been making arrangements for a grand fiftieth wedding anniversary party. But at the last minute, he canceled the event, in order to answer the "President's call."

FDR had named Uncle Henry, at seventy-seven, a "wheat delegate"—not to the London summit, but to the Geneva talks. The elder Morgenthau, Roosevelt knew, had no expertise in wheat, but his son had wrangled the offer. (FDR made sure to shore up Henry Sr. by adding to his party, on the eve of their sailing, Fred Murphy, the Republican publisher of the Minneapolis *Tribune*, who not only knew a good deal about wheat, but boasted that he owned "the record butter-producing cow in the world.")

At midnight on May 2, before the *Bremen* left New York Harbor, Henry Sr. called a press conference to heighten the drama. "The whole world has dominant men, tremendously anxious for a solution to the wheat problem," he said, but together they would find a way "to win this war against depression." He would sail with Josie and his favorite granddaughter. At twenty-one, Barbara Wertheim (daughter of Alma Morgenthau and Maurice Wertheim, who in marriage would become Barbara Tuchman) skipped commencement at Radcliffe to make the trip. The aspiring historian adored Grandpa Morgenthau: "He was fascinating to be with because he was so open. He talked to me the way my father never did."

In Geneva, the talks stalemated almost at once, but Henry Sr. was thrilled. On May 21, he shared his delight in a letter to his children at home: "It is strange that at my time in life I should have a repetition of my experiences in Turkey and Greece. I have again been catapulted right into the midst of the international arena." Toasting his golden anniversary with the League delegates, "itching to talk" with the Germans in their midst, he decided to stay on, as the wheat talks moved to London, in the shadow of the larger economic conference. "I won't write another book," he assured his family, "and will not burden with long letters again." He only "wanted you all to know that the Old Man is himself again, and feels much younger than I have in years past."

At home in Washington, Henry Jr. had been making good on a promise to liquidate all federal wheat holdings, selling off the last of 30 million bushels in futures. He also kept nudging FDR about his father. At lunch on May 22, he asked if Henry Sr. might be promoted, joining the main delegation in London. "I am only sending six delegates, two senators," Roosevelt replied. "Your father will be a member of the Advisors commission." A week later Henry Sr. again cabled his son, asking that his "status in London . . . be announced." FDR then told reporters there would be an additional three "technical experts": Bernard Baruch, Joe Kennedy, and Henry Sr. Kennedy declined, and Baruch offered to monitor the talks from New York. Even young Barbara Wertheim understood the offer was "a gesture—be nice to the old man," but Henry Sr. was overjoyed.

The London Economic Conference, at least on its opening day, bore out the promise of a grand event. King George V welcomed the world's top importers and exporters to the marbled Geological Museum in South Kensington. Thousands had come: a king (Feisal of Iraq), six prime ministers, twenty foreign ministers, eighty cabinet officials and central bank chiefs—in all, representatives of sixty-six nations. FDR had also toyed with coming, but chastened by his memories of Wilson in Paris, he stayed home.

Roosevelt had chosen the American delegation more for political balance than a unified economic vision: Hull, a believer in free trade and sound money, would be its official head; Warburg, the chief financier among the group, would lead the talks with the European bankers; and finally, when catastrophe loomed, Ray Moley, the brains-truster eager to play umpire, would be dispatched on a rescue mission. None had represented their country abroad, and from the start, nearly all seemed at odds: Senator Key Pittman, a hard drinker from Nevada, had long lobbied for inflation and high silver prices to please the miners of his home state; Secretary Hull wanted, if anything, greater exports; and Moley, going over Hull's head, appeared all too eager for the spotlight. To make matters worse, Pittman had been on a binge since leaving the ship; he lurched about the hotel corridors with a pistol, threatened to stab a fellow delegate, and, at a dinner hosted by Lady Astor, leered at the ladies.

Amid this crowd, Henry Sr. stood apart. Officially, he had come to talk wheat (his mandate: to set quotas on exports), but no one could stop him from making the most of his return to the world's high table. There were parties, luncheons, and an audience at Buckingham Palace. (Barbara Tuchman remembered Grandma Morgenthau arranging urgent necessities: a feathered headdress, bespoke pearl-laced gown, and lessons in curtsying.) At a garden party at Windsor Castle, Henry Sr. created a stir. As the Americans lined up to pay respects to the king and queen, Henry dared to hold a conversation. When George V thanked him for tending to British interests in Constantinople during the war, Henry had stood in place, bandying words with the royals. The delegates were shocked: No one was to exchange more than pleasantries to their majesties. When the press got wind of the faux pas, Henry Sr. erred again—quoting the king in public. "He had been too long out of the swim," his granddaughter judged.

Not content to restrict himself to wheat matters, Henry Sr. met with old acquaintances from Turkey, dined with H. G. Wells (who was covering the talks as a reporter), and as a gloom darkened the negotiations, without a word of guidance from Washington, took matters into his own hands. No U.S. official had had contact with a Soviet official since 1919, but on June 21, as the secretary of state and the American delegation sat at the monetary talks, Henry Sr. called on Maxim Litvinov, the squat, bespectacled Soviet commissar of foreign affairs. He found a ready interlocutor: Litvinov not only spoke fluent English (having lived in London and married an English writer), but he had come on Stalin's orders to secure a much-needed trade deal.

The two men enjoyed a "quite frank talking," as Henry Sr. recorded in a pocket diary. Litvinov was "very anxious to know why US opposes them"—"they feared your propaganda," Henry Sr. replied—but the commissar "agreed to a fixing of export limit" on the proposed U.S.-Soviet trade. Henry Sr. took pride that he had "tried to force the issue," but when news of the secret meeting leaked, Washington backtracked. The Roosevelt administration had made clear it would welcome Soviet purchases, but Uncle Henry had been unable to contain himself: Moscow might place orders amounting to a billion dollars "in the near future," the news reports held, and recognition of the USSR was "a possible, indeed a probable" by-product of the London conference. The State Department rushed to tamp down expectations, even as Henry Sr., flush with a return to the game, told all in his midst to await great developments.

| | | |

At home, FDR was eager to remove himself from Washington, and from the battle in London. With his envoys floundering—"Hull had absolutely no authority over the delegation," Warburg would recall—the president left for Campobello, sailing from Massachusetts on a friend's sloop, the *Amberjack II*. The president may have feigned nonchalance, but the trip would be momentous—this was the first time he had been to Campobello since 1921, when polio struck.

Henry Jr. had rushed ahead, flying to Nova Scotia, arriving in time to accompany Mrs. Roosevelt in a small launch, sailing out in the harbor to meet the president as he sailed in. "A thrilling experience," he would write. At FDR's house, Henry Jr. found an intimate crew: Marion Dickerman and Nancy Cook were there; Missy LeHand and her brother; Johnny Roosevelt, the president's youngest child, and Jimmy Roosevelt's wife, Betsey; and Louis Howe. Almost at once, Howe seized on Morgenthau, no doubt welcoming the arrival of a pliable ally.

Pulling Henry aside, he said pressure was "building on the President" to agree to a "stabilization operation"—for the United States to lead the way on stabilizing exchange rates. Norman Davis, a veteran of Wilson's Treasury, who'd sailed to the island with FDR, had been lobbying for a deal on currency rates. "I am against it," Howe said, but "we will be discussing it on the way back," and wanted to know Morgenthau's stance. Henry was caught off guard: "Not knowing an awful lot about it, I sort of felt my way but told him in principle I agreed."

All those at the Roosevelt home on Campobello had one goal: to make the days seem, as much as anyone could, like the old family gatherings, when FDR could still clamber over the rocky shores and sail its bays at will. In the evenings, as the young people headed out, "only a half dozen of us" remained at the house, Henry recorded, and FDR "mixed cocktails for all and was very jolly." Friday lunch was a picnic on the beach—Eleanor Roosevelt roasting hot dogs over an open fire—and the president seemed to unwind. But that evening serious talk threatened the idyll.

Marvin McIntyre, FDR's traveling secretary, brought the news from London, a draft plan of action that Hull had sent for approval. When McIntyre asked how should he reply, Roosevelt was dismissive: "Send word to Hull to say nothing, do nothing and agree to nothing."

That evening, as "Franklin, Eleanor Roosevelt, Marion and Nancy, and I sat around and talked for a couple of hours," Henry recalled, he stepped into the fray. Howe, half-asleep on the couch, said little, as Henry attempted a discussion of foreign exchange, gold, and exports. He'd done some quick homework: reading a cover story in the *Saturday Evening Post,* an opaque article on trade by a prominent business reporter. Henry tried his best to make sense of it—the writer, Garet Garrett, was known to challenge orthodoxies. "Does foreign trade promote prosperity," Garrett had asked, "or is it prosperity—the prosperity of individual nations—that produces foreign trade?" The writer, Henry told FDR, makes the case for taking care of one's own house first, and opening markets to foreigners second. Throughout it all, the president listened closely—just as Henry sensed he would.

For months, FDR had fallen prey to a rosy promise: the notion that if the Depression had deepened as prices fell, the way out was to "*reflate*"—to force prices to rise again. The "brains-trusters" had tried to dissuade FDR, gently explaining that he'd inverted the relationship: Rising prices would come after the recovery, not bring it about. But the tutoring did no good; Roosevelt would not budge. He'd come under the spell of a new economic guru—George Warren, a little-known agronomist from Cornell whom he'd first met in Albany.

"The Professor," as FDR called Warren, had entered the president's circle thanks to Henry Morgenthau, Jr. Roosevelt was no great student of finance: He'd endured a bit of economics at Harvard, but proven himself, more than once, a dreadful investor. Sensing an opening, Henry had recruited Warren. The day after the inauguration, Warren boarded an airplane—the first flight of his life—and within hours found himself at Roosevelt's side, detailing with a stack of charts and graphs how the bright future would come to pass.

Warren was nothing if not an optimist. At fifty-nine, raised on a Nebraska sheep farm, he now raised Holsteins and chickens on five hundred acres near Ithaca. Although "nearly self-taught" in economics, as his biographer would concede, Warren claimed to have discovered an essential relationship between commodity prices and gold: Commodity prices, he argued, rose and fell in response to the amount of gold held in government reserves. And for years, he'd painstakingly compiled a massive trove of statistics to prove it. In 1932, Warren co-published *Wholesale Prices for 213 Years: 1720–1932,* a dense academic work that reappeared, after Roosevelt's election, under a revised title aimed at the New Dealers: *Prices.*

Warren's theory was beguilingly simple, and, as one commentator later wrote, "unknown to the world of orthodox economics." He'd studied the gold-mining booms in California and Australia, and concluded that commodity prices rose as new gold entered the market. The opposite trend also appeared true: When the gold supply slowed, commodities sank. Most economists greeted Warren's theory with bemusement; commodity prices *did* often fluctuate with the gold price, but they argued that commodity prices were the cause, not the effect. Henry Morgenthau disagreed: He found Warren's charts and graphs convincing and, above all, essential tools to convince a willing audience.

Henry had come to Campobello not only with the magazine article, but with a new set of Warren's props. As FDR waited downstairs, Henry went up to his room—returning with "my charts," diagrams hastily drawn up by his staff, based on the theories of Professor Warren. As Henry unfurled the numbers, the president sat rapt.

| | | |

On Saturday, July 1, Mrs. Roosevelt and her friends left Campobello early in the morning by car for New York. The president, Henry, Howe, and FDR's son Franklin Jr. boarded the USS *Indianapolis,* a cruiser bound for Washington. The men around Roosevelt had tried to prepare: "They [had] sent me up in a Canadian Patrol Boat," Henry wrote, "to try to buy some rum and gin for FDR at the Canadian Liquor Store. It took me one hour to get there only to find out it was Dominion Day, and the bank and liquor store were closed." Onboard, the sailors put on a dry "happy hour," an evening of stunts and "prize fights."

On the following afternoon, the lazy days of Campobello behind him, FDR "took off his coat," as Henry recorded, "sat down at his desk for a couple of hours, and wrote his message to London on money." Howe had tried a draft, but Roosevelt rewrote it. FDR read them aloud his reply, and they had giggled like schoolboys, imagining the reaction of the delegates in London. But none of them, least of all Henry, could have predicted the fallout.

In London, the Americans had worked through the night, desperate to get the Europeans to sign a joint declaration setting a course on exchange rates—and a vague aim to return, "when the time comes," to an "international gold standard." They needed only FDR's approval. Roosevelt, though, had set a second team of advisors to work in New York, in an effort to monitor the London talks: Baruch; Woodin, the Treasury secretary; and Dean Acheson, his thirty-nine-year-old undersecretary. Given the delays in communication, and the widening rift among delegates, it was not easy. The transatlantic telephone calls, still a novelty, were trying. On the afternoon of June 30, Moley phoned the New York advisors at Woodin's house—where the secretary, suffering from cancer, had retreated. During the call, Woodin fainted. With Baruch and Acheson fearing the worst, and Moley desperate to announce FDR's approval in

London, Acheson tried to reach the president, but could not. Campobello had no telephones. When at last FDR received the messages, he learned that the New York group had approved the proposed joint declaration, but Moley and the others in London remained in the dark.

As the clock wound down, Roosevelt appeared to stall. When he finally sent his cable across the Atlantic, on Monday morning, his men in London—Hull, Moley, and the rest—had scarcely slept for days. It was late at night when they read it. From the sea, FDR had written, in longhand, one of the most scathing communiqués of his political career. In the "bombshell message," as the press dubbed it, he rejected the London proposal, even before receiving the final text.

Roosevelt had launched an assault on exchange stabilization, the very purpose of the London talks—and the goal he'd been professing for months. "Old fetishes of so-called international bankers," he chided, "are being replaced by efforts to plan national currencies." The United States would not be entering any new exchange scheme, nor would it return any time soon to the gold standard. The delegates, FDR wrote, had revealed a "singular lack of proportion and a failure to remember the larger purposes" for which they had been called together.

In London, at the time FDR's cable arrived, the American delegates were preparing to leave for a weekend at Cliveden, the Astor estate. Senator Pittman was drunk, Hull attempting to hold him in check, and Moley unable to imagine how he could explain the president's cable to the conference—and to the horde of reporters. Once the news hit, Moley knew, all hope for a deal would vanish.

At first, the U.S. delegates were stunned, but they soon figured it out: Howe and Morgenthau had had the president's ear to themselves. "It was," Moley would write, "all that we needed to know." Howe "didn't know beans about monetary questions," and Morgenthau owed his "rudimentary knowledge of monetary problems" to Professor Warren. In fact, things were worse than Moley feared. A third force had also influenced the president: From London, the elder Morgenthau had kept his son informed, predicting that the talks were doomed.

The world's financiers recoiled in shock, but the British rushed to the Americans' aid. John Maynard Keynes welcomed the move, gilding it as a step toward a managed currency: "President Roosevelt Is Magnificently Right," declared the headline over his *Daily Mail* column. (FDR had cut "through the cobwebs with such boldness," Keynes claimed.) In the House of Commons, Churchill—still struggling to find a road back to power—also rose in support. "Conferences exist for men," he said, "and not men for conferences." Walter Lippmann, too, sought to tamp down Roosevelt's about-face: "To safeguard his programs," he wrote, "the President has wisely rejected all proposals which would interfere with it." All the while, Ramsey MacDonald, the prime minister, fumed that the move would topple his government. In the end the London conference "rose to nothing," as H. G. Wells wrote in his parody of the grand failure, *The Shape of Things to Come*. "It began at its highest point and steadily declined."

Sitting in a basement office at the Commerce Department, compiling yet more graphs and charts, George Warren read the reports from London and smiled. For months, he'd remained a cipher, a faceless counselor shuttling in and out of a rear door to the White House. But now the professor from Cornell, as those in Roosevelt's closest circle knew, was on the ascent. And just ahead of him, leading the way, was his former student, Henry Morgenthau, Jr.

| | | |

On September 21, *The Washington Post* carried a front-page story that caught Washington unawares: FDR intended to "appoint" Henry Morgenthau, Jr., to take charge of negotiating a massive trade deal with the Soviet Union, one totaling "upwards of $50,000,000." In London Litvinov had made it clear: The Soviets were eager to buy American goods—heavy machinery, cotton, and other commodities—but would need U.S. loans. At lunch at the White House the following Monday, Morgenthau could not hide his nervousness. Since his first days in office, FDR had spoken of Russia, and of late, FDR talked more and more about wheat and cotton, and about bumping up U.S. exports—a reprise that to Henry hinted at a plan hatching in Roosevelt's mind. Given the news leaks, he asked, did the president still want him "to go ahead and make any loans to Russia"?

Roosevelt suggested a shortcut: "What would you think of bringing this whole Russian question into our front parlor instead of back in the kitchen?"

"That is fine, if you want to do it," Henry said. "But that is up to you."

The president laid out an idea: an exchange of letters, drafted in secret by both sides, that would lead to face-to-face talks. "Send for Skvirsky," he told Henry. Boris Skvirsky, officially the head of the Soviet Information Bureau, was known as "Stalin's man" in Washington. A half-bald native of Odessa, barrel-chested and with passable English (he'd come by way of Australia), Skvirsky had been in the capital since 1921, quietly operating out of a red-brick house on Massachusetts Avenue.

Henry first sought out Bill Bullitt, the State Department man handling Soviet affairs. Since Versailles, no one in government had pushed harder for a warming with the Russians. In 1919, Wilson had sent Bullitt, a twenty-four-year-old junior diplomat and son of a wealthy Philadelphia businessman, on a secret mission to strike a deal with Lenin: to broker a deal to end the Russian Civil War and the Allied blockade of the nascent USSR—allowing the Allies to withdraw the interventionist troops sent in 1918. Bullitt won approval from the Bolsheviks, but not from the Allied leaders at Versailles. In the years since, unable to escape the shadow of the failure, Bullitt had yearned to become the first U.S. ambassador to the Soviet Union. Morgenthau knew Bullitt would back any opening, but over lunch that day he learned that the State Department wouldn't go for it.

Cordell Hull, Bullitt explained, could never get past "the religious issue": the Bolshevik refusal to guarantee that Christians would not be persecuted. Yet as Bullitt went on, tallying all the reasons for State's opposition, Henry recognized much more was at stake than exports and imports. American aid, Bullitt explained, would allow the Soviets to break away from economic dependence on Germany. It would also help curb a new fear in Washington: Japanese expansionism. To Henry, FDR's scheme was coming clear. He was not merely chasing a trade deal; the president wanted to recognize the Soviet Union.

As word of Morgenthau's secret talks spread throughout the cabinet, opposition mounted. Henry Wallace cried the loudest, insisting to FDR that he feared "the religious effect on the voters": The Soviets, many in Washington and across the country feared, not only proselytized atheism but persecuted believers, regardless of faith. The conversation, Morgenthau wrote, left the president "thoroughly puzzled."

Bullitt, meanwhile, began walking Morgenthau to work in the mornings, eager for news. "At first this annoyed the President," Henry would recall, "on the ground that Bullitt was going over Hull's head," but in time, as the talks developed, Roosevelt gradually entrusted the negotiations to Bullitt. Henry would serve as the bridge: On October 18, after considerable trouble, he found Skvirsky in New York and asked him to come to his office at 10:30 the next morning.

Skvirsky arrived on time, and FDR had drafted the script; Morgenthau and Bullitt only had to act it out.

"Several weeks ago," Henry told the Russian, "I told you that for the time being our negotiations were off, pending consideration by the White House. You asked me if this was a friendly move and I said yes. I will now give it to you. In about five minutes Bullitt, from the State Department, will come here with a piece of paper unsigned, and show it to you."

Right on cue, Bullitt made his entry, and turned to Skvirsky. "I have a piece of paper in my hand, unsigned," he said. "This document can be made into an invitation for your country to send representatives over to discuss relations between our two countries. We wish you to telegraph the contents of this piece of paper in your most confidential code, and learn if it is acceptable to your people."

If acceptable, Bullitt went on, the president would sign it, and both letters would be released at once by Moscow and Washington. But if the drafts were deemed unacceptable, Skvirsky would have to give his word never to speak of the offer, nor of their meeting.

Skvirsky agreed, but before rising to leave, he asked a question: "Does this mean recognition?"

"What more can you expect," said Bullitt, "than to have your representative sit down with the President of the United States?"

On November 16, 1933, after months of secret negotiations led by Henry Morgenthau, Jr., and a final intercession by FDR himself, the United States recognized the Soviet Union. Within hours, Bullitt was named ambassador.

||||

In mid-October, Henry Jr. had been enjoying a rare quiet evening with Ellie when the phone rang. It was the president, and he was impatient. "We have got to do something about the price of wheat," he said. "I can't take it any longer. . . . Can't you buy 25,000,000 bushels for Harry Hopkins, and see if you can't put the price up?" Hopkins now ran FERA, the federal relief agency charged with buying mass quantities of hogs, sheep, apples, beans, and other foodstuffs for states in dire need. Falling commodity prices—by October wheat had fallen 90 cents a bushel since the inauguration—threatened far more than the farm belt. "The whole recovery program," as Henry would recall, "was jeopardized by this galloping palsy."

Henry Wallace, Morgenthau knew, had the wherewithal to do the buying. He called up the agriculture secretary and, finding Harry Hopkins with him, invited both to his home that night. If Hopkins would take the wheat off Farm Credit's hands, they could avoid the mistake of the Hoover years: getting stuck with a surplus that rotted as prices fell. Wallace at once said he "could use 30 million bushels"—and on the following morning, Morgenthau launched "the buying game," as he called it. "Wheat was perched precariously at 64 cents when I placed the first order for 1,000,000 bushels," he would write. By day's end, he had ratcheted the price up by 10 cents.

"We accomplished what the President wanted," Henry wrote that evening, "and I felt . . . one of the big moments of my life."

By September, it had become a routine: Nearly every weekday morning, Morgenthau, Professor Warren, and Jesse Jones, the Houston banker atop the Reconstruction Finance Corporation (RFC), would call on the president in his bedroom. Henry would usually find Roosevelt lying comfortably on his old-fashioned, three-quarter-size mahogany bed. "A table stood on each side," he wrote in his diary, "on his left would be a batch of government reports, a detective novel or two, a couple of telephones. On his right would be pads, pencils, cigarettes, his watch and a plate of fruit." Refreshed after a night's rest, FDR would eat his soft-boiled eggs while his guests relayed the latest changes in gold and commodity prices.

As Roosevelt finished up his breakfast, they would set the price of gold for the day. The price established on any given day made little difference: They needed only to keep it going up, just higher than the world price, in anticipation that commodity prices would follow. To confuse speculators, they would vary the daily increases, gradually, and by purely arbitrary means. Keynes would call it "the gold standard on the booze," but Warren had won a chance to try a national economic experiment. He'd persuaded Roosevelt that substantial government gold purchases would trigger inflation and raise the price of farm commodities, a major objective of the New Deal and a political necessity for the president.

Once Roosevelt was done with his meal, Morgenthau would ask, How much gold should we buy today?

"One day," Henry recalled, "when I must have come in more than usually worried about the state of the world—Hitler had just come to power in Germany—we were planning on increasing the price from 19 to 22 cents." Roosevelt took one look at Morgenthau and suggested a rise of 21 cents. "It's a lucky number," FDR said with a chuckle. "Three times seven."

The price was within the range set a week earlier, but Henry realized the absurdity of the scene. "If anybody ever knew," he wrote, "how we really set the gold price through a combination of lucky numbers, etc., I think they would really be frightened."

| | | |

At nine o'clock on Monday morning, November 13, Henry again stood before the president in his bedroom. After FDR had agreed on the new price for gold, he asked Henry to stay on a minute.

The president remained sitting up in bed. He had said he wanted to discuss Farm Credit, but after a moment raised his real subject. "I had a very interesting and confidential conversation with Mr. Woodin," Roosevelt said. "I have suggested to him that he take a leave of absence without pay." In five months, the ailing Woodin had visited his office in the Treasury only fourteen times.

Henry listened intently, without a clue as to what was to come.

"I am going to write him a letter," Roosevelt said, "in answer to one which he has written to me suggesting that we get somebody to become Acting Secretary who knows government and knows finance." The president paused. "I have decided that that person is Henry Morgenthau, Jr."

Henry was dumbstruck. He knew he had an iron supporter in the White House—Mrs. Roosevelt—but although she would come to his aid time and again in the years to come, their friendship had little to do with this advancement. It was a matter of track record: Under his guidance, Farm Credit had swelled into a reservoir of $4 billion in credit. In eight months, Henry had scrapped Hoover's dismal Farm Board, creating an efficient agency that now pumped $1 million a day into the farm economy. He'd lent $425 million to debt-burdened farmers, and still had $355 million in the kitty. He had also served FDR well in several of the president's riskiest moves.

Henry broke out in a cold sweat, struggling to follow the president's words.

"You made good for me in Albany," FDR continued, "and you are one of the two or three people who have made an outstanding success here in Washington. . . . So let's you and I go on to bigger things. We will have lots of fun doing it together."

24. "To Swim with the Tide and Not Sink"

WINTER-FALL 1934

I n Henry Morgenthau, one columnist observed, President Roosevelt had installed at the Treasury "the kind of friend [he] needed most"—one who could "take the rap" for monetary experiments like setting the price of gold over his soft-boiled eggs. Republicans warned that with an obedient secretary FDR would only pick up the pace in his hazardous ventures. "FDR will be his own dictator of American monetary policy," predicted one writer.

The big farm associations, though, rejoiced. "We are delighted," the head of the American Farm Bureau wired Roosevelt: Morgenthau, who had pumped out more than $1 billion to save mortgages, was "the friend of we folks," sure to "give us an honest dollar." Walter Lippmann, writing in the Republican *Herald Tribune,* found "a sense of assurance" in the appointment, while Ochs's *Times* had already delivered a glowing profile in November, smoothing out the rough patches in Henry's résumé. Yes, the new secretary had quit Cornell without a degree, but only because "his health failed him." There were further distortions; the finances of Fishkill Farms, always a sore subject between father and son, had become a political liability. The *Times* brightened the picture, reporting that Morgenthau could boast, for the first time, of "farm profits." In truth, Henry's land—he'd now consolidated 1,400 acres—had gained enormously in value (he cited a figure of $500,000 to his father in 1930), but the farm had yet to break even.

Woodin would resign two weeks before Christmas, and Henry Morgenthau, Jr., was sworn in on January 2, 1934. On Wall Street, Henry's appointment was a testament to loyalty and fool's luck. Morgenthau was not only young—at forty-two, one of the youngest of the fifty-two men to run the Treasury since Alexander Hamilton—but lacking in experience. Even the *Times* conceded Henry's "only banking experience" had come in the "last nine months." For his part, he professed no market expertise; as years passed, others would call him a "banker," even a "financier," but Henry never made the claim.

The cabinet met the news with a mixture of fear and fury. Morgenthau now sat to FDR's left—"second in command of the Cabinet," he would say, "after the Secretary of State." The Treasury secretary, worried Ickes and Wallace, had an "in" that no other cabinet member enjoyed. They saw in Henry's ascension further evidence, when none was needed, of the boss's reliance on old friends. His rivals might snipe, but Henry had done well at Farm Credit. He had displayed a gift for pushing through the president's agenda. He had proven, too, as no one else close to Roosevelt had, that he could reform and run a sprawling bureaucracy. Hoover's farm board had been demoralized and outmoded. Henry rebuilt it into an aggressive agency that seemed to double in size each month—with five hundred employees when he departed, controlling $4.5 billion in capital. Henry had become, as trumpeted in the *Times,* "in effect the president of the world's largest bank."

Above all, Henry enjoyed even greater access to FDR. Each Monday, as noon neared, he'd leave his large oak desk in his large office at Treasury, descend in a narrow private elevator, exit a door on the west side of the building, and walk a hundred yards to the East Wing of the White House for lunch with the president. From the first, others resented Henry's lunches with FDR: The two men, almost always, ate alone. Henry could still try Roosevelt's patience—of late a self-righteous stubbornness had come to the fore. But FDR delighted in the lunches; he knew he had a new weapon in the cabinet.

| | | |

"When I was thrown into this thing . . . ," Henry would confess in June 1934, "I was glad to be able to swim with the tide and not sink."

He had inherited an empire. The Treasury was the longest arm of the government. More than 37,000 men and women worked in its agencies, services, bureaus, units, and divisions. They kept the government's books, printed dollars, stamps, and bonds, supervised the banking system, upheld the financial laws of the land, inspected cargo, oversaw federal construction projects (from post offices to courthouses), ministered to the immigrant millions, oversaw national health standards, and, most important, gathered in and doled out billions of dollars. The budget was enormous; Henry rarely had to ask for more funding.

Treasury's law-enforcement powers were immense as well: 70 percent of all prisoners in federal jails had been put there by the Treasury. Henry would oversee nearly 6,000 T-men, as the Treasury enforcement agents were dubbed, and not just the Secret Service. He inherited the White House police, the Special Intelligence Unit, Bureau of Narcotics, Internal Revenue Service, and the guards and officers in the Mint, Assay Office, Bureau of Engraving and Printing, and Customs. There was more: The Treasury oversaw the Coast Guard (a vestige of Prohibition, when the government patrolled for bootleggers), and an in-house legal staff, one of the biggest in Washington. In the federal government, only the generals and admirals could claim to have more money at their disposal.

And yet, Roosevelt had done his friend no favor. The Treasury in 1934 was still reeling from FDR's early gold-purchasing scheme. With Wall Street in turmoil, many—including the U.S. Chamber of Commerce— demanded a return to the gold standard. By 1934, as forty economists denounced the "soft-money heresies," Al Smith rushed to their side, add- ing a populist's megaphone to an esoteric argument: "I am for gold dol- lars as against baloney dollars," Smith announced. "I am for experience against experiment." As Henry arrived at the Treasury, the once-sleepy field of fiscal policy had become a battleground. It was a national debate, "the most intense," Arthur M. Schlesinger, Jr., would write, "since the Bryan campaign of '96."

On November 27, Carnegie Hall hosted a "sound-money" protest, while on the same night, thirteen blocks to the south, thousands packed the Hippodrome to hear the fiery retort of a chubby-faced priest from Detroit. Father Charles E. Coughlin—the "radiorator," as *Time* called him—had come to boost the gold-buying program, forgoing his Sunday sermon at the Shrine of the Little Flower outside Detroit, which was broadcast to millions of radio listeners. Coughlin had hardly disguised his political ambitions, diverging from liturgical matters to the heat of the gold debate. Now he had warmed to FDR ("It's Roosevelt or ruin"), a one-sided embrace that would not last long.

Outside the Hippodrome, the crowd jostled to enter the hall, as mounted police tried to keep order. Inside, the stage was crowded with politicians—Senator Thomas, former governor Sulzer, former mayor Hylan, dozens of others. As one man, slow to get up from his chair, rose to the lectern, the crowds quieted. At seventy-seven, Henry Morgenthau, Sr., was not fooled by Father Coughlin's collar; he knew the dangers of embracing a populist demagogue. And soon enough, Coughlin would reveal himself as an anti-Semite—denouncing Henry Jr., and defending silver as a "Gentile" metal—but the about-face would not come for months. On this winter evening, as the orchestra played and hundreds lined the avenue outside, the former ambassador, eager to defend the Roosevelt course and spur support for his son, stood center stage.

He had heard the president take the oath of office, Henry Sr. reminded the crowd, and was certain FDR would keep his promise to restore the people's faith in themselves. "Nothing is fouler or meaner," he said, "than for people at the present moment to attempt to destroy the confidence in our country."

Roosevelt warmed to the battle. Here was the chance, he told aides, to up the ante: He cast the debate as a conspiracy, led by Republicans and desperate Wall Street bankers, to rein in reform. Soon the fighting became moot. The gold buying had proven a temporary expediency. Cheapening the dollar did bolster trade and, for a time, strengthen domestic prices, but Professor Warren's grand promise—a rising tide of commodity prices—proved illusory. In short order, FDR struck a bargain: Congress passed the Gold Reserve Act, and on January 31, 1934, the president signed a proclamation returning the country, as Henry Jr.'s aides told the stunned reporters, to "a modified gold standard." The Treasury would fix the weight of the gold dollar at "15 5/21 grains nine tenths fine," reducing the gold in the dollar to 59 percent of its former weight, and setting the price of gold at $35 an ounce—a bar that would remain in place until 1971, when Richard Nixon lifted it entirely.

| | | |

Henry Jr. rose each day by six, and despite bouts of ill health—the migraines came more frequently now, often knocking him low for hours—worked long days. In the mornings at home, he scanned the newspapers and reviewed the stack of reports he'd lugged home the night before. After breakfast, Henry continued his habit of walking two miles down Connecticut Avenue to the Treasury. Sometimes, he was joined by a colleague, but more often he would walk with Dano, the Great Dane he and Ellie had given their daughter Joan as a puppy. The sight of the secretary, well over six feet tall, striding to keep pace with the giant dog drew stares, and photographers. Some days Dano would stay at the office.

(When a group of Southern senators mistook his giant water bowl for a spittoon, the secretary taped a sign to it: "Dog.") Usually, though, Dano got a ride straight home, in a Treasury limousine.

By 8:45 A.M., Henry had entered his office, an elegant room—old oils, well-worn carpets—more than thirty feet in length. First off, he checked the exchanges (London and Paris); he had had two tickers installed, one for news, the other for financial quotations. Then, after a second coffee at his desk, he would gather his closest aides—"the 9:30 group," he came to call it—six or so men forming a half circle before him. The 9:30 group was the inner circle: part personal brains trust, part political shield.

The script rarely changed. Each morning, the secretary would attempt casual banter, and fail. A look of concern would take over his face, and he would turn to the agenda for the day. Henry's closest advisors would remain unknown to the country, but Washington insiders soon grasped their influence. Several had been with Henry at Farm Credit: Herb Gaston, the public relations man; Herman Oliphant, the general counsel; and William McReynolds, his staff assistant. McReynolds was the Washington veteran: He had spent decades in the civil service—starting in 1906, as a post office clerk.

Henry had also won recruits from the best and the brightest in finance: Earle Bailie, partner at the New York firm J. W. Seligman and Company; Marriner Eccles, scion of a Salt Lake fortune and an independent-minded western banker; Jacob Viner, a brilliant economist from the University of Chicago; T. Jefferson Coolidge, a Boston Brahmin banker; and Roswell Magill, a Columbia professor and one of the few tax experts who knew the code inside and out. Henry would continue to rely on back-channel advisors—men he had known since boyhood, such as Frank Altschul, rising at Lazard Frères, and Harold Hochschild, now head of American Metals. But he tried to surround himself with men who were young, dedicated, and above all untethered to Wall Street.

The Albany veterans would be Henry's first line of defense. Gaston, his PR man, proved adept at policy work, rising to be deputy commissioner. Born in Oregon, Gaston had started out as a reporter in Fargo and Minneapolis before coming east. Henry liked to talk of Gaston's muckraking days out west, his crusade against gambling bosses and the politicians who sheltered them, but his early career had, in fact, been radical. In 1920, he'd written a 325-page defense of the activist farmers' movement—the "prairie fire" that threatened the Midwest—and in

1923, when the garment workers' unions launched *The New Leader*, he'd come to New York to work for Norman Thomas. Though Gaston had since shifted to the center, much of the old radical remained.

Henry's days became an endless succession of meetings: bankers and economists, financiers and diplomats, congressmen and senators. They started early and carried on, almost without respite, until evening. Mrs. Klotz kept strict time. Each day the cast changed, but Mrs. Klotz remained: She now carried the title of "Secretary to the Secretary," but from her first day at Treasury, her reach extended far beyond her desk. In every meeting, she would sit in a corner, knees pressed primly together, taking precise and exhaustive notes. It would become a stenographic vigil without precedent in the history of the federal civil service: Mrs. Klotz attempted to record every word. She would also empty the secretary's in and out boxes, collecting the reams of reports, memoranda, letters, news clips, even tiny hand-scrawled notes, that crossed his desk. The "Morgenthau Diaries," as the enormous compendium came to be called, include, as well, transcripts of the secretary's conversations with cabinet members, White House aides, Wall Street barons, generals and admirals, and politicians of all parties. In the end, the "Diaries" would stretch to nearly nine hundred bound volumes. In time, Henry would also order that Mrs. Klotz create a subset of documents: the "Presidential Diaries," summaries, as retold by Henry in the afterglow of each meeting, of his conversations with the president.

Henry enjoyed Henrietta Klotz's company. She was honest, and fiercely loyal. He enjoyed, too, how visitors remarked on her good looks. To his dismay, though, Mrs. Klotz soon gained the notice of the press: A glowing news profile featured a studio portrait testifying to her beauty, drawings depicting the range of her many tasks, and a headline calling her the "Best Secretary in the New Deal." The reporter noted not only Mrs. Klotz's allure but her blunt willingness to protect the man she respected above all others—including the president, whose inscribed portrait hung opposite her desk.

There was gossip of a romance, but anyone who knew Henry's prudishness scoffed at the idea. And yet there was, as he knew well, a devotion that bordered on obsession. Mrs. Klotz, as the boss always called her, always remembered an event from the early days, when Joan was a baby, when she discovered the red line. "I went over and I touched Joan's feet," Mrs. Klotz would recall years later. Nana, the family nurse, had taken her outside and left her carriage uncovered. Her feet were cold.

"She'll get sick," Mrs. Klotz had warned, but Ellie quickly shut her down. "I learned to be good, mind my own business," she would tell one of the Morgenthau children years later. "But you know, I felt as though, when you were little, that you all belonged to me."

In 1929, Henrietta and Herman Klotz had had their own child, a daughter born with a rare condition—her eyes lacked irises. Henrietta named the girl after the boss's wife, Elinor. As the daughter grew up, and excelled despite the eye disorder, her mother would do all she could to have her follow in Joan's footsteps: She would attend the same exclusive schools, even the same college. It was "this strangest thing," Joan Morgenthau would say, of her new shadow.

The secretary, who had arranged a sinecure for Henrietta's husband (first at the RFC, then at the Treasury), reaped the reward of the affection, but strict boundaries ruled their relations. Whenever the secretary would give Mrs. Klotz a lift home in his limousine, he asked the driver to let her out blocks from her apartment building, lest an observer get a false impression. If the feelings were not reciprocal, the devotion certainly was. To Henry, his secretary was indispensable: No one else could run such a tight ship. No matter how early he arrived at the office, Mrs. Klotz was at her desk to greet him. No matter how late he stayed, she never left first. Together, Henry assured Mrs. Klotz, they would strive for bureaucratic perfection.

He would need a loyalist. In the cabinet, even though he had been among the first to back Hopkins, Rosenman, and Wallace, Henry won few friends. He suffered, Ickes wrote in his own diary, "an inferiority complex": "If one disagrees with him, he doesn't take to it kindly but, rather, takes it in a personal way and feels you are opposed to him personally." If he was temperamental, Henry was also exacting. In his first days as secretary, Henry had issued new orders to the guards at the Treasury building: They were to keep their clothes clean and buttoned, shoes shined, refrain from smoking or reading on duty, and "show respect for official superiors by standing at attention when approached or being addressed." When Henry issued "General Order No. One," forbidding "loose talk" by staff to reporters, the press cried censorship. As their plea reached the president vacationing in Warm Springs, Henry had just arrived: He caught a tongue-lashing from FDR in the therapy pool, and promptly reversed course.

On policy, few knew where the new secretary stood. "Political philosophy" was a phrase rarely employed with regard to Henry Morgenthau, Jr. Even Democrats feared that he was too left-wing—a socialist or, worse, a Bolshevik at heart. His father liked to tell the story of a dinner party in early 1935, at the home of Louis Wiley, Adolph Ochs's close friend who ran the business side of the *Times* for decades. Conservative Long Islanders had dominated the evening, speaking of the New Deal with cautious apprehension, before fixing, over cigars, on the new Treasury secretary. They had been careful not to offend, but Henry Sr. cut to the chase: "Gentlemen, you need have no fear of my son's being a Communist," he said. "I have seen to it that he is a man of means."

Henry would also be accused of being a capitalist in disguise. In March 1935, Ickes recorded the concern in his diary, quoting John Nance Garner: FDR's vice president feared Henry did not have "any sympathy with progressive ideas." Garner, he went on, "believes that in his heart [Morgenthau] is against the bill to abolish the holding companies, and that in general his sympathies are with the big interests of Wall Street."

By early 1934, as Henry marked out his own path, the assumptions began to shift. As he had at Farm Credit, Henry took the reins without fanfare but with a firmness rare among the New Dealers. He consolidated dozens of departments, cut the dead timber, delegated the details to his new army. Above all, as he built a hierarchy of command, even his rivals realized that Henry would refuse to be an easy target. For a man who still struggled with public speaking, none of the president's men seemed to have gained as much confidence, as quickly, on the job.

Within months, the change was noted. "He doesn't bite his lower lip anymore," one reporter wrote. "What Mr. Morgenthau didn't know," he added, "he learned." Even Jim Farley, the party boss turned postmaster general, never a great fan, commended Henry, if only in private: "Secretary Morgenthau has grown considerably in his job," he wrote in his diary, "and his mental attitude seems to have changed." The shyness remained, but Henry had grown accustomed to the expanded horizon, and not a year into the job, he reached a public milestone. Ellie beamed quietly, but made sure the children and everyone at home in New York saw it: In September 1934, a finely etched portrait of the secretary of the Treasury—pince-nez, stern gaze, and half grimace in place—peered out at the nation from the cover of *Time*.

25. "We Have Just Begun to Fight"

1932-1934

Only in summer, during August, did the Morgenthau children—Henry III, Bob, and Joan—stay with their parents for more than a few days. The two boys were packed off to Deerfield Academy in western Massachusetts, and Joan to the Madeira School in Virginia.

In this, the Morgenthaus were hardly unusual: Many Our Crowd families had long followed patrician expediency, sending children to the boarding schools of New England. Yet through the years of the Roosevelt administration, as the Morgenthau children came of age, they not only lived apart from their parents but often separate from one another. On weekends in New York, they would see Grandma and Grandpa Morgenthau, as well as Grandma Fatman, Ellie's mother, Settie. The grandparents would indulge them: Grandpa Morgenthau loved nothing more than to host family parties at the sprawling apartment at 1133 Park Avenue, his new base of operations, while Ellie's mother, Settie, now a widow, treated them to fancy teas in her suite at the Savoy-Plaza, the grand hotel on the southeastern edge of Central Park. And Ellie did her best to shore up the children. She wrote long letters to the boys at Deerfield and Joan at Madeira. She relayed the latest from Washington: the parties, the secretary's battles, and on occasion news of a victory. Their father wrote less often, first in a hurried scrawl, then by dictation to Mrs. Klotz. But even as the letters continued (Ellie would often write several times a week), the distances remained.

Henry and Elinor, too, struggled into the new life. Edith Wilson, the former president's widow, lived nearby. At a White House dinner, she told Henry, "We would be glad to have you as neighbors." They'd found a house in one of Washington's best neighborhoods, a stately, two-story brick Georgian on Kalorama Road. The house had four large bedrooms and came with elegant furnishings, but the Morgenthaus were renting—and never knew how long they would stay. They missed the country, too—Henry terribly. In early 1933, coming into the administration, he'd had to sell the *American Agriculturalist*. (A young publisher, Frank Gannett, had picked it up, acquiring his first magazine.) But Henry longed for time on the farm. He had tried to run things from afar—tracking egg counts, fertilizer deliveries, apple orders—but was forced to turn to a caretaker. Still, he returned as often as possible. On a Saturday morning, he might decide at the last minute to fly up—FDR lent him a Navy plane—to the tiny New Hackensack airport, a little-used airstrip in Dutchess that FDR had paved as governor. Even being on the farm a few hours, Henry would say, was worth it. "The place looked beautiful," he wrote in his diary in June 1933. "And I hated to leave it."

Above all else, Henry and Ellie prized evenings at the White House. On May 1, 1934, Franklin and Eleanor hosted the Morgenthaus—including Uncle Henry—at a family dinner. "It was just 'The Pres.',", Ellie reported to her boys, joined by Mrs. Roosevelt, Malvina "Tommy" Thompson (Eleanor's secretary), Missy LeHand, and the Morgenthaus. Visiting Ellie and Henry en route to a mineral spa in West Virginia, Grandpa Morgenthau was seated next to FDR, who, Ellie noted, "was in A no. 1 form." She worried about her father-in-law, and her mother, too, her incipient dementia worsening. But Ellie and Henry had grown used to it: An evening with the Roosevelts, its stream of private jokes, easy laughter, and political gossip, could always lift their spirits.

| | | |

In her first weeks in the White House, the first lady had decided to make good use of the White House stables, and invited Elinor Morgenthau to join her. Like their husbands' lunches, their early morning rides became a routine: The usher would summon the horses from Fort Myer across the Potomac, and then deliver them by van to Rock Creek Park. In jodhpurs and boots Eleanor and Elinor would ride side by side, trailed at a polite distance by a Secret Service man, trotting through the woods along the shallow creek. Returning to the White House disheveled and smelling of horse, the first lady would never fail to incur the disapproval of a staff already nostalgic for the prim ways of the Hoovers.

"The two Eleanors" had begun to work closely on social evenings as well. Since Grover Cleveland's day, the Gridiron Dinner had been a fixture on the White House calendar, a male-only drunken fest for the president, cabinet, and congressional leaders. In 1933, Eleanor Roosevelt staged her own party, the Gridiron Widows' Dinner. She invited all the cabinet wives—and Frances Perkins's husband. It would become an annual tradition, an all-female evening of silly skits, and Eleanor asked Ellie, whose drama skills she admired, to stage it.

Still, the "political work" remained foremost. One weekend in May 1934, they drove out to West Virginia to inspect a woman's prison in Alderson. Mrs. Roosevelt had never been so far south. They listened as the inmates spoke of their travails, and heard the warden, Dr. Mary Harris, talk of rehabilitation: giving the women skills and returning them to husbands and children. The prison pilgrimages became a near-annual tradition.

Mrs. Roosevelt never seemed to lack energy, and also had the gift of being able to fall asleep at once in any car. Ellie, though, tired easily—and the trips were draining. "Mother traveled with Mrs. Roosevelt so much," her daughter, Joan, would recall, "she used to come back and have to go to bed for a couple of days." First ladies had long enhanced their husbands' political image, but the public now saw modern women at work, and not merely in support of their husbands. Besides prisons Eleanor and Ellie visited nursing homes, poor houses, tenements, orphanages, grammar schools, universities. They went down into coal mines, and up into the Appalachians. It became a kind of social justice tour, always impromptu and unscripted, just the two of them.

A late-summer visit in 1934, though, threatened a breach. On August 14, a date Eleanor Roosevelt always disliked—the anniversary of her father's death—she came to see her friend. Ellie was morose and irritated, a rarity. Her mother was failing, but there was something else. She felt shut out, that Eleanor in recent months had avoided her. But Ellie blamed others: So many, she told Eleanor, were monopolizing the first lady's time. (Ellie did not need to name the offenders: Nancy and Marion, Mrs. Roosevelt's constant companions.) Why had Eleanor not seen more of her over the summer? Ellie asked. What had she done to deserve the distancing?

Eleanor found the sulking incomprehensible—if not silly. "I can't think what I did to make you feel I didn't want to hear from you this summer," she wrote Ellie days later. "In fact," she went on,

*I did very much and missed having no letters and thought of you
often. . . . I'm so sorry about your Mother and I know how you are
feeling for it is much worse to watch someone you love suffer than
suffer yourself. Poor darling, you have so many troubles and never
seem to get a real rest. I'm going to try to plan in early Nov. to take
you away for a long week end! Friendships are always important to
me and please don't ever think the opposite no matter what stupid
things I do which hurt your feelings. It is never intentional.*

Ellie was little relieved; the jealousies remained. As she saw Eleanor's
attentions turn elsewhere, she would continue to stew.

| | | |

That summer, it seemed as if all of Washington went on holiday. In July,
the capital emptied. When Roosevelt set sail for a fishing cruise in the
Caribbean, nearly everyone, it seemed, followed him out the door.

Henry III, seventeen, had gone to Europe with his best friend, Jerry
Straus, a scion of the Macy's fortune, and the boy's parents. The rest of
the family enjoyed a month at a dude ranch, an hour outside Bozeman,
Montana. They went to Wyoming, too. The Interior Department was
still enlarging the Grand Teton Park and the Morgenthaus got a private
showing: riding horseback to the edge of Jackson Lake to take in the
Tetons. At eleven, Joan learned to ride bareback through the streams. On
a pack trip into the backcountry, a wrangler took the secretary and his
son hunting: Bob, days shy of his fifteenth birthday, held a .25-35 pump-
action Winchester, and with one shot—the wires spread the news—
brought down a grizzly. As would become her custom, Ellie had chosen
the vacation; guardian of her husband's fragile health, she demanded
that he rest. The ranch promised isolation: no aides, phones, rail station.
After two weeks, the secretary nearly managed to relax.

Publicly, no one but the president, the first lady, and *The New York
Times* gave Henry much credit for bringing authority, and direction, to
the Treasury. Jim Farley had begun to see another side: the principles
behind the stubbornness. "He apparently is desirous of cooperating
more with the other members of the cabinet and others in the administration," wrote Farley in his diary. "As time goes on," he added, Henry
"will continue to improve" in the job. Yet the odds, he conceded, were
stacked: "Of course, the fact that he is a New York Jew and the fact that

the financiers do not feel that he has had sufficient financial experience will always be held against him."

Survival, Henry knew, would depend on money: how fast he could fill the federal coffers. Henry faced the biggest public debt on record, more than $27 billion. The Fourth Liberty Loan, 4¼ percent bonds dating from 1918, was also set to mature in 1934—a bill of $6.3 billion. The move would require a tricky refinancing: The Treasury announced two successive early redemption calls, offering new bonds in exchange for the old, with a catch. In the first call, the Treasury offered to exchange a 12-year bond for the Fourth Liberties that would carry the same 4¼ percent interest in the first year, but drop to 3¼ each year after. The first year "sweetener," as Henry's economists called it, was meant to encourage bondholders to exchange their old paper. The bond, a split-coupon issuance, was a one-off, an experiment Morgenthau's Treasury would never repeat. But it worked: The Treasury had to pay out less than $400 million in cash.

Still, all the while government spending skyrocketed at a rate unseen in the nation's history. Lew Douglas, the hard-edged Arizonan who had served as budget director since Roosevelt's first day in office, could take no more; for months, he had refused to support the grand relief schemes, warning of catastrophe. In late August, he came to Hyde Park on an urgent visit—and resigned.

The next morning, FDR summoned Henry. It was the day of the Morgenthau clambake—Ellie and Henry, knowing how Roosevelt relished the gatherings, had made it a Labor Day fixture. Henry drove the half hour north to the house, taking along three aides, but at the door was told FDR wanted to see him alone. "I found him taking a bath," Henry recounted days later. "He sat up straight in the bathtub and looked me straight in the eye and said, 'Henry (with great emphasis) in the words of John Paul Jones—"We have just begun to fight." ' "

Douglas's quitting was not just a betrayal; the timing could derail the fall congressional campaigns. Roosevelt had pleaded with him as a patriot, and a Democrat, to stay on. "Ten years from now," he'd warned, Douglas "would be sorry for what he had done." (Douglas had held firm—and later would join the Liberty League and turn against Roosevelt.)

FDR was left "terribly upset and hurt"; from the bath, he issued an order: "Henry, I give you until midnight to get me a new Director of the Budget."

In Douglas's departure, Henry saw an opening. He'd had little love for the budget chief but did share his worries. The lessons learned at his father's knee were unshakeable; Henry Jr., too, feared the pace of spending and demanded a balanced budget. Henry, in fact, had been miscast as a founding New Dealer: He believed passionately in the ideals, but was never comfortable with the means; he would crusade for relief, but could never stomach the federal government's spending its way out of the Depression.

When Roosevelt suggested a successor—Tommy Corcoran, a Washington operator whom FDR had nicknamed "Tommy the Cork"—Henry rejected him. "Out of the question," he said. Corcoran was "a first-class lawyer, a first-class political operator, a first-class accordion player," and "an intellectual crook." Moreover, he knew little of finance and could "not be relied upon to keep a tight rein" on spending.

Roosevelt seemed surprised, but without waiting for a reply, Henry tossed out a name: Daniel Bell, a twenty-three-year Treasury veteran who had started out as a stenography clerk. Bell was a quiet, sallow-faced cog in the vast machinery, who had met with FDR no more than a dozen times. To Henry's shock, Roosevelt at once accepted the idea. He even drafted, in his own hand, an immediate press release. FDR would make Bell's rise the news, not Douglas's sudden departure.

That evening at the clambake, Roosevelt joined Henry for cocktails. The two sat alone. "You could tell," Henry wrote, "a great weight" had fallen from "his shoulders." As the evening went on, the president began to sing old ditties. "A great load and worry was off his mind," Henry noted. Eleanor Roosevelt saw it, too. "Somehow," she wrote her confidante Lorena "Hick" Hickok, "he worked his rage out by having a grand time!" Those around FDR, Henry recorded with pride, were also struck by the sight. Since Roosevelt had moved into the White House, Henry heard all say, "they had never seen him sing and be so jolly as he was that night."

With Bell named budget chief, many in Washington expected that his former boss would rule over the budget as well. No one imagined that Henry could outgrow his patron's shadow, but Henry had established dictatorial rule in the Treasury, and his administrative circle of power, always tethered to the president, was expanding. When Eugene Black, the Federal Reserve chair, quit, Henry floated a name—Marriner Eccles, the Utah banker he had recruited to Washington—to succeed Black, and once again Roosevelt approved. There was more. That fall reports surfaced of a plan afoot to establish a central bank that would supplant the Federal Reserve—a scheme, the rumors held, aimed to bring the entire banking system under control of the Treasury. "If these things come to pass," *Time* worried, "Henry Morgenthau Jr., who has possibly less financial training than any of his predecessors, will have far more financial power than any of them."

In the spring of 1935, Henry unveiled a campaign to raise billions, giving the American people a chance to own a slice of the New Deal, and at the same time make a small profit. On the morning of March 1, he joined FDR at the White House to unveil the first United States Saving Bonds—"baby bonds," the public dubbed them. As floodlights filled the Oval Study, the president, Henry, and Postmaster General Farley acted out a skit:

"I wish you would tell me about these United States Savings Bonds which went on sale today," FDR began, as the newsreel cameras whirled.

"The Treasury," Henry said, "has decided that every citizen should have a chance to buy sound government securities and become a partner in his government. These bonds are issued in denominations as low as $25. . . . The $25 bond will cost you $18.75 today. It grows in value every year, and if you hold it for the full ten years you will increase your investment by one-third."

Roosevelt: "But suppose I want to cash my bond before that? Suppose I need the money in a hurry?"

Morgenthau: "In case of emergency, the Government will redeem your bond at any time after 60 days from the date of issue."

Roosevelt: "Sounds like a pretty good proposition to me. . . . I want to buy from you six of the $25 bonds, one for each of my five grandchildren and one for myself. I hope that my arithmetic is right."

Producing his billfold, FDR laid out five rumpled bills: a $100 note, a $10 note, and three singles. "Now you owe me 50 cents," he said with a chuckle. "And I am sure, there will be analogous sales of these bonds all over the country." There were; by spring, with demand booming, the presses at the Bureau of Engraving and Printing worked through the night to churn out the "baby bonds."

||||

At the Treasury, Henry also got to play cop—"I love to be a policeman," he would later admit. To start, he went after a big fish: Huey Long, the imperious former governor, now a U.S. senator, of Louisiana, whose disdain for the democratic process, and inscrutable ties to the corrupt powers of New Orleans, were notorious. Long was a target for another reason, too: His improbable campaign alliance with FDR had long since turned into one of the president's worst rivalries.

Three days after becoming secretary, Henry had sent for Elmer Irey, head of the Intelligence Unit, the investigator who'd unearthed the tax dodges that led to Al Capone's conviction in 1931. Henry had been briefed: Several years earlier, the Treasury had opened an investigation into corruption in New Orleans, probing for income tax evasion—but the case had been shut. "Why have you stopped investigating Huey Long, Mr. Irey?" he asked. Ogden Mills, Hoover's secretary of the Treasury, had told him to stop, Irey said. "What's the matter, Mr. Irey," Henry went on, "are you afraid of Huey Long?" No, Irey said, "I'm awaiting instructions."

Roosevelt and Long had history. Long had wanted one thing from Roosevelt: patronage, jobs for his machine. For a time, it appeared as if the president would bring Long to his side and keep him close. The dance continued for more than a year, but ended abruptly when Long visited the White House in June 1933. Long wore a summer suit and straw hat, which he only briefly removed to touch FDR's knee, or elbow, as he made a point. The impudence was not lost on his host. Long again pushed for control of the political appointments in his state, but Roosevelt would not yield.

Leaving the White House, Long had pretended the sting did not hurt. He'd learned a lesson, he said, about such men, and told the reporters a story. His grandfather once had had a worker who could pick twice as much cotton as anyone on his farm. He'd fired him, of course. "If you stayed around here," his grandfather had explained, "fust thing I know I'll be working for you." Said Long, "That's the way I feel about Roosevelt, he's so doggone smart that fust thing I know, I'll be working for him—and I ain't goin' to."

Irey's investigation had been stalled for nearly two years—but now, Henry told him, "Get all your agents back on the Louisiana job. Start the investigation of Huey Long, and proceed as though you were investigating Joe Doe. And let the chips fall where they may."

The secretary instructed Irey that he was to report to him once a week, entering through Mrs. Klotz's office, "not the main reception room."

Irey did so, for almost a year. Once when he fell short of information, he skipped a meeting. On the next morning, Henry called him. "This is the Secretary," he said. "You haven't been to see me in eight days."

A strategy took shape. Instead of going directly after Long, they would encircle him, taking out his top men one by one. In October 1934, Abe Shushan, head of the Levee Board in New Orleans, was indicted for income tax evasion, and in December, Joseph Fisher, a state representative, followed. Henry would offer regular updates for Roosevelt: If both of Long's men were convicted, they would strike at the heart of his court: either the New Orleans mayor, Robert Maestri—"Red Light Maestri," as he was known locally—or Seymour Weiss, hotel operator and Long's golfing partner and unofficial business manager. The investigation made headway: Fisher was convicted in April 1935, and Shushan would soon face trial. Irey pressed on, laying the groundwork for a full-scale investigation into Long himself. In July, Irey sent his top agent to New Orleans, and throughout the summer, as the evidence accrued, updated the Treasury secretary. By September, Irey had uncovered an illicit scheme that the prosecutors believed might stick: It had to do with the Win-Or-Lose Corporation, the prospecting of Louisiana oil and gas fields, and a self-enrichment conspiracy orchestrated, the documents and witnesses said, by Long himself. The prosecutors scheduled the case for the grand jury to begin on October 3.

The Treasury's crusade, after a year and a half of investigation, would lose its chief target. On September 8, the day after Irey presented the collected evidence, Huey Long was shot on the steps of the state capitol. A day and a half later, at forty-two, he was dead. Still, Henry pushed on, even after Shushan won an acquittal, and the Justice Department, without warning the Treasury, abandoned the trail in 1936—dismissing all eleven of the remaining Louisiana criminal cases. (Part of the rationale was a lack of evidence, and part of it was pragmatism: Long was gone.) But Henry took a series of civil cases to the Board of Tax Appeals, which in 1937 convened a special court to hear them. "The word went from Morgenthau," Irey would recall, " 'No compromises.' " Each defendant whose case the Justice Department had deemed too weak would plead guilty—and more than $2 million in taxes and penalties would be collected from Long's lieutenants (including Weiss, Shushan, and Maestri), as well as from Long's own estate.

Henry had been determined to clean up corruption and crime across the country—and at every juncture, FDR backed him. If Henry was uncomfortable with the economists and lawyers, struggling to track their labyrinthine explanations of the department's security transactions and tax reforms, he got on well with the T-men, the Treasury agents, and championed their work. He rose even earlier, getting up at five in the morning to study the investigative reports. He added an Alcohol Tax Unit to the Internal Revenue Service, a corps to combat the lingering bootlegging trade. He vowed to go after the Chinese and Japanese opium smugglers, too, and even the biggest organized crime bosses.

Henry set his sights on Arthur Flegenheimer, aka Dutch Schultz, then still on the run. A federal grand jury had indicted Schultz two years earlier for tax evasion, but to get him, Henry had to fend off both the FBI and the New York Police Department. On November 1, 1934, he called J. Edgar Hoover and the new mayor of New York, Fiorello La Guardia, who had won office as a crime fighter. Schultz had enjoyed impunity for too long, Henry said. He had his suspicions, but refrained from accusing anyone of protecting Schultz. "The point is," he warned La Guardia, "the Treasury wants this fellow." The mayor assured Henry that he shared the same goal, but conceded there could be "sabotaging" among the lower ranks of the police force: "Some of these things that I've observed," La Guardia said, "I think that this gentleman has very strong connections." With Hoover, Henry was equally blunt: Schultz was "the last of the big income tax gangsters," he said, and it was time to end the charade.

Hoover promised to make Schultz a priority. "We here," he told Henry, "will just put him down as kind of Public Enemy No. 1 secretly, so we can find him."

For weeks, Schultz managed to remain at large. All the while, Henry tracked the case, keeping up the pressure. In late November 1934, Schultz decided to surrender: In Albany, he turned himself in to the local U.S. commissioner, a federal official. Schultz's lawyers attempted a clever ploy: The commissioner would arraign their client, and release him on a low bail. But as the federal prosecuters debated their next move, Hoover called Henry to give him the good news.

Their conversation on November 28 revealed an unlikely affinity between the secretary and the FBI director, one that stretched for decades, in times of alliance and enmity. Hoover proposed an unusual deal: that the federal prosecutors arraign Schultz, secure as high a bail as possible, and then hand the case to the Treasury.

Henry didn't like the sound of bail. "Now I'm not a lawyer," he said, "but isn't there some way we can hold that fellow in jail after all these months?"

Hoover tried to explain: Schultz's lawyers would likely fight a move to bring Schultz to New York City—where "you folks of course can interrogate him." If "his lawyer wants to be technical," he added, "they can block you every way."

To Henry, the process sounded overly complex, and time-consuming. "Can't you kidnap him?" he asked, not entirely joking.

"Well, I simply won't hesitate if I get the opportunity," Hoover said.

"I mean all this damn legal red tape," Henry went on.

"It's the most exasperating," Hoover agreed. "The whole thing is our legal procedure protects the criminal but it doesn't help the law enforcement office."

"Not a bit," Henry concurred.

Although Hoover promised to insist that "the bond be fixed at the highest figure possible," Henry fumed. Many bootleggers, he said, had jumped bail at $100,000.

For months, Schultz remained free, thanks to a tangled series of legal maneuvers. But by fall 1935, the debate became moot. Thomas Dewey, the New York special prosecutor, wanted a third trial, and this time, he assured Henry, he'd try Schultz himself. Henry gave his blessing. Yet before Dewey could start, in October 1935, Schultz was shot dead.

If Long and Schultz fell to assassins' bullets, the Treasury did score successes, most notably among Henry's favorite target: tax cheats, big and small. Roosevelt, too, loathed them. The urge to name, shame, and punish the cheaters—it was an instinct the two men shared. As targets, Henry chose the giants: Andrew Mellon, his own predecessor at Treasury; Charles Mitchell, head of the National Citibank; A. P. Giannini, lord of the Bank of America, the behemoth of California; Moses Annenberg, the magnate who owed his fortune to the *Racing Form*. The cases would come in succession, a series of prosecutions over several years that brought a storm of publicity and pressure from Wall Street and the Congress that only strengthened Henry's zeal.

"Somebody over here has to be the S.O.B. on taxes," he would tell his men, "and I am perfectly willing to be it."

Mellon did not go down so easily. In March 1934, Henry charged Hoover's Treasury secretary with fraudulent returns, claiming Mellon owed the government more than $3 million. To plead the case before a

Pittsburgh federal judge, Henry brought in Robert H. Jackson, the future attorney general and Supreme Court justice. Jackson complained to Henry that the Republican press was accusing him of ruthlessness.

"You can't be too tough in this trial to suit me," Henry told him.

"Thank God I have that kind of boss!" said Jackson.

"Wait a minute," Henry replied. "I consider that Mr. Mellon is not on trial, but Democracy and the privileged rich and I want to see who will win."

The Mellon investigation did not begin well: The press decried the case as a vengeful attack on a political opponent—"weak from the start," wrote one columnist, and "aired with a maximum of ballyhoo and a minimum of good taste," added another. But on the first day of the trial, Henry got good news from the courtroom: Mellon had sworn that he had signed his tax return in Washington, D.C., but it was notarized in Pittsburgh—rendering it invalid.

"They have been forced to admit that this return was a false return from the very beginning," Jackson told Henry.

"Well, I'll be damned," said the secretary.

"It's just horseshoes," Jackson said, admitting surprise. "Of course, we'll have to claim we knew all the time."

"That's all right," Henry said. "It reads awfully well in the paper."

There was more, Jackson went on: The defense had "admitted that while Mellon was secretary of the Treasury he was selling short in the market." Now they had the "evidence," Jackson added, "that justifies everything we've ever done and more, too."

The case ended in a draw. Mellon won in court, avoiding indictment, but was forced to pay a civil fine.

The Annenberg case, however, would prove to be Roosevelt's favorite. At lunch with FDR on April 11, 1939, Henry asked if he had anything on his mind. "He said only one thing—He wanted to make sure that I was going to 'get' Moe Annenberg." "I assured him I felt very confident that we would." The new tax code, Henry had explained, cut deductions for incorporated yachts, racing stables, and mistresses; Annenberg's deductions—his daughter's wedding and his girlfriend's trip to South America among them—had been denied, but he kept his accounts in code. Irey's men worked for five years before they cracked it. In the summer of 1939, a grand jury indicted Annenberg, who by spring would plead guilty, pay an $8 million fine—the largest ever for an individual charged with tax evasion—and receive three years in jail.

| | | |

It was a bright morning in New Hampshire when in June the Treasury secretary gave his first address in public—to the graduating students, teachers, and parents at Deerfield.

Ellie, Bob, and Joan sat nearby, on hand to see the eldest of the three Morgenthau children graduate. In the fall, Henry III would go to Princeton. The secretary had given a number of radio speeches, but those who heard him on that afternoon heard a different man. Maybe it was the setting, or the timing, but Henry gave a personal speech.

For years, he said, he had enjoyed passing "among these hills and valleys that you know so well and that have come to be another home for my two boys." He had thought about talking about "monetary policy, or budget making, or major governmental financing," but decided to address something more urgent, "more fundamental." Henry spoke of scoundrels, the men and their advisors who would "cheat their government and their neighbors." The troublemakers belonged to two classes, he said, "those who are in the upper world and think themselves worthy of respect, and those who are in the underworld and don't care whether they are respectable or not." It was a refrain that would echo for years at the Treasury, and in the Morgenthau family. "I say," he added, "they are the gangsters of both the upper and the lower world."

Henry had kept a tally. He told of "a physician who for years had gathered a very large income by dispensing narcotics illegally to addicts"—a "sort of case that fills me with disgust and wrath." He warned of those "who sharpen their pencils and use trick devices to understate their income"—not just the bootlegger but "the bankers who handle his 'dough.'" And the lawyer who "knows just what he is doing and yet 'fronts' for him." "What of the politicians who stand by and let him operate?" he asked. "And finally, when a Treasury enforcement unit does what local authorities have not been able to do and indicts him for a Federal penitentiary offense—evading his income taxes—what of the influential, respectable citizen who comes down to Washington with a message that the gangster is really quite a fine upstanding fellow who may have done a little technical wrong but ought to be let down easy?"

Such men, Henry told the boys, are "the dark side of the picture."

It was nothing less than a defense of American democracy, against the rising tide of fascism and the attacks on the New Deal as no more than a vehicle for the personal fiat of Roosevelt. To Henry, his work entailed more than raising money: It was about preserving democracy. "When we seek to cheat and nullify and evade," he said, "and help others to evade . . . we are in truth undermining the main foundations of our government."

"You boys," he told the graduates, "will soon be working shoulder to shoulder with us," and will learn the virtue of "self-sacrificing labor." He had seen it, he said, in the T-men's faces. He had learned it, though, at his father's knee. "One is unfortunate if he hasn't learned it early in life," he said. "I began to discern it as a boy when I sat in a corner of my father's office," and years later, when he "saw him laboring to protect the Armenians from annihilation." Some men cut rock to build roads, others enforce laws—but each serves the public good. Self-sacrifice, Henry said, was "a password to a great brotherhood." "In spite of occasional exceptions and violations . . . it is a rule that is a part of the American spirit and character."

26. "I Went Over Him and Under Him and Around Him"

FALL 1936–SPRING 1939

F DR and his Treasury secretary could not shake the sense of an approaching war—and the enemy, for both, had a face. Both men shared a drive—years ahead of nearly anyone in Washington and against the high tide of isolationism in the country—to stand against the Nazi threat. Both knew something of the German people and their martial spirit. Henry had the lineage, and Roosevelt the boyhood memories.

FDR had gone often with his parents to Germany—at least eight times—on Sara's insistence that her husband, James, rest his weak heart at the Bavarian spas. For six years, when FDR was between nine and fourteen, they went each summer; for a time, he even went to school there. In Bad Nauheim, young Franklin had been made to wear a sailor suit, and the rules were strict. Memories of uniformed schoolchildren marching would never leave him. He could remember, he would write, how when Wilhelm II came to the throne, "the talk among us children became stronger each year towards an objective—the inevitable war with France and the building up of the Reich to the greatest world power." By 1914, Roosevelt's distaste had turned to disdain: He spoke out against "Kaiserism," and "Prussianism"—and in 1918, touring battlefields in France and Belgium, he wrote in his diary of "stolid, stupid" German prisoners and the "little pile of dead *Boche*"—French slang for Germans—that offended "our sensitive noses."

Neither man's knowledge ran deep, nor were their experiences all negative, yet as the Nazi specter grew, FDR's and Henry Jr.'s memories would quickly darken: Roosevelt would remember only bullies and boors, and Henry would forget the hospitable officers and diplomats of Gallipoli and Constantinople.

In late 1915, on his final trip to Turkey, Henry had gone to the front. His father the ambassador had been against it, sending his son with the Constantinople police chief and a military attaché from the embassy. For the first time, Henry Jr. saw war up close. At Gallipoli, he'd seen "nearly all the buildings ruined." He donned a Turkish uniform to tour the trenches nearby—some fifty feet apart, and only days earlier abandoned by the British. At the peninsula's southernmost point, he saw a "perfectly gorgeous" view ruined by artillery fire—shells shrieking overhead. (Henry Jr. would tell Ellie how he'd felt "a sort of tingling feeling somewhere in my chest.") And everywhere, Henry saw the wreckage: the abandoned British helmets, tin cans, and tents; the empty tunnels that still held poison gas; and the bomb craters that had rendered the earth a lunar landscape. Henry would never forget his time among the German officers. He'd visited General von Sanders in his *Hauptquartier,* from which he commanded the Turkish Fifth Army, and joined a victory party. As the general rose to drink to the kaiser, and his officers bobbed up one after another, adding their toasts, the American guest had joined in, but the scene would never leave his mind. It wasn't just the ruins of war—for the first time, Henry would say, he'd felt the unshakeable certitude of the German military.

By the time he reached Washington, Henry had also been hearing his father's warnings for years. Since Versailles, Henry Sr. had made it a refrain: The world, he insisted in speech after speech, was only enjoying a respite; Prussian militarism would surge again.

One evening in May 1919, Henry Sr. stood in a Liberty Hut in Coblenz and became one of the first American public figures to warn of a "new world war." Days earlier he had visited the Krupps factory and asked a worker if Germany would fight again. "Next time," came the reply, "we will have to go after them with our nails." "Do not go home and tell the people the war is over," Henry Sr. had told the American soldiers in Coblenz in a speech that made the front page of the *Times.* "The young men of America may yet have to fight. I believe that within fifteen or twenty years America will be called upon to save the world."

By 1933, Henry Sr.'s forecast had only grown darker. Over the Labor Day holiday, he entertained John D. Rockefeller, Jr., in Bar Harbor, Maine. Rockefeller had come to Mizzentop, Henry Sr.'s three-story granite house amid the WASP "cottages," seeking advice about a German concern's proposal to lease a building in Rockefeller Center. Henry Sr. said he'd be "very much opposed," but not because he feared a boycott, as the Rockefellers did. "A war is inevitable in the near future," he said, offering a vastly different reading of European politics from the one Rockefeller's aides had been feeding him. The conflagration, Henry Sr. added, would leave Germany "dismembered," in such a state it would not become "a world power for many years to come."

Roosevelt, too, from his first days in the White House, could also see the far horizon. As they sat down to lunch on May 15, 1933, Henry Jr. had raised the subject of Germany: "You know, I am really the only 100% Jew in your administration," he said, a rare reference to Judaism. "As a personal favor, I would greatly appreciate it if you would let me check anyone whom you were thinking of appointing as Ambassador to Germany."

He would be glad to, FDR said.

Over lunch, Henry probed deeper. "What is the likelihood of war with Germany?"

"A very strong possibility," Roosevelt said.

"Will the U.S. have to go in and defend its treaty rights?"

"We won't have to send any men abroad anyway," FDR replied with optimism.

But the next day, operating on little more than instinct, Roosevelt sent a message to the heads of fifty-four countries attending the disarmament conference in Geneva, ahead of the economic conclave that summer. He called for the "complete elimination of all offensive weapons." Earlier in May, FDR had told Hjalmar Schacht, the Reichsbank head then on a Washington visit, to pass a message to Hitler: The United States considered Germany the "only possible obstacle" to a disarmament treaty. On the following day, Hitler delivered his "peace speech" to the Reichstag, standing for ninety-eight minutes to deny he would subjugate any nation to German domination. To a world unaccustomed to the Führer's propaganda, Hitler's response to the Roosevelt entreaty brought admiring headlines.

Roosevelt, too, allowed himself to imagine that his words had been heard. On May 22, he greeted Henry buoyantly: "I think I have averted a war," he announced. "I sent word through the German ambassador to Hitler that I was going to send a message and that if his message [to the Reichstag] was of the same character as von Papen's [the German vice chancellor's inflammatory speech at Munich days earlier] that I would not blame France if she went to war."

In foreign affairs, Roosevelt may have been Wilsonian at heart, but his clear-eyed sense of political realities often surpassed his idealism. When FDR spoke of Europe, the future seemed hostage to inevitability. Two weeks before Christmas, in 1934, he stunned Henry with a blunt prediction. They'd been discussing Japan when FDR switched the topic to Germany. The Nazi plague, he was concerned, would spread—and the United States would have to come to Europe's aid. FDR's words so startled Henry that as soon as he left the Oval Study, he took a piece of White House stationery and scrawled them down:

"If the Nazi inhuman policy should be extended to England because her back was to the wall," Henry wrote, summarizing their conversation that day, "he, the President, believed the U.S. would, of course, go in and help England."

| | | |

From the start, as in nearly everything Henry and FDR did together, there was no strategy, blueprint, or plan. There was only an agreement: The country needed to prepare for rearming its allies in Europe. The United States would also need to mobilize its own armed forces. The question, though, was not merely one of political or popular will. No one knew if America's factories and plants, atrophied by years of the Depression, could build enough airplanes, tanks, ships, rifles, and munitions to halt a Nazi onslaught. And given the popular fear of yet another European war, few in Washington were interested in learning. Faced with the opposition of Republicans, his own party, and many in his cabinet, Roosevelt would turn yet again to the Treasury.

Just as in the first year of the New Deal, when Henry had served the president on secret plans far beyond the bounds of his department, so he would be called on again. As the threat of Nazi aggression grew, FDR would come to rely on his friend to find every way possible to go around the Neutrality Act of 1937, an enlargement of the first such act passed by Congress two years earlier, as the fighting spread in Europe. The president charged Henry with the effort to rearm Great Britain and France in spite of the law. With Roosevelt in the lead, they would move out ahead of popular opinion, and wait for the country to catch up.

In these years of mounting tension, a battle was waged to prepare the Allies, and America itself, first for defense, then for war—and the Treasury became a critical command post. The work would take place in secret, at times stretching the legal boundaries of his office, but Henry would help lead the campaign for mobilization. The risks were enormous, and the strain immense, but he would call it his most important work in Washington. "If we had ended with Germany winning, I would have ended hanging from a tree," Henry would say years later, before boasting: "We at the Treasury Department were ready for war almost before anybody else."

They had to run against popular opinion. In the spring of 1938, as the Nazi march began, the country remained defiantly isolationist, and the New Dealers, with the recession unrelenting, were on the defensive. Wall Streeters and industrialists declared they saw no cause for alarm. Many in the administration were equally blind: Ickes, Wallace, and even Hopkins—men who would go on to play leading roles in the war effort—were preoccupied with the home front. At the State Department, Cordell Hull insisted on keeping the United States on the sidelines. To Henry, State was always too "timorous, conventional and correct." "It was dominated," he wrote, "by what I used to call the 'foreign-office mentality'—the notion that you got things done in foreign policy by being a gracious host at diplomatic banquets." "They are all appeasers: never ruffle anybody. Always smooth everybody, keep everybody happy. You must never offend anybody." The polite talk, Henry warned, could not last long.

In March, Hitler took Austria, and by summer, he had turned his sights on Czechoslovakia. As German troops mobilized around the Sudetenland, the provinces where ethnic Germans predominated, the Czechs mobilized in turn. England and France, the latter bound by treaty to defend the Czechs, were desperate for arms, airplanes, and munitions. Henry saw the coming storm clearly: "Seldom in recorded history have tensions been so great," he said in a speech that month. "Seldom has the world prepared so madly and so rapidly for a war which all hope to avoid."

By fall, the fault lines surfaced. In Paris, Ambassador Bullitt still believed the British would not yield. Hitler had signaled to his generals his intention "to smash Czechoslovakia by military action in the near future." In London, though, Ambassador Joe Kennedy sided with the appeasers. FDR had recently named Kennedy to the Court of St. James's, and he had fast made a habit of testing Roosevelt's patience—and become a thorn in Henry's side, routinely volunteering his own ideas on fiscal policy. On August 31, as Chamberlain signaled his assent to the German annexation of the Sudetenland, Kennedy cabled the State Department a draft speech that he hoped to deliver in Scotland. The speech veered into direct contention with administration policy—highlighted by the claim that "for the life of me, I cannot see anything involved which could be remotely worth shedding blood for." FDR confided in Henry his outrage: It was as if Kennedy wished to say "I can't for the life of me understand why anybody would want to go to war to save the Czechs." "The young man needs his wrist slapped rather hard," Roosevelt told Henry. State cut the line, and Kennedy acquiesced this time, but he would persist in bucking the president.

On September 8, Georges Bonnet, the French foreign minister, proposed that Roosevelt referee the Czech crisis. Days later, he urged him to plead with Hitler not to use force. Throughout it all, the administration kept silent. By September 13, with war imminent, Henry ordered all stocks of U.S. gold—up to $200 million worth—in London returned to the United States, arranging for a U.S. battleship in London to store the bullion. Hull, who feared the Treasury was overreaching, fumed, but Henry told FDR he had only one worry: that London would be bombed.

On September 15, Chamberlain flew to Berchtesgaden, in southern Germany, for the first of three talks with Hitler. The French premier, Édouard Daladier, soon joined him, as did Mussolini. Hermann Göring, Joachim von Ribbentrop, Martin Bormann—names that meant nothing to Americans—would make appearances. Within two weeks, Chamberlain had gone to Munich and returned to London, holding aloft a slip of white paper, an agreement signed by Hitler pledging that England and Germany should never go to war again. "Czechoslovakia has been served up to me by her friends," Hitler exulted.

On September 19, as the British and French sought to convince the Czechs of their wisdom, Henry conferred with the president. The Czechs would fight, Roosevelt said. Henry agreed. He ought to get word to France, Roosevelt said: In case of war she should not attack but stay behind the Maginot Line, and "with other countries surrounding Germany" fight a defensive war, shutting off German supplies. A defensive war, properly executed, Henry concurred, "had a 60–40 chance of bringing Germany to her senses." FDR saw no alternative. If the neighboring countries now attacked Germany, he said, they stood only "a 40–60 chance of being successful."

Henry listened in agreement: The need for a line of defense was urgent. He remembered Gallipoli, the German officers in Turkey. "You know, Mr. President," he said, "if we don't stop Hitler now he is going right on to the Black Sea—then what? The fate of Europe for the next 100 years is settled."

| | | |

FDR liked to say he needed camaraderie in his cabinet. But nearly everyone in it had a rival, and many had more than one. For Henry, it was Harry Hopkins. He had long envied Roosevelt's cozy relations with Hopkins, but as Europe slid closer to war than at any time since the Armistice, a new worry crowded his mind. Once war came, Roosevelt would lose interest in the Treasury and Henry would be pushed aside. Hopkins would be the president's chosen heir. Still, Henry knew, FDR's affections could be fleeting: Just when he singled Hopkins out for praise, at the next cabinet meeting he would go out of his way to chasten him. No one in Roosevelt's shop, Henry told himself, was ever safe. "He never let anyone around him have complete assurance that he would have the job tomorrow," he would later say. "The thing that Roosevelt prided himself the most about was, 'I have to have a happy ship.' But he never had a happy ship."

As was often the case, Henry was unnecessarily fearful. After the Munich Agreement, Roosevelt only came to depend on him more: No one in the cabinet cared more deeply about the problems of military preparedness. To FDR's surprise, the stiffest resistance to gearing up for war came from the War Department itself. Secretary of War Harry Woodring, the forty-six-year-old former governor of Kansas, a Democrat in a Republican state, had learned to be cautious. The press, if it noticed him, called him the "common man" of the cabinet. A high school dropout, he'd started out at a local bank as a janitor and retired early at its helm, cashing out on the eve of the 1929 crash. Neither visionary nor schemer, if Woodring had any agenda it was to keep America's arms and equipment at home for America's troops.

Woodring not only played down the Nazi threat, he denied it existed. In a cabinet stocked with isolationists, he became the most vocal opponent of rearmament. Even his own chief deputies would come to resent his intransigence. Woodring's "myopia," as Henry called it, prevented him from seeing the danger to America's own national security. In September 1939, after German troops and tanks invaded Poland, and Britain and France declared war, Roosevelt called an urgent cabinet session.

What did the War Department need? he asked. "Several million blankets," Woodring replied.

It was a line Henry never forgot. He resolved to outmaneuver Woodring and the War Department: "I went over him," he wrote, "and under him and around him."

Without consulting Woodring or FDR, Henry quizzed friendly deputies at the War Department, probing for statistics on stockpiles and production capacities. He also instructed his staff to use the Treasury's power to shore up antifascist governments. Henry demanded new weapons for economic warfare: He pushed for credits to China, raised duties on German and Japanese imports, and froze all funds in U.S. banks held by the Germans, Japanese, and Italians. He asked his aides to draw up a list of all the metals essential for war, and devise ways to keep them out of the fascists' hands. He halted U.S. sales of scrap iron and aviation gasoline to Japan, and when Roosevelt asked him to corner the market on molybdenum, a metal essential to armaments production, he turned to his boyhood friend Harold Hochschild, head of the American Metals Company. After one lunch with Henry, Hochschild agreed to suspend all sales to the USSR—which the United States feared was reselling the metal to Germany—and soon persuaded all other U.S. producers to halt shipments to Germany and Japan as well. The Treasury secretary had launched an unspoken war on the fascists.

After Munich, Henry trespassed openly into foreign policy. "Let us not repeat the short-sighted mistakes of Britain and France," he wrote Roosevelt. "Let us *while we can peacefully do so* try to check the aggressors." Henry quoted a speech Churchill had given months earlier, before becoming prime minister: " 'If we do not stand up to the dictators now, we shall only prepare the day when we shall have to stand up to them under far more adverse conditions.' " "I know you are firmly convinced, as I am . . . that the forces of aggression must be stopped," Henry concluded. "By whom if not by us?"

A White House lunch with FDR on November 14, 1938, turned "momentous," as Henry put it. After FDR and Henry had finished, Hopkins and several Army men joined them, only to hear Roosevelt propose a rapid escalation of production: 10,000 planes a year, with the capacity to produce twice that number. He said that the rise of German power at Munich had "completely reoriented our own international relations," and "that for the first time since the Holy Alliance in 1818 the United States now faced the possibility of an attack on the Atlantic side in both the Northern and Southern Hemispheres." He went on to demand "our providing immediately a huge air force so that we do not need to have a huge army to follow that air force," and considered "that sending a large army abroad was undesirable and politically out of the question."

Roosevelt then offered a history lesson: In 1917, it took the United States thirteen months after Wilson declared war to put the first plane on the European front. This time, he warned, there would be "no such period of grace." He conceded a second reason the country needed the planes: "I am not sure now that I am proud of what I wrote to Hitler in urging that he sit down around the table and make peace. That may have saved many, many lives now, but that may ultimately result in the loss of many times that number of lives later. When I write to foreign countries I must have something to back up my words."

Within weeks, when Jean Monnet, the French political economist, arrived in Washington eager to buy planes, Ambassador Bullitt ushered him into Henry's office. The Frenchman found his way to the Treasury, and not the Army, Navy, or State Department, because Treasury's Procurement Division served as the government's lead general purchasing agency. There was another reason, one FDR appreciated: The Treasury stood above the rivalries between the Army and Navy, and was run by a friend who could be relied upon to keep a secret mission secret.

When Monnet announced a desire to buy a thousand airplanes, Henry, ever cautious, was skeptical. Before meeting with Monnet, he called over to the State Department—and checked that the mission was indeed authorized. He also studied the plan for payment. When he learned that the French proposed sending the monies through a sham company in Canada, Henry refused. The Neutrality Act, he said, was clear: Any payment must come from one government to another. "I had something of a phobia about the role which private bankers had played during the first World War," he explained. "I was determined to keep war profits to an absolute minimum."

When Woodring learned of Monnet's visit at a cabinet meeting on December 21, he was outraged. Henry lingered by FDR's desk after the meeting that day. Roosevelt looked tired and drawn as he listened to Henry relate what he'd offered the French: They could inspect and test the Curtis P-40 Warhawk, the Douglas bomber, and a Martin bomber, model 166. FDR had heard from the General Staff: The P-40s, General Hap Arnold and his men insisted, were the best the United States had.

They also contained secret components, not least a bombsight. But how could we let another country buy the aircraft, they argued, before we had them ourselves?

As Roosevelt told Henry he was reluctant to offer the P-40s, Henry couldn't mask his anger. "Mr. President, think about it again," he said. "If it's your theory that England and France are our first line of defense . . . let's either give them good stuff or tell them to go home, but don't give them some stuff which the minute it goes up in the air will be shot down."

Roosevelt relented: So long as the French orders did not interfere with the Army's own, the Monnet mission could proceed. Woodring, in turn, tried to get Henry to guarantee the French would buy every aircraft that they inspected—an impossible demand, Henry knew, that was merely a ploy to send the French home empty-handed. "Since I cannot undertake to guarantee the French orders," he wrote the president, "I am unable to proceed further in this matter, so long as Secretary Woodring maintains his present attitude."

Henry had forced Roosevelt's hand: Woodring retreated, even calling Henry later that day to apologize. The generals were at fault, he said. Worse, he feared the Congress would raise hell over the sale of American planes.

"All I wanted to do, Henry," Woodring said, "was simply to protect you in the matter."

"I don't want to be protected," Henry replied.

On January 20, three French experts, accompanied by a U.S. Navy officer, flew to California. At the Douglas plant in Santa Monica they were shown a newly built test aircraft. And on the morning of January 23, once the engineers had stripped the bomber of its secret devices, a Frenchman climbed aboard. In private, the secretary of the Treasury had called it "the best plane in the world," but the test flight would prove a catastrophe: The new bomber went into a spin while attempting a bank at 400 feet over the Los Angeles municipal airport. It crashed in a parking lot, nearly crushing ten people in their cars. At 200 feet, the pilot's parachute failed, and he fell to his death.

Henry heard the news and felt horror. Not only had the pilot died, but rescuers had pulled an injured passenger from the hulk before it burst into flames. The survivor was clearly a foreigner, but the Douglas Company, acting on U.S. Army orders, identified him only as "a mechanic named Smithins." Soon, the reporters learned the truth: Captain Paul Chemidlin, a French Air Force officer, had been on a secret mission, testing out "America's most modern light bomber."

Henry's worst fears had come to pass. He knew the revelation would have consequences: Congress and his rivals would demand answers, and if the truth of the French sales came out, outrage would follow. But what Henry could not foresee was how his friend the president would react.

27. "About the Future of Democracy and the World"

FALL 1937–WINTER 1940

Each fall, for as long as anyone could remember, the Deerfield Academy boys advanced down the road, enrolling at Amherst by the dozen. Bob Morgenthau had long set his heart on Amherst, the small liberal arts college thirteen miles south of Deerfield, but the move nearly did not happen. For a few weeks in the fall of 1937, he thought he would follow his brother to Princeton. In fact, in September, the newspapers announced he'd enrolled at Princeton. By then, Bob was already a freshman at Amherst.

His mother had taken him up, delivering him in the family Chrysler. They went right away to Morrow Hall, Bob's dormitory, to unload his trunk. There were no events for freshmen, no meetings for parents, and no place on campus open to eat dinner. Ellie dropped Bob off and left. He walked down Main Street, found a Greek restaurant, and sat down to eat his first dinner at Amherst by himself.

At eighteen, Bob had been away from home for four years. At Deerfield, he did not so much excel as glide. He played sports year-round—soccer had become his strong suit—and remained a prankster, a boy of privilege never in danger of becoming a hooligan. He did well in the classroom, without exerting discernible effort. He was not much good at languages and revealed little patience for literature, but history and politics held his attention. He wrote essays on the devaluation of the franc, global trade policy, Alf Landon vs. FDR, and the false dreams of fascism. "As Hitler and Mussolini have shown," he wrote in one essay, "Fascism is based on nationalism which leads to war. Hitler may have reemployed many men, but he is preparing only for war—leading Germany to a dead-end."

At Deerfield, success had come almost in spite of his best efforts to forestall it. He was Bob Morgenthau now, no longer "Bobby, the younger son of the Treasury boss." The family name was known: Bob could not escape it, nor did he try to. His father had returned to Deerfield often to give talks—"You've been selected from a specialized group," he told Bob's classmates, "be worthy of your privilege." Grandpa Morgenthau, too, did not miss the chance to appear before the students. But if the Morgenthaus were known on the small campus, they were hardly revered. The student body was overwhelmingly Republican, and Mr. Boyden, the headmaster who had ruled the school since 1902, was unmoved by celebrity, political or otherwise. Bob had stood on his own.

By senior year, he would be voted editor in chief of the yearbook, join the Cum Laude Society, and be elected class president—even though he did not run. For all the record of achievement, Bob had almost not fulfilled his ambition to go to Amherst. A successful collegiate career, Mr. Boyden liked to say, was built of a series of ascending endeavors, challenges overcome on the threshold to manhood. The foundation, though, was simple, and essential: membership in a good fraternity. At Amherst, Bob was told, only one fraternity was worth joining: Alpha Delta Phi. His father, as he always did, agreed with Mr. Boyden. There was one hurdle: The fraternity had apparently never admitted a Jew.

At Amherst, the Class of 1941 comprised 240 students—and only 5 were Jews. To Mr. Boyden, the hurdle was not insurmountable. Before classes began, he enlisted two Amherst alums, Bill Avirett, a Deerfield history teacher, and Dick Ballou, a Harvard graduate student, to plead Bob's case at the fraternity house. It fell to H. Stuart Hughes, the Alpha Delt president, and grandson of Charles Evans Hughes (now chief justice of the Supreme Court), to hold a vote.

Amherst, like Deerfield, was a Republican reserve, dating back generations. One alumnus, Charles Whitman, former Republican governor of New York and member of the Class of 1890, stood hard against young Morgenthau. The governor's son was Hughes's classmate and fraternity brother. "The old man," Hughes would recall, "used to come back to Amherst and join in drinking bouts." The stand, though, may have had as much to do with politics as religion. Avirett and Ballou vouched for the candidate, as did Mr. Boyden, a rock-ribbed conservative won over by Mrs. Roosevelt only when she persuaded FDR to appoint him to a national youth commission. Opposition ran fierce, but in the end, Bob won.

The initiation came on a Friday night, November 5, 1937. Bob Morgenthau stood in a dark suit and tie, one of thirteen initiates in the chapter's 105th delegation. Beside him stood his fellow pledges: Bob Wiggins, Ed Johansson, Royal Cornelius Van Etten, Jr. Like nearly all of his classmates, they came from well-to-do families, raised in tree-lined towns within reach of the big cities along the Eastern Seaboard. They were jocks or legacies, often both.

The Treasury secretary decided not to attend the banquet—he had no wish to rile the alumni—but Boyden's emissaries reported back to Ellie and Henry. "I watched him during the solemn ritual of initiation last night," Avirett wrote, "and felt a sense of tremendous pleasure, when at the conclusion I caught his eye and for a fleeting second saw a smile of recognition flash across his face."

The secretary had been wise not to come: The crowd was decidedly conservative. The speakers' table, Ballou quipped, "resembled a Landon campaign troupe." Yet Bob held his own among the Republicans: He "meets people very easily," wrote Ballou, and "carries himself with the air of a gentleman." Their son had mixed in easily, the alums reported, tossing jokes, and sharing in the banter. "Bob looked," Ballou added, "as though he would become the vital force in his delegation."

The Alpha Delt house, the alums had made clear to Henry and Ellie, was enemy territory, but the challenge could stand their son well. It is not a "bad education," Averitt wrote, "to be thrown with some whose prejudices are typical, however regrettable." Bob had already taken

a courageous step in joining so exclusive a group. There will undoubtedly be moments that are unpleasant and times when he may wish that his father was less famous—but he had to face that situation wherever he goes. . . . Meanwhile, he has already handled himself with a fine dignity and poise, he has already begun to win the respect and warm liking of not only other boys but older men who were watching him critically—and I believe has begun to learn some more of the inevitable lessons of leadership which will pay him handsome dividends as life goes on.

His studies, at first, did not go as well. He had never taken to books, and few courses seized his interest: In his freshman year, Bob earned B's and C's, taking English, French, history, Latin, and public speaking. In the first term of his sophomore year, he had added economics, fine arts, and political science. But he was spending more evenings at the *Student,* the college newspaper. The reporters took the work seriously: Richard Wilbur, a freshman from New Jersey with ample literary gifts, may have been sharpest among them. That fall, Bob had also helped to found the Amherst Political Union, a club that would bring speakers to campus— "a ruse," he would say later, "to become president of something." But he wanted fiery debates, and saw that he could use his parents' ties to recruit big names: Norman Thomas, the Socialist leader; Louis Bromfield, the writer; and even the Chinese ambassador.

The Alpha Delts, the Union, and sports—they would dominate his first years at college. Yet of late there had also been a shift: Like so many of his classmates, Bob now read the newspapers with purpose. After the Munich Agreement, the events unfolding across the Atlantic had invaded the campus. As the sense of foreboding grew, one professor above all others sounded the alarm: Karl Loewenstein, a political scientist who'd begun his career in Germany, taught the sociology of dictatorships and revolutions. As a Jew in Munich, he had watched Hitler's rise, fled to the United States in 1933, and three years later arrived in Amherst.

In the autumn term, Bob got to hear the professor for himself. "I learned last week that your son is one of my students in a course on Elements of Modern Politics," Loewenstein wrote in an introductory letter to the secretary of the Treasury in October 1938. Days earlier Bob had stayed after class for a long talk. "Although his political horizon is far more extended than that of most of his colleagues in my class," the professor wrote, "I hope he will get something out of my lectures." Loewenstein was clear-eyed about Germany's path. He tried to remain optimistic, if only for the students' sake, but as he watched in horror the events unfolding in Europe, as he admitted to the Treasury secretary, he was forced "to conceal some deep misgivings about the future of democracy and the world."

| | | |

That fall, Bob had moved into the Alpha Delt fraternity house. His prized trophy joined him in his room at the back: The grizzly bear from Montana, stuffed and mounted, assumed a place of honor beside the fireplace. Bob had joined nearly fifty "brothers." Few would become friends, even fewer confidants. He was already well known across campus, and well liked, but Bob also kept a guard up. There was, some would note, a certain distance. Some saw it as aloofness, others as conceit. It had already become second nature: Bob kept his own counsel. In part it was modesty, and in part self-preservation. He could not embarrass his family; he had to protect the family name. But there was another reason: a growing sense of guilt.

Henry and Ellie invariably skirted the subject in their letters and at the dinner table. During the years in Washington, though, an understanding had begun to form. It started within the family, though soon relatives and anyone who knew the Morgenthaus well could see it.

Henry III had many talents. He was a good horseman and swimmer. At Princeton, he ran cross-country, and served on the editorial boards of the *Daily Princetonian* and the literary magazine. He sang in the glee club, and composed music. He entertained, for a time, the thought of becoming an architect. But as a youth Henry III had an awkwardness that had only become more pronounced as a young man. His feet were so large, Ellie had taken him to the family doctor, who prescribed a pituitary gland extract. (The idea, he would recall, was to stimulate growth— "so my body might catch up with my feet.") In college, he was nearly six feet, just slightly shorter than his brother, but the unease remained— evolving in a sensitivity and shyness, he would say, unshared by his siblings.

At Deerfield, the boys had been a study in contrasts. Henry III, often ill, had needed, Mr. Boyden reported to his parents, "to be pressed to accomplish the best work of which he is capable." For Bob, no pursuit seemed to pose trouble. "Bob does his work easily and is an outstandingly able student," Mr. Boyden added. He had jumped into "all the activities of the school. . . . He does all this without the slightest difficulty or prodding on our part." By the time both were in college, it had become part of the family narrative: Henry III, people would say, took after his father, but it was Bob who had his mother's confidence and resolve. The boys did not feel the competition, but among the family it seemed almost natural: In a growing divide, two avenues, separate and increasingly distinct, led to the future—and only one would be favored.

If Ellie and Henry Jr. avoided the issue, Grandpa Morgenthau confronted it head-on. He nurtured the boys, as he had his son: He took them to Eagle Nest (the Adirondacks club that he'd bought with two Our Crowd friends), to Mizzentop, let them stay with him at the apartment on Fifth Avenue. Eleanor Roosevelt sensed it, too. She was fond of all the

Morgenthau children but formed the warmest bond with Henry III. She felt the need to protect him—as if she could foresee the future. Bob had overcome his illnesses, and now seemed marked by a sureness of purpose. Friends saw it in his step; they noted how the attention shifted when he entered a room. The dynastic line had become clear: The wrong boy had been cast as the designated heir. Henry would carry the burden, and Joan would fight for her own ground within the family, but Bob was the son his parents and grandfather would count on to attain great things.

| | | |

In January 1940, the whole family was in Washington, enjoying the tail end of the Christmas break, when the secretary got word that the Douglas bomber had crashed in Los Angeles. Ellie had known little of the secret French mission, but she knew her husband's rivals and enemies would call for his head. The children could not predict the fallout, but for the first time they worried about their father. They imagined, though, that the president would rush to his aid.

The first days followed the expected turns: Editorial writers demanded an explanation, Republicans and America Firsters cried foul, and the Senate launched an investigation. But the White House kept silent. At the Treasury, and in the Morgenthau home, a shocking question settled in: Could Roosevelt have decided to let his friend dangle?

On January 26, the Senate Military Affairs Committee opened the hearings behind closed doors. General Arnold was among the first to testify. Senator Bennett Clark of Missouri, son of Champ Clark, Wilson's old rival, and a leading isolationist, led the witness. How could a *Frenchman,* he wondered, end up in a secret plane?

"He was out there," the general replied, "under the direction of the Treasury Department, with a view of looking into possible purchase of airplanes by the French mission."

The press had a field day. Arnold had let loose a bombshell: Permission for the French to see the bomber "had not been obtained from any officer of the Army or from the War Department, but from the Treasury." The general conceded that all the secret components had been removed, and the Army had known of the mission, but he was sufficiently vague, allowing the senators to think the mission had been the work of the Treasury alone.

Henry immediately called Woodring. "I'm not going to have it smeared all over the front pages that I did this," he said. "I know who signed the order to go over there. We have a copy of it."

That afternoon, Henry was called to testify on the Hill. He summoned his steadiest voice, and tried to lay out the chronology of the mission. But the senators kept interrupting, demanding to know the extent of Roosevelt's role. Had FDR known the French would see the aircraft? "I thought I made it plain," replied Henry, "that we did it at the request of the President." Senator Gerald Nye, an avowed isolationist from North Dakota, took up the attack. Nye had gained fame chairing the committee that revealed the vast profits American companies had made selling arms in World War I. "The airplane deal with France . . . constitutes, in my opinion, a military alliance," he said.

Woodring himself, Henry said, had sent an order from General Arnold to the Air Command in California, authorizing the test flight. And "just so that there can be no possible misunderstanding," he added, he produced the general's order, showing it to the committee. "As I always say . . . the Treasury backyard is big enough for me," Henry said. "I am very, very careful not to go over to somebody else's territory, and when I do, I only do it on written instructions."

At the White House, the president was offering his own version of events. The cabinet found it "desirable to get French orders as soon as possible" to spur American factories into production, he told the press, as Henry testified. Why, a reporter asked, had he given the job to the Treasury? "Two very simple reasons," Roosevelt said. "First, the Treasury Department was interested in building up American industry . . . and second . . . the Procurement Division worked in close cooperation with the Army and the Navy in the procurement of many types of supplies."

Roosevelt did not wish to get into a scrap with the isolationists. He did not fear them, but Henry was the far softer target.

On the morning of January 31, the two had a rare face-off at the White House. "I want to talk to you about the French planes," Henry insisted, but Roosevelt shrugged it off: "I don't want to go into all the details." Henry pressed on: "You haven't even heard my side of the story."

"You had a terrible row with Woodring," FDR said, repeating what McIntyre had passed along back in December. Not so, Henry countered, he had merely disagreed with Woodring's deputy—"never even raised my voice." Well, FDR went on, Henry had been foolish, too, "to flash that order"—moving responsibility for procurement to the Treasury—in front of poor Woodring—"that was too much of a shock." Worse, Henry had no right to tell the senators that FDR had given him a letter.

"Mr. President, I didn't," Henry protested. "You told me that I could say that you had given me instructions, which I repeated to the Committee but I scrupulously refrained from saying I had any letter from you . . . it was Harry Woodring who let that cat out of the bag."

It was wrong just the same, Roosevelt insisted, to show the committee General Arnold's order.

"I was confronted with two alternatives," Henry said. "I could . . . say that General Arnold was a liar or I could produce the orders." He had chosen, he told FDR, the dignified response.

||||

At the height of the fight, as Father Coughlin again lambasted him on the airwaves, Henry assured the 9:30 group at the Treasury that he had done the right thing.

"On account of all the criticism," he began, "I just want to say this for the benefit of this group: that what I have done for China . . . what I have done to assist the French [to] get planes—I am delighted I was able to do it; if I had to do it, I would do it all over again. . . ." Even among his closest aides, Henry felt the need to justify himself. Aware that Mrs. Klotz was taking it all down for posterity, he added: "Everything that I did was with the knowledge and approval of the President of the United States."

The senators refused to give up. They sensed Roosevelt had made a mockery of the law, and of Congress. They demanded the "letter" Woodring had spoken of, Roosevelt's written approval of the deal. When Roosevelt said there had only been "chits," they turned the heat on Henry. Searching for a way out of the scandal, the secretary asked Gaston to draft a letter to the committee. "Since your request relates to a confidential communication for the President," wrote Gaston, "I regret that lacking specific authorization from him, I am not at liberty to comply with it." FDR liked the letter, but amended it slightly, in his own hand: "Since your request relates not to one but to many confidential communications, written and oral, between the President and Departments of the Government . . . I am not at liberty to comply with it."

FDR's edits, Henry said, made "all the difference in the world."

It soon became clear the mission would be a success. By mid-February, the French had signed deals with almost every leading U.S. manufacturer: They would buy air frames and engines, and take an option to buy five hundred fast bombers, more than double the number their own industry could produce. On March 23, Monnet returned from Paris to express his gratitude. "The whole outcome of the mission," he told Henry, "mainly due to the support that has been given here by you, has had a very great effect in France." And the French deals were only the start: A flood of foreign purchases followed. The orders, as Edward Stettinius would write, were "almost revolutionary in their effect upon our aviation industry, and laid the groundwork for the great expansion that was to come."

The scandal would subside, but the lessons remained. Henry had never wavered. He refused to have his name ruined, refused to let others speak for him. Only in private did he fume, telling Ellie he did not understand how Roosevelt could let him twist in the wind. "For a month I went through hell," Henry would say. Roosevelt had shown his worst side: He had pushed Henry to the edge of abandonment, knowing that he would return to the fold. And yet the secretary was loath to blame his patron. "I think something is happening that none of us know about," Henry told Gaston, "because I have never seen him act like this, in six years." Searching to regain his faith, he told himself the final destination would make everything all right.

The Monnet mission, though, marked a change. For months, the two men would regard each other with an uncertain distance. On Mondays, they would still lunch at the White House, but a chill had set in around the table.

28. Again, at the Brink

1939-1940

I t had become increasingly clear that FDR was uncertain about running again. Mrs. Roosevelt had no desire for him to do so. He was tired—often going to bed well after midnight and rising early. He wanted most to relax in Hyde Park and fish in Florida and, one day soon, build a cottage near his mother's house, and write.

If the president did run for a third term in 1940, Henry was sure FDR would name Harry Hopkins as his running mate. In 1936, FDR had given Mrs. Roosevelt reason to believe he would back Hopkins, and by 1938, she'd begun to drop public hints: Hopkins "has an inner conviction that his job needs to be done and that he must do it," she wrote in one of her "My Day" columns. "I think he would be that way about any job which he undertook." Then in December FDR named Hopkins the secretary of commerce, an attempt, Henry was sure, to harden the image of a softhearted social worker in advance of an upcoming run. Even in precarious health (cancer surgeons at the Mayo Clinic had removed much of his stomach in 1937), Hopkins, Henry felt, had stolen his place in the cabinet—and become the Most Trusted Friend.

Throughout the spring of 1939, Henry found himself wrestling more than ever with the president. At lunch in April, he asked Roosevelt to read his draft statement on the new tax bill—a departure from New Deal policy that cut individual and corporate taxes and pushed for private investment. Roosevelt revealed little interest: He'd be tied up until June with the historic visit of the king and queen of England. And yet, in the coming days, as Henry persisted, FDR seemed to toy with him. The president kept revising Henry's statement, bit by bit, until little of the original remained. Morgenthau took it personally: "You know," he told Missy LeHand, "the President put the roller over me. And then he saw a little bit of Morgenthau sticking out, so he ran the roller over me again."

At noon on May 18, Henry decided he could take no more. He went to see Mrs. Roosevelt. The old fears—he was being boxed out, punished unfairly—had resurfaced. As the two sat for an hour, Henry made a confession.

"Franklin," he said, had "been bullying me" for months, "brow-beating me and being thoroughly unpleasant." Mrs. Roosevelt was not surprised. FDR had "really not been feeling well," she said. And "when he is like that, he takes it out on people close to him who he knows will take it."

"I was beginning to think," Henry went on, "that the President was trying to get rid of me. And I would be tickled to death to go home."

"Of course, you would," said Mrs. Roosevelt. "I understand perfectly. You have no reason to stay." But you must not read too much into her husband's mood, she warned. Just the other day she had suggested to FDR that the Morgenthaus, including the children, go with them to San Francisco, to the World's Fair. The president was delighted, she said. "If he had anything in mind about getting rid of you," she went on, "he could have thought of half a dozen excuses to say no." And yet, when she had spoken about inviting Hopkins for supper, he gave "a number of reasons why he did not want to have him."

Henry was unconvinced. After all the "torture," Henry was sure of it: Roosevelt never wanted the tax bill. Mrs. Roosevelt urged him on: "Why don't you take in your statement," she offered, "and say to him firmly, 'Now this is your last chance to make some suggestions, because I am going up to the Hill.'"

No, Henry replied, he would just tell him he was going to the Hill with the statement as is. "And if he did not approve, he could get another secretary of the Treasury."

| | | |

Throughout the months of Henry's cold peace with FDR, he and Ellie clung to Mrs. Roosevelt. A first lady like no other, she held her own press conferences (ladies only); wrote her own daily column, "My Day" (syndicated in 135 newspapers); published a bestselling autobiography; and was now paid to give speeches. She chided her husband's rivals and, nearly as often, his defenders. Above all, thanks to her family name and the singular elasticity of her marriage, Eleanor Roosevelt had carved out a life of rare opportunity, on her own. She not only had her own circle of friends and intimates, she had a private sanctuary in New York City: a third-floor walk-up in Greenwich Village that she rented in a brownstone off Fifth Avenue.

On the second day of August, after leading the Morgenthau children—Bob, Henry III, and Joan—on a visit to the World's Fair in Queens, Eleanor Roosevelt escorted the whole family to the pier on the West Side. The Morgenthaus would sail on the *Normandie,* to spend August, and the first half of September, in northern Europe—just a family trip, the secretary assured the reporters. If there were any official meetings, he said, it would be to thank the Finns—the rare nation paying off its old war debts—and to "study Danish agriculture." Henry did, in fact, hope to see the Danish farms, but he had another reason, as Ellie and the children knew, to spend six weeks in Scandinavia: Henry wanted to get a closer view on events inside Germany.

Wherever the Morgenthaus went—from London to Copenhagen to Helsingør—the press hounded him; no one believed that Roosevelt's Treasury chief had come to Europe merely to enjoy a family vacation. In Stockholm and Helsinki, Henry did have a swirl of meetings: foreign ministers, finance chiefs, industrialists. As he moved across Scandinavia, Henry felt the tensions running high.

And then the thunderbolt struck.

On August 23, Stalin and Hitler stunned the world with their non-aggression Pact. "Molotov-Ribbentrop," as the accord became known for the foreign ministers who signed it, paved the way for Hitler's invasion of Poland and Stalin's seizure of the Baltic states. The Morgenthaus arrived in Oslo just as word of the Soviets' about-face came, and the city's main square was flooded with people. "It was as if everyone in the city had come out," recalled Joan—sixteen at the time. The Norwegians sang patriotic songs until late in the night.

By August 25, Roosevelt had cut short his summer holiday, and returned to the White House. In Oslo, with the *Normandie* remaining in port (its captain fearing German U-boats), the secretary had taken the precaution of ordering a Coast Guard cutter to stand by. On August 28, Henry canceled the rest of the family tour, and the cutter steamed into Bergen harbor to pick up the secretary and his son Bob—"the most seaworthy member of the family," his brother would write. They left the pier in darkness, and given the proximity of the German submarines, they would maintain radio silence throughout the voyage.

On September 1, the secretary's cutter was tossing about on the North Atlantic when the Nazis rolled into Poland. The family was separated and unable to communicate. "Mother was very, very nervous," Joan would remember, "but they couldn't take us along with them." Instead, Ellie, Joan, and Henry III had scrambled onto a small Norwegian liner for a rough voyage home. Two days out, their ship was stopped on the open seas, as a British cruiser, its name and numbers painted out, forced the Norwegians to verify themselves. Aboard the U.S. Coast Guard cutter, meanwhile, the secretary and his son Bob scarcely slept: The captain and crew kept the speed as high as possible, even in rough weather, fearful of the German submarines close by.

The fear was soon borne out, though Henry did not know it at the time: On September 3, a German torpedo sunk the *Athenia,* a British ship with 1,400 aboard, off the Hebrides—killing 112 passengers, including 28 Americans. Hours earlier, the secretary's cutter had docked near St. John's, Newfoundland, where his usual Coast Guard pilot, Lieutenant Dick Burke, picked him up in a seaplane and flew him to a base on the Massachusetts coast. Landing after midnight, Henry Jr. and Bob were greeted by Mrs. Klotz and Gaston. They drove to Logan Airport, where Lieutenant Burke again took the controls to fly to Washington. They landed at four in the morning on September 4, and before dawn, Henry was back at his desk.

| | | |

Europe, again, prepared for war. In London and in the Treasury, it was clear that the patchwork system, improvised and hardly seamless, that Henry had relied on to supply matériel would no longer work. Nor would it be needed. In November, once Congress amended the Neutrality Act, erasing the legal hurdles, the British and French launched a joint purchasing mission (with separate offices) in New York—run by a headstrong Scotsman, Arthur Purvis.

Henry and Purvis, to everyone's surprise but Roosevelt's, hit it off. At forty-nine, Purvis would become "Churchill's arms buyer." To the prime minister, Purvis was an ideal candidate: He knew Washington and the Americans, and he had begun his career in the United States during the last war, when he was sent to buy naval equipment. Purvis and Henry, despite the difference in their backgrounds, fell into an easy, close partnership. "He was not only the ablest British representative in Washington," Henry noted, "but one of the rarest persons I have ever known."

Tall and lean, with gray hair and bushy black brows, Purvis spoke in a deep Scotch burr and drew on a store of anecdotes, relating to Scottish triumphs over the English. "It always takes a Scotsman to pull England out of a hole," he assured Henry. And whenever a rival in London tried to undercut Purvis, Henry came to his defense. The secretary "took every opportunity to make clear to London . . . that he was the man we proposed to deal with."

Even as Woodring and Arnold resisted, FDR saw the horizon clearly. The arms purchases were not only good for the Allies, they were the catalyst for American preparedness. Henry could foresee yet another benefit: the political dividends. FDR had of late begun to tell aides he was unlikely to run for a third term. On January 24, 1940, he made it clear to Henry that he would not, "unless things get very, very much worse in Europe." Days later FDR hosted the editor of *Collier's,* introducing him as "my future boss." The two struck a memoirs deal, to begin in 1941: $75,000 a year for twenty-six articles. But with the Nazis set to attack France, the harder it became to imagine FDR leaving office on his own. By March, Henry was overjoyed: Roosevelt had come fully around to Henry's project of aiding Britain and France. "These foreign orders mean prosperity in this country," FDR told Henry, "and we can't elect a Democratic Party unless we get prosperity."

In April, the Germans launched their blitzkrieg. Denmark fell in a day, then Norway, and on May 10, tanks crossed into France. The next morning at the White House Henry cornered General George C. Marshall. How many troops, he asked, could he put into the field today? "80,000," Marshall replied. On the front page of the *Times,* the maps had grown ominous: Large dark arrows depicted the onslaught. At the Treasury, the 9:30 group had grown worried: U.S. supplies to the Europeans were flagging, and everywhere, both in the private sector and in government, there seemed hurdles to increasing the speed of delivery. In the first months of 1940, the British and French had ordered 8,000 planes and 13,000 engines—a buying spree that would bring in $84 million to build U.S. plants. And though Purvis now revealed the ceiling of London's budget to Henry—one billion dollars—the War Department refused such large buys. Woodring had not budged in his isolationism. The day after Norway and Denmark fell, Henry called up Louis Johnson, Woodring's deputy. Had he made progress? Henry asked. "No," Johnson replied, disgust in his voice. "I'm having all kinds of trouble with Woodring."

FDR hated to fire anyone, but Henry was determined to get rid of Woodring. For nearly a year, he'd urged the president to fire his secretary of war, even spending the better part of an afternoon making the case on a long drive with FDR upstate. At last, the president promised to do it that evening. The next morning, Henry asked, "Have you fired that man?" Roosevelt, looking sheepish, replied, "I was so busy and tired last night I couldn't get around to it." Exasperated, Henry joked that the government had no need for a pension system, if everyone who worked for him never had to worry about their future. Roosevelt laughed—and Woodring stayed in place.

Within days, Hitler's troops approached the English Channel, forcing the British to abandon Dunkirk. The British left the northern fields of France clogged with their abandoned tanks, trucks, artillery, and rifles. Within a month, the French resistance collapsed. Great Britain now stood alone. What was once unimaginable had become inevitable: The Germans were poised to make a final push across the Channel.

On May 15, Churchill—in his first week as prime minister—cabled Roosevelt: "The small countries are simply smashed up, one by one, like matchwood. . . . The scene has darkened swiftly," Churchill wrote in the first of nearly two thousand cables he would send to FDR during the war. He asked for help "with everything short of actually engaging armed forces." Immediate needs were "the loan of forty or fifty of your older destroyers," and "several hundred of the latest types of aircraft." Churchill spared no words. "If necessary," he added, "we shall continue the war alone, and we are not afraid of that. But I trust you realize, Mr. President, that the voice and force of the United States may count for nothing if they are withheld too long."

On June 20, FDR at last rid himself of Woodring, and replaced him with a pillar of the East Coast establishment, Henry Stimson. It was a daring move, typical of the Roosevelt style. Now seventy-three, Stimson had been Taft's secretary of war, and had served every president since McKinley. He was also, as leaders in both parties noted, a Republican. Roosevelt had long admired Stimson, and the feeling was mutual.

On the same day, Roosevelt brought in another prominent Republican, Frank Knox, as Navy secretary. The timing was dramatic: The Republicans were soon to hold their convention to pick a nominee for November. Knox, the party's vice-presidential candidate in 1936, out of loyalty to the Republicans asked for a delay until after the convention. FDR refused. Stimson, too, had a request. After Henry had warned him of the infighting at the War Department, Stimson asked to be allowed to bring in his own deputy. When Grenville Clark, FDR's old friend, who'd floated the idea of Stimson's return, offered the name of another Republican, Robert P. Patterson, Roosevelt at once agreed.

Henry did not know Stimson, but he'd heard the stories from his father. He knew, after the Triangle fire, how they had worked together. He knew, too, that Stimson had long fought the isolationist tide. He abhorred Nazism, and disdained the defeatists who proclaimed the Germans invincible. "At last," Henry wrote, "we had a Secretary of War who measured up to his job in every way."

Stimson soon discovered that Henry had usurped many of the "normal functions" of the War Department. For months, the Treasury's Procurement Division had undertaken a clandestine campaign to deliver airplanes to Europe. The idea originated with Roosevelt: If the Neutrality Act forbade direct shipments to a combatant, why not send the aircraft by way of Canada? Henry arranged to have the planes flown to Plattsburgh, New York, fifty miles south of Canada. From there they were transferred to tractor-trailers and driven across the border. The scheme was repeated elsewhere: Lockheed bought several acres along the northern edge of North Dakota, quietly built a grass airstrip, and began to fly in the planes. Horses then towed them across the frozen prairie into Canada.

Roosevelt knew the urgency. On May 16, he had gone to Congress to demand "stupendous appropriations," as it seemed to Patterson, the new assistant secretary of war. FDR set a target of 50,000 airplanes to roll out each year, far beyond current capacity. After Dunkirk, the War Department found a loophole: "Surplus" war supplies could be sold to the British. Within forty-eight hours, the Army had gathered 500,000 rifles, 900 field guns, 130 million rounds of small-arms ammunition, and another 100 million rounds for the field guns. Shipments sailed within a week. Roosevelt, though, knew the British could not afford the pace of its purchases, and Washington did not want Jamaica, Trinidad, or British Guiana as payment. Imperial wealth, Henry kept saying, was irrelevant. To buy guns, ships, and planes, the British needed dollars, gold, convertible securities. The orders, though, were draining the British Treasury.

To give any loans, FDR knew he would be forced to seek the blessing of a still largely isolationist Congress.

IIII

Roosevelt was soon aided by the British themselves. On November 5, FDR, with Henry Wallace as his running mate, won an unprecedented third term, defeating Wendell Willkie, but with a far lower popular vote than he'd trumped Landon with in 1936. To Roosevelt, it scarcely mattered: He'd gained almost 5 million more votes than in 1932. Yet FDR would have little time to rest. Two weeks later, Lord Lothian, the British ambassador, arrived back in the United States. At La Guardia Field, he emerged from a Pan American Clipper to greet a swarm of reporters— and drop a bombshell: England was in desperate need of defense supplies—and the money to pay for them.

Two hundred lives are lost daily to the bombs, Lothian said. The next year would be long and hard. "England will be grateful for any help," he added. "England needs planes, munitions, ships, and perhaps a little financial help." As he spoke, cameras flashed and applause swept through the crowd. Surprised, he looked up and smiled.

Lothian spoke without authorization, as he confided to Henry days later. The secretary chided him that he had done the British no favors. Not only had he played into Nazi hands—"The Cry for Help of a Beggar," a Berlin headline proclaimed—he had made the president's job of rallying Congress nearly impossible.

FDR had also heard Lothian, but was eager to relax after his victory. As he left Washington for a Caribbean cruise on the *Tuscaloosa,* his first holiday since the campaign, he promised Henry he would mull over the British problem. FDR was at sea five days later, taking in the sun, when a letter arrived by seaplane from Churchill. The prime minister's plea was eloquent, long (more than four thousand words), and dire.

"The moment approaches when we shall no longer be able to pay cash for shipping and other supplies," he wrote. "While we will do our utmost and shirk from no proper sacrifice to make payments across the exchange, I believe that you will agree that it would be wrong in principle and mutually disadvantageous in effect, if . . . after victory was won with our blood, civilization saved and time gained for the United States to be fully armed against all eventualities, we should stand stripped to the bone." Churchill would later call the letter "one of the most important I ever wrote." Hopkins would recall how FDR had sat in a deck chair, reading and rereading the letter, turning the pages in his lap for hours. And how, for two days after, the president brooded in silence, weighing something in his mind.

29. "Not Far from Armageddon"

1940–1941

On December 17, Henry sat across from the president at lunch in the White House, and found him "in a very good humor, very quiet and self-possessed, and very proud of the fact that he hadn't looked at a single report that he had taken with him from Washington." In FDR's absence, Henry had spoken to Purvis of "a gift to England." At a press conference, he'd trespassed further: "I don't know any way of giving them financial assistance without formal approval of Congress." Roosevelt, Henry knew, had been told of his comments, and been irked by the boldness. But as they sat across from each other at the president's desk, Henry could sense something of greater concern weighing on FDR.

"I have been thinking very hard on this trip about what we should do for England," Roosevelt said. "And it seems to me the thing to do is to get away from the dollar sign."

FDR began to unfold for Henry the idea that had been forming in his mind. "We should build up our own production," he said, "and then say to England: 'We will give you the guns and the ships that you need, provided that when the war is over you will return to us in kind the guns and the ships that we have loaned to you.'"

What did Henry make of the idea?

"I think," the secretary replied, "it is the best idea yet. . . . If I followed my own heart, I would say, let's give it to them; but I think it would be much better for you to be in the position that you are insisting before Congress and the people of the United States to get ship for ship when the war is over."

That afternoon in the Oval Office, Roosevelt unveiled the plan. "Suppose my neighbor's house catches fire," he explained to the reporters, "and I have a length of garden hose four or five hundred feet away. If he can take my garden hose and connect it up with his hydrant, I may help him put out the fire.

"Now, what am I to do? I don't say to him before that operation, 'Neighbor! My garden hose cost me fifteen dollars; you have to pay me fifteen dollars for it.' No! What is the transaction that goes on? I don't want my fifteen dollars—I want my garden hose back after the fire is over."

The idea, Roosevelt went on, was to get rid of the "silly, foolish, old dollar sign." He could not yet offer the details, but the deal would hinge on "a gentleman's obligation to repay in kind." He was speaking selfishly, he assured the reporters, "from the American point of view— nothing else." But Roosevelt knew he had found a way out. Whatever was "loaned" might well never come home, yet the administration could skirt the politically untenable hurdles: There would be no need to repeal the Neutrality Act, or for any statement of a formal "gift" to the British. Henry was elated. It did not have a name yet, but the proposal was pure Roosevelt: a solution, equal parts preposterous and self-evident, to a problem that had weighed so heavily for so long.

"We made sure at that moment," Henry would reflect years later, "that we were going to win the war."

| | | |

In a rural corner of western Massachusetts, on the thousand-acre campus of Amherst, Bob Morgenthau had taken to living between two horizons. College life was filled with fraternity parties, sports, and, for at least a few evenings a week, books. Yet even at Amherst, the turmoil roiling Europe was inescapable. By his junior year, Bob had made a private vow: He would do all he could to do his share.

Hitler's rise, though, did not preclude dating. There'd been several girls in the city, nearly all from the narrow circles of Our Crowd. One from his old school, daughter of a Rothschild partner, and an associate of his grandfather's, was particularly keen. Delia Heming was one of his sister Joan's best friends. She had gone on to Smith, and wrote letters almost weekly. But it was another "Smith girl," Bob reluctantly told his brother, who had taken her place.

Martha Pattridge stood apart. They had met by chance. Martha was in her third year at the women's college, an outgoing, athletic girl from Minnesota. She had an open face, widespread blue eyes, and light-brown hair that curled when cut short. At Smith, anyone who knew her—and just about everyone did—liked her. She was "sporty," they would say. Golf and tennis were favorites, but Martha could play almost any game well. To Bob, she seemed the ideal girl-next-door, open and warm unlike girls he'd known in New York. But she was quick, too, and decisive, and as her closest girlfriends knew, she could deploy a wickedly droll sense of humor. She did not reveal it often, but Martha seemed driven by a "granite determination," a friend would say, a legacy of her Puritan roots.

Her parents were New Englanders transplanted to Minnesota. Both were Vermonters. Her father—a no-nonsense Presbyterian, principled Republican—traced his roots in the state back five generations. Pat Pattridge had studied at the University of Vermont and followed his father into dairy farming, but as the French Canadians flooded the state, he could not compete. He had gone to Minneapolis, found work—starting as a cashier for a grains trade paper—and waited five years before coming home to marry his sweetheart, Hazel Gates.

They'd built a home outside Minneapolis, in Wayzata, a quiet town on the northern edge of Lake Minnetonka. The house was big enough, but not too big, especially amid their wealthy neighbors. (The Pillsburys lived close by.) Martha had no sisters, only an older brother, Jim. They attended preparatory schools, but local ones, not eastern boarding schools. For years, Martha's father had run the *Northwest Miller,* and although the publication had once brought a good profit, the milling business had long since moved south to Kansas City. Still, Pat and Hazel Pattridge were not ones to complain. Neither were their children. It had been an upbringing with few cares, whose happiest hours were spent out of doors.

Martha was uncertain about the Morgenthau boy. Interested, yes, of course, she would say years later, but in no rush to commit to anything serious. They'd been introduced by one of Bob's fraternity brothers, a Minnesotan a year ahead of her, who'd driven her down to Amherst. They had enjoyed a picnic all together, and a single date followed before summer came.

In June 1940, at the end of his junior year, Bob had moved in with Sissie and Irving Lehman, Bob's great-uncle. Irving was the chief judge of the Court of Appeals of New York and the older brother of Governor

Herbert Lehman. (The judge had followed the Our Crowd model. "Keeping it in the family," he had married Sissie Straus, sole daughter of Nathan Straus, the Macy's heir.) Bob would spend the summer at the Lehmans' leafy estate in Port Chester, just north of the city, "reading law," as they called it, gaining a sense of the legal profession. He would sit in his great-uncle's library, studying briefs in cases pending before the court. In part, he'd agreed to the arrangement out of interest, but in greater measure, he acquiesced to the wishes of his mother. The Lehmans had no children. At Christmas and Easter, they would join in the Morgenthau gatherings. In summer, they'd invite Henry and Ellie's children to their house on the Cape. Bob, though, was their favorite; "Uncle Irving and Aunt Sissie" treated him nearly like an adopted son.

By summer, Bob and Martha were corresponding. Sissie saw the mail coming in, and offered a warning. "I hope you're not getting serious about a girl," she told Bob. "It would be a big mistake at your age." Martha wrote several times a week—at times, twice in a day. Bob listened to his great-aunt and begged her not to mention the letters to his parents, but he also made sure to answer each one.

One morning in early July, Bob was driving the Buick into the city, on his way to the dentist. He had made it onto the West Side Highway when he heard an announcement on the radio that made him pull over. On a news station, Charles Edison, the Navy secretary, and son of the inventor, announced a new Navy Reserve officer-training program—"the V-7," they called it—that would lower the standard age requirement, and accept college juniors.

For months, Bob had given much thought to enlisting, and had even tried the Army. He wanted to become a reserve officer, to be ready for the war. He'd first tried to attend the Army Civilian Military Training Camp at Plattsburgh, upstate, but was rejected because he didn't have a college degree. He then sought to become a reserve officer in the Canadian army, but they were only accepting college graduates for officer training.

Bob drove at once to the Naval Militia dock at 135th Street—two exits away. The USS *Illinois,* a decommissioned hulk, sat moored on the Hudson. The V-7 program, the officials said, was designed for men "just like you"—with at least three years of college. He filled out the form, but needed to take it home to the farm. Not yet twenty-one, Bob would have to get his parents' consent. His father was all for it, but his mother hesitated. There was also the hearing test: A botched surgery for a mastoid infection he'd had as a teen had left permanent damage. All but deaf in his right ear, Bob had to cheat. In line for the checkup, he asked the guys coming out what the doctor had asked—and repeated the same answers.

Consent in hand, Bob joined the V-7's first class, 500 "college-grade" enlistees. By July 20, 1940, as newsmen and photographers recorded the leave-taking, he boarded the USS *Wyoming* for the first part of the training, a thirty-day shakedown cruise along the Eastern Seaboard to the Caribbean. After the graduation, if all went well, Bob would undergo a ninety-day program at a midshipmen's training school, emerging as the lowest rank of naval officer: ensign. Given the miraculous pace, the V-7 graduates would be dubbed "90-day wonders."

When his ship reached Virginia Beach, Bob wrote home. "We get to Quantanigo by July 28," he told his parents. "Quantanigo" was Guantanamo Bay, home to a U.S. Naval base since the Spanish-American War. On July 31, the *Wyoming* was moored in the middle of the bay. The V-7 boys tried to look busy: They polished and repolished the rails while the crew ran the ship. That morning Bob boarded the mail boat, and eased out into the bay under a cloudless sky. One of his shipmates had come up with a crazy idea, but Bob leapt at the chance: He wanted to say he had stepped foot on Cuban soil. It was his twenty-first birthday.

| | | |

Eleanor Roosevelt had become a most unorthodox first lady, yet she remained a child of the aristocracy—and to her way of thinking, a young woman's "debut" was an important landmark. If Eleanor loved anything more than a party, as her friend Ellie knew, it was a chance to cast aside fusty traditions. As such, in the fall of 1940 when she and Ellie discussed Joan Morgenthau's impending coming-out, Ellie was only slightly taken aback when Mrs. Roosevelt suggested, Why not have the party at the White House?

"It has been decided this year not to hold the diplomatic reception," the first lady warned the lady reporters in November. The war in Europe, she allowed, could make a social gathering of the diplomatic corps an awkward affair. Instead, she proposed an alternative: "I'm going to attend a young people's dance in honor of Joan Morgenthau—her debut." It would be a small party, "sort of a coming-out."

It was not the first time Eleanor Roosevelt had flouted convention out of respect for her friends, the Morgenthaus. In 1937, she had quit the Colony Club, a social group in New York that she had helped to found.

Neither she nor Ellie publicly revealed the reason; neither desired a scandal. But Eleanor had proposed Ellie for membership, and the club had blackballed her Jewish friend. The White House dance, too, would break tradition. In 1902, T.R.'s daughter, "Princess" Alice, had come out at the White House, and in 1938, Eleanor's own niece and namesake had followed. But a party for Joan Morgenthau would mark the first time a girl unrelated to the presidential family had enjoyed the privilege.

All the Morgenthaus were thrilled, except the guest of honor. "I dreaded the idea," Joan would say later. "I thought: Could there be a greater horror?"

| | | |

The festivities began at eight o'clock in the evening on the day after Christmas, as the president and Mrs. Roosevelt hosted a small dinner upstairs at the White House. Henry and Ellie, Bob and Joan sat amid seven boys and five girls, friends from Amherst, Deerfield, Madeira, and the Upper West Side of Manhattan. Stuart Hughes, Bob's college friend, sat beside the president. (His grandfather, the chief justice, would soon swear in FDR for a third term.) Franklin Jr. flirted gently with Delia Heming, while Henry Morgenthau and Harry Hopkins, the only other cabinet member present, traded turns teasing the young people. Hopkins seemed renewed. In May, he had looked so ill at a White House dinner, FDR had asked him to stay overnight. Hopkins had never left; he now lived down the hall, in the room that had once been Lincoln's study.

Ellie had warned Bob and Henry III to prepare for a busy social season. She sent long lists detailing the debutantes' parties, hostesses, and dress codes. Over the two-week Christmas break, there would be nine dinners, dances, and teas, but the main event would be Joan's fete at the White House. For weeks, Ellie and the first lady had worked on the battle plan. The East Room must be packed: Five hundred were invited. "Boys should outnumber girls," Mrs. Roosevelt instructed, "3 to 1." There were to be no wallflowers, and above all, Joan must be partnered, and kept dancing throughout the night.

As the Morgenthaus dined upstairs at the White House, the remaining hundreds on the guest list gathered across Washington in a daisy chain of dinners. Rarely had the elite of Washington and New York's Our Crowd commingled so intimately: The Nathan Strauses hosted one party, the Robert Guggenheims presided at another, while FDR's cousin, Laura Delano Houghteling, hosted a third. At the pre-party dinners—several others were scattered among the mansions of Georgetown—few made mention of the rarity of the occasion. Fewer still spoke of the strangeness of it all: a Jewish girl, a studious collegian who revealed little interest in such affairs—Joan's brothers would call her "a rebel"—feted at the White House, by America's reigning Knickerbocker dynasty.

After dinner, the president insisted on greeting the first rush of guests. As the White House driveway grew clogged with roadsters and limousines, FDR had himself wheeled into the foyer while Joan stood outside beside Mrs. Roosevelt. She wore a gown of white tulle, embroidered with silver sequins. (Joan had refused to go to New York to shop for a gown, so Ellie and her brother Henry had brought down five to try on.) On her wrist was a bracelet of pearls, and around her neck cut crystals and a pearl necklace.

At ten o'clock, the dancing began. As Sidney's Orchestra, the favorite in Washington's ballrooms, played, the floor filled with long tulle skirts. The colors, Mrs. Roosevelt would write, had turned the East Room into "a summer flower garden." No one enjoyed the party more than Mrs. Roosevelt; she danced with Franklin Jr. and others for much of the evening. Sidney's musicians, she would say, were "particularly kind to me," playing many waltzes. The young people also danced the conga—a first for Mrs. Roosevelt. The party, *Time* would report, was "informal but not rowdy." Between dances, the guests sat on the floor, sipped pink lemonade, ice water, and "a mild sauterne punch that would not have harmed a milk barfly."

When the president was wheeled into the ballroom, everyone rose in respect. When he came face to face with Joan, he threw his arms around her, kissed her and said, "I am sorry I cannot have the first dance with you." Those close enough to hear the president were in tears. He stayed for nearly two hours, watching the dancing, before heading upstairs. "I was sorry," the first lady would write in her "My Day" column, "he could not have stayed away from work longer." FDR retired to his study. As the orchestra played below, he worked on a draft of a fireside chat. At midnight, supper was served.

The dancing resumed, but by three in the morning, Franklin Jr. told Henry III and Bob the music was disturbing his father. Bob ordered the band to play "Goodnight Ladies," but as Mrs. Roosevelt told the country the next day, "No one paid any attention, and finally Sidney and his orchestra played the 'Star-Spangled Banner.'" Everyone had to stop dancing and join in the singing. "That ended what, for me, was a delightful evening," the first lady told her readers.

Henry and Ellie read the society pages with relish. Each year, Eugene Meyer, owner of *The Washington Post*, held a party on the twenty-sixth—Henry was delighted to see it bumped from the center of attention. Joan's party, the *Washington Times-Herald* reported, had given "the final burnish to one of the brightest holiday seasons that has ever dazzled the Capital's younger set." It would also be, as many had come to suspect, one of the last grand parties at the White House for years to come.

|| ||

The president had worked hard on his radio address, trying to recapture the magical force of his first fireside chats of eight years earlier. Three days after Joan's party, FDR spoke to the American people. As he had in 1933, when he spoke of the banking crisis, Roosevelt tried to explain to "my friends" what the growing crisis in Europe meant to "their daily lives." "If Great Britain goes down," he said, "the Axis powers will control the continents of Europe, Asia, Africa, Australia, and the high seas. . . . It is no exaggeration to say that all of us, in all the Americas, would be living at the point of a gun."

At noon the next day, Henry and Arthur Purvis arrived at the White House. "FDR was at his best," Henry would recall, "charming, witty, his eyes sparkling and his face beaming." Purvis took his time arriving at the subject, but in a quiet voice he at last came to it: The British would ask for ships and arms that could cost more than $15 billion. The figure was double his highest expectations, but Roosevelt did not blink. If that were the price of saving civilization, so be it. Turning to Henry, he gave the job of drafting a bill to the Treasury.

"Lend-Lease," they were calling it now in the Treasury, would be no easy sell. Henry knew the America Firsters on the Hill would not concede easily, but first he had to win over his fellow cabinet members. Within a week, on the evening of January 7, he was back in the Oval Study. Henry put the bill—initialed by Hull, Stimson, Knox, and Bill Knudsen, the General Motors chief recruited to head the production of war matériel—on the president's desk. At 5:15 P.M., Roosevelt picked up a pen and beneath the other initials wrote "O.K., F.D.R."

Three days later, as the hearings opened, and Senator Nye and his isolationist cohorts on the Foreign Relations Committee again raised resistance, FDR attempted to stop them short. The president pulled yet another stunt: Having learned that Wendell Willkie, the Republican he had trounced in 1940, was heading for London, he asked Willkie to help sell the new program. Roosevelt knew that like Stimson and Knudsen, Willkie—a lapsed Democrat and an internationalist—stood firmly against fascism. FDR could forgive the campaign cries—Willkie had called him a "warmonger" with a "dictatorial complex"—if his former opponent could support aid to Britain. On January 12, Willkie accepted. "Appeasers, isolationists, and lip-service friends of Britain," he said, would only sabotage the British defense. Willkie would serve as FDR's envoy, touring the ruins of London, Coventry, and Birmingham, descending into the Underground and playing darts in the pubs. He would win the respect of Churchill, demonstrate bipartisan American support to the British, and help to win the publicity battle at home.

But Roosevelt had left it to his Treasury secretary to sell Lend-Lease on the Hill. Before leaving for a weekend at Hyde Park, FDR had reassured Henry that he would survive even Senator Nye's grilling. At the Treasury, though, on the eve of Henry's testimony before Congress, a state of panic set in.

After dinner on the evening of January 13, as word spread of Willkie's support, Henry hosted half a dozen of his top aides at his home for an urgent strategy session. For hours, the men debated how best to shield their boss before the Senate. Ellie joined the circle in the living room. Coffee was served, then drinks. As the discussion went on—the men did not depart until after ten P.M.—Henry worried about revealing the extent of Britain's defense needs and the dire state of London's finances on the Hill. He demanded clarifications, confirmations of facts, dates, and figures. His nerves were running high: "I want to memorize these things," he declared.

Ellie listened as the secretary's aides arrived at a decision for him: Henry must confine himself to facts, and only those concerning the bill's "financial aspects." Having settled on a consensus, the men seemed to relax. Yet before they could adjourn, Mrs. Morgenthau interrupted.

The advice was misguided, Ellie said. She seconded her husband's insistence—"the opposition," she said, "are going to try to embarrass him." For years, Henry's aides had suspected Mrs. Morgenthau's influence. Her closeness to the first lady, it was said, was the crutch the boss could rely on. They had seen glimpses, too, of her intelligence, but rarely had they witnessed her forcefulness firsthand. The secretary must make the politicians' job easier, Ellie said. The isolationists and the waverers would have to sell such an extraordinary bill at home; Henry's job was to render it plain and simple. Don't give the senators, she said, "an awfully sort of jumbled thing which they can't piece together." She added a jibe: "You assume they will only ask him questions that are purely financial?" Then she added, turning to her husband: "I think you ought to have a very strong first statement . . . something in your own language."

The next morning, his wife handed him a single typewritten page—notes on his best pitch to the Congress. Henry had to be more than a mere "statistician and dispenser of figures, with no opinions." And he had to avoid sounding a "note of despair like [Ambassador] Kennedy." "As our fiscal advisor," Ellie argued, "I think you must evaluate the figures, not on behalf of what they will do for the British economy, but for American democracy." The secretary's testimony had to get across one theme above all others: "We are buying time to rearm." The bill might be unprecedented, and complex, but the idea was simple, Ellie wrote: "Keep England Going, in Order to Let Us Prepare."

It was advice that the Treasury secretary took to heart, and he followed it, as best he could, first before the House committee, then the Senate. He endured Senator Nye's cross-examination, his brow sweating and voice rising, and then hit back. "Lacking a formula by which Great Britain can buy supplies here," he told Nye, "I think Britain will just have to stop fighting—that's all." Lend-Lease, Henry insisted, would not only ensure British orders for American planes, it might save Britain itself.

| | | |

Since childhood, the Morgenthau boys had scarcely been made to feel their Judaism. They had been schooled in a world of morning chapel, choir, and Christmas, and yet at Princeton, Henry III suffered. In his first week on campus, he had returned to his room one day to find a note under the door. "Despite your ham-eating propensity," it read, "you have something you cannot conceal." At Amherst, Bob felt no such anti-Semitism. He'd never attempted to hide that he was Jewish, neither did he give it much thought. At least not outwardly.

From the first, Bob had fit in almost too well at Amherst. He never felt any dislocation or loneliness. He lettered in soccer. (At right halfback, he was better, he would say, "at getting up and down the field than scoring goals.") And at the *Student*, he rose to editor in chief. (For his deputy, he chose Richard Wilbur, the sophomore with a literary bent.) Still, by senior year, a new consciousness of his Jewishness took hold: It was not a matter of spirituality or religious ritual, but an increasing sense of obligation. The war overseas had consumed him. Bob had always read the newspapers closely, but now he began to ask his father for help: He hoped someone at Treasury could look into assisting Professor Loewenstein (whose brother was interned in France); he requested any government reports on the rising numbers of Jewish refugees fleeing Hitler; and in late 1940, he invited Mrs. Roosevelt to speak on campus.

Eleanor Roosevelt and Ellie drove north in the first week of February, up the snowy Merritt Parkway. On campus, the trees were bare, and the sidewalks icy. Bob, as president of the Political Union, introduced the first lady to an overflowing hall. Mrs. Roosevelt had prepared for the event with the seriousness of an appearance before a gathering of hostile Republicans upstate. She wore a cream dress that draped to the toe, and a double string of pearls wrapped tight. Her theme was "The Future of American Youth," but she spoke only of Europe, and if America would go to war. "If we were under Hitler," Mrs. Roosevelt said, "all we would have to say is 'I obey.' . . . In a democracy, however, responsibility is the first virtue and self-discipline is vitally important." Some things, she added, were more important than peace. Mrs. Roosevelt chose her words with care, but left little doubt. "We gave the peace away," she said, "because we wouldn't take responsibility for anyone other than ourselves."

Eleanor Roosevelt loved listening to the students, she told Ellie afterwards. They gave her hope. "The times are such that youth today is taking life very seriously," she wrote in "My Day" of the visit to Bob and his classmates. "I think this younger generation is going to face the realities of the world situation and the changes that have come about here and abroad with a more realistic understanding than ever before."

| | | |

Bob Morgenthau, too, had gained new focus. Throughout the winter he had been at work on a long term paper, researching what the papers now called "the refugee problem." Hoping to write "an intelligent discussion of solutions," he'd gathered the government reports on the situation in Germany, Austria, and Czechoslovakia that his father had sent. Bob quoted a broadcast by Sir Herbert Emerson, the League of Nations commissioner on refugees: More than 350,000 Jews had fled Germany and

Austria. He read, as well, a confidential report of the Intergovernmental Committee on Refugees that depicted a landscape far grimmer than the public reports. The State Department, displeased with its findings, had fired its author, but a lawyer in the Interior Department—at the Treasury secretary's urging—had shared it with Bob. Still more official documents— the sketch of a plan to resettle European Jews in Alaska, another to send them to the Dominican Republic—found their way from Washington to the Alpha Delt house in Amherst, Massachusetts. And yet, by the time he sat down to write, Bob saw few solutions.

He homed in on the end of 1938—"For it was in that year that the last chance for international action was lost." He wrote of the Nuremberg Laws (decreeing "a Jew is a person with two Jewish grandparents re- gardless of the religion professed"), the aftermath of Munich ("the per- secution of minorities grew acute in a steadily widening circle"), and the murder in November 1938 of Ernst vom Rath, the twenty-nine-year-old secretary of the German Legation in Paris ("the signal for anti-Jewish outbreaks throughout Germany"). By the spring of his last year in col- lege, Bob's vision of the horizon was crystal clear. He feared for the Jews under German domination; he feared for America's willingness to defend them; and he feared for the future of his own generation.

In a valedictory letter in the Amherst yearbook (he was the editor), Bob wrote: "The class of 1941 has the bittersweet satisfaction of know- ing it goes out with an epic."

Much in recent months has been said about the American way of life. That American traditions and privileges in this small New England college, in the outcropping of a sturdy devotion to democratic insti- tutions, we have had a chance to experience all these. We have been among the few who, during the past year, have had the opportunity to learn freely, in a free country at peace. It has perhaps been im- pressed on us that we, above others, should have an abiding faith in democracy, and we should always remember Amherst as more than a place filled with the pungent memories of youth. We should re- member Amherst as the place where we learned to appreciate the values inherent in Western civilization. As the last year draws to a close, the Greeks and British have fallen at Thermopylae, America stands not far from Armageddon, and the class of 1941 prepares to do battle for the Lord.

Bob wasted little time: Hours after graduation, he drove down to New York, and the next day, he reported aboard the USS *Prairie State* to continue his accelerated naval training. He and his Amherst friend Brooks Beck joined five hundred enlistees, each hopeful for an "emergency" commission as a Naval Reserve ensign. (Among them: Sargent Shriver, who had graduated from Yale three years earlier.) The "90-day wonders" wore sailor suits: white blouses, white trousers, and round midshipman's caps. Space was limited; they slept in three- and four-tier bunks. Instruction moved at a brisk pace: The V-7 candidates learned navigation, seamanship, and communications—plowing nearly halfway through the Navy coursework that required four years' study at Annapolis. Wednesday afternoons were "Ropeyarn Sundays," their only hours off. And by fall, it was over.

On the morning of September 16, 429 young men—their numbers winnowed—graduated aboard the ship moored at the 136th Street Pier. Bob Morgenthau received his commission, flanked by his father and grandfather. The graduates wore white, ensign's gold-striped shoulder boards proudly affixed, as they listened to the assistant secretary congratulate them with a warning: "Events of the last few days strongly indicate that war may be forced upon us." The entire family would drive over to the Biltmore Hotel for a supper dance at its rooftop restaurant. Within days, though, the boys split up: Some sailed for England, to study the new navigational technology—a device called "radar"—and some went to Noroton, to the Navy radio school on the Connecticut River. Bob was among them. He and four others rented a house in Stamford owned by a cousin. There would be drinking bouts, poker, and talk of girls, but they would also learn the equipment and rules of the CAC—the communications and command center on a Navy destroyer.

Throughout the fall, Martha wrote often. She had returned to Minneapolis, moving in with her parents in a new apartment on Lake Harriet. For weeks, she did not hear from Bob, and when she did, she often teased him. "I am very impressed with you writing two letters in two days," she wrote. "It's fun hearing what the Navy does to you day by day." She told of her father, his admonishments to clean up her room, and her relief when the family went out for long walks around the lake. There were evenings at the symphony, cocktail parties, sporting games, and her new work, a job at the Junior League, but it all left her bored. In her letters, Martha allowed her hidden sardonic self to come through. Of a gala she wrote: "It's pretty much one of those bow and speak to people you know affairs." Of her work downtown: "My job of this week consists of answering a telephone in our office from 9 to 5, taking reservations, etc. It's sort of fun, because you can say, 'Hello, Junior League Hotel, Day,' in lots of different ways."

Throughout it all, she missed Bob. She knew that the future, once far off, would soon draw near. "Sometimes," she wrote, "I feel silly rattling on about inconsequential things when life for you seems to be on the serious side, but every time I get a gloomy or solemn thought, I can hear you calling it 'cheap stuff' and then feel better."

By October, Bob had told her the next step: The Navy had asked all "90-day wonders" to fill out a form, giving their top three choices of vessels. Bob had written "Destroyer," "Light Cruiser," "Heavy Cruiser."

"I wish you good luck in your orders," Martha wrote. "If one wishes one good luck in one's orders. Can't quite say I hope you get a Destroyer, because it sounds awful, but you seemed to want one. Let me know when you hear."

Officers could also request a fleet: the Pacific or Atlantic. Next to each of his choices, Bob asked for the same destination: EAST, EAST, EAST. He was intent, even before college, on fighting only one enemy: "Thought about it every day," he would tell an interviewer years later. "I wanted to kill Nazis."

| | | |

On Sunday afternoon, December 7, at 1:40 P.M., FDR sat at his desk wearing an old sweater belonging to one of his sons. He and Harry Hopkins had just finished lunch in his study. Roosevelt had deliberately kept his schedule light: He'd fallen behind on his stamp collection, a favorite hobby, and he hoped to catch up. The telephone rang, and the White House operator said apologetically that Frank Knox, secretary of the Navy, insisted on being put through. A report had come from Honolulu. Hopkins watched as Roosevelt listened to the receiver for a moment. And he sat dumbfounded as the president suddenly said, "No!"

The Morgenthaus, Henry and Ellie, Joan and Henry III, were in Manhattan for the weekend. On the night before, the secretary had presided at a special "Treasury Hour" radio broadcast: the NBC Symphony Orchestra, led by Arturo Toscanini, called out of retirement for the occasion. Henry III flew in from Cleveland (where his father had won him a job at the federal housing authority), and Grandpa Morgenthau had joined them, alongside Uncle Herbert and Aunt Edith, the governor and his wife.

Bob could not make it. He had just reported aboard the USS *Warrington,* a destroyer docked at the Charlestown Navy Yard in Boston. Three days earlier, though, he'd been in Washington, and his father had given him a surprise—bringing him in to see the president. Henry and FDR now spoke often of their "boys"—Bob and Franklin Jr.—who'd both chosen the Navy. Franklin Jr., five years older, was already at sea. "Is it not fine?" FDR had told Henry, Bob got his wish? Perhaps, he'd added, Bob and Franklin Jr. might end up in the same division? Roosevelt, Henry would write in his diary, had brightened at the sight of Bob— "He really seemed more pleased to see him than I have seen the President pleased over anybody in a long time."

By Sunday afternoon, Henry and Ellie, Joan and Henry III were just leaving Voisin's, the French restaurant on Park Avenue. The secretary was due to fly to Arizona on a holiday at a ranch near the Mexican border, before Christmas. Joan had knocked his glasses off, and broke them—he was furious. It was Charles Frazer, the secretary's chauffeur listening to the radio in the car outside, who'd heard the staggering news first. Unnerved, Charles started to drive off, leaving everyone on the sidewalk. "Daddy," Henry III would write, when he finally found time to sit down and record the events of the day, "was in a 'tizzy.' "

In Boston, meanwhile, standing on the deck of the *Warrington,* Bob Morgenthau heard it on the loudspeakers. "Pearl Harbor has been bombed by the Japanese," came the voice. "This is not a drill." Everything came to a halt: Officers and ensigns stood still. "Repeat: This is not a drill. Pearl Harbor has been bombed by the Japanese."

||||

FDR had spent eighteen minutes—Harry Hopkins would count them— doing "nothing whatsoever." He seemed to be frozen. For weeks, the president had read a succession of military reports on Japanese movements: They appeared to signal an offensive in the Pacific, but none of the Navy men could say where. Since the spring, the Navy had joined the Treasury in calling for measures to cut off all supplies to the Japanese. "The Navy confirms our opinion," an aide had written Henry, "that Japan is receiving all the aviation gasoline she wants from the U.S." For weeks, Roosevelt had also pushed for negotiations with the Japanese.

Days earlier, he had sent Hull and his deputy Welles a directive: "I should like to know the intention of the Japanese government." On November 17, Hull had consulted the top two Japanese envoys in Washington and escorted them to a meeting with FDR, but Tokyo's plans remained a secret.

On that Sunday, after hearing the news from Honolulu, the president at last acted. At 2:05 P.M., as Hopkins watched stunned, Roosevelt finally put in a call to Hull at State.

The Morgenthaus returned to the hotel to find a call from the White House waiting. The president came on the line at once, and in a calm voice told Henry that the cabinet would convene at 8:30 that evening. His Coast Guard plane was standing by, Henry said. He would come straightaway.

In the car on the way to the airfield, Henry, Ellie, and their son heard that the president was expected to see the congressional leaders after the cabinet meeting. They all knew what would come next: In the morning, FDR would seek a declaration of war. As the secretary boarded the plane, Ellie and Henry III piled into the remaining seats of a commercial flight. In Washington, Ellie and her son drove straight to the Treasury.

The inner circle had taken up their chairs in the secretary's office. Emergency orders, long since studied and prepared, were discussed and signed without delay. Henry summoned the heads of the Secret Service and the Coast Guard. He called the secretary of state and the attorney general. He instructed his staff to safeguard the exchanges and the markets. That night the chairman of the Federal Reserve in New York slept on a couch in his office.

Henry called Mike Reilly, head of the Secret Service men at the White House. Henry and Reilly had developed something of a feud. For six years, Reilly had been at Roosevelt's side, but the secretary (who was his boss) had heard repeated tales of Reilly's drinking. Each time, FDR would rise to his defense, but Henry had no patience for the security man's "blowing off steam," as Roosevelt called it. To Reilly, Henry now gave orders: He "screamed as though stabbed," Reilly would recall, instructing him to double the White House guard. Henry hung up immediately, only to call back ten seconds later, demanding that he quadruple the guard, and issue machine guns to each man.

At 6:35 in the evening, Henry called Gaston and the Secret Service chief Frank Wilson into his office. As they listened, Henry called the president.

"We are freezing all Japanese funds," he said.

"Yes."

"We are not going to let any Japanese leave the country or to carry on any communications."

"I see."

"Well, our responsibility is the border."

"Yes, yes. That's right."

"And we're putting people into all the Japanese banks and business houses tonight and we're not going to let the Japanese get in there at all."

"That's good."

"Now the other I would like—Chief Wilson and Gaston are here."

"Yes."

"We would like permission to put a detail of soldiers on the White House grounds."

Roosevelt was reluctant to call in the Army. "Well, wait just a second," he said. "Suppose you get some additional White House guards?"

"We've done that," said Henry. "We've already doubled the guard force."

"You've doubled the guard. That's all you need. As long as you have one about every hundred feet around the fence, it's all right."

"But you think that's enough?"

"That's fine."

"Well, the guards have been doubled."

"What you could do is this: block off both Executive Avenues . . . put up barricades between the White House and the Treasury, and also on the one between the White House and the State Department."

"We will do that tonight. All right, sir."

Throughout the evening, Henry would not relent, insisting that every possible protective measure be deployed.

The emergency cabinet session stretched on past ten P.M. Henry had never seen such grim faces. Roosevelt called it the most important cabinet meeting since 1861. As the reports from Hawaii came in, and grew more precise, Henry heard more of the devastation and its significance. Secretary Knox was anguished—he "feels something terrible," Henry would tell his aides—and Stimson "kept mumbling that all the planes were in one place." As the men spoke, the shock remained. But the mood in Roosevelt's study had already begun to shift. There was relief, too, Stimson would later say: for the president, and for themselves. Now at least they knew what had to be done.

At the White House, Henry again berated Reilly. To the Secret Service man, Henry seemed paranoid—he "kept peering," Reilly would recall, "through the White House windows in search of enemy aircraft." Henry saw no humor in it: He was worried about the president and insisted that a company of soldiers surround the White House.

At 11:09 P.M., Henry returned to the Treasury. "It is just unexplainable," he told his aides. "I just can't say—much worse than anyone realizes." The secretary kept going: "They have the whole fleet in one place—the whole fleet in this little Pearl Harbor base." The Navy, he added, "will never be able to explain it." He worried, too, about his own family, ordering blackout curtains for his house. Henry kept his aides late, checking and rechecking the precautions, until one in the morning.

| | | |

The attack on Pearl Harbor caught America unawares, but as a nation now bound for war, it was willfully unprepared. Isolationism still ran strong. Since the spring, warnings from Washington of the hardships to come—the Office of Price Administration had called for cutting automobile production by half within six months; Ickes predicted gasoline shortages on the Eastern Seaboard—had only brought outrage. In May, 12,000 machinists had struck in San Francisco's shipyards, and Newark became the first American city to test a blackout system. (It was a failure: The lights went out, but the crowded streets downtown turned into a carnival, what a reporter described as a "mardi gras atmosphere.") Above all, on December 7, the U.S. Army was "weak indeed," as Bob Patterson, assistant secretary of war, would say: 1.6 million men, 27 infantry divisions only partly trained and equipped, fewer than 200 air squadrons, and a mere 7 divisions "sufficiently hardened to go overseas."

On Monday morning, as the horror sunk in, and the extent of the damage became known—the Japanese had also attacked the Philippines, Wake Island, Guam, Hong Kong, and Malaya—the markets held steady, without any Treasury support. Wall Street relied on "patriotism and horse sense," Henry would tell reporters. He'd also begun, as he'd promised the president, a first sweep of Japanese and German assets in the United States. By morning, the Treasury's law-enforcement men had arrived at the doors of almost every enemy-owned factory and business across the country, including I.G. Farben's subsidiaries, and shut them down.

Ellie had joined Mrs. Roosevelt at the OCD headquarters on Dupont Circle, the Office of Civilian Defense. Since the summer, the first lady had been all but running the new outfit. It had originated as her idea; she had seen how the British organized the home front, with preparations for air raids, sandbags, and blackouts. She wanted to work with women and young people, to prepare for war and maintain morale. FDR had appointed Mayor Fiorello La Guardia to run it, but the mayor quickly lost interest. So Mrs. Roosevelt took over, organizing the headquarters and recruiting a staff. Ellie served at her side, setting up a volunteer corps. That morning Mrs. Roosevelt spoke calmly, giving the order to shift to a wartime footing. She told Ellie she'd be flying with La Guardia that evening to California, to "what may turn out to be the next danger zone of the war." She asked Ellie to take over the headquarters in her absence.

Shortly after eleven o'clock in the morning, Eleanor and Ellie left separately, the first lady in a White House car, for the Capitol. At noon, the president was to address the Congress. Ellie brought Henry III along, stopping first at the Treasury to join her husband. At the Capitol, the crowds were quiet and orderly, but Secret Service men and police had lined the grounds. The secretary left his wife and son to have a cup of coffee in the House restaurant before he marched in with the cabinet to hear Roosevelt's speech.

Mrs. Roosevelt had made sure that Henry III would have a place to sit, on the steps of the aisle in the White House gallery. It was nearly empty, although the floor and every other gallery was packed. Mrs. Woodrow Wilson sat alone in the front row. At 12:15 P.M., Mrs. Roosevelt entered the gallery with her party and was seated next to Mrs. Wilson. Harry Hopkins sat on the step beside Henry III, calling out the arrivals, and everyone in the gallery rose as they entered. "Here comes the Senate," he said. "Here comes the Court, all except Jimmy [Byrnes] . . . now here comes the Cabinet. . . ."

As the president entered, he was greeted with a burst of applause, and the cheers resounded above the clapping. The president's voice had the clear resonant ring of earlier days. He spoke fewer than five hundred words, finishing in six minutes. America had suffered a day that would "live in infamy," he said, but he pledged that this "form of treachery shall never endanger us again." He called on Congress to declare that since the attack on Pearl Harbor "a state of war has existed between the United States and the Japanese Empire." Those present were struck: The simplicity and brevity of his message made its gravity even stronger.

Within half an hour, the Senate had left for its chamber to take action, and the secretary of the Treasury returned to his office.

"The President's words," wrote young Henry days later, when he sat down to record the swirl of events, "had begun to revive us from the stunned effect of the first shock." The secretary's elder son had joined him in his office. At the Treasury, a strange limbo set in; the world had shifted on its axis, but no one knew just what to do first. "I sat in my father's office and listened," Henry III wrote. At about 3:30 P.M., the secretary held a press conference. Henry Morgenthau, Jr., sat at his desk, his back to the window that faced the White House. The view over-looked Roosevelt's study. Outside, the police and soldiers stood post. The president had protested, but Henry had again ordered the guard doubled. The barricades were up, and the streets were silent.

The half circle of reporters stood in front of the secretary's desk. One of the reporters said the president would soon be signing the Declaration of War, which had just been sent down from the Hill. Young Henry turned to the window in time. He looked out across the narrow walkway and saw "the bright flashes of the cameramen's bulbs," as he would re-cord, "darting out of the windows of the president's office and disap-pearing into the grayness of the late afternoon."

30. At Sea

As the USS *Winslow* eased out of San Juan Harbor in Puerto Rico, bound again for the South Atlantic, Bob Morgenthau had come to appreciate its beauty and power. Known as "tin cans" for their thin hulls, destroyers had become the Navy's workhorses, its most versatile vessels. Bob would serve the next four and a half years on destroyers—aboard seven ships, under seven captains, spending forty-six months at sea in the Mediterranean and Pacific theaters. His first tour, though, came on the South Atlantic: a long year and a half, nearly unbroken by time off, from the winter of 1942 until the spring of 1943.

Five weeks after Pearl Harbor, Bob had set sail from Boston. In San Juan, he'd reported to the *Winslow,* sister ship of the *Warrington* and one of seventy-nine destroyers of the U.S. Atlantic Fleet. He joined a corps of officers that had seen an eventful six months: Since the spring of 1941, the *Winslow* had trained with submarines along the Maine coast, kept watch over quarantined Vichy ships at Martinique and Guadeloupe, and escorted the *Augusta,* the cruiser that carried FDR to Newfoundland for a rendezvous with Churchill, their first meeting, at which they signed the Atlantic Charter. By November, they'd picked up a convoy in Halifax (Dunkirk troops bound for Singapore), cleared the Cape of Good Hope, and been just off Cape Town when news of the Honolulu attacks came. The men knew the danger, and the importance of guarding convoys: Six weeks after Pearl Harbor, German submarines had been spotted on the supply lanes along the approaches to New York Harbor. Before long, dozens of oil tankers and freighters, steaming without escort, had been sunk—one four miles off the New Jersey coast.

By the time Bob stepped aboard in early 1942, the *Winslow* had joined Rear Admiral Jonas H. Ingram's South Atlantic Fleet, one of the first U.S. Navy units to direct aid to the Allies. Since June 1941, as part of Roosevelt's push to aid the British with all "methods short of war," the fleet had patrolled the South Atlantic, hunting German submarines, blockade runners, and raiders. The raiders—German warships disguised as merchants—had preyed on cargo ships headed for London, sinking dozens. The South Atlantic was too vast and the British navy too small to stave off the attacks. Ingram's Task Force 3—four old light cruisers and five destroyers—had lent a hand, helping the British cover the vast triangle of ocean between the Caribbean, Brazil, and Africa.

Ever since Bob declared his intention to enlist, Henry Jr. had walked a tightrope between worry for his son's safety and disdain for anyone in government who sought favors. For all his restraint, though, the virtuous secretary always gave way to the worried father. In November 1941, days after Bob got his first orders, Henry made an inquiry with the Navy. He was on the phone with Admiral Harold Stark, ostensibly to learn the status of a rusting U.S. icebreaker the Soviets had their eye on (Ambassador Gromyko had just come to see him about it), when Henry abruptly changed the subject.

"Now, I'm going to ask you—as long as I have you—a very indiscreet question," he said. "And if you don't answer, I'll understand."

The admiral kept silent.

"If I could be told—in strictest confidence—where the *Winslow* operates," Henry went on, "I'd appreciate it."

Stark could not answer offhand, but promised to check.

Again, Henry tried to soft-pedal. "If you tell me, 'Morgenthau, you'd better not know,' I'll understand perfectly. . . . I'm just a father, in this case."

For years, Henry had reassured his sons that he would never use his office to meddle in their lives. But when it came to the war, he could not help himself. In January, Henry cabled Rex Tugwell, the New Dealer recently posted to Puerto Rico as governor, again asking for news of his son. Tugwell sent "an eye-witness report": He had hosted Bob at the governor's mansion in San Juan. Young Morgenthau, he reported, had taken to visiting on his off nights. At the Tugwell family's rummy game, Bob had come out "best man," and amiably chatted with the local commanding officer's daughter—a young lady, Tugwell added, "much more entertaining than a card game with the family."

If at the Treasury, with the legion of bureaucrats at his disposal, Henry could not help himself, he knew better than to attempt any direct communication with a ship's captain. Not that it would have done any good. From the start, the *Winslow*'s skipper, Captain William J. Marshall, was blunt: He would make no fuss over the secretary's son.

For Bob, the Navy opened a new world. The crew, like the officers, came from all corners of the country. For the first time, Bob was "thrown in with this great range of folks": a farmer's son from New Orleans, two brothers from Little Rock, a big band horn player from the Bronx.

Bob had come aboard as the assistant communications officer and soon settled into the officers' wardroom. They were close-knit veterans, "old men" in their thirties; though they rarely spoke of it, many had been at Pearl Harbor. Some were Annapolis graduates, others were "mustangs"—officers who had come up through the ranks as enlisted men. Only a few, like Bob, were fresh out of college, just months out of training. Had Hitler not intervened, they would have been on their way to becoming lawyers, doctors, finance men.

Bob's closest friends, though, had not gone to college. Frank Tuggle, the chief gunner's mate, had enlisted after high school in Virginia. Tuggle grew up in a large family, hunting squirrel and rabbit from a young age. His father would hand him two shotgun shells, and say, "If you don't kill something, we don't eat." Tuggle was a physical man who could take offense easily—he had boxed on occasion—but he possessed a quick mind. He had come aboard in December, and the two had formed a fast bond. At night, as Bob manned the bridge, Tuggle stood out on the foredeck in the narrow No. 2 gun turret. Throughout the dark hours, connected solely by headsets, they would keep each other awake reciting Tennyson's "The Charge of the Light Brigade."

The chief radioman became another close friend. Bill Lambert, an Irishman from Springfield, Massachusetts, was one of the most experienced men on the ship. He had signed up for the Navy while Bob was still at Deerfield.

Still, the old divisions of civilian life—race, class, education, and religion—carried over to the ship. Nearly all the men were white, Irish and Anglo-Saxon in the main, with a scattering of Italians, Poles, and Greeks. There were five Black men on the ship—two cooks and three mess attendants, who wore white "mess jackets" with tight collars and served the meals, both in the main crew's mess and in the narrow wardroom that served as the officers' dining room. All slept in segregated berths and were steward's mates, first, second, or third class. Prior to June 1942, a Black sailor could not advance to the Navy's lowest rank, apprentice seaman.

Within a few weeks, as the lead officer transferred out, Bob became the communications officer, responsible for all messages on the ship and ship-to-shore communication. Before long he also became the boarding officer. It was not a job to be envied. He was in charge of taking out the whaleboat and boarding suspicious merchant ships. The danger came not from the men one encountered aboard a suspect ship, but from the rope ladder dropped down its side. The men had to grab ahold of it at the top of a ten-foot swell and pull themselves up, making sure to climb aboard before the whaleboat surged back and slammed against the hull. If a man's timing was off, he could end up with a broken leg.

In May, the men of the *Winslow* finally got their first taste of action. They were escorting the oiler *Patoka* from Brazil to Trinidad for refueling, when the alarm sounded near the mouth of the Amazon. It was nearly eight o'clock in the evening. The sea was smooth and the overcast sky fast darkening. The *Patoka* could scarcely make nine knots cruising. The *Winslow* was about 2,500 yards ahead, zigzagging and preparing to drop back into a closer position for the night, when the bridge picked up the sound of propellers. The *Winslow* lacked radar, but the sonar caught the echo portside, no more than six hundred yards off. Captain Marshall ordered depth charges dropped off: six at ten-second intervals. At the same time, he ordered a sharp turn to the left, flank speed on the starboard engine, so as to avoid the explosions. As the whorl of the second charge reached the surface, the men on the bridge caught sight of "a dark snub-nosed object" breaking the water's surface at a seventy-degree angle. Amid the shock wave of the third charge, it slipped back under.

The bow of a German submarine stood twenty-five yards from the center of the detonations. Marshall opted not to drop a marker buoy, fearing that the smoke float—a target used to guide a bomber—would illuminate the ship. Instead, he slowed the engines and asked his men to wait. When a radioman picked up the call signs of a Spanish ship, Marshall offered an explanation: The German subs had been waiting to rendezvous with a supply ship. After nearly two hours, and no further contact, the captain ordered the ship to rejoin the oiler he'd left without an escort. Over the roar of the engines, Marshall congratulated all on the bridge: They would be credited with sinking a U-boat. Yet as the oil bubbled to the surface, Marshall quietly wondered if the Germans had not pulled off a ruse and escaped. For Bob, it was an early lesson in the uncertainties of war at sea.

| | | |

By June, months overdue for repairs, the *Winslow* returned to South Carolina. The ship would also be outfitted with more firepower: 20 mm guns and K-guns, which could launch depth charges from the side of the ship, rather than off the stern in racks, a practice that had changed little since World War I.

In Charleston, the officers won four-day passes. Rather than head for the city, Bob would take a train to the farm for a long weekend. He was eager to see his parents and hoped that Joan, too, would be at home. Yet above all, he wanted to see his girl.

Martha would arrive from Washington, where she had moved with three Smith friends into a large rented clapboard house on the city's northwestern edge. She'd never been "political," as she would tell friends. But in 1940, during Roosevelt's reelection campaign, Martha had carried FDR placards at Smith, and after graduation, determined to leave the Junior League girls behind, she'd gained her father's blessing to move to Washington. Like so many of her college friends, Martha wanted a part in the war effort. Her brother, three years out of Dartmouth, was in Europe; Jim Pattridge had enlisted, becoming an Army artillery spotter. She thought of joining the WAVES—Women Accepted for Voluntary Emergency Service—but won a job with the new British Ministry of Supply and Information. She'd found work as a secretary in the office set up by Arthur Purvis, Henry Morgenthau, Jr.'s Scottish friend and partner. She wrote Bob of her joy: It marked an entrance into the working world, and the war—and best of all, she'd got the job on her own.

Bob and Martha enjoyed the long weekend at Fishkill Farms, but the couple's reunion was interrupted on Sunday when FDR and a distinguished guest—Winston Churchill—arrived from Hyde Park for an afternoon of drinks. They settled into the chairs in the garden—avoiding the front steps and the unseemly sight of a president being carried across the threshold. On the lawn at the rear of the house, the men sat in low wicker chairs, Eleanor and Ellie beside them, in a half circle under the maples.

Bob, buttoned to the neck in naval whites, was called on to fix cocktails. Roosevelt asked for his "favorite." It was a summertime tradition: Whenever the Morgenthaus hosted the Roosevelts, the president knew

Bob could be relied on to make mint juleps. Once Bob mixed the sugar, mint, and a good bit of bourbon, Roosevelt savored the drink. Churchill took a sip and asked for scotch.

Ellie did her best to entertain. She wore a short-sleeve dress, tight gray elastics on her legs. For years, she'd been having trouble with her legs—they would swell up and the pain would become too intense to walk. In April 1940, she'd had emergency surgery. Henry had sent her by ambulance to the hospital, registering her under an assumed name. The doctors diagnosed phlebitis, but the surgery had done little good. Of late she felt drained, unable to keep up. Throughout the summer, a private nurse, prim in a white dress and bonnet, would hover close. The doctors kept running tests, while Henry worried.

Bob had brought a lightness back to the farm. Thanks to him, Henry would tell Ellie, the afternoon with the Roosevelts and the prime minister had gone off so well. Henry hated to see him go. At the last minute, he offered to escort him—flying from New York—back to his ship. In Charleston, he wanted to see Bob off, but he also wanted to meet Bob's new skipper.

Captain Marshall had left the ship in June. It had come as something of a surprise, but Marshall was deemed too senior to waste on South Atlantic patrols. Promoted to commander, he transferred to the Atlantic Fleet headquarters at the Brooklyn Navy Yard. The new skipper, "Doc" Mowatt—his given name was Warren, but no one dared called him that—had little trouble settling in. A lieutenant commander, he was a Naval Academy graduate who had been serving on destroyers since the 1920s. Mowatt made an effort at diligence, at least when sober. But when he drank, which was often, he could become a monster—racist, vengeful, and, given the close confines, dangerous.

If his dinner arrived late, or not piping hot, he would lash out at the mess attendant: "Lock up that n****r, and throw the key away!" The *Winslow,* though, had no brig. It fell to Bob to instruct two crewmembers to convert a paint locker, a small supply room, into a makeshift cell and put a lock on the door. After Mowatt had inspected the new "brig," Bob searched out the mess attendant. "Stay out of sight for a couple of days," he advised. It was the same each time: When he sobered up, the captain would relent.

As the *Winslow* resumed the patrols of the previous spring, Bob faced an urgent concern: Captain Mowatt was becoming unbearable. In early 1943, acting on a rumor, he ordered the ship south to the Falklands, an impulsive expedition to search for a Nazi submarine base. In Rio, as Mowatt returned aboard ship with a prostitute, Bob conspired with another officer to remove the captain from duty.

They were aided by his poor health. Mowatt was not only a hard drinker, he suffered from a bad heart. In the second week of February, Mowatt suddenly began to complain of chest pains. As they grew more acute, a plan took shape. It was risky—if caught, they could face a court-martial. Bob's co-conspirator was Brooks Beck, his friend from Deerfield and Amherst, who'd recently come aboard, thanks to a switch of officers arranged by Bob. Beck sought out the captain and delivered the bad news: "You've probably had a heart attack," he said. Beck, who made a hobby of reading medical textbooks, advised Mowatt to rest in his cabin, and seek a medical leave. On February 22, Bob informed his father, with deliberate subterfuge, that the captain "has been sick and will probably be relieved."

In truth, Bob and Beck had pulled off a "special operation," ridding themselves of the rogue captain. On the orders of the ship's doctor, Mowatt was confined to his cabin, and soon he was relieved of his command. The executive officer, W. T. Samuels, became acting captain. Bob, at age twenty-three, and a lieutenant j.g.—junior grade—became the acting executive officer—"the exec," in Navy parlance.

When a new captain came onboard, the acting captain reverted to being the executive officer, and Bob became a surplus "exec." As no ship could have two executive officers, Bob knew he would have to leave the ship, and by June, the orders arrived.

On July 4, Bob left the *Winslow,* boarding a DC-3 on the first leg of a long trip home. He was the lone passenger on a transport from Belém, Brazil, to Georgetown, British Guiana. During the flight the Navy pilot came back to the cargo area and challenged Bob to a game of cribbage, leaving the plane on automatic pilot and his co-pilot in the cockpit. They were above the Amazon jungle when both engines went out. The pilot bolted for the cockpit, found the co-pilot asleep, and put the plane in a dive to restart the engines on fresh gas tanks. Two days and two flights later, Bob was back in the States.

| | | |

In the third week of August, he sailed from Norfolk to Curaçao, and reported for duty aboard a new ship, the 347-foot destroyer USS *Lansdale.*

By the summer of 1943, the "destroyermen," as those who served aboard the "tin cans" were now known, had gained notoriety in the Navy. Their swagger was known as a "destroyer roll," and their behavior on land, on rare days of recreation, as "the bane of the Shore Patrol." Destroyers were small ships stripped of many of the comforts enjoyed aboard carriers, battleships, and cruisers. On the big ships, layers of rules and regulations separated the officers and crew. On a destroyer, officers and crew alike slept in cramped quarters. "There is no canteen," a naval historian would write, "or ship's service booth where a man might get a coke, an ice cream or western story pulp magazine." On a destroyer, an ensign on the *Lansdale* would say, "You knew every man, good and bad sides. And they knew you."

On the *Lansdale*, to his surprise, Bob remained an executive officer, the second-in-command. He now had a captain, though, who commanded respect. "Val" Havard had something of an aristocratic bearing, and a thicket of silvery hair. Valery Havard, as he told the new men in his command, was born to serve, and he laid down the rules. "Everyone likes to give candy to children," he told Bob on his first day aboard. "But if this ship is to survive a war zone, one of us has to be an S.O.B. And I've decided that's you."

On that first night, the *Lansdale* sat in port, fueling in the darkness before heading out on August 26 to escort a tanker convoy to Ireland. It was an old route. In the fall of 1941, the ship had been one of the first U.S. destroyers to escort a westbound convoy across the Atlantic from the MOMP—the "Mid-Ocean Meeting Point," just south of Iceland. Ever since, it had remained on escort duty, taking convoys from the Caribbean and U.S. ports to the British Isles and North Africa—along the sea routes that Churchill himself had set. As the North African campaign drained British oil supplies, in late 1942 the prime minister had proposed to Roosevelt that the United States should deliver oil to the front. Thus had begun a supply operation without precedent: millions of barrels of oil, and thousands of tons of guns and ammunition, tanks, jeeps, and half-tracks—battle gear and K-rations—transported to keep the fires of "Operation Torch" (the invasion of North Africa) burning. By January, the Navy had laid out three new tanker routes: (1) "CU–UC," Curaçao and Aruba to the United Kingdom; (2) "OT–TO" ("Oil Torch"), Curaçao and Aruba to Casablanca, with a Gibraltar branch line; and (3) "USG–GUS," New York and Norfolk to Casablanca. The new oversea pipelines, Churchill instructed, would yield an extra 100,000 tons of oil a month, and every gallon was essential to keeping the British forces at work.

Convoy duty was trying. "Riding herd," as a naval historian in 1945 wrote, meant running like a tough sheepdog, "breathlessly and tongue-lolling around her flock, shooing stragglers into line, and then tackling, in the manner of good and faithful sheepdogs anywhere, all enemies regardless of size and number, whether aircraft, surface squadron, or wolf pack."

For months, Bob's routine aboard the *Lansdale* changed little. The convoys could be slow (nine knots) or fast (more than twenty), headed for Ireland or Casablanca. But the danger remained high. The German subs were gunning for Allied ships. If a tanker fell behind, the *Lansdale* would have to slow and patrol around the straggler. In December, as the ship headed back to the United States from Casablanca, the seas were rough. Gale-force winds and high waves caused the convoy to scatter, but in two days it had re-formed and Bob found cause to celebrate. On December 17, the crew caught sight of New York Harbor. At 8:20 that evening, the *Lansdale* settled back into home port.

||||

Bob and Martha had not intended to rush things. They had scarcely had time to get to know each other, let alone decide on a life together. The war, as both had begun to suspect, might change the schedule. In summer, they'd even spoken of it: It had seemed remote then, an unlikely chance, but both recognized how accelerated their relationship had become. They were both twenty-four years old. Three years had passed since their first picnic, but all told, Bob and Martha had spent only a handful of days together before he went to sea. For months, though, they had thought of little else. And throughout the year, Martha had written to Bob of the news: So many friends from college—"Smith girls" and "Amherst boys"—had gone ahead of them and already married.

For Bob, the two weeks in New York would be his first time off in months. His family knew he'd spend Christmas and New Year's with Martha, but within five days of his arrival at home he took all by surprise, making it official: He proposed. Bob had considered it since the summer, but a sudden shift sealed his decision. The *Lansdale* stood in the dry dock of the Navy Yard, having come into Brooklyn for repairs and to be outfitted with a top-secret addition, the latest in American military technology: radar that could search the skies for enemy bombers. Bob knew little of the new equipment, but he'd learned that the Navy had abruptly changed its plans for the *Lansdale*. The ship was in the middle of getting a new paint job—camouflage for the Pacific theater—when new orders arrived: Instead of heading for the Pacific, they would sail for the Mediterranean.

On the European seas, the likelihood of getting wounded, or worse, was far higher. The wedding would have to be simple, and fast. Bob knew it meant asking Martha to sacrifice, but he had made up his mind to ask for her hand, out of fear that he would not be home for a long time—if at all. For Martha, marrying a man only days before he returned to sea was not an act of patriotism, nor did she imagine it a "war marriage"—the urge to seal bonds and celebrate life that seemed to be sweeping across their generation. Martha was marrying for love.

On December 27, Henry and Ellie made the announcement public. And on December 30, the day Stalin boasted of a new Soviet offensive, a drive to retake a thousand towns and push twenty-two Nazi divisions back to the Polish border, Bob and Martha got married.

The wedding would, after all, be a hurried affair. Henry Morgenthau, Jr., was not up to hosting a grand event but he ascribed great meaning to the day. For months, as the news from Europe grew darker, Henry had had trouble sleeping. He worried about the turns of the war, and the horrors, if the reports could be true, visiting the lands already under Hitler's boot. Ellie worried about her husband's health, so much so that she confided in friends, and even consulted her own doctors. Ever since they heard of the *Lansdale*'s return to New York, Henry could speak of little else, and when Bob told him of the sudden proposal, his father was overcome. The wedding would be more than a break from the war: It would bring the hope, Henry imagined, they all desperately needed for the future.

At first, there was talk of FDR attending, but given the rush, it was out of the question. Mrs. Roosevelt, though, insisted on coming. The marriages of her own children had left the first lady disillusioned with matrimony: Anna had divorced after eight years, and remarried within six months; Jimmy Roosevelt had followed (he would have four wives in all). Eleanor would confess to Ellie her envy, how pleased she was for her friend's daughter-in-law, and two days before Christmas, she sent a note to "Lt. Morgenthau."

"Dear Bob," she wrote, "I can't tell you how happy I am for you and Miss Pattridge."

I have known you so many years and have watched you grow up, and I have a feeling that someone in my own family is being made happy.

My congratulations to you and every sincere wish that the years will bring you real happiness, and that you and your fiancée will achieve the relationship which your father and mother have had during their married life.

> *Affectionately,*
> *Eleanor Roosevelt*

Ellie's uncle, Chief Justice Irving Lehman, hosted the wedding at his brownstone on the East Side. On Thursday afternoon, the Morgenthaus arrived early, ahead of Martha's parents, who came by train from Minneapolis. The welcome appeared warm, but all remained keenly aware of the distance between the families. Pat and Hazel Pattridge were reserved, and Republican. Few of their friendships strayed beyond the world of the midwestern establishment: business, sport, the Junior League. But the Pattridges were not overly religious; they themselves had been married by a Unitarian in Vermont. Henry and Pat could also find common ground: Both had started out as farmers and found their footing as publishers. The men managed convivial talk—grain futures and dairy prices were favored topics—even as the discomfort was never far.

The bride entered the living room, descending a long curved staircase. Sewn into a gown of white satin (a dress she'd bought and paid for in cash herself), Martha carried a bouquet of white cornelias and white sweet peas at her waist. Joan, midway through her third year at Vassar, served as maid of honor, while Betty King, Martha's closest friend from Minneapolis, was the lone bridesmaid. Henry III, now a lieutenant and having rushed home on leave from Fort Jackson, South Carolina, where he was training with the Second Cavalry, was best man.

Within an hour it was over. The rounds of champagne toasts ended, the cake was finished, and Bob and Martha left the party early. A Treasury car waited to take them down to the St. Regis, for their first married night together. In the morning, the newspapers carried a sunny photograph from the wedding: the first lady, in rare elegance in satin and pearls, beaming beside the newlyweds. A honeymoon, though, as Ellie confided to Eleanor, would come only when Bob got leave.

On Sunday morning, the groom was due back aboard the *Lansdale.*

31. Civilization Fails the Test

SUMMER 1942–FALL 1943

FDR was rarely ambivalent about anything, but he was especially decisive when accused of a bias, whether it be a prejudice or partiality. When critics hounded him for being too close to the Jews, the president had been known to return fire. All too often, though, the Roosevelt counterattack relied on wit and charm—words, and no more. The anti-Semites had long slurred "Rosenfeld" and his "Jew Deal." The Nazi propagandists had made the point explicit, drawing big-nosed caricatures of Morgenthau, Rosenman, Frankfurter, and others among the president's Jewish advisors. Hitler went further, telling a Spanish diplomat he had proof of Roosevelt's "Jewish ancestry." The president had heard such claims before. In 1935, during the first reelection campaign, he answered questions about his ancestors with perfect pitch: "In the dim, distant past they may have been Jews or Catholics or Protestants. What I am more interested in is whether they were good citizens and believers in God. I hope they were both."

It was one thing to defend the rights of American Jews, and quite another to protect the Jews of Europe. Roosevelt had only been a few days in the White House, when Irving Lehman, Ellie's uncle, told him of the dangers facing Jews in Germany, and urged that the United States open its doors. Since 1929, a quota system had allowed some 150,000 immigrants to enter each year, with nearly half of that number reserved for those coming from England or Ireland. During the Depression, Hoover had tightened the restrictions, reading expansively a 1917 clause barring entry to any foreigner "likely to become a public charge." The standard of admission became, de facto, independent means or the guarantee of a job. With one-quarter of American workers without jobs, and Congress adamantly opposed to any increase in immigration, Roosevelt could do little to alter Hoover's reading of the law: By 1933, the number of new arrivals from Germany sank to a record low as the "public charge" clause kept out Jewish refugees. Even the narrow quota—25,957 immigration visas for Germans—went unfilled. Only 1,241 German émigrés—an unknown number of them Jews—were admitted.

Judge Lehman had urged FDR to relax the Hoover-era stance, and within weeks, Felix Frankfurter, then a professor at Harvard Law School, came to the White House to echo the appeal. Frankfurter left FDR believing that he had "set the train in motion." Days later, though, Justice Brandeis wrote Frankfurter that "F.D. [Franklin Delano] has shown amply that he has no anti-Semitism. . . . But this action, or rather determination that there shall be none"—no shift from the Hoover policy— "is a disgrace to America and to F.D.s administration." Frances Perkins, who oversaw the Immigration and Naturalization Department, would also try, but no matter how hard they pushed, the State Department stood firm. It was not only Sumner Welles, the patrician assistant secretary of state, who worried about the floodgates opening. An entrenched corps of isolationists—the president's old friend Billy Phillips among the most vocal—warned of dire consequences: the infection of the body politic, the threat of foreign allegiances, and the loss of jobs.

The majority of Congress and the American people opposed a mass influx of immigrants, especially impoverished Jews. At the same time, the country's Jewish leaders could not agree on tactics. Some, like Judge Lehman and his brother Herbert, were loath to pressure FDR; others worried that a public outcry would only strengthen Hitler's hand. Zionists feared any U.S.-led resettlement program would threaten their dream of a homeland in Palestine. If the United States became a haven for Jewish immigrants, Rabbi Stephen Wise argued, who would settle for a desert half a world away? As a result, few Jews raised the refugee question at the White House, and few said a word in public. Instead, throughout Hitler's first years in power, America's Jewish leaders retreated into the silence of official Washington.

Still, by 1938, even before the Nazi march across Europe, the plight of Europe's refugees had moved to the forefront of Roosevelt's mind. New ideas, as always unconventional, began to stir: What if the United States, FDR wondered, could find land elsewhere to move the Jews en masse out of Europe? Over lunch in January 1938, the president took up the idea with Henry. Why not look at the old German colonies in West Africa, or in Mexico, or Venezuela?

In March, once Hitler annexed Austria and the refugee tide rose again, Roosevelt returned to the subject: Why couldn't the United States take in more Austrians? he asked at a cabinet session. Henry's notes from the meeting make clear FDR's reasoning: "After all," Roosevelt said, "America was a place of refuge for so many fine Germans in the period of the 1840s, why can't we again offer them a place of refuge?" "He suggested," Henry recorded, "that we combine the quotas of Germany and Austria and let the Austrian refugees come in under the combined quota." Some among his aides raised fears that Congress would object, but before long FDR found the legal authority and merged the German and Austrian quotas. He also put forth a compromise: Why not set up a commission to explore resettlement options in foreign lands? As Perkins and others embraced the idea, Roosevelt asked Secretary Hull to invite thirty-three governments to a conference on the refugee problem.

The administration faced an economic recession, midterm elections, and isolationists and anti-Semites in both parties. But the president was determined: On April 13, with Wilsonian optimism and an eye on the domestic political benefit, he hosted an "interfaith" meeting, bringing eleven non-Jews and three Jews to the White House. Henry Jr. had stood at the president's bedside that morning, sounding him out on a new tax bill. His father arrived at the White House just as he was leaving. Bernard Baruch and Rabbi Wise joined Uncle Henry, who was two weeks shy of his eighty-second birthday, and a trio of clergymen who brought Protestant and Catholic clout. Henry Sr. was pleased to see that FDR had made the talks more than a publicity stunt: Perkins and Hull joined Welles and George Messersmith, now the highest-ranking man at State with firsthand knowledge of Nazi Germany. They were joined by an American who may have known Hitler and his motives best, James G. McDonald. A former League of Nations high commissioner (Uncle Henry had lobbied State to back him for the job), now on the *New York Times* editorial board, McDonald had been one of the first Americans to meet with Chancellor Hitler in 1933.

Hitler was "a maniac with a mission," FDR told the group, but he announced a countermission: a campaign to save the refugees trapped in German-occupied lands. Roosevelt's audience heard a hedge: No one should use the term "Jewish refugees"; instead, the group would be named the president's Advisory Committee on *Political* Refugees. Not all present were keen to sign up: Baruch and Raymond Fosdick cited busy schedules, and Henry Sr. also begged off. He was wary, as always, of the Zionists, and with the odds stacked against success, he did not wish to taint his son.

Despite the opposition, in the summer of 1938 FDR's idea became a reality. In Évian-les-Bains, the French resort town on Lake Geneva, envoys from twenty-nine "Nations of Asylum" joined diplomats and reporters at the luxurious Hotel Royal. On the eve of the Évian conference, Anne O'Hare McCormick, the *Times* columnist, called it a "test of civilization." FDR made scant public mention of the conference, his secretary of the Treasury even less, and at Évian, "civilization" failed: Only the Dominican Republic made a public stand to open its doors. Rafael Trujillo, the Dominican dictator, eager to improve his reputation after massacring thousands of Haitian farm laborers months earlier, pledged to take in 10,000 refugees. But no other Central American nation matched the offer. The United States, meanwhile, continued to raise the accepted objections to welcoming a European exodus, and as envoys spoke of an oversupply of "traders" and "intellectuals" amid the refugees, the undercurrent of anti-Semitism was inescapable.

The Évian talks were a "terrible experience," Golda Meir, who attended from Palestine, wrote. Forbidden to speak, she sat in the gilded hall "listening to the delegates of thirty-two countries rise, each in turn, to explain how much they would have liked to take in substantial numbers of refugees and how unfortunate it was that they were not able to do so." Delegates "took pleasure cruises on the lake," the hotel concierge said decades later. "They gambled at night at the casino. They took mineral baths and massages at the *Etablissement Thermal.* Some of them took the excursion to Chamonix to go summer skiing . . . it is difficult to sit indoors hearing speeches when all the pleasures that Évian offers are outside."

Italy joined Germany in not sending an envoy; Mussolini's propagandists denounced the project from the start. *La Tribuna* declared it a sham convened by FDR only because, "as is known, he is of Jewish origin." Still, Mussolini's spokesman may have come the closest to telling the truth. Months later, as the conferees reconvened in London, Virginio Gayda said the message was unmistakable: "Nobody, not even those who might think seriously of opening their doors and making room for Jews in their national, or imperial territories . . . wants the Jews."

|||||

In Washington, the president had grown impatient with the "lukewarm attitude" of foreign governments. In October 1938, FDR appealed to Prime Minister Chamberlain, convinced that England, having secured the postwar mandate after the Great War and become the gatekeeper of Palestine, could solve the crisis. At lunch on October 25, Roosevelt let Henry in on the secret: Hours earlier he had summoned the British ambassador, Sir Ronald Lindsay, and drawn the line. He'd been stern, FDR assured Henry: "He just would not stand for any nonsense."

"The British," FDR insisted, "would have to give a permanent homeland to the Jews," and this time, unlike the infamous Balfour Declaration, "they would have to keep their word."

Roosevelt saw only one way to solve the Palestine problem: divide the Arabs and Jews, and segregate them. "There are 400,000 Arabs that are working for the Jews," FDR told the British ambassador, offering a plan of action. It was a typical Roosevelt solution: plain to see, hard to enact. "Let them get out of this section," he suggested, and have the Jews "keep out of the section occupied by the Arabs."

"We want to keep the friendship with the Arabs," Sir Ronald replied.

"You can buy that for about 50,000,000 pounds," Roosevelt said. "And the United States will be glad to chip in."

FDR was already looking beyond Palestine. A devotee of maps since boyhood, he had scoured the world, looking for regions that offered a hospitable balance of population, climate, arable land, and politics. Harold Ickes had suggested Alaska, or even the Virgin Islands, but Roosevelt looked further afield. On October 14, 1938, he had just finished reading a new book on the virtues of "pioneer agrarianism," *Limits of Land Settlement,* when he summoned its author: Isaiah Bowman, a leading geographer. After graduating from Harvard a year ahead of FDR, Bowman had directed the American Geographic Society, before serving as president of Johns Hopkins University. He had also been the map man at Versailles—the "scientist" at Wilson's side when the victors redrew the borders of Europe. Roosevelt asked Bowman to recommend lands that could take in a mass resettlement of refugees. "Frankly," he wrote, "what I am looking for is the possibility of uninhabited or sparsely inhabited good agricultural lands to which Jewish colonies might be sent." He was thinking in the range of "fifty to one hundred thousand people."

In Germany, as Roosevelt was casting about for far distant corners to resettle Jews, the Nazis unleashed a pogrom. Beginning in the early hours of November 10, 1938, the mobs, led by the storm troopers of the SA (the Sturmabteilung), attacked Jewish shops and homes across Germany. In the worst violence since Hitler's rise, no city would be spared. By morning, at least a thousand synagogues had been set afire, and more than 30,000 Jewish boys and men aged sixteen to sixty had been rounded up in Germany and Austria. In the United States, no one yet knew where those detained had been sent, but the horrors of Kristallnacht, the Night of Broken Glass, filled the newspapers. FDR recalled his ambassador in protest—the only world leader to do so—and at his next press conference, he expressed outrage. He'd been handed a draft statement, just three sentences long, but Roosevelt had given it force with his own words: "I myself," he added in pencil, "could scarcely believe that such things could occur in a twentieth-century civilization."

Still, FDR's condemnation of the attacks in Germany only went so far; he did not utter the word "Jews," and again affirmed the quotas. At the Treasury, Henry refused to believe that his friend would not show compassion. He knew that political expediency may yet hold sway, but six days after Kristallnacht, Henry insisted to his chief aides that they could not afford to sit idle. He was sure of it: The president had an urgent desire to save the refugees, and since "nobody is helping him," Henry added, "I am going at least to do the spade work."

The secretary turned to Isaiah Bowman, the Johns Hopkins geographer Roosevelt had contacted, and whom Henry Sr. had known since the 1920s. Bowman produced a detailed report on prospective regions in South and Central America for resettling the Jews. On the evening of November 20, 1938, Bowman joined Henry Jr. at his home in Washington for a Sunday supper of roast duck. They spent the evening studying maps, going through a list of countries that FDR had drawn up in his own hand. The president was keen on northern Venezuela, especially the plateaus north and south of the Orinoco River. As Henry and Bowman went country by country, the geographer pasted scraps of paper on the maps, summaries of each nation's suitability.

"It is an exciting search," Bowman wrote FDR on the following day. But he was pessimistic: "Northern South America," he reported, "offers no place for colonization, on a large scale, of people such as we have in mind."

Bowman might have seemed a natural ally, but neither the Morgenthaus nor the president seems to have inquired about the geographer's own attitude to the Jews. A believer in the virtues of pioneer farming, Bowman was a eugenicist who considered Jews, like Blacks, an urban race ill equipped to build settlements in inhospitable climes. His biographer would paint Bowman as an unabashed anti-Semite, yet his relations with the Morgenthaus, at least as revealed in the correspondence and documents, were not only cordial but mutually enhancing. Just as Henry Sr. had allied in the Wilson campaign with Charles Crane, the Chicago industrialist who would become a Hitler apologist, so Henry Jr. managed to work side by side with a man who disdained Jews.

| | | |

The Roosevelt plan remained short on action, long on fact-finding. But its objective, a distant foreign resettlement for the Jews, seemed likely to hold, until the spring, when a German steamer, the *St. Louis,* approached Cuba with 937 refugees onboard—most of them German Jews, many survivors of Dachau and other of the earliest concentration camps.

In November 1938, Colonel Fulgencio Batista, the Cuban strongman, had visited the White House and in exchange for a promise of lower sugar tariffs, offered to take in Jewish refugees. The voyage of the *St. Louis,* though, would end any romantic dream of an island paradise for the refugees. By May 13, 1939, when the ship sailed from Hamburg, Cuba, a country of 4.5 million, had accepted fewer than 6,000 Jews. Many onboard the *St. Louis* carried landing permits issued by a corrupt Cuban official, papers they believed would grant them entry to the island. Seven hundred thirty-four of those onboard were on waiting lists for U.S. visas.

In Havana, harbor officials allowed only twenty-eight passengers from the *St. Louis* to come ashore. While it remained at sea, the Cuban government had invalidated the landing permits, and a standoff ensued. The passengers knew their fate if the ship were forced to return to Germany. One refugee, a survivor of Buchenwald, could take no more: He cut his wrists and dove into the Havana harbor.

On the Friday afternoon of May 26, 1939, when the ship entered Havana harbor, Roosevelt was headed to Hyde Park. It fell to Sumner Welles, now the undersecretary of state, to handle the affair. Henry Morgenthau, Jr., knew what to expect from the men of the State Department: Welles had once told Henry that he considered Mussolini "the greatest man that he had ever met." As Henry watched the crisis unfold, the pleas from Jewish leaders grew more urgent before finally, on the eleventh day, he took action. The *St. Louis* had left Havana harbor and was heading north toward Miami when Henry urged Hull and Welles to allow the ship to dock in the Virgin Islands, but the State Department insisted no refugees could be allowed on U.S. soil. Hull had kept in close contact with the Cuban ambassador, who assured him, as late as June 5, that a deal could be struck: Cuba would allow the refugees to disembark in return for $500 a passenger, a bond intended to be repaid to the depositor. The Joint Distribution Committee (JDC), a U.S. Jewish organization, attempted to negotiate on behalf of the passengers, but lost contact with the ship. It fell to Henry to take action.

On June 6, 1939, at 3:59 P.M., he spoke with Commander E. G. Rose at Coast Guard headquarters:

> MORGENTHAU: I've seen in the papers that out of Ft. Lauderdale you've been tracking the German ship, the *St. Louis*.
>
> COMMANDER ROSE: Yes, sir.
>
> MORGENTHAU: Do you know where she's located now?
>
> COMMANDER ROSE: I haven't seen anything on it today, but I believe the first was off Miami and the vessel turned back from trailing her somewhere down toward Key West.
>
> MORGENTHAU: Well, I'd—I'd like to know if you can find out where she is. Hello?
>
> COMMANDER ROSE: Yes, sir.
>
> MORGENTHAU: I don't—I want you to treat it confidentially, you see, so that nothing gets out that I'm interested.
>
> COMMANDER ROSE: I see.
>
> MORGENTHAU: But I—I spoke to Mr. Hull about it and I understand they can't locate the boat, you see.
>
> COMMANDER ROSE: All right, sir.
>
> MORGENTHAU: Now, I'd like—if you can handle this mission confidentially send a—a radio [message] both to Lauderdale and Miami, would you? . . . But handle the thing so that there will be no kickback and no publicity on it. . . .
>
> COMMANDER ROSE: I see. Well, we can send it in a tight code and safeguard it, I'm quite sure. . . .
>
> MORGENTHAU: Yes, and see if they can locate the *St. Louis*.
>
> COMMANDER ROSE: All right, sir. And would you like to be notified . . .
>
> MORGENTHAU: Yes, I want to be notified right away.

The commander signed off: "We'll do all that we can."

The secretary's attempt at intervention—if only to ensure the safety of the ship—would remain unknown to the country, and the Jews agitating for action across the country. From late May to early June, newspapers blared the scandalous headlines of the ship forced back into Hitler's grasp—"Ship Steams Away to Return Refugees to Reich"—yet in fact Henry did not ask the Coast Guard to block the ship from entering U.S. waters. On the contrary, he tried to buy time to negotiate. In Havana, though, the JDC representatives got nowhere. They also ignored offers from Honduras and the Dominican Republic. (The Dominicans, too, asked for $500 per passenger.) In New York, the JDC officials were prepared to pay the ransom, but their attorney in Havana demurred. On June 7, the White House told the Cuban government it would not allow the refugees to enter the United States, leaving the Cubans to reaffirm their refusal.

Unwanted in the Americas, the *St. Louis* headed back across the Atlantic. Through the urgent efforts of the JDC and the Intergovernmental Committee, FDR's commission on refugees, Belgium, England, France, and the Netherlands agreed to accept the refugees; none were forced back to Germany. Two-thirds survived the war, with half of them eventually immigrating to the United States. Two hundred fifty-four were killed in Europe—those who fell prey in occupied France, Belgium, and Holland and were gassed in Auschwitz or murdered in other camps.

The *St. Louis* haunted Henry: The tragedy laid bare the grim truths of the refugee crisis. On June 19, 1939, at lunch in the Oval Study, he again prodded the president. "A year has passed," he told FDR, "and we have not got anywhere on this Jewish refugee thing. What are we going to do about it?"

Roosevelt stopped and pondered the question. "I know we have not," he said, but he was determined, he assured Henry, to see the thing through. In fact, he raised the question again at lunch with the president-elect of Paraguay, who pledged to "take 5,000." Roosevelt, as ever, was convinced of his powers of persuasion. "I am sure," he told Henry, "I could get two or three people together and we could work out a plan."

Roosevelt repeated an argument Henry had heard earlier: that even if one managed to resettle the refugees from Germany, then Poland, Romania, and Hungary would only force their own Jews out—and the Allies would have "to take care of 4 or 5 million people."

"But Mr. President," Henry countered, "don't you think that is what we have to face anyway?"

"Absolutely!" FDR said. "That's what I have been saying, but I can't make any headway. I am willing to go so far, if necessary, to have them even call it the Roosevelt Plan."

Money, too, remained a problem. Even if Roosevelt could find countries to host the Jews, resettlement would cost millions. Get me, he told Henry, "a list of the 1,000 richest Jews" in the country, and "I am willing to tell them how much they should give." Roosevelt had names in mind. "A man like Zemurray"—Sam Zemurray, president of United Fruit, known as the New Orleans banana king—"ought to give $5 million," he said. "And a lot more like him."

"Mr. President, before you talk about money you have to have a plan," Henry said. "And if you don't mind, I would like to keep after you."

Allowing himself to believe once again in a Roosevelt rescue plan, that afternoon Henry recorded in his diary: "He is really tremendously interested. The great trouble is . . . nobody . . . is following him."

32. "War Rumor Inspired by Fear"

1942–1943

As the months passed, and pressure to rescue the Jews built, the nation's leading newspaper maintained a discomfiting silence about the suspected annihilation of a people.

For Adolph Ochs, Henry Sr.'s old friend and the *Times*'s owner, Hitler's rise seemed to speed a personal decline. "Toward the end of 1933, Ochs seldom appeared in public," Meyer Berger, a *Times* reporter, wrote in a commissioned history of the paper. "He was now broken mentally as well as physically. The spread of intolerance, the ever more melancholy case of the international situation," had taken a toll. Ochs had died in April 1935, at age seventy-seven. Within a month, his son-in-law, Arthur Hays Sulzberger, assumed the throne.

Arthur and Henry, boyhood friends, had stayed in close touch. In 1934, as Henry was settling into the Treasury, Sulzberger wrote with a complaint: *Fortune* had called, seeking Sulzberger's insights for a profile on the new Treasury secretary. "I am a little disturbed," Sulzberger wrote Henry, "at the way in which you, the Jews and the *Times* are linked together." He had hoped to shake the interviewer from jumping to foolish conclusions. "I tried my best to steer *Fortune* away from it," Sulzberger told Henry, "when I refused to comply with their request for one of my pictures to use in the article."

Ochs and Sulzberger long feared the *Times* being derided as a "Jewish paper"—it must never be seen, they held, as offering Jewish news written by Jewish reporters for Jewish readers. The instructions went unwritten, but the boundaries were understood. Jewish reporters saw their bylines shortened, initials replacing any name that sounded "too Jewish." Top editors' jobs, too, were reserved for non-Jews. Ochs and Sulzberger could not ignore the Jews among their readership, but they feared alienating the WASP establishment.

Sulzberger's first years as publisher had coincided with a wave of anti-Semitism that surged in the Depression's wake. Whether among the devotees of Father Coughlin or the German-American Bund, Hitler's message had gained currency in dark corners of America. In 1938, Sulzberger ventured beyond New York, traveling the country to get a sense of popular opinion. "Anti-Semitism is difficult for a Jew to check up on," he wrote to Henry from the train. "I have the feeling however that it is following the normal course of bad times which is when it always flourishes." And yet, as the Nazis crowed about the rising power of Jews in America, the publisher knew that his paper could ill afford to feed the propaganda.

Sulzberger expected more, though, from the Roosevelt White House, and did not shy from asking his friend to intervene. In October 1939, Sulzberger fumed when FDR spoke of the "Jewish race" in reporting progress in his Intergovernmental Committee on Refugees. The president had let slip an unfortunate choice of words, Sulzberger chided Henry, as "any anthropologist will, I believe, destroy the theory that there is such a thing as the Jewish race." Even people of goodwill must exercise caution, the publisher insisted, lest they "all too unwittingly help to play Hitler's game."

In December 1939, Sulzberger also called on Henry to broker—just as Henry Sr. had once done for Ochs—a date with the president. Over lunch at the White House, FDR told the publisher of his ideas for resettling the refugees. He relayed Bowman's findings, detailing the advantages of the eastern slope of the Andes, and reporting that he, like Sulzberger, favored a remote locale. Sulzberger had returned to New York relieved. At lunch, the president had employed a new term: "those of the Jewish faith."

Language, though, could not hide the underlying problem. The *Times* did all it could to appear neutral, the national model of objectivity. Anne O'Hare McCormick, a devout Catholic, could ask on the eve of the Évian conference: "Can America live with itself if it lets Germany get away with this policy of extermination?" But the *Times* editorialists, fearful of drawing attention to the paper's Jewish ownership, could not demand that the stringent immigration quotas be relaxed, let alone lifted. The paper did run an editorial on the *St. Louis,* but only after it had been forced to return to Europe. Even then, it neglected to mention that the refugees—all but five—were Jewish.

In August 1939, Sulzberger had visited Germany, and he would speak of an "unforgettable three-hours' talk" with Leo Baeck, chief rabbi of Berlin. Two weeks later, after the German invasion of Poland, the *Times* ran its first story on the deportation of Jews from Austria and Czechoslovakia. Datelined Berlin, the story reported "intimations" that "a solution of the Jewish problem is on the German-Polish agenda in Poland." Dozens more would follow. Otto Tolischus had reported from Berlin for the paper since April 1933. Born in East Prussia, Tolischus was a naturalized American citizen, Columbia graduate, and one of the *Times*'s three main correspondents in Berlin during the Hitler years. He had not shied from reporting the escalating attacks on the Jews. Tolischus became such a thorn in the Nazis' side, in fact, that they refused to extend his residency permit. In March 1940, from Oslo, following the German onslaught into Denmark and Norway, he wrote Sulzberger a prescient memorandum. "The Poles, like the Jews," Tolischus wrote, "are marked for extermination—physical extermination for the Jews and for those Poles who cannot reconcile themselves to German rule." Sulzberger considered the report of such value, he breached a sacrosanct wall: He sent a copy to Henry, who in turn soon passed it on to FDR.

Two years passed, though, before the *Times* at last gave credence to the macabre reports circulating in Europe. On a Saturday, June 27, 1942, a first story mentioned "gas chambers" and "concentration camps" in just two stunted paragraphs near the end of an article on page 5. Three sentences long, with no headline, it was a dry paraphrase of a statement from the Polish government-in-exile in London: 700,000 Jews had been murdered in "probably the greatest mass slaughter in history." For the first time, an American news story reported the use of "gas chambers": "Every death-dealing method was employed," the Polish exiles relayed, "machine-gun bullets, hand grenades, gas chambers, concentration camps, whipping, torture instruments and starvation."

In fact, the *Times* only reported the news after the BBC and CBS had broadcast it, but its silence had ended. A week later, the newspaper provided more details: "The Germans were methodically proceeding with their campaign to exterminate all Jews," and had already sent "special gas chambers on wheels" to western Poland. The report was hardly vague—"In the village of Chelmno near Kolo ninety persons at a time were put in the gas chambers"—but still few Americans noticed. The report ran on an inside page, while the front page foretold doom on two fronts of the war: The Nazis had seized the port of Sevastopol in the Crimea, and Field Marshal Erwin Rommel stood only seventy miles from Alexandria and the Suez Canal.

| | | |

Five weeks later, on August 8, 1942, Gerhart Riegner, a thirty-year-old German refugee who had studied law at the best universities of Germany and France, and once dreamed of becoming a professor, walked into the U.S. consulate on the Swiss shores of Lake Geneva. The young lawyer had agonized for months, but his decision to speak to the Americans, to relay the secret communiqué he'd been entrusted with, would shake the Roosevelt administration to the core. It would also cause Henry Morgenthau, Jr., to question his faith in his own government, and nearly all that he held dear.

The Riegners had been fixtures in the elite political and cultural circles of Berlin. During the Weimar Republic, Gerhart's mother had served on the central committee of the German Democratic Party, and his father, a liberal scholar, had worked with the legal architect of the Weimar Constitution. The family also had deep ties to Jewish culture: Louis Lewandowski, the nineteenth-century composer whose music had filled synagogues across Europe, was a relative. Gerhart studied at the universities of Berlin, Heidelberg, and Freiburg, before reading law at the Sorbonne, and had hoped to follow in his father's path, when the war intervened.

In exile in Geneva, Riegner found work as the local representative of the World Jewish Congress. For five years, he'd managed the congress's affairs from a small office in the former Hotel Bellevue. "I had one of the most beautiful landscapes before my eyes," he would recall, "and I knew that all over Europe the most terrible things were happening." If at first his work involved gathering reports for the League of Nations, once the war came, and the League all but died, Geneva turned into a vital listening post in Nazi-occupied Europe.

The name "World Jewish Congress" sounded grandiose, as if it were a secret society of Jews in pursuit of world domination—the nightmare of all who believed the fiction of the Elders of Zion. In truth, the congress had no official power, little money, and only a few staffers in New York and London. It sought to protect the rights of Jews in eastern Europe, but riven by division and shunned by rivals, it more accurately reflected the weakness of world Jewry in the face of the Nazi threat. Still, for all its failings, the congress could claim a forceful leader: Rabbi Stephen Wise. The connection to Wise led two Swiss intermediaries—Isidor Koppelman, a Jewish businessman in Zurich, and Benjamin Sagalowitz, press liaison for the Swiss Jewish communities—to tap Riegner as their messenger to the Americans.

The news that the men asked Riegner to deliver had come from a secret source, a prominent German industrialist—and was so horrific in its magnitude it left him dazed. Walking the shore of Lake Geneva for hours with Sagalowitz, Riegner tried to overcome the shock: "Was it conceivable?" he asked. "Was it credible?" It took two days to convince him.

Riegner went to see the American consul, but as he entered the consulate, he was greeted by a junior officer. Howard Elting, Jr., a tall, clean-cut Princeton graduate, had shuffled through a series of postings before the war: Dresden, Istanbul, Batavia, The Hague. Geneva was a step up, but he remained in the lowest rank of the service. Elting was only filling in; the consul was on holiday, skiing in the Alps.

Elting at once noted Riegner's "great agitation," and sought to reassure him, but as Riegner began to relay what he had been told, he refused to name the secret source. He would only call him a German businessman of "considerable prominence," one of the country's biggest industrialists, who employed more than thirty thousand people. The man had connections in Berlin's political and military circles, even access to Hitler's headquarters. The industrialist, Riegner said, had given information previously—and always been proven correct. As Elting listened, Riegner relayed what he had heard. The young diplomat would write in the cable to Washington:

> There has been and is being considered in Hitler's headquarters a plan to exterminate all Jews from Germany and German controlled areas in Europe after they have been concentrated in the east (presumably Poland). The number involved is said to be between three-and-a-half and four millions and the object is to permanently settle the Jewish question in Europe. The mass execution if decided upon would allegedly take place this fall.
> Riegner stated that according to his informant the use of prussic acid was mentioned as a means of accomplishing the executions. When I mentioned that this report seemed fantastic to me, Riegner

said that it struck him in the same way but that from the fact that
mass deportation had been taking place since July 16 as confirmed
by reports received by him from Paris, Holland, Berlin, Vienna, and
Prague it was . . . conceivable that such a diabolical plan was
actually being considered by Hitler. . . .

The messenger had in fact tempered the message, omitting the worst—
that "a giant crematorium" had already been built. Riegner made one
request: Elting must at once forward the news to Washington and send a
coded message to Rabbi Wise in New York as well. "I told Riegner," Elting would write the State Department, "that the information would be
passed on to the Legation"—the U.S. diplomatic post in Bern—". . . but
that I was not in a position to inform him as to what action, if any, the
Legation might take."

In Washington, the men at State, doubting the veracity of the report,
decided not to relay it to Rabbi Wise. Elting had sent it on to Bern, where
Leland Harrison, the chief U.S. diplomat in Switzerland, appended his
own dispatch that undermined the Riegner report, as having the "earmarks of war rumor inspired by fear."

Rabbi Wise soon learned about it, all the same, as Riegner had also
gone to see the British diplomats in Geneva. (The British had cabled the
news to the Foreign Office, which passed it on to the British MP who
headed the London office of the World Jewish Congress.) At once, Wise
sent an urgent letter to Undersecretary Welles, informing him of the extraordinary report from Geneva, and asking that he request the "conservative and equable" Riegner to substantiate "the appalling rumor."

Welles picked up the telephone, politely asking that Wise refrain from
publicizing the Geneva report until the department could confirm it. For
nearly three months, Rabbi Wise sat mute. Only on November 24, 1942,
did Welles at last meet with Wise, and hand over the Riegner materials,
telling him to make them public. On the following day, the *Times* revisited the story of the mass murder of the Jews: "Himmler Program Kills
Polish Jews," read the headline on page 10. The articles remained brief
reports on inside pages, but as they multiplied, a momentum built.

"One is almost stunned into silence," Edward R. Murrow told the
nation on CBS radio on December 13. "But it's eyewitness stuff supported by a wealth of detail and vouched for by responsible governments. What is happening is this: millions of human beings, most of

them Jews, are being gathered up with ruthless efficiency and murdered. . . . The phrase 'concentration camps' is obsolete. . . . It is now possible to speak only of extermination camps."

| | | |

Henry Morgenthau, Jr., had gained fame, though not the kind he sought. Derided as FDR's loyal servant, he was parodied as a scowling, stumbling public speaker—the only man in the cabinet who refused to testify before Congress without aides at either side. The caricature was unfair, but based in truth: "I never went to the Hill," he would later concede, "without ten experts." Henry knew well how he appeared in the popular imagination, and feigned not to care. At the Treasury, no one believed the pretense. His own men, though, had come to see a different man—awkward and shy, but a master bureaucrat, indefatigable and dogged in pursuit of the president's policies. Yet even at the Treasury, as the reports of genocide became inescapable, a new mood set in. Throughout the fall of 1942 and in the winter, Henry would face a new siege, and this time the challenge came not from the Hill, but from his own men.

At Treasury, the scope of the refugee crisis in Europe had become the preoccupation of a team of young lawyers under Henry's charge. The four of them—Randolph Paul, Ansel Luxford, Josiah DuBois, and John Pehle—led Foreign Funds Control, a little-known division that dated to the War of 1812. When the Nazis invaded Norway, the Roosevelt administration had relaunched "Foreign Funds," as it was known. As Washington sought to wage economic warfare against Germany, Foreign Funds led the way—laying down trade restrictions and import controls on enemy assets. The division, in short, was tasked with starving the German war machine of cash, and under Henry's guidance, it became the Treasury's war room.

It was a small circle at the top, but Foreign Funds comprised several thousand employees and by the end of 1942 it had frozen billions in assets. Since the first reports of mass murder leaked out from Europe, the Treasury lawyers had sensed something amiss at State: a distaste for refugee matters. In recent months, though, distrust of the diplomats had given way to outrage. The lawyers were unlikely allies: Some were "Oliphant boys," recruited by Herman Oliphant, the Columbia professor who had run Henry's brains trust until his death in 1939; others the secretary himself had lured to Washington. Some were midwestern arrivistes, others veterans of the East Coast establishment, but all, despite their boss's austere manner, had grown fond of the man they only ever called "Mr. Secretary."

John Pehle led the team. Known in Washington as Morgenthau's fair-haired boy, he *was* blond; in his midthirties, he looked even younger. A midwesterner, Pehle had arrived at the Treasury in 1934, straight from Yale Law, and carried himself with the air of an academic outsider in Washington: He smoked a pipe, favored three-piece suits, and kept a gold watch on a chain in his vest pocket.

Joe DuBois was the unit's lead counsel and cheerleader. Also in his early thirties, he had been cycling in and out of Washington since the 1930s. He had wanted to stay at his small firm in New Jersey, but Henry had lured him back into service. "Things were getting hot," DuBois would say of the secretary's call in early 1941, when he had acquiesced, offering to stay "for a short while." DuBois worked at Henry's side for six years in all.

Luxford, a year older than DuBois, was an Iowan regarded as the in-house stoic. He wore rimless round glasses, bow ties, and his hair brilliantined straight back. Luxford had first come to the Treasury in 1935, and left for a time before the war, taking his wife and young daughter to St. Paul, where he set up a private practice, only to be recalled to Washington. He, too, had returned on a "temporary basis," but, like DuBois, would stick it out for the duration.

Randolph Paul, general counsel of the Treasury, was the group's elder. A year older than the secretary, Paul had been in private practice in New York and gained renown as one of the city's sharpest tax attorneys. Tall, lean, and patrician, Paul had a habit of taking off his thick-rimmed eyeglasses and chewing on the end of an earpiece to mull over a question. Grandson of a butcher, he had gone to Amherst and New York Law School and taught at Yale Law. Five days after Pearl Harbor, he had joined the Treasury—and led the drafting of the new tax code that would shape the government's fiscal policy not just for the war effort, but for the postwar economy.

To the surprise of those who regarded him as an empty suit, Henry Morgenthau, Jr., had united men much younger than himself, and far cleverer, in a common fight. The war had changed the Treasury: A sense of purpose now pervaded the marble corridors. Henry's lieutenants had seen his shortcomings—the public fumbling, private hand-wringing, and tender ego. Yet they had come to share a commitment, though they would have laughed at the notion, that bordered on the sacred. They knew, too, that however awkward and fretful, Henry was determined to lead them.

The Treasury men were conformists, not activists. For years, the business of government—bureaucracy, statistics, legislation—had consumed them. None had demonstrated any interest in refugee matters, much less in the fate of the Jews, but the secretary had given them wide autonomy. Oliphant had helped Morgenthau to design Lend-Lease, establishing the legal ground to arm Britain, France, and the USSR. Several had even visited the front. "One of the things about Treasury, under Morgenthau," Pehle would say, "was the ordinary jurisdictional bounds were not regarded as applicable." By the fall of 1943, the four lawyers had become seized by a new mission, an initiative that others in the federal government would soon call an insurgency. For months, they had sought to grant Riegner, the desperate messenger in Switzerland, a Treasury license to receive U.S. funds to support—by sheer bribery, if necessary— the refugees' escape. It would be a complex campaign, bound up in legalese and red tape, but for Henry's men the aim was clear: to force open a legal door to save Jewish refugees.

Riegner had told of an opening: It might be possible to save the remaining Jews in Romania and France. The Romanian dictator, Marshal Ion Antonescu, long an eager accomplice to Hitler, feared an Axis loss was approaching. He offered to let the Jews out—at a price of at least $50 a head. It was also possible, Riegner had added, to save tens of thousands of Jewish children in France, Belgium, and the Netherlands. An underground—sympathizers, mercenaries, bribable officials—was in place. Riegner only needed the funds. He sent this appeal to Leland Harrison, the U.S. envoy in Bern in April; it reached Henry's men in June. They had seen a paraphrased version of the appeal, but had demanded to see the entire, original cable.

For months, as they petitioned the State Department for details, they received only vague denials. All the while, their counterparts at State insisted that they had sent over all the cables pertaining to economic matters. DuBois, Pehle, and the others sensed that State was stonewalling, and soon found the source: the Division of European Affairs, a bastion of old-guard Foreign Service officers who presided over the third floor of the old State, War and Navy Building—"an antiquated home," the editor of The Nation wrote in 1942, of the "faded and moth-eaten tradition of Victorian diplomacy." The diplomats, sons of the East Coast establishment, worried openly that the foreign aliens would saddle the government with dependents. The State Department, they insisted, had complied with Roosevelt's wishes. The "refugee problem" was no concern of the Treasury's, they argued, but belonged in the realm of European Affairs and on the floor below, in the office of Breckinridge Long, the assistant secretary in charge of granting U.S. visas to those hoping to flee Europe. Any decision to take action, whether relief or rescue, was theirs and theirs alone.

Henry's lawyers were sure, as Joe DuBois wrote, "It was Treasury business, all right." They had become obsessed with funding a rescue mission—to find a way of "financing these escapes," DuBois would recall, "that wouldn't at the same time benefit the enemy." Could the United States send money to aid the escape without feeding dollars to the Nazis?

On July 16, 1943, the Treasury signaled that it was prepared to issue the license to Riegner's group, the World Jewish Congress, but at State the lawyers met another wall. The more they probed, the more their suspicions grew. Finally, they took matters into their own hands. From the unlikely corner of Foreign Funds, quietly and without any formal brief, Treasury undertook to investigate another arm of the federal government. Their boss counseled caution: The secretary feared the hunt would boomerang, hurting his standing with FDR—and dooming any chance of saving the refugees. The Treasury lawyers soon got glimpses behind the curtain from two "moles" at State. It took months, but as DuBois, Pehle, Luxford, and Paul sorted out the history, they uncovered a second trail of documents, one that exposed an ugly—if not criminal— chronology of delays and denials, of lies and cover-ups.

By the winter of 1943, Henry's men had the goods on the old guard at State. The trouble was, they had ensnared their own boss as well.

33. "Courage First"

"Clear the way for those rabbis!" The stationmaster at Union Station was trying to make himself heard over the crowds. A parade of dark figures wearing black coats and Old Testament beards, they came from New York, Philadelphia, and Baltimore, nearly four hundred rabbis converging on Washington, just after noon, on October 6, a few days before Yom Kippur.

As the rabbis marched up First Street to the Capitol, Peter Bergson led the way. By the fall of 1943, Bergson was well known to Henry and FDR. Blessed with intelligence and a quick tongue, he had quickly become the voice of radical Zionism in America, threatening to eclipse the more moderate Stephen Wise. Born Hillel Kook, Bergson had grown up in Jerusalem, a nephew of a former chief rabbi of Palestine. At twenty-eight, he was a secular Jew and an agent of the Irgun Zvai Leumi, an underground paramilitary group created by Ze'ev Jabotinsky, a Russian exile who had first conceived of a Jewish Legion in World War I to free Palestine from the Turks. Jabotinsky's death in 1940 had not slowed the movement: Bergson had come that summer to the United States to raise money for the armed struggle. Kristallnacht, though, had forced him to change course: The U.S. government, Bergson now argued, would never save a single Jew without a mass-scale propaganda war to shame it into action. He had launched the Emergency Committee to Save the Jewish People of Europe, an agitprop machine with one goal: to embarrass the Roosevelt administration into rescuing the Jews.

"The March of the Rabbis" was not Bergson's first stunt. A born impresario, he had attracted a wide circle of allies—"the Bergson Boys," FDR and Henry called them. Months earlier, they had placed a series of full-page advertisements in the *Times*. On February 16, 1943, one played on the shocking news from Romania:

FOR SALE TO HUMANITY
70,000 Jews
Guaranteed Human Beings at $50 a Piece

Roumania is tired of killing Jews. It has killed one hundred thousand of them in two years. Roumania will now give Jews away practically for nothing.

In March, Bergson had also organized a mass spectacle in Madison Square Garden. *We Will Never Die,* scripted by the playwright Ben Hecht, drew 40,000 people to a double premiere. Moss Hart directed Stella Adler, Edward G. Robinson, Dean Martin, and Frank Sinatra, amid hundreds of others, in a "pageant" that featured music by Kurt Weill. "These are the two million Jewish dead of Europe today," Robinson, the narrator, said in a prelude, and at its end, he declared: "Of the six million Jews in German-held lands, the Germans have said none shall remain. . . . When the time comes to make the peace, they will have been done to death." It was not great theater but it proved a public relations coup. Within weeks, Bergson had reprised the pageant in Washington, where Mrs. Roosevelt, six Supreme Court justices, and dozens of senators and congressmen took it in.

On the morning after seeing the show, Eleanor Roosevelt devoted a "My Day" column to praising it. FDR, though, had no intention of granting the rabbis an audience. In his bedroom on the morning of the march, Roosevelt told Marvin McIntyre, his appointment secretary, that he, and not the president, would receive the delegation. (McIntyre said he'd see the rabbis, but "four only.") In fact, FDR could claim an urgent engagement. As the rabbis arrived at the White House, the president ducked out a side entrance and headed for Bolling Field to dedicate four new Liberator bombers, destined for the skies over Yugoslavia.

||||

With the outrage building, Bergson lobbied Congress for a special agency to lead the rescue of the Jews. Rabbi Wise and the Zionist leaders chafed at the upstart's crass tactics—but Bergson would not relent. He stepped up the advertising barrage: "HELP Prevent 4,000,000 People From Becoming Ghosts," cried an ad in the *Times* in November. Another, three weeks later, asked, "HOW WELL ARE YOU SLEEPING? Is There Something You Could Have Done to Save Millions of Innocent People— Men, Women, and Children—from Torture and Death?" Bergson won over Congressman Will Rogers, Jr. (he got to his wife), and even William Randolph Hearst. "This is not a Jewish problem," Hearst wrote in his newspapers. "It is a human problem." Then on November 9, 1943, Bergson got his wish: Congressman Rogers and Senator Guy M. Gillette introduced a resolution calling for the creation of a United States Commission to Save the Jewish People of Europe.

In the middle of this three-way fight among Bergson, Wise, and the White House, was Henry Morgenthau. Throughout Thanksgiving week, the Treasury's lights were aglow deep into the night as the secretary's lawyers again tried to sort through the State Department's cables. For days, they tried to piece together the correspondence, and marshal the evidence that their colleagues at State had not only thrown hurdles in their way, but followed a deliberate path of obstruction. The Treasury men hoped to convince their boss, so that he might convince his.

"May I make a point?" John Pehle asked, at a meeting in the secretary's office on the evening of November 23. In his hands was a file of official correspondence on the refugees.

"If you please," said Morgenthau.

"This file is full of cables," Pehle said, "which we have originated and which State has sent, which are full of little remarks like, 'the Treasury wants this,' 'the Treasury desires you to do this.' . . . And Harrison [the U.S. minister in Bern], unless he is just a dumbbell, can see through that, that State is in effect saying, 'This is what the Treasury wants you to do.'" The undercurrent was clear, Pehle argued: State did not have to do the Treasury's bidding.

Go slow, the secretary said, fearful of overreach. "We are on new territory when we are taking up a matter of refugees." Ever hesitant, he urged caution. "Gentlemen," Henry went on, "I can say on the record that I am delighted at your motives. No one would like to see this come out in the open more than I. Unfortunately, you are up against a successive generation of people like those in the State Department who don't like to do this kind of thing [opening the door for refugees], and it is only by my happening to be secretary of the Treasury and being vitally interested in these things . . . that I can do it. I am all for you, not that I am a cynic or discouraged, but . . . don't think you're going to nail anybody in the State Department—"

"I am not sure, Mr. Secretary," Luxford interjected.

"—to the cross," said Morgenthau, finishing his sentence.

After months of delays, in the first week of December, Secretary Hull replied to the Treasury's repeated questions as to why no action had been taken on the Jews. State, Hull insisted, bore no responsibility for the delays. The trouble was Riegner: The Swiss lawyer had no plan of action. As his aides fumed, Henry remained wary of taking the issue straight to the president. "I admire you people for getting excited about it," he said. "God damn it! It makes me feel good." But he worried about repercussions.

Randolph Paul, the reserved tax attorney who rarely spoke in personal terms, interjected: "Well, I feel especially sore at all these Jewish episodes in the State Department, and I'm convinced it's just a gang in there that are blocking everything and so . . . I get a little bit extra hot on that account."

"Well, I of all people," said Henry, "appreciate the sympathetic interest of you boys. On the other hand, I've got to be a balance wheel."

Any move on State, the secretary feared, would be seen as an attack on Hull—and though Hull may have been an anachronism, Henry did not think him dishonest. Hull could be misled, but he would not lie about the reasons behind the reluctance to grant the Treasury's license for the rescue effort. There had to be more to it, Henry told his aides.

The secretary, though, was already plotting an indirect route to FDR: If he complained to Hull, the president was sure to hear of it.

"It's like that story Henry, my boy, told me," he told the aides. "His men didn't have enough to eat . . . on maneuvers, so he went into his Colonel's tent and addressed himself to the Major, with the Colonel lying on the bed 10 feet away . . . at the tops of his lungs . . . whereupon the Colonel got up from the bed and said, 'What the hell is all this? I want to hear about this!' And he investigated."

"The Treasury boys" did not have to wait long: Within two weeks, a clue to the reason behind the intransigence at State emerged. All that fall, official London had struck an ambivalent pose on a rescue plan for the Jews. The British government seemed divided: The Ministry of Economic Warfare appeared willing to offer support, but the Foreign Office held back. On December 15, Morgenthau and his men learned the ugly truth:

The British had only hardened the State Department's anti-refugee line. London was "concerned," FDR's ambassador, John Winant, cabled, "with the difficulties of disposing of any considerable number of Jews, should they be rescued from enemy occupied territory." The Foreign Office, Winant relayed, "foresee it is likely to prove almost if not quite impossible to deal with anything like the number of 70,000 refugees whose rescue is envisaged by the Riegner plan."

The news from London shocked the Treasury: The opposition ran deeper than anyone had realized.

"Amazing cable," DuBois would say a few days later, as the men sat in a semicircle before the secretary's desk.

"The British are saying, in effect," Pehle added, "they don't propose to take any Jews out of these areas."

"Their position is," said DuBois, " 'What could we do with them, if we got them out?' Amazing."

"Mr. Secretary," Pehle said, "the bull has to be taken by the horns." Someone had to "get this thing out of the State Department."

Before the men left, Henry spoke not as their boss, but as a human being.

"Again, I can't say how much I appreciate your sympathetic interest in these things," he said.

"We appreciate yours, too, Mr. Secretary," Luxford said.

"Sympathetic?" said Paul. "God!"

"It is our gain that you feel that way," added Luxford.

After the meeting, Joe DuBois returned to his desk and found a telephone message: A State Department contact had asked if he could drop by his office that afternoon. The friendly diplomat was not the Treasury boys' only source at State. Two other, lower-level officials had offered help, but no one had expressed such urgency. DuBois had long known there were gaps in the State correspondence. Scouring the cables that the Department had forwarded to the Treasury, he'd noticed a reference to a cable from February: "No. 354," a reply from Washington to Harrison, the U.S. envoy in Switzerland.

DuBois sensed that the earlier cable might hold significance, and brought the discovery to Morgenthau, who demanded to see the original cable from State. Later that day Breckenridge Long, the assistant secretary of state, sent over a copy, but it was only a paraphrase of "No. 354." According to the paraphrase, State had asked that Harrison refrain from using diplomatic channels to send reports to "private persons"—like Wise—in the United States. "Private messages," the cable instructed, circumvented "the censorship of neutral countries," and could cause those countries to cut off all diplomatic mail. At Treasury, the paraphrase heightened suspicions; for weeks, Henry's aides had demanded to see the original cable but been rebuffed. And so, as DuBois headed to State after lunch, to see his contact in the department, he had a sense of what might be on offer.

Donald Hiss was an assistant to Dean Acheson and head of State's own office of Foreign Funds Control. One of the New Deal's bright young men, Hiss was a Harvard Law graduate who had clerked for the Supreme Court justice Oliver Wendell Holmes. He was also the younger brother of Alger Hiss, another State Department official, who would gain infamy after the war, charged with spying for the Soviets. Until his death in 1996, Alger Hiss denied taking part in espionage, but in 1950 he would be convicted for perjury. His brother Donald would fall under the same suspicion, though he was never indicted. In December 1943, on the day DuBois entered his office, the younger Hiss was acting, to judge by all available evidence, on his conscience alone—defying his superiors and State Department protocols.

Hiss was on edge. His telephone was tapped, he was sure, and his "conversations with Treasury were being listened to." Straight off, he told DuBois of the risks: "If it were known that I have shown you cable 354," he added, "I might well lose my job."

When Hiss handed DuBois the two cables, and DuBois placed them side by side, the subterfuge leapt out. The original cable, No. 354, bearing the date February 10, 1943, confirmed the accuracy of the paraphrase State had shared. But no one at Treasury had known what the "suppression cable," as Henry's aides would soon call No. 354, referred to: What was the "private message" that State did not want sent to "private persons"? To his horror, DuBois learned the answer when he read the second cable on Hiss's desk. No. 354 was a reply to Harrison's cable of January 21, 1943, No. 482—a communiqué that relayed Riegner's report of the mass murder of Jews in Poland and the "indescribable" condition of the Jews in Romania.

The cable upbraiding Harrison had been signed "For Hull by S.W."— Sumner Welles—and initialed by four State officials. These four, DuBois surmised, must have sent it without Welles's knowledge. Because on April 10, two months after the "suppression cable," Welles again asked for the details he had requested in January. In response, Harrison expressed confusion. "While I have not transmitted more of R.'s [Riegner's] messages," he wrote,

in compliance with the terms of your 354, February 10, I have at the same time felt that information which he is able to furnish and which appears to be reasonably authentic should be in your hands. . . . May I suggest that messages of this character should not (repeat not) be subjected to the restriction imposed by your [cable] 354, February 10, and that I be permitted to transmit messages from R [Riegner] more particularly in view of the helpful information which they may frequently contain?

DuBois had found the smoking gun. The State Department had deliberately tried to stop the news of the mass murder from reaching anyone in the United States—and then lied to the Treasury about it. When DuBois relayed the discovery to the secretary, Henry called an urgent meeting.

At the Treasury on the following evening, a Sunday, Henry made sure to have his wife there as well. Ellie interrupted often, unafraid to joust with her husband's aides.

"Gentlemen, this is some memorandum," Henry said, as he held a draft that his aides had prepared for Henry to deliver to Hull, by hand, the next day. The memo concerned the U.S. response to the British refusal to aid in the rescue of the Jews, and Henry's aides had put ferocity in his mouth: "To me, Mr. Secretary, this position is astounding," the draft read. "In simple terms, the British position is that they apparently are prepared to accept the possible—even probable—death of thousands of Jews in enemy territory."

The lawyers made clear the Treasury's demands. "I propose for your consideration," the document continued, "that we cut the Gordian Knot *now* by advising the British that we are going to take immediate action to facilitate the escape of Jews from Hitler and *then* discuss what can be done in the way of finding them a more permanent refuge." The memo offered a final plea: "Even if we took those people and treated them as prisoners of war it would be better than letting them die."

| | | |

The following day, December 20, Henry marched over to State, taking Pehle and Paul along for ballast. They had spent the morning rehearsing a script for the showdown. Henry's aim was not only to deliver a stern warning, but to get all the cables. Only the originals, all agreed, could convince FDR of the State Department's deception. Henry's aides had coaxed him into a scheme to play Hull: to ask for a copy of cable 354, casually, without revealing its importance.

Sitting in Hull's elegant office, Randolph Paul felt the weight of the occasion. Morgenthau, he would say, "was taking his political life in his hands." Hull was "known as a killer," and he could be counted on to seek revenge. Yet the secretary of state also knew, Paul added, that "Morgenthau had a personal hold on the President."

Before Henry could present his letter on the British refusal, Hull spoke. To Pehle, the secretary of state seemed worn out, a man on the defensive, but Henry knew there would be no easy concession.

"I've already sent a cable to Ambassador Winant," Hull said, handing Henry the reply on a pink-copy sheet. Henry was taken aback—the wind, he would say, had been knocked from his sails. He had never seen stronger official language. Hull read aloud his reply to Winant, letting the words sink in. The department expressed "astonishment" at the British position. London's stance, he assured Henry, was not in line with the policy of the State Department, but at times, he conceded, such matters did not get his attention. When they did, he found it necessary to take them in hand, skirting the people down the line who raised objections. To get action, Hull said, you had "to rip" through the complaints.

At Hull's side sat Breckinridge Long, the State official who had caused the Treasury such consternation, doing all he could to slow the granting of a license to rescue the refugees. Long interrupted: "I don't know if you're going to like it . . . but I drafted personally a license Saturday, and issued it and cabled it to Switzerland." He had issued the license to Riegner himself, Long said, but had not had time to consult Treasury. Long had obviously prepped for the meeting. He ran through a list of State's efforts: They had tried to rescue Jews from Germany and occupied Europe, he said, in hopes of sending them to the United States, Sweden, Madagascar, and Palestine—but the Germans had succeeded in "thwarting most of these rescue attempts."

As if by way of reply, Henry handed Hull the Treasury report, which charged his department with a deliberate hindering of Treasury's efforts to save any remaining Jews. Hull read it quickly, without comment. Only when the secretary of state sent his aides to retrieve the cables did Henry make his move.

"By the way," he said, "I have a cable in my hand from Harrison, No. 2460, in which it mentions a cable, No. 354. While you're getting all the other cables, would you mind getting that one for me?"

"Make a note of that," Hull told Long. "And just give it to him."

As the men rose to leave, Long approached Henry. "I want to talk to you privately," he said, ushering him into another room.

Henry and Long had known each other since the Wilson years, having crossed paths when Henry's father was in Turkey. At sixty-one, "Breck" Long was on his second tour at State. His education in world affairs, other than a course or two at Princeton, dated to a master's thesis unfortunately entitled "The Impossibility of India's Revolt from England." Long had practiced law in St. Louis before marrying the wealthy granddaughter of Francis Preston Blair, Jr., the Democratic nominee for vice president in 1868. Availing himself of his wife's resources, he delved into politics, giving generously to the Wilson campaign in 1916. In 1917, the debt was repaid: Long became a third assistant secretary of state.

Lacking discernible expertise, Long had been put in charge of Far Eastern affairs. "I am surprised," he confessed in his diary, "how much can be done without any knowledge of it on my part."

In 1920, Long had quit State to run for the U.S. Senate from Missouri, only to lose in the Republican landslide. He had returned to the law, weathering the Depression years in Montpelier Manor, a horse-breeding estate in the Maryland hills. In 1932, he again gave lavishly, backing Roosevelt. Again, the largesse was returned—in 1933, FDR named him his envoy to Italy. Long would live to regret his writings from Rome. Mussolini, he wrote to a fellow diplomat, was "one of the most remarkable persons," and his rule, "the most interesting experiment in government to come above the horizon since the formulation of our Constitution."

Long had also explored Nazi ideology. "Have just finished Hitler's Mein Kampf," he wrote in his diary in early 1938. "It is worth reading. . . . It is eloquent in opposition to Jewry and to Jews as exponents of Communism & chaos." He added, "My estimate of Hitler as a man rises with the reading of his book." After his Italy posting, Long had returned to private practice before FDR, in 1940, brought him back to State. Now as assistant secretary, all matters relating to the European Jews crossed his desk. At Treasury, he was seen as the instigator of the logjam on saving any refugees.

The war years had taken a toll on Breckinridge Long. "My physical and nervous resources have been taxed to the point of exhaustion," he complained in his diary early in 1941. He railed against the enemies at home: leakers, "Fifth Columnists," stubborn ambassadors. When the issue concerned the Jews, Long's pique rose. "The refugee problem is a thorny one," he wrote in 1942—and their plight was raised by interlocutors like James McDonald, Rabbi Wise, Mrs. Roosevelt, and even Sumner Welles (who saw him "as an obstructionist"). Visits from Wise left Long derisive: "The Jewish organizations are divided," he wrote after the rabbi had come to ask for assistance, "there is no cohesion nor any sympathetic collaboration. Rather rivalry, jealousy and antagonism."

For years, he'd deemed Henry Morgenthau no more than an annoyance, a placeholder who owed his survival to the mercy of the Roosevelts. Now, Long realized, he faced a different man.

Henry had Long cornered. Long's recent lying before Congress was the talk of Washington newsmen. In secret testimony on the Hill—"a 4-hour inquisition," Long called it in his diary—he said there was no need for any Bergson-backed agency to save the Jews, reciting an extensive record of rescue: "We have taken into this country since the beginning of the Hitler regime and the persecution of the Jews, until today, approximately 580,000 refugees." Many in his audience believed Long, even those who should have known better. According to the immigration service, of the 476,930 aliens who had entered the United States in the decade since 1933, only 165,756 had self-reported as "Hebrews"—or Jews. Of these, about 138,000 had escaped persecution. (While it would remain impossible to give a precise figure, the best estimate for the number of Jewish refugees who could have been admitted to the United States in the years 1933 to 1941, as the persecution mounted, is derived from the number of unused German quota visas: a total of some 165,000.)

Henry braced himself, refusing to let the opportunity go.

"I just want to tell you," Long started in, once the two were alone, "unfortunately the people lower down in your Department and lower down in the State Department are making a lot of trouble." Long raised the issue of anti-Semitism, alluding to underlings who had "been spreading this stuff," and "raising technical difficulties."

At last, Henry seized the opening.

"Well, Breck, as long as you raise the question, we might be a little frank. The impression is all around that you, particularly, are anti-Semitic!"

Henry looked him in the eye.

"I know that is so," said Long. "I hope that you will use your good offices to correct that impression, because I am not."

"I am very, very glad to know it," said Henry, adding, "Since we are being so frank, you might as well know that the impression" at Treasury was that State shared the British position on refusing any rescue plan.

Long protested: He hoped they could work together. Of course, Henry said. "After all, Breck," he replied, "the United States of America was created as a refuge for people who were persecuted the world over, starting with Plymouth." As he offered the history lesson, Henry tried hard not to condescend. Instead, he repeated his father's vow to President Wilson and to the Young Turks in Constantinople: "As Secretary of the Treasury for one hundred and thirty-five million people," Henry Jr. said, "I am carrying this [rescue effort] out as Secretary of the Treasury, and not as a Jew."

"Well," Long said, "my concept of America as a place of refuge for persecuted people is just the same."

Henry said he was "delighted to hear it."

||||

The final piece of the puzzle would not reach the secretary until Christmas. After his showdown with Long, the mood at Treasury was celebratory, and Henry's team of lawyers nearly giddy—then they got the cables Hull had promised Henry.

Something was amiss. In the copy of the "suppression cable" that State sent over, someone had deleted one phrase—"Your 482-January 21." In the absence of the reference to the earlier cable from Switzerland—the dispatch relaying Riegner's report of the mass murder of Jews in Poland and the mortal threat to the Jews in Romania—the reply seemed innocuous. Henry's aides, though, had heard from their "information termites" at State that the omission was deliberate. Long himself, they learned, had done the editing. The men at State were trying to cover their tracks: hiding that they had not only ignored the dire warning, but scolded the messenger. Henry now had all the evidence he needed to go to FDR.

The Treasury team worked nonstop, with Joe DuBois spending most of Christmas Day drafting the report. When they handed the first draft to Morgenthau, its language was stark. DuBois, Luxford, Paul, and Pehle accused the State Department of a war crime—burying a report, from a reliable source, of genocide: "We leave it for your judgment," they wrote, "whether this action made such officials the accomplices of Hitler in this program and whether or not these officials are not war criminals in every sense of the term."

Henry was startled. "What did you people think I was going to do with this?" he asked.

"I think there is only one thing to do," said Paul. "This is the ideal opportunity to get three of the most vicious men [Long and two underlings] removed from their offices in the State Department that you will ever have."

"You still haven't answered my question."

"I think you have to talk to Hull about it."

"I mean," Henry said a few moments later, "when you call these people 'accomplices of Hitler in this program,' they are war criminals in every sense of the term. . . . You are finding them guilty without trying them."

Henry sent the men back to revise the document. He refused to convict the State Department without a fair hearing: You can't be judge and jury, he insisted. For days, as the team wrestled over how, and when, to take their case to Hull, Henry searched for a way out. At one point he even considered asking the chief justice of the Supreme Court, Harlan Stone, to be the messenger. He and Ellie had gotten to know Stone and his wife. "He feels this thing very deeply," Henry assured his aides, but they argued against it—and redoubled their efforts on the draft.

By the second week of January 1944, the secretary was growing anxious for action. "Do you know you have been on these memoranda about two weeks?" he asked his staff.

"It is a very difficult memorandum to write," Paul said.

DuBois had changed the report's title, now calling it with deliberate audacity "Report to the Secretary on the Acquiescence of this Government in the Murder of the Jews."

Henry again urged caution, but his men gave little ground: The new draft accused the State Department of "willful attempts to prevent action from being taken to rescue Jews from Hitler." Cast as a letter to the president, the report drew the boldest line of the secretary's tenure: "Unless remedial steps of a drastic nature are taken, and taken immediately, I am certain that no effective action will be taken by the Government to prevent the complete extermination of the Jews in German controlled Europe, and that this Government will have to share for all time the responsibility for this extermination."

The Treasury report also called for Henry to make explicit the charge that the State Department officials had intended to deceive the American people: "In their official capacity they have gone so far as to surreptitiously attempt to stop the obtaining of information concerning the murder of the Jewish population of Europe. . . . The evidence supporting this conclusion is so shocking and so tragic that it is difficult to believe."

||||

On January 13, Henry consulted Ben Cohen and Sam Rosenman, two men whose advice FDR had long trusted, and who, not coincidentally, were also Jewish. When Henry had broached the idea of a meeting with the president, Rosenman warned him off. He was concerned, above all, about a leak.

"The thing I am thinking about is whether when you talk about refugees you want to have three Jews?" Rosenman said—referring to himself, Cohen, and Morgenthau. "If there were to be publicity, I think the choice of the three people is terrible."

"Don't worry about the publicity," Henry had replied. "What I want is intelligence and courage. Courage first, and intelligence second."

Rosenman and Cohen had tried to dissuade Henry from going to the president, yet Henry had committed to using all his weapons. He was prepared to mention that a "nasty scandal" was sure to ensue, should word leak about the State Department cables.

On Saturday, January 15, Henry and the "9:30 group" rehearsed for hours.

"The President has two Cabinet officers, and he has to decide between them," one aide said.

"He calls Hull in—and says, 'Cordell, this is—' " offered Pehle.

"You don't know the President," Henry interjected.

"That may very well be," Pehle said, trying to go on, but the secretary had heard enough.

"I think this is a very weak and compromising way to do it. If I go to Hull in the first instance . . . then he has a chance to get his case to the President before I do."

"That is the point," Pehle said.

Ben Cohen had joined the group, offering cautious advice, not only how to bring FDR around, but how to sell any rescue plan to Hull.

"Wait a minute; I have an answer," said Henry, as he laid out a plan: He would ask to see the president tomorrow, and give "him all the dirt."

FDR, he was all but certain, would say, "Make this easy for me. See Cordell."

Cohen was not sure: "It might be that the President will be willing to ask Hull to come over to talk it over with him and you."

"I don't know," Henry snapped back, "but I know the President well enough to go to him and say, 'I want to see you on a matter that is very, very close to my heart. I want your advice. How would you handle this situation?'"

Mrs. Klotz, taking it all down in her corner, could not contain herself: "That is wonderful."

"You can sit around and worry, but you just don't know until you face the President what kind of mood he is in," Henry said. "He may say, 'I will relieve you of this, Henry.' He may say, 'You have got to relieve me. You do it.' You just don't know. The only way to find out is for me to go over there and see him and ask his advice: 'There are the facts, Mr. President, the most shocking things I have found since I have been in Washington. Here we find ourselves aiding and abetting Hitler. How can we at this very late date try to make up for lost time?'"

|| || ||

Early on Sunday afternoon, January 16, Henry, John Pehle, and Randolph Paul arrived at the White House. They climbed the stairs to the second floor and entered the Oval Study, beside the president's bedroom.

Henry Morgenthau had suffered weeks of sleepless nights; his nerves were shot and the migraines had come back. To meet the supreme moment of his life, he would have to abandon the caution that had guided him since childhood, and steel himself for rejection.

Henry had dreaded this meeting. "It was a wretched time," his daughter Joan recalled, who had remained home from Vassar for the holidays. "All throughout that winter Daddy was beyond anguish. . . . I saw it every night, written on his face. He'd always had migraines, but the worry and fear nearly crippled him. He knew it, he even told us: 'It's too late, but someone's got to do something.' To sit there and remain silent— it would have killed him."

Henry feared what his best friend would say, but after enduring a "terrible eighteen months" since learning of Hitler's plan to exterminate the Jewish people, he had reached the breaking point.

The meeting would last less than an hour.

Henry began by telling the president that the time had come to confront the hard question: How to save as many of the Jews still alive in Europe as they could?

"Henry, I would prefer that the facts be summarized orally," Roosevelt said, declining to read the long document the secretary had brought.

"Mr. President," Henry said, "I am deeply disturbed about the failure of the State Department to take any effective action to save the remaining Jews in Europe." Treasury, he said, had "uncovered evidence" that certain State officials "were not only indifferent, but they were actually taking action to prevent the rescue of the Jews."

FDR held the report in his hands, but he did not even glance at it. One of the final lines begged for a solution: "The matter of rescuing the Jews from extermination is a trust too great to remain in the hands of men who are indifferent, callous, and perhaps even hostile."

When Henry mentioned "children in box cars," the president spoke up. Yes, the refugee situation was dire but weren't there reasons, he countered, we had not taken in more? For years, FDR had listened with sympathy to the fears of a "Fifth Column"—pro-Nazi saboteurs infiltrating the home front. (In 1940, he'd given a speech on the "threat," warning of "peaceful visitors" who were "actually a part of an enemy unit of occupation.") Hadn't we heard about refugees coming over, he said to Henry, and causing trouble? FDR seemed disinclined to believe that Breck Long would intentionally create obstacles, but he conceded that Long had somewhat "soured on the problem" after Rabbi Wise "got him to approve a long list of people being brought into this country." Many of them, Roosevelt added, "turned out to be bad people."

The president's fear of letting in the "wrong" immigrants might have caught some off guard. But Henry knew precisely what FDR was referring to and did not hesitate to tell him he had the facts wrong. "Mr. President," he said, "at a cabinet meeting the attorney general said that only three Jews of those entering the United States during the war [more than 100,000 by the best estimates] had turned out to be undesirable." Roosevelt merely grumbled that he had been told the "number was considerably larger."

||||

FDR did not feign a fight.

When Henry asked that Pehle present the case, the president listened intently as the aide read aloud from the report, moving with calm precision through the tangle of State Department cables. Henry had come, as well, with a draft executive order in hand. It called for the president to establish a War Refugee Board—charged with the "immediate rescue and relief of the Jews of Europe and other victims of enemy persecution"—that would have as its members Henry, Hull, and Leo Crowley, head of the Foreign Economic Administration.

Roosevelt glanced through the proposed order, and made one change. He saw no reason to include Crowley; Stimson, the secretary of war, he said, should be the board's third member. Further, he wondered, had they consulted Stettinius, Hull's number two? FDR gave the impression that they need not consult Hull, but they should go and see Stettinius—the president's idea, as Randolph Paul would explain, was to "get him to agree, so that Hull not only had the president and Morgenthau to contend with, but his own undersecretary."

Mrs. Roosevelt cut the meeting short, leaning into the study to remind her husband of Sunday lunch. Whether planned or not, the interruption played to Henry's hand: There was no time for debate.

Before leaving, the secretary wanted to make certain the president understood him: This was no turf war—he was not seeking revenge on the State Department. "Effective action could be taken," Henry insisted. He spoke of the Armenians—how his father had succeeded "in getting the Armenians out of Turkey" and "saving their lives." FDR agreed, wondering if they could move any Jews "through Romania into Bulgaria and out through Turkey"; such channels, he thought, were "wide open." You could help Jews to safety, he imagined, "out over the Spanish and Swiss borders."

On Monday Henry was scheduled to deliver a national radio address—"Let's All Back the Attack!"—to launch the Fourth War Loan Drive. He would serve as emcee, hosting on the air General Dwight D. Eisenhower (who a month earlier had been named the supreme Allied commander of all forces in Europe), Admiral Nimitz, Bing Crosby, Captain Glenn Miller, and Captain Ronald Reagan. Henry had fretted terribly about his speech, worrying to Ellie—and Henry III and Joan—that FDR might "sour" on him. One line about the Nazis' future caused the greatest anxiety—about "stringing up the ring-leaders of hate and letting them hang there until they are dead"—but he was desperate to hold on to it. Over the phone that Sunday evening, he asked Roosevelt if the line went too far. FDR liked it, but gibed that "You might want to add the word 'proven' before 'ring-leaders.'"

Henry hung up relieved: He had heard the old "grand humor" in the president's voice. Before going to bed, he would look back and realize that he had staked everything on the meeting that Sunday morning. Never had he so directly made the case for saving the Jews. Never had he so boldly stood up for his convictions before his best friend.

Six days later, FDR acted. On January 22, 1944, he ended the State Department's obstruction, signing Executive Order 9417 to establish the War Refugee Board. Roosevelt instructed the secretaries of Treasury, State, and War "to take action for the immediate rescue from the Nazis of as many as possible of the persecuted minorities of Europe—racial, religious or political—all civilian victims of enemy savagery." The creation of the War Refugee Board, though, signaled a dramatic policy shift. Breckinridge Long was stripped of the refugee portfolio. "Let somebody else have the fun," he wrote in his diary, adding, weeks later: "What can they do that I have not done I cannot imagine. However I think it is a good move—for local political reasons."

At fault, Long wrote, were the "4 million Jews in New York & its environs, who feel themselves related to the refugees." He stood by his record; the State Department had done all it could. "This will encourage them in the thought the persecuted may be saved and possibly satisfy them—politically," Long wrote, "but in my opinion can not save any persecuted people we could not save under my recent and long suffering administration."

John Pehle, an architect of the Treasury campaign, would head the new refugee board. Within weeks, Pehle had at his disposal money and the U.S. government's largest network of field agents in Europe, men and women with the knowledge, and ability, to force open any remaining escape route. From France, the Balkans, Bulgaria, Romania, Hungary, and North Africa, agents of the Refugee Board helped free Jewish survivors. It united spies and smugglers, local officials and diplomats to feed, fund, and arm underground networks in the hopes of opening doors to freedom. The board also entertained ransom negotiations with Nazis.

In one ambitious proposal, though, the War Refugee Board would be stymied. Pehle would push for an Allied bombing of the rail lines to the largest of the death camps, Auschwitz-Birkenau in Poland. In June 1944, Pehle received a cable from the board's representative in Geneva, Roswell McClelland, detailing intelligence from the Czech and Hungarian underground on the five primary deportation routes from Hungary. His sources, McClelland added, urged "these lines be bombed . . . as the only possible means of slowing down or stopping future deportations." Pehle forwarded the intelligence to the Pentagon but was rebuffed: Any bombing would be "impracticable," John McCloy, the undersecretary of the Army, replied, and would divert "considerable air support essential to the success of our forces now engaged in decisive operations."

For Henry, the establishment of the War Refugee Board was a triumph. His men would join Mrs. Klotz in presenting him with a certificate testifying to their pride in him. But he knew it was a small victory—too little, too late. Instead, he would be haunted by the State Department's record of inaction, deception, and, though he loathed to say the word, lying. "The God-damnest thing," he called it.

The Refugee Board saved as many as 200,000 Jews—no one would ever tally the true number. And yet, in the years that followed the war, among the six million, they were invisible.

34. In the Med: April 20

WINTER 1944–SPRING 1944

t was New Year's Day 1944 when Bob shipped out again on the *Lansdale*. Within hours of the ship's leaving Brooklyn, an explosion in New York Harbor shook the ground as far away as Manhattan. The concussion blew out windows on the coast of northern New Jersey and Long Island; Henry and Ellie felt it at home on West Eighty-first Street. The radio bulletin came almost at once: A destroyer had blown up, but few details could be given. "Our latest word," Frank Knox, the Navy secretary, said, "is that the vessel was at anchor."

The USS *Turner* had blown up at the mouth of the harbor, off Rockaway Point. Maneuvering through a dark snowy squall, it had dropped anchor near Ambrose Light, just beyond the submarine net protecting the harbor. After nine months at sea, it awaited clearance to proceed into the channel. The blast had come at 6:18 A.M. A new shift had just entered the mess for breakfast, while on deck others had begun to unload the ammunition, a laborious routine required of ships before coming in to Fort Lafayette, the old naval base on Staten Island's eastern edge. What caused the explosion would never be determined: Some thought it a mine, others an enemy submarine. Most likely, it was the ammo: With the ship's shells piled on the deck, a lit cigarette could have provided the spark.

Months would pass before the death toll became public: 15 officers and 138 enlisted men. But in those first anxious hours, even the secretary of the Treasury did not know which ship had been destroyed. When the *Turner* blew, the *Lansdale* stood a few thousand yards away.

Henry and Ellie did not know Bob's fate, and would not know for three days. Only when the Navy at last reported the demise of the *Turner* could the Morgenthaus return to Washington relieved. Those aboard the *Lansdale,* though, could not know the scale of the disaster. Only much later did Bob hear the news: "Howie" Murray, a good friend at Amherst, had been aboard the *Turner.* A twenty-four-year-old from outside Chicago, Murray had captained a gun crew on the Lend-Lease convoys to the Russian Arctic. On one harrowing Murmansk run, he and his men had faced more than a hundred waves of Luftwaffe bombers. Murray would not be Bob's only Amherst classmate to die. Friends from Deerfield were lost, too. Yet on that first day of January, as the *Lansdale* set out again in harm's way, the sinking of the *Turner,* and its untold wake of death, weighed heavily on Bob, his fellow officers, and the crew.

||||

The *Lansdale* was headed back on convoy duty, this time in the Mediterranean. "Med Duty," Captain Douglas Swift warned his officers, offered little joy. The *Lansdale* would follow the sea road that the Allies had cut through the Strait of Gibraltar, hewing close to the North African coast and moving through the Tunisian War Channel to swing northward through the Tyrrhenian Sea north of Sicily. When asked about the dangers, Swift only grinned.

The call to battle stations came twice a day: just before dawn, and again in the evening, before sunset. A piercing siren, it would resound throughout the ship, sending the men rushing down passageways and up ladders to their posts, where, in helmets and life preservers, they stayed each time for two and a half hours.

"We were at GQ"—General Quarters—"at dusk every night," Marion Porter, one of the few Black members of the crew, recalled. "It was the favorite time for attack by the Nazis." The planes came as the last light disappeared, when it was too dark to see an object against the western sky. The Luftwaffe "liked to swoop in low," Porter said, "just skimming the water, coming out of the blackness of the mountains on shore." Each evening the air was heavy with dread. "Could never know quite when" the attack would come, "but it was sure to come."

In mid-February, new orders came: The *Lansdale* would move from convoying to "shore bombardment," joining the naval vessels supporting the Allied assault in Italy. For months, the U.S. Army had been fighting northward from Naples, desperate to move on Rome and pry open the Nazi grip. The drive, though, had stalled. The British, on the Adriatic side, had not fared much better. On December 2, the Luftwaffe bombed the port of Bari, sinking sixteen transport ships. Churchill, though, saw the chance for a turning point. An amphibious landing on Italy's western coast, he argued, could outflank the Nazis, catapulting Allied troops behind the Gustav Line, the noose the Germans had drawn across the width of Italy, and landing them just south of Rome. Eisenhower considered it risky, but in early 1944, as he left for England, to become supreme commander of the Allied Expeditionary Forces, a British general took charge in the Mediterranean—and Churchill won out. "Operation Shingle" would zero in on the little port of Cape D'Anzio.

The assault began almost too well. When the first troops went ashore on January 22, the German defenders were caught off guard. Facing no opposition, a patrol advanced nearly forty miles to Rome—and began to unload equipment, but the Germans rushed in troops from the north and gained the high ground. As the Wehrmacht artillery pounded the beaches and the Luftwaffe bombed the Cape, the Americans at once saw the battle shifting—and before long could foresee that the toll at Anzio would grow far higher.

For the sailors in the waters off the coast, it was hell—thirty-two bombing attacks in the first ten days. The Allied armada had assembled in Naples, with French, Dutch, and Greek vessels bolstering the U.S. and British ships. On February 13, the *Lansdale* joined them, taking up its assigned position in Destroyer Squadron 7, in a division under the command of Val Havard, Bob's old captain. Their orders were clear: to provide cover for the GIs to make it ashore. From there, the Americans would attempt a rear attack on the Germans' right flank.

The *Lansdale* moved alongside the *Philadelphia* and the *Hilary P. Jones,* blasting the German emplacements that lined the shore. "The big guns," Bob would say, of the five-inch guns that could reach twelve miles. Although they fired the guns nearly without pause, the Nazi counterattack was relentless. On February 18, the HMS *Penelope,* a British cruiser, was sunk by a U-boat. The *Lansdale* raced to get closer—at times the men could see the soldiers on the beach—as they hoped to lend support for the GIs trying to cross the Rapido River, the narrow waterway that divides Naples and Anzio. The first time the ship approached, they were stopped by fog; on the next day, the Germans were waiting. Nazi gunners "straddled" the ships—firing a series of salvos to the left and right of the *Philadelphia* and the *Lansdale,* forcing them to retreat.

The *Lansdale* remained in the waters off Naples until February 27—bombarding German targets on shore, fighting off German bombers at sea, and witnessing Mount Vesuvius belch out its biggest eruption in seventy-two years. On March 18, the *Lansdale* was ordered south, first to Castellamare, then to Capri, before sailing once again for Algiers. It took a week to reach Mers-el-Kébir, just north of Oran, where the ship would tie up for repairs and to get more firepower. At launch, the *Lansdale* had had five five-inch guns, and torpedoes. In the Mediterranean, though, the threat was not submarines but bombers. At the base in Algeria, the *Lansdale* would lose half of its torpedo tubes, and gain four 20 mm Oerlikon guns and two twin 40 mm guns. The ship remained in port a week, testing out the new hardware.

The *Lansdale* left port on April 18, at six o'clock in the evening. Half a dozen new crew members, young men fresh from boot camp, had come aboard, joining another seventeen who'd joined the ship in late March, survivors of the *Mayo*, a destroyer hit badly at Salerno. The captain and Bob questioned the look of the new crew; four were growing beards—a barbershop quartet, they were preparing to sing for the wounded at a Red Cross quarters once the ship returned to port.

It was nearly ten A.M. on April 19, when the ship met up with the new convoy. UGS-38 was a massive ship-train: eighty-eight ships in ten columns, headed for Bizerte, the port on the northern edge of Tunisia. Nearly all were merchant vessels, except for two tankers and one Coast Guard cutter, the USS *Menges*. The escort contingent comprised sixteen warships, but the *Lansdale* was its sole destroyer. As the "jam ship," she was charged with fending off any glider bombs—radio-controlled bombs launched by high-altitude bombers—and hunting for U-boats. Their position would be Station 6 on the isolated edge of the outer screen, a few thousand yards off the port bow. The men called it the most dangerous spot on Mediterranean convoys, "the coffin corner."

On the afternoon of April 20, Hitler's birthday, the crew gathered on deck and Bob joined them at the rails to watch the porpoises below. It was still light out at 7:40 P.M., when the red alert sounded and another "sunset serenade" began, the men rushing to General Quarters. Morgenthau manned the CIC, the combat information center that had replaced the charthouse and become the ship's "brain": the nexus of all data—radio, radar, and sonar—that had to be interpreted and relayed to the control stations throughout the ship, as well as to neighboring ships. George Fritzel, headphones on, listened close to the scanning receiver.

Fritzel, an engineer from California, couldn't be certain, but it sounded "like Germans talking." At once he told Morgenthau, who dispatched a radio tech with good German. The tech heard it clearly: German pilots discussing an attack on the convoy.

Dusk was falling—the bombers' hour. The attack that followed would be recorded, in each nerve-racking turn, across the convoy's radio transmissions:

At 7:50 P.M., the minesweeper *Sustain* reported an interception of enemy radar transmissions.

At 8:08 P.M., the *Lansdale* got an unexpected "All Clear."

At 8:15 P.M., the *Menges* received the first report from a coastwatcher: unidentified planes, twenty-one miles north, approaching the convoy.

At 8:18 P.M., the planes, now seven miles out, were identified as enemy.

Max Pecherer, a thirty-two-year-old radioman from Detroit, was sitting high above the main deck in the Flying Bridge—the lookout's perch, a revolving chair riveted to the deck and equipped with binoculars, a bearing dial, and an elevation indicator to spot enemy planes. Every lookout—the ship had four, one for each 90-degree sector—wore a helmet with earphones attached that linked him to the bridge. Pecherer heard the planes, the U.S. Air Force ones first: "Looking skyward I saw American Airacobras flying very high in the same direction as our ship was moving." Pecherer notified Morgenthau in the CIC: a pair of P-39s, he said, U.S. fighters, passing at 2,500 feet.

At 8:26 P.M., the sun dipped below the horizon. Only traces of light remained in the west, and to the south, the mountains along the Algerian coastline had become a silhouette. The convoy had reached the waters where a previous convoy, UGS-37, had been intercepted on April 11—"Torpedo Junction," the veterans called it.

At 8:30 P.M., a second alert sounded. Captain Frank McCabe of the *Menges* announced it first: "Planes on your port bow."

They came out of the darkness, emerging not from the north, but from the shore.

"The Germans could see us, but we couldn't see them," Chuck Wales, a torpedo officer from western Massachusetts, said. "Perfect timing for a torpedo raid."

At 9:00 P.M., the USS *Lowe*, on the convoy's starboard side, reported five planes: the first wave of Junkers Ju 88s, attacking from dead ahead.

A minute later, they were picked up again: The *Joseph E. Campbell,* the destroyer escort leading the outer screen, radioed, "They are ALL around me . . . they are enemy, they are enemy."

Then, at 9:03 P.M., it came: a brilliant wall of light that Bob Morgenthau never forgot. All across the convoy, the sailors saw it before they heard it: a blast that sent a tower of fire thousands of feet skyward. The SS *Paul Hamilton,* a giant Liberty ship—one of the nearly 3,000 U.S. cargo ships built during the war—at the convoy's center, had been loaded with ammunition, demolition charges, aviation fuel, and troops. The blast lasted several seconds, killing all onboard. The *Hamilton* had been carrying 504 men of the Army Air Corps, including a demo squad bound for Anzio. With an additional 47 men in the crew and 29 Navy Armed Guards, the toll would reach 580 dead—one of the greatest losses of life suffered by a Liberty ship in the war. Only one body was recovered.

As the explosion of the *Hamilton* lit up the waters—"making us a beautiful target," recalled George Sinclair, the chief petty officer—a second wave struck: Seven Junkers hit the convoy's starboard flank, damaging two merchant ships, one fatally.

At 9:03 P.M., the bombers zeroed in on the *Lansdale,* swooping in low from the starboard side. "One let loose with a fish too soon," Marion Porter, one of the mess attendants in the crew, recalled. As Captain Swift ordered the ship to starboard, the torpedo whizzed past the bow. Pecherer heard the command "full right rudder" as the ship turned hard into the convoy, but a second later an explosion rocked the ship. Pecherer's chair lifted clear off the deck: "Next thing I knew, I was floating through the air."

A second plane had come straight at the *Lansdale* amidships. It dove in low, a dark blur a few feet off the water.

Porter was at his new battle station, the portside 20 mm guns. A sweet-faced nineteen-year-old, just over six feet tall, he'd been raised in Spartanburg, South Carolina. Leaving school after the seventh grade, Porter had always worked—as a grocer's clerk, dishwasher, cutter in the local marble yards, and most recently, a janitor in a PX. At seventeen, he had joined the Navy "to learn a trade," marrying a girl from Knoxville, Tennessee, before shipping out. In Norfolk, Porter and his fellow mess attendants had gone to "Cooks & Stewards School," getting training in cooking and serving meals—the only roles available to Black men enlisted in the U.S. Navy since 1932, when the Navy reopened its doors to Black men. (In 1940, Navy Secretary Knox saw no reason for change. "I am convinced," he wrote, "that it is no kindness to Negroes to thrust them upon men of the white race. One branch of the Navy is reserved exclusively for Negroes, and that is 'Messmen.'")

For two years Porter had run the bakery on the *Lansdale,* making pies, cakes, and breads for the officers—until the ship entered the Mediterranean. Only the demands of battle could break the race barrier. At least two *Lansdale* mess attendants had been trained as gunners, but it fell to Lieutenant Morgenthau to assign them new battle stations: He had put six stewards on the guns. "Breaking that rule was no small thing," Morgenthau would say, but he hadn't thought about the consequences, good or bad. There wasn't time: The Nazis were "a pretty good catalyst."

The second plane had dropped a torpedo 500 yards off the starboard beam of the *Lansdale,* before climbing suddenly to pass across the forecastle. As the plane went up, "I was firing all the while," Porter said. "We got him in the belly." The plane keeled over and crashed into the sea, just as the explosion rocked the ship. Porter was still firing when the torpedo hit amidships, "right below our gun."

The torpedo hit the No. 1 forward fire room, cutting a gash in the hull and opening both sides of the ship to the sea. The *Lansdale* had two fire rooms (holding the boilers that generated steam for the turbines) and two engine rooms—one in the stern, the other in the bow. A half-inch of steel separated the rooms, and at least eight crew members manned each fire room. Beyond the bridge, just near the middle of the ship, and directly under the whaleboat, the deck had warped upward, and a hole, five to eight feet wide, now exposed the forward fire room.

When the explosion came, Lieutenant Jim Bever, a twenty-three-year-old from Bellingham, Washington, "bounded against the rail, then back and my head hit the bulkhead." "The lights came on again," Bever recalled. "There was a second explosion and the lights went out. This time, for good."

Marion Porter kept firing: "Something hard crashed into my right leg after the explosion, and then my gun jammed. I got up to change the barrel and realized I was hurt more badly than I had thought. My arms were numb and my right leg just gave way completely. I collapsed, helpless."

| | | |

The *Lansdale* took a 12-degree list to port. Bob Morgenthau remained in the CIC, trying to assess the damage, but all light and power at the forward part of the ship, in front of the damage, was out. The bridge had also lost steering control, and the communications—the engine-room telegraph and annunciators—were dead. The 40 mm guns had lost power, and the radar in the CIC was out. As the rudder jammed at 22 degrees right, the ship, steaming at 13 knots, began to spin in a clockwise circle.

Below deck was chaos—bent metal, noise, water, panic. The torpedo had struck deep inside the hull, precisely in the area designed for maximum protection, cut through the ship's steel ribs, and ripped a hole that stretched from the main deck to below the waterline. The forward bulkhead had been blown into the IC, the interior communications room, and "the plot," the plotting room that housed the treasured Mark 1. The size of a modern dishwasher, the Mark 1 Fire Control Computer—all gears, cams, and shafts—was a mechanical analog computer, one of the most complex machines of the day.

Sal Rizzo had been in the forward engine room, manning the evaporator—the device that turned seawater into water for the boilers. On the other side of a quarter-inch of steel, at least eight men had been manning the fire room when the torpedo hit. "It more or less blew up the boilers," Rizzo would say. At least twenty men died instantly in the fire room and the plot alone.

Those still alive below now saw the dark sky through a hole in the plot's rear bulkhead. The men escaping the room left the door open, and within seconds oil flooded in, filling the mess, the dining area. It rose to nearly two feet, and then doubled. The pumps no longer functioned, and the forward fire room was smoking. A fire had started, but it had been quickly extinguished by the water rushing through the hole in the ship's side.

On the other side of the bulkhead, Doug Brewer had been manning the phone in the engine room. He kept his headset on after the torpedo hit but heard only silence from the bridge. Brewer was not a swimmer, but he had no choice. Each man aboard had two life preservers—one a rubber belt and the other a kapok jacket that could be inflated in the water—a Mae West, they called it, after the buxom Hollywood star. "Here, take my jacket," Brewer heard a shipmate call out. "I'm hurt too bad."

Ben Montenegro, a gunner's mate from outside Boston, was standing near the tail of the ship when the torpedo hit. Montenegro was one of the vets: He had enlisted three days after Pearl Harbor, as a high school senior. Boot camp had been five days, and then he boarded the *Lansdale*. When the first torpedo hit, the stern gunners had lost communications, but they knew the steering on the bridge was out. "We were going in a circle," Montenegro would recall, "and the ship kept turning over to the side." Montenegro could get up on his legs, but struggled to move forward. Unable to keep his balance, he "got washed over the side."

Captain Swift and Lieutenant Morgenthau gave orders to lose all topside weight, but the port anchor and chain would not budge. The torpedoes, too, could not be jettisoned: The tubes, fore and aft, were jammed. Nor could they lose the depth charges. The captain and his exec realized that the damage amidships would prevent the rear repair party from coming forward to stanch the flooding. Soon they also learned that there would be no *forward* repair party; that group—thirteen men tasked with doing battle repairs—had been in the galley. As the big guns sounded, they had run up to the main deck and been standing directly over the forward fire room when the torpedo hit. All but two were killed.

One man had stayed below: the "talker," Bob Dott, a twenty-year-old from Philadelphia. Dott had been on the line with Morgenthau in the CIC, and only remained belowdecks because he was plugged in—the line could not reach the deck. Dott got blown down the ladder and knocked out. When he came to, he saw the ship's doctor—Bill Neal, who'd also been knocked out by the explosion—trying to help a shipmate. The man was burned so severely Dott could not recognize him; he was conscious but could not move. "As water flooded in, I got him up into the ward room," Dott would recall, "and the doctor got down from the bridge. We were trying to work on him, keep him alive."

Dott saw it was no use. "We better get out of here!" he yelled. "We can't leave him," Neal said. But the ship had begun to roll, the water streaming down the ladder from the radio room into the wardroom. They rushed out, leaving the burn victim behind. "I didn't want to leave him either," Dott would say years later, "but we could hardly stand—the water was coming in so fast."

By 9:20 P.M., as Captain Swift regained control of the rudder, the ship began to settle. "For about 12 minutes the ship never had more than a 15 (degree) list," Lieutenant Morgenthau wrote in the battle report to Washington, "and it seemed highly probable that she would remain afloat." But in a moment, the ship buckled at its midpoint, and within seconds, the deck was listing at a 45-degree angle.

Morgenthau feared the worst, and the crew sensed it too. Within three minutes, they heard the call: "Abandon ship." There was little panic, but with the ship approaching a right angle to the water, they could not launch the starboard life raft. They struggled, too, with the floater net. Ever since leaving Norfolk, it had hung on the ship's side, sheathed in canvas, untouched. Unable to free the net from its holder, the men furiously cut it loose. "We had a terrific list to port," Fred Gehlmann, an officer from Chicago, would recall, "so we had to clamber down the starboard side."

The ship was fast breaking in two—like a book opened facedown, a survivor would say, its spine on the edge of a table, one half flat on the surface, the other dangling off the edge.

Chuck Wales, the torpedo officer, ended up next to Porter, the mess attendant on the gun. Porter's leg had been shattered, broken in more than one place. Wales had tried to help him up on his feet, but they got separated. "At least I got him on his feet, so he could get over the side," Wales would say.

Porter's gun crew had shot down two planes. At the call to abandon ship, Gehlmann recalled, the Black gunners had "sort of half-mumbled, 'Yes, sir,' and went right on shooting." Lying on the deck as the water rose, Porter hung on to a gun mount. "As I tried to get around him," Gehlmann recalled, "he said, 'Pardon me.' And then got up again to aim."

Marion Porter would be one of the last to leave. Years later he would recall how "Lt. Morgenthau came over to me and asked if I was hurt." Morgenthau told Porter to inflate his life preserver, but Porter was unable to move. So the lieutenant grabbed a kapok and tied it around Porter's chest—and by then, as Porter would recall, "I was in water up to my back."

"Are you ready to go?" Lieutenant Morgenthau asked.

"He got me free and sort of moved me around into position," Porter would say, "and then pushed me into the water."

Lieutenant Jim Bever grabbed his tin hat when he heard the call to abandon ship. Before scrambling over, he asked Lieutenant Morgenthau, "Aren't you coming?"

"Later," Bever heard the exec reply.

Almost everyone was off the ship, but Lieutenant Morgenthau returned to help the captain.

IIII

The men hit the water together. They jumped in, six, ten, fifteen at a time. They sank in a heavy layer of bunker oil, and then tried to swim to the floater net. Nearly two dozen struggled to hang on to a single net.

Some did not jump. They slid down the hull of the ship, barnacles tearing into buttocks, ripping life belts.

George Fritzel and Vince Moravec, the radio jammers, strapped inflatable belts to their waists, but feared "they might be punctured" on the way down. In the cold water, though, a boot camp lesson returned: "Get away from the ship as quickly as possible, don't get sucked down with her."

Peter Soler, who'd come aboard only three weeks earlier, heard a voice. "Ski" was yelling: "Soler, you alright?" Jerry Wroblewski—the crew knew him only as "Ski"—was a radio tech from Chicago, a popular man on the *Lansdale* who'd been aboard since early 1941. Soler struggled to tread water amid a cluster: "13 of us together," he would recall, "my belt supporting two others and me."

Karyes Barclay, a cook, was an overgrown kid from Birmingham, Alabama. Cooking or eating, he was always smiling. Barclay had gone overboard, but try as he might, he could not kick free of the ship. "The suction of the screws," his fellow cook Raymond Quirion recalled, "pulled him right in."

Back on the ship, the captain and his exec knew what had to be done. They worked quickly, without speaking. A radio tech, Marshall Geller, took care of the code books, following procedure: "Publications carried to CIC at General Quarters were placed in a heavy metal box, which was locked and thrown overboard," Lieutenant Morgenthau would record. The Fleet Code, Aircraft Code, Fleet Signal Book—all were secured. The men also bundled together the bridge and radio room publications, locking them in two safes.

By 9:30 P.M., twenty-seven minutes after the torpedo struck, the list had grown to 80 degrees. The *Lansdale* was splitting apart. In the dark water, the men could hear it: screech of metal against metal, hatches bursting in geysers. Geller, the radioman, stayed with Captain Swift and Lieutenant Morgenthau. Now all three kicked off their shoes and much of their clothing, and went over.

Morgenthau had seen George Haines, the gunnery officer, go over. Ray Miller, the gunner's mate, slid down alongside him. "George was one of my closest friends on the ship," Morgenthau remembered. "Bright, capable, eager." Schooled at Hotchkiss and Yale, Haines was a child of the East Coast elite. He'd married in his junior year at Yale, and had graduated in his Navy uniform. A son, George Eddison Haines III, had arrived in August 1943.

"While I was taking my shoes off," Miller said, he heard Haines shout that he was going back to look for others. "I yelled at him not to go."

From the water, the men watched as the ship broke apart. The stern went first, as the bow lifted almost vertically, before sinking slowly out of sight. They could see the ship's screw and rudder—and men still clinging to the bow. The *Lansdale* was going under in 1,100 fathoms, the 159th ship of the U.S. Navy, and the 43rd destroyer, lost since the start of the war.

| | | |

The skies had cleared. The German planes, having sunk a destroyer and a merchant ship and damaged at least three others, would not return. At 9:44 P.M., Captain W. H. Duvall, the task force commander aboard the Coast Guard cutter *Taney*, at last radioed a rescue order: "Pick what you can." The Coast Guard ships in the convoy, biding their time in nearby waters, now had permission to begin a search.

As the *Menges, Newell,* and *Chase* steamed closer, the survivors took shape: darkened bodies struggling in the water. The water was cold, no more than 50 degrees. They struggled to keep close, clutching arms, legs, an inch of canvas or net. "Let's stay together," Al Caplan yelled, "to make a radar target." Before long, many, like Caplan, passed out, and the lucky ones floated unconscious.

"You could hear people crying, hollering and praying," said Sal Rizzo, who had broken two ribs. Across the blackness you could also hear song—men singing "The Battle Hymn of the Republic," "How Deep Is the Ocean"—"trying to stay warm," recalled Montenegro, "to keep spirits up." They all heard the *Menges* before they saw it; the bullhorn blasted: "Come this way, don't get excited."

At 10:10 P.M., the *Newell* radioed Captain Duvall: "We are picking up men from 'the Pheasant' [the *Lansdale*'s code name] and I think she cannot be saved. Just a small portion is up."

At 10:34 P.M., the *Newell* called across to the *Menges:* "We have quite a lot of men to pick up here." One cutter asked the other to come closer. "We dare not move around because there are too many single swimmers that may get caught in our screws."

"We would see the faint outline of a ship near us," Fritzel remembered, "and we'd all shout to get their attention, then it would be gone." It happened over and over again, as the men drifted, trying to tread water. Some were helped up a cargo net and onto the cutter's deck; others could not take the cold and gave up. "You'd see them one minute," Fritzel would say, "and they'd be gone the next."

By 11:00 P.M., the rescuers had put in the whaleboats. Those in the water could be hoisted aboard on bowlines tied to crew members on the Coast Guard ships, but the small boats could only hold two dozen men at a time. They would have to return to the ship and unload before shoving off again. Every so often a searchlight flashed across the black swells. "Swim toward the ship!" the voice cried above the whaleboat's motor. Some managed to grip the edge of the boat, pulling themselves up. Soler landed facedown in bilge, almost at once emptying his stomach of seawater and oil.

Max Pecherer could hear voices, but as the waves came, a silence settled. He made it to a whaleboat: "They grabbed me by my trousers, threw me across bodies that seemed dead." Pecherer would be the last one picked up.

Wroblewski, the radio mate, had found a friend from the radio room in the water. Clinton Neuman, a short kid from upstate New York, had worked the line at a plastics factory before enlisting on the first weekend after Pearl Harbor. Like so many, he'd joined the rush to war: three weeks of training before the sea.

"Let's stay close," Wroblewski yelled to Neuman, "and find us a life net."

"No, Ski," came the reply, "I can't handle this." In the darkness, Neuman undid his belt. Ski yelled to the men just beyond. They dove down, groping in vain. Neuman would be listed as "missing in action." At twenty-two, he left his mother, seven siblings, and a wife and son.

Lieutenant Haines was one officer, the survivors agreed, who did all he could to save the others. "George swam for almost three hours," Morgenthau said. "He gave away his life preserver, he tried to keep everybody around him afloat, but by the time the whaleboats arrived, he was gone."

Many of the men would speak, years later, about God. "There are no atheists swimming in the open ocean," Marshall Geller would say. They were young and strong, but they had prayed in the frigid darkness, some treading water for as long as four and a half hours.

Bob Morgenthau, who had also slid over the hull with the captain, spoke of the divine, too. "I made a deal that night with the Almighty," he would say, "as I was trying my damnedest not to go under. I promised the Almighty, 'If I ever get out of here, I'll do something with my life bigger than myself'—that was the bargain."

||||

The *Menges* had eased to 15 knots as the search slowed. Captain McCabe caught sight of a red flare and a white light blinking on and off about a half mile to the northwest. Grabbing his bullhorn, as they came alongside, he shouted: "Put out the light! . . . We see you, are coming to you. Put that light out!"

It was a life raft, with two men onboard: Germans, an observer and a radio operator. The Americans seized their raft, equipment, and provisions. They were hurt: One had an injured leg, and the other a gash across his face and half of his teeth knocked out. Both were gaunt in the face and looked undernourished. They said they had been hit and had crashed before they could launch a torpedo. (Later, they would be interrogated: The bombers had taken off from southern France, and the attack had been unusually large: three units forming a total of sixty planes.) Now they were stripped and given first aid before being led at gunpoint to bunks on the mess deck. Captain McCabe assigned two men, armed with submachine guns, to guard the room.

The stench aboard the Coast Guard ships was terrific; the survivors were soaked in oil. Fearing a fire, an officer opened the hydrant on the main deck to wash off as much of the oil as possible. There was no place to sleep: Every passageway, corridor, and compartment was coated with oil, and the bulkheads and decks were crowded with soiled clothing. Some of the men could not walk; many could not stop shivering. They were given blankets, long underwear, dungarees, and whiskey. For many, though, the shock took hold at once. The doctor and the pharmacist's mate gave two emergency blood transfusions, and revived several men with artificial respiration, but for two of those pulled from the water, it was too late.

||||

By 12:42 A.M., the *Newell* had picked up the last survivor. At 2:25 A.M., the *Menges* hoisted its whaleboat aboard, moving along the path to Algiers. By then, the Coast Guard vessels had rescued 232 men.

At dawn, the ships stood at the pier, side by side. Men reached across the rails, smoking cigarettes in their oily clothes. The rescued had trouble making it down the steep gangplank. Some wore Coast Guard khakis, but dozens were in long johns. All reeked of bunker oil. They huddled in small groups, a new habit that would last for weeks. The German prisoners were handed over to Allied Headquarters, and their equipment to Naval Intelligence in Algiers. The Coast Guard ships did not stay long; they inspected their magazines, guns, and smokeless powder, and by 9:00 A.M., both had left to rejoin the convoy.

The *Lansdale* survivors were bussed to a U.S. Army base outside of Algiers. They would sleep on straw mattresses in tents in the desert, taking meals outdoors, and lining up with canteens for water. The base stood alongside a makeshift POW camp: Behind barbed wire Italian soldiers tended sparse garden plots.

In the United States, the sinking, like the details of every military engagement, was a secret. FDR, though, had learned of the attack within hours. On April 21, a naval cable from Algiers reported the news— "Please inform Secretary Morgenthau that Exec Officer is safe and well"—which Roosevelt at once forwarded to Henry. "Elinor and I," came the wire in reply, "deeply appreciate your having us notified that Bob is well and safe."

In Algiers, in the heat of an Army tent, Lieutenant Morgenthau got to work. Captain Swift could offer no instructions: He had suffered superficial wounds—a cut cheek, an injured leg—but he would remain in the hospital tent for weeks, spending his days in an iron bed, bare bulb overhead, smoking Chesterfields. His officers sensed something amiss. "You could see it at once," Bob would say. "Something was troubling him." Swift could not sleep, and his hands shook so violently, he couldn't light his own cigarettes. The doctors called it "battle fatigue." "The Captain no longer talked much, he kept to himself," Morgenthau said of him. "A man so capable had all of a sudden seemed incapable of doing much of anything—let alone his job."

Swift was required to file a series of detailed after-action reports for Washington, but the job fell to Morgenthau. William Nielsen, quartermaster mate third class, had carried the quartermaster's book into the water, but lost it in the cold darkness. The secret codes and reciphering pads, at least, were safe. "There is not a possibility that the enemy could have boarded and salvaged any secret or confidential pubs or equipment," Lieutenant Morgenthau wrote.

Like all the officers, Bob had to inventory his losses: cuff links, eyeglasses, suspenders, and his texts: Dutton's *Navigation and Nautical Astronomy*, Bowditch's *American Practical Navigator*. He also had to tally the dead. In all, forty-nine men had been killed and seventy-six wounded. He would organize the burials, as well. On April 22, Bob presided over the farewell amid the cleared dirt of the base. Under a tall row of palms, their fronds twisting overhead, the survivors looked on solemnly in a half circle. Two caskets—holding the sole remains recovered—lay before them: plain wood on saw horses, draped with the Stars and Stripes. A minister offered a prayer, and the Coast Guardsmen gave a ten-gun salute.

In an Army jacket and khakis, Lieutenant Morgenthau stood opposite the priest, slightly apart from the officers. Four of the dead were officers he had come to know well and admire deeply. Newton Thatcher Westhill had served as Bob's navigational assistant. Westhill was the chief petty officer and, at thirty-nine, nearly bald, and older than almost any of the others. In the water, he had suffered a heart attack. Like Bob, Westhill had gotten married just before the ship departed for the Mediterranean. John Cronin, the second sailor buried, was an enlisted seaman from Chicago, one of those who had survived the sinking of the *Mayo*. Cronin had suffocated, oil filling his lungs. The funerals were brisk, and formal, but as the survivors tried to adjust to a new life, many resorting to sleeping pills, the ritual would be repeated. By week's end, five more bodies had surfaced in the waters offshore.

At home in the United States, three weeks passed before the Navy released the news. As word spread that the secretary of the Treasury's son's ship had been sunk, Henry fielded calls from reporters wondering if Henry III, then en route to the Second Cavalry in Europe, had gone down? Only on May 10 did NBC's Lowell Thomas announce it on the evening news: "An exciting story is told about the sinking of the United States destroyer *Lansdale*. . . ." The Navy, Thomas reported, said "most of the crew was saved, including Lieutenant Robert Morgenthau, son of the Secretary of the Treasury." On the following day, the *Times* reported it, as well. "Morgenthau's Son Is a Survivor," read the front-page headline, above a photograph of Lieutenant Morgenthau escorting survivors down the gangplank.

Within a month, Bob was at home and could tell the story for himself. At the pier in Norfolk, the crew and officers rushed for the phones, newly installed by the Navy for the occasion. (In the days since the headlines appeared, families across the country had been panic-stricken, fearing their sons among the dead.) Martha—red flowers behind each ear—had come to the dock, escorted by Henry. They could hug only briefly before being ushered off into a waiting room; for the reporters, Bob Morgenthau was the star attraction. He would take a seat beside Captain Swift to pose for the photographers and answer questions. Swift spoke haltingly, preferring instead to listen as Bob told of the blitz attack and long rescue.

In a gray office at the Bureau of Naval Personnel in Washington, Bob did little else but write the families of the dead. He did visit his captain at St. Elizabeth's, the mental hospital in Washington, and he went to see Marion Porter, who was being treated for his fractured leg. Bob would put Porter up for the Silver Star. The mess attendant who had manned the guns would walk with a limp.

That August, Bob Morgenthau received the Bronze Star, pinned on his chest during a ceremony in Norfolk, as hundreds of "bluejackets," sailors in training, stood at attention. He found little to celebrate. In the years to come, the men of the *Lansdale* would hold reunions. They would chase an urge to stay close, fearing the loss of what they had gained: a sense of the horror, and luck, that bound them. They would also track down the German former POWs, bringing the men together after decades. By then, though, the survivors had formed a tradition, a gesture born of instinct that hardened into habit.

April 20, Bob Morgenthau would say, was their second birthday. For decades, they would pick up the telephone and wish one another "Happy Birthday."

35. "And I Mean the German People"

SPRING 1944

n the spring of 1944, everything seemed to be going Henry Morgenthau's way. With the founding of the War Refugee Board, the secretary had surmounted the challenge of the State Department and reached new heights of power. But still, the ego remained ailing and the skin dangerously thin.

Henry had always fretted over his image in the popular imagination but in March he railed at the appearance of a new book, *Washington Broadcast*, an assemblage of satirical profiles of the Roosevelt court, published anonymously by an old Washington hand. Yet the author, Wythe Williams, the reporter who wrote a popular column under a pseudonym—"The Man at the Microphone"—had Henry pegged with precision:

> *Henry the Morgenthau sat at his desk,*
> *Henry the Morgenthau stared into space—*
> > *What did he see?*
> > *Why did he frown?*
> > *Was he disturbed*
> > *By the talk of the town?*
> *Henry the Morgenthau wrinkled his face—*
> > *Why was he pained,*
> *Haggard and strained?*
> *Henry the Morgenthau sat at his desk*
> *Wilted and wan like a man in disgrace—*
> *Why was he somber, shorn of all hope?*

Why? Because Congress had called him a dope,
*   Censured him, spanked him, applied the old ax*
To Henry the Morgenthau's plan for a tax:
*   Sneered at him,*
*   Jeered at him,*
Grimaced and leered at him.
What could he do in his grief and despair
But sit in his sumptuous Treasury chair
And take in the neighboring air with a state.
That's what he did
*   And he did it so well*
That all who observed him
*   Agreed he was swell!*

As the profile made a splash among the press corps, Henry went to FDR to plead for assistance: "They paint a picture of me sitting at my desk gazing out the window and not doing anything!" he complained. "The only thing I have to do on War Bonds"—the vast Treasury program to fund the war effort—"is shake hands with the movie stars."

Roosevelt just howled; few knew better how easily Henry could be offended. The secretary, though, offered a solution: "If occasionally I do something good, like the Fourth War Loan, you would say so publicly, then it would be some answer to the people who say I don't do anything." Roosevelt, for example, might send him "a telegram which I could read over the radio, complimenting me on the thing." The request, FDR said, was within reason. Henry was relieved: "The people around me advised me not to do it, because it seemed too forward to ask you."

| | | |

Henry extended his run of success in July, at Bretton Woods. For three hot weeks, as the Allies pushed on across Europe, the Treasury would host the biggest talks on international finance since the debacle of the London Conference a decade earlier: 730 representatives from 44 nations attempting to do nothing less than avoid the errors of Versailles, and forge a plan to shape the postwar world monetary order. Henry and his aides had chosen the setting of the once-grand Mount Washington Hotel, a ski resort in New Hampshire's White Mountains, because the scenery was spectacular, the air cool, the remote locale ideal for security—and because the hotel allowed Jews.

From start to finish, Henry presided. Ellie, however, could not be his main support as usual. For months, she had shuttled in and out of hospitals, the doctors at a loss. "She began to show signs of a disorder," Henry III would recall, "a tendency to develop blood clots." The doctors diagnosed thrombosis but could only offer stopgaps. All the while, the pain increased. To shore up his wife, and himself, the secretary brought along Joan, their daughter, who was interested in foreign affiars, and eager to support her father.

Henry held marathon meetings with the finance ministers, retreated to recalibrate his goals with his aides, and in the evenings ingratiated himself with the star of the talks: John Maynard Keynes. Keynes and his wife, the Russian ballerina Lydia Lopokova, stayed in the suite above the Morgenthaus. (At night, Henry was kept awake, his ears battered by Baroness Keynes's dancing overhead.) As ever, he obsessed over details: the seating arrangements at meals, cajoling the favored reporters in their midst, and even, on the closing night, moving his speech forward half an hour—so the live radio broadcast would be heard across the country.

Throughout the conference, Henry would indulge in wishful thinking, revealing a private insistence that cooperation would win out and that the allegiances forged in war would endure beyond the exigencies of the present urgency. The talks at Bretton Woods, though, opened and closed with a showdown between the British and the Americans. Keynes, leader of the British delegation, sparred frequently, and bitterly, with one of Henry's chief deputies, Harry Dexter White. White had studied at Stanford and Harvard, but grown up in an immigrant Jewish household, one of seven children, at a rough edge of Beacon Hill in Boston. His parents had come from Lithuania; his mother died when he was a baby, and his father—the original surname was Weit—went into the hardware business. White had faced a hard climb—there were years working in the family store, World War I service as an officer (he'd adopted a mustache, to "look older"), limbo as a college dropout, and a stint teaching in the Midwest—but at forty-one, the New Deal had saved him. In 1934, Jacob Viner—Henry's first head economist, "the Chicago genius," he called him—had recruited White to the Treasury, where White, equal parts economist and fighter, had proved dogged and efficient, the loyalist Henry needed. White had been by the secretary's side for more than a decade.

In Baron Keynes, White faced the most formidable economist of the day. In myriad ways, the two were nearly opposites. White was short, and Keynes nearly a foot taller, but the distance in temperament was greater: Keynes had little use for blunt Americans and brazen Jews, while White—blunt and brazen, but by all accounts brilliant—despised the classism of the British aristocracy. The two's contentious talks only mirrored the general sessions, the marathons marked by outbursts, interruptions, even walkouts.

Both men had brought drafts of their competing plans to New Hampshire. The Treasury sought a postwar system of trade and exchange in which the U.S. dollar held sway, while London hoped for the revival of imperial trade practices and relaxed exchange rates. For years, Keynes had pushed for an International Clearing Union, a worldwide bank with its own currency—"Bancor"—that would seek to support the postwar Western economies that were burdened by war debt, including Britain's. White had come with his own plan: an International Stabilization Fund that would instill a new exchange rate mechanism, anchored to the dollar and pegged to the price of gold—a bold revision of the gold standard FDR jettisoned in 1933.

The war between Keynes and White dominated the conference. Keynes's anti-Semitism, however visceral, did not emerge in the meetings. In private, though, he railed against the trio of American Jews running the show: the Treasury secretary, White, and White's deputy, Edward Bernstein. After one meeting, Keynes fumed "Bernstein is a regular little rabbi, a reader of the Talmud, to Harry's grand political high rabbidom. . . . The chap knows every rat run in his local ghetto, but it is difficult to persuade him to come out for a walk with us on the high ways of the world." As the weeks went on, the talks grew heated—and at more than one point seemed destined for a dead end. In the end, though, there was little the British economist could do; politics and the monetary power of his hosts won the day.

The Americans and the British agreed on a blueprint for a managed system of exchange rates. Bretton Woods would create two institutions to govern the postwar financial order: the International Monetary Fund (IMF) and the World Bank, as the new pillars of global finance would become known. Keynes, if White had his way, would lead the work on developing the World Bank, which was intended as the junior partner of the IMF; the latter was envisioned as the mightier, an unprecedented reserve of funds set aside to enable nations suffering trade deficits to settle their international accounts. When it came to determining the site of these new financial behemoths, Keynes cried foul (he lobbied for London), but both the IMF and the World Bank were to be headquartered in Washington.

Harry White was overjoyed. And his boss, the Treasury secretary, claimed the victory as his own.

For all the fighting over economic theory, the battle at Bretton Woods had come down to money. Neither the Americans nor the British could predict if the Soviets would ante up for a global fund. The question hung over the talks until the last hour, when with rare dramatic flourish Henry announced that Moscow would pay in $1.2 billion, far more than the $900 million every other delegation pledged. Bretton Woods, Henry declared, would stand as proof that the nations of the world could cooperate. A near disaster had turned into a celebration.

At the final session, Henry gushed that he hoped the enemies in Europe were listening. "I like to think," he said, "that in this enormous amount of words that has gone over the air through short wave, that the German people will realize that what we have done here at Bretton Woods on the economic front must make them realize that to continue to fight on the battlefields is useless."

Henry had saved the farewell speech for himself. It was nearly eleven in the evening when he rose to the microphone, pince-nez affixed, in a white linen suit. "We are at a crossroads," he said, beaming at the center of the world's attention, "and we must go one way or the other." The conference had "erected a signpost—a signpost pointing down a highway broad enough for all men to walk in step and side by side. If they will set out together, there is nothing on earth that need stop them."

| | | |

The triumph at Bretton Woods, coupled with the founding of the War Refugee Board, emboldened Henry. "It might've been the height of his confidence in himself," his daughter Joan, who had enjoyed a front-row view in New Hampshire, would say.

That summer, Henry again stepped beyond the bounds of the Treasury. Even as he instructed aides to map Europe's economic future, he waded into the military endgame. A fierce debate was brewing in Washington—a struggle over how the Allies should treat a defeated Germany—between advocates of a "hard" or "soft" peace. The conflict, at heart, was about morality: After the unprecedented horrors of the Nazis, what should justice look like? How should the victors treat the vanquished? FDR had said, time and again, he would not brook a soft peace, yet he avoided, whether by design or accident, setting in place an interagency plan for postwar Germany. Henry Morgenthau, Jr., knew which side he stood on, and newly fortified, he was hell-bent on seeing Roosevelt beside him.

The secretary had always relied on "the people around" him. Now more than ever, he needed them: Dan Bell on the budget, Randolph Paul on taxes, and on nearly any question of international finance, Harry White. Yet when it came to Germany, and how the victors should treat the Germans in the postwar era, FDR's Treasury secretary would listen, above all, to himself. Henry's ideas on Germany would provoke a battle so divisive and impassioned, stretching from Washington to Europe and back, and causing such rancor within the Roosevelt administration, as well as its successor, so as to color indelibly his role in history. In the end, all the other trials would fall to the side.

The driving force among FDR's inner circle in shaping the future of Germany, Henry would become known as the architect of "the Morgenthau Plan," a vengeful and misguided scheme, the civilized world would say, to reduce postwar Germany to a "pastoral" state.

| | | |

In his first meeting with FDR after the Fourth of July holiday, Henry raised the idea of going to France on an inspection tour to see how the "occupation currency"—U.S.-printed francs used by U.S. troops since D-Day—was "getting along." It was an excuse to sound out the Army's thinking on Germany, and to Henry's surprise, Roosevelt gave his blessing.

On August 5, Henry boarded a military transport plane, a C-54 Skymaster, at Presque Isle, Maine, for a grueling sixteen-hour flight to Prestwick, Scotland. Accompanying him were three aides: Harry White, Joe DuBois, now headed for a Treasury posting in London, and Fred Smith, a former newsman asked to come along to handle the press. During the flight, White pulled from his briefcase a State Department memorandum discussing the Allies' future economic demands on a defeated Germany: "Report on Reparations, Restitutions, and Property Rights in Germany." Henry settled back to read it—"first with interest," he would recall, "then with misgivings, and finally with sharp disagreement." The State recommendations failed, in Henry's eyes, to come to grips with "the basic question": how to "prevent Germany from imposing devastation and terror on a helpless Europe for the third time in a single century?" He was dumbfounded: Could the memo truly reflect State's thinking? Henry was determined to learn all he could about the Allies' plans for Germany's future.

Landing after midnight at an air base on the Scottish coast, Henry and his aides boarded a special train that took them through the night to the south of England. By morning, they arrived at Southwick House, near Portsmouth, General Eisenhower's headquarters in England. The Allies, it seemed, were days from entering Germany, Henry learned over lunch with Eisenhower. As Henry and the general ate, Harry White wasted no time, pressing Eisenhower on the wisdom of the War Department's thinking on postwar Germany. As Smith took notes, White recited the current orders: The Army's Civil Affairs division ("G-5," the office set up to ease administration in Allied-occupied territory) was "to move up and bolster the economy quickly," keeping the Army from getting bogged down in chaos. That may have worked elsewhere, White said, where the goal had been to rebuild and repair—providing transport, utilities, social services as fast as possible, to keep the Allied drive going. But once Berlin fell, Eisenhower's forces would face a vastly different task. Germany was not a thoroughfare; it was the end of the road. And yet, White went on, the War Department had not shifted its plan at all: The troops would move into Germany, and begin rebuilding as soon as possible.

As Eisenhower listened, his face tightened. "I am not interested in the German economy," he said, "and personally would not like to bolster it, if that will make it any easier for the Germans." The Germans deserved the punishment that would come, he said. That morning, Eisenhower had learned of yet more Nazi atrocities: "The ringleaders and the SS troops should be given the death penalty without question, but punishment should not end there." The German *people* had supported the regime, and, Eisenhower went on, he would like to "see things made good and hard for them for a while." Those demanding a soft peace, he argued, were people who feared Russia. They saw a revived Germany as a bulwark against an expansive Russia in the future. "This is a problem," he told Henry, "because the strength of Russia is fantastic."

Eisenhower said there was no use in treating a "paranoid" gently, and the "whole German population was a synthetic paranoid." He went on: "All their life the people have been taught to be paranoid in their actions and thoughts, and they have to be snapped out of it. . . . I certainly see no point in bolstering the economy, or taking any other steps to help them."

Knowing his boss's delight with the general's tough stance, White warned, "We may want to quote you on the problem of handling the German people."

"I will tell the President myself, if necessary," Eisenhower shot back.

Throughout his trip, Henry would replay General Eisenhower's words. In London, as Henry met with Churchill and ventured into the Underground to tour the bomb shelters, Eisenhower's phrase "synthetic paranoids" would echo. The general, as Fred Smith would recount, had "set the spark." Henry had long imagined only one permissible future for Germany: as a humbled nation of farmers. "As a farmer myself," Henry would write in 1947, "I knew that people who lived close to the land tended to be tranquil and peace-loving by nature, to be sturdily independent and hostile to outside tyranny. Why not make Germany a nation predominantly of small farmers? Why not solve the problem of the itching trigger finger by removing the trigger?"

| | | |

After London, the secretary visited Normandy. He spent time with the wounded before the cameras, but in truth he'd come to glimpse his older son. Henry III had arrived in England that spring as a second lieutenant with the Second Cavalry, just as the Cavalry was to join the new Third Army, commanded by General Patton. Three days after D-Day, as the Third Army was sent in to take Brittany, Henry III had suddenly received new orders. He was sent, along with a platoon, to provide "a security guard" to SHAEF, the Supreme Headquarters of the Allied Expeditionary Force.

"Assigning a specific junior officer by name was rather odd," Henry III remembered, "as was indeed the entire operation." His platoon would be posted at SHAEF headquarters in England before moving soon to the Allies' "Forward CP" base in France. The command post at Reims "was not all that forward"; it featured three trailers parked in a row—housing for Eisenhower, Kay Summersby, his driver and secretary, and Air Marshal Arthur William Tedder. The trailers had little need for security: Neither the general nor Miss Summersby was ever present. Henry III and his platoon were instead shown a dump truck of crushed gravel and instructed to shovel it out carefully, along a path connecting the Eisenhower and Summersby trailers. "It was upsetting," Henry would recall.

"I was made an executive officer of the troop—and I'd never wanted any special treatment." (The son feared his father had pulled strings, but it was a deputy, seeking to please, who had arranged the transfer.)

On August 9, as the secretary toured Cherbourg—"to hell and gone," he said of the damage wrought by German mines and Allied bombs—his son received orders to join him at General Omar Bradley's headquarters in Normandy. General Bradley hosted father and son at lunch. "This is an opportunity that comes to a commander not more than once in a century," Bradley said. "We're about to destroy an entire hostile army." A week earlier, Patton had committed the Third Army to the Normandy fight; Henry III "felt like a deserter." His father, though, was overjoyed. The secretary had wanted to see the front, and, as he had in Gallipoli, he got close to the action: "within 5,000 yards of the Germans," he wrote Ellie. He'd also spent "a wonderful 31 hours" with their son: "Henry was with me where ever [sic] I went," he told Ellie. They slept side by side on cots—"no sheet, no pillow"—and still the secretary had enjoyed the "best nights rest that I can remember."

"The war is going unbelievably well," he added. "I felt awful when I left Henry and was glad I had on my dark glasses. Let us pray and hope that this terrible war will be over soon."

||||

The secretary flew back to Washington on August 17, and two days later he was at the White House to meet with the president. "I stayed for a half hour," Henry dictated to his diary, "but I couldn't do justice to my subject because I felt that I was under such pressure, and I talked terribly fast." To his relief, he found FDR in a good mood—"very attentive and tremendously interested and most friendly."

Henry had worked in Washington for more than a decade, but he had never enjoyed a day without fearing for his standing with the president. FDR had been his best friend for more than three decades, yet it was always a lopsided friendship: Henry feared asking indulgences of the Chief, or falling from his good graces. He had long since learned, though, how Roosevelt governed: "The Roosevelt way," he would say, was to defy expectations. For all their years in Washington, he and Ellie had never put much stock in any future plans. Throughout the years in Washington, they never bought a house. Each time Roosevelt won reelection, they rented—believing every extension would be the last. Yet over time, a shift emerged. If once Henry would have languished and sulked for weeks, waiting on Roosevelt's deliverance, now gloom did not last long. The need for reassurance, for the president to clear the clouds, would remain, but even Ellie remarked on it: Henry and Franklin never seemed closer.

That day at the White House, Henry had come to relay the news from London—but he also hoped to sound out FDR on the plans for Germany. He began by recounting his afternoon with Churchill. The prime minister had given him a thrill, a tour of his "war room," showing him a model of the British landing at Normandy. Churchill had taken Henry into his confidence: England was broke, he'd blurted out. The prime minister had said he would wait, though, until the end of the war "to lay the whole thing before Parliament." They would call for his head, he expected, but it no longer mattered. Churchill was nearing seventy, and it was time, he'd said, that he "made peace with my Maker." The PM had seemed hurt, almost vulnerable—and, to Henry's mind, desperate for a new loan. And for some reason, he feared the secretary had soured on England. Why had Henry "turned against us"? Churchill asked. Why had he become "rather hard in your attitude toward us?"

Henry hoped that Roosevelt might decode the questioning. But FDR could not get past the news that England was broke. "I had no idea," he kept saying. He joked that maybe he should "go over there and make a couple of talks and take over the British Empire." Roosevelt knew how popular he was with the British soldiers, he said, and how unpopular Churchill had become.

In London, they'd discussed the future of Germany too, Henry went on gingerly. At lunch with Sir John Anderson, chancellor of the Exchequer, he'd even aired an idea—"purely my own": "I think we could divide Germany into a number of smaller provinces," Henry had said, "stop all industrial production and convert them into agricultural land holders." Sir John had fallen silent. The next day, though, Churchill had listened intently; it may have been flattery, or the hunger for a bailout, but Henry took it as interest.

There was more. He'd seen Anthony Eden, too, Henry told FDR. Over tea with the foreign minister, as he'd again probed for details of the Brits' plans, Eden had seemed puzzled. Germany's future, Eden said, was all settled—FDR, Churchill, and Stalin had taken care of it at the Tehran talks. Henry was taken aback, but before Eden could figure out that FDR had kept the Tehran deal a secret, Henry asked him to read from the minutes of the talks in Iran. It was true: At Tehran the Big Three had agreed to divide Germany, tasking the EAC (the new European Advisory Commission, made up of representatives from the USSR, United States, and United Kingdom) with divvying up the zones of occupation. The news jolted Henry. To Roosevelt's way of thinking, the EAC, Henry knew well, might be little more than a convenience to buy time and lure the Soviets into postwar cooperation, but he was stunned to have been left in the dark.

The EAC, Henry now told the president, was sitting idle. In London, Winant, the American ambassador, and the U.S. member of the EAC who had been at Tehran, had confided in Henry that despite repeated attempts, he'd received no instructions from State. The EAC had not formulated any plans. Worse, parallel groups had cropped up, pursuing their own initiatives. "Mr. President, here in the State Department," Henry said, a man named "Pasvolsky"—a White Russian émigré who had gained Hull's ear on European economics—"has been making a study, but he didn't know about the Tehran Conference agreement."

As Henry marched on, Roosevelt fell silent.

The day before, almost as soon as he'd landed, Henry had rushed to the State Department to complain to Hull. The secretary of state, too, was in the dark on the Tehran deal. "Henry, this is the first I have ever heard this," Hull swore.

As Henry recounted Hull's astonishment, FDR did not say a word. He only "looked very embarrassed," and the secretary repeated it "so that he would be sure to get it." Henry said, "As far as Winant goes, I can't quite understand it because he had a group study this, and Winant claims he knew what you did and still the group under him were not carrying out your instructions."

To Henry, the road map was coming into focus, and it was not one he could accept: State was considering the idea of bringing Germany back into the family of nations; the Brits were looking to Germany as a postwar market; the War Department wanted to do its own work; and the EAC, flouting direct instructions, was planning for a united Germany.

"The sum and substance," Henry told FDR, "is that from the time of the Tehran Conference down to now, nobody has been studying how to treat Germany roughly along the lines you wanted."

"We have got to be tough with Germany," the president said, "and I mean the German people, not just the Nazis. You either have to castrate the German people, or you have got to treat them in such a manner so they can't just go on reproducing people who want to continue the way they have in the past."

"Well, Mr. President, nobody is considering the question along those lines in Europe," Henry said. "In England they want to build up Germany so that she can pay reparations."

"What do we want reparations for?"

"He left no doubt in my mind," Henry recorded in his dairy, "that he and I are looking at this thing in the same way, but the people down the line aren't."

As Henry walked back across the narrow roadway to the Treasury, he felt reassured that FDR "wants to be tough with the Germans." Henry had further cause for relief. The president, headed to Hyde Park on Saturday evening, invited him along. He and Ellie, FDR had assured, "would be the only people on the train." He was going down to the train early, the president added, so they "would have more time to talk." To others in the cabinet, the offer might have been no more than a friendly invitation. To Henry, though, it was a resounding signal: His best friend was firmly on his side.

36. "Unnatural, Unchristian, and Unnecessary"

AUGUST 1944

" could not get the German question out of my mind," Henry wrote, recalling these days in an article (ghosted by the historian Arthur M. Schlesinger, Jr.) that appeared in the *New York Post* in 1947. "If no one else was going to try to carry out the president's wishes in the matter, then I would." Sensing an opening, Henry set up a Treasury committee, tasking White, Pehle, and Luxford to analyze "the German problem."

The battle over a U.S. blueprint for postwar Germany would be a three-way tug-of-war. Given FDR's distaste for long-range planning, and his fondness for setting one advisor against another, Henry faced off against not only Hull but a more formidable opponent: Henry Stimson, the secretary of war.

On August 23, Stimson hosted the Treasury secretary at the Pentagon for lunch, asking John J. McCloy, the assistant secretary of war, to join them. Henry had not requested the date: Harry Hopkins had sent word to Stimson, urged on by FDR, that a "talk" with the Treasury secretary over how to deal with a conquered Germany would be in order.

In his memoirs Stimson remembered his lunch with Henry as the beginning of the "most violent single interdepartmental struggle" of his long career. Stimson had just returned to his office from the White House. He and the president had not met for two months—FDR had gone on an extended tour of the Pacific, while Stimson was visiting the fronts in Europe and Africa. At seventy-six, Stimson was the cabinet's elder statesman, the sole member whom FDR could not engage in banter. It had been a short visit, twenty minutes of "rapid fire talk," but Stimson managed to get his concerns across. Refusing to let "the meeting turn into a description of the two trips," he stood to deliver the warning: "A decision on what we are going to do to Germany," Stimson told FDR, "was of primary importance in the peace settlement." Roosevelt said he was to hold talks on the matter soon, with Churchill in Quebec. Within weeks, he assured Stimson, he "expected to settle all these questions" about Germany.

At the Pentagon, Stimson and Henry showed little interest in their meal. In Europe, the tide, on so many fronts, was turning. "A great day in war news," as Stimson recorded in his diary. "Paris has been freed." Within hours, they would learn of Romania's turn from the Axis. "This is the first big crack in Hitler's machine," one that "deprives him of his main source of oil," Stimson wrote that evening. "The end seems to be approaching on a galloping horse."

In Stimson's office, Henry could sense the opposition stiffening. The secretary of war took no pleasure in the Treasury wandering into the preparations for the occupation. Further, Stimson had heard that Henry was already advocating, in private, summary executions for Hitler's top officers. As Stimson weighed in on the future of Germany, the "distaste for a cold peace" was clear. Stimson was "thinking along the lines of a long Armistice," Henry recorded in his diary, "or a period of at least 20 years to police Germany."

"If you let the young children of today be brought up by SS Troopers," Henry countered, "aren't you simply going to raise another generation of Germans who will want to wage war?" It was true, Stimson allowed, but he seemed to hedge. As Henry put forward his idea of "removing all industry from Germany and simply reducing them to an agricultural population of small land owners," Stimson said that would in effect return Germany to 1860, when "she only had 40 million people."

"You might have to take a lot of people out of Germany," he said.

Henry was blunt in reply: "Well, that is not nearly as bad as sending them to the gas chambers." The secretary left dejected; the War Department would be no ready ally.

That afternoon, back at the Treasury, Henry told his aides to devise a way to win over Stimson. The secretary of war remained a larger-than-life figure, a legend from his father's past, but he "tires very easily"— recent back surgery had left Stimson in pain. Age was taking its toll: "You know," Henry told the aides, "you have to tell Stimson these things two and three times over before he gets it." But Stimson, he felt, could be brought around. And Henry already had a plan, one he was eager to put to the president: Perhaps FDR wished to get "State, Treasury and War working" on a plan together?

Early in the morning on August 25, Henry was back in the Oval Study. He would not wait for Hull or Stimson; he'd brought FDR a hastily written memorandum, highlights from the Army handbook that he had picked up in England, the guide for the U.S. military's governance in Germany. It revealed, Henry was certain, the War Department's myopia.

Henry entered sensing that FDR's health had taken a turn. At a dinner for the president of Iceland the night before, Roosevelt had given a long, warm toast. His guest then rose and spoke, but once he had sat down, Roosevelt had offered the same toast, all over again. "Everyone was so stunned," Henry wrote, "hardly anybody got up when he proposed the toast the second time." In the Oval Study, the secretary "was shocked for the first time" to see "a very sick man." FDR, Henry wrote hours later, "seems to have wasted away."

He handed the president the excerpts from the handbook, and watched as Roosevelt's eyes scanned:

Your main and immediate task, to accomplish your mission, is to get things running, to pick up the pieces, to restore as quickly as possible the official functioning of the German civil government in the area for which you are responsible. . . .

The first concern of military government will be to see that the machine works and works efficiently. . . .

The highly centralized German administrative system is to remain unless otherwise directed by higher authority. . . . The food supply will be administered so as to provide, if possible, a diet on the basis of an overall average of 2,000 calories per day. Members of the German forces will be rated as normal consumers. . . .

Roosevelt looked up. "Well, you can read this thing two ways," he told Henry. The instructions might favor a "hard peace" or a "soft," depending on your interpretation.

"Look, Mr. President," Henry said, the handbook "will go into operation unless there is some directive from the top down." Stimson knew, he went on, that Henry was going to lobby Roosevelt. "But I understand you are seeing him"—the war secretary was due for a White House lunch that day—"and I don't want to annoy him, so I think maybe you better give me back the memorandum and handbook."

"No," FDR said. "If you don't mind, I would like to keep it and read it tonight and then I will return it to you."

Before Henry left he added one last thought: his own view of the postwar world order. The president was clearly ailing; it would not hurt to remind him.

"I don't know how much you know about Bretton Woods," Henry said, "but in England you can see the thing much clearer." The monetary deal had revealed a divide over the Soviets, he told FDR. "There are two kinds of people," he explained. "One like Eden, who believes we must cooperate with Russia and that we must trust Russia for the peace of the world," and then there was "the other school," represented by Churchill, who asked him, "What are we going to have between the white snows of Russia and the white cliffs of Dover?"

"Well put," Roosevelt said, adding that he was with Eden: He wanted to work with the Russians.

Henry took the chance to speak of the summer's successes. "I know that, Mr. President," he said, "and I was able to work with Russia at Bretton Woods. . . . Dean Acheson said I seemed to have 'a sixth sense' on those things. At first he told me he thought I had handled the Russian situation entirely wrong, and then he was man enough to come around at the end and say I was completely right. And Keynes said the same thing. I think I could be used along those lines, and I am not being used."

FDR listened attentively: "He was interested," Henry told himself, "but what will come of it all I don't know." As always, he feared unsettling his treasured relationship. "I am going to continue to feed the President suggestions," Henry recorded in his diary, "but it is quite obvious that he wants to keep me very much in the background, and wants to do it his own way as usual."

In the evening, Roosevelt mustered the strength to read the handbook. By morning, he sent a stinging memorandum to the War Department; McCloy would call it a "spanking letter." "This so-called 'Handbook' is pretty bad," FDR wrote.

> I should like to know how it came to be written and who approved it down the line. If it has not been sent out as approved, all copies should be withdrawn. . . . It gives me the impression that Germany is to be restored just as much as the Netherlands or Belgium, and the

people of Germany brought back as quickly as possible to their pre-war estate. . . .

It is of course of the utmost importance that every person in Germany should realize that this time Germany is a defeated nation. I do not want them to starve to death, but, as an example, if they need food to keep body and soul together beyond what they have, they should be fed three times a day from Army soup kitchens. . . . The fact that they are a defeated nation, collectively and individually, must be so impressed upon them that they will hesitate to start any new war. . . .

There exists a school of thought both in London and here which would, in effect, do for Germany what this Government did for its own citizens in 1933 when they were flat on their backs. I see no reason for starting a WPA, PWA or a CCC for Germany where we go in with our Army of Occupation.

Too many people here and in England hold to the view that the German people as a whole are not responsible for what has taken place—that only a few Nazi leaders are responsible. That unfortunately is not based on fact. The German people as a whole must have it driven home to them that the whole nation has been engaged in a lawless conspiracy against the decencies of modern civilization.

It would be days before Henry read the letter, but as Labor Day approached, he sensed that although the fight was not over, the two stood in firm agreement. There would be no "coddling" of Germany.

Over the holiday weekend, the Morgenthaus were to host the president and Mrs. Roosevelt at the farm. In advance, Henry asked Harry White to rush an early draft of the Treasury's plan—what would become known, infamously, as the Morgenthau Plan. The memorandum called for destroying Germany's military plants, for the Allies to take control of the industries in the Ruhr and Rhineland, and for resettling those Germans displaced in the process. On Saturday, September 2, with the Roosevelts driving over for tea, Henry prepped himself to talk, "quietly and uninterrupted," on Germany.

As the two couples sat beneath the trees, Henry handed FDR the draft: six typewritten pages and two pages of a Rand McNally atlas—a map of Europe, divided by hand-drawn black borders. On the map, the bulk of Germany had been nearly split in two, and marked: "North German State" and "South German State."

The president seemed in good humor, on the rebound. As he turned the pages slowly, reading with care, FDR teased, "I wonder if you have the three things in it that I am interested in." When he had finished, he told Henry the points that he felt were "psychologically and symbolically extremely important." First, Germany should not be allowed aircraft of any kind, not even a glider; second, no one should be allowed to wear a uniform; and third, there should be no marching of any kind. The ban on uniforms and parades, FDR felt, would do more than anything to drive home the defeat.

The president also told Henry of his stinging letter to Stimson—"putting them in their place." Henry could not have asked for more. Once again, he seized a chance to push Roosevelt. "I don't think it goes nearly far enough," Henry said of the Treasury draft. "Where this memorandum falls down," he said, "is that the heart of the German war machine is the Ruhr"—marked an "International Zone" on the map in the president's hands—"and I would like the Ruhr to be completely dismantled, and the machinery given to those countries that might need it.

"I realize," he told FDR, "this would put 18 or 20 million people out of work, but if we make an international zone out of it"—governed by a United Nations mandate—"it is just time before Germany will attempt an *Anschluss*." There would be a bonus: England and Belgium, so badly hurt by the Germans, would see their rival coal and steel producer decimated, guaranteeing "their prosperity for the next 20 years."

They had spoken on Germany for more than an hour, Mrs. Roosevelt holding her tongue. The president, Henry felt, was not only in "complete sympathy," but might go even further. Roosevelt assured him that he would take up the plan with the prime minister soon, in Quebec. "It will be tough sledding with Churchill," he warned.

| | | |

Monday was a holiday, but Morgenthau gathered his aides early to regale them with his progress—and spur them on. "The President is entirely agreeable to the suggestion of closing the Ruhr," he said. "And I want something on that, do you see?"

Time was of the essence. "The man is hungry," Henry told his aides. He had gone to see Mrs. Roosevelt, too, after the tea. He wanted to be sure that Mrs. R., so "pacifist" early on, was on his side. The first lady, he told his aides, was all for closing the Ruhr: "Put the thing under lock and key and shut it down completely," she had said.

Henry talked on, as John Pehle and the others struggled to interrupt. White had gone back to the draft plan, trying to fold in the president's desires. The prohibition on military dress presented a hurdle. "The uniform is to be troublesome," Harry White said, "probably five million people have nothing else to wear."

The Ruhr, too, posed a problem. "It is your view that it should be locked up or wiped out?" White asked. But what would you do, the aide went on, "with the population?"

"Excuse me," Henry cut in. "The President is in complete accord on this, and the thing that he likes particularly about it is the idea that this would help put England back on its feet."

"Well," replied White, "I think that somebody is going to be confronted with what to do with fifteen million people."

"You can't put a fence around the Ruhr and keep all the people out," ventured Herb Gaston, the press aide.

"The only thing you can sell me," Henry insisted, "or I will have any part of, is the complete shutdown of the Ruhr."

"You mean vacating the whole thing?" asked Gaston, incredulous. "Driving the population out?"

"Just strip it!" said Henry. "I don't care what happens to the population."

"But there is some intermediate thing, between those two things," said Gaston. "I don't understand—"

Henry turned impatient. "I would take every mine, every mill and factory, and wreck it."

"Of every kind?" asked Gaston.

"Steel, coal, everything. Just close it down."

"You wouldn't close the mines, would you?" cautioned Dan Bell.

"Sure," said the secretary.

"You would leave agriculture?" asked Gaston.

"Yes."

"Leave it in international hands?"

"Yes."

Morgenthau was speaking in a voice the men had rarely heard. They knew well how he could speak in false starts, sputtering in vacillation and frustration, but now the words cascaded with momentum—and outrage. The secretary was adamant, as always, to break through the lethargy, to get ahead of the generals and diplomats. But in the rush of declarations, there was something more: a force bordering on audacity.

"I am not going to budge an inch," Henry said. "I find the President is adamant on this thing. Sure, it is a terrific problem. Let the Germans solve it! Why the hell should I worry about what happens to their people?"

On that Monday in early September, as Henry held forth, he offered an example that he had "lived through in the eyes of my father." Henry was always reluctant to bring up his father—or lay claim to his legacy in Constantinople. Yet as he spoke of the Ruhr, and what to do with the millions displaced, Henry returned to Turkey, and to a lesson, as he saw it, that did not arise from the slaughter of the Armenians.

"One morning," Henry told his aides, "the Turks woke up and said, 'We don't want a Greek in Turkey.' They didn't worry about what the Greeks were going to do with them. They moved one million people out. They said to the Greeks, 'You take care of them.'"

In that mass deportation, Henry saw a precedent. He ignored the aftermath: the burning of Smyrna in 1922, and his father's work to help resettle the refugees.

"Whether it is one million, ten million, or twenty million, it has been done; a whole population was moved. The people lived. They got reestablished in no time."

His aides sat in silence, as he plowed ahead.

"If you can move a million, you can move twenty million. . . . It seems a terrific task. It seems inhuman; it seems cruel. We didn't ask for this war. We didn't put millions of people through gas chambers. We didn't do any of these things. They have asked for it." He went on: "Now, what I want to say is, for the future of my children, and grandchildren, I don't want these beasts to wage war. I don't know any way than to go to the heart of the thing, which is the Ruhr, and I am not going to be budged."

The silence had become a wall as the secretary dug in.

"I can be overruled by the President, but nobody else is going to overrule me. I am not going to worry what happens to them, and nobody is going to overrule me, except the President.

"Go along with me," Henry said, almost pleading, "and make the Ruhr look like some of the silver mines in Nevada."

"Sherman's march to the sea!" Bell cut in, attempting levity.

"No—some of the ghost towns," the secretary corrected. "Make this a ghost area."

The president was eager to act, as well. The trick, of course, as Hopkins had warned Henry over lunch that day, was to get FDR to commit quickly—"before somebody else changes his mind."

| | | |

On the same day, Stimson and his wife, Mabel, had returned to Washington from Highhold, their country estate on Long Island. He had risen early to fly, eager to see General Marshall for an update on the progress in Europe. Stimson remained more than unsettled by Morgenthau's meddling: In part it was annoyance—what business was it of Treasury's?—but his concern ran deeper. Stimson could not abide Henry's call for summary executions of top Nazis—as many as 2,500. Listening to Marshall, Stimson was relieved to hear a military man's humanity for the conquered. "It was very interesting," he wrote in his diary, "to find that Army officers have a better respect for the law"—in terms of investigating and punishing the Gestapo—"than civilians who . . . are anxious to go ahead and chop everybody's head off without trial or hearing."

Stimson was exhausted, but he was resolved to engage in the battle. He went home, took a long afternoon nap—restoring his energy for the next round. Henry and Ellie had made a routine of holding informal dinners at home, where cabinet members, visiting dignitaries, and men from across the administration could mingle. Stimson had never been a frequent guest, but that evening, he and Mabel came to the house in Kalorama for a long meal, joined by their top aides—John McCloy and Harry White—to discuss it again: what to do once the troops entered Berlin.

"We had a pleasant dinner," Stimson wrote, "but we were all aware of the feeling that a sharp issue is sure to arise over the question of the treatment of Germany."

Cordell Hull and Harold Ickes, even Harry Hopkins, had earned Henry's derision. But Stimson stood apart. He was a statesman, a public servant Henry had admired since his father's years with Wilson. Henry had "met no finer man," he would later write, "in all my years in Washington." Stimson, for his part, might bitterly disagree with Henry on Germany, but remained sober in his estimation of the secretary's endeavor: "Morgenthau is, not unnaturally, very bitter," he wrote that evening after the dinner, "and as he is not thoroughly trained in history or even economics it became very apparent that he would plunge out for a treatment of Germany which I feel sure would be unwise." They had talked the thing over, Stimson said, with "temperateness and good will." They could succeed "in settling with perfect agreement" on the currency rate for postwar Germany; but on the big picture—how Germany must be governed—the distance between them had only grown.

Henry, though, had stacked the cards. Playing to FDR's propensity to adopt a semblance of balance, he'd proposed that the president set up a committee of State, Treasury, and War "to prepare how to deal with Germany." Roosevelt had agreed, naming Hull the chair. But it was Henry who took the lead, sending Hull and Stimson the Treasury plan.

At 9:30 the following morning, Hull convened the new "Cabinet Committee" of Hull, Stimson, Henry—and Hopkins, who had been added by FDR. On his desk the secretary of state had a draft agenda. An encouraging sign, Stimson imagined, but something was amiss. "Hull has been rather crotchety about the whole thing and showed it," Stimson noted in his diary. Hull, Stimson feared, deemed the initiative an intrusion onto his turf, but "the truth of the matter," Stimson felt, "is that the situation has been drifting into a chaotic situation."

As Hopkins sketched the advantages of destroying Germany's industrial potential over allowing it to continue, Henry could not tell which way Hopkins was leaning. Yet when Hull weighed in on Henry's side, Hopkins leaned toward joining them. Stimson seemed alone in his outrage: "This is just fighting brutality with brutality," he insisted. "We can't solve the German problem except through Christianity and kindness." Stimson and Morgenthau squared off: The war secretary spoke of the Bible, and Jesus, in an awkward tone, or so it struck Henry. ("He seems to be afraid to talk about Christianity in front of me," the Treasury secretary told his aides. "I don't know why.") Stimson seemed unlikely to win out, but Henry found his "soft" talk infuriating. "All you've got to do is let 'kindness and Christianity' work on the Germans!" he would say later that day, mocking Stimson's words on a call with Hopkins.

The battle, though, was wearing on the war secretary. Stimson had come home late from dinner at the Morgenthaus, stayed up studying the Treasury documents, and then risen early to read them again. Returning to the Pentagon from Hull's office, he appeared spent; McCloy had never seen him so depressed. "In all the four years that I have been here," Stimson would write that evening, "I have not had such a difficult and unpleasant meeting. . . . We were irreconcilably divided." Hull had surprised him: The secretary of state sounded "as bitter as Morgenthau against the Germans," making it evident that "Morgenthau had been rooting around behind the scenes." For the rest of the day, Stimson had worked on "hammering out . . . a vigorous statement." "I feel that I had to leave a record for history," he wrote, "that the entire government of this Administration had not run amok."

The meeting in Hull's office had left both Stimson and Morgenthau disappointed. The four had reluctantly agreed to let the secretary of state draft the main plan, with recommendations from all others. But as Stimson went to bed that night, the words he had heard in Hull's office unsettled him. "It was very singular," he wrote in his diary, "that I, the man who had charge of the Department which did the killing in the war, should be the only one who seemed to have any mercy for the other side."

| | | |

In the morning, the president summoned Morgenthau. It was time to bolster the fragile ego. "Don't be discouraged about yesterday's meeting," FDR said, before Henry could open his mouth. "I had Cordell trembling."

"I don't know what he meant by that," Henry later dictated, "because Cordell certainly was not trembling. . . . But the amazing thing was that he should have greeted me the way he did, because he must have realized the way I felt, and this was most encouraging."

Roosevelt knew how to massage his friend. "The German question" had sparked the secretary's old anxieties, and FDR could foresee the likely path to come: As War and State demanded their own plans, the cabinet skirmishes would only grow. To raise tensions even higher, Henry was again beginning to see Hopkins as his chief rival for FDR's ear. The president could sense it—and knew better than anyone that fear never worked in Morgenthau's favor. He had to get Henry to slow down on the Ruhr. "The whole question," FDR said, "seems to be about closing down the plants, and we have got to do the thing gradually." When Henry asked for a longer audience soon, Roosevelt agreed: The "Committee on Germany," as FDR now called it, would get two hours on Saturday.

That morning McCloy warned Stimson: Morgenthau "sticks to his guns and has been to the president again and demanded a rehearing of the talk that we had." Morgenthau, McCloy added, was "turning the entire forces of the Treasury" to "demolish" Stimson's revision of the

Treasury draft. "So I fear," Stimson concluded, "we are in for some fireworks."

The showdown came, as expected, at noon on Saturday, September 9. At the White House, Henry, Hull, and Stimson met with the president. Instead of two hours, Roosevelt gave them forty-five minutes, "taken up mainly," Stimson noted, "by the President's discursive questions and remarks." FDR seemed worn out, unable to shake a cold, but as he was soon to leave for Quebec, the men knew the gravity of the moment. "We were all trying to get our licks in," Henry recalled. He had come with black binders filled with copies of a revised, even bolder plan—"a new diatribe on the subject of the Nazis," Stimson called it, "an enlargement of his previous paper on how to deal with them."

As Henry handed out the plan, Stimson fumed. "None of us had seen this until we got into the room," he later complained, "and therefore it was impossible to answer it intelligently."

Roosevelt half listened, half read the Treasury memo. At one point, he read aloud the title of a supporting brief: "It Is a Fallacy That Europe Needs a Strong Industrial Germany." He looked up and said coyly, "This is the first time I have seen this stated." Everyone seemed to disagree on the point, FDR went on, "but I agree with this idea. Furthermore, I believe in an agricultural Germany."

Henry struggled not to rejoice. "I evidently made a real impression on the president the time he came to my house," he crowed in his diary. "The more I talk to him, the more I find he seems to be coming around to our viewpoint."

Hull "took no leading part as chairman," Stimson recorded. Instead, as Hull sat silent, Stimson spoke up. The Morgenthau scheme would "breed war, not peace," he told the president. "It would arouse sympathy for Germany all over the world; it would destroy resources desperately needed for the reconstruction of Europe."

Stimson had come with his own memo. It was not, he wrote, "a question of a soft treatment of Germany or a harsh treatment of Germany." "We are all trying to devise protection against recurrence by Germany of her attempts to dominate the world." But Stimson could not stomach either closing the mines ("I cannot conceive of turning such a gift of nature into a dust-heap") or such harsh treatment of the top Nazis. If Henry insisted on executions, no matter how many thousands, Stimson would insist on trials by a tribunal.

Stimson stood on moral grounds Henry could understand. It was Hull who left him puzzled: "Hull just won't get in on the discussion," Henry wrote, "and just what his game is I don't know."

Back at his desk at Treasury, Henry was nearly beaming. In front of them all, FDR had backed him. Two topics were sure to be raised at Quebec, the president had said. "One is the military and the other is the monetary, because Churchill keeps saying he is broke. If they bring up the financial situation, I will want Henry to come up to Quebec." For Henry, his hopes continued to grow. "This is the second time he has said that," he recorded in his diary.

Stimson, on the other hand, left the meeting "rather low," and concerned about FDR's ability to govern. At the meeting, Roosevelt was "distinctly not himself," and days later, Stimson worried, "I have been much troubled by the President's physical condition." The Quebec talks now carried a disturbing specter. "I rather fear for the effect of this hard conference upon him," Stimson wrote. "I am particularly troubled . . . that he is going up there without any real preparation for the solution . . . for how to treat Germany."

| | | |

That afternoon Stimson boarded a military plane for a weekend back at Highhold. Onboard, as McCloy sat beside him, he thumbed through Henry's "black book." The revised Treasury plan, he lamented, was "full of the bitter spirit of his old paper," only now "buttressed by alleged facts." In the margins, he attacked claim after claim: *Childish folly! A beautiful Nazi program! This is to laugh!*"

Henry, meanwhile, had secured a seat on the presidential train for Saturday night to Hyde Park. When they arrived at Highland Station in the morning, Roosevelt drove on to Springwood while Henry left for the farm. The president wished to spend the weekend preparing for Churchill. In his new fieldstone library, Roosevelt worked at Woodrow Wilson's old mahogany desk, the one he had used to draft the League of Nations Covenant aboard the *George Washington* as he sailed for Paris. As the summit with Churchill approached, Versailles weighed heavily on Roosevelt's mind.

On Monday, September 11, the president's train arrived in Quebec. Almost at once, the northern air refreshed his spirits—"typically fall sunny weather," Grace Tully, FDR's personal secretary, noted, "clear, cool and most invigorating." Twenty minutes later, Churchill emerged on the platform, cigar lit and kitted out in his favorite blue uniform, the formal dress of an "Elder Brother" of Trinity House, the British corporation, dating to 1514, of harbor pilots. The scene, noted Lord Ismay, the PM's chief military aide, seemed "more like a reunion of a happy family starting on a holiday than the gathering of sedate Allied war leaders for an important conference."

For Eleanor Roosevelt, the summit seemed "such a waste of time," as she confided to Elinor Morgenthau. "The ladies' duties are all social," she wrote. She could go shopping with Mrs. Churchill, or journey into the countryside for a tea, but she failed, she told Ellie, to develop a rapport with the prime minister's wife. "It would be boring," she wrote, "except for the meals with a few people when the PM and F are entertaining."

The monotony would soon end. On the following evening, Henry received his long-awaited summons. At the farm, a Secret Service man handed him an urgent telegram:

PLEASE BE IN QUEBEC BY THURSDAY,
14 SEPTEMBER, NOON.
ROOSEVELT.

Henry packed at once. He knew "how easily the President could be sidetracked," his aide Fred Smith wrote. "This time no one was going to get the chance."

On Monday, back in Washington, Stimson again sought out Justice Felix Frankfurter, inviting him to dinner "to cheer us up." Frankfurter told Stimson to ignore Morgenthau's onslaught. "It would not go anywhere," he predicted; FDR would "catch the errors," realize "the spirit was all wrong." Stimson remained unconvinced: "I wish," he wrote, "I was as sure."

By morning Henry had flown to Canada, arriving a day early. In Quebec, the Roosevelts and the Churchills were to stay in the Citadel quarters, where they had convened a year earlier. The stone fortress offered elegance and commanding views of the St. Lawrence River. Built by the British after the War of 1812, the fort was intended as a refuge against an American onslaught.

Henry would stay nearby, at the Chateau Frontenac. Mrs. Roosevelt, though, made sure he was invited at once for afternoon tea. As Henry entered the presidential suite, Roosevelt smiled, and turning to his Scottish terrier, Fala, said, "Say hello to your Uncle Henry." This time, Henry took the teasing as a welcome sign: He noticed that FDR already held in his lap a black binder, the documents detailing the Treasury plan.

In Roosevelt's mind, a way forward had taken shape. "I have asked you to come up here," he told Henry, "so that you could talk to the Professor"—Churchill's nickname for his current confidant and aide, Lord Cherwell. He and Churchill were "doing shipping" at dinner that night, and though Vice Admiral Emory Land would be on center stage, FDR invited Henry to join them.

How freely could he talk with Cherwell? Henry asked.

"You can talk about anything you want," FDR said.

"Anything?"

"Well, let me look at that book."

As the president looked over the Treasury plan, he said, "I wouldn't discuss with him the question of the zones to be occupied by our armies. That's a military question. Nor would I discuss the question of partitioning, as that's a political question. But you can talk about the fact that we are thinking of internationalizing the Ruhr and the Saar, including the Kiel Canal. If Holland has a lot of land inundated by Germany we can give her a piece of Western Germany as compensation."

Roosevelt kept reading, and then said, "I have sent for Eden." The prime minister had not seen it necessary to bring his own foreign minister, Anthony Eden, but the president now encouraged him to do so. "Churchill, Eden, yourself and I," FDR told Henry, "will sit down to discuss the matter."

Morgenthau brightened. If the president was keen to bring Eden over, he thought, it was because of what Henry had told him after his London trip: Eden wanted a "hard peace."

"Don't worry about Churchill," FDR said. "He is going to be tough [with Germany], too." As Henry was leaving, the president motioned to Grace Tully. "Put that book"—the Treasury plan—"right next to my bed," he said. "I want to read it tonight."

| | | |

By morning, the Washington papers had Stimson fuming. "It is an outrageous thing," Stimson wrote in his diary. The president had "invited Morgenthau up there, or Morgenthau has got himself invited." McCloy tried to console his boss, but he, too, refused to believe that FDR would "follow Morgenthau's views." "If he does," McCloy said, "it will certainly be a disaster." Stimson was boiling. He wrote: "Here the President appoints a committee . . . in order that it may be done with full deliberation and, when he goes off to Quebec, he takes the man who really represents the minority and is so biased by his Semitic grievances that he really is a very dangerous adviser to the President at this time."

In Quebec, Henry was thrilled to be included at the state dinner. He had not expected, though, to be the star attraction. Arrayed around Roosevelt and Churchill were Admirals William Leahy and Emory Land, Lord Cherwell, Lord Leathers, head of British shipping, and the president's and PM's physicians. Yet despite the admirals' presence, there was little talk of ships. Germany took center stage.

FDR announced that he had asked Morgenthau to come up to discuss postwar plans. Henry, he said, would meet with Cherwell in the morning.

Churchill cut in. "What are my Cabinet members doing discussing plans for Germany without first discussing them with me? I intend to get into the matter myself." The PM was impatient: "Why don't we discuss Germany now?"

Roosevelt asked Henry to explain his program. But as Morgenthau dove in, revealing the heart of his plan—dismantling the Ruhr—Churchill stirred. "I had barely got under way," Henry would say, "before low mutters and baleful looks" told him "the Prime Minister was not the most enthusiastic member of my audience."

All that was necessary, Churchill said, was to cut off the armament production; what Henry was suggesting was "unnatural, unchristian, and unnecessary."

"I am a great admirer of Churchill," Henry would write, "but I have never seen him more irascible and vitriolic than he was that night. It is quite an experience to be on the receiving end of one of Churchill's blasts." The PM, Henry wrote, "turned loose on me the full flood of his rhetoric, sarcasm and violence." The Treasury plan, Churchill said, was "like chaining his body to a dead German." Churchill's attack came at full force; it was, Henry would say, full of "the most foul language." "I have never had such a verbal lashing in my life."

As Henry attempted to highlight the advantages for England, Churchill cut him short: Even if the British managed to get the steel business Germany had once claimed, he said, it would not be much of a boon.

Admiral Land, on the other hand, backed Morgenthau, even thumping the table for emphasis. After dinner, Land told Henry that his proposal had liberated him. The president, Land said, had been talking to him along those lines for a long time, but this was the first time that Land had had a chance to say what he felt. Admiral Leahy, though, seemed to side with Churchill. Leahy thought the only way to assure the peace would be if the United States, the United Kingdom, and possibly Russia—"if she behaves herself," as Harry White, Henry's notetaker, recorded—were to "crack down" on any nation that trespassed the border of any other.

Throughout Churchill's outburst, FDR had kept silent. Morgenthau tried to interject, insisting that he wasn't for starving the Germans. Slouching in his chair, Churchill reddened with anger. At one turn, he asked Roosevelt: "Is this what you asked me to come all the way over here to discuss?"

Roosevelt tried to save the evening. He reminded Churchill of Stalin's words at Tehran: "Are you going to let Germany produce modern metal furniture? The manufacture of metal furniture can be quickly turned into the manufacture of armament."

Years later, Henry would try to recast FDR's performance on that first evening. The president had merely let Churchill "wear himself out attacking me"; he had "used me," Henry wrote, "to draw the venom." And then, as calm returned to the table, FDR could rejoin the conversation, with his charm and humor, to regain the momentum. All the same, Henry went to bed that night deeply unsettled and endured a sleepless night.

||||

At ten o'clock the next morning, Henry hosted Lord Cherwell in his suite. "The Prof," as Churchill called him, had become one of England's most influential scientists—the prime minister's "one-man brain trust," in Henry's view. An Oxford physicist and celebrated tennis player (he had played Wimbledon), Cherwell seemed an aristocrat's aristocrat, yet remained a man of mystery. Born Frederick Lindemann to an American mother and Alsatian father in Baden-Baden, he had grown up in Germany, graduating from university in Berlin. In 1919, he had moved to England, taking up a chair in physics at Oxford. Tall, dapper, and wealthy, Lindemann had come to know Churchill on the tennis courts—as a doubles partner to his wife. Clementine adored him, and "the Prof" found himself a favored houseguest at Chartwell. In 1941, raised to the peerage, Lindemann became Baron Cherwell, after the river in Oxford.

By the time he rose to national attention, the Prof had become more English than the English—he drove a Rolls-Royce to his lectures, and his arrogance bordered on the xenophobic. And yet, the German accent remained, and though he preferred not to speak of his origins, it was said, on both sides of the Atlantic, that the Prof was not only "foreign," but Jewish.

In one of several biographies to come after the war, Cherwell's Oxford friend, the economist Roy Harrod, wrote, "The question of whether the Prof was a Jew was a subject of frequent discussion," and "it will always remain something of a mystery." Many, like McCloy, held on to the rumors. In 1947, McCloy quoted Churchill as damning "Morgenthau and the Prof," in relation to the Quebec agreement: Both "were Shylocks." Whatever his background, Cherwell would find an affinity with Henry. The Prof, as a Churchill aide testified, "detested Germans."

Whether or not Henry was curious about Cherwell's religious background, he asked Mrs. Klotz to gather intelligence: Ellie's cousin at Oxford, he told his secretary, was sure to know the Prof. Arthur Goodhart, who'd accompanied Henry Morgenthau, Sr., to Poland as a young legal scholar, was now a don at Oxford. Mrs. Klotz cabled his reply to Quebec: Cherwell, he reported, is "almost the Prime Minister's most intimate friend." Goodhart offered more: The Prof was "conservative" and, given his snobbish airs, "not popular" with the British public. Lindemann had befriended Einstein and helped a number of Jewish scientists to flee Hitler, but of his Jewish roots, Goodhart said nothing.

In Quebec, the Prof tried to calm the waters, even managing to cheer Henry. When the two met on the morning after Churchill's tirade, as Cherwell scanned Henry's "black book," he admitted that the PM had caught him off guard, too. Churchill did not get Henry's intended meaning, the Prof said. Wasn't his opposition about something else? Henry countered: Didn't Churchill wish to see "a strong Germany" stand between the "white cliffs of Dover" and Communist Russia? Yes, the Prof conceded, "that was it."

Cherwell was all for dismantling the German industries, he told Henry, and distributing them to "the countries she had devastated." The Germans, he said, "would, of course, not starve."

The Prof had offered to make a pitch, and by afternoon, as Churchill and Roosevelt reconvened, he had managed to bring the prime minister around. "I will take it," Churchill said, adding there was "a good deal to be said for this approach." The Russians, moreover, "would probably in any case insist on obtaining any machinery available . . . to restore the factories which Germany had ruined in her advance into Russia."

Henry charged ahead. Dismantling the factories, he said, "should be undertaken as soon as possible, say within the first six months of our troops entering the Ruhr." FDR seconded him: It would be no "undue hardship," he said, "to require Germany to revert towards" the agricultural state "such as she had enjoyed up to the end of the last century."

The prime minister and the president agreed to set up a committee on postwar planning for Germany. They would keep it informal for now, in the hands of a chairman both could work with. "How about Harry Hopkins?" Churchill asked. "No," said Roosevelt, "I want Morgenthau."

| | | |

By Thursday evening, Foreign Secretary Eden arrived. Henry and Cherwell spent the following morning conferring, before being summoned to see FDR, Churchill, and Eden.

The discussion did not open as Henry had expected. For days, the British had hoped to focus Roosevelt's mind on their primary concern: American aid to England. Desperate to extend Lend-Lease, Churchill had been the one to suggest that FDR bring Morgenthau along to Quebec. Yet by week's end, a draft agreement—on a $6.5 billion deal for the first year after the war—remained unsigned. In his memoirs Churchill would claim that Henry drew out the talks, attempting to arm-twist the PM's approval for the Treasury plan on Germany. Morgenthau and Roosevelt, men "from whom we had so much to ask," he would write, were "so insistent." On Friday afternoon, as Roosevelt spun story after story, Churchill reached the breaking point: "What do you want me to do?" the PM blurted out. "Get on my hind legs and beg like Fala?"

When FDR at last got around to signing the deal to extend aid, Churchill's gratitude revealed England's dire need. With "tears in his eyes," Henry remembered, the PM said they were doing this for "both countries."

Yet when they returned to the German question, Churchill again flashed his anger. "Where are the minutes of this matter of the Ruhr?" he demanded, asking to see the record of what Morgenthau and Cherwell had discussed in their absence.

Henry and the Prof had begun talks on the Treasury plan, but the secretary had convinced the Prof "to say we had no minutes." (The Prof had in fact written notes summarizing their discussion, but Henry thought they "presented much too weak a case"—he was sure they could get Churchill to go further.) The PM was taken aback, but before he could launch another attack, FDR broke the ice. There were no minutes, Roosevelt quipped, because Henry had insisted on telling "too many dirty stories."

"Well, I'll restate it," Churchill said, offering a vision for Germany's future. When he'd finished, the PM suggested that Henry and the Prof remove themselves to another room and try again. "It only took us a few minutes," Henry would recall, before they returned with the new draft.

Churchill read it aloud:

> At a conference between the President and the Prime Minister, Mr. Churchill said that he would sum up the discussion that we had been having in regard to the future disposition of the Ruhr and the Saar. He said that they would permit Russia and any other of our Allies to help themselves to whatever machinery they wished, that the industries in the Ruhr and in the Saar would be shut down, and that these two districts would be put under an international body which would supervise these industries to see that they would not start up again.
>
> This programme for eliminating the war-making industries in the Ruhr and in the Saar is part of a programme looking forward to diverting Germany into largely an agricultural country.
>
> The Prime Minister and the President were in agreement upon this programme.

Churchill was not pleased: "No, this isn't what I want." As he turned to Cherwell and Morgenthau to insist on his own version, Henry saw an opening. "I don't know what the rules are," he said, "but is there any reason why we can't have a stenographer present? Then you could dictate directly to her."

"By all means," Churchill said. Cherwell produced the PM's secretary, and Churchill launched into an improvised dictation, holding in one hand Henry and Cherwell's draft "as a sort of a text." Roosevelt offered only one change: When the PM reached the sentence on the industries, FDR had him insert "in Germany." The ban, he insisted, should not be limited to the Ruhr and Saar.

Churchill now dictated with force and few pauses:

At a conference between the President and the Prime Minister upon the best measures to prevent renewed rearmament by Germany, it was felt that an essential feature was the future disposition of the Ruhr and the Saar.

The ease with which the metallurgical, chemical and electric industries in Germany can be converted from peace to war has already been impressed upon us by bitter experience. It must also be remembered that the Germans have devastated a large portion of the industries of Russia and of other neighboring Allies, and it is only in accordance with justice that these injured countries should be entitled to remove the machinery they require in order to repair the losses they have suffered. The industries referred to in the Ruhr and in the Saar would therefore be necessarily put out of action and closed down. . . .

This programme for eliminating the war-making industries in the Ruhr and in the Saar is looking forward to converting Germany into a country primarily agricultural and pastoral in its character.

Roosevelt signed the document—"O.K.," "F.D.R."—and Churchill added "W.S.C." and the date, "15.9."

Years later, the prime minister claimed duress: Morgenthau's persistence and the hunger for American aid had got the better of him. Eden had already blamed Morgenthau—at once. "You can't do this!" he told Churchill. "After all, you and I publicly have said quite the opposite." But Churchill would not hear the criticism. "The future of my people is at stake," he shot back. "And when I have to choose between my people and the German people, I am going to choose my people." Stung by Churchill, Eden took it out on Morgenthau. The foreign minister felt "irritated," he wrote in his diary, "by this German Jew's bitter hatred of his own land." That fall Eden would write in a Foreign Office memo analyzing Allied plans for Germany: "Morgenthau's interference is a piece of gratuitous impertinence. These ex-Germans seem to wish to wash away their ancestry in a bath of hate."

Henry would suffer the consequences of the Quebec agreement more than anyone else present in the Citadel that day. The deal's final sentence, regarding the aim of "converting" Germany into a nation "primarily . . . pastoral in its character," would haunt him. Yet as those who worked beside the Treasury secretary could have guessed without knowing, "pastoral" was a literary adjective absent from the secretary's vocabulary. It was Churchill who had inserted the term.

| | | |

On Long Island, in Huntington, Stimson faced "a scene of desolation." His country house, set on a hundred rolling acres, commanded views north and south, to Long Island Sound and the Atlantic. A hurricane had swept through days earlier, leveling locust and apple trees, cutting all electricity. The Stimsons had no telephone, "except for our own wire," a long-distance cable dating to the Hoover era, when Stimson served as secretary of state. On the weekend, McCloy had managed to deliver the bad news from Quebec—the president was decided "flatly against us."

Stimson found it incredible that FDR, as he wrote in his diary, had "gone over completely to the Morgenthau proposition." Cherwell must have done it, he surmised, for the Prof was "an old fool," a "pseudo-scientist," "who had loudly proclaimed we could never cross the Channel." The news left Stimson on edge. "It is a terrible thing," he wrote, "to think that the total power of the United States and the United Kingdom in such a critical matter as this is in the hands of two men, both of whom are similar in their impulsiveness and their lack of systematic study."

Ever since he first heard Henry's plan, Stimson had sensed an echo—of the Roman peace imposed on Carthage. "I have yet to meet a man who is not horrified with the 'Carthaginian' attitude of the Treasury," he wrote. "It is Semitism gone wild for vengeance, and, if it is ultimately carried out (I can't believe that it will be) it as sure as fate will lay the seeds for another war in the next generation."

| | | |

Back at the Treasury, Henry was giddy. "The thing up in Quebec," he told the Treasury boys, "was unbelievably good." Wresting the blessing from the president and Churchill, he said, was "the high spot of my whole career in the government." FDR had even thanked him. He'd been "groping for something," Roosevelt said, and "we came along and gave him just what he wanted."

Henry then rushed to the State Department to tell Hull and Stimson of his victory at Quebec. They would differ as to his tone: To Hull, Henry was "wildly enthusiastic" as he waved the deal aloft, while to Stimson, Henry had spoken "modestly and without rubbing it in." But both resented the turn: The Treasury had again moved on their turf, and FDR had left them in the cold. The "whole development at Quebec," Hull would write, "angered me as much as anything" in all his years at State. Roosevelt's actions—"such irresponsibility and deviousness"—left him fuming, and drained.

For the old men of the administration, Henry sensed, battle fatigue was setting in. Stimson in his diary called Henry's news "the narration of a pretty heavy defeat for everything that we had fought for." If Stimson was in retreat, Henry sensed that Hull was "on the verge of resignation." Nursing a bad cold, Hull seemed increasingly feeble. Henry was sure of it now: Treasury could straight-arm State and the War Department. The Brits, too, would come around. "The fellow Cherwell is a breath of fresh air from the sea!" Henry told his aides. "You can get further with him in fifteen minutes than anybody they have sent over here since Purvis." Moscow, too, posed no great challenge: He could handle the Soviets, Henry was certain, just as he'd brought them to the finish line at Bretton Woods.

Only one hurdle remained.

Born into a poor, devout family in southern Germany, Lazarus
Morgenthau married Babette Guggenheim (whom he had known
since childhood) in 1843. Babette would give birth, in all, to fourteen
children over twenty-three years.

Family portrait, before America: Lazarus and Babette in Mannheim,
Germany, with their children Pauline, Minna, Siegfried, Gustave,
Recha, Ida, Bertha, and Maximilian, in 1855, a year before the birth
of their ninth, Heinrich, who would be known as Henry in New York.

An inventor with zeal, Lazarus owned a cigar factory and a mansion in Mannheim by 1860. (The home is shown here during the poet Friedrich Schiller's centennial celebration, which Lazarus helped to stage in 1862.)

Lazarus with a Golden Book of Life, 1871. A fundraising tool he patented, the ceremonial books found favor with charities such as orphan asylums and hospitals, offering donors recognition—akin to having their names "entered" into the Book of Life at the Jewish New Year.

At eighty, Lazarus, ever the gambler, printed cards declaring himself an "eighty-year-old youngster."

Lazarus would suffer flights of fantasy—dying in 1897, alone and a pauper. But in his diary, written at age twenty-seven, in 1842, he recorded his humble origins, so that "neither pride nor arrogance may gain a foothold in my family."

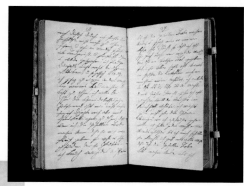

Henry Morgenthau, Sr., and Josephine Sykes, who was born in 1863, wed in New York in 1883. (Her father had immigrated to Detroit from Europe a decade before her birth.)

Wedding eve: Josephine (standing center) with her widowed mother, Helen Himmelreich Sykes (third from left), and sisters as bridesmaids, 1883.

Henry Sr. (center) and Woodrow Wilson (third from left), then the governor of New Jersey, at dinner in New York City to celebrate the fourth anniversary of the Free Synagogue, April 24, 1911. That evening, Henry told Wilson that should he run for president, he had the real estate mogul's "unreserved moral and financial support."

Henry Sr. would help run Wilson's 1912 campaign for the White House. Eager for a cabinet job, he was instead offered the ambassadorship to the Ottoman Empire—deemed the "Jewish" position in any administration. He declined the post, but Wilson, his political guru, Colonel Edward House, and Jewish leaders convinced him to reconsider. Said Wilson: "Remember that anything you can do to improve the lot of your co-religionists is an act that will reflect credit upon America."

The American ambassador: Henry Morgenthau, Sr., arrived in Constantinople on Thanksgiving Day 1913, and would serve until the spring of 1916. Henry Sr. is surrounded on the U.S. Embassy steps by staff and crew of the gunboat *Scorpion* in 1915. His son Henry Jr., on the last of three visits to Turkey during his father's tenure, stands far right.

WITNESS TO GENOCIDE

When Turkey entered World War I in October 1914, the Armenians were deemed a threat to the war effort. A May 1915 decree ordered Armenians expelled to the Syrian Desert, resulting in mass arrests, deportations, and widespread death.

Ambassador Morgenthau received urgent dispatches from across the empire, as well as photographs revealing the horrors. On July 11, 1915, one consul wrote: "Everyone knows it is a case of going to one's death."

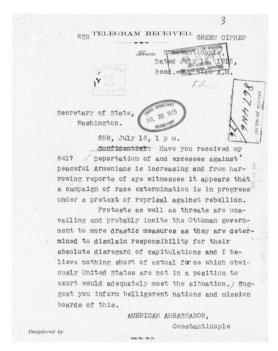

On July 16, 1915, Morgenthau sent an urgent cable to Washington: "it appears that a campaign of race extermination is in progress under a pretext of reprisal against rebellion."

"Scenes like this were common all over the Armenian provinces in the spring and summer of 1915," Morgenthau wrote in his 1918 memoir of his years in Turkey.

AMBASSADOR HENRY MORGENTHAU IN THE HOLY LAND

He Visits Palestine and Syria and Is Given Special Privilege to See the Mosque Over the Cave of Machpelah.

HENRY MORGENTHAU, American Ambassador in Constantinople, has just made an extensive trip through Palestine and Syria. He long desired to see the land which once belonged to Israel, and felt that once having been through the Turkish provinces he could, in his official position, better handle problems which might present themselves.

He was accompanied by Mrs. Morgenthau and Miss Ruth Morgenthau, their daughter, as well as by the legal adviser to the Embassy and a uniformed cavass as bodyguard. In Jerusalem the party was joined by Dr. Hoskins of the American Mission in Beirut, Mr. Peet of the American Mission in Constantinople, and later by President Bliss of the Beirut College. A reception at the United States Consulate in Jerusalem in honor of Mr. Morgenthau was given by Samuel Edelman, the Vice Consul in charge, and a dinner by the Governor of Jerusalem. The Ambassador himself later gave a large dinner.

One of the incidents which marked the stay was a trip to Hebron and an inspection of the mosque over the Cave of Machpelah. This ancient Hebrew burial place of the Patriarchs is today most jealously guarded by the Moslems, who control it, and those of other faiths are not permitted to enter the sacred precincts. Less than a score of persons are today living for whom this rigid rule has been relaxed, and it is several years since any one has been thus favored, as was the small party admitted with the Ambassador.

The trip from Jerusalem to Hebron, 22 miles, was made by carriage, with Turkish cavalry as outriders. At Hebron a triumphal arch spanned the road and Jewish school children sang songs of welcome. Within the mosque once a Christian church, parts of which go back to Hebrew times, are shown the catafalques of Abraham and Sarah, Isaac and Rebecca, Jacob and Leah, while through a small hole in the floor one gets a view of the cave of Machpelah itself, in which, says legend, the Patriarchs were buried, and which is perhaps the only authentic Hebrew burial place still shown in the Holy Land. A special firman issued at Constantinople to Mr. Morgenthau made it possible for the party to enter this sacred shrine. While the party was in the mosque a double row of Turkish infantry was drawn across the entrance to keep out the fanatical mob.

Mr. Morgenthau went from Jerusalem to Mount Gerizim. The party drove first to Ramallah, where they saw the school for boys just erected by the American Friends' Mission. On the way were seen many places of Biblical interest.

Mr. Morgenthau and his companions examined the ruins of Samaria, lately uncovered by Dr. Riener with funds furnished by Jacob Schiff. Remains of the palaces supposed to be those of Omri and Ahab were seen, as well as the ancient gateway through which the spoils of Benhadad's blighted army were brought into the starving city. The next day Jacob's Well and Joseph's Tomb were visited, as well as the Turkish Hospital, soap factories, and bazaars.

After spending a Sunday at Nablous, Ambassador Morgenthau proceeded via Zamarin to Haifa, by which route he visited several of Baron Rothschild's colonies and the new American Agricultural Experiment Station near the foot of Mount Carmel.

On the Summit of Gerizim.   *Mr. Morgenthau Being Shown the Spot Where Abraham Was Prevented from Slaying His Son, Isaac.*

Pilgrimage to Palestine, 1914: In the Holy Land, Morgenthau won a rare visit to the Tomb of the Patriarchs in Hebron—one of the world's most ancient sites, known to Jews as the Caves of Machpelah, and to Muslims as the Sanctuary of Abraham.

"There we stood, Moslems, Christians and Jews—all of us conscious of the fact that we were in the presence of the tombs of our joint forefathers . . . the ten minutes to which this prayer extended were undoubtedly the most sacred that I have ever spent in my life." —Henry Morgenthau, Sr.

The ambassador (third from left), his wife, Josephine, daughter Ruth, American missionaries, and staff of the U.S. consulate in Jerusalem. In an August 1914 cable, Morgenthau warned of "serious destruction" of the Jewish colonies, and urged leaders of the American Jewish community to raise direct aid—the first such American effort.

Father and son return: Morgenthau Sr. and Jr. arrive in New York Harbor on the *Frederick VIII* from Turkey, February 22, 1916.

The former ambassador would remain at the forefront of politics. Here, at a City Hall mass rally, Morgenthau (bow tie) plays power broker, standing with Charles Evans Hughes, the former governor of New York and 1916 Republican presidential nominee (far left), and Theodore Roosevelt (center) to back "the boy mayor," John Purroy Mitchel (right, in tan suit), in a failed reelection bid, October 1, 1917.

Roving ambassador: In 1919, President Wilson sent Henry
Morgenthau, Sr., to investigate reports of pogroms against Jews in the
new Polish republic. Henry Sr. is flanked by U.S. officers and his wife's
cousin Arthur Lehman Goodhart (back row, third from left), who
served as counsel to the commission. The fact-finding mission covered
2,500 miles across Poland to visit Jewish communities, but proved a
public relations failure. Critics called the Morgenthau report—
minimizing the Polish government's culpability—a whitewash.

Henry Morgenthau, Sr., would help lead the Near East Relief Committee to aid
the Armenians, and in 1923, after the destruction of Smyrna brought an exodus
of Greek refugees, he chaired the League of Nations Refugee Settlement
Committee. Here he visits an orphanage in Athens, 1923.

Old Wilson Democrats come early to FDR's side: (left to right) Senator David Walsh, Colonel Edward House, Governor Franklin D. Roosevelt, Boston mayor James Michael Curley, Senator Marcus Coolidge, and Henry Morgenthau, Sr., June 1931, in the seaside resort town of Manchester, Massachusetts.

Three generations: Henry Morgenthau, Sr., at eighty-nine, with his son Henry Jr. and grandsons Robert (far right) and Henry III (far left), recently returned from the war, Bob from the Pacific, Henry III from Europe, at a B'nai B'rith gala dinner to honor the former secretary of the Treasury, New York City, November 1945.

Henry Morgenthau, Jr., and Elinor Fatman, daughter of Settie Lehman Fatman and Morris Fatman, a textile baron, wed on April 17, 1916, in her parents' brownstone, 23 West Eighty-first Street in New York City. They had grown up on the same street, even sharing a tutor as children.

The Lehmans, circa 1888: Mayer Lehman (center), one of three brothers atop Lehman Brothers, the banking empire built on cotton, and his wife, Babette (to his left), maternal grandparents of Elinor Morgenthau, the Treasury secretary's wife. Back row, standing, left to right: Arthur Lehman, Philip Goodhart, Clara Lehman (Limburg), Morris Fatman. Middle row, sitting, left to right: Hattie Goodhart with Helen (Altschul) on lap, Howard Goodhart (standing), Mayer and Babette Lehman, daughter Settie Lehman Fatman with baby Margaret on lap. Seated on lawn: Herbert and Irving Lehman.

Henry Jr. with his sisters: (left to right) Alma, Helen, Ruth. The sisters were "bitterly jealous of the unabashed favoritism" shown their brother by their father, Henry Morgenthau III would recall. At the same time, "they all adored 'Pa.'"

Henry Jr. (far left), at twenty-four, in the trenches at Gallipoli, December 1915, on his third trip to his father's side in Turkey. Henry Jr. journeyed to the front lines with Bedri Bey, Constantinople's police chief (far right), just ahead of the British forces' ignoble withdrawal.

FDR and Henry Morgenthau, Jr.,
1930. The two met as early as
1914 and worked side by side
throughout Roosevelt's years as
governor. Henry worked each
campaign as FDR's advance man
in New York State starting in
1920, when FDR was a vice
presidential candidate. A tradition
formed: Henry would make a
final election-day tour with the
candidate and wait out the returns
by his side. When FDR was
stricken with polio at age thirty-
nine in 1921, he allowed few men
to help him; "Henry the
Morgue," as he teasingly called
his friend, was an exception.

FDR loved little more than to relax in private with his few close
friends: a picnic in the fields of Dutchess County, Pine Plains, New
York, August 1940.

"From one of two of a kind," FDR inscribed this 1934 photograph of himself and his friend to Elinor Morgenthau. Close in Democratic politics, Roosevelt and Morgenthau grew closer still as residents of Dutchess County, gentlemen farmers who shared a love for the rolling hills of the Hudson River Valley.

Henry Morgenthau, Jr., sworn in as FDR's commissioner of conservation, with the governor and the Morgenthau family looking on, January 1, 1931. (The future district attorney, age eleven, stands at far right.)

Rivals and allies: Henry Jr. (far left) at the White House to discuss relief, with members of FDR's cabinet: (left to right) Joseph P. Kennedy (who coveted Morgenthau's job), Harry Hopkins, and Harold Ickes, April 1935. Henry never felt as close, or as confident, with his fellow cabinet members as he did with the Roosevelts. "I am a juggler," FDR confided to his friend. "And I never let my right hand know what my left hand does."

Biggest bond harvest in history: Since the spring of 1933, no one in FDR's cabinet worried more about the gathering storm in Germany than Henry Jr. On the evening of April 30, 1941, seven months before Pearl Harbor, FDR launched the first bond drive with the secretary of the Treasury. Roosevelt called the defense bonds "visible tokens of partnership" and asked that all Americans help to "swell the coffers of the federal Treasury."

Elinor Morgenthau, former star of the Vassar drama society, was the real orator of the family. Elinor, who assisted Eleanor Roosevelt in the federal Office of Civilian Defense, is shown here at the Chrysler plant in Detroit in January 1942. When Secretary Morgenthau suffered a migraine attack, she took his place, and despite a sprained ankle climbed atop a tank to rally the workers.

Elinor Morgenthau was an adept writer and political strategist; here she helps the Treasury secretary prepare a radio address. "My father never made a move without consulting my mother—with good reason," Henry III said. During the war, as Mrs. Roosevelt's deputy in Civilian Defense, Elinor not only assisted the first lady with her *Over Our Coffee Cups* radio program, but presented her own USO radio talks.

Elinor Morgenthau and Eleanor Roosevelt enjoyed a morning routine of riding horseback through Rock Creek Park in Washington, D.C. Close friends, they often traveled together, highlighting the first lady's causes: They visited striking workers—mostly women—at a factory in Brooklyn, toured a women's prison in West Virginia, and promoted a homesteading project for destitute coal-mining families. In October 1944, they inspected the first U.S. refugee camp for survivors of the Holocaust in upstate New York.

Joan Morgenthau, at fifteen, with her father on the farm, 1938. "Raising purebred cattle would be viewed as a rich man's hobby," an advisor warned, but Henry Morgenthau, Jr., was proud of his Holsteins. By 1922, his bull, Dutchland Colantha Sir Inka ("Dutch"), had sired eighty-seven daughters—forty-three of whom stayed on the farm, producing milk and fat. The war, though, spelled the dairy's end: In 1943, Morgenthau sold the whole herd (fifty Holsteins, fifty Guernseys).

Joan Morgenthau became a debutante at a Christmas dance given to her by Eleanor Roosevelt in 1940. Joan became the first daughter of a cabinet member "presented to society" at the White House. As the elite of Washington and Manhattan's "Our Crowd" mingled, FDR threw his arms around the guest of honor, telling her, "I am sorry I cannot have the first dance with you." All the Morgenthaus were thrilled, except Joan: "I dreaded the idea," she would say.

Elinor and Henry Jr.'s daughter would become a noted pediatrician, founding, in 1968, the Mount Sinai Adolescent Health Center, one of the first such programs in the United States. Amid the 1970s heroin epidemic, Dr. Morgenthau also pioneered the city's first substance abuse prevention programs for teens—operating out of a trailer in a parking lot in East Harlem.

37. "For 48 Hours, I Was on the Top of the Heap"

FALL 1944

"I don't think Pa would really mind defeat," Mrs. Roosevelt wrote to their son James early in the 1944 campaign. "If elected he'll do his job well. . . . I think he can be kept well to do it but he does get tired so I think if defeated he'll be content."

FDR seemed increasingly aloof—above all, from the looming campaign for a fourth term. The longer he remained on the sidelines, the darker the political prognosis grew. Thomas Dewey was the consensus of the press. To the shock of the cabinet, Henry had declared himself ready to lead the charge on the domestic political front. Even before Quebec, he'd had the Treasury boys compile another big "book"—ordering up Gallup polls and asking aides to map the numbers. When he learned how close the race seemed—sixteen states hung in the balance, Gallup claimed—Henry sent the polls each week to the president.

From Boston (where he had gone to witness the commissioning of Bob's new destroyer), Henry called the White House. He asked Grace Tully to get word to the president. Roosevelt, he said, must convene a session at Hyde Park, something along the lines of Quebec, but "devoted entirely to politics." The president should call in the top men, he told Tully, "just to sit around and plan a campaign." If Henry could solve postwar Germany, he imagined, he could head off any domestic discontent in the weeks before the election. He asked Tully to tell the president he had given a speech in Chicago recently and been shocked to find "complete apathy." Americans were "satisfied with the President's conduct of the war," but they hungered to know what FDR was "going to do about jobs after the war is over?" And if Roosevelt wished him to draft a speech, Henry said, he'd get ahold of the "right people" at once. In truth, he had already instructed his men to bring in the speechwriters.

It was not to be. Just as Henry Morgenthau was starting to indulge the intimacy earned in his decades at FDR's side, just as he was beginning to savor his hard-earned success, a leak brought him crashing down to earth.

On September 22, the secret Quebec deal burst into the press—and "like angry bees," Henry wrote, "the newspapers began buzzing around me." On September 22, Arthur Krock, Joe Kennedy's favorite *Times* columnist, asked if Henry had "become the President's advisor on foreign affairs instead of Mr. Hull?" FDR had sided with Morgenthau on a hard peace for Germany, Krock reported, and split the cabinet. Henry would blame the fallout on Krock, but Drew Pearson had the scoop a day earlier—thanks, in all likelihood, to Henry's own staff. On September 21, Pearson reported that FDR "blew up" when Morgenthau had shown him the draft Army handbook. "Feed the Germans . . . !" Pearson quoted Roosevelt as saying, "I'll give them three bowls of soup a day, with nothing in them." Pearson, it seemed, had the whole backstage drama: the Treasury plan, Roosevelt's "blistering" riposte to Stimson, and even the copies FDR had sent to Hull and Morgenthau, replete with his "penciled notations."

With the cabinet threatening open warfare, FDR tried to placate the dissenters. On September 21, Stimson's birthday, he sent roses. On September 22, he invited Ickes for lunch. The interior secretary was a rare lunch date. As the men ate outside, joined by Anna Roosevelt, the president's eldest child and only daughter, Ickes was struck by how Roosevelt had weakened. FDR, he wrote in his diary, revealed "the wear and tear of the past eleven and a half years." Anna had become her father's gatekeeper. As the vigor ebbed, Anna—in tandem with her second husband, John Boettiger, a former newspaper man from Seattle—had tried to cut off the flow of supplicants. Even Mrs. Roosevelt would complain of having to go through her daughter to see FDR. If Anna had her way, Morgenthau and Hopkins—"always the difficult ones," as his appointments secretary Marvin McIntyre would say—would be kept at a distance.

Ickes cut to the point: The "soup for the Germans" story would play "very bad politically," and he didn't care for Morgenthau's growing influence. Could it be true, he asked, that Henry was going to go "across the country," stumping for the president? Morgenthau as a surrogate made no sense, he warned. "The feeling of anti-Semitism" in the country was "intense," Ickes said, and Morgenthau was deeply "disliked." Henry's tour was only another war bond campaign, FDR replied, but Ickes remained doubtful: Had not Morgenthau "slipped up to Quebec to get the jump on Hull and Stimson?"

"Morgenthau is taking advantage of his personal relationship with the President," Ickes concluded in his diary. "The situation is not a good one."

As the leaks and counter-leaks grew, the cabinet war spilled into public view. On September 23, an aide barged into Henry's office with a copy of *The Wall Street Journal*: What Henry had called the Quebec Agreement, the paper now christened the "Morgenthau-sponsored policy," reporting that it was not yet official policy, and the cabinet was at odds. Dorothy Thompson, a columnist Henry had long admired, soon joined the battle. In a column entitled "Morgenthau's Carthagean [*sic*] Peace," she asked, "Have we gone crazy?" "Mr. Morgenthau's plan is not original," Thompson wrote. "There is a model for it. It is the Nazi plan for defeated countries." As Henry read the attacks, Thompson's words stung the hardest: "Hate is an emotion," she wrote, "that should be confined to the heart. When it rises into the brain the result is insanity."

"The pack is in full cry," noted Stimson, a day before lunching at the White House. On October 3, he sat between Anna and the president in the family quarters upstairs—the setting ordered by the doctors, so as not to sap FDR's energy. It was Stimson's turn to be taken aback by Roosevelt's appearance: "for the first time" he looked so "unwell." Yet almost before Stimson could open his mouth, the president "grinned and looked naughty," and said, "Henry Morgenthau pulled a boner." Stimson sensed a retreat: Days earlier, when Roosevelt had called, he seemed eager to mollify his war secretary. Now across the table, Roosevelt tried to backtrack. FDR, Stimson surmised, knew "he had made a false step and was trying to work out of it." Roosevelt would never bless anything so drastic as the Morgenthau Plan, he assured Stimson. "He didn't really intend to try to make Germany a purely agricultural country," Stimson would record in his diary, but offered an "underlying motive"—"the very confidential one that England was broke."

Still, Stimson would not let the president off lightly. He produced from his pocket the agreement FDR had initialed in Quebec.

"I read him the three sentences beginning with the one saying 'the industries referred to in the Ruhr and Saar would therefore be necessarily put out of action and closed down' down to the last sentences saying that 'looking forward to converting Germany into a country . . . pastoral in its character.' "

Roosevelt was "staggered." He had no idea, he told Stimson, how he could have initialed the document. Stimson was not sure if FDR was playing coy, or truly had been misled, but pressed on. There was much about Morgenthau to admire, he said; Henry had been "so kind to me when I first came into the Cabinet." The Treasury secretary may have trespassed beyond bounds, but he was a good man. That was why, Stimson went on, he had "shuddered" when Morgenthau launched his "campaign against Germany, knowing how a man of his race would be misrepresented for so doing."

Stimson felt he was making ground: "The President and Mrs. Boettiger," he wrote in his diary, "both strongly agreed."

"Throughout the war," he told FDR, your "leadership had been on a high moral plane." The postwar policies must not "poison this position." Before leaving the president, Stimson handed him a copy of the Drew Pearson column that had ignited the fire now engulfing Morgenthau. FDR, though, did not have to read it; their lunch had settled it— Stimson would never have to raise the idea of a "pastoral Germany" again. After leaving the White House, the secretary of war was driven back to Woodley, his estate in the woods at the center of the city, where he enjoyed "a massage, dined and spent the evening alone."

| | | |

With the cabinet arrayed against him, Quebec burned in Henry's mind. "For 48 hours, I was on the top of the heap," he told the Treasury boys. "I wish I could ever get there again." To make matters worse, the Republicans soon took up the cry.

On October 18, Governor Dewey made the Morgenthau Plan a campaign weapon. In a speech in New York, Dewey ridiculed Roosevelt for taking Morgenthau, "whose qualifications as an expert on military and international affairs are still a closely guarded military secret," to Quebec. Dewey cut deeper: Goebbels, he railed, had seized on the "episode to terrify the Germans into fanatical resistance." German morale had risen "almost overnight," he charged, and the surrender was no longer imminent. "They are fighting with the frenzy of despair. We are paying in blood for our failure to have ready an intelligent program for dealing with invaded Germany."

Dewey was not altogether wrong. Three days later, Goebbels declared that "it hardly matters whether the Bolsheviks want to destroy the Reich in one fashion and the Anglo-Saxon in another. They both agree on their aim: they want to get rid of thirty to forty million Germans." In his 1945 New Year's address, Hitler would rail against the Treasury plan—decrying "the uprooting of 15 or 20 million Germans and transportation abroad, enslavement of the rest of our people, ruination of our German youth, but above all, starvation of our masses." In short, "the Morgenthau Plan," as Albert Speer would write, "was made to order for Hitler and the Party, insofar as they could point to it for proof that defeat would finally seal the fate of all Germans."

Henry was stricken with near panic. The headlines at home had brought shame, but his notoriety in Berlin, he feared, could lead the Nazis to capture his son, Henry III—and once they learned his identity be "extremely cruel." Henry III had managed a transfer, rejoining the Second Cavalry. Now attached to Patton's Third Army, the cavalry group tanks were moving across France, advancing rapidly, but engaging in frequent skirmishes. The secretary asked Eddie Greenbaum, his old friend and lawyer, what could be done: Might Henry III be given a false identity, and even fake dog tags? Greenbaum consulted the War Department, but McCloy warned him off the idea. The Nazis often gave their spies false papers, he said, and should they capture young Morgenthau with fake tags, the Army would have no choice but to "completely disown" him.

Greenbaum instead suggested that Henry ask a favor of Walter Bedell Smith, Eisenhower's aide: to have SHAEF "pull Henry out of his outfit and send him to a quiet sector." The secretary knew better. "Henry would never forgive me," he said. "I do not want to have the boy touched."

| | | |

On the third Saturday in October, three weeks before America went to the polls in the first wartime presidential election in eighty years, FDR finally joined the campaign trail—making his first public appearance as a candidate. On a rain-soaked Saturday, he made a grueling all-day tour of New York City. Roosevelt was determined to make a stand on Dewey's home turf, and he wished, as well, to quell the ugly rumors of his failing health. On the train from Washington, for the first time since Pearl Harbor, FDR had invited reporters and photographers—thirty-seven in all—to come along. The New York tour was intended as a grand show, orchestrated for the press as much as the onlookers, more than two million who lined the streets in the wet chill.

Roosevelt rode in a black Packard, roof rolled back, exposed to the weather, as the motorcade threaded the drenched streets. From morning until the afternoon, they crisscrossed the boroughs—covering fifty-one miles—before arriving at Ebbets Field. The storm had gained force. As the president's physician and White House aides scanned the skies, FDR took in the packed stadium. As if relying on instinct alone, he threw off his old Navy cape, and then—after an aide snapped his heavy braces straight—rose to his feet. The president, standing bareheaded in the storm, captivated the crowd. It was his first time at Ebbets, he announced, though of course he'd rooted for the Dodgers in years past. As an image for the front pages, it was genius. "His very presence in the storm," Hassett wrote that evening, had put "the lie to his detractors" and their "vendetta . . . against his health."

Henry had been among the president's party throughout the day. He'd insisted on setting the tableau—ensuring that Senator Wagner, up for reelection, and Herbert Lehman, the former governor and Ellie's uncle, hovered close to the president. In the evening, after a brisk massage, change of clothes, and a lie-down, FDR was to give a foreign policy speech at the Waldorf. Henry would sit near Stimson and McCloy and hear Roosevelt rise to Dewey's challenge to deliver "even the pretense of a plan for the future." For a man who had opened his campaign reliant on the radio, the marathon day in New York was a triumph: Roosevelt had answered Dewey and demonstrated vigor. By day's end, as the motorcade pulled up at Mrs. Roosevelt's apartment on Washington Square—FDR's first and only visit to his wife's refuge—Mayor La Guardia stood outside in a soaked hat, assuring reporters, "I think I'm tough, but he took it better than I did."

For Henry, it was a coup: After the firestorm, he imagined himself safely returned to the inner circle.

The relief, though, was short-lived. On November 3, four days before the election, Arthur Krock again stoked the fire: "Lend-Lease II," the new loan for England, he charged, had come in exchange for the Morgenthau Plan—Roosevelt and Morgenthau had all but bribed Churchill at Quebec. Reading the *Times* at the farm, Henry found it too much to stomach. "How Arthur Sulzberger, who wants to see the President elected, could run a story like that!" Henry cried to an aide. "Today is Friday. Dewey can use it tonight or tomorrow."

On Saturday, Henry's fear turned to reality. A reporter called to warn that Dewey was planning to "skin" him that evening, in his wind-up speech at Madison Square Garden. Dewey, the word was, would claim that the Morgenthau Plan had only prolonged the war. Burning with dread, Henry urgently tried to reach Roosevelt. The president, or even Stimson, would have to back him up, denying the Treasury plan had hurt the boys at the front. At 8:15 P.M., Henry tried to raise FDR on the phone, but his train had already left the station, headed for a final speech in Boston. Henry reached the White House telegraph operator, asking to get word to Grace Tully and Rosenman: Dewey was going to blame the Morgenthau Plan for extending the war, he said, and "Stimson or General Marshall should deny" the accusation at once.

At 8:45 P.M., Henry spoke with Stimson at Cold Spring Harbor, pleading for him to "do something." Dewey's charge was "ridiculous," Stimson assured Henry. "Our soldiers have not changed their fighting one bit," he said; the advance had been slowed by a "lack of port facilities." All the more reason, Henry said, to put out a statement. Stimson promised to consider it, but wrote in his diary that such a move would be "foolish." He could not allow "the Army to enter last-day politics."

That evening at his final rally, Dewey did slam the Morgenthau Plan. He decreed it "so clumsy that Mr. Roosevelt himself finally dropped it. But the damage was done." The Treasury secretary's "private plan for disposing of the German people after the war," Dewey charged, rejuvenated the Nazis, giving them a boost as great "as ten fresh German divisions." "Almost overnight," he charged, "the headlong retreat of the Germans stopped." What had become of Eisenhower's vow, repeated that fall, to end the war in Europe in '44? Dewey asked. America had paid for such "improvised meddling," the Republican challenger said, with the "blood of our fighting men."

Dewey did not mention Morgenthau by name—he called him only "that master of military strategy and foreign affairs," echoing Goebbels— but the blow landed hard.

| | | |

For as long as anyone in the Hudson Valley could remember, FDR had capped every campaign with a long drive, winding his way through the river towns, with Henry Morgenthau, Jr., by him. On Monday, November 6, the eve of the election, Roosevelt would enjoy what he called "another sentimental journey." For all the noise over the Morgenthau Plan, FDR reverted to tradition, and his most loyal friend. He donned a fur-lined overcoat—a gift from Stalin—and took Henry along again, riding once more in frigid weather in an open car, newly equipped with bulletproof windows, along the old Post Road.

At Wappingers Falls, FDR stopped to address the crowd. They went on to Beacon, and then took the ferry to Newburgh to shake hands at the Eureka Shipyards. The president seemed to withstand the cold better than his companion. Henry wore only a light topcoat: By Newburgh, his teeth were chattering and he'd turned "a cobalt blue." A Secret Service man ran back to the press cars, asking if anyone had a drink. There was one, but a quart bottle, and no one could imagine the secretary, a reporter would write, "taking a pull at the jug in front of several thousand people." But Henry found a hotdog stand, poured himself "a two-inch jolt into a cup of coffee," and in minutes, the whiskey and "a lot of ungentle kidding from the President" had restored circulation to his face.

On election night, Henry and Ellie drove up to Hyde Park to wait out the returns with the Roosevelts. The vote soon became clear—FDR won reelection handily, 432 to 99 electoral votes, though the popular margin would be the narrowest since Wilson's reelection in 1916. Still, Dewey stubbornly made it a long night—conceding at 3:16 A.M. Even then, he offered no words for the victor. At four A.M., the president left the party, being wheeled off to bed, but Hassett caught him in the corridor. As the aide offered congratulations, FDR roared back, "I still think he is a son-of-a-bitch."

In the months since Quebec, Henry had cleaved to Roosevelt more closely than ever; he made sure to be at his side as often as possible, and scarcely raised a challenge on policy. In Washington, they would try to stop Henry: Stimson, Hull and Ickes, Anna and her husband—they would try to drive a wedge between him and FDR. Giving in, though, was an impossibility now; if in the first years in Washington, Henry had recoiled at the barest slight, threatened to quit whenever he sensed a rival invading his turf, a confidence had set in. He had tasted glory in Quebec, and for all the resistance and ridicule, he was determined to see his plan through.

An idea had taken root. If Washington could not be trusted, he would take his case to the American people: He would publish "the Morgen-

thau plan" as a book—to appear "on the day that Germany collapses."
The president, he was sure, would back him. Henry had told his aides of
the book idea at a meeting on the election's eve. Mrs. Klotz said she
would bet "two bucks" that Roosevelt would stop him.

"I'm going to do it with or without consent," the secretary vowed,
warning of an emboldened Morgenthau to come: "You people," he said,
"have to be prepared for a lot of new things from me after the election."

38. In the Pacific: "Undivided Attention"

Long before Maine became a state, the village of Bath had built the first seafaring vessel in America. On the Maine coast, three hours' drive from Boston, Bath had first gained fame for its tall-masted schooners. By 1943, the war had swollen the ranks of the Bath Iron Works: nearly twelve thousand men and women churning out destroyers, from keel-laying to launch, in as few as four months. Bath built more destroyers than any other U.S. shipyard—and more than all the shipbuilders in Germany or Japan. During Fourth of July week in 1944, the iron works launched the USS *Harry F. Bauer,* one of twenty Sumner-class destroyers built in rapid succession, and readied the ship for a fall sendoff at the Boston Navy Yard.

By summer's end, Lieutenant Bob Morgenthau would sail aboard the *Bauer,* bound for the Pacific, but he had skipped out on the temporary bachelor quarters at Bath, waiting out the weeks with Martha in a rented apartment in Cambridge. Bob had made sure to "stock the pond"— seeing to it that many of the best men from the *Lansdale* and the *Winslow* joined him on the new ship. Each had received an invitation with strict instructions: "Do not discuss this with anyone" and "No cameras allowed." They arrived at the commissioning ceremony in Charlestown to find the top local brass in dress whites, and Henry Morgenthau, Jr., presiding. Wearing a dark-blue suit and sunglasses, Henry stood stiffly on the main deck beside the commandant of the First Naval District and Mrs. Harry F. Bauer, widow of the war hero for whom the ship was named, who had died off Guadalcanal. The secretary stood in the shadow of the five-inch guns as Bob joined him on deck to address the officers and crew standing below.

At 2,200 tons and 376 feet, the *Bauer* was bigger than the *Winslow* or the *Lansdale*. It was also deemed more seaworthy and boasted more, and more powerful, guns. Laid down as a destroyer, the *Bauer* would be among the dozen Sumner-class destroyers converted to minelayers. The change meant only one alteration: The years of war had taught Admiral Nimitz, commander of the Pacific Fleet, to lose the top weight, replacing the heavy torpedo tubes with mine tracks. The crew would train on the ship as if it were to be deployed as a minelayer, but they would never use the mine tracks. In the Pacific, the Navy had found a more efficient, and more accurate, way to drop mines: B-29s. To its crew of 327 and its 20 officers, their ship remained, in essence, a destroyer.

The *Bauer* sailed south along the Atlantic coast on a shakedown cruise. By November's end, she was escorting two transports to the Panama Canal, before entering the Pacific to give a submarine screen for the USS *Alaska,* a new cruiser. On Christmas Day 1945, they were in San Diego for still more training, before crossing the Pacific and reaching Pearl Harbor in time for New Year's Eve. At Pearl, the officers at last got their orders: Lieutenant Morgenthau's ship would join the amphibious force bound for the next stop in the Navy's island-hopping campaign: Iwo Jima.

The *Bauer*'s executive officer had not looked forward to the Pacific. "Europe was much closer to my heart," Bob Morgenthau would say. "You felt the immediacy of it; you were in the heart of the war—facing the Germans." There was also a sense of uncertainty. The Pacific was a foreign world: "Europe was all the places we knew, or had heard of: Gibraltar, Naples, Sicily. But who'd ever heard of Ulithi or Okinawa?"

By the time the *Bauer* reached Hawaii, Morgenthau had learned that his new captain would pose trouble. Commander Richard C. Williams, Jr., was a veteran skipper, a wiry man with a thin face who had survived Pearl Harbor. (He had been at home that morning with his wife and newborn son when the attack came.) Williams was well educated—the son of a Latin teacher, grandson of a judge, and an Annapolis graduate. But he was also a drinker and a brawler. Morgenthau saw the drinking early on, and before long, at a supply stopover on Saipan, the fighting. Captain Williams ended up in fisticuffs with another captain, the son of Admiral Jonas Ingram. Nine years Morgenthau's elder, Williams had been born and raised in Baltimore, and gone to sea in the year that FDR was elected. The drinking was one thing, his feelings about the war another. Williams, according to Morgenthau, "was pro-Nazi." "We're fighting the wrong enemy," Williams would say. "The Germans are our allies. We should be fighting the Russkies." The captain's biggest sin, though, was incompetence.

Morgenthau had brought nearly forty men with him. In Washington as he awaited orders, he'd pinned a note to the bulletin board at the naval gun factory, and recruited a loyal core from the *Lansdale*: George Sinclair, Jr., the yeoman; Lieutenant J. J. ("Jack") Haffey, Jr., the gunnery officer from a farm in Missouri; and "the Senator," Marvin Eubanks, the communications officer. He also reached back to the *Winslow,* bringing several other former shipmates, including Frank Tuggle, the Texan with a fondness for Tennyson, as the plotting room officer.

The men had become close. "Of course, we knew who Bob was," Sinclair said of Morgenthau. "We knew his father was sitting with the President most days, but on a destroyer at sea, facing submarines and kamikazes, that didn't mean a helluva lot."

"We didn't care about the father," Alex Weinberg, a machinist mate from Chicago, would add. "Everyone on the crew knew Lt. Morgenthau was a regular guy. And only one thing mattered: he kept the ship going."

Bob would again run the CIC, but now he also became the ship's navigator. Normally, a captain would have two officers performing the two jobs, but the designated navigator had missed the ship in Norfolk—a long night of drinking—and Captain Williams had relieved him of his duties. In the Pacific, Morgenthau would work nearly around the clock. This time, though, he had an advantage: "The Senator," his friend Eubanks, also served as the officer of the deck. A direct wire connected the men: Morgenthau "could talk with Eubanks without going through the Captain," a shortcut that "saved me from an awful lot of trouble."

The *Bauer* joined Mine Squadron 3, a unit of twelve Sumner-class destroyers, each converted to a minelayer, and led by Captain Frederick Moosbrugger, veteran of Guadalcanal and the Solomons. The squadron would form the backbone of sea support for the Iwo Jima assault, and later, in what would become the most dangerous duty in the U.S. Navy during the war, serve along the "radar picket" line at Okinawa, the sixty-mile-long island that loomed as the largest target in the drive on Tokyo.

Morgenthau's ship left Honolulu at the end of January, making rushed stops at Eniwetok and Saipan. The men conducted target drills, loaded supplies (food, ammunition, fuel), and, on at least one afternoon, anchored in the blue-green waters off Saipan, enjoyed a swimming party. They arrived at Iwo Jima just before dawn on February 19.

For the Navy, the "tin cans" remained at the core of the arsenal. A destroyer's "speed, maneuverability, relatively high firepower for their size, and comparatively low building price," a maritime historian wrote in 1945, had made them "not merely the most versatile, but ton for ton the most efficient, naval craft ever devised." In the Mediterranean, the destroyers had performed rescues, thrown smoke screens around cruisers, and blasted the shores to soften up the ground for the beachhead assaults. In the Pacific, to protect the fleet against Japanese air attack, the Navy devised a strategy of "picket stations"—creating a curtain of radar that encircled Okinawa, interlocking the radar from one ship to the next, and assigning, at least at first, one destroyer to every station. Soon, once it had become obvious that the destroyers would need help, the Navy bolstered the stations with "small boys," landing craft that would attempt to pick up "the swimmers"—survivors from ships that had been sunk. And then, at the height of the Okinawa campaign, when the attacks came nearly without pause, the commanders added a second destroyer to each station.

At Iwo, the *Bauer* was sent in to do shore support for the Marines—blasting machine-gun pillboxes, fuel tanks, ammo dumps. As Morgenthau talked to the forward observer to set the targets, the ship stood just out in front of the *North Carolina*. "They were lobbing 16-inch shells over us," Morgenthau recalled. "Sounded like a freight train every time one went." Although the *Bauer* got straddled by the Japanese gunners, the Marines faced the greatest danger—the first wave went in at 8:30 A.M. "I remember seeing an LCI [landing craft, infantry] with Marines ready to land," Dave Garcia, a radio mate from Los Angeles, remembered. "They were not gung-ho like you'd see at the movies. They were solemn. They knew some of them were not coming back."

In those first days, as the *Bauer* faced scattered hit-and-run nighttime air attacks, Lieutenant Morgenthau was surprised at the relative quiet. The officers used the radio sparingly; Morgenthau instructed them to relieve the burden on the voice circuits and rely instead on "visual communication"—semaphore flags or a blinker light. Navigation, too, was fairly easy: "The Japanese charts," either prewar or captured, Lieutenant Morgenthau recorded, "were accurate and sufficient."

The *Bauer* joined a unit of five minesweepers, zigzagging several miles south of Mount Suribachi. Morgenthau watched the radar in the CIC, but those up top could see the enemy with binoculars—or the naked eye.

For the first time, the men experienced a kamikaze attack. The Japanese planes came in low, at times no more than five hundred feet off the water.

"It was terrifying," Morgenthau would say, "a world of difference from the Med." If a German bomber had been hit, the crew would bail out. When the kamikazes got hit, though, even in flames, "they'd just keep coming right at you."

Captain Williams not only revealed pro-Nazi sentiments, he was a "racist, just a blind racist." As he had on the *Lansdale,* Morgenthau intended to deploy the Black mess attendants on the guns. He had asked them all to join him on the *Bauer,* but Marion Porter had been laid up in the naval hospital in D.C., his shattered leg requiring more than a year of surgeries. Yet again, Morgenthau would assign the messmen to the 20 mm guns, a pointer and loader on each.

"These men are veterans," he told Williams. "They've been on the 20 mm guns." But Williams would have none of it: "Oh, Bobby, you can't do that. You can't put n****rs on guns."

For weeks, the men feuded until a deal was struck: Morgenthau could have a Black gun crew on the sponson (the gun platform) on the forward stack, as long as he put a white gun captain and a white gun crew beside them, "to steady them," as Williams put it.

Days later, when the ship faced its first kamikaze attack and the plane exploded right over the stack, once the smoke cleared, Captain Williams had a surprise. The Black gun crew had stood by their gun, but the white crew, Morgenthau would say, "had jumped clear," at least twelve feet to the main deck.

On February 23, the Marines raised the flag on Suribachi. For Bob, the capture was all the sweeter, given the news he had just received: On February 21, Martha had given birth to their first child, Joan (soon to be known as Jenny). Bob and Martha were both twenty-five years old. At sea, he would mark the day: "D+2," two days after the Marines went ashore on Iwo Jima. Bob had learned the news on the Armed Forces Radio; at a press conference in Washington that day, his father had deliberately turned personal—"I'm the proud grandfather of a little baby girl, my first grandchild"—hoping that the news would reach the Pacific.

Within two weeks, the *Bauer* sailed for Ulithi, preparing for what would prove the last, and largest, of the island operations: Okinawa. On Ulithi, no more than a series of sand spits, the men won a brief window of "liberty"—time off for recreation, beers, and the captains' brawl. In the last week of March, as the Okinawa invasion neared, the *Bauer* served as "den mother" for a group of minesweepers, moving into Kerama Retto, the archipelago of islands west of Okinawa, that would serve as the repair base for the amphibious forces.

"She is believed," Captain Williams would write in the action report, "to be the first major war vessel flying the Stars and Stripes to enter these straits."

The *Bauer* also took on the biggest risk: The minesweepers were small (136 feet long), and made with light wooden hulls, but Morgenthau's ship was iron-hulled, the only vessel in the group heavy enough to set off a mine. "We'd got a report of torpedo boats hiding in Kerama Retto," Bob would recall, "so we headed in." The Japanese, the Navy believed, were set to use the small torpedo boats as "suicide craft." The *Bauer* moved in close among the islands, providing cover for the little wooden-hulled boats that swept the straits ahead of the troops' landing.

The sweep of the Kerama Retto's channels seemed to catch the enemy unawares: Captain Williams would write that the "Japanese reaction to our efforts were not as determined as has been expected." But the *Bauer* did come under attack. In their first three months in the Pacific, the men had faced only single attacks—and downed four planes—but on the night of March 28, just as the Navy closed in on control of the entire cluster of islands, Japanese bombers came at the ship. The attack lasted six hours, without pause, until morning—the *Bauer* gunners shooting down three planes, and driving another away, heavily damaged.

On the day of the invasion, the *Bauer* joined the picket ships offshore, one of 88 destroyers. In all, in the ensuing three months, 206 ships and more than 36,000 men would serve on "picket duty" to form a ring around the island—service that would become known as the most dangerous job in the Navy. Between April 6 and June 22, the Japanese launched at least 1,465 suicide aircraft against the U.S. ships, sinking 36 of them, and damaging 368 others. In the battle, the Navy lost 4,907 men—and another 4,824 were wounded.

From the first, it was clear to all onboard that the Okinawa invasion—in the planning since the fall of 1944—would demand even more men than had been sent into Normandy. In all, 183,000 U.S. troops, four

Army divisions and three Marine Corps divisions, would be deployed in the ground assault, with nearly twice the number of men in support— a total of 548,000 troops taking part in the biggest invasion of the war.

At 4:06 in the morning, Vice Admiral Richmond Kelly Turner, commander of the Amphibious Forces, Pacific Fleet, gave the signal, and at 5:30, 10 battleships, 9 cruisers, 23 destroyers, and 177 gunboats opened the shelling. At H-Hour, the time operations were set to begin, the first wave of troops hit the beaches. The Navy would land more than 60,000 men on the first day. On shore, they discovered little resistance.

The Tokyo high command, having lost their entire fleet at Midway, would gamble, allowing the U.S. troops to land almost unopposed. The Japanese forces, nearly 80,000 strong, fell back to the south, forcing the Marines to come and get them. The goal was simple, if brutal: Their demise foretold, the Japanese would make a last gift to the emperor, bogging the Americans down on the island in order to win time for Tokyo to launch a new kind of kamikaze raid, a series of mass-scale suicide attacks that would be called *kikusui* (later known to naval historians as the Floating Chrysanthemum raids, after the flower adorning the imperial crest). In a last-ditch attempt to stave off the American armada, hundreds of suicide planes would take off from the island of Kyushu, 350 miles north of Okinawa, and from Formosa to the south, to attack in an orchestrated swoop.

Lieutenant Morgenthau and Captain Williams kept the batteries manned at half strength at all times, "so that only a short warning would be necessary to have all guns firing." Lookouts were on constant duty, and gunners never left their stations. In one early attack a Japanese bomber, detected at 6,000 yards coming in low, was shot down at "about 3500 yards." In the Hellcats and Corsairs overhead, the U.S. pilots soon learned, as one would later write, to stay out of range of the "hair-trigger gun crews."

Once the Marines had gone ashore, the *Bauer* took up its picket station. The Japanese air raids had commenced in earnest. "Three times, three or more planes," Williams would write, attacked the ship "in a concerted raid." And it was only the beginning: For more than two months, the *Bauer* would face "almost continuous attack."

April 6 brought the first swarm in a series of ten rounds of *kikusui* raids—totaling an estimated 1,900 sorties, in all—directed against U.S. ships off Okinawa. (In the initial attack alone, the Navy would record sightings of 355 Japanese planes in forty-eight hours.) "We were just south of Ie Shima," Morgenthau recalled—the tiny island where Ernie Pyle, the famed war correspondent, would be killed—"when we got the undivided attention of a couple hundred planes."

The *Bauer* was patrolling picket station No. 15, one of the stations closest to Kyushu, the southernmost of Japan's four main islands. At a quarter to four in the morning, the skies were still dark, but the crew could see a plane dive in low over the ship—and keep going, passing over the bow. "We couldn't understand why it didn't crash into us," Morgenthau would say. "Because we were firing, there was a tremendous racket." Every gun was going: 6 five-inch guns, 14 40 mms, and 12 20 mms. "There was always so much noise and vibration, we could've been hit and we wouldn't have heard it."

The *Bauer* had, in fact, sustained a hit. Hours later, at the seven o'clock report, the first lieutenant, Frank Morrow, came up to the bridge and told Morgenthau, "We've got water up in the forward peak tank."

"Put the pumps on," Morgenthau said. "Pump it out."

Morrow returned minutes later.

"Something's wrong with the pumps," he said. "We can't get the water level down." Several more minutes would pass before he came back to the bridge. Morgenthau could see that his face was white.

"There's a hole on either side of the bow," Morrow reported.

From the bridge, the officers could not see the waterline, but a torpedo had passed through the ship—without detonating. Lieutenant Morgenthau, on the TBS headset (used for ship-to-ship communications), tried to raise the squadron commander, Captain Moosbrugger, who oversaw command of the picket stations—but another voice broke in: "This is Anzac"—the code name for Vice Admiral Turner, commander of the Amphibious Force in the Pacific.

"Don't wait," Turner instructed. "Proceed to base. Repeat: Do not wait to be relieved, proceed at best possible speed to base."

"We didn't think we could do more than about 10 knots without collapsing the bulkhead," Morgenthau would recall. So he turned the ship around, and slipped safely into the repair base at Keramo Retto. The ship was there overnight, and the repair crews worked around the clock. Only after they'd pumped the water from the bow did they discover the cause of the damage: Stuck inside the ship, just forward of the paint locker, was an impeller, the torpedo's propeller. The *Bauer* had been remarkably fortunate: The torpedo had either detonated on the other side or it was a dud. "We were pretty happy," Morgenthau would say, "that it didn't explode in the ship."

By the next evening, once the repair crews had welded steel patches over the holes in the bow, the *Bauer* was back on a new station.

||||

On Wednesday, March 1, exhausted from his 14,000-mile journey to Yalta and back, President Roosevelt addressed a joint session of Congress. Four months after his valiant performance at Ebbets Field, FDR had to sit behind a row of microphones at a small mahogany desk in the well of the House floor.

"I hope that you will pardon me for this unusual posture of sitting down," Roosevelt began, "but I know that you will realize that it makes it a lot easier for me not to have to carry about ten pounds of steel around on the bottom of my legs."

Nervous laughter followed. It may have been the first, and only, time that the president spoke of his disability in public.

While FDR said he had come home "refreshed and inspired," to Henry Morgenthau, Jr., sitting six feet away, the president looked "very tired" and "had lost a great deal of weight." Even those who did not know FDR well noted the change. After Yalta, according to Herbert Feis, the State Department economist, Roosevelt's "eyes, gray with fatigue, looked out vaguely from the shrunken flesh of his face." Harry Truman, the new vice president, listened to the speech from the House rostrum. In the four months between the convention and the election, FDR and his running mate had met only two or three times. Years later, Truman confided that as he watched Roosevelt on that afternoon he came to the conclusion "the President wouldn't last."

FDR mustered the strength to speak for nearly an hour, setting forth his vision of the "unconditional surrender" that at last seemed within reach. Germany would be divided into zones of occupation, and the surrender would mean "the end of Nazism"—"and of all its barbaric laws and institutions." To avoid the mistakes of the last war the Allies would claim reparations in kind, not money. There would be, too, no flooding of the Ruhr—"We do not want the German people to starve"—but Germany could not "retain any ability to wage aggressive warfare." The German people, he said, only stood to gain: "It will be removing a cancer from the German body politic which for generations has produced only misery and only pain to the whole world."

Roosevelt had worked through several drafts, but his critics would see the speech as evidence of a man losing pace. They noted the long, rambling digression on the destruction of Yalta, as FDR described the czar's palaces and villas ruined, and the "great navy yards" of nearby Sevastopol. "I think he must've ad-libbed fully one third of his talk," Henry noted afterwards. Yet the tales from Crimea offered a vivid firsthand report from the war and led FDR to a condemnation of the "reckless, senseless fury of German militarism"—and the speech's greatest applause. "I'd read about Warsaw and Lidice and Rotterdam and Coventry," he said, his voice rising, "but I *saw* Sevastopol and Yalta! And I know that there is not room enough on earth for both German militarism and Christian decency!"

| | | |

The president may have adopted Stimson's language, but by his own indecision, inattention, and propensity to play one cabinet member against another, he had set in motion yet another battle in the administration's unending civil war.

In the months since the demise of the Morgenthau Plan, the War Department had been at work on its own directive, a set of instructions for General Eisenhower to shape the military governance of Germany. Stimson, demoralized and by his own admission worn out, had handed the job to John McCloy, a bureaucratic battering ram whom Morgenthau called "a bundle of energy and drive." Stimson's deputy saw a way forward: In autumn, soon after FDR and Churchill had departed Quebec, the Joint Chiefs of Staff had rushed out an "interim directive"—clearing it in one day. The document would become known after its file number, "JCS 1067." Morgenthau embraced the plan as "a clear statement along the lines favored by the Treasury." "You will take no steps looking toward the economic rehabilitation of Germany," the document instructed, "nor designed to maintain or strengthen the German economy"—other than for the purpose of facilitating the occupation. In JCS 1067, Morgenthau allowed himself to believe, the aims of the Morgenthau Plan would live on.

At the State Department, the old guard faced a new hurdle: Cordell Hull, slowed and ailing, was receding into the background. After Quebec, Hull had all but begged Roosevelt to allow him to resign, but FDR asked that he stay on until after the election. "I can't tell you how poor Mr. Hull grieved over" the Morgenthau Plan, an aide would recall. Hull had gone to the White House to win the president over, only to enter the hospital within days. By November, Roosevelt caved to the realities: Hull was through. "The Morgenthau business," Hull's wife told Arthur Krock, "was the final blow."

FDR had named Edward Stettinius, the former president of U.S. Steel, as his new secretary of state. Stettinius may have looked the part—square jaw, white hair, bespoke suits—but few in the cabinet considered it a wise choice. Stimson lamented that Stettinius, who'd been acting secretary of state for several months, seemed "pretty ignorant of international history." Henry, though, liked Stettinius. He told Eleanor Roosevelt that he considered him "the best I could think of from the President's standpoint," as FDR "liked to be his own Secretary of State, and what he wanted was merely a good clerk." At State, where many officials considered him a glad-hander out of his depth, Stettinius inherited a staff unwilling to accept the War Department's JCS 1067. They had their own plan—a "Draft Directive for the Treatment of Germany"—and Roosevelt had even put his signature on it. Unlike JCS 1067, the State plan did not call for Germany's dismemberment, advocating instead a centralized occupation government that could take charge of the German economy.

To Henry, State's blueprint was anathema—"at cross-purposes with everything I have stood for," he told aides. It was also, Henry was convinced, against all that the president envisioned. But a new source of opposition was mounting. Anna Roosevelt and her husband, John Boettiger, had strengthened their influence with FDR, and as the Allies gained ground in Germany, both feared Morgenthau would attempt a second Quebec. Boettiger, at forty-two, was a former newspaperman who'd faced a hurdle in the first family. He had served in the First World War and been too old to be drafted after Pearl Harbor, but all the Roosevelt sons were in the service—and he had felt the glare of the boss. In early 1943, he'd told FDR how he wished he could join him at Casablanca, when the president had said, "But John, you're not in uniform!" So Boettiger enlisted in the Army, leaving Anna and their four-month-old son. He had taken part in the landings in Sicily and Salerno, and after serving as a functionary at the Tehran talks, he won a desk job under McCloy.

Newly promoted to lieutenant colonel, Boettiger had visited Aachen that winter, the first Allied-occupied city. He saw the grim conditions among its 14,000 residents (down from a prewar population of 160,000), heard the American officers debate a "hard" versus "soft" peace and detail the failings of the improvised occupation—the Allies were handing out rations of bread, meat, and potatoes that were "higher than under Hitler." To Boettiger's untrained eye, the need for "guidance" was obvious: The officer in charge of Aachen, a Florida policeman, had no "training in MG or CA"—military government or civilian affairs—and was "hopelessly incompetent to cope with situation."

At the White House, the tour had lent Boettiger an air of authority; he was glad, he confided in his diary, to have "some mud on my boots." But the intervention of the president's son-in-law, his lack of official standing, and his eagerness to undermine the blueprint of even his own War Department infuriated Henry.

At one o'clock on March 20, the Treasury secretary was scheduled to lunch with the president. Three hours before arriving, he learned that Anna and her husband would join them, "to keep me from making my case." Henry had first met Boettiger during his time atop Farm Credit. He'd been a police reporter in Chicago, the secretary told aides, a "star" at interviewing, who'd "gone after" him—and "they don't change." Fearing a leak, Henry asked that the White House lunch be off the record.

As Henry predicted, the pleasantries almost at once gave way to an argument: The Germans, the president's son-in-law told Henry, mustn't be left to "stew in their own juices." Germany, Boettiger had insisted to Henry since his return from Germany, couldn't be left to fend for itself; the Allies would have to run the economy—"supervise lower-down wages, prices, and distribution"—or "complete chaos" would ensue.

Boettiger went further, even criticizing the Pentagon plan, JCS 1067, as too vague for the Army men "down the line." "It wasn't workable," he insisted; there had to be clear instructions. The Allies would have to ensure the population got enough food.

Henry fumed at the audacity: A low-level official with no expertise dared to come between him and the president. As Boettiger railed on— "we must regulate prices, we must tell them how much they eat, we must tell them how much coal they mine"—Henry volleyed in return and Anna came to her husband's defense. Henry felt sorry for the president, caught in the middle, but took heart as FDR interjected.

"Let them have soup kitchens!" Roosevelt said. "Let their economy sink."

"You don't want them to starve," his son-in-law countered.

"Why not?" FDR shot back.

After lunch, Boettiger led Henry to a sofa. "I want to say something to you nobody else can hear." He pleaded with him to change his mind on "letting the Germans stew." He raised the specter of Quebec and the political backlash. "You are going to start the whole thing all over again," Boettiger said. "And look at the mess you are going to get the President into."

"I won't change my principles," Henry said. "If I'm annoying the President, I can get out of town."

||||

Once again, Henry was in danger with the Roosevelts. "It's getting lonesomer and lonesomer," he'd worried aloud to his aides, after an earlier bout with Boettiger. FDR's grasp of the details was fading, and Boettiger had proximity on his side. "When you go up against a fellow like that," he said, "you can't forget that he eats one or two meals a day with the President." Henry, though, may have won the upper hand without knowing it. That Boettiger was even arguing with the secretary in front of the president meant that he had tried with FDR—and got nowhere. At lunch, as Henry railed against the State Department March 10 plan, Roosevelt said he had no recollection of having seen it. Henry's fears could be true, he now realized: The president had not understood what he had signed. "They had whipped something across his desk," Henry would tell Grace Tully, "which was just what he didn't want." At the White House, FDR had offered a compromise: If Henry and Stimson could strike an agreement with Stettinius, he would withdraw his approval of the State plan.

Three days later, on Friday afternoon, March 23, Henry forced the issue with the president. The War Department had delivered a revised plan (again largely the work of McCloy) that closely resembled JCS 1067. The new draft carried much of the spirit of the original Morgenthau Plan: "All economic and financial international transactions, including exports and imports, shall be controlled with the aim of preventing Germany from developing a war potential. . . . Recurrent reparations should not . . . require the rehabilitation or development of German heavy industry." It was a welcome turn, but Henry knew timing was of the essence. The president would have to give his assent, in writing, before Anna or Boettiger intervened.

FDR seemed ready to end the battle among State, Treasury, and War. He was prepared to sign, he told Henry, but Henry wanted to ensure there would be no questioning Roosevelt's intentions: He asked FDR to add a clarification in his own hand, allowing no uncertainty that the new plan "should supersede" the State directive of March 10. FDR may have been distracted, or worse, his stamina failing. He asked Henry how to spell "supersede"—and as Henry admitted he did not know, he worried that while Roosevelt "was thinking about it, he might not write it in." Henry, though, was not above taking advantage of an opening. He made certain that the president did as asked, scrawling, beneath the final line of the four-page plan: "O.K. F.D.R., *super seding memo of Mar 10, 45.*"

Who were the drinks on? Roosevelt asked when he had finished.

"Me!" Henry said.

| | | |

The day would end as earlier triumphs had, back at the Treasury, under darkening skies. Henry summoned his aides that Friday evening before they could leave for the weekend, to offer an update that was part locker-room speech, part talk therapy. Rarely had the secretary ever been so personal. The president and he had had "one of the most important conferences that I have ever participated in," Henry said. "I have never been under such pressure in my life to give way on principles, and I didn't." And now, victory was in sight. It had to stay "very much in the room here," but the secretary announced "the first step toward a kind of peace which I think will last."

Six months after Quebec, many around FDR could not see beyond the failed "Morgenthau Plan." In their eyes, and for millions of Americans and Europeans as well, Henry would forever carry the taint of the Quebec proposals. Yet even Stimson, who bemoaned the "fantastic 'pastoral Germany' program," could abide by the new directive, judging it a "fairly good paper."

As Henry spoke with his aides that evening, he saw the continuity: Whether it was preparing for the war, fighting for the refugees, or refusing to accept a "soft" peace, his team had held together. "We stand for something worthwhile," he said, while "the State Department crowd" had tried to get the president "to change, and they couldn't." Sooner or later, he went on, "the President just has to clean his house. I mean, the vicious crowd over there, and people for cartels, for appeasement, and for building up Europe . . . they are Fascists at heart."

The next afternoon, Grace Tully asked Henry, "You think it has worked out satisfactorily all the way around?"

"Entirely," he said. "It's more than a relief. After all, what we are arguing about . . . is the future of the world."

39. "Henry, I Am with You 100 Percent"

APRIL 1945

Three was much to admire about the hotel suite in Daytona Beach, but the most alluring feature was the veranda, its view opening onto the white-sand shore, empty of people in the early morning when Henry took his coffee.

On March 24, the day after lunching with the president, Henry and Ellie had boarded an overnight train to Miami. Henry was worn out from the battles over Germany and the fight for congressional approval of the Bretton Woods agreements. For weeks, after moving house yet again, first to a hotel, then to a large apartment on Connecticut Avenue, he and Ellie had been trying to get to Florida. They had taken two rooms, and the vacation opened well. Henry would rise at half past seven and go for a swim. "Then I come back," he told his boys, "and have breakfast, usually with Mother, and then I take a little nap. Then I go in for another swim again, then we have lunch, and then I have another nap." Afternoons, they would go for "a little walk, and then we come home and . . . we have a little drinky." The routine took hold: In a week, Henry had telephoned the office only twice.

Gertrude Leiner, a local woman in her thirties who worked in her husband's drugstore downtown, had tried to warn Morgenthau about the hotel. She had read a news item on his visit and left a letter at the front desk: "You are probably not aware," Leiner wrote, of the Sheraton Plaza's policy: no Jews allowed. "We Jews in Daytona resent this discrimination bitterly as being pro-fascist." The community was pushing a boycott, and she urged him, "as an outstanding citizen of the United States," to "take a stand." Henry did not. He did, though, attend his first

Passover seder—a large affair held at the town hall to honor local Jewish men in uniform. Henry, like his father before him on his travels abroad, rarely took joy in the embrace of the Jewish community. In Florida, they had seized on him: "They saw him as FDR's favorite Jew," his daughter, Joan, would recall, "the man who'd led the charge in Washington to save the Jews." If once Henry had recoiled at the attention, now he accepted a minor role.

The seder would be the trip's highlight. Within days, Ellie, at fifty-three, was hit again by illness. For years, the Morgenthaus had kept her condition quiet; only close family and the Roosevelts knew. It was a blood concern—"insufficient circulation," the doctors said—and though the root cause remained elusive, the weakening was clear. "My mother had this blood trouble that ran in the Lehman family," Henry III would say. "Several relatives would face similar symptoms." Throughout the war years, Ellie's condition only worsened. In the spring of 1943, she underwent another operation—this time, a hysterectomy. Her husband kept mute on the subject, only joking with Roosevelt: "They say she will be a new woman, and . . . I will have to perk up a bit." Yet her son Henry III would recall years later that the surgery was "unnecessary"—the doctors had failed to find a proper diagnosis. It also proved of no help: Ellie endured a series of complications, and the pain and fatigue continued. For Henry, Ellie's condition became an uncomfortable subject. "We do hope Ellie is much better," Governor Lehman wrote in July 1943, and then again in September, he gently asked, "How's Ellie?" Each time, her husband's reply remained the same: Fine, fine.

For months, the secretary had worried the press would find out. As the blood clots worsened, and her strength drained, Elinor Morgenthau sought treatment in secret. At times, her health seemed to improve, only soon to darken. The tests continued, the diagnoses shifted, but Ellie found no relief. "Because of all these clots," daughter Joan, then finishing her final term at Vassar but headed for medical school, would say, "Mother was in a lot of pain and discomfort."

In the fall of 1944, Ellie returned to the hospital in Washington. On Thanksgiving Day, she was operated on a third time. The surgeon tried to lessen the inflammation in her legs and arms. Bob had come down—he was still awaiting the launch of his new ship—to be at her bedside, but again, the recovery was slow. For months, as Henry waged battle over the plans for Germany, Ellie struggled to hide the pain. After the inauguration, Henry was determined that she take a break. Some sun and time away from Washington would do her good, the doctors said. Ellie had arrived in Daytona exhausted and suffering from laryngitis. In Florida, her condition only worsened.

The heart attack came on April 3.

Henry frantically called for an ambulance, and Ellie was taken to the hospital. The attack had come without warning, as a clot moved to the heart, causing an obstruction. "Mother had a very mild heart attack and she's getting along fine," Henry wrote Bob and Henry. The doctors expected a fine recovery, he insisted; she would even be able to ride a horse again. His sons, though, could read the worry between the lines. "Mother in fact was confined to an oxygen tent," Henry III would say, "and she was gravely ill."

Bob Patterson, the secretary's closest associate at the War Department, set up a teletype line between the hospital and the Treasury for urgent communications. Yet as the doctors spoke in grave tones, Henry fell into a kind of shock—and the migraines returned.

Ellie's illness shook Mrs. Roosevelt as well. With the president in Warm Springs for Easter, she had gone to Hyde Park to help get "the Big House" in spring shape. When FDR called on Saturday evening, he found Eleanor half asleep, worn out from unpacking china. The next morning, she realized that she had neglected to share the news of the day: "I forgot to tell you," she wrote her husband, "that Elinor Morgenthau had a serious heart attack at Daytona and Henry has been terribly worried." "The war strain," Eleanor feared, was taking its toll.

FDR at once told Daisy Suckley, his devoted distant cousin who'd become a near-constant companion, of the attack—and telegraphed Henry how sorry he was, asking that Henry keep him informed. When it came to calming fears, the Roosevelts were masters. Eleanor wrote her friend in the hospital: "You must just rest and get well," she told Ellie, "and then perhaps we can all have a quiet summer in the country! I'll promise to hoard my gas and come and stay."

As word spread, Henry was inundated: Governor Lehman called, Stettinius called, and Edith Lehman, the governor's wife, flew to Daytona, as much to steady Henry as to cheer his wife. The Lehmans had lost their son Peter, a pilot, to the war—killed in a crash the year before. Peter Lehman's death had hit his cousins, Henry III and Bob, hard, but only now did the secretary recognize its toll on the young man's mother. "We never think in terms of the women," Henry chided his aides over the phone on April 10. A new war bond drive was coming up, he reminded them, and Mrs. George Patton had been so good at pitching the bonds: Why not add more mothers who like Mrs. Lehman had lost their sons to the campaign? The Treasury boys should have seen her fury, he added, when she discovered German POWs working in the Army hospital in Daytona—"she'd make even Joe DuBois pale." The governor's wife, he explained, had seen "some German prisoners . . . fat as hogs, working around the hospital, and the guard with his back turned smoking a cigarette." The Treasury would do well, Henry said, to harness the mothers' power to sell a "hard peace" to a skeptical America.

With victory over Germany on the horizon, Henry refused to be away from Washington long. Publishing his "book"—a thinly veiled elaboration on the original Morgenthau Plan—had become a chief preoccupation, and he assured his staff that if Elinor improved "for another 24 hours," he'd fly up at once. Whether it was the pressure of his wife's illness or his first encounter with the German prisoners of war—Florida would host as many as 200,000—Henry now insisted that the book come out as soon as possible. He wanted to set the record straight and, though he dared not say it, to clear his name.

On March 23, before leaving for Daytona, Henry had sought the president's blessing on the eve of his departure for Warm Springs. He had arrived at the White House early that Friday morning, taking the elevator up to the family quarters. As FDR had not yet finished his breakfast, Eleanor decided it unwise to send Henry in. Instead, she offered to pose the question for him. Franklin was not opposed, Eleanor said when she returned, but he had asked, "Why a book now?" And when she assured the president that Henry would wait until the war was over, FDR had acquiesced: "That's all right. Let him go ahead and make the study."

Henry had seized the opening. "Since you are going away for a time," he wrote Roosevelt that same day, "and events are moving fast, I should like your permission before you go to get some facts on the German economy ready for publication in book form. When Germany falls . . . the people of this country are going to need information on this at once."

By March 28, FDR had given it more thought. "The plan you outlined," he wrote Henry, "is laudable in purpose, but I find it difficult to know just what to say. The people of the country are going to need information on the German economy. The spirit of the Nation must be given articulate expression. But it's not so easy to say when the Nation will or can speak. Timing will be of the very essence. We must all remember Job's lament that his enemy had not written a book. . . . Anyway, we'll have to keep thinking about it."

It was not an answer that Henry could accept.

By April 11, Elinor Morgenthau appeared to be gaining strength, her appetite returning. Ellie was not out of danger, the Army doctors cautioned, but Henry could get back to the Treasury. Before leaving, though, he placed a call to the president. He was headed to Washington, Henry told FDR, but asked if he might make a stop en route, in Warm Springs.

||||

President Roosevelt was losing weight—as much as twenty pounds—at an alarming rate, and his face took on an ashen pall. The heightened concern had begun in Quebec. Churchill, on the final night in Canada, had asked Admiral Ross T. McIntire, the president's doctor, to his rooms for a confidential update on FDR's health. The admiral relayed the results of the summer checkup: There was nothing "organically wrong," but Roosevelt was certainly showing his age, sixty-two, and the "constant strain" of the past twelve years. McIntire made no mention of high blood pressure, let alone an enlarged heart, nor the fact that for months Dr. Howard Bruenn, a cardiologist at the Navy hospital outside Washington, had been a fixture in the presidential entourage. In March 1944, Anna Roosevelt had insisted that McIntire—an eye, ear, nose, and throat specialist—bring in a heart doctor, and by August, as FDR returned from the long trip to the Pacific, Anna's worries had been borne out.

Roosevelt had stopped in Seattle, giving a speech at the Bremerton Navy Yard. For the first time in months, he strapped on the heavy braces to stand on the forecastle of a destroyer, just ahead of a five-inch-gun mount, to tell the yard workers, and the country listening on radio, of his talks with Nimitz and MacArthur. As the metal dug into his legs, his daughter watched anxiously at the rail, and to many it was clear something was wrong. After the half-hour speech, FDR came belowdecks. "I had a helluva pain!" he told Dr. Bruenn. They stripped him down, performed a cardiogram, and drew blood. Dr. Bruenn would call the chest pains a "transient episode," but one, he would add, offering "proof positive" that FDR was suffering "coronary disease, no question."

The president had arrived in Warm Springs on March 30, Good Friday. As his entourage settled in at the Little White House, several of his aides and staff felt an uneasy tension. The Secret Service man, Reilly, had noted a change: At the station, as FDR was lifted into the car, he had been unable to help the men carrying him—Roosevelt was "absolutely dead weight," Reilly said. That evening, Bill Hassett, FDR's secretary, told Dr. Bruenn, "He's slipping away and no earthly power can keep him here." FDR had wanted a small traveling party: his cousins and confidants, Laura Delano (known as "Polly") and Daisy Suckley, Hassett and Grace Tully, Dr. Bruenn, and a second Navy doctor. There was, as well, the usual team of Secret Service men, and attendants—Arthur Prettyman, a former Navy mess attendant who had been the president's valet since 1939, and "Joe" Esperancilla, the steward who'd served meals at the White House since the Hoover years. Roosevelt, too, always took particular delight in the women at the center of the cottage's working life—Daisy Bonner, the cook who spoiled him with Southern specialties, and Lizzie McDuffie, the Atlanta native who'd worked as a maid at the White House since 1933—and whom FDR had known since he discovered the therapeutic waters of Georgia.

The president wanted quiet. He also wanted privacy. FDR was looking forward to a visit from his friend, confidante, and—since 1913, when Eleanor hired her as a social secretary—object of his deep affection, Lucy Mercer Rutherfurd. Mrs. Rutherfurd was newly widowed; her husband, twenty-nine years her elder and long incapacitated by a series of strokes, had died nearly a year earlier. On April 9, Roosevelt insisted that the Secret Service drive him to the town of Macon, eighty miles away, to meet Lucy and her friend "Shoumie," Madame Elizabeth Shoumatoff, a White Russian émigrée artist, whom Lucy had commissioned to paint his portrait—a gift for her daughter.

Lucy would be the star attraction of the week, but Daisy and Polly were as close to the president as anyone alive. Polly Delano, the unmarried daughter of FDR's uncle, Warren Delano, was known across the Hudson Valley for her outlandish style. She wore red nail polish, weighed down her wrists and each finger with jewelry, dyed her gray hair purple, and thrived, it seemed to many, on flouting convention among the river families. Polly lived alone in Rhinebeck, and bred Irish setters. Daisy Suckley, FDR's far more distant cousin, was in so many ways opposite to Polly—but both women were united in their worship of the president.

On the following day, after FDR spun stories for the four ladies at lunch, he emerged from a nap to announce that he wished to take Mrs. Rutherfurd for a drive. In the Ford convertible coupe, sitting in back, a blanket over his legs, FDR drove out to a favorite lookout with Lucy.

The car went slowly over the Georgia roads so as not to toss Roosevelt around, to Dowdell's Knob on Pine Mountain, a spot Roosevelt had shown Lucy the previous fall. They enjoyed a wonderful afternoon out, Lucy would tell the ladies at the cottage. They had sat on a log "in the sun, talking, for over an hour," Daisy Suckley wrote in her diary, "& he came back with a good tan."

For a week, they savored days of cloudless skies and warm weather. FDR played foolish games, spun jokes and old yarns, intent on putting all at ease. He was well aware of his ill health; Dr. Bruenn had made clear the gravity of his condition and set strict dietary rules. "He should gain weight but hates his food," Eleanor wrote a friend after speaking with FDR that week in Warm Springs. "I say a prayer daily that he may be able to carry on till we have peace & our feet are set in the right direction."

The doctor had instructed that the president eat supplements of oatmeal to spur the appetite. The cousins, Polly and Daisy, teased FDR about his "gruel," but he took delight as each night Daisy ladled the oatmeal and cream mixture into his mouth. The president lay in bed, enjoying the "little act of helplessness!" Daisy wrote in her diary. Covers up, he "relapsed into babyhood . . . it amuses him to be fed, and I love to feed him," she confessed. "On paper it sounds too silly for words and it *is* silly—but he's very funny and laughs at himself with us."

Despite his weakness, FDR shared confidences, too. He spoke of the United Nations conference in San Francisco, set to open in two weeks—as Daisy put it, his "part in World Peace, etc." Whether a daydream or plan, the country would never know, but months earlier, returning from the Pacific, FDR had confided to his Treasury secretary the same idea for their future:

"Now look, Henry," the president had said, "you and I will gradually ease out of present jobs and become country gentlemen, and you and I will take an interest in this new world organization."

"What do you mean, Mr. President?"

"Well, there is going to be an organization of United Nations with which I expect to be associated, and you should go with me."

In Warm Springs, FDR went further. On Friday, April 6, he told Daisy he could "probably resign sometime next year, when the peace organization—the United Nations—is well-started."

By Wednesday morning, April 11, Roosevelt's blood pressure had risen slightly, but he "seems pretty well," Daisy noted. Dr. Bruenn had seen him, leaving with the admonition "Keep lazy, Sir!" Daisy made certain to remind Lucy that the president must not strain himself, but he soon had the card table set up, opened over his legs, eager to get to work. There were cables to draft to Stalin and Churchill, an itinerary to set for the train trip to San Francisco, and a speech to give Friday evening, by radio hookup, to the Democratic Party's annual Jefferson Day dinners around the country.

Among the ladies, the staff, and the doctors, there was also "some excitement," Mme. Shoumatoff would note, about the arrival that evening of the dinner guest, the secretary of the Treasury.

IIII

At seven o'clock that evening, Henry entered the Little White House and found the president sitting in a chair with his feet up on a large footstool, the card table drawn up over his legs. The paperwork done, Roosevelt was busy mixing cocktails.

FDR was in good spirits, but Henry was taken aback at his physical state. "I was terribly shocked," he noted in his diary that night. Henry had seen Roosevelt less than three weeks earlier, but he had "aged terrifically and looked very haggard." His face was drawn and hollowed, his body frail. "His hands shook so that he started to knock the glasses over," Henry would note, "and I had to hold each glass as he poured out the cocktail."

Yet as always, FDR made a show of Henry's arrival. He called for a giant tin of caviar, a gift from Stalin he had been saving since Yalta, and Henry offered to serve some to Roosevelt. Daisy, the cook, had laid out sliced onions and eggs on a plate, but Henry knew better.

"If I remember correctly Mr. President, you like it plain," he said.

"That's right," FDR said.

As Henry spooned out the caviar, he watched the president anxiously. "I noticed," Henry would write, "that he took two cocktails and then seemed to feel a little better." But Roosevelt's memory seemed to fail him—"he was constantly confusing names." They could all feel it: "an encompassing tension," as Mme. Shoumatoff would say. She had been the first to interrupt the two men enjoying their cocktails, and "I was a little embarrassed to find only Roosevelt and Morgenthau in the room, apparently in deep conference." The artist apologized and left, "wondering what it was all about." When she reappeared a short time later with

Lucy, the cousins, Daisy and Polly, had joined the men, and FDR was "again acting as bartender behind the card table."

The frostiness between the secretary and the women, though, remained. "Morgenthau glanced at me without enthusiasm," Mme. Shoumatoff would recall. "I felt very strongly that he was preoccupied with something quite disturbing. He later made a telephone call, the reason, the president said, was his wife's illness."

As they moved to the dining room, there was more of a commotion than usual. Henry winced as the valet and butler shifted the president to a chair: "I have never seen him have so much difficulty transferring himself from his wheelchair to a regular chair," the secretary wrote his sons, "and I was in agony watching him."

At dinner, FDR tried to keep the talk lighthearted. They joked about the early Val-Kill furniture that filled the rooms, a vestige of Mrs. Roosevelt's attempts at an artisanal cottage industry, but the conversation "picked up momentum," Mme. Shoumatoff would remember, when "Roosevelt and Morgenthau began recalling different amusing and entertaining incidents about Churchill." Throughout it all, the president seemed preoccupied with Lucy, paying little attention to the other end of the table. Henry assumed it was because FDR could not hear the talk, but even when Polly's large Irish setter interrupted the meal, vomiting beside the table, "it didn't seem to upset the President at all." There was more talk of the San Francisco conference, and of the chocolate waffles—Daisy and Lizzie had made the dessert in the new waffle irons, a birthday gift from the Morgenthaus—and of FDR's lament that the California trip had become something of a nuisance, delaying his return to Hyde Park "until May 1st."

After supper, as the ladies retired upstairs, and FDR and Henry were left alone again, the secretary at once brought up his book project. Henry spoke of the letter he'd sent the president asking his blessing before they left Washington. He showed FDR a photostat of the president's reply to him, pointing to the final, abstruse command: "We must all remember Job's lament that his enemy had not written a book."

"Where did you get that from?" FDR asked. "I have never seen it before."

"Well, the reason I am bringing it to your attention is because I want to know what it means."

"I don't know what it means," Roosevelt said. "Hassett or somebody told me you wanted to get a book out right away, and I thought it was a mistake."

Henry was not about to stop. "What I want to do," he said, "is to get out a textbook after V-E Day." *Harper's,* he said, were prepared to gamble $5,000 on it. "For example, I would like to write a chapter on how 60 million Germans can feed themselves."

"I said they could," Roosevelt insisted.

"Well, I have written a chapter on that," Henry said.

He would show the book to the president, of course, Henry said, even hoped that FDR might write the preface—or, should he prefer, get Stettinius to do it. But he wanted his permission, to get the book out to the American people.

"I think that is fine," Roosevelt said. "You go ahead and do it. I think it is a grand idea."

"I have a lot of ideas of my own," FDR added, musing on the memories he'd like to add. The president went back to the early days, as only Henry could allow him to do, recalling how Dr. Schacht, Hitler's banker, had come to the White House, "weeping on his desk about his poor country." It was a tale Henry had heard often, but he indulged FDR: The two shared a laugh. The president, Henry would write, "seems to enjoy telling it."

Above all, Henry would leave grateful to have received a blessing.

"I asked the President if he wanted me to interest myself in the future treatment of Germany," he dictated to his diary that night. "He didn't answer me directly. I said, 'Look Mr. President, I am going to fight hard, and this is what I am fighting for. . . . A weak economy for Germany means that she will be weak politically, and she won't be able to make another war.' "

"Henry, I am with you 100 percent," he quoted FDR as replying.

"You may hear things, because I am going to fight for this," he told Roosevelt. The president kept silent, but Henry had put him on notice, repeating the vow several times.

When they were nearly done, Polly entered the living room. "Are you gentlemen through talking?" she asked. "Will another five minutes be enough?"

Ample, Henry said.

Soon, as the ladies returned, Henry went upstairs. He took the phone—with its extra-long cord that allowed the president to take calls in any room—into Polly's bedroom to call Edith Lehman, eager for an update on Ellie. When he returned downstairs, Henry went in to say goodbye to the president. It was nearly 10:30 P.M. Henry had sent his plane ahead, to Atlanta, and faced a long drive from Warm Springs. It would be midnight by the time he reached the airport, yet as Henry lingered at the door, looking into the room, the foursome, FDR surrounded by Lucy, Polly, and Daisy, were sitting before the fire, laughing and chatting.

"And I must say," he would recall, "the President seemed to be happy and enjoying himself."

It would be their last meal, their last conversation, and, as Henry would look back and recognize, the beginning of the end of his public career.

On the morning of April 12, FDR awoke with "a slight headache and a stiff neck," as Daisy recorded. Dr. Bruenn massaged his neck and ordered a hot-water bottle, and the president was given a roundup of the latest military developments: The Ninth Army had advanced to within sixty-five miles of Berlin. Dr. Bruenn phoned Admiral McIntire with good news: FDR had "gained back 8 of his lost pounds," and was looking forward to attending "an old-fashioned Georgia barbeque" that afternoon at the home of the local mayor.

It was nearly one o'clock when the president emerged from his bedroom, dressed in a double-breasted gray suit and a crimson tie, to sit for Mme. Shoumatoff. "His colour was good," Daisy would note, "& he looked smiling & happy & ready for anything." His valet and attendant lifted him into his favorite chair. Roosevelt had asked several times for the morning mail—the plane from Washington had been delayed. He got to the newspapers as Mme. Shoumatoff began to sketch. His suit hanging limp, his frame now shrunken, she decided to paint him in the grand Navy cape. Even now, FDR could not sit idle. As she painted, he made his way through the papers that Hassett had set before him, signing documents and letters, as the secretary laid them out around the room for the ink to dry. "The laundry," FDR liked to call the daily routine.

"Here's where I make a law," he said, signing a bill for a credit corporation. While Esperancilla began to set the table for lunch, FDR glanced at his watch. "We have 15 minutes more to work," he told Shoumie. She heard the words clearly, but watched in horror as the president "suddenly raised his right hand and passed it over his forehead in a strange jerky way." Daisy would hear more words: "I have a terrific pain in the back of my head," FDR said, before slumping over in his chair. The valet and butler carried him to the bedroom nearby. Within minutes Roosevelt had lost consciousness.

Dr. Bruenn was summoned from the pool, and Admiral McIntire in Washington urgently dispatched a specialist from Atlanta, but there was nothing to do. Dr. Bruenn diagnosed a hemorrhage in the brain, and to the reporters who raced along the country roads, he would liken the stroke to "a bolt of lightning, or getting hit by a train." Daisy Suckley would wait until midnight, as the lights still burned in Warm Springs, to mark the precise time: "3:35 P.M.," she wrote, "Franklin D. Roosevelt, the hope of the world, is dead."

Henry had arrived back in Washington at 3:45 A.M. on the 12th after traveling all night from Georgia.

He learned the news first from Mrs. Roosevelt; she called him at a quarter to six that evening, asking him to come at once to the White House. Eleanor wanted to tell Henry herself; she'd already called the hospital in Daytona, asking the nurse to remove Ellie's bedside radio. (With Eleanor by his side, Henry got Ellie on the phone, but he was so worried about her reaction he asked her doctor to deliver the news.) The memorandum he dictated of his final visit to the Little White House was dated April 11, but once back in the apartment on Connecticut Avenue he recorded another telling of the events in Warm Springs on the Ediphone machine.

Alone after being "in a sort of daze all day," he dictated a letter to his sons, telling Henry III in Germany and Bob in the Pacific, how it happened—how he had lost the man at whose side he had stood, and whom he had loved, for more than three decades. He would never say a word about Lucy having been at Roosevelt's side. He would hold the secret out of love for Mrs. Roosevelt, and respect for the president's privacy. But on that night, sitting alone in the darkness of the new and unfamiliar apartment, he began quietly to set down the record of the final meeting.

"Around 7:30 P.M. Eastern War Time," he began, "I called on the President. . . ."

40. Trouble with Harry

SPRING 1945

With FDR's death, Henry Morgenthau, Jr., "had lost his sponsor," as the historian John Morton Blum would write, "his chief, his closest friend." Roosevelt's death leveled Henry: The personal toll, he would realize only months later, was like a tidal wave. For days, Henry remained in shock. In Washington, though, he felt another sudden loss, an immediate and total vacuum of support for any of his urgent policy drives.

The first cabinet meeting with "the new man," as Henry would call Truman, came within an hour of the news from Warm Springs. FDR's death had brought them all low: Despite "his idiosyncrasies," Secretary of War Stimson wrote, "every one of us felt very keenly the loss of a personal friend." Truman spoke of the death, and his own grief, vowing there would be no change of direction.

"I want every one of you to stay and carry on," he said, "and I want to do everything just the way President Roosevelt wanted it."

"Mr. Truman," Henry said, "I will do all I can to help. But I want you to be free to call on anyone else in my place."

Within two days, Henry was back at the White House, for a first private conversation with President Truman. Right off, Truman had told Henry how he, too, was grieving: "I think I admired Mr. Roosevelt as much as you did."

"I don't think that's possible," Henry replied.

Once again, the Treasury secretary opened the door to his leaving: "I want you to feel that you are untied as far as I'm concerned," he said.

Truman would have none of it. "That's what everybody has been telling me," he said, but added, "I need the help."

"I feel this war very strongly," Henry said. "I have one son with General Patton and another in the Pacific, and his ship has just been torpedoed for the second time. . . . My first idea is to win the war and then I want to win the peace."

"That's what I want to do," Truman replied.

Whether Truman was improvising, stalling, or merely baiting the hook, Henry let the president into his thoughts, revealing the extent of the plans he and Roosevelt had been cooking up—much of it unknown to Truman. "I have been doing a lot of things which Mr. Roosevelt has encouraged me to do that aren't strictly Treasury business," Henry said. He drew back the curtain. "In my job," he went on, "I am very vulnerable because we moved the financial capital from London and Wall Street right to my desk at the Treasury."

"That's where I want to keep it," Truman said.

"Well, the big boys will be after me," Henry added, "and I can't do what I have been doing unless I have the complete backing of the President."

"You will have that from me."

Pleased by the words, Henry took a bold step. "I have some very definite ideas" about Germany, he said, "and I would like to explain them to you and explain the Morgenthau Plan."

"I would like to know about it," Truman said.

"There are no differences between Stettinius and me," Henry went on, "but the differences are down the line. They haven't carried out the President's orders." Too many of the State Department veterans were Hoover holdovers, he said, men not "in sympathy with the New Deal and Mr. Roosevelt."

"Well, I will get rid of them if they give us any trouble," Truman said, but added that he had already discussed Germany with the secretary of state—and hoped to head off a confrontation: "I don't want any fussing between you and Stettinius."

"There is no fussing between us," Henry replied, "but what I am worried about is the people under him."

As Truman walked Henry out, his parting words sounded stronger to Henry: "Now I want you to stay with me." In reply, Henry yet again tried to be humble: "I will stay just as long as I think I can serve you."

"When the time comes that you can't," Truman said, "you will hear from me first direct."

The new man, Henry concluded, "has a mind of his own." Truman had been "most courteous with me," he wrote that evening, "but, after all, he is a politician, and what is going on in his head time only will tell."

| | | |

On April 20, Eleanor Roosevelt left the White House for good. She filled twenty trunks and sent them off to Hyde Park. In New York City, she greeted a crowd of reporters quietly: "The story is over," she said.

Mrs. R. was on her own now, telling friends that she would keep to herself, taking time for the family and refraining from public speaking. In a letter to Ellie four days after FDR's death, she confided that "readjusting is not so hard physically but mentally. I realize I counted much on Franklin's greater wisdom & it leaves one without much sense of backing."

In those first days, though, Eleanor did not remain alone. On the afternoon of May 1, she returned to Washington as a private citizen for the first time since FDR's death—and on Henry's invitation set up camp in the secretary's rented apartment on Connecticut Avenue.

"I told her that our home was her home," Henry told his sons, but he did his best to give Mrs. Roosevelt and her secretary, Miss Thompson, wide berth. "We have breakfast together every morning, dinner together one night alone." Her host was more in awe than ever: "She certainly is an amazing woman."

Henry relished the company. In Florida, Ellie's recovery had hit one hurdle after another. The doctors had moved her back into an oxygen tent, hoping to ease the strain on her heart. They assured her husband that she would be able to travel soon, but Ellie had yet to even sit up in bed. Amid the gloom, Mrs. Roosevelt's presence was a welcome distraction. Janet and Helen, the Scottish sisters who remained cook and cleaner for Henry and Ellie, reported that "Mrs. Roosevelt putters around in the morning, takes it easy, and then in one case went to sleep after lunch sitting on the couch."

"I really believe," Henry wrote, "it is the first peace and quiet she has had in many, many years, and she agrees."

As Mrs. Roosevelt worked in the living room, drafting her "My Day" columns, Henry began to think of his own future. On May 4, he wrote his sons after the fall of Berlin and the Germans' surrender in northern Italy, "I don't see how the war against Germany can keep up very much longer." He had followed the Second Cavalry, he wrote Henry III, "clear across Germany since you jumped off, Henry, from the Moselle." The Army, he said, had been "kind enough to tell us from time to time about where you are . . . somewhere around the Czechoslovakian border. It certainly must've been a most thrilling experience."

Henry said he would try to see his way through until the Japanese surrender, but not beyond. The reconstruction period could be left to a successor. "Because the wear and tear on me during the last 12 years," he wrote, "has been pretty hard." Henry offered, too, a rare confession: He was "pleased that I've been able to carry on as well as I have. . . . What with the President's death, and Mother ill in the hospital, and Bob's ship being hit by a torpedo—it is enough to give anybody plenty of worry."

By Tuesday morning, May 8, Truman had proclaimed Victory in Europe—V-E Day, as it would be popularly known—on the president's own birthday. America rejoiced, and New York City was awash in jubilation. Henry Morgenthau, Sr., could not contain his joy. The secretary had seen his father days earlier, flying up for the night to celebrate his eighty-ninth birthday. The old man looked "amazingly well and in excellent spirits," Henry Jr. had written his sons, his health intact. To the patriarch, V-E Day was a family triumph not to be overlooked amid his son's struggles.

"My dear Henry!" he wrote to his son in Washington, "On this important day, I am thinking of your approaching birthday"—Henry Jr. would soon turn fifty-four.

> You have so much to be thankful for—such a wife and such three
> fine children and all well except dear Ellie. . . . With Ellie's illness
> and your sons among the combatants and Ellie's present siege—and
> also Franklin's loss, you certainly had a dark spell. Now everything
> looks better and so I am wishing you a happier year and years to
> come. . . . This is a period when we all have to be philosophical and
> count our blessings and belittle our troubles.

Henry Sr. had heard Truman's proclamation on the radio and was proud to learn Henry Jr. had stood next to the president as he delivered his remarks. He heard, too, how Senator Wagner had been won over, and was now set to lead the Senate push for "the Bretton Woods plan—

which promises to be adopted." And soon, the secretary's father added, "the Morgenthau plan is also favorably considered"—so in all, "you will have accomplished a lot."

At the Treasury, though, would be no gloating.

"I am not going to make any speech," Henry told his aides when they reconvened, "but I would like to say this much: I think that those of you have been associated with me since Pearl Harbor and before . . . can all feel we have had a little share in this victory. . . . We gave them some orders to start with—the French engines." The orders, he said, had given the Air Corps a "year's head-start": Thanks to the Allied orders across the country, the production of planes and engines had gone into high gear, "and all of that was done from this office." He recalled, too, his Scottish ally, Arthur Purvis, and how FDR had positively glowed when "he got the idea of lending the ships to the English, rather than selling them . . . the idea of Lend-Lease was sort of born there that day."

If elsewhere in America politicians and the families of GIs in Europe hosted victory parties, Morgenthau's Washington was little changed. "V-E day has come and gone," Henry Jr. wrote Bob and Henry III. "Everybody took it very quietly here. Nobody left their desks, and there was no celebration in the streets at night." He and Mrs. Roosevelt had said it often that week: There was nothing to celebrate until the Pacific was won. "Some of my own sons," Mrs. Roosevelt wrote in her column the day after Truman's announcement, "with millions of others, are still in danger."

Henry took the same message to his chief aides. "We have got another very tough one ahead of us," he warned, "and when . . . the Japanese quit, then I think for the first time in my life . . . I think I will get drunk."

| | | |

Even victory in Europe could not ease the loss of FDR. Henry had no ability to grieve, and no time to try, before the new challenge took hold: Truman, and how to win him over. He had never been forced to gain the confidence of a politician, much less a stranger.

The fall of Berlin had given the new president a respite, but Henry knew he would be hard-pressed to get him to pay attention to his ideas for Germany. With the U.N. conference continuing in San Francisco, and urgent preparations for the next round of talks with Stalin and Churchill in Europe—the German capital was said to be venue of choice—Truman faced too many distractions.

On May 4, the president had asked Henry to stay after a cabinet meeting and handed him back a chapter Henry had given him from his manuscript on Germany, "The Road to Peace." Truman had read it twice, he said, and could not sleep for hours from worry. He had gone back over the Yalta Agreement, Truman explained, "and Churchill, Stalin and I have to agree on a plan." "I like everything that's in there," he told Henry, speaking of the draft chapter, "but it's up to me to say that."

Take it, Henry said, and put your name on it.

That wasn't the point, Truman said. "You have to give me time. I am new at this thing."

"I'm not going to take it," Henry soon told his aides, fuming at Truman's stonewalling. "I was willing to take it from Roosevelt because I was his friend, but I want a little more now."

On May 9, Henry again brought up his book with Truman. He decided to force the issue. "Mr. President," he said, "I realize you don't want me to publish this thing . . . but I have accepted your decision."

Not so, Truman said, he just wanted to keep "all the cards" in his hand—and the U.S. plan for the occupation was one of the aces. He led Henry to a map that showed a Germany marked by dividing lines—"I just wanted to show you," Truman said, "I am studying this myself."

"I got the impression," Henry interjected, "you liked my plan."

"Yes, by and large, I am for it," Truman said.

Henry again brought his papers: showing the president "the part on agriculture," and the charts detailing how Germany ranked fourth in the European production of wheat, rye, beets, and potatoes. Truman was amazed, saying: "That's contrary to what everybody has told me."

Once again, Henry would return to the Treasury relieved: "I went away again with the distinct feeling that the man likes me and has confidence in me." But the distrust lingered. The following morning, on May 10, at 10:09 A.M., Henry did something that he had never dared, or felt the need to do, with Roosevelt: He taped the president of the United States. Whether fearing a retreat or an imminent reprisal, Henry did not turn off the office recording system. The conversation—as transcribed in Henry's diaries—concerned the budget (Truman vowed not to lower taxes in 1946), but the secretary wanted to draw out the president on his plan for Germany.

The battle over the occupation blueprint had come down, in large part, to the distance between Harry Truman and Henry Morgenthau, Jr. It would have been hard to imagine two men of greater contrast in background and character. Each felt that the other had come from the opposite end of America. Yet they shared, at heart, a set of fundamental values: an allegiance to Democratic politics, a fondness for homespun wisdom, and, above all, a distrust of pitchmen—whether in business or politics. In meeting after meeting, Truman had heard Henry out. Soon, he would again: Henry came to the White House to discuss a "plan for rehabilitation of Germany," Truman recorded in a note to himself, "to which I listened with interest." And yet, the president had leaned, from the first, closer to the countervailing forces, the views of the War Department and State.

Henry, though, would claim the final victory. On May 10, when Truman at last signed a directive for Eisenhower, the U.S. plan for the military occupation—a revision of JCS 1067, the War Department draft—Henry privately boasted that the document retained much of the Treasury's original language and thrust. It left the responsibility for the German economy to the Germans. "This is a big day for the Treasury," Henry told his aides that evening. "If I hadn't been there, I don't think he would've signed it." For the secretary, it was the first triumph of the new era. Truman, he gloated, had greeted him with "Congratulations!" The news would soon hit the papers, Henry was certain, and to his press aide, he offered a final suggestion: "If somebody doesn't recognize it as the Morgenthau Plan, just rub his nose."

41. In the Pacific: "A Quiet Station"

SPRING–SUMMER 1945

Bob Morgenthau was standing on the bridge of the *Bauer,* off the southern coast of Okinawa, when the news of FDR's death came over the Armed Services Radio. The ceremony at sea would be brief: The officers and crew gathered on deck, beneath the flag at half-mast, for a moment of prayer. Neither Captain Williams nor Morgenthau spoke, although their silence did little to mask the disbelief.

Unable to send a cable, Bob could not send word to his parents. He was left to mourn alone. "I cried," he would later say. "I cried for the first time in my adult life."

By late April, the kamikazes had not only changed the nature of the naval warfare in the Pacific, the suicide bombers had delivered a new level of fear. It was not only in the dusky twilight or predawn murk—the attacks could come just as easily in the blue sunlight of day. The raids terrified the men, officers and crew alike. One morning, Lieutenant Morgenthau found an assistant engineer from Missouri hiding in a laundry bag on the main deck. Another evening, the *Bauer* was on picket duty alongside the destroyer *O'Bannon,* when a call came in the middle of the night: The ship's exec asked Morgenthau to "send over your doctor." The *O'Bannon* had been hit and several men wounded, but a night transfer was dangerous.

"What's the matter?" Morgenthau asked over the radio. "What's happened to your doctor?"

"Jumped overboard," came the reply.

On April 29, as the *Bauer* stood northwest of Okinawa, close to Japan's southern tip, she faced the largest raid yet.

Overhead, the lookouts caught sight of the planes coming out of the afternoon clouds. The Japanese approached on a straight path: at least seven planes, including four "Zekes," single-engine fighters, and one "Lilly," a twin-motored bomber. (The U.S. generals and admirals had given the Japanese planes nicknames: Fighters tended to get male names ["Zeke," "Oscar"] and bombers, female ["Betty," "Val"].) The *Bauer* had air support; they'd seen the Hellcats and Corsairs overhead all afternoon. But at 3:10 P.M., two Corsairs were ordered back to base, and as they were relieved, the attack began.

The Zekes ducked into the clouds, hidden from sight, until the Lilly reemerged, in the lead—and the bomber made a run at the *Bauer*. The plane exploded in midair, plunging into the sea. The action report, drafted days later, described the downing: "We splashed her using partial radar control. . . . She burst into flames with a terrific explosion throwing the pilot and parachute clear." Later, the parachute would be found, but no body.

The gunners next took out a Zeke coming hard at the ship. "He dived directly and almost vertically," Captain Williams recorded, crashing twenty-five yards off the starboard beam. From the bridge, the officers could see the bomb—"a 100 lb. variety with a point detonating fuse"—that exploded as the plane hit the water, shaking the ship but causing no damage.

At the same time, two more Zekes broke from the clouds. One made a run on the port bow. The two 40 mm quad guns took it under fire, turning it away in flames. The other Zeke attacked from the north and caught fire at 2,000 yards, but made it through the flak. The gunners had knocked out the engine and killed the pilot: "His controls locked, and the plane glided over the number two stack, a riddled mass of flames." The kamikaze cleared the ship's stacks by ten feet, crashing into the sea. As it hit, the second downed plane also exploded, with as great a force as the first.

The attack lasted only minutes, but the *Bauer* gunners never paused, firing 284 five-inch rounds, and nearly 2,000 rounds of 40 mm and 20 mm ammunition. "The only way of combatting such an attack," the captain would tell headquarters, "is to disregard the cease firing buzzer and keep shooting!"

For Morgenthau, and the men of the *Bauer*, there was no respite. Late into the evening, enemy planes were still circling overhead. By midnight, though, the ship had won a congratulatory dispatch from Vice Admiral Turner, commander of the Amphibious Force: "WELL DONE FOR PROTECTING THE TASK FORCE THIS AFTERNOON."

| | | |

The morning of May 11 opened serenely, with no sense of foreboding. The weather was good, as the yeoman recorded: "high broken clouds, flat sea, good visibility, gentle, southeasterly winds." For Lieutenant Morgenthau, the day carried special significance: It was his father's birthday. When Bob awoke that morning at 5:43 A.M., he could think of only one thing: "I don't want to get killed on my father's birthday."

Three days earlier, as the *Bauer* patrolled a new picket station, they had got word of the victory in Europe. "We were obviously pleased," Morgenthau would remember, "but we knew we could not relax." The Tokyo command, as the last member of the Axis Pact, was sure to step up the attack: "We knew something big was coming. Just had no idea how big."

It would begin early in the morning on May 11 and last nearly half an hour, as the *Bauer* endured its second kamikaze swarm in clear daylight. They had been on picket station #5, patrolling alongside the destroyer *Douglas H. Fox,* four LCS(L)s (landing craft supports [large])—the small ships that had proven a staple of the Pacific, earning the sobriquet "the Mighty Midgets"—and one gunboat. Twice on the previous morning, the ships had been called to General Quarters, but each time no Japanese planes had appeared overhead.

At 7:40 A.M. the first report came: a cluster of fighters coming in from the north. By 8:01, the *Bauer* opened fire on a "Dinah," a twin-engine reconnaissance craft, managing to turn it away. Lieutenant Morgenthau called the CAP (Combat Air Patrol) at Yontan Airfield on Okinawa— and within minutes eight Corsairs were in the skies to the north. At 8:03, the *Bauer* spotted two more Japanese planes, closing in low. The gunners shot down the first, hit the second hard. It was heading for the conning tower of LCS-88, a ship from Portland, Oregon, when it peeled off, going down in flames. The pilot, though, had let loose its bomb, which hit the "Mighty Midget," igniting fires and blasting the aft twin 40 mm gun mount clear off the ship. Shrapnel shot to the tower, hitting the commanding officer in the head, killing him at once. The explosion took ten men, including the gunners who had downed the bomber.

The *Bauer* had turned bow in, to allow its forward and aft guns to fire at the incoming planes. The barrage was constant, but Morgenthau's ship shot down three planes, including one that "bounced off the deck in a suicide dive." None of the *Bauer*'s crew was killed, and when the smoke cleared, the doctor discovered only one man wounded.

Their colleagues would not be so fortunate. The VMF-221, the Marine pilots stationed on the carrier *Bunker Hill*, had left at 7:00 that morning, heading out to fly patrols over the picket ships. Within an hour, they had downed several Japanese planes, but as they returned home, by 9:15, their carrier was under attack. A pair of Japanese fighters dove directly into the *Bunker Hill*, causing the greatest number of casualties of any kamikaze attack in the war: 396 men killed and 264 wounded.

After the attack of May 11, Bob Morgenthau would remember a strange calm settling in. The crew had started to call the *Bauer* "the luckiest ship in the Navy." The exec, if only privately, allowed himself an indulgence. "I'd survived the *Lansdale*," he would say, "but I didn't consider that lucky. The Pacific was different—the intensity of the kamikaze attacks wore you down. We didn't have time to think, but it would've been natural to count the odds. So after May 11th, I began to feel it too—Lady Luck sitting on my shoulder."

The first week in June brought the last major raid. The attacks had left the *Bauer* unfit for picket duty, but the ship could still be put to use: The *Bauer,* and another destroyer minelayer, the *J. W. Ditter,* joined several gunboats on "flycatcher patrol." Since the spring, the Japanese had resorted to a last-ditch strategy. As the American ground forces closed in on the southern reaches of Okinawa, they had found a means to escape: loading their troops onto barges and moving out at night. The Navy had assigned cruisers, destroyers, and gunboats on flycatcher patrol to strike at the barges that slid up the coast in the darkness.

"We thought they were putting us on a quiet station," Morgenthau would say, "giving us a break."

At dawn on June 6, on patrol twenty miles off the southwestern tip of Okinawa, the *Bauer* arrived to relieve a destroyer. They patrolled the area at fifteen knots in a northerly direction, a thousand yards astern of the *Ditter.* The clouds were low, offering coverage for the enemy planes, but the day passed without event—until just after five o'clock in the evening.

Lieutenant Morgenthau was in the CIC when the call to General Quarters sounded. If the men had learned that the picket stations closest to Japan saw the most action, now they found out that patrols to the southwest of Okinawa, those closest to Tokyo's bases on Taiwan, had it no easier. "It was a swarm," Morgenthau would say, "from port and starboard—all directions." By 17:13, the *Bauer* and the *Ditter* were under attack by at least eight planes. On a cargo ship across the waters, the men watched the attack and saw the *Bauer* and the *Ditter* each bring down three Japanese aircraft. Two planes, however, had crashed into the *Ditter*, killing ten and wounding twenty-seven.

The *Bauer*, though, seemed to have been spared yet again. A kamikaze had come in on its starboard beam, crashing into its side—just short of the main deck by about five feet. There was a sudden smell of diesel, but no explosion. The plane had hit at the waterline. Morgenthau got the first report: "The forward emergency diesel room was flooding with fuel and water." He sent a team down to survey: There was "a significant hole," nearly twelve feet wide, in the side of the ship.

In the morning, a team of experts came aboard to assess the damage. There was no cause for alarm, they concluded. "Repair experts and divers who examined the holes in the side," the action report would record, "thought them to be caused by engine parts or the plane's landing gear." The *Bauer* would head in for repairs to Leyte, the big base more than a thousand miles to the south in the Philippines. Sailing on the edge of a typhoon, the ship arrived more than two weeks later.

In Leyte, repair crews welded plates over the holes and pumped out the compartment, but once the fuel tanks were emptied, they made a startling discovery: A 550-pound, semi-armor-piercing bomb was lodged up against the bulkhead of the forward fire room, just underneath the forward magazine. The kamikaze had been so close, no one noticed that an aerial torpedo had struck the ship. "The 'tail' of the 'fish,'" the Navy would tell the press, "was left hanging inside the ship."

"That was the day," Morgenthau would say years later, "I learned never to trust an expert."

The *Bauer* had carried the bomb for seventeen days. The disposal crew soon revealed how great the men's luck had been: Three threads in one fuse were all that had prevented the firing pins from dropping on the charges, which likely would have killed all onboard. The news spread quickly among the men of Halsey's Third Fleet, even reaching a *Philadelphia Inquirer* reporter on a carrier in the middle of the sea. The myth of the "luckiest ship" would grow: The *Callahan*, the ship that took over the *Bauer*'s patrol, would get hit by a 250-pound bomb aft, blowing apart its magazine. Sunk on July 29, the *Callahan* was the last U.S. destroyer lost in the war.

In eighty days of nonstop action, from March 25 until June 11, the *Bauer* had sustained thirty-seven air attacks, and its gunners had shot down at least thirteen planes—the crews would insist they scored three others and assisted on another three "splashes." It was a record to be proud of: The officers and crew would be awarded the Presidential Unit Citation, one of only forty-three destroyers so honored in the war.

42. Big Man Falling

SPRING–SUMMER 1945

At a White House press conference on May 23, as Truman announced three new cabinet members, a reporter shouted: "Mr. President, did Mr. Morgenthau offer his resignation this morning?"

"No, he did not," Truman replied. "And if he had, I wouldn't accept it."

Henry was thrilled to hear the affirmation: The president, he told his aides that afternoon, "had said it twice!"

The secretary remained uncertain of Truman's plans for him, but he took it upon himself to instruct, even cajole, the new president. At the White House on May 23, Henry offered unsolicited advice from the Pacific—his son Bob's. He showed Truman a letter from Bob—"and read him the parts I'd marked in red." Henry also told him "how to run the Cabinet," and suggested he trim it "to 10 members." Above all, Henry pushed him on Germany. He derided Truman's plan to put Supreme Court justice Robert Jackson in charge of the tribunal that would try Nazi war criminals. "I think he was a conscientious objector during the war," he told aides, "and I don't think he will carry this out." Henry knew the old charges surrounding his "Carthaginian" plan would arise, that his critics would say he was seeking retributive justice, but he felt he could weather the attacks. "My motives are not revenge," Henry insisted, "but one hundred years of peace in Europe."

By June, most of Washington knew that Truman would soon be heading to Europe, joining Churchill and Stalin for the talks in Berlin. Weeks earlier, though, Henry had told the president of an invitation to France—

Jean Monnet had asked the secretary to open a war bonds exhibit in Paris. Several times, Henry gingerly reminded Truman of the invitation, eager for his approval. He wanted to go, Henry said, not only to support the French, but "to see my son." The mention of Henry III played on Truman's sympathies: He seemed to consent, even offering a plane, as FDR had done. Henry assured the president there was no rush: He would have to wait until Mrs. Morgenthau was able to come home.

Emboldened, on June 13, Henry reminded Truman how he'd gone to Europe in the previous year—and discovered that "the Army was for building up . . . a strong Germany." He would like to do so again, to see what they were planning for the Ruhr and the Saar. The idea did not land well. "The President seemed very much distracted and fidgety," Henry recorded, "and sort of jumped around the room and paced up and down."

Truman tried to wriggle free: "I just haven't had time to think this thing through," he said.

"Well, the French feel that it would help to teach democracy to their people," Henry said, returning to the bonds exhibit.

"Just let me read the thing," Truman said of the invitation. "I want to take it home and read it. I want to think it through."

At that, Truman ended it: "When I make up my mind, I will put all my cards on the table."

"I certainly expect you to do that," said Henry.

| | | |

By early June, Henry had escorted Ellie back to Washington, yet as she rested at home, Henry had only one person he could turn to for relief: Mrs. Roosevelt.

After the tense exchange with Truman about his trip to Europe, Henry had flown up to the farm, rushing when he arrived to Mrs. Roosevelt's cottage. She had assured the public that she was "not going to parties of any kind," but Henry convinced her to attend one event, offering to escort her to a local speaking engagement. He went with Mrs. Roosevelt to the Nelson House, the grand Poughkeepsie hotel that FDR had used for political gatherings since his days as governor. It was Flag Day, June 14, and the men of Elk Lodge No. 275, several hundred in dark suits, had filed in early.

Mrs. Roosevelt had insisted she would not attend the dinner, only the speeches afterward, when she would accept on FDR's behalf a posthumous Medal of Valor. She and Henry arrived together, Mrs. Roosevelt wearing a black dress and a black hat, a short black veil at its back. The dining room was stifling, and amid the crowd of Elks, Henry felt distinctly ill at ease. He and Mrs. Roosevelt found Dean Thompson, the Vassar president, and settled in at the head table.

Mrs. Roosevelt had to wait out half a dozen speeches, and a labored introduction by the Grand Master of the Elks, but when she took the lectern, the heat in the room seemed to rise and Henry was nearly moved to tears. For the first time in public, Mrs. Roosevelt spoke of her husband in the past tense. She was in mourning, but the weight she carried now was not grief: It was a sense of uncertainty, of not knowing the future course that her life would, or could, take. Yet she spoke not of herself, her own loss and uncertainties, but of the nation's.

"We must get over fear," Mrs. Roosevelt said. "If we start out with fear, we are not going to have the peace that we hope to gain." She had never heard her husband express fear, she said, in either his personal or professional endeavors. Even in the first hours after Pearl Harbor, as so many worried, FDR had been confident that the Navy would "come out on top." Her husband had always said we must win the war, but "having won the war," she told the crowd, "we must make very sure . . . we also have won the peace."

There would be so much to do, even once the war in the Pacific was won. "We are going to have discouragement and times when our high ideals have setbacks, times when we do not achieve what we want without effort." If Americans could not have perfection, she asked, shouldn't we "take what we can get and keep going?" That was the spirit that drove her husband, and it was the spirit that we must adopt. "We must have patience and a sense of our responsibilities," she said; the country could not afford, as it did after 1918, "to listen to the voice of fear and caution." She offered a plea: Remember that "peace is worth the sacrifice that we have put into war." It was the most beautiful speech, Henry wrote his sons, he had ever heard her give.

| | | |

Henry returned to Washington determined to try a new tack. Truman saw him as only a Roosevelt man—try to get personal, Henry assured himself, and he might win the president's confidence more easily. Did Truman ever play poker? he asked. He told him of Ellie's illness—and "how lonesome" he'd been while she was in the hospital. Truman had reached the end of his sympathies: "I am the lonesomest man in Washington," he shot back. "I have nothing to do but walk around by myself."

By June 18, the change was unmistakable. Henry arrived at the White House for another private meeting, prepared "to make a little speech . . . that my going to France wasn't a matter of life and death." But as soon as he entered, the president opened up on him "very direct": "I have been thinking about your going to France," Truman said, "and I don't want you to go. . . . I don't want you and myself over there at the same time. When I come back you can go any place, anywhere you want to in September."

Henry got the point. "He didn't want me messing around over there at the same time," he wrote, as it "might make it difficult for him."

"Stalin has invited me," Truman went on, confiding new details on the upcoming talks in Potsdam on postwar Europe, "and I have got to work out a plan with Stalin and Churchill for Germany." He added, "I don't want you to be out of the country while I am."

Henry saw another opportunity to school the president. He reminded Truman that when FDR went to Yalta, Roosevelt had told him that if an emergency arose, it would be up to him to convene the cabinet.

"That's so," Truman agreed. "I want you to be here, you are the ranking man by law." (Truman as yet had no vice president, and the secretary of state, whomever he appointed, would accompany him to the talks in Germany.)

"I would much rather have it come from you, than by law," Henry said. "I would like you to say something to the Cabinet before you leave."

Truman promised he would do so.

It was a setback and, seen in retrospect, a signal of what was to come, but Henry tried to see it as a sign that he and Truman could work together. He appreciated the new man's candor, even sensed a budding kinship. "Truman said he felt like a brother towards me," Henry recorded in his diary that day, "and he wished I would feel that way towards him. I said that I would like to."

Even as the secretary attempted new avenues to ingratiate himself, another sharp turn came when Truman named Jimmy Byrnes as his secretary of state. A venerable Southern power broker with a long political résumé—a former congressman, senator, and governor, early ally of Wilson, and close cohort of FDR—Byrnes had served briefly on the Supreme Court, moved into diplomacy, and nearly been tapped as FDR's running mate in 1944. For much of the war, he had masterfully run the Office of War Mobilization, the supra-agency that oversaw defense production.

Henry could not stand the man. The two had squared off for years; on the funeral train from Hyde Park, Henry had even bid Truman's men to pass on a message: "I don't like Byrnes, and I don't get along with him. . . . I think Truman would make a great mistake" if he chose Byrnes. Henry added prophetic words: "Maybe I will be cutting my own throat."

By July 3, Byrnes had been sworn in. When Truman called him "my able and conniving Secretary of State" in his diary that week, he meant it as a compliment.

That afternoon, Truman met again with Henry Stimson to devise a game plan for the Potsdam talks. Truman had come into office knowing little of FDR's secrets—and nothing of the War Department's "S-1" project to build the atomic bomb. Truman was eager for a script for what he should tell Stalin about the bomb. Should things go well, Stimson said, you can tell him "we were pretty near ready and we intended to use it against the enemy, Japan." But the secretary of war had a second vital issue on his agenda: "the German question." As the two went over the maps, Stimson warned that the occupation would pose enormous challenges, and "the only way" to make "it go right was to not allow the element of vengeance to come into the problem at all."

Stimson tried to head off any attempt by Morgenthau to reenter and fill a policy vacuum. As Truman listened, he went further: "I told him of the problem of our Jewish people here and I recounted informally the episode of last summer at Quebec." Truman said that he had heard about it, and laughed. Stimson, though, was dead serious, recounting his October lunch with FDR and his warnings about the plan for a "pastoral Germany." "The danger," Stimson added, "was not yet over," pointing to a recent statement by Bernard Baruch. Of Morgenthau and Baruch, stand-ins for the country's Jewish leaders, Truman offered the conclusion that "they were all alike—they couldn't keep from meddling in it."

The next morning, Stimson called Byrnes to assure him he had no interest in "encroaching on his ground," and Byrnes made clear that he stood with Stimson on the plans for Germany. As they spoke, Byrnes let drop that "Henry Morgenthau was on the prowl," and likely "to turn up in Germany just on the chance that he might be needed." "Byrnes and I," wrote Stimson, "laughed over it together."

Even as the word spread throughout the cabinet and the Hill that

Morgenthau's days were numbered, Henry was intent on stalking the president. On the morning of July 5, he went to see Truman, clutching a handwritten list of agenda items, the last a dark scrawl: *"who is in charge while he is away."* It was a habit—writing a list and keeping it close— that Henry had formed long ago, in Albany. He returned to it whenever he feared his nerves might get the best of him.

"Look, Mr. President," Henry began, "the last time I was here you said you felt like a brother to me. . . . I would like to reciprocate that feeling and have an official family talk. . . . You are leaving, and there is all this gossip . . . about my being through, and I would like to raise the question with you before you leave because I am assuming a great responsibility while you are away."

In the morning Truman was to board a train bound for Newport News, where the USS *Augusta* awaited to take him across the Atlantic— his first trip to Europe since 1918.

The president assured Henry that he was "going to say that you are the man in charge while I am gone."

Henry pushed harder: "Well, I would like to know whether you want me to stay until V-J Day."

"Well, I don't know. I may want a new Secretary of Treasury."

"Mr. President, if you have any doubts in your mind after my record of twelve years here, and after several months with you and when I have given you my loyal support, you ought to know your mind now, and if you know it, I want to get out now."

"Well," Truman said, "let me think this thing over."

"Mr. President . . . either you want me or you don't, and you know it now."

"I can't make up my mind."

For Henry, that was more than enough.

"Well, Mr. President," he said, "I am going to write you a letter of resignation. . . . Would you like me to stay while you are abroad or would you like to have it take effect immediately?"

"I would like you to stay while I am abroad."

"Well, I will write you a letter. Do you want me to put in a draft of an answer for you?"

"Yes."

"Do you want me," asked Henry, "to break in Vinson as my successor while you are gone?"

Fred Vinson, a former congressman from Kentucky, had served five years as a Circuit Court of Appeals judge, and since 1943, he had stood, alongside Byrnes, at the helm of the war economy in a series of posts, chiefly atop the Office of Economic Stabilization. Washington insiders might have snickered at his basset-hound look—he had a long face, and dark, sad eyes—but Judge Vinson was deemed a steady hand at economics. And to Truman, he was political kin: a plainspoken "country politician" you could trust. It was an open secret that the judge stood in line to take over the Treasury.

"Oh, Vinson is going with me on account of Lend-Lease," Truman said.

Henry again asked for a public statement of support, reiterating that he would be willing to stay on until after the president returned, but Truman cut him short: "You are rushing it."

Even as the president repeated the phrase several times, Henry barged on: A White House statement had to go out that evening, he insisted.

"If you don't give it out tonight," he said, "I will be forced to give it out tomorrow. And I wouldn't like to do that while you are on the high seas."

Truman again said he wanted to think it over. But Henry would not relent. Whether it was a new assuredness, or a realization that, perhaps for the first time in his life, he had nothing to lose, he refused to be left in limbo.

"Either you want me to stay until V-J Day or you don't. . . . After all, Mr. President," Henry said, "I don't think it is conceited to say that I am at least as good or better as some of the five new people you appointed to the Cabinet, and some of them I think you definitely made a mistake."

Truman was taken aback. "Well, this makes me feel very badly."

"Well, don't feel badly."

Within hours, Morgenthau had repaired to his office to recuperate. He sat with a circle of aides, Pehle and Luxford, Gaston, Dan Bell, and Harry White, men who had been by his side for decades. "I feel sorry," Henry said, "only on account of the great disturbance it will cause you people." As for himself, he added, the real "disturbance" had come "when Mr. Roosevelt died. . . . This doesn't disturb me now. In fact, I am beginning to feel kind of good.

"Nobody," Henry went on, "especially after being Secretary of the Treasury for twelve years . . . can take that, and I don't see why I should have to. . . . I couldn't hold my head up and have this man say to me he was uncertain about me."

| | | |

Henry had seized the upper hand. He found Truman "very weak and indecisive," but as he told Eugene Meyer, the owner of *The Washington Post,* that evening, "I just thought I would call the cards rather than letting someone else do it." *He* had picked the time, not Truman. Yet Henry had underestimated "the Missouri crowd." Before leaving town, Truman announced the Vinson appointment, and Henry, knowing that Vinson would be going to Potsdam, thought he would have weeks left in office. But in the days that followed, he found out otherwise.

Ten days later, once the dust had cleared, Henry sat down and again tried to settle his nerves. He held the microphone of his Edison Voicewriter close and drafted a letter to Bob and Henry overseas: "My dear sons, This will most likely be the last time I dictate a letter of this kind to you, because I imagine that by tomorrow I will no longer be Secretary of the Treasury. I'm going to write you quite frankly what happened and I suggest that you destroy this letter . . . It won't do any good to leave it laying around."

On Friday evening, July 6, the day that Truman left for Potsdam, Henry had called to congratulate Vinson. "Well, that's awfully sweet," Vinson had said, before letting slip news that staggered Henry: "between you and me I'm not going."

"You're not—you're not going."

"No, I'm not going."

"But the President said you were."

"I know, but he changed his plans."

Truman's men had pulled Vinson off the boat that afternoon; his luggage had gone on ahead. Henry had been led to believe he had time, a month at least, and would run the cabinet while the president was in Potsdam. Now Henry saw no reason to delay. Neither did Truman, who sent Sam Rosenman to do the dirty work—to tell Henry that he was through.

Rosenman would regret that the task "broke their long friendship," but he had taken it on because it was "a Presidential directive." He also thought the move inevitable: Morgenthau, Rosenman would write, was "temperamentally unsuited to Truman's style of operation. . . . Truman

would not suffer pressure." For Henry, though, it was an act of coward-
ice never to be forgiven—a president sending an old friend, a Roosevelt
man who happened to be a fellow Jew, to push him out.

It was not personal, Rosenman told Morgenthau. All day long, Truman had said before leaving town, people had been calling, worried
about what might happen if he, the president, and Byrnes should die
while they were out of the country—"not very complimentary to your
old man," Henry would write his sons, "but what you might expect."
Truman had related to Rosenman the story of his fight with Henry,
nearly as Henry remembered it: Henry had wanted to quit at once, but
Truman had insisted he stay on until he returned from Europe. Truman
did not want to change his position, Rosenman explained, but he was
under pressure now; the standoff had become "a matter of public relations." The president, he insisted, had not given Rosenman an order,
only a wish: If Morgenthau chose to resign immediately, Truman would
be "very happy."

What did Henry have in mind for his future? Rosenman asked, attempting to soften the blow. The White House counsel, it seemed, would
be one of the few Roosevelt men to join Truman's team; he let on that he,
too, would be at Potsdam.

"Nothing," Henry said.

"I can't promise you anything," Rosenman said, "but if you did resign
he would be under obligation to you."

Truman already had Morgenthau's resignation letter. Now Henry
drafted another letter for the president's signature. He composed two
draft replies for Truman: one in which he thanked Henry for his service,
and another in which the president would name him governor of the new
bank to be created under the Bretton Woods agreement—the financial
agency to become known as the World Bank.

"I made it perfectly clear," Henry would insist to his sons, "that this
letter had nothing to do with the exchange of the other two letters"—the
first resignation letter, and draft reply that Henry had sent for the president's signature.

As Rosenman promised to cable the letters at once to Truman, who
was now at sea, Henry rushed to make plans. A week earlier, sensing the
end, he had ordered a Secret Service guard to protect his files around the
clock. Now he told Vinson of the idea that he might become the bank
governor, and aides that he would stay in Washington at the apartment
until Mrs. Morgenthau was strong enough to be moved. By evening, the

president's cable had arrived from the *Augusta*. Truman had accepted the resignation letter, and consented to the draft reply. As for the third letter, proposing that Henry be named the American governor of the new bank, Truman wrote: "I concur only in the exchange of the first two cables. . . . Do not . . . release third cable."

It would be the last official word Henry would hear from Harry Truman. Years later, Truman told Jonathan Daniels, the newspaper editor who would briefly serve as his press secretary, "Morgenthau didn't know shit from apple butter," and further, in an unsent letter to Daniels, he called Morgenthau a "block head, nut—I wonder why FDR kept him around."

It would take Henry years to recover. It had been such a long struggle— more than a decade of supplicating and self-doubt, hedging and prevarication, had finally given way to a clarity of vision, and the will to see it through. Henry had just begun to feel the full power of his office, and get comfortable in it, when he lost it.

At Vinson's swearing-in at the Treasury, Henry stood in the corner of his own office, alone. No one approached him and he approached no one.

43. Home Is the Sailor

FALL 1945–WINTER 1946

T he officers of the *Bauer* thought they would be in the Pacific another three years. The kamikaze waves, to those defending the
destroyers on the picket stations, knew no end. Worse, the men
had come to see a final campaign in the Pacific as inevitable: U.S. troops
would have to take the fight to Japan's main islands and launch a full-
scale amphibious invasion. "'Golden Gate in '48,'" Bob Morgenthau
would say, "that was the slogan." No one expected to see San Francisco,
the Navy's favored destination, until then. "We were not looking forward to the invasion of Japan," Bob would recall, "and then one morning we got the news."

On August 6, President Truman had turned to the "S-1" project, ordering the atomic bomb dropped on Hiroshima. In Washington, as a
dark rain fell, General George Marshall phoned Secretary of War Henry
Stimson to report the "success of the operation." From his estate on
Long Island, Stimson sent word to the president, then aboard the USS
Augusta, crossing the Atlantic on his return from Potsdam. In Hiroshima, more than 146,000 people would die.

Bob's ship had stood two dozen miles off Okinawa, and though he
and the crew could not know the human toll of the bomb, years later he
could remember thinking only one thing: "Thank God."

"No one at home," he would say, "realized what a shellacking we
were taking at Okinawa." The kamikaze attacks had peaked by July, but
none of the men on the *Bauer* was looking forward to the landings at
Japan.

Two days after the Hiroshima bombing, Secretary Stimson woke up at five o'clock in the morning with "a rather sharp little attack"—a heart attack that led him to raise the idea of resigning with Truman. He did not, and on the next day, August 9, the U.S. Air Force dropped a second bomb, this time on Nagasaki. At least 74,000 Japanese were killed—all but an estimated 150 of them civilians.

Five days later, a Tuesday in New York, Joan Morgenthau, recent graduate of Vassar, boarded a train and left the city. She had gone out to Long Island with her brother Henry III, who was just back from Europe. The trip out of the city, Henry's first since coming home, had been his idea: He asked his sister to join him for a day of sailing. "It was a Coast Guard loaner, surplus," Joan would remember. "We were putting it near the end of Long Island, at Greenpoint, and all of a sudden, the bells started going. That was it. That's how we learned the news." Japan had surrendered.

At Fishkill Farms, two weeks later, Elinor Morgenthau wrote daughter-in-law Martha a long, unusually personal letter. Martha had sent photographs of the new baby in a red-leather frame that Ellie had kept on her bedside table in the hospital. She was overjoyed, she wrote Martha, to have the photographs—and asked for more: Other "than the wedding one . . . I haven't any picture of you."

"Bob has been very good about writing since my illness," Ellie wrote. "And it has meant so much." She wondered about Martha's plans: If Bob got a thirty-day leave, would she come from Minneapolis? (She'd been alternating between an apartment in that city and her parents' place on the lake at Wayzata.) Ellie offered a proposal: "When Bob first comes back to the East if you want to be free to come and go with him whenever this may be, or if you want to take a little vacation with him from both of your families and leave the baby with me," they could come "for a few weeks or months." The baby could stay with her at the farm, Ellie wrote, as long as there was someone to look after her. "Unfortunately it will be at least a year before I myself could lift a baby or do much of anything except look at her adoringly."

Lieutenant Morgenthau had not let anyone at home know, but he'd already received the orders to detach. Two weeks earlier, Captain Williams got the word: The Navy had a complex formula, based in part on age and length of service. Bob at age twenty-six was married with one child and had served, since July 1940, a total of fifty-two months. By September, he would have accrued the forty-nine points required for a release from active duty.

At five o'clock in the morning on September 2, 1945, Bob stepped off the *Bauer,* transferring to another ship to head home. Sending a cable to Washington, alerting his parents, would have been a breach of protocol— Bob declined. Eleven minutes later, the *Bauer* sailed on, bound again for Buckner Bay. Within days, it would move north to sweep the minefields of the South China Sea. Bob would always recall his "mixed feelings"— he had wanted to be there at the end. He also felt torn, leaving so many of the officers he'd grown close to, and leaving them so far from home. But on the Sunday that Bob Morgenthau left his ship, the world's attention was fixed on the USS *Missouri,* a U.S. battleship anchored off Tokyo.

"The surrender terms," as the log of the *Bauer* recorded, "were officially signed in Tokyo Bay"—and the war in the Pacific had ended.

||||

On September 24, Bob stepped foot on American soil in a daze, at the Naval Shipyard in Bremerton, Washington, an hour's ferry ride west of Seattle. He walked up the steep streets alone, lugging a sixty-pound duffel half a mile in search of a cheap hotel. In the morning, he would take the first train out. It took nearly two days to reach Minneapolis. Martha had been staying in Wayzata, at her parents' house. The sight of her, their daughter in her arms, brought tears. Martha had come home with the baby, alone. That summer, she had already taken to calling her by a nickname, to avoid confusion with Bob's sister: Joan had become "Jenny." At the station, Bob held his eight-month-old daughter for the first time.

"I was left speechless," he would say. "And it wasn't the exhaustion: it was happiness beyond words."

||||

Mornings on the farm, the orchards would be covered in mist. In autumn, the breeze carried the sweet smell of the apples almost to the front steps of the Old Homestead. By the first of November, though, the sky of the valley turned gray, the bare branches emerged again, and the cold moved in. There it would stay for winter.

Henry Morgenthau, Jr., had served longer than nearly any other cabinet member in U.S. history, but he always insisted his true calling lay elsewhere. Since the 1920s, the line in Henry's passport listing his "occupation" had not changed—it still read "farmer." Like his son, he, too, was exhausted, deflated by the battles with Truman, but having been thrust so suddenly from power, Henry was relieved to be back on the farm.

Joan may have understood her father better than the boys did. She had known how he loathed Jimmy Byrnes, and had seen his shock at how quickly the Roosevelt men had shifted allegiances. "The moment Truman brought in Byrnes," she would say, "that was it for my father." Joan had seen the new club forming, and closing its doors, before her father could recognize the turn.

She had watched, too, as he struggled to adjust to a new life. "After my father left Washington, it was very difficult for him. He went from being a big shot to—really, not being. It was a big downfall. Roosevelt's death was a tremendous shock for *me*. For him, it was a new life. It was very hard to adapt to all of a sudden not being important."

Henry had come back to New York empty-handed. He never expected a flood of invitations, the lucrative propositions from financial houses and big banks that his predecessors at the Treasury had received. The New Deal had so radically rearranged the order of things, Wall Street would never see Morgenthau, or his men, as allies. There was the timing, as well: the advent of Truman, the end of the war, and his own abrupt departure—none of it helped Henry. He would join a board or two—and did serve for a time as president of the Modern Industrial Bank, but it was hardly a sinecure. Instead, in those first months, Henry remained at the farm, insisting that he missed nothing of Washington. He only wished for his family to be close, and well—home together at last.

| | | |

Bob stayed only a few days in Minneapolis. By late October, he and Martha and the baby had reached New York. Once he arrived on the farm, Bob disappeared into his old bedroom and slept for twenty-two hours.

For months, Henry had dreamed of seeing the children together again at the Homestead. It was not a fleeting reunion he envisioned, but a return to a life that had left them all. Bob, Henry III, and Joan, he'd written to each a year earlier, should come back once the war ended to live at the farm for at least six months. The dream now seemed within reach. Joan, after two summers of laboring through science classes at Columbia, had started medical school—one of 22 women in a class of 125. With Henry III returned, and Bob as well, their father allowed himself to imagine they could pick up life where it had been interrupted, four years earlier—"on that Sunday after the Toscanini concert," as Henry III would say.

That fall, the former secretary also released his book, *Germany Is Our Problem,* which he dedicated to his sons "with the hope that neither they nor their children will have to fight in another war." The reviews saw the book for what it was: a desperate attempt to set the record straight. Henry had made sure to include, as a preface, "a photographic copy"—still marked "Top Secret"—"of the memorandum summarizing 'The Morgenthau Plan' which President Roosevelt took with him to the historic conference at Quebec." He knew the taint would remain on the family name, but Henry was pleased that at last the country could see his plan's foundation in facts and figures—and as he told Ellie, at least a few reviewers had seen it in a new, more positive light.

At the farm, for a time, an uncertain calm settled. Ellie still could not go on long walks, or undertake strenuous exercise—but she was overjoyed to welcome the baby. She had rearranged a bedroom upstairs, hired a baby nurse, and set up a nursery. There was a return, too, to a favored routine of the old days—even though all knew everything had changed. In early November, Mrs. Roosevelt came for a weekend, and this time, she spent the night. At breakfast they sat together looking out of the picture window at the farm: "The line of the hills was clear-cut against the blue sky," Eleanor would write in "My Day," "and the great oak in the foreground looked majestic," reminding her "of the many times my husband and I had sat beneath it" with Henry and Ellie. No one who had attended "those happy parties" could forget them, she wrote, "any more than I can ever cease to be grateful for our years of happy friendship." It was Mrs. R.'s way, Ellie knew, of bucking up the Morgenthaus.

Even before Bob left the Pacific, Captain Williams had sent a commendation up the chain of command: "Extremely brilliant, industrious, and resourceful," he wrote of his executive officer, deeming him "fully qualified for command of a destroyer." By October, Bob would become a lieutenant commander, and be awarded a Gold Star, in lieu of a second Bronze Star.

Days later, he would make his first, and only, appearance in New York City wearing his dress uniform. At the Astor Hotel, at a B'nai B'rith gala to honor the former secretary, three generations of Morgenthau men sat on the dais: Grandpa and Henry Jr. beaming in tuxedos, Henry III and Bob at their sides. The former secretary stood before the crowd of 1,300 to receive a gold medal, the same award his father had received thirty years earlier. Henry Jr. also took the occasion to deliver his first speech as a private citizen, speaking as he rarely had in Washington, with emotion rising in his voice.

"A few months ago," Henry said, "a wave of horror swept the civilized world." The photographs and newsreels had revealed how Germany treated "slave labor and persecuted prisoners." "Everywhere," he said, "men stood amazed, enraged, horrified." Yes, the "bestial system" had been overthrown, but the images from the camps only confirmed "what we at the War Refugee Board had long known."

With two members of the Truman cabinet sitting close by, Henry issued an urgent plea: "I am convinced there is only one solution for the homeless, stateless Jews," he said, "the immediate admission of at least 100,000 to Palestine." It was a demand to Truman, and the new British prime minister, Clement Attlee, who was due to arrive in Washington within days. " 'Displaced Persons,' " Henry said, "is a pitifully inadequate phrase" to describe the refugees. "Those emaciated walking skeletons" remained in Germany, and "before midwinter they will be dying by the thousands."

"While we have been enjoying this excellent dinner," he went on, "with nothing more serious in our lives than to fret about than when are we going to get a new car, a new refrigerator, or a new pair of nylons, men have been dying of starvation and exposure."

That fall, Bob Morgenthau moved through the days as if his life had become someone else's. Everything seemed to have changed, he would say: "People seemed quieter, the country smaller." The Navy had left him changed, too. He had returned home having met "men from all across America—rich and poor, from big cities, small towns, all races." He thought for a time about staying in the service, yet after fifty-four months, seven ships, and as many captains, Bob left the Navy, "released to inactive duty." For months, he did little: slept in the afternoons, appeared at odd hours only to eat, and soon returned to bed. "It was a kind of numbness," Bob would say. All the while, law school loomed. He had assured himself, and his parents, that once he came home he would apply. Years earlier, in his last fall at Amherst, Bob had sought advice on the profession from New York's chief justice, his great-uncle, Irving Lehman, and Felix Frankfurter, the Supreme Court justice. Frankfurter had warmed to Bob at once—"he's got maturity and good sense . . . a superior article"— and encouraged him not to rush: The law would be there.

IIII

In his declining years, Henry Morgenthau, Sr., had made a tradition of sitting for birthday interviews. Each year, a *Times* reporter would make the pilgrimage to the apartment on Fifth Avenue. It may have been a Sulzberger indulgence, rather than a reflection of Uncle Henry's influence, but each year the articles seemed to get longer. On his eightieth birthday, in 1936, the commemoration was enhanced by a half-page portrait sketched by S. J. Woolf, longtime illustrator and writer for the *Times* Sunday magazine. Woolf came from the same small circle of German Jews and remembered the slightly odd, officious dandy of his youth: Lazarus Morgenthau—"a tall, erect, silk-hatted old German," who always wore a white tie and black formal coat, and who, despite the years in New York, never progressed beyond broken English.

Henry Sr. would receive the journalists in his study, a dark-paneled room overlooking Central Park. Tall glass-doored bookcases lined two walls. Against another stood a large ornately carved desk, a small bust of Napoleon at its center. Henry would sit on a chromium chair—a deliberate modern addition to the prewar decor. As he spoke, a thin hand rubbing his sparse beard, the elder Morgenthau reveled in the memories.

Each year, Henry offered almost regal proclamations, predicting the state of world affairs to come, and adding to his tally of the errors of the past. At eighty-seven, he reported one remaining desire: "to live long enough to see the destruction of Hitler and Hirohito and all that they stand for." At eighty-eight, he confessed to enjoying his mocha cream cake, and recalled how in Kiel as a young man, he had witnessed the launching of the first German battleship. Now, he added, he "was waiting for the sinking of the last." At eighty-nine, two weeks after FDR's death, he spoke of the peace to come. He warned against a return to the mistakes of Versailles, and the "carving up" of Germany. And he predicted, as well, the postwar boom to come: the "billions in unused resources" that "are going to start us off on a real era of prosperity."

For years, Henry had lived alone. In the first year of the war, his wife of fifty-nine years had become too ill to live at home. Too often, at seventy-six, Josie wandered out—a call would come: "She's lost." What the doctors termed "hardening of the arteries" in another era would be called Alzheimer's. Her mind failing, Henry had sent Josie to Four Winds, the Our Crowd sanatorium in the woods of Westchester County.

Henry Sr. had long stood at the center of the family, although twenty-three years had separated the oldest and youngest of Lazarus and Babette's children. He had made a set of the leather-bound albums for every branch of the family—each bound in soft leather, its pages edged in gold leaf, and covers embossed with two words in gilded letters: MORGEN-THAU FAMILY. He had paid for the studio portraits and the calligrapher. Each of Lazarus and Babette's fourteen children was carefully recorded, as were their progeny. Henry Sr. had outlived his brothers and sisters—all but one by decades. The narrowing had come with remarkable swiftness: Even before he turned forty, Henry had lost more than half of his brothers and sisters. Seven had not lived to see the twentieth century. Only one sibling—Max, who died in 1936—had lived to see a Morgenthau in the cabinet.

Whenever anyone asked the secret of his longevity, Uncle Henry's answer rarely varied. "My recipe," he said, "has been ever since my boyhood that I have been moderate in everything except work." At ninety, Henry Sr. had relaxed his regime. He never rose before ten A.M., took a short walk before lunch and, afterwards, a nap, followed by an afternoon stroll. On most days, someone came along, a grandchild or two, but he rarely made it farther than ten blocks. At four o'clock, he drank a glass of orange juice. Late afternoons were spent in the study, where he returned to the books of his youth: Arnold, Emerson, and Franklin. He reread Thomas Huxley and the memoirs of Carl Schurz, the first German-born American elected to the U.S. Senate, and took delight in dipping, at random, into *Bartlett's Quotations*. In the evenings, he could no longer "attend meetings," nor could he give speeches, "and enjoy the stimulation of being heckled." His bedroom was spare: nearly without furniture, other than the outsized four-poster bed. Portraits of his wife, son, grandchildren, and great-grandchildren nearly covered one wall. The maid had long ago learned to feature the newest arrival: A portrait of the youngest baby in the clan stood alone atop the walnut dresser.

|||

On a Monday night in November, Henry Sr. suffered a stroke at home. He slipped into a coma, and died a week later, on November 25, 1946. He had spent July and August at Lake Mohonk, the old Quaker resort near Poughkeepsie, returning on Labor Day. He had not noticeably slowed, but complained of fatigue. His children had not imagined the end was near. In the last hours, Henry Jr. and his sisters, Alma, Helen, and Ruth, were at his bedside. Henry Sr. had awakened on the last day and surveyed each of their faces, but he could no longer speak.

Within hours, the *Times* announced the names of fifty-six honorary pallbearers. (The patriarch had set the list long ago.) Some—Albert Einstein, Cordell Hull—could not attend, but Bernard Baruch and Lieutenant General Harbord, the man Henry had recruited for his failed dream of an American mandate to protect the Armenians, would lead the procession on the morning before Thanksgiving. Among the five hundred mourners who filled Temple Emanu-El were many celebrated names of politics and finance, figures from the Roosevelt years and the Morgenthaus' extended family: the Lehman brothers, La Guardia, Sulzberger, Josephus Daniels, Ed Flynn, Eugene Meyer, the Filenes, and old real estate partners. Even Stephen Wise could not stay away. For a moment, old enmities were overlooked. Whether they had known him as Uncle Henry or Ambassador Morgenthau, those gathered came to see off one of the last "big men" of the old era. Henry had been one of the city's few survivors, whose career had spanned the centuries, from the Gilded Age to the rise of New York City and the corporate trusts. Born in the shadow of the European revolutions of 1848, he had come to New York as America rose from the ruins of the Civil War, and lived to see the grand ambition of the New Deal as well as the horror of modern warfare. "He played many parts in a long lifetime," the *Times* wrote, "but it was as a kindly and mellow philosopher that Henry Morgenthau was known best to the present generation."

The mahogany coffin, draped with gardenias, orchids, and white roses, lay at the altar. Eleanor Roosevelt sat beside Henry Jr., his sisters and their husbands. The organist played Beethoven, and a soloist from the Bronx House sang Mendelssohn. The service was not only "an hour of sorrow," but "also an hour of triumph," said Raymond Fosdick, president of the Rockefeller Foundation, in his eulogy. Fosdick had been a friend of forty years; they had met long before Wilson's ascent, downtown among the social workers at the Henry Street Settlement. Fosdick tallied the accomplishments, but sought to bring out the elder Morgenthau's philosophy of service. Uncle Henry always tried to rise above sectarianism, Fosdick said. "He was a civilized human being. Everything that he did in the course of a life crowded with good deeds can be deduced from this single fact."

Sitting with a reporter six months earlier, Henry Morgenthau, Sr., had sounded serene. "To have lived is a great experience," he said, "and to have left some little mark in the world is a source of great satisfaction." Yet Henry confessed one regret, a rare note for the man of ego, will, and means: "I feel somewhat like Cardinal Wolsey"—Henry VIII's cast-out and doomed lord chancellor—"when he said, 'Had I but served my God with half the zeal I served my king.'" Asked to explain who his "king" was, Henry replied at once: "Material things."

"It is the spiritual side of life that is satisfying," the patriarch said in the final interview. "But it took me a good many years to find this out."

PART IV

THE SOVEREIGN DISTRICT

44. After the Fall

1945–1948

Sitting at his oak desk at the farm, Henry Morgenthau, Jr., scrawled out an eleven-page letter to Mrs. Klotz. An attempt to express gratitude, the letter revealed Henry's struggle to speak from the heart: "When President Roosevelt died, my time in the Treasury was up," he wrote. "Unfortunately we did not realize it right away. If we had we both of us might have had time to plan our future together. It would have made me *very happy* if we could have continued working together. But to my everlasting sorrow it did not work out that way. But I will continue to hope and plan that in the not too distant future we will be working side by side once again."

> During the past 23 years you have given me the best of your working life. I have tried many times to show you how much I have appreciated it. I don't know if I can put into a few words or pages how much I appreciate your complete devotion to my interests. Your unselfish giving of your time and thought to assisting me in whatever I was devoting myself to at the time. I realize well that you have had to carry a more than full burden as a wife and mother . . . [which] made it all the more remarkable what you have been able to do for me. . . .
>
> God help anyone who in your opinion was disloyal to me. . . .
>
> The Jewish people in this country have been kind enough to say that I helped in saving the lives of some Jews abroad. Whatever credit I deserve in this matter I want you to know that I want to share it equally with you.

With nothing more than the habit of stubborn will, Henry tried to cobble together a new life in the city, taking over his father's old apartment on Fifth Avenue. He would never lack for money: Henry Sr. had left an estate worth nearly $1.5 million, and his wife's inheritance would top his own. He retained, as well, a scattering of real estate holdings across the city, yet Henry struggled to find purpose. Ellie, too, felt the disappointment. She had hoped Henry would get a diplomatic post, but nonetheless encouraged him to try to replicate the structure of his Washington life. He took an office on Madison Avenue, in the firm of his old friend and lawyer, Eddie Greenbaum. Henry would set up shop, hire a handful of assistants, and oversee the writing of his memoirs. He also brought back Mrs. Klotz—at first she refused, opting to stay at Treasury. But she was "a marked woman," as she put it, and in time, Henry's daily phone calls worked. In the fall of 1946, she rejoined him in New York. Even in exile, Henry let his habits lead him: He read "memos" late at night, kept them in a stack by his bedside, and rose early to telephone "aides" at dawn.

Although FDR had built the first presidential library at Hyde Park, in the winter following his death Henry took up a new project, helping to turn Springwood into a national historic site and organizing the Roosevelt Memorial library. But the venture, a reprisal of his father's project to honor Wilson, failed to fill his days.

His departure from Washington had been so abrupt, a rupture he struggled to surmount. "He was not the same man," his son Henry III would say. "He felt a loss beyond anything he could express." But the new chapter, Henry told himself, would bring what he needed most: time to restore his nerves, and resume a life with his family. He left Washington with goals—the work on FDR's library, and his own memoir—but with no long-range plan other than to live again on the farm. It would be a quiet life, removed from politics and immersed in the business of his orchards. Yet for all his professed wish to resume his old life as a gentleman farmer, Henry soon found himself drawn back to the fire.

||||

The diary scandal was the first interruption. In October 1946, William Shawn, editor of *The New Yorker*, published a scoop. Henry had entrusted Shawn, under the guise of a breezy Talk of the Town item, to reveal the existence of a Morgenthau "diary": 900 typewritten volumes "containing over 60 million words"—encompassing countless official documents, as well as the transcripts of his meetings and telephone calls, from nearly every day of the secretary's service from 1933 to 1945. It was a paper trail without precedent, and Henry had granted *The New Yorker* an exclusive preview. The "diary"—872 volumes, the *Times* soon corrected—now filled the shelves along three walls in Henry's makeshift office on Madison Avenue. A team of six researchers, directed by Professor Allan Nevins of Columbia University, were at work, condensing the volumes into "a workable source for *My Twelve Years in the Treasury*, a book of memoirs he plans to publish."

The ensuing news reports piqued interest on Capitol Hill. One scholar on the Nevins team, Jonathan Grossman, a thirty-one-year-old historian at City College, pronounced the diaries "candid and honest." "Mr. Morgenthau pulls no punches and does not try to hide his own mistakes," Grossman told the annual meeting of the American Historical Association. "But there is sufficient [evidence] in the Diary to lessen the reputation of important men and to provide a field day for Mr. Roosevelt's bitter opponents."

As his old critics and rivals in Washington cried foul, and Henry feigned astonishment, Truman asked John W. Snyder, the new man atop the Treasury, to investigate how the papers had left the department. Snyder, a close friend of the president, had succeeded Vinson in the summer of 1946, when Truman elevated Vinson to the Supreme Court. Snyder insisted that the documents, as federal property, be returned. Henry asked "for a little time to go into the matter." Smelling scandal, the press pounced. "Never had such a man," *Time* opined, "squirreled away so great a hoard of data against the long, cold winter of private life." Snyder questioned the legality of removing the papers, letting on that the diary had been bound at the Treasury.

Henry bluffed. His so-called "diaries," he said, "could more appropriately be called a scrapbook." Most of the papers, he said, were "photostats." He had embarked on a risky game. "President Roosevelt was a careful student of history," he told the press, "and firmly believed that those in public life owed a duty to the public to keep the material they had accumulated." Scholars, he offered, deserved the right to see the history that crossed his desk. Mrs. Klotz knew the truth. Roosevelt, in fact, had repeatedly asked his cabinet to abstain from taking notes in their meetings. The ban, naturally, led to meticulous recordkeeping, perhaps the most prodigious in presidential history. Ickes, Stimson, Wallace, Forrestal, even the agriculture secretary, Claude Wickard—they all kept detailed diaries. "The New Dealers," John Morton Blum would say, "were scared to death that if they didn't keep a record, someone would knife them in the back." None, however, approached the obsessive depths of Henry's.

Henry had, in fact, been mulling what to do with the "diary" for years. For a time, he thought he might open it to Joseph Gaer, the ghost-writer he'd engaged for a would-be official biography; he also thought of donating the papers to the National Archives. He did not, though, ever consider leaving them behind at the Treasury. Just how he managed to spirit nearly nine hundred volumes out of the Treasury building—a truck was required—never became known. Blum, the Yale historian who would spend more than a decade working with the records, attributed the transfer to a well-placed "consulting fee"—a poorly disguised bribe. (Jimmy Roosevelt, Blum learned, was the beneficiary.)

In his last months in Washington, Henry put a plan in motion. He would set up a private shop—historians, economists, and writers, culled from academia, Treasury, and State, who could troll the volumes, un-tangle the threads, and weave a history of his service to Roosevelt, and the country. Their brief: to publish a one-volume version of the secre-tary's memoirs. Henry was not interested in anything remotely personal, he said. The publication should consist only of his record in government: how he and Roosevelt propped up the banks, saved the farmers, and pulled the country out of the Depression; how he had helped prepare the country for war; how he had led the fight to save the last Jews of Europe; how he had been hastily dismissed by the man sitting in his best friend's seat in the White House.

In a clash of personalities and objectives, the project soon fell through. But Henry also came to a realization: He did not want to look too deeply into his own record. He "realized that he didn't want to live in the past," Mrs. Klotz would recall. "And he couldn't." Returning to the years with Roosevelt "was too painful."

Henry opted, instead, for a faster route—and one that circumvented any attempt at objectivity. In 1947, portions of the diaries started to emerge. That fall, Collier's ran a six-part series, a behind-the-scenes look at the hard-fought struggles of the Roosevelt White House: the battles against isolationists on Capitol Hill and greed on Wall Street, and with the generals and diplomats in Washington to prepare the country to fight the fascists and save the Jews of Europe. Each episode, not surprisingly, featured Henry at center stage. The articles caused a stir, but Henry was not done. In November, he upped the ante. He again mined the diaries to publish under his own name a four-part defense of the Morgenthau Plan in the *New York Post*—ghostwritten by a young historian, Arthur M. Schlesinger, Jr.

The debut of the Morgenthau Diaries, even in scrupulously edited glimpses, produced a sensation. Republicans and Democrats were less taken aback by the "exposés" than by the existence of such a massive trove of documents—the most detailed record, some ventured, of decision-making at the highest levels ever produced. Only a select few previews had been published, but politicians and historians were eager to see what else the diaries held—and former rivals from the Roosevelt years feared the secrets yet to be revealed.

Henry, though, considered his first foray into the limelight a success. He did not seek exoneration, only his rightful place in history. At last he had been permitted to make his case. The truth always comes out, he told friends. He gathered his team of writers and historians again, newly steeled in pursuit of redemption.

| | | |

Even as the diaries scandal seemed ready to fade, another ghost, Harry Dexter White, reappeared. By common consent White was a brilliant economist. But as John Morton Blum would say, "Anyone who ever met him could agree on only one thing: Harry White was a royal S.O.B." Henry Morgenthau, Jr., knew White as well as anyone in Washington. The economist had come to the Treasury in 1934 and stayed by Henry's side until the end, rising to assistant secretary. White had crafted the blueprints for the World Bank and the International Monetary Fund, yet in the years since his triumph at Bretton Woods, another storyline emerged. After the war, as Stalin turned from ally to adversary, a Red Scare gripped Washington—and White would soon gain infamy.

Elizabeth Bentley and Whittaker Chambers, two of the leading witnesses to Moscow's infiltration of the Roosevelt administration, had told congressional investigators, and successive rounds of FBI agents, of a double life. On November 7, 1945, in an FBI interview in New York, Bentley, who had acted as a spy courier in wartime Washington, said White had long been a source, and inside supporter, of the clandestine Soviet operation in Washington. For a time, the accusations disappeared into a well of silence. Six weeks later, on January 23, 1946, President Truman nominated White to be the executive director of the newly founded IMF, and on February 6, the Senate confirmed him. By then, though, the rumors had begun to circulate. In early December, FBI director J. Edgar Hoover had sent a memorandum to the White House, warning General Harry H. Vaughan, a military aide to Truman, of the accusations against White. After White's nomination, the FBI director attempted again to get word to the White House—warnings that Truman would later say reached him too late.

As the accusations went unheard, or unheeded, White assumed the post, but after a year in the new job, his health declined. In March 1947, he announced his resignation. Yet on June 19, White was still at the IMF when Truman's new attorney general, Tom Clark, announced an investigation into the Bentley accusations. Within days, White vacated his office.

By the summer of 1948, Hoover had delivered Bentley and Chambers to the House Special Committee on Un-American Activities (HUAC). On July 31, Bentley testified that White had been a conduit for secret information. Three years later, Bentley would repeat her claims, and exaggerate them in a sensational memoir, *Out of Bondage:* "I was able through Harry Dexter White," she wrote, "to arrange that the United States Treasury department turn the actual printing plates"—for the U.S. occupation currency—"over to the Russians!" Bentley never claimed to have met with White, nor could she offer any physical evidence. Chambers, though, did.

On August 3, 1948, Chambers testified that White had been a "fellow traveler," and given him government documents—four sheets of lined yellow paper, purportedly in White's handwriting. The pages were less a memorandum than a hodgepodge of notes from early 1938 gleaned from cables, internal documents, and the writer's own observations. Chambers stopped short of claiming that White had been in the Communist Party. The Treasury aide had proven to be a difficult character, and one of his least productive contacts. "His motives," Chambers would write, "always baffled me."

Ten days later, White himself sat before the congressmen. During the long summer of testimony, the stolid economist, bespectacled and balding, offered the most gripping performance. As J. Parnell Thomas, the HUAC chairman, led the charge, White pleaded that he was the victim of circumstances. The logic, he said, was simple to sum up: "a) There are Communists, b) I have many friends, and c) those friends might be Communists. I mean, that is silly."

White relished the confrontation. With each question, he counter-punched, refuting the accusations made by Bentley and Chambers. "He put HUAC on the defensive," his biographer, R. Bruce Craig, would write. The performance, though, would be most remembered for the moment when White recited his "American Creed." He had pulled a note from his suit coat, an ode to New Deal values that he recited aloud:

> I believe in freedom of religion, freedom of speech, freedom of thought, freedom of the press, freedom of criticism, and freedom of movement. I believe in the goal of equality of opportunity, and the right of each individual to follow the calling of his or her own choice, and the right of every individual to an opportunity to develop his or her capacity to the fullest. . . . I consider these principles sacred. I regard them as the basic fabric of our American way of life, and I believe in them as living realities, and not mere words on paper. That is my creed.
>
> These are the principles . . . I have been prepared to fight for in the past, and am prepared to defend at any time—with my life if need be.

When White had completed the dazzling rhetorical pirouette, the room broke into applause.

Four days later, Harry White was dead of a massive heart attack.

Watching it all—the barrage of charge and countercharge, the testimony, and the sudden death—Henry Morgenthau, Jr., was in shock. On the Hill, few had leveled any direct charges, and even the press—except for the most conservative columnists—had shown restraint. But Henry knew that each time his name was publicly uttered in the company of White's, the taint grew. He struggled to find a strategy to fend off suspicion, but he was floundering: He could not conceive that a spy ring had operated under his nose, nor could he bring himself to believe that White had worked for the Soviets. "White never did anything," he would say, to arouse his "slightest suspicion." Still, the fear tormented him. He canvassed the members of the old "9:30 club": None believed the allegations. Yet Henry kept silent; he did not publicly defend White in his hour of trial. He only drafted a letter, filled with rare emotion, to White's widow. "I was shocked to read in the newspapers of Harry's untimely death," he wrote.

> *I am sure you know how I feel about my association with Harry . . . but I want to try to put it into words in the hope that it*

*may be of some comfort to you at this time. . . . Starting with
Sept. 3, 1939, when England went to war with Germany, Harry
was ceaselessly doing his part to see that the United States would
have a preparedness program. . . .*

*After we got into the war, Harry was most helpful in seeing that
everything was done to wage war successfully against the enemy.*

*It was Harry and his associates who worked as a labor of love
on my book* Germany Is Our Problem. . . . *To sum it up, Harry was
a topflight public servant who served his country well. If I get
around to writing the real story of my life in the Treasury Harry
will occupy an important place in the book.*

Years later, Henry would fume when White's widow, Anne, released the
letter to the press. Yet even as he wrote, Henry knew the costs of the
scandal surrounding his former deputy would be enormous. If the spy
charges were proven, the fallout could be fateful. Relations with the Soviets, already darkening, were sure to worsen. And yet, in the first flush
of retirement, Henry allowed himself to think the White controversy was
an eclipse that would pass.

He faced a greater challenge: filling the emptiness of life after Roosevelt. "He didn't know what to do with himself," Mrs. Klotz would recall. "Nobody wanted him."

45. "No Sense of Proportion"

1946-1949

After nearly a year of solitude, Henry found a new calling.

The creation of a Jewish homeland would be his refuge. The entreaties had begun even before he'd left office, but in the spring of 1946, the line of unwanted suitors had become a parade. Meyer Weisgal, a short gruff Polish immigrant who had become the Zionist leader Chaim Weizmann's man in New York, arrived at Henry's office with an urgent plea. Someone was needed, he said, "to awaken the Jews of America." For the first time since he left Washington, Henry felt flattered. "He needed that affection just at that time," Mrs. Klotz would say, "because Wall Street wanted no part of him."

By the fall of 1946, the offer had become clear. The United Jewish Appeal (UJA) wanted Henry as its chairman. Since its founding in the wake of Kristallnacht, the UJA had been the chief fundraising machine for Jewish causes. It was a national organization, but one of several—and riven by internecine battles. The struggle was over priorities: whether American Jews should devote their efforts on behalf of their fellow Jews at home, repatriating those who had survived the horrors in Europe, or realize the long-awaited dream of building a new homeland in Palestine.

Henry had spent his life avoiding Jewish causes and feared becoming a pawn. His father's words weighed heavily. "Don't have anything to do with the Jews," Henry Sr. had told his son in one of his last admonishments. "They'll stab you in the back." For months, Henry vacillated. His suitors finally reassured him of their intentions. They wanted the Morgenthau name, but they also needed his managerial skill. The first challenge would be to forge a united front. In January 1947, Henry accepted the offer and became the new chairman of UJA.

Within weeks, he was back in Washington. Standing before several hundred Jewish leaders, with President Truman and General Eisenhower at his side, Henry announced a new fundraising campaign: The UJA was upping its annual goal to $170 million, money that would relieve the conditions of the Jews in Europe, the 1.5 million survivors. "There is no word that can exaggerate the urgency," General Eisenhower said. "Only one who has seen, as I have, the mental and physical effects of savagery, repression and bigotry upon the persecuted of Europe, can realize the full need for the material help." For Henry, it was a revival. He was back on the podium.

Henry put the appeal in plain language. The Jews of Europe had yet to find freedom. They remained in "camps," he said, as his brother-in-law, Herbert Lehman, who during the war had answered FDR's call to lead the refugee relief effort, listened in silence. Europe's Jews, robbed of their homes and property, cold and hungry, now languished in the Displaced Persons camps. Henry sketched the numbers: In 1946, given the strict quotas, only 26,000 Jews had legally reached Palestine, while at the same time, the number of Jewish DPs had swelled from 85,000 to a quarter of a million. The United Nations, he went on, was failing in its job. The U.N. teams were restricted to the DP camps in Germany, Austria, and Italy; in Hungary, the UJA would have to be the primary provider, feeding more than half of the country's surviving 200,000 Jews. Who could answer the call? Only those who had the means to offer relief: the Jews of America.

In March 1947, Henry took to the road, touring the country at breakneck speed. In seven days he delivered speeches in seven cities. He also helped fashion a new technique: "card-calling." The evenings would be called "big gift" dinners; guests would be asked to fill out pledge cards, and then be called on to stand and read the cards aloud. The ploy played on the pride (and guilt) of American Jews, and it worked.

For years, as he led the war bond drives, Henry had learned the art of the sale. He could stick to a script, even force a smile for the cameras. But now he spoke off the cuff, and from the heart. Before one appearance, he was warned that the audience "would never part with a dime." It was not a large crowd, no more than a hundred people. "He made a speech and I looked around," Mrs. Klotz recalled. "Icicles sitting in each seat." But when he had finished speaking, he did something new. He approached the tables. He put his arm around one man, and said, "I know you will contribute." "Oh yes," came the reply. "I'll give $5,000." Henry worked the entire room. "They raised a fortune," Mrs. Klotz said.

The checks got bigger. In one night in Dallas, he pulled in $650,000. In New Orleans, he coaxed $250,000 from Edgar Stern, the heir to a cotton fortune who had married a Rosenwald, an heiress to the Sears, Roebuck fortune. In Richmond, Atlanta, and Houston, Henry doubled the previous year's totals. A month later, Henry hopscotched from St. Louis to Omaha to Wilkes-Barre in three days. He didn't know it, but his pleas carried an echo of his grandfather Lazarus of more than half a century earlier. The aggressive techniques once deployed in the service of suspect nineteenth-century philanthropy would now be used to build the new homeland.

| | | |

It was one thing to force a semblance of unity at the UJA, but Washington remained an island of intransigence. Years later, once the State of Israel had come into being, and its bloody birth—the war Israelis call "the War of Liberation" and Palestinians call "al-Nakba," the Disaster— receded from memory, politicians and propagandists on all sides would say that without Harry Truman there never would have been an Israel. Since 1939, they would note, Palestine's fate had been frozen in limbo. Roosevelt had never committed to a firm position. He could promise in his final months that "full justice will be done to those who seek a Jewish home." But he had long taken care to reassure the Arabs that no postwar plan would be set without their consultation.

By 1947, though, as the full horrors of the Holocaust emerged, the pendulum had swung to the Zionists. It was not only the welfare of the 600,000 Jews of Palestine. Where else could the survivors of the Nazi camps find refuge?

The trouble, as Henry knew well, was that Truman could not stand the Zionists. In 1944, he had broken with his party, declining to back the Democrats' pro-Zionist platform. Truman was known, as well, to make wisecracks at the expense of Jews. "Jesus Christ couldn't please them when he was here on earth," Henry Wallace quoted Truman as saying in a July 1946 cabinet meeting, "so how could anyone expect that I would have any luck?"

Henry Morgenthau tried to get Truman's ear, but was rarely granted more than a cursory meeting. He had, though, won accommodations.

Before he was kicked out of the cabinet, as reports mounted about the miseries of the U.S.-run DP camps in Germany, Henry pushed for an investigation. He got Truman to accept a proposal to send Earl Harrison, dean of the University of Pennsylvania Law School and a former U.S. immigration commissioner, on a fact-finding mission to Germany. By all accounts, Harrison's findings, submitted in August 1945, deeply moved Truman. Conditions in the camps were wretched, the president wrote in a letter to General Eisenhower, enclosing the Harrison report.

"'We appear to be treating the Jews,'" Truman wrote, quoting Harrison, "'as the Nazis treated them except that we do not exterminate them.'"

At Potsdam, Truman had ventured further. He came out in support of resettling Holocaust survivors—as many as 100,000, the figure Harrison recommended—in Palestine. But Truman hated nothing so much as pressure, especially from someone now out of government. In his diary, Truman revealed his true feelings. "Had ten minutes conversation with Henry Morgenthau about Jewish ship in Palistine [sic]," reads an entry. "Told him I would talk to Gen[eral George] Marshall about it." (In January 1947, Marshall had taken over the helm of the State Department.)

Henry had called Truman to discuss the *Exodus 1947,* the ship bearing 4,515 Jewish refugees bound for Palestine that the British Navy had rammed and boarded days earlier. After reaching Haifa, the British forced the refugees—including 655 children—onto three prison ships, and sent them to Cyprus, ostensibly for a holding period before they could enter Palestine. Instead, they were locked in cages below deck, and returned to Europe. Truman was outraged at the audacity of Henry's attempt at lobbying. "He'd no business, whatever to call me," Truman wrote after he hung up. "The Jews have no sense of proportion nor do they have any judgement on world affairs."

The president could not control his anger, venting his frustration in his diary. "The Jews, I find are very, very selfish. They care not

how many Estonians, Latvians, Finns, Poles, Yugoslavs or Greeks get murdered or mistreated as DP as long as the Jews get special treatment. Yet when they have power, physical, financial or political neither Hitler nor Stalin has anything on them for cruelty or mistreatment to the underdog.

Put an underdog on top and it makes no difference whether his name is Russian, Jewish, Negro, Management, Labor, Mormon,

Baptist he goes haywire. I've found very, very few who remember their past condition when prosperity comes.

It was an extraordinary outpouring—equating vengeful Jews with Hitler and Stalin—but the private words reflected a belief that Truman did not elsewhere conceal. "I fear very much that the Jews are like all underdogs," he wrote Eleanor Roosevelt that August. "When they get on top they are just as intolerant and as cruel as the people were to them when they were underneath." Unfortunately for Henry, Truman saw him as the embodiment of the overzealous and misguided Jew.

On the question of a Jewish homeland, Truman would grow increasingly exasperated. In November 1947, the U.N. debated Resolution 181, a plan, years in the making, that would end the British Mandate and partition Palestine into a Jewish and an Arab state. The Zionists hoped to sway the last of the fence-sitters. Chaim Weizmann met with the French, while Henry worked the New Zealanders—and every friendly contact he still claimed among the world's prime ministers and finance ministers. The lobbying, until the final hour, was unrelenting. "I don't think I've ever had as much pressure put on the White House," Truman wrote. On November 29, when the General Assembly approved the resolution, Henry sent the president an exultant telegram, expressing his gratitude. Truman recoiled. "I wish you would caution all your friends," he wrote Henry, "who are interested in the welfare of the Jews of Palestine that now is the time for restraint and caution." The U.N. vote, Truman went on, "is only the beginning and the Jews must now display tolerance and consideration for other peoples in Palestine with whom they will necessarily have to be neighbors."

Within days, General Marshall announced that the United States would embargo all arms shipments to the Middle East. At the U.N. and in New York, the factions were pleased. But in Palestine, as the Arab League and the Arabs of Palestine rejected the resolution, the conditions were set for war.

||||

Nearly three years out of office, Henry Morgenthau had become something he had spent most of his life avoiding: a power broker in the American Jewish community. In early 1948, he played host to Goldie Meyerson—later famous as Golda Meir, then the little-known head of the Political Department of the Jewish Agency, the would-be Foreign

Ministry of the would-be state. She arrived in New York on an emergency mission, without luggage or a dollar in her pocketbook, only a winter coat shielding her dress.

Henry would offer access to a new money pool: the "White Jews," as Henry Montor, a UJA leader, called the German Jews, many of them non-Zionists. With Henry's help, Meyerson addressed the Council of Federations and Welfare Funds' annual conference in Chicago. It was not a Zionist organization, and its leaders were not particularly supportive of a Jewish Palestine. The group, in fact, had opposed putting Meyerson on the conference schedule. To her audience in Chicago, the visitor was unknown, yet they listened rapt as she reported on Israel's urgent struggle with the Arabs.

America's Jews "cannot decide whether we will fight or not," Meyerson said, but they could decide if "we will be victorious." She recounted a recent ambush. Thirty-five Jewish boys had tried to rescue a settlement besieged by Arabs. Unable to use the roads, they had skirted the surrounding Arab villages, crossing the hills on foot at night. "They fought for over seven hours, fought back hundreds of Arabs, fought to the very end." Every one of the boys was killed. The story—its details, she said, came "from an Arab"—had a coda. "The last one was killed with a stone in his hand. He had no ammunition left." Within days, a new UJA slogan appeared in a full-page advertisement in the *Times*. The ad featured a drawing of a young man laid low under a stark headline: "After Seven Hours . . . he died with a stone in his hand."

Publicly, Henry Morgenthau would couch the purpose of Meyerson's visit in terms of relief and resettlement, but Ben-Gurion had sent his emissary with one goal in mind: to raise money for arms. It fell to Henry to sway the fundraisers. Moe Levitt, one of the heads of the Joint Distribution Committee (JDC), was blunt: "We can't get involved in this." To head off a crisis, a meeting of the elders was called in New York. Henry sat beside Meyerson at the table, and they were joined by Jonah Wise, Bill Rosenwald, Edward Warburg, Levitt, and Montor. The five men controlled, in effect, the three largest Jewish groups in America. After Meyerson now again made her pitch, Rosenwald repeated Levitt's concern: The UJA, he said, could never get involved in arms purchases; any such move would destroy the group's hard-earned credibility among their own citizens. As he spoke, Montor noticed that "tears began to roll from the eyes of Golda Meyerson." She knew Rosenwald's sway among American Jews.

Henry Morgenthau had heard enough. "I feel just as deeply about America as you do," he said. "I tried to serve my country. But the United Jewish Appeal is here for the purpose of saving the Jewish people, and we can't save the Jewish people unless the Jews in Palestine are able to defend themselves. . . . If Golda Meyerson says that they have to have arms and we are the only place where they can get the money to buy the arms, I'm afraid, Bill, you'll have to accept my decision."

There would be no more debate. What he had done for France and England before the war, Henry would now do for the Jews of Palestine. If arms, munitions, and military equipment were needed for the Haganah, the Yishuv's underground military organization since 1920, the Jewish Agency would get them. Meyerson returned to Israel on March 19 with $50 million—twice the amount Ben-Gurion had requested. The money, as Golda Meir recounted in her memoirs, was "turned over at once for the Haganah's secret purchase of arms in Europe."

The intervening months saw the turning point in the civil war that had raged since the U.N. Resolution. The British, facing the flood of illegal immigrants and the rising terrorist attacks, had decamped. By May 14, the Jewish Agency made it formal: The Yishuv had become the State of Israel. The next day, as long expected, the Arab forces—legionnaires and irregulars from Transjordan, Egypt, Syria, Lebanon, Iraq, and Saudi Arabia—invaded the country.

| | | |

By October, Henry was in Israel. On his first trip to the Holy Land, he came under the wing of Weizmann and Ben-Gurion, and witnessed the arrival of the survivors, the DPs who had made the long journey across closed borders to Palestine. Ben-Gurion and Weizmann treated Henry royally. Both spoke of his father. Ben-Gurion had grown fond of retelling how Henry Sr. had saved his life in 1914—intervening when the Turks had taken the young Zionist prisoner and threatened him with execution—and Weizmann did his best to forget his distaste for Wilson's former ambassador. Weizmann found the son warm, if not brilliant. A far more capable man, he would tell aides, than his pompous old man.

Henry was determined to see as much of the land and the front as possible. Ben-Gurion sent Yigael Yadin, the young archaeologist who had become chief of operations for the Haganah, to serve as tour guide. Each day, Ben-Gurion set the itinerary. "Morgenthau wants to visit," the prime minister wrote in his diary, "Jerusalem, the Negev, and the arms industries." They traveled the "Burma Road," a makeshift road cut through the craggy hills around Jerusalem, and nicknamed after the road the Allies cut around Japanese positions from Burma to China during World War II. They stooped low through trenches and scrambled through a dark tunnel to glimpse the Arab-occupied Old City. One afternoon, they visited the Cathedral of Notre Dame. While inside, two mortar shells fell sixty feet off. Amid the exchange of gunfire that followed, the Haganah minders rushed the party away.

At dinner that night, Henry pleased his hosts. Many around the world, he said, opposed including Jerusalem in the Jewish state: the Arabs, the heads of the Christian churches, even his own government. But he vowed to fight. "After traveling over the Burma," he said, "I am convinced more than ever there can be no State of Israel without a Jewish Jerusalem."

As the days passed, Henry sounded a different, deeply personal note. In Tel Aviv, he joined Ben-Gurion at the prime minister's residence on Simchat Torah, the first celebration of the holiday (marking the end of the year's Torah readings) since Israeli statehood. Days earlier, the Israeli forces had taken the Negev town of Beersheba and were sweeping across the northern border into Lebanon. The victories brought the crowds into the streets. Hearing the noise, Ben-Gurion led Henry out of his house. The crowds engulfed them, holding aloft Torahs and banners. Henry attempted to join the singing and dancing. He understood little of the day's religious significance, but was caught up in its emotion. In his diary, Ben-Gurion wrote of his guest: "He is a naïve, decent, and good Jew." As few among those standing nearby failed to notice, Henry was wiping away tears.

Everywhere in Israel, Henry felt the echoes of the past. In Haifa, he saw the masses coming off the overcrowded boats from Cyprus. The refugees, he said, "looked more like animals than human beings": "If there were 12,000 cats or dogs being treated like the Jews are in Cyprus," he said, "the world would rise up in protest." The scenes, he kept saying, reminded him of his father's time in Turkey. The Armenians were no different, he said. Oppressed people deserved a homeland.

On one of his last days in Israel, the convoy stopped in the desert. They pulled off the narrow road leading from Tel Aviv, just before it began the climb through the Judean Hills toward Jerusalem. It was a chill day, early in the afternoon. The settlers had been at work since before dawn. By noon, the frames of two houses had emerged, the rough beginnings of a *moshav*—an agricultural collective—beside the ruins of an Arab village. Weizmann and Ben-Gurion announced a surprise: The settlement, one of thirty-two in their new campaign, would be named in honor of their American guest: Tal Shahar, or Morning Dew—"Morgenthau" in Hebrew.

| | | |

After years of illness and failed treatments for a growing list of ailments that defied diagnosis, Ellie ate little, slept poorly, and could not concentrate for long. By the summer of 1949, the pain had become severe, and constant. On Wednesday, August 31, she entered the New York Hospital. It was the liver this time, the doctors said. Throughout that first week, the family maintained hope. It was nothing new, the children told themselves; she had not felt well all summer. By the weekend, though, her condition worsened; by Sunday night, Ellie was acutely ill.

Henry scarcely left her bedside—and then he, too, became a patient in the hospital. Nine days after his wife checked in, he had nearly collapsed during an emergency meeting of the UJA. The family put out a cover story: Mrs. Morgenthau was suffering from "pneumonia," and her husband had entered the hospital with "suspicion of pneumonia." In truth, Henry, in a room down the corridor from his Ellie, was suffering shortness of breath and heart palpitations—the result, the doctors said, of extreme stress. As they continued to monitor his heart, a new press release was issued: The former secretary would be "discharged," but remain as "a guest in the hospital." Their mother's condition worsening, the children took turns by her bed. That summer, Joan had been interning at Maimonides Hospital in Brooklyn, but came as often as she could and stayed as long as possible. Ellie lay in an oxygen tent, suffering abdominal and chest pain. She had not only thrombosis but a bloated abdomen. At last, years late, it was becoming clear: Ellie was suffering from a rare and acute blood disease: Budd-Chiari syndrome. "I diagnosed it," Joan would say. "Fluid in the abdomen. That was the final clue."

On September 21, after three weeks in the hospital, at fifty-seven, Ellie died.

At Emanu-El, more than a thousand people filled the pews, but Henry Morgenthau, Jr., did not speak. Eleanor Roosevelt delivered the eulogy. The organist played Sibelius, the choir sang a setting of a John Donne poem, and a young soprano from the Met, a beneficiary of Ellie's largesse, sang Mendelssohn. Mrs. Roosevelt, dressed in layers of black, called her an uncommon friend, and a champion of all the right causes in the world. She spoke in rare intimate terms. She told of her friend's regret: how in recent years, her health failing, Ellie could not maintain the pace. She recalled the early days, the campaign tours upstate, the speeches at the women's clubs, the camaraderie of their work at Civil Defense. "She would have wanted to give every ounce of her strength to help do the things of the world which she felt it was important to do," Eleanor said.

To the Morgenthau children, Mrs. Roosevelt would agree with Henry, confiding a private belief: The war had taken their mother. To the audience, she spoke of love. Ellie, she said, "gave of her worldly good with generosity, but what she gave without stint was herself and her own affections and love. And that is what those of us who loved her are grateful for today."

Once again, as she had so often done in interceding on his behalf with FDR, Mrs. Roosevelt found the words that Henry Morgenthau, Jr., could not.

46. "A Little Righteous Indignation"

1948-1952

At Yale Law School, in early 1946, Bob Morgenthau joined a class of young men, sudden adults—the victors of the struggle against fascism. Some had been at Guadalcanal, or with the Office of Strategic Services (OSS, a wartime intelligence agency) in Europe, or in signal intelligence in Japanese waters. Some had even served on neighboring ships, fought in the same campaigns, along the same front lines. Yet to a man, no one spoke of his service. No one asked, "Where were you?" "What did you do?" "How did you make it out?" Their war stories had yet to become memories.

It was "such a quiet time," Louise Ransom, one of Bob and Martha's closest friends at Yale, would say. The homecoming brought a slowing down, and a suspension of fear. It was an abrupt return to living on a narrow scale, caring about the simple concerns forfeited to the war. At the same time, they drew a bolt across the years of military service—locking it away, while their wives, eager to move on, did all they could, or so they imagined, to hasten a return to normalcy.

Yale Law had long attracted the brightest graduates of the Ivies, but Bob's classmates stood apart. Years later, professors would look back and marvel: Dozens of Yale Law graduates from the first postwar classes had become eminent scholars, politicians, federal judges, high-ranking members of government. One became mayor of New York, another a Supreme Court justice. For Bob, though, the years at Yale were not about sitting with the tall stacks of casebooks. He and Martha had gone through the years of war as if through a snowstorm—head down, feet forward, rarely lifting their eyes to the future. At Yale, he would absorb the concepts of the law—and be taught by giants of constitutional law, contracts, and labor law. (William O. Douglas presided at moot court; Felix Frankfurter came to speak.) But Bob did not immerse himself in the arcana of statutes and regulations. He joined an exclusive eating club, Corbey Court—effectively ending its unwritten Gentiles-only policy. "At Corbey," a classmate would write at the time, evenings "always happily concluded in the masculine atmosphere of cigar smoke and beer." In joining the club, and quietly recruiting other Jewish students, Morgenthau helped to "knock out one quite divisive institution in the law school," recalled another classmate, Lou Pollak, who would later become dean of Yale Law. There would be exams, but years later few would recall ever seeing Bob in the library. The years in New Haven offered, instead, a chance at a delayed beginning, a respite to begin to come back to life.

Bob walked into his first class three days before Jenny's first birthday. He and Martha would stay in New Haven only two years—it was an accelerated course for veterans—but for the first time they made a home of their own. They arrived with one child, and left with two. A second daughter, Annie, was born in April 1947, and the Morgenthaus settled on the northern edge of town, in North Haven. They bought a modest two-bedroom home, for $11,000—borrowing the money from Bob's mother.

During the war the law school had nearly closed—enrollment sank to a low of fifteen students (women and wounded, chiefly)—but now the veterans came flooding back. Most were married, and lived in a Quonset "colony"—rows of huts Yale had set up in the fields around the Yale Bowl. If the law school was a narrow community, Bob and Martha, living outside of town, saw their world close even tighter, to revolve around two other families: the Ransoms and the Whites.

Bob Ransom, who now lived around the corner with his wife, Louise, had been friends with Bob Morgenthau since Deerfield. A fellow New Yorker, and the son of a corporate lawyer, Ransom came from a Republican, Presbyterian family in Westchester County, north of the city. He'd also gone to Amherst, where "the two Bobs" were inseparable. Ransom was one of two classmates invited to the White House for Joan's coming-out. The war, and marriage, had intervened; but the friendship endured.

Bob Ransom had spent a semester at Yale before entering the Army. At Fort Bliss in El Paso, he had married Louise, a Vassar girl four years ahead of Joan Morgenthau. Louise Ransom knew little of her husband's war—only that he had survived narrow escapes and ended up a captain in the OSS. A succession of base postings had followed, and two children had been born, before Ransom returned to Yale Law. Louise, with her intelligence and candor, became fast friends with Martha.

"We were partners," she would say, "in almost everything we did."

If Yale brought a reunion with an old schoolmate, it would also unite Bob Morgenthau with a new friend, Byron White. Tall, handsome, and with muscles that his boxy suits could not hide, White stood out. To most at Yale, and football fans across the country, he was known as "Whizzer." Bob never used the nickname; White disliked it, and urged friends to abandon it. They had met on the first day of term, and Bob had found White a house for rent down the street in North Haven. Byron White and his longtime girlfriend, Marion Stearns, completed the trio of young couples. The Ransoms already knew Byron and Marion—she had been a classmate of Louise's at Vassar. By June, White and Marion were married.

At first blush, White seemed Morgenthau's near opposite. Raised in the rural north of Colorado, White had come from a hardscrabble Episcopalian family. He grew up amid cattle ranches, fields of sugar beets and wheat, and little else. The Depression left many in White's generation without prospects, but he had made it to Denver on a scholarship to the University of Colorado. White had starred in baseball and basketball, but football was his real sport. In 1937, he'd led the nation in scoring and rushing—and in his senior year, he carried Colorado to an unbeaten season, and the Cotton Bowl. His team lost, but he was MVP of the game. "Whizzer" White had become a national star.

In the classroom, he was equally spectacular: Phi Beta Kappa, valedictorian, and a Rhodes scholar. He was headed for Oxford when the Pittsburgh Pirates (later, the Steelers) dangled a salary of $15,000—an unprecedented sum—for a single season. White postponed his graduate study for a term, opting to try professional football. During the 1938 season, he led the league in rushing—and in 1939, he went to Oxford. After nine months in England, he'd come home and enrolled at Yale Law. White would interrupt his studies a second time, joining the Detroit Lions. In 1940, he led the league in rushing, and he played a second season—commuting on weekends from Yale. Once Pearl Harbor came, though, he joined the Navy.

White and Morgenthau were at Yale together only two terms, but they formed an immediate kinship. Both had survived the Pacific. White had served at Okinawa; he had been aboard the *Bunker Hill* when the kamikazes nearly sank it. They shared, too, a disposition that some mistook for snobbishness. In White's case, it was a misapprehension, bred, as one reporter would note, by his "total incapacity for carrying on, or enduring, small talk." They were alike, too, in their quiet geniality, but neither White nor Morgenthau suffered fools. Each kept his circle of intimates to a chosen few.

In his second year, Bob settled on labor law. He studied under Harry Shulman, who had umpired the infamous labor disputes between the Ford Motor Company and the United Auto Workers. Bob enlisted John Lindsay, another classmate and Navy veteran from Manhattan, to help organize a labor law conference, using a campus forum to lure big-name speakers. But his interests soon drifted. As Byron White stayed late after seminars, eager to engage the great minds at every chance, Bob was more likely to be spending his afternoons on the tennis courts.

Decades later, Bob would say, without a trace of humor, that he'd learned only one thing at Yale: "You have to read the statute." The advice had come from J. W. Moore, a leader of the Legal Realism movement and author of the thirty-four-volume *Moore's Federal Practice*. To Moore, a self-described "country boy" with a Montana drawl, it was a mantra: Read the law, and always return to it. It was singular wisdom that Bob employed to get through his studies. The first term was rough, but for the remainder of his time at Yale, as he would say, "I coasted."

Bob Morgenthau would graduate in the bottom half—46th in a class of 80.

||||

"After the war," for nearly everyone in America, had become the marker. Since the end of the fighting, sleep came more readily and car trips in the countryside ceased to be a luxury. The future had come closer. For the Morgenthaus, though, even the two brothers who had returned from the Pacific and Europe, the time marker was "After Washington." In the first years of his father's return to New York, Bob watched as he stumbled to find his way again. Yet he and his siblings struggled to help him. They all faced their own distractions—and Bob had obligations. He and Martha, and their two little girls, Jenny and Annie, were in the throes of a new life. He'd always seen politics as an inevitable turn—that Bob go into politics, Joan would say, was "assumed from birth." But as he finished up law school, he had not yet made up his own mind. Political office would have to wait.

After his last exams, Bob had made the rounds at the big firms downtown. At Winthrop, Stimson, Putnam, and Roberts, they spoke of afternoon tea and charity work, and warned that they did not usually "see people off the street. . . . Normally, we have people entered at birth." The partner raised the question of Morgenthau's "origins," wondering why he did not seek out a firm "in the green goods business"—finance. Sullivan & Cromwell, he suggested, the white-shoe firm that had opened its partnership to Jews, would seem "a good fit."

Most of the interviews ended sharply when Bob spoke of his interest in public service. "I'd like to do some good," he told the managing partner at Paul Weiss. "I'd like to, as well," came the reply. "But I want associates who can work late at night, so I can go home for dinner—maybe then I'll have time to think about public service."

Robert P. Patterson, the former federal judge who'd served at the War Department since 1940, and Henry Morgenthau, Jr., had enjoyed a Washington alliance. They had joined forces to fight for military preparedness in the early days when "Woodring's blankets" were deemed sufficient support of the Army. Patterson had been the secretary's partner at the Pentagon, and Henry had brought him onto the board of the Modern Industrial Bank. But they had never been close. The secretary's son arrived at the door of Patterson, Belknap and Webb on his own terms, drawn by the judge's legal brilliance, renowned independent streak, and faith in public service. Patterson himself had only returned from Washington in February 1948. Bob joined the firm two months later.

Born upstate in rural Glens Falls, New York, Bob Patterson was raised among farmers and lumberjacks. He graduated from Union College in Schenectady, then went to Harvard Law. He had excelled in the first class taught by Felix Frankfurter, been elected editor in chief of the law review, and graduated tops in his class. In 1915, he joined the famous New York City firm of Root, Clark, Buckner and Howland.

By the 1920s, Patterson had won a national reputation. He helped found his own firm, and twice turned down a chance to return to Harvard Law as dean. In 1930, President Hoover had named him to the federal bench, to succeed Thomas Day Thacher in the Southern District of New York. In 1939, Roosevelt promoted him to the Second Circuit Court of Appeals. Patterson was that rare political figure, a Republican so staunchly independent and undaunted by patronage that both parties revered him. Yet neither controlled him. "The establishment claimed the Judge," Morgenthau would say, "but he was never part of it."

As Stimson's deputy at the War Department—he'd been promoted to undersecretary not long after his arrival—Patterson proved a demanding boss. He pushed his staff to the edge, as he wrote in a memoir discovered decades after his death. They "would never do more than admit that 'the impossible takes a little longer.'" Patterson led the drive to raise an army of 3.5 million men, and the race to equip them. "When I look back across those crowded five years," he wrote, "it sometimes seems a miracle to me that we won the war." He had spent $100 billion, overseeing all fronts of domestic production, everything from the atomic bomb to the laces for the GIs' shoes—the "shit-kickers," he called them, that he wore long after the war's end. He had done it all without ego, and without scandal.

Patterson would never speak of it, but he had nearly joined the Supreme Court. The appointment was even announced, but Stimson had just resigned as secretary of war and Walter Reuther called Truman, vetoing McCloy as a replacement for Stimson. Truman instead tapped Patterson, offering him a deal: "You're going to become Secretary of War," he promised, "and then get the next vacancy" on the Supreme Court.

If he had any regret, Judge Patterson never let it be known. Two years later, Truman wanted to appoint him as the first secretary of defense, but after seven years in the War Department, Patterson did not wish to assume a position that he'd helped to create. "Never," wrote Truman, "have I accepted a resignation with more poignant regret." The judge returned to New York City. Time and again his name was floated for high office: mayor, senator, or governor. But in 1948, he joined Chauncey Belknap and Vanderbilt Webb's firm, creating Patterson, Belknap and Webb (PBW).

Morgenthau considered himself absurdly lucky: Almost from the first, he knew it would be the apprenticeship of a lifetime. Bob would serve less as an associate at PBW than as the judge's personal law clerk. Patterson served on corporate boards and carried a full load of federal cases. He also routinely argued before the Supreme Court: Within months of his arrival, Bob, though not yet admitted to the bar, would find himself drafting briefs to be filed in Washington.

Patterson and Bob Morgenthau established an easy rhythm. Often, they worked late into the night. There were weekends, too, at the judge's farm, seventy acres along the Hudson in Garrison, New York. Patterson would introduce everyone who came to visit. Bob met the doughboys, five veterans of the Argonne, whom the judge credited with saving his life, and watched in silence as he passed them envelopes of cash. (Not all, he would say, had weathered the years as well as he.) In the firm, the closeness between tutor and disciple did not go unnoticed. It was as if, they would say, the judge had found a second son.

| | |

Bob and Martha called it their "lucky strike"—winning an apartment in the new cluster of red-brick mid-rise buildings on East Twentieth Street and First Avenue in Manhattan. The Morgenthaus were among the first to move into Peter Cooper Village, which had only opened in 1947. The apartment was small, but at $120 a month a bargain. The city planners hailed the complex, later to be joined by the Peter Stuyvesant buildings, as a by-product of America's triumph in the war: a gigantic housing project built during the war years for union workers and veterans, and set aside for the middle class. Still, the complex was exclusive—and "no Blacks" was an unwritten rule.

The nest would not last long. Peter Cooper Village enforced a strict rule: Only two children were allowed. But in the spring of 1951, when Jenny was six years old and Annie four, a third daughter was born: Elinor Gates Morgenthau. The Morgenthaus would be forced to move—to Riverdale, the leafy neighborhood overlooking the Hudson just north of Manhattan. It was the Bronx, but in name only. Long a Republican stronghold, Riverdale was a realm of the wealthy. Its prewar houses, outsized and judiciously varied, remained separated by green, and spread at a remove from the postwar apartment blocks, low and humble, that lined the main thoroughfares. The Morgenthaus' house was nearly five thousand square feet, at the heart of a tangle of quaint streets lined with trees. A short walk from the steep banks of the river, it stood on the same street as the mansion where in the 1920s Joe Kennedy had parked his brood.

Each weekday morning, Bob commuted down the West Side Highway to his office at PBW, on the forty-third floor of the granite skyscraper at One Wall Street. The firm comprised only eight associates and eight formidable partners, and Morgenthau would learn more "from them than in all the classes at Yale Law." A big case came almost at once: In 1946 and 1947, a host of wealthy stockholders had filed a flurry of lawsuits against Twentieth Century Fox, the Hollywood giant, and its chain of cinemas. The suits charged securities fraud—an insiders' sale of stock, by which unseemly means the company's own chief executives had made a killing. The chief targets were the Skouras brothers, Charles, Spyros, and George, the Greek-Americans who'd founded the company in 1935 but still ran the now-sprawling conglomerate as a family shop.

Patterson represented Charlie Skouras, eldest of the brothers, and the executive at the heart of the dispute. (In the suspect stock deal, Charlie had made $4,281,000.) He put Morgenthau in the middle of the case, asking him to prepare a list of possible questions their client would likely face in an upcoming deposition. They met with Skouras in the comfort of his own Midtown office, rather than in the firm's conference room. The brothers' accents remained thick.

"Don't aska me all dees questions," Charlie said, as they worked their way through the possible questions. "It's all Greek to me."

"Very funny," Patterson said. "Just don't dare try that in the deposition."

Days later, as the deposition was postponed, Patterson told his young assistant, "You can handle this, Bob"—and turned to another case.

Three months out of law school, and Morgenthau was up against some of the most prominent lawyers in the country. Sam Rosenman, FDR's former speechwriter, represented the company and National Theatres. Milton Pollack, a brilliant lawyer known for aggressive posturing, was lead counsel for the plaintiffs. Pollack was "all elbows," a colleague would recall. Once during a deposition in Spyros's office, without asking, he took a cigar from a humidor—and lit it. Skouras fumed: "Mr. Pollack, I don't remember offering you a cigar."

"Those aren't your cigars," Pollack replied, "those are the stockholders' cigars."

It fell to Bob to learn what he could about the origins of the company. Charlie had been the first to come over from Greece, settling in St. Louis, where he had worked as a hotel dishwasher before embarking on a meteoric rise in Hollywood. Bob would spend days with Skouras, walking him back to the 1930s. Charlie loved to tell the old stories, but one afternoon in the course of reminiscing about the earliest days, he dropped a bombshell. From the beginning, he and his brothers had divvied up all earnings according to a secret agreement—"50 percent of everything goes to me," Charlie explained to Morgenthau matter-of-factly. "Spyros and George, they get 25 percent each." What was once a family business had long since become a giant conglomerate, but not only did the off-the-books formula continue to govern their operations, the brothers had failed to disclose it in the requisite filings with the Securities and Exchange Commission (SEC).

Morgenthau could not believe it: "It meant one thing. Fraud." The surprise admission left the brothers open, at the least, to a charge of filing false corporate documents. A settlement, a surprise to all, soon followed.

Decades later, Pollack, who went on to serve as a distinguished federal judge and had since retired, confronted Morgenthau. "Boy, did I take you to the cleaners on Twentieth Century Fox," he said.

"Milton, you're old enough to know," Morgenthau replied, and spilled the brothers' secret deal. "You got taken, not me."

| | | |

Judge Patterson, in a city of grandstanding defense lawyers, was an outlier. A quiet moral stance, he'd learned, could often suffice to put people on notice. "A little righteous indignation," he would tell Bob, "can be a big help."

In September 1948, months into his apprenticeship, Bob saw Patterson become one of the few Wall Street lawyers to take on HUAC, the House Committee on Un-American Activities. As president of the city bar association, he presided at a forum that condemned the hearings, seconding a law professor who termed HUAC "an example of the inquisitorial system run riot." The judge would also take on so-called "loyalty cases," defending those caught in the sights of Senator Joseph McCarthy, coming to the aid of both the celebrated (actor Edward G. Robinson) and the unknown (Dorothy Kenyon, a former New York magistrate).

Patterson's involvement came with personal consequences: In the summer of 1947, he himself came under attack. Republican congressman George Dondero of Michigan—he had served as mayor of Royal Oak, Father Coughlin's town—had named ten former War Department men as "Communist sympathizers," charging that Patterson had failed "to ferret them out." Many of the men Dondero accused were Jewish, and two were former Treasury men: Josiah DuBois, then a prosecutor at Nuremberg, and Colonel Bernie Bernstein. The undercurrent was clear: Their association with Henry Morgenthau, Jr., newly under a cloud for relying on Harry White, carried a taint.

Patterson, though, had little time for politics. He insisted instead on maintaining an old-fashioned sense of "duty," especially when it concerned the obligations of citizenship. When Walter Rice, general counsel of Reynolds Metals, one of the firm's top clients, asked him to represent J. Louis Reynolds, the company's vice president and a son of the aluminum giant's founder, he refused. The Internal Revenue Service was investigating Reynolds, but Rice assured Patterson there was nothing to it.

"Walter, if what you say is true, you do not need me," Patterson said. "And if it isn't true, I don't want to represent him."

The judge was willing to represent unpopular clients, but he believed that taxes were "the price to pay for civilization."

| | | |

It evolved naturally, not by plan, but Bob and the judge became close. In the country, they were neighbors, too—their family farms fifteen miles apart. Each fall, Patterson would take Bob to the Army-Navy football game. At the same time, Bob was keeping his father at arm's length. He and Henry Jr. remained close—"My father," he would say, "was my best friend"—yet as the war receded, a wall emerged between them. He continued to admire his father, and respect him. But even if he did not recognize it at the time, Bob had set a new boundary. As the 1950s opened, he still came to his father with news—Martha's doings, or the children's. But no longer did he consult him—"not on family matters, not on private matters," he would say. "And sure as hell, not on anything to do with the law or politics."

Each day, instead, working with Judge Patterson, Bob now faced the embodiment of all that he hoped to become. Patterson was fearless, principled, utterly without pretension. There was the quiet defiance, too, the independence built on an impeccable record of achievement. The judge, as Bob would later see, had become a kind of second father.

On the afternoon of January 22, 1952, Patterson was in Buffalo, in federal court. A new client had retained him to navigate an antitrust case and it was their first hearing. Patterson had also recently been retained to represent U.S. Steel before the Supreme Court. The judge rarely left Bob behind when he traveled, but Morgenthau had explained that if he went to Buffalo, he would not get the U.S. Steel brief drafted in time. And so, he had stayed in the city. The judge would fly back alone that afternoon.

When, after a late lunch, Bob returned to the office, the receptionist did not smile. Marie Gaselman not only greeted visitors, she served as the firm's switchboard operator. In the office, Marie was the one who always knew where everyone was. She and her husband, Joe, the office manager, lived across the river, in Elizabeth, New Jersey. A neighbor had just called, relaying the news.

"A plane's gone down in Elizabeth," Marie said.

When he reached his office, Bob looked out the window, and saw the storm. "What kind of crazy son-of-a-bitch would be flying on a day like this?" he wondered.

It had happened minutes earlier. At 3:44 P.M., American Airlines Flight 6780 had begun its descent, the twin-engined Convair dipping its nose and heading for the Newark airport. The weather had been deemed "pilot's option"—bad, but manageable. The pilot, Thomas J. Reid, was experienced, just home from an airlift in Japan. The airline, though, did not know that he was in a hurry. His wife, Henrietta, waiting with their little girls, eighteen months and three and a half years old, was at home. She was pregnant; Reid wanted to make it home. The plane crashed four blocks away from the family house.

All twenty-three people onboard, and nine others on the ground, were killed. Patterson was only the most celebrated of the victims.

The judge was sixty years old. The sudden loss left his protégé without bearings. Bob had known loss: His mother had died two years earlier, and friends and classmates had been killed in the war. But Patterson was a giant, one he had grown close to and learned from each day. The judge, too, had been his own patron—not his father's, nor his grandfather's—an advocate and coach who had entrusted him with the privilege of responsibility from the first.

At the funeral, President Truman would sit among the family at the National Cathedral. As the honor guard carried the flag-draped casket, Henry Morgenthau, Jr., would stand on the cathedral steps, alongside the other honorary pallbearers, who included Secretary of State Dean Acheson, Speaker Sam Rayburn, Generals Omar Bradley and George Marshall, and Justice Learned Hand. The obituary writers struggled to sum up Judge Patterson's gifts. In war and peace, one editorialist wrote, he'd been "an example of the public-spirited citizen."

47. "This Thing He Married"

1950-1955

When Henry Morgenthau, Jr., met Marcelle Puthon Hirsch, a Frenchwoman, his long-suffering assistant, Henrietta Klotz, would insist that she felt no jealousy—only regret and guilt. After all, Mrs. Klotz had encouraged Henry to date, and as she would say, she'd been the one who led him directly to "this thing he married"— she was unable to utter her name.

Henrietta Klotz could never forgive herself for allowing the new woman onto the scene. In the years since they'd left Washington, Mrs. Klotz if anything spent more time in her boss's company. Their relationship, after more than three decades of working side by side, had only grown more perplexing. Yet since Elinor's death, Henry had taken to speaking of his assistant in a new tone. His children noticed it, too: "Mrs. Klotz and I" had become "Henrietta and I." They seemed closer than ever, almost intimate. In October 1950, they had gone together to Israel. Morgenthau had hired Robert Capa, the famed Magnum war photographer, to make a UJA propaganda film. *The Journey* would be the only movie Capa ever directed. Together, Henry and Henrietta had toured the country: the landmarks of Jerusalem, the beach at Tel Aviv, and of course, the *moshav* at Tal Shahar. Henry appeared elated: flying over the mountains in an Israeli Air Force plane, seated in the co-pilot's seat, hand on the throttle, chewing gum. He wore his overcoat collar turned up, sunglasses, and a fedora. Wherever they went, his former assistant was at his side, often on his arm.

Decades later, Mrs. Klotz would insist that the relationship had been strictly professional. The rumors, though, persisted, and Morgenthau's children believed they held some truth. "Mrs. Klotz wanted more," Henry III claimed. "She was utterly devoted to him, almost slavishly. That devotion may well have crossed over into love." Joan agreed: "No question, for Mrs. Klotz it was an obsession." But none of Henry's children could imagine their father crossing the line. "He couldn't do it," in the words of Henry III, "even if he'd wanted to."

Mrs. Klotz, for her part, would cite sympathy as her sole motive: She'd wanted the secretary to be happy. "Your father was lost after your mother died," Mrs. Klotz told Henry III. "He didn't know what to do with himself. Bob went off with his wife to one of the islands. They didn't want to take him along."

She had worried that Henry's isolation would deepen, and sought out social engagements for him. She turned to Bill Weintraub, a publisher of *Esquire* in the 1930s, who had left to found an advertising agency that claimed a floor in Rockefeller Center. "I knew Bill fairly well," Henrietta recounted, "enough to say to him, 'He's so lonely. . . . Why don't you invite him to your house? You have a house out on Long Island.'"

In the summer Weintraub invited Henry out to a party at his weekend place in Southampton. Afterward, Henry returned to the city bewildered but transfixed.

"I met the strangest women," he told Henrietta, describing the party-goers.

"Why? What do you mean, the strangest?" she asked.

"They didn't listen to the radio, they didn't read a newspaper, they . . . What did they do? They kept changing clothes."

Amid the crowd at Weintraub's house in the Hamptons, Henry had met Marcelle. She was not only Catholic but, until October 1951, married. Thanksgiving week 1951, the engagement was announced. For Bob, his brother Henry, and sister Joan, the headlines did not make for pleasant reading: "Morgenthau to Wed Mrs. Hirsch," the *Times* declared, as the AP announced, "Morgenthau to Wed French Divorcee." "Mrs. Morgenthau," the press reported, had recently obtained "a Virgin Islands divorce."

The wedding took place on November 21, in an apartment on East Sixty-second Street. Henry, at sixty years old, stood in a rare glow. The bride wore "an afternoon costume of navy blue," its neckline plunging and stiff collar jagged, and adorned only by a gold brooch. Although the bride had lived in New York for decades, becoming a naturalized American, she did not appear to have many American friends. Her sole attendant was Mrs. Pierre Moulin of Guadeloupe, French West Indies.

The newspapers reported Marcelle's age as forty-seven. She was, in fact, fifty-three.

The new Mrs. Morgenthau would not have to move far. Her first husband, Stephen G. Hirsch, a wealthy French Jewish importer, lived on Park Avenue around the corner from Henry. Marcelle had taken steps toward becoming Jewish. It was "some kind of conversion," Henry III would say. As his father, now chairman of the UJA, wished to have a Jewish wedding, Dr. Julius Mark, senior rabbi at Emanu-El, presided. There were few guests, only the family and the visitor from the Caribbean.

Bill Weintraub stood beside Mrs. Klotz. "My God," he whispered. "I feel responsible. He could have had her as his mistress but marry that woman?"

At six P.M., after a brief toast, the newlyweds left for the airport. After a week in Paris, Henry would take his new bride to Israel—his fourth trip there in three years.

Henry was besotted, and he soon assumed a life that few of his friends or family could recognize. The secretary had been "blinded," Mrs. Klotz judged. He had always been a frugal man, never one for fancy restaurants, let alone the 21 Club; but now he and Marcelle dined out nearly every evening. Henry was on the credit register at his local stops near the farm: the Wiccopee General Store, Fishkill Hardware, and Ketcham's Garage. Marcelle opened accounts by the dozen: jewelry at Cartier and Van Cleef & Arpels, crystal at Baccarat & Porthault, dresses at Bergdorf Goodman and Bonwit Teller, winter coats at Frederica Furs. The local salon, florist, liquor shop, French bakery, and French laundry—all soon had "Morgenthau" accounts. And above all, she urged her new husband to travel. Each season brought a new destination: Europe, Southeast Asia, the Caribbean.

Henry's children could not fathom what had come over their father. Mrs. Roosevelt, on the other hand, understood it perfectly. "Your father," she told Bob, "has found a woman who's one-third wife, one-third nurse, and one-third mistress."

||||

All the while, the ghost of Harry White haunted Henry's mind. Was White a spy? Since 1947, Henry had tried to get answers from Washington—

first from the Justice Department, then from Patterson, when the judge was still at the Pentagon. In January 1952, as the old claims surfaced again, Henry could take no more: He called FBI headquarters and demanded a meeting with J. Edgar Hoover. He wanted to know what "definite evidence" the FBI had that White was "disloyal." He had read the news accounts of Elizabeth Bentley's allegations, and years earlier, when he'd asked Tom Clark, Truman's first attorney general, Clark had called Bentley's story "a lot of bull." Henry still wanted "concrete evidence." According to the FBI report, he left "very much upset to learn that there appears to be no question but what White was working for the Russians."

For Henry, though, the fight to clear his own name was hardly over. The Republicans, now ascendant after the 1952 election, again charged that the Morgenthau Diaries might contain evidence of White's treasonous undermining of U.S. policy in the Treasury. On November 6, 1953, Eisenhower's attorney general, Herbert Brownell, gave a speech in Chicago, claiming that White had been "a Russian spy" who "smuggled secret documents to Russian agents for transmission to Moscow." It was not new news: Brownell had merely recycled the old Chambers-Bentley claims, but the Senate Internal Security Subcommittee, chaired now by Senator William Jenner, Republican of Indiana, renewed the hunt for the diaries. Henry had donated them to the FDR Library, but retained control over their publication. In 1951, Hoover had dispatched agents to the library, their "covert operation" to cut out, literally, any materials that may be seen as "unfavorable to Mr. Hoover or the FBI"—a task they fulfilled. Now two Senate investigators took up residency at the library to comb the nearly nine hundred volumes for nine months, from October 1954 until June 1955. The investigators searched for White's subversive fingerprints, copying excerpts from the diaries—more than four thousand pages in all—that the subcommittee insisted on making public.

Still, it would not be until the summer of 1955, after the Democrats had regained control of Congress, that Henry would testify before the senators. His son Bob accompanied him, serving as his attorney. There would be no advance notice for the press, and the secretary would appear behind closed doors.

Hoover fumed that the fix was in: He suspected a conspiracy between Morgenthau and the subcommittee's Democratic chair, Senator James O. Eastland. Hoover had a source: J. G. Sourwine, Eastland's counsel and no friend of Morgenthau. A former newsman from Reno, Sourwine would make a name for himself accusing a host of reporters—many of them *Times* men, and most of them Jewish—of Soviet sympathies. Sourwine would keep in close contact with his friend at the FBI, Louis B. Nichols, the number three man at the Bureau. On the eve of Morgenthau's testimony, Sourwine urged caution. "His attitude is excellent," he reported of Morgenthau's early talks with Eastland. "He is mad at White and those who played him for a sucker. He will be a friendly witness."

Hoover remained skeptical—"I would never be too certain of Morgenthau's sincerity"—and ordered a man to tail the secretary.

As Hoover feared, Senator Eastland went out of his way to praise Morgenthau in the portion of the testimony made public. Henry had followed up with a thank-you note to Eastland: "I would not want anything better on my tombstone than your statements."

When Sourwine reported Henry's gratitude, sending a copy of the letter to the FBI, Hoover scrawled a note in the margin: "Time will tell. I see no purpose to be gained in going to Eastland. This statement re Morgenthau speaks for itself."

By July, the FBI director was irate. He had got word that Henry would not be handing over the diaries. "Reversal by Morgenthau doesn't surprise me," Hoover wrote to his men. "It serves the Committee right, which went all out in nauseating commendation of Morgenthau."

All the while, Hoover could only watch as the dance continued.

In October, Henry was back on the Hill to meet with the senators—his son Bob again at his side. "He was desperate," Bob recalled. "He wanted to avoid the appearance of wrong-doing, but he feared they'd just dirty his name." Henry spoke with the reporters gathered outside Senator Eastland's office. He wore a pinstriped suit with a white pocket square. At the impromptu press conference in the corridor, the film cameras whirled as Morgenthau spoke.

"My meeting with Senator Eastland and Senator Jenner ended on a very happy note."

As the reporters scribbled in their notebooks, he weighed each word.

"As far as my diary, the Morgenthau Papers, are concerned, they're in the hands of Mr. Mansure, who's the head of that department under which the archivist comes." Henry spoke without notes, shifting his weight from foot to foot. "And if any Senator, or committee, or anybody connected with the government, wants access to my papers . . . the complete right, authority, rests with Mr. Mansure."

"I'm going back home content," Henry said. "Senator Eastland and Senator Jenner treated me most courteously, most kindly. I'm going back feeling relieved. I go back to my job, of being a farmer and harvesting and selling my apple crop. And that's quite a job this year. Prices are not too good."

As the reporters chuckled, the secretary, so ill at ease in his return to Washington, brightened, the relief seeming to wash over him. Bob stood nearby. He refused to speak to the press, but a photograph of the meeting—his father standing by the two senators, his "attorney," Bob, head down, behind them—ran across the front page of the *Times*.

The senators, though, had been clear: The Morgenthau Diaries were of national import; they could hold clues to White's, and others', spying for the Soviets. "These papers are of far-reaching importance to the workings of this committee," Eastland had said in the hearing. "Eventually this question will have to go to the President."

⏐ ⏐ ⏐ ⏐

Henry wished for "all the noise" to die down. He wanted to retire to Fishkill—on his marriage license, he'd again listed his occupation as "farmer." Henry did what he could to convince his new wife, but Marcelle would have none of it: The farm would have to wait.

In the city, instead, he returned to an old project. Even before leaving Washington, Henry had set a goal to write a book—or, more precisely, to commission a book to be written on his Treasury years. (Joseph Gaer's manuscript, half finished, sat yellowing among his Treasury papers.) Henry wanted to right the balance, to make sure that his side of the story, as he saw things, was told in full. It had to be a sober retelling of events and policy debates and decisions, with only the briefest of biographical details revealed. The chronicle, he insisted, must hew as close as possible to the massive paper trail—the millions of Treasury documents preserved in his diaries.

The search for a historian capable and willing to embark on such a Herculean undertaking proved difficult. It was not so much a question of scholarship, or academic stature, but of fear, doubt, and distrust. Henry had kept his diaries and papers as a private reserve, granting access to a precious few. He was wary, above all, of someone rummaging through them—and fearful of opportunists out to make a buck.

Since leaving Washington, Henry had cycled through a series of historians, mostly Columbia people. Eddie Greenbaum, his lawyer and trusted fixer, did the casting calls. Allan Nevins took a crack, but turned it over to a crew of graduate students. ("Just dreadful," a scholar would remark of the result.) Henry Steele Commager then tried his hand, also to no avail. By late 1953, at the recommendation of Arthur M. Schlesinger, Jr., who had seen enough of the diaries to know the riches they contained, Henry had settled on the historian John Morton Blum, then teaching at MIT.

"Henry Morgenthau was a very, very suspicious man," Blum would say. "There was something glowering about him, the old 'Henry the Morgue' "—FDR's old nickname for his friend. "My wife and I, behind his back, called him Eeyore, but we did grow fond of one another. And when after years, he grew to trust me, he was just about the sweetest man on the planet."

Blum began with a visit to the Roosevelt Library. Herman Kahn, the archivist in charge, offered a warning. "John, before you take another step," he said, "I want you to read the efforts of everybody else who's agreed to do this." Kahn wheeled out a truckload of manuscripts. "And all those who gave it up."

It would be a four-way arrangement that did little to ease Henry's fears. Blum would "consult closely with me at all times," Schlesinger assured Morgenthau in a letter laying out his terms. "I would supervise his work; but, as I see it, I would not (and could not) do any of the actual writing." Morgenthau insisted on a contract with a publisher, but also that he pay Blum out of his own pocket. He was to pay "$10,000 a year for a period of three years," Schlesinger wrote, "this sum to be distributed by me to the writer, to the expenses of the project and to myself as editorial supervisor."

Blum saw trouble ahead. He remembered the *Post* articles. "Arthur had a great knack for capturing [Morgenthau's] tonalities," he would say, "so the prose reads much more like [Morgenthau] than it would have with a less gifted ghost." Blum made clear to Schlesinger that he neither needed, nor desired, "a third author." There was another, bigger concern that Blum asked be conveyed to the patron: Morgenthau needs to understand, he wrote Schlesinger, that he (Blum) is "a professor and not a publicist." His terms agreed to, Blum set to work. Or tried to.

Working for Morgenthau would prove exacting. Not only was the former secretary unrelentingly wary, but the true scope of the job soon became clear. Over the next twelve years, Blum would try to tame the diaries into a book. Early on he saw the impossibility of a biography, and instead he would produce a miracle of scholarship: a chronicle, elegantly told and layered with political and economic context, compressed into a mere three volumes.

| | | |

It was an act of historical retrieval, but also of retrospective gilding. The experience would prove notable as much for what Morgenthau demanded that Blum leave buried as for the discoveries he unearthed along the way.

Blum started with the sisters. For decades, as Henry rose to prominence, he had kept his distance from Helen, Alma, and Ruth. And they had returned the favor. Two had been divorced, one twice. And one, Alma, Henry and Josie's second child, had died. Since Alma's death, and Marcelle's arrival, Helen and Ruth, eldest and youngest of the sisters, had grown ever more distant from their brother.

"There were a lot of angry women in the family," according to Henry III. Iphigene Ochs Sulzberger, Ruth's friend since childhood, called her "a very, very angry woman." She had felt herself "an unwanted child," Iphigene told Henry III. It was "pretty clear, at least, that they were shooting for another boy." At root, the cause of the anger was "male chauvinism," Ellin London, Ruth's daughter, would say. "Grandpa professed love for his girls, but never considered them as worthy as his son."

Henry's sisters had tales to tell, stories that Blum was eager to hear. He went to see Ruth and Helen, and didn't tell Henry about it. He sat for hours, listening to them speak of the early years, how Josie had nurtured them in the arts, and how their father never imagined his daughters would work.

Blum drafted a first chapter, on Henry's childhood, and sent it to Fishkill. He soon received one of those "Henry-the-Morgue, 5:30-in-the-morning telephone calls." Even at the farm, the former secretary maintained his Treasury habits.

"John," he said, "this is Henry Morgenthau, and I am very upset."

The chapter just wouldn't do, Henry said, and insisted that Blum come up to the farm right away. "Everything his sisters told me he wanted out," Blum recalled.

"I want nothing personal in this," Henry said. "Only the record, the political record of my government service, from beginning to end."

He demanded that Blum tear up the chapter.

| | | |

There were other forbidden zones. Any overt anti-Semitism, whether in words or actions, would be off-limits, as Blum learned when he tried to include a story that he considered revealing. Decades later, he recalled it vividly:

"Henry Sr. and Henry Jr. had been on a train, heading back to New York from the White House, after the Ambassador's return from Turkey, when on the same train they run into Jacob Schiff. Schiff asks the younger Morgenthau, 'What do you do?' To which, the father, Henry Morgenthau, answers, 'My son's a farmer.' Schiff continues. 'What's he farm?' 'Well, apples, corns and hogs,' says Henry Jr. 'Are the hogs profitable?' 'Yes they are, sir,' says young Henry. 'Then they're kosher,' says Schiff."

Henry refused to allow Blum to use the story in the book.

"But Mr. Morgenthau," he protested, "you told it to me yourself."

"I know," Henry replied, "but sometimes I'm anti-Semitic."

Henry's limits were strict, and his sense of decorum rooted in the atavistic German-Jewish fear of offending anyone in the Establishment. Even Breckinridge Long, his old nemesis at the State Department, was not to be chastened. Blum had no recourse: Morgenthau may have believed that Long had resisted the Treasury's fight to aid the last Jews of Europe, but he "didn't think Long was anti-Semitic"—and the diplomat's diary, which made clear his thoughts on "the Jews," had not yet been published. There was, too, the piquant line of President Truman's. It had come, Blum would explain, when "Truman was heading to Potsdam, and Henry wanted to go along, and Stimson came to Truman in a white heat and said, 'If Morgenthau's going, I'm not.'" To which, according to Blum's research, Truman had replied: "Don't worry, neither Morgenthau, nor Baruch, nor any of the Jew boys will be going to Potsdam."

When Blum quoted the line in a draft, Morgenthau demanded it cut: "I don't like the phrase 'Jew boy' in the mouth of any President of the United States.'"

Elinor, too. Blum "wasn't allowed to mention her in the book. Nothing, except he was married and she was ill. There was nothing in between." Still, Blum found willing sources among those close to the family. Henry's "two wonderful Scottish retainers"—the Crawford sisters, Helen and Janet, the women who had cooked, cleaned, and minded the Morgenthau children for decades—remained on the farm. As Henry's heart condition worsened, he could not concentrate for long. "We'd work for two hours at a time," Blum explained. "Then he'd go rest and

I'd go walk about the orchards." After lunch, there would be a nap. The Crawfords would take Blum aside "and read me the riot act about Marcelle." Mrs. Roosevelt, too, would come for Sunday supper. She made sure that her car collected her at ten o'clock in the evening. Henry went to bed at nine P.M., so Blum and she always had an hour together. "And Mrs. Roosevelt could not be restrained; she talked freely about Ellie."

Henry would say that he only wished to set things straight, to give a "balanced rendition" of how Roosevelt ruled and he had led the Treasury. If there was a score to settle, Blum came to learn, it was a deeply personal one. Henry wanted to establish, in print, his independence. He wanted to separate himself first from his wife. "Elinor's friendship with Eleanor Roosevelt was of critical importance," Blum would say, but Henry "was deeply afraid everyone would think that was the key to his success." He also wanted to distance himself from his father: "He didn't want his father to get any credit for what he'd done."

The father, even long dead, haunted the son. Even though he had outpaced his father's legacy—"Junior's work, especially in pushing through on Lend-Lease," Blum believed, "will give him a reputation a century hence far greater than his father's"—Henry still yearned to escape his shadow. That was "the real reason" Henry had gone into farming.

"It was the one thing he could find about which his father knew nothing."

48. "To Hell with It"

1959–1961

To take "the overnight" in the postwar years meant only one thing among the legal guardians of Wall Street: Important business awaited in Washington. At ten in the evening, the queue for the night train would form at Penn Station, a line of gray suits carrying dark briefcases. The train arrived in the early morning, just across from the Capitol building and ahead of office hours on the Hill. On a chill evening in December 1959, two weeks before Christmas, Bob Morgenthau boarded the train, taking the overnight to see an old friend.

Bob Morgenthau and Jack Kennedy had rarely seen each other since they were boys on summer vacations: Their fathers may have been rivals, but the families had crossed paths since the 1930s. One summer, the Morgenthaus stayed on Cape Cod, near Hyannis Port, and young Jack and Bob had raced "Wianno Juniors," the local yacht club's sixteen-foot sailboats. In the evenings, the children had attended dances at the club, and movies at the Kennedy house. In August 1938, when Jack was twenty-one, and his father the U.S. ambassador in London, they'd met again—on the French Riviera. The summer meetings seemed to come as if by coincidence, but Bob was never sure: There was little that his father left to chance.

Bob admired Jack, considered him worthy of higher office. Kennedy, a decorated hero for his exploits in the South Pacific, had the war record. He had the charisma, looks, money, and, almost impossibly, a common touch. But what drew Bob to Jack above all was the chance his candidacy offered to overcome the religious barrier. "I grew up in a house where so many stories of Al Smith's career were told," he would say.

"And Smith had been smeared as a Catholic." It was time, Bob believed, "a Catholic got a shot at the White House." "Kennedy for President" was not yet a groundswell, but if a campaign was about to take flight, Bob Morgenthau was not going to let it pass him by.

||||

Since Robert Patterson's death, Bob had taken on much of the judge's old practice. Bob had made partner in 1954, but in the absence of a mentor to encourage and inspire him, much of his work at the firm had begun to lose its allure. Private practice, he reminded himself, was never meant to be the far horizon. Bob remembered, as he often would, his grandfather's words about the virtues of public service, and an obligation to take advantage of his "head start." It was less a suggestion than an order.

At home, too, Bob and Martha faced another struggle. The baby, Elinor—they called her "Nellie"—was "not right." Martha saw it first, and Bob much later, only reluctantly conceding to the reality. For more than a year, the family pediatrician counseled caution and little more. If he knew, he told the parents nothing. They had gone to see a series of specialists, and had the child spend months at a leading diagnostic center in Rochester, before a pediatrician at last put it bluntly. "Get her out of the home," he said.

The words shook Bob, but he knew the doctor was right. "I was the coward," he would say. "Martha knew. It was the only way to preserve the family." Almost five years old, the child, the doctor said, had an IQ of an eighteen-month-old. It was not "a borderline case." Nellie did not speak. She was also violent. She would yank down the drapes, strike out at her siblings. She paid no attention to either parent. The greatest danger, though, was to herself. Bob had insisted on keeping her at home, against the advice of doctors. "But she was intent on hurting herself," he would say. "Nothing we could do to stop her."

They had visited several schools—"many of them were terrible, frightening"—before settling on Lochland, a former farm on Seneca Lake, in the Finger Lakes region upstate. The school, founded in the 1930s, offered a beautiful setting: a large white house overlooking a coppice of chestnut and oak trees and manicured lawns sloping down to the lake. The caregivers were skilled, and the director compassionate—she would write letters, detailing Nellie's days. Bob and Martha would visit, yet each time they would carry home the same emptiness: Nellie never said a word, nor did she show any sign of recognizing her parents.

For Martha, the loss of her youngest daughter was irreparable. Yet for her, and especially for her husband, there would at least be a kind of renewal. In March 1957, at the close of winter, Martha gave birth to a boy. Robert Pattridge Morgenthau, known as Bobby—"never Junior," his father would correct—arrived six years after Nellie's birth. Martha and Bob, both nearing thirty-eight years old, could not suppress their relief. A boy, at last. "For twelve years," Jenny, their firstborn, quipped, "I was the oldest son."

IIII

Bob Morgenthau had arrived early in Washington, and come straightaway to the senator's office on Capitol Hill, where the forty-two-year-old Jack Kennedy greeted him as an old friend. On the big mahogany desk were copies of the senator's books, *While England Slept* and *Profiles in Courage,* and the walls were covered with photographs of boats. A model airplane stood atop a bookcase—a replica of the one his brother Joe was flying when, packed with explosives to attack a German submarine pen on the French Coast, it blew up over England.

They spoke of their fathers, New York, and the Democratic Party. Kennedy worried openly about Mrs. Roosevelt—Could he win her over? If so, how? She remained a Democratic powerhouse, and to many, the soul of the party. Few families, as Kennedy knew, were closer to her than the Morgenthaus.

"If you run," Bob said, "just know I'm eager to help. Any way I can."

IIII

Bob's old friend Byron White had known Jack Kennedy for years—and JFK had made sure to keep in close touch. They'd met first in England the summer before the war. White had been at Oxford and Kennedy in London, on an extended visit to his father, the ambassador. In July 1939, they toured Europe together. Their paths crossed again in the Pacific in 1943, where both served in the Navy. Lieutenant White, by coincidence, was assigned to write the official report on the sinking of Kennedy's torpedo boat, PT-109. And they would meet a third time, in Washington. In his final term at Yale, White won the brass ring of the graduates: a Supreme Court clerkship. When he arrived at the offices of the chief justice, Fred Vinson, Kennedy was settling into his new office on the Hill, as a first-term congressman. Kennedy would often cross the street, from the Capitol to the Court, to come by and chat, and they grew close.

Joining the Kennedy campaign marked a return to the public arena for White. For a decade and a half, "Whizzer White" had all but disappeared from the national horizon. In 1947, he had turned down offers from the top Washington firms and returned home to Colorado, enjoying a quiet practice in Denver. The Kennedys, eyeing Colorado as a key to success in the West, saw his gifts as a campaign surrogate. In Denver, White helped to outflank the old guard at the state convention, winning 27 of 42 delegates for Kennedy. He had surprised Old Joe Kennedy and won the respect of younger brother Bobby. At the Democratic convention that July in Los Angeles, they would not forget White's able maneuvering—and they would keep him in the inner circle.

Bob Morgenthau made it onto the convention floor. He cadged a press pass from a friend, a *New York Post* reporter, and scribbled his own name on it. At Kennedy headquarters, Morgenthau found Byron White, and for the first time since childhood, he met with Bobby Kennedy.

Bobby and White explained that the campaign wanted to try an experiment: to launch a national organization—even setting up a parallel organization to the party, if necessary—to lure independents, and even Republicans, to JFK's candidacy and the broader cause of reform it represented. White would head the group, but explained that the New York arm would carry special importance. As Bobby laid out the plan, it became clear: He wanted Morgenthau's help. White nodded: "You'll head up the branch in the Bronx."

At that moment, Morgenthau understood that the Kennedy campaign could have far-reaching consequences for New York politics. JFK would carry the city with or without the younger reformers, but Bobby, Morgenthau saw, was not merely intent on sending a signal to the party overlords, the old-time rulers of the machines, from the district to the county to the state level, still known by all as "bosses." What he was talking about would mean taking a far greater risk—he was attempting to break the stranglehold, once and for all, of the old Tammany machine in New York City.

||||

Some called it suicidal: The Bronx was Buckley turf.

Charles Buckley, born in the borough in 1890, had inherited the Democratic machine from Ed Flynn, FDR's old party operator, and almost single-handedly preserved it as the most powerful political apparatus in the state. A congressman since 1935, Buckley chaired the all-important

Committee on Public Works, dispensing billions of dollars in federal program money. He was a short, bug-eyed Irishman who could charm any political clubhouse, cut low an impolite reporter, and sniff out a slice of patronage anywhere along the Eastern Seaboard. A chain-smoker with a salty tongue, Buckley often sounded as angry as he looked. He had not distinguished himself on the Hill, but Congress was only a day job. From a modest house on West 192nd Street in the Bronx and the nondescript borough headquarters on Courtlandt Avenue, Charles Buckley oversaw an empire—"the organization," he called it. Just where the limits of the Buckley "organization" lay—how far the politician's reach extended into the local school boards and unions, church groups and neighborhood associations—remained a mystery. Unless you tried to fight it.

In the summer of 1960, the bosses stood at the peak of their power and Joe Kennedy had a plan for how he would engage them. He would cut deals, one-on-one, in the old style, with Eugene Keogh, the longtime congressman from Brooklyn; Peter Crotty, the Buffalo boss; and most eagerly, the city bosses: Buckley of the Bronx and Carmine De Sapio, the Manhattan party leader who had recently seen his stature grow nationally. Joe Kennedy saw De Sapio as his son's natural ally, and he knew Buckley, a friend, would swear fealty to the Irish. If the old man had anything to do with it, the bosses would stand front and center in the New York campaign.

At the Los Angeles convention, though, Jack and Bobby had vowed to join forces with the mounting insurgency in New York. The Kennedy brothers had pledged to stand with the so-called "Reform Democrats," a new group of young voters and activists. The reformers hardly constituted a movement, but the more often Buckley and his fellow bosses called them "amateurs" bent on a mutiny, the greater their numbers grew. And Bob Morgenthau stood in the vanguard.

Morgenthau had long been committed to overturning the bosses' reign. In law school, he'd joined the AVC, the American Veterans Committee, a new group founded by the generation returning from war. Neither liberal nor conservative, the AVC hoped to give a political voice to the young veterans, serving as a counterweight to the VFW and American Legion, their fathers' associations. At Yale, Bob helped found a local chapter, and alongside William Sloane Coffin, then an undergraduate, recruited classmates to its ranks. In New York City, he'd stepped up the fight. In 1948, Bob helped to form a political alliance of young professionals, veterans in the main, united by an urgent desire for reform. They called themselves the "Young Democrats," and vowed to challenge Tammany, "to maneuver around the machine," as Morgenthau would say. "We knew it would be near-impossible," Justin Feldman, a young lawyer also at the forefront of the group, would recall. "But we knew someone had to try." By 1954, coalescing around Averell Harriman's victorious run for governor that year, they would gain numbers, and a new name: the Reform Democrats.

In Los Angeles, the New York reformers had announced their enthusiasm for the JFK-LBJ ticket, but declared that they "could not and would not work for it under Tammany Hall." The group had forced the Kennedys to choose sides between the bosses and the young reformers. The Kennedys, of course, wished to have it both ways. "When the convention was over," John Seigenthaler, a close Kennedy aide, would say, "there were really two campaigns in New York. And Bob Morgenthau found himself in the middle of the war."

It fell to Bobby to broker a truce: On August 1, at the Kennedy apartment on Park Avenue, he met with Mayor Robert F. Wagner, Jr. (the senator's son), for forty minutes. As Bobby laid out his plan to ally with the reformers, the mayor warned that the bosses would not go quietly. For the rest of the day, as the press waited outside in the heat, Bobby remained indoors, working the phones until after midnight. The next morning, he convened a close group of advisors to hash out the new organization: "Citizens for Kennedy."

The campaign would be a radical departure. Byron White would run things nationally, while Bill Walton, a former newsman, would serve as JFK's chief liaison in New York. Bob Morgenthau would head up the Bronx, and advise on strategy across the boroughs. As the four men gathered close, Bobby read off a list of forty recruits, many of them former Adlai Stevenson backers. Mrs. Roosevelt, Herbert Lehman, and Bernard Baruch headed the list.

Forty-eight hours later, they had failed to win the bosses' support for a single united campaign operation, and Bobby turned to the press. In the middle of the crowded living room, he announced the heresy. Citizens for Kennedy, he said, had arisen out of "the peculiar situation in the City of New York." White and Walton stood by his side, and Morgenthau behind him. "It will be independent of the regular Democratic organization," Bobby vowed. "It will be answerable to Senator Kennedy's organization, will take orders and instructions from the Kennedy organization, and will follow the procedures of the Kennedy organization."

It was not quite a truce, but the bosses tried to save face. "This is going to work out," said Michael Prendergast, the state party chairman. De Sapio, too, tried to look a winner. Under the Kennedy plan, he insisted, "everybody helps." Only Charles Buckley said nothing.

||||

Citizens for Kennedy opened the door to public life for Bob Morgenthau.

He concentrated on winning over community leaders and registering Latino voters—the overwhelming majority of whom would support Kennedy. The Bronx group increased registration by 44 percent. Bob also escorted the campaign proxies across the Bronx: He brought Mrs. Roosevelt, who had been coaxed into an endorsement by two generations of Morgenthaus; Abraham Ribicoff, the Connecticut senator who had been among the earliest to come out for Kennedy; and, in September, Rose Kennedy, who arrived with white orchids pinned to a turquoise suit. At every stop, Rose extolled the virtues of "my son Jack," and ended her remarks with the same words: "We think it would be hazardous to continue four more years of stagnation. With Jack in Washington, no other nation would approach us. Then only will the United States be a great power again, respected by all the world."

Morgenthau also brought Bobby Kennedy and the candidate himself. On the final weekend before the election, he stood beside Jack and Bobby as they stumped in the Bronx. It was a campaign tradition, the end-of-the-race visit to the Irish neighborhoods of Rose Hill, heart of the Fordham University campus. The senator was going door-to-door, a dozen reporters in tow, when out of nowhere a priest appeared. He came out on the sidewalk and started to follow Bobby. Ever fearful of an anti-Catholic riptide, Bobby would have none of it. "Too many reporters," Morgenthau would recall, "and they were too close." Morgenthau stood by his side as Bobby turned and shouted, "Get the hell away from here, Father."

||||

Soon it was over, in one of the narrowest victories in U.S. history. On November 8, 1960, Kennedy defeated Richard Nixon, winning the popular vote by 118,550 of the nearly 69 million votes cast. It was the big cities that gave him the electoral college majority—303 to 219 for Nixon. At forty-three, JFK would be the first Catholic, the youngest man ever elected president, and the first one born in the twentieth century.

Within days of the election, rumors swirled. The president-elect, resting in Palm Beach and receiving candidates for the cabinet, was considering the unheard-of: naming his brother attorney general. Bobby had made his own reputation as a fearless Senate investigator who had run one of the most effective campaigns in political history. But the reports brought a storm: A president's brother had never been awarded a cabinet position. Bobby, moreover, was not only preposterously young—thirty-five years old—he had never even practiced law. The Kennedys rushed to calm the fears. On December 16, Bobby assured reporters that he would have a steady hand on deck: Byron White would be his chief deputy.

For weeks, White and Morgenthau had been in almost daily contact; now White asked him to come down to Washington. When they met, White at once relayed the news: The Kennedys wanted to put Morgenthau's name forward as the U.S. attorney for the Southern District of New York, the most powerful federal prosecutor in New York City. Would he accept?

Bob had told Martha serving as U.S. attorney was his dream.

"Of course," he said, "I'd be honored, if—"

White raised a hand. "Before we do anything, it has got to be taken up with Buckley."

Within days, Bobby made clear his instructions: "We still can't go over Buckley's head," he told Morgenthau, "but would you go see him and try to work it out?"

Morgenthau knew the reception at Charles Buckley's headquarters would not be warm. For years he had sought to steer clear of the machine. Now he had to face its boss directly and pay homage. On the way, he remembered something Bobby had said. Buckley still lived in a modest house, but he allowed himself a few luxuries. He treasured his seventy-one-acre horse farm across the Hudson. Bobby and Buckley had once stood together at a fence on the farm and talked. "Notice how the horses don't talk," Buckley had said. "That's how I like people to be when they're around me."

Making matters even more delicate, the Bronx boss had already weighed in on the plum U.S. attorney position, putting forward six names—and Morgenthau was not among them. Yet Bobby Kennedy had rejected each one in turn; none had passed his investigators' vetting.

At his headquarters overlooking East 149th Street, Buckley greeted Morgenthau with a cigar in his mouth. He wasted no time reminding him of the Kennedys' debt—his arm-twisting of the state's delegates at the Democratic convention remained foremost in his mind. Buckley said nothing to Morgenthau about his own preference for U.S. attorney. He mentioned no other candidates, but he made one thing clear: "I'll select the staff."

If Morgenthau "had difficulty grasping the meaning of this," for Buckley it was business as usual. As many as sixty-five assistant U.S. attorneys would be appointed in the Southern District, and "Buckley felt it was only natural they all should be good clubhouse Democrats cleared through him."

Morgenthau struggled to reply.

"I'll tell you what," Buckley said. "If you don't like them, let them go after six months."

Morgenthau recoiled. Ethics aside, to give a man a job and fire him after six months was "grossly unfair." How could he do that to the men, their cases, the whole office? As he walked out of Buckley's office, Morgenthau wondered how many U.S. attorney offices around the country were ruled like this. Too many, he feared.

"I reported all this to RFK," he would write. "But he was still not ready to push Buckley aside."

An entente ensued, even as Morgenthau struggled to understand what had happened. It was an initiation into the Byzantine ways of New York politics, but it seemed a dubious manner of conducting business, he would write in a note to himself, "between a Congressman and a lawyer who happened to have worked on the winning campaign." Yet the closeness of the election, as much as the old political loyalties, was to blame: "Every hand was needed to help unify," Morgenthau wrote. "The stronger the hand, the more it was needed."

In time, Buckley would be left one last move. He offered a final name: William S. Gaud, Jr., a New York lawyer who lived in Greenwich, Connecticut. Bobby decided to play a trump card. He leaked Gaud's name to the *Times,* where the story appeared on the front page. There was a terrific outcry: How could New York City's chief federal prosecutor live in Greenwich?

"To hell with it," Bobby told Morgenthau. "You will fill the position."

49. "You Should Have Known Me When I Was Somebody"

1952-1967

On Bob's desk in Riverdale, the letters from his father piled up. Henry and Marcelle rarely seemed to rest; Bob's father and his new bride were traveling around the world. They flew, they sailed, they took ocean liners. The itineraries were varied—Rome and Haiti in 1952, Cuba, Bermuda, and Peru in 1953, Hong Kong in 1956—but France became the chief destination. Henry always fancied himself a Francophile, and now they went to Paris three times a year. Wherever he went, Henry sought the embrace of officialdom. Diplomats, royals, financiers—he took comfort that they would still see him, that in his sixties he still remained a figure worthy of attention and confidences.

On their travels Henry might meet with diplomats and royals, but his attentions were elsewhere. Marcelle had him entranced. The passion that went into working on behalf of the Jews, those left in Europe and those trying to build the fledgling state in Palestine, had begun to wane. Marcelle pulled her new husband away from the charity work—"the Jewish stuff," Joan said, "left her bored."

Henry's children were certain of the source of the new lassitude, as was Mrs. Klotz. "It went down the drain when he married Marcelle," she would say. "All of a sudden, he wasn't wearing a watch. He kept joking, telling everybody, 'Well, now that I married a French woman, I have to come home in the afternoon.' It killed me."

There was the question of money, too. Elinor Morgenthau, who had grown up a Lehman, had never gone in for anything lavish. She stored her jewelry in a vault, too uncomfortable to wear it; Mrs. Klotz knew its contents and value better than she. But Marcelle loved gems. She bought it all—rings, earrings, necklaces. And she made demands: Henry would even buy her a canary diamond. By 1954, he had set up the Puthon Morgenthau Trust, a fund to provide for his new wife after his death. To Joan, Henry III, and Bob, the worst was coming to pass: Marcelle was driving a wedge between the father and his children.

After their wedding, Henry and Marcelle had moved into his father's apartment on Fifth Avenue. She had tried to enliven the décor. "It was almost unreal," Mrs. Klotz would say. "I've never been in a house of ill repute but that's the only thing I could think of." The children loathed visiting—"It was no longer Grandpa's place," Joan would say—and soon Henry had sold it. Weekends on the farm, too, became tense. "There was a long narrow table," Henry's granddaughter Jenny recalled. "He'd sit at the head, Marcelle next to him, and all the children were always at the other end. Segregated."

By the late 1950s, Henry had reached a decision: Politics, Washington, New York even, were no longer his world. In part, it was a recognition of the obvious. In the years since Washington, Henry had seen so many plans come undone. In 1947, when he first spoke publicly of the diaries, and his idea to mine them for a book, he vowed that "any money such a book may bring" would go to the Morgenthau Foundation for Peace. The foundation had been a project of Ellie's—with her gone, it, too, faded. There had been, as well, the embrace of the Jews. By 1951, he had led a massive UJA fundraising drive, $500 million in Israeli bonds, but soon after, he quit the organization.

Marcelle had won out. In 1959, they announced a move to France. The former secretary called it a dream come true. Henry had bought an acre in Cap Ferrat on the Riviera, a stunning cliffside lot overlooking the Mediterranean, down the road from the famed Hôtel du Cap, where the family had stayed before the war. For his new life with Marcelle, Henry would build a modest house, two bedrooms, no pool, but christen it grandly "Villa Morning Dew," in an homage to the family name. When a neighbor filed suit, claiming her view was ruined, the judge in Nice ruled that the half-built villa be demolished. Construction was delayed until Henry won a reversal. As they waited, Marcelle ordered tapestries from Paris, and Henry brought over a big yellow Cadillac—"We can barely get through these tiny streets," he wrote home. As his children expected, Henry came to regret the move.

A compromise was reached: They would split the year between New

York and the Riviera. But even at home, Henry found his new life hard to accept. The invitations to the benefits and club luncheons slowed to a trickle. His name appeared less and less in the papers. The Poker and Pretzel Club—a club he'd formed in childhood with old friends Arthur Sulzberger, Harold Hochschild, and two others—rarely convened. Hochschild found Henry's new wife florid and base, worried she would take him to the cleaners. The Treasury gang, too—DuBois, Pehle, Paul—had moved on, each deep in new professional worlds. (They remained close, held regular "9:30 group" lunches, but Henry was not among the guests.)

Henry was out—outside of politics, a world, before Roosevelt, that he had never aspired to conquer, and outside of finance, a world he had never known before Washington. By 1958, he had given up keeping an appointment calendar altogether.

What he feared most, though, was the distance that had come between him and his children. Joan was deep in her own career; she had married in 1957. She had known Fred Hirschhorn, Jr., for years—the families had long been friends—but waited until she was in her thirties and had her medical degree. Fred was a son of Our Crowd, heir to a fortune in the cigar business. He had grown up in the same building where Henry and Josie lived, a floor below. As a boy Fred attended the Punch and Judy puppet shows that Grandpa Morgenthau hosted on Sundays for the children. Fred had also attended Joan's coming-out at the White House, the escort of Governor Lehman's daughter. They met again one summer, at a Straus family barn dance, and began to date. When Fred went to the war, he asked Joan if she would "wait." He returned in 1946, but it was "Dr. Joan," one of twenty-two women in the Class of '49 at Columbia medical school, who made her groom wait—more than a decade.

Henry III, too, had waited years to marry. He'd moved to Boston, become a producer for public television, the forerunner of PBS, and convinced Mrs. Roosevelt to play host of a series on world affairs, *Prospects of Mankind*. (They'd taped the first show the week of her seventy-fifth birthday.) He'd sought out Ruth Schachter, a professor then teaching in the African studies program at Boston University, as a guest to appear on the show—"We were looking at the Congo's civil war." They met in early 1961 and were married within a year. Ruth had fled Vienna as a young girl after Kristallnacht. She had grown up in an Orthodox household; Henry feared how she and his father would get on. He only informed his father of his intentions three weeks before the wedding.

The former secretary by then had slowed. In part, it was a physical deterioration. In September 1961, at seventy, he would suffer a serious heart attack. He spent ten days at Vassar Hospital, and assured a reporter when he left that he felt great, but a boundary had been crossed. To John Morton Blum, the Yale professor at work on turning the Morgenthau Diaries into history, "after the first attack, he was never really the same."

It was not only a matter of health. To his son Henry III, he seemed a hollow man, stripped bare and without direction. In 1962, when Henry III introduced his father to his bride-to-be, the former secretary sounded a pathetic note: "You should have known me when I was somebody."

| | | |

Henry Morgenthau never considered himself an expatriate, but by the mid-1960s not only did he spend summers in France, he and Marcelle would stay at Villa Morning Dew for long stretches during other times of the year. The former secretary preferred to live in what his daughter Joan called the "Marcelle cocoon," protected from any derision stemming from his marriage to a woman who preferred boutiques and resorts to political conclaves and farms.

Henry pretended that he did not miss Washington, but, after twenty years, his fall still hurt. In France, he could enjoy the afterglow of power—dining with ambassadors and financiers in Paris, and in the south, spending evenings with vacationing celebrities. Ed Sullivan threw a party for him; Rudolf Nureyev offered an evening out. Along with "the news" of his new life, he sent his children photographs—himself with the television and film stars—"as I think you will be pleased to see your old man laughing and enjoying himself."

Henry's eyes, never good, had grown bad. Blum would recall "a curious ballet with spectacles." For all of Henry's preference for the pince-nez, which he always wanted to be photographed in, he kept more than a dozen pairs of glasses. "There was always a fuss," Blum recalled. "He'd change them constantly, trying to read." His cataract-clouded eyes were going, but that did not stop him from getting out. Each day he made a pilgrimage to the grand Hotel Negresco in Nice—for a swim and a massage, and in the evenings, there were daiquiris to mix. "We can't do much," he would say, "but we can eat well."

Henry tried to play the role of an old Roosevelt man in exile, but he knew the party would not last. The Riviera lacked the simple virtues of the farm. And in his quietest moments, he felt the void. Writing to Henry III, he struggled to be direct. The villa was an expensive endeavor, and he missed his family. "If you should pass through Nice," he wrote his son, "maybe we get a glimpse of you." (Henry III had seen the villa under construction, but would never spend a night there.) "PS," he added in a faint scribble, "I am nearly blind."

| | | |

By the fall of 1965, Henry and Marcelle had returned to the farm, and in late November, he was rushed to Vassar Brothers Hospital. Henry left after a week of tests, but returned to file a complaint—$100 had been stolen from his hospital room, he told the police. Some in the family saw a characteristic vigilance; others feared the onset of paranoia.

In the spring, as Henry's seventy-fifth birthday approached, "the children" began to plan a party. They got Marcelle to agree and persuaded her to hold it at the farm. Invitations were printed but not sent: Henry was again in the hospital. Whether it was the strain of his second marriage or the toll of his years in Washington, his decline—another heart attack, this time followed by a stroke—accelerated.

The health troubles were no longer restricted to the circulatory system. "By then, the emotional problems really grew," Joan would say. For nearly a year Henry III had refused to visit the farm; he thought his father did not approve of his marriage. (Ruth, the Orthodox believer, was "too Jewish.") So Joan and Bob took to visiting their father as often as possible, taking turns, "almost every other day, to take him out for a drive."

Henry's condition worsened. "His mind was going," Joan said. By the summer of 1966, his doctors had sent him to a clinic in White Plains. Joan, Bob, and Henry found their father in a locked ward amid a cluster of red-brick buildings, a treatment center founded in the nineteenth century as the Bloomingdale Insane Asylum—the same institution where his grandfather Lazarus Morgenthau had been sent in 1883.

"They packed him off as a mental patient," Henry III would say. "Certainly he was depressed, but it was directly a result of his circulatory problems. When they got him there, they stopped treating the circulatory thing. They took him off the medicine he'd been taking for his heart . . . and, of course, at that point he began to get very ill, physically."

| | | |

As Henry declined, Marcelle revealed herself.

The last years, Bob said, "she made his life miserable." Once, while Henry was in the hospital, he wanted to give Marcelle something special. He asked Bob to buy a ring and a bracelet, and expected her to choose.

"Which do you want?" Bob asked.

"Both," she said.

"She was cruel," Mrs. Klotz told Henry III. "Common and cruel."

Marcelle left her husband in the mental hospital and went to France. "She went for two weeks," Joan said, "and stayed two months."

That fall Bob brought his father back to the farm, where he was tended to by private nurses. His children did what little they could. Marcelle remained in the South of France. Their father had them sign papers deeding the villa on the Mediterranean to Marcelle. Still, Mrs. Klotz insisted that her boss had come around: "He hated himself for not seeing her as she was, because she left him when he was most sick." Years later, his father's anguish still rankled Bob: "He was in a pretty bad way, but he could see what was going on."

He even spoke of divorcing Marcelle.

In time, she returned. Marcelle arrived at the farm, assuring the children that she was in charge. But she let their father go off his treatment plan.

As his health worsened, suspicion overtook him. He suffered from Marcelle's "insatiable demand for affection," Henry III would say, and "became mistrustful of his children, of everybody."

| | | |

The last stages brought a drift into isolation, and helplessness. At Vassar Brothers Hospital the nurses had trouble drawing blood. Henry had severe arteriosclerosis and deepening circulatory problems—in that final winter, the doctors had to amputate a leg.

"I remember going up to the farm," Joan recalled, "with one of my daughters, to cut a Christmas tree and bring it down." Joan had three daughters now: seven, six, and five years old. Elizabeth, the eldest, accompanied her to see Henry. They found him, confined to the house, in bed. "And she was fascinated," Joan would say, because "he was having his stump dressed." Of the eleven grandchildren, many of the grown ones came, too. They were shocked to see the patriarch so ill. To Anne, Bob and Martha's second-eldest daughter, "it was horror."

In the end, Bob and Joan were there together. "I don't want anything more done to me," Henry told them. "I only want to die with dignity."

That night, against Joan's insistent advice, Marcelle gave permission for the doctors to administer dialysis. Joan started to drive up on the Taconic, but found a section of the parkway closed off under more than a foot of snow. She lifted the sawhorses from the on-ramp and drove on alone. Her husband stayed at home with their girls. But she got there too late.

On February 6, 1967, a Monday night, following a succession of heart attacks, Henry Morgenthau, Jr., died at the hospital in Poughkeepsie. He was seventy-five.

"For thirty years," the *Times* wrote, "Mr. Morgenthau was Mr. Roosevelt's confidant, cranky conscience, intensely loyal colleague, and unabashed, but occasionally outraged, admirer."

The family asked John Morton Blum to give the eulogy. Bob handled the press, the funeral, and the estate. At Temple Emanu-El, the pews were packed. Marcelle did not join the family; weeping loudly, she sat apart, two friends attempting to calm her. For Bob, Joan, and Henry III, the funeral marked a double ending. With Henry gone, they would never see Marcelle again.

| | | |

In his later years, Henry Morgenthau, Jr., who had so assiduously preserved almost every minute of his years in power, did not always find solace when he looked back. The crushing end—the loss of FDR, the break with Truman—remained raw.

On a visit to the villa in France, near the end of their long journey together, Blum had presented a chapter on the Morgenthau Plan. As always, he read it to Henry aloud. To Blum, it was not only a question of eyesight: "There was also a reading problem, which he confused with a vision problem. I don't think to the day he died, Henry Morgenthau was comfortable reading." This time, the recitation hit a roadblock. The draft included—a rarity for the historian—a personal critique, slight but unmistakable, of the plan to destroy the Ruhr industries. The rebuke was instant: "I want that sentence out," Henry demanded. "You're too young to know whether or not the Morgenthau Plan was a mistake." The ire was at full flame: "And I will bet you, though I won't be around to collect, that you're going to have to fight Germany again before you die."

Morgenthau would die assured that his lasting achievement had come with Roosevelt. The battles of the 1930s, fought hand in hand with his greatest friend, had yielded the sweetest victories. "They were selfish," he said of the Wall Street titans who derided him as an interloper, dim-witted and foolhardy. "The only flag they followed was their own gain. Franklin and I moved the money capital from London and Wall Street to Washington, and they hated us for it, and I'm proud of it."

He was fearful, right up to the end, of sounding self-serving. Yet he had his pride, and he demanded that the record of the time when the world was at risk of collapse reflect his successes. The fight against Hitler remained his greatest feat. "If Hitler had won," he told Blum, "there wouldn't be any democracy anywhere, here or in England or in Europe. We were all too weak; we were all too slow to wake up. And then we had to move fast, and the United States had to supply all the armies that fought the Axis."

"I don't know how we did it," he said. "I don't think we'll ever have time enough to do it again. But we did do it. And Franklin gave me a chance to do a lot of it, to stick my neck out and be the whipping boy if I failed. And we got the airplanes produced, and the goods to Churchill, and Lend-Lease; and none of them, not the English or the Russians or the Chinese, could have fought without us, and we didn't get much thanks after it was over. But it was worth it, more than worth it."

50. **Bobby and Bob**

1961–1964

In a city of lawyers, no destination inspires more expectancy or dread, depending on the degree of confidence in any single case, than Foley Square, the triangular expanse of concrete and trees just north of City Hall in lower Manhattan. The square, named after a saloonkeeper who had little to do with law, has been "the scene of as much drama as any place in our world," wrote Milton S. Gould, a legal giant who spent half a century in the courts that line its edges. "Here, little men have become kings, and great men have fallen into ruin. Fortunes have been passed by judicial *Diktat* from one hand to another; the squalid scandals of rich and poor, high and low, have been sorted out. If there are ghosts, they must foregather in Foley Square."

No building so dominates the square as the District Court for the Southern District of New York. "The Mother Court," as it is known, is the country's oldest. Its interiors were encrusted with bronze and paneled in oak, but the federal prosecutors, nearly forty men and one woman, worked in a rabbit warren of offices, aided by two dozen secretaries and a handful of clerks, beneath ancient ceiling fans that as summer neared threatened to fall with each turn.

On the morning of April 19, 1961, Bob Morgenthau, forty-one years old, raised his right hand to be sworn in by the chief judge, Sylvester Ryan. Bobby Kennedy remained in Washington, fighting back inquiries concerning the invasion of Cuba, by some 1,400 Cuban exiles, CIA-trained and -funded—the next day Castro would declare the "mercenary troops" "crushed." Although the Bay of Pigs fiasco gave the attorney general a good excuse to be absent, Bob Morgenthau stood before nearly three hundred spectators, flanked by Martha and their children. The girls, Jenny and Anne, stood behind their father, while little Bobby jumped up, reaching, as the cameras clicked, to kiss a cheek.

The U.S. attorney's salary was $20,000 a year, less than the children's tuition, and Nellie's care upstate—she was ten now—ran $10,000 a year. Before Jenny and Anne could protest about leaving private school, their grandfather promised to cover the balance. Still, Bob knew the job would come at another cost: It would leave him little time at home. Since 1927, twenty-two men had served as U.S. attorney in the Southern District. Only three had lasted longer than three years. At Patterson, the hours had been long, but now early each morning he would have to drive downtown in the family station wagon and rarely return home before late. He would work Saturdays, and often Sundays. Yet, as Morgenthau would say, looking back years later, there was no other place in the world he'd rather have been, and "no better place to learn how to be a prosecutor."

The Southern District of New York was the crucible.

The first steps along the path to becoming the nation's preeminent prosecutor, though, were neither easy nor obvious.

All Bob Morgenthau's life he had seemed to glide into success: As a boy on the farm, whether on horseback or ice skates, hammering together a chicken coop or planting saplings—the accomplishments came without much discernible effort; at Deerfield and Amherst, classmates rarely saw him with a book; in the Mediterranean and the Pacific, he had endured the worst of the war at sea, for months on end, and come home without a scratch; at Yale Law, he'd finished in a sprint without any sweat; and in private practice, he'd won a gilded place, right from the first, at the knee of one of the country's foremost legal warriors. To others, the unseen force was clear: The family ties were always there, a safety network of men and women in the Democratic Party, finance that reached back even beyond the Wilson years, to his grandfather's rise.

It was implicit: Here was a Morgenthau, next in the line. The unspoken awareness bore Bob Morgenthau along, right up until the day that Bobby opened the door to a new career, the one Bob had been in training for since he'd met President Coolidge at age six: "public service."

Morgenthau made his opening moves fast—first to work through the backlog, then, even as he was learning, to set an agenda. He spoke more of "concerns"—the issues of crime and corruption facing the city and the country at large—than "cases." He would stay up late reading stacks of

"302s"—the stream of FBI surveillance reports. He would learn the names of Mob enforcers or heroin importers, quiz an agent about what had happened on a specific street corner or at a union hall in the Bronx, but even studying the particulars, he spoke of the larger landscape: the toll of crime on the city's economy, local politics, and, above all, the chances for "common folks" to make ends meet.

With Bobby Kennedy at his back, Morgenthau could not just enforce the law; he had to attempt to make it—to innovate. He would try out novel legal tactics, deploy old statutes in new ways, experiment: "Bob was always strategizing," Pierre Leval, one of his chief assistants, recalled. "It was, 'Let's try this, let's try that'—whether it'd been done before or not." "He was looking to move the law forward," said another assistant, Paul Rooney, "and that's how he operated: it was a series of 'firsts.' " And when the law came up short, when the prosecutor could not close newfound loopholes in the federal code or when the code had failed to anticipate new varieties of crime, he would head to Washington and lobby as none of his predecessors had, to change the law.

Over the years to come, the struggles would be epic. He would face loss as well as success, but he would redraw the boundaries of power in New York, as he built, cornerstone by cornerstone, a career without precedent in the history of American law enforcement. And the lessons he learned on Foley Square—the levers of state power that a prosecutor could rely on, and those he could not—never left him.

| | | |

Bobby Kennedy and Bob Morgenthau, at least in their public personae, appeared near opposites, but they found an easy kinship.

Bobby seemed to understand Morgenthau as few did. He could look past the shy and stolid exterior to the detective and strategist inside. He sensed a desire to win, a drive and determination that would be invaluable. "The one thing that I think bonded Bob Kennedy to people with whom he interacted was the unwillingness of the person to be a yes man," said John Seigenthaler. "He had opinions, and you could change them, but if you didn't try, if he sensed that you had something to say but didn't say it, you could find yourself not being asked again. Morgenthau's great quality was saying something that was straight, that was from the shoulder."

At the Justice Department, Kennedy had brought in Byron White (who had turned down higher jobs) as chief deputy. White in turn recruited the Yalies: Several of Morgenthau's law school classmates would head key divisions in the department. Not all were Ivy League New Englanders: To run the all-important Criminal Division, RFK chose a midwesterner, and a Republican, Jack Miller. The message was clear: At "Kennedy Justice"—as the department under his reign would become known—brains, not patronage, ruled.

Morgenthau followed suit. In 1961, he faced a raft of vacancies—thirteen of fifty-two jobs, normally all the province of patronage. The first fight was for the plum slot of chief assistant. A congressman from the Upper West Side insisted that Morgenthau hire his son-in-law, "or he'd vote against an aid-to-education bill." Morgenthau refused. A second candidate presented himself: William J. vanden Heuvel, a former counsel to Governor Harriman, who lacked prosecutorial experience. But he'd served, he said, under "Wild Bill" Donovan, the OSS founder, at the U.S. Embassy in Bangkok. "Donovan was incompetent," vanden Heuvel explained. "I ran the embassy." Again, Morgenthau balked.

Instead, he gave the job to Vin Broderick, a former deputy police commissioner—a move that was, at least in part, a conciliatory nod to Charles Buckley. "Buckley trusted the Brodericks," Justin Feldman, Morgenthau's old friend from the Harriman campaign in 1954, would say. Vin and his older brother, Joe, who would become a priest, had joined Morgenthau in the Young Democrats. "The Brodericks were Bronx boys who could've eased into Buckley's machine," Feldman would say, "but instead they chose to fight it."

Within weeks Morgenthau had filled in the ranks. At a time when the Southern District offered none of the allure of the white-shoe firms, either in money or prestige, Morgenthau poached from their Ivy-pedigreed ranks. But he looked, as well, to the "city schools"—Fordham, St. John's, Brooklyn Law—for those who had worked their way to their degrees. When John Adams walked in, Morgenthau hired him at once. Adams, who would go on to found the Natural Resources Defense Council, the country's first environmental law advocacy, had no criminal experience. But he'd grown up in the Catskills and earned his way through law school moonlighting on repair crews for the state water system. "Morgenthau loved that," Adams would say. "A construction worker in the office."

The district court did not have a single Black judge, but Morgenthau sought out Black prosecutors. It was a deliberate decision to shake up the staid office of the Southern District, and expand the boundaries of the acceptable. R. Harcourt ("Harry") Dodds had grown up in Harlem and graduated from Dartmouth and Yale Law. Franklin Thomas, who came by way of Columbia and Columbia Law, rode the subway in each day from Bedford-Stuyvesant. In time, Morgenthau would also hire Sterling Johnson Jr., a veteran of eight years as a New York City cop. But another bright young lawyer from Harlem, a decorated Army veteran, arrived first.

Charles Rangel had fought in Korea before entering St. John's Law. His grandfather, the uniformed operator of the DA's elevator in the Criminal Courts Building, had helped him gain entrée to Frank Hogan's office. For two years Rangel interned in the DA's office, but when a vacancy arose, Rangel, who had made dean's list in law school, was denied an interview. When the *Amsterdam News,* the city's leading Black newspaper, got wind of it ("Rejected," read the headline), Morgenthau sent an invitation. "I couldn't get my dream job," Rangel would say, "but I got a better one—the U.S. attorney himself rescued me."

There was something else: Many of the young men in the office were veterans. "Virtually everybody had some military experience," Paul Rooney would say. "And the military takes the whine out of you."

The new U.S. attorney also drew a new line. In Morgenthau's first week on the job, Congressman James Healey, one of Buckley's boys from the Bronx, called. He wanted to come in and talk over a case. "I don't know about anything that's pending," Morgenthau said, but Healey insisted. The next day, as Morgenthau settled into his office—the walls bare, boxes on the floor—Healey turned up. Two "constituents" had been arrested, he explained, but had not yet been indicted, under the Trading with the Enemy Act—for importing hog bristles from China. "All I want you to do," the congressman said, "is kick the case around for six months." Morgenthau got the file and discovered an intriguing history: Each time an assistant verged on bringing the case to a grand jury, his predecessor's chief assistant had transferred it to another assistant. He'd done so six times. Morgenthau did not think twice: He expedited the case, gaining an indictment within days. Healey called again, screaming. "Couldn't you at least have kicked it around for 30 days?" he asked. "So I could collect my fee?"

To Morgenthau, the divide was clear: "You could never let the elephant into the tents."

Before long, his office would become known as *primus inter pares*— first among equals, across the ninety-three federal judicial districts. "He runs a little Department of Justice," soon gibed the U.S. attorney for Maryland at the time. The exceptionalism, and the freedom that came with it, became plain to see, and though Bobby Kennedy was loath to admit it in public, among his chief aides at Justice he made no attempt to deny it. Under Morgenthau, the Southern District of New York would gain a nickname: the Sovereign District.

51. "Our Thing"

1957–1963

RFK entered the Justice Department with a battle plan. His critics would call it a settling of scores—the list of enemies, headed by Jimmy Hoffa and the Teamsters, was long, and his Senate investigations had made headlines for years. Now Kennedy wanted to galvanize the power of federal law enforcement: Kennedy Justice would be activist, the bulwark of reform in his brother's administration. Bobby worried, too, about civil rights; since the late 1950s, he had come to see a mounting conflict between the races. But his schooling as a Senate investigator had lent him a singular focus: He wanted to expose and, if at all possible, curb the growing power of organized crime in the United States.

"Bob Kennedy," as those who knew him best often called RFK, came ready to do battle. "Bob planned a war," Jack Miller, his Criminal Division chief, would say, "and Morgy"—the nickname Bob Morgenthau had acquired among the Kennedy men—"was going to be central to it."

RFK oversaw an army of U.S. attorneys across the country, but none faced more organized crime than the chief federal prosecutor in New York. First, as Bob Morgenthau saw things, they would have to motivate the troops. He relied on the Kennedy ethos. "The fellows in my office," he would say, "felt they were working for Bob Kennedy."

On trips to the city, Kennedy made Morgenthau's office his first stop. He liked to poke his head into the offices, quiz the assistants. He soon formed a tradition, holding court at Gasner's, the bar that had stood on Duane Street, across Foley Square, since 1933. "Gasner's was our clubhouse," Mike Armstrong remembered. It was, a legal scribe would note, "as close as the New York lawyers ever came to an inn of court." Morgenthau understood the importance of the barroom sessions: Bobby, not much older than most of the assistants, would sit for hours and grill them. The attorney general of the United States wanted to know the questions and details, no matter how small, at the heart of their cases. The assistants were not only entranced, they were inspired.

If Bobby and Morgenthau agreed on the main front, they first had to draw the lines. "Bobby Kennedy was the most aggressive A.G. we've ever had," Stephen E. Kaufman, a Morgenthau assistant at the time, would say. Kaufman had joined the U.S. attorney's office at twenty-six. Known in the office for his soft edges and sharp mind, Kaufman would soon become Morgenthau's closest confidant. "Kennedy desperately wanted to put in 'strike forces,' guys who'd only be accountable to Washington," he recalled. "And Morgenthau wasn't going to allow it."

Two months in office, Morgenthau discovered a pair of Department of Justice attorneys on his turf, working a big narcotics case out of the Dixie Hotel in Midtown. He called the department and spoke to Ed Silbering, a Justice aide and an ambitious Long Islander who was fast becoming a nemesis. "I told Silbering we'd handle it ourselves," Morgenthau would recall. "I might have used language a little less polite."

Within minutes, Kennedy called, sounding "less than pleased."

On June 14, Bobby took an early-morning flight and came to see Morgenthau. The war on crime, Kennedy said, would be run out of Justice. Morgenthau stood his ground. "Very tactfully," as an FBI official in the meeting recorded, he assured RFK that all requisite legal matters involving any New York investigation could be handled "most satisfactorily" by his office. Afterward, Kennedy and Morgenthau stood outside on the courthouse steps, posing for photographers. Neither man mentioned the dispute, yet both knew who had won. The men from Justice were sent packing.

Bobby had done more than compromise. He summoned the heads of every federal investigative body in New York to Morgenthau's office: the FBI, IRS, Alcohol and Tobacco, Bureau of Narcotics, Secret Service, Customs, Immigration. "Nobody had ever done this kind of thing before," Morgenthau would say. Each had always run its own dominion. To Bobby, the need to communicate was common sense: "Let's get all of the agencies to cooperate," he told Morgenthau, "to exchange information, and to work together."

Kennedy and Morgenthau knew the challenges. Above all, they would have to find investigators and enforcers willing to commit to the fight against organized crime. The FBI, both men knew, would offer more resistance than help: Since the end of the war, J. Edgar Hoover had ceaselessly warned of the "Red threat" but scarcely mentioned "organized crime." FBI agents were all but banned from uttering the word "Mafia"— no such organization, Hoover insisted, existed in the United States.

The FBI director, of course, knew better. In 1957, two state troopers in upstate New York had been investigating check fraud when they overheard the son of a local baron, Joseph S. Barbara, Sr., at a motel reserving rooms for a "convention of Canada Dry men." Barbara, a soft-drink distributor, was better known as a bootlegger with deep ties to organized crime. Intrigued, the troopers staked out the motel, as well as Barbara's sprawling estate in the nearby village of Apalachin. They soon witnessed the "convention": Dozens of luxury cars, many from out of state, delivered sixty-three men to the urgent conclave at Barbara's house. In Manhattan three weeks earlier, crime boss Albert Anastasia had been shot dead in the barbershop of the Park Sheraton Hotel—and in the ensuing power vacuum, the bosses feared an all-out war. When someone caught sight of the troopers, Barbara's guests fled, only to be rounded up and arrested.

"Apalachin," as the bust became known, was the Rubicon. Hoover would still plead ignorance—when Justice circulated a report detailing the spare facts known about the Mafia, he ordered it destroyed. But after Apalachin, the FBI had adjusted its language. "They had to say, 'Yeah, this is organized,'" Bill Vericker, an FBI agent who'd interrogated two of those arrested, would recall. "Only then did we become the 'organized crime group.'"

Instead, counterintelligence predominated: In New York in the late 1950s, the Bureau had 150 agents working a single spy case. "We were up to our necks with the Soviets," Richard McCarthy, a veteran FBI counterintelligence agent, would recall. "But the Italians? Not even on the radar." Few in federal law enforcement had studied the state of organized crime across the country, let alone attempted to curb its rise. But Kennedy and Morgenthau shared a sense as to where they might find allies. In 1957, on the day before the arrests in Apalachin, RFK, as counsel to the Senate rackets committee, had asked a witness, an undercover agent, "Is there any organization such as the 'Mafia,' or is that just the name given to the hierarchy in the Italian underworld?"

"That is a big question to answer," Joseph Amato replied. "But we believe there does exist today in the United States a society, loosely organized, for the specific purpose of smuggling narcotics and committing other crimes."

Amato was not a Hoover man. He worked for the Federal Bureau of Narcotics, the FBN. Morgenthau, too, knew their work—his father had supervised the FBN when the agency was housed at the Treasury—and he agreed: The narcotics men might be more responsive. In the war to come, they could be natural allies.

On May 17, 1961, Bobby launched the first salvo. He went to Congress to push for legislation to fight the "hoodlums and racketeers," who in "many instances have become so rich and so powerful, that they have outgrown local authorities." As Kennedy drew the line in Washington, Morgenthau followed suit in New York.

Before dawn on that same day, federal agents fanned out across the boroughs in a blitzkrieg of raids. By day's end, Morgenthau, having been in office just weeks, could claim a record haul: Eighteen men had been arrested, including five in Italy. In all, the new U.S. attorney would announce the indictment of twenty-four "associates" engaged in "organized crime."

The sweeps yielded national headlines, and Bobby reported that he was pleased. But still Hoover did not relent. Anyone who spoke of a national crime syndicate, the director said as late as 1962, was selling "baloney."

Successive rounds of the battle would follow; the mass-scale raids in New York would continue. Together, Bobby told Morgenthau, "we'll fight this war—and we are going to win it." But given the odds, if they were going to succeed in making inroads against the Mafia, both men knew they needed luck on their side. The big "break," as Morgenthau would call it, fell right into his hands, in the wake of a murder in the Atlanta Federal Penitentiary.

| | | |

The exercise yard of the Atlanta prison was half-filled on the morning of June 22, 1962. A dozen men watched as Prisoner Number 82811 swung the old pipe—two feet of galvanized iron, attached at one end to a broken brass faucet. Joe Valachi was no giant, but he packed 188 pounds into his five-foot-six frame.

The blows came in rapid succession. Valachi had bashed in the skull of another prisoner before he could turn to see his murderer.

On that morning only the most seasoned veterans of New York's

criminal underground, those who had made a profession of gang violence and the narcotics trade, knew Valachi's name. Before the year was
out, though, his name would become known to households across America. Valachi was a New Yorker, born in East Harlem in 1904. He had a
seventh-grade education and few known skills, but he could handle a car.
Among his compatriots, his exploits were legendary. He could spot a tail
and give it the slip like few men; thanks to his skill behind the wheel,
Valachi had become "a made man."

Valachi had spent decades in the family of Vito Genovese, head of the
most powerful organized crime syndicate in New York. "He was never
the triggerman," an investigator would say. "Always the driver, the spotter, never the one over the body." And yet, in all, Valachi would admit to
having taken part in at least thirty-three murders.

He had not been in the Atlanta prison long, but each day he lived in
mortal fear. Genovese, his former boss, was there as well, and had engi-
neered it so that Valachi was assigned to his cell. He had seen to it, as
well, that Ralph Wagner, a "kid" from the neighborhood who had been
Valachi's delivery boy, was another cellmate. For days, a rumor had
spread in the prison that Valachi had turned, become a "rat." In the mess
hall, he would switch food trays with another inmate, fearful of poison-
ing.

One evening days before the attack, Genovese had grabbed Valachi's
face—and kissed him. "The kiss of death," mumbled Wagner from the
next bunk. Valachi took it as fact: The boss had ordered him dead.

Valachi had killed John Joseph Saupp—a check forger from a small
town in Ohio—by mistake. When Valachi saw Saupp coming at him in
the yard, he mistook him for a Genovese enforcer from home, "Joe
Beck," Joseph DiPalermo. Valachi did not hesitate. "There was some
construction work going on," he recalled, "and I saw a piece of pipe
lying on the ground." After the blows, he had turned back to take a
closer look, to make sure he'd got the right man—but it was too late:
"With all the blood, who could tell who the hell he was now?"

||||

Within days, Morgenthau got a call from Atlanta. Menahem "Menny"
Stim, a New York defense attorney of considerable repute, had an urgency in his voice. His client was in a bind. "Valachi's just killed an inmate in the Atlanta pen," he said, and "he fears for his life and will
cooperate fully."

The offer was without precedent. At first Morgenthau doubted it: "It was beyond anything you could imagine, getting a man from the inside." For decades, since the founding of the Mafia in Sicily, all members of Italian organized crime had sworn a blood oath to maintain a vow of silence—*omertà,* they called it. Violators faced a death sentence. U.S. investigators did not yet know of the vow; they only knew no one had ever come forward.

As Stim detailed his client's predicament, Morgenthau began to believe his motives. The U.S. attorney, Stim was certain, would want Valachi to testify against his crime bosses in New York. Valachi understood, but had one condition: He would only talk to the FBN—the Federal Bureau of Narcotics, and to one agent in particular: "the Italian guy," the agent who had first questioned him back in the spring of 1959.

Morgenthau knew who Valachi meant. Wary of the FBI, he had turned to the narcotics agents. They were rough-edged, closer to the action, and, above all, "New Yorkers—guys who knew the neighborhoods . . . even many of the wiseguys." The FBN had seventy-eight agents in New York—and the U.S. attorney had found one who could deliver. Frank Selvaggi had met Morgenthau driving him around the city, on "protection duty." A Bronx native, the third of four sons, Selvaggi had joined the FBN in 1958.

Selvaggi did not need a prosecutor to convince him of the reach of Italian organized crime. "When I was a kid, you got your face smacked in if you ever said the word 'Mafia,'" he would say. He'd grown up in Pelham Bay, frequented the Irish bars where the Mob guys reigned, and knew a number of the local bosses by their first names. Given the history, Selvaggi was only mildly surprised when the U.S. attorney of New York called and asked him to come by his office.

Soon it would be known in the headlines as "the Valachi case"—once the former Genovese soldier testified on national television, the first "made man" to offer a look inside the Mafia in America. Later, others would take credit: the FBI, the Senate investigators, Robert Kennedy, even Morgenthau. But from the first, even long before the murder in the Atlanta prison yard, the case belonged to Selvaggi.

‖ ‖

It had begun with Helen Streat, a Black sex worker in her twenties, who lived just north of Central Park. In the winter of 1960, Selvaggi arrested her after she emerged from a "plant house"—an apartment where a dealer stored drugs—with ten ounces of heroin lining her ankle-length leather coat. Streat flipped. Her dealer, in turn, led Selvaggi up the chain, to "the Italian connection"—a wholesaler whose name he did not know, but who had a girlfriend in the Bronx. For days, Selvaggi drove across the Bronx, with only a vague description of where the girlfriend lived— until at last he found it. Staking out the apartment house, he caught sight of "the Italian connection."

He had recognized Valachi at once. Growing up in the Bronx, Selvaggi had seen him in the neighborhood—seen "him punching a guy out on the corner where I lived."

Valachi's criminal odyssey began early. He'd done his first stretch at eleven years old in the Bronx Catholic Protectory, for throwing a rock at a teacher. The rap sheet grew long: robbery, extortion, burglary, assault— by 1923, he was in Sing Sing. Once released, he worked a crew that raided furrier warehouses. In one robbery that went bad, Valachi was shot by a beat patrolman, the bullet lodging "in the base of his skull." His crew returned, put him in a baby carriage, and wheeled him to a local doctor, who managed to remove the slug. By 1930, Valachi was a "made man." Soon, he married up: His bride, Mildred, was the daughter of Gaetano "Tommy" Reina, a mobster with sufficient standing to have been murdered two years earlier. Vito Genovese served as best man.

Selvaggi knew Valachi ran a jukebox business, and surmised he would not leave town without arranging for someone to collect on the jukebox earnings. When Valachi fled upstate, Selvaggi followed his hunch, and got a line on the neighborhood kid tapped to make the jukebox rounds. Ralph Wagner was a onetime boxer from East Harlem in his late twenties, whose life ambition was to join the Mafia. "The kid worshiped the Mob, but couldn't get 'made,'" Selvaggi would say. "Ralph was half-German, half-Italian. And you had to be one-hundred-percent Italian."

Wagner told Selvaggi that the jukebox handler always called Valachi on Friday nights, around eleven o'clock. He had the telephone number, too: It belonged to a telephone booth somewhere on a two-lane rural road west of Hartford.

"We knew where the phone-booth generally was," Selvaggi would recall, "so we kept driving back and forth down the road." It was pitch-black, no lights. "Suddenly a single bulb goes on in a dark phone booth." In the darkness, "you couldn't miss the big shock of white hair." That evening, even before they'd made it back to the city, Valachi stunned the agents—revealing a willingness to cooperate. Nearly out of gas, Selvaggi had stopped at a firehouse. When they entered the bathroom, Valachi had turned to the agent: "Your partner's a Jew," he said. "Let him talk to the Jews. We're Italian, I can talk to you."

It was the first opening. Within days, Selvaggi went to Morgenthau and asked him to set a low bail. Once out, Valachi would take to calling Selvaggi, usually in the dead of night. "I'd be laying on my kitchen table," the agent recalled, "trying to stay awake, waiting for his call." They would go out driving, for hours all night. "That's when he started talking—he wouldn't tell it all, but he wanted to talk about the history, how it all began in New York."

Valachi also gave up the name of his "Italian connection." "For the first time," Morgenthau recalled, "we had a direct line on the heroin coming out of Southern Europe"—the route that would gain fame as the French Connection. Selvaggi's sleuthing soon paid off: In May 1961, Bobby Kennedy announced the indictment of twenty-four traffickers, suspected of importing "at least $150 million" worth of heroin—grown in Turkey, processed in France, and sold in New York. Morgenthau would fume as three of the ringleaders jumped bail and fled to Europe, but in time, he got another break: A wiretap caught one of them on a call to Lucky Luciano, the Mafia boss then in exile in Naples. U.S. agents were closing in when Luciano suffered a fatal heart attack. The three who'd jumped bail, though, were convicted, and sentenced to fifteen years in prison. Valachi, too, eventually received a twenty-year sentence on narcotics trafficking—and was sent to Atlanta.

| | | |

When he learned of the murder in Atlanta, and Valachi's sudden eagerness to talk, Morgenthau knew how to proceed. First, he called Bobby Kennedy, asking the attorney general to arrange a transfer. Then he called Selvaggi, asking him to get to Atlanta as soon as he could. On July 17, 1962, Valachi pled guilty in Atlanta to a lesser charge, second-degree murder. On the same day, Selvaggi escorted him, handcuffed, on a flight home.

Morgenthau feared leaks. Get Valachi out to Westchester, he told Selvaggi. His thinking was strategic: Register him under an alias, someplace where "they"—the Mafia *and* the FBI—would not look. The Mafia would know the moment that Valachi left the prison that he had become an informer, and were sure to be on the hunt. As for the FBI, Morgenthau knew Hoover would also be fuming—and searching for his prized witness. At best, the FBI director would try to steal the case; at worst, he would denigrate Valachi as a witness, if only to spite Bobby Kennedy.

Selvaggi and Valachi flew to New York and drove directly to the Westchester County Jail. It was in a secluded corner of Westchester, with few prisoners—almost "a little country club." He registered the prisoner as Joseph DeMarco.

It would not be easy to break the code of silence. Valachi was not the courageous type, but gradually, he began to open up. Selvaggi and Valachi met daily, alone in the warden's office. In time, he began to speak of Vito Genovese, and the deals. Valachi had placed a bet: Behind bars, his odds of survival, though slim, were better.

Selvaggi carried with him the FBN's "Mafia" book, an archive of photographs. As they turned the pages, Valachi attached names to the faces. Some were famous: Luciano, Joey Bananas, Three-Finger Brown, Tony Ducks, and Jimmy Blue Eyes. Others were not: Big Pat, Little Moe, Tough Tony, The Shadow, Benny Squint, Dom the Sailor, The Gap, Tea Bags, Felix the Cat, Tony Bender, Pip the Blind, Sally the Blond, and Jimmy Legs. And there were the Joes: Joe Adonis, Joe Diamond, Joe Sweet, Joe Babes, Joe the Baker, Joe Palisades, and Big Nose Joe. And the Charlies: Charlie Bullets, Charlie Four Cents, Charlie Lucky. And the Jerrys: Jerry the Bug and Jerry the Lug—the latter once "very friendly" with Meyer Lansky. And the De Martino brothers: Tony the Bum, Benny the Bum, and Teddy the Bum.

Throughout the weeks of interrogation, Valachi had yet to give a name to the overall organization—it was Selvaggi who called it the "Mob"—but he described, for the first time, its power structure: "Five Families" controlled organized crime in New York and beyond. The groups carried the names of the men who ran, or once ran, them: Lucchese, Genovese, Gambino, Bonanno, and Profaci. The Five Families, he said, constituted a small army—"about 5,000 men" all told, with 2,000 of them "active." In all, Valachi would offer 317 names—enough to fill ten typewritten pages, and prepare a wall-sized chart to hand-deliver to the attorney general.

And then the FBI intervened.

On September 10, Agent Jimmy Flynn appeared at the Westchester jail, demanding to join Selvaggi in the interrogation. Morgenthau pushed back, but Bobby Kennedy had made a strategic decision: He would give in to Hoover's demands for access to the witness in order to shame the FBI director into action. As Morgenthau protested, Jack Miller, the

Criminal Division chief in Washington, made the goal clear: If Morgenthau turned Valachi over to the FBI, Bobby might get Hoover and his men "to admit there *is* a Mafia, and then we can say to them, 'What are you doing about it?'"

Morgenthau acquiesced: The FBI took charge of the interrogation. For Agent Flynn, the first matter of importance concerned semantics. By September 14, he had found a way to allow Hoover to save face: "When asked whether the organized criminal element had a name today," Flynn wrote in a report to Washington, Valachi "stated that there was not a 'Mafia.'" But "when pressed regarding an actual Italian expression that symbolized this organization, he volunteered the title, '*Causa Nostra*'"— Our Cause.

Selvaggi, shut out and left to stew, fumed when he heard the Italian phrase. The FBI agent, he would insist, had simply made it up. "He had to—because the boss had said, 'there's no organized crime.' So Flynn cooked it up," Selvaggi would say. Hoover would add "La"—and from that day on, the FBI files on Italian organized crime were renamed accordingly: "La Causa Nostra," or LCN. In time, the name took a Hollywood turn, *La Cosa Nostra*—Our Thing.

Morgenthau's men would remain skeptical. "The FBI did all they could to avoid calling it 'the Mafia,' because Hoover had denied it for so many years," said Andy Lawler, who would spend years prosecuting the Lucchese family. "But *Cosa Nostra*? He could live with that."

| | | |

In September 1963, Valachi would testify as the star witness at the Senate's McClellan Committee hearings on organized crime. The televised proceedings proved a national sensation, yet Valachi was a less-than-perfect witness. The gravel-voiced canary, Jack Anderson wrote, "sang like a crow." He looked the part of a henchman—square head and graying buzz cut—but offered a confessional short on particulars. At times, he stumbled. When a senator from Nebraska asked, "Can you tell me about the state of organized crime in Omaha?," Valachi turned around to William Hundley, chief of the Justice Department's organized crime section, seated behind him, and asked, "Where the fuck is Omaha?" Still, Valachi put the lie to Hoover's blindness in vivid detail: Americans heard the witness speak of bodies, bullets, and millions of dollars reaped in illegal profits. There would be no turning back.

The news that the U.S. government had claimed its first Mafia turncoat had come on the eve of the hearings, in August 1963. It may have seemed like a leak, but the headlines were part of Bobby Kennedy's careful, if risky, orchestration. That summer, as his sixtieth birthday approached, Valachi had begun to scribble out his life story. He used a ballpoint pen and yellow notepaper to draft a mountain of a manuscript—1,180 pages, when typed up by the Justice Department steno pool—that he entitled *The Real Thing*. The attorney general knew a good story when he saw one. He handed the manuscript to a favored reporter, Peter Maas, who would use it as the basis for *The Valachi Papers*, a bestseller—the first paperback run was 1.75 million copies—that also became a Hollywood film. For all Kennedy's efforts, Miriam Ottenberg, an investigative reporter at the *Washington Star*, scooped Maas. In a front-page exposé, she identified Valachi: "For the first time," she wrote, "the witness is not a committee investigator or a narcotics agent on the outside looking in. The witness is on the inside looking out."

Hours before the news hit, an FBI agent called to warn Valachi's wife. "He must be crazy," Millie said. "He knows the rules."

Bobby Kennedy had created a celebrity witness, but Selvaggi felt betrayed. "Not by Morgenthau," he would say. "By my own people—the guys up top, they screwed me." Soon, he would be forced out—"they considered me too close to the wise guys"—and in time, he was transferred to the Westchester sheriff's office. A string of jobs followed, but Selvaggi would never escape the shadow of his biggest case. In a draft of her scoop, Miriam Ottenberg had given the FBN agent credit, but after a Kennedy deputy intervened (fearful of Hoover's wrath), Ottenberg awarded the glory to the FBI.

Even Bobby Kennedy did not utter Selvaggi's name. He gave the credit to Morgenthau for taking out a ring that had, "conservatively speaking," imported $150 million worth of heroin into the country. For Bobby, it was a first victory. He had laid bare the existence of the Mafia, and set himself apart from his older brother. For Morgenthau, though, Valachi's testimony was only the beginning. The end of *omertà*, to the U.S. attorney, meant that Morgenthau's war on the Mafia had just begun.

52. "A Lehman Candidate"

1962

When it came to politics, Jack Kennedy trusted few men beyond his father, his brother Bobby, and Ted Sorensen. But Lou Harris had found that ever since the primaries in 1960, whenever he spoke, JFK listened. And in the wake of the election, the president had all but appointed his former pollster in charge of the Democratic Party in New York.

Kennedy knew he would need a resourceful strategist in the state. The elections of 1961, when Mayor Wagner, sensing the winds of change brought by the Reform Democrats, broke with Tammany to win reelection, had left the party machine in ruins—and De Sapio, Buckley, and their fellow bosses licking their wounds. The Kennedys would have to find a new tack, as New York posed a particular danger: Governor Nelson Rockefeller was facing reelection, and already positioning himself to take a run at the White House. "Rocky was the one the Kennedys feared," Harris would recall. Taking him out of contention for 1964 was out of the question, but they hoped, at the least, to wound him.

The question loomed: Who could best serve as their proxy, someone who could put up a decent fight with Rockefeller, and leave him a less formidable opponent to JFK in a reelection bid? "Lou, we've got a problem," the president had said early in the winter of 1961, confiding in Harris the fears of a Rockefeller juggernaut. The list of New York Democrats eager to challenge the governor had grown long, but none suited the Kennedys. By Christmas, Harris had found a possible solution—a first-time candidate, and a strategy for how he could win. It might sound crazy, he told JFK, and he was still running the numbers, but when the president next visited New York, he would lay the plan out for him.

On January 19, 1962, JFK and a half-dozen White House aides arrived at the Carlyle Hotel, his preferred rest stop in the city. He summoned Mayor Wagner and Harris. The meeting began, and ended, in tension. "Wagner and Kennedy didn't like each other," Harris would say. "They came from different parts of the political spectrum, and had absolutely no rapport." The president had called on his pollster to serve as the bridge.

In the weeks since JFK first expressed concern about the gubernatorial race, the chances of a Rockefeller landslide had only grown. "Rocky," as the press had taken to calling him, had the money, the charm, and, as increasingly became obvious, strong bipartisan appeal. On civil rights and welfare, Rockefeller had carefully hewed close to the center, attracting sufficient numbers of minority and urban voters. Harris, though, had come prepared with new polls. The window, he told Kennedy, had opened: The odds remained long, but Rockefeller was vulnerable. There was the family trouble—a divorce after thirty-one years of marriage— and a clutch of Albany scandals beginning to emerge. Harris had polled all sixty-two counties of the state and was surprised to see the top potential Democratic candidates hitting 42 percent upstate. In the old days, when party control ruled New York City, any Democrat polling so well upstate stood a good chance. Yet 1961, as Kennedy knew well, had altered the landscape: They could no longer count on the party machine that Citizens for Kennedy and Morgenthau's young reformers had done so much to weaken. Harris, though, saw hope. "If we could find someone who could bring in just 5 percent more," he said, setting a goal of 47 percent of the vote, "we'd have a horse race."

Charles Buckley was pushing the candidacy of Frank O'Connor, the DA of Queens, but if it had to be an Irishman, the Kennedys preferred Frank Hogan, DA of New York County. No one, it seemed, was considering the man Harris had in mind—a close friend and Riverdale neighbor. Before offering the name, Harris laid out the strategy: "We need 'a Lehman candidate,'" he told JFK, someone in the mold of Herbert Lehman, the four-term governor and former senator who'd served New York from 1933 to 1957, "both in terms of appealing to Jews, but also as a civilized politician." Lehman, at eighty-four, remained hugely popular among the city's Jews. Days earlier, the pollster had floated the balloon in a call to Mayor Wagner. The mayor, he was certain, could be swayed; the president, though, would be harder going. Wagner, who'd deployed Lehman to great effect in the mayoral race, at once saw the logic: Only a Jew could come close against Rocky. At the Carlyle, Harris laid out the polling numbers on the table: You needed a Jewish candidate, he told the president, ideally one from the city, and one who could attract minority voters. Only a few were qualified.

"It's got to be Bob Morgenthau, whether you like it or not," Harris said.

| | | |

Months passed, as party insiders pushed for safer candidates—Jim Farley, FDR's old party chair, or Franklin Roosevelt, Jr.—but Farley had gone to work for Coca-Cola and Franklin Jr. had opened a car dealership in Washington. By August 1962, the names had faded, and the phone call came.

Morgenthau's first reaction was to worry. At forty-three years old, he had never run for office. Worse, he had no chance; he would have to forfeit the job he had loved from day one; he would let down the office. There was also the family. Martha, who would turn forty-three in October, was pregnant.

The Kennedys, though, did not like to wait. New York demanded resolution. On August 15, the president tried to mediate, summoning Mayor Wagner and Congressman Buckley to the White House. They met with the president on the same day, at different times. Buckley, defiant in the face of Wagner's turn toward the reformers, pushed O'Connor, while hours later, Wagner warned that the bosses would never give up. The party needed rebuilding, a feat that only a compromise candidate could pull off.

The following day, the *Times* headline announced, "Democrats Consider Robert Morgenthau." The would-be contender himself, finding the wrangling unseemly, had left for Martha's Vineyard, joining Martha and the children on vacation. Four days later, though, Bobby Kennedy summoned him to the Kennedy family compound on the Cape. Morgenthau and Bobby spent the evening of August 19 in Hyannis Port debating his chances. "It was not a Bobby Kennedy move," Morgenthau would later say. "It was a Wagner move more than anybody else. But it had the approval of JFK. I don't think Bobby Kennedy was that enthusiastic about it."

The attorney general knew better than to push too hard. Yes, he conceded, he and the president had first favored Hogan, but the Democrats needed someone who could restore the party to its former strength under Lehman: in short, a Jew.

The Kennedys knew that the Republican power brokers were worried. Rockefeller had not only divorced in March, but rumors were swirling of "another woman." Nearly eighteen years Rockefeller's junior, Margaretta "Happy" Fitler Murphy was the wife of a Philadelphia virologist; she was on the staff of the Rockefeller Institute and a good friend of the governor's. Rocky and Happy had met on the '58 campaign and until recently had worked together nearly each day. Happy Murphy had joined the governor's personal staff. Republican strategists were terrified—and Democrats hopeful—of the damage that the affair might do to Rocky.

"It'll be a very tough fight," Bobby told Morgenthau. Yes, he was young, but "people had said Jack was too young to run for President." The name Morgenthau, Bobby added, carried weight: He'd be sure to get plenty of press, nearly all of it good. Above all, Bobby argued, he would be seen as a reformer—a man of the new era, not the party. The logic was dubious, but Morgenthau, whether out of blindness or ambition, swallowed it.

"I was old enough to know what I was getting into," he would say.

| | | |

The convention would come late that year—pushed back to early fall by the bosses in a final attempt to buy more time—but the wheels were already in motion. Before Morgenthau could give his assent, the Kennedy camp was speaking to friendly reporters. Three days after the meeting with Bobby on the Cape, Morgenthau listened as the president faced the press.

> QUESTION: Mr. President, after your conference with Mayor Wagner last week, there were reports that you had agreed to endorse Robert Morgenthau as the Democratic Gubernatorial nominee in New York. This, presumably, is an election of some considerable importance to you. Can you tell us, do you have a preference for this election and who it might be?
>
> THE PRESIDENT: No, and I wouldn't take any position on the matter until the Democratic Convention meets in mid-September. I think the choice ought to be made there.

By August's end, the reformers had found a receptive audience in the press. As a Morgenthau boom mounted, O'Connor, the Queens DA and eager contender, decried the return of "bossism." No one, not even the Kennedys, could squelch him. "Right here in New York all of us are being made second-class citizens by a small group of willful men who are not responsible to the people but only to those who pay them," O'Connor railed. "I can match fourteen years of public service to Mr. Morgenthau's one year. I have won five elections—he has never run for office."

On September 5, Morgenthau resigned as U.S. attorney. He stood before the cameras—tanned from the Vineyard, square glasses folded into his suit pocket—in the law library of the prosecutor's office. He had only made up his mind the night before. "Widespread support for my candidacy" had led him to run, he said. To a reporter's shout—"Can you tell who told you that?"—he answered, "I'm just basing it on conversations with friends and with other people." It was a less than auspicious beginning. On his first morning as a candidate, Morgenthau was on the defensive.

The state convention opened in the cavernous Onondaga War Memorial Auditorium in Syracuse on Monday, September 17, amid a fraught atmosphere, and by evening had devolved into intraparty warfare. Morgenthau could claim at least 350 of the 570 votes needed for the nomination. Charles Buckley had warned the Kennedys that there would be a battle, at least through the first ballot. In the first hours of the convention, Morgenthau's backers worked to split Erie County's 72 delegates. The majority still supported O'Connor, but Peter Crotty, the power broker who had dominated the upstate party since 1947, wrested 26 delegates for Morgenthau. Two big blocks remained in the balance: 185 delegates from Brooklyn and Buckley's 110 from the Bronx.

Mrs. Roosevelt, too ill to come to Syracuse, had let her desires be known. If her own son could not rise beyond the House—Franklin Jr. had lost to Jacob Javits for Senate in 1954—it would be sweet consolation to see young Morgenthau make it to Albany. Other elders in the state party, though, played coy. Farley and Harriman flew to Syracuse on the same flight as the city bosses Buckley and O'Connor, and allowed themselves to be photographed together on the tarmac. They had appeared, too, at an O'Connor press conference, as the Queens DA insisted he alone could win.

By nine o'clock in the evening, Herbert Lehman rose for Morgenthau. He praised the prosecutor's unique gifts, noted the stellar war record, and failed to mention that his candidate was the son of his niece. As the men tapped to give Morgenthau's seconding speeches took turns at the microphone, hyperbole filled the hall: "There is a new star rising," announced Bill Luddy, the Westchester chair, son of an upstate drayman; Morgenthau, said Fred Eggert, a Bronx assemblyman, was "a man who can be trusted to give his mind and soul for the next four years to the destiny of this state"; the U.S. attorney, thundered Albert Hecht, the Dutchess County chair, "has the fighting qualities of another county son, Franklin Delano Roosevelt!"

O'Connor's backers refused to go quietly. They cursed and yelled, booed and rushed the platform. A riot nearly broke out: The lights were turned out, and a police detail was ordered in. Still, O'Connor's camp did not calm down. Instead, they got a second wind, as two upstate politicians orchestrated a "Stop Morgenthau" movement. Within hours, Abraham Beame, the city comptroller and longtime Brooklyn party figure, threw in his hat. The power brokers worried: Never in the history of the state party had a gubernatorial nomination required a second ballot.

On the first ballot, Morgenthau fell short by seven votes. Round after round of procedural battles ensued. At one point an O'Connor lieutenant jumped onto the stage to demand a roll-call vote for an adjournment, but Buckley was only biding his time. That morning, a call had come from Bobby Kennedy: The administration wanted Morgenthau. At 3:15 in the morning, a second ballot was held—and Morgenthau went over the top. At 5:00 A.M., he appeared before the weary reporters.

"BOB AND FRANK SLUG IT OUT," screamed the front-page headline in the Syracuse Post-Standard, while the Binghamton Evening Press announced, "Morgenthau Nominated to Tune of Boos and Jeers." The convention would be called the "most unruly" in the history of the state party. "Probably never before," an upstate reporter wrote, "has the name of a winner been so violently and consistently heckled and booed as was Morgenthau."

Lou Harris had stayed at home, monitoring events upstate by telephone. "Everybody was complaining," he would recall, " 'Morgenthau's too inexperienced, he's never run before.' But I kept saying, 'He's just what the doctor ordered.' " As concerns grew, Harris brokered a deal, maneuvering John J. Burns, mayor of Binghamton, onto the ticket. "It became apparent, because I was an upstate Catholic," Burns recalled, "that it would be a good balance on the ticket."

At 8:02 in the evening, Morgenthau was steeling himself to walk onto the stage and accept the nomination when the president called from Newport, where he and Jackie had gone to watch the America's Cup races. JFK offered congratulations, but they spoke only briefly. The president had called as much to wish him well as to check the candidate's pulse.

"Bob wanted it very much," Harris would say, "but he was entirely untested. I was looking for an upset—and I really thought Bob just might do it."

I I I I

The campaign would be a seven-week sprint. On Sunday night, September 30, Morgenthau appeared on "Race for Governor," the first of the candidates' interviews on WNEW television. He sat behind a small desk, facing a panel of three journalists.

He did not laugh, scarcely smiled, and spoke haltingly, measuring his words with undue care. But for half an hour, the candidate, looking his most handsome, critiqued the Rockefeller record: his lack of enthusiasm for job creation, his inability to attract federal money for new space programs, and, above all, his "impossible" pledge not to raise taxes. But throughout the candidate's polite and precise exegesis of the governor's record, the reporters kept returning to one issue.

"Mr. Morgenthau, politics, largely through the impact of television, has become such a highly personalized business recently," said Herb Kamm of the *World-Telegram & Sun*. "Governor Rockefeller is an extremely personable man. Has a lot of glamour. You have been described as a rather unflamboyant type. Do you feel your campaign is going pretty well now? Has a lot of momentum?"

Again and again, Morgenthau was asked about his persona in allusive terms as the reporters struggled to edge the bounds of courtesy. Each time, he seemed to blanch.

"I think the candidate is probably the last person to know that," he answered. "But I think it *is* going well—and I think the issues are in favor of the Democratic ticket. And we intend to wage the campaign on the issues."

"Are there any plans," Kamm parried, "to use a word that even Rockefeller would appreciate, to *schmaltz* up the campaign a little bit?"

"No, no plans," he said.

"How do you stand on the feud between the 'regular' and the 'reform

Democrats' of New York City?" asked Lawrence Barrett of the *Herald Tribune*.

Morgenthau dodged: "Everybody's united."

"Still, there is a conflict going on," Barrett said.

"My job now," Morgenthau said, "is to concentrate my fire on the Republican Governor, the incumbent."

In a calm tenor, the candidate quoted Department of Labor statistics, spoke of the dire need for technological improvements, and reprised the Kennedy administration's plan for "a long-range solution" in education. And still, the questioners circled back to personality.

"Do you feel you've gotten off to a halting start? You don't feel that there's a great deal of apathy around?"

"May not have been noisy," said Morgenthau, "but it's early . . ."

| | | |

It was not only a question of time. Rockefeller, America's first self-financing politician, would outspend Morgenthau by five to one. He spent more in Westchester County than his opponent spent in the entire state. Yet the greatest liability remained the candidate himself. Morgenthau was not only a novice, he lacked basic skills on the stump. "He was a horrible speechmaker," his daughter Jenny would recall. "Just dull, not nervous." Morgenthau was "an absolutely incredible choice," Robert Novak, the conservative columnist, would write. "Never was there a more inept campaigner."

Rockefeller, on the other hand, was a natural—a born millionaire who managed to affect a commoner's touch. Reporters loved him. The governor's "appeal to the youngsters is indeed great," wrote one. "But his celebrated magic, undiminished since 1958, seems still to captivate voters . . . In rapid, unpredictable sequence, he doles out winks, V-signs, boxers' clasps, crossed fingers, and—when fitting—a little chatter in Spanish for the Puerto Ricans." The press ascribed to him the same "presidential aura" that had surrounded JFK in 1958.

Morgenthau, meanwhile, as one reporter wrote, possessed a "slow smile and faintly palsied wave." Every time he attempted a bold step, he appeared to stumble. No matter where he went, he found few crowds, and when he did, he often got lost in them. " 'Which one is Morgenthau?' they ask," wrote a reporter on his trail.

The Democrats had the edge in registered voters—nearly 500,000 more than the Republicans—but the party failed to activate the troops. Even the big guns, like Farley, fell silent. Morgenthau was left in the hands of a half-dozen aides. Harris and Justin Feldman, Bob's old friend, were the main forces. A handful of young prosecutors from the U.S. attorneys had quit with Morgenthau to help on the campaign. Hank Walter, a *World-Telegram* political reporter, took a leave to run press. And Bobby Kennedy sent up a young political science professor, late of Syracuse University, Pat Moynihan, then working in the Labor Department, to add ballast.

Soon Moynihan would be churning out speeches, but the press, as he would recall, proved "uncooperative." Rockefeller's acceptance speech at his convention ran on the front page of the *Times*. Morgenthau's speech in Syracuse was buried on page 26. Each week, Rockefeller issued an edition of "Morgenthau Mistakes"—a sharply worded position paper to rebut his opponent's proposals. Undeterred, Bob put nearly everyone he knew on the stump. The prosecutors of the U.S. attorney's office could not be enlisted, but he could recruit the survivors of the *Lansdale*. Morgenthau was reluctant to play to the war record, but Harris and Feldman overruled him. Marion Porter, one of the mess attendants who had manned the guns on the *Lansdale,* joined other veterans on the stump. They appeared alongside the candidate atop a mock-up of the sunken destroyer and paraded throughout the upstate counties. Bob leaned on his brother Henry, too. He and his wife, Ruth, ran strategy sessions. The one notable absence was the former secretary of the Treasury, even at summer's end, after his annual return from the South of France; he would never appear in public with his son.

Everyone was waiting on JFK. Bobby had assured Morgenthau that the president would campaign vigorously for him. October offered two landmarks of any New York campaign, Columbus Day and Pulaski Day—opportunities to showcase the candidate before two essential Democratic blocs, the Italian- and Polish-American communities. JFK promised to stump for Morgenthau at a series of rallies, first in the city, then upstate. But events intervened—"the Cuba thing," Justin Feldman would call it.

On September 28, Morgenthau rose before dawn to fly to Washington. He joined Jim Donovan, the Brooklyn lawyer who had been tapped to run for Senate against Jacob Javits. The Kennedys liked Donovan, who had gained fame defending, as "a public service," the Soviet spy Rudolf Abel. Donovan had been tasked to negotiate the release of the

Bay of Pigs prisoners, 1,113 American-trained paramilitary fighters held by Castro since the failed invasion of April 1961. JFK spoke briefly with Morgenthau before a photographer interrupted, capturing the two clasping hands in the Oval Office. The president, though, seemed distracted. The White House was mired in round-the-clock deliberations, girding itself for the greatest national security test faced by the United States since World War II, the Cuban missile crisis.

It was late on Wednesday night, October 10, when the White House called Morgenthau headquarters—the president's trip was uncertain: He might be delayed, and he might not come at all. JFK was hunkered down, deliberating with his national security team. Morgenthau was due in Buffalo, to speak at a state civil service employees convention. But he had no choice. Forced to stay behind in New York City to await the president, Morgenthau looked for a substitute to step in for him: his wife. The next morning, Martha flew to Buffalo.

||||

"Mrs. Morgenthau" would prove to be the campaign's chief asset. Yet few in the campaign appreciated her true gifts or desires. She did not profess opinions, did not make demands. She had not grown up amid men and women who lived in the White House. Yet Martha, behind the faint half smile that was her first resort in the company of strangers, even among the men with whom her husband spent his days, possessed an acumen, and farsightedness, that often went beyond the candidate's.

"Mom," her daughter Jenny would say, "had good political sense."

"She was unencumbered by political knowledge," her daughter Anne would add, "but she knew better what people, people out there, would think." She was a quiet person, but not as reserved as her husband. "He was quite quiet and wooden and non-projecting. Mom was more available, more socially comfortable."

Martha did not measure it, but the distance was evident to her daughters: how far she had traveled from her parents, the Pattridges, transplanted Vermonters and rock-ribbed Republicans. For Martha, it had been a gradual process, begun at Smith. "Stepping away," her eldest daughter called it. She had made the decision to raise her children as Jews—at least to the same minimal degree that her husband had been brought up in the faith. Martha had been raised as a Protestant; her father was Episcopalian and her late mother Unitarian. "Her parents were definitely anti-Jew," Jenny would say. "And anti-Roosevelt and anti-

Black, but she'd never met any Blacks, Jews, or Democrats. When she met Daddy, she didn't think he was any different from anyone else."

Only days before she first stepped out alone on a political stage, Martha had made her press debut. "Mrs. Morgenthau Gives Interview in Her Charming Home in Riverdale," announced the headline in the *Albany Knickerbocker*. In a two-hour chat, the society reporter paid much attention to appearances. Martha wore a blue sweater, black skirt, and low-heeled shoes—"I like to look at clothes," she said, "but you couldn't say I'm interested in fashion." After offering a cup of coffee, the candidate's wife answered questions "slowly and directly." She pronounced herself "a little surprised to tell her life story to strangers."

Anne had just left for boarding school, her choice, at Concord Academy. "I thought it was wise," Martha explained, "to help Anne build an identity of her own." She spoke, too, of Nellie, then eleven and still at Lochland, hiding nothing. She toured the house—the children's sculptures on the fireplace mantel: a clay horse, wooden whales; the watercolors of the farm done by friends; the piano, an old upright, in the corner ("No one plays it now"); and the gateleg table between the windows, on which sat an autographed portrait of the president and Mrs. Kennedy, opposite a copy of the inaugural address. She even introduced the family pets, but she revealed no fault lines.

Martha presented a picture of patriotism, public service, and healthy living. The Morgenthaus, she said, were athletic—"like another prominent Democratic family," the reporter noted. They liked to swim, ski, skate, and play tennis and ice hockey. She had no staff, only "one good woman" to do housekeeping and cooking. Martha had never seen the Executive Mansion in Albany, she confessed, but given the baby coming soon, she added, "we sure could use the extra room."

As she stepped to the dais in Buffalo, Martha looked out on nearly eight hundred civil service employees, jammed into the ballroom of the Statler Hilton for their fifty-second annual meeting.

"I'm terribly sorry I'm me, and not Bob," she began. "About 9 o'clock last night they called me out of bed at home and asked me to sub for Bob here today. I said I would and immediately washed my hair and switched a car pool assignment." Wearing a herringbone maternity dress, she read her husband's words, but emphasized all the right notes, and hit all the dramatic pauses.

"The present Republican administration," Martha read, "broke faith with its employees when it voted a pay increase for them but postponed the effective date. . . . The only reason it was postponed was to enable Gov. Rockefeller to present an apparently 'balanced' budget to use for campaign purposes." Such actions, she said, "would not be condoned by a Democratic administration."

As the audience cheered, Martha moved on. Led by Peter Crotty, the county boss, and trailed by a dozen local sovereigns and secretaries, ladies and gentlemen of the party and labor apparatus, she stumped across the city, charming nearly all whom she encountered, according to the reporters in tow. At Main and Genesee, she cut the ribbon at a new Morgenthau headquarters. In the ballroom of the Hotel Buffalo, she addressed an overflow crowd at the Citizens Committee for Morgenthau luncheon. At the local Chevrolet factory, Mrs. Morgenthau joked with the reporters: "My five-year-old son would have loved to tour the plant because he knows more about motors than I do. He has said that he'd rather be a mechanic than a lawyer because lawyers can't fix anything." She shook hands with the workers, some two hundred of them, as they finished their shift at the plant.

Rockefeller, as usual, was on the hustings nearby. He had also addressed the civil servants that morning, and gone on to open a bridge outside the city. Mrs. Morgenthau, though, won the day. With less than a month to go, the campaign had found a spark. Morgenthau, wrote an upstate reporter, had at last "unleashed a mighty potent campaign weapon . . . his attractive and urbane wife, Martha."

||||

JFK at last arrived in New York City on October 11. At the Marine Terminal at LaGuardia Airport, Morgenthau tried to meet the president but was stopped by his Secret Service detail, who had no clue who he was. After a White House aide interceded, Morgenthau climbed atop the rear of the open Lincoln-Mercury Continental convertible, and sat beside JFK.

They rode together all the way into Manhattan, sharing the jubilant reception along Second Avenue to Seventy-sixth Street and Park Avenue. At the Carlyle Hotel, the two made their way through the throng and into a suite on the mezzanine. Sitting close, the president and Morgenthau made a series of television ads, taking turns reading from the electronic prompter. If the candidate sounded wooden—"Fellow citizens, it is a privilege to have President Kennedy with us"—JFK was in peak stride. His voice was strong and cadences smooth: "Bob," he said, "I want to express my congratulations to you for the campaign you're conducting here. . . . New York's the richest and most influential state, and I wish you every success."

On the following day, JFK spoke at a breakfast fundraiser for Morgenthau, shaking hands and offering praise, before setting off for the main event, the Columbus Day parade on Fifth Avenue.

At the reviewing stand at Fifty-ninth Street, Morgenthau stood beside the president. Yet Kennedy seemed subdued. Even at the parade, the heightened Soviet threat weighed heavily. A banner draped over a Studebaker announced "WE WILL BURY KHRUSHCHEV!" Later that day, amid the streets swollen with celebrants, JFK would speak of his mother's father, Honey Fitz, and the story that the old man would tell of having Venetian roots. "I've never had the courage to make that claim before," Kennedy said, with a wide grin. At each word, the crowd roared. But it was a civic day, by tradition a day of nonpartisan celebration. The most dramatic moment came as JFK arrived at the parade's reviewing stand by Central Park. Finding Rockefeller, he reached out for a warm greeting—dozens of photographers capturing the president and governor smiling widely—as Morgenthau and Mayor Wagner looked on dourly.

Kennedy exerted scant effort on behalf of the Democratic candidate for governor. At the parade, he called Morgenthau "an able and distinguished candidate." Later, at Idlewild, as Bob saw the president off, bound for a speech in Pittsburgh, JFK told the press, "A candidate has been chosen of which the people can be proud." Morgenthau heard it clearly: The silence was strategic. The Kennedys would not risk political capital on him.

| | | |

The campaign hoped for a better day on Sunday, October 14, when the president rejoined the candidate in Buffalo.

At the Pulaski Day parade, JFK received one of the biggest welcomes since the inauguration. The reporters, astounded, estimated that 400,000 had come out. As the presidential motorcade formed a slow-moving wedge, winding its way through the crowded street, Morgenthau stood waiting at City Hall, facing the sea of people that had filled Niagara Square.

The loudspeakers sounded—"He's on the freeway, he's coming in six minutes"—as the crowd waited, long since ready to erupt. The Secret Service had told Hank Walter, Morgenthau's press man, to sit onstage and stay put. But when JFK finally arrived, Walter, ran to the photographers in front. "Kennedy walked out onto the stage and went down right to the front, to the edge of the crowd," Walter would recall, "but Bob just stood there, 15 feet away, frozen."

"I was yelling at him," Walter would say, " 'Get closer! You want to be seen with the President!' " At last he caught on. By then, though, JFK had stepped to Morgenthau's side, moving the candidate in front of the cameras.

Morgenthau would speak only briefly. He recounted that General Pulaski, hero of the Revolutionary War, who gave his life at the battle of Savannah, "represents the contribution of the Polish people to culture and to the freedom of the United States." But when JFK rose to approach the microphone, the crowd again came to life.

As the president sat reading over the draft of his speech to the Polish-American crowd, he had a new reason to think of the Soviet threat, but he could not disclose it in public. That Sunday, the Pentagon had received the first photographs that would lead the country to the brink of a nuclear conflict. Taken from a U-2 spy plane, the images presented evidence that Soviet missiles had arrived in Cuba, missiles that could carry nuclear warheads and were capable of striking the United States. In Buffalo, even with the intelligence reports on his mind, JFK did not mention Cuba. Poland was in a Soviet prison, he said, but it would not be so forever. If in New York the president had seemed subdued, his voice now carried thunder. "As the old song says, as long as you live, Poland lives." "*Jeszcze Polska nie zginiela!*" he shouted, referring to the Polish national song, "Poland has never been lost."

The president made no mention of the election.

| | | |

Morgenthau knew the odds. But he did not anticipate how hard Rockefeller would play. Alton Marshall, a top aide to the governor, rounded up the troops—enlisting men from the Rockefeller organization, as well as the private aircraft to ferry them around the state.

The unfolding crisis over Cuba also further diminished Morgenthau's chances. Kennedy had vowed to come again to New York, but by the third week of October, the White House made it official: No one would be coming to Morgenthau's aid. Not JFK, RFK, LBJ, or even any cabinet members. As the stakes in the Cuban standoff climbed, there was no room, the president said, for partisan politicking. To make matters worse, even the *Times,* despite the deep family ties to its publishers, came out for Rockefeller—"an able Governor," the endorsement declared.

Morgenthau knew he only stood a chance if he could face Rockefeller one-on-one, but the governor held off. Rockefeller's "refusal to debate Robert Morgenthau," Gore Vidal wrote, was "well calculated." "He would have been facing a first-rate lawyer and he knew he would be in trouble."

On Sunday evening, November 4, two days before the election, Morgenthau and Rockefeller would finally appear together before the television cameras. The WNBC "face-to-face exchange," though, was no debate. Instead, the five candidates crowded the stage: the two contenders, and three unknowns from fringe parties. Still, for one hour, neither the governor nor his challenger held back.

For Rockefeller, it was a chance to grandstand. A clear-cut victory could solidify his dream to take on Kennedy. For Morgenthau, there was nothing to lose. Throughout the show, as tensions rose, the two pummeled each other. For weeks, Morgenthau had hammered the governor on taxes, tenants' rights, and unemployment. He'd painted Rockefeller as a man with little interest in the business of state governance, and far more in running for president. "I'm going to move the capital back to Albany," Morgenthau had said. "Governor Rockefeller spends less than a quarter of his time in Albany. Most of the business in the state is carried out in a private office of the Rockefeller family." He needled the governor, too, to make a pledge: that if reelected, he would serve out his four-year term. Rockefeller refused. New York governors, he said coyly, had a tradition of running for the White House. Who could rule it out?

Now at last sharing a stage with Rockefeller, Morgenthau attacked on education, the economy, taxes. As he charged that 72,000 jobs had been lost in the state, and wages and economic growth had sagged during the governor's administration, Rockefeller erupted. "That's a complete misrepresentation of fact," he shouted. Morgenthau did not hesitate: "That's an absolute representation of fact, Governor, and you know it!"

The thrust and parry became a bit too lively: The station was forced to delay a break for station identification for four minutes. Rockefeller alleged Morgenthau was showing a "disregard and contempt of the truth." But when he charged that the Democratic platform would, if adopted by the state, force a tax increase, it was Morgenthau's turn to interrupt: "That's absolute bunkum, and you know it." Finally, he charged that Rockefeller "has had a phony pay-as-you-go system." Turning to face the governor, he delivered the best line of the campaign: "It means we pay, and you go—to Washington."

At the program's outset the two had shaken hands and smiled. By the close, they avoided speaking. "I think I really got to him," Morgenthau would tell an aide.

||||

On November 6, Bob walked hand in hand with Martha before the cameras and into P.S. 81, the local grammar school, in the Bronx. As they entered the polling station, he raised his right hand in a V sign. He stopped, smiled, took questions, and said all the things a candidate is expected to say on Election Day. By evening, though, the outcome was clear: The Republicans, as predicted, swept the vote.

Bill Pfeiffer, Governor Rockefeller's campaign manager, liked to speak of a million-vote margin. "They were very successful at putting out the story," Morgenthau would say, "Rockefeller was going to win by a million, two hundred thousand votes." Morgenthau had, in fact, done better than expected. Rockefeller won by 529,000 votes—40,000 fewer than his 1958 margin over Harriman. "This was no disaster for Rockefeller," Novak would write, "but it was nothing to brag about."

For all the unseen footwork, and repeated promises, of the Kennedys, JFK had had little, if any, effect on the campaign. "They say it's difficult," Rockefeller had quipped, "to rub one person's personality off on anybody else."

Morgenthau did not feign surprise, and yet the loss took a hidden toll. Within a week, he was back at work, at his old desk overlooking Foley Square. (President Kennedy had kept his end of the deal, reappointing Morgenthau two weeks after the election.) But he felt something was missing from his life. "There was the ego," his daughter Jenny would say. "But it was never about ego for him. Ambition, yes. But this was different: Governor was always the one job he really thought he could do. And do damn well."

Years later, reflecting on the campaign with the Rockefeller biographer Cary Reich, Morgenthau spoke of 1962 as an achievement. "Considering the shortness of the campaign, my lack of experience, lack of funds, I think 44 percent of the vote was pretty incredible."

In the aftermath, asked Reich, did Morgenthau harbor a grudge? Did he ever think that he had been used, that Wagner and the Kennedys had known he stood no chance, but they "wanted to gore Rockefeller a bit"?

"I don't know," Morgenthau said. "I mean, you've done something, and that's it. You're not going to sit back and cry about it. I'm the kind of person, once something's over, it's over."

53. "White Whale"

1962–1964

Defeat was followed, overnight, by a greater loss.

Eleanor Roosevelt had been in the Columbia-Presbyterian Hospital since late September. She had long complained of fatigue, but two years earlier, at age seventy-five, her condition markedly deteriorated. Dr. David Gurewitsch, Mrs. Roosevelt's physician who had become one of her closest confidants, learned she had a blood disorder, aplastic anemia—her bone marrow could not produce sufficient red blood cells. She'd undergone two procedures, yet the relief proved only temporary. Hospitalization, it was clear, was a must. But Mrs. Roosevelt begged off: She was, she insisted, "too busy to be sick." By September 1962, as the bruises, and the pain, spread, she at last acquiesced.

Just before Eleanor Roosevelt entered the hospital, Henry Morgenthau III came to visit. He found her at the apartment on Seventy-fourth Street in bed—"a great white mountain of bed clothes & pillows and a tired intent cheerful face." Mrs. Roosevelt sat propped up in the sunny room, its walls a clutter of photographs, reminders of that "combination of family friends and the great figures of the world who crowded into her life." On the hearth sat a white china cat, life-sized and sleeping. It was one of the very few objects she had taken from the "big house" at Hyde Park.

Even now, Mrs. Roosevelt professed herself "ready to work." "The strenuous life was no longer an easy matter of course," Henry III wrote, but Mrs. Roosevelt was not about to quit: "She had only conceded to some greater degree of planning and conservation of energy." A new television series was in the offing, to be called *An American Experience*.

The concept remained vague—the former first lady would converse with guests, who'd speak of their role in the vital events of the day—but she was eager to get it going. "The talk . . . seemed in part honest and real," Henry III would write of the visit, "while there was the concurrent sense of playing a game."

All the plans masked a truth: As the pain endured, Mrs. Roosevelt could foretell the end. On October 11, she celebrated her seventy-eighth birthday in the hospital, and begged Dr. Gurewitsch to let her die. She refused additional tests, demanding to go home. On October 18, she got her wish. And on November 7, after suffering a stroke, Eleanor Roosevelt died at home.

Bob Morgenthau was devastated. "Mrs. R.," as he called the former first lady, embodied the "soul of the party." She was the last tie to the old days, the world before war and the height of his parents' happiness. But for Bob, the loss was personal: Mrs. Roosevelt had taken care of him as a boy when he'd convalesced after his ear surgeries; she'd been a guardian angel when he was away from home, first at school, then at college, and finally, in the war; she, not his father, had been his essential political guide and benefactor. Losing an election brought a temporary hurt, disappointment, and a bruised ego; losing Mrs. R. left a void he could never fill.

That evening, Bob drafted a statement. He remembered the private kindness—"her reading to me in the hospital when I was a small child"—but also the country's most famous woman: "To millions of people Mrs. R. became the symbol of kindness, understanding and dedication to the service of others. The whole world has lost a great friend."

| | | |

On November 22, President Kennedy, in Hyannis Port for Thanksgiving, announced that Bob would be reappointed the U.S. attorney in New York.

Later, when one term grew into a second, and the cases had multiplied into a record tally, and the victories shone more brightly than the defeats, Bob Morgenthau would claim that he had followed no prosecutorial model. "Trust your gut, follow your instincts," he would often say, when asked his formula. The reporters accepted it, so did the assistants. But most knew there were unseen traits and tactics, an entwining of personality and pedigree that yielded power. To nearly all except a few intimates, Morgenthau was inscrutable. Private audiences were rare; he preferred the company of his own mind. He had never been a talker, and the deep gravel of his voice, and his manner of speaking, mouth half-open, often lent his spare instructions a biblical gravity. He had a habit—whether by design or nature, no one could be sure—of speaking in a fugue: He might hold three conversations at once (someone across his desk, someone at the door, another on the phone), and when intrusions arose—a phone call, an elevator ride, a jury's return—he would only pause, switch tracks, and carry on. Those stranded at a crossroads soon learned to practice patience.

Morgenthau wielded another weapon: a droll humor, but one so dry, as his close friends would recall, it was rarely appreciated by many in his audience. The assistants, however, could not help but hear the saltier side of his vocabulary, and the bluntness of his commands. They could attribute it to the Navy, although it had been with him since childhood. Bob Morgenthau did not become the champion of the victims, of those who lost their savings, jobs, and lives, solely because of compassion or a genius for administration. That force which the courthouse reporters and assistants came to call "confidence" was an aggressiveness that had been there all along.

He had learned so much in the war, he would say. He'd come to know and rely on so many men from across the country, and when he said they had come from such a range in "background," he meant race and class. In the war, he had learned the divides of the country, and seen the hatred they engendered. But it was the fight—the bravery and work ethic of the officers and crew—that he carried with him.

Bob Morgenthau could not rule in the style of his father. He was neither grandiose nor defensive. He was free, too, of the mood swings—rarely buoyant, never giddy. Bob had set his own, minor key: He had launched the office on a course, and made sure it had consequence.

| | | |

From the first, Bob Morgenthau and Bobby Kennedy had seen eye to eye: They had agreed on the main fronts of the federal war on crime, but now, in the wake of the failed gubernatorial bid, Morgenthau found himself with new leeway. It was as if, having served as JFK's sacrificial lamb, the U.S. attorney had won, by way of consolation, even greater autonomy.

Morgenthau would seize the chance to expand the agenda. He would remain Bobby's lead general in the fight against the Mafia, while also opening a second front, a battle of his own design. He would go after the criminals on Wall Street, in Midtown, and in boardrooms everywhere, the men who wore suits and ties—men, he would say years later, who were "as dangerous to society, if not more so, than the guys on the street with a gun or a knife."

In part, he acted on impulse. Bob Morgenthau had "an instinctive hatred for the fixers, the wheeler-dealers, the promoters, the men with connections," an assistant would say. But the new campaign also owed a rare debt to his father. Before his swearing-in, he had received just one bit of advice from his father: "Remember the Mitchell case." Thirty years earlier, Henry Morgenthau, Jr., had overseen a tax investigation that yielded criminal charges against Charles E. Mitchell, chairman of the First National City Bank. His son regarded it as "one of the first landmarks of my father's term as Secretary." The criminal case failed, but the government won a civil case, forcing Mitchell to pay more than a million dollars. Morgenthau's father cited it as the sole instruction of any value that he could offer: "Make sure you get those thieves on Park Avenue—anybody can get the others."

America's postwar boom had brought a heyday for confidence men. The country, awash in money and aspirations, saw a new generation of swindlers and sellers, fraudsters and stock manipulators—and nowhere were they more active than in New York City. Yet since 1934, when the Securities and Exchange Commission was founded, the SEC had failed miserably to live up to its charge. William O. Douglas, then teaching at Yale Law, had criticized the act, even as he helped to defend it from Wall Street attacks in 1933: "I saw just enough of the horrors of Wall Street," he wrote to Felix Frankfurter, "to know that adequate control of those practices must be uncompromising." Douglas himself would later head the SEC, and yet for nearly three decades, the agency had proven toothless.

From the end of the war to 1958, the Southern District had not successfully prosecuted a single securities fraud case, and by 1960, the office had won just three cases. Morgenthau was determined to reverse the tide. "My most basic conviction when I became U.S. attorney," he would write, was that "society cannot operate under two sets of rules—one for the poor, and one for the high and mighty." The jails were filled with the "economically disadvantaged," while "little attention had been paid to the affluent and influential."

"White-collar crime" was a new phrase in 1961, but Morgenthau would do more than any other prosecutor in the country to introduce it into the American vernacular. He would establish a division devoted to securities fraud—the first in the United States—and bring a raft of indictments against deal-makers and financiers, bankers and executives. To lead the fight, Morgenthau poached a baby-faced attorney with a mop of curls, a rising associate at Paul, Weiss. Arthur Liman knew the name Morgenthau: The Treasury secretary had been a hero of his growing up. Liman was drawn to his new boss: "Bob was shy, almost grave, but utterly without pretension, and he radiated energy."

Still, when Morgenthau called him, Liman doubted he could do the job. "I know almost nothing about stocks, let alone stock fraud," he said. He had studied no securities law at Yale; he had not even read the statutes.

"But Arthur," Morgenthau replied, "neither have the crooks."

With Liman as his field general, the U.S. attorney would score a series of securities fraud cases, landmarks coming in lightning succession. Morgenthau would indict the chairman of the New York Stock Exchange, the executive vice president of Manufacturer's Trust, and the treasurer of the Democratic State Committee. He would purge the New York branches of the Internal Revenue Service and the U.S. Post Office—indicting more than two hundred accountants, inspectors, and auditors. And in a string of cloak-and-dagger investigations, he would bring to federal court the first of a new kind of criminal: the shadowy, if well-pedigreed, bankers and brokers who specialized in the shell corporations of Switzerland.

In time, the targets would expand. Morgenthau's war on white-collar crime would last nearly a decade. But of all the well-heeled offenders who entered into the prosecutor's sights, none could claim a higher profile—and none, he would say, deserved greater scrutiny—than Roy Marcus Cohn.

| | | |

Cohn had first appeared on the national stage a decade earlier, as the snarling, flame-throwing counsel to Senator Joseph McCarthy. If there existed a man in New York who embodied the antithesis of Bob Morgenthau, it was Roy Cohn. From the zeal he displayed in sending the Rosenbergs to their execution, to his enthusiasm for smashing legal taboos and social mores—Cohn represented all that Morgenthau despised. Yet the two shared more professional alliances and personal associations than either would care to realize.

Born in the Bronx in 1927, Cohn had grown up amid Roosevelt loyalists in the New York Democratic Party, the adored only child of respected, if not quite Our Crowd, Jews. His father, Albert Cohn, was a state judge who owed his position to Ed Flynn, the Democratic machine man. Judge Cohn, though, was a reserved, dutiful man who rose by dint of service. His son owed his ambition and arrogance, relatives would say, to his mother, Dora, who came from a wealthy family of clothiers. "Mutti," as Cohn called her, had always predicted great things for her son. She lived with him in the family apartment on upper Park Avenue until her death.

Cohn was a precocious child. "A little kingmaker," a friend would recall. He took delight in orchestrating the election of friends to office at his school—Horace Mann, the elite high school of the Bronx—but abstained from running himself. He finished school early, at sixteen, and negotiated college and Columbia Law in just four years. By twenty, Cohn had a law degree but would have to wait a year until he was old enough to sit for the bar examination. In 1948, his father easing the way, Cohn became the youngest assistant U.S. attorney in the history of the Southern District of New York. In 1951, Cohn brought a bloodlust to the prosecution of the Rosenbergs. With their conviction, the young prosecutor caught the eye of the Red-baiting senator in Washington.

Joe McCarthy hired Cohn—"the most brilliant young fellow I've ever met"—over a son of Joe Kennedy, the senator's patron, as chief counsel on his subcommittee. (RFK would serve as the assistant counsel.) In part, McCarthy realized he could use Cohn's sharp tongue, but he also wished, as one reporter close to Cohn observed, to ward off charges of anti-Semitism. McCarthy needed a Jew.

Bob Morgenthau would lead the way in investigating Cohn, but Bobby Kennedy was never far behind—"the two Bobbies," Cohn called them. If at times the attorney general hedged, pausing to weigh the political costs of any probe—few men counted as many well-placed cronies in Washington as Cohn—Bobby always backed Morgenthau. The U.S. attorney, though, could not have foreseen it: how "an instinctive sense," as Morgenthau put it, would lead to a legal campaign that lasted years. And in the end, he would wonder whom it had haunted more: Cohn or himself. The U.S. attorney would bring indictment after indictment— three in all, leading to four trials—on charges ranging from blackmail and extortion to bribery, conspiracy, securities fraud, and obstruction of justice. And each time, Cohn would walk.

"The Cohn thing," as the young assistants called it, would stretch for more than a decade, outlasting Morgenthau's tenure as U.S. attorney. "To many, it made little sense," Andrew J. Maloney, perhaps the only man to work for both men, would say. "It was a 'prosecution obsession,' or it was 'a persecution complex.'"

"But one thing was clear," Maloney added, "Roy Cohn was Bob Morgenthau's white whale."

| | | |

The hunt had begun even before Morgenthau's swearing-in. In early 1961, Morgenthau decided to follow his suspicions and probe the fast rise of one of the country's more colorful stock wheeler-dealers. Alexander Guterma, a balding bear of a man, had arrived in the United States from the Philippines in 1950, and catapulted himself into the top tier of the country's securities players. Guterma had grown rich, but remained a man with a mysterious past. (He spoke "like Brooklyn," a reporter noted, but boasted of having been born in Siberia, the son of a czarist general.) Guterma traded almost anything that crossed his path—stocks, bonds, debentures—yet paid scant attention to what the companies involved actually made or did. In 1956, he controlled assets worth more than $25 million. By the decade's end, he would be better known as a convicted stock manipulator and mass-scale swindler—and would lead prosecutors from one swamp to another.

As Morgenthau's office looked into Guterma, Cohn's name floated up in the murk.

Guterma was the mastermind behind a financial "labyrinth" that would become known in the office as "United Dye." The United Dye & Chemical Corporation traced its roots to a nineteenth-century silk-dyeing company, one of the largest textile concerns on the East Coast. It had debuted on the New York Stock Exchange in the 1920s, and under Guterma's reign become a "diversified holding company." By the time Morgenthau arrived at Foley Square, though, it was little more than a shell. "United Dye was a ghost vehicle," Gerald Walpin, a Morgenthau assistant, would say. "No more than an entity for fraud used by a handful of swindlers to get out stock to innocent purchasers."

Walpin was a holdover from the old, predominantly Republican, regime. At twenty-nine, a Yale Law graduate from the Bronx (his father ran a fire extinguisher repair company), he inherited the case. A tangle of dodgy characters and long-gone assets—dead coal mines in Illinois, a half-dead pipeline in Wyoming—"United Dye" was at heart a massive stock fraud: the sale of 575,000 unregistered shares that cost the public more than $5 million. In 1959, a grand jury had voted to indict, but "it was a very limited indictment involving a technical violation." Four men—"Las Vegas major players"—had loomed large in the investigation but somehow managed to escape indictment. This was odd considering that the SEC had recommended criminal prosecution of the four.

"Something's amiss," Walpin sensed. "And right away, I took it to Bob."

Morgenthau called in the SEC agents who had led the initial investigation. "Boy, did they let off steam," Walpin recalled. "They told us the story of how the assistant"—Leonard Glass, a young prosecutor in the U.S. attorney's office before Morgenthau's arrival—"who'd brought the indictment, had ignored them." Morgenthau grew more interested as he heard the men relate what had happened to the case in the hands of his predecessor, the Republican Hazard Gillespie. The SEC men's tale pointed beyond incompetency to corruption.

The SEC investigators said that prosecutor Glass had sabotaged the case before the grand jury in 1959, undercutting evidence against the Vegas swindlers and their partners. Worse, they said, when they demanded to make their case to Gillespie, Glass had brought them to Morton Robson, the clean-cut young prosecutor who had briefly served as acting U.S. attorney while Morgenthau awaited confirmation. Robson kept them standing, allowing the SEC investigators only a few minutes to argue for indictments.

In July 1961, Walpin launched a new grand jury investigation, and Morgenthau soon filed a superseding indictment charging twenty-six men and seven corporations with fraud, including the four "Vegas people" previously omitted. The trial commenced in early 1962, with the defendants whittled down by guilty pleas to twelve men and four corporations. Morgenthau had no inkling that it would become the longest (until then) federal trial in history.

| | | |

Guterma, mastermind of the scheme, had pled guilty and became the government's prime witness. On the stand for several weeks, he detailed how the defendants had sold a massive block of shares through boiler rooms, while at the same time manipulating the stock price through a series of nominee buyers. Walpin, whom Morgenthau had tapped to prosecute the case, was pleased. The trial was going well, but after more than a month of testimony, things took an unexpected turn.

In midstream, the "United Dye case" suddenly became the "Roy Cohn case."

One weekend morning, Walpin was at home when William Mulligan, the lead defense counsel, called. "Jerry," he said, "I'd like to plead my four."

Walpin was taken aback.

"But I want you to understand," Mulligan continued, "they have some serious information to give you—and if it turns out to be true, I'd like you to take it into account at sentencing."

Walpin listened intently.

"Sam Garfield"—one of the Vegas four—"met with Roy Cohn in New York, and agreed that he was to be given $50,000," the attorney said. "Two-thirds was to go to the assistant U.S. attorney"—then the acting U.S. attorney, Robson—"and one-third to Roy. So that the four of them would not be indicted." Another of the four, Allard Roen, manager of the Desert Inn and Stardust Resort, had delivered the cash to the federal prosecutor in an elevator in a Las Vegas hotel.

"Obviously," Walpin would recall, "this was rather interesting information on corruption in the U.S. attorney's office." It was also evidence of "a serious crime by Cohn."

At the next court date, three of the "Vegas" defendants pled guilty, seeking lighter sentences and removing themselves from the case. (The fourth would soon follow suit.) On April 2, 1962, Walpin convened another grand jury to probe the Cohn allegations, while the United Dye trial continued. He would spend several months "juggling two balls": In the mornings, Walpin tried "United Dye," and in the afternoons, he conducted the new investigation before the grand jury. And he summoned Cohn to testify—three times.

Still, "we weren't really investigating Roy Cohn," Morgenthau would tell an interviewer in 1968. "He was on the periphery."

By the summer of 1962, Bobby Kennedy got word that Cohn was demanding a sit-down with Morgenthau. George Sokolsky, the conservative columnist, complained to Kennedy that Cohn was being harassed. Bobby assured Sokolsky "nobody would railroad his friend to jail," but he picked up the phone.

"Would you see Cohn?" Bobby asked Morgenthau.

"Of course," the U.S. attorney said, reluctantly.

When Cohn called to arrange a meeting, Morgenthau's distaste only grew. He had heard from the attorney general, Cohn said, that the prosecutor had wanted to see him. "No," Morgenthau corrected him, "but I'd be happy to see you."

On July 11, 1962, five men gathered in Morgenthau's large office overlooking Foley Square. Sil Mollo, head of the Criminal Division, and Vin Broderick, the chief assistant, sat at the long conference table on either side of the U.S. attorney. Opposite them, attorney Paul Windels, Jr., sat beside Cohn. During the Eisenhower administration, Windels had run the SEC office in New York. He had brought the criminal recommendation against Guterma in 1959. Now Cohn had enlisted him as his lawyer in the Morgenthau investigation. A bold move, its gall was not lost on Morgenthau.

Cohn adopted a genial stance. He "recognized" that the U.S. attorney could not always know what his "subordinates" were up to, but saw it as his duty to inform Morgenthau that his men were trespassing into dangerous territory. Everyone, Cohn said, from his partners to his clients to his rabbi, were wondering what he had done to deserve such scrutiny. An investigation was one thing, but the leaks to the press went beyond the pale. His law practice was hurting, so were his fledgling business dealings—Cohn had not only formed a firm to promote professional fights but taken a number of high-flying corporate stakes. He knew the game, Cohn said: The Department of Justice was "out to get him." He was "thick-skinned," but "when one receives this type of information from so many different sources, one becomes concerned."

Morgenthau said that neither Justice nor the U.S. attorney was out "to get" anyone. Cohn was suggesting the office "would suborn perjury—and we wouldn't." When allegations are received, though, they are investigated.

Windels attempted to lower the temperature. He and Cohn, as former prosecutors, could well understand that "when you investigate you have to hit hard," he said. "But you shouldn't suggest information to informants." He realized, of course, "overenthusiastic assistants can go overboard." Still, he had to let Morgenthau know, the investigation was already being attributed by some people "to a 10-year-old feud between Mr. Cohn and a highly placed person in the Department of Justice."

"Mr. Kennedy!" Cohn clarified.

"You're a public figure," Mollo interjected. Hence, "the publicity."

"While 10 million people might think I'm a fine fellow," Cohn said, "there's another 10 million who think the opposite." Morgenthau and his men shouldn't think he was being too sensitive, Cohn added, but the examples of prejudice against him were mounting.

Cohn knew he was getting nowhere, yet before he got up to leave, he offered a warning: His friends "were waiting for the word from him."

Who's that? Morgenthau shot back.

"My friends in the news business," Cohn said. "The Newhouse chain, the Hearst chain."

Morgenthau knew well that Si Newhouse, scion of an empire in newspapers and magazines, had been one of Cohn's closest friends since their days together at Horace Mann.

Morgenthau, too, held cards. Even as Cohn complained of one investigation, Morgenthau saw no reason to tell him that his name was, in fact, swirling in three other investigations—cases fast developing with far-reaching leads, and potentially farther-reaching consequences.

| | | |

In February 1963, after eleven months and five days, the United Dye case at last wrapped up, with each of the remaining defendants found guilty. Soon Walpin also completed the grand jury investigation of Cohn. But Morgenthau knew he faced tall odds.

Walpin had been called down to Justice. Nicholas Katzenbach, the senior Justice aide, questioned the wisdom of charging Cohn with conspiracy to obstruct justice: They lacked evidence to corroborate Allard Roen's statement that he'd given money to Robson in the elevator of the Las Vegas hotel. Both Robson and Cohn had denied it before the grand jury. The witnesses, too, were hardly ideal: "All were either confessed felons," Walpin would say, "or admitted perjurers." For Katzenbach, there was only one thing to do: Drop the indictment. Everyone knew that Bobby Kennedy and Roy Cohn had a feud dating to 1953 and their time on McCarthy's Senate subcommittee. (Cohn and RFK had squared off— associates spoke of "fisticuffs" in the Senate corridor.) The press, Katzenbach said, "will just throw mud at Bobby."

On Labor Day weekend, Morgenthau was in Connecticut, returning from Martha's Vineyard on his boat, when he got word from the attorney general: "You'd better come to D.C.," Bobby said on the phone as Morgenthau listened, standing in a harbormaster's office. "The sooner the better." Morgenthau brought Walpin and a second assistant to see RFK at Hickory Hill. Ethel Kennedy greeted them, and coffee was brought out to the living room in silver service.

"Bobby wanted to be sure we had the case," Morgenthau recalled in 1968. "Many in the Department warned him not to go ahead with it, and he wanted to know: 'Is it the *right* thing to do?'"

Bobby at once asked for the details: "Your facts."

The men began to kick the case's tires: how things stood, how it might play in court, how they could defend against Cohn's defense. "He was trying to punch holes," Walpin would say. "He was direct, and, I thought, brilliant."

"You've got a very difficult case," Bobby said. "Do you believe they're guilty?"

After four hours of debate, the attorney general came to a resting place. He looked at Morgenthau, then Walpin.

"Nick's right," he said. "I'll get lots of mud. But that's what I'm here for. You bring it."

| | | |

Roy Cohn could not wait to get into court. On the morning of September 4, 1963, he showed up at Foley Square to plead not guilty.

He'd come a week early, but let the press in on the secret. "Biggest crowd I've seen since the Army-McCarthy hearings," Cohn announced, unable to suppress a smile as he strode toward the courthouse. Reporters, photographers, and television cameramen filled the steps.

Morgenthau had made good on his promise to Bobby. After eighteen months, on its final day of existence, the grand jury had returned an indictment. Cohn, at thirty-six years old, was "caught up in the toils of an intricate and infamous device," as *Life* described the case in a cover story, "set into motion 8 years ago by a clique of master swindlers, to rob the corporate body of an old American firm and cheat its stockholders." An irony lay at the heart of the charges: Morgenthau had not implicated Cohn in the fraud itself, nor suggested that he profited from it. Rather, Cohn stood accused of conspiring to save the four Vegas participants in the fraud from prison, and then, as *Life* put it, "conspiring to save himself from the consequences of his first conspiracy." Lest Cohn had any doubt, the indictment made it clear: Morgenthau had turned Bill Fugazy, a New York travel agency magnate. The Cohn loyalist, a pal since childhood, would testify against him.

Cohn faced not only the obstruction of justice charge, but perjury, and if convicted, up to forty years in prison.

To the defendant, there was no case—only "an official vendetta."

Making his way up the stairs, Cohn entered a packed courtroom—the same courtroom in which he had convicted the Rosenbergs twelve years earlier. He appeared calm, nodding to acquaintances among the courtroom personnel, before taking a deep breath and, in a voice loud enough for those outside to hear, pleading "not guilty."

Morgenthau stood on the right side of the prosecution table. He spoke softly to Judge Dudley B. Bonsal: "In the matter of bail, the government is willing to release the defendant in his own recognizance."

Afterward, Cohn reprised the attempt at one-upmanship: If Morgenthau hit him with a ten-count indictment, Cohn offered his own eleven countercharges, distributing the "bill of particulars" to the press. The defendant, one reporter noted, "wanted to try the U.S. attorney rather than be tried by him."

Morgenthau, Cohn said, had offered "immunity to gangsters and racketeers, in order to get perjured evidence against me," hiring "a freelance, international bounty man" (an apparent reference to a former FBI man) at a cost of "thousands of dollars" to search for information on him at home and abroad. "I am prepared to name names," he said. "I have certain documents." Cohn demanded a hearing before an "impartial forum"—the New York Bar Association would do—on the charges that "Morgenthau and company" had solicited false testimony. The prosecutors had put out the word through the prisons, he said, that anyone "willing to tell his story implicating me could look forward to mitigation of his sentence or perhaps freedom."

Cohn basked in the glare of the press. "I challenge Mr. Morgenthau," he said, "to back up his charges by personally appearing as the prosecutor at the trial."

Did the attorney general have anything to do with the indictment? a reporter shouted.

"History speaks for itself," Cohn said. "I have never been invited to any of his swimming parties."

Bobby Kennedy, though, was only part of the problem. As Cohn explained it, the animus went back to Bob Morgenthau's father, the former Treasury secretary. The U.S. attorney was retaliating, Cohn insisted, for his role in embarrassing his father. Cohn said that in the McCarthy investigation the elder Morgenthau's name had surfaced. "When I was first in the Justice Department," he wrote in a statement quickly mimeographed, "and then chief counsel to the Senate subcommittee, it was my duty to investigate Soviet infiltration in the Treasury Department. It dealt with the delivery of United States occupation currency plates given to Russia at the direction of Mr. Morgenthau, Sr., on the advice of Harry Dexter White."

"I had no personal malice toward Morgenthau, Sr.," Cohn continued, speaking of the former Treasury secretary. "I never met him. But Morgenthau, Jr., has harbored a feeling about this. The feeling here is somebody up there just doesn't like me."

Morgenthau could not countenance the charge. Five years after the indictment he was still fuming. "Complete horseshit," he told Victor Navasky, then a young freelance writer. "My father was unaware of Cohn's role in the Treasury investigation. [He] was never called before the McCarthy subcommittee, was never interrogated by them, and if he was investigated by Cohn, never knew anything about it until Cohn's statements. And neither did I. I might add I never felt it necessary to vindicate my father's reputation."

Yet as a defense strategy, the vendetta charge was brilliant. Morgenthau's prosecutors would have a hard time disproving it. Cohn, moreover, had managed to hire Frank Raichle, a defense attorney from Buffalo who was forever short on trial preparation, but magical before a jury. The trial consumed Gerald Walpin, the assistant U.S. attorney. He worked on it seven days a week, sleeping at the courthouse. Each night he went to bed in a narrow bunk in the "infirmary" (a small room on the ground floor), waking at five in the morning to shower in a judge's chambers.

The climactic witness for the government, Allard Roen, the Desert Inn manager, had told investigators that he had handed the money to Robson, then an assistant federal prosecutor, in an elevator at the resort. Roen said it had occurred on August 23, 1959, but Robson—who would not be charged—countered that on that day he was in the Bronx, helping his wife unpack furniture in their new apartment in Riverdale.

Walpin had to strike back. Cohn had told the grand jury that he hardly knew Sam Garfield, one of the four Vegas players implicated in the original United Dye case—and who had mysteriously managed to escape indictment. Their relationship, Cohn testified, had only been as attorney and client. Walpin, though, had unearthed an old SEC case from 1960, in which Cohn had testified he had known Garfield only "as a friend," not as an attorney.

"That evidence was dramatic," Walpin would say, but rather than deploying it in the direct case, he intended to spring it on Cohn on cross-examination. Yet Walpin feared a leak. "Things that we did got to Roy Cohn," he would later recall. Cohn had a mole inside the U.S. attorney's office, Walpin believed, and he was not alone in the suspicion. Morgenthau was sure of it, too—and he would be sure to root him out.

Walpin told only Morgenthau and the assistant second-seating him—a second prosecutor in the chair beside him as backup—about Cohn's testimony in the earlier SEC case. When Cohn took the stand, Walpin was ready: "I got him to make the bed, to reaffirm that he had only represented Garfield." Several times Walpin repeated the question, before handing Cohn the earlier, contradictory, testimony. Raichle attempted a redirect, but for once Roy Cohn was at a loss for words.

| | | |

The end came abruptly and, as befit the turns of Cohn's life, in preposterous fashion.

On Sunday evening, the jury was ending its fourth day of deliberations. "We were heading for conviction," Walpin would say. "Bob, I, my wife—and a few others, went to dinner. A pre-victory dinner." That afternoon, the jury had sent in questions for the judge—asking for clarification on two counts—before breaking for dinner at six o'clock. Cohn, too, had gone out to eat. A victory for the defense seemed remote. "But Roy insisted we all go to Lüchow's for dinner," a friend recalled. "It was like a funeral. But Roy said, 'Fuck it! We'll win on appeal.'"

When Morgenthau and Walpin returned to the courthouse, they found Judge Archie O. Dawson waiting at the top of the steps. He waved for them to hurry up, ushering them into his robing room. As Walpin walked in, he saw Cohn and Raichle already sitting there.

"I've got to dismiss the jury," Judge Dawson said. "The father of one of the jurors has died."

Walpin jumped out of his seat. "Judge, I'll take a jury of 11," he said. (New York State at the time did not require alternate jurors during deliberations.)

"We can have a jury of 11," the judge said, "if Mr. Cohn will agree."

Cohn would never consent to a verdict by an 11-person jury, Morgenthau knew, but each side rushed to the law library, searching for a precedent. When they returned, Walpin tried one last time: "At the very least, Judge, will you tell the jury that they will be dismissed, unless they're able to bring their verdict in tonight?"

"I can't do that," Dawson said. "That would be pressure."

The jury returned after their dinner, and at 7:15 P.M. resumed deliberations. At 9:05 P.M., the foreman sent a note to the judge, asking to retire to a hotel. At 9:20 P.M., as the jurors filed back into the courtroom, the woman who had lost her father was weeping. All the jurors looked at the edge of exhaustion.

Was the jury ready to return a verdict? Judge Dawson asked.

"No," replied the foreman.

The judge relayed the "very sad news," explaining that the juror "properly wants to go home and I think she should."

At 9:25 P.M., he declared a mistrial.

The foreman struggled to understand. "We are making good progress," he said. Until that afternoon they had stood at 11 to 1 for conviction, and by evening they had at last agreed. Yet in light of the seriousness of the case, they had decided to sleep on it.

"I'm sorry," the judge said. "I've discharged you."

| | | |

The retrial would not hold the same drama, but it, too, yielded the inevitable dead-end. A rehearsal of the evidence often favors a defendant, but Cohn had another advantage: "Cohn knew my cross, and could prepare for it," Walpin would say. On July 16, 1964, a jury of eleven men and one woman acquitted Cohn of all charges. "I thank God for the United States of America," he said, "where no matter who in high places moves against you, there is recourse to a jury of 12 Americans."

Morgenthau would not let up. "It's not that I wanted to dig into Cohn's affairs," he would say, "his name kept coming up in one investigation after another. Was Bobby Kennedy interested? Of course he was, even after Jack was killed. Cohn was dirty, we knew that. But we did have this trouble—the problem was finding the evidence to make a case."

Over the years to come, the prosecutors interrogated Cohn's friends and associates, law partners and clients. Morgenthau also got the Post Office to set a "mail cover," tracking the names and addresses of the letters Cohn, and his attorney and partner Tom Bolan, received at his office and home. Cohn feared his telephone was tapped, too. Cohn would decry Morgenthau's hunt as beyond control, encompassing "700 persons," "more than 1,000 subpoenas," and "more than $1 million" in costs.

When the *Times* Sunday magazine published a profile of Morgenthau in 1968, Cohn sent its author, Victor Navasky, a scathing telegram. Navasky had quoted a Morgenthau assistant as saying that "the Harry Dexter White thing has nothing to do with Bob's prosecution of Cohn." To Morgenthau, the assistant had said, "Cohn is a hot-shot, *nouveau riche parvenu*. If anything, that has more to do with it."

"*Nouveau riche parvenu*," Cohn seethed in his riposte, "apparently this means that Mr. Morgenthau feels that my ancestors didn't make it to American shores soon enough to make me sufficiently family-treed."

Once again, Morgenthau would ignore the counterattacks, and not let up. "A man is not immune from prosecution," he had grown fond of saying, "merely because a U.S. attorney happens not to like him."

54. After Dallas

1964

November 20, 1963, was Bobby Kennedy's thirty-eighth birthday. At Justice, they had held an impromptu party in his office. Bobby had climbed on the desk in the enormous office to deliver a mock oration. He spoke of his successful but politically controversial run— managing Jack's campaign, playing the lead in his cabinet, championing civil rights, leading the fight against Hoffa, and pushing for a bill to authorize FBI wiretapping—with irony. He'd built a record, he joked dryly, sure to be a boon to his brother's reelection. Ramsey Clark would remember Bobby being "melancholic—almost hopeless-sounding." It seemed as if he was done as attorney general, and Kennedy Justice— from RFK's own zeal and outsized role in the administration to the re- cent headlines over his hunger for more FBI bugging—had become a political liability. Another aide recalled saying, "I guess Bob won't be here by Christmas."

The next day, Bobby presided over an organized crime conclave—U.S. attorneys had flown in from across the country. Morgenthau had come down to D.C., bringing with him Sil Mollo, his Criminal Division chief. In the wake of the Cosa Nostra revelations, Kennedy decided it was time for the next phase. One day was not enough: Bobby had asked the men to stay on, the meeting continuing on Friday morning. Bobby wore a light-gray suit, two-buttoned, long lapel—"a Kennedy suit," as it was now called. As usual, he had tugged open the tie, tossed the coat on a chair, rolled up his shirtsleeves. Bobby liked what he heard. Progress had been slow, but it was coming.

"It was a good meeting," Jack Miller would say. "You could really feel we were getting somewhere."

At a quarter past noon, Kennedy looked at his watch, and said, "What do you say? Shall we make it back here at 2:15?" The meeting adjourned, and the young prosecutors of the department headed back to their offices on the second floor.

| | | |

Bobby had made no secret of his desire to move on from Justice. Three weeks later, once he'd found the strength and returned to the office, he would call in his closest aides and hand each a set of gold Tiffany cuff links, inscribed with the seal of the Justice Department, RFK's and the man's initials, and the dates "1961–64." Bill Geoghegan would recall Bobby telling him, as early as 1962, when JFK named Byron White to the Supreme Court, how surprised he was that White, at forty-four, would go to the Court: "I'll be moving on," he'd said, "and he can have this job." Bobby often aired the options. "At one point, he wanted to be Ambassador to Vietnam," Ted Sorensen would say. "At another, he would become Secretary of State. He thought one way or another, 'I'm going to be leaving the Justice Department: I can't stay on as A.G. and run my brother's campaign.'"

All that fall in New York, in the office of the Southern District, many of Morgenthau's men had heard the whispers. "There was a rumor RFK planned on quitting soon to run JFK's reelection campaign," Bob Arum would recall, "and Morgenthau was slated to take over as the new A.G."

"Of all the U.S. attorneys with whom Bob Kennedy interacted," John Seigenthaler adjudged, "if you asked him: Who was the best among peers, who stands out? it would be Morgenthau. No question."

| | | |

On that Friday in November, as Bobby led his guests from New York out of the department, he took his own car, a Ford Galaxie, the top down in the unseasonably warm weather. Morgenthau was not surprised: The attorney general cruising alone in the convertible along Pennsylvania Avenue was not an uncommon sight. They drove out across the Potomac to Hickory Hill, the family home in nearby McLean, Virginia. Bobby had called ahead to tell Ethel that Morgenthau and an assistant would be coming out for lunch. She was pleased, eager to present the new baby—

Christopher, born that July. When the car pulled up, Ethel was there to greet them in gray slacks and a green sweater.

A table had been set on the terrace near the pool. Bobby asked Morgenthau and Mollo if they'd care for a swim, and even when they declined, he went in for a few minutes, then changed into dry shorts. They sat at the small table to eat a simple lunch: clam chowder and tuna fish sandwiches.

The conversation was congenial, informal. Beyond the wide lawn, at the top of the gentle hill, workmen were painting a new wing on the far side of the house. Morgenthau watched as one performed a balancing act: hanging shutters with one hand while holding a transistor radio in the other. They had just finished the clam chowder and were about to start on the sandwiches. Bobby glanced at his watch, and told Morgenthau and Mollo, "We'd better hurry and get back to that meeting."

It was about a quarter to two o'clock when a maid came over to the table and said to the attorney general, "Mr. J. Edgar Hoover is on the White House phone."

Kennedy excused himself and walked over to the telephone at the pool house, by the shallow end of the pool about forty feet away.

"I kept talking with Mrs. Kennedy," Morgenthau would say, "but I could see the Attorney General at the phone."

At the same time, the workman came over. He was wearing overalls and a painter's cap, and he held the transistor radio in his hand. "It says on the radio that the President was shot."

Somehow, it did not sink in.

Morgenthau's first reaction "was that this is some sort of nut."

Mollo and Ethel also heard the workman. Bobby did not. He was standing near the far end of the pool. The call with Hoover did not last more than twenty seconds. "There was a look of shock and horror on his face," Morgenthau would recall. Ethel saw it, too. "At the telephone, Bobby just clapped his right hand over his open mouth." He hung up the phone and turned away. Ethel had run over to him, and threw her arms around him. Bobby could not speak for another fifteen seconds. Then he turned, almost forcing out the words.

"The President's been shot. It may be fatal."

Bobby ran up to the house. Ethel followed, inviting Morgenthau and Mollo to sit in the living room, by the stairs, and watch the television. There were bulletins from Dallas: No one knew how the president was, but they were giving hope. "They were still reporting that he was in the emergency room," Morgenthau would say.

After a time, Bobby came back downstairs. He stood for a moment by a door to the living room, looking in.

"He died," Bobby said, and then he left.

| | | |

In the days that followed the assassination, Washington and the nation fell numb, mourning and in shock. "Bob Kennedy did not come back to the office for a long time," said Jack Miller, chief of the Criminal Division at Justice. Decades later, Miller remembered the days with pain. "Bob was in a kind of fog—we all were."

If anyone could lift the cloud, it would have to be Robert Kennedy himself. Just before Christmas, he attended a Christmas party for an orphanage—he had promised to go long before the assassination. The journalist Peter Maas went with him, and on the walk from the Justice Department they had bought toys. As Bobby walked in, the children were screaming and playing, but suddenly there was silence, as everyone stood still. When Bobby moved to the middle of the room, a little boy, no more than six or seven, darted forward, stopping in front of him. "Your brother's dead!" he blurted out. In the frozen silence that followed, the boy nearly began to cry, but Bobby bent low. "That's all right," he said quietly, as if to reassure himself, "I have another brother."

In early 1964, RFK would travel again to Asia, visiting Indonesia, Malaysia, and the DMZ between the two Koreas. For Bobby it was a "peace mission"—an attempt to broker a ceasefire in the guerrilla war in Borneo, along the Indonesian-Malaysian border. But it was another whirlwind tour, the kind he once took delight in: around the world in thirteen days. At President Lyndon Johnson's behest, he had met with the leaders of seven countries. Back home by the end of January, on his first morning in Washington RFK went directly to the Oval Office to brief the president for nearly two hours. He then flew to New York to meet with the U.N. secretary general. At the White House and at the U.N., Bobby presented his findings from the trip. Yet before leaving New York, he stopped at Foley Square.

Morgenthau knew Bobby was preoccupied with Asia: His mind was on Borneo and guerrillas, far from Valachi and the Mob. But Morgenthau could sense it: The high-stakes diplomacy had given Bobby a jolt.

He was coming back to life. Yet Morgenthau wondered, too: Could he ever return to fighting form, and be the attorney general again? As Bobby listened, Morgenthau relayed the progress: The office had pushed ahead in the war on the Mafia; new avenues for investigation were emerging. Morgenthau's men produced charts and surveillance photographs, as he walked Bobby through the myriad relations among the crime families—and their reach across New York and the country.

The Mafia was booming. Revenues in gambling, loan-sharking, and narcotics now approached $9 billion a year. Morgenthau's men had combed the property records and the FBI 302s: Organized crime ran bowling alleys, jukebox and vending machine operations, meat-packaging plants and bakeries, trucking outfits and construction companies. The Five Families maintained control of the old mainstays—restaurants, nightclubs, and bars (especially those, as the *Times* would report, that "cater to male and female homosexuals"), but they were eating their way into finance: union pension and welfare funds, broker-age houses, and banks.

Organized crime had spread deep, as well, into real estate. They were still working the paper trails, Morgenthau said, but the Mob appeared to have a stake in a swath of prime Manhattan properties: from the *Wall Street Journal* offices on Broad Street to the Chrysler Building, and even the Midtown building on East Sixty-ninth Street, home not only to the New York telephone company but the FBI's headquarters in the city.

And yet, the crackdown was showing early returns: In the first six months of 1963, Justice had indicted 171 racketeers—compared with 24 for the same period three years earlier. The FBI, too, at least in his district, was cooperating. In an outreach that would become characteristic of his long tenure to come, Morgenthau had forged a new alliance with the Bureau. He'd befriended the head of the New York field office, and the information flow was running high: The Bureau had collected more than a thousand names to track and deployed a floor of agents in the fight.

He'd devised a strategy, Morgenthau went on, to take the investigations to a new level. A team of assistants was working to sort the names, assigning each man to one of the Five Families. He would launch a series of grand jury investigations; every crime group would get its own probe. Once his assistants had mapped the names, they would subpoena them all, en masse—and apply pressure on the bosses as never before.

Bobby sat by Morgenthau's side as he went through the charts. But as the meeting ended, the doubts flooded in: Morgenthau wasn't sure how much of it the attorney general had heard.

On the next evening, though, Bobby called Jack Miller at home, late in the evening: Where were they, he wanted to know, on "that investigation in Chicago"? Miller was delighted and called Morgenthau straightaway. "It meant," he would say, that "Bob was back in business."

| | | |

Morgenthau readied his men for war. Each boss of the Five Families—Tommy Lucchese, Joseph Bonanno, Vito Genovese, Carlo Gambino, and Michael Miranda, caretaker of the Profaci group—would meet his scrutiny.

In February 1964, Morgenthau impaneled a grand jury to target the Lucchese family, the crew that in the first decade after the war had introduced strong-arm tactics to the city's politics. At sixty-five years old, five-foot-two, and dapper as ever, Tommy Lucchese had long claimed to be no more than a successful "dress manufacturer," but nearly every beat cop in New York, and every crime reporter, knew him as "Three-Fingers Brown" (a machine-shop accident had cost him a finger)—a Sicilian-born gangster who had begun his underworld climb almost as soon as he arrived in the city, at age eleven. With Lucchese at the helm, the family had moved into Tammany politics (a son had entered West Point, recommended by a congressman), and it had recently expanded its portfolio, muscling into the garment district. Morgenthau saw an opening: Of the Five Families, the Luccheses had the most street soldiers (the prosecutors tallied more than three hundred names), young men likely to talk.

The grand jury rooms on the fourteenth floor of the federal courthouse became the main theaters of play. Morgenthau would run as many as six grand juries at a time: The long corridor was lined with witnesses and the defense attorneys, forced to wait outside. The prosecutors brought a raft of Lucchese wiseguys before the grand jury—among them, John ("Johnny Dio") Dioguardi, James ("Jimmy Doyle") Plumeri, Carmine ("Mr. Gribbs") Tramunti, all potential heirs apparent. It became a routine, and for months, it worked: They subpoenaed the top ranks of the family to testify before the grand jury, granted them immunity, and if they refused to talk, held them in contempt. In short order, five Lucchese lieutenants had gone to jail.

Still, the prosecutors could be stymied. Vincent Alo presented a memorable case. Better known as "Jimmy Blue Eyes," Alo was a dashing son of East Harlem who had worked on Wall Street as a teen, befriended Meyer Lansky, and developed a profitable expertise in opening casinos (first in Florida, then in Cuba)—before being publicly identified by Valachi. A captain in the Genovese family, Alo also served as a liaison between Lansky and organized crime families across the country. Yet when Morgenthau's men brought him before the grand jury, in an hour and a half of testimony, Alo would plead "a memory lapse 134 times." "The performance of a lifetime," Gary Naftalis, the twenty-eight-year-old prosecutor who suffered through the testimony, would say.

As the battle went on, threats arose. Judge Lloyd MacMahon found a dog's head on the porch of his house in White Plains. When Vincent Rao—"counsel" to the Lucchese family, as the *consigliere* would be described in court—went before the grand jury, Andy Lawler, lead prosecutor of the group, heard that someone from the neighborhood had approached his father. "Your son's getting publicity," the man had said, "this is a good opportunity for him." Lawler recognized it as a "none-too-subtle" warning.

By the second week of February 1964, Tommy Lucchese himself arrived at the U.S. Court House. Bobby Kennedy flew in for the event; Morgenthau met him at LaGuardia.

As Lucchese entered the grand jury room, the police held back the throng of reporters—and the U.S. attorney walked the corridors with the attorney general, only pausing to ask an assistant for the latest news from inside.

Morgenthau would long remember the day as the abortive start of a marathon: Lucchese pleaded the Fifth and was on his way out of the grand jury room within ten minutes. Yet he would be summoned again, and again. In July 1965, called back before the grand jury, Lucchese seemed to suffer under the questioning. In one session, he excused himself to confer with his attorney eighty-three times in three hours. Morgenthau's men would plead with a judge to stop the obstructionist parleys, but to no avail.

The standoff continued. Lucchese appeared at the courthouse so often, and was chased by reporters each time, that once he and Morgenthau had come face-to-face—and promptly turned their backs on one another. Morgenthau subpoenaed nearly three dozen members of the family, but the boss eluded him. In the summer of 1966, Lucchese was diagnosed with a brain tumor, and within a year, at age sixty-seven, he was dead.

| | | |

Bobby Kennedy's return to Justice would be short-lived. For months, he had mused openly to aides, and to Morgenthau, about a possible new turn: running for vice president with President Johnson in the fall of 1964. But in late July 1964, a day after meeting with Bobby, the president went before the television cameras to rule out any further such talk. "No cabinet officers would be considered for the Vice Presidency," LBJ said. It was hardly a surprise.

Bobby, in turn, was already thinking of moving on—and running for the Senate. For months, Kennedy had been paying more attention to New York, and he began to sound out Morgenthau on matters beyond Justice. RFK knew the U.S. attorney as a native New Yorker with deep ties to the party men, labor bosses, Wall Street leaders, and enough of the city's Jewish leaders to gauge the atmosphere. "Bob relied on Morgenthau's advice and information that was political in 1964," Seigenthaler would say. "He'd consulted Morgenthau and had many conversations, before Bob made the decision to run"—and Morgenthau was there at Gracie Mansion in late August, when Bobby announced his campaign for the Senate from New York.

The U.S. attorney worried that RFK had yet to recover from the assassination. The two saw each other often that summer: As Kennedy geared up his campaign against the incumbent Republican, Kenneth Keating, they discussed how best to navigate the New York party—and to escape the taint of carpetbagging. In the early stages of the race, Morgenthau accompanied Bobby on trips around the state; he would recall "how difficult it was for him to focus on the campaign." Bobby was "still so preoccupied with his brother's death," Morgenthau would say, and "not sure whether he was doing the right thing." The campaign, he sensed, was less a drive for political change than an act of personal recovery.

For Morgenthau, one line was clear: The other campaign, the crusade that had bound him so closely with RFK, was over. "I saw him often," Morgenthau would say, "but we never spoke about organized crime again."

55. The Junkman

1966–1968

As Bobby Kennedy moved to the Senate, Bob Morgenthau was forced to find new allies. He'd known Nick Katzenbach, RFK's deputy who took over as attorney general, since Yale Law, but the relationship was fraught on both sides. "Bob had more autonomy than any other federal prosecutor," Katzenbach would say. "And he enjoyed that." Fault lines emerged: a tax matter here, a fraud investigation there. In the daily calls from main Justice, Morgenthau began to feel an unspoken but discernible force, a pressure that he would soon welcome as a sign of confirmation: He was unsettling the right people. Yet Bobby could no longer shield him, and LBJ, Morgenthau came to believe, wanted to rein him in.

It was too late.

Morgenthau could see it now more clearly: If in his first years in office he had moved forward by trial and error, at times by default, now he had a map and could chart, or so he considered, his own way. He still conferred with Washington, first with Katzenbach, and then with Ramsey Clark, who took over Justice when Katzenbach, in 1967, moved to State. But he no longer hid his disdain for both men. He could not help poking fun at the pedigree, invariably referring to Katzenbach by his full name— "Nicholas deBelleville Katzenbach"—and pausing on each syllable for maximum effect. His distaste for Clark was of another order entirely: "Nick was a stuffed shirt," he would say, "but Ramsey owed his career to LBJ's attempt to please the old man"—Clark's father, Tom Clark, the Supreme Court justice, and a Texan whom LBJ had known since the 1930s. Katzenbach and Clark, from Morgenthau's vantage, scarcely differed in purpose: Both existed to throw obstacles in his way. And after five years in office, he had come to enjoy little more than riding rough-shod over Washington.

Dominance was not in his nature; it was a skill that he had acquired on the job. "Bob was never callous, but he was merciless in pursuit of a goal," Steve Kaufman, one of his closest assistants, would say. Rarely did he give an order, demand, or ultimatum. He offered an invitation, a suggestion, a proposition—and he kept coming back. "When he wants something out of you," his former assistant Pierre Leval would say, "he comes at you again and again and again." It was "a perseverance like none I've ever known." He wore people out. He had discovered a means to bend aides, politicians, and opponents to his will. A list of "all the people who said no to Bob Morgenthau," Leval added, would make for "one of the world's greatest fables—and the world's shortest book."

Morgenthau was finding his way: what kind of prosecutor he wanted to be, and above all, even unwittingly, the way in which he could forge his own path. "Power—he never called it that out loud," Kaufman, who rose to head the Criminal Division, would say. But Morgenthau's words now carried a force, never overt, but implicit, that was growing. Each day he considered the calculus: How can a federal authority, a man who spent his days behind a big desk in a granite fortress downtown, and who was obliged to pledge fealty to Washington, extend his reach across the city, and beyond?

And in the fall of 1966, Morgenthau decided it was time. He would up the ante, redoubling his efforts on the second front, which now gained focus: corruption on Wall Street and in corporate boardrooms—or, in the phrase born of his prosecutions, "white-collar crime."

| | | |

That October, he filed criminal charges—for the first time in the history of U.S. jurisprudence—against three members of Lybrand, Ross Bros. & Montgomery, one of the "Big 8," the country's largest accounting firms. *U.S. v. Simon,* as the case would be known, had begun when an assistant had paid careful attention to the footnotes in an annual report. A single offending note, in the balance sheet of the Continental Vending Machine Corporation, hid some bad news: To fund his own stock dealings, Harold Roth, Continental's president, had siphoned off more than $3 million from the corporation, and the "marketable securities" purportedly se-curing the debt amounted to Roth's "own controlling interest in the company itself." Morgenthau charged not only Roth but also the three Lybrand men with creating and certifying a false balance sheet.

The firm's clients included Ivy League universities, AT&T, and Mobil Oil. But Morgenthau was caught off guard: When he announced the indictments, the entire accounting industry came after him. It would not prove easy going; a first trial ended in a hung jury. (Accountants, he'd learned, also had a code of silence: None would testify, until he pressed his own accountant to enlist a colleague.) A second jury deadlocked, only returning to the jury room on judge's orders. Morgenthau, in a rarity, sat at the counsel table for the closing argument. Five men had dominated the jury, each a corporate executive, including the treasurer of IBM's world trade division and the chief of Chase's petroleum department. As the jury went out the last time, the jury warden overheard one of the female jurors say to the IBM executive, "What in the world is wrong with you, can't you understand what this case is about?" Within twenty minutes, the jury had returned a verdict: guilty. No longer could "accepted accounting principles" be used to conceal a client's fraud.

Soon another Morgenthau case broke another barrier: Lawyers, too, could be charged for aiding a stock promoter on a crooked deal. In 1964, Judge Henry Friendly, considered by many the greatest legal mind on the bench, seconded Morgenthau's drive on white-collar crime: "In our complex society," Friendly wrote, "the accountant's certificate and the lawyer's opinion can be instruments for inflicting pecuniary loss more potent than the chisel or the crowbar." It was a line that never failed to bring a smile to the prosecutor's lips.

And yet the war on Wall Street would prove far harder to wage than the war on the Mob. It was difficult getting any federal agency to initiate an investigation of the high and mighty. The FBI claimed they lacked jurisdiction, and the SEC had only a handful of investigators—men who were told to sit at their desks in Washington. To lure the feds Bob Morgenthau needed a big fish.

| | | |

Louis Wolfson was one of the country's first "conglomerateurs"—and the U.S. attorney, trusting another of his "educated guesses," was sure he was a crook. By 1964, few men in America could claim as great a fortune: Wolfson proudly wore the crown, awarded by a financial journalist who had chronicled his improbable rise, as "the most spectacular corporate raider of modern times."

Handsome as a Hollywood star, Wolfson commanded boardrooms as easily as shareholder arenas. Tall and always impeccably dressed, he had a rugged face that bore the scars of a youthful career as the Jacksonville, Florida, boxer known as "Kid Wolf." But he had long since outgrown Florida and the corporate world, producing movies and Broadway shows and socializing with actors and athletes. In 1959, he dared to open a horse farm in central Florida, challenging the dynasties who had bred Thoroughbreds for decades. In 1965, when Wolfson's horse Roman Brother placed third at Laurel Park, he was handed the trophy from an avid track-goer, J. Edgar Hoover.

"Wolfson had immunity for a long time," the columnist Jimmy Wechsler said. "That immunity passed when Bob took over."

Few corporate titans were more closely tied to the Johnson administration. Wolfson had not only been a donor, he had relied on the legal counsel of Abe Fortas, one of LBJ's closest and longtime advisors, who had been named to the Supreme Court in the summer of 1965. As Morgenthau investigated Wolfson, Attorney General Katzenbach hungered to claim new cases. Jack Rosenthal, the Justice spokesman, told Morgenthau, "I think we should get involved in announcing some of your big cases."

"Be my guest," Morgenthau said. "But the next big case is Wolfson, and I don't think you want to announce that one."

Why not? asked Rosenthal.

"Ask Nick," Morgenthau replied, referring to the attorney general.

"Never," Morgenthau said decades later, "did I get as much pressure on anything else."

||||

The son of Jewish immigrants from czarist Lithuania, Wolfson seemed born to the role of maverick raider. His father had come by steerage to Baltimore and worked the streets, peddling fruit and hawking ice. By 1914, Morris Wolfson had moved the family to Jacksonville, where he discovered the junk business.

Louis started in junk at fourteen. With his father and brother Sam, he put together a small construction outfit, Florida Pipe & Supply Co. They survived the Depression, and profited—like many in metals—from the war. By 1945, after an acquisition spree, Florida Pipe had topped $4.5 million in annual sales, and Wolfson called himself "a turnaround man"—a virtuoso able to rebuild any company. In truth, he had targeted poorly run companies, bought them on the cheap, and sold them off for parts. Two shipyards were his chief prizes: Tampa Shipbuilding and St. Johns River Shipbuilding—once manufacturers of Liberty ships, now government war surplus, each company came with a federal stipulation that it be kept intact. Wolfson had liquidated both at a fat profit. His true talent, as a writer noted, was an ability to see which businesses were "worth far more dead than alive."

In the 1950s, as Wolfson gained fame on Wall Street as "the Junkman," Morgenthau had come to know something of the company at the heart of his conglomerate: Merritt-Chapman & Scott Company, itself a marriage of construction and salvage giants. In 1953, though, Wolfson launched a series of proxy wars—"ingesting," in Arthur Liman's words, "whatever companies swam within his reach." In short order, Merritt-Chapman added disparate manufacturers—steel, paint, chemicals—as well as businesses in transport, banking, and entertainment. By 1964, Merritt-Chapman had climbed high on the Fortune 500.

Even as a young clerk for Judge Robert Patterson, Morgenthau had heard the rumors. In 1946, Wolfson was said to have won the St. Johns River shipyard with a $25,000 bribe. Accusations flew, but the investigation (by the Justice Department and a House committee) stalled when the alleged recipient, a maritime appraiser, died. Then in 1954, when Morgenthau was a young advisor to Averell Harriman's campaign for governor, the raider again raised eyebrows—arriving at headquarters, it was said, with a suitcase filled with cash. Yet what remained foremost in Morgenthau's mind was the egregious episode with American Motors four years later—when, he believed, the government "should've brought criminal action" against Wolfson (at the time the largest shareholder in the carmaker) for manipulating its stock.

By 1964, a twenty-seven-year-old accountant at SEC headquarters in Washington had decided to take a closer look. "It came by accident," Stuart Allen would say. "I was scouring the documents, and there it was: something did not add up." Allen would spend years on Wolfson's trail, following illegal stock sales in companies he controlled. Allen first found "irregularities" in Continental. Once a part of Capital Transit, operator of Washington, D.C.'s streetcars and buses, Continental's "enterprises" ranged from an amusement park outside D.C. to movie theaters in Florida to a licensing deal with Propel-Pak, a chocolate drink featuring an "aerosol process."

Allen would learn that Merritt-Chapman had drawn suspicion before:

In a series of private deals, it had bought back its own stock at a price at variance with the market. The SEC had started an investigation, only to abandon it. Allen, though, convinced his boss to reopen the case. He wasn't sure how far it could go, but he sensed an ally: "Morgenthau had sent the signal. He'd take on the fight, no matter how wealthy and connected the other side might be."

In the fall of 1966, Morgenthau indicted Wolfson in two front-page cases. The first charged Wolfson and Elkin "Buddy" Gerbert, his chief corporate understudy, and five co-conspirators, with selling 690,000 shares in unregistered stock of Continental. The second case struck at the heart of the empire, Merritt-Chapman. "A more traditional criminal" affair, as Morgenthau called it, was centered on a conspiracy to defraud the SEC and shareholders.

The stock case came first. By law, the Continental shares should have been registered with the SEC. While the sum involved (a $1.5 million profit) was "not peanuts," quipped a reporter who had chronicled the raider's rise, it must have been "a blow to his ego to be indicted in connection with such a low key chisel." At trial, Wolfson pleaded ignorance: "Anyone who violated a rule or regulation has to be insane. Especially a man in my position." In reply, Mike Armstrong, one of Morgenthau's best men in court, and the new head of his securities fraud unit, cited Wolfson's hubris: "If you're going to steal, steal big."

Armstrong called to the stand a former SEC official who recounted explaining to Wolfson, for two hours in 1950, the registration requirements. He also produced an ace: Alexander Rittmaster, Wolfson's finance man, who would testify for the prosecution. During the investigation, Armstrong had learned that Rittmaster had a prior conviction—bribery of a city official—and flipped him.

"Boss, we got the brains of the operation," Armstrong told Morgenthau. "We've got them nailed."

"Now, you've got a chance," Morgenthau replied.

From the start, Morgenthau feared what he called "the Robin Hood thing." In his corporate raids, Wolfson had gained a certain popular following. "Strange as it seems," Morgenthau would say, "many saw him as a folk hero. We feared, too, the Southern charisma."

It got worse. Wolfson counted a long list of stars as friends: Bill Shoemaker, Eddie Arcaro, Bill Hartack, the top jockeys in the country; football coaches Bear Bryant and Wally Butts; professional athletes like the former Yankee Al Rosen. And Joe DiMaggio. The Yankee Clipper had

had stock dealings with Wolfson. "Just sound him out," Morgenthau counseled. When Armstrong learned that DiMaggio was scheduled to play in the annual Old Timers Game at Yankee Stadium, he sent a note: "Come and talk to us." If he failed to come in voluntarily, DiMaggio would get one of Morgenthau's "office subpoenas" at the game. "An office subpoena," Armstrong would explain, was "one of the illegal things we used to do—it looked like a subpoena, had no force of law whatsoever, but people got impressed by them."

DiMaggio came to the office. They let him in the back entrance, a half-dozen young prosecutors piling into the interview room. "He was delightful," Armstrong recalled. DiMaggio said he'd only been given the shares in Continental; he didn't really know Wolfson. He *did* know his brother Cecil, and had even joined him on his honeymoon to Europe. Armstrong warned DiMaggio he might be called to testify for the defense as a character witness. The prosecutor went over a list of possible questions, but DiMaggio insisted he could not answer them: "I don't know him that well. We've had dinner maybe one time."

And so it came as a surprise when, as the trial was nearing a close, Morgenthau got a call from Edward Bennett Williams, the famed defense attorney: "My client Joe DiMaggio is going to appear as a character witness tomorrow." On the stand, DiMaggio was asked the same questions by Wolfson's attorney that Armstrong had put to him. But now the answers had shifted: Yes, DiMaggio said, he had known Wolfson a long time, and of course, he knew his reputation in the community to be stellar.

Room 110, the largest courtroom in the building, was packed. Morgenthau assistants filled the benches. Armstrong decided to attempt a cross-examination.

"Mr. DiMaggio, remember we met last spring in my office?"

"Oh yes, Mr. Armstrong."

It was no use: The prosecutor at once understood an attack would only hurt his case. As DiMaggio left the stand, he turned to the judge: "May I shake Mr. Wolfson's hand? I've not seen him in a long time."

In fact, the two had lunched together that day.

"Only a lunatic cross-examines a national hero," said Tony Sifton, the Morgenthau assistant, and future federal judge, who second-seated Armstrong. DiMaggio would return to the courtroom and sit in the front row until the trial's end. Armstrong asked the judge to instruct the public not to move before the jury left the courtroom. "I don't want DiMaggio running up to Wolfson every time," he pleaded.

The case stood up: The jury convicted Wolfson and Gerbert of nineteen counts involving the sale of unregistered stock. Once told by his lawyers the worst he could suffer were civil penalties, Wolfson faced a possible maximum of ninety-five years in prison.

| | | |

A month after the indictment in the Continental case, Morgenthau dragged Wolfson back into court on the Merritt-Chapman charges. A "10b-5 case," named after the rule of the Securities Act of 1934 proscribing "manipulative or deceptive practices," it centered on a scheme to defraud by failing to disclose a set of secret "buy-back agreements" Wolfson and his cronies had used to raise money.

Armstrong left the office in late 1967, and passed the files to a thirty-year-old prosecutor named Paul Grand, who had come to Morgenthau's office two years earlier. Raised in Missouri, he knew Wolfson's ruthless corporate practice firsthand: Grand's father had served on the board of a St. Louis company that fell prey to the former junk king. Grand went to Morgenthau, worried he could be accused of bias. "Do your job well," Morgenthau said, "and it won't matter."

For Morgenthau, the pressure only increased. "The Friends of Lou Wolfson Committee" took out a full-page advertisement offering support. Fred Vinson, Jr., the assistant attorney general atop the Criminal Division, who was close to LBJ and Fortas, would call, complaining "we were abusive to Wolfson, not giving him a fair shake." In Washington, the twin cases against Wolfson would have consequences. Days after the second indictment, Morgenthau found himself in Katzenbach's office at Justice, when an aide whispered in the attorney general's ear: "The White House is on the phone." Katzenbach left to take the call and, when he returned, announced, "I guess I'm no longer the Attorney General." In his memoirs Katzenbach would claim he was out because LBJ needed him at State, where he became an undersecretary, tasked with defending the escalation in Vietnam. Morgenthau would insist otherwise: "It was about Wolfson—LBJ had had enough."

In August 1968, after nearly two months of testimony, Wolfson was found guilty in the Merritt-Chapman case and sentenced to an additional eighteen months in prison. The case would be overturned on appeal—

and retried twice, each time resulting in a hung jury. As a third retrial loomed, Wolfson pled nolo contendere to one count of filing a false corporate statement, in return for the government dropping all other charges.

In the first case, Continental, Judge Edmund Palmieri had sentenced Wolfson to one year on each count, to run concurrently. Wolfson would move for a new trial based on new evidence: The SEC's eight-page letter introduced at trial was a forgery, he claimed. "Government's Exhibit 21," his lawyers argued, was "prepared on a date later than the October 16, 1950 date it bore." The watermarks on the SEC document, they argued, did not yet exist. Morgenthau sent Paul Grand to Wisconsin to the factories that produced the federal letterhead. "I became the world's expert on the 7-star, 9-arrow government watermark," Grand would joke. Mrs. Pearl Tytell, whose husband had testified in the Alger Hiss case, led the document team for the defense. The author of the SEC letter had died, but Grand brought in his stenographer: a young mother of three, who distinctly recalled Wolfson visiting the office, and identified the putative forgery as having been typed by her, from a number of details peculiar to her style and spacing.

Judge Palmieri denied Wolfson's motion, and his conviction was affirmed on appeal. And still, Wolfson vowed to fight on. Morgenthau expected an epilogue to the prosecution: He knew Wolfson had powerful friends. What he did not know was that one of them sat on the U.S. Supreme Court.

56. "Joe Bananas"

1964–1985

Joseph Bonanno, at fifty-nine, his widow's peak gone gray, had tried his best for more than a decade to enjoy the warmth and quiet of Arizona. He was an investor in real estate, his associates told the prying reporters, owner of 109 acres of beautiful desert north of Tucson, and a dozen lots downtown. Yet in 1964, Bob Morgenthau summoned him to come before a grand jury in Manhattan, to explain the origins of his growing property portfolio.

For more than thirty years, "Joe Bananas" had run one of New York City's original Mafia families. In his testimony, Valachi had given Morgenthau eighteen names; his men identified hundreds more: all soldiers of the Bonanno crime family. One by one, he had brought them before the grand jury, impaneled with one sole purpose: to take down the entire syndicate.

"It was a dragnet," Jerry Walpin, the assistant U.S. attorney handling the investigation, would say. Hundreds of subpoenas went out to every known Bonanno family member. Once again, Morgenthau repeated the grand jury strategy he'd deployed in the Lucchese investigation: Grant the witness immunity, and compel him to testify. "The tactic itself caused a great deal of conniptions," Walpin recalled. "This had never been done before. There was real fear: Nobody in the higher echelons, or the lower, could be sure that everybody wouldn't talk. Or that somebody might not be given immunity, and what happened then?"

Bonanno had tried to evade Morgenthau's hunt, fleeing to Canada. In May 1964, he'd driven north from his dairy farm in upstate New York, crossing into Quebec as a "visitor." He applied to stay permanently, announcing plans to buy into a local cheese company. The Canadians saw through the ruse and arrested him, in part, for lying to Immigration about his criminal record. (Bonanno had neglected to note a 1942 arrest for underpaying employees at his Brooklyn sweatshop, the state's first conviction under the "Wage and Hour" law, and a violation that set him back a $50 fine.) The Canadians announced a deportation, and by late summer, after months of legal wrangling, Bonanno was kicked out of the country.

Morgenthau moved fast, issuing a grand jury subpoena.

On the morning of August 4, Bonanno entered the Federal Court House by a side door, accompanied by his attorney, William P. Maloney, and rode the elevator up to the fourteenth floor. Bonanno remained in the grand jury room nearly an hour, before Maloney requested an adjournment of several days, so that his client might "refresh his recollection" in advance of his testimony. The judge allowed the request.

Bonanno knew how Morgenthau was waging the grand jury war; he feared that he'd be given immunity, and once he refused to talk, he would be jailed for contempt. Morgenthau did plan on reprising the tactic, but not right away. "In fact, we had not decided to do it on that day," he would say, "but Bonanno didn't know that." If on the first day of testimony he was not given immunity, and he took the Fifth, Morgenthau would explain, "he would've been free to walk."

The legal chess game soon became moot.

On October 20, 1964, on the eve of his testimony, New Yorkers awoke to bombshell news: Bonanno had disappeared. His lawyer Maloney addressed the reporters, standing in the foyer of his Park Avenue apartment building to replay how it had happened: He and Bonanno and a second defense attorney had gone out to dinner, and all returned late by cab to Maloney's apartment on Park Avenue South. It was just past midnight when they stepped onto the sidewalk, and two men suddenly appeared and kidnapped his client.

"C'mon, Joe," one of the men had said, Maloney explained. "The boss wants to see you."

They were each six feet tall, and weighing about two hundred pounds.

"Where are you going?" Maloney said he yelled after them. "That's my client!"

He'd started to give chase, but one of the men had turned and fired—the bullet hitting the pavement in front of him. The men had rushed

Bonanno around the corner, and thrown him into a beige sedan waiting on Thirty-sixth Street.

By morning, Maloney said he worried that a gangland execution awaited his client, but the police were still searching for the bullet and the doorman confessed to seeing nothing. As Morgenthau rushed to call Washington first, the press was feasting: "JOE BANANAS," the *Daily News* headline declared, "CALL HIM DEAD."

| | | |

Later, when it was all over, and the nineteen-month period of Bonanno's "alleged fugitivity" had come to a close, the U.S. attorney would call it "a pretty dark patch" of his tenure. He had known that the Bonanno group would be harder to crack than the Lucchese family. But Morgenthau had managed to put the fright in the Luccheses—"bring 'em to heel," he would say—and he imagined he had momentum on his side. Bonanno's flight, though, had taken him by surprise, and it would prove a source of enduring embarrassment. In the months to come, Morgenthau would need all the help he could get to find him.

When it came to the Mob, Sil Mollo and Bill Tendy had long since become his indispensable guides. Holdovers from the previous regime, both were veteran prosecutors with outsize personalities. Mollo, his first chief of the Criminal Division, was foul-mouthed, short in stature, and imperious—"Field Marshal Mollo," the assistants called him. The U.S. attorney's office was his family; he'd been there since 1939. He knew every assistant, judge, and case—and how best to align them to Morgenthau's advantage. If Mollo was the office's administrator, Bill Tendy was its star prosecutor. Bald and four years older than Morgenthau, Tendy was the "old man" of the U.S. attorney's office, head of the "Junk Unit"— Narcotics. He'd graduated high school at twenty-seven, skipped college, and at forty, enrolled at Fordham Law. Tendy came from East Harlem— a "dees and dems" guy, as Morgenthau would say, who sang Verdi.

Tendy had been born "Tedesco." His Italian father had died when Tendy was a toddler, and his mother had sent him and a sister to Ireland to live with their grandmother—and twelve other children. At seven, he'd been found wandering the fields and been delivered to an orphanage. (The nuns treated him well: His voice led the choir.) When his mother had remarried and found work cleaning houses, she'd called the children home. Tendy had made it through evening high school, and started Fordham, before volunteering to fight in the Philippines. After law school, he opened a solo practice in the old neighborhood—"home of the wiseguys," his wife would say. Rao's, the famous restaurant, was a few blocks away, and the Eaglette, a favored Mafia bar, around the corner. At the bar Tendy met Vincent Velella, De Sapio's Republican counterpart, who offered a tip, hoping to seed an alliance: "You oughta try the U.S. attorney's office."

Morgenthau would begin each day with Tendy and Mollo. He admired both aides, relied on them, and needed them more than ever. The grand jury investigations were continuing apace, but Bonanno remained at large. Morgenthau insisted that the agents—FBI, Customs, and Internal Revenue—"shake the trees." The raids continued across the city: Bookmaking joints, gambling houses, loan-sharking outfits, anywhere the Bonanno family appeared to rule, was hit. The FBI reported 180,000 leads, "items of criminal information." Morgenthau sent federal agents to Europe. In Germany, they joined Interpol officers on the trail. In Sicily, the Italians hauled in suspects in Castellamare, interrogating them about the Mafia boss who'd gone missing in America. And all the while, the U.S. attorney would assure eager reporters that Bonanno was merely scared, and on the lam.

For a time, it worked. Morgenthau could run his own feint. But as the months passed, and the headlines multiplied, it became apparent whose ploy was more likely to win out. Mollo would stand firmly against it, but Morgenthau knew what he had to do: He now signaled that his door was open—that he was willing to consider terms of surrender for Bonanno, who he had no doubt was in hiding, waiting for a sign.

| | | |

Albert J. Krieger had witnessed Morgenthau's war on the Mafia firsthand. A bear of a man with an outsized bald head and a courtroom baritone, Krieger could intimidate, but he had never intended to become a defense attorney for one of the leaders of the Five Families. He'd started out in real estate—"far from fancy: in the Bronx"—and quickly become known. He moved "from the Puerto Ricans to the Italians," and into East Harlem. He'd never tried a criminal case until a small-time dealer was arrested with a quarter ounce of heroin in his pocket. A near riot ensued, and by the next morning a group of local real estate men appeared in Krieger's office. "They were begging for calm, and asked me to help." Krieger won the case, and the real estate work ended. "Most days the line formed early, often it went out the door."

Morgenthau did not care for most of the Mob lawyers: "the black-collar defense bar," he called them. Krieger was an exception. In court he emanated a formality—in speech, bearing, and decorum—that more than matched Morgenthau's. He did his homework, too: He could stand and deliver an hour-long opening without notes. Unfailingly polite to judge and jury, on cross-examinations he was merciless. "There was no trickery," Morgenthau would say. "He was an honest guy—but he could gut a witness." Few defense lawyers had squared off with the U.S. attorney in more cases; none did he hold in higher esteem.

In January, Morgenthau's investigators heightened the pressure on the Bonanno family, gaining yet more wiretaps and informers. The prosecutor also went after Bill Bonanno, the elder of Bonanno's two sons, having the FBI arrest him in Tucson for failure to appear before a Manhattan grand jury as a material witness to the kidnapping. Bill Bonanno, in turn, had approached Krieger to represent him.

"Bill was raised to be legit," Gay Talese, who chronicled the son's rise and fall in *Honor Thy Father*, the 1971 bestseller, said. But the feudal ways of the Mafia took hold: In 1956, Bill had wed Rosalie Profaci, daughter of another family boss in a union that attracted as many Mafia leaders as the Apalachin conference. In the early 1960s, Bill Bonanno became increasingly involved in the family activities, to the degree that on the eve of his father's disappearance, his father considered him his rightful second-in-command.

Not everyone in the Bonanno family—now numbering more than four hundred men—agreed. The "family" split: "Some understood his thinking," Krieger would say, "and backed the son, but others, let us say, were reluctant." Whether the boss's disappearance caused the rift, or was a consequence, few outside the Five Families could tell, but the schism soon became abundantly clear.

Bill Bonanno would appear twenty-one times before the Morgenthau grand jury during January and February 1965. Against the advice of his lawyer, Krieger, he "answered nearly every question"—all but two. For that rare silence, Morgenthau held Bill Bonanno in contempt: The son spent ninety-six days in jail.

Upon his release, Bill was summoned to a meeting; it was time, the anonymous caller said, for loyalists and disloyalists to compromise. On a Friday night in late January 1966, Bill arrived at Troutman Street in Ridgewood, Queens. It was after eleven o'clock, and cold. Bill had come with several of his father's closest men; they had picked the location, even the house. As they neared the address, bullets flew. The gunmen fled; Bill narrowly escaped. The neighbors had heard more than twenty shots, but no one called the police. The lines were now drawn—the ambush opened the "Banana War."

Krieger had not readily accepted when Bill asked if he could see if there could be a way to negotiate his father's surrender. Krieger knew that "the Old Man," as he had taken to calling Bonanno Sr., would be safer in the government's hands. It was his own liability that concerned him: "Dealing with a fugitive is very dangerous," he would explain, "especially one on the front page of the newspapers." He feared "exposing myself to a potential prosecution" as a participant in the obstruction of justice.

But the attorney thought he might be able to strike a deal with Morgenthau, and he told Bill so: "If I can get clearance from the government, fine. If I can't, I'm not accepting."

Krieger first wanted a blanket of immunity—for himself.

So began a series of secret negotiations with the U.S. attorney. All the while, the press kept printing FBI "sightings"—Bonanno was in Sicily, Tunis, Haiti, Mexico, and back in Canada. In early May, six days before he entered Judge Marvin E. Frankel's courtroom, a government source insisted he was in Europe.

In truth, Bonanno had never stepped foot out of New York City, and for months he had lived in a colorless high-rise in Queens, in a distant relative's apartment off Flushing Avenue.

| | | |

On the May morning in 1966 that Krieger delivered the most wanted man in America to justice, he parked his white Lincoln off Foley Square, and entered the courthouse through a side entrance—the same door that Joe Bonanno had used nineteen months earlier. Krieger had played handmaiden, but it was Bonanno's decision: The time had come to answer Morgenthau's call.

Bonanno and his attorney headed for Room 318, the largest chamber in the courthouse. A handful of spectators sat scattered in the pews, more than one of them asleep.

Krieger rushed to a phone booth in the hall outside. Finding Morgenthau's line busy, Krieger ran up the back stairs, and into the U.S. attorney's office. Told he was out on "morning rounds," Krieger raced again down the stairs.

If Judge Frankel recognized the silver-haired man entering his court-room, he did not show it. The judge even appeared taken aback when the man, apologizing for the interruption, stood before him, gave his name, and said, "Your Honor . . . I understand that the Government would like to talk to me."

The judge peered over his spectacles.

"*You* are Joseph Bonanno?"

"Yes, Your Honor."

Judge Frankel paused, taking in the room—the pews were filling, any-one dozing now alert—before saying, "Please be seated."

Bonanno, holding his gray fedora before him, sat in a front row. Krieger soon returned, his stony face revealing nothing of his conference with Morgenthau, who, in shirtsleeves, himself now entered the court-room.

As Bonanno and his two attorneys sat in a front row, the routine suc-cession of the morning's cases before Judge Frankel continued. Soon, though, the courtroom filled: Off-duty bailiffs, clerks, detectives, and as-sistant U.S. attorneys rushed to join the reporters. An hour had nearly gone by, without any sign of action from Morgenthau. As the lunch break loomed, Morgenthau abruptly left the courtroom.

"It was as if the government," Gay Talese wrote, "after investing so much time, effort, and money in its worldwide search for Bonanno, did not really know what to do with him now that it had him."

At 11:40 A.M., three federal marshals slid into the bench behind Bonanno. One whispered to Krieger: "Albert, we've got to arrest your client."

"Not a problem," Krieger said, annoyed it had taken so long. "You have a warrant?"

"Yes."

Krieger knew what to expect. They would be led downstairs, to the holding pen on the ground floor. As the marshals escorted Bonanno and his attorney out, they noticed that Morgenthau had reappeared—now wearing a dark suit jacket, and accompanied by his top lieutenants, Mollo and Kaufman. Morgenthau approached the bench and handed Judge Frankel a sealed manila envelope—the Southern District's case against Mr. Bonanno.

Downstairs, two FBI agents sat across from Bonanno and began to probe. They asked outright where he'd been hiding. Met with silence, they asked to inspect his clothes, his hat, his tie, and searched for a laundry ticket, a coat check, a lapel, any clue as to where he'd been. His outfit was exactly what he had worn on the night of his "kidnapping": the same shoes, suit, shirt, tie, and socks.

Once the defendant reappeared in the courtroom, Morgenthau took over the stage.

"Your Honor, we move that the sealed indictment be opened."

Did Mr. Bonanno, Judge Frankel asked, waive the reading of the one-count indictment? (The charge: obstruction of justice for willingly failing to appear before a federal grand jury.)

Krieger interjected: "He does." When the Judge asked how his client wished to plead, Bonanno spoke in a loud voice: "Not guilty."

Morgenthau now stood.

"Judge, in the matter of bail," he began, "Joseph Bonanno was born on January 18, 1905, in Sicily, Italy, and he is married to Fay Bonanno, and they have three children . . . he has no known legitimate occupation, and . . . has a criminal record, which includes arrests in connection with attending a meeting in Apalachin, New York, together with major criminal figures from throughout the entire United States. He was also arrested in Tucson, Arizona, in 1956, for failing to appear before a grand jury. He was arrested in Brooklyn for two violations of the Wage and Hour Law. He was also arrested and convicted in Canada in 1964. . . .

"The government started to look for Joseph Bonanno in the summer of 1963 in order to serve him with a grand jury subpoena. He was not found in Arizona or in New York, and was finally located in Canada after he had filed his application for permanent residence. After his arrest and conviction in Canada he was then deported to the United States, and upon his arrival in Chicago was served with a grand jury subpoena from this District. He did appear before a grand jury in August of 1964 and was directed to reappear on October 21. According to reports from his attorney, he was allegedly kidnapped in the early hours of the morning."

As he spoke, Morgenthau was not blind to the irony: The recitation was a litany of failure. Bonanno had slipped his grasp and hidden in plain sight. Worst of all, he had come in on his own terms.

The government would have to prove its case—that Bonanno had *willfully* failed to appear before the grand jury. Morgenthau and his men would have to disprove the defense's story of the kidnapping. And if the months of meetings with the prosecutors had revealed anything, it was that they could not.

"We believe that he is the head of one of the five major criminal organizations operating in and around New York City," Morgenthau went on. "We believe that he is a man who has shown that he has complete disregard for the processes of the court and for the law. And we believe that at least since December 19, 1964, he has been free and able to come into the court at any time that he wished, and he is only coming in now because it suits his own personal convenience."

As he finished, Morgenthau elicited gasps—"Under all of these circumstances, we ask for bail in the amount of $500,000."

Bonanno pretended to be shocked. His attorney joined him in feigned disbelief.

"If Your Honor please," objected Krieger, getting to his feet. "I am not asking for his parole, but bail must be realistic, and bail must be sufficient to assure the government and the court of the return of the defendant, but not so unrealistic that it amounts to a request for no bail."

"Are you saying that he can't make $500,000?" the judge asked.

"He cannot, Your Honor. He cannot."

"With the property you have described, what bail would you recommend?"

"Well, I think that $25,000 bail, Your Honor, would be reasonable and realistic."

Morgenthau could hold his silence no more.

"Certainly, Mr. Krieger has known for many, many months, during which he has represented Mr. Bonanno, that we have been looking for him. He certainly has not been with his family, or at his residence for that period of the last year and a half."

The words "family" and "residence" hung in the air, Morgenthau's frustration surfacing.

"Why he has come in at this particular time of course we don't know in detail," he said, "but I don't think that anybody who is under a Grand Jury subpoena should be permitted to select the time in which he wants to come in and appear before a Grand Jury or before the court."

Krieger cut him short.

"The defendant's wife is ill," Krieger countered. "Regardless of any charges against him, he is a human being and he is entitled to simple, basic—"

"I appreciate that, Mr. Krieger," Judge Frankel said. "The question is, what amount of bail will ensure the appearance of this human being in the court when he is expected." He then set bail at $150,000.

Morgenthau gathered the papers before him, Mollo and Kaufman following him out of the courtroom. Afterward, Bonanno and his attorneys made their way through the scrum.

"How do you feel?" one reporter asked.

"Under the circumstances," Bonanno replied, smiling widely, "as well as could be expected."

Morgenthau knew he had lost the day. He didn't know that Krieger had entered court that morning with a bail bondsman and a certificate authorizing a bond up to $500,000.

57. Amid Darkness, "Sunlight"

1967–1970

I n the first week of June 1968, Morgenthau was in a New York hospital, laid low by fatigue and stomach pain—"the worst colitis attack of my life." On the morning of June 5, he was still feverish when Martha called. During the night, she said, Bobby Kennedy had been shot in Los Angeles.

RFK had begun thinking seriously about a run for the White House in the winter of 1967, and after three months, pushed by the party's left flank to challenge President Johnson and end the war in Vietnam, he finally made up his mind by March. Bobby got a late start, and faced strong, seasoned competition: Eugene McCarthy, the Minnesota senator with a soft voice and sharp wit, who'd won New Hampshire with an astonishing 42 percent in March, and Vice President Hubert Humphrey. But on April 4, on the dark night when Martin Luther King was assassinated, Bobby had found his voice. Near midnight, as a largely Black crowd awaited the candidate at a park rally on Indianapolis's north side, he climbed atop a flatbed truck to deliver the news: He spoke across the deep racial divide, quoted Aeschylus—"even in our sleep pain, which cannot forget, falls drop by drop upon the heart . . ."—and mentioned his brother's murder for the first time in public. Bobby that night confessed the temptation to hate, but spoke of healing: "What we need in the United States is not violence and lawlessness, but is love, and wisdom, and compassion toward one another, and a feeling of justice toward those who still suffer within our country, whether they be white or whether they be Black." Across the country, riots broke out; Indianapolis remained quiet.

If Bobby had begun his campaign with a vow on Vietnam ("to rid ourselves of . . . those illusions which have lured us into the deepening swamp"), King's murder added the race war to the moral imperative. After the run of spring primaries—RFK had won four states, as well as the District of Columbia—the campaign seemed to coalesce in California in the first days of June. Bobby had gone to the Ambassador Hotel on primary day to await the returns. By midnight he'd learned that he had won big—with 46 percent—and entered the ballroom crowded with supporters. He took the stage and spoke again of "the division, the violence, the disenchantment" plaguing the country, but a buoyancy now filled his voice—"Now it's on to Chicago, and let's win there" were his final words from the microphone.

Bobby was making his way through a hallway to the hotel kitchen, when he was shot three times by a twenty-four-year-old Palestinian immigrant, Sirhan Sirhan. Twenty-six hours later, on June 6, at 4:44 A.M., New York time, he was pronounced dead.

From his hospital bed, Morgenthau would send words of condolence to Ethel. He'd always been grateful for her help on his failed run for governor. Ethel had joined Martha on the stump: Both had been pregnant, but they'd traveled across Manhattan and the Bronx, touring the political clubs, wooing the reporters and voters. The crowds had warmed to the women—a rare highlight in a grim campaign—and even in his defeat Ethel had extended unusual kindness.

He also called Bill Barry. A former FBI agent, Barry had been at Bobby's side—he'd served for years as his driver and bodyguard. Barry was among the first to leap from the crowd, helping to wrestle the killer to the ground. Throughout the campaign, Barry had been Morgenthau's point of contact. Years earlier, he had brought the two together: Since Bobby's first days as attorney general, Morgenthau had made sure Barry served as his chauffeur and bodyguard whenever he came to New York. "Bobby liked him so much," Morgenthau would say, "and not just because they both hated Hoover." Four years earlier, when RFK ran for the Senate, Barry volunteered to protect him—using vacation days to be at his side. Hoover took revenge: transferring the agent to Alabama. Barry would not be cowed, and instead, after fourteen years with the Bureau, he quit. Morgenthau found him a sinecure (a job in bank security), but when RFK announced his White House run, Barry returned. In Los Angeles that night, he'd stood with Kennedy as he left the podium. "Take care of Ethel," Bobby had told him, before heading for the kitchen.

Morgenthau had seen Bobby months earlier, in April. It had been a tumultuous week: LBJ had stunned the Democrats, announcing he wasn't running, and King's murder had shaken the country. Bobby, after criss-crossing the country, was back in the city, eager to craft a media campaign in short order. One evening he'd asked Morgenthau to come by a studio on the West Side, and Morgenthau arrived to find the candidate and his chief aides in a huddle, reviewing rough cuts of television ads. "The brain trust was there," he would recall, "and Bobby was giving his thoughts."

As Morgenthau listened to Bobby weigh in on the ads, he allowed himself to imagine the future. When RFK had announced his run, few among Kennedy's former army of prosecutors had been more pleased than Morgenthau—his children would recall a rare show of "elation." By spring, some in Bobby's circle—including Steve Smith, his campaign manager and an old Morgenthau friend—would say a second Kennedy in the White House could mean a cabinet post for Morgenthau, most likely attorney general. Morgenthau's enthusiasm, though, had little to do with his own career. "Daddy really believed in Bobby," his eldest daughter, Jenny, would say. "It was more than an affinity, it was adoration."

In the studio that evening, the chief federal prosecutor in Manhattan could not help but think back to Kennedy Justice—and how far his former boss had traveled. The television ads made clear the campaign's focus: civil rights and Vietnam. The war on the Mafia, Morgenthau understood, would be relegated to the past, and not featured in the campaign. Yet as the editors cut the footage, he thought of Bobby's years as A.G. It was a record of accomplishment, and a tenure, he was sure, that would stand without peer for a long time. Above all, though Hoover could never admit it, RFK had forever altered the FBI, shifting the Bureau away from the Soviet threat to fighting organized crime.

And yet, after leaving the department for the Senate, Bobby had changed much of his thinking on criminal justice. In their last meetings, Morgenthau had seen it: Kennedy was less interested now in putting people behind bars. Bobby wanted to learn, as he told Morgenthau, about "what happened to defendants after they were convicted" and "whether going to jail brought them out as better members of society or . . . hardened criminals." The warmth and charm remained, but a new expansiveness, and empathy, had emerged in his thought. "He'd evolved," Morgenthau would say. His politics had changed, and the shift, he realized, could attract an even broader base. Sitting in the TV studio with Bobby that spring, a conviction had settled for the first time in Morgenthau's mind: *He might just win.*

||||

After MLK, after RFK, the country, and New York City, had little time to wait. America convulsed with protest. For Morgenthau, the tumult of 1968 would pose new challenges. The Southern District had long ranked as the pressure-cooker of the nation's federal prosecutorial districts, but the U.S. attorney in Manhattan faced a new threat. By summer, with Richard Nixon, the former vice president, running for the White House, and winning every Republican primary he entered, Morgenthau sensed a confrontation looming. And yet, he only redoubled his efforts.

By now it was a record the newspapers loved to recite: Cohn, Wolfson, Lucchese, Bonanno, the Big Eight, the IRS, political parties on both sides. From fraud to embezzlement to conspiracy, Bob Morgenthau had indicted fat cats and mobsters, as well as their legal and financial abettors. He had not won every case; too often, he would say, the convicted found a way to walk on appeal. But he had sent a message to Wall Street, to the unions, and to the Mafia: The days of impunity had ended.

The U.S. attorney loved to win, but he was willing to take on any sector of criminal activity and risk losing, if only to curb its growth. You didn't always open an investigation to get a jail term, Morgenthau would tell his assistants. Often you brought a case to "throw light"—to bring crime out of the darkness. The assistants had come to call it "the Morgenthau line": "Sunlight," he had grown fond of saying, in a paraphrase of Justice Brandeis, "is the best disinfectant."

The foundation—the underpinning of a prosecutorial drive that would last nearly half a century—had taken shape. But one battle remained: the fight against official corruption. Morgenthau had a personal dislike for all criminals, but he reserved a particular disdain for those who abused the public trust; they struck at the institutions of democracy, undermining faith in what he considered his own domain: public service. New York City, as he'd learned even as a child, knew few rivals when it came to dirty politics; long before Boss Tweed, a parade of confidence men had feasted at its trough of municipal contracts. And as Morgenthau would set out to prove, the tradition continued.

||||

It had begun in the previous winter.

On Sunday evening, December 17, 1967, Bob Morgenthau called one of his closest friends from law school, the mayor of New York City, John Lindsay. He was calling as a courtesy, to deliver a heads-up before the hammer came down: "I'm sorry," he said, when Lindsay came on the phone, "the arrest is coming tomorrow." Morgenthau considered it the least he could do.

Mayor Lindsay, in his second year in office, had seen his reputation rise and his political base broaden. On the night that Dr. King was killed, as America's cities erupted in flames, Lindsay had walked the streets, trying to be a conciliator. The mayor, increasingly a Republican in name only, seemed to hunger for higher office. Many, his aides and rivals alike, spoke openly of a run for the White House.

But on Monday, December 18, Morgenthau delivered the blow: The FBI arrested James L. Marcus, the mayor's recently departed water commissioner, after a grand jury voted to indict him for playing a central role in a kickback scheme that struck at the heart of the city's governance. The affair involved a $40,000 bribe to secure an inflated contract to clean and repair a vital link in the city's water supply, the Jerome Park Reservoir in the Bronx.

Morgenthau's call had stunned Lindsay. Marcus had already resigned, six days earlier, and though the mayor had heard of a county investigation, the DA, Frank Hogan, had assured him that his former commissioner was not a target. Morgenthau, though, hauled in not only Marcus, but an unlikely trio of accomplices as well: Tony "Ducks" Corallo, a Lucchese family underboss; Danny Motto, head of Queens Local 350 of the Bakery, Confectionary and Food International union; and Henry Fried, president of S. T. Grand Construction, a contractor long the beneficiary of public works deals.

"I hated to have to tell John," Morgenthau would say, "but Hogan had assured him Marcus was clean—that he'd been cleared." On the phone, Lindsay's shock was genuine: Morgenthau had stolen the case from Hogan, the long-serving Manhattan DA, and taking advantage of Bobby Kennedy's anti-racketeering statute, made it a federal one. The mayor had reason to fear: A Morgenthau probe would have no boundaries. "John knew better than to ask [about the case]," Morgenthau would say. "But he knew without asking we'd follow it wherever we had to go."

Lindsay had brought in a new generation of talent to city politics. Amid a team of "Boy Wonders," as the press dubbed the Lindsay men, James L. Marcus seemed to fit right in; he had enjoyed a meteoric rise to the top of city government. He had come out of nowhere, or so it seemed. Even those who had worked closely with him during the campaign would have been hard put to describe his past—or to offer examples of his experience or expertise. The *Times* only ran its first profile of the commissioner and his rapid climb after word spread of an imminent Morgenthau arrest. At thirty-nine, Marcus, the paper reported, was "all gray—his hair, his face, his suit." In retrospect, his near invisibility—the first quality many recalled—was no accident.

Marcus was a man happiest at the edges of a political gathering. He seemed destined for the comfortable career of a middling financier, until he married, in 1962, a pretty young woman hoping to become an actress, a graduate of the Royal Academy of Dramatic Art in London and summer stock in Maine. Lily de Pourtales Lodge was the daughter of John Davis Lodge, former governor of Connecticut, and a niece of Henry Cabot Lodge, Jr., former senator from Massachusetts. Marcus had come from a different world: He grew up in Schenectady, the only child of a middle-class Jewish family. He attended military school, before Union College and the University of Pennsylvania. He failed to graduate from either institution. But in 1964, when Marcus met John Lindsay, then a congressman from Manhattan's "silk-stocking" district, the details of his origins were already obscured: In the Lindsay circle, where such status carried currency, Marcus was introduced as "one of the Lodge family."

After Lindsay's victory, Marcus joined the administration as "a volunteer aide"—coming to City Hall without pay and allowing others to believe that family wealth afforded him the independence to do so. Lindsay made Marcus the administration's troubleshooter on "the water supply." It hardly seemed a plum sinecure: In the summer of 1965, New York's water had become a heated campaign issue. The region was mired in a drought, and the water system was antiquated and overdue for an overhaul. Water was slow to arrive, brackish, and foul-smelling. Lindsay had assured voters he'd solve their concerns and assign a top engineer to the task.

At first, the mayor named Marcus to negotiate with the Delaware River Basin Commission, tasking him with extending a deal to deliver more water to the city. Marcus seemed to take to the job, and within months announced a resolution: The city would be allowed to take "490 million gallons of water a day" from the Delaware River. "Things are in good shape," he said, adding that the city's reservoir system would soon be full for the first time in five years. Lindsay, in turn, rewarded him with the top job: At thirty-five, with no expertise or experience, Marcus was named commissioner in charge of New York City's water, gas, and electricity. And still, neither the mayor nor his aides bothered to vet Marcus; no one had confirmed even the degrees that he claimed.

The U.S. attorney had noted the sudden rise. Water commissioner was a position with power. It wasn't just about water, Morgenthau would say: You couldn't dig a hole in any city street without getting "a Water Commissioner's permit." Few seats in City Hall offered closer proximity to the levers of governance: patronage, favors, and bribes. Morgenthau could see how the mayor fell for Marcus: He was handsome with an easy smile, ever eager and youthful—"always had a suntan," an associate would say, "always looked like he just came out of the shower." But Morgenthau would soon come to know, as he read the FBI reports, the real résumé: Marcus had cycled through a series of short-lived, one-man ventures in finance, chemicals, and advertising—"a young man," Morgenthau would say, "susceptible to seduction."

As Marcus settled into City Hall, he found himself in financial quicksand. In 1966 he'd made a large stock buy "on margin"—putting up less than a quarter of the purchase price in cash. Within days, as the share price sank, Marcus faced margin calls; the brokerage house began to press him. He took out loans, but his losses mounted.

| | | |

Since the first days of the Lindsay administration, the complaints about Manhattan's water had only multiplied. One cause was clear: The Jerome Park Reservoir in the Bronx, 96 acres holding 773 million gallons of water, had never been cleaned. To do so, it would have to be drained, scrubbed, and repaired—a restoration job larger than any the city had ever attempted. The contract, cast as an "emergency" measure, would sidestep public bidding, and at $1 million be the largest such deal ever awarded.

Danny Motto, at fifty-seven, lived in Greenwich, Connecticut, but he had run a Queens union (a local of the Bakery and Confectionary Workers) since the war. Among law enforcement, Motto had earned a shady reputation that dated to 1944, when he was caught dealing in rationed gasoline. Long before Lindsay took office, the union boss had come across a labor lawyer with an unusually broad range of friendships. Herbert Itkin, a Brooklyn-bred attorney in his early forties, kept a desk in a Midtown office where he pursued claims of personal injury, mostly among Teamsters men. But Itkin had enjoyed a second life, as he would later detail for Morgenthau and his investigators, as an informant for both the CIA and the FBI.

"Herbie Itkin," Morgenthau would say, "was one of our toughest witnesses—certainly the strangest." Itkin had come to the attention of the New York FBI field office by way of the CIA: None other than James Angleton, the famed CIA counterintelligence chief, made the introduction. Itkin had stumbled into a CIA operative in New York, Mario Brod, a fellow lawyer who, as Angleton told an FBI agent, Bill Vericker, had long served as "a chief conduit for information on the labor circles and the Mob." Itkin and Brod had formed an ad hoc working relationship—and had delved deeply into the shadowy world of "Teamster loans," union loans notorious as a source for fraud and corruption. The CIA chief made a pitch, and the FBI accepted: Itkin would go to work for the Bureau as an informant—and over the course of five years, during which he "proved hard to handle," Itkin delivered. He infiltrated the Mob: In 1967, he could say, with little exaggeration, "I am almost a Mafioso myself. I have been with them a long, long time."

By 1967, Itkin had made another friend: the mayor's recently appointed water commissioner. It was Itkin who introduced Motto, the union boss, to Marcus—and four months later, Motto in turn introduced the Lindsay aide to his "cousin," Tony "Ducks" Corallo—an underboss high on Morgenthau's chart of the Five Families. The water commissioner's new friends had united around one sole interest: the "fat contract" to repair the Bronx reservoir. A deal was struck: a kickback scheme in which all, including Marcus, were guaranteed a cut. Itkin's take alone, as the middleman would say, was to be "$75,000 in green."

Eight months later, on May 11, 1967, Lindsay and Marcus arrived by helicopter to preside at the refilling of the Jerome Park Reservoir. Standing side by side, the mayor and the water commissioner obliged the press photographers who had waited for hours, smiling in unison as they opened the giant sluices.

| | | |

Days before Christmas 1967, Morgenthau indicted Marcus for his role in the kickback scheme. Marcus, who pled guilty, was sentenced to fifteen months, and after a trial, "Ducks" Corallo would be sentenced to three years, and Motto and Fried to two years each.

"The Marcus affair" captivated New Yorkers. Amid the sensational news reports, names of prominent politicians and executives swirled. If Marcus had been selling city contracts, who else had tried to profit from the racket? For months, reporters and city insiders played a parlor game: Who would fall next?

On December 20, 1968, a year after the Marcus arrest, Morgenthau answered the question: indicting none other than Carmine De Sapio, the famed former head of the Tammany machine, and the kingmaker who had put Wagner in City Hall and Harriman in Albany, and who served as a power broker at more than one Democratic National Convention. Itkin had told the U.S. attorney of a second deal—one involving Consolidated Edison, a city permit, and a construction contract to build a power line over a city-owned aqueduct in Westchester. De Sapio had stepped in as the "umpire," offering to lend a hand (for $12,500 in cash), encouraging Marcus to delay the permit sought by Con Ed until it awarded the construction deals to contractors of De Sapio's choosing— namely, those at the heart of the reservoir scheme.

Morgenthau had indicted De Sapio on three counts of conspiracy and bribery; he had also brought new charges against the mobster Corallo and contractor Fried. (Corallo would get a four-and-a-half-year prison term in the Con Edison case, to run concurrently with the time he had already begun to serve in the reservoir case.) Yet it was the fall of De Sapio, "last of the bigtime bosses," that signaled the end of an era, and delivered to many in the city a sense of consolation. A once-indomitable force in the city, famous for his dark glasses, gray pompadour, and uncanny ability to survive scandal after scandal since 1952, was now called to justice.

On the eve of sentencing, De Sapio would launch a final drive for leniency on health grounds. Yet the judge would conclude that the evidence he had heard was "overwhelming . . . and, sad enough to say, from the lips of the defendant himself." Asked by a prosecutor about his role in the Con Ed conspiracy, De Sapio had cried, "I wouldn't do that thirty years ago, when I was an amateur!" Asked to stand and speak, the fallen kingmaker offered only a confused dialogue with himself, an inchoate dance of fits and starts, that ended, as if on cue, with pride: "I tried to prove I was innocent. I was telling the truth . . . but I just don't understand . . . perhaps I have been the victim of an aura, a climate that is concerning many people relative to organized crime . . . I have done everything to the best of my ability to maintain—preserve the kind of reputation I think I earned for my family and friends. I am sorry it has turned out this way."

The former boss of Tammany got two years in prison.

||||

President Johnson, from the first, had revealed an antipathy for the U.S. attorney in New York. LBJ wanted to see Morgenthau gone and to install his own man in the Southern District: the son of his own favored lawyer and a longtime party insider, Eddie Weisl, Jr. More than once, the president had called Morgenthau to dangle a federal judgeship, a position in Washington, anything to get him to move on. Johnson had only kept Morgenthau in place because Bobby Kennedy had demanded it. (RFK, as his friend Peter Maas would write, "promised a nasty, public fight if he didn't.") With Bobby gone, Morgenthau was left without a protector, yet Johnson's displeasure had not slowed him—in particular, when it came to matters close to the White House.

For years, Morgenthau had been trying, as discreetly as possible, to chase the loose ends still dangling from the Louis Wolfson investigation—accusations that, if true, were political dynamite. He'd heard them first from his assistants, the prosecutors who had run the Wolfson cases. The charge, and its time frame, were sufficiently specific to warrant concern: The Junkman, it was said, had sought—at the height of the SEC's probe into his securities maneuverings—the legal assistance, and intervention, of a sitting justice of the Supreme Court. The justice in question was Abe Fortas—and Fortas, as Morgenthau knew all too well, had been an LBJ confidant, friend, and advisor since 1939—"somebody," as Wolfson would say on his way to prison, "as close as anybody could be" to the president. If Wolfson had made such an entreaty, and if it had found a receptive embrace, Morgenthau knew what the two facts amounted to: a crime without precedent in the annals of the Supreme Court, and a case that he would have to send up the chain of command.

||||

For three years, Morgenthau had known about "the Huffnagel file." He told his assistants to keep it hidden, stored until it gained maximum value.

That day would not come until the spring of 1969, when the Supreme

Court ended the long line of appeals by Wolfson and Buddy Gerbert, his "right hand man and first lieutenant," hoping to reverse their conviction in the Continental stock fraud case, the first charges that Morgenthau had brought against the Junkman. As the lawyers and reporters scanned the Court's denial of the writ, hardly anyone noted that a lone justice had "recused" himself: Abe Fortas.

On one hand, it made sense: Fortas's old law firm, Arnold, Fortas & Porter, had represented a Wolfson company when Fortas was a partner. Even after Fortas left, the law firm had continued to defend Gerbert, Wolfson's co-defendant in the two criminal trials in New York. The justice, as some noted, was right to remove himself from considering the Wolfson appeal. Morgenthau, though, knew otherwise.

Since the summer of 1966, the Huffnagel file had remained in the forefront of his mind. It dated to the early days of the investigation of Wolfson, led by assistant U.S. attorney Mike Armstrong and Stu Allen, the SEC man. For weeks, they had pushed Alexander Rittmaster, Wolfson's crony, to cooperate. Morgenthau made it clear: "No Rittmaster, no case." One afternoon in August 1966, Rittmaster grew exasperated: "I don't know why you guys are working so hard," he said. "Everything's been taken care of in D.C. . . . Mr. F is on it."

"Who the hell is 'Mr. F'?" Stu Allen asked.

For weeks, Rittmaster would not say, but by fall they had dragged it out of him: "Mr. F" was Abe Fortas. Even as Morgenthau began his investigation, Rittmaster claimed, Fortas had visited the Wolfson horse farm, a sprawling ranch in Ocala, Florida, and Wolfson had assured his chief lieutenants not to worry: "Mr. F was on the case." "The word was," Rittmaster said, the SEC investigation would "be taken care of in Washington."

If Morgenthau doubted the tale, he knew it contained a detail that needed checking out: Rittmaster had said Buddy Gerbert, Wolfson's number two, had picked up Fortas at the Jacksonville airport and driven him to the farm in Ocala. When Morgenthau learned that Fortas might be called as a character witness for Wolfson at trial, he did not hesitate: They needed to dig further. "There were no words," Armstrong would recall, but the next move was clear. "We had to prepare a cross"—in case they had to cross-examine a sitting Supreme Court justice.

Critics, and even friends, who knew about "Mr. F" would assess the risks and caution Morgenthau: Was it necessary to take a man down—a Democrat, and a legal scholar? His answer never wavered: "Of course."

In December 1966, Stu Allen, the SEC investigator, flew to Miami and began a search for a record of the justice's trip. Directed only by logic, he went to the records office of Eastern Airlines, the airline with the most flights from Washington, D.C., to Jacksonville. The hunt was not simple. Some filing boxes held used tickets from as many as fifty flights. Allen, moreover, did not know the day; Rittmaster had only said "summer." But Morgenthau and Armstrong had a hunch: The trip was likely to have come near the date that the SEC referred the case for criminal prosecution to the Southern District. On the fourth day of searching, Allen unearthed the gold he sought: a round-trip ticket, in Fortas's name, for June 14–16, for $105.84.

When Morgenthau heard the news, he issued a warning: "Keep it under wraps." Armstrong made a file—labeling it "Charles Huffnagel," a code name for Fortas—and put it in a desk drawer, where it remained for three years, until the Wolfson appeal reached the Supreme Court—and Justice Fortas recused himself.

||||

Morgenthau could not recall meeting Fortas. He may have done so during his father's Washington years; Fortas had been prominent in the city since the New Deal. But he was a lawyer of the genus Morgenthau distrusted, often going on little other than instinct: the Washington "fixer."

Fortas had come to the capital as a legal scholar, serving under William O. Douglas at the SEC, where he had met Lyndon Johnson. They were both Southerners, but differed in vital ways—Fortas had gone to Yale Law, played the violin masterfully, collected modern art. Yet as LBJ rose, Fortas became a close advisor—the closest, some said. He had served as LBJ's counsel in the White House, his gatekeeper and fixer. Whenever a scandal flared, Fortas could be relied upon to quash it. He could also fend off the unwanted: supplicants, reporters, rivals. Fortas provided this informal service even after LBJ appointed him to the Supreme Court in October 1965. He offered counsel on the federal judges Johnson should pick, who should staff the highest ranks of the State Department, and, most controversially, how the generals should run the war in Vietnam.

When the investigators told Morgenthau of Wolfson's possible tie to Fortas, he sensed a turn of good luck. Since the earliest days of the Wolfson investigation, Morgenthau had felt the pressure from Washington—"the most heat I ever got," he would say. LBJ, he was certain, was a man who had been used to cutting corners since his early years in West Texas. Morgenthau had felt the Johnson "touch" at work: He would remember Bobby Kennedy, then in his last days at Justice, calling after Morgenthau brought the first charges against Wolfson: Could they move the case to Miami, he'd wanly asked. "Why?" replied Morgenthau, incredulous. "So you'll have a chance to put in the fix?" It was a poor joke, but Bobby's retort had taken him aback. "No," he said, "so *they* could have a better shot at putting in the fix."

Morgenthau knew Wolfson's ties to the Democratic Party ran deep, but even he had been surprised—"floored," he would say—to learn of the Fortas connection. Rittmaster had proven a star witness: After caving, Wolfson's former cohort had pled guilty, and made the trial. But the story he'd blurted out to Morgenthau's men—Wolfson asking Fortas for help—was not aired in court, neither in the first case nor in the second. Morgenthau had sat on it. He had made sure, though, to test the tale's accuracy—and been more than pleased to see it come out airtight: On June 14, 1966, during a Supreme Court recess, Fortas had indeed flown to Jacksonville, visiting Wolfson at his horse farm. The SEC's investigation was advancing, and even as Fortas and Wolfson conferred, it had become public. (On June 15, an SEC attorney mentioned it before a New York state court judge, as he asked for a delay in the settlement of several unrelated Merritt-Chapman stockholder suits, pending the probe's outcome.) The following day, Fortas flew home, but within days Wolfson told Rittmaster that the justice had been "furious" the SEC had gone back on its word, and not given Wolfson's lawyers another chance to explain before sending the case to Morgenthau. Still, Wolfson was confident, as Rittmaster heard, that Fortas would handle it.

Morgenthau had the evidence—not only Rittmaster's words, but the plane ticket. Still, he bided his time. "It was too damn hot," he would say, years later. "Where would you go with it?"—an accusation of a Supreme Court justice intervening in an SEC investigation.

He first tried to bring the Huffnagel file out in the summer of 1968. In the wake of Earl Warren's retirement, as LBJ nominated Fortas to become chief justice, Morgenthau knew he had to act. Fortas would become the first sitting justice nominated to be chief justice and thus forced to appear before the Senate, where he would be grilled about his extracurricular activities on Johnson's behalf: Republicans and Democrats alike pounded Fortas with questions on his frequent Oval Office consultations.

Morgenthau told Fred Vinson, Jr., chief of the Criminal Division at Justice, about Fortas's trip to the Wolfson horse farm. Vinson was the son of the man who had replaced Morgenthau's own father at Treasury. If there was animus, Morgenthau would insist it had nothing to do with his father—"and everything to do with sucking up to LBJ." Vinson Jr. took no action. But the Fortas nomination hit another hurdle: The justice had accepted, the hearings revealed, a $15,000 fee for a seminar at the American University Law School. One of Fortas's former law partners tried to explain away the speaker's fee, which was exorbitant for the time, but as the Judiciary Committee declared an intention to probe further, Fortas announced he would not appear before the senators.

His nomination doomed, Fortas at last asked the president to pull it. Within a week, LBJ had persuaded Warren to stay on, at least until the presidential election the following month.

||||

Abe Fortas would not become chief justice, but LBJ could not forestall an investigation. The fuse was burning: An anonymous letter had arrived at the Senate Judiciary Committee, claiming to reveal a consultancy agreement between Fortas and the Wolfson Family Foundation—and a $20,000 payment to Fortas. Morgenthau soon caught wind of the letter, and took it as sufficient cause to try again. That fall, as Fortas returned to the Court, Morgenthau again attempted to deploy the Huffnagel file. He returned to main Justice, but Vinson Jr. and now the attorney general, Ramsey Clark, too, did LBJ's bidding: They stonewalled him. They promised to look into it, and warned him about trespassing beyond his jurisdiction.

In the face of the increasing resistance, Morgenthau struck back. If his father, Henry Jr., had loathed the Washington columnists and the proxy battles waged by the Roosevelt factions, Bob Morgenthau shared with his grandfather Henry Sr. a deft ability to work the press. The *Times,* of course, was a favored avenue, but the main conduit was Bill Lambert, star investigator at *Life* magazine. It was Lambert who'd told Morgenthau of the anonymous letter—either the reporter had written it or Stu Allen had. Lambert had handed over the details, gleaned from an IRS source, of the Wolfson payment: On January 1, 1966, three months after Fortas was sworn in as an associate justice, a check for $20,000 was made out to him on a Jacksonville bank account of Wolfson's foundation. It was endorsed with Fortas's name and deposited into his personal account. Lambert saved the best for last: Fortas had not declared it on his tax returns.

On Friday, November 8, 1968, days after Nixon's election, Morgenthau again called the attorney general. "*Life*'s on this thing," he told Ramsey Clark. "Lambert's not going to let go and it's damn serious." Clark claimed to know nothing of it; the news, he would say years later, "hit as a shock." When Clark went to Fortas's house in Georgetown the next day, the justice tried to explain the check away—it had "something to do with integrated housing." Clark waited as Fortas went to call his secretary at the Court, Gloria Dalton, who handled his finances. After the call, Fortas returned to tell Clark that he had not reported the fee because "I paid that money back. I decided that I couldn't do it."

His law clerks knew better. At least two were aware that Fortas flew on occasion to Jacksonville, and that he had an association with the Wolfson Foundation. One of them, Dan Levitt, received a call one Saturday night from the White House operator: "Johnson wanted to talk to Fortas, and I told him that he was in Florida." The message was clear: The justice had gone to see Wolfson. The clerk was "a little troubled by the fact that Fortas and Wolfson had this relationship," because "if you read the *Journal* or *The Washington Post,* you knew Wolfson was under SEC investigation." To warn the justice, Levitt left on Fortas's desk a copy of Title 18, "Crimes and Criminal Procedure"—circling the statute that covered the conduct of judicial branch officers.

Ramsey Clark, meanwhile, was relieved not to have to spend the last days of the Johnson administration fighting a fire at the Court. In an irony of history, the airing Morgenthau sought would come at the hands of the new regime in Washington. Attorney General John Mitchell and the incoming head of the Criminal Division, Will Wilson, were eager to hear more of the Fortas-Wolfson connection. Wilson sent men to scour Morgenthau's files, and summoned the assistants who had worked the Wolfson cases, Armstrong and Grand, to Washington. Before leaving they met with Morgenthau. "Bob, who had a lot of respect and regard for Abe Fortas, put it all aside," Grand recalled. "He said simply, 'Do what you got to do, but be as fair-minded as you can.' It was not 'Gild the lily.'"

Whether it was blindness or a foolhardy self-assurance, Fortas allowed himself to imagine that the Morgenthau mess had subsided. Yet in the first months of the Nixon administration, as a new law clerk, Walter Slocombe, recorded, "It became evident in the office that something was afoot." In Fortas's chambers, the reporters' calls gained urgency; Mitchell and his men were leaking to several newsrooms at once. The AP called about an IRS investigation of Fortas's taxes. Another reporter asked when Fortas would quit. As the siege set in, Wolfson, heading for prison, could not restrain himself—and nearly told all. Morgenthau hardly believed it when in late April, he read Wolfson's last newspaper interview as a free man—days before he entered a federal prison in Florida. Wolfson boasted that he could have won a pardon from LBJ, had he asked for it, from someone "as close as anybody could be" to the president.

Lambert, the *Life* reporter, encouraged by Morgenthau, plowed on. In late April, he'd sent Fortas a letter, asking for comment on a new revelation: The deal with Wolfson, Lambert had learned, was in fact a "lifetime agreement" for $20,000 a year. As Fortas attempted to explain, Lambert prepared a cover story for May. Nixon's men were eager for the exposé: John Ehrlichman, the White House aide, would write that "Nixon cleared his desk of other work to focus on getting Fortas off the Court."

On Friday, May 2, Bill Moyers, LBJ's former press secretary, called Fortas to warn him that the *Life* story would appear on Sunday, May 4.

Fortas spent the weekend in his office. He was agitated and, when he spoke of the arrangement he had with Wolfson, "not particularly coherent," a clerk would record. At last, he issued a three-hundred-word statement that raised more questions than it answered. Fortas said he had returned the fee to Wolfson, but made no mention of the amount, nor of the eleven-month lag between receipt and repayment. In Congress and in the press, the calls grew louder: Fortas should either give a better explanation, or resign.

The Nixon men knew they had been given dynamite. On May 7, Mitchell secretly met with Earl Warren, ostensibly to warn the chief justice. In fact, the attorney general tried a bluff: The Justice Department, Mitchell implied, had tapes of Fortas talking to the SEC chairman on Wolfson's behalf. No such evidence existed, but the next day, two FBI agents paid a visit to Wolfson in prison. "Wolfson not only confirmed the agreement for life," Lambert reported in his next exposé, he "revealed that he and Fortas had discussed the SEC case."

On the evening of May 14, as President Nixon prepared to address the nation on Vietnam, Fortas sent a letter of resignation to the White House.

The announcement ended, Lambert wrote, "ten days of the most feverish press and political activity that Washington has seen since the

Cuban missile crisis." Bob Morgenthau saw the irony: He had handed the incoming Republican administration a dream opportunity to get a liberal Democrat off the Court, and one intimately involved in the making of Johnson's Great Society. Morgenthau allowed himself no satisfaction in Fortas's demise, nor would talk of the justice's end ever elicit a sign of pleasure. The U.S. attorney did, though, enjoy the tales from Florida, relayed by FBI agents who made the trip to see the former junk king in prison.

Louis Wolfson had been sent to the "honor camp," minimum security, on the Eglin Air Force Base in Florida. Among the 450 convicts, mostly moonshiners and bootleggers, Wolfson would encounter James Marcus, John Lindsay's erstwhile wonder boy. Marcus would serve most of his eleven months in the rough barracks that dated to the war. "Mr. W," as America's former chief corporate raider was known, and the former water commissioner of New York City ended up working side by side, on the same shift, in the prison laundry.

58. "Sinewy Fingers"

1969

Martha Morgenthau had always kept a distance from "downtown." It was less a matter of duty than of instinct: She maintained a midwestern reserve and never hungered for the Manhattan limelight. Little of the city's social calendar—the theater, the galas, the carousel of political dinners—was her world. She believed in her husband, believed, as she told her children, that he would "do good." But Martha was a private person, and it was her private confidence that her husband relied on.

At home, Martha set the calendar. The days revolved around family, and weekends around a small circle of friends: the Thachers, Ransoms, and Resors. The couples were close, though the others were Republicans, descendants of old patrician lines: Bob Ransom, whom Bob had known since Deerfield, was a corporate counsel at IBM; Tom Thacher, son of Hoover's solicitor general and grandson of one of the most famous name partners at Simpson, Thacher & Bartlett, had married an Auchincloss and served in Governor Rockefeller's cabinet; Stan Resor, son of a former head of the J. Walter Thompson advertising agency, had married Jane Pillsbury, Martha's friend from Minneapolis. (In 1965, LBJ had named Resor his secretary of the Army, and he'd stayed on under the new Nixon administration.) Politics, though, was kept to the side when they gathered for cocktails, dinners, or ski weekends away. The partisan divide never seemed to matter; what mattered was the war, Yale Law— the men, and their wives, had survived both—and the children. (They were all big families—the Thachers had two girls and four boys; the Ransoms, six boys; the Resors, seven boys.) The Thachers lived nearby, the Ransoms in Bronxville, and the Resors in New Canaan. But they had formed an easy set; they were families abounding in natural gifts, inherited wealth, and every other feature of good fortune.

Riverdale had become the Morgenthaus' idyll. The neighborhood—born "River Dale" in the eighteenth century—was one of the last corners of country in the city: The roads were curving and riven with asphalt cracks. The Morgenthau house stood by the woodlands, at the bend of Independence Avenue. From outside it seemed imposing, but inside the house was rambling, noisy with kids, friends, and animals. In the evenings, though, they could count on quiet, broken only by the train from Grand Central running north along the river. The house in Riverdale, intended as a haven for Martha and the children, had become a refuge for Bob as well. "If she was private, he liked that," their son Bobby would say. "She was his wall—Mom kept us, the family, walled off from whatever troubles he could be facing at work."

They had fun, too, and weekends were for sports. "She was a real old Minnesota girl," her daughter Annie would say. "A terrific athlete. She played hockey, swam, waterskied, was a really good golfer and tennis player—it was a big part of their life" before the war. Her father was a huge baseball fan, and her nickname growing up was "Charlie," an homage to a favorite Minneapolis Millers minor-league third baseman. For decades, sports had been a bond: Martha and Bob loved to play together, and to compete. At tennis, they were doubles partners—never indomitable, always formidable. Only the snows would keep them from the local courts down the hill, by the Hudson. The Riverdale Yacht Club was, in fact, yachtless and so small a commuter could travel the rails beside it for years and not notice it, but its pair of courts afforded the Morgenthaus a reassuring view of the water, breezes even in midsummer, and long seasons of round-robin competition.

| | | |

It was on the tennis court that Martha felt it for the first time—a numbing pain in her arm, near the shoulder. She tried to rub it away, but could not. The pain persisted, and though she was loath to mention it to Bob, let alone the children, she went to see the doctor. In early 1969, she was diagnosed with breast cancer. The doctor offered scant specifics—such was the state of the science at the time. He spoke only of a need for tests, and time to wait and see.

For months after Martha told him, Bob pretended nothing had

changed. Each morning he drove down the West Side Highway to work; each evening he came home late. All the while, Martha remained "the wall"—now aiding Bob in keeping up the façade that nothing was wrong. She'd led the PTA and the local Red Cross chapter, joined the fight for a neighborhood library, and, above all, helped to transform Wave Hill—the estate overlooking the Hudson that her husband and other local attorneys had rescued from development—into a public garden and environmental center.

At home, it was Martha who maintained the routine: She ran the big white rambling house, tended its garden—she'd planted the roses herself. She would take the kids—only twelve-year-old Bobby, and Barbara, six years old, remained at home—to the local pool a half block away to swim. Annie was finishing up at Radcliffe, due to graduate that spring.

Martha would come to understand that surgery was inevitable, but she wanted to forestall the telling—and she did not want to ruin the graduation. "She was kind of self-effacing," Annie would say. "When she went in for the operation, neither she nor Dad knew she was going to have a mastectomy." The surgery was supposed to take an hour or two. After four hours, Bob heard the words "radical mastectomy." He had never heard them before.

Martha had no choice, her eldest daughter, Jenny, would say, "that's just what they did then." The doctors expressed relief: They had found no evidence of the cancer's spread. In the months after she came home, there would be no follow-up: no chemotherapy, no radiation.

That summer, after graduating, Annie had come home, too. Her father offered her an internship in the office, but her main work was at home. "I drove Barbara to camp, and I was like junior Mom." Annie had yet to devise "a plan" for her life. She thought of pursuing economics—her Radcliffe major—or perhaps city planning, or law school, but "the illness shifted all that—we could think of little else."

Her father at least could pretend to preoccupy himself with the looming battles. But something had shifted. Martha had been, from the first, *his* confidante. She did not advise; she listened and consoled. Bob, she knew, could deny reality, or at least persuade himself to delay the inevitable arrival of logical conclusions—as he had done with their gravest challenge, the decision to say goodbye to their little girl, Nellie. And when he verged from fear toward dejection—though she had never known him to descend all the way there, and doubted that he even could—she would reassure him, lifting him up again. Still, Martha knew one thing about her husband: He might be riddled with concerns, but he did not know indecision or self-doubt. He knew "things would work out"—for Bob Morgenthau they always had.

And so, in the fall of 1969, a new certitude settled in: If anyone would have to plan for the future, something other than the one they'd dreamed of, the gently flowing life of enduring prosperity and well-calibrated challenges, Martha would have to be the one to do it.

| | | |

Few took notice, but the charter hanging on the wall of the fourth-floor office of the U.S. attorney had made clear the end date: Unlike that of nearly every other federal prosecutor in the country, Morgenthau's tenure would outlast LBJ's. U.S. attorneys serve four-year terms, yet because he had left office to run for governor, and been confirmed in an off-year, Morgenthau's current term would not expire until June 1971. Few expected it to pose a problem—until Richard Nixon moved into the White House.

Since the close of 1968, Morgenthau had known the clock was ticking on his tenure. And when he surveyed his office's investigations, he saw much unfinished business. His men, for instance, were in midstream on a new probe of an old nemesis.

| | | |

No one got Morgenthau's goat like Roy Cohn. He fumed openly to aides that Cohn was the most corrupt man in New York City. Cohn, he would complain, got a box of cigars from J. Edgar Hoover every Christmas, kept a direct phone line to Lou Nichols, Hoover's number three, and could curry favor across the city with whomever he wished—bankers, attorneys, clergymen, even Cardinal Spellman. Morgenthau had never stopped investigating Cohn, and by 1969, he was more intent than ever to make a case—and Cohn, as the prosecutor saw things, was practically daring him to.

Cohn had used his influence to block every investigation, Morgenthau was sure of it. "He's a little paranoiac about Cohn," Morgenthau's former assistant, Arthur Liman, told a writer working on a magazine profile in 1968. "He felt Cohn had so much influence with the FBI. We had a cooperating witness who had a meeting with Roy, the FBI bugged the room with the permission of the tenants. They put the bug in the bathroom and all it picked up was interference from the light." Morgenthau insisted that Cohn had interfered and got the Bureau to bungle the bugging.

And in the summer of 1969, Morgenthau was certain that Cohn had persuaded Hoover to transfer three FBI agents out of New York, just to spite the U.S. attorney. The three agents, who were given thirty-six hours' notice, had been working on Morgenthau's most recent attempt to nail Cohn: investigating what would become known as the "Fifth Avenue Coach case." In January 1969, Morgenthau had indicted Cohn for the third time in five years—now on charges of bribery, conspiracy, extortion, and blackmail—having gathered evidence that he had bribed a city appraiser to help a valued client, the Fifth Avenue Coach Lines. Cohn had paid six bribes, totaling $25,000, in 1964, Morgenthau charged, including one in the corridor of the federal courthouse, outside Courtroom 110 where Cohn had been on trial in the earlier case. The trial in the new case would start in late September 1969.

On the eve of trial, Cohn dropped a bombshell. He told reporters, and the court, that the judge in the case, Inzer B. Wyatt, could not be impartial—and must be removed. That summer, Judge Wyatt, Cohn charged, had hosted Paul Perito, a Morgenthau assistant prosecuting the case, in his private beach tent in Monte Carlo. The judge had previously disclosed the encounter—a gesture of generosity after an accidental meeting on a Riviera holiday. But Cohn was intent on making the most of the last-minute gift from his courthouse spies: Morgenthau's "vendetta" had lasted six years, he said, and now "they are more like hunters, with me the hunted."

If Morgenthau saw Cohn's influence everywhere, Cohn in turn saw Morgenthau's reach behind every obstacle he faced. He would compile a litany of complaints: A Morgenthau cousin was clerking in Wyatt's chambers; "a squad of ten Internal Revenue agents . . . were assigned to Morgenthau"; Morgenthau's men had put out the word through the jails that any convicted swindler would win a reprieve if he helped the government "get Cohn." The cousin did clerk for the judge, but had nothing to do with the case; the IRS men were chiefly tasked with investigating corrupt fellow agents; and although one inmate did offer to help Morgenthau ensnare Cohn, he was rebuffed.

The Fifth Avenue Coach Lines trial lasted nearly three months, and offered a drama that only elevated Cohn's showmanship. On the eve of closing arguments, Joseph Brill, Cohn's attorney, was returning to court from lunch when he collapsed on the courthouse steps. "A heart attack," Cohn would insist. Morgenthau, and the court reporters, would call it a convenient illness: His attorney's sudden absence allowed Cohn to rise in his own defense—without facing a cross-examination. The move would only enhance the Cohn legend: The defendant offered a summation, without notes, that lasted nearly seven hours.

The jury came back late on a Friday night, after only three hours, to acquit him on every count.

"Thank God," Cohn cried, "we put juries between the type of tyranny that Morgenthau perpetrates on his enemies!"

| | | |

By tradition, U.S. attorneys offer to resign upon a change of power in the White House. Not Morgenthau. He let it be known that he intended to serve out his term.

LBJ may have failed to wrest Morgenthau from office, but Nixon presented a challenge of a higher magnitude. The Republican made no secret of his distaste for the Kennedy-appointed prosecutor in Manhattan. Days after Nixon's election, Morgenthau joked to a reporter: "Do you think I should prepare my memoirs: *I Was Fired by Richard Nixon*?"

And yet many believed that Nixon could find a way to live with Morgenthau. The two might even find common ground: Morgenthau, after all, was no civil libertarian. "Bob never really thought about civil liberties," Arthur Liman would tell a reporter in 1968—agreeing to be quoted only anonymously. And at the height of the battles over civil rights and Vietnam, Morgenthau had drawn the ire of the American Civil Liberties Union (ACLU). When he convened a grand jury to probe a draft-card burning in Union Square, the Reverend A. J. Muste, a radical activist, called it "an inquisition into political beliefs." Aryeh Neier, head of the New York Civil Liberties Union, hired two stenographers and positioned them outside the grand jury room, as the witnesses retold what they had been asked by Morgenthau's men. He and Muste aired the prosecutors' questions—on the protesters' views on Vietnam, they claimed—at a press conference. "It made Morgenthau very angry; he called every one of our board members to get my head," Neier recalled. Above all, as Nixon knew, the U.S. attorney respected, and relied on, the FBI.

By the summer of 1969, it was clear an accommodation was not to be. Nixon signaled that Morgenthau had to go. Roy Cohn would claim a hand in the final act, but Morgenthau refused to believe that even Cohn could wield such power. Later, he would look back and say his firing was due to "a whole bouquet of trouble." He'd been pursuing "so many investigations that Nixon could not stand—and we were not about to stop short."

||||

Bob Morgenthau had long nurtured his father's distaste for tax cheats, and in his final months he would chase them to a realm where no U.S. prosecutor had ventured: offshore. For years, Morgenthau had lobbied to curtail the growing allure of overseas tax havens—pressing the accountants, bankers, and politicians to defend the Treasury's coffers, and prevent the country's richest from sheltering their wealth in the numbered bank accounts long available in Switzerland, and increasingly in the Caribbean as well. Nixon's victory would only add urgency to the fight.

Since the mid-1960s, Morgenthau had been hearing about the financial evolution of the organized crime families: They had learned to launder their profits in Swiss banks. Wall Street had an even closer relationship with the offshore world. As he chased the leads to the tax havens overseas, Morgenthau's attention soon turned to Randolph Guthrie, a name partner in the firm Nixon had joined in 1963. Guthrie, long a counsel to a Geneva bank, had worked both sides of the Atlantic, as the muckraker Jack Anderson would reveal, in a "multi-million-dollar Swiss bank deal." No other federal body bothered to investigate, the columnist would write, leaving "the Swiss bank with their shady deals in the hands of the kindly, indulgent SEC and Federal Reserve," instead of the "sinewy fingers of a tough prosecutor."

Morgenthau was also following a paper trail to Key Biscayne, Florida—Nixon's favored holiday destination since the early 1950s. Days after his election in 1968, Nixon had celebrated at an island compound among old friends, ensconced in a bungalow adjoining an "unprepossessing pink brick house"—the bachelor home of a Florida banker, one of Nixon's most generous supporters, and his best friend, Charles G. "Bebe" Rebozo. Nixon had been born poor, and raised, as he liked to remind audiences, in a clapboard cottage built by his Quaker father. In the fall of 1968, though, he tallied his net worth at $515,850—$401,382 of which was invested, at Rebozo's hand, in Florida land. The close relationship with Rebozo would soon grow even cozier: Within weeks of his election, the incoming president purchased the first of two small oceanfront homes in the same Key Biscayne compound—and "the Florida White House" was born.

Even before the real estate deal became known, Morgenthau had had more than suspicions. A number of sources, he would say, had "led us to Nixon." For more than a year, he had scrutinized the Cosmos Bank, a Zurich financial house that had exhibited an enthusiasm for the Bahamas, drawn to the region by the advent of casino gambling, and a near-total absence of taxes. In particular, Morgenthau focused on a new resort near Nassau: a casino and hotel on Paradise Island, a tiny and aptly named jet-set locale. Probing Cosmos, he had been only mildly surprised to learn of its ties to several of the financiers in Nixon's inner circle.

The details of the deal remained obscure, but the outline was clear: Cosmos had loaned money to a company that built a bridge linking Paradise Island with the nearby city of Nassau. It was the bridge's ownership in particular that caught Morgenthau's eye: The majority stockholder was the chairman of the casino's holding company, and a heavy Nixon contributor, but the Swiss bank claimed to have retained a 20 percent stake. The blueprint seemed flawless: Tourists would flow across the bridge, and the casino would reap the tolls. In the first days of January 1968, the resort held a gala opening that featured a raft of Hollywood stars—and the former vice president, Richard Nixon.

To Morgenthau, Nixon's appearance at the resort's grand opening could not have been a coincidence. In early 1969, Morgenthau was intent on opening an investigation into the finances of the Paradise Island bridge. He wanted to learn, above all, if there was a hidden beneficiary owner of the 20 percent share that the Swiss bank claimed to hold. "We had the bank people before the Grand Jury," he said. "When asked, 'Who owned this 20-percent investment?' They insisted they did, but we had learned they'd never made another such direct investment." Morgenthau could never "run it to ground," as he would say, but he was "convinced it was true": The bank was holding the stake for Nixon, in Switzerland.

New leads would arise. Days after the inauguration, as the president made his first trip overseas, Morgenthau got word of a secret breakfast meeting in Paris. Nixon spent a week there, long days filled with official meetings. The private breakfast, though, did not appear on the White House calendar, nor was there any notice in the press. Nixon, Morgenthau was told, had met with an American lawyer who was a Harvard Law graduate, and an expert in setting up Swiss bank accounts.

The suspicions would not die. Morgenthau would receive, two decades later, an anonymous letter that left him convinced he had been right all along. The envelope contained a single page, on which appeared a stark typewritten message:

Nixon's Swiss Bank Account
Bank Cantrade, Bleicherweg 30, Zurich 8039
051-36 23 60 as of early 70
Subsidiary of UBS, Baerwald & Deboer Florida (Rebozo).

It was plausible: The bank, its address, the connection to Bebe Rebozo, were accurate. "Baerwald & Deboer" was the now-defunct securities firm run by Franklin DeBoer—Rebozo's number two at the Key Biscayne Bank. Morgenthau would attempt to trace the letter, find the whistleblower, and confirm the ownership of the account—to no avail.

| | | |

In the summer of 1969, the White House raised the pressure on him to leave. Attorney General Mitchell, who had managed the Nixon campaign, led the way, pressing Manhattan's Republican leaders for successor candidates. Morgenthau dug in his heels, growing more vocal in his opposition to the tax havens and "white-collar crime." As Nixon bemoaned "crime in the streets," Morgenthau threw down a gauntlet in a speech to industrialists at the Waldorf: "We even find persons who publicly denounce crimes of violence while privately committing more 'socially acceptable' white-collar crimes." By early December, he was testifying in Washington, railing against the evils of Swiss bank accounts before an obliging House Banking Committee.

As Nixon's opposition mounted, so did Morgenthau's victories.

For six months, he had been investigating one of the most powerful men in Washington, Speaker of the House John W. McCormack, a Boston power broker first elected to Congress in 1928. McCormack wouldn't be indicted, but Morgenthau did ensnare two close associates: his chief assistant, and a lobbyist who had long posed as a member of the Speaker's staff. He charged both with influence-peddling and perjury in a securities probe that threatened to touch Hamer Budge, Nixon's new man atop the SEC. Morgenthau drew Nixon's ire, first by sending two assistants "to interview" the SEC chairman, then by summoning him to New

York to testify before a grand jury. The Speaker and the SEC chairman would both claim failing memories—McCormack, asked to explain the goings-on in his office, replied, "I am not an inquiring fellow"—yet the case would yield convictions for the Speaker's associates, and soon force the end of one of Washington's longest political careers.

The final days of Morgenthau's tenure would bring both disappointment and delight: Two pivotal trials that had run for weeks in parallel ended with opposite results. On December 12, as one jury deliberated the fate of Carmine De Sapio, another had delivered the Cohn acquittal. Even as his nemesis celebrated another victory, Morgenthau could find some solace: On the following day, De Sapio was convicted.

Still, Morgenthau knew he could not outpace the inevitable.

Five days later, at 9:40 in the morning, the elevator doors opened on the fourth floor of the federal courthouse, and an FBI agent strode down the long hall and into Morgenthau's office. He carried with him a letter from Attorney General Mitchell, the formal invitation for the U.S. attorney to resign. Before Morgenthau could reply, and even as New York's two Republican senators called on Nixon to keep him, the president told a reporter the prosecutor had been fired. A Republican, the White House said, Whitney North Seymour, Jr., onetime assistant U.S. attorney, would replace him.

After Morgenthau had read the Mitchell letter, he emerged to speak to the press. His sentences, in rare fashion, were clipped. He hinted there were unseen forces behind the move, "the rich and well-placed."

Asked to clarify, Morgenthau said, "Well, we do have investigations into people in business and finance."

"High Republicans?"

"We don't look at their political affiliation," he said, smiling.

Morgenthau added that he would give "the Attorney General's request consideration." For a tense week, as Nixon grew irate, he stayed put.

On December 22, Morgenthau finally gave in. Across the country, the evening news programs announced it: The U.S. attorney had tendered his resignation in the face of administration pressure. "To continue to resist the will of Washington," he said, "can only lead to the disintegration of the office."

JFK had appointed him, Morgenthau reminded the reporters who filled his office, and RFK had told him "Do what is right." For nine years, he said, "I have tried to be faithful to that commission. . . . Men thought by the public to be beyond the reach of the law because of their wealth, power or position were investigated, tried and convicted."

The voice was strong, almost proud, as he stood beside portraits of his father and Mrs. Roosevelt.

"The Presidents who appointed me, and resisted pressures to replace me, recognized the value and importance of an office free from political, economic, and personal considerations." He spoke of the case of James Landis, former dean of Harvard Law, "a close friend and confidant of the Kennedy family," convicted of failing to pay his taxes. He spoke, too, of the record: "10,000 prosecutions" and a success rate of "90 percent." He had convicted union men and mobsters, fixers and accountants, bankers and stock swindlers, dirty politicians and judges. He sought to give any credit to the men and women—the number of the latter had swelled to two—on his staff and the federal agents, who were "paid little, work long hours, and often receive abuse." Without such public servants, he said, "I find it doubtful that our concept of a free society could survive."

But he could not work "under these conditions"—"cannot function with full effect when I serve at the sufferance of superiors who have announced publicly that I can only continue on borrowed time."

His independence "has been undermined," he concluded, and "nor do I wish to lead a fight in which the principal casualties will be innocent by-standers."

They gave him until January 15 to clear out.

PART V

THE BOSS

59. "A Job That I Know"

1970–1974

" t was worse than after the war," Bob Morgenthau would recall of the days after he was fired as U.S. attorney. "I felt a little lost, disoriented."

Days after leaving, Morgenthau did something he had not done in more than twenty-six years of marriage: He booked plane tickets for himself and his wife, and flew to Puerto Rico. Martha had convinced him a few days of sun and walking the beaches would be restorative. Martha had not regained her energy, and both knew she, too, could use the time away.

The showdown with Nixon had left Bob unmoored. He could now claim more popular support than ever, but he was unsure how to capitalize on it. He had no precedent to follow. When RFK was killed, he reacted with willpower, redoubling his efforts, lest he fail to carry out a legacy. But when Nixon fired him, Morgenthau first thought of politics: Bobby's old Senate seat—occupied by a Rockefeller-appointed Republican—would come open in 1970, as would the governorship. Few among the state Democrats could claim his popularity. The stand against Nixon had made him an emblem of national resistance; *New York* magazine named Morgenthau to its list of the Top Ten most powerful New Yorkers. The president had made him a martyr—and a candidate with unique allure.

In San Juan, the Morgenthaus stayed in one of the old quarter's finest hotels—he knew its bar from his Navy days. He and Martha played tennis, enjoyed the warm evenings, but wherever he went, as Bob weighed running for a Senate seat against the governorship, the sense of limbo hung close.

He saw, too, another opening coming into view: a chance to enter politics without running for office. Even in San Juan, he could not avoid the headlines: John Lindsay was in desperate need of shoring up. A Republican in a city of Democrats, the mayor had been bruised by the series of City Hall scandals. Yet his ambition remained undiminished: Lindsay wanted to be governor, or senator, and in Morgenthau's standoff with Nixon he saw an opportunity. "Morgenthau's name was on New Yorkers' lips," the pollster Harris recalled.

The mayor had called days before the trip to Puerto Rico and offered a job: deputy mayor, in charge of crime-fighting. In San Juan, Morgenthau toyed with the idea: Riding into City Hall as a crusader on a rescue mission had its appeal. If things went well, Lindsay would owe him. And the sinecure that the mayor dangled would buy him time to survey the political landscape, and a reasonable perch from which to launch a campaign.

The *Times* announced Lindsay's "coup," days after Bob and Martha returned home. After a whirlwind courtship, the mayor appointed Morgenthau, at fifty, to his first political job. Lindsay now had a trio of deputy mayors—the first in city history—and each representing a different party: Republican, Democrat, and Liberal. "This puts the kind of nonpartisan, fusion coalition cast to the government that I'd really like to see," a beaming Lindsay said. The slap at the unpopular president was loud and clear: "Nixon loses," a Democratic insider said at the announcement, and "Lindsay wins."

Amid a flurry of news conferences, Morgenthau was designated the city's first "drug czar." Four of his best young federal prosecutors joined him, setting up shop in a municipal building near City Hall. But Morgenthau had scarcely settled into the new post when they sensed their boss was distracted—more eager to play muckraker than bury himself in the drug-policy minutiae. His instincts, part principles and part self-defense, took charge: He saw nefarious deeds afoot everywhere, and unable to investigate, he leaked. In February, he launched a poorly disguised attack on the new city council president, Sanford Garelik. (He had seen two cops sitting outside Garelik's office: Arthur Schultheiss, head of a detective squad, whose brother, Morgenthau told reporters, was a powerful monsignor in the Bronx, and Cyril Regan, a police inspector known among cops, Morgenthau insisted, as a "bagman.") He kept calling the reporters: A Bronx judge was on the take, and the party bosses of Manhattan and Brooklyn were making bribes. By spring, it was clear: Lindsay would not abide Morgenthau long, and sensing the limit of his time in City Hall, Morgenthau was laying the ground for a run for office.

Some urged a challenge to Lindsay—but Morgenthau had no interest in the job. Being mayor, he told Martha, was "impossible." In truth, as only Martha knew, Morgenthau had never stopped dreaming of a second run for governor. Going to Albany meant the chance to do good that might just last.

If he chose to run, Morgenthau would face more than one hurdle. By early 1970, the Democrats had already settled on a Jewish candidate: Arthur Goldberg, the former labor secretary and Supreme Court justice. Yet where many party insiders saw an obstacle, Morgenthau saw only further motivation. Few men, not even Roy Cohn, got under his skin like Goldberg. "It's the hubris—Arthur insisted on taking himself so damn seriously," Morgenthau would say. Morgenthau liked to recall that when Goldberg quit as LBJ's ambassador to the U.N. in 1968 and joined the firm of Paul, Weiss, he ordered a steel wall built in his corner office, which was painted over as faux brick. "They got Jack, and then Bobby," Goldberg would say. "I could be next."

Morgenthau never managed to settle into City Hall. From the first, it was an ill fit: Lindsay had given him, as the *Times* put it, "a basically nonexistent job" and one "with nonexistent duties." And Morgenthau had his sights set elsewhere. On March 26, after just forty days at Lindsay's side, and without receiving his first city paycheck, he made it formal: Morgenthau announced that he would challenge Goldberg in the Democratic primary for governor. "I ran 8 years ago and fell flat on my face," he told reporters. "But 8 years ago I ran as part of an aged political process. Today 8 years wiser, I run as a direct challenge to that process." Behind the bluster Morgenthau held, or so he thought, a pair of aces. He believed he could bank on the support of the *New York Post,* and its staunchly liberal editor, Dorothy Schiff. He had also been assured he could rely on the support of Alex Rose, leader of the Liberal Party—and the key to any victory in 1970, given the fractured state of New York politics.

"Dolly" Schiff was an old friend. As a confidante of FDR—some would say they were even closer than that—Schiff had watched Bob Morgenthau grow up. The granddaughter of Jacob Schiff, master financier in the banking firm Kuhn, Loeb & Co., Dolly had been at the helm of the *Post* since before the war. At sixty-seven, she was at the height of her publishing power. "The *Times* was the *Times*," Lou Harris would say, "but Dolly Schiff could launch, or kill, almost any campaign."

Schiff had long tried to get Morgenthau to come work for her—as publisher of the *Post*. Since the first days after Nixon's election, she had been wooing him. Over lunches and late-night phone calls, they had grown close, but never come to terms. Now Harris was serving as intermediary. He, too, considered Schiff's support essential, sensing a compatriot in making Morgenthau a stronger candidate.

In the wake of his firing, as he tried to gauge his best political shot, Morgenthau had sounded out an old friend, the *Post* columnist Jimmy Wechsler. Wechsler in turn shared his thoughts with his boss: "Jimmy thinks Bob," Dolly wrote in a note to herself, had "not gotten over the bad showing he'd made against Rocky, wants to prove his manhood by winning one."

"Why hadn't you told Bob that he was a hopeless political candidate?" Schiff had asked.

"Only a mother could tell him that," Jimmy replied. "Not a brother."

"I would be glad to," Dolly said.

By early May, Schiff could not sit idle and watch the political suicide. She invited Morgenthau to lunch, and for the second time, she urged him to join her at the *Post*.

"I told him," Schiff recorded in a note to herself that evening, "that, like Adlai, he was not a handshaker or a backslapper, nor a pizza eater (like Rocky), [but] that he was made to order for us. He knew about skullduggery in Wall Street and politics. He was a lawyer, which we badly needed here. His politics and ours were similar. He had a marvelous reputation for integrity and he was respected by both the editorial page editors and the City Room editors."

The lunch did not go well. Schiff had stunned Morgenthau, revealing that one of the city's chief power brokers had turned away from him—a move that Morgenthau would later call "the double-cross."

||||

Alex Rose was a labor leader of the old needle-trade school, head of a small union, the United Hatters, Cap and Millinery Workers. Polish-born, he had survived the ghettos of Eastern Europe and sweatshops of the Lower East Side to enter New York politics in 1936, helping to found the American Labor Party. But in 1944, Rose and David Dubinsky, the garment workers' boss, broke with the party and founded the Liberal

Party. In the years since, Rose had reigned as boss of the Liberals, developing the party into a force in city, state, and national politics. Rose had not always succeeded as a kingmaker, but his influence, as Morgenthau knew, could prove decisive.

It was Rose who had first come to Morgenthau, days after Nixon had fired him, to float the idea of running for governor. In early January, Morgenthau had taken the bait: He was confident that with the Liberals behind him, and the backing of the *Post,* he could win the primary. Yet as more candidates declared, a hurdle arose: Rose believed Morgenthau could win in a two-way race—not a three-way one. In April, as Howard Samuels, a wealthy businessman from upstate who had coveted the governorship since 1962, gained momentum, Rose decided to switch horses: He would save Morgenthau for something better.

"Rose saw Morgenthau as having a real future," Bruce Gyory, an Albany strategist whose father was close to the Liberal leader, would recall. "He believed, and he was not alone, Morgenthau could be a rare candidate in New York City—the man to succeed Lindsay in '73 as Mayor." Rose knew the calculus of New York politics: You could afford one loss, but two could kill a career. And so the Liberal leader had made an about-face; though he would later regret it, he went with Goldberg.

The trouble was, no one informed Morgenthau—until he sat down to lunch with Dolly Schiff.

Schiff blurted it out. Rose had changed his mind, she told him: Morgenthau would not get the Liberal Party nomination. The news "shocked" Morgenthau, as Schiff would write that night, so much so that he did not believe it. By evening, when he called the publisher at home, Morgenthau had confirmed the betrayal. "You were right," he told Schiff. The Liberals, he'd heard, were about to nominate Goldberg.

Yes, Schiff said, trying to console Morgenthau, it was a blow. And Rose, she was sure, had placed a side bet from the first, encouraging Goldberg to run as well. "Alex probably was at the bottom of the Goldberg thing, anyway," Schiff said. Before hanging up, Morgenthau had one question: Did she think he ought to withdraw from the primary race? If he did, he said, he had to "do it tonight." May 13 was the legal deadline—another day, and he would be on the ballot for the June primary, and assured of a crushing defeat.

More than thirty aides gathered that evening at the hotel on the East Side, the makeshift campaign headquarters. Martha arrived at eleven P.M. By then, the aides had taken a poll, voting to urge the candidate to carry on. Martha, though, could say aloud what the others could not. She weighed in decisively. "We're not going to do this," she told those gathered in the room. "This is unwinnable."

At 11:47 P.M., Morgenthau held a press conference, announcing he was quitting the race. He was "disappointed and relieved," and cited "money" as the sole factor. The truth cut too deeply: Rose, the man whom Morgenthau had imagined his patron, had become his destroyer. The "campaign" had lasted barely five weeks.

||||

That fall, Governor Rockefeller won a fourth term with ease, Goldberg faring worse even than Morgenthau had in 1962—losing by 200,000 more votes. Even Ted Sorensen, a close colleague of Goldberg's, would joke: "Arthur said for a long time that he wanted to be a candidate for governor in the worst possible way—and he was." The defeat sent Goldberg back to Washington, and to private practice. But Morgenthau remained empty-handed.

The failed sprint for Albany burnt all Morgenthau's bridges at City Hall, but other avenues opened. Senator Javits, one of the Republicans who had backed Morgenthau in his standoff with Nixon, spoke again of a judgeship. Wall Street, too, was an option—Goldman Sachs beckoned, as did Loeb, Rhoades & Company. But the most pressure came from his old friend and chief client at the Patterson firm, William G. Maguire, chairman of the Panhandle Eastern Pipeline Company. In the decade after Judge Robert Patterson's death, Maguire more than once made clear his desire to poach Morgenthau. "He didn't want Bob as in-house counsel," Justin Feldman, Morgenthau's old friend, would say. "He wanted Bob to be his successor." And for nine years, Maguire had held the job open—in vain.

Morgenthau spurned all offers, and returned to private practice, only now as a solo practitioner. In a sequel to his days at the Patterson firm, he sublet an office on Park Avenue, in the forty-seventh-floor suite of Bill Matheson. Matheson, whom he had come to know as an associate at his old firm, had long been a source of solace—and funds. (Matheson, in a compact arranged by Morgenthau and Maguire, had taken over Michigan Gas Utilities.) "Every time we ran out of money, Bill would come up with it," Feldman would say of the man who had been Morgenthau's chief political backer since 1962.

Nominally, 277 Park Avenue was the New York headquarters of

Michigan Gas. Another tenant, across the hall, was Steve Kaufman, Morgenthau's former chief of the Criminal Division at the U.S. attorney's office. Matheson may have "worshipped Morgenthau," as Kaufman would say, but Kaufman was his closest confidant—"the *consigliere*," former Morgenthau assistants called him. Morgenthau moved into the office adjoining Matheson's, intent on returning to oil and gas legal work. Yet few considered that the arrangement would last. "I don't think Bob ever intended to stay put for long," Kaufman would say. "I mean: what kind of solo practitioner never bothers to put his name on the door?"

| | | |

"We did not discuss it," Jenny Morgenthau, eldest of the five children, would say of her mother's illness. "No one spoke of it. Not my siblings, not my father. Nobody."

Two of Martha's daughters were newlyweds. Jenny had met Chris Wadsworth at Columbia in 1969: She'd been studying urban planning, and he was training to be an architect. Wadsworth had grown up outside Boston, his father a lonely Republican in a family that dated to 1638. Jenny and Chris were married at Fishkill Farms, in the spring of 1970, four days after Morgenthau quit the governor's race.

Annie wed four months later. "I got married pretty fast," she would recall. "We'd started going out in March, and got married in September." Paul Grand was thirteen years older, and had worked at the U.S. attorney's office under her father. Grand had been out of the office a year when he met Morgenthau's daughter. Still, he would remember driving out to the family home in Riverdale, stopping and saying to himself, "Paul, what are you doing? This is madness!"

"I was able to fly through the radar," Annie recalled. "My father was running for Governor, and Jenny was engaged, so nobody seemed to notice—great for us—how old Paul was."

Yet for Bob and Martha, the year of joy, the parental delight and respite that had followed the two weddings, would be cut short. By summer, Martha sensed that the cloud had returned. In August 1971, the family was at dinner when her arm again gave her pain. Annie and Jenny could see it: She was starting to rub it. Martha did not tell anyone—not her children, and not even Bob, but she knew the symptoms. Her own mother had died of breast cancer, at sixty-nine.

In September, Martha returned to the hospital for tests. Annie would only learn it by chance: She had a doctor's appointment of her own that day at Columbia-Presbyterian. "We didn't know yet what was going on," she recalled, "but when I went up to her room, the doctor was in there with her. I had to wait in the hall."

Annie had found out that morning that she was pregnant, but did not mention it to her mother. She stood outside the room, while the doctor sat with Martha—telling her that the tumor had come back.

Afterward her daughter confronted her.

"Why didn't you tell us earlier?" Annie asked.

"I wanted everyone to have their vacations."

Bob told no one outside of the family. "Once Martha got really sick, he never spoke of her illness in any depth," his friend Nick Gage, the *Times* reporter, would say. Jenny's husband, Chris Wadsworth, would remember a distinct lack of details. "There was no talk of it, other than 'She's going to get better.'"

Within months, Martha was horribly sick. This time, she underwent chemotherapy. Bob took her to the hospital, but kept the appointments quiet. "How many times did she have treatments?" Annie wondered. "We never knew."

Bob had nowhere to turn. He tried to maintain the family routines, but it proved impossible. At home, no one discussed Martha's condition, let alone the future. The preference was clear, even to the newcomers: "It was 'You keep your thoughts to yourself,'" Wadsworth said. "But everyone could feel it: A sadness surrounded the family—it sat there."

In August, Martha insisted that the family go to Martha's Vineyard, as always, for the month. "I think she knew she was horribly ill," Annie recalled, "but that was the thing she was going to do: 'The family needs a vacation.'"

"Talk to me in the morning," Martha would tell the children. "That's when I feel my best."

Years earlier, Martha had bought a Sunfish, a small sailboat, just for herself, and named it *HERS*. One day in that last month on the Vineyard, she went down to the dock with a paintbrush. She added, in crude yellow paint, two letters: a "T" and an "I"—making it *THEIRS*.

In those weeks in August, Martha was having terrible trouble breathing. She was waking up in the middle of the night, "gasping for air," Annie would recall, "and scared." Yet she did not go to the Vineyard hospital. Bob had formed a plan for going back home: He would drive the car down to New York with the youngest children, Bobby, a teenager at fifteen, and Barbara, not yet ten, and Martha would fly. All knew she was not well enough to drive, yet Bob had not consulted her about the plan to travel separately. Martha was furious enough to spend the night without him. No one slept. "She was gasping so loudly," Annie would remember, "struggling for breath."

Martha entered Columbia-Presbyterian on September 6, two days after Labor Day, and on September 28, she signed a will. She also composed a note, several pages long, crystal clear in its wit and foresight: an inventory of her jewelry, and how to divvy it up. Above all, what to keep from the "*W.S.*"—two initials that her children at once decoded: the "Wicked Stepmother." Martha not only expected Bob to remarry, she told him that he would.

> engagement ring—Bobby.
> wedding—left on me
> star sapphire ring—Jenny
> sapphire and diamond—*Bobby's child?* wife?
>   If none—give to niece. *Must* stay with blood rel.
> diamond pin with sapphire stones—
>   give to Bobby's wife if Daddy likes her—given to me by EFM
> [Ellie Morgenthau]—came from Morgenthaus when she married.

When it came to her necklaces, about one in particular Martha wrote that her husband should "give to wicked stepmother. I hardly wore it—only to JFK ball." All others were to be "divided among Jenny Anne Barb," and not "to go to any child of W.S. or any child of RMM & W.S."

For weeks, they kept a vigil. Bob came to the hospital every morning and evening; Jenny and Annie remained at their mother's side. None of them believed that she could die. Some days, Annie carried her baby with her. In the final week, their father had brought first Bobby, then Barbara, to say goodbye.

Bob spent the last night, with Jenny and Annie, by Martha's side. "It was the most shocking thing that had happened to any one of us," Annie would say, when on the morning of October 5, eight days short of her fifty-third birthday, Martha Pattridge Morgenthau died.

When they returned home, Bob went upstairs to tell the other children. He went first to Bobby, then to Barbara. The older daughters waited outside as he spoke to each child. In a moment, the world had pivoted. "Jenny and I took over," Annie would recall, remembering how their new role began. "And then we all had breakfast."

||||

It was a subdued memorial, at the farm. They gathered out back under the tall maple trees, behind the old white-and-black-shuttered house. The children spoke, as did Bob.

The words aligned in a single portrait: Martha had faced the end as she lived, not with cold stoicism but, as a close friend said, "common sense and selflessness." "She had all the granite qualities of her tough Puritan ancestors," Barbara Thacher said. "But Martha had more than stern devotion." She'd been able "to face and overcome fear—and what's more, to help others do the same."

The sadness that had invaded the family for more than a year now had a home, a defined locus. Yet there was no relief. "We didn't really even have time to grieve," Jenny said. "Someone had to take care of Bobby and Barbara—and Dad."

Bob seemed to exist in a world apart, even from himself. "He was frozen," Jenny said. "Numbed," Annie would add. Martha's death opened a chasm impossible to fill. Yet their father remained at the core of the family. "He was the center, always the center," Jenny's husband, Chris Wadsworth, would say. The marriage would not last long—four years—but in the aftermath of Martha's passing, the two men got to know each other. "Bob calmed people down just by his being there. The loss was enormous for the family, but there was no conversation of it; the emotions were not exterior."

Morgenthau had no intimates, other than Martha. Her death left him undone. He had been so unready, "utterly unprepared," Jenny would say. His few close friends—Pierre Leval and Steve Kaufman from the U.S. attorney's office, Lou Harris from the neighborhood—urged him back to life. Within days, he was in his new office, but just what he did, or who his clients were, had lost importance. "He got income for *something*," remembered Annie's husband, Paul Grand. "But it didn't hold his passion like the cases had. He'd lost the office, and then Martha—he was sort of adrift."

Morgenthau knew there would be a next step, but had no notion just what. He thought again about the mayoralty: Lindsay's unsuccessful bid for the presidency in 1972 had left the seat open, and many urged Morgenthau to run. He thought, too, about Washington; McGovern's people had made an overture, however unlikely, about the attorney generalship. With Nixon's landslide reelection all but assured, and the children needing his attention at home, Morgenthau moved the idea to the edge of his mind. His next opportunity would come; he would bide his time.

| | | |

Frank Hogan had ruled the second most powerful public office in New York City for more than three decades—he had been sworn in three weeks after Pearl Harbor. At seventy-one, "Mr. District Attorney," as Hogan was known, was considered "inviolable," as one court reporter put it. One of the first men hired by Thomas Dewey for his special rackets investigation in 1935, he had eased into the head job at thirty-nine, in 1941 (when Dewey decided to launch a second campaign for governor), and as 1973 opened, he relished the opportunity to run again—for a ninth term. Hogan embodied the Irish old guard. He wore bow ties, pinstripes, and French cuffs with gold cuff links, and beneath a great shock of white hair his blue eyes seemed to twinkle. He rarely spoke in public, never held a rally, scarcely appeared before the press. One of the city's longest-serving public servants, he was among its most private.

Hogan had come up as a homicide prosecutor, but he had not tried a case since the war. He maintained the public image of "a Calvinist crusader"—a protagonist, as a *New Yorker* profiler wrote, "out of the gangbusters movies of the 1930s and 1940s." In truth, Hogan was a man of nuances: equal parts shy and tough, puritan and proud. "Hogan saw himself as the bridge to the Dewey era, not as any kind of modernizer," Mike Pearl, who for three decades covered the criminal courts for the *Post,* would say. "The last thing he would want would be radical change."

Hogan had built an institution in his image: The Manhattan DA's office, long a backwater to the federal U.S. attorney's office, had gained in prestige and professionalism. Yet in recent years, Hogan had seemed in retreat: No investigations of City Hall, Albany, Wall Street, or the Mafia had captured the headlines. "The dirty doings simply aren't being uncovered," Paul Hoffman, a court reporter, wrote. "Observers offer three reasons for the slowdown in Hogan's rackets-busting: inertia, overload and outmoded ideas and methods." Some had even begun to wonder aloud, Hoffman noted, "whether Hogan was more interested in covering up corruption or exposing it."

For months, the challengers circled. In early 1973, rumors of ill health swirled, but Hogan refused to give in, pledging "to campaign as vigorously as I know how," against his first opponent since 1941: Bill vanden Heuvel, now forty-one. Many among the political establishment knew Hogan was ailing, but still deemed it an insult that the upstart vanden Heuvel, Lindsay's reformist chief of corrections and a onetime Senate aide to Bobby Kennedy, dared to mount a challenge. Hogan won the June primary handily.

On August 10, Hogan was rushed to the hospital. He'd been admitted by ambulance, but his wife attempted to downplay it, saying he'd gone in for "routine tests." In truth, Hogan had suffered a stroke. He remained in St. Luke's Hospital for six weeks, as the DA's office tried to keep the press in the dark about his condition—conveniently allowing the deadline for any independent contenders to file for the November vote to pass. Still, in good health or not, Hogan, nominated for reelection by all four major political parties, would be on the ballot. In November, even as Hogan's condition worsened, he won, with 97 percent of the vote.

Two days after Christmas, Hogan faced the inevitable, announcing he would resign.

Morgenthau knew that Hogan had two heirs in the office: Al Scotti, his chief assistant, at sixty-nine, was the inside favorite; John Keenan, the revered head of Homicide (he'd served Hogan since 1956), stood a close second. In the end, a far more unlikely candidate would get the nod. Richard Kuh, another veteran of the office, won a leg-up thanks to the ego and ambitions of Nelson Rockefeller. In late 1973, Governor Rockefeller had resigned with an eye on a run for the White House, appointing a placeholder, his stalwart lieutenant governor, Malcolm Wilson, as governor. In early 1974, Wilson bypassed Scotti to appoint the fifty-two-year-old Kuh to serve out Hogan's term as district attorney.

For many, the notion of Dick Kuh running the Manhattan prosecutor's office was an impossibility. Kuh may have been brilliant (Phi Beta Kappa at Columbia, followed by Harvard Law) and a Democrat, but he remained best known as the DA's enforcer of the hard line: Kuh had gone to Albany (where he'd met Wilson) to lobby for the "stop and frisk" and "no knock" laws—allowing police to search citizens on the street and enter their homes without prior notification. Kuh had served Hogan for eleven years, trying many of the DA's most controversial cases. Most notoriously, he led the prosecution of Lenny Bruce in 1964.

Kuh was smart and a master of the courtroom, but his conservative past would be hard to shake. "Quite possibly, the law has an obligation in some areas to legislate morality," he had said at a 1971 *Playboy* panel on homosexuality. "I think we could agree that if a man with homosexual tendencies never meets a practicing homosexual, it's unlikely that he himself will become one. The law can assist in reducing the likelihood that he will meet one. We have quarantines against scarlet fever, quarantines against other diseases." Critics called him a "holy warrior," "a hanging DA," and warned of rough edges. A *Times* editorial noted Kuh could be "assertive in ways that many find abrasive." Colleagues who admired his trial work spoke of a penchant to speak of himself in the third person. Still, Kuh pushed on, boasting to the *Post* "that no Democrat would be so foolish as to run" against him. Tradition at least was on his side: Running for DA, an uncontested post since 1939, was unheard of in Manhattan.

Kuh stood poised to defy the pundits, but as Hogan lay ailing, the field quickly grew. The Harlem leader Basil Patterson was eager to run, as was Mike Armstrong, the former Morgenthau assistant who had become chief counsel on the Knapp Commission, and two former Hogan assistants, Burt Roberts, now a judge, and Nick Scoppetta, the investigations commissioner. Even Roy Cohn, a registered Democrat, taunted that he might run as the Conservative Party candidate. Kuh, though, retained pole position.

Until Nat Hentoff started to make calls. Hentoff was a fixture of the New York press, a columnist at *The Village Voice,* known for searing commentaries in defense of civil liberties. In February 1974, he published the first of a three-part series revealing the divisions and despair roiling the district attorney's office, "The Idealistic (sic) Prosecutor"—a jibe at a recent *Times* profile of Kuh, similarly entitled (minus the "sic"). Hentoff had made his name as a jazz critic; he did not ordinarily cover the DA. But the state of Frank Hogan's office had Hentoff incensed. Morale was dismal, and Kuh loomed as the only successor.

Hentoff was particularly outraged about Lenny Bruce (for whom he'd testified as an authority on the First Amendment). Bruce, as anyone knew, had not merely been prosecuted. He had been hounded off the stage: No cabaret would host him. Kuh had not merely fulfilled the law. He had helped to orchestrate a stakeout of the comedian, dispatching an inspector with a hidden microphone to Bruce's act at the Cafe Au Go Go. Two years after his conviction, at age forty, Bruce was dead—overdosing on morphine. The Bruce case, Hentoff quoted Ed Koch as predicting, would prove Kuh's albatross. "Well," Congressman Koch said, "it's not easy for people to forget that a man was tortured to death."

One evening in Riverdale, in a study half lit by a single desk lamp, Hentoff's first article on the malaise at the DA's office caught the attention of the former U.S. attorney. Morgenthau picked up the phone. "What you wrote about Kuh," he asked Hentoff, "was it all true? Did you really speak to all those people in the DA's?"

Hentoff had never met Morgenthau, never even spoken to him. "I knew him as the former U.S. attorney," he would say, "and I knew who his father was, of course. So I was taken aback."

Hentoff rarely used blind quotes, but in the series he did, almost exclusively. "Of course, it's true," he told Morgenthau. The Hogan assistants had talked openly.

After the second article appeared, Morgenthau called again, seeking more details. "I was so surprised," Hentoff recalled. "He just wanted to be sure it was reported fairly," the columnist would remember, "that this was the feeling inside the DA's, and that it was widespread. He was interested in one thing: Was the opinion of Kuh that *bad*?"

Hentoff ended the last article of the series with a plea: "I hope that Robert Morgenthau will come forward, and soon."

| | | |

On Tuesday, April 2, 1974, at ten minutes after noon, Frank Hogan died at age seventy-two.

This time, Morgenthau was prepared.

Even as Hogan had lay ailing, Morgenthau had begun mobilizing to launch a campaign. He began with a letter to the publisher of the *Post*. "Dear Dolly," he wrote after reading Schiff's glowing pre-endorsement, disguised as an editorial, in March. "That was a great editorial. Its message was unmistakable, and I deeply appreciate it. I think it is already having a substantial impact on prospective candidates." He hired, too, a PR man, and began to make the rounds. He sent an emissary to Hogan, and went to see Al Scotti, the veteran who'd run the office after Hogan fell ill. "I liked Scotti and I didn't want to get in his way," Morgenthau would say. "But when Wilson appointed Kuh, Scotti came to see me and asked me to run. I had never considered it seriously before, but I thought, 'This is a job that I know.' "

The plot only lacked a backroom of brokers. As it happened, the scene of the political scheming was a far cry from the smoke-filled clubrooms of Tammany: a one-bedroom apartment on the East Side, filled with Persian rugs and climbing plants. Donna Shalala, a thirty-two-year-old junior professor at Teachers College, hosted the conclave. Shalala had worked for Bobby Wagner, the mayor's son who'd proven too shy to live up to the mantle of "heir apparent," but who had managed to win a seat on the city council. Her star was on the rise: Governor Hugh Carey would soon name her to the Municipal Assistance Corporation, the only woman among the Wall Street team led by Felix Rohatyn and Judge Simon H. Rifkind, tasked with delivering the city from financial catastrophe. The *Times*, in turn, would hail her as "one of the most powerful women in New York City."

The crowd in Shalala's living room was an impressive circle of Democrats: Wagner, "the two Johns" (Connorton, Jr., and LoCicero, party leaders), Richard Wade, the historian, and Pierre Leval, Morgenthau's former assistant and close friend. In time, they opened the door and welcomed the candidate to the group. The vetting was not formal: "a couple of meets," Shalala would recall, "with a very cautious Robert Morgenthau, who listened intently but did not say much." Then they checked the statute. To be a candidate, he needed a Manhattan address. As luck would have it, there was a place at the San Remo, the landmark building on Central Park West—a sublet from a relative. It was on a low floor, in the back, and dark. "Not the San Remo at its best," Jenny would recall, but it was furnished.

| | | |

The primary—the governor had called a special election to succeed Hogan—would be in September. From the start, there were moments of sharp conflict. On the evening of May 20, the day he announced his candidacy, Morgenthau ran straight into Roy Cohn at the Mid-Manhattan Democratic Club, as Cohn was leaving the packed meeting room. It was their first encounter since Morgenthau had tried to send Cohn to jail. Cohn had spoken to the club of his own possible run, but more urgently attacked Morgenthau: the man "palming himself off as a liberal."

Morgenthau had Downtown and the West Side, he knew. But he sought broader support, coming out against the death penalty: The new laws permitting capital punishment for those convicted of killing policemen and corrections officers, he said, were unconstitutional. He claimed support in Harlem, too: standing beside Percy Sutton and Charlie Rangel, his former assistant in the U.S. attorney's office. Cohn, though, persisted. At a debate at an East Side political club, when Cohn, Kuh, and Morgenthau were slated to face off, Morgenthau asked Mike Armstrong to stand in for him. "I got the shit kicked out of me," said Armstrong. "Cohn had a real bone to pick with Morgy, because of the three trials. Kuh went first, and then Cohn got up, and said, 'If I were running against the man I am now debating, this guy's tremendously qualified, but he's standing here because the man who's running doesn't have the guts.' "

A dark rumor, too, spilled into the press, fed by Cohn and Kuh.

On the eve of the vote, the *Times* ran a story accusing Morgenthau, during his time in private practice in the 1950s, of having resorted to illegal wiretaps on behalf of his client, Panhandle Eastern. He was accused of hiring Robert Maheu, a Washington private investigator and former FBI agent known for his ties to Howard Hughes, to bug a consultant to a rival gas company, which had won a string of battles decided by the Federal Power Commission (FPC), the industry regulatory body. "Kuh mentioned it in the press," Justin Feldman would remember, "but it was Roy's deal. He'd dug up the Maheu stuff." Morgenthau, Cohn told reporters, shared "a great similarity" with John Mitchell, Nixon's attorney general: namely, a fondness for bugging and opening mail.

The allegations, first aired in a 1966 Senate investigation, had to do with Morgenthau's suspicion that Panhandle had lost each time before the FPC because members of the commission were on the take. For years, Morgenthau had denied knowledge of the bugging—and he did so again, however unconvincingly: "Indecent and irresponsible," he called Kuh's accusation. Yes, he'd hired Maheu to gather evidence of corruption, but any wiretaps had been undertaken without his "approval or authorization."

Still, no one could do as much damage to the candidate as Morgenthau himself. He remained a dismal speaker, and an even worse campaigner. One evening in Inwood, in upper Manhattan, an attempt to greet commuters at the 207th Street subway station proved disastrous. "It was just amusing to watch," recalled Andy Lawler, a former assistant who worked the campaign. "He had no great desire to stand there and shake hands." A man appeared on the sidewalk who began to regale Morgenthau with a story about his father, the Treasury secretary. And that was it—the candidate was lost in conversation. Lawler kept yelling at the passersby, "Step up and meet Robert Morgenthau," and "all Bob wants to do is talk to this guy, get away from having to meet a whole lot of other people, and have an intelligent conversation."

Downtown was no better. An encounter with Judge Irving Lang outside the Criminal Courts Building laid bare the problem. At a sidewalk cart, Judge Lang was grabbing a bite, having a knish. Morgenthau walked by and they had an exchange that became legendary among party insiders:

"Hey, Irving," the candidate asked, "what's that you're eating?"

"Bob, if you knew what I was eating, today you'd be Governor."

New York politics had its bruisers, natural heirs to the La Guardia school of sidewalk stumping. If Morgenthau did not have a loud voice, Bella Abzug did. Running for reelection to Congress, Abzug took him under her arm. Together, they worked the Upper West Side. Ed Koch, the congressman from the West Village, also led the candidate by the hand—at times, literally. On a Saturday morning that summer, as Koch recalled it, "I took Morgenthau on a walk down the East Side of Manhattan." As they made their way down Lexington from Eighty-sixth Street to Fifty-ninth, shaking hands, stopping at times to talk, "I introduce Morgenthau, and I have a style about it: I say to people, 'This is Bob Morgenthau. You know Morgenthau. You know that name!' And they look at me sort of wide-eyed. And I say, 'That's him!' Morgenthau doesn't know what to do. If he could, he'd creep under a manhole cover, he's so embarrassed by it."

Morgenthau's "team"—half a dozen aides, nearly all former assistants from the U.S. attorney's office and veterans of the abortive 1970 governor's race, had tried a few polls, but doubted them. "We regarded ourselves as being in a tough race," Pierre Leval would say. "Kuh was the incumbent, and a forceful figure, who was getting a lot of press." The first time they ordered an in-house poll, it came in at nearly 80 percent for Morgenthau. "The Nixon bonus," they called it, referring to the president's resignation that August. Yet week after week, as they repeated the polls, each time they'd get nearly 80 percent for Morgenthau. "I can't believe that," Leval would recall thinking, "can't be true." Sure enough, though, the Democratic primary results proved the polls correct: Morgenthau won with more than 75 percent of the vote.

Trounced in the September primary, Kuh would persist, to Morgenthau's eternal annoyance, running as a Republican in the special election in November—and again getting drubbed. "Kuh's Achilles' heel," Koch recalled, "was that he was a sonofabitch—and everybody knew it."

60. Riot

1975–1978

Bob Morgenthau never had to look hard for money; whether he had earned it or inherited it, he'd always enjoyed more than his fair share. But as he settled into office, the new district attorney, at fifty-five, found himself with an unfamiliar focus: "the money hunt." Before he could begin to plan how he'd fight crime, he would have to come up with the funds to do it. As the *Times* would ask: "Is he a good scrounger?"

Morgenthau faced an array of unattractive challenges. Violent crime was soaring, while the city's resources continued in a historic freefall. The murder rate was spiraling higher: 1,554 homicides in 1974, with nearly half of those murders in Manhattan alone. He had learned first-hand, too, of the rise in police corruption: Frank Serpico, a West Village detective who'd dared to name dirty cops, had gone to Morgenthau long before appearing at the Knapp Commission's televised hearings that transfixed the city in 1971. The NYPD was under siege—morale was at a new low and public trust even lower. At the DA's office, Morgenthau faced another hurdle: Among the corps of two hundred assistant district attorneys (ADAs), the turnover rate was rising. During the short-lived Kuh interregnum, many veteran prosecutors had fled for the exits.

Money, though, would have to come before anything else. The city was nearing bankruptcy. Mayor Abe Beame had entered office in 1974, a year before Morgenthau. A Brooklyn clubhouse Democrat since 1929, Beame seemed the right man to fix the city's fiscal woes. In a quiet four-decade climb through the ranks, Beame had risen from accountant to budget examiner to budget director to comptroller. In City Hall meetings, he would scribble figures to himself, the small memo pads filling up with numbers. Beame knew the budget better than anyone else, but he seemed to suffer, quipped Nick Pileggi, then a young City Hall reporter, from "a 45-year addiction to caution." To fund the DAs, and stave off a mass exodus, Morgenthau would have to fight Beame for emergency funding, and look elsewhere.

Morgenthau knew the job would not be easy. Yet he had abundant faith in his own abilities and never doubted he could attract the men and women needed to seal his success. New hires, though, meeting him for the first time, would be taken aback: Morgenthau seemed frail, and aloof, too shy to meet your eye. It was a tradition the DA would hold to in all his years in office: A new assistant on the first day would be invited up to the sprawling office on the eighth floor; there'd be a handshake, a camera's flash, and a moment in which the DA attempted a smile. Yet as they left the room, many young assistants in those first years would remember thinking what they dared not ask aloud: *Was the new man up to it?*

| | | |

Morgenthau would get an early challenge: A case late in the summer of 1976 that would be all too soon forgotten, but that for a year and a half, as the DA tried to find his bearings and calm the city's restive factions, would preoccupy his mind and set the course for the future of his office. A spectacle of violence, ten minutes of mayhem that left one man dead and nearly three dozen injured, the case soon grew into a New York story, and like all big New York stories, it was awarded a name: the Washington Square Riot.

For months, the riot and its aftermath would play out on the front pages of the tabloids and in the neighborhood bars and diners, as the city's residents once again claimed a right to lay odds, long before any judge struck a gavel, as to which way the scales of justice would tip. But right from the first, it offered a stage on which the city's disparate cast of actors—uptown politicians, downtown shopkeepers, Black ministers, Italian nuns, schoolteachers, and police bosses—could form opposing camps, and demand not only a fair hearing, but an overdue reckoning. The riot, in short, became Morgenthau's first big headache.

| | | |

It began on the afternoon of September 8, 1976, as the word went around the West Village: *Meet in the park tonight.*

The first boys arrived just before six in the evening. Some knew each other from school, I.S. 70, up on Seventeenth Street, or Our Lady of Pompeii down on Bleecker. Some played hoops at the Carmine Street Gym, others, stickball on Eleventh Street, on the long block between Greenwich and Washington. Some lived to the north in Chelsea, others as far south as Houston. But "we were all Village kids," one would say. "We hung out in Greenwich Village, though we never called it that. It was 'The Neighborhood,' and it was *ours*."

Some belonged to the Go Club, a crew of Irish and Italian junior high kids who liked to spray graffiti and talk tough. Others were of Portuguese or German descent. A few were Jewish, at least two were Latino, and one was Black. Nearly all came from good homes, parents who worked hard and once dreamed of having a better life than their own parents who had left the old country.

The boys had their own landmarks: Andy's, the corner candy shop on Bleecker; George Hertz's place at Twelfth Street, home of the local numbers game; and the White Horse, the bar on Hudson where they could count on getting served. They had their own nicknames, too, and their own language and, within it, a code. Some of it was habit, some was tradition, and a lot was for the sake of honor. If you smoked on a stoop, you left matches in the rusting mailbox by the front door—for the next guy. If you played stickball past sunset, you didn't lie when a window got broken. And above all, you never ratted anyone out.

By 7:30 on that Wednesday evening, the park, nestled between Seventh Avenue and Hudson Street and known officially as James Walker Park, in honor of the mayor who once lived nearby, was crowded. In the twilight, the boys had filled the baseball field. Later, when it was over, when the violence had ended and an unnatural silence filled its wake, no one could give a precise total: Some said they numbered at least 50, others put it as high as 100.

They gathered on the patch of cement near the bocce court. Mikey Doyle was riding a bike through the crowd. Joey Chiappetti, Chucky Boutureira, and Andre Sanchez stood near the tables painted black and white for chess. Andre and Chucky had led the recruiting. Chucky had gone down to get the kids on MacDougal, to Noah Lipman, Gary Cangelosi, and Ronny McLamb of the Go Club. The plan was set: Tonight, they'd take back Washington Square and reclaim the park.

The circle grew close, and several boys hoisted McLamb, the sole Black kid in the crowd, up on the table. "Be sure not to hit him!" someone cried. "He's with us." As the boys shouted, they tied a red bandanna around McLamb's head—a sign to leave him alone once the action began.

Richard Rizzo, at eighteen among the oldest, stood by. It was all happening so fast, he would later say. Rizzo watched as they put "the Black kid" on the table.

Are you coming along? Chucky asked Rizzo. Do you want a bat?

"Yeah," Rizzo said.

They began to split up into groups, the most vocal shouting "Go to the Fourth Street Park"—as they called Washington Square—and wait until everybody showed. They moved quickly, fifteen or twenty boys at a time, along the four blocks east to the square—stopping only at tiny Minetta Park, to pick up more kids.

On the southwestern corner of the park, they filled the streets, even the spaces between the parked cars. Sanchez went into the park on reconnaissance—went in, many would say, carrying a stick, to see if he could find "the guys." He returned disappointed: The targets were not there.

"What are we doing here?" Gerard Botros yelled to Mike Andriani. Mike shook his head. "This is crazy," Andriani said. The crowd was too big, too hungry.

Chucky Boutureira climbed up on a car. At eighteen, Chucky was tall, a Bedford Street boy who'd gone from the nuns at Our Lady to the priests at La Salle, a big kid with a wide smile, whose father cooked seven days a week at a Spanish place for $500 a month. Chucky stood atop the sedan, a soldier rallying the troops. Let's take a vote, Joey yelled: We going in? Hands shot up, and voices drowned him out. A witness would hear the vote: "Anyone who wants to get the n****rs out of the park, say Aye." They began to yell, and jumped the fence to get into the park. Later many would say they'd turned around, fled, and run away as fast as they could. Most, though, did not.

The "Village kids" had set in motion, whether by plan or not, a chain of events, the fatal consequences of which would within days preoccupy the new district attorney, and threaten to upend the social balance, always precarious, not only of the neighborhood they shared, but of the city itself.

| | | |

Morgenthau had been fighting his own battle. To fund the office, he would have to do more than demand—he'd have to get creative. By the fall of 1974, New York City could not pay its debts. As the municipal bond market threatened to close its door to New York, Mayor Beame was forced, first, to freeze all hiring. The municipal unions revolted, but it was not enough. The mayor would have to shed 12,000 of the city's 300,000 employees. Beame gutted the city's workforce, something unheard of since the Depression, and slashed the budget by 8.5 percent.

The district attorney's office received next to nothing: $5.5 million out of a criminal justice budget of $1.2 billion. Legal pads were rationed, as were pencils. Morgenthau considered it beneath him to beg, but on most days of his early tenure on Centre Street, he would arrive at his desk brimming with ideas of how to wrangle more funds—from the feds, the state, and above all the city.

"Let's go over to City Hall," he would say, bringing John Keenan, his first chief assistant and top holdover from the Hogan years. Morgenthau recruited, as well, three protégés from the U.S. attorney's office: Mollo would be the drill sergeant to the troops; Leval, his cerebral confidant, would oversee the trial bureaus; and Peter Zimroth, a dry cleaner's son who'd clerked at the U.S. Supreme Court, would run appeals. The hardest job, though, fell to Keenan. Morgenthau planned a series of radical reforms—not least dismantling the Homicide Bureau, a coterie of veterans who had long stood at the center of Hogan's office. Keenan would be the bridge to the forces who, amid the rush of changes, threatened mutiny. "Without Keenan," Morgenthau would say, "I'd have had the legs cut out from under me."

Together they would walk across Foley Square and march into City Hall. Almost weekly, they went in search of "D.M.'s," "dispensations of the Mayor." Morgenthau rarely set an appointment—whenever he and Keenan arrived at City Hall, Mayor Beame would be "stuck in a meeting." "We would find a seat in the corridor," Keenan recalled, "and wait for the Mayor to come out." Once Morgenthau caught sight of Beame, he pounced: "He would grab Beame by an elbow, and not let go." The office needed money, the DA would insist, and despite the financial crisis, he would get it. "He'd get Beame to sign the D.M.'s, just to be rid of him."

Morgenthau's wrangling also extended to Washington. As always, he relied on a friend to help get him there: In his first week in office, the DA reached back to an Amherst and Yale classmate, Jack Chester, a Republican lawyer, who'd served as a counsel in the Nixon White House. By 1975, Chester had returned to private practice in Ohio, but his friend Bill

Saxbe had stayed on as attorney general. When Morgenthau asked Chester to broker a meeting, he soon found himself in Saxbe's office.

"Why on earth should we be helping out the DA of New York City?" the attorney general asked, as he greeted Morgenthau. Amid Gerald Ford's uncertain interregnum, Saxbe himself was a transitional figure, and would leave within weeks. Morgenthau, though, knew there was money to be had: In the upheaval of the late 1960s, the race riots that roiled American cities had led Congress to make a show of funding law enforcement. A pot of gold remained, he'd been told: an untapped bonus of the omnibus crime bill of 1968, the Law Enforcement Assistance Administration (LEAA). The agency offered grants, but a local official would need friends on the inside. Saxbe turned out to be a surprise ally: He insisted on leaving no fingerprints, but acceded to Morgenthau's wishes. The DA left Washington with a promise of federal funds.

By the spring of 1976, tens of thousands of civil servants had lost their jobs. But Beame's budget men opened up new "lines"—line items in the budget that meant new hires—and restored old ones that had gone unfilled. The money had arrived from Washington as well. Morgenthau had found a way to hire forty new assistant prosecutors, and even give first-year assistant DAs a small raise.

Then, on April 20, he announced a sweeping reform, the first restructuring of the office in four decades. "A revolution," an aide would call it. Morgenthau inaugurated "ECAB," as he called the new vertical system of prosecution, short for Early Case Assessment Bureau. He termed it a "customized" approach, and it was a complete dismantlement of the hierarchy that had ordered life in the DA's office since Tom Dewey. For decades, cases had moved along an assembly line: Some assistants would handle complaints, others arraignments, and still others trials. From now on, senior lawyers would work the Complaint Room, where prosecutors did an "early case screening," evaluating the quality of felony arrests to determine whether they merited prosecution, and if so, on what charges. If the assistants decided the cases merited an indictment, they would now handle them all the way through to trial.

The old chain of command, with its invitation to pass the buck, was broken. As a case progressed, the same assistant would develop leads, interview witnesses, and present it in court. The goal was not only to streamline the massive caseload of the office, but to build in accountability. A bureaucratic reform, one of many he'd make in quick succession, it also spoke to a Morgenthau instinct: the need for fair play. The shift ruffled Hogan's old guard, yet Morgenthau went further, making good on his plan to scrap the Homicide Bureau. "The unit was a throwback," Keenan, one of its veterans, would concede. "All male, macho, and wedded to the old ways." Insulted, many left.

In the months that followed, Morgenthau fended off a backlash from the Hogan disciples, leaning on his top aides. But he also found a bridge to the old guard, and a gatekeeper with a peerless store of office intelligence: Ida Van Lindt, his predecessor's secretary. Ida had come to the DA's office in 1956, at seventeen. She started work on the day after her high school graduation, and planned to stay a year, and to go to college at night, but Hogan had soon spotted her at the elevator—and asked her to stay.

Ida had worked at Hogan's side for nearly two decades when Morgenthau arrived with his own secretary, a veteran of the U.S. attorney's office. There'd been fights—a stapler nearly flew—but Ida warmed to "Mr. Morgenthau." ("Such different styles," she would say, "such different men.") She ran the DA's personal switchboard, set his calendar, kept his confidences. Above all, Ida chased paper. She sorted, indexed, filed without end, and yet the mountains—letters, case files, court filings, news clippings—grew. Beneath the towering papers, only the contours of the DA's desk, a steel battleship filling a corner of the room, remained visible.

Morgenthau moved methodically, pragmatism winning out over idealism. But reform, of course, came at a cost. Thanks to the end of the seniority hierarchy, many prosecutors now trying cases were less than a year out of law school. A decade earlier, Hogan's bureau chiefs—six out of six—had been there at least twenty years. Another unintended consequence of the restructuring would soon become apparent: 60 percent of all the DA's cases never got to trial but were disposed of at arraignment—pled out, often for reduced sentences. "Probably too high a figure," Morgenthau would tell a reporter. "But we have to have priorities. I was elected to concentrate on violent, more serious crimes. On serious crimes, we're doing a pretty effective job. Not perfect, but effective."

The DA feared the dangers if the crime surge were allowed to continue unchecked. He decided to take Mayor Beame on a series of field trips, attempting to convince him of the need for reforms in the DA's office, and for more resources. Morgenthau began with a trip uptown, to a heroin supermarket. The mayor, Morgenthau, and the police commissioner drove to one of the city's biggest open-air drug markets, at Eighth

Avenue near 116th Street, and watched the dealers hawk their wares. Sterling Johnson, Jr., the special narcotics prosecutor, oversaw the mayor's trip uptown. Johnson had been one of Morgenthau's favorites in the U.S. attorney's office: Raised in Bedford-Stuyvesant, he'd served in the Marines and then in the NYPD—before going to Brooklyn Law, at night. Morgenthau had not only hired him as a federal prosecutor, but later put his name forward to run Special Narcotics.

Beame was shocked by what he saw and heard. As the unmarked van sat at a street corner, a dealer approached, offering the mayor whatever he desired: cocaine, pot, pills. The district attorney had made his case. Morgenthau in those lean first years may not have won as much of the city budget as he demanded, but Beame would never again need convincing.

|| ||

In Washington Square on that warm September evening in 1976, the boys had rushed in, a blurred mass in red and white tank tops. In seconds, they'd flooded the southwest corner of the park.

The park was getting dark. Young people were finishing picnics, meeting dates, playing catch, drinking quarts, smoking dope. Until *they* arrived. Later, some would call them "white youths," others "Gambinos," but nearly everyone with the courage to speak out afterward said they were boys and they were all white, or so it seemed. They ran north across the park, past the fountain at the square's center toward the arch, the marble gate that since 1892 had marked the start of Fifth Avenue.

At the arch, Joey Chiappetti seemed to yell the loudest. He was a short kid with a sweet face that could open in a wide grin, and, a sergeant would testify, a skull tattooed on one arm and a black rose on his left wrist. "Charge," Joey yelled, and the kids had gone running. They split into two groups, one flooding the concrete around the fountain, the other coming down the cement ramps, before they rejoined and fled to the south, out of the square. In all, they did not stay long, the witnesses would say: ten minutes, at most.

Some, like Michael Andriani, would say they had no plan, but had only come to watch "a one-on-one fight." Many, to be sure, were unprepared for the bloodshed to come, but to the witnesses, sitting on the benches, lying on the grass, the cries were unmistakable: "N****rs out of the park!" "All n****rs and Spanish, get out of the park!"

Nancy Trichter, a twenty-five-year-old white student at Rutgers Law, was crossing the park with a friend, a young Black woman, when the mob arrived. "It was so sudden," she would say. "They were chasing all of us, but the only people they hit were Black."

Shirley Bradley was sitting on a bench near the fountain. It was getting dark, but she could see clearly: One of the boys swung and hit a man with a bat, and then, by the corner of the playground, he kicked a pregnant woman in the belly. The pregnant lady, she would say, was dark-skinned and wearing a maternity dress—"5 or 6 months showing."

Carl Warren knew several of the women in the square that evening—"park friends," he would say. Warren yelled at them to leave. He was not one to run from a fight. Known to friends as "Bonecrusher," Warren was a big, bearded Black man with a barrel chest. As a teen, he had served time for auto theft and robbery, and in the fourteen years since had held down two jobs: Mornings he worked on Long Island as a clammer, and nights as a clerk in a liquor store near the park. Warren, standing near his friend "Cotton," could see what was coming: white kids everywhere, and in their hands they carried pieces of pipe, chains, baseball bats, and table legs—many studded with nails.

The blows fell fast. Everywhere, it seemed, the boys found a victim: Dijuan Philyan, a thirty-three-year-old construction worker and a park regular, was hit in the eye and chest, cracking his collarbone. Bernard Jones, a twenty-two-year-old physical therapist, was walking through the park when a white kid ran up: "We don't want any n****rs in the park," he said. Jones was struck with a bat, from behind—first in the head, then on the arm.

Mario Peraza they caught near the arch. "Get him! Get him!" they yelled. He'd just entered the park on his bicycle, a prized Japanese ten-speed. With his goatee and long black ponytail, Peraza stood out. "I was scared because they were crazy," he would say. "They were hitting everybody who was dark." The first blow to his head made a horrific sound—"like a watermelon popping," Bill McKenna, a railway worker in his thirties who stood nearby, would say. As more swings followed, Peraza was thrown from his bike. He fell to the ground and passed out. Later he said, "I thought I was dying."

Charles Febee had been by the fountain when the mob arrived. At thirty-one, he'd recently left the Army and was looking to go back to school. That afternoon he'd gone to the park, to hang out, as he often did, with friends. By eight P.M., he had heard the roar behind him: "about one hundred white kids with bats and clubs."

Febee ran to the raised plateau, to get the best vantage point. When he saw them, he rushed toward the two biggest people he knew in the park: Cotton and Bonecrusher. Standing beside them, he saw a member of the mob come at them and heard him say, "There are some more of them up there."

Shirley Bradley also saw what Febee saw: Bonecrusher did not run away; he charged a group of boys carrying bats. "What's going on?" he yelled. One of the white boys yelled back: "All n****rs out of the park."

Febee, from about four feet away, saw two boys start to hit Bonecrusher across the head with a club. He was hit twice in the back of the head, once in the knee.

Febee ran, and ran right into ten others. He came face-to-face, he would testify, with the boy he'd later pick out: Mikey Doyle. Doyle passed him, then swung around, and cocked his bat. Febee veered right, but could not duck. The blow landed on Febee's face, pounding his right eye.

The worst came last. Natividad Montilla had caught sight of the group even before they made it to the arch. He took off toward his friend, Marcos Mota, who was the reason he ever came to the park. In the afternoons, you could be sure to find Mota there: playing volleyball. Mota was compact, five-foot-nine, but strong. Born in the Dominican Republic, Mota had played on the Dominican national team, and on a local Dominican team in the Village. When the city recarved the park a few years earlier, adding a volleyball court, Mota had found a second home. At twenty-two, taking classes at a community college on Staten Island, and working for a West Side moving company, Mota lived in Brooklyn with his mother in a fourth-floor walk-up, but came almost every afternoon to play.

"Marcos was a very clean guy," Montilla would say of his friend. "No drugs—never even smoked pot, unlike most of us." They'd been hanging out with two girls when the boys swarmed in. One of the girls yelled to Mota to leave, but he headed for the arch to see what was happening. Montilla was running to catch up with Mota when, in the floodlights of the volleyball court, he saw his friend get hit—and fall. He ran to his side, but Mota was not moving.

Throughout it all, the park was empty of police. The two patrolmen usually on duty were nowhere to be found, nor were the radio cars that often circled the square. By the time any officers appeared, the mob had left.

At 8:13, central dispatch put out the call: "Any six-shooters at Washington Square Park?" Several witnesses called for ambulances, too, and when at last one arrived, its driver insisted the dispatchers send police. "I gotta protect the bus, too, hon," an operator told a patrol car, referring to the ambulance. There's a "riot down there."

By the time they arrived, the only thing left to do was tally the wounded: At least thirty-five people were injured and thirteen were sent to hospitals. "Ambulance attendants were picking up bodies," a passerby said, "and the other people were looking away."

| | | |

From the first, Morgenthau knew he had trouble on his hands. As U.S. attorney, Morgenthau had developed a sixth sense—"Bob was the most suspicious person I know," Pierre Leval would say, "and his hunches were invariably correct." The DA could also read the press corps: He knew when a case could explode into a headline, and thought he knew how to get ahead of it. Given the racial overtones, the city could ignite. Within hours, the violence had hit the tabloids, and his phone, Morgenthau knew, would soon be ringing.

He had only been in the job twenty months, but he had brought with him one of his most valuable assets: his network. Morgenthau not only knew judges and defense attorneys, he knew dozens of local leaders across New York City. Since 1948, and the rise of the Young Democrats, Morgenthau had worked the city's political circles. He never much enjoyed the circuit—breakfasts at the neighborhood clubs, cocktails with the district leaders, long party dinners—but he made sure never to forget a face, and to connect it with a name and a position. At the U.S. attorney's office, his secretary had filled several address books. Ida Van Lindt added the names from Frank Hogan's orbit, several hundred in all. Before long, her single Rolodex would grow to a set of five. Some might have considered it a habit, or a procedural custom, but the DA possessed an instinct inherited from his father and grandfather: He relished little more than information. He knew the cost of a single false step, and believed, above all, in the power of information, timely and confirmed.

From the start an uncertainty hung over the riot case. It was Morgenthau's first question: *Why?* Why had they done it? In those first hours, as the mayor talked and the police searched for witnesses, the ambiguity grew. And the DA's fears mounted: The early storylines were sufficiently contradictory to be dubious, but given the various factions involved, they were sure to gain credence. The cops moved first, leaking a report based on rumor: "A fight over bad drugs," park habitués said, had set off "the incident." A Black dealer, unnamed witnesses said, had sold "oregano" to a white kid looking for marijuana. The story took hold, gaining detail by the day. Still, other reports, like one of the first in the *Post,* pointed to a larger specter: "a long-standing feud," as described by locals, "between the Italians who live in or near the area and Blacks who use the park . . . for evenings of drinking, card playing and pot smoking." What the tabloids left unsaid, others did not. Tensions had been building for years.

The police signaled an intention to get to the bottom of it. They posted a dozen officers to patrol the park all night, and set out on a sweep. They went to the schools and the churches. They walked into Our Lady of Pompeii, the Catholic school in Little Italy, and pulled out the fifth and sixth grades. One by one, they questioned the children. "Who was in the Square?" they asked. "Give us the names, the older guys who were in the park."

Two days after the riot, nine young men were in custody. They ranged in age from sixteen to twenty. Many were from the five-story tenements that blighted the blocks around the station house, from walk-ups where their families had lived for decades. Many of their parents knew the local cops by name. That afternoon, their supporters had gathered in the narrow streets. They formed an all-white parade to march on the precinct house. Some carried hand-drawn signs: "Don't blame our youths!!! CURB YOUR JUNKIES." Others shouted: "Don't arrest our kids for doing your job!"

They lined the sidewalk by the station house, before turning south, to 100 Centre Street, arriving in time for the arraignments. Michele Andriani had joined the women. Her brother Mike was among the detained. Steve Durnin was there, too. His little brother Michael had also been picked up, arrested with another guy on Twelfth Street. After the court hearing, the reporters asked the same question: Why? "Outsiders" had taken over the park, came the reply. Which outsiders? New people, from another part of town, who had no rules. "Mothers can't take their children to the park anymore," one woman said. After the boys were arraigned, the police did not return them to the local station house. "They feared another riot," Steve Durnin would say, "so they moved 'em up to Harlem."

| | | |

Four days later, the riot became a homicide. At 8:15 P.M., on Sunday, September 12, without regaining consciousness, Marcos Mota died. Mota had come to New York at age twelve, with his mother, in 1966. His mother could not bear to go to the morgue. She asked a friend to handle the arrangements.

At the DA's office, the case fell to a young ADA named John Moscow. Moscow had joined the office four years earlier, in his first summer out of Harvard Law, and had already earned a reputation as a brilliant eccentric. His mind followed a nonlinear logic that few could fathom; charting a case, he would start in the middle, paying no heed to chronology, to zig and zag across a fact pattern. But it was his physical presence that people remembered more. Moscow had a way—tic or habit, no one could say—that was unforgettable: As one knee jackhammered up and down, his upper body rocked back and forth. In the courtroom, it had the effect, some said, of a lawyer davening before the jury.

At twenty-eight, Moscow had tried more than two dozen cases, and done "fairly well," but never run a case so big. In the days following the arrests, he made an unfortunate habit of reporting his progress to the DA. Charging into Morgenthau's office one afternoon, Moscow interrupted him leafing through a stack of papers. Seeing him, the DA cocked an eyebrow.

"How you doing on the homicide?" Morgenthau asked.

"So far," Moscow said, "the only guy we've got a case on is the only Black kid in the crowd."

"So I hear," Morgenthau said. "Why is it when the victims are all Blacks and Hispanics, you round up the Black guys?"

"Relax, Boss," Moscow said. He was still young, but he had never been shy. "I assure you, that's not the way it's going to be."

| | | |

On Monday morning, as news of Mota's death spread, the DA tried to calm the storm. It would become a Morgenthau tradition: Each time a significant turn came in a big case, he would walk down the long broad hall of the eighth floor, past the offices of his chief assistants, and into the narrow library. There he would sit behind a square table, facing the television cameras, the reporters arrayed in rows. The DA's press conferences could be tense, but no one dared cross an invisible line.

"Morgenthau could get away with saying the most amazing things," Mike Cherkasky, who would serve him for more than sixteen years, rising to be investigations chief, recalled. "Anyone else—no chance. But the Boss? He could announce something that raised a hundred questions, and no one'd question him." Whether it was the historic lineage (fabled and presumed "patrician"), the reputation for integrity that preceded him, or the public nature that could instantly turn imperious, the DA knew that he possessed a natural command. Morgenthau could just say, "Can't discuss it," and the curtain would fall.

On the Monday morning after Mota's death, the pressure was rising. The number of young men in custody had grown to eleven, the DA announced, but contrary to the police claims, he had "no immediate plans" to seek a murder indictment against those defendants. "Right now," he said, he'd established "no legal link" between them and the death. He was trying to slow down the clock, undercut the false narratives, and be sure not to misstep. "Fifty percent of the information gathered in the first 24 hours of an investigation," he had already grown fond of reminding his assistants, "is usually proven wrong."

The DA was concerned. The legal case, as all could see, had grown cloudy—embarrassingly so. All the youths arrested were released without bail, except one: Andre Sanchez, seventeen, held on a $15,000 bond or $5,000 cash—money he did not have. Sanchez, whom Moscow called "the ringleader," was Puerto Rican; another defendant, Boutureira, was said to be of Spanish descent; and a third, McLamb, as Moscow had warned, was Black. That three defendants were young men of color appeared to undermine the motive—the claim that a mob of "white boys" had stormed Washington Square to rid the park of undesirables. The diverse defendants, as the *Post* wrote, "tended to quell the original fears that the rampage had racial overtones."

Morgenthau knew the office would have to present a clearer story in court. For weeks, though, the investigation went nowhere: The police unearthed few leads. Moscow did have one promising thread: the rumored drug deal that had gone bad. Two girls had said that on the night before the riot they'd seen a fight. A white kid had tried to buy dope, and somebody had broken his jaw—somebody named "Blue." Moscow called in the cops: "Guys, think you can find a dealer, a Black kid named Blue?" It was not much to go on, but the prosecutor pressed on. He drew up lists of names—more than a hundred, anyone identified as having been in the park that night—and called them in. Nearly all refused to talk.

One afternoon in October, Moscow summoned four detectives to his office. At four o'clock they left to serve subpoenas on three Jewish girls who lived in a New York University (NYU) tower south of the park— each a potential "alibi witness": Three boys, who Moscow heard had been in the square during the violence, claimed to have been with the girls at a party. At five o'clock, Moscow went to a retirement party for his supervisor in the Trial Bureau. As he approached the DA, the words came without notice.

"I hear," Morgenthau said, "you're subpoenaing the Jews now."

The speed at which the news traveled back to the eighth floor stunned Moscow. He traced the only possible route: The police had served the subpoenas, the girls complained to their parents, and their parents reached someone in City Hall.

Two other young women subpoenaed, Theresa Cowan and Diane Brown, who had witnessed the fight on the riot's eve, would testify before a grand jury. They had seen the boys who came to the park for drugs: Frankie Vales and Andre Sanchez. Theresa knew them from the neighborhood, just as she knew Blue, the dealer. And she remembered hearing something: "We'll be back to get you tomorrow."

Blue was the one who had broken Frankie's jaw. The police found the records at St. Vincent's Hospital. But there was more: The fight had only accelerated the timetable for a plan that had already been in place. Several witnesses, when pushed, conceded that as early as two days before the riot, several of the boys arrested had spoken of taking back the square—and stockpiled weapons. Moscow had found further damning evidence: On the night of the riot Ronny McLamb had been on his way back to the neighborhood when he ran into two acquaintances. McLamb, they said, had boasted about the fight, and that he had "smashed someone."

In time, Morgenthau would hear more. Witnesses spoke of a conspiracy: It wasn't just the Village boys, the police had been in on it, eager to have help in "cleansing" the park. Shopkeepers told of being hit up for money to pay off the cops. The Sixth Precinct, Morgenthau would learn, had been warned in advance, too. Detective Kingsley had taken the call: A male voice said that "one of the neighborhood kids got his jaw broken last night in Washington Square Park by a Black guy, and that his friends would be back tonight with bats and clubs to take revenge against the n****rs." Detective Kingsley had noted the warning—the logbook read 5:45 P.M., September 8—but his colleagues who came on duty after him, the prosecutors learned, either ignored it, or changed their own entries to the log. At 7:00 P.M., David "Doc" Brown, the lone officer on duty in the park, was given the okay to leave for dinner. Brown would express ignorance of the warning. There was more: Dr. Nita Karp, a psychologist who lived just off the park, happened to be treating one of the boys detained after the riot. He told her that he'd been warned—just ahead of the violence—by a policeman in an unmarked car to get rid of any weapons fast, as they'd only have "two minutes to clear the park."

Morgenthau decided to question the police. In all, thirty-eight officers from the Sixth Precinct would appear before the grand jury. As one officer after another pled a poor memory, the investigation into the suspected police complicity proved futile.

The violence in Washington Square, though, had brought the neighborhood representatives to the DA's door. At 10:30 in the morning on October 22, they filled every chair around Morgenthau's long conference table: members of the city council, the state senate, the assembly, the local community board, and the institution perhaps most exercised by the grim state of affairs in Washington Square, NYU. The phrase "race riot," it was clear, did not sit well. The politicians started slowly: "It's too bad somebody got killed," one said, "but there's all these drug problems in the neighborhood." The undercurrent of their entreaty was clear: "There's no need to be too hard on the kids involved." The politicians were heading to an unseemly conclusion, that the DA should not prosecute a homicide—"an embarrassing thing to have in the air," one of those present would note—when Morgenthau intervened.

"You know, you're right," he said. "The drug problem is a serious problem, and I'm glad you're all here." He went on, taking the opportunity to chide the civic leaders: "Of course, I can understand you don't want to be asking questions about a homicide investigation, that would cross a line. But you can of course help—you can help me get the money and resources to go after the drug dealers."

Throughout the fall, John Moscow plowed ahead with the main investigation, bringing a parade of witnesses—participants in the mob, victims, bystanders, parents, and siblings—before the grand jury. More than once, Morgenthau caught word that the young assistant had presented evidence and posed questions with an eagerness that stretched prosecutorial decorum. The DA, though, had little to fear: Judges rarely returned indictments for excessive zeal. And by December, Morgenthau was able to announce an indictment that pleased few among the Village's politicians, neighborhood associations, or police precincts—charging ten young men with a conspiracy "designed to drive Blacks from the park."

||||

By the late 1970s, New York City's criminal justice system was under pressure, perhaps as never before in its history, to keep pace with the rise in crime. Heroin use had risen to epidemic proportions by 1970, and it had not yet abated. Crime in the city mirrored the state of affairs in urban centers across the country: The arrests seemed without end. In six years, from 1972 to 1978, the number of people behind bars in federal and state facilities rose by 50 percent—to 450,000. Almost 60 percent of those incarcerated were held in state prisons. Even as state officials rushed to add beds, prison conditions—health and safety standards, overcrowding, and, above all, unrest—grew into a public and political concern. Since the Attica uprising in 1971, Morgenthau had studied conditions in the state jails; he'd helped to staff the panel that investigated the cause of the protests. He had also played a key role, even before becoming DA, in shaping the future of the country's response to the rising trade in illicit narcotics.

Morgenthau had placed a succession of former protégés from the U.S. attorney's office in key positions, both in Washington and in New York: In 1970, he'd secured a job for Paul Perito (one of the prosecutors of Roy Cohn) as chief counsel to the powerful House Select Committee on Crime; in 1973, he'd placed another, John R. Bartels, Jr., as the first head of the newly created Drug Enforcement Agency; and in 1975, he'd seen to it that Sterling Johnson, Jr., was named to the new city office of Special Narcotics Prosecutor. As such, long before Ronald Reagan declared a "War on Drugs" in the fall of 1982, Morgenthau men were already in place, eager to lead the fight.

The dominant influence, though, remained Governor Rockefeller. In 1973, Rockefeller, hoping to ride a "tough-on-crime" sentiment to the White House, pushed through a set of statutes requiring long mandatory minimums for drug offenses—the most draconian sentences in the United States. (A sale of two ounces, or possession of four ounces, of a narcotic drug became a Class A felony, carrying a fifteen-years-to-life sentence.) From the first, and throughout the next three decades, the Rockefeller laws would cast a shadow over Morgenthau's tenure. There would be a seemingly endless string of attempts to revise the state's sentencing laws—blue-ribbon panel after gubernatorial commission, each claiming the high-minded goal of "reform."

It began in 1977, when Governor Hugh Carey created an Executive Advisory Committee on Sentencing, naming Morgenthau as its chair. "The Morgenthau Committee" would argue that the goal of rehabilitation, widely accepted as "the primary purpose of punishment" in the state until the late 1960s, had lost its consensus support. At the time, virtually all felony sentences in New York were indeterminate. It proclaimed the current system "a failure" and "parole release a charade," endorsing instead a legal concept known as "the parsimony principle." "The mainstay of the liberal determinate ideal," as a later commission would write, the principle held that sentences should be "the *least severe sanction* necessary [italics in original] to achieve legitimate sentencing objectives."

The Morgenthau Committee called on the state to devise "a grid" of sentencing guidelines: setting forth "a narrow range of sentences for each combination of offense and prior criminal record category, with the higher term not exceeding the lower term by more than 15%." The guideline sentences were not to be mandatory: A judge could depart from them, imposing a sentence of his choosing "if aggravating or mitigating factors were found." Yet Albany balked: Amid strong lobbying by judges and parole officers, the reforms were rejected—and the Rockefeller laws remained. And so, two years into his tenure, the DA had offered his first fundamental contribution to the evolution that would, within two decades, turn a vast swath of the rural dairy lands upstate into prison boomtowns.

||||

At the same time, Morgenthau faced more than enough troubles in his own office. The DA in 1977 remained, as the *Times* put it, "in the throes of transition." He faced an "avalanche of urban crime, perilous budgetary problems and continuing turnover" among the troops, as seventy assistants had already quit, unable to endure the increased workload on miserly salaries. He'd entered office eager to try to replicate on the county level the big investigations in fraud and organized crime that had become his trademark at the U.S. attorney's office. But given the lack of resources, he'd been forced to hold off. Still, as Morgenthau looked to November and charted his reelection (to a first full term), he spoke of the positive. He had, in fact, become a "good scrounger," and the backlog of felony cases was diminishing. The numbers were also getting better: Even as the caseload grew, his office boasted a higher conviction rate, lower dismissal rate, and, most significantly, a rise in the percentage of convictions that carried prison time.

That the job was difficult Morgenthau had expected. But nothing could have prepared the DA, or the city, for what an aide would call "the Summer of Hell": the long hot months in 1977 when New York City endured a five-borough power outage, a serial killer on the loose, and the most contentious and turbulent mayoral race in decades—the chief contenders Ed Koch and Mario Cuomo. Throughout it all, the Washington Square riot case would continue to simmer, and only at the summer's end, once the fever broke and the election neared, did it return to dominate his days—this time, despite his confidence in the indictment, with the addition of a hurdle offered up by an obstinate judge.

61. City on Edge

1977

The blackout hit on July 13, a sweltering evening at the height of the mayoral campaign. At 9:34 P.M. a cargo pilot aloft in the skies above Queens, en route to a landing, watched as the runway beneath him vanished. He radioed the control tower: "Where's Kennedy Airport?" In an instant, ten thousand traffic lights also went dark. The city, and most of Westchester County to the north, had lost power. With the exception of the flashing red aircraft-beacons atop the Citibank building and the World Trade Center towers, and the flame in the Statue of Liberty's torch, the urban eclipse was total.

For the next twenty-five hours, until 10:39 P.M. on the following day, New York City saw an explosion of violence: more fires, looting, and arrests than ever in its history. The totals, however incomplete, had the city reeling: 1,037 fires, 1,615 stores damaged in looting and rioting, and 3,776 arrests. Hardest hit were East Harlem, the South Bronx, Bedford-Stuyvesant, and Bushwick. The cost would top $300 million, but the toll extended far beyond. "Night of Terror," *Time* would call it.

When the lights went out, Morgenthau was at home, still in the sublet at the San Remo. From the apartment at Seventy-fourth Street, Central Park had become a dark mass, but along the Upper West Side, the diners at the few restaurants still open ate by candlelight, and at the bars, patrons took their last drinks to the sidewalks, joining the impromptu block parties.

The DA had come home unsettled; a conversation with John Moscow in the afternoon had him concerned. The young ADA was smart, but he did not seem to appreciate the danger at hand. In the Washington Square case, Judge Robert Haft was sifting through the grand jury testimony; a decision was pending on whether he would accept the indictment. Leval, the DA's right-hand man, had told Moscow not to worry: Judges may like to cause a stir, but they rarely turn back an indictment. But Morgenthau did worry: Judge Haft was "a tricky one." He might prove the exception.

On Thursday morning, the day after the city had plunged into darkness, Morgenthau arrived at the office earlier than usual. He expected mass arrests to have come in overnight. With nearly half of his staff on vacation, the office, he said, would remain open for as long as it took to clear the arraignments from the night before. He called for volunteers to work the 6:00-P.M.-to-midnight shift and "the lobster" (from midnight until morning) after that. He would long remember that the female assistants, still vastly outnumbered by men, all raised their hands. "None of us would have batted an eye over working all night," Nancy Ryan, who had joined the office in 1975 after graduating Yale Law, would recall. As the cases flooded in, the ADAs filled the complaint room, typing up the complaint forms themselves, as much of the secretarial staff could not make it in. They faced a huge wave of cases to process, and had little time: Grand jury indictments—if the DA wanted to keep in jail any felony defendant held on bail—had to come within six days of an arraignment. Everyone pitched in, but it was slow going. The day was extremely hot—the building, without air-conditioning, was sweltering.

Morgenthau met with Benjamin Malcolm, commissioner of corrections. Malcolm had been up all night. He had gone first to Rikers, where several prisoners had used the darkness to escape. He went next to the Bronx jail, where violence had broken out. Every cell in the city's seventy-three police precincts was full, as were the prisons. There was no alternative, Morgenthau agreed, but to reopen the Tombs, the cells attached to the courthouse that had been ordered closed in 1974 for their inhumane conditions. At 10:30 A.M., Malcolm crossed the square to the federal building, where he proceeded—since no elevator was working—to climb nineteen flights to get the judge's order.

Morgenthau turned to the massive arraignment rooms—AR-1 and AR-2—that flanked the eastern end of the lobby, each packed with defendants. He entered the complaint room with Leval, his chief assistant, who wore the same suit, shirt buttoned, tie knotted, as the day before. At one table that had been pushed near the only window to catch the sunlight, assistants strained at typewriters. Others were typing by flashlight, held by police swearing out complaints. Morgenthau was there to bolster the troops. Many had come in from vacations and now faced the deluge. He and Leval told the assistants to "DP"—decline to prosecute—any of the 651 cases in Manhattan that appeared to lack sufficient evidence. They would have more than enough work; only a few of those arrested would be allowed to plead to misdemeanors. (A year earlier, as the backlog of cases in the court system eased, the DA had begun to restore commercial burglary to its former status of a felony.) Up the stairs, as Morgenthau toured the courtrooms, at each turn they rushed to him: assistants, witnesses, victims. One woman demanded he punish "the animals who destroyed" her store. Morgenthau met with the bureau chiefs, and above all Dick Lowe, his assistant managing the operations. Lowe was a son of Harlem, his father a police officer and his mother a clerk in the women's jail. He could not hide it: Lowe was saddened so many of the looters were Black. But he advocated a hard line: The blackout might prove a "blessing in disguise," if it made the office more "reluctant to offer misdemeanor pleas for felony crimes."

As of 3:00 P.M. on July 14, the Bronx had processed two cases—two more than Brooklyn. At 100 Centre Street, at 4:30 P.M., as the corridors turned pitch-black, the courts closed on account of darkness. Morgenthau's office had prepared 250 felony complaints, but the judges could not read them. Still, in the tropical darkness the patrol wagons kept coming, and the arrested were shunted off, first into the "feeder pens" on the ground floor, and then into the cells belowground. In the windowless basement, a supervisor had set up a gasoline-generated spotlight, turning the miserably hot cells hotter yet.

In the hours between the time the lights went out and when they came back on Friday morning at 7:23 A.M., the police had arrested more than 3,500 people—eight times the number of the 1968 riots. By Saturday, the civil liberties groups had learned of the squalid conditions in the cells: Not only was there no bedding to cover the steel benches, but hundreds of the accused, displaying welts from nightsticks and cuts from glass, needed medical attention. One holding pen, twenty by nine feet, held thirty-six men.

In the darkness of AR-2, Judge Edwin Torres admired the scene: prosecutors and defense attorneys taking turns in front of him, trying to decipher their paperwork in the glow of a police flashlight taped to the microphone stand. Even as the lights came back on, Torres did not pause—the first defendant before him was a Black woman wearing a white sun hat and blue jeans rolled to the knee. As the judge ordered her remanded, she looked back at a friend in the gallery, a woman who leaned forward, and glowering at the judge, the Legal Aid attorney, the young prosecutors, and Morgenthau, said, "All. You. Whiteys. I ain't seen no *whiteys* come through here!"

Morgenthau had held to the hard line: no slippage. Days later, Lowe would call the experience "our proudest hours in years." The prosecutors had resisted "the temptation to permit low pleas to clear the system." Instead, he wrote, "Working by candlelight, in overheated rooms, under wretched conditions . . . members of this office demonstrated to the public and to ourselves that the myth of the bankruptcy of the criminal justice system is just that: a myth."

| | | |

Two weeks later, as forewarned, a serial murderer who had been terrorizing the city for a year, claiming eleven victims (five dead, six wounded), struck again. In June, the killer had sent a letter to the *Daily News* columnist Jimmy Breslin, mocking the police—"PS: Please inform all the detectives working the case that I wish them the best of luck."—and signed off with a name that became infamous: "Son of Sam." On the last Saturday night in July, he struck again. In Bensonhurst, at 2:35 A.M., a young couple parked on a lover's lane on their first date were shot. The boy lost an eye; the girl was killed.

Three days later, another New Yorker was killed—the victim of a terrorist bombing. For years, Morgenthau had read the FBI reports: A terror group, the FALN, had long been at work in the city, eager to advance the cause of Puerto Rican independence. (Two years earlier, days after his swearing-in, they'd blown up a pub near Wall Street, killing four.) On August 3, they struck again: Two bombs exploded in Midtown office buildings, one a block from Grand Central—killing a twenty-six-year-old man. By August 5, the *Times* sounded despondent. New Yorkers had suffered another "deeply disturbing week": "This time it is the madness of men, not the madness of machines, that strains the pride and the patience of the city's inhabitants." Is New York City, the paper asked, "a failed ultra-urban experiment"?

At the DA's office, the pressure increased. The serial killer, the bombings, the blackout across the boroughs—for months, the violent havoc seemed to grow without limit. Each day Morgenthau faced new demands to help restore a semblance of civic order. The NYPD had three hundred officers devoted to finding the serial killer, but Mayor Beame, in his final months, called almost daily. Koch, the Village congressman who'd long had good relations with Morgenthau, helping him get elected, pressed harder: "The city's verging on chaos," he yelled at the DA. "If the cops can't do anything, can't you?"

By the second week of August, the police got lucky, as a number of threads came together at once. The Brooklyn couple would be Son of Sam's final victims. An eyewitness had seen the shooter run off, and was able to help the police make a sketch of the suspect; the ballistics found at the scene matched those of previous attacks; and improbably, the killer had used his own car, parked near a fire hydrant, and gotten a ticket. On August 10, 1977, David Berkowitz, a Postal Service worker from Yonkers, was arrested.

Just as Morgenthau was emerging from the summer's madness, the judge in the Washington Square riot case, Robert Haft, had done precisely what the DA feared he might: throw out John Moscow's first indictment. The *Times* headlines were merciless: "10 Freed of Charges in 'Village' Killings"; "Justice Criticizes 'Excessive Zeal' of Prosecutor . . ." Morgenthau was hard put to imagine worse press. Haft had accused the DA of abusing the grand jury system, ruling that his young assistant had revealed his "inexperience" and "ignored his responsibility" to present evidence in a "balanced and impartial manner." The judge had tossed out two months' worth of grand jury testimony, and returned the indictment. Morgenthau took the blow—and returned fire. He impaneled a new grand jury and instructed Moscow to re-present the case; by the end of October, they had won a second indictment. The case was to be heard in January.

The DA had weathered the summer's storms, and would sail to reelection. In November, Ed Koch won the mayoral race, defeating Mario Cuomo (running as the Liberal candidate) by fewer than 80,000 votes. Morgenthau, on the other hand, won handily: 205,337 votes to 8,750 for his Conservative opponent, a patent attorney and lead counsel for the local chapter of the National Rifle Association. The DA's tenure had reached a new stability: For the first time in years, there would be raises and soon, additional lines. The staff would grow, and recruiting women, he vowed, would be a priority. In 1975, when he took over, only 19 of the 190 assistant DAs were women. Two years later, 56 of 229 were women. Kuh had started a sex crimes unit, and Morgenthau, with renewed federal funds, promised to bolster it and to inaugurate a raft of new units, including one in Family Court, to handle juvenile offenders, the DA said, accused "of murder, rape and robbery." There were new federal funds, too; of the office's now $12 million budget, only $7.7 million came from the city. Ever mindful of the hurdles faced by victims and witnesses, he used the new money in part to hire the office's first Spanish-speaking prosecutors and interpreters, at a time when, as the *Times* would later note, "such actions registered as at least mildly revolutionary."

After two years in office, Morgenthau also had his share of critics. Although his predecessor Hogan had not argued a trial for decades, the critique would become a refrain: Morgenthau did not appear in court. It was true: Only once had he stood before a judge—to oppose bail in a rape case. The DA was unfazed: "You can't try cases," he said, "and run an office of this size." Morgenthau, a reporter noted, "had come to personify the professional prosecutor." Morale was on the rise, and yet, the DA would say, he felt "like I'm running a vocational school." For too many of his young assistants, it was still on-the-job training. The office lacked skilled prosecutors, and the staff to support them—let alone the resources to attempt a return to his prized investigations, the "big cases" that might last years, and devour his budget, but could bring real and lasting change.

Amid the tumult of the mayoral race, it was one of the few points of agreement between Koch and Cuomo: Morgenthau not only needed to stay, he would need all the help he could get.

||||

The DA had also fallen in love. They had met in an interview, five years earlier. He was still in private practice when Lucinda Franks, a twenty-six-year-old reporter for UPI, insisted on interviewing him for a story. She came with a good calling card: Two years earlier she'd won a Pulitzer—the first woman, and the youngest reporter, to win for national reporting. The award had done little to dampen her natural ambition; she'd been chasing a story on the Watergate figure Maurice Stans—who, along with John Mitchell, would soon stand trial—and caught a rumor that Stans had laundered campaign funds in Mexico. Go see Morgenthau, someone had told her: The U.S. attorney fired by Nixon had the goods.

By that time, Morgenthau had begun to date—"a lot," Jenny would say. "Daddy dated a lot of different women," she remembered, "but he wasn't really searching." A series of fix-ups—evenings out with former Miss America Bess Myerson, Barbara Walters, the widowed daughter of an older friend—ended almost at once. By the time he reached the DA's office, though, the journalists had come to dominate his social calendar. Morgenthau revealed a weakness for reporters—including two women assigned to cover the courts, one from the *Times,* the other from the *Post.* "They were funny, and smart, and accomplished," he would say. Most were blond, his daughters would note, and younger—considerably so.

Lucinda arrived at the office on Park Avenue on a rainy day in April 1973, and soon ended the string of girlfriends. If he had not been looking for a new partner, from the first Morgenthau sensed he had found her. "It was never going to be simple," he would say, "but I felt it might just work." By the time they wed, in the summer of 1977, Bob was fifty-eight, and Lucinda, thirty-one.

"Cindy" Franks, as she was then known, had been born in Kankakee, Illinois, and grown up in Wellesley, Massachusetts, outside of Boston. Her parents were midwesterners, and Republicans, her father an executive at a failing steel company, and her mother head of the Boston Opera Guild, president of the local Junior Service League, and a trustee at the local hospital. Wellesley was a "hateful town," Lucinda would recall, "full of men in yellow pants and red jackets who belonged to the John Birch Society and housewives who planted themselves in garden clubs." She had entered Vassar in the mid-1960s, and thrown herself into radical politics. She helped found the SDS chapter on campus and rarely missed an antiwar march. Graduating in 1968, she was the image of the flower child: a blue-eyed English major, long blond hair parted in the middle, as she would note, "just like Joan Baez."

She went overseas at once, talking her way into a stint at the all-male UPI bureau in London. She covered the radical underground there, always straddling the line, she would later say, between activist and observer. She joined an anarchist club, read Kropotkin, and fell in with a group of young radicals headed for Belfast. They went on a march for Catholic rights, camping out in churches along the way, two to a sleeping bag, until they were ambushed by Protestant bullyboys. She sustained a "photogenic scalp wound," before being ordered back to London.

In the spring of 1970, she landed her biggest scoop. In New York, three members of the Weather Underground, the militant radical organization, had been killed when a pipe bomb they'd been assembling blew up a brownstone in the Village. Lucinda's mother, eager to aid her daughter's career, made the connection: Diana Oughton, one of the young women killed in the explosion, came from a town near Kankakee, her own hometown. Her mother's best friend, as luck would have it, knew the Oughtons.

From London, Lucinda saw her opening. She and Diana were both children of privilege, who had attended elite colleges and embraced radical politics. Her parents, Lucinda imagined, might want to learn how the turn had come. Convincing UPI to send her to Illinois, Lucinda was soon at the Oughtons' home. "You remind me of Diana," Jim Oughton said. She would spend five weeks on the road, living with Diana's parents (sleeping in her room), meeting her friends, reading her letters, and trying to see into the closed world of the Weathermen. Lucinda ended up "identifying" with Diana so much, she would write, she nearly threw her "notebook in the trash and joined the groups that shaped her." When she returned to UPI's headquarters in New York, her bosses teamed her with Tom Powers, one of the agency's best reporters, who'd been writing on the student protests at Columbia and Berkeley. "Lucinda thought of herself as being on the side of the revolution," Powers remembered. "We argued a lot, struggled a bit, but she was dogged." Their five-part series ran around the world and won a Pulitzer in 1971.

Lucinda was twenty-four, three years out of Vassar. From London, she could have chosen any beat. She elected to investigate the draft dodgers, the young American men who had sought refuge in Canada and Sweden. Although few knew it, Lucinda had already delved into the resistance movement. In London, she had met Roger Williams, an American who had written a book on draft resisters and now ranked on the FBI wanted list. Among the radical expatriates of London, Williams was something of a celebrity. He was newly married, but the relationship was faltering. He and Lucinda had struck up an immediate romance and lived together in London for six months. After the Pulitzer, when UPI moved Lucinda to New York, he followed.

It was Roger Williams who sent her to interview Morgenthau. No ordinary draft dodger, Williams may have been the only indicted resister who had gone to Vietnam as a newspaper correspondent. In New York, he'd found work at NBC News, where he spent weeks calling everyone on Nixon's enemies list. Morgenthau had told him of the "loose ends" of his final days as U.S. attorney—specifically, the Nixon money that had gone overseas. In April 1973, in her first audience at Morgenthau's private practice office, Lucinda heard much of the same story. But she'd also made an impression. "It all began with a simple, white, knit poncho," she would remember. "I wore it while interviewing Bob for a story about the fall of the Nixon administration. . . . After I left, he had the peculiar experience of being haunted by the garment."

Morgenthau began to talk her up with friends. This girl, he would say, should be at the *Times*. He mentioned her to Nick Gage, his friend and one of the paper's top investigative reporters. "Bob kept after me," Gage would recall, "until finally, I called Arthur"—Arthur Gelb, then the metro editor at the *Times*. Lucinda's first byline appeared in the *Times* on March 2, 1974.

For more than a year, the relationship remained professional. As Morgenthau launched his campaign for DA, Lucinda was still living with her antiwar boyfriend, but Morgenthau would call her at work. At her desk, Lucinda would pick up the phone and hear the familiar voice. "Bob Morgenthau," he would say. "Got a pencil?" Before long, he'd taken to calling her at home, too. Her boyfriend, she would say, would neglect to pass on the messages. The turning point came in the summer of 1976, as Lucinda was preparing to leave New York and join Williams in Telluride.

On the night before her flight to Colorado, Morgenthau called again. "There's a party at Arthur Schlesinger's," he said. "And I'd like to take you." Lucinda begged off. She was on deadline on a freelance story for *Rolling Stone*. "I'm sorry," she said, "I've got to finish this piece."

"You'll get it done," he said, leaving her no choice. "I'll pick you up at 7."

| | | |

The party at the Schlesinger townhouse on East Sixty-fourth was to take place during the Democratic National Convention. The room was packed with political and press luminaries from the Roosevelt and Kennedy eras: Ben Bradlee and Sally Quinn; Swifty Lazar and Joe Kraft; Adlai Stevenson and Pamela Harriman. In the middle of the party, everyone seemed to freeze, their eyes turning to the door, as Jacqueline Onassis, still known as a recluse, entered. Jackie appeared to glow as she crossed the room, seizing the attention. Lucinda would always remember the moment, and how Morgenthau was more taken with her than with the star of the party: "I looked up at Bob," she would recall, "and he was smiling too, but not at Jackie O."

A month after their first date, Bob asked Lucinda to his house for dinner. Bobby was away at Amherst, and his two older daughters, Jenny and

Annie, now lived on their own. Nellie remained upstate, never to return to the family. She could dress and eat, but required constant vigilance. Bob would still visit, yet would not bring the other children. Only Barbara, at thirteen, remained at home. Lucinda saw her circumstances clearly. Morgenthau had always done his best: He had attended the kids' school events and sports, knew their closest friends, and every summer led the sailing and fishing expeditions on the Vineyard. But Martha had been the one most intimately involved with their upbringing; he had been more remote—at work, or with his work at home. Now he faced unfamiliar territory.

"Since Martha's death," Lucinda would recall, "he had tried to become all things to his youngest." Barbara, as she learned at that first meal in his house, held a special place. "He knew the names of her teachers, knew she talked to an imaginary squirrel, researched the type of skis she needed for winter holidays together." He always took her calls. Ken Conboy, his executive assistant, would remember a conference with the mayor when the DA excused himself in midstream. He kept Beame waiting, as he spoke with Barbara. "He was asking her about her new jeans, how they fit, what color they were, did she like them." Lucinda would look back at the first dinner in the Morgenthau home and realize that "the invitation was primarily to see how his daughter Barbara . . . and I got along." She felt, she would write, "as if I were being brought home to meet his parents."

It was not only Bob's teenaged daughter. He and Lucinda would meet the cold embrace of his older children, and their spouses, as well. In August 1976, the family would again retreat to the Vineyard. One weekend Lucinda joined them. There were no songs around the bonfire or picnics on the beach; the time together was strained. Even the family border collies, Hiram and Hannah, regarded her with suspicion. Years later, the elder children would cringe remembering that first summer; choosing their words with care, they called their relationship with their father's new girlfriend "hard," "troubling," and "doomed."

Lucinda might exaggerate the differences between herself and the DA, heightening the drama of their union. (She was wont to portray herself as younger, and more radical, than she was.) But she was in love. "He's quite handsome," she wrote her grandmother. "And he has this to-die-for little half-moon smile. There's one other thing—he's Jewish, but the highborn kind. . . . His blood is as blue as yours." She wrote of his "wicked, hilarious, really dry sense of humor," and added, "Gram, be happy. I think my wild days are numbered. This I know because if there's one thing Bob is not, it's wild."

For months, they lived rootlessly, shuttling among Lucinda's apartment, the house in Riverdale, and the sublet at the San Remo. In the summer of 1977, Lucinda talked him into buying a place of their own: 41 Charlton, a townhouse five blocks south of Washington Square, built by John Jacob Astor in 1827. They would sell the Riverdale house, Lucinda would move out of her apartment, and Bob would give up his sublet.

Bob's children were taken aback. The proposed move downtown seemed wildly impractical—how would Barbara commute to school in Riverdale? But more important, it signaled an end to the closeness with their father that had filled the years since Martha's death five years before. They had enjoyed more than just time. In those first years after their mother's death, the children had felt an intimacy with their father they had not previously known. It had been an unexpected consolation: The bonds had tightened, the relationships grown easy.

Bob's children, in retrospect, would call the break inevitable. And as is so often the case in New York, it came over real estate. "I'd wanted to live in the Charlton Street house with friends from college," Bobby would recall. "Dad said, 'No.' And he'd never said 'No' to anything." At once, Bobby sensed the wall going up. So did his siblings: As the move downtown grew closer, their opposition mounted. By then, both the children and their father knew they were entering a new phase in their relations.

Morgenthau's sister predicted disaster. Dr. Joan Morgenthau Hirschhorn, professor of medicine at Mount Sinai, founder of one of the first adolescent youth clinics in the country, member of the boards of private schools, foundations, and Vassar, could appreciate a working woman. But Lucinda, Joan would say, seemed like "a wild working woman." "What the hell was Bob thinking?" she wondered.

Morgenthau years later would stop short of answering the question. He would concede the obvious: Lucinda was so much younger, and in many ways the opposite of Martha. But in her youth, ambition, and spirited playfulness, he found great attraction. Even his closest friends, the few from his years as U.S. attorney, would later raise their shoulders and speak of "love."

Still, he was in no hurry to marry. Lucinda, though, insisted on it. "Wanna go to Vegas?" she asked once. He stalled: "Let me ask Barbara what she thinks." In the end, he did not consult the children.

The wedding took place on November 19, 1977, two weeks after the DA's reelection, in the sunken garden behind the house on Charlton Street. Lucinda wore an old-fashioned ivory chiffon dress, and a cap of Belgian lace refashioned from her grandmother's gown. The DA looked pale, uncertain what he was doing there—a month before, he had still been wearing Martha's wedding ring—until his bride appeared. Lucinda was beaming. As she came down a set of makeshift stairs, she nearly fell—a heel caught between the slats. Judge Sidney Asch, a Morgenthau neighbor and old friend, kept things rolling, presiding over a blend of Episcopalian and Jewish rituals. The Morgenthau children, to Lucinda's surprise, accepted it all blithely. Bobby stood next to his father, bearing the ring, his best man. "I was prepared to see them staring at their feet," she would write, "unwilling to witness what they feared the most."

The newlyweds expected to move into the Charlton Street house. Lucinda had bought furniture, and Bob filled the wine cellar, but in the end, they heeded the children's objections—and never moved in. "The Boss wanted a love nest," said Peter Fiorillo, the DA's bodyguard and driver at the time, "but his kids, they were dead-set against it." Instead, the newlyweds retreated to the Upper East Side, moving—"thanks to a real estate friend of Bob's," Lucinda would say—into a large penthouse, rent-stabilized but in considerable disrepair, on Eighty-eighth Street.

62. "The Color of His Skin"

1978

At 2:20 in the afternoon on January 30, 1978, eighteen months after the riot in Washington Square Park, John Moscow stood before the jury. The young assistant DA opened his case by recounting "the People's" version of the events on "that night," when every Black and Hispanic man was driven from the park—except, as a reporter sitting in the courtroom would write, "two who had been rendered unable to depart because one was paralyzed and the other was dying."

Moscow spoke to a jury of seven men and five women—three of whom were Black. His words were heard as well by the nine defendants, their nine lawyers, and the presiding judge, Robert Haft. Haft had already demonstrated his independent streak, and in returning the first indictment, he had revealed no fondness for Moscow.

Haft was one of six "calendar judges" in the Criminal Term of the Supreme Court; nearly all were acting Supreme Court judges. Thanks to the patronage that had long held sway in the selection of judges, only a handful were deemed competent to preside over trials, and even fewer of possessing the wherewithal to keep a caseload moving. The judiciary, in turn, devised a shortcut: The ablest Criminal Court judges were elevated to "Acting Supremes"—ostensibly on a temporary basis, though many would stay for decades. Calendar judges were selected for their prowess in clearing a docket. Once a case was ready for trial, common practice held that the calendar judge would pass it on to another judge. Haft, however, had not. Much to Morgenthau's chagrin, he had assigned the case to himself.

Moscow at once fought back. During the voir dire, jury selection, he insisted that the proceedings be recorded. Given their history, Moscow was after Judge Haft—"setting him up for an Article 78," seeking to dismiss him from the case for bias—and Haft knew it. By then, though, the prosecutor also faced another problem: moving the venue for the pretrial hearings. The hearings, held behind closed doors, had taken place not in the main Criminal Courts Building, but across the way, in the Civil Court Building, at 111 Centre, a grim limestone edifice built in the 1960s. The reason was simple: Given the sheer volume of criminal cases, new "parts"—as courtrooms are called in the legal parlance of Manhattan—had been opened in the Civil Court Building, and lower court judges brought in from upstate to ease the backlog. Moscow was irate when Haft announced that the trial, too, would be heard in Part 106, on the seventh floor, now devoted to criminal cases.

"Got to get a change of courtrooms!" he'd shouted to Morgenthau, again barging into his office. The case had to be tried at 100 Centre, not 111. He needed, he insisted, a courtroom with access to the judge's elevator. Security demanded it: These kids feared for their lives. "I've got to get my witnesses into the court, and out, without being public," he told the DA. "No private access, no case."

Morgenthau reached for the telephone. He had known Dave Ross, the administrative judge in charge of the operations of all city and state courts in New York City, for decades. Ross was known as a doer—"his brusqueness and crudeness and even rudeness," an observer told the *Times*, "make Ross almost the perfect leader." As citywide administrator, Ross had the authority to assign, or reassign, any one of more than four hundred judges to any case in the court system.

Ross would not take Morgenthau's call. "Dave was nobody's fool," Moscow knew. "He wasn't touching this case." Instead, he redirected Morgenthau to his deputy, Jawn Sandifer. Judge Sandifer was a native of North Carolina, one of nine children; segregation had forced him north. He had studied law at Howard University during FDR's second term and gained prominence as an NAACP lawyer. In 1950, Sandifer had won a case that would help to set the stage for *Brown v. Board of Education*. In 1964, Mayor Wagner named him to the bench, and four years later, he'd won a Supreme Court seat. In Sandifer, Morgenthau had found a welcome audience—and the deputy administrative judge agreed to relay the DA's concerns.

Even in his sixties, Judge Sandifer was a striking presence. As he entered Haft's courtroom, jury selection came to a halt. "Your Honor," he said, "may I speak with you for a moment?" The two disappeared into the jury room, and when they emerged, Haft tried not to wince as he spoke. His displeasure, though, was evident. Sandifer had conveyed Morgenthau's demands, and Haft had been forced to cave: Moscow would get his change of courtrooms, and access to the judge's elevator. Haft, moreover, had heard a warning: The administrative judge would be watching his conduct in the upcoming trial.

Morgenthau had played a trump, though he did not explain the move to his assistant, nor did Moscow ask. "Clarity," the DA would say, had come to Haft's mind as Judge Sandifer painted the broader landscape. When the two judges spoke, Morgenthau would say, Sandifer reiterated the need, when it came to John Moscow, to wipe the slate clean—to treat the young ADA "fairly." And Sandifer, the DA would add, had also made clear that Haft would never be nominated to a higher court without the support of the Black Democrats of Harlem.

| | | |

On the opening day of the trial in late January, a makeshift cardboard sign hung outside the court, indicating it was now Part 106—Judge Haft's new courtroom. Outside, the family and supporters of "the baseball team"—as they called the nine defendants—rallied, carrying hand-painted signs. From the neighborhood, the schools, the church they had come, as they would every day of the trial. Inside the courtroom, Moscow proceeded to name the defendants, one by one. "None of you have scorecards," he told the jurors. "But I'm sure that by the end of the trial you'll be able to distinguish them.

"These people did not come together spontaneously," Moscow went on. He spoke of "conspiracy," a plan hatched two days before the violence. He ran through the chronicle: A core group of boys, all white, had gone recruiting. They had rounded up volunteers at the local parks and playgrounds, before gathering in the Leroy Street Park. They had stockpiled weapons—anything hard enough to hurt that could be carried in one hand.

Moscow spoke, too, of motive. "The People will prove that the intent was to strike what the people there called 'n****rs,'" he said. Not everyone in the mob knew the plan. Some went along, he said, "for what they thought was the legitimate purpose of driving the dealers out."

The prosecutor laid out the charges—conspiracy, riot, manslaughter, and six assaults.

The families of the accused filled the gallery. Nearly all had come from the Village; many had lived there for decades, in the five-story tenements. It was "a longshore neighborhood," one of the elders would say. All the men seemed to work the piers, and the streets were divided by where your people came from. "The longshoremen on the 11th Street Pier were Spanish," Steve Durnin, defendant Michael's brother, twenty-seven years older, recalled, "and everybody who lived on 11th was Spanish." Over time, borders blurred: "Spanish married Irish." In the 1960s, as the land turned valuable and the developers wanted it, Mayor Wagner cut a deal and Lindsay saw it through. "They had to get rid of the longshore people," Durnin would say. "Most of the Irish went up to Chelsea. They moved them north, and made sure they didn't come back."

Throughout the trial, the families would keep vigil. Steve Durnin made sure to arrive early to get a good seat. Joey Chiappetti's sister, Maryann, would rush to the courthouse after waitressing, or whenever she could get someone to cover her shift. Many of the families would blame the dealers—"The Black guys were selling drugs down there," Steve Durnin would say, "terrorizing the people in the park"—but some would not. Still, all who came to lend their support knew how hard growing up in the neighborhood had been. Only two of the defendants had had steady jobs, and just one had graduated from high school.

Morgenthau had known it would not be easy going. It would be hard to distinguish the prosecution's witnesses from the defendants, Moscow had warned. Many of the boys had been in the park, some had taken part in the melee, and several barely escaped indictment. All were disinclined to testify. As predicted, the first days of trial did not augur well. Moscow was tense, revealing, some in the office would say, the political pressure on his shoulders. He had a mind that raced, and he seemed to struggle to focus. Worse, his relations with Judge Haft again veered toward confrontation. Moscow, at least to the judge's mind, was hellbent on forcing evidence into the record without a legal basis. The faster he barreled on, the less Haft disguised his displeasure. "Mr. Moscow," he said at one point during the second week, "I think I should inform you—the judges have a pool on when I'm going to be forced to declare a mistrial in this case." Morgenthau took note; he asked that Jim Kindler, a senior assistant, lend a hand. For a time, Kindler took a chair beside Moscow, "second-seating" him. Moscow's mind just worked too fast, Kindler would say: "He was always four steps ahead of the jurors. My job was to put on the brakes."

At the Treasury, with a swell of reporters and his longtime assistant, Henrietta Klotz (at his left), January 1935. From his first day in office, Morgenthau dreaded the press. He also deemed leaks one of Washington's worst sins, fearing them among rivals, his own staff, and even his family.

From 1941 until his firing by President Harry S. Truman in 1945, Morgenthau led seven War Loan Drives, delivering more than $200 billion for defense—"more money," FDR said, "than has ever been spent by any nation at any time." A wretched public speaker, Morgenthau would get help from celebrities—among them James Cagney, Bing Crosby, and Orson Welles. Here he is seen with Captain Ronald Reagan, ordered into temporary duty, broadcasting a play to launch the Fourth War Loan, January 17, 1944. By war's end, more than 85 million Americans had bought war bonds.

Amid the ruins of Normandy, in the village of Perrières, August 8, 1944. Morgenthau met with General Dwight D. Eisenhower in England, flew to Cherbourg ("to hell and gone," he told aides), and was briefed by General Omar Bradley. "This is an opportunity that comes to a commander not more than once in a century," Bradley said. "We're about to destroy an entire hostile army."

Final victory lap: Morgenthau and FDR on their last election-eve tour, Beacon, New York, November 6, 1944. Roosevelt, gaunt and pale, insisted on riding in the open-air car, promising the crowd, "I'm back again—still going strong!" five months before his fatal stroke in April 1945.

Riding high before the fall: In July 1944, Morgenthau chaired the Bretton Woods Conference on the postwar monetary order, trying to keep pace with John Maynard Keynes. The British economist brought intellectual star power (and his Russian ballerina wife) to the New Hampshire talks, which established the International Monetary Fund and, in time, the World Bank. It was a summer of success—until news of the "Morgenthau Plan," and the secretary's desire to return Germany to an agrarian state, leaked. "For forty-eight hours," he would say, "I was on the top of the heap."

Morgenthau receiving a medal for his wartime service from President Truman, December 12, 1945. In truth, after FDR's death, the two had a short, tumultuous relationship: Morgenthau, Truman wrote, was a "block head, nut," who "fired himself from my cabinet for threatening what he would do to me." Within days, Morgenthau, after nearly twelve years in office, was gone.

The Morgenthau family
on horseback at Fishkill
Farms, 1934. Left to right:
Robert, Henry Jr., Joan,
Elinor, and Henry III.

Henry Morgenthau, Jr., at his
farm, May 14, 1944. Fishkill
Farms had fruit trees and, for
a time, grapevines, but its
apple orchards were his first
love. In spring, he loved to
walk their rows, taking in the
sweet blossoms.

After the death of his first
wife, when Morgenthau, at
sixty, married a
Frenchwoman, the *New York
Times* headline brought
scandal: "Morgenthau to
Wed Mrs. Hirsch." With
Marcelle Puthon Hirsch
Morgenthau, at their
apartment ceremony,
November 21, 1951. (The
newspapers reported her age
as forty-seven; she was in fact
fifty-three.)

When Henry Morgenthau, Sr., quit the Free Synagogue in 1919, he became America's leading anti-Zionist. ("Zionism is a surrender," the elder Morgenthau wrote, "not a solution.") But after World War II, his son embraced the new Jewish state, visiting Israel in October 1948. Here he films immigrants at Tal Shahar, a village renamed in his honor (Morning Dew in Hebrew, Morgenthau in German), as Robert Capa (back to camera) films the scene, 1950.

At Lake Tiberias, Morgenthau (second from left) with Mrs. Klotz (far right), his loyal assistant; Eliezer Kaplan, the Israeli finance minister; and Golda Meir (then Meyerson), the future prime minister, 1950. In 1948, Morgenthau had aided Meyerson's fundraising tour of the United States, during which she collected more than $50 million—for relief and arms. As chairman of the United Jewish Appeal, Morgenthau would raise $465 million to resettle Jews in Israel. But he soon tired of the fights among American supporters of Israel and retreated with his second wife to a new home, Villa Morning Dew, on the French Riviera.

The future DA with his father in a photo booth, circa 1927. That year, Henry Morgenthau, Sr., always eyeing the future, licensed a new invention, the Photomaton, a "quarter-in-the-slot automatic photographing device." The early "selfie" machines appeared on Broadway and Coney Island, as Henry Sr. led a group of eager investors that included FDR with plans for a national rollout, but the crash of 1929 ended the venture.

Eager "to kill Nazis," Robert Morgenthau enlisted at age twenty, joining a Navy officers' training program in the summer of 1940. He would serve fifty-four months, in both the Mediterranean and the Pacific. In his Amherst yearbook, Morgenthau, president of his class, revealed prescience: "The class of 1941 has the bittersweet satisfaction of knowing it goes out with an epic. . . . We have been among the few who, during the past year, have had the opportunity to learn freely, in a free country at peace. It has perhaps been impressed on us that we, above others, should have an abiding faith in democracy."

Robert and Martha Pattridge Morgenthau on their wedding day, December 30, 1943. On home leave from the Mediterranean, Bob had proposed before shipping out again.

At dusk on April 20, 1944—Hitler's fifty-fifth birthday—German torpedo bombers swarmed in low over an Allied convoy off the coast of North Africa, sinking the USS *Lansdale*, a U.S. Navy destroyer carrying 282 men, including a twenty-four-year-old executive officer, Lieutenant Robert M. Morgenthau. In all, 49 men were lost. Survivors, covered in bunker oil, were pulled in the darkness from the frigid waters of the Mediterranean.

Lieutenant Morgenthau (hands in pockets, lower left) checks his crew as they leave the USS *Menges*—along with the USS *Newell*, one of two Coast Guard ships that worked through the night to rescue more than 200 survivors.

Two German bombers were captured, and a funeral for two of the *Lansdale* dead was held at a U.S. Army base in Algeria, with Lieutenant Morgenthau (third from right) presiding. Seven officers and crew members were buried at the North Africa American Cemetery in Tunisia. Morgenthau would soon head for the Pacific, where his ship, the USS *Harry F. Bauer*, survived wave after wave of kamikaze attacks, as well as direct hits from a torpedo and a bomb (both failed to detonate). Its officers and crew received a Presidential Unit Citation.

Young corporate lawyer turns federal crime fighter, 1961: Robert Morgenthau with family—his wife, Martha, and their children Jenny, Anne, and Bobby. Not pictured: daughter Elinor, who, born with a severe developmental disability, had since a young age been cared for in state facilities in upstate New York. "I was chicken," her father would say, to send her away, but the doctors "at last convinced me."

New frontiers: The new U.S. attorney for the Southern District of New York with Attorney General Robert F. Kennedy on the steps of the federal courthouse in Foley Square, Manhattan, June 14, 1961.

At the attorney general's side, planning the war on organized crime: RFK at the head of the table, Morgenthau to his right, encircled by Department of Justice prosecutors, 1961. Different in many ways, the two men became close. "That was one of his great gifts," Morgenthau would say of Bobby Kennedy, "to make people feel they were part of the team."

Running for governor: with President John F. Kennedy in New York City, Columbus Day, 1962. JFK tried to boost the long-shot campaign to unseat the incumbent, Nelson Rockefeller, a moderate and popular Republican who charmed crowds and reporters. It was far too little, too late: Morgenthau was a disaster on the stump—a candidate, as one reporter wrote, who possessed a "slow smile and faintly palsied wave," and was too shy to stand next to Kennedy for the cameras.

"The Sovereign District," as the Southern District of New York became known during Morgenthau's tenure as U.S. attorney. In 1967, among the ranks: one woman, Patricia Hynes (third row, center, behind Morgenthau), who would go on to head the city bar association, and one Black prosecutor, Sterling Johnson, Jr., a U.S. Marine veteran and former police officer, who would become the city's special narcotics prosecutor before being appointed to a federal judgeship in the Eastern District of New York.

Morgenthau '62: the campaign, the first of two failed gubernatorial runs, produced a comic book to highlight the candidate's wars—against the Germans, the Japanese, and the Mafia in America. It was no use: As the Cuban missile crisis heightened anxieties, JFK and Bobby Kennedy could not campaign, and New York voters were loath to unseat Rockefeller. "I personally feel," the head of the FBI's New York office told J. Edgar Hoover, "it will be somewhat a lamb being led to slaughter."

"The fixer"—Roy M. Cohn, formerly legal counsel to Senator Joseph McCarthy during his anti-Communist crusades, on trial for perjury and obstruction of justice, April 17, 1964.

"Joe Bananas": Nineteen months after his "kidnapping" and a worldwide FBI manhunt, Joseph Bonanno (light suit) reappears at the federal courthouse and is released on $150,000 bail with legendary Mafia defense lawyer Albert Krieger (left, with glasses), May 17, 1966.

On December 12, 1969, Cohn, after four trials in six years, would walk. But on the next day Morgenthau got one of his biggest victories: Carmine De Sapio, once the all-powerful boss of Tammany Hall, was convicted of conspiring to bribe Mayor John Lindsay's water commissioner, and to extort contracts from Consolidated Edison. (De Sapio, in trademark dark glasses, is seen here leaving court, December 13, 1969.) Days later, President Richard Nixon declared that Morgenthau must quit or be fired. A standoff ensued, but on January 15, 1970, after nearly a decade in office, the prosecutor gave way, and Nixon's chosen replacement, a Republican, moved in.

Becoming "the Boss": Sidney Asch (right), justice of the State Supreme Court, swears in Robert M. Morgenthau as DA of New York County for the first of nine terms, January 2, 1975.

Voting with his second wife, the journalist Lucinda Franks, and holding son Joshua, two years old, election day, 1985. Nearly three decades the DA's junior, Franks in 1971, at age twenty-four, had become the first woman to win a Pulitzer Prize for national reporting. It was a marriage of love, and trade in two of New York's passions: "I gave him political gossip," Franks would say, "and he sniffed out stories for me."

A key unit: Trial Bureau 50, 1983, featuring the future U.S. Supreme Court justice Sonia Sotomayor (second row, center), future federal judge Roslynn R. Mauskopf (second row, far right), and Nancy Ryan (front row, far right). In 2002, Ryan would help lead a painstaking reinvestigation of the Central Park Jogger case, resulting in the sentences of the Central Park Five being vacated. Sotomayor joined the DA's office in 1979, serving as a Morgenthau assistant for five years. The DA played a pivotal role in her rise, from recruiting her when she was a student at Yale Law to championing her appointment to the Supreme Court.

The one that "will never go away," Robert Morgenthau's heir, Cyrus Vance, would say of the Central Park Jogger case. In the days after a twenty-eight-year-old white woman was found near dead in Central Park, the tabloids and *The New York Times* feasted: It was a " 'Lord of the Flies' rape," wrote a *Times* reporter, and the boys, "neither drug crazed nor from broken homes, could not be written off as a feral fringe of the underclass."

The defendants in court on February 23, 1990, the day Judge Thomas B. Galligan ruled "incriminating videotaped and written statements" admissible as evidence in their trial. The boys, aged fourteen to seventeen at their arrest, would become known as the Central Park Five: Antron McCray, Kevin Richardson, Yusef Salaam, Raymond Santana, and Kharey Wise. Also charged were five others who remained less known, among them Jermaine Robinson. In October 1989, Robinson pled guilty to one count of robbery, while all other charges against him were dropped, in exchange for turning state's evidence. At the two trials, however, Robinson was never called to the stand.

"You Can't Prosecute Crime in the Streets Without Prosecuting Crime in the Suites"

As U.S. attorney and as district attorney, Morgenthau led wars against the Mafia and, for the first time, against "white-collar crime," investigating:

- BCCI, the "greatest banking fraud in history," and its U.S. representatives, Clark Clifford and Robert Altman (top left: Clifford, the former secretary of defense, and his law partner Altman testify at congressional hearings on BCCI, September 11, 1991)

- the Gambino organized crime family's "Mob tax" on the garment industry (center photograph: Joseph Gambino and brother Thomas Gambino, behind him, indicted on antitrust charges, June 23, 1992)

- the rising trade in narcotics that Morgenthau had witnessed over half a century (bottom: the DA with more than six hundred pounds of uncut cocaine, November 9, 1992)

Politics and philanthropy: with Ed Koch during his last campaign, Upper East Side of Manhattan, in 2005. In his final race for DA, Morgenthau faced rare, strong opposition in the Democratic primary, but won handily—and went on to win with 99 percent of the vote in the general election.

Jumping rope, in 1981, at Playstreets, the sports and cultural program sponsored by the Police Athletic League, a nonprofit Morgenthau had chaired since 1962. As his grandfather had done for Woodrow Wilson and Near East Relief, and his father for war bonds and Israel, the DA recruited New York's wealthiest—from George Steinbrenner to Donald Trump—to support the city youth programs. In the 1980s, the DA gained a second cause, helping to build the Museum of Jewish Heritage—A Living Memorial to the Holocaust in lower Manhattan, which he chaired from 1982 to 2014.

"Operation Rotten Apple": The DA (center), police commissioner Raymond W. Kelly (left), and the DA's longtime investigations chief, Daniel Castleman (right), announce another Mafia sweep: eleven members and associates of the Genovese and Lucchese organized crime families indicted for running a gambling and numbers ring in the Bronx, 2006.

"The Boss never quit": Lucinda Franks with the DA at their Martha's Vineyard home, August 2014. In retirement, Morgenthau would join one of the country's top law firms and go to the office every workday until shortly before his death—at age ninety-nine, ten days shy of his centenary—in July 2019.

On the tenth day of the trial, one of Morgenthau's fears came true: The prosecution was starting to lose witnesses. That morning Anthony DeFranco, known to the defendants as "Dif," had left his house telling his mother he was heading for court, where he was due to testify for the state, but DeFranco did not arrive. ("A Witness Disappears in Village Killing Case," the *Times* headline would announce.) In court, Moscow again fumed. Subpoenas, he insisted, would not suffice to ensure his witnesses made it to court. As Haft dismissed the jury from the courtroom, the prosecutor rose and put a challenge to the Judge: "I ask the court to inquire of the defendants who the next People's witness is," Moscow said.

"Is that a serious request?" asked Haft. The defense attorneys, too, looked taken aback.

Yes, Moscow said, he was serious: The judge should ask the young men on trial who his next witness was—after all, they seemed to know the names of his witnesses in advance. Moscow had provided the defense attorneys with the Rosario material—the pretrial witness statements—the night before. One of them, Moscow went on, his voice dripping with irony, must have "inadvertently" let slip the witness's name to the defendants, who in turn ensured that he would not testify.

Moscow made a further startling request: He asked that the judge take into custody McLamb, Chiappetti, Sanchez, and Boutureira—the four defendants who would have been implicated by DeFranco—"to dissuade elements in the community . . . from engaging in rash and improper steps."

The judge was stunned. "That's one of the most drastic remedies I've ever heard," said Haft. "There's no evidence that any one of those you've named has committed any unlawful act."

"The alternative is to lock up the witnesses," Moscow replied, "and let the defendants go free, which is a far more drastic remedy."

It soon became clear that Moscow was managing to build a case. Over the course of a year and a half, the prosecutor had come to understand the "old neighborhood." He'd interviewed more than 150 witnesses and got a few of them to talk.

But it was the victims who made the case. Carl "Bonecrusher" Warren told how he had seen Andriani hit Mario Peraza. "I saw him as clearly as I see you," Warren said. "He was less than 12 feet away from me. And I don't intend to forget a person who calls me n****r." The best witness, though, was the man who had suffered the most serious wounds among the survivors. The riot had cost Charles Febee a fractured skull and the use of his right eye. On the night of the riot, Febee had been a thirty-six-year-old disabled veteran. He had served a dozen years in the Army, only leaving after suffering an injury—severing the tendons of a hand, trying to break up a fight. He had recently decided to return to work: That morning, in fact, he had registered at the Technical Career Institute, and afterward, he was walking down to Washington Square.

On the stand, Febee was neither vengeful nor spiteful. "I started running toward the ramp," he said. "I ran into two other kids, and passed one. Then I got hit." The "two other kids," Febee said, were Michael Doyle and Anthony Paolini. The defense would argue that he could not have identified the right men. But Febee had been trained to identify men. He spent five years as an MP in Bangkok—tracking down GIs who had gone AWOL. Each day, Febee would look at mug shots and scour the bars of Bangkok for American soldiers, until he got his man. He had made eight arrests that had led to eight convictions.

When the bats started to fly, he had gone to the plateau—the "best lighted" area in the park, and "the one with the clearest field of vision."

The defense argued that it was impossible: Febee "saw too much"—"one eye, 5 seconds, no way," Moscow would sum up the objections. Febee, they said, was framing the five men in order to gain a million dollars in a civil suit. "I suggest to you," Moscow countered, "that the mind is like a camera, better than any camera that has been built, that we are constantly taking in multiple, multiple images." "The film is retained," he said, "the memories were retained, but the lens was shattered."

| | | |

After nine weeks of testimony, the jury began its deliberations. Every so often, they sent out a note, requesting that testimony be read back, or a legal point clarified. At the end of each day, the judge ordered them sequestered for the night. On day 6 of deliberations, they filed into their seats after lunch and asked a final question on a point of law. Morgenthau took this as a good sign. Then at 3:32 P.M., the courtroom filled again, and Judge Haft took the bench.

As the forewoman stood to read the verdict, Moscow drew a deep breath. The prosecution had lost a quarter of their witnesses: Sixteen, even with warrants to bring them in as material witnesses, could not be found. As the forewoman, Ruby Wilson, spoke, eleven court officers stood together behind the defendants, a wall to shield the spectators. The gallery remained crowded with friends and family, but no longer were they alone in fearing the outcome. "It would have been awful if that September evening had gone unpunished," the columnist Murray Kempton (who'd observed much of the trial) wrote. "Now it seemed awful that it would not."

Six of the nine were found guilty.

Family members collapsed in one another's arms. The most severe penalties would fall on Sanchez, whose quarrel initiated the assaults, Chiappetti, who the prosecutor said had done the organizing, and Ronnie McLamb, who was said to have struck the worst of the blows. Three of the boys were set free, judged to have only tagged along. Rocco Areena, newly released, walked out of the courtroom well and moved to a front-row seat, throwing down the book he had been reading—a boxing history—loudly on the bench. Edward Burns heard "not guilty," leaned back, and exhaled. Tony Paolini was the last to be acquitted. As the three boys sat together, they neither whooped nor laughed—"they wore their innocence," Kempton noted, "almost as a kind of guilt."

Within days, the protests outside the courthouse would begin anew. The supporters carried new signs: "6 Out of 100"; "Moscow Is Not a Hero"; "Stop Anti-Italian Press Coverage." The Village politicians, too, returned to see the DA. Throughout it all, Morgenthau absorbed the criticism. Whether in public or private, he did not reveal any celebration, but the DA had already paid his young assistant his compliments: Moscow had faced a hostile and tight-lipped neighborhood, a vanishing pool of witnesses, and a contrarian judge—and he had salvaged the case.

||||

At noon on May 12, nearly two years after the bats flew, Judge Haft prepared to deliver the sentences to five of the six convicted. Haft took no joy in meting out the jail terms. Moscow had pushed for the maximum: "Sentences of imprisonment must be required," he said. "There appears to be a feeling among youths in the area that such attacks can be carried out with impunity."

One by one, the defense attorneys rose. "Nobody is happy when a person dies," said Chiappetti's counsel. "Nobody is happy when a person is maimed." But that was not the intent, they insisted. "This incident may have reflected a sense of frustration by people, in general. To select six individuals and make them the scapegoats for all the evil in New York is totally unfair."

Andriani was the only defendant to speak on his own behalf. "I'm innocent, I didn't do this," he said. "If I'm guilty of anything, I'm guilty of being stupid enough to follow."

The judge rose, poured himself a glass of water from a jug on the bench, and switched eyeglasses to read from the paper before him. His audience was not the defendants, but their supporters. "Some of the community—not the majority, I am sure—seek to excuse the defendants' actions. There can never be justification for vigilantes. . . . Those who claim this incident was not racial," Haft went on, "are totally naïve or don't wish to see the truth." "All who were struck were Black or Hispanic. . . . The sole reason that anyone was struck was the color of his skin." As he spoke, he wiped tears from his eyes. Others may have participated, but that "doesn't expiate" the guilt of the defendants. "They are not martyrs. They were part of a raging mob."

The judge said Chiappetti deserved "the severest sanction": four to twelve years in prison. Boutureira, the "most enthusiastic follower," would get three and a third to ten years, and McLamb, the same. Andriani, who "ran with the crowd," got a maximum of six years, while Doyle received four years.

The reprisals in prison, the families warned, would come. "Reception parties will be waiting on Rikers Island," one attorney predicted after the trial. Haft ordered special security precautions: Four of the defendants would be kept in protective custody apart from the prison population, and two others in a cell of their own. Boutureira, twenty years old, one of three facing years upstate, had been beaten by Black inmates shortly after his arrival at Rikers. "They'll all be killed before they've been in jail a year," said Chiappetti's sister.

In the emptied courtroom, after the spectators had filed out, Murray Kempton found the prosecutor. John Moscow's first words were about McLamb, the seventeen-year-old who, the columnist wrote, "must be the first Negro ever convicted for his part in the lynching of a Negro." "Did you know," said Moscow, "McLamb was born in prison?" His mother had been incarcerated, and "pregnant when she got there." The prosecutor was trying to lend context, to make sense of it. "Can you conceive of the hatred?" he asked. Yes, the reporter said. But he could also conceive of "the need to belong to *something*."

| | | |

That afternoon, as Judge Haft was preparing to deliver the sentences, Morgenthau lunched with the mayor.

The ugly saga, Morgenthau assured Koch, had come to a close. Not all would be happy—he could expect a backlash from the Italian associations, and the civic activists, from the Village to Harlem, would decry the verdict as flawed, but overall the outcome was good. The neighborhood's residents and its largest real estate holder, NYU, would be pleased. So, too, would Koch. The mayor had lived in the Village since the 1950s, and still slept most nights in a rent-controlled apartment just off Washington Square. Koch had never hidden his desire to get rid of the vagrants, junkies, and dealers. The police promised greater patrols, and the park, at last, might yet be cleaned up.

Soon the DA would move on, his attentions called elsewhere. There'd be a big arms-smuggling case—an escapade involving a New Jersey gunrunner, a rogue CIA agent, and foreign despots—that would lead him to chase the offenders to Europe, and beyond. There would be, too, a grim succession of headline murder cases. In what the tabloids dubbed "the Phantom of the Opera" case, in July 1980, with the Berlin Ballet in town and Nureyev dancing at the Metropolitan Opera House, during intermission a thirty-one-year-old violinist, Helen Hagnes, was sexually assaulted, bound, gagged, and thrown from the roof. (By summer's end, a young stagehand had been arrested, and confessed.)

Three months later came the thunderclap heard around the world, as just before eleven P.M. on December 8, 1980, a man stepped from the shadows at one of the city's finest addresses, pulled out a revolver, and shot John Lennon dead. Before Christmas, the DA faced the press throng to announce the indictment: He was charging Mark David Chapman, a former security guard from Honolulu, found at the scene holding the murder weapon, with murder in the second degree.

Morgenthau, though, displayed a distinct lack of interest in murder. Violent ends with their attendant forensics—fingerprints, blood, semen—held little allure. He liked cops; he respected their work, and relished their admiration. It wasn't just the mess of it, the muck, the broken bodies. Violence lacked mystery. There was something else: The last two years had been a steady churn of murder and riots, and he had managed to guide the office through it all, but his heart lay elsewhere. Above all,

Morgenthau yearned to return to his natural waters, the big sprawling investigations.

The Washington Square case, though, was something different: The case had so many pieces, a jigsaw puzzle of facts, factions, and blurred allegiances. The office had made mistakes, but the case had proven to be a useful test. He considered the undercurrents of the riot and its after-effects—racial enmities and neighborhood loyalties, police connivance and the drug trade, and civic pride masking a campaign of bigotry—and sensed they would all come back into play. In fact, he was sure of it.

For most New Yorkers, the case of the Washington Square riot would soon recede, an aberration of episodic violence that had been resolved, even as its root causes—racism and gang brutality—remained unaddressed. For the DA, though, it would stand in his memory for more than a decade, a bookend awaiting a twin: another night of mob violence in a city park.

63. "Failure After Failure"

1983–1989

Bob Morgenthau had refused to be a widower. He'd never wanted to be consigned to a life alone, and now he and Lucinda, despite the twenty-seven years between them, had defied all the expectations of disaster. They became more than companions; they became partners who shared an intimacy few understood. "I gave him political gossip," she would recall, "and he sniffed out stories for me." In fact, she did much more. She helped him stay young, and focused on the work ahead. Even in his fifties, he'd been plagued by a forgetfulness concerning the mundane details of life—it was less an absentmindedness than an obsessive fixation on pressing cases. One morning, he called Lucinda from the office: "My God," he told her, "I've come to work with one brown shoe and one black one. Can you bring me the other black one?"

Still, a silence had remained since the first days of their marriage. Bob never spoke of Martha, never shared stories about her, and never told Lucinda what it had been like to lose her. Martha, Lucinda had learned, was "forbidden territory." Early on, though, a month before her wedding, Lucinda had been rummaging around in the old Riverdale house when she discovered a letter Martha had left for her husband a month before she died. Its crux, as best as Lucinda could recall: "You will want a wife and you should have one. Then you finally have a complete marriage. She should be a nice woman, who is attentive to you. She should be someone who fills the house with people, your friends and neighbors, because you need people around you."

Martha had foreseen Bob's desires. Even at home, he would need to keep busy, to have the house full of people, and Lucinda had come to agree. She enjoyed as well, far more than Martha had, joining his social world—dinners with Mayor Koch, New York Yankees owner George Steinbrenner, real estate barons, the occasional movie star. If others continued to worry about the age chasm, Lucinda did not: "Bob became my island of calm and stability," she would say. "Marriage for me meant freedom." Lucinda had always wanted to write books, and the year before their wedding, she had quit the *Times* and become a freelance writer. But a new desire emerged. It was so sudden and strong, she would say, it took her—"a former radical feminist"—by surprise: She wanted more than anything to have a child. Pregnancy would not come easily, but in 1984, a son, Joshua, was born. Bob, at sixty-five, carried the baby everywhere, first in a sling, then a backpack. Her husband was enchanted. "Caesar," Lucinda would say, had "arrived."

"Our lives have been taken over by Joshua," Lucinda wrote in her diary that spring. "If I go out of the house, I come home in a panic desperate to see him. Bob works hard as usual, but part of his mind is devoted to making up stories and songs for the baby. He comes home early now to see the spectacle of his son winding up for his evening meal"—nursing. "Bob is amused. Delighted that Josh has inherited his big appetite. He holds him and sings, 'I am a pig, a very big pig, and I don't care who knows it. All I do is eat, eat, eat, 'cause I'm a barracuda.'"

The timelines of their lives, as Lucinda had known, would soon catch up with them. Josh had become a big toddler, and one day, Bob, as he'd often done, was carrying him on his back when he had to stop. "You'll have to take him," he said. "I'd been dreading those words," she would say. The decades between them were beginning to show: Bob was nearing seventy, and the demands of parenthood were wearing on him.

And yet Lucinda, despite her husband's age, wanted another child. She was determined to have a girl—and in the summer of 1990, Amy Elinor would come, adopted as a baby when her brother was six. "Bob was less physically active with our second child," Lucinda would say, "but he lavished his jokes, his songs, and his impish smile upon her."

On weekends, they'd still go up to the farm. In the first years together, they'd camped out in Henry and Ellie's house, "the Old Homestead." Little about the house had changed: The high-ceilinged rooms remained filled with the same overstuffed couches and dark-wood furniture, and its walls covered with the pastoral murals that had been hand-painted by WPA artists. In the closets upstairs, Henry Jr.'s suits and coats still hung, and in the basement, his wine cellar remained stocked. But in 1984, Bob and his brother and sister divided up the orchards and sold the house. Henry and Joan had conceded to what they'd long since considered inevitable: Bob would be the one to carry on the family farm. He would keep the heart of the old farm, 150 acres of orchards, as well as the tractors, cider press, apple graders, the red barns, and the ramshackle farm store. For years, the operation had been limping along; it rarely broke even.

Bob would face an annual battle to maintain the orchards, many of whose trees were as old as the New Deal. He'd convinced Lucinda to move to a far corner of the remnants of the orchards, across the road from his parents' house, and into what she referred to as a "dung-colored mobile home"—a trailer. She'd endured her pregnancy there, without air-conditioning, her husband admonishing her in summer to cool off in the "rubber ducky"—the inflatable pool he'd bought her. When Amy arrived, Lucinda lobbied, as she would say, "for a real house." Now with the second baby on her hip, she worked with contractors to install "touches that would remind Bob of the old house where he grew up"— wainscoting and bay windows that looked out on the apple trees.

The farm offered a safe haven, too, for all to gather together—for Bob to host his older children, Jenny, Anne, Bobby, and Barbara. Barbara, Bob and Martha's youngest, and still a teenager when her father remarried, had gone on to boarding school, and then to Amherst. She'd been in her second year at college when her father and stepmother arrived to announce that Lucinda was pregnant. Bob's youngest had reacted "accountably," Lucinda would remember, by "laughing." Her father, though, could foresee the trouble to come. A second marriage, Morgenthau would say, was hardly ever easy on children, and given Lucinda's youth (Morgenthau's new wife was a year younger than his oldest daughter), the challenges were sure to be even greater. "Things with the kids," he'd say, "would never go smoothly."

He tried to keep abreast of their doings—and their spouses. Bobby had married the summer before Josh was born, and Annie and Paul Grand had two teenaged children of their own. He made sure to have dinners, almost daily calls, and time together at the Vineyard in summer. And every October, they would all dine together to celebrate Martha's birthday. But the divide was firm: Jenny, Anne, Bobby, and Barbara, within years of their father remarrying, were calling themselves "the first family."

| | | |

While he tried to calm the waters at home, at work, too, the DA faced a time of troubles. In 1979, New York City had led the nation in violent crimes and muggings, with 82,572—on average, 226 a day. The murder rate had only skyrocketed, reaching historic highs: from 390 murders in 1960 to 1,117 in 1970, and to 1,787 in 1980—a 60 percent rise during a decade that saw the city's population fall by one million. Morgenthau had championed Robert McGuire, a former protégé in the U.S. attorney's office, to become Ed Koch's police commissioner. But McGuire had to contend with cutbacks and inertia. In 1980, the clearance rate for rape cases was 31.5 percent; for robbery, 13.8 percent; and for burglary, 6.5 percent.

The courts, meanwhile, were paralyzed. In 1978, in the Manhattan Criminal Court an average of 17 judges were assigned a total of 85,512 misdemeanor cases. Things were so bad that year the Criminal Court held only 164 trials—0.2 percent of its cases. By 1980, Criminal Court judges had to handle up to 120 cases a day, an average of one every four minutes. "Madness," Morgenthau called it at the time, adding that the Criminal Court had "in fact ceased to function as a court." The state of affairs at the state Supreme Court, where felony cases were heard, was no better. "The system works better than we have any right to expect," said one judge, Harold Rothwax, "but worse than can really be imagined."

Amid the grim landscape, Morgenthau faced another challenge.

That summer, at age sixty-six, he would be running for a fourth term, and it would prove a rare contest: "The one real race we had," Mike Cherkasky, a longtime top assistant, recalled. "The Boss considered getting less than 70 percent a race; most politicians don't." Until then, Morgenthau had had only token opposition, if any. But two recent cases, each among the most contentious and publicized in his career, had combined to open the door to a challenge.

Six months earlier, days before Christmas, a thirty-seven-year-old white resident of lower Manhattan, named Bernhard Goetz, shot four Black teens on the subway. The teens had approached him, asking for $5—"I have $5 for each of you," he was heard to say, pulling out a .38 caliber revolver and shooting the boys. Goetz claimed self-defense. After two rounds of grand jury investigations, four months of jury selection, and a three-month trial, Morgenthau had managed to win conviction on only a single charge: carrying an unlicensed gun. "I underestimated the anger," Morgenthau would say of the groundswell that supported Goetz. The "Subway Vigilante" had fled to New Hampshire, only to return to the city, in handcuffs, as a national folk hero, the New Yorker who finally stood up to the street violence plaguing the city. "Goetz-mania," as the tabloids called it, reigned; Mayor Koch announced he'd received 240 letters on the case, 237 in sympathy with the shooter.

Morgenthau had done his best to slow the rush to excuse Goetz, even leaking a confession to the press: Having fired four times at the boys, he'd stood over the body of one of them, and before firing again said, "You don't look so bad, here's another." Still, the popular support grew. The DA would hear it wherever he went: "Women," he'd recall, "lots of women, furious with me—but most of all, spewing hate on those Black kids."

At the same time, Morgenthau was confronted by an even greater backlash. It was another subway case, but this time the perpetrators were cops. In June 1985, as the DA prepared to run again, six transit police officers, all white, were due to stand trial, charged in the death of a twenty-five-year-old Black graffiti artist, Michael Stewart. Stewart, a former art student at Pratt, had been arrested for scrawling three-foot-high letters on a wall at the First Avenue station. He had tried to run, been beaten unconscious, fallen into a coma, and, after thirteen days, died. Initially, the cause of death was ruled "cardiac arrest," and only later was it amended to a "spinal-cord injury in the upper neck."

The Goetz and Stewart cases brought forth public outrage, led by but not limited to the Black communities of the city. It was more than enough to raise calls for a new man in the DA's seat. C. Vernon Mason, a Harlem attorney, the thirty-seven-year-old co-counsel to one of Goetz's victims, rose to the challenge—turning the three-month race into a referendum on Morgenthau's tenure. The DA took the measure of his ten years in office, and ran as a man of law and order: "There are 53,000 people who may not be voting for me," he said, "not because I have not done my job but because I have done it so well." He was referring, he told voters, to the number of convicted felons that his office had prosecuted. He took pride in the record: He had convicted 52,831 felons, and indicted more than 150 public officials and 50 police officers. By primary day, Mason would do better than the rest—getting 32 percent of the vote—but still fall short.

Morgenthau was chastened. "It shook him," an aide to Governor Mario Cuomo said at the time. "He's always seen himself as this bastion of progressivism and suddenly here were Blacks kicking the shit out of him." More than his pride, or ego, he worried about morale and, for the first time since taking office, the state of the city. The tenuous peace that had held since the Washington Square case was gone. The neighborhood activists and community leaders had never declared a truce, but now across the city, their most volatile factions threatened an uncivil war. Morgenthau knew he had repair work to do—and little time. In November, after a trial that dominated the news for five months, each of the officers in the Stewart case won acquittal.

| | | |

When the transit cops walked, Morgenthau faced the expected consequences: the bad press and the protests of civic leaders. Even as he weathered the storm, he could not ignore the need for change. Soon he would build up the in-house investigations division, winning a fierce bureaucratic battle to hire retired detectives who answered to the DA, not the NYPD. He would set up, as well, a unit to fight police corruption, and before long, another devoted to the twin categories of crime that had long gone underreported and under-prosecuted: domestic violence and child abuse. At the same time, he looked to upper Manhattan, and sought to curb the rise of crime among the residents of Washington Heights, Inwood, and Harlem. He would open a DA's branch on 125th Street, an office that would find scant success; few citizens knew of it, fewer still came in to report crimes. He'd grown sensitive, too, to the rise in bias crime, seeking out leaders of the emergent gay and lesbian communities, realms where law enforcement had long been derided. (He lunched regularly with Ermanno Stingo, an openly gay activist who wore a pink triangle to sit in court, monitoring cases of anti-gay and -lesbian violence.) Yet above all, Morgenthau was looking to reenergize the office, give it new direction, and he needed "an engine."

He also had to contend with a newcomer to the world of New York law enforcement. In 1983, a reedy Italian-American prosecutor from East Flatbush had become the U.S. attorney for the Southern District of New York, setting up shop three blocks from the DA's office, in Morgenthau's old post. In his first two years on the job, Rudy Giuliani had racked up a string of successful Mafia prosecutions, stealing headlines and threatening to eclipse the DA. In the two decades since becoming Bobby Kennedy's federal warrior, Morgenthau had not seen such competition from another prosecutor. Giuliani's ambition, and his press savvy, threatened to encroach on his territory. "Rudy was out tearing up the town," a Morgenthau deputy would say, "while we were looking at our empty hands." In law enforcement and city politics, a fear began to spread: Had the district attorney lost his hunger for the big cases?

"I will not cede turf to anyone," the DA told Mike Cherkasky, his new chief of the Rackets bureau. And in defending his turf, Morgenthau would return to his prosecutorial roots—taking on organized crime again, but this time opening a new frontier: He would adapt an old legal theory—New York State's antitrust law, which dated to 1899—to pursue a new strategy. No longer would he throw the bad guys in jail for a few years, only to watch their proxies keep their seats warm until they got out. Now, he would attempt sweeping reforms, moving sector by sector in a series of cases in the years to come, to force the Mob out of entire industries.

Cherkasky arrived at the DA's office in 1978, the year of the riot trial, but he'd known "the Boss" since childhood. Morgenthau, he'd say, was *the* mentor in my life." Cherkasky grew up in Riverdale, went to Fieldston, the elite private school that the older Morgenthau children also attended. Annie had been Cherkasky's sister's best friend, and his mother one of Martha Morgenthau's closest friends. At age twelve, during Morgenthau's second run for governor, Cherkasky walked to school wearing Morgenthau buttons on his jacket. In 1985, he had done so again, running the DA's reelection campaign.

Public memory, Morgenthau reminded Cherkasky, was quick to fade. He'd not won a major victory in some time. Worse, the new federal prosecutor—he had taken to avoiding Giuliani's name—seemed intent on poaching on his territory: moving into narcotics, city corruption, and even, for a time, the Goetz case, before recognizing the dangers of a turf war. Giuliani had backed off, but Morgenthau was certain the respite would not last long.

In the months since his reelection, the DA had not rested. He took stock of the biggest pending cases, and discovered a gaping hole: investigations. Ironically, Morgenthau had neglected what had been his former strength as a federal prosecutor. "We'd had failure after failure," an assistant would say. "We just weren't making cases." The Rackets and Fraud bureaus were well-stocked—twenty-seven ADAs in all—but their lack of success had become a joke. As one assistant noted: "We used to laugh about them . . . the line was 'the Rackets bureau is a fraud and the Frauds bureau is a racket.' "

The humor did little to mask the trouble. To his lead assistants, it had become clear: Giuliani had become an unavoidable rival, and Morgenthau would have to go head-to-head with the U.S. attorney. In part, it was pure ego—a contest for the biggest cases between the city's top prosecutors. But for Giuliani, there was history underlying the rivalry: He had long looked up to Morgenthau. In the summer of 1968, Giuliani had clerked for a federal judge and been awed by the way Morgenthau ran the Southern District. "I saw him not as a model, but *the* model," he would say. He'd even tried for a job in Morgenthau's U.S. attorney's office. In 1977, he would try again—this time, hoping to become the DA's chief assistant. (Giuliani, then an official at the Department of Justice in D.C., soon faced unemployment.) He would later say that Morgenthau had begged him to bolster his team, but Giuliani's résumé, sent to the DA in January 1977, made clear his desire: "Any assistance you can render," read the cover letter, "would be greatly appreciated." The DA had never extended a job offer.

A decade later, Morgenthau had never ceded ground to another prosecutor, and he was not about to start. Especially given the stakes. Across New York, as Bobby Kennedy had once forewarned, the Five Families had come back from the prosecutions of the 1960s with a vengeance. The Gambino, Lucchese, Bonanno, Genovese, and Colombo organizations had returned like weeds, choking an entire range of industries in the city—from the construction of its tallest buildings to the carting of its trash—and spreading into New Jersey and Connecticut. By the mid-1980s, organized crime was said to reap more than a billion dollars a year from private business in the city—and Morgenthau was struggling to fight back.

To Cherkasky, the confluence of events—"the rise of Rudy" and the return of the Mob—meant one thing: "It was going to be a war."

||||

Morgenthau would begin by ordering a review of all racketeering cases across New York State. He was looking for the state of the art in Mob prosecutions, and to his surprise, Morgenthau discovered one agency was making headway. The State Organized Crime Task Force, OCTF, was the brainchild of Ron Goldstock, son of a Bronx liquor wholesaler, and a man Morgenthau loathed. "Lotta ego," the DA would say. "And even more trouble." Goldstock had been Frank Hogan's chief of Rackets when Morgenthau arrived in 1975. The two had clashed, and within months, Goldstock left. He spent the next five years in a variety of jobs (for a time in academia—at the Cornell Institute on Organized Crime, the first think tank on the Mafia in the United States—and then the federal government), before settling, in 1981, at the OCTF in White Plains.

In Mario Cuomo, Goldstock had found a governor eager to appear tough on crime, and on the Mafia in particular. With Cuomo's backing, Goldstock got not only tough but innovative: deploying the state version of RICO, the federal Racketeer Influenced and Corrupt Organizations Act, to fight the Mafia. Congress had passed RICO in 1970, but given its complexities, few prosecutors had used it to full strength—especially on the state level. Goldstock had tested the state law in a series of cases, found success, and, to Morgenthau's chagrin, made a name for himself. With Giuliani encroaching on his turf, the DA could not waste time. A single case would not suffice—he needed a campaign.

A new ethos took hold. "No more sitting and waiting for a tip," Morgenthau announced to his top assistants. "We're going to identify areas where New York City is being hit by corruption and we're going to investigate." He gave his Rackets chief carte blanche. "Go and create the best investigation group you can," he said. "Take anyone in the office, recruit anyone. We're going to play in this space."

Cherkasky dove in. He got a squad of NYPD investigators and filed for his first wiretaps. Morgenthau, as his assistant Dan Castleman would say, "was interested in *industry-wide* cases"—cases that threatened the lifeblood of the city. In the office, a new phrase—"the economic and social viability of New York City"—would become a Morgenthau mantra. "Garments, Construction, Carting," he told the assistants. "We're going to take the industries back, one by one."

In 1986, Morgenthau set up the Labor Racketeering Unit, a team of nearly thirty members—attorneys, investigators, accountants, analysts— that would focus on unions, politics, and organized crime. Then he proposed a plan of action: The assistants should study the union-dominated industries, plot the points ripe for corruption, and begin to dig. Labor Racketeering would move quickly, probing the unions that fed on city contracts and bringing more than a dozen cases in short order. Morgenthau would move sector by sector: In 1989, it was the plasterers; 1990, the Newspaper & Mail Deliverers' Union; 1992, the carpenters; and 1993, the plumbers and an array of other unions in the construction trades. "Morgenthau loved it," Rob Mass, the first head of the unit, would recall. "He relished being back in the game. And the office felt alive again."

| | | |

New York's garment district had always been a world within a world, an urban labyrinth of grand showrooms, narrow storefronts, and upper-story sweatshops. Morgenthau had seen it as a boy; he'd always enjoyed touring the district with his grandfather. They would walk the streets, Henry Sr. regaling him with stories of the old family emporiums: Ehrich Bros., Abraham & Straus, and, of course, Morgenthau Bros.

As U.S. attorney, Morgenthau had seen, too, the industry's extraordinary growth in the years after the war. By the 1960s, the garment center had expanded from a few square blocks to a maze of shops that ran from the Thirties into the Forties, along the spine of Seventh Avenue. In the following decade its sweatshops had expanded south, deep into the Chinatown tenements. On nearly every block, new immigrants toiled in the dark, airless lofts, bent low over machines to stitch together mountains of cloth. No one knew the precise figures, and few officials had conducted any thorough study, but by the 1980s, the best estimates held that at least 60,000 New Yorkers worked in the sweatshops, attempting to eke out a living with little pay and no legal protection. The district, so long cloaked in rags-to-riches nostalgia, was ruled by an unwritten code of behavior, and rules, that perpetuated one of the city's most inequitable economic environments.

Amid the rapid growth, and without reform, the production cycle remained as it had been for decades: Along Seventh Avenue, the manufacturers designed sample garments and cut fabric according to design; the "cutwork" (cut clothing material) and "trimmings" (buttons, belts, zippers, snaps, hooks, eyes) were then trucked south to Chinatown, where the bulk sewing was done; and in the journey's final leg, finished goods were trucked back to manufacturers or wholesalers. At every stage, with a premium on timeliness, no manufacturer could survive without a trucking company to move the product. And the Five Families either owned or controlled the companies.

Since the 1930s, organized crime had forced an unseen, and illegal, confederacy among the unions in the garment industry—controlling the Master Truckmen of America, the International Ladies Garment Workers Union Local 102, and the Greater Blouse, Skirt and Undergarment

Association. In the postwar years, garment industry leaders, eager to fend off Communist encroachment into the unions—real or perceived—embraced the racketeers. In the 1960s, Morgenthau had made inroads into the industry, but stopped short of an all-out investigation; the Bonanno, Genovese, Lucchese, and Colombo families—those most heavily involved in the narcotics trade—had preoccupied his time. In the years since, the families' trucking companies had only dug in deeper, divvying up the sweatshops. By the 1970s, each loft was "married" to a trucking company, and the truckers, in turn, were controlled by muscle.

"The garment district," the DA told his chief assistants, "let's take a closer look and see if we can't find a way in." The scope of the industry and the risk of failure, though, presented a challenge of a new order of magnitude; Cherkasky needed help. Years later, all would say there had been no favoritism. One name, they insisted, "just rose to the top."

||||

"Eliot Spitzer is a creation of Bob Morgenthau," Cherkasky would say. Spitzer, too, was a child of Riverdale. Morgenthau knew his parents well—Bernard Spitzer was a wealthy Manhattan developer best known for erecting a row of grim towers along the Upper West Side—but the DA did not know the son. After Harvard Law, Spitzer had clerked for a Morgenthau law school classmate, Judge Bob Sweet, before joining a white-shoe firm. At Paul, Weiss, he'd started on a low rung in Mergers and Acquisitions but soon distinguished himself—as a climber.

He apprenticed to Arthur Liman, one of Morgenthau's favorite protégés. In the years since leaving the U.S. attorney's office, Liman had become a powerhouse in securities law. Spitzer had not been at the firm a year when he walked into Liman's office and confessed discomfort. He loved constitutional law and debate, but money, he said, stirred no intellectual curiosity. Liman did not hesitate. "Go work for Robert Morgenthau," he said. Within a month, Spitzer was at the DA's office.

He arrived at the end of August 1986, just as Morgenthau was gearing up his new campaign on organized crime. Spitzer was assigned to Career Criminal—a plum post—and thrown into trial work. He had just turned twenty-seven, and had never tried a case. He started with "Rob-1," first-degree robberies that were Class B felonies. Colleagues were amused when Spitzer asked if he should move his "portfolio" into a blind trust to avoid any conflict of interest. "The cockiness," Cherkasky would say, "was huge."

Spitzer climbed fast. After less than a year in Career Criminal, he was called up to Rackets and put on an investigation into malfeasance in Albany, the state capital. Morgenthau had directed the unit to look into an old upstate trick, using the public payroll to run political campaigns. For the first time Spitzer would witness what he would later term "the classic Morgenthau—this combo of intuition, single-mindedness and fearlessness." The trail would lead to a number of top Democrats. When Cherkasky and others informed the DA that some of the biggest names in the state party could be indicted, Morgenthau shrugged. "The law," he said, "goes where the law goes."

The new kid in Rackets had done well; it would not be long before Cherkasky walked in to extend an offer.

"We want to make a case against trucking companies, the garment industry," he said.

"Okay, what's the case?" Spitzer asked.

"That's the job: You figure it out."

||||

The investigation would have no precedent. Spitzer was a lowly junior assistant DA, but Cherkasky, his former supervisor, would say Morgenthau saw the potential—"not only the big brain, but the even bigger ambition."

Spitzer would devote the next four years to the investigation that would come to define his tenure at the DA's office—and open up a whole new field of opportunity for Morgenthau. It was not even a case at first, but "an *idea*," Spitzer would say, a theory built "on a premise that . . . the organized crime families collectively controlled trucking and the garment district. So the first question became, 'Is it true?' If it's true, how do you prove it? What harm flows from it? How do they enforce it? At first, it was nothing more than that." Initially, the garment center investigation was just one of many that Rackets pursued. "The case wasn't considered anything special," Spitzer recalled. "But for me, it was my life."

By January 1988, they found their targets: Joseph and Thomas Gambino, sons of Carlo Gambino, one of the more enduring patriarchs of the Five Families. Tommy, at age sixty, and nearly seven years older than his brother Joe, professed to be a businessman. Morgenthau, though, had long seen his name near the top of a chart in the DA's office, a schematic that matched up surveillance photographs with surnames in an attempt to map the twenty-one captains of the Gambino organized crime group.

The FBI now deemed their "family" the largest and most powerful in the country, but the Gambino brothers were no longer the organization's most notorious members: John Gotti claimed that honor.

The forty-seven-year-old Gotti could strut before the cameras and roam about town with impunity, or so it seemed. Tommy and Joe shunned nightclubs and newsmen, and spoke in measured terms, but they were the earners: They controlled at least a dozen trucking concerns that by the mid-1980s grossed upwards of $10 million a year. If Gotti and his adjutants relied on the more traditional pursuits of Mafia enforcers—arm-twisting, knee-capping, murder—Tommy and Joe had never been accused of violence. Joe had never even been arrested.

Yet as Spitzer wrote in a memo to Cherkasky, an extensive "foundation of information" existed on the family's domination of the garment center. Working out of a narrow office, a converted elevator shaft, Spitzer amassed a tower of paperwork, the remains of old—and failed—investigations. What he found amazed him: "Despite the fact that 'everybody knows' that the Mob controls the industry," Spitzer wrote, "there have been no cases brought against the primary figures and no real efforts to loosen the Mob's grip on a critical New York industry."

Spitzer took his case to the DA—who saw the obstacles, but also "the big idea."

"It was a cartel," Morgenthau would say. "Not always as orderly as the economists would describe, but a cartel that set prices and made sure no one stepped out of bounds." Such was the Mafia's dominance that conflicts hardly ever erupted in violence. Power relationships were enforced not with muscle, but with intimidation: Many of the Chinatown shop owners, new immigrants surviving on thin profit margins and wary of intrusive officials, had little choice but to bow to the unwritten rules. That the arrangement was criminal, and its scale enormous, Morgenthau could see. But the question arose: Could they prove it?

"Boss, let me try," said Spitzer. "If you give me enough time and resources, I'll give you a case."

| | | |

It began as a routine sting. A thirty-year-old Asian-American undercover police officer, Kim Lee, would pose as a gypsy trucker: "David Chan" of "Lock-Kee Transportation." Lee would drive an old truck (repainted with a fresh logo, and almost immediately blanketed with graffiti) around Chinatown. He would wear a wire and tour the sweatshops, attempting to solicit business. Within days, he gleaned that each shop worked with a "regular" trucking company—most often, Consolidated Carriers. One sweatshop owner explained the system of "double-billing," unknown outside of the industry. According to the terms of a long-standing "arrangement," even if an owner used his own truck or a gypsy trucker, he still had to pay his "regular" trucking company. Hearing the explanation, Lee feigned surprise: That meant the manufacturers are forced to pay twice?

"That's right," one owner said. "As you know, Gambino has a lot of power."

"Gambino?" asked Lee.

"Gambino's uh . . . whatever, the Mafia," the owner replied.

And the independent truckers? Lee wondered.

"They run into problems," the owner said. The trucking companies kept tabs on every sweatshop; they employed minders.

"What kind of people?" Lee asked.

"Company people."

As Lee made his way around Chinatown, the contours of the scheme emerged. The "marriage system," as the investigators called it, was maintained by "salesmen," company men who tracked which goods were moved where, and by whom. (The Gambinos, it appeared, favored the shops that their trucking companies were "married to.") Searching for a legal theory to make a case, Spitzer soon found it: "It's about freedom of choice," he told Cherkasky. The sweatshop owners could not choose the truckers. It was an antitrust case, Spitzer said. And the cost was clear: The Gambinos levied a "mob tax"—a cut the shop owners had to pay to organized crime to deliver the goods, whether they in fact did or not.

Spitzer sent a second undercover into the field. As "Chan" continued to visit the sweatshops, Angel Rivera, another police officer, worked the Consolidated freight terminal on Twenty-fourth Street near the Hudson River. This time, the undercover would be on the inside—working within the Gambino garment empire. Before Rivera could load cargo, he heard the rules from Joe Gambino himself in a hiring interview: No drugs and no stealing. If anyone got caught stealing, Rivera would quote Gambino as saying, "We don't call the police—we take care of it ourselves."

Still, even with two stings under way, the investigation stalled. "Nobody would talk," said Spitzer—neither the sweatshop owners nor the manufacturers. In part it was fear, and in part economics. Some may have conceded a "Mob tax" existed, but argued it was paid by every-body in the industry. "Nobody was at a competitive disadvantage," Spitzer would say of the early returns. He'd have to come up with some-thing stronger: something he could act on. "We just couldn't get what the Boss needed, the P.C."—probable cause.

In late 1988, Spitzer upped the ante: "We will need," he wrote in a new memo, "to control a sewing contractor being victimized by the Gambino family's extortionate scheme." With no contractor willing to cooperate or in a position to be forced, he argued, "I believe it is worth purchasing a sewing contractor in the garment district." He insisted on making the pitch in person.

In Morgenthau's office, Spitzer came to the point quickly—he wanted to set up a sweatshop. A state trooper had seen an ad in *El Diario:* A place had gone bankrupt, a loft near Chinatown. The price, he noted, was not cheap: $20,000. At that point, The Scowl—as Morgenthau's children and closest aides called it, the DA's favored expression of disap-proval, when he tightened eyes and curled his lips—began forming. But the young ADA went on: The prosecutors would not just own the sweat-shop, they would operate it. "We'll make real clothes, genuine schmattes," he explained. "The undercovers can run it, but we'll have to employ seamstresses."

The idea appealed to the DA's imagination. Spitzer had counted on it: Cloak-and-dagger operations, he knew, were a Morgenthau forte. "The Boss loved our stuff," a colleague in Rackets would say.

Just before Christmas, the DA gave his blessing. Cherkasky escorted Morgenthau over to the LRU, the Labor Racketeering Unit, a small of-fice set up across from the courthouse at Broadway and Leonard Street. With a boost from Albany, Morgenthau had recently gained funds to launch a strike force to target the construction industry. The LRU team comprised not only ADAs but DA squad detectives and eight forensic accountants, most of them retirees enjoying a career extension. The case was clearly beyond their purview, but as the LRU crew listened to Spitzer's pitch, they knew they had little choice. "We had jobs, they had careers," recalled Tony Carro, one of the accountants. "And they were always looking for the big case that would make hay, give a start to a political career." In the end, Spitzer won them over. "Eliot was Eliot," Carro would say.

Before giving the green light, Morgenthau made one revision. They could set up a sweatshop, but only if they froze out the NYPD. "The fewer people who know, the better," he said. Use the state police instead, he instructed. "Troopers who can do the intel, run surveillance, everything you'll need." At 100 Centre Street, the idea of state troopers running around the city raised eyebrows. Troopers could catch speeders and deer poachers, but organized crime families? "The FBI and NYPD used to make sophisticated cases," Roz Mauskopf, a senior assistant assigned to the case, would say, "but the New York State Police, a 3,000-man agency that patrols rural upstate New York, down in the city making one of the most innovative cases in years? Unheard of." Yet Morgenthau had tapped an investigative source with prowess, and one he would not have to share with either Rudy Giuliani or Ron Goldstock, the state organized crime prosecutor. Looking back on the choice, Mauskopf called it "visionary."

Dan Wiese had been a state trooper for nearly a decade. When in the spring of 1989, Morgenthau had arranged his reassignment to the LRU unit, he had never led an undercover investigation in the city. Morgenthau had asked Wiese to form a team—lock picks, wire men, investigators— eighteen men in all. Within weeks, Goldstock got wind of Morgenthau's move, and summoned Wiese and his men to White Plains. He gave the troopers his take on prosecution—there were two models: " 'the Model T,' which was Morgenthau, and 'the Ferrari,' which was him," Wiese recalled. "And once he'd finished explaining the differences, I stood and walked out."

By spring, Morgenthau's sweatshop was open for business. To a visitor, Chrystie Fashions resembled most any other of the hundreds of sweatshops in lower Manhattan: an open 1,500-square-foot shop crammed with sewing machines, on the ninth floor of an old building at 195 Chrystie Street on the Lower East Side. Inside, twenty-five women, nearly all Latina, bent low over their machines, sewing skirts and blue jeans, children's jeans and pleated skirts.

Ronnie Rivera had been writing tickets on Long Island when the call came from Morgenthau's office. The state trooper had also been moonlighting for years, as one of Wiese's men remembered, in the garment industry. Rivera had worked nights as a production manager at Monterey Beach Wear, a sweatshop on Thirty-fifth Street—as luck would have it, just above the Gambinos' office. To run Chrystie Fashions, he would grow his beard thick, braid his long hair into a ponytail, and recast himself as "Maximo Rivera"—a "Jewish Hispanic" sweatshop owner with an easy smile and big laugh. Rivera quickly became known in the neighborhood. He would begin each workday at 6:00 A.M. downtown at the LRU office, then change into a jacket and tie before heading to the shop. In the office, he wore a gray fedora and glasses—"little specs," he recalled, "to give an air of manager-smarts." The seamstresses called him "Max." A Gambino associate in the industry gave him another nickname: "the Spic-Jew-fuck."

The troopers had inserted a bug inside the phone jack of Rivera's telephone line and embedded a video camera in a wall of his office. Across the hall, rotating shifts of unseen troopers would keep vigil, listening and recording. The adjacent loft, conveniently vacant, was made to resemble a telephone repair office; Rivera hung a sign on the door: "U.I.S."—United Intercom Systems. Each day, as the building filled with Puerto Rican and Dominican workers, a handful of six-foot Caucasian "phone repairmen" rode the rickety elevator and disappeared behind the door across the hall.

The operation did not come cheaply. Every two weeks, Spitzer would return to the Boss with payment vouchers. The sweatshop had become a real business with a real payroll to meet—and, as Morgenthau had feared, a cash drain.

Everything from the working conditions to the wages had to be aboveboard. Morgenthau was less concerned with the workers' well-being than with burdening the prosecution to come. "No point sinking tens of thousands of dollars," he said, when he did not know how high the total would go, "to set a trap, if we're burned because you broke the law."

Running a legal shop, though, would prove a challenge; a sweatshop that treated its workers fairly would draw suspicion. "We had to pay 'em well," Rivera would say, "but we couldn't blow our cover." When the workers started to bring in friends, he had to tell them to keep their good fortune quiet.

It would be four months before Chrystie Fashions received their first visit from a Gambino representative. "We were hoping for somebody in the Consolidated operation to come in and tell us how things were run," said Carro. "And that's exactly what happened." One fall morning, Rivera greeted a middle-aged man with a graying mustache. Roger Kunka announced himself as a Consolidated "salesman," and offered a business card with an address on Thirty-fifth Street—the Gambinos' office. His "boss," Kunka said, was Joe Gambino, and Gambino was not pleased to see the shop had been using gypsy truckers. "We'd like you to go to the office," he added. "And say hello."

On Thirty-fifth Street, the younger Gambino brother was direct. "'These are our people,'" Rivera would recall Joe saying. "'You're in a Consolidated building, and anyone in a Consolidated building uses Consolidated trucks.'"

The message was clear. "Anything delivered in that tone," Rivera would say, "you don't need to tell me twice."

An opportunity to test the system was not long in coming. The Gambinos were not giving the sweatshop enough work, only crumbs. So they went to Baruch Rabinowitz, an Orthodox manufacturer in Brooklyn. Kim Lee, the undercover officer working as gypsy trucker "Chan," would move Rabinowitz's goods, carrying cutwork to and from Chrystie Street.

One day in the spring of 1989, Kunka, the Gambino salesman, returned. Using one of the shop's tapped phones, he called Rabinowitz. "Hear me out," he told Rabinowitz. "We are the truckmen of this shop here. Okay?"

Rabinowitz called Rivera at once. He was shaken. "I know that they are connected with the Mafia," he said. "I don't want to start with them."

Days later, on April 12, 1989, a second Consolidated salesman, Sam Andrew, arrived at Chrystie Street unannounced and saw Lee headed for Brooklyn with a rack of goods. "Doesn't he know this is a Consolidated shop?" Andrew asked. Grandfatherly and balding, Andrew hardly fit the bill of a Mob henchman. (He was so soft-spoken, the troopers nicknamed him "Andrew the Marshmallow.") Yet to Rivera, his meaning was clear: He was muscling the gypsy trucker. The evidence, though, was not on videotape. The men were standing in the shop, and the video cameras were inside Rivera's office. Rivera coaxed the two men into his office, closed the door, and tried to get Andrew to repeat his threat.

"It would be much easier for you, much easier," Andrew told Lee, not to compete with the Gambinos, or any other company. When Lee left the office, Andrew added, "I'm trying to keep polite, and help the man out." But if he kept trying to circumvent the marriage system, he went on, consequences would follow.

"Maybe my guys won't do it," Andrew said. "But somebody will."

"Yeah," said Rivera.

"You know," Andrew continued, "I don't want to say he's gonna get his ass kicked, but he will. Sooner or later. One of the fucking truckers will take him apart, and he'll be spending the next six months in the fucking hospital. They'll break his legs."

| | | |

"We've got the P.C.," Spitzer nearly shouted. Extortion would be hard to prove in court, Morgenthau reasoned. But he listened to what the sting had gathered, and agreed: After fourteen months, they had the requisite evidence. They could get to work on a plan to wire the Gambinos' office. "Eliot was overjoyed," Wiese recalled. "He was bouncing off the walls. But I was wondering if we had a prayer of getting in there and out alive."

The turn meant shuttering the costly sweatshop. The only way to close up the operation and not draw suspicion, all agreed, would be to stage a public arrest: "Maximo" Rivera had to be dragged out in a take-down. On August 11, 1989, a dozen agents crashed through the door of the loft on Chrystie Street. Guns drawn, they searched the office and, in a visible flourish, discovered a bag of white powder (flour passing for cocaine) and a handgun in a desk drawer. The seamstresses grew hysterical. Seeing their boss hauled off in handcuffs, many cried. It had all gone according to plan, Rivera would say—"And we knew it'd get back to the Gambinos."

64. "To Change an Industry"

1989-1991

"You gotta figure a way to get a bug into their offices."

Dan Wiese, the state trooper on the receiving end of the request, foresaw the dilemma. "When Eliot first said it," Wiese would recall, "I went home and didn't sleep."

For months, Wiese and his men would clock the Gambinos' every move. Joe Gambino rose each day at five in the morning and headed for the Consolidated office. "This had been Joe's job—for decades," a friend of the Gambino brothers would say. "He'd answer the phones, deal with issues, deal with problems, hire people. It wasn't a charade. He was in that office every single workday, and often on weekends." Tommy, too, for much of the day, was at the headquarters on Thirty-fifth Street. "Tommy kept everything running on time," the family friend would say. "If these guys were in the city, chances are they're at their desks."

Morgenthau's investigators faced other hurdles. "Their headquarters were a fortress," the DA recalled. After hours, an alarm company came by the office every hour to check on the premises. Each time, they would lift the gate with a steel rod, and slip in signed notices attesting to the time they had been there. Wiese knew, though, that the electronics and locks presented the biggest problems. He had brought in Jack Breheny, a retired NYPD lock-picker, famed for bugging the Jaguar of "Ducks" Corallo, the mobster who fell in the Marcus case. In all, five people would be on the entry team: An alarm expert, a wire man (a former telephone company worker), and two detectives from Morgenthau's squad would join Breheny. First, they had to devise a way to get a look inside the office. Morgenthau pulled strings: Two of the DA's detectives would go in with two firemen on a routine "inspection." Second, they had to learn the configuration of the alarm system. To do so, they knocked out the phones, and intercepted the repair call to the telephone company. When the Gambinos called in the repair, Wiese sent in his own phone man.

On Halloween night 1989, the troopers staged the first attempt to enter the building. They would have to cut the padlocks off the roll-up doors, and cover their tracks. They bought identical locks, so that if they had to cut the existing locks off, they could replace them with new locks, and fill them with Krazy Glue. They would fill in all the locks on the block with the glue, as well. "That way, they'd think: 'Halloween, it's a prank,'" Wiese would explain. Breheny faced nine locks going in, four coming out—including several deadbolts that he had to re-pick in order to re-lock. On that first night, he got inside, only to discover a silent alarm and have to retreat.

Ten days later, on a Sunday night, the team returned. On Broadway, two Con Edison trucks blocked the entrance to the one-way street, a repair team feigning to fix a gas leak. Wiese had also sent a man across the street, to the Macy's flagship store. He told the managers that the police had learned of a drug deal that would take place at Florsheim's, and asked that Macy's redirect their video cameras to the store at the far end of the block. "I didn't want them filming our guy picking any locks," Wiese explained.

Thirty-fifth Street was deserted—two troopers had cleared it hours earlier, offering $20 bills to the homeless, and warning of an "inspection" —as a middle-aged man dressed in black shuffled along the sidewalk. Midway down the block he stopped, fished a flinty tool from a pocket, and bent low to get to work. A rolling steel gate, twelve feet across, covered the entrance to the Gambinos' office. The "potato locks," the fat padlocks anchoring either end of the gate, would demand time. When at last the gate went up, a car approached. Four men got out, and disappeared inside.

This time, the troopers managed to disable the alarm. They planned on being inside the office for forty minutes, but remained for nearly four hours. When they emerged, the sun was rising.

The plan had been to install a transceiver, but in midstream the troopers were forced to improvise, planting a Brady bug instead. "We got lucky," Wiese would say. "They had an old phone system that they'd upgraded, but like most people do, they'd left the old wires in the wall."

The wiretap specialist was able to run a wire from the Consolidated of-fice to the basement next door, and on south to 349 Broadway, the LRU office around the corner from the DA's.

Wiese and his men worked swiftly. Before they shifted the desks and removed the ceiling tiles, they took Polaroid photographs, marking where each item lay. The wire man had packed dozens of different col-ored wires, so as to duplicate the existing wiring. Throughout the night, Wiese stayed on the phone with Spitzer, giving updates to the prosecutor, who was in his apartment in the Corinthian, the East Side building his father had built. Spitzer's wife, Silda, was expecting; their first child was due within days. "So there was Eliot, an expecting father, at home and desperate for this thing to become real," Wiese would recall. "He was going nuts."

| | | |

Years later, Morgenthau would marvel at their fortune. "Bugs are never easy," he would say, "but this was a beaut." At 349 Broadway, they set up a wire room. From six in the morning to seven in the evening, the hours that the Gambinos and their associates were in the office, the troopers listened in. The DA's office made duplicates of the tapes, and assigned four analysts to pick out the voices. Wiese got an old cassette deck from a junkyard, installing it in the dashboard of his car for his commute. Each morning, he and Spitzer would compare notes. "We lis-tened and listened and listened," said Spitzer.

The tapes made it clear, Spitzer would argue, the Gambinos were run-ning a cartel, orchestrating control of the city's trucking industry.

Morgenthau filed for a search warrant and, after ninety days of listen-ing and recording, let the NYPD in on the operation: On January 30, 1990, the troopers and nearly a hundred officers moved in. Wiese and his men went to Thirty-fifth Street. The search at the Gambinos' headquar-ters yielded four truckloads of company files. They seized financial records from ten garment district trucking firms—seven controlled by the Gambinos, two others tied to the Lucchese crime family. And in the safe, they found—to the DA's amazement—statements relating to a money management account holding $75 million.

The raids also turned up a ledger kept by Roger Kunka, a tally of the system of double-billing, payments made even by those manufacturers who did not use Gambino trucks. Spitzer used the notebook to flip Kunka. Boxed in, both he and Sam Andrew, the soft-spoken would-be enforcer, became witnesses for the prosecution. Kunka at first was so dumbfounded—how did the prosecutors know so many details?—he thought his dentist had conspired with the DA, planting a bug in a filling.

And even after the raid, the investigators continued to listen. Morgenthau had made the call: Leave the bug live for a few more days at the Gambinos' office. Tommy and Joe would know about the search warrants, not the bug. "You never know," the DA told Spitzer. "It's always possible: These guys are talkers, maybe they'll keep talking."

After a week, as the troopers returned to Thirty-fifth Street to retrieve their Brady bug, Spitzer followed his characteristic flair for the dramatic. Three investigators went in. "Oh, not again," said Tommy Gambino. "What are you doing here now?" The troopers cut a hole in a ceiling tile, brought in a ladder, and pulled out the bug. Tommy's face went gray. "That look," Wiese would say, "was worth a year's pay." The Gambinos "knew they were done the minute we pulled that tile."

| | | |

Morgenthau's team had put together a fifty-five-count indictment. Tommy and Joe Gambino, two employees, and four of their trucking companies were charged with racketeering, under the state's Organized Crime Control Act, OCCA, and Tommy would be indicted as the mastermind of the conspiracy that imposed "a Mob tax" on every item of clothing manufactured in Manhattan. Morgenthau had also added a twist: "The common purpose of the defendants was to control the trucking of garments in the New York metropolitan area through extortion, coercion, and illegal agreements *in restraint of trade* [italics added] and thereby to reap the financial rewards of this criminal conduct." The Gambinos not only faced organized crime charges. By their allocation of customers and territory, the DA alleged, they had also violated the Donnelly Act, the state antitrust law—which was little known, was rarely used, and had never been applied to the Mafia.

If convicted, the Gambino brothers each faced sentences of twenty-five years to life.

The trial opened on February 4, 1992, at 111 Centre Street before Judge Thomas B. Galligan, son of Irish immigrants (his father tended bar) and a Navy veteran of the war in the Pacific, who at sixty-seven lived alone in the Bronx. Each morning, the Gambino brothers arrived ten minutes before the start of the proceedings, unaccompanied by wives or children. Dressed in double-breasted Armani suits, they climbed the stairs and, on entering the courtroom, approached the scrum of reporters awaiting their arrival. Joe never uttered a word, but Tommy would approach the first row. He would pause before the reporters and offer a "Good morning, gentlemen," one newsman remembered, "as if measuring our faces for future reference."

Spitzer's opening statement would last nearly three hours. "You will hear about tapes, and documents," the prosecutor said, as he paced from one corner of the jury box to the windowsill on the edge of the courtroom. "You will hear witnesses. You will learn more about the garment industry, probably, than you ever wanted to know." The case, he said, may seem inordinately complex—the mountain of evidence had filled eighty-eight boxes in the DA's office. But at heart, it was about common sense.

The legal theory demanded time to unpack, but he would work slowly, methodically, to unfurl the catalogue of alleged misdeeds.

"You can't manufacture anything in New York without trucks," Spitzer said. "If you control the trucks, you control the industry." He was attempting to keep it simple. "And they"—he pointed to the Gambino brothers sitting at the defense table—"control the trucks. And their partner is organized crime. They control what factories in the garment industry use what trucks, which destroys competition and destroys freedom to choose." The financial arrangement comprised many layers, but its consequence would be clear, he said, to a grammar school student: "a tax"—a hidden cost to the industry and anyone buying clothing made in New York City—"that flows through the pockets of Thomas Gambino and Joseph Gambino," the brothers "known in the industry as members of the Gambino crime family."

The crime, Spitzer said, came down to "a simple idea": "This case, ladies and gentlemen, is ultimately about a Mob tax, dollars, and the right to choose truckers, in exchange for enforcing an agreement which eliminates competition for the manufacturers."

Spitzer pointed to a large chart covered with lines drawn in four colors, a schematic that revealed how the Mob divvied up the sweatshops. All the "cutwork" and all the "trim" that entered New York's showrooms or department stores got there by way of the Gambino family trucks, he said, because they controlled the routes. "Most criminals," he went on, "don't wear suits. These defendants do. Don't let that fool you. These defendants are businessmen. You'll hear that and you'll see it. But these are businessmen with a powerful partner, organized crime. It wields an iron fist inside a velvet glove."

| | | |

Across the aisle sat seven defense attorneys, a team with a formidable résumé of success. Mike Rosen, representing the elder Gambino, launched the counterattack. Rosen's words came slowly, his voice deep and wide, redolent of Williamsburg, and his rakishly long silver hair combed behind the ears. A partner of Roy Cohn's for nearly two decades, Rosen knew how to draw in an audience. He began with three short sentences: "My name is Mike Rosen. I represent Tommy Gambino. And this is America."

Rosen had spent the better part of a year in preparation, jettisoning every other case in his practice. Addressing the jury for the first time, he scoffed at the "nasty names" the young prosecutor called the defendants. Tommy Gambino, Rosen said, "built his business the old-fashioned way." "Consolidated Carriers is like the oil which keeps the various components of the garment industry running smoothly." "The extortionists," Rosen said, his voice rising, "give contractors $10,000 loans. They find them loft space. They loan them racks and hampers. They give them work." The proof will show, he said, "they offer a service."

Yes, Rosen went on, the Gambinos are the sons of their father, and they socialize with other reputed Mafiosi. "Yes, Tommy Gambino is a friend of John Gotti," he offered. "They met. They talked. Frances and Tom Gambino are friends with Vicky and John Gotti." But they had done nothing "to be ashamed of."

Rosen stood as he ran down the list. "You will not find any baseball bats," he said. "You won't find any broken bodies." The Gambinos were businessmen, he repeated, now adopting the first-person plural: "We built our business the old-fashioned way: by putting in time, effort, and dedication."

Jerry Shargel, one of New York's most celebrated criminal-defense attorneys, stood next; he represented "Brother Joe," and would serve as lead attorney for the defense. Shargel and Morgenthau had a history, a string of high-profile cases. Two years earlier, Shargel had opposed Cherkasky in the DA's murder trial against Gotti, a case involving a contract hit on John O'Connor, the Carpenters' Union boss, that Morgenthau had lost, reinforcing the famed Gotti nickname, "the Teflon Don."

The DA's case, he told the jury, was "built on images and distorted facts." In a voice as thick with sarcasm as Rosen's, Shargel dismissed Chrystie Fashions, the DA's undercover sweatshop, as "a joke." Morgenthau's men, he said, had been so focused "on the prize," they had become "blinded, like with psychological cataracts."

Shargel turned to the defense table, bent low to pick up a cardboard sign.

"Mr. Spitzer . . . made mention of the fact as to who Joseph Gambino's father was, Tommy Gambino's father. . . . They told you about a man named Carlo Gambino, a man who died some fifteen years ago." He paused to hold aloft the sign, nearly three feet wide. The attorney raised it before the jurors. It read, in large black letters, "GAMBINO."

"This," Shargel said, "is what the case is all about." The DA, he said, could not have brought such a case against anyone else—his client's sole crime, he concluded, was that he'd been born a Gambino.

| | | |

The tabloids, as Morgenthau had expected, were distracted. The New York press corps and a good share of the world's was preoccupied with the other Mob trial under way across the bridge in Brooklyn. Each weekday since January 20, John Gotti had sat, growing ever more impatient, in an airless federal courtroom in the Eastern District of New York. Morgenthau had foreseen that the new Gotti case could influence the Gambino trial, but he had weighed the potential consequences and decided to proceed all the same.

The Gotti case, as the press was quick to point out, presented a study in contrast. If Gotti leapt at the chance to verbally assault his prosecutors, the Gambinos maintained a steadfast decorum. If Gotti arrived in court each morning from jail, the Gambinos went home every evening. If in Lower Manhattan, the jurors heard scant evidence of violence (a few threats, no acts), in Brooklyn, Sammy "the Bull" Gravano, Gotti's deputy and co-defendant, made a sudden, dramatic decision to turn coat, and testify against his former boss—spilling the unseemly details of nineteen murders. Morgenthau knew by the first week of the Gotti trial that he'd miscalculated: Rather than reinforcing the bloody ruthlessness of the Mafia, the daily headlines coming out from the federal court in Brooklyn threatened to make the Gambino trial seem a tepid white-collar affair. "A business case," as Mike Rosen called it.

By the second week of the Gambino trial, Morgenthau was worried. Spitzer was a force in the courtroom, but still green. In a long trial, Morgenthau would say, caution, not zeal, was at a premium. So the DA had assigned two assistants to help on the case: Rob Mass, who had assisted Cherkasky in the Gotti murder trial that the DA's office had lost, would second-seat Spitzer. In addition, Roz Mauskopf, a Morgenthau favorite, would "babysit," ensuring, as a colleague would say, "Eliot did not come off the rails."

Spitzer felt like he had a good case going. The prosecution's third witness would be Ronnie Rivera, the trooper who had run the sweatshop. His testimony was pivotal, and Mass would handle the direct. Rivera did his best to explain how the trucking companies controlled the market, retracing how he'd gone to AAA Garment Delivery, a trucking company not controlled by the Gambinos, to see if they would carry goods for Chrystie Fashions. The trucking executive had told him, no, they could not; Chrystie was a Consolidated shop. Once Rivera had left, the trucking official had called Joe Gambino to report the approach.

As Rivera recounted it, the jury heard the taped call. They also heard another call, one that carried the threat of violence. A Consolidated employee spoke of the harm that might befall "David Chan," the undercover police officer posing as a gypsy trucker: "He'll be spending the next six months in the fuckin' hospital."

On the stand, Rivera had seemed uncomfortable, but managed to get through the direct. He still had to face Shargel's cross-examination, and that is when Spitzer, and soon Morgenthau, realized things were in danger of falling apart.

"This is a tape case," Shargel told the jurors. No matter how elegant the DA's theory, the tapes were the heart of the case. The troopers had recorded nearly 60,000 conversations, but only a handful would be introduced as evidence. Rosen, however, had learned from previous cases: "You've got to listen to 'em all, closely, and more than once."

He and the Gambino brothers had studied every recording in the state troopers' oeuvre. "Tommy camped in my office for a year," Rosen would say, as they listened to "thousands of hours"—1,279 cassettes. They would sit, headphones on, throughout the long days, tethered to a little Panasonic machine—"a $10 drugstore job" that Rosen had borrowed from his daughter. As they listened, the attorneys wrote on index cards, notes on each tape. In time, they built a cross-index that Rosen called "the Beauty Pageant"—a list of conversations, coded by name of speaker, topic, and possibilities for rebuttal. "It was literally all we did for months," Rosen recalled.

As a result, Shargel, who parachuted in weeks before the trial, would enter court with far sharper tools than the prosecutors. "We knew every tape, and that really broke their confidence," he recalled. "Every day we would come into court with this huge stack of tapes and transcripts and they'd just sort of be eyeing them."

It was the Beauty Pageant that did in Ronnie Rivera. Years later, those who witnessed the decimation would recall it as "wrenching." It was, Shargel would say, "a peculiarly effective cross." Rivera seemed to grow confused under the questioning. "I just kept kicking the shit out of him, minute after minute, hour after hour."

Careful pretrial spade work also paid off for the Gambinos' defense on another note. On the Sunday night before the trial's start, Shargel had had an idea: He would check with the former owner of the DA's sweatshop. He got the telephone number of the woman who had sold the loft to the DA's office. "Those bastards never paid me!" she yelled. Rivera had given her half of the purchase price before they set up shop, but not, she said, the remainder. On the cross, Shargel put the question to Rivera: "And isn't it a fact, sir, that you never paid her the rest of the money? . . . You cheated Bolivia Cascante, didn't you sir?"

Years later, the defense attorney would still savor the moment. "Trial work is hard work, hard fucking work," Shargel would say. "But sometimes you have pearls of joy."

Spitzer tried to salvage Rivera's testimony, but fell short. "I debated putting Ronnie on," he would say. "He'd never testified in a major trial before, and to have your trial by fire be Jerry Shargel, with Tommy Gambino looking on, was not going to be fun."

Shargel had also committed Rivera's daily reports to memory, and spent hours correcting his testimony. "Look at your report of September 7, 1988 . . . Does that refresh your recollection? . . . Look at September 30th . . . One P.M., if you can't find it, Trooper Rivera." By the end, Rivera faltered. "How can I be accurate?" he pleaded. "There's too many details."

The defense had shredded much of the undercover's testimony. Spitzer knew, too, that the taped evidence posed a problem: The threats might have been recorded, but could be seen as sufficiently vague. After Rivera left the stand, Spitzer's demeanor shifted. The man Shargel had deemed arrogant, vicious, on a crusade—"a little Eliot Ness"—was now humbled.

The prosecution was about to begin the second half of its case, the organized crime part. The next scheduled witness was Larry McDonald, the retired state trooper who served as Morgenthau's chief organized crime investigator. McDonald's brief was to tie the case together: He had charted the family tree with Tommy and Joe and their father, Carlo, and was set to detail the historical and current ties among the Gambino organized crime family. But as McDonald prepped his presentation, something happened. It was unexpected, and sudden, and no one in the courtroom, had they been privy to the knowledge, would have believed it.

On the morning of Wednesday, February 19, Shargel and Spitzer both dropped their guards. Spitzer was fifteen years younger, and though he and Shargel had come from different worlds—Princeton and Harvard versus Rutgers and Brooklyn Law—they were in many respects twins. Both were cocksure and press-savvy, brimming with ambition and wound tight. Since the trial's start they had stood side by side, only a few feet between them. Yet Spitzer would not speak to Shargel, nor walk over to the defense table.

By the second week of trial, though, the two had found a square foot of common ground, the neutral zone between their respective tables. On occasion, during the breaks in the proceedings, one man would drift over, and for a moment, a truce would hold. The banter was brief, never more than a line or two. But it had become clear: Each had found something to admire in the other, each saw something of himself in the other. There would be room, each considered, should the need arise, to talk.

The occasion came on that Wednesday in mid-February, after the midday break. Larry McDonald was about to take the stand. Returning from lunch, Shargel and Rosen found Spitzer in the middle of the courtroom well, standing by the wall. The prosecutor approached, moving quicker than usual.

"Hey, guys," he said, "can I talk to you?"

65. "A New Endgame"

1992–2015

Morgenthau's team had arrived at the midpoint of their case. They had put on their antitrust witnesses and aired the videotapes—evidence, Spitzer and Mass had said, of the threats of violence. In the remaining weeks, they would hope to prove the organized crime charges. When Spitzer made the overture after lunch, Shargel had agreed to a chat. They went slowly, feigning candor to trade opinions as to where they thought the jury stood. The extortion charges were "a toss-up," Shargel said. Given the paucity of evidence, the jurors would likely side with the defense.

Spitzer knew Shargel was right. He went out on the limb first, uttering the word "disposition." "I'm surprised," Spitzer said, "somebody from your camp never broached it with us."

Shargel would say he heard it as "a joking question." "Mike," he said, turning to his co-counsel, Rosen, "you better come over and hear this!"

When Spitzer repeated the question, Shargel tossed back a joke: "Well," he said, "what if we plead to the antitrust with no jail?"

Spitzer did not consider the offer seriously. Still, the door had opened. After court that evening, Rosen discussed the idea with his client. Go ahead and talk, Tommy Gambino said, but any negotiations had to abide by one proviso: "No jail time. Not even a day."

Spitzer and Mass left court and rushed to Cherkasky. "You won't believe this," Spitzer blurted. "They're interested in a plea!"

"I'm not sure I *do* believe it," Cherkasky said, but he considered the options. "Eliot, do you really want this? Because if you do, we have to do it now." Spitzer was preparing to fax the defense a list of the "O.C.

witnesses"—the organized crime experts—set for the following week. Timing was of the essence, Cherkasky reasoned. He knew the next witnesses faced a tough sell, and the defense had not yet had an opportunity to do any damage to them. "We have to act quickly," he told Spitzer. "Because we will never, ever have this much leverage."

On the eighth floor, Morgenthau listened intently. For days, he had been receiving grim reports from the courtroom. "We knew we had them *legally* cold on the antitrust counts," Cherkasky would say. "But . . . our extortion case was very, very weak to begin with, and only getting worse at trial." A new concern rankled Morgenthau: a runaway jury—a jury that would heed neither the prosecutor nor the judge, and one that would be unlikely to convict on a technical antitrust violation. Still, he liked the chances: The DA weighed the odds of conviction on the extortion counts at "75 percent."

Morgenthau quizzed Spitzer on the witnesses to come. McDonald, the office O.C. expert, would also draw out Tommy's ties to Gotti. The prosecutors had the surveillance photographs enlarged and mounted on boards for the jury: Tommy and Gotti strolling near the Ravenite Social Club. Morgenthau considered the cases from the 1960s, the stream of Mafiosi he had dragged before the grand jury. He knew the lineage: Tommy and Joe, in their second-generation aspirations, would dread it, the DA said. The last thing the Gambino brothers wanted was "all that Cosa Nostra stuff to be aired in court. . . . Tommy Gambino had stood trial before. But he'd beat that one. Now here for the first time he was going to see himself depicted as a mobster in a courtroom. We didn't have a lot, but what little we had wasn't at all befitting the self-image he preferred."

To the defense, the opposite seemed true. Shargel was certain the Gambinos would be convicted on the antitrust counts, but he felt they were winning on all the other counts. Still, he sensed the risk. "What if running through the barbed wire, we got unlucky and got nailed on . . . three extortion counts? Then our clients faced the maximum, with some real serious jail time."

On February 20, the parties met behind closed doors. They also had to take Judge Galligan into account. Rosen needed no reminding: When it came to sentencing, Galligan was known for handing down the maximum. As Cherkasky and Spitzer conferred, they knew they held an ace. Within days, Sammy "the Bull" was due to testify in the John Gotti case in Brooklyn, helping to put Gotti in prison for the rest of his life. "Tommy

Gambino and his brother did not want to go to state prison, not even for a second," Cherkasky would say. "You're talking about two little sixty-year-old white men who did not like the idea of Attica."

That afternoon, after court, the prosecutors met the defense team in Cherkasky's office, adjacent to Morgenthau's, to set down conditions. For the Gambino brothers, avoiding jail time was non-negotiable. Any deal, the prosecutors countered, would have to bar Tommy and Joe from the garment center—for life.

They had to be "out, out, out of the industry," Spitzer said.

"No way," replied Rosen. "No can do!"

After nearly an hour, the terms emerged: Tommy and Joe could agree to a fine, even get out of the business. But they would not acknowledge threats of violence, extortion, or any Mafia involvement. From the first, Rosen made clear the Gambinos would never plead to extortion.

"Let's do this," Spitzer offered. "You have a talk with your clients, and I have a talk with Bob Morgenthau."

| | | |

The DA polled the assistants: Mass thought they had a chance, so did Mauskopf. Cherkasky again argued that the timing was on their side: They would never have greater bargaining power.

On Friday morning, Morgenthau met with Cherkasky for thirty minutes. His feet as always on the trestle's edge beneath the conference table, Morgenthau kept his eyes on the yellow legal pad in front of him. He did not touch the pencil. The words were coming together in a single phrase; he could see the finish line: It would be "a new endgame." The memories remained fresh: Tommy Lucchese, fleeing the grand jury room, disappearing into the men's room with his lawyer. Vincent Alo, cohort of Meyer Lansky and better known as "Jimmy Blue Eyes," invoking the Fifth 134 times. All the *capos* and *consigliere*s he had sent to jail, only to see new soldiers take their places. There would be heat, of course. The press would bark, the politicians carp. The defense bar, too, would hoot—never had a prosecutor agreed to such a thing. But he could take it.

The critics only needed a little help to figure it out. He would have to provide context, tools to understand the bargain, its simplicity and historic consequence. For all the noise, the office would obtain just what he had desired: The objective had always been to remove the Gambinos from the industry. To get the same relief that the plea would deliver would have demanded five years' work, at least, and it would have been costly. Now if the cards fell into place, if everyone checked their temper and Spitzer managed to stick to the script, he would arrive at the original goal and set a precedent. In one move, the DA would accomplish more than exacting punishment. He would "change an industry."

"Okay, no jail," Morgenthau said at last. "But we need two things: money and the lifetime ban." The Gambinos would have to agree to be barred from any trucking business in the garment district. They would have to sell every last truck in the city. "And there's got to be a victim fund," he said. The Gambinos would have to pay a fine—"a fat one"—to make good on the victims, the sweatshop owners who'd been forced to pay the Mob tax all these years.

Cherkasky returned to his office and called Spitzer. "Green light," he said, and hung up.

||||

On Sunday afternoon, Cherkasky was in Connecticut, coaching his eleven-year-old daughter's soccer team, when his beeper rang. It was Spitzer: "We're on." He raced to Manhattan in time to join nearly a dozen lawyers, both trial teams, in Morgenthau's office. The sun was setting as they took their places around the vast conference table. Jim Kindler and Dan Castleman, two of the DA's top assistants, joined Spitzer and Mass. Morgenthau, at dinner with Lucinda and his friends Steve and Marina Kaufman, would call in for updates.

Rosen reiterated the Gambinos' insistence: They would never plead to extortion. "And bear in mind," he added, "any talk of jail, and we'll continue with the trial."

It was dark outside when they started to talk money. Spitzer and Cherkasky tried to set the Gambinos' fine, first demanding $30 million, then $20 million. As they negotiated, the men could hear the bells of Trinity Church. When Cherkasky threw out a number—"How's $12 million?"—the defense agreed. It was late, nearly midnight, when Judd Burstein, a defense lawyer, and Spitzer sat at a computer to draft the agreement. At one point, Burstein pushed Spitzer aside. "I'm the better typist," he joked.

To ensure that the Gambinos adhered to the deal, Morgenthau would ask the judge to appoint an overseer, a neutral party mutually agreed upon, to manage the sale of the Gambino-related trucking companies. "We called it a 'Special Master,'" Castleman would say. "But it was essentially a monitorship—the first one we did." Morgenthau proposed Bob McGuire, his old friend and Koch's former police commissioner.

McGuire, who had returned to the private sector to run Kroll Associates, the investigation company, seemed a good candidate: He was cerebral, fair-minded, and no grandstander. Rosen and Shargel offered their own candidate: Elkan Abramowitz—a prominent defense attorney. Ironically, Abramowitz was another former Morgenthau assistant, friend, and law partner of the DA's son-in-law, Paul Grand, Anne Morgenthau's husband. In the end, they compromised: Abramowitz would serve as McGuire's deputy.

On February 26, Shargel entered Joe Gambino's plea: "guilty to Count 2." Five defense attorneys rose, one by one, to repeat the plea. Judge Galligan asked Tommy and Joe to give their consent.

"Your Honor," Tommy began, before the judge cut him off: "You'll have to speak loud enough for the reporter to hear you, the court reporter."

"Between 1982 and 1989," Tommy began again, "I agreed with certain other trucking companies . . . that we could not compete with each other for the trucking of garments to and from contractors located in Manhattan's Chinatown and elsewhere in the New York metropolitan area."

As Spitzer drafted the paperwork on the Special Master, Morgenthau worked the phones. "Will you back it?" he asked Ron Goldstock. The DA was concerned about the fallout, and as news of the deal spread, Morgenthau was coming under attack. "Yes, we gave up jail," he conceded. But the plea, Morgenthau said, would help save "a dying industry." The deal accomplished what his predecessors extending back to Dewey had not: an end to the Mob's stranglehold on the garment district. "This takes them out in one fell swoop," Morgenthau told the *Times*. Goldstock backed him up. "It's a terrific settlement," he said. "Certainly the public is better off with the garment industry taken from the hands of racketeers than with a person sent to prison."

And yet, a coda nearly upended the deal. In March, the Gambinos returned to court for sentencing. Judge Galligan, who took no pleasure in the plea, watched as his clerk handed the Gambinos a "green sheet," the document setting forth the standard conditions by which any defendant in New York County agrees to a conditional discharge.

"What the hell is this?" Tommy asked Rosen.

The single piece of green paper stated that "the undersigned" agreed to live "a law-abiding life," not to associate with known criminals, and not to visit establishments known to host criminal activity.

"There's no way my client's signing this thing," Rosen told the judge.

"Look at it from their point of view," Rosen would say later. "Morgenthau and his people considered them organized crime. This 'green sheet' was telling them who they could see and who they couldn't." To Tommy and Joe, the restrictions were insulting.

Spitzer had not seen it coming. He called Cherkasky. "Mike! You won't believe this," he said. "You gotta get down here. They won't sign the green sheet."

Judge Galligan's voice was laced with anger. "No one's ever walked out of my courtroom without signing a supervision," he said. But for the prosecutors, there was no going back; the Special Master had hired investigators. Within an hour, Cherkasky got the confirmation from Morgenthau: If the defendants did not wish to sign the sheet, the DA would not object.

Judge Galligan fumed. "Nobody leaves my courtroom without at the very least agreeing not to commit felonies or misdemeanors!" he demanded from the bench. "So even if they don't sign the sheet, they have to agree to that!"

Tommy and Joe did, and were pronounced free to go.

| | | |

The Gambino case would become a landmark, shaping much of Eliot Spitzer's career to come. He adopted Morgenthau's phrase—"to change an industry"—and the case would serve as his model for innovative law enforcement: the bold move that brought headlines and promised dramatic change, even as defendants walked. The case also fed, as one Spitzer biographer would note, the prosecutor's growing hunger for the "adrenaline rush he got operating in the realm of cloak-and-dagger." Most significantly, the Gambinos had given him a platform for his ample political ambitions.

In the fall of 1992, Spitzer returned to the white-shoe world. He joined the elite firm of Skadden, Arps, Slate, Meagher & Flom. Within two years, he would resign to run for attorney general of New York. At thirty-five, as Spitzer launched his first campaign for public office, he sought the counsel, and financial backing, of his wealthy father, but he turned first, he would say, to "the Boss." He sought the Morgenthau blessing—and was refused. "Too early, Eliot," the DA warned. "Learn to bide your time. Pay a few dues."

In the 1994 primary, Spitzer spent $4.3 million—and was decimated. In a four-way race, he finished last.

|||

Bob McGuire made quick work of enforcing the Gambinos' withdrawal. In the summer of 1993, the Gambinos' interests were sold off to four trucking companies. McGuire would audit the books each quarter, and dole out $3 million of the Gambinos' fine in compensation to the victims overcharged.

By 1995, Morgenthau could speak of "new competition." Three years into McGuire's monitorship, the *Times* heralded the success on the front page: Manufacturers reported shipping costs had dropped, as dozens of new trucking companies entered the market. "For the first time in decades," said McGuire, "customers are shopping for truckers." Retail prices, too, had fallen. And McGuire's work would yield still more indictments: A dozen others would be charged, including Joseph "Little Joe" DeFede, acting boss of the Lucchese family. By 1999, more than seventy-five independent trucking firms were working in the garment industry.

Morgenthau had observed Mafia men, the bosses and their soldiers, for nearly forty years. Tommy and Joe Gambino had stood out. On the tapes, they could be heard lamenting the family business and its travails: "The Life," they called it. Joe enjoyed little more than cooking—it was reported he made pastries on weekends for a Brooklyn restaurant. Tommy, the DA would say, reminded him of Michael Corleone, the youngest son in the *Godfather* trilogy. "Tommy was the smart one," Morgenthau would say. "He enjoyed culture." He went to Carnegie Hall. He dined at the Columbus Club on Fifth Avenue, a prominent stage for the city's notable Italian-Americans. "He wanted something better for his kids. He wanted out."

In time Tommy and Joe would "retire," and Dynamic—the interstate trucking company the settlement deal had allowed them to keep—would become the leading interstate trucking company in the United States. Tommy's son, Thomas Jr., would serve as an executive at Dynamic. Tommy Sr. doted on his grandchildren, attended galas as a philanthropist. In 1991, Tommy and Joe had established the Gambino Medical and Science Foundation, and they would donate at least $2.5 million to a pediatric hospital on Long Island, opening the state's first bone marrow transplant unit for children. Dynamic, too, had a tradition of giving. In 2015, at an annual fashion industry gala, the trucking giant, now with a division in China, donated $25,000 to the UJA Federation of New York.

It was like every generational transformation, Morgenthau would say. Lucchese, Bonanno, and even poor Joe Valachi had not managed to get there. But the Gambinos, and so many of the men who once ruled the Five Families, would. The DA liked to trace the evolution. Every ethnicity had indulged in organized crime at one point in its passage into American history. It may not be the old men of the Cosa Nostra, Morgenthau predicted, but one day their heirs would go "full white-collar." And then, the conversion complete, they would face the same troubles with the law "as anyone else who tried to cut corners to make a buck."

"Did we succeed?" Spitzer would later ask. The undercover operation, he was certain, had done its job. "We managed to push the system and trigger a response, because the system in steady state doesn't need to manifest what it's doing. But you push it, you get a response that is the evidence of what the system is—a monopoly enforced by threats of violence." The Gambino case, he would add, was "a premonition" of what he would try to do with Wall Street, and "what Morgenthau tried to do in terms of systemic change." Looking back, Spitzer would conclude, "I think at the fundamental level we did succeed. We broke a monopoly structure, created choice, and our theory was always, 'Look, these sweatshop owners will run their own trucking companies, other people will come in, and certainly there'll be price competition.'"

"The conclusion is so Morgenthau," Cherkasky would say. "We were only the disciples." "It was one of the things he preached: Putting people in jail is fine, but particularly in the white-collar area, you have to change the institutions that allow the corruption." Morgenthau made the calculation and accepted the risk. "He could take the heat for a longer-term view. He *always* had the long-term view. He was never caught up in 'today.' It was never: 'I need to have the headline today,' or 'I need to have the applause today.' When we settled the Gambino case, we knew we were going to get criticized for not putting someone in jail, but we were going to change the institution. That's what we were about: 'changing industries.'" Had Tommy and Joe just gone to jail, Cherkasky said, "there would've been people lined up from here to Bayonne" to replace them.

For Morgenthau, the case marked the first in a trilogy: In the absence of RICO, the federal anti-racketeering law, the DA would pursue "systemic cases" using state law. Morgenthau would tackle the core industries long suffering under Mafia control—the carpenters, construction, and carting sectors. These "industry-changing" cases, Roz Mauskopf would say, were an unseen cornerstone of "the Morgenthau legacy." The garment district case, contended Mauskopf, who would become a federal judge, revealed the DA's strongest suit. "We were trying to shoehorn these sophisticated notions of crime into archaic laws like larceny, 'scheme to defraud'—that had more to do with confidence games," she recalled. "Morgenthau was responsible for the localization of federal law, what had traditionally been exclusively the province of the federal government and the U.S. attorneys, because of statutes, money, and reach of jurisdiction." But beginning with the Gambino case, the DA would turn it all on its head: He approached the "industry-changing cases" as if from a federal perspective, Mauskopf would argue, investigating and prosecuting them in the same manner—and though he faced "more archaic laws, less resources, and limits to his jurisdiction," he'd make these cases "as successfully as any U.S. attorney."

66. "The Bank of Crooks and Criminals International"

1992-2019

Shortly after eleven in the morning on July 29, 1992, the rear door of the sprawling office on the eighth floor opened, and in walked the DA, leading a trail of nine men: his chief assistants and investigators, as well as a quartet of officials from the Justice Department and the Federal Reserve Board. In two days, Morgenthau would turn seventy-three. Reporters, photographers, and television crews crowded the office, the air heavy with his stale cigar smoke. "A New York County grand jury has returned two indictments," the DA announced, the basso deep as ever, but now muted and grave. The shutters clicked as he detailed the allegations, the "criminal conduct arising out of the operation" of the Bank of Credit and Commerce International—BCCI. Throughout its nineteen-year history, Morgenthau said, the bank had "operated as a corrupt criminal organization," one that "bribed central bankers, government officials, and others worldwide to gain power and money."

Six individuals were charged, but the reporters had turned out to hear the names of only two: Robert A. Altman and Clark M. Clifford. At eighty-five, Clifford reigned as Washington nobility, "elder statesman" of the Democratic Party, and one of the most respected men in the capital. Altman, his forty-five-year-old protégé, Washington-born and -bred, had risen as his law partner, and now stood as one of D.C.'s most ambitious super-lawyers.

Morgenthau detailed before the assembled press a few highlights of the global criminal enterprise:

—Twenty-one bribes paid to finance ministers, central bank regulators, and regional development officials in ten countries, ranging from Pakistan to Argentina.

—Four other BCCI executives, including the bank's charismatic founder, Agha Hasan Abedi, and his loyal cohort and successor, Swaleh Naqvi, were charged with fraud and bribery, and with operating a corrupt enterprise.

—Ghaith R. Pharaon, a Saudi financier with deep ties to the Saudi Groyal family, and Faisal Saud al-Fulaij, a Kuwaiti, were also accused of acting as front men for BCCI in its secret purchase of First American Bankshares, the banking group that had grown to become the largest in Washington, D.C., and two other U.S. banks.

At the heart of the case stood the allegation that the two Washington lawyer-bankers had defrauded regulators, federal and state, covering their tracks and enriching themselves over a fourteen-year period, as they did their utmost to ensure that BCCI's secret ownership of a prominent bank in the nation's capital remained secret. The charges were complex, involving a scheme to defraud the Federal Reserve and the New York State Banking Department into granting a license to operate a U.S. bank, as well as to engage in bribery, conspiracy, and false business filings. But it was the naming of Clifford that shocked the DA's audience. Even among Morgenthau's lead assistants, many were caught off guard. "Few of us," one would say, "could believe the Boss would go that far."

Morgenthau would pause as he delivered news of the indictment, as if he, too, was surprised by its magnitude. "One year ago today," he recalled, "we said that BCCI was the biggest bank fraud in world history. Now we know it is also one of the biggest criminal enterprises in world history."

Amid the cascade of questions, Morgenthau would concede ground. The evidence, he allowed, was often circumstantial. In some instances, his investigators found witnesses, but not documents—and in others, documents, but no witnesses. After forty-five minutes, he was done.

Would there be further indictments? a reporter shouted.

"You know better than to ask me that," he shot back.

Could the DA name names?

The investigation, he assured, was far from over.

Had elected officials been bought off?

"I'm not ruling out anybody."

| | | |

Since his final day as Manhattan's chief federal prosecutor, Morgenthau had missed them, the cases he called "the big ones": the sprawling securities investigations that might begin with a curious federal clerk or a footnote in an annual report, but would lead out of New York City, allowing him to make a stand against fraud and corruption, be it on Wall Street or in Washington, establish a legal precedent, and even on occasion win. The complex financial shenanigans of Louis Wolfson, Roy Cohn, Richard Nixon—among so many others—had held a singular allure. Like his father, Morgenthau loved little more than the hunt: to follow the money, and keep tracking it, until the trail laid bare the untoward political machinations he had suspected from the first. If along the way, he expanded his jurisdiction and enhanced his power, all the better. But the aim remained the same: to trust his instincts and root out the bad guys.

After seventeen years as district attorney, although Morgenthau had brought scores of financiers, bankers, traders, and brokers to book, he had yet to deliver a financial case to match the blockbusters of the 1960s. In July 1992, that changed: Decades later, BCCI would stand as the most ambitious and far-reaching investigation of his career—a journey into the netherworld of an international bank that at its peak had 417 branch offices in 73 countries. It had begun like any other banking case on his turf: "My jurisdiction," he was fond of saying, "is set by any dollar that crosses any bank in New York County."

To some, though, the BCCI case was another instance of prosecutorial overreach, and worse: a global labyrinth of financial legerdemain so complex—of double- and triple-dealing—no judge or jury could ever make sense of it. Morgenthau knew it wasn't going to be "duck soup," but from the first felt the need to "get digging." For years BCCI, as the millions it defrauded and anyone else watching the evening news would soon learn, had been known to the world's despots, drug lords, and even the director of the CIA by a nickname: the "Bank of Crooks and Criminals International."

The investigation, all agreed, had presented unique challenges: Morgenthau oversaw years of digging, including sixteen months of grand jury testimony—the minutes had run 10,000 pages. During that time he had antagonized officials not only in Washington but a good number in London, Luxembourg, and the Grand Caymans and across the Middle East. Even many of his own prosecutors had grown exasperated. Still, he barreled on. It had been, in characteristic fashion, a lonely stand—against Wall Street, the European banks and financial regulators, and ultimately, the highest officials at the Justice Department. Yet no one else, his supporters would say in the end, could have pulled it off. "In Morgenthau, you had a combination of integrity and experience," said Chuck Schumer, an ambitious congressman at the time. "You needed somebody who had both, and the experience to be able to smell before even the evidence was there, that there was something big here."

|||

The case had been brewing for three years when on that July day the DA gathered the press to drop his bombshell.

Clark Clifford had been a friend and advisor to every Democratic president since Truman, and several Republicans, as well. With his white hair, craggy face, and mellifluous voice—the honey thickened considerably since his youth in St. Louis—he seemed to eminence born. It was as if human biology and Washington politics had conspired to create a prototype of the presidential confidant. Clifford embodied the role of "lawyer-lobbyist"; he had almost single-handedly crafted it. Just recently, he had published his memoirs, a certain bestseller. But, instead of a victory lap, Clifford now faced charges of helping BCCI hide its illegal ownership of First American Bankshares and of bribe-taking—charges that carried a maximum penalty of eight years in prison and $80 million in fines. Altman, his younger partner, stood in greater trouble (for filing false reports, the DA charged, with the Federal Reserve Board and state banking authorities): a possible sentence of twenty years in jail.

To Clifford, Altman was more than the heir presumptive in his law firm. He was the son Clifford never had. Both men had served as executives of First American, BCCI's chief subsidiary in the United States: Clifford as chairman, and Altman as president. They had stood, the New York grand jury alleged, chief among the bribe-takers. In the bank's maze of illegal schemes, the DA said, Clifford and Altman had reaped tens of millions of dollars.

The investigation had been, as the DA would recall, "one helluva mess." He had never seen anything like it. Not Tammany Hall, not the Mafia, not the most ingenious of the stock swindles of the 1960s. "Nothing compared," he would say. "Nothing prepared me for what we'd see, and learn, in the end." But in a sense, the case, the most sprawling, laborious, preposterous, and contentious of his career, had been there all along, waiting for Morgenthau to find it. "BCCI was the essence of Bob," his good friend Pierre Leval would say. It was not just the chicanery and hubris, and the cloak-and-dagger. Compounded by complexity and enormity on almost every level—including the risk of overreach, for himself and the office—the case, recalled Leval, "almost seemed tailor-made."

Morgenthau years later would insist it had all been worth it. BCCI's paper trails of fraud, bribery, and money laundering—the practice of using banks and daisy-chain companies to hide the origins of ill-gotten cash—crisscrossed the globe. By the time Clifford and Altman were charged, the two elite Washington lawyers would take their place among a host of notorious rogues who had been BCCI clients. The names had filled the headlines—despots and terrorists, drug traffickers and arms dealers: Saddam Hussein, Ferdinand Marcos, General Manuel Antonio Noriega, Adnan Khashoggi, Abu Nidal and his Fatah Revolutionary Council, Pablo Escobar, and even Khun Sa, reputed lord of Burmese opium. Yet BCCI had not only invited criminals to launder illicit profits as depositors. It courted politicians and power brokers, West and East: Jimmy Carter, James Callaghan, Javier Pérez de Cuéllar, Deng Xiaoping, Henry Kissinger, Andrew Young, Jesse Jackson. Morgenthau could trace the lines in the shadows, too. The CIA had used BCCI to fund covert operations—not least the infamous Iran-Contra scheme. So, too, had the ISI, Pakistan's intelligence service. And the bank, it was said, had helped nurture Pakistan's drive to develop a nuclear weapon.

In BCCI's coffers sloshed millions from Persian Gulf royalty, central banks in Africa and Latin America, European aid organizations, and, as Morgenthau liked to remind his assistants, the savings of at least one million depositors from across the developing world. So varied and obscure were the bank's connections and customers, it would be no surprise when reports surfaced, thanks to a French intelligence brief, that it had also been used to shield the fortune of a young entrepreneur recently expelled from Saudi Arabia, Osama bin Laden.

To Morgenthau, BCCI represented the future: electronic cash, porous borders, geopolitical battles—Israelis with Arabs, the CIA with ISI, even a U.S.-Soviet proxy war. Amid it all, the regulators and auditors were at best incompetent. There was more: a cover-up, as Morgenthau had feared almost from the first, that extended to the highest levels of power in Washington, and beyond. Appearing before the Senate in May 1991, Morgenthau revealed his exasperation: "We are finding problems at every step of the way"—from BCCI's auditors (Price Waterhouse UK), its would-be, last-minute regulator (the Bank of England), and even the U.S. Justice Department.

The indictments of Clifford and Altman had come a year to the day after Morgenthau had brought the first charges against BCCI. On July 5, 1991, the bank—operating at the time with 19,000 employees and $22 billion in assets—was seized. Three weeks later, Morgenthau charged BCCI's founder and chief executive officer, Abedi and Naqvi, in "a $20-billion-dollar fraud" to "defraud its depositors." It was a feat, he said, that required skill, chicanery, and abettors on each continent. But from beginning to end, from the bank's registration in Luxembourg to its infiltration of the U.S. banking system, it had relied on a group of ultra-rich Arab investors to play front men—the DA termed the ploy "rent-a-sheikh"—and to mask nothing less than the largest crime in financial history.

| | | |

The criminal investigation of BCCI had begun one afternoon in Florida, in 1987, when Bob "Musella"—an undercover Customs agent whose real name was Bob Mazur—had been driving a palm-tree-lined boulevard in Tampa when an outsized sign on a building caught his eye. "BCCI"—the large gold letters glittered from an upper window. At once, he pulled in. "It just screamed 'offshore,' " Mazur would recall.

Since the previous summer, agent Mazur had done his best to live the good life on Florida's Gulf Coast. Masquerading as "Musella," a man of obvious means and shadowy connections, he threw himself "into the circuit," and ran a tangle of enterprises: an air charter business, a jewelry-store chain, a mortgage company, and a financial consultancy. He had a long list of influential friends, a circle, it seemed, born of a powerful "family" in New York, relatives who ranged from Mafia enforcers to Wall Street operators.

"It was simple enough at first," he would recall. "I just had to play the game, keep up appearances." He wined and dined associates in strip clubs and penthouse suites, flew on private jets and the Concorde, and made sure to be seen, as often as possible, in his dollar-green Mercedes 500 SEL, the car of choice in late-1980s Tampa. Within months, Musella had become known as a player, with partners in Colombia, Panama, and the Caribbean in need of washing capital; the details of the trade remained obscure, but the goods were clear enough—coffee, weapons, and drugs.

In truth, Mazur was an Italian-American, not yet forty, who grew up on Staten Island hearing tales of how his grandfather drove trucks for Lucky Luciano. Mazur, who had long worked the front lines of the war on drugs, had won a new brief: "to find a way in," a back door to Colombia's cartels. In the first days of the undercover assignment, he'd been scouting the scene, "just meeting with all kinds of different folks," when, as he put it, "I stumbled on the Pakistanis." The men from places Mazur had never visited—Islamabad, Lahore, Peshawar—had come to Florida to grow a new "global Muslim bank."

He opened an account at BCCI; in time, he would move $14 million in narcotics proceeds from Colombia through the bank. In his meetings with the Pakistani bankers, "Musella" wore Italian suits and carried a buckskin briefcase. His suit jacket and briefcase hid recording devices, and as he secretly captured hundreds of conversations on microcassette, Mazur built Operation C-Chase—so named after the Caliber Chase Apartments, the Tampa condo complex where he'd launched the sting— into one of the most successful undercover operations in the annals of U.S. law enforcement.

Mazur had struck gold. For the cartels of Medellín and Cali, the late 1980s were a time of astonishing growth; top traffickers, reaping millions a *week,* were desperate to launder their profits. Unable to keep up with the flood of cash, the Colombians searched out safe havens. When Mazur first shook hands with his "Pakistani friends," the Latin Americans were already looking to the new cash-based centers of the Middle East: Abu Dhabi, Bahrain, Dubai, and Oman.

Amjad Awan, a smooth-talking executive in BCCI's Miami branch, was pleased to meet "Mr. Musella." From the first, Awan and his colleagues made little pretense. "It was all about deposits, they needed cash on hand," Mazur would say. At each juncture, lest there be doubt in a future courtroom, the agent was explicit: As the tape rolled, Mazur made clear his "clients" were Colombian, and his "service" was to obscure the origins of their drug-trade profits. After his first meeting with Awan, when Mazur called Laura Sherman, a fellow case agent, "she almost fell off her chair." "That guy is huge!" she said. Sherman, who had been working the federal investigation of General Manuel Noriega, the Panamanian leader, could not believe Mazur's luck. Awan, she said, was "one of the number one people of importance" in the Noriega probe.

Like so many at the top of the BCCI "family," Amjad Awan belonged to the Karachi elite. His father, Ayub Awan, had once headed the ISI,

Pakistan's intelligence service, and Amjad's marriage to the daughter of the man who had built Pakistan's air force, chaired the national airline, and led a political party only enhanced his prospects. By the 1980s, Awan had achieved the pinnacle for a Pakistani banker—a career in the West. He had worked for the Bank of Montreal before coming to the attention of BCCI.

It was Agha Hasan Abedi, the founder of BCCI and the revered dreamer at its helm, who had lured Awan from the Canadians, grooming him for a special task. Mazur could guess what it was: In Awan's Coconut Grove ranch-style house he'd seen a framed photograph of the banker with Noriega in dress whites, an inscribed memento of a visit with the general. Since the day Noriega opened his numbered accounts with BCCI—the secret coffers, the agent would learn, that the general used to hide millions and to pay out bribes in Panama—Awan had run them.

With good fortune, Mazur managed to infiltrate the bank, convincing the Pakistani bankers of his clientele and winning the trust of the Colombians. Within months, he was sending millions to BCCI and watching it ricochet around the world through its "family" of offices and affiliates. Mazur grew close to Awan and the banker's colleague and closest friend in Tampa, Akbar Bilgrami—the two BCCI representatives, both in their thirties, who oversaw the bank's strategy in Latin America.

To Mazur, the BCCI game plan was clear: Awan and Bilgrami had a mandate to expand, as fast as possible. Money laundering, Mazur came to realize, was no side deal by a few rogue officials. "Marketing dirty money and building 'relationships' with politicians—that was it," he would say. "For BCCI, there was nothing else." Abedi was determined to spread his "family" around the world. In each country, BCCI's chairman would seek out the power brokers and curry their favor. Abedi's list of "friends" was long and growing: Jimmy Carter, the Bush family, including George W. and Jeb Bush, and several of their associates, including William Casey, the CIA chief. The stated goal—the world's preeminent Muslim bank—seemed admirable.

The sting developed so fast that Mazur, and his superiors, could scarcely keep pace. He was soon introduced to BCCI's bankers in Central America. In Panama City, another Karachi expatriate schooled him in the latest laundering products: Luxembourg's numbered certificates of deposit. In Paris, Mazur was feted by Nazir Chinoy, BCCI's senior officer in Europe, a veteran of Bank of America and Citibank, who managed more than $1 billion in client funds. Wherever he went, the agent heard the same pitch: BCCI was happy to wash his would-be clients' drug profits. At the same time, he also had a host of cartel members, and their aiders and abettors, on the hook. Soon, Mazur would make his biggest move—hoping to place "a $100 million nest egg for Medellín" in the hands of BCCI.

But just as the end appeared in sight, the undercover agent sensed trouble—from his own superiors.

In the spring of 1988, as Mazur and his colleagues charted avenues to develop, their bosses at Customs in Washington had drawn a line: There would be no future cases. The sting would end in October. No explanation was offered, but the reasoning behind the cutoff soon became clear. Ronald Reagan had made the "War on Drugs" a cornerstone of his administration, and George H. W. Bush, his vice president, was now running to succeed him. A historic drug bust would be a publicity boon. It would also serve, Mazur was shocked to learn, his own boss at Customs. Should Bush win, Senator Jesse Helms told William von Raab, the Customs chief, Helms would push for the creation of a federal drug czar— and von Raab would occupy the throne. And so, as Mazur discovered, Washington had set the date for the denouement of C-Chase, and von Raab, eager for the limelight, cut a deal with NBC News to film it. Mazur was livid: Any leak, let alone on national television, could prove lethal to the undercover agents working the case.

||||

The takedown came on October 8, 1988, a Saturday. For months, Mazur and undercover agent Kathy Ertz had been seeding the ground. They had posed as a love-struck couple, as they wined and dined a string of BCCI courtiers, and by summer, they had announced their engagement. When Mazur and Ertz set the date, inviting each of their targets, nearly all accepted.

They flew in from Colombia, Panama, France, New York, and Miami. Customs and FBI agents posed as limousine drivers to ferry them to a resort outside Tampa. With the ballroom decorated and gifts piled high, the stage was set. A Medellín trafficker sent $20,000 worth of red Colombian roses; two BCCI officers from Paris gifted the couple a $40,000 Persian rug. The NBC cameramen posed as wedding videographers. For Mazur and Ertz, though, a problem emerged. Many of the bankers and traffickers had become so close to "Bob" and "Kathy," they brought their families. The agents refused to make the arrests in front of wives and children. So they improvised. On the eve of the wedding, the guests were invited to the groom's bachelor party atop a high-rise downtown, near the federal courthouse. Yet as the limousines pulled into the garage, the bankers and traffickers found no strippers. Instead, as each emerged, they were handcuffed.

By morning, European authorities raided the BCCI offices in London and Paris. Agents recovered truckloads of records, including a road map to Noriega's fortune. The Tampa and Miami offices, too, yielded a trove of paper. At the time, BCCI was the seventh-largest private bank in the world, with assets exceeding $20 billion. In all, the Tampa indictments would charge eighty-five individuals and four businesses—including the bank itself—with money laundering and narcotics trafficking. Five bankers, including Awan and Bilgrami, would be convicted in Tampa, two others in London, and by 1990, the bank had pled guilty to money laundering and agreed to pay a $15 million fine.

Mazur, though, knew there was more to the case. "I could have had the top guys," he would lament. "A meeting with Naqvi"—Abedi's successor—"was on the table." But his bosses at Customs, looking for a quick resolution, had put the clamps on. He remembered being chided at a February 10, 1988, law-enforcement conclave in Tampa. From across the region, investigators and officials had convened. His supervisor, new on the job and eager to climb the ranks, had almost screamed.

"Mazur, don't you worry about anything but the drug money," Bonni Tischler said. "Keep your nose out of everything else!"

"My sense was there's CIA accounts in this bank," Mazur would say. "And the powers that be in D.C. didn't want some little guy snooping around their business."

| | | | |

Morgenthau did not know much about the rumpled investigator, but what he did know was a fact generally held by the man's admirers and detractors alike: Jack Blum, an old Senate hand, was one of the keenest bloodhounds in Washington. Nothing about him seemed to fit the part. Blum was a large man with an unrushed air, who wore outsized black-framed glasses and baggy suits that had long since lost their creases. But as a generation of political reporters and congressional staffers knew, Blum was a man of stories, chronicles of deception and wrongdoing that he could deliver like a prewar radio bard, the singsong patter taking a listener out across the plains of corporate greed, through valleys of dimly lit contraband—drugs, arms, chattel—only to emerge in the pristine landscape of a governmental whitewash. Little animated Blum more than when the bad guys and the good guys joined forces to waste The People's money. In his office, amid the mountains of clutter, hung a poster of his favorite film, *Casablanca*.

Jack Blum had graduated from one of the best investigative schools in Washington history: the Senate Select Committee to Study Governmental Operations with Respect to Intelligence Activities, better known as "the Church Committee" for its chair, Idaho senator Frank Church. Until 1976, Blum had helped Church probe the illegal activities of U.S. corporations working with the CIA and other intelligence agencies. He'd done a stint in private practice, before Senator John Kerry, in 1986, coaxed him back to serve as special counsel on his Subcommittee on Terrorism, Narcotics, and International Operations. At forty-five, Kerry was a first-termer, a liberal Democrat who had come to Washington in the shadow of Senator Ted Kennedy and remained largely unknown. But Morgenthau had watched Kerry's rise. A former prosecutor and a decorated Vietnam veteran, Kerry had come to prominence as the telegenic leader of the veterans' antiwar movement. Morgenthau admired the record—a Navy lieutenant, Kerry commanded patrol boats in the Mekong Delta and was wounded three times. Even more, the DA remembered the courage that Kerry had exhibited when he returned home. In Washington, Kerry had won the chairmanship of the Senate subcommittee, and been given a mandate to probe the drug trade and money laundering in Central America. Kerry had homed in on Noriega, taking up the hunt with a vigor that gained notice. Here was a senator with a hunger for complex investigations and a relish for public shaming, qualities in demand ever since Watergate. On the Kerry subcommittee, Blum ran the Noriega investigation. Throughout the long hearings on Panama, he sat beside Kerry—and it had been his idea to invite the Manhattan DA back to the Senate to testify on offshore banking.

In Washington, Morgenthau was still seen as a Kennedy man, and the DA knew Kerry wished to curry favor: The former antiwar activist was at heart a Boston Brahmin eager for the Kennedy luster. Yet there was more behind his outreach to Morgenthau. "Kerry felt an affinity," an aide at the time would say. "He'd been a DA, too. He prided himself on putting away bad guys, and much of what he did first in the Senate—it came from that DA instinct." There was awe, too. "The Senator knew the name Morgenthau," another Kerry aide would say. "All that history, from party politics, the New Deal, the war, Watergate—it was magic." Their meeting proved mutually rewarding, with Kerry basking in the aura of the country's most prominent prosecutor, and the DA gaining a national platform for a favored cause, closing offshore loopholes.

It was in the midst of "that swamp," as Blum would call the two-year investigation into the Panamanian dictator, that he came across the shadowy Pakistani bank filled with Arab money. He had probed BCCI for more than a year, and made headway, but by 1989, Blum had grown exasperated. Roadblocks kept reappearing, whether from the work of Senate colleagues, federal agencies, or unseen actors in dark corners, he could never be sure. Worse still, the subcommittee's mandate was coming to an end, and in March, Blum's contract would be up. BCCI, with its trails of corruption that circled the globe, was too explosive to offer to the wrong hands. Blum was ready to give up when he remembered "something very important from my legal education: We have the federal and state levels." And on the state level, he would say, "I knew there was only one guy to go to. . . . I knew what the man stood for. . . . This was someone with fortitude, and if anyone in American law enforcement had it, enough power to carry this thing forward. If anyone got in the roadway, he was going to bulldoze on."

| | | |

On April 14, 1989, at just after eleven in the morning, the district attorney motioned Blum toward the conference table, to the far end unshingled with papers. Morgenthau sat in his usual chair, last on the left, and offered a Te Amo. Blum declined the cigar, but the DA lit his own. He sat beneath a framed copy of a Pat Oliphant cartoon, blown up to three feet wide. Published in newspapers across the country two years before Watergate, it depicted Morgenthau costumed as Sherlock Holmes, a bloodhound dragging him along a trail of footprints leading to the door of a Swiss bank—where Nixon barred his way, saying: "Ridiculous, Morgenthau—you're fired!"

Morgenthau had cleared an hour. Before him lay a yellow legal pad. He turned a page, and leaned back.

"This is not a simple case," Blum began, "it's the biggest bank fraud in the history of the world." He had not even been looking for it, he said, but the bank "kept cropping up." BCCI had been hiding in plain sight, ready for the taking, for years. Why no one had done so, he said, remained a mystery.

Blum began by reprising the tale of C-Chase and the rushed takedown in Tampa. The Customs case, he said, was only "the tip of the iceberg." BCCI was a vast international bank without a physical headquarters. He had found a few key officers of the bank. They feared for their lives, but had met with him, one in the last few days. The story was murky, but its contours sufficiently clear: BCCI was deep in the drug trade, money laundering was its corporate policy, and the bank had only survived by buying influence—protection from friends in high places—around the world.

Morgenthau needed no enticing. Everyone in the DA's office had heard the speech about "crime in the streets" and "crime in the suites." Its memorable line—"You can't prosecute upper Park Avenue [in Harlem] without prosecuting lower Park [Downtown], too"—had come from his father, one of the few inheritances he would admit to. Morgenthau needed no reminding of the endless "war on drugs." Since his time as a federal prosecutor, he had decried the turnstile arrests of small-time dealers. Few knew better the cost to the overburdened criminal justice system. His office now handled the highest caseload in the United States, more than 100,000 cases each year. Nearly a third of those carried narcotics charges. And the figures, the DA liked to remind politicians, masked the true toll. Drugs, more often than not, played a role in many other cases—murder, larceny, child abandonment. For years, he had tried to convince others to see the bigger picture: Narcotics was a market, Morgenthau would say, and the market's oxygen was money. Who controlled the money? The banks. "You can't stop the flow of drugs," Morgenthau liked to say, "without policing the banks."

As he listened to Blum, the DA interjected a question: "Is there evidence of laundering here in New York?"

"I wouldn't be sitting here otherwise," said Blum. BCCI owned First American Bankshares, he said, and First American owned First American Bank of New York—with forty-eight branches upstate and three offices in Manhattan, including a headquarters on . . . Park Avenue.

There was more. Clark Clifford and Robert Altman, Blum said, had helped BCCI's founder, Abedi, secure the bank's entry into the United States. The origins of the bank, and the Middle Eastern sources of its billions of dollars in assets, remained obscure. Yet the Washington lawyers had represented BCCI at a decisive Federal Reserve meeting, vouching for the foreign investors and assuring that they had no link to BCCI. There had been plenty of doubts, but the Fed had blessed the sale. Leads now abounded, Blum explained. A raft of lawsuits had yielded depositions, documents, witnesses. Worse, Clifford and Altman had also handled the Tampa cases—securing "special detention" for the BCCI players convicted, allowing them to live in condos, under private guard, paid for by the bank. Blum had tried and failed to move the investigation further in Washington. "My work's over," he said. "The bank's going to get away with it."

Mike Cherkasky listened to the tale "with skepticism." "Blum was a straight shooter, but he came in here telling a story like a lunatic on the subway." "Africa, England, the entire Middle East—they were all in on it, and then to boot, you had prime ministers, presidents, central banks conspiring as well. This crazy bank had bought and sold governments—it was impossible to believe." The office was deep in the Gambino investigation, and Cherkasky could not fathom how the Boss could even consider taking on another case so complex, and risky.

Yet Cherkasky would have no chance to speak. Even before Blum had left, Morgenthau yelled for Ida Van Lindt. She called down to the library and soon delivered a copy of *Moody's Bank Stock*. The DA was already leaning hard, but as he read the entry for First American Bankshares, he made his decision. The bank was not only a Washington bank. "I saw it was a wholly owned subsidiary of First American Corp. Holding, which was a Delaware corporation, that was a wholly owned subsidiary of Credit Commerce American Investment, which was incorporated in the Netherlands, and that was a wholly owned subsidiary of Credit & Commerce American Holdings, incorporated in Curaçao." He had not finished reading—the entry added, "These companies are controlled by a group of Mideast investors"—before saying to himself, "It looks like somebody's trying to hide something."

The press would raise a red flag and New Yorkers fume that their DA, at a time of unchecked violent crime, was merely wasting tax dollars. Morgenthau faced obvious questions of jurisdiction, too, but brushed them aside. "If New York is the banking center of the world and the money is laundered through here," he would say, "there is our jurisdiction. If the United States attorney is not doing it, I'm doing it."

67. "Either . . . Stupid or Venal"

1989–1992

Every August, Morgenthau would make the pilgrimage to Martha's Vineyard. He loved to sail; he had been aboard boats in the waters off Cape Cod since his earliest years. As a youth, he had soloed to Nomans Land, an island three miles off Martha's Vineyard, and at sixty-one, he had led Lucinda on a circumnavigation of New York State on his thirty-two-foot wooden fishing boat: up the Hudson, through the Erie Canal, across Lake Ontario to Canada, and back. (If Lucinda worried about making it back to the 23rd Street Pier in Manhattan, Bob did not: He'd navigated "1,100 miles, 60 locks, four canals, four lakes, three rivers and two countries," he said; "42nd Street in August will be easy.") After the sinking of the *Lansdale,* though, after treading water for hours in the dark and chilly Mediterranean on the night that forty-nine members of his crew had died, he was done with ocean swimming. On the Vineyard, he would rarely go in the water.

Josh, now a teenager in full form, loved little more. At summer's end in 1998, he was fourteen, and each morning he got up early eager to do one thing: ride the surf on his boogie board. Most mornings, he managed to convince his mother and sister Amy to join him at the beach. On Labor Day weekend, Barbara, Lucinda's youngest stepdaughter, came along. Josh was a good swimmer, but the surf could grow rough. When Barbara joined him in the water, a giant wave suddenly arose, swallowing her. Lucinda scanned the surf, relieved to see her head bob up, neck-deep in the water. Soon, though, Amy began "punching my arm, yelling at me," Lucinda would remember, "saying something about Josh."

Thrown by a strong wave, he had been slammed to the sand and seemed to be flailing on the shore.

"He's just clowning around," Lucinda thought at first, reassuring Amy. But they both ran to him.

"I feel funny," Josh told his mother. "Something hit me." Lucinda called an ambulance. In the emergency room at the island's hospital, they took X-rays and diagnosed a broken rib.

"Don't leave me," Josh said to Lucinda, almost whispering. His skin had turned a dull gray. It was a holiday weekend; the sole doctor in the hospital was in surgery. The nurses checked Josh's blood pressure. "He's fine," they said. "His vitals are normal."

Lucinda, though, sensed something deeply wrong. No sooner had the surgeon at last been convinced to see Josh—leaving an assistant to finish the procedure—than the boy's blood pressure plummeted. Within minutes, the doctor offered a new reading: "No broken rib. This boy's spleen is ruptured. Badly. He's losing blood as quickly as we can replace it." He had seen such cases before, survivors of car accidents.

Bob and Lucinda conferred, as panic set in. He called every doctor he knew in New York. Josh could be helicoptered off the island, taken to a larger hospital. "By the time you get him to Boston," the doctor said, "he'll be dead." He told them, "I have to go in there now or I can't save him."

Bob had closed his cellphone. "Go in," he said. "Operate."

"The spleen was cut right in two," the doctor said. There was no way to sew it together; they had removed it entirely. "We used every bag of his blood type"—replacing the boy's blood three or four times. "It's a miracle we had enough."

Weeks of convalescing would follow, and Josh would recover. His father did not speak of providence or fate. He preferred, as always, to credit "Lady Luck." It was another instance of rare fortune, Morgenthau would say, that the surgeon had been trained in trauma and recognized at once the gravity of the injury. "We could've lost Josh, right then. Again—just damn good luck."

| | | |

At the office, though, the DA rarely, if ever, admitted to believing in chance. When it came to Clark Clifford and Robert Altman, he was sure of it: They had known that BCCI was a scam, and right from the beginning, they'd known BCCI needed the American lawyers to mask their illegal acquisition of the D.C. bank.

"Stop at nothing," Morgenthau told his top assistants in the spring of 1989. *They had to have known.*"

The DA had never crossed paths with Clifford or Altman, but he disliked their breed. "It was the hubris," Morgenthau would say, the half-scowl forming. "The self-importance—the pomp." But personal distaste, he would insist, had nothing to do it. "Guys who go for the money, sooner or later, they get in trouble."

Clifford had led a charmed life. For decades, he'd enjoyed a perch in Washington that overlooked the White House: a corner office in Clifford & Warnke, the firm he founded with Paul Warnke, a former Pentagon official who would become a giant in the field of arms control. Clifford had been in Washington since July 1945, arriving just as Morgenthau's father was exiting. He was one of the original masters of the art that would come to be called "damage control." The ascendant John F. Kennedy hired him as his lawyer: Clifford handled property matters, tamped down the storm over the authorship of *Profiles in Courage,* and grew close to JFK and his wife. Not long after the 1960 election, Kennedy poked fun at his lawyer's ego. Clifford, he told an audience in Washington, did not want a job. "You can't do anything for me," Kennedy quoted him as saying. "But if you insist, the only thing I would ask is to have the name of my law firm printed on the back of the one-dollar bill."

The inside joke soon wore out. Clifford was no longer a "fixer," but one of Washington's "wise men." He was at Kennedy's side after the Bay of Pigs, and Johnson's as he searched for an exit from Vietnam. In 1966, along with Abe Fortas, he helped craft the State of the Union speech, and two years later, he succeeded Robert McNamara as secretary of defense. By 1969, although he served less than a year at the Pentagon, the reputation was sealed: Clifford was known, as James Reston put it, for "rescuing American Presidents from disaster."

At seventy-five, with most of his friends long ago retired, Clifford had found a new career. At First American Bankshares, he would be a working chairman. He'd brought along Altman, now a partner in Clifford & Warnke, and installed friends on the board: Stu Symington, the former Missouri senator, and two retired Army generals. Vowing to raise First American's profile, and spare no expense, Clifford asked his wife, Marny, to redecorate the bank headquarters in a patriotic hue, filling its rooms with Early American furniture and lining its walls with Currier and Ives prints—twenty-seven American presidents on horseback. Clifford toured each subsidiary bank and, Altman at his side, interviewed the staff. He oversaw construction and the new advertising campaign. He even appeared in one television commercial, becoming the face of the bank.

Clifford and Altman would insist it was never about the money. As chairman, Clifford said, he earned a nominal salary of $50,000 a year, less than chairmen at comparable banks. Altman said he took none. Yet from BCCI and First American they would collect more than $15 million in fees as the bank's lawyers. They had enjoyed, as well, hobnobbing with the Saudis and sheikhs—and grown close to Abedi and Naqvi, BCCI's founder and its CEO. In 1984, when Altman married Lynda Carter, the actress who played Wonder Woman, politicians and Hollywood stars had attended. So had Abedi—his wedding gift, a black Jaguar.

The more Morgenthau learned, the more his suspicion grew into certainty: Clifford and Altman could not have been so blind. But still the DA had no smoking gun, no unimpeachable evidence that Clifford and Altman had lied—that they'd not only known BCCI secretly owned First American, they'd been in on the takeover scheme from the start. Morgenthau convened a grand jury, sent out subpoenas to First American and BCCI in New York and Washington, and again gave his troops their rallying cry: "*They had to have known.*"

| | | |

The television news anchors would term BCCI "a Pakistani bank," but in fact its origins, and largest shareholders, were more deeply rooted in the petroleum-rich shores of the Arabian Peninsula.

Hasan Abedi was a born courtier, a conjurer of illusions. He had founded a bank, he said, that breathed "humility and dignity, beauty, love and creativity." BCCI conclaves featured marathon seances of Abedi-speak: pabulum that was part Werner Erhard, part L. Ron Hubbard. Yet his genius lay, two decades earlier, in winning the trust of a middle-aged sheikh, uneducated and unburdened by Western tastes, who lived in the vast desert that would come to be known—in large part thanks to his Pakistani advisor—as the United Arab Emirates. In 1966, Abedi had crossed the Arabian Sea in a two-seat airplane, carrying "an exquisite hand-knotted carpet" to embark on an audacious courtship. Abedi would offer a series of entreaties, not least escorting the sheikh on falconry hunts in the deserts of Punjab, where, as the enterprising banker in Karachi had learned, the Arabs' prized prey, the houbara bustard—long since hunted out on the Arabian Peninsula—remained abundant. By 1972, he'd managed to win over Sheikh Zayed, last of the four sons of Sheikh Sultan bin Zayed al-Nahayan. At fifty, the sheikh was oil-rich and wholly inexperienced in high finance; until the arrival of the Western prospectors, he'd counted his wealth in camels. Abedi's considerable efforts paid off, as Zayed entrusted him with his newfound fortune.

One good turn, for Abedi, had led to another. Abu Dhabi, largest of the tribal fiefs, then still known as the Trucial States, was home to only 160,000 souls, mostly Bedouins. For the enterprising Abedi, though, Sheikh Zayed could offer entrée to his neighbors. In the late 1960s, the Middle East was still emerging from colonialism. Gamal Abdel Nasser's dream of pan-Arab unity was fast vanishing, but in the wake of the Six Day War in 1967, King Faisal of Saudi Arabia had discovered a groundswell of solidarity among his neighbors, and in Zayed, a partner. As the sheikh turned to the House of Saud, his Pakistani banker followed.

In Jeddah, Abedi would befriend two prominent operators: Kamal Adham, founding chief of Saudi intelligence, and Ghaith Pharaon, whose father, a royal physician, had been a confidant of King Faisal, and who had sent his son to study in Europe, and then Stanford and Harvard. The terms of their alliance would never emerge, but Adham and Pharaon formed a compact with Abedi. Their first project would be the construction of a Hyatt Hotel in Jeddah. A partnership bloomed, one that would serve each man's disparate interests for decades to come.

From the start, the DA had known the investigation would stretch even his own expansive view of his jurisdiction. He would have to dispatch investigators to Pakistan, Abu Dhabi, and Saudi Arabia. The trips would bring rewards: Morgenthau's men ruffled feathers with the local authorities, the State Department, the FBI, and the CIA, but they returned with witnesses and documents connecting First American with BCCI.

Still, they needed a bigger break, Morgenthau said, an insider willing to step forward. He had a hunch: Someone still at work in the bank, someone high enough up, would come out of the shadows. And that someone, he suspected, would be found in London. New management had taken over BCCI's London headquarters, and mass layoffs followed. Among those let go, Morgenthau wagered, were senior people willing to talk.

| | | |

In the spring of 1989, Morgenthau oversaw 571 assistants. That summer he would hire John F. Kennedy, Jr.—another in the line of sons and daughters of the well-known (politicians and newsmen, in the main) to join the Morgenthau ranks. But John Moscow, whether he intended to or not, had made himself known.

"In the office, John was already larger than life," Steve Kaufman, one of the DA's closest confidants from the U.S. attorney years, would say. Few had forgotten his prosecution of the Washington Square riot, but at forty, Moscow had tried more cases than he could count. Outside the office, he had also earned an outsized reputation. "Zealous" and "obsessive" were the words colleagues often used to describe Moscow. And no one, they would add, better understood what animated Morgenthau: the big financial cases, the ones that started slow, and then built over months, even years.

Acting on Morgenthau's intuition, Moscow coaxed a reporter, Jonathan Beaty of *Time*, one of those on the hunt to reveal BCCI's secrets, into taking a trip to London: "It's a shame," the prosecutor said, "no one over there's willing to listen." He offered Beaty three names in England, knowing the reporter—notorious at the magazine for his expense account—could not resist. Beaty was soon on a plane.

Masihur Rahman was one of the names. He had known Abedi, the BCCI founder, since 1966. In the winter of 1990, at fifty-seven, he now feared for his family's safety. He had never intended to go into banking but had risen to become BCCI's chief financial officer. "Masi," as Moscow would call him, "gave us what we'd been digging for—and more." He was not yet thirty when, having trained as an accountant in England, he met Abedi—who at the time was only beginning his courtship of Sheikh Zayed—and had served at his side ever since. He'd married an American woman and lived in a suburb of London, but remained tethered to Abedi. Rahman referred to the bank's founder as "Agha Saheb"— invoking a term of respect reserved for a master or father. Abedi was less a boss than, as Rahman would say, intending it in the familial sense, "a kind of godfather."

In 1989, the Bank of England and the Luxembourg regulators had asked Price Waterhouse to review the bank's books—and BCCI, in response, had put Rahman in charge of triage. His research for the auditors soon led to panic: "I got to know many, many affairs of the bank," he recalled. "And this disturbed me very much, and because I was the professional in the bank and these were items which horrified me, I wanted to resign forthwith as soon as I finished my report."

The bank insisted Rahman stay on, even enlisting his wife to convince him, but on August 1, 1990, he quit. A campaign of intimidation followed—he and his wife got threatening calls. Scotland Yard offered patrols, and the local police installed an alarm, but Rahman could take no more. He was ready to talk.

In early 1991, he agreed to meet the *Time* reporter at Brown's Hotel in central London. They spoke for nearly five hours. It was midnight when Beaty challenged Rahman: Your story is intriguing, he said, but "too incredible to be put into print."

"I can show you," Rahman protested. "I have copies of all the audits in the trunk of my car!"

Outside in the dark of the street, he pulled "an armload of folders and papers" from a gray Mercedes. Flipping through the records, the reporters recognized immediately what they had. "There were scores" of loans, Beaty would write in a chronicle of the BCCI scandal, "hundreds, thousands of loans in staggering sums for which there had been no repayment for years." The "loans" had been cash outlays, and the documents offered proof: Abedi and his backers had used the bank as a private kitty—and BCCI's depositors, victims of the multibillion-dollar fraud, had been left in the dark.

"Mr. Rahman, you need more than *Time* magazine's help," Beaty said. "The only person I can think of who can give you the kind of protection you need is Robert Morgenthau. . . . Take the audits to him. You need a powerful protector."

Rahman made only one request: that Morgenthau bring his wife and children to the United States. The DA took care of it, cajoling officials at State and Justice.

Morgenthau's men weren't prepared for Rahman's trove: The Price Waterhouse audits revealed how BCCI—previously stymied in buying a U.S. bank openly—had acquired First American through a series of secret loans, totaling $854 million, to shareholders in CCAH—Credit and Commerce American Holdings, the holding company of First American. The sole collateral for the loans, moreover, was stock in CCAH. In all, the audits showed "misappropriated deposits" and "false loans"—used to cover losses—totaling more than $1 billion. Price Waterhouse had given the audits, Morgenthau and Moscow were unsurprised to learn, to the Bank of England months earlier. The DA had his smoking gun.

Morgenthau, though, had not spent the winter waiting idly. In November 1990, he used his knowledge of the Price Waterhouse audit to send out a new round of subpoenas and goad the Federal Reserve in Washington into action. In December, William Ryback, a Fed official, had flown to London to meet with BCCI's new managers, who refused to hand over the audits, but offered a peek at the October 3, 1990, summary. "Bill feels BCCI has been lying to us for years," wrote Tom McQueeney, who accompanied Ryback, in a December 1990 memo, "and he would like to have Clark Clifford and Robert Altman investigated for their role in withholding that vital information from us." Still, the Fed remained wary of Morgenthau. "Bill hasn't committed anything to writing on this," McQueeney added, "lest Mr. Moscow of the N.Y. DA office subpoena such records."

On January 4, 1991, the Fed at last opened a probe of BCCI's alleged control of First American, and referred a criminal investigation to the Justice Department. Soon *The Washington Post* published its first investigative story on BCCI—headline: "Who Controls First American Bankshares?"—and Clifford and Altman denied any wrongdoing. "There has been no participation, directly or indirectly, by BCCI," Clifford said. He insisted, as he'd told the Fed in 1981, that it had been only a "limited, arm's-length relationship." By March 4, though, the Fed at last took a stand, declaring BCCI had illegally acquired some 60 percent of First American through the hidden loans, and requiring that the bank sell its shares and exit the U.S. market.

Two weeks later, Clifford went on *60 Minutes* to decry a campaign of defamation. "If the Fed has been deceived," he told Mike Wallace, "if Mr. Morgenthau has been deceived, if the banking commissioner in New York has been deceived, I have been deceived." Days later, weighing his predicament, Clifford conceded the obvious: "I have a choice of either seeming stupid or venal."

| | | |

On Sunday morning, May 5, 1991, Paul Warnke, co-founder of Clifford & Warnke, had awoken at home but not yet come downstairs, when his wife went outside to collect *The Washington Post* from the front step.

"Jesus Christ," she yelled as she brought the paper inside, "you won't believe this."

A front-page story revealed Clifford and Altman's purchase of First American stock—and their subsequent sale of the shares at a $9.8 million profit. The lawyer-bankers had bought the stock in 1986 and 1987, the *Post* reported, with $18 million in loans from BCCI, and in 1988, they had sold 60 percent of their holdings for $32 million. Clifford had made a pretax profit of $6.5 million and Altman $3.3 million. The attorneys had sold the shares at three times the price they had paid, after eighteen months, and were left with debt-free ownership of a remaining 3,368 shares. BCCI, moreover, had delivered not only the stock but the buyer: a Lebanese merchant named Mohammed Hammoud, who borrowed the money to pay for the stock, putting up the shares as collateral. Rahman, the BCCI executive, would call Hammoud "one of our most flexible fronts." "The stock transactions," wrote the *Post* reporters, Jim McGee and Sharon Walsh, "are the first public indication that Clifford and Altman profited personally through their private dealings with BCCI."

Clifford might truly have believed, as he told his family and partners, that the storm would pass. But Warnke, the reserved disarmament negotiator who'd long since been surpassed in the firm that bore his name by the brash Altman, knew better. He turned to his wife and said, "The wheels are going to come off now."

||||

In the wake of the stock-deal revelations, Morgenthau's hunger increased. To him, the stock deal that so handsomely enriched Clifford and Altman was no more than a bribe. "That transaction told us everything," he would say. "It was lawyers getting their pockets lined." The news of the fat profits BCCI's lawyers had made spurred on the DA and his team. Others in the office might raise concerns—going after lawyers was always hazardous, going after an icon of the Democratic Party even more so. But Morgenthau, as his investigations chief, Mike Cherkasky, would say, "was not going to bend."

The opposition only mounted. The hints and nudges came from all corners, sometimes blatant, sometimes half-veiled. They could also be personal. At a Deerfield reunion, one of Morgenthau's old classmates, Jim Reed, told him to "lay off Clifford." Reed, who had been a close friend of JFK (he served on the same PT boat, and later became an assistant secretary of the Treasury), said Clifford's cousin had been a class-mate of theirs at Deerfield. "Let the old man be," he said.

In Washington, the forces were darker. The CIA, the DA had learned, knew a lot about BCCI. Jack Blum had heard first of the CIA's accounts, a financial back channel to the mujahideen fighting the Soviets in Afghanistan. Amjad Awan had been one of the officers handling those accounts, but the Agency had also resorted to BCCI in Iran-Contra. The CIA itself had heard that the bank was corrupt—"a terrorists' laundro-mat," one official said—and that it had long been eager to control an American bank. In January 1985, the Agency had sent its liaison at Treasury a warning, relaying a report that BCCI secretly owned a Washington bank. Douglas P. Mulholland, the former CIA official at Treasury who received the one-page report, recognized it as "dynamite," and took it at once to Donald Regan, the Treasury secretary. Mulholland asked the CIA for the name of the bank and learned it was First American. Regan paid no heed, but the warnings continued: James Baker, Regan's successor, received one in 1986, as did Nicholas Brady in 1989. Neither took action. At the CIA, the bank had become so notorious that in 1988, when von Raab, the Customs chief overseeing the Florida sting, called Robert Gates, the deputy head of the CIA, Gates told him that of course he knew about BCCI. At the Agency, Gates said, the bank was known by its "Crooks and Criminals International" moniker.

Morgenthau was incensed by the roadblocks. An assistant attorney general in the frauds section had called, asking what it would take to end the DA's investigation. Morgenthau could not understand the question: "Look, it's an important case—the bank was laundering drug money. We can't just turn our eyes. It's not just the fraud, it's about the drugs."

The official was undeterred: "Well, suppose we gave you a hundred narcotics cases, good ones?"

At the time, Morgenthau only felt it as a suspicion, but years later, it would harden into a belief: The DA had heard the government had formed an interagency task force on BCCI, working at the sub-cabinet level and comprising representatives from State, Defense, Treasury, and Justice. Their goal, he would say, was "to stop me."

Senator Kerry, too, felt the forces coalescing. "There were efforts to try to slow us down," he would say. In 1990, as criticism mounted of the plea deal in Florida, Senator Orrin Hatch came to BCCI's defense. The Republican Hatch called for a "proper perspective": The troubles, he said in a speech on the Senate floor, "arose from the conduct of a small number of B.C.C.I.'s more than 14,000 employees." (Hatch would come to regret the words—conceding that Altman had drafted them.) The Senate leadership, though, did not wish to give Kerry another stage.

By May, he had found a way around the Senate bosses: Kerry would secure time from a fellow Democrat, Alan J. Dixon of Illinois, chair of a banking subcommittee, and give Morgenthau center stage at a public hearing. The DA's testimony, on May 23, 1991, would be an orchestrated spectacle, but even his assistants could not be certain what he would say:

KERRY: I have heard through the grapevine . . . of an instance or instances, in which the Justice Department has access to, or custody of, a witness with material information regarding this case, which your office would like to interview, but they have refused to provide your office with access to such a witness. Is that accurate?

MORGENTHAU: With this correction. They have said that he may be available in a year.

KERRY: In a year?

MORGENTHAU: Yes. Not at this time. We've said, when? And they said, well, he should be available in a year. I don't want you to think that they have refused to let us see him. [Laughter]

KERRY: Was there any rationale attached to the need to delay a fellow law enforcement authority from having access to a witness for a year's period of time?

MORGENTHAU: I don't know the answer to that, Senator.

The DA had prompted Kerry, and asked the senator to join him in the televised dance, hoping "it might do the trick." It did. On the day after Morgenthau testified, he finally got word from London. For more than a year, the Bank of England had refused to hand over the Price Waterhouse audits of BCCI. Only after Morgenthau had testified in the Senate and accused the British regulators of stonewalling did Eddie George, deputy head of the Bank of England, pick up the telephone and offer the documents.

| | | |

Morgenthau had dealt the final blow.

On Friday, July 5, 1991, without notice, the Bank of England ordered the closure of BCCI. The raids came in a coordinated fashion around the world. In New York, at 8:30 in the morning, officers from the New York Fed locked the doors at the BCCI offices in the city. In Los Angeles, it was not yet dawn when the regulators sealed the doors, and in the U.K., where it was lunchtime, bailiffs cordoned off the bank's twenty-five branches. In Luxembourg, where the entire judiciary had gone out to the countryside on a picnic, it would take time to track down a judge to authorize the closure of the bank's headquarters. When the regulators arrived, they discovered Sheikh Zayed's men in the conference room, unaware of the unfolding drama and attempting one final time to devise a rescue. By the end of the weekend, the bank had been shuttered—its branches closed in eighteen countries, and under restriction in forty-four others.

That Friday, John Moscow stayed late at the office. The phone was ringing constantly, past and present BCCI staffers eager for a deal. But one call came from Morgenthau: A New York bank, he said, had $30 million on deposit with BCCI. The money, now frozen, would "in all probability" be lost. Here was a victim, Morgenthau said, genuine and convenient. The loss, strong evidence of fraud, would add essential local ballast to the far-reaching indictment.

And yet, the victims knew no borders. In a day, more than a million depositors had been cut off from their money. In Bangladesh, where four branches had collected deposits from 40,000 customers, more than $10 billion was frozen. In Hong Kong, where $1.4 billion was held in BCCI accounts, riots broke out. (The Hong Kong deposits included $200 million from the government of China.) By July 22, the closure hit Tokyo, as well—the first liquidation of a foreign bank since World War II. In the United Kingdom more than 120,000 British residents had deposited $400 million in BCCI. Fifty-five thousand small business owners, the majority of them immigrants from Asia, lost their savings. Local councils did, too; dozens of regional governments had fallen prey to the bank's tempting interest rate.

The DA knew the unraveling of BCCI would be a messy, protracted affair. But Morgenthau had set a timetable. By the summer of 1991, he upped the ante, forcing his counterparts in Europe and Washington to act. On July 23, the DA placed two urgent calls to Robert S. Mueller III, the assistant attorney general in charge of the Criminal Division at Justice. Morgenthau was blunt: He would move to announce the first charges in the case, with or without the backing of the Department of Justice. And the indictments, the DA vowed, would come within days.

For months, Morgenthau and Mueller had been snarling at each other. The DA liked the assistant AG—"a straight-arrow with guts." That made the inaction all the stranger. Justice had handled BCCI, Morgenthau considered, with at best "benign neglect," and at worst, deliberate obstruction. Clifford, he told assistants and reporters alike, had cowed the federal prosecutors. In a series of off-the-record interviews, Morgenthau had blamed Mueller for the delays, and Mueller, who could guess the source, was incensed. "Nobody has ever accused me of . . . lacking aggression," he told a reporter. At Justice, there had been no "foot-dragging," and certainly, no "cover-up."

In June, Mueller had attempted a truce. With five federal investigations of BCCI under way, he summoned the U.S. attorneys from Tampa, Miami, Atlanta, and D.C. The attorney general, Dick Thornburgh, also invited Morgenthau and his team to Washington, but when the New York prosecutors assembled on the train, the DA was absent. "The Boss isn't coming," Jim Kindler, the most senior among them, said. "Yes," he nodded to the incredulous young faces, "he's standing up the Justice Department."

The turf war grew uglier. Morgenthau accused Mueller of resistance— telling reporters the Justice official had even instructed British intelligence to stop cooperating with the DA's grand jury investigation. In reply, the attorney general had raised his voice on the phone with the DA more than once. Thornburgh would also go on television: "There's a difference between what a local prosecutor like Mr. Morgenthau has to investigate and . . . the arena . . . that we're in, which involves nationwide and international offenses," he said on *Face the Nation*. "We don't deal in sound bites. What we have to do is present evidence in court."

For Morgenthau, it was more than enough to provoke him to act.

On July 29, he announced the first indictments: twelve counts against BCCI, Abedi and Naqvi, and two of the front men in its acquisition of the D.C. bank, Ghaith Pharaon and Faisal Saud al-Fulaij. The charges, the DA said, represented "maybe 20 to 25 percent of what will ultimately be the result of the investigation."

Senator Kerry, meanwhile, raced to catch up. In August, he launched a new round of hearings, three days of televised drama that riveted Washington. Masihur Rahman, the financial officer from London, took center stage, recounting the rise and ruin of the bank. A small man with thick glasses and a soft voice, his tale of survival, in the months since he had reached out to Morgenthau, seemed straight out of John Le Carré.

"My wife and children were suffering greatly," Rahman said. They had pulled the children out of school, and tried to hold on, but each night they would "put the children under the bed . . . for fear of some physical violence or some gunshots." In the dark, the cars would come, sit in the driveway, and turn off their headlights. He had convinced his wife to leave, and in spring, Morgenthau had brought the family to the United States. Rahman had stayed in London: He found a job, moved to a small flat, lived alone. He was hoping for a new beginning when a warning came.

"If you open your mouth," said the man from BCCI, "I've personally killed people in my life and I'd use the same gun on you."

| | | |

On the Hill, Kerry would continue his hearings (holding thirteen in all), and in October, the House Banking Committee joined the chase. At Justice, too, Mueller at last swung into action, announcing the indictment of BCCI in Florida and the District of Columbia on November 16. A month later, the feds and the DA appeared to have formed an alliance, announcing a deal: BCCI pled guilty to criminal charges in both the New York and federal cases, and agreed to surrender $550 million in assets—a record forfeiture at the time. In Washington, Mueller was pleased. Yet for all the official enthusiasm, Blum, now on the sidelines in private practice, asked an inconvenient question: "The real criminals are still sitting in the Persian Gulf and in Pakistan watching the proceedings somewhat bemused," he told reporters outside the Washington courthouse. "When is anybody going to go after them?"

For months, Morgenthau had been looking hard at "the Saudis"— Ghaith Pharaon had been indicted, but a raft of eminent targets remained. Leading the list: Kamal Adham, the former Saudi intelligence chief, and Khalid bin Mahfouz, heir to the National Commercial Bank, the Saudi kingdom's largest bank, founded by his father. The bin Mahfouz family had long been bankers to King Fahd, and in 1985, after BCCI suffered huge losses in options trading, Abedi had gone to them for a bailout. Khalid and his three brothers paid nearly $1 billion for their stake in BCCI, and he had served, from 1986 to 1989, as a director of BCCI.

Throughout the spring of 1992, Morgenthau chased leads that BCCI deposits—"in the realm of hundreds of millions," the DA would recall—had gone astray. Bin Mahfouz's bank had not only branches across Saudi Arabia, but one in New York. For the DA, it was an opening. John Moscow received documents that revealed more than $200 million had gone to accounts in the name of Adham and one of his aides, who had remained at Saudi intelligence after Adham's departure.

On July 1, 1992, in another stunning turn in the saga, Morgenthau accused bin Mahfouz of stealing $300 million from the bank, and indicted bin Mahfouz and his Pakistani associate, Haroon Kahlon, for defrauding BCCI. In doing so, Morgenthau became the first prosecutor in the affair to take action against the Saudis.

The DA had discovered the importance of the Saudis to BCCI, their prestige and entrée having formed a bridge to the West. And as he let it be known that he had other Saudis in his sights, the Saudi establishment was stunned. King Fahd called the U.S. ambassador, Charles W. Freeman, Jr., insisting that the State Department offer a statement vouching for the stability of the Saudi banking system. Ambassador Freeman demurred. There was nothing he could do, he explained: U.S. law, or in this case, a "maverick prosecutor's office," had to run its course.

68. "Only Good People"

1992

For Morgenthau, the denouement was in focus. For nearly a year, the DA had fixed his sights on Clifford and Altman. At Justice, Mueller and the new attorney general (a conservative New Yorker named William P. Barr) could embarrass themselves, and stop short of chasing the "big fish" in Washington and in the Persian Gulf, but the Manhattan DA's office would finish what they had started.

John Moscow had a theory of the case. It had been a conspiracy, and Clifford and Altman were not unwitting conspirators. They'd known from the beginning, he assured Morgenthau: Abedi, Naqvi, Adham, and Pharaon—the entire cast had been in cahoots to hide BCCI's control of First American. The hurdles, Moscow conceded, were high: The evidence remained largely circumstantial, and many of the bank's former senior officers were abroad—Morgenthau had little hope of getting depositions from them, let alone bringing them to court. But Morgenthau sensed an opening: Altman. Clifford, the DA believed, might be willing to sacrifice him.

In early 1992, Clifford appeared at the DA's office for six days of questioning. Moscow battered him with pointed queries—"who knew what when"—trying to get him to deliver Altman. Clifford, though, waved away the bait. "I don't think Mr. Altman would have known that," he would counter. "He would have told me if he did." The prosecutors exhausted Clifford, but he stoutly maintained that neither he nor Altman had had any inkling of anything untoward.

Morgenthau would allow one last hearing. In early June 1992, Clifford and Altman's redoubtable attorneys, Bob Fiske and Bob Bennett, arrived at Centre Street to meet with Morgenthau. Cherkasky and Moscow flanked the DA in his office. Fiske was a pragmatist: Clifford, he would later say, was "going to take a hit either way. . . . He had to either say he knew the real truth about BCCI, or he didn't. And if he knew about it, there was a fraud, and if he didn't, whatever happened to this guy that was the ultimate wise man in Washington?" The defense attorneys had come with a long memorandum, replete with exhibits. They pleaded with Morgenthau for three hours—arguing there was no evidence that Clifford and Altman knew of the alleged ownership of First American by BCCI, and that they had run the bank well. The DA, they insisted, had no case. Morgenthau listened patiently but was unmoved.

By July, Mike Cherkasky's initial worries were being borne out: More than a few legal experts were now decrying the extended probe as a case of an overzealous prosecutor who had lost his way. Morgenthau, though, had even more ambitious plans: Years later, he would admit that Clifford and Altman were not the ultimate targets. If he could bring the two lawyers to court, he believed, the "worst crime" of the case—how BCCI had bought and exploited government officials in the United States and around the world—would come to light. "Call me a fool," Morgenthau would say, "but we wanted the names."

On the critical question of whether or not to indict Clifford and Altman, the DA would hear opposing arguments from his two most trusted assistants. Cherkasky insisted that going after the lawyers was a mistake, an error that would overshadow the success the DA had had in exposing and closing BCCI. Moscow, at the same time, remained hell-bent on indicting the two lawyers. In response, Morgenthau devised a two-track strategy: Cherkasky would open talks with Clifford and Altman's attorneys, Fiske and Bennett, while Moscow forged ahead toward an indictment.

Bennett, one of the most celebrated defense lawyers in Washington, loathed Moscow—"fucking nuts," he would say of the prosecutor—but in Cherkasky, he found a ready ally.

In midsummer, Cherkasky called Mueller at Justice—the talks had yielded a possible deal. Mueller would have to consult his new boss, Barr, but Justice could agree to the terms: Clifford would avoid criminal charges and be allowed to plead no contest in the civil lawsuit the Federal Reserve was intent on filing. Altman would plead guilty to two misdemeanors; spared prison, he'd be banned from the practice of law for five years. After he received the blessing of Justice and the Fed, Cherkasky took the plea to Morgenthau.

"We've done an unbelievable job against BCCI," Cherkasky began. "We've climbed to the top of the mountain. Don't take the next step and indict, because it's a long way down."

Moscow, sitting across the table, was furious: "Whitewash," he said. The office could not back down. Clifford is "a fixer and an influence peddler and we have to go after him."

Morgenthau drew the line: It was criminal, and the stock deal that enriched Clifford and Altman was the crowning offense. Cherkasky would have to end the talks: "No deal," Morgenthau announced. "We're indicting, as soon as possible."

Later, Clifford would insist he'd never made any such deal. "Under no circumstances," he said, "was I going to plead to anything." Publicly, he had always insisted on a trial, but his attorneys had met with Morgenthau several times. They'd also come to recognize that Mueller had no hunger for the case. "Justice was happy to let Morgy go forward," Bob Bennett recalled, "because they thought it was weak." Yet once the DA was set to indict, Mueller followed suit. "We think we have the evidence to support this case," he told Barr. "We're comfortable with it. It is narrower than Morgenthau's case."

| | | |

To be sure, the DA's horizon extended to the Middle East. In London, the Serious Fraud Office was pursuing Kamal Adham, the former Saudi intelligence chief enmeshed in BCCI. Adham, who owned extensive assets in the United States and England, had signaled a willingness to talk. On Monday, July 27, Adham stepped off the elevator on the eighth floor of the DA's office, trailed by his lawyers. Morgenthau knew the purpose of the visit: Adham had come to sign a deal. The Saudi financier pled guilty to aiding BCCI in its crimes in the United States, agreeing to a $105 million fine. Most important, he offered to cooperate. For Morgenthau, it was a coup: Few knew more of BCCI's secret dealings than Adham, who had been privy to its inner circle almost since its start. But the DA also knew he had gained leverage over Clifford and Altman. If for months they had kept up the insistence on going to court, the prospect of Adham on the witness stand, Morgenthau believed, would catalyze their inclination to cut a deal.

On the following day, as Morgenthau edited the press release announcing the indictments of Clifford and Altman, their lawyers arrived at his office. Carl Rauh, a Clifford attorney, insisted his client could not stand trial: Clifford had suffered a heart attack decades earlier, and although he had taken medication ever since, the drugs no longer worked. Clifford's heart was fragile. A trial, Rauh said, "would kill him."

That evening, Morgenthau obtained a court order to freeze Clifford's brokerage accounts in New York: The DA would hold nearly $19.2 million in cash and securities ransom. Moscow called it "routine," but the action infuriated Clifford. Years later, Bob Bennett remained angry. "It was an outrage," he would say, "beyond the pale." If Bennett could not understand it, his client claimed to know the motive: It went back decades, to the Treasury under Truman, and some perceived slight of the DA's father. Morgenthau would deny it, but Clifford would echo Roy Cohn's claim: The prosecutor was on a vendetta, out to destroy him.

The accounts, Clifford pleaded, held "practically everything my wife and I had." He would have trouble, he said, maintaining his household—his driver, cook, and maid.

| | | |

On the same July morning that Morgenthau announced the indictments of Clifford and Altman in New York, the Federal Reserve commenced its civil suit in Washington, accusing the two lawyers of lying, and seeking fines of $80 million. Morgenthau and the Fed had formed an alliance, and their sleuths recovered enough of the paper trail—"planeloads of documents from Abu Dhabi," one investigator would recall—to set forth with forensic precision Clifford's and Altman's alleged violations.

Clifford foresaw the worst. He had defended himself before the Kerry Senate subcommittee, a House banking committee, the federal grand jury in Washington, and in the Manhattan DA's office. What had begun as "the trouble" he would soon call "two and a half years of hell." Throughout it all, he insisted he was innocent. He had made concessions, carefully crafted, now at the Senate, now before the grand jurors. His "judgment" that the bank he'd chaired had had no link to BCCI had been "questionable," he had said. "I guess I should have learned it some way. I guess I should have sensed it. I did not." Of the fat profit he and Altman made on the shares' sell-off, he said, the deal had been in the bank's benefit, a means to ensure he remained at First American. "We'd had four years of stellar performance," he said. "We had taken this out-

fit and really turned it around, and they wanted an additional induce-
ment for me to stay on."

Still, Morgenthau's pursuit took its toll. In the fall of 1991, when the
Library of Congress hosted a dinner to honor Averell Harriman's centenary, Clifford was left off the dais; at the party, hardly anyone spoke to
him. By the summer of 1992, Clifford told a friend: "I've become a social
pariah in this town." The troubles hit at home, too. "As I'm getting into
bed," Clifford said, "it's with a certain sense of dread, because sometime
during the night I'm going to wake, and I lie there and try the case."

In early 1993, as the drumrolls in New York and Washington grew
louder, Clifford feared Morgenthau's case more than Mueller's. He and
Altman wanted a trial in Washington to come first. And if the federal
trial came first, whatever its outcome, the judge might "jeopardize" them
out of the state charges, ruling that the DA's case constituted "double
jeopardy." But if Morgenthau came first, Clifford would seek to be severed from his co-defendant.

Ironically, Clifford's bad heart saved him. Three arterial systems were
90 percent blocked, and the fourth was almost in as poor shape. Clifford
was in urgent need of bypass surgery; his doctors said he could not endure a long trial in New York. The judge appointed a panel of five doctors to make an independent determination—and they concurred.
Although the surgery would be postponed, Clifford won a reprieve: Altman would go it alone, and Clifford would be granted a delay for his
own trial—an event that all knew would never come. Clifford would
undergo a quadruple bypass on March 22 and return to the clapboard
house in Bethesda, Maryland, outside Washington. By May, he was recovering well, and keeping close track of his former junior partner's trial,
which was now unfolding in a Manhattan courthouse.

| | | |

Even before Altman's trial began, the case took a strange turn. On
March 2, State Supreme Court justice John A. K. Bradley, when he ruled
that Clifford's case would be delayed, had spoken of "possible plea bargains" under consideration for Altman. The judge was quoted in the
press as referring to such talks under way—including, according to a
Washington Post report, "the option that he would plead guilty to all the
charges against him, in return for being allowed to avoid jail time."

Altman's attorney was outraged. Gustave Newman, a criminal lawyer
known for decades as a formidable defender, was not particularly expert

in white-collar crime. Newman's forte was "the hard stuff," as he would put it: "rape, murder, general violent mayhem." He termed Judge Bradley's public comments "extraordinary" and "inexcusable." There were no plea talks, Newman insisted. "While I have discussed possible dispositions with the district attorney," he wrote in a motion, ". . . Mr. Altman has never considered pleading guilty to the indictment and has rejected plea offers made by the district attorney." He demanded Bradley recuse himself: The judge, he argued, had "treated Mr. Altman as if he is presumptively guilty and has assumed the role of prosecutor." Newman's fury would endure, but the case remained in Judge Bradley's hands.

John Moscow had spent nearly two years readying himself for the trial of his career. In sixteen months he had brought 120 witnesses before the grand jury—a record that would stand for years. Still, there were doubts. Even a prosecutor who helped on trial prep would claim to have seen it coming: "John's the best investigator in New York City, if not the English-speaking world," the assistant would say. "But John's not a trial lawyer. I couldn't say anything. I should have, but I couldn't." The fault, some in the office believed, lay not with Moscow, but his boss. "Bob Morgenthau doesn't have many failings," Cherkasky would say, "but one of them became clear in BCCI. He's intensely loyal to his people, and at rare times, loyal to a fault."

On March 30, 1993, Moscow opened the prosecution's case against Altman for defrauding regulators and accepting bribes. Moscow stood before the jury—eight women, four men—and warned them of the journey ahead. It was a complex case, he said. It would take time to sort out—months. Many witnesses would testify, the topics might seem impenetrable: They would hear about shares deals, about offshore accounts, about subsidiaries, and about holding companies around the globe. Moscow seemed in danger of winding too many circles in the air—but BCCI had been a beast, and the case would be, too. Mapping out the labyrinth, he cautioned, would demand the jurors' attention. A fraud of historic proportions deserved no less.

When the prosecutor, after three hours, finally sat down, Gus Newman rose. He begged the judge's forgiveness, but might he perhaps be allowed to start his opening? All glanced to the clock: It was nearly lunchtime, seemingly a good point to take a break. But Newman offered to make it quick—just "fifteen minutes." In retrospect, it would be all the time that he needed. As Judge Bradley nodded his assent, Newman unfurled in big, simple strokes how misguided the entire case was. Altman, he argued, was "being prosecuted for political reasons," and "the evidence would show" it. Newman did not speak long; he kept to his allotted time. But it was a smart ploy: to give a quick overview of his case, right after Moscow's extended prelude. And when the judge gaveled the lunch recess, it was Newman's voice—and not Moscow's—that lingered in the jurors' ears. It was "the move that changed everything," the defense lawyer would say. "Right there, we won the case."

Newman had made the trek to Morgenthau's office several times, trying to avoid a trial. The DA's intransigence—"obstinacy," Newman would call it—stung. In court, he quickly succeeded in reframing the case: Politics, and not greed, had landed Altman in his predicament. (Newman accused the "prosecution and the bank regulators" of a "cover-up," contending that they'd only sought "a scapegoat" to deflect their own failings.) The trial would be epic, five months of witnesses, documents, and financial minutiae that challenged the jurors' patience, and depth of civic duty. To the end, Newman's voice, and his first salvo, would resonate.

Early on, Judge Bradley again revealed a tendency for the unexpected move, this time against the prosecution. It was as if, some would say, the judge, having spoken out of turn before the trial—of plea options and "overwhelming" evidence—was attempting to right the balance. "The Judge kicked us in the ass, repeatedly," said one assistant who worked the trial. The prosecutors lost motion after motion. Doggedly, Moscow waded through the swamp, putting forty-five witnesses on the stand, and three hundred exhibits into evidence. When at last the defense's turn arrived, Newman rested his case after twelve minutes—repeating, almost verbatim, the "political prosecution" cry of his opening.

On the trial's final day, Judge Bradley delivered a last blow to the prosecution, dismissing what Clifford would term "the most dishonest and most manufactured charge"—the accusation that he and Altman had received a bribe in the First American stock deal. That afternoon, Clifford ventured out in Washington for the first time in months, lunching with Richard Holbrooke, the longtime diplomat and D.C. insider, at the Metropolitan Club. Holbrooke, who had helped Clifford write his memoirs, would recall the defiance: "He wanted to show everyone he was alive and well."

On Saturday evening, August 14, it was nearly seven o'clock in New York when the jury returned after four days of deliberations. Clifford was upstairs in Bethesda, asleep since the afternoon. His wife reached the telephone first. From the courthouse, Altman blurted out, "Marny, they've freed me." She raced to wake her husband. Soon, he would be standing in pajamas at the back door, speaking to an ABC News crew. "The jury considered the case," Clifford said, "and found there was no case."

Barbara Conley, the jury forewoman, wept as she read the verdict. "I felt insulted by the prosecutor's case," she would say.

Morgenthau was in the South of France with Lucinda, at the end of a two-week holiday. John Moscow had the unfortunate job of waking him up in Nice—"not a pleasurable call." That night Morgenthau issued a statement: "We accept the verdict, of course. Justice has been served," he said. "However, our investigation of BCCI continues." The DA said little to Lucinda, and not much more to his assistants, but all knew: The ego was bruised, and time would do little to ease the loss. Yet Morgenthau did not linger on it. As always, he refused to question the righteousness of the case. There remained, too, the mystery of the money: At least $12 billion was still missing from the BCCI coffers. And the DA wanted to know "where the money went, and how we might get it back."

| | | |

The liquidators—appointed by the courts in 1991, when BCCI was shuttered—moved swiftly. They set out to recoup the billions, and commenced litigation in the United States, moving in concert with the state and federal government. First American had become the largest bank in D.C., and they would sell it. The authorities were going to keep the proceeds—"let the money disappear into a black hole," one lawyer recalled—but Morgenthau insisted, in a meeting at the Federal Reserve, "No, that's not the way it's going to work." He brought in an old friend, Harry Albright, former head of the Dime Savings Bank in New York, as trustee. Albright pulled off a miracle, selling First American for $550 million. The DA was adamant that the Fed maximize the sale for the victims, and that they create a victim restitution fund.

In London, the bank's court-appointed liquidator testified that all creditors stood to recoup ten cents on the dollar, or less. In early 1994, over a long weekend at the Le Richemond Hotel in Geneva, Sheikh Zayed came to a settlement. There were dozens of lawyers, teams from Justice and the Federal Reserve, the liquidators, and First American's trustees, but the crew from the Manhattan DA's office, Moscow at its helm, ran the show. Sheikh Zayed, who claimed to have been duped by his Pakistani bankers, vowed to extradite to the United States Swaleh Naqvi, who had succeeded BCCI's founder Abedi as its chairman. The sheikh also vowed to pay $500 million in restitution and give access to the trove of BCCI documents—more than a million pages—hidden in Abu Dhabi warehouses, in exchange for assurances that he would not face federal or state charges. For Morgenthau, it was the long-sought opening. He had secured eleven plea deals and recovered $1.2 billion for BCCI's retail depositors, but the day after the deal was announced, the DA sent his team to Abu Dhabi. The hunt had begun—and would last for decades. By 2013, all told, the authorities would recover some $8.5 billion—nearly 86 percent of the deposits lost when the bank was closed.

| | | |

No one walked away unscathed.

John Moscow never regretted it, but BCCI would be the cloud forever hanging over his head. "Moscow could've tried a simpler case, one the jury could understand," said Eric Lewis, an attorney hired by BCCI's liquidators, who would spend a decade chasing the missing money. "But John's mind doesn't work that way, he doesn't think linearly."

Ghaith Pharaon, the Saudi power broker and one of the most prominent "Arab investors" in the case, paid $37 million in fines to the Federal Reserve for his role in BCCI's illegal takeover of First American. He retained, though, extensive holdings abroad, including the Attock petroleum conglomerate in Pakistan. And at his death, in Beirut in 2017, Pharaon still faced the criminal charges brought by the Manhattan DA.

Kamal Adham, the former Saudi spymaster and another central player in the BCCI case, pled guilty, and paid more than $100 million in fines.

Masihur Rahman, the bank's former chief finance officer, would divorce his American wife, leaving their children in the United States. He took up residence in Accra, Ghana, where for years he vowed to set the record straight. His memoir, *The Rise and Fall of the Largest 3rd World Bank,* would tell a story that diverged from his testimony. BCCI's demise, Rahman wrote, was due to the Manhattan DA's "plan . . . to entrap me," a plot born of a greater conspiracy. "New York is the hub of Jewish power," he explained, "and Morgenthau is a father figure of this big community."

Swaleh Naqvi, Abedi's successor atop the bank, was sentenced to eleven years in prison. In all, with credit for three years in an Abu Dhabi cell, and a further two years' reduction for cooperation, Naqvi served five years in Allenwood, the minimum-security facility in Pennsylvania known as The Farm.

Agha Hasan Abedi, the conjurer who had wrought all the magic and the troubles, who had lured the sheikhs to the Pakistani deserts for falcon hunts, and won billions with dreams of a global "Muslim bank," would recede from the world. He lived out his last days inside a walled compound in Karachi, rarely receiving visitors.

Clark Clifford, five years after his former partner's acquittal, and two weeks after he and Altman abandoned their claims to $18.5 million in legal fees and First American stock, to settle the remaining civil lawsuits arising from the BCCI case, died at home, at age ninety-one. "He was smart enough to know his reputation would never be the same," his attorney Bob Bennett said. "He should've stuck to what he knew, but they played him like a violin." The sheikhs, Bennett said, had treated Clifford "like a God—and he loved it."

John Kerry had staked much of his Senate career on BCCI, yet during his 2004 run for the White House, he rarely mentioned the case. The candidate, former staff members would say, preferred not to make enemies. The aides would recall the summer day in 1992 when Morgenthau indicted Clifford and Altman. They'd sat in the senator's office and heard Kerry talk of politics and money—and how they united in the BCCI affair. The two Pakistani bankers from the Miami sting, by then federal prisoners, had just testified before the Senate. Kerry seemed in disbelief. Four years earlier, Clifford had visited him, offering to save him time. "Clifford sat right on that sofa," Kerry told aides, "and said, 'BCCI's a good bank.'"

It wasn't just the bribes, the money laundering, the secret control of banks. It was the curdling power of lobbyists, the senator said: BCCI's reach seemed without end. Ed Rogers, an aide to President George H. W. Bush, after leaving the White House was hired by Kamal Adham—on a $600,000 contract. Even Kerry was not immune: A Florida banker caught up in the BCCI scandal had given generously to the Democratic Senatorial Campaign Committee—led by Kerry. "The amount of money that floats around this city is grotesque," the senator said that afternoon on the Hill.

Could anyone, an aide asked, be relied on to protect the public?

"Only good people," Kerry said, "the Robert Morgenthaus—people who see their duty and do it."

69. The Jogger

1989

Joe Walsh could hear the gurgling coming from down in the ravine. It was nearly 1:30 A.M. on April 20, 1989, and the moon three-quarters full, but in the damp thickets of the northern reaches of the park, it was pitch-black. Two men had come running at the squad car, shouting that they had seen someone in the woods: "A guy," lying prone, thrashing in the darkness.

Walsh had spent nearly twenty years on the force, the last nine in the Central Park Precinct. He and his partner, Bobby Calaman, had been in an unmarked car, idling under the streetlamp at the bend where the 102nd Street crossdrive meets the East Drive, doing the crossword, when the two men, Latino construction workers, came out of the dark, visibly unsettled. Carlos Colon and Vinicio Moore had been cutting across the park, heading back to East Harlem after a night of Budweisers on the West Side. The men had followed the path along the creek below the 102nd crossdrive, an asphalt S that runs between the two curving roads, the West and East drives, that frame the park. The path limns the southern edge of the North Woods. The crossdrive is at its most narrow here; the San Remo apartments—Morgenthau's first home as DA—stand on the horizon to the southwest, and the Schomburg Towers to the northeast. All weekend the rains had been heavy and the tall grass was wet. Officer Walsh was not eager—"It's a perfect place to end your life," he'd say—but he eased the car off the pavement and, turning on the brights, drove down the hill until, where the trees ended in a small stream, the headlights caught it clearly: a body writhing in the mud.

"The guy" was a woman, Walsh saw, as he approached, and he could hear her moaning. "First thing I saw was just she was severely beaten," he would say. "Her head, one of her eyes was really puffed out, almost closed. She had cracks in the side of her head. The side of her head was cracked, sort of covered with blood."

"Who did this?" the officer asked. "Can you speak?" The woman could not respond. She had been tied up—"pretty wonderfully, believe me," he would say. "I tried to pull the knot out of her mouth, and I got her untied, but when I saw how she was tied . . ." Whoever had done it had bound her with elaborate complexity. Her T-shirt, long-sleeved and bearing the letters "CC" beside an image of the U.S. flag, had been twirled into a tight rope—"a ligature," a prosecutor would call it. Wrapped around her neck, the shirt had been stuffed into her mouth, and tied around her wrists—locking her hands close to her face. Her palms forced together and fingers clenched, the hands left Walsh with a paradoxical impression: "It actually looked like she was praying."

As Walsh tried to help her, she began to kick wildly. "She was struggling, still struggling, moving her hands up and down, trying to bust them loose," he would recount. "She seemed to be in some type of shock. She was looking right at me. She seemed to be not seeing me, she seemed to be looking right through me."

The woman appeared to be in her late twenties. She was naked, except for a jogging bra. It, like the rest of her body, was covered with mud and blood. At 2:11 A.M. an ambulance arrived, twenty-five minutes after the initial call. The victim had lain bleeding in an inch or two of water for nearly four hours. Her body temperature had dropped to 80 degrees, and she had lost more than 75 percent of her blood. At 2:29 A.M., when the victim arrived at Metropolitan Hospital on East Ninety-seventh, she was near death.

The victim had a career in finance, retired parents, two brothers, a storybook childhood, and a résumé of excellence, from Wellesley College (where she was a Phi Beta Kappa) to graduate school at Yale, earning a joint degree in business and international relations. In New York, she had moved a few months earlier, to a fifth-floor walk-up on East Eighty-third, a sublet she hoped to buy. Her neighbor on the floor below, James Lansing, would call her "the nicest girl you could meet." She was twenty-eight. By morning, she was rechristened the Central Park Jogger.

She arrived in the intensive care unit "functionally exsanguinated"— she had nearly bled out. Her blood pressure was so low, the technicians could not get a good reading. Her brain, its normal surface wrinkles flattened with the swelling, was at risk. The doctors spoke of "severe brain damage." "Most people having lost 80 percent of their blood," the chief doctor would testify, "they're dead." Her skull was fractured, forehead and scalp lacerated with five deep cuts. Her left eye socket was crushed, and the eyeball forced backward.

To Ramon Rosario, midway through his fifth year on the midnight shift in Manhattan, and the first detective to see her, the bruises on her knuckles told the story. She had fought back. In the ICU her wrists and ankles were wrapped in gauze, and strapped to the gurney, yet she continued to flail.

By morning, as the tide of joggers and cyclists returned to the park, the prosecutors and cops had paced off a crime scene, and the tabloids, fed by leaks from the precinct houses, were feasting. "Nightmare in Central Park," screamed the front page of the *Post*. "Teen Wolfpack Beats and Rapes Wall Street Exec on Jogging Path." "Central Park Horror: Wolf Pack's Prey," seconded the *Daily News*. "Female Jogger near Death After Savage Attack by Roving Gang."

| | | |

Within two days of the attack in Central Park, the police had hauled in thirty-seven boys, aged fourteen to sixteen, all residents of the "PJs," the housing projects just beyond the northern edge of the park. In all, twenty-nine detectives had done the interrogations, and ten boys were arrested. In those first hours, the disclosures fueled a tabloid war that would stretch through the summer. "Rape Suspect's Jailhouse Boast: 'She Wasn't Nothing,'" blared the *Daily News*. The *Post* countered: "Rape Suspect: 'It Was Fun.'"

On the first Monday after the attack, the *Post* ran a photograph of Governor Cuomo on its front page. The headline: "None of Us Is Safe." "A visibly shaken Governor Cuomo," the article announced, had spoken out "on the vicious Central Park rape: 'The people are angry and frightened—my mother is, my family is. To me, as a person who's lived in this city all of his life, this is the ultimate shriek of alarm.'"

"New Yorkers learned a new word for fear," the *Post* reported on the day after the attack. "We were going wilding," one of the boys said. The chief of detectives professed ignorance; he had never heard the term before. Even for Manhattan, it was a new specter, a force threatening social order. "Wilding," the *Post* explained, was "like something out of *A Clockwork Orange,* packs of bloodthirsty teens from the tenements, bursting with boredom and rage, roam the streets getting kicks from an evening of ultra-violence . . . like an animal, which had caught the scent of blood, the mob—buoyed by the excitement of the chase—gets out of control."

"Wilding." It was a word "that chilled and titillated," wrote J. Anthony Lukas in the *Times*. "In two staccato syllables, it encapsulates the slithery dread many New Yorkers feel at the menace lurking out there in the dark."

Root causes of the night of terror diverged. It was a " 'Lord of the Flies' rape," added *Times* reporter Sam Roberts (in an article headlined "When Crimes Become Symbols"), and the boys, "neither drug crazed nor from broken homes, could not be written off as a feral fringe of the underclass." In the *Post,* Pete Hamill drew the front lines of class and color: "They were coming downtown from a world of crack, welfare, guns, knives, indifference and ignorance. . . . They were coming from the anarchic province of the poor. And driven by a collective fury, brimming with the rippling energies of youth, their minds teeming with the violent images of the streets and the movies, they had only one goal: to smash, hurt, rob, stomp, rape. The enemies were rich. The enemies were white."

By May 1, Donald Trump took out full-page advertisements in the *Times, Daily News, Post,* and *Newsday*—at a cost of $85,000—to decry the "roving bands of wild criminals," and call for the return of the death penalty. "Many New York families—White, Black, Hispanic and Asian— have had to give up the pleasure of a leisurely stroll in the Park at dusk," Trump wrote. A "dangerously permissive atmosphere" had created a world in which "criminals of every age" could "beat and rape a helpless young woman and then laugh at her family's anguish." Trump had seen a recent newscast, an exploration of the "anger in these young men." "I no longer want to understand their anger," he wrote. "I want them to understand our anger. I want them to be afraid."

| | | |

The district attorney first heard of the body in the park when he got a call at home early on Thursday morning. He and Lucinda had enjoyed a quiet Passover dinner at Steve and Marina Kaufman's on Sullivan Street the night before, and after an early breakfast with a favored reporter, he faced a full day at the office. The highlight was lunch with an old *Lansdale* shipmate. April 20, the anniversary of the ship's sinking, was still celebrated each year as the survivors' "second birthday."

As he entered the office, Ida Van Lindt stopped him short with more messages.

By 1989, the district attorney, fourteen years in office, had reset the order of things in the world of New York law enforcement. He had faced disappointments, most notably the highly publicized cases of Bernie Goetz (released from jail on the gun charge, and unrepentant) and Robert Chambers (who admitted to strangling Jennifer Levin, but pleaded guilty to first-degree manslaughter in a deal). Yet if a few years earlier, critics had seen him as either too lenient, or too tough, or playing catch-up with Giuliani, the complaints now had become few and in general were attributable to "immodest rogue bastards." Time and again, his prophecy had been borne out: Public memory, indeed, faded quickly. He had spread his power, liberally and equitably, at least to his liking, over the vast office, which had grown beyond assistants, to include investigators, accountants, secretaries, and one photographer. The hierarchy was not vertical, but more closely resembled a pyramid: A single arbiter sat atop an archipelago of divisions, units, and bureaus—each a fiefdom run with as much autonomy as its ruler could get away with. Morgenthau never explained the system of power sharing. He never revealed its intricacies, the ever-present balancing acts of loyalty and forbearance, trust and forgiveness. He did not need to. The limit of his tolerance was known: Trials could be lost, investigations could go awry, but when a case blew up—a subpoena leaked, a jury misled, a victim deceived— there was nowhere to hide.

The jogger case, Ida knew, was not one Morgenthau would leap at. "The terribly bloody, brutal ones," she would say, "were not his cup of tea." The "big ones" were the cases where the connections were seemingly invisible and the opportunities for intelligence gathering limitless. Harpoon a big case, like the Gambinos, BCCI, even wrongdoing in Albany, veterans of the office knew, and you could ask for time and money. Embezzlement, stock fraud, political shenanigans—the Boss's appetite for corruption in high places was boundless.

Murder was another matter. Morgenthau had never been able to muster the same keen interest for cases of extreme violence. They demanded an aptitude less cerebral; the dots were too concrete. There were exceptions, of course, ones he did savor. Bierenbaum, the plastic surgeon who dismembered his wife and flew a Cessna from New Jersey out over the Atlantic and threw her body parts from the plane. Morgenthau loved that case. And another: the mother-and-son grifters, Sante and Kenneth

Kimes, sixty-nine and twenty-nine at the time, who strangled Irene Silverman, an eighty-two-year-old widow and onetime Radio City Rockette, in the vain hopes of stealing her East Side brownstone. Even then, it was the challenge of making an impossible case that Morgenthau enjoyed: More than once, his office had won murder convictions without a body.

And yet, the jogger case would draw his attention as no other. Few New Yorkers remembered the riot in Washington Square of more than a decade earlier, but Morgenthau did. They were not mirror cases, but both unfolded on fields of violence, roiling the city's sense of security and stability, even its founding myth. Each would be seen as evidence of the melting pot gone wrong, and in each, the same corrosive forces surfaced—police bias, a rabid press, and, from start to finish, a racist bloodlust—as Morgenthau stood at the center, trying to keep, or at least feigning to keep, an impossible balance. The case would threaten to rend not only the city but, in time, the close relationship between the DA's office and the NYPD. And, as it spread to his own office, it would force a final divide between two of his closest and longest-serving assistants.

Morgenthau could not be sure, but he expected a rush to assign blame, and an urge to offer a seamless narrative. Some would point to social ills with deep roots; others, to a frame-up. The DA would have to hold the line, even as he understood, and would later concede, that one factor, unspoken if hardly hidden, motivated nearly every argument: the color of the victim's skin. If in Washington Square, the victims had been Black and Brown, now the city had a victim who was not only white but a woman who would be held up as a paragon of its promise.

For all the talk about New York City as a liberal bastion, the jogger case would feed a climate of political reaction. The case would tap outer-borough anxieties about Manhattan's spiraling violent crime, helping to launch Rudy Giuliani's career in politics and Donald Trump's debut on the same stage. Thirteen years apart, taken together the nights of violence in Washington Square and Central Park would preview, as well, the politics of the American future: the wars among the discontented and forsaken. Throughout it all, as the calls for law and order grew, those with clear eyes and hindsight could trace a color line: white fear of young Black men.

| | | |

On the morning of April 20, Morgenthau asked Ida to get John Fried, head of the trial division, on the phone. To the DA, there seemed one likely destination for the investigation, and Fried did not hesitate: Believing that the jogger was unlikely to survive, and the case would become a homicide, the trial division chief would hand it to Peter Casolaro, one of the office's most experienced homicide prosecutors. By the end of the day, though, Morgenthau had changed his mind: It would go to Sex Crimes.

In the spring of 1989, Linda Fairstein, at forty-one, stood at the apogee of a remarkable career. Few, if any, prosecutors in the country could claim a deeper well of experience in, or aptitude for, sex crimes. None had a higher profile than the former Vassar English literature major. She predated Morgenthau at the office. Hogan had hired her out of the University of Virginia law school in 1972, one of 7 women in an office of more than 150 ADAs.

Fairstein was more than one of Morgenthau's most trusted prosecutors. She was a pioneer. She not only enforced the law, she had helped create it. Before the mid-1970s, under New York state law a victim of a sexual attack was not considered a credible witness. The statute demanded corroboration. The law governed "every material fact essential to constitute the crime," and was deemed the most restrictive in the country. "If someone walked out of my office and had a purse stolen and then was raped by the assailant," Fairstein would explain, "the victim's testimony could convict him of the theft but not of the rape." Under Richard Kuh, Leslie Crocker Snyder had founded the Sex Crimes bureau, but Snyder preferred the "stranger rapes," it was said, cases with a weapon and corroborating evidence, the ones considered easier to prosecute. Fairstein, then not yet thirty years old and an ADA in the felony bureau, had been handed "the problem cases": date rapes and acquaintance rapes. With Morgenthau, it all changed. "He just went places where a lot of people in law enforcement were not willing to go," she would say. Gay rights, child abuse, domestic violence—he wanted to extend the DA's reach to embrace the widest range of "special victims." In 1976, Morgenthau asked Fairstein to take over Sex Crimes. She had started with four assistants, and by 1989 had added ten. (Before retiring in 2002, she had built the bureau to forty prosecutors.) "No DA in the country," she would say of Morgenthau, "put resources into it as he did."

Fairstein carried herself, and was seen by many, as more of a successor than an assistant. Few if any in the office were more loyal to Morgenthau. It was not only a matter of professional stature. Her husband,

Justin Feldman, at seventy, was one of Morgenthau's closest friends. Morgenthau and Justin went back to 1948, when both had been at the forefront of the Young Democrats. The DA had not played matchmaker; for some time, they even dated behind his back. She would never forget the day when he let on that he knew. He had reached her at an airport. It was a Friday afternoon and she told him she would be heading up to the Vineyard. With whom? he asked—the French restaurateur she'd been dating, or Justin? She would never know his source, but Fairstein would not forget the call—a reminder of one of her cardinal rules of survival. Morgenthau, she knew well, lived on information. "Don't ever let him be the second to know."

| | | |

The jogger case was assigned to one of the unit's most experienced prosecutors, Elizabeth Lederer. Lederer was a thirty-four-year-old native New Yorker who demonstrated economy in her speech and movements. At the DA's office, Lederer did not belong to the garrulous crowd, nor was she a loner. She emanated a sense of purpose, of energy stored in reserve—a competitive runner between races. Meticulous in gathering facts and marshaling a narrative, she had rarely lost a jury trial.

Lederer arrived at the 20th Precinct on West Eighty-second Street at eight o'clock on the evening after the attack. Humberto "Bert" Arroyo, of the Central Park Precinct, was put in charge of the investigation. Within forty-eight hours, the detectives had few facts at hand. They had not been to the crime scene. They were interrogating, a prosecutor would say, "blindly." Still, before long a timeline took shape, and it extended the investigation far beyond a single victim. Within one hour on the night of April 19, at least seven people had met violence in the park.

One of the boys interrogated explained how it began. In the gathering darkness, two groups of teenagers had formed: one from the Schomburg Towers, and the other from the Taft Houses, the projects just north of the park. As they converged, their number swelled to nearly three dozen. At the northeastern corner of the park, as they were about to leave the sidewalk, they stopped—one boy made a head count and another shouted the "rules of the night": "Don't bother no women, no couples, no old people."

Between 9:05 and 9:15 P.M., as they moved south, the boys set on four people, each a block or two south of the last. Michael Vigna was barreling north on a bike on the East Drive, just above the 102nd Street crossdrive, past the hill, when he met the group. Vigna, at thirty-one, was a competitive cyclist. He knew the time: He had marked his pace by the clock atop the Newsweek building below Columbus Circle. Biking in the park was a source of sustenance. He was going to school at night, trying to finish college, but in the evenings he would cycle in the park—"as much as my body would allow." Most nights, it was calm and peaceful; he would be alone on the road. Now he encountered "30–40 young kids," fanned out across the road. On the hill to the left, a rock outcropping almost came over the asphalt. He had no choice but to go straight. "I wanted to avoid them, but as I did, someone tried to reach out and punch me in the face. Something whizzed by my ear." There was no room to spare. The boys screamed and tried to block him, but Vigna swerved hard to the left, just by the granite that edged the narrow road.

Around 9:10 P.M., Antonio Diaz, a Latino in his early fifties with no home, no job, and a history of drug dependency, was walking by himself, carrying a bodega bag filled with dinner: a sandwich and a can of beer. The boys knocked him to the ground, kicked him, snatched the bag, and dragged him off the road. They left him unconscious.

Gerry Malone and Patricia Dean, a newly engaged couple riding a tandem bicycle, were on a second lap around the park, when they encountered the group on the East Drive south of the 102nd Street entrance to the park. The boys again tried to block the cyclists. Malone bore down, tried to ramp up his speed as he headed straight for them, scattering the group. Still, several of the boys, Dean would testify, grabbed at her. There was yelling, too. The couple could remember two cries: "Whitey," and "Fucking white people."

Within minutes, just to the south, a taxi driver, Ronen Rubin, taking a fare to Harlem, saw two youths on the East Drive near 102nd Street when something hard hit his cab. "It sounded like a bullet," he would say. When Rubin got out to investigate, he saw the dent below his window, and another six or seven boys standing beside the road. "Get back in the car," one said. "If you're not going to get back in, we're gonna kill you."

| | | |

The boys moved on, past a young couple on a bench. Yet when they reached the reservoir, and its jogging path, and the boys encountered four male joggers in succession, the rage seemed to gain strength.

David Lewis, a thirty-year-old banker at Manufacturers Hanover, was on his nightly run. He had run in the park for years, and nothing ever happened. The first voice came from the woods: "Ready," someone shouted. One boy threw a rock. "Wanna run with me?" Lewis taunted. "Yeah, we'll run with you all right," came the reply. Then Lewis looked in front of him, and saw "10 or 11 guys fanned out." Lewis, who had run track in high school, managed to sprint away, and head for the police headquarters on the Eighty-fifth Street crossdrive. By then, an officer had found Diaz, confused, bloodied, and wandering along a path. He radioed the alarm—a mob was roaming the park.

Robert Garner, at 140 pounds, was scarcely larger than many of the boys. A thirty-year-old British Airways consultant, he was on his second lap around the reservoir when he was surrounded. He would recall nearly two dozen boys, and a lot of yelling. He thought somebody cried out "Merry Christmas!" before he was hit by a rock. A tall kid began punching him in the face and chest, while others held him.

"What do you want?"

"Money, of course," came the reply, amid laughter.

They'd pushed him down an embankment, one boy punching him in the face and torso, Garner testified. "No money," he'd yelled. "Get out of here!"

"I was terrified," he would say. "I thought I was going to die."

Between 9:45 and 9:50 P.M., John Loughlin, a forty-year-old physical education teacher, on his usual run, counterclockwise around the reservoir, came across a group of boys who seemed to be in a fight: Someone was lying on the ground, and about "a dozen or more people" seemed to be attacking him. At six-foot-four and 190 pounds, he was a former Marine, who had taught at a middle school in upper Manhattan for four years. "It looked like someone was in trouble there," he would say, "so I stopped."

Loughlin was jogging in a green Army jacket and camouflage pants and carrying a Panasonic radio and headset. Some of the boys mistook him for a "D.T.," an undercover detective, one would say, or a Guardian Angel, the self-proclaimed warriors for order who had recently taken to the subways and streets.

Loughlin, testifying later in court, would recall one of the boys saying, "What are you looking at?" "What are you, one of those vigilantes?" He'd recall, too, other boys closing in, picking "up the cry."

As the blows came, Loughlin fell to the ground. He'd put a "hand up to ward off one of the blows" to the back of his head, he would remember. And he yelled out, "Stop, fellows, why are you doing this?"

| | | |

Jermaine Robinson, at fifteen, lived with his grandmother on 116th Street. Both parents were corrections officers—his father for the state, his mother for the city. That evening, she was working at the Bronx House of Detention. Like many of the boys in the group, Jermaine was a bright kid who earned good grades in school. But he stood out: He wore gold caps—fruit of his labor. Since he was fourteen, he'd worked for his uncles in the drug trade, first as a lookout, then in "hand-to-hand" in the street. (That afternoon, he'd finished his "bundles," selling $10 baggies of heroin to white kids, and put at least $80 in his pocket.) He'd also gained a reputation for having a history of violence—"leveling" a junkie, earlier that spring, who'd harassed him for money.

He picked Loughlin up off his feet, and threw him to the jogging track. Others joined in, rushing him, but Robinson stood over the prone body. Loughlin resisted—tore a pocket of Robinson's coat—a goose-down hoodie. Jermaine lunged back, enraged. A cousin and others tried to hold him back, but Robinson "slammed him." Loughlin was also hit in the chest and head repeatedly with a heavy instrument—a baseball bat, he thought. ("Something hard, heavy and smooth," he would say.)

David Good, a geotechnical engineer in his early thirties, had entered the park at the Engineer's Gate, at Ninetieth Street and Fifth Avenue, at 9:35 P.M. He'd been going at a "crisp 8-minute mile pace," when he, too, ran into a circle of boys. They gave chase, throwing sticks and stones. "You better run faster," they screamed. Good doubled his speed, but a stick hit his leg. He got clear, but not before turning and calling the boy who'd thrown it "a miserable piece of shit."

Michael Vigna, one of the first cyclists attacked, had shaken it off. The kids were menacing, but he considered it "gang-related activity." He'd gone on to do two or three more laps. He stopped one of the police cars, on the road, going the wrong way. He leaned in, telling the cop he had been "attacked by a bunch of kids," and saw in the back of the car a victim, his face covered in blood.

By 9:55 P.M., the police had found John Loughlin. The PE teacher had regained consciousness and was staggering along the bridle path, holding his bloodied head. Forensics would show that he had been kicked, punched, and beaten with a metal object to the head. At the hospital, they would stitch his head and hand, and photograph the blackened eyes, swollen face, and welts across his body.

Years later, many of the participants would agree: There were many strange goings-on in the park that night. A fire burned on the West Side, in the same latitude where the attacks on the cyclists and joggers took place. Sirens blared, as the fire trucks raced to the scene, while police scooters, squad cars, and unmarked vehicles seemed to be circling everywhere, their searchlights whirling.

By 10:30 P.M., the police had five boys in custody, arrested just west of the park, near 102nd Street. Eric Reynolds and his partner, Bobby Powers, had been patrolling in a green Parks Department van, one of two plainclothes units in the park that night. The park had been so saturated with radio cars, "headlights everywhere," that Officer Reynolds thought: Maybe the kids are "not in the park any more. Maybe they've left." The radio call had stated that Loughlin had been found on the west side of the reservoir, so he figured they'd gone west. "When we came out at the 100th St. exit and the West Side Drive," Reynolds recalled, "there they were: 20 or 30 of them, in a pack." Reynolds and Powers would arrest five boys, including Raymond Santana and Kevin Richardson.

Jermaine Robinson would be arrested on the morning of April 21. When the detectives found him, he was wearing a "Corrections Guardians" sweatshirt emblazoned with an eagle and the words "Dare to Be Black." Interrogated, Robinson admitted to taking part in the attack on Loughlin. He signed a statement written out by a detective, but he did not make a videotaped statement. He did not acknowledge any attack on a female jogger. Robinson was taken downtown to Central Booking, held in the Tombs before being charged with assault and robbery—but not with rape. He was released on $7,500 bail.

All told, the night of havoc and violence would lead police to collar more than three dozen boys, all Black or Latino. In time the number would whittle down to ten, then five, who stood accused of the rape and other attacks that night—none of whom had ever been arrested before.

| | | |

They attended schools across the city, high schools named in honor of heroes: Jackie Robinson, A. Philip Randolph, Adlai Stevenson, Fiorello

La Guardia. They were children of hardworking New Yorkers: One was the son of a postal worker, another of a fashion designer, a third of a born-again Christian and a longtime therapist's aide. In the days and weeks that followed, though, the newspapers, and the world, chose not to focus on the lives of the defendants, but on the one person who had nearly lost hers.

At the hospital, against nearly all predictions, the doctors said the victim was responding to light, and to her mother's touch.

70. "A Brilliant Job"

1989-2002

Linda Fairstein arrived at the station house on West Eighty-second after eight P.M. on April 20, not long after Elizabeth Lederer, an assistant district attorney in the Sex Crimes Unit. "I was in the precinct for 38 hours—without closing my eyes," Fairstein would recall. She was there to supervise, while Lederer and the detectives carried out the questioning. Fairstein would never waver in her estimation of Lederer's work. "Brilliant," she would say. "It was a brilliant job."

Bert Arroyo and his colleagues from the Central Park Precinct had jurisdiction, but the Manhattan North Homicide Squad ran the interrogations. Throughout the police department, and the DA's office, the detectives carried a reputation. One of the squad's leaders, Mike Sheehan, an NYPD veteran of two decades, had worked the Robert Chambers case with Fairstein and gained a measure of fame. Manhattan North was known as the best. "That's what we do," one former member of the squad would say. "We get confessions."

Raymond Santana and Kevin Richardson were taken in shortly after ten o'clock on the night of April 19, even before the jogger was found. Antron McCray's mother brought him later that night, after another boy's mother reported her son had been arrested. Yusef Salaam and Kharey Wise—their names given up by others—were brought in on the following day. None of the boys, police would tell reporters, showed remorse. Instead, the cops said, they were "laughing and telling jokes and whistling at policewomen."

It was nearly 5:30 A.M. on April 20 when the detectives began the interrogations, successive rounds of questioning that stretched into the next evening. The boys were interrogated over a span of thirty hours. (McCray, Santana, and Richardson each had a parent or guardian present; Wise, the eldest at sixteen, was not required to have a parent by his side.)

At first, no record other than a few scant notes was made of "the interviews," as the police would call them. The detectives pressed them, using any tool they could: They spoke of nonexistent evidence, played the boys against each other; they cajoled, they yelled, and, at least one of the boys would later claim, used their hands. Above all, they led the boys to believe that the more they talked, the sooner they would go home.

In the early hours of the morning on the second day of interrogations, once the boys also confessed to participating in the worst attack of the night—the assault and rape of the jogger—the videotaping began. At the 24th Precinct, Elizabeth Lederer, the ADA assigned to the case, worked with methodical care to record the boys' statements. As she spoke, a detective, or often more than one, sat nearby. Four of the boys—McCray, Richardson, Santana, and Wise—would make confessions on camera. (The fifth, Salaam, was being videotaped when his mother arrived and, convincing the prosecutors that he was underage, ended the session.)

All five implicated themselves in several of the evening's attacks. Richardson would say that he had met up with friends to go into the park to "beat people up"; Santana, that they had gone in to "rob bicyclists and joggers"; and McCray, that he had participated in the attack on "the bum" by hitting him. None of the boys admitted to rape—to penetration. But each incriminated himself as an accomplice to the attack on the jogger.

McCray, fifteen: "I grabbed one arm. This other kid grabbed one arm. And we grabbed her legs and stuff. Then we got a bunch of turns getting on her, like getting on top of her."

Santana, fourteen: "He was covering her mouth. Any time she would talk, he would smack her, he was saying, 'Shut up bitch.' And he kept smacking her."

Richardson, also fourteen: "When he pushed her, he ripped her blouse off."

Kharey Wise, sixteen: "This is my first rape. I never did this before. This will be my last time doing it."

The tabloids did not hold back: "Pack Ignored Her Cries, Called It Fun," *Newsday* announced.

| | | |

On June 25, 1990, fourteen months after the crime, the first of two trials in the case commenced. McCray, Salaam, and Santana appeared before Judge Galligan—the same judge who would preside in the Gambino case. All who came before him, defense attorneys or ADAs, needed no reminding of the judge's fondness for long sentences. Outside the courtroom, the streets held almost as much drama as inside it. If in the first days after the jogger was found, Morgenthau could call Congressman Charlie Rangel and ask him, once again, to calm the seas, they were too turbulent now. Each day, protesters lined the sidewalks, decrying a railroading. Led by the Harlem community leader the Reverend Al Sharpton, the Supporters, as they came to be known, paraded signs and chanted, at times blocking the entrance to the courthouse. Unlikely allies stood opposite: a red-beret brigade of Guardian Angels and feminist activists in pink T-shirts.

Each morning, Elizabeth Lederer walked the plank, enduring the reporters and the Supporters, who baited her with slurs: "bitch," "white devil," "whore," and "slut." Lederer was an experienced trial lawyer, considered one of the best in the unit. Yet Morgenthau did not know her well—she was reserved, even a bit standoffish, and lived on Long Island. It was a demeanor, the DA told a deputy, that would serve her well. Still, even as the trial opened, the strain was apparent. Trial prep had lasted more than a year—fifteen hours a day, often seven days a week. She suffered migraines and complained of exhaustion. Lederer herself had been a jogger, but now she stopped. She started smoking again, lost weight, and dark bags began to shadow her eyes.

Her marriage, after two years, was foundering. Yet the family troubles—a protection order in April, a divorce petition in May—would not become public until after the trial, and Morgenthau had little cause for concern. He could count on her commitment to the case, and he could also count on Fairstein. As "a fact witness," his Sex Crimes chief would testify as to what she had seen and heard in those first days after the attack. Deploying her prosecutorial skill from the witness box, she commanded the facts, and, at times turning to the jury, conjured word pictures that lingered. In court, Fairstein gave, as a reporter would note, "a vivid, incriminating picture of the suspects' behavior" at the precinct house. She had heard "whistling, screaming, raucous laughter, as though a party was going on."

Fairstein testified, too, how on the next morning, at dawn, she accompanied two Manhattan North homicide detectives as they took Richardson and Wise to the crime scene. She recalled "a large tree, surrounded by a lot of leaves and branches and an astounding amount of what appeared to be dried blood." A detective had asked Richardson if he recognized the scene. "This is where it happened," Richardson had replied.

" 'What happened?' " she quoted the detective as asking.

"The raping," Richardson said.

At the sight of the "large area of matted grass, with a lot of bloody-looking matter," she said, Wise said, " 'Damn, damn, that's a lot of blood.' " Fairstein let it sink in, repeating the phrase: " 'Damn, this is really bad, that's a lot of blood.' " When a detective had asked, Why did it surprise him?, Fairstein remembered Wise replying, " 'I knew she was bleeding but I didn't know how bad she was.' "

The case was hardly open-and-shut. It was "extremely complicated," Fairstein would write, "in no small measure because it had been a 'riot' (as the law defines it), with multiple victims and multiple defendants." Morgenthau knew it, too: There were scant, if any, forensic ties to the defendants. DNA, first used in a criminal case in the United States in 1987, remained in its infancy. Testing was expensive and took months. Juries had trouble parsing it, and judges did not deem it foolproof. The police had made no matches to the bloodstains found in five sites.

In April, the prosecutors caught a break: A newly discovered stain on one of the victim's socks yielded a semen sample. "New Evidence Delays Jogger Trial," *Newsday* trumpeted. The trial was pushed back seven weeks, as the prosecutors waited on the FBI. Morgenthau had curled his lip at the results: The semen did not match any of the defendants. "I feel like I've been kicked in the stomach," Lederer told a colleague, Harlan Levy, the DA's point man on DNA. "This most composed woman," Levy would remember, "was visibly shaken."

They would have to rely on the defendants' words: the videotaped confessions that each had made, with the exception of Yusef Salaam. Salaam was soft-spoken, a good student who carried himself with a preternatural solemnity. His mother, who taught part-time at the Parsons School of Design, had made sure he enrolled at LaGuardia, the city's premier public high school for the arts. Salaam would pose a challenge on the stand, but Lederer was unfazed. In her cross-examination, she directed attention to the tentative claims, and candid admissions, of his memory of the night:

"You were walking with a group of about 50 people, is that right?"

"Yes."

"You get to the Conservatory Garden, everyone starts walking up that path in the park?"

"Yes."

"And then suddenly everybody is gone?"

"We was walking up the hill," Salaam said, "and in walking up that hill I got real tired, and I was walking—I was sort of lagging behind. Before I got to the top of the hill, everybody had already moved out of that area. I don't know where they went."

"As you were walking the hill," the prosecutor soon said, returning to the thread, "there looked to be what were 50 up the hill, is that right?"

"Yes."

"And then all of a sudden at one point you can't see them anymore?"

"Like I said, they kept walking."

Salaam said he had decided to walk away from the group at that point "for no reason."

"I kept on walking," he continued. "I didn't get to the East Drive yet. Then I saw a man laying on the ground."

"You saw somebody, is that the person you thought was dead?"

"Yes."

"And you walked over to that person?"

"No, I didn't."

After several more questions, Lederer asked: "And you decided to run away?"

"Yes."

"Did you go call the police?"

"No."

"Did you go over to see if he was bleeding?"

"No."

"You just decided to run away from him?"

"If I touched this person, my fingerprints would have been on him."

"Listen to the question," the judge interjected.

"You just ran away from him?"

"Yes, I did."

Moments later, the prosecutor added, "You didn't leave the park when you saw this person who you thought was dead, did you?"

"No."

"And you didn't go and call for help, did you?"

"No."

"You ran further into the park, is that right?"

"I ran down south, further down south."

"You stayed in the park, is that right?"

"Yes, I did."

Minutes later, Lederer returned to a potent piece of evidence, what she would call a "pipe"—but which others would describe as a solid metal bar, at least twelve inches long, wrapped in black tape from end to end, once used to keep the door in the Wise apartment securely locked.

"And you had that pipe in your pocket?"

"Yes, I did."

"You always carry a pipe in your pocket?"

"No, I don't. I don't have a pipe of my own."

Soon, Salaam was recounting for the prosecutor that on the night of his arrest he'd told a detective, "I thought it would be fun going into the park."

"You went into the park that night. You weren't going there for a picnic, were you?"

The accused were not blessed with the most accomplished defense attorneys. Years later, the disinterested legal assessments would cite a range of inadequacies, from negligence to incompetence to opportunism. Still, each attorney did argue that his client was innocent. They also sought to dispute the validity of the confessions, arguing that they had been coerced. But Judge Galligan allowed the tapes to be played in court.

The jury watched as Lederer on the video asked McCray, "And did you hit her?"

"Yes, kicked her," he replied.

"Okay, where did you kick her?"

"I don't know. I just kicked her."

"And who else kicked her?"

"Um, Kevin, um Steve, all of us," he answered, referring to Richardson and Steve Lopez, who along with Wise were due to face the same judge in the second trial.

"Okay, she was screaming. Is that how you could tell that she had been hit?"

"She wasn't screaming," McCray said. "She was hurt, though."

"She was hurt?"

"Yeah."

"How could you tell she was hurt?"

" 'Cause she was lying there."

"Everybody started to hit her. Did anyone have a weapon?"

"Yeah, this black pipe."

"Who had that pipe?"

"I don't really know, but I think it was the tall Black kid."

Several questions later:

"After she was hit in the head with the pipe, did somebody take her clothes off?"

"Yeah."

"Okay, who took her clothes off?"

"All of us."

Demonstrating how he held the woman, McCray said, "I had her just like this."

"And was she trying to pull away?"

"Uh huh."

And then:

"Did somebody have sex with her?"

"Yeah."

"Did a lot of people have sex with her?"

"Yeah."

Lederer paused to note that the videotape showed McCray's parents beside him before, with deliberate care, she had read him his rights.

On July 16, 1990, the prosecutors called the jogger herself to the stand. Her recovery stunned all in the courtroom. In fifteen months, she had relearned how to walk and talk. She would call it "a second childhood." Still, she had no memory of the attack. Her testimony lasted only twelve minutes. She could not identify any of the boys on trial, but she achieved Lederer's goal. After the trial, a juror would make Lederer's strategy clear: "I mean, I felt sorry for the lady," Ben Meal said. "She looked like she could hardly make it up to the stand."

In the end, the confessions proved overwhelming. Each trial lasted nearly two months. In the first, the jury deliberated for ten days, and in the second, eleven. The first jury comprised four whites, four Blacks (including the foreman, a onetime NAACP employee with a law degree), three Latinos, and one Asian-American—all male except for two women. The second: five whites, three Latinos, three Blacks, and one Asian-American. They had struggled—but in both instances voted to convict.

By Christmas, it was over: Four defendants were found guilty of rape, and one of sexual abuse. One was also found guilty of attempted murder.

All five were convicted of assault, riot, or both in the other attacks in the park that night. All verdicts were upheld on appeal—except Santana's: He never completed his appeal case.

|||||

"Justice has been done," Morgenthau announced to the press after the first trial. "Coming as it does after 10 days of deliberation, this verdict presents the considered judgment of 12 citizens who scrupulously reviewed the evidence and searched for the truth." That evening, he reserved several tables at Forlini's, his favored restaurant across the narrow street behind the office, and assembled the prosecutorial team. Finding several of the Manhattan North detectives in the restaurant as well, Morgenthau invited them to join the crowd in the back room.

The DA would refuse to entertain questions of race. "From the beginning," he told reporters, "I have insisted this was not a racial case." He spoke of those who, in his view, wanted "to divide the races and advance their own private agendas," and of how the city was "ill-served" by those who had so "sought to exploit" this case.

A year earlier, Mayor Koch had lost his reelection bid to David Dinkins. An urbane lawyer, Dinkins favored bow ties, spoke softly, and preferred to remain above the fray. But he had come up through the Harlem Democratic club—a member, with Rangel, Percy Sutton, and Basil Patterson, of the Gang of Four, the politicians who ruled Harlem. On the jogger verdict, Dinkins struck a conciliatory pose. "It's not a racial incident—that could have been my sister, my daughter," he'd said as a candidate. "We ought not to permit it to be made into something else."

|||||

Five boys were sent upstate. For Morgenthau, the victory marked a turn. The guilty verdicts, as the *Times* noted, broke the string of setbacks that his office had suffered. (In addition to the Goetz and Chambers sagas, John Gotti had been acquitted earlier in the year in the DA's assault and conspiracy case.)

Elizabeth Lederer, though, did not celebrate. Four days after the first verdicts were announced, the *Post,* on its front page, revealed the "Secret Agony of Jogger DA": "Brave Prosecutor's Marriage Failed as She Put Rapists Away." Between the two trials, Fairstein had offered a respite, hosting Lederer on the Vineyard. But the divorce battle had taken a toll.

The questions, too, lingered. To Tim Sullivan, who sat in on both trials, chronicling them in his book, *Unequal Justice,* the holes were obvious. Between the first and second trial, Lederer elided the problem with the timeline of the attacks. If in her opening statement at the first trial, she highlighted the attack on the female jogger, putting it early in her chronology of the assaults that night, in the second trial Lederer left the timing of the rape obscure.

And then there was the obvious hole in the evidence: the semen. In court, an expert testified that the DNA extracted from the victim's cervix and sock had come from the same source, a single source. Only one person, it seemed, had ejaculated, and he was not on trial.

||||

By 1990, some 55,000 New Yorkers were behind bars, on parole, or on probation. Two years earlier, corrections officials had declared a state of emergency at Rikers Island, where the number of inmates had grown to 14,150. (Capacity was 12,858.) The overcrowding demanded a radical experiment. The legislature moved to allow 200 prisoners to await trial under house arrest—monitored by a new invention: an electronic ankle bracelet. It was, of course, too little, too late. In the rush to house those incarcerated, the walls were already going up.

When it came to law and order, even Nelson Rockefeller had been outdone by the great liberal from Queens, Mario Cuomo. Entering office in 1983, Governor Cuomo faced many of the same troubles that the DA had: The state coffers were running dangerously low, while the Rockefeller drug laws had more than doubled the prison population. Cuomo was only a week in office when he faced his first crisis: Sing Sing, the decrepit prison in Ossining, erupted in a riot. Cuomo, unlike Morgenthau, opposed mandatory minimums for narcotics crimes, yet the new governor would claim no alternative: Ronald Reagan's War on Drugs had stolen any would-be reformist momentum, while New York City would soon face the advent of a new drug epidemic, crack cocaine, and an attendant surge in violent crime. With public opinion strongly favoring incarceration, and politicians of nearly every stripe forming a supporting chorus, Cuomo—not yet a month in office—announced plans to add seven thousand cells to the state's inventory. In the years between the passage of Rockefeller's drug laws and Cuomo's construction boom, the population of New York's prisons would rise nearly fivefold. Mario Cuomo, in his three terms as governor, would add twenty-nine prisons to western and central New York, as well as to the bucolic landscape of the Adirondacks.

Todd Clark had become a guard at the Auburn state prison, north of the Finger Lakes, in Governor Cuomo's last term. By 2001, at thirty-seven, he'd worked at Auburn for thirteen years, and long dreamed of running his own car shop. All that time, Clark ran the same "company"—forty-four men, nearly all lifers. He began his days at seven A.M., with the count: He would open the cells, checking to see if the men were alive, before leading them first to breakfast, and afterward either to the yard, the school, or the shop, where they made desks and license plates.

Clark never had cause to pay particular heed to Matias Reyes. He was one of the "old-timers," in his company at least five years. Many of the Latinos were Cripps, or Ñetas, the gang born in Puerto Rico's jails that had grown across America's prisons. Not Reyes. He was short, somehow baby-like, with a round face and rounder cheeks. He kept to himself, rarely complained, even gained weight behind bars. But beginning in late November 2001, Clark began to sense that something was amiss. "He never said, 'Boo,'" Clark would recall, but Reyes "just didn't seem right." In his cell, or in the yard, it was the same. He looked troubled, Clark would say, "like he had to get something off his chest."

The guard brought him to the chaplain, but Reyes returned, saying it was no good. Clark tried again: Thinking the inmate might have suffered a death in the family, he sent him to a counselor. When Reyes again returned, Clark asked, "How'd you make out?" Reyes shook his head: "No use." Finally, the guard asked, Was there anything he could do to help? Even though he could never fully explain it, and many COs—his fellow corrections officers—let alone strangers in the village, would curse him for it, Clark would not regret the offer. Reyes nodded: "Give me ten minutes."

That day, during lunchtime, Clark assembled his company, and instead of leading them to the mess, he locked them in. He took Reyes down the cellblock, and into his "office." As they sat in the guards' break room, scarcely larger than a cell, Reyes blurted it out: "I saw this guy, in here. He's doing time for something he didn't do. They said he did the Central Park Jogger. But he didn't. That was me."

Todd Clark had never heard of the jogger case. In the spring of 1989, he'd been twenty-four years old, living near the prison. As he listened to

Reyes, he had no idea what to do; he had never had an inmate admit to a crime.

"Oh, whoa," he managed.

"Guarantee me protection," said Reyes, "and I'll tell you much more."

Matias Reyes had seen the other inmate, a recent transfer, in class. The New York State Department of Corrections had adopted a policy, a drive to ensure all inmates pass their high school equivalency exam. He had also run into this same inmate in the fall of 1989, at Rikers. They had fought over the television, each wanting a different channel. But Reyes did not know his name, only his prison nickname.

Clark set out to investigate. He prepared an array of mug shots of six inmates. When he put the photographs before Reyes, the inmate did not hesitate. Clark was not in the habit of pulling files on his company. ("Don't want to judge them," he would say.) But he checked the rap sheets. Kharey Wise, the eldest convicted in the jogger case, had been sixteen when he received a term of five to fifteen years. Reyes, at thirty-one, was serving a sentence of thirty-three and a third years to life. Later, some would say Reyes had an ulterior reason. "That's the funny part," the guard would say. "He wouldn't get anything out of it. He wasn't going to get less time. In fact, he could've got *more*." Above all, Reyes was afraid. "The guy was all fear," Clark said. Whether it was Wise or someone else currying favor, Reyes worried that "they'd come back and kill his ass."

| | | |

Morgenthau knew who Reyes was—half the office knew "the East Side Slasher," as the tabloids called him.

In the spring of 1989, Reyes had a job of sorts, helping out at the counter in a bodega on Third Avenue near 102nd Street. The 23rd Precinct station house stood on the corner. If anyone asked, Reyes gave his address as the Washington Houses, across the avenue. His mother lived there, but on most nights, Reyes slept in an old van that belonged to the bodega's owner. People in the neighborhood felt sorry for him. Many of the detectives from the "2-3" knew him, too: He was "Tony," the counter boy at the deli where they got coffee, donuts, and cigarettes—and where they'd found a "cooping room," a backroom where cops could drink beer.

Reyes's childhood, by his own account, was a series of traumas and catastrophes. Born in a coastal town in Puerto Rico to unwed parents, he'd been handed off at two—"sold," as his grandmother put it—by his mother to his father for $400. His mother had moved to New York, leaving him behind with his father, a handyman. At age seven, he snuck out to play in a river, when two older boys threw him into the water, beat him, and sexually abused him. The humiliation continued. For a time, he went to live with his mother in East Harlem, but did not make it past the ninth grade. He returned to Puerto Rico, where again at the river, on the Fourth of July, he suffered an accident. He tried to dive from a tree, "to impress girls," he would tell a court-appointed psychologist, and broke his neck. He spent months in a "halo"—four screws in the skull holding a steel ring around his head. After recovery, he again visited his mother in New York, when a "tragedy had occurred." He had no memory of it; he was drunk, he would say. But an aunt had told him: He had raped his mother. He saw her again only once.

By seventeen, Reyes was on his own. Most nights, he was on the streets. He had taken to cocaine, and mugging, but the worst would come later, in a brutal spree in the summer of 1989.

On June 11, 1989, he stalked, raped, robbed, stabbed, and beat a twenty-three-year-old white woman in her apartment on 116th Street, between Park and Lexington.

On June 14, 1989, he attacked a twenty-four-year-old Latina in her apartment on East Ninety-seventh, just off Madison Avenue. Lourdes Gonzalez lived in the basement apartment, with her fiancé, the superintendent. "Your eyes or your life," he said before stabbing Gonzalez ten times. "I kept on stabbing her and I don't know in what places I got it," he would say. "Her babies was screaming, too." Gonzalez had three children with her: her boyfriend's seven-year-old, Tony, her own six-year-old, Carlitos, and her three-month-old daughter, Amanda. The attacker had locked the two boys in the bedroom, and she persuaded him to let the baby go with them. After he fled, the boys ran upstairs to a neighbor's. Gonzalez managed to get on the elevator and ride it to the lobby, before collapsing. She died that evening. Gonzalez was nearly eight weeks pregnant.

On the afternoon of July 19, Reyes followed Amanda Eisley, a twenty-year-old white college student living with her parents on Madison Avenue, near Ninety-fifth Street. He beat her, raped her, and tied her up with a telephone cord, binding her wrists to her ankles. He had begun to cut her eyes, but when she collapsed, he took her ATM card and abandoned her. Before he left, though, he called 911 to summon help.

On July 27, 1989, he struck again. He attacked a twenty-eight-year-old white woman in the hallway of her apartment building on Lexington, at the corner of Ninety-fifth Street. He was unarmed but he punched her, robbing her of her purse, before a neighbor interrupted.

The attacks came to an end on Saturday afternoon, August 5. Reyes followed Elizabeth Reynolds, a twenty-four-year-old white woman, to her apartment on East Ninety-first. Again, he took her bank card, and forced her to give him her PIN. He was intending to tie her up, but Reynolds managed to flee. In the lobby, a building porter and another tenant restrained Reyes until the police arrived.

Charged with the serial rapes and the murder of Gonzalez, Reyes would plead guilty and be sentenced—by Judge Galligan, the same judge who would preside over the jogger trials—to thirty-three and a third years to life.

|| ||

It took nearly six weeks for the word to wend its way downstate through the labyrinth of the penal system, but when at last it reached the DA—on the final day of February 2002—alarms went off.

Morgenthau did not "believe the sonofabitch for one minute," he told his closest aides. "Gotta make sure," he said, "this guy isn't just looking for a quick way south." He remembered visiting the hellish prisons upstate, a boyhood tour with FDR and his father. And he'd seen it before: inmates coming down to the city, even for interrogations, even if they couldn't see the sky: "They know they're back, and they like it."

"Let's be damn certain," Morgenthau said. "Let's go slow." The veterans knew Morgenthau's Law: The first information gathered in any case, he would say, usually ended up being 50 percent wrong. Every fact had to be tested, and tested again. Each assertion this inmate makes, the DA said, prove it twice. "We can't go anywhere," he said, "without a statement that's airtight." The jogger case was already high-stakes, and now, with a reversal without precedent hanging in the wind, it threatened chaos. If they got it wrong, no one would ever forget.

"Get the DNA test," he ordered. "No fuckups."

The Reyes trial had turned, in part, on the DNA evidence—and Peter Casolaro, the ADA who had prosecuted Reyes, had kept it. Casolaro, who had spent two decades in the office, never let go of evidence. The technology was not yet advanced—RFLP, they called it, a technique that produced autoradiographs, X-ray-like films in tiny strips. The "auto-rads," as the DA's office called them, revealed a DNA profile, and Caso-laro had kept Reyes's autorads—blown up large for trial, and stashed behind a filing cabinet. The prosecutors would not need, at least initially, to ask Reyes for a DNA sample; they could ask the FBI laboratory to compare the old autorads with the DNA sample that remained in their database from the jogger trials. They did, though, have to dig for the evidence from the jogger trials; it would take months to find the victim's bra, shirt, tights, and the blood and semen samples.

On May 8, a preliminary match came back: Reyes's semen was found on one of the jogger's socks. As the tension on the eighth floor rose, Mor-genthau decreed that the circle of information be kept closed—one leak, and hell would break loose—and he declared that the reinvestigation would be run by Nancy Ryan, one of his chief deputies, and Casolaro, but that Liz Lederer, as the lead prosecutor of the original trials, would also be on the team. Ryan since early 1990 had been chief of the trial division. It was the heart of the pyramid: The division handled—either by trial or plea-bargaining—the majority of the 100,000 cases that the office encountered each year. Morgenthau knew well her reputation in the office: She did not focus on the victims, it was said, she focused on the cases. But time and again, the DA had called on her in crises. She had shut out the noise, gathered the facts, and cleaned up the mess. Morgen-thau considered her his best investigator, and "one of the smartest and toughest" assistants he'd ever had. The DA knew a reinvestigation would roil the office, and he knew there was no love lost between the chiefs of his Trial Bureau and his Sex Crimes Unit: "Linda versus Nancy," one of his top assistants would say. "You could've sold tickets." But Morgen-thau had no need to give Ryan instructions; she knew them.

"We had to verify both halves of the statement," he would say. "One, that Reyes raped the jogger, and two, that he *alone* did it."

The DA's team called upstate. The prison guard, Todd Clark, had taken Reyes into protective custody, locking him behind a glass door, alone, in the infirmary. Now they asked that he be moved out; Reyes feared for his life. In March, the prison administrators made a mistake, moving Reyes to Attica—where the threat of reprisal loomed greater. But by late June, he was moved again, to the Clinton Correctional Facility in Dannemora, near the Canadian border, and held in solitary.

On May 16, Morgenthau requested help from the Manhattan North Homicide Squad. Liz Lederer had selected two detectives, and the DA and Ryan blessed the choice: Rob Mooney and Tommy McCabe, even-keeled veterans, partners for more than a decade, professionals you could rely on. And in 1989, McCabe had worked the jogger case.

In the third week of May, Morgenthau requested that the prison authorities deliver Reyes to the DA's office. On May 23, 2002, after a six-hour drive in a prison van, he was led to the "lineup room" on the ninth floor, down the hall from where the grand juries met. The room was small, and one wall had a large window of one-way glass. Mooney was to do "the initial interview," as they called it. When Mooney and McCabe entered the room, ADAs Ryan, Casolaro, Lederer, and another ADA, Daniel McNulty, as well as a third police official, remained behind the glass, watching.

The interview seemed to begin well. Reyes reprised his story, but it soon became apparent that he was not prepared for his new audience. Sixteen years on the force, Mooney took pride in his tough-guy reputation as a veteran of Manhattan North, the city's prime real estate for Homicide. The detective let Reyes retrace his steps—from the chase to the rape—but challenged him, questioning every claim: What had he been wearing? How'd he dragged her? Had he pulled his pants down?

Under the barrage, Reyes, as Mooney recorded in his notes, "got a little impatient."

"I don't know why you're asking me all these questions," he said. "I'm telling you I raped her!"

"My problem is I can't see how you could have done this alone," Mooney said.

The detective went further, telling Reyes that his DNA had matched, but he also said that the statute of limitations had expired. This was true—no charges could be brought in the case.

By four P.M., it looked like Mooney was headed for a dead-end; detective and prisoner were locked in a shouting match. As the detective pressed him, Reyes had grown increasingly frustrated; now he was agitated.

"I'm sitting on a chair with rollers," Mooney would recall. "I'm rolling around, sliding, and he's moving around. A lot. Can't sit still. At one point I'm after him, and he's up on one leg, backed into the corner of the room. And I ask him, point-blank: 'You didn't actually do this alone, did you?'"

You don't believe me? Reyes shouted. Fine. Just take me back.

Outside, the prosecutors caucused. Lederer had left, but Ryan, who returned to her office several times during the afternoon, had rejoined the group at the glass. "We have to stop this," Casolaro said. McNulty agreed: They had to send somebody else in. Mooney would record in his notebook that Ryan feared "he [Reyes] would completely shut down & we would lose him." Casolaro was the logical choice: His method was gentle, methodical, and Reyes knew him. When Casolaro had interrogated Reyes in 1989, at one point the defendant had put his head on the table—"I can't go on," he'd cried—before Casolaro brought him back to life, and elicited the confession. Casolaro agreed that he would take over the questioning, but feared he'd only further antagonize Reyes.

"He doesn't want to see me," he said. "I'm the guy who sent him to jail." He turned to Nancy Ryan: "Nancy, you go in and get Mooney."

As Ryan went into the room, trying to speak to Mooney, Reyes looked to her.

"Are you a DA? Can I speak to you?"

Ryan's presence seemed to calm Reyes down.

When she left the room to confer with Casolaro and McNulty, they concurred: "You're in, Nancy. He wants to talk to you."

She returned and took a seat. As they talked, Reyes's shoulders fell, and with the detective out of the room, his words flowed more freely. Ryan stayed in the room awhile, nearly an hour. Casolaro and McNulty recorded the interview on video, and when Ryan emerged, they adopted a plan: She would do another video with Reyes, trying to lead him through the story from start to finish. With the details memorialized, should he refuse to speak again, they would have it on tape.

After a break for dinner—Chinese takeout—Reyes opened up. He offered hints from his past, a string of clues that could be followed up on. It took time; he spoke in fits and starts. But as Ryan and Reyes fell into a rhythm, he eventually told the story: his version of the events of the night of April 19, when he found a young white woman jogging along the 102nd crossdrive.

Central Park was dark when Reyes left the bodega and headed south. He entered the park at 102nd, and caught sight of the jogger on the East Drive, jogging on the east side of the road, in the runners' lane. She wore running tights—black or blue, he could not remember. But they were tight. That was part of the attraction, he said.

"I just had to have her," he would later say.

In pursuit, he started "zigzagging" in the grass off the road. She wore a headset, a Sony AM-FM radio. The music was loud, he could hear it. He waited to see if she took the long way—if she would go up, until the road looped around, or if she would cut across, taking the crossdrive, which was narrower, with fewer streetlamps. She turned left, along the shortcut.

"She makes the turn," Reyes would recount. "All this time, there's no sounds, no cars. Nobody's going by. So next thing you know, as she proceeded to jog along, 'cause it's a pretty long stretch here, right on the, on the right-hand side, around the grass, I see a tree branch . . ."

He caught sight of a "stick" or branch, he told Ryan, lying on the ground on the north side of the road. He picked it up. It was heavy: He had to use both hands to hold it. He raced to catch her. Her ears were covered; she couldn't hear his footsteps. He came from behind, hitting her in the back of the head. She was conscious but stunned. He dragged her from the roadway. She was talking, trying to protest. She held her hand to the back of her head. She was bleeding, she cried. He saw the blood, on the right shoulder of her T-shirt. He pulled off her tights, he said, and her shoes, and raped her.

There was so much that he could not remember. He kept repeating it: I wish I could remember more. He was frustrated, but the details were gone. At some point, he said, she broke away. She tried to run. He was sure of it, because he had an image of her running, naked below the waist.

They went over it again and again, Ryan switchbacking with questions. As they went forward, and then in reverse, moments would resurface, and flow by with new fragments of detail. Yes, he said at one point, "I think I punched her." He had hit her in the face and head. He used his hands, and a rock, and other things. What other things, he could not remember. He'd found her keys. There were two, he thought, in a little black case. It had a zipper, and Velcro. He had demanded her address; he wanted to steal. She had refused. That made him angry, and the violence grew worse.

When he left her, Reyes told Ryan, the jogger was bloody. Unconscious. But he knew that she was alive. It was the breathing—she was making a hard sound, as though something had broken in her throat. When he reached the crossdrive, he saw the headset. He put it on, walked up onto the ball fields to the south, and headed out of the park.

Reyes had emerged at the 102nd Street entrance on Fifth Avenue.

He'd come across an undercover detective he knew from the 23rd Precinct: "Blondie," everyone called him. The cop was in a yellow cab (in fact, an unmarked police car), sitting beside a partner Reyes did not know. "Blondie" was a good-looking detective, Charlie Freitag, and he deemed Reyes harmless—the kid from the bodega. Had he seen any trouble in the park? Reyes would recall the officer asking. None, Reyes replied, and the detectives moved on. Years later, the detective would not recall the encounter, but would add that if he'd seen Reyes "with blood on him, he probably would have thought he was the victim."

71. "One Good Thing"

2002-2003

The sphinx had come back to life. Morgenthau refrained from a public tallying, even among his closest aides. He was never one to think out loud, but all along, as Ryan and Casolaro kept digging, they could feel it: The Boss had doubts. "He kept his cards very close," Casolaro would say. "Others may have known which way he was leaning, but I didn't."

Morgenthau tried to chart the avenues—how it could play out. Never had the office gone back on so major a case. Many, he knew, would refuse to believe it: The boys confessed; videotapes could not lie. The press would have a field day. And the assistants, Fairstein, Lederer, all who'd worked the first trials, would fight him. The convicted, too, once the scent got out on Foley Square, would have their pick of lawyers. The city, the state, the police department, and the DA's office—all had "exposure," the legal code word that foretold, depending on your side of the desk, a nightmare or a fat fee. They could come after individual cops, and even prosecutors. Lord knows, Morgenthau had been sued before— hundreds of times; he never cared to count. The city would cover him, but this was different.

"We can't rush this thing," he said every time he convened the team. "Can't afford a single mistake."

It was also a matter of not rankling the other power center in the universe of New York City law enforcement. Ever since word had leaked among the upper echelon of the city's law enforcement about an inmate with a bad conscience upstate, the NYPD had struggled to find its footing. Officially, Ray Kelly declared a willingness to help. Few could imagine a more unlikely candidate for a partnership. Kelly was known for dictatorial tendencies: He ran the department, swollen since 9/11 with new purpose and conviction, as a state within a state. He'd first served as police commissioner in the early 1990s, under Dinkins. Now returned to the top job by the new mayor, Michael Bloomberg, Kelly had won a free hand. In the aftermath of the terror, he became a symbol of the city's resurrection.

The press spoke of a feud, but in truth, the DA and the commissioner got on well. Morgenthau had outlasted ten commissioners, but Kelly—Irish Catholic, son of a milkman, former Marine, platoon leader in Vietnam, sixty-one years old in 2002—was his favorite. Kelly might strike the pose of a dandy, model for magazines wearing bespoke suits and pastel ties from Charvet, the French shirtmaker, but the DA liked the Marine Corps style, the get-it-done ethos. It did not hurt, either, that the two shared a rival: Rudy Giuliani. In Kelly, Morgenthau saw a vital ally—and a hedge against an ambitious mayor: Bloomberg was untethered by party, patrons, or constituency.

Kelly gave way. The DA could run the reinvestigation of the jogger case, but the NYPD would be involved at every stage. He put Deputy Chief Bob Giannelli in charge of the case at "1PP"—One Police Plaza, the NYPD headquarters a block south of the DA's. Giannelli, in turn, would assign a supervising lieutenant and the two detectives. The police task force would work alongside Morgenthau's team, following the DA's lead. Morgenthau heard the signal. He had made the calls: Giannelli, an old friend of Kelly's, had once been his radio car partner. The commissioner would be paying attention.

Morgenthau did not expect the most explosive news in the recent history of the NYPD to remain a secret long. But on June 12, 2002, it leaked. Three weeks after Nancy Ryan's first interview with Matias Reyes on the ninth floor, the *Times* had the scoop: "Manhattan prosecutors are investigating a claim by a convicted murderer and rapist that he attacked the woman who was raped and badly beaten in the racially charged Central Park jogger case." The *Times*, though, took care with its footwork. The tests were "preliminary," and had only shown "that the man's genetic material is consistent with some of the evidence." The DA did not yet have "a conclusive match."

To Ryan and Casolaro, leading the reinvestigation, the *Times* report was a disaster. But Morgenthau saw it as a catalyst—the ball was in play. Now he could reach out. He placed two calls: The first, as always when

Harlem verged on edge, was to Charlie Rangel. The other was to Bill Perkins. Three of the five boys convicted in the jogger trials had lived in the Schomburg projects. Perkins, a city councilman since 1997, had been president of the Schomburg tenants association at the time of the attack. Over the years, Morgenthau had cultivated Perkins. He knew everyone in the projects, including the families of those convicted. The DA did not tell Perkins the details of how far they'd come in the reinvestigation, but he told him enough. Perkins spoke with the families, and then called an old friend, Michael Warren.

At fifty-eight, Warren was known as a savvy defense attorney. In the 1960s, he had been a radical at the edges of the Black nationalist movement. He had been expelled from college—the charge was threatening the president—before William Kunstler, the famed activist lawyer, picked up his case and won a reinstatement. Warren had represented Tupac Shakur on a sexual abuse case, and the family of Amadou Diallo, but he was best known for defending Sheik Omar Abdel Rahman, "the blind sheik" indicted in the 1993 World Trade Center bombing, and El Sayyid Nosair, assassin of Meir Kahane, both convicted of terrorism. Warren worked out of a brownstone in Brooklyn, a portrait of Che Guevara hanging over his desk. He enlisted, as well, Roger Wareham, a fifty-three-year-old lawyer with a national reputation in the fight for slavery reparations.

Warren seized on the case, at once sending a private investigator, Earl Rawlins, upstate to interview Reyes. Rawlins came back with his own notes and audiotapes. Warren spent three weeks preparing a motion; he would ask a judge to throw out the guilty verdicts. On Friday, August 30, he filed it. The following week brought a flood of reports in the newspapers, culminating, on September 26, with an ABC News exclusive interview on camera: In lurid detail, Reyes sketched the story that he had told Ryan in May. Of the five boys convicted, three had been released, having served their sentences. Only one, Kharey Wise, remained in jail for his conviction in the jogger case. All had long since recanted their confessions. (Except Salaam, who never signed a confession.) They had been coerced, they said, deprived of sleep, led to think they could just go home—if only they talked. They had lied. "Just to give them what they want to hear," Wise had told ABC. "And I fell for it. The 'okey doke.' I fell for it."

And yet the reversal was far from clear. For Morgenthau, "the thing still did not hang together." Like many criminals, Reyes was not an ideal witness to his crime. There was much that he could not remember, if he had ever been cognizant of it. The DNA was not enough. Warren and Wareham would take the forensics match, but the city's lawyers (the office of the corporation counsel), the NYPD, and many on the DA's own staff would look for any holes no matter how small. Morgenthau was sure of it: Too much was at stake. Anyone convinced of the veracity of the two verdicts in the case would exploit any distance between fact and statement, prying open just enough room for doubt, whether to a judge, a jury, or the readers of the tabloids, to seep in. The skeptics would try to build a case for a "third alternative," as a homicide prosecutor would later put it: a combined attack. Reyes had committed the rape, they would say, but the boys had been there, too, whether before, during, or after.

| | | |

Nancy Ryan's marathon was far from over: The phone calls from Matias Reyes—more than two dozen in all, nearly always coming in the evening—had stretched for months. No sooner had she cleared one hurdle, when another arose: There were leaks from the police department, reporters turning up to see Reyes in prison, rumors among inmates, and even the attorneys for the five men convicted for the 1989 rape, as she would tell Reyes, "don't necessarily trust us either." And the man at the storm's center was growing despondent: Reyes struggled to remember anything that could help Ryan, as she put it, prove "this to everybody." He demanded to see a hypnotist, take a lie detector test. When Ryan demurred, his mood darkened: "I never in my whole life done something good." The prosecutor heard a refrain. Reyes had said it in one of their first talks, by way of explanation: He "wanted to do one good thing" in his life, "just one good thing." Depression set in—and fear. Others in the prison were sure of it: It was "political"; there'd be a "cover-up."

Reyes struggled, too, to get a sense of the old man he'd finally seen on TV for the first time—he'd only ever heard "people talk about him"— "Mr. Morgenthau": "I seen the stress a little bit in your face," he told Ryan in a call in early fall. "And I saw it in Mr. Morgenthau's." He'd been "honored" by what the DA said: "'There'd be no rock or nothing left unturned.'" He wanted to believe Ryan's boss: "I don't know his background. All I hear is what people say, and I think that for his age to be up there, still in office, he must've done a good job." He feared, too, the worst: Someone might assassinate the DA. "Even guys in here," he said, were "shouting things like that: 'It'd be nice to see that man go down.'" Reyes was desperate to prove he wasn't lying—and he did not want to disappoint the top man. "I'm not out to flatter anybody, but I wish I'd had the opportunity to meet him. Maybe he would've listened to me, and I—"

Ryan cut him short: "Let me tell you a couple of things. First of all, about Mr. Morgenthau. This is a guy who was in combat in World War II; he actually commanded a ship." Ryan told the story of the *Lansdale*—how they'd sunk the ship, and "he and everybody in his command went into the water . . . and he went back to fight the Japanese some more." As she spoke, her cadence quickened, the certitude coming forth. "So this is not a guy who's going to back down from any kind of pressure, or from any kind of opinions from people who don't know what they're talking about."

| | | |

"I remember punching her."

To the DA's team, Reyes's memory of the violence was essential. If true, it could indicate that at the time that the jogger was with Reyes, she was still struggling. He had not found her unconscious, as some would later argue, rendered pliant by a gang of kids who attacked her first, had their fun, dragged her to the woods' edge, and left her there, temptation for a serial rapist.

"I popped her with something," Reyes said. "I think I might have hit her with the hands, too." Ryan and Casolaro would connect it to a question that had long lingered: They remembered a wound on the jogger's face. It was an oddly shaped cut on her left cheekbone: a tiny cross, the arms curved upward. In court, Lederer had never been able to explain how the victim had received that wound. Maybe it was the corner of a brick, they thought. They had checked each defendant for jewelry, as it seemed to have been made by something sharp and small. In September, nearly five months after her first interview with Reyes, Ryan got her answer.

They were talking to Reyes in Clinton again, when she asked, Had he ever owned any jewelry? He drew a little picture, as he was in the habit of doing, of a ring. It depicted a cross. Reyes, who was left-handed, said he used to wear it on his left hand.

"Do you know what happened to it?" she asked.

When I was arrested, he said, they took it.

Casolaro checked his office: He still had the ring. Affixed to the band was a crucifix, with a raised figure of Christ.

It was a process: The prosecutors would continue to try to corroborate the shards of memories, testing what Reyes told them. Toward the end of one early interrogation, Ryan asked one of her standard questions: Had Reyes committed any other crimes, ones he'd not been tried for? Reyes did not hesitate; Ryan heard about two additional attacks.

The first had come in the fall before the summer rampage. The victim, like nearly all the others, was in her late twenties. She was on her lunch break, sitting alone, on a pew in the Church of Heavenly Rest, the granite church on Fifth Avenue across from the park. "I thought that it would be a peaceful 10–15 minutes," she would say, "I wanted to say a prayer for my mother and father." He had appeared out of nowhere, asked if she worked at the church. Unnerved, she moved to leave, but before she could make it to the street, he grabbed her from behind. He told her not to scream: He had a knife. Choking her, he dragged her down a stairwell, forced her to remove her clothes, and was set to rape her when she managed to ward him off. She had an infection, she lied. He struck her in the head, took her money and jewelry, hit her again—and fled.

For the second attack, also on a young woman, Reyes could not give a precise date, but he knew where it had happened. He drew a map, even diagrammed it. The location—in Central Park—was precise. Ryan asked the detectives on her team to see if a record existed of a sexual assault occurring near that location in the spring or summer of 1989. For months, neither the police nor the prosecutors found any report. They went to the Central Park Precinct, but a basement flood had ruined their records, so they searched at 1PP.

The DA's investigators did not yet see it, but in time they would: The NYPD, at best, was not keen to share discoveries. In retrospect, there had been clues: In May, during one of Ryan's first conversations with Reyes, Detective Mooney, who was not in the interrogation room, had asked Ryan to ask Reyes "about a scar under his chin." Reyes said that he'd had stitches, but not under his chin: He'd been throwing bottles on the sidewalk, watching them pop, when one caught him under the lip. He even remembered which hospital he'd gone to.

What were "the stitches" about? Ryan had asked Mooney. The detective said that he'd only been told to ask about the stitches by a senior police official; there'd been word that Reyes might be tied to an earlier rape case. The question, to the prosecutors, seemed odd, and it lingered.

It had long been a tradition in post-conviction investigations: The DA and the NYPD would form a partnership, with the DA's office as the lead agency. Now Morgenthau's assistants felt a shift. If the reinvestigation had begun as a collaboration, a rift had opened. It remained more of a fear than a certitude, but the prosecutors sensed an advancing competition.

It would not be until August when the police handed over the file from the earlier rape that had occurred in the same week as the attack on the jogger. Mooney entered Ryan's office and plunked down a copy of the microfilmed DD-5s, the police report, pulled from the archives at police headquarters. The attack had taken place, as Reyes had said, in midafternoon near a cement and rock circle in Central Park in the area called Fort Fish, remnants of a War of 1812 fortification, above the skating rink near 106th Street. The victim was in her mid-twenties, blond, and athletic—similar to his others. She had gone to the park to do tai chi, and after twenty minutes had been sitting on a rock when a young man in a blue jeans jacket and pants approached. He tried to chat her up: He lived in the Bronx, where he also boxed, but was staying at his aunt's on Park Avenue in the Hundreds. He worked in the park, at the skating rink, though he wanted to be a lifeguard. Something in his manner made her uncomfortable, and when she moved to leave, he leapt. He carried no weapon but began punching her in the head. He dragged her across the high weeds, pulled her pants down, and had started the rape when another man, hearing screams, intervened. The attacker got up and walked away.

The woman was taken to St. Luke's Hospital, with bruises, abrasions, and cuts about her face and torso, but she was able to recount the ordeal. He had called himself "Tony," she told the police. And she recalled a physical detail: three fresh stitches on the right side of his chin. He had told her he'd been cut boxing.

To Ryan, Reyes had not called it a "rape." He could not remember if he had completed the act. The victim remembered her attacker screaming "Get off, get off!"—as if, she said, he could not ejaculate.

Irma Rivera, the Sex Crimes detective who interviewed the victim at the hospital, had tried to do her job. She knew where to begin: The day after the assault, Rivera canvassed boxing clubs in the Bronx and ERs on the East Side, and soon learned of a man fitting the description who had had stitches on his chin a day before the attack. A nurse gave her the name and an address—but a police records check yielded no photograph.

Matias Reyes's grandmother lived down the block from "the 2-3," Rivera's precinct, on 102nd Street in the East River Houses. The grandmother hadn't seen him in a while, and said she had no photographs of Reyes. Still, on April 18, Rivera put together a photo array, but the victim could not identify anyone. On May 23, the detective tried again, hoping to show a new set of photos, but the victim did not appear at the precinct. In June, the detective tried to reach her again, but the victim had left for California and disconnected her home phone.

By the end of June, the investigation stalled, and on July 2, ten weeks after the crime, Rivera's sergeant recommended that the case be marked "CLOSED."

| | | |

Morgenthau could not believe what he was hearing. The earlier assault in the park had come on April 17—two days before the rape of the jogger. He asked his new head of Sex Crimes to check the property storage at 1PP: Did the police still have the rape kit—a package of evidence collected in a sexual assault forensic examination—from the earlier attack? Morgenthau had yet to receive any word on the serology report, and for six months, he had made certain not to tip his hand. The reinvestigation posed a "kind of crossroads," his investigations chief, Dan Castleman, would say. "The Boss was caught in the worst case of his career, and it was not at all clear where things were going."

Morgenthau had always brought the big cases home, but the reinvestigation was keeping him up at night. There were the ruined lives of the boys convicted—a tragedy that weighed heavily. And there was something else: the growing sense that he had been at fault. Since his years as U.S. attorney, he'd made it a Morgenthau hallmark: "Hire the best, and give them the room to do their best." The DA could not shake the growing regret: He should have kept a closer watch on Sex Crimes.

On July 1, Morgenthau had received the new DNA results, tying Reyes with greater certitude to the jogger attack.

"The thing was racing ahead," Morgenthau would recall. "And if I couldn't slow it down, least I could do was take control of how it would play out."

| | | |

"Your boss is gonna make the front page," Jim Dwyer, a reporter who had covered the jogger trials for *Newsday* and since moved to the *Times,* told Jim Kindler, Morgenthau's chief assistant. To some, it may have sounded like a gift, but at the DA's office it was taken as a warning. Dwyer's article came out on the Saturday of Columbus Day weekend, the front-page headline setting off a shockwave: "Likely U-Turn by Prosecutors in Jogger Case."

Morgenthau had greeted the reporter days before sitting down, in shirtsleeves at the far end of the conference table, ready to go on the record. The transcripts of the two jogger trials stretched nearly 15,000 pages. The DA had before him a single handwritten line on the yellow legal pad as he prepared to lead Dwyer through the labyrinth. He covered every critical juncture, beginning with Reyes's first interview, and ending with the discovery of the April 17 rape. He made sure to back his staff, and at the same time he attempted to lend support to the police department. The boys' confessions may have been flawed, the DA said, but anyone who watched the videotapes could see there had been no coercion. "I don't think anyone's leaning too hard on them," he said. He had not made up his mind, he cautioned, but Reyes's claims were holding up. And if they continued to, he was leaning to acceding to the defense request to set aside the convictions. He could make the move on legal grounds alone: The police report of the attack two days earlier, he said, could prove more than sufficient cause.

"Read the statute," he'd told his chief assistants. "If there's newly discovered evidence," he would say, "and a reasonable probability that it would have led to a more favorable verdict, the original verdict has to be set aside. That's the law."

It was, of course, convenient legal ground. New York State law afforded him a dodge: He could assume a moral stance without having to weigh in on the guilt or innocence of the five boys convicted. There would be no talk of exoneration, much less an apology. To Morgenthau, the case, "this whole enormous mess," had gained a sharp focus. "I have no choice," he told his aides. "It's not even a decision."

| | | |

In the years since the jogger trials, Linda Fairstein had only risen in stature. The prosecutor who pioneered sex crimes investigations in the United States had become an international expert in the field, pushing for greater forensic science and testifying for stronger legislation. ("Linda," said Senator Hillary Clinton, welcoming Fairstein back to the Senate in 2002, "has really, I think, opened the door to the prosecution of these terrible crimes.") In her off-hours away from the DA's office, she had also nurtured a dream: writing murder mysteries. The series featured a female prosecutor, Alex Cooper, intrepid, brilliant, and loosely modeled on herself, she would say, only "younger, thinner, and blonder." To no one's surprise, the heroine's boss was a wily old district attorney who chewed unlit cigars, munched on red apples, and weighed in on every case. As the thrillers became bestsellers, Fairstein gained a multi-book publishing contract. She remained, as well, in the public eye. Often, when high-level law-enforcement posts opened, her name was floated. She spoke of accepting, if offered, the job of police commissioner, and she was vetted in 1993 to become the first female attorney general of the United States, before Bill Clinton gave the job to Janet Reno. And for years, she was ranked among the candidates to succeed Morgenthau.

Fairstein had been kept in the dark about Reyes's emergence. "I was overjoyed," she would recall feeling when she learned of the inmate's confession. "We always knew one guy was missing"—the DNA the prosecutors could not match. To her, Reyes merely completed the picture: "That this guy was a rapist, but these other kids went in to wild and beat people up, I don't think it was a coincidence." The boys' confessions, she insisted, were genuine. "When was the conspiracy formed by the police?" she would say. The first kids were picked up before the jogger's body was even found. "And one of them," she would claim, "said, 'I didn't kill that woman.'" There were too many cops, she said, pulled from everywhere: They did not know each other. It was not, she said, "the French Connection crew, who're standing in a locker room, saying, 'Let's go get the first 39 Black and Hispanic kids we can find.'"

Fairstein could only draw one conclusion. "I think Reyes is part of this pack . . . the 13- and 14-year-olds aren't becoming aroused in a group, there's blood everywhere. . . . I think he stays, after the others run on, drags her, and does exactly what a rapist would do."

The jogger case and its aftermath, the attendant circus and fallout, would become Fairstein's bête noire. Many years later it would come to be seen as a stain on her record; it would impugn her integrity. She and Nancy Ryan, many in the office felt, had long nurtured something of a rivalry; now the press would drive the wedge. Reports surfaced that the feud stemmed from the jogger case: Ryan, the articles falsely held, had claimed it for Homicide, only to lose out to Fairstein's hunger for a headline case. Both women denied a rivalry, and yet it was apparent each disliked the other. It was a divide due, in part, to personality. Both were commanding presences who loved their work, but one was a popular member of the city's social circuit, while the other shied away from the office parties. Yet Morgenthau was also to blame for the acrimony. From the first, his operational style had borrowed from FDR's: "Never let your left hand know what your right is doing."

It was no oversight: Morgenthau had intended to shut Fairstein out of the reinvestigation. The DA learned about Reyes's confession by February 13, but Fairstein, who had left the office that month, did not hear of it until the spring. Only then, she said, did Morgenthau call.

The DA assured her that they wouldn't "close this out" without speaking with her. When Morgenthau's chief assistant, Jim Kindler, repeated the words, Fairstein heard a promise: As she had been a "fact witness" in the original case, they would not complete the reinvestigation without interviewing her.

There would be further calls throughout the summer, and a last one in October. The DA called and reached Justin, Fairstein's husband and one of his oldest friends. As Justin spoke on the phone, Fairstein listened on a handset within eyesight in another room. Morgenthau had reached his decision, he said: The filing would come within weeks. He conceded a political motive, Fairstein would claim—"I need Harlem," she'd recall hearing him say.

The DA, for his part, would insist that politics played no role, and that he had tried throughout to reason with his former chief of Sex Crimes. He wasn't interested in her "opinion"—they had what they needed—but he hoped to bring her onboard.

Justin, in turn, had sought to head the DA off. Both men recalled a heated exchange, something of a joust:

"You're making a mistake on this one, Bob."

"Justin, this is serious," Morgenthau had said. He spoke of the attack two days earlier—"so similar" in its victim, location, violence. "It was Reyes." The NYPD had even known who it was, had looked for him.

Morgenthau was fuming at the lapse. Fairstein had always taken great pride in how she supervised Sex Crimes. Yet the *Times* had even reported the earlier attack—the May 29, 1989, article sought to give space to all the other women raped in the same week as the jogger, the "28 Not in the News." And the first person, Morgenthau added, whose name appeared in the article: Fairstein. (Later she would say she had not read the story.)

Justin met the fury. "You mean to tell me, Bob, if there's a mugging on

96th and Broadway, you'd check to see if there was a mugging in that same week on 94th Street?"

"Goddamn right I would."

| | |

The *Times* forecast of Morgenthau's "U-Turn" lit up police headquarters. The higher-ups at the NYPD, it seemed, felt they could not afford a reversal. It was more than a matter of embarrassment, of honor or principle. The emergence of Reyes, and news of the earlier case, left the department vulnerable, exposed to criticism—and much more. They hoped "to undermine Reyes's credibility," a Morgenthau assistant would say, "and to bury the earlier, April 17th, attack."

On November 1, Commissioner Ray Kelly announced a fact-finding commission, ostensibly to determine if "police procedures" needed improving in light of the case. Kelly appointed a three-man panel: Two were attorneys, Mike Armstrong and Jules Martin, and the third, Steven Hammerman, was the deputy police commissioner for legal affairs. Kelly's choices reflected care; each had long-standing ties to Morgenthau. The commission would soon make public its own findings, but its conclusions were based in large part on an unpublished NYPD report that, in the words of its author, "they watered down and took what they wanted" from.

Detective Rob Mooney had traveled to "every prison in the state," he would say, to reinterview Reyes's cellmates and fellow inmates. The orders were clear: Find any holes in the confessor's story. Mooney traveled with two other detectives, and as Christmas week neared, had begun to draft the internal report for the department. At a holiday party, the brass formed a line to greet the commissioner. At the far end of the room, a supervisor approached Mooney: "The Commissioner wants a word."

Kelly approached: "So?" he asked.

"We're good," said Mooney. "No egg on our face. It's all looking good."

| | |

The district attorney, though, could apply pressure as fiercely as he withstood it. He cut to the chase with the police commissioner. Morgenthau called Michael Warren, lead attorney for the five convicted in the jogger trials, and announced that they had reached a finish line. New York law did not permit the DA to move "to vacate" (to set aside the convictions),

Morgenthau explained to the defense attorney—"not after 90 days have passed after a judgment's been entered." But he offered a way out: He would have no trouble acceding to a defense motion asking a judge to throw out the convictions.

Morgenthau had faced another option: He could have agreed to a defense motion asking the judge to set aside the convictions, but stopping short of dismissing the charges. In other words, as many of his most loyal and long-serving aides would note—sorely wishing that he had—Morgenthau could have asked for a new trial. What of the other attacks in the park on the night of the jogger's rape and assault? many in the office asked. Should those assault charges be vacated as well? Two men had been severely beaten—one with a metal bar, lacerating his face, hand, and head—and been left unconscious.

The decision weighed heavily on the DA. It was the one case, his wife Lucinda would say, that until it was resolved brought anxiety. "Once Reyes came forward—Bob may not have talked about it, but he knew where it might end." The DA considered the factors: Even at the time of their trials, the evidence linking the accused to the other attacks had not been strong; moreover, they certainly wouldn't have served such long sentences. Morgenthau saw it clearly: "No useful purpose would be served by a retrial." For him, the earlier attempted rape remained paramount: Had the juries known of the April 17 attack, they would not have voted to convict.

On December 5, 2002, Morgenthau made good on his word. He could not foresee all the trajectories of the fallout, but as he filed a motion "not to oppose," no one knew better the magnitude of it all. The DA filed, too, a fifty-nine-page affirmation, setting forth the myriad facts of the reinvestigation in meticulous detail. Casolaro and Ryan had drafted the report, but the Boss read each word and, ever the precise editor, crossed out many. The convictions would be vacated—on all the charges. "We conclude," the affirmation held, "that there is a probability that the new evidence, had it been available to the juries, would have resulted in verdicts more favorable to the defendants, not only on the charges arising from the attack on the female jogger, but on the other charges as well." "Other crimes committed on April 19 were grave and inexcusable," Ryan wrote in the document. They were "unprovoked attacks on strangers, apparently undertaken for the fun of it, which left some terrorized, two knocked into unconsciousness, and one seriously injured." In prison interviews, Richardson and Santana had candidly acknowledged involvement in the violence. But several of the DA's top assistants, Caso-laro and Ryan among them, had convened a last-minute meeting with the Boss on the day before filing the affirmation, and convinced the Boss of their position: If you denied the validity of the confessions regarding the attack on the jogger, you had to deny the confessions entirely.

State Supreme Court justice Charles Tejada did not have to agree with the district attorney. Morgenthau, though, had taken an extraordinary step: visiting the judge in advance. "It was unusual," the DA would say. "But he was under a lot of pressure to hold a hearing. I wanted to empha-size the importance of this case, and underscore, if needed, how exhaus-tively we'd reinvestigated it. . . . I wanted to make sure he understood, and that nobody tried to confuse him. I went to see him so that he recog-nized our position: There was absolutely no legal need for a hearing."

Justice Tejada paid heed. On the morning of December 19, even as the Detectives' Endowment Association, one of the city's largest police unions, filed for an injunction to halt the proceedings, and an appellate court judge reviewed it, Judge Tejada did not wait. In fewer than five minutes, he sealed the DA's move to set aside the verdicts of thirteen years earlier. "The motion is granted," the judge announced to a court-room packed with friends and family of the five men who had spent so much of their youth behind bars: Antron McCray, Kevin Richardson, Yusef Salaam, Kharey Wise, and Raymond Santana. Amid the cries of exultation, the judge strained to make his voice heard, wishing all "a very Merry Christmas and a happy New Year."

| | | |

At 1PP, Commissioner Kelly was grim. The detectives had carried on their upstate tour, searching out Reyes's former prison neighbors, chas-ing leads, even re-running the jogger's route, desperate to find any hole in the confessor's story that might undermine his credibility. The police had also fed a steady stream of attacks in the press. As Morgenthau ex-pected, the tabloids again weighed in, this time with even greater venom: "Jogger Detectives Rip DA for Buying 'Lie,'" declared a *Post* headline.

The NYPD had cause for concern: In the time between rounding up the boys from East Harlem and arresting the East Side Slasher, four women had been raped and one killed. It was called a "mistake"—either negligence or incompetence. But no one at the DA's would go further and claim that the police had intentionally buried the paperwork on the April 17 attack. To many, the oversight made sense. "It would not have been at all unusual," said one prosecutor on the reinvestigation. "Violent crime was soaring in '89, they couldn't chase every lead in every rape."

Not long after Judge Tejada's ruling, the civil war broke out. He was loath to do it, but Morgenthau saw no recourse, other than "to take on the P.D." The DA would meet with the Armstrong Commission, as the three-man police panel had become known. He also traded blunt letters with Kelly, who now accused the DA of withholding evidence. "We *did*," Morgenthau would concede, "but only after we concluded the P.D. was not on the level." The police, he had reluctantly come to believe, and only after repeated prodding by his chief aides, "were just looking for ways to discredit our reinvestigation." Morgenthau rarely set down sharp words on paper, but he sent the commissioner a blistering letter— "the Kelly return-of-fire," an aide would call it with relish: "There is simply no point to our assisting a re-investigation conducted for the purpose of impeaching our conclusions."

"The hat" was the final straw. For months after their first meeting, Ryan and Reyes would speak on the telephone. During one conversation on August 22, Casolaro and John Capers, a DA investigator whom Morgenthau had long considered his best detective on difficult cases, listened in. They told Ryan to ask Reyes if he owned a red hat. They had seen it in the file: a red baseball cap was left at the scene of the April 17 rape. Reyes couldn't remember, but that evening, before Ryan left her office, he called her back. He'd been thinking: He and his friends had stolen some sports team hats from a rack, and he'd taken one—with the logo of the San Francisco 49ers. What color was it? Ryan asked. She could hear other voices as Reyes turned to ask the other inmates. Red and gold, he said, those were the 49ers' colors.

"Bullshit," said Mooney, when Ryan reached him. "He's just trying to please you."

Morgenthau had asked the NYPD to find the hat—his assistants harbored the hope that it would retain a sample of Reyes's DNA—and for months, the police reported that they had searched without luck. The DA's review was long over, and the sentences thrown out, but the detectives had continued to canvass Reyes's former fellow prisoners—and in Morgenthau's office, the questions still churned. Too many loose ends remained; Ryan would not let go. Morgenthau kept asking about the rape kit from the earlier attack, for example—and it had yet to be found. The property clerk said it had been destroyed, a routine matter, in 1995, without being analyzed. Then, in May 2003, Ryan had a thought: Perhaps the kit had not been destroyed, but in fact been sent out of state? In past years, Morgenthau had made an effort to send old rape kits out for testing, in hopes that the DNA results, once entered in a database, might find the culprits in unsolved cases. Ryan got a record of all such kits that had been sent out of state: a few dated to 1989, and each was listed with a storage number. She asked a twenty-two-year-old paralegal, Chris Prevost, to look into it. After several rounds of calls, Prevost learned that the rape kit from the April 17 attack had indeed been destroyed in the course of regular police business, but one piece of evidence remained: "a hat."

At 1PP, the paralegal received a cold greeting: "That guy's here for the red hat," said a male voice from the rear of the clerk's office. Prevost had taken care not to mention why the DA was interested in the property, but as he waited to sign it out, one officer told another that it related to "that Central Park jogger rape case." The baseball hat had surfaced in police storage, held inside a clear plastic bag, its top unsealed, and the edge "uneven"—as if it had been cut open. Someone had recently stapled the bag closed, and attached a note. It was a request written by hand: "HOLD"—underscored three times—"DO NOT RELEASE WITHOUT AUTHORITY OF PROPERTY CLERK." The note was signed "C.O."— the commanding officer. Eight slides, too, emerged, containing hairs from the hat. On May 22, 2003, Ryan and Casolaro received the evidence, but neither the hat nor the hairs had ever been analyzed. They ordered the tests; the hairs were Reyes's.

The prosecutors were shocked. They had taken it as a given that when the police came upon evidence they would hand it over. And to Morgenthau, it had become clear: The police had attempted a cover-up.

72. "No Guile"

2003-2014

To no one's surprise, the accused became the accusers.

Korey Wise, as he now called himself, was the last of the five young men to walk free. He left Auburn in August 2002, after thirteen years in jail. They were all in their thirties now; it would be a struggle to return to society. Yusef Salaam had become a communications specialist at a hospital. He had returned to Harlem, still wrote poetry, and planned to write a book. But his former co-defendants could not get good jobs. They did maintenance work or manual labor—or worse. Vacating the convictions, the five said, was not enough. They wanted justice. They were looked on as liars, they said. "At the end of the day, people think you are guilty," Raymond Santana added. "Robert Morgenthau has been district attorney for over 30 years. He doesn't just let anyone off. It wasn't a technicality."

In December 2003, the five men filed a civil rights claim against the city, the police department, the DA's office, and twenty-five law-enforcement officials. Morgenthau and Ray Kelly headed the list, followed by Fairstein, Lederer, and the detectives who had worked the case. They accused the police and prosecutors of "false arrest," "false imprisonment," and "malicious prosecution." Jonathan Moore, a prominent civil rights attorney now representing three of the five, would term it "the most racist prosecution that occurred in the City of New York." As compensation, they sought $250 million. Mayor Bloomberg had no interest in speeding the case along, and for years the federal judge, Deborah A. Batts, sat on it. Appointed by Bill Clinton in 1994, Batts was the first Black, openly lesbian judge to serve on the federal bench. To the surprise of all parties, she revealed no interest in the case. "The slowest judge in human history," an attorney called her. Batts waited nearly four years before ruling that the case could go forward. Only in 2011, almost eight years after the lawsuit was filed, did she set it on a fast track to trial.

| | | |

At the DA's office, and throughout the extended Morgenthau family, camps divided and the internecine warfare broke out. Linda Fairstein let her feelings be known. After Morgenthau's reversal, she'd call Kindler, the chief assistant. "She sounded as if she was crying," he recalled. She cursed, and spoke of betrayal.

Fairstein blamed Nancy Ryan: "When I left in 2002," she would say, "the only person who had the balls—it was probably my most important job—to confront Nancy Ryan about anything was me." There was no one left, she would say, who would "stand up" to Ryan. In time, Fairstein was appalled to watch a videotape of Ryan interrogating Reyes. Ryan, she said, voice near fever pitch, "was seduced by this guy."

Above all, Fairstein blamed Morgenthau. In September 2011, Justin Feldman, her husband of twenty-four years, died at age ninety-two. She did not invite the DA to the funeral, or the memorial. Later, she would attempt an explanation when none was sought: Morgenthau, she wrote in a note, was "the kind of 'friend' who never once called Justin in the last years of his illness to simply say hello and ask how he was. A great user, RMM is."

Resentment, though, seemed the governing emotion. "He was a lot closer to me than Nancy," she would say of the man she still called "the Boss." "I can't tell you how many times he spoke to me about firing Nancy. But he chose to believe her, and throw me by the wayside. It was the path of least resistance and political expediency."

Morgenthau would hold his ground: From the first, the investigation, with so many suspects and police involved, was bound to be chaotic, but the police had made so many missteps. He'd grown irate when he learned that documents had gone missing—even crime scene photos, including close-ups of the naked victim. The Manhattan chief of detectives, Aaron Rosenthal, had taken them home. The DA would also blame his Sex Crimes chief: "I shouldn't have given Linda so much leeway," he began to tell close aides. "Linda should've known," Morgenthau would say of the earlier rape in the park, and "should have made the connection."

The detectives would demur: "Pattern cases" can take you only so far.

The East Side Slasher was known to do "push-ins"—follow women to their apartments, force them inside, and rape them at home. The jogger case seemed to diverge. (Even Peter Casolaro, who had prosecuted Reyes in 1991, did not make the connection.) Still, at least one detective, Mike Sheehan, and one ADA, Harlan Levy, worked both cases, and the same judge had presided over the jogger trials and Reyes's, yet they had failed to connect the two.

With hindsight, Morgenthau could insist that the April 17 rape should have caught someone's attention.

Irma Rivera, the detective who'd chased an elusive "boxer" with "fresh stitches," and found a name but no photograph, would hear the alarm—but too late. In August 1989, when the East Side Slasher was caught, her sergeant called: "Matias Reyes, name ring a bell?" "Yeah," Rivera said, "my guy from April 17th, the Central Park rape." Rivera had also worked the summer's worst attack, on Lourdes Gonzalez, the pregnant mother raped and murdered in front of three children. When the detective saw a mug shot, she recognized Reyes at once: "It's that weird nose, like a boxer, almost flattened, as if he's missing cartilage." Rivera, too, had known "Tony," the bodega kid. Weeks earlier, after interviewing the two boys who'd seen Gonzalez's assailant—her fiancé's seven-year-old, and her own six-year-old—the detective had taken them for ice cream at the same bodega. "If Reyes is there, they'd have recognized him," she would say. For months, the question would haunt her: "What would've happened if I'd have caught Reyes on my case?"

Misstep, or bad luck, Rivera wasn't sure, but as Reyes sat in jail, she'd kept digging. When she learned he'd bitten his victims, she went back to the files: "I started pulling all these other cases: crackheads, girls raped on rooftops, cases no one'd ever solved." She consulted another detective in the precinct, the veteran running the Reyes case, and she made the connection: "This guy did my April 17th case." It was true, she would concede, the MOs differed—"my case was a rape outdoors, in plain daylight"—but she found no enthusiasm. "They had their case"—the East Side Slasher—"all wrapped up, they told me, 'on a silver platter.'" To Rivera, it seemed a matter of expediency: There was no need to add another case, with a divergent fact pattern. Yet Rivera had made her conclusions known—and they would be remembered.

In 2002, once Reyes confessed, the brass had come up to the Bronx to see her. She'd just had a baby, and was "very nervous," when the two higher-ups, one the deputy chief, Giannelli, took her out to an expensive lunch, and asked her to go over the April 17 case again. When she was done, they asked one question: "Who else you tell about this?"

| | | |

For nearly a decade, Mayor Bloomberg held firm, refusing to settle the civil case brought by the five men convicted in the jogger trials. The Bloomberg era had become known as the age of social engineering at City Hall. Whether the trouble was snow removal or the school system, one goal reigned in the city bureaucracy: innovate and prototype at will, in order to minimize idle capacity and maximize efficiency. Paying off the wrongfully convicted, no matter how well publicized their legal travails, did not rank high on the mayor's priorities. "In terms of what actually happened" in Central Park that night, "maybe we'll never know," Bloomberg had said when the sentences were vacated. The mayor, above all, was in no rush to antagonize his closest, and most powerful, ally in city government, Ray Kelly.

If some contended it would be cheaper to settle, Bloomberg's plan soon became clear: Stall as long as possible, either to exhaust the plaintiffs' attorneys or, at the least, to leave the embarrassment for his successor. Michael Cardozo, the mayor's corporation counsel, head of the city's Law Department of more than seven hundred lawyers, led the effort. Cardozo had little fondness for Morgenthau. (The animosity was mutual, and dated to a contretemps over Morgenthau's tradition of keeping and apportioning, as he saw fit, the millions of dollars in fines that his office reaped.) Cardozo marshaled the city's legal forces, enlisted a raft of private attorneys, and remained silent on the subject of Judge Batts's inertia. Throughout the years of the civil suit—Cardozo would serve Bloomberg from beginning to end—the matter remained an albatross, costly, but hidden and largely forgotten.

But in the summer of 2011, the jogger case returned to the headlines. Sarah Burns, a recent Yale graduate, who as an undergraduate had become interested in the case as a summer intern in the office of Jonathan Moore, one of the defense lawyers, published *The Central Park Five: A Chronicle of a City Wilding*. The *Times* termed the book "slim, but ambitious." (Fairstein called it "bullshit and the unsupported opinions of a college kid.") Burns, the daughter of the filmmaker Ken Burns, soon released a documentary, a collaboration with her father and husband. The Central Park Five made appearances at a law school panel, film screenings, and a City Hall rally. A generation of New Yorkers who had not known the original case had found a cause célèbre.

In 2013, the pace quickened. Bloomberg, after three terms, was timed out. New Yorkers would see the first free-for-all Democratic primary since the World Trade Center towers fell. Even in the early stages of the fight to succeed Bloomberg, the jogger case took center stage. The NYPD had become a target, its long-standing policy of "stop and frisk" under attack by white liberals and communities of color across the city. Nearly a dozen candidates vied for the Democratic nomination, and on the stump few failed to mention "justice for the Central Park Five." No one spoke of money, but the call was clear, and nowhere did it sound with greater force, or frequency, than at the Reverend Al Sharpton's head-quarters in Harlem. The city, declared candidate Bill de Blasio, the fifty-two-year-old public advocate, had "a moral obligation to right this injustice."

After narrowly coming in first in the September primary (with 282,344 votes of the city's nearly 3 million registered Democrats), and then claiming a landslide victory in November, Mayor de Blasio entered office with a host of promises. The settlement of the Central Park case was one of the first that he kept. As his corporation counsel, de Blasio chose Zachary Carter, a former prosecutor and judge, who in 1993 had become the first Black U.S. attorney in the Eastern District of New York. The appointment signaled the end of the lockstep relationship between City Hall and the NYPD; in the Eastern District, Carter had successfully prosecuted several high-profile civil rights cases against police officers. The slow march of the civil case was over: By September 5, 2014, a judge signed off on the settlement. "We can finally put this case behind us," Mayor de Blasio said, "and these five men and their families can begin to heal these wounds and move forward." The five would share $41 million—about $1 million for each year spent in prison, with their lawyers receiving one-third of the cut.

The settlement rankled many in the NYPD and at the DA's office—and even two of the doctors who had first treated the jogger remained convinced that the forensics did not allow for a single attacker. Lederer became a scapegoat, once again receiving death threats. At the DA's, the divide deepened, and would last for years. The trials were riddled with holes; everyone knew that. Tim Sullivan, the Court TV reporter who sat through the months of testimony, knew it as well as anyone. There were "so many contradictions among the defendants' accounts," he wrote a decade before Reyes stepped forward, "that it is impossible to know conclusively what occurred." The confessions were clearly flawed, Sullivan had understood, but even in the wake of the trials he'd probed deeper. He listened as Elizabeth Lederer told him, in a moment of candor more than a year after the second trial: "You weren't there. I wasn't there. . . . You work with what the defendants say to you," she went on. "I don't think it's my job to go in and say, 'This is what happened.' I mean, I can tell you, 'This is what the evidence says happened . . . and I find this compelling, or this to be a very persuasive argument.'" But as to what exactly happened, the prosecutor conceded, "I can't tell you."

| | | |

"Morgenthau was integral to this case, on both sides: good and bad." Jermaine Robinson was nearly forty-eight years old, and ready to speak. He'd spent eight and a half months upstate—held for a stretch in a cell across the way from "an Italian kid from that Bensonhurst crew," one of the teens convicted in the murder of Yusef Hawkins, the sixteen-year-old Black boy killed four months after the jogger was found. Jermaine had come back to the city, graduated high school, found a good job. He did not want to advertise it, but he spoke of working for a time abroad. Still, he'd never been able to return to Central Park.

"Everything that happened that night changed my life. Changed the way I think, changed the way I look at the world, changed the way I look at my own skin," he would say. "Those five were railroaded, and I hold Morgenthau responsible. But he had to push it forward, answer to the agenda at the time. It was the whole city: the media, the cops, the people."

Robinson had been "lucky," he said. He had not implicated himself in the rape, nor had any of the boys put him at the scene. Further, his blood had failed to match the DNA from the victim's rape kit. He alone had been identified by John Loughlin, the PE teacher who'd gone out for a jog that night, but in the fall of 1989, Lederer had offered a plea deal: a one-year sentence for first-degree robbery in exchange for cooperating with the prosecutors. But he'd stood by his story: Yusef and Antron had taken the train back to Harlem with him, and he'd seen no blood on their clothes. Despite the plea deal, Robinson had not been called to testify in the 1990 trials.

In 2013, the city's lawyers did depose him in the $41 million civil case, but he received none of the settlement money. He wanted one thing: "to apologize to everybody, whether they had a bad place in that case, or a good place in the case." It was strange, he would say, looking back. "It all started with a few friends passing the word around the housing projects in East Harlem, that we were meeting up because the next day we didn't have school. It was a holiday"—Passover. "So it was planned: 'We're gonna bug out tonight, everybody get ready.'

"I did that beating," Robinson said. "I can call it 'a temper,' or say 'something set me off,' but that was me." (He'd used his hands, he would insist—not a "pipe.") Something else weighed more heavily: "I led those gentlemen into the park that night, and I've got to live with it for the rest of my life."

| | | |

The city would move on. For a time, at the 102nd crossdrive, near the grassy slope where the jogger was attacked, the NYPD erected a guard booth and posted an officer, twenty-four hours a day, seven days a week. By the time Mayor de Blasio announced his "fair resolution," it was long gone. On a warm spring day, the sweet smells of the greenery at the edge of the North Woods would lift into the air, and the crossdrive again fill with joggers and baby strollers. By then, nearly a third of the city's residents had arrived in the previous decade.

The ones who did remember, though, were left with the same uncertainties as the jogger herself. Her name, as the world had learned, was Trisha Meili. In the spring of 2003, at forty-two, Meili published a memoir: *I Am the Central Park Jogger: A Story of Hope and Possibility.* She sat down with Oprah, Katie Couric, and Larry King. The book became a bestseller, and Meili began a new career. She hoped, she said, to help those facing the tall odds of physical and psychological recovery. The doctors considered Meili's own return something of a miracle. The only visible sign of her ordeal was a scar near one eye. She still had headaches, and at times she had trouble walking. She had lost, as well, her sense of smell. Eight months after the attack, she had returned to Salomon Brothers. She could no longer manage complex math, but she had done research for the firm. In 1998, though, she left Wall Street; she had long imagined she would do something else, something more. Now it made the best sense: She moved into the nonprofit world.

Meili had become a runner again. Her first jog had come three or four months after the attack. She could scarcely walk, but she had made it around the parking lot of a rehabilitation center in Connecticut. Running "felt so good," she would say. "It filled me with such hope and it made me think I could conquer anything." She had also found love: Meili met her future husband on a blind date in 1995 and two years later they were married.

"Part of my being at peace with the events of April 19, 1989," she wrote in her book, "is accepting that I will never know." Still, even three decades later, the not-knowing lingered. "I so wish the case hadn't settled," she said on the thirtieth anniversary of the attack. "I wish that it'd gone to court, because there's a lot of information that's now being released." Meili would spend each day of her life in an act of reclamation, transforming herself from a victim, one of the world's most famous. She was a survivor—and she would dedicate her life to the hard work of healing other survivors. And although she did not carry any memory of that night—"blessedly so," her lead surgeon would say—she would always bear the trauma. In 1995, completing the New York Marathon, she ran once again through Central Park.

| | | |

Throughout it all, the DA had tried to skirt the precipice, avoiding public condemnation of the police or his assistants, past and present. But he would point out that he had not "exonerated" the five young men wrongfully convicted of the rape and assault on the jogger—and he had never issued a public apology. In private, though, he would concede that had he known then what he knew now, he never would have charged the boys in the jogger attack. It was not a matter of pride, he would say; he could admit a mistake—and did. But an apology would take him out of the reassuring realm of "the statute," and into the personal, the discomfiting province of regret, shame, guilt. "Convicting an innocent man," he would say, "is the ethical prosecutor's worst nightmare." Emotions, though, were transient; they would recede, and the law remain.

In time, Morgenthau would come to speak of the phenomenon of false confessions—"something more law schools need to teach"—and concede a miscarriage of justice, one of the gravest in the history of the city. It was not only about the boys who had lost so much of their youth to jail, or even the jogger: He had to consider the integrity of the office. The NYPD had made mistakes, and in their effort to save face, they had overreached. But the DA's office had as well—including, above all, Morgenthau himself. He knew the case would cast a long shadow that he could not escape. It would be, he'd say, "written on my tombstone."

One of the attorneys on the defense team would call it "the DA's finest hour." Barry Scheck had founded the Innocence Project in 1992, and done as much as any lawyer in the country to exonerate the wrongfully convicted in America. "Morgenthau faced enormous pressure" in the reinvestigation, he would say. "It threatened everything: relations with the police, with City Hall, and especially with the people in his own office. But this was Morgenthau at his best—he, and he alone, made the decision. And no one else could have."

Even the *Times,* which had not always applauded the work of the DA in the case, would in the end heap praise: "No one goes through life without making mistakes, but not everyone can figure out what they were, or own up to them," wrote Jim Dwyer. There was "no guile," he added, in the DA's "blunt exercise of principle." Morgenthau had cleaved to the safety of the statute. "I had no choice," he would repeat, "given the new evidence." The reversal was never a point of pride, but another landmark of his demand that the office conduct itself, in the phrase borrowed from his grandfather's friend, owner of the *Times,* "without fear or favor."

73. "The Price of Liberty"

1995-2009

Morgenthau would face a rare challenge, at eighty-six: Leslie Crocker Snyder, a former assistant, dared to run against him. Snyder was a pioneer: the first woman under Frank Hogan to try a homicide case, and the head, under Morgenthau, of the nation's first sex crimes unit. She had gone on to serve on the bench for twenty years, presiding over a string of headline cases. For decades, no one had mounted a serious fight against the DA, but in 2005, a formidable campaign loomed.

To Morgenthau, that Snyder even dared to run was an outrage. "Goldilocks," as he derisively called the blond Snyder, was out of step with New Yorkers. A rarity among the state's judges, she was all for the death penalty—once saying of a convicted murderer, "I would have been willing to give him the lethal injection myself." Morgenthau was revulsed. Since the first years of his tenure, when he called it unconstitutional— eight years before the New York Court of Appeals so ruled—the DA had led the fight against the death penalty in the state. He pointed out with pride that he'd never sought it in any case. To Snyder, this was a sign of undue leniency. When she went further, doubting Morgenthau's stamina (Snyder, at sixty-three, was twenty-three years his junior), he dismissed her as "uncouth, unethical, and unqualified."

From the first, Snyder signaled an intent to go on the offensive. The line of attack was hardly radical, but New York's criminal justice system seemed poised to enter an era of reform, and she cast herself as the agent of change. After a decade that had seen crime fall precipitously—led by a historic drop in the city's murder rate—a political rationality had come to Albany. In 2004, the legislature voted to relax, if only incrementally, the Rockefeller drug laws, eliminating the life sentences carried by some drug charges and reducing mandatory minimums for others. As critics decried the move as falling short, Snyder seized an opportunity. Morgenthau, she charged in a television ad, was to blame "for the slow pace of reform."

The gauntlet was thrown. "Things have changed so much since 9/11," Snyder told an interviewer. "They're so different now from when Richard Nixon was in office. There's the Internet, identity theft, child porn. The main thing is, this is the 21st century."

For the DA, it got worse. Once-appreciative journalists also began to raise their voices against him. "Age isn't the issue," the columnist Sydney Schanberg wrote. "Holding the same powerful office for 32 years is." Morgenthau, Schanberg argued, had "built an unseen empire"—looking after "the New York City establishment, the political and moneyed ruling classes. . . . He is, after all, a charter member." By August, even *The New York Times* had turned on him. On the eve of the Democratic primary, the *Times* drew the curtain in an editorial headlined "When to End an Era": "In the last 30 years, Robert Morgenthau has given Manhattan a world-class district attorney's office. It pains us not to be able to endorse him for re-election." To some, the *Times* might be the paper of record. To the DA, it was almost family: The friendship between the two clans that had begun with Adolph Ochs and continued with the publisher's son-in-law and successor, Arthur Hays Sulzberger, had lived on among the successive generations. The reversal at the *Times* was not a slight. It was a betrayal.

Still, Morgenthau fended off the insurgency. In the September primary, Snyder gained 41 percent of the vote—a scare for the DA. But in the general election, running unopposed, he won 99 percent of the vote.

At the DA's office, the 2005 election seemed more of a boon to the Boss than any other. Aides spoke of the blessings of "a real contest"—and its unexpected consequences. Morgenthau's blood had hit a high boil again, and he'd found a new fighting form. Many in the inner circle remarked on it: His voice had regained vigor—and to the surprise of all his speeches had a new force. "Bob's actually become a good speaker," said his older brother, Henry III. In the office, where some had begun to track the tabloid rumors—Morgenthau was catnapping on his couch, losing interest, pondering retirement—he rose to the occasion.

Now reelected and renewed, he had pushed the horizon back another four years—for himself, and the assistants, now more than five hundred, who worked for him. Relief pervaded every floor of the office. Morgenthau, who had entered the DA's office at age fifty-five, would not leave before his ninety-first year. If he ever did.

| | | |

Before he was through, Morgenthau would make one last stand. He would take the measure of a preposterously long career and embark on one last "big one"—a case that would return him to many of his early goals and old frustrations, and become one of his tenure's most far-reaching investigations. The trail ran from an overseas foundation in Midtown Manhattan to a labyrinth of shell companies, to a myriad of financial relations among a dozen of the West's most eminent banking houses. But it all centered on Iran. And to Morgenthau the goal, from first hunches to final charges, was clear: "to keep Iran from going nuclear."

The hunt would not be welcomed by liberals in New York, much less by the Obama administration, but to Morgenthau, Iran had become the greatest threat to world peace. To some, it revealed a loss of perspective—even in the office echoes would resound of the criticism leveled at his grandfather in 1917, and his father in 1945: that they'd been blinded by obsession. In truth, it was a conviction born of World War II: Israel held the promise of all that the Allies had won. And when the DA spoke of Tehran's ambitions, his words echoed his father's. As he warned of the Iranian threat of a "nuclear holocaust," in his mind he saw a twenty-first-century sequel to the Holocaust. The U.S. must never let its guard down, he would say, quoting a line once favored by America's nineteenth-century leaders: "The price of liberty is eternal vigilance."

At the DA's office, if anyone dared question the wisdom of the chase, Morgenthau would hear none of it. A door had opened, and though he would later call it a windfall—the hand, again, of "Lady Luck"—it was all here, the forces that had propelled him for nearly half a century: a novel legal attack; a self-righteous view of his fiefdom and its expansive jurisdiction; an opportunity for a public whipping of Wall Street; a lonely stand against Washington; and a chance to remind the mayor, and a half dozen of the country's most renowned white-shoe law firms, of the power of the district attorney.

It would begin in the fall of 2005, days after he was elected for the ninth time.

||||

Eitan Arusy had recently arrived in New York with his wife and their two young boys, trading a small apartment in Israel for a smaller one in Queens. He'd moved with no guarantee of finding work, but a friend had put in a word, and that friend's friend—a rackets prosecutor who'd fought in the Yom Kippur War and had worked for Morgenthau for decades—won him an audience with the DA. Arusy did not possess a law degree, and knew little of the American legal system. But within days, he had a new job: "investigative analyst" in Morgenthau's office.

The world, Arusy would say, changed overnight. He had spent fourteen years in the IDF, the Israeli Defense Forces, rising to major and later gaining a measure of fame. In Israel, he'd become a mainstay on television; an Israeli officer who spoke Arabic, Arusy had served as the IDF spokesman to the Arab world. At the DA's, he was led to a small cubicle among a warren of offices. He assumed the prosecutors would assign him work. Instead, they said, "You need to bring us cases."

"I don't have any."

"Find them."

"How?"

"Build them."

A supervisor had explained the concept of "jurisdiction," and left him to dig for "something we can chase."

Arusy would join the Investigations Division Central, the DA's unit at the forefront of the fight against international white-collar crime. Born of the BCCI case, and the stubbornness of its first chief, John Moscow, the unit was known in the office affectionately as "DANY-Overseas." The nickname reflected the team's ethos, and Morgenthau's goal for it: "We know no geographical limits." The unit, Moscow would say, "was all Morgenthau—his brainchild, his ambition, and his beyond-the-sky reach." The men and women of DANY-Overseas were revered by their colleagues, and enjoyed the pedestal; in the long corridors of One Hogan Place they wore navy blue windbreakers emblazoned with the moniker in bold yellow letters across the back.

By 2006, Moscow had left for private practice, and Adam Kaufmann, a veteran of the DA's office for more than a decade, had become deputy chief of the unit. Kaufmann assured Arusy that he would have the quiet, and the time, to find leads. Arusy took over a conference room, and began to read whatever he could get his hands on: academic journals, newspaper clips, out-of-print books. He sought out experts, too, never quite telling them what he was after. He did not lie; he did not know the answer.

One day, he stumbled on a 1998 lawsuit, a federal case in Maryland, *Flatow v. Islamic Republic of Iran*—the first suit brought on behalf of an American victim against Iran for state sponsorship of terrorism. "Initially, I didn't recognize the [plaintiffs'] name," Arusy would recall, but as he read on, the memories returned.

In the spring of 1995, Arusy, at twenty-one, had been assigned to his second military posting—in Gaza. After Yitzhak Rabin and Yasser Arafat's awkward handshake at the White House two years earlier, the Oslo talks had opened an avenue to limited self-rule in the West Bank and the Gaza Strip. The Israelis and the PLO had attempted an experiment: joint patrols. Operations started in Gaza and Jericho and after a year and a half were extended to the rest of the West Bank. The accords had established three district offices in Gaza. Arusy worked in Khan Yunis, south of Gaza City and just north of Rafa, the main border crossing with Egypt. He lived in a compound, a scattering of barracks made of aluminum siding. It was home to the Israeli and Palestinian soldiers, about a dozen of each, who worked and lived side by side. For nine months, the experiment in Khan Yunis proved a success; there were anxious days in the operations room, but also evenings out for pizza in the nearby Jewish settlement.

On April 9, a Sunday, the soldiers were in the compound, about to have breakfast, when the sky above them seemed to buckle. The Israelis and the Palestinians could even see the smoke. Their joint operation room received the word: a suicide bombing.

That morning, nearly six thousand miles away in the northern New Jersey town of West Orange, Stephen Flatow was backing out of his driveway, late for synagogue, when he heard the news on the radio. His daughter Alisa, twenty years old, a junior at Brandeis, was abroad, studying in Israel. A bus had been bombed in Gaza, the news announcer said. "I knew it at once," Flatow would recall, but he drove on, going to the Sunday service at synagogue. Within a half hour, his wife called: Alisa had been on the bus. That night her father flew to Israel. At the hospital in Beersheba, Alisa could no longer breathe on her own.

"Yes, I like America," she'd written her father in her last email.

I'm going to the Zudicks for lunch on the second day of Yom tov
so Shaindy can call me sweetie all afternoon.
That's about it for now, I'll call soon—maybe.

love, Alisa

The shrapnel had lacerated her brain, severing the stem. She was brain
dead, the doctors said. Flatow spoke with his wife, and two rabbis, before consenting to the doctors' request. Alisa's organs, in an act rare
among Orthodox Jews at the time, would be donated. Her heart, liver,
kidneys, lungs, and corneas went to six Israelis.

That night, President Clinton called. He was awed at how Alisa's father was holding up. He and Hillary had spoken about it: "We don't
know," Clinton said, "if we'd be so brave, if something happened to our
daughter."

Flatow had not slept for thirty-six hours. "Mr. President," he said,
"would you do anything for your daughter?"

"Absolutely," Clinton replied.

"Just because Alisa is no longer here with me," said Flatow, "doesn't
mean I stop being her father."

| | | |

Arusy had reached the blast site within minutes: Kfar Darom, a settlement ten miles south of Gaza City and just north of Gush Katif, an Orthodox resort on the Mediterranean—the destination of Alisa Flatow
and two American girlfriends. The bus was smoking, leaning to one side,
as if it had a flat tire. They at once saw the bloodbath—the debris of flesh
and bone, burnt metal, remains of a donkey. The soldiers moved as fast
as they could, gathering wounded, carrying stretchers—one bearing
Alisa—to the helicopters.

At the DA's office, as he read through the Flatow case in December
2005, Arusy came to recognize the name—and he was taken aback. He
was a rational man, a Zionist, and an officer, but some other force seemed
at work. It was as if, he would say, he had been "sent" to New York to
discover the case, and to gain closure for himself, and so many others.

Stephen Flatow, Alisa's father, was a title insurance attorney who for
years had helped run his sister's office in Jersey City. He had never sued
anyone in his life, but in February 1997, he decided to try the impossible.
He filed a federal lawsuit, the first to take advantage of a new anti-
terrorism law allowing Americans to seek compensation from Iran, as

sponsors of Islamic Jihad—the terror group that claimed credit for the suicide attack. Flatow asked for $150 million. He would have settled, though, for no money. His real goal, as he said, was merely "to send a message." He had also been persuaded by the economic arguments: The courts, Flatow believed, could work in conjunction with the U.S. government, its diplomats and intelligence agents, "to cut the money supply" from Iran. The aim, he would say, was "to get Iran out of the terrorism business, so others would be spared."

The Iranians had failed to respond to the lawsuit. At the court hearings in Washington, D.C., the defense table remained empty. In March 1998, a federal judge awarded the Flatow family $247.5 million.

Outside the courthouse, Alisa's father permitted himself an indulgence. "I think Alisa is smiling on us," he said. "I think she is having a good laugh." Yet Flatow knew the battle was not over: An American judge had delivered an American verdict. He would again consult the attorneys, and again they would predict a dead-end. The fine, they said, could not be enforced. Flatow refused to concede, but for seven years the consensus held. Even members of his own synagogue would say he had lost his way.

| | | |

In the years since BCCI, DANY-Overseas had grown by every measure that mattered in the DA's office: staffing, budget, and the affections of the Boss. By 2006, the unit had investigations under way in more than a dozen countries. Each case shared an essential element: the involvement of a bank in the County of New York. The Israeli analyst knew little of the U.S. financial system, but he had learned the Morgenthau rule: "Follow the money and you'll find our jurisdiction."

Within months, Arusy could hardly move in his office; the boxes were stacked high. He had culled the cases of the late 1990s, when a series of civil litigants, terror victims, won wrongful death judgments against Iran. The Flatow case, he discovered, was one among many. The 1996 anti-terrorism law allowing Americans to sue foreign governments for criminal acts beyond U.S. borders had opened the floodgates.

Digging into the court filings of the Flatow case, Arusy came across an Iranian charity, the Alavi Foundation, that appeared to own a string of properties in the United States. The foundation's headquarters was at 650 Fifth Avenue, a thirty-five-story glass-and-granite tower at Fifty-second Street. It stood near Rockefeller Center and St. Patrick's Cathedral, and amid a string of Midtown showcases of luxury goods. Since the 1980s, the foundation had remained a cipher, even as U.S. law enforcement considered it a front for the Islamic Republic of Iran. Stephen Flatow had made the same claim in his lawsuit, but the court found that his lawyers had failed to prove Tehran's control. By the time Arusy stumbled onto the foundation, it had been all but forgotten.

The story of the foundation's gleaming tower in Midtown dated to the summer of 1973, when the shah of Iran paid $8.6 million for the old De Pinna department store, a nineteenth-century emporium that had closed its doors in 1969. In December 1973, the shah set up a U.S. arm of the Pahlavi Foundation, a charity he had established in Iran in 1958, five years after the CIA-led coup that reinstalled him as Iran's ruler. Given the bleak state of the city's economy, Mayor Lindsay opened his arms to the Iranians: In 1976, the De Pinna building was demolished, and construction commenced. The tower had risen by late 1978, and the foundation had begun to acquire assets across the United States (schools, mosques, building lots in four states), just as the mass street protests swelled in Iran.

On January 16, 1979, as Tehran erupted in unrest, and Washington signaled an end to its support, the shah fled Iran. On February 1, Ayatollah Ruhollah Khomeini returned home—after more than fourteen years in exile—to a celebration of millions in the streets. In one of their first acts, Khomeini's revolutionaries established the Bonyad Mostazafan—*Bonyad* being the Farsi for "foundation," and *Mostazafan* meaning "those who are oppressed." A state-run charitable trust, the Bonyad was a convenient vehicle to take control of the shah's assets, including the Pahlavi Foundation. By October 1979, the directors of the shah's foundation had resigned, supplanted by new men, emissaries of the Ayatollah. "It was like a Mafia operation," an Iranian-born historian, exiled to the West, would remember. Jafar Sharif-Emami, a former prime minister of the old regime and the shah's proxy atop the foundation, quit. "He had little choice," the official recalled. "They essentially took his wife hostage."

By the end of 1979, Manoucher Shafie, an Iranian exile who ran a small construction company in upstate New York, found himself in the president's chair. "Manny" Shafie had big plans, but first the foundation would change its name: from Pahlavi to Alavi—to honor Ali, first imam of Shiism. The new directors, though, feared sounding a Shia alarm in the United States, and held off; they had had enough trouble leasing the

Midtown tower's street-level retail space. The ayatollahs in Tehran would have to live with the anachronism: More than a decade would pass before the name was finally changed—to Alavi.

|| ||

The money trail, for Morgenthau's investigators, always began with the red flags: the reports of suspicious activity that U.S. banks were mandated to send to "FinCen," the Treasury's Financial Crimes Enforcement Network. The DA knew something of the federal clearinghouse; half a lifetime ago, he had helped to create the law that gave birth to it.

On December 9, 1968, Wright Patman, the amiable Texan who chaired the House Banking Committee, held a hearing on the Hill. At times, congressmen invite witnesses to testify, and sometimes, witnesses invite congressmen to hold hearings. Morgenthau, as U.S. attorney, had not only testified, he had prodded the congressman, his chief patron on the Hill, to act. For hours, Morgenthau had laid out the litany of cases that the Southern District of New York was investigating, enumerating in detail the "ingenious ways" an American tax cheat could "have the use and enjoyment of the money which he has concealed in a foreign bank." He did not restrict himself to Switzerland but talked about the Bahamas, Lichtenstein, and Panama. Something needed to be done, Morgenthau urged, to enhance transparency. On that day, Chairman Patman declared his intention to introduce what became the "Banks Records and Foreign Transactions Act," a law passed in 1970—once Morgenthau had returned to the Hill to testify, and edited successive drafts of the legislation. The Patman bill would, in time, become better known as the "Bank Secrecy Act."

The act would be amended several times, and FinCen would be born in 1990. By 2001, in the aftermath of 9/11, the Treasury bureau saw its powers enhanced, to fight money laundering and safeguard national security. As Arusy probed the Alavi Foundation, he learned that the records of its financial transactions were incomplete, but seemed to confirm his suspicion: The foundation was a front. It claimed to promote Persian culture, in particular Ahl al-Bayt—a Shia strain as radical as Wahhabism is among the Sunni. It did support a mosque and school in Queens (among its students were the children of Iran's diplomats at the U.N.), as well as mosques and schools in Texas, Maryland, and California. It also paid for the distribution of Shia Korans to prisoners across America. But

Arusy sensed an undercurrent: The initial $42 million "loan" from the government of Iran to build the tower was never repaid. If true, an investigation might reveal not only tax fraud but, more important, evidence that the foundation remained under Iranian control.

For weeks, Arusy fought Adam Kaufmann to open an investigation. At forty-one, the deputy head of DANY-Overseas had worked the spectrum of financial crime: Ponzi schemes, tax evasion, private placement fraud. Now Kaufmann was running his own cases, half a dozen at once, "nonlinear investigations," in the tradition of his former boss, John Moscow. He was not eager to take on Iran. "Adam thought it was a personal thing," Arusy would say. "That I was seeking revenge against the Muslims."

The big break came when Arusy unearthed a forgotten lawsuit. In 2004, a former Alavi president had sued the foundation for breach of contract: Assa Corp., owner of 40 percent of 650 Fifth Avenue, he claimed, had reneged on a deal to sell its share of the building. Amid the legal wrangling, Arusy was drawn to one fact: The case had settled quickly, quietly, and the former president had won a $4 million judgment. To the analyst, it was clear: The foundation was loath to expose its finances to scrutiny.

Arusy was eager to bring his findings to Morgenthau, but Kaufmann urged caution: The 2004 lawsuit might be a sham, a legal contrivance whose hidden goal was to siphon money from the foundation. It could be simple greed, he warned. They would need more. Only when the FBI attained a warrant to search the Queens home of a representative of Bank Melli, Iran's state bank, did they get it. The banker had moved, but he left behind nearly forty boxes of records; the paper trail revealed ties to half a dozen shell companies.

| | | |

By March, Arusy had won an audience on the eighth floor. Morgenthau sat at the far end of the conference table in his favorite chair, the aquamarine leather worn two shades lighter than any other seat in the room. The DA leaned back, right foot on the trestle, its varnish rubbed clean by decades of his shoe resting on it, and listened.

Kaufmann spoke first. A case was developing, he said, but they needed leads—and above all, a crime. "Something we can actually charge."

What about the NYPD? Morgenthau asked. David Cohen, the deputy commissioner for Intelligence, a CIA veteran recruited after 9/11, was a favorite of the DA's. Morgenthau checked in with him as often as he could. "Cohen's guys come up with anything?"

"They searched the trash," a DA investigator said, but found little of use.

Only when Arusy told of "the wires"—where the money had gone and who had received it—did Morgenthau's eyes light up. Hossein Mahallati, the former president of the foundation, appeared to have used a series of accounts "to layer money," sending funds overseas to individuals at Iranian institutions and embassies around the world. Four checks bore the name of one beneficiary—an employee, a Google search revealed, of the Iranian mission to the U.N. in Geneva. The man, listed as a "driver," had received $300,000.

The Israeli had the DA's attention. To Morgenthau, the logic was clear: There was only one reason why Iranians at consulates and embassies would receive camouflaged payments. Arusy spelled it out: "They're behaving less like diplomats, and more like intelligence officers," he said. "It's an operation—and the recipients are agents."

Arusy knew his audience: When it came to protecting Israel, Morgenthau stood with the hardest of the hardliners. Ariel Sharon, the former prime minister, had come to Morgenthau's farm in Dutchess County, and Morgenthau had visited Sharon's in the Negev. Even as liberal New Yorkers accused Sharon of war crimes, dubbed him "the Butcher of Beirut," the DA called him "my friend." For years, as well, he'd nurtured "friends" in the CIA, Mossad, MI6, anyone in intelligence services around the world who believed, as he did, that Iran was determined, whether by long-range missiles or a nuclear weapon, to destroy the State of Israel.

Morgenthau had heard enough. There was a case here to be made, and quite possibly more than one. The paper, though, could only get them so far.

"In the old days," he interrupted, "you'd get a bug." Short of a bug, you needed someone on the inside. At the foundation, or damn close. They needed a mole.

Kaufmann and Arusy exchanged nervous looks: The Boss had asked for the moon.

"What about the Shah?" Morgenthau said suddenly. As often happened of late, when the DA offered a wild suggestion, no one in the room knew quite what to make of it. He was nearing ninety, yet it was not a question of age. For decades, his sense of humor, bone-dry, had flown over the assistants' heads.

"Anyone talk to the son?" Morgenthau went on. He had read a piece in the newspaper not long ago, an interview with the shah's eldest son. "A long shot, but he may have someone."

Arusy braved the silence.

"You know what?" he said. "Not a bad idea."

||||

Reza Pahlavi was forty-five years old in 2006, and mired in a life of contradiction. The shah's son lived as a semi-recluse in a mansion in Maryland, but he remained a vocal opponent of the Islamic government in Iran. Pahlavi had set up a website devoted to the counterrevolution to come, authored a memoir, and, on rare occasions, won a few minutes of airtime on CNN.

Making contact proved harder than the DA imagined; the shah's old guard stayed in touch, but they seemed bound more by fear than any romantic notion of a return. Months would pass before the investigators won an introduction to a former member of the shah's intelligence apparatus, an older Iranian émigré now selling rugs in Washington, D.C.

In the summer of 2006, he welcomed Kaufmann, Arusy, and another ADA on the team, Laura Billings, to his shop. The day was hot and humid, and the conversation stiff. Yet in time, as the shah's former aide served cold watermelon slices, he opened up about his days in Tehran. When he spoke of the years that followed the ayatollah's return, the apprehension was unambiguous: After the revolution, he said, everyone he knew faced the threat—and a colleague had been killed in Paris. "Mullahs, Europe, murder," Billings thought. "This is a new world to me."

The exile knew the story of the Alavi takeover: how the men had come to New York and told the old board members, "Sign these papers— You've got family in Iran, sign these papers or something may happen." Information, even far from Tehran, carried a heavy price, he'd learned. "They don't care where you are," he told the prosecutors, "they will get you." Still, the shah's former aide promised to try to help.

A month later, he called. "There's a guy in Europe," he said. A former officer of the foundation had moved and taken documents with him— "a lot of documents." The shah's man did not elaborate. He only asked two things: "Would you like to meet him?" and "If you do, you must promise me that you will help him."

By June, Kaufmann, Arusy, and Billings walked into Forlini's, the DA's haunt a block away from the office, in the shadow of the Tombs. They were seated at the table when he entered, the man whom they would henceforth call "the German" in all their internal communications, lest his identity leak. He at once stood out amid the lunchroom crowd: He had, it seemed, neither shaved nor showered in days. He seemed exhausted from the long flight. But he had come alone, they were reassured by the two detectives on watch outside, and he had not been followed.

"Salaam," Arusy said, extending a hand. "A pleasure."

Within minutes, the German pulled a file of documents from a thin briefcase. As Arusy began to turn the pages, he tried to keep the shock from registering on his face. He shot a look at his boss. "Impossible," thought Kaufmann, but did not utter a word. "You see the document," the Israeli would recount, "and you see it's an Iranian document." Arusy could read the Farsi. "You see the official stamps. You see it's a secret document, and it's from the 1980s. You see names, and entities, and immediately you understand."

The German had not brought the entirety of his cache. "The rest," he said, "are under my bed." Many bore the stamps of the Bonyad Mostazafan, the foundation formed during the Iranian revolution to channel much of the new regime's finances, exports, and charity; others had come from the then Iranian prime minister's office. The documents went back years, as far as 1979. Taken together, they laid bare the relations between the foundation's officers and the Bonyad. The documents appeared to confirm a hidden ownership, and the infusions of money that had kept it alive.

The German's real name—as he would in time reveal from the witness stand, before disappearing into witness protection—was Seyed Mojtaba Hesami-Kiche. Born in Isfahan, in central Iran, he'd been raised in a middle-class family, and in the days of the shah, he had won a scholarship to attend university in the United States. In the 1980s, after serving in the Iranian army, he had found a degree of privilege, working in comfortable government jobs. Hesami had been lucky, he explained at that first lunch in lower Manhattan, to gain an introduction to an important man: Sayeed Mohsen Tabatabai, head of the Bonyad. Tabatabai liked him: He could speak English, he knew America, and he understood how things worked in the two worlds. The Bonyad chief had given Hesami a job at the foundation in 1982, as the coordinator between the Tehran foundation and its New York branch. He'd seen it all—correspondence, financial documents, internal records—and kept as many copies of the documents as he could stuff into his briefcase each day. The paper trove became an insurance policy: He, too, had a family to protect.

||||

Morgenthau saw a path emerging. First, he wanted to check the German's bona fides, then he wanted to get the motive clear. Years earlier, Hesami had tried to be a whistleblower: He'd walked into the FBI field office in Atlanta—only to be rebuffed. Infuriated, and scared, he fled to Germany. He had maintained his ties to Iran, even worked for an Iranian front company, but his conscience did not go quiet. In 2003, he tried again to offer information, first calling the U.S. Embassy in Berlin, then the consulate in Hamburg. Each time, he got nowhere. "The Americans," he would say, "never took me seriously." Hesami was neither vengeful nor greedy; he was ashamed. He looked at the ayatollahs in Tehran and said they were "crooks." He had one motive: "I love my country."

The DA was more than pleased. An insider like the German could tie together so many loose threads: He could corroborate bank accounts, names of individuals, and even the story of the tower on Fifth Avenue.

At the next conclave on the eighth floor, Morgenthau delivered the news as a fait accompli: He was going to bring in the feds, the CIA and the FBI. The German could prove to be a significant source, he said, by way of explanation, not just for the Alavi case, but for untold other national security investigations. His aides had expected the turn: Some were relieved, others infuriated. Morgenthau had picked up the charge. "Let me be clear," he added: The collaboration would be information-sharing only; the investigation remained the DA's. The CIA and FBI, he added, with a half smile, "can wait for the leftovers."

74. "'Judas' Morgy"

2009

"The Iran thing" had become more than a favorite case. By the fall of 2008, Morgenthau had come to see that the Alavi probe, and the banking investigations it would give birth to, offered a grand stage to showcase the hallmarks of his tenure. "These cases are as complex as any he's done," said John Moscow. "But they're different: the Boss is in the final battle of a long, long war."

After months of scouring the Alavi bank accounts, Arusy and Billings discovered numerous transactions that seemed to have originated in Europe. They also found a curious three-letter notation in a data field: "BMI"—the acronym, they would learn, for Bank Melli of Iran. Soon, the investigators went further, asking Morgenthau if they could get a judge to demand the foundation's emails. Subpoenaing electronic correspondence was a rare, if not unprecedented, step. But Morgenthau did not hesitate. "No one, as far as I know, has done it," he told the team, "and before they take the tool away, you'd better hurry." He was no fan of the Patriot Act; he thought Congress after 9/11 had overreached. But it did promise what he had long fought for: greater financial transparency. All U.S. banks now had to file regular "KYCs"—Know Your Customer forms. And from the KYCs, as the DA's investigators knew, you could assemble a database of email addresses.

Morgenthau signed the search warrants, and Yahoo, Google, and Hotmail complied. The result, he would say, was "a gold mine": More than 15,000 emails, diligently copied onto CDs, arrived at Hogan Place. "Rarely in my experience," the DA would say, "have we gained so much detailed and concrete evidence so simply." The correspondence, he added, "broke this thing wide open."

The emails had contained attachments: wire transfers showing both ends of a transaction, sender and recipient. The transfers also revealed that Iranian money was coming to banks in the United States—in contravention of U.S. sanctions.

Morgenthau's response was immediate: "Are we ready to go after the banks?" Within weeks, he'd sent out 150 subpoenas, and the banks had delivered hundreds of thousands of pages of records. As the DA's team studied the haul, a puzzle emerged: The New York banks were operating "blind," meaning that their computers could not see that the money had come from Iran.

"It seemed a mystery," Morgenthau would say. His team knew about anti-money-laundering systems, screens, and filters. "But none of us had heard of 'stripping.'" In the world of global banking, though, it was a term of art. "Stripping" denoted the removal from a wire transfer of the numbers required by SWIFT—the Society for Worldwide Interbank Financial Telecommunications, the clearing system in Belgium that since 9/11 has stood as a firewall for the world's banking system. "Stripping," in short, was an act of camouflage, a deliberate attempt to circumvent the post-9/11 checkpoints, and speed money, in this case lots of money, to a destination where U.S. law forbade it to go.

| | | |

Nearly three years into the Iran investigation, the DA had reached a juncture. He could only take the investigation into the Alavi Foundation so far, but by the summer of 2009, an ambitious U.S. attorney, Preet Bharara, had assumed office in the Southern District of New York— a man Morgenthau liked and could trust. They struck a deal: The Southern District would take over the Alavi case and bring federal charges for asset forfeiture, hoping to seize the tower on Fifth Avenue, but Morgenthau would keep the banking cases.

Beginning in 2007, Morgenthau had targeted in quick succession nearly a dozen banks for violating the sanctions on Iran. Lloyds, first on the list, did not claim ignorance. The bank conducted an internal investigation, and even sent an employee from England to the DA's office, to walk the prosecutors through the stripping operation. Lloyds had run a "strip club," the investigators would quip: a room at a payment processing center in Birmingham, England, where employees learned how to strip wires of any trace of their origins. Lloyds had prepared a how-to, an instructional memorandum for new personnel.

Once again, to Morgenthau's surprise, Washington stonewalled. The more he demanded that someone go to jail, the more the attorneys from Justice and the Treasury spoke of a "deferred pros"—legal shorthand for a deferred prosecution agreement. "We didn't even know what it was," Kaufmann recalled, "because we don't have it." A recent innovation by the Department of Justice, such deals had come into vogue. A company could skirt a criminal indictment by agreeing to cooperate, reform, and pay a hefty fine. From the first, Morgenthau did not take to the idea. " 'Deferred,' " he said, "means only one thing: 'Ain't gonna happen.' "

Throughout the summer of 2008, the DA and the federal lawyers squared off. By fall, as the stock market collapsed, whatever latent enthusiasm remained in Washington for a public chiding of the banks soon faded. As the world learned of "mortgage-backed securities," and politicians spoke of the Great Recession, the Bush administration dug in. Justice and Treasury locked arms. They would concede that the New York prosecutors had the evidence, but insisted on "a noncriminal resolution." The banking collapse had changed everything, the federal lawyers said. Bob Hoyt, the Treasury's general counsel, was blunt: "It's not the time for this."

In the fall of 2008, after the election of Barack Obama, the outgoing chiefs at Treasury and Justice still seemed intent on stalling.

By the first week of January 2009, Morgenthau could take it no more. "The feds are dragging their feet," he said. "What a bunch of fucking idiots." His office had drawn up its own draft agreement, yet for months the competing parties in Washington kept quibbling. "We thought everything was done," Morgenthau said. But Justice and Treasury refused to sign off. "If I get to see Obama," the DA fumed, "I'm going to tell him to keep a guy with a baseball bat nearby, to knock the heads off those bureaucrats."

Two days later, the arguing ended. On January 9, 2009, the DA declared the first victory in the Iran probe: Lloyds—the bank that had not only done stripping for the Alavi Foundation, but also cleared billions of dollars in wire payments on behalf of clients in Iran, Libya, and Sudan— had settled, agreeing to a $350 million fine. Half of the money would go to New York State and half to Washington. Morgenthau could find solace in the $175 million: "That's real moolah," he said.

| | | |

Robert Morgenthau had never met Romeo Cerutti. As they faced one another across the dark-oak conference table at the Department of Justice, down the hall from Bobby Kennedy's old office, an uneasy chill hung in the air. Lanny Breuer, chief of the Criminal Division, took the seat at the head of the table, Morgenthau to his right. Adam Kaufmann sat beside the DA, and the rest of the lawyers—and two FBI agents—took their seats around the long table. As Morgenthau had entered, his step now slowed to a shuffle, nearly two dozen attorneys awaited him. Several of them, now in private practice or in the government's employ, had once worked for him.

Cerutti was known as a fastidious man. His accent was hard to place, but his diction and carriage marked him as an anachronism. He seemed a man from another time, a gentleman from Mittel Europa. For much of his adult life he had lived in Zurich, but he was not a banker. Cerutti, who had earned a doctorate at Fribourg and a master's at UCLA, and had survived two years at a firm in Los Angeles in the 1990s, was the chief general counsel of Credit Suisse. Promoted months earlier, he had quickly learned it was not an enviable position.

Kaufmann's team had moved on to the next bank, Credit Suisse. (Lloyds had exited the Iranian business in 2004, but, the prosecutors had learned, Credit Suisse had taken its place—illegally handling at least $700 million of Tehran's money.) The DA's men thought they could wrap up the case by fall, but Morgenthau refused to relent. He had steadfastly pushed for criminal charges. Yet again, Washington feared an indictment. "This is crazy," a Treasury official said. "What're we going to do? Blow up Credit Suisse?"

The DA had come to the Justice conclave with a script in mind. "He didn't say much at first," recalled Kaufmann. "He listened, and listened, and then he spoke."

"One thing I'd like to know . . . ," Morgenthau began with deliberate slowness. "How much did you have on deposit? How much, in all, can you tell me please, did you have of Iran's money?"

The Swiss and their American lawyers were taken aback. So, too, was the assistant attorney general. The investigation had run nearly two years, but no one had asked the question. "We never even considered it," one investigator conceded, "but it was the question at the heart of the thing."

Kaufmann knew where the DA was headed: The lesson of "the gold goalposts" was an old favorite of Morgenthau's from his U.S. attorney days. On the train to Washington, the Boss had told it again. Banking was all about the "gold goalposts," he'd told the assistants. He had learned it from Tom Wilcox, who'd started in banking as an errand boy in 1934 and by the late 1960s was in line to take over Citibank. Morgenthau had buried Citibank with subpoenas, hunting cash that fled offshore. And in reply, "poor Tom" offered a proposal, the DA went on, as he and his team headed for Washington:

Tom gets me on the telephone and says, "There's an easier way. Why don't you just come by the office? Our senior guys meet every morning for coffee at 8 A.M. Let's see if we can't get you your records, rather than subpoenaing all these guys." So I arrived early, and as I'm sitting there waiting, I notice all these guys walking by with little gold goalposts in their lapels. I asked Tom: "These the guys that won the football pool this week?" "No," he says. "They're the guys who made their goal in deposits." That's when I came to appreciate that banking is all about deposits. You reward the people who get the deposits.

Banking had changed some since the 1960s, Morgenthau allowed, eyes fixed on the lawyers across the table. "But one thing remains true: It's still about the deposits, isn't it?"

He tried again:

"How much of Tehran's money did you have on deposit?"

Well, Cerutti answered, it varied.

Morgenthau pressed. "What are the parameters, from what to what?"

I don't know, came the reply.

Bullshit, Morgenthau thought to himself.

The question "threw them," Kaufmann would recall. "They didn't know what to make of it." No one in the investigation knew how much Iranian money the Swiss, or the English, or the French who came later, had on deposit.

At Morgenthau's interjection, Breuer, their host, was showing red. Moments earlier, they had stood outside the conference room and set a game plan. Breuer, too, had once been a Morgenthau assistant. He had stayed four years in the 1980s, arriving amid the Bernie Goetz mess and leaving shortly after the jogger case. Morgenthau knew Breuer to be smart and diligent, but always remembered him as "a poor Jewish kid from Queens." Breuer had long since become a legal star. On Capitol Hill, on K Street, and in the elite firms of Connecticut Avenue, his name carried clout. Breuer had served in the Clinton White House, defending the president in the Monica Lewinsky case and the impeachment hearings. The district attorney had been his first mentor, though, and he, too, still called Morgenthau "the Boss." Yet before the prosecutors entered the conference room, *his* room, Breuer stopped short. His hand touched Morgenthau's arm. "You're going in there to listen, right?" Breuer said. "So we're clear: No threats."

The question about Iranian deposits, though, yielded the desired effect. Morgenthau took control of the table. His words had momentum now, and gravity. He asked for their indulgence, to tell about the war. He spoke of the night that the *Lansdale* was hit. He told how the ship had gone down, how he and the others had been left in the frigid Mediterranean to tread water, and how ever since, he had had a habit some might deem discourteous: "I don't like waiting around for help," he said.

Not only could he go it alone, he intended to.

"Gentlemen, I hate to tell you, we can do this another way," he said. Morgenthau had not come to Washington to make a stand or draw a line; he had come to warn the U.S. government and the Western financial world to act. But he found himself explaining how jurisdiction worked in the United States. "We're sort of like Switzerland," he said. "We, too, have a federal system." Laughter crossed the table, faces tightened. "But we're a bit different," he went on. "We've got a second level of jurisdiction—the *state* level." In New York, he said, he could bring a criminal indictment without anybody's approval, except the grand jury.

"I need these guys," he went on, with a wave to Breuer and his Justice Department staff, "to do a 'deferred pros.'" Looking at Cerutti, the DA added, "But I don't need them to *indict* you."

A new grand jury, he added, would be impaneled in two weeks.

The Swiss seemed to recoil. There was nothing, they believed, that they could not negotiate. They'd foreseen a different game plan: Reckoning on the DA's advanced age, they considered Morgenthau eager for a resolution. He would be willing to settle on the cheap, they thought, before heading out the door.

Morgenthau gave the Swiss ten days to decide: Settle or face criminal charges in Manhattan. Then he turned to his right, informing his aides: "This meeting is over."

In the coming days, Morgenthau's assistants plowed ahead, six attorneys and six paralegals working twelve hours a day, six days a week. It was not a bluff. "We proceeded as if we were putting the case on," Kaufmann said. "We would try Credit Suisse."

On day 4, the Swiss blinked. They signed two agreements, one with the federal government and another with Morgenthau's office, and consented to a fine. On December 15, the DA beat the feds to announce the deal. Morgenthau invited the Treasury and Justice officials to join him in front of the cameras. "I'm going to thank you," he said, and they replied, "Please don't." Few in Washington wished to be associated with any punishment of the banks. Since the Thanksgiving showdown, though, Morgenthau's assistants had acquired a new bravado. "To resolve this," they said, "the money has to be north of $500 million." Treasury came up with $536 million, based on a penalty matrix, and Morgenthau consented: Credit Suisse would pay it all—with one-half again going to New York State, the largest fine in the history of the state.

||||

Eitan Arusy left the DA's office long before the Swiss settled. A family of four, he'd come to believe, could not live in the city on a $70,000 salary. He joined a security firm, and moved for a time to Switzerland, where the Iranians, he was certain, watched his "every step." At the FBI, many still believed him an Israeli plant, but Arusy was unbothered: He had started it all, he had kept the pursuit alive, and his work had come to fruition.

Bharara's prosecutors worked fast, and the FBI had made a good case. On May 11, 2009, they had searched a house on Long Island, the residence and office of Alireza Ebrahimi, secretary of the foundation's board since the early 1990s, and its note-taker. In a notebook marked "Summer 2003," one entry confirmed Arusy's earliest suspicions. The notes—in Farsi with a scattering of English—made clear that the Government of Iran controlled the foundation. A July 25 entry recorded a debate on the possible sale of Assa's 40 percent interest in the foundation's headquarters: "Assa share → Sell it → 30,000 → . . . Assa dangerous → Get rid of it . . ."

Two days later, Ebrahimi kept jotting notes. He wrote, in part: ". . . Collusion and illegal arrangement . . . → Foundation shares → Public prosecutor → . . . Assa → Bank Melli 40% share → I cannot sleep at night . . ."

Iran, it appeared, would have to pay. In September 2013, nearly two decades after the bus bombing in Gaza, federal prosecutors in New York won a civil forfeiture case against the Alavi Foundation. The United States would claim title to the tower on Fifth Avenue, and the families of the victims of terrorism would share in the assets. The Alavi building, the real estate firms estimated, could sell for as much as $1 billion.

The proceeds would go—as Morgenthau had insisted from the first—to the American victims of Iranian terror. Still, the celebration, it soon transpired, was premature: The Iranians would appeal the verdict in the federal case—and win. In 2019, the Second Circuit voted unanimously to return the "tower case" to the Southern District—chiding the judge for a "troubling pattern of errors" on procedural issues—to consider bringing a new trial.

Morgenthau also sought a settlement from a second British bank: In August 2010, Barclays would be fined for handling Iranian money, and paid $298 million. Still others would follow: HSBC, ING, Standard Chartered, Commerzbank. And BNP Paribas, France's largest bank, would be hit the hardest. BNP had been among the first banks to draw the scrutiny of Morgenthau's team, but it had won a temporary reprieve. Bob Bennett, the French bank's lead American attorney at the time, the celebrated lawyer who defended Clark Clifford and Robert Altman, had assured the DA's assistants there had been no wrongdoing. Bennett, Morgenthau would say, "was either misinformed or lying." In 2014, BNP was fined nearly $9 billion.

By then, though, the federal authorities would claim the lion's share of the credit, and few remember the probe that started it all, the look into a secretive foundation on Fifth Avenue. By then, it was the money that stole the attention: The banking cases, all told, had yielded a harvest of more than $14 billion.

||||

Morgenthau was drained. Throughout 2009 he had been forced to divide his single-minded focus: Even as he fought Treasury and Justice in Washington, he had had to orchestrate a final electoral campaign in New York. The Iranian cases had sapped his strength. At times, Morgenthau would compare "the Iranian thing" to BCCI: Once again, he had led a hydra-headed investigation, dispatched prosecutors to Europe and the Middle East, and opened a chase that would last more than a decade. BCCI, though, belonged to another universe, to the crimes of political corruption and greed at the expense of the common man. In the Iranian cases, Morgenthau had always seen a far more dangerous threat: Tehran's hunger for a nuclear weapon.

All along, Morgenthau had looked at the maze of transactions and seen a nuclear shopping spree. "The banks," he said, "were a way to open up the investigation, to get jurisdiction." He had in fact wanted to go after Iran's suppliers, purchasers, shipping lines, even its intelligence agents around the world. In the spring of 2009, the DA had warned Congress: The urgency of these cases was not about money laundering or profiteering bankers. Iran was desperate to build a bomb, and someone had to stop them.

Morgenthau also brought his concerns to the attorney general, the Treasury, and the White House.

"You may not remember Pearl Harbor," he told officials half his age, "but I do."

In Washington, some considered it Morgenthau's folly, chalking it up to age. Not everyone, though. In the summer of 2009, the Stuxnet virus, a computer worm devised by the CIA and their colleagues in Israel, began to invade the mainframes of Iran's uranium-enrichment centers. Hundreds of centrifuges went haywire, setting back Iran's nuclear-weapons program years. A sabotage campaign was under way. Soon a series of Iranian physicists would suffer early deaths in unexplained explosions. It was a secret war—whether the work of the Americans, the Israelis, or both, few knew. But Morgenthau, ever the friend of the CIA and Mossad, was eager to join the fight.

In December 2009, as the DA announced the Credit Suisse settlement, he saw an opportunity to be blunt. "You've done so many offshore investigations since the 1960s," a reporter asked. "What was particularly troubling about this case?"

"Here," the DA replied, "it's a danger of destabilizing not only the Middle East, but the entire world." The banking cases, he said, had revealed Iran's ultimate goal: The Iranian government, through a labyrinth of shell companies, was intent on searching the world for the requisite ingredients for long-range missiles and nuclear weapons. "Now more than ever," he said, "we need to be tough on Iran."

The fear was rooted in his life: It was the "goalposts" of Wall Street, the intolerance of Tehran, the blindness of Washington. And it ran darker—to Pearl Harbor, the kamikazes, the German torpedo bombers. His assistants and allies might wince, but Morgenthau believed it in his bones. With the world at risk of a nuclear holocaust, he had to speak out.

||||

It was still dark in Queens on the Friday morning in February when the cellphone of Morgenthau's bodyguard buzzed on the bedside table. A friend had seen a story in the *Post*. "Is it true?" asked the voice.

By the time Morgenthau arrived at the press conference at One Hogan Place on the morning of February 27, 2009, the whole city knew the DA was retiring. On the eighth floor, the reporters and TV crews had filled the library. Lucinda took a seat in front of the cameras at her husband's side. For months, Morgenthau had kept silent about his decision. As he turned it over in his head, he told no one.

At eighty-nine, the DA could still intimidate. His eyes, once aquamarine, had paled to gray-blue, and if the physique did not dominate, even now he retained the intensity of a man on guard.

He had considered another run, he told the assembled reporters, and even mentioned a possible slogan that he liked: "90 in '09." But in the end, he realized the time had come. As the gravelly bass rumbled from the thin frame, everything in the room seemed to change, taking on a charge of history.

"What will you do?" a reporter asked.

"I don't know yet," he said.

||||

Over breakfast on Eighty-sixth Street, and on weekends at the farm, Lucinda could sense that he was narrowing in on a decision. In the end, it was no longer a question of *When?* he told himself, but of *Who?* It had come down to settling on a successor.

Out of a field of many, Morgenthau had winnowed it to two: Dan Castleman, his chief assistant of more than two decades, and Cyrus Vance, Jr., a patrician scion of old New York and the Democratic establishment. Neither man exuded charisma; neither had ever run for office.

Castleman had served Morgenthau since 1979: chief of Rackets for three years, and chief of Investigations for the last fifteen. Vance was a dark horse; the fifty-three-year-old son of the esteemed lawyer who had served as Jimmy Carter's secretary of state, he had worked for Morgenthau in the 1980s for six years, but left New York, seeking to escape the shadow of his father. He moved to Seattle, where he worked as a defense attorney, and in sixteen years on the West Coast, he added high-profile murder cases to his résumé. Vance defended the "Sudafed killer," Joseph Meling, accused of killing two people with the cold medicine laced with cyanide, as well as Indle King, Jr., a man accused of strangling to death a Russian mail-order bride—and lost both cases. It was not, as many in the office grumbled, a record to run on for DA.

Morgenthau heard the negatives but paid little heed. "I knew the father," he said, "and I knew the family." Castleman, for all his experience, had disappointed. He was as good a soldier as Morgenthau ever had, and a fixture of the office, yet something was lacking. At heart, he was a behind-the-scenes guy. "Dan wouldn't get out and do the political work," Morgenthau would say. "Breakfasts at the clubs, dinners at the neighborhood associations—that's what you've got to do. Dan was reluctant to make the rounds. Cy needed no instruction."

That morning, Castleman was frozen out of contention. Forced to stand behind Morgenthau, he attempted to avoid the cameras. Seconds earlier, he'd sensed that he was "dead." He had approached Lucinda in the hallway before going in to face the press scrum, and she had looked right through him. For Castleman, the about-face left him numb; he had been one of the few Morgenthau confided in. As early as 2005, when the two had their first conversation about the inevitable end, Morgenthau swore him to secrecy: "This is my last election," he had said.

It was not long, though, before the chief assistant balked, and began to test the job market. With two teenaged children in private schools, and a wife urging him toward the private sector, Castleman cast about. When he made the short list for a $400,000-a-year job, Morgenthau got word—thanks, as Castleman would say, "to the closed circle in which everything gets back to Morgenthau." For the DA, the possibility of losing his chief assistant was a catalyst. Over the coming months, Morgenthau began to speak with Castleman about the future. The conversations traced a series of hints and clues, rather than a strategy or plan. Yet as Morgenthau spoke, Castleman came to see his thinking: The Boss wanted to retire, and was desperate to deny Leslie Snyder—now in private practice, and sure to run again—any chance to succeed him.

A shortcut was needed. During Eliot Spitzer's abortive reign as governor, Castleman had dared to float the idea of a midterm appointment. "One thing you could do," he told Morgenthau, "is step down, and then the Governor could appoint me." Castleman even gamed it out with Spitzer. Instead, the DA had offered Castleman an alternative, hinting that he would name an heir before the election. And yet, in public, Morgenthau insisted that he would run again. Castleman had no illusions: "I knew the Boss was never going to give up the reins one second before he had to."

Nearly a year before the election, signs began to emerge: Vance reappeared in Manhattan; Michael Cherkasky, the former Morgenthau top assistant who remained a confidant, hosted fundraisers; and by February 2008, a campaign structure—"Cyrus Vance for District Attorney" —was in place. All the while, Vance maintained that he was merely a candidate-in-waiting; he would join the race only if the DA chose to bow out. "I'm running to succeed Bob Morgenthau," he said, "not to oppose him or attack him." By the year's end, with Morgenthau raising money for a reelection campaign, the jockeying yielded four candidates: Snyder, Vance, Castleman, and Richard Aborn, a defense attorney and a prominent advocate of police reform. Each was a former Morgenthau assistant.

As the field solidified, Castleman pushed Morgenthau harder. "If he held back his endorsement, it would be fatal," Castleman would recall. "How could I explain that my boss and mentor for 30 years wasn't coming out and supporting me?" Time and again, Morgenthau balked. When at last the DA point-blank refused, Castleman could not contain himself. There were no raised voices—neither man was a shouter, but the conversation grew heated.

"You made promises to me," Castleman said. "And I stuck around because of that promise, and now you're gonna renege?"

Morgenthau announced his retirement on that chill Friday in February. By Monday, Castleman had quit. The *Post* headlined the turn: "'JUDAS' MORGY BACKS CY OVER AIDE." On the same day, Morgenthau tried to defend his decision: "When I think of my successor," he told reporters, "I've got to think about who's the best qualified to deal with the outside and inside. 'Mr. Inside' and 'Mr. Outside' are two different talents."

For years to come, dozens of loyal Morgenthau assistants would speculate on the real reason behind the decision, and disagree. Castleman, too, searched his mind. He would replay the conversations. The Boss would do anything he could to deny Snyder. "In a race with three men and a horse, the horse wins," Morgenthau told Castleman. "In a race with three white guys and Leslie, Leslie could win, and I'm not gonna let that happen." He needed to thin the field: You could have two white guys, but not three. "And at the end of the day," Castleman concluded, "the only one he could get out of the race was me."

Politics, though, were only part of it. "Hubris," said Morgenthau days after his announcement. "Dan thought the job was his, that he was entitled to it." In Morgenthau's world, there could be no entitlement—except his own. Over the decades, the DA had told more than one person that he, or she, would be his successor. "There'd been at least four or five 'heirs,'" Cherkasky would say. "But everyone knew it all along: Only one person on the planet was going to choose the successor—the Boss." After nearly thirty-five years in office, Morgenthau was not going to let anyone else dictate the future. "Dan put a gun to his head," said Cherkasky. To the DA, it was unforgivable. "Castleman's position," Morgenthau said, "was that I owed it to him after all these years of faithful service. What he didn't take into consideration was that maybe he owed *me*—for rewarding him all along through all those years."

| | | |

The DA, who had won nine elections in an unbroken string, would triumph in his emeritus campaign. Vance won the September 2009 Democratic primary handily, with 46 percent of the vote. On election night, at the victory party at a Cajun restaurant off Times Square, Vance thanked his supporters, including David Dinkins, Caroline Kennedy, and Gloria Steinem. But everyone present knew who had elected the candidate. The bar was crowded with assistants, past and present—"the Morgenthau Army," one quipped—and the shouts grew loudest as the district attorney, ruddy-cheeked from the Vineyard and sporting a tan suit, made his way to the microphone. Morgenthau would stay late that evening, until long after the speeches ended and Vance had left. He wanted to linger, as he had so often as a boy on election nights. He wanted to enjoy the noise and the lights of triumph. Vance's victory, as all knew, had been his as well—his last.

Outside in the darkening night, as the DA walked down a deserted Forty-sixth Street, a lone well-wisher approached. Morgenthau would be missed, she said.

"You can sleep easy," he replied. The black Suburban was idling, door opened. Morgenthau offered the words softly, as if to himself, in reassurance. "The city's in safe hands."

75. "On the Outside"

2011-2018

In retirement, there would be no crosswords, puzzles, or painting classes for Bob Morgenthau. Shortly after New Year's in 2010, he was welcomed, with the official title "of counsel," into the corporate firm Wachtell, Lipton, Rosen & Katz. Still, he was determined to make a good show of it, trying to prove to his wife and family that he knew how to relax. But soon enough Morgenthau would fail to convince anyone.

By the second year of an unquiet retirement, he could no longer contain his anger, or his regret. The snarl had returned, and the stumbles of his heir Cy Vance, as he saw them, had become irredeemable blunders. It was inevitable, many who knew him best would say: "The Boss has only reaped what he sowed" was a common refrain. No one, former aides would say, could meet his expectations, nor could he sit idly on the sidelines. Morgenthau found a near-daily cause for irritation, but of particular concern was the case of the French banker Dominique Strauss-Kahn.

In the spring of 2011, Strauss-Kahn was the managing director of the International Monetary Fund, an overlord of global banking, celebrated in financial and political circles around the world. He was also the undeclared, but widely presumed, Socialist candidate for the presidency of France. But on Saturday, May 14, 2011, detectives escorted Strauss-Kahn off an Air France plane at Kennedy Airport, minutes before it was to depart for Paris. By 2:15 A.M. on Sunday, Vance had charged the banker with the attempted rape of a thirty-two-year-old housekeeper, an immigrant from Guinea, in a luxury suite of a Midtown Manhattan hotel on the previous afternoon.

Within days, Morgenthau was fuming. His successor seemed intent at every step, as Morgenthau put it, "to fuck things up." First, Vance had allowed Strauss-Kahn, haggard and unshaven after a night in jail, to be paraded before the world's press. The spectacle turned Morgenthau's stomach: The demand for a "perp walk" had arisen in the mid-1970s—and though others loved it, he had rejected it, considered it beneath the office.

Above all, Morgenthau could not believe Vance's carelessness with the case. "He was rushing, and took a huge risk," he said two days after the arrest. Once again, he invoked the old rule: "Fifty percent of all the information you get in the first 24 hours is usually wrong."

Morgenthau tracked the case by the hour. He could tap former assistants on both sides for information: Strauss-Kahn had hired Ben Brafman, one of the city's most celebrated defense attorneys, who had spent four years in the DA's office. As Morgenthau learned about Nafissatou Diallo, the hotel maid who accused the banker of the sexual attack, he offered the same advice to both sides: "Vacuum up the paper trail—employment, immigration, travel, housing—all of it." Diallo seemed a compelling witness: An asylum seeker from West Africa who could not read or write in any language, she claimed to have no knowledge of Strauss-Kahn's position and wealth. Yet when Morgenthau learned that her asylum application had holes—she would later admit to fabricating, at the urging of an immigration lawyer, a gang rape as the reason she sought to emigrate—he saw the case collapsing. Why had they rushed? he fumed. In any case, especially the high-profile ones, you had to build it carefully; you couldn't make rash decisions. The last straw came on May 19, as Strauss-Kahn was indicted. The judge set a $1 million bail, demanded an additional $5 million insurance bond, and returned the banker for a sixth night in jail. Morgenthau was outraged: "There's no risk of flight, the guy's got a huge house in D.C., he's known around the world, there's no place he can hide. It makes no sense to keep him locked up."

Morgenthau could not yet bring himself to admit it, but the banker's case had only proven what he had long feared: Vance was not up to the job. He'd seen signs of the failings during the campaign, but they'd shared so many values, he'd chosen to overlook them. It was not a matter of politics, or intelligence, and certainly not decency. It was a lack of curiosity, and engagement with people. He'd seen it in the way Vance failed to look at a waiter when he gave his dinner order. And since Vance had settled into the eighth floor, in the way he had others do his bidding,

especially the firing, as Morgenthau had heard time and again, of prosecutors who had given decades of service to the office. Morgenthau now
saw a detachment, and a lack of perspicacity, that he'd only glimpsed
before. Once a promising project, the new DA would be kept at arm's
length. Vance would not hear, at least not for months, and not directly,
what the few close to Morgenthau already surmised: The Boss was ready
to disown his heir.

IIII

But Vance needed his patron—perhaps now more than ever.

After filing the indictment against Strauss-Kahn, the new DA came
calling. On the afternoon of July 5, he visited Morgenthau's Midtown
office at the firm, seeking his advice. On July 13, he and Morgenthau
lunched at the Century Association, a private club a few blocks from the
hotel where the incident had occurred. And on July 27, at 10:30 A.M.,
Vance called again. "He wanted me to come down to the office," Morgenthau would say, "to return and to show the flag. But I wouldn't play
any games, not for his benefit at least." Morgenthau refused the invitation.

"Take your time," Morgenthau had counseled Vance on the Strauss-
Kahn case. "Get an adjournment. They can't complain about an adjournment."

The assistants handling the case didn't believe there *was* a case, Vance
told Morgenthau. They worried about Diallo's credibility.

"Who doesn't lie about their immigration?" Morgenthau countered.

There was more, Vance said. She'd told diverging stories about the
attack.

The case had already folded, Morgenthau realized: "You couldn't be
certain which story she'd tell."

"Only one thing to do," he told Vance. "Dismiss the charges."

Vance held firm until the second week of August, when he flew to the
Vineyard to see Morgenthau. He came seeking a blessing: He was weighing a final determination on whether to bring charges and wanted Morgenthau "onboard."

The team was against going forward, Vance said. "I'm the only one
who still wants to do it." He said he'd been thinking of bringing in other
people to try the case.

Morgenthau foresaw the fallout at the office: doubt, division, and discontent. "Suicide," Morgenthau said. "Don't do it."

Vance had only one reason for the show of deference, Morgenthau thought: "He doesn't want to be out there alone."

The supplication on the Vineyard did not go well. On the evening of his visit from Vance, the former district attorney was still incensed: "I will not be used," he said.

Five days later, in a stunning about-face, Vance dismissed the charges. The tabloids and talk shows erupted, and Diallo's defense attorneys, civil rights activists, women's rights leaders, and many among the DA's own staff fumed. Morgenthau agreed with the decision, but rued how the case had been handled, from start to finish. "A disaster," he called it, and one that Vance would have trouble recovering from. Morgenthau no longer cared about the fortunes of his successor; he cared about only one future: the survival of the office—*his* office—in all its competency, integrity, and sovereignty.

| | | |

Even in retirement, Morgenthau refused to believe the fight, political or legal, was over. As he struggled to adapt to civilian life, the old battles raged on. In the exit interviews with the press—they would stretch for months—he returned to Iran. "Everyone has dropped the ball on" the sanctions, he said. He did not spare Obama, either: "The president is smoking pot or something if he thinks that being nice to these guys is going to get him anywhere." Well into his nineties, Morgenthau had not slowed: He moved from cause to cause, trying to serve them all before his time ran out.

He returned, as well, to the death penalty fight, focusing his energies on one case: William Kuenzel, a former auto mechanic with an eighth-grade education, who had spent more than two decades on Alabama's death row. Gene Anderson, a lawyer who'd worked for Morgenthau in the U.S. attorney's office, and later married his daughter Jenny, had carried the case pro bono for years. When Anderson died in 2010, Morgenthau picked up the cause. Alabama, Morgenthau knew, had the highest per capita death penalty rate in the country, and Talladega County, in which Kuenzel had been convicted of murder, had sentenced more men to death than any other in the nation. To Morgenthau, the case echoed the jogger reinvestigation: "Newly discovered evidence" demanded that it be reopened. But he did not take it as a pretext to score a legal point: He wanted to see an innocent man walk. "The guy didn't do it," he said.

Linda Offord was a thirty-nine-year-old clerk working the night shift at Joe Bob's Crystal Palace in the town of Sylacauga, Alabama, when she was shot to death in an apparent robbery gone bad in 1987. Kuenzel was found guilty on the word of his roommate, who admitted that he himself had been involved in the murder, and who had the victim's blood on his clothes. The sole corroborating evidence of Kuenzel's involvement was a witness whose grand jury testimony contradicted her identification of him at trial—a contradiction the prosecutor did not disclose.

Morgenthau had a fondness for Alabama, and did not shy from speaking of the family ties—the Lehmans had made their first fortune in cotton there—but to his astonishment, the state courts had dismissed the case on procedural grounds, because Kuenzel could not be conclusively exonerated. The decision caused Morgenthau to quote a favored line from Dickens: "The law is an ass." "In essence," he would explain, "they said there's presumption of guilt because he was convicted once—without the newly discovered evidence. If that's not nonsense, I don't know what is."

Morgenthau recruited the former DAs of Los Angeles and Milwaukee to join him in a "friend-of-the-court" brief to the U.S. Supreme Court. He also brought in Edwin Meese, Ronald Reagan's attorney general, who filed an amicus brief of his own. In time, the lobbying—he would call Alabama nearly each week—opened a door: The governor's legal aide, on the eve of leaving his post, sent word to Morgenthau—"You remain a legend among legal public servants"—that he would recommend the governor to "look with favor" on a request for commutation, lessening Kuenzel's sentence from death to life.

The Alabama State Supreme Court issued a stay of execution, but relief was not forthcoming. After months of correspondence, in a long telephone call to the inmate on death row in April 2016, Morgenthau tried to persuade Kuenzel—"Let us save your life"—but he declined to request a commutation. If granted, the concession would have gotten him off death row, but kept him in jail. Morgenthau tried to convince him, but Kuenzel insisted on fighting for a reversal of his conviction.

The end of the legal battle, for Morgenthau, grew near. For months, as their appeal for certiorari sat at the U.S. Supreme Court, he'd heard "good rumblings"—and hoped the conservative, right-to-life justices might support it. But the appeal, based on the Court's system of sorting death penalty cases by federal circuits, fell under Justice Clarence Thomas's purview to distribute it—with a recommendation to review the case or not—to his fellow justices. The result did not surprise Morgenthau: "We got screwed, without a word." The request was not granted; Kuenzel would remain on death row—awaiting execution. In the years that followed, the condemned man's hopes, and his own failure to see them through, would haunt the former DA of New York County.

||||

It had long been a lament: As DA, he'd never had enough time to write. Now he would. He did not seek a ghostwriter for self-adulatory memoirs, like his grandfather, or a historian, like his father, to weave the mountains of paper that had crossed his desk into a legacy-burnishing chronicle. Instead, he attempted a return of sorts—even though he did not recognize it as such—to the prewar days, to his editorship at the *Amherst Student,* his college paper.

Week after week, Morgenthau offered opinion columns—unsolicited Op-Ed articles—to the *Times,* the *Journal,* the *Daily News,* he was not choosy. The words revived him. A first column appeared in *The Wall Street Journal* six months into his "retirement": "Ending the Stigma of War-Related Stress." Morgenthau wrote of the American military veterans, more than 300,000, who suffered from PTSD and depression—and the curse of suicide, an issue he'd experienced with his fellow officers in World War II. "Eighteen veterans commit suicide every single day," he noted—"more than 6,500 a year."

Iran remained a focus, and the fight against offshore havens that fed the global drug and weapons trade. After drafting one article on Iran, he grew frustrated with a *Times* editor who dared question the veracity of his statistics regarding the Cayman Islands. He'd claimed that the tax haven had two trillion U.S. dollars on deposit—more than in all the banks in New York City combined—and that a single building in the territory had "more than 19,000 companies listed there."

"What's your source?" the editor asked. "How do you know that?"

"I read it in *The New York Times,*" he replied.

Ida Van Lindt, still at Morgenthau's side, faxed over a copy of the article; published four years earlier, it quoted Senator Carl Levin offering the statistics. When the editor called back to thank him, Morgenthau kept silent. "What I did not add is, I'd only read about it there because I'd given the numbers to Senator Levin—and asked him to put them out."

His mind, agile as ever, filled with new ideas and causes: legal aid for undocumented immigrants; medical benefits for veterans; amnesty for those serving draconian sentences for drug offenses. He worked, too, with the top jurist in the state, Robert Katzmann, chief judge of the Second Circuit Court of Appeals, to help found the Immigrant Justice Corps—a legal clinic, staffed by young attorneys from the top schools, to serve the city's undocumented immigrants. The "Corps," he explained, could offer free help—assisting the immigrants to gain visas, green cards, citizenship.

In the decade after leaving the DA's office, Morgenthau published seventy-four articles, but he had always felt words could not do enough. His mind still churned with ideas to spur real action in the criminal justice system. The rising threat to the city's newest immigrants had become a constant worry: At night he lay in bed, figuring how he could "run a dummy"—to see, from the inside, how the system treated the undocumented. Would it be possible, he wondered, to deploy a paperless immigrant, have him jump a subway turnstile, and be sent to Rikers? Could he keep him safe? Could he protect a "plant" long enough so that he could get out, and report what he had seen? It could be done, he reasoned. But he would need cover: the blessing of a trusted judge. He wanted to expose not just the brutal fiat of the guards, but how the officers of ICE, the federal Immigration and Customs Enforcement agency, contrived to deport men and women, mothers and children, from a "sanctuary city." Immigration was the city's lifeblood; without new arrivals the city would never endure. Again and again, he returned to the past, and thought of his own grandfather, Henry Sr.: "He came to this country at 10 years old—what if he'd been turned away?"

||||

There was no anguish over his record as DA, but there was a returning instinct for reform. Few knew the statistics better. Each year more than 10 million Americans were arrested. The criminal justice system had become little more than a conveyor belt: In 90 percent of cases nationwide those arrested went to sentencing—without trial. In New York, the numbers were higher: In 2017, more than 98 percent of the felony arrests that ended in convictions had "pled out." Yes, the city had seen a historic drop in violent crime. During his tenure the number of homicides in Manhattan had fallen by more than 90 percent—"a drop," as he wrote in his final year-end report, "not due simply to the dawn of gentler times." "Serious crime," he noted, including robberies and burglaries, had fallen dramatically across the board. Even though the office had lost nearly a quarter of its cases, Morgenthau could claim a historically high "success rate." But who had gone to the state's jails? It weighed on him. Communities of color, he knew, were ground through the system at a vastly disproportionate rate.

He knew, as well, the tally: Morgenthau had likely put more people behind bars than any other American in history. Three and a half million prosecutions, by his own rough count, bore his name. He liked to speak, of course, instead of the lives ruined, of the reforms made. Morgenthau in retirement was hailed as the "most innovative" prosecutor in the city's history. It went beyond his pursuit of financial fraud and political corruption. He'd increasingly devoted resources to cases of domestic violence and child abuse. He'd tried, as well, to fight bias crime; he had seen crimes of "prejudice," as the NYPD patrol guide once termed attacks on gays, lesbians, and minorities, double. At a time when New York State had no law that defined bias crime, he'd long pushed for one—testifying as early as 1988. (It was not until 2000, after a decade of Republican opposition, that the state's Hate Crimes Act was passed.) Over the decades, he had also changed the profile of the office. From 1975 to 2009, the number of lawyers of color had grown fivefold, from 4 percent to 22 percent, and the number of women had risen from 11 percent to 52 percent.

But Morgenthau may have been most proud of the "John Doe" convictions, a combination of technology and diligence that despite the long odds had delivered justice for survivors of sexual violence. In 1970, the city had over a thousand rape cases, and only eighteen convictions. "Old laws," he said. "That was the problem." The courts demanded corroboration, a vestige of the sixteenth century. "The law protected the man, held women to a higher standard of evidence." When he'd become DA, the office had one ADA assigned to Sex Crimes. By 2009, they had fifty-three. He had studied the New York law and abhorred that it deemed rape in the first degree a "B violent felony," on a par with first-degree burglary and first-degree grand larceny, and set a five-year statute of limitations. "When you're burglarized or robbed," he'd argued, "you get over it." But when you're raped, "I don't see how you ever got over it." Any system of criminal justice, he considered, must allow special consideration for such crimes.

He had known that the statute on rape could be extended to ten years, if the perpetrator's whereabouts were unknown. In 2000, when the medical examiner joined the federal DNA databank, Morgenthau set up a cold case unit, and became the first prosecutor in the United States to indict a DNA profile—with the defendant "to-be-arrested-later." "John

Doe indictments," he called them. The prosecutors would use DNA evidence gleaned from a victim, or crime scene, and should an assailant ever be apprehended—he could be prosecuted. By 2019, the office had obtained sixty-two such "John Doe" indictments, nearly all for sexual assault.

He had also led the campaign to change the rape law, fighting in 2006 to raise the charge to a "Class A" felony—alongside murder, first-degree kidnapping, and first-degree arson. No longer would every rape case face a statute of limitations. He traveled to Albany, taking with him two survivors of sexual assaults who had identified their attackers, but only after too much time had passed. The DA and the women met with Sheldon "Shelly" Silver, Speaker of the State Assembly and, for more than a decade, invincible boss of Albany. Silver could back the change, he'd told the DA, but demanded a horse trade—on the civil statute. Morgenthau was blunt: "Shelly, shut the hell up." To the surprise of all, Silver did. The law passed, 139–1.

And yet, there was no denying it. Throughout his years in office—across the most consequential period for criminal justice in U.S. history—the system had grown exponentially by every measure. It had also grown crueler, he would concede, and less resistant to reform. But in the decade that he'd spent "on the outside," in retirement, he'd come to see that change was long overdue. Too little, too late, many would say. Yet he railed against the rise of private prisons—much to the chagrin of his new law partners, who represented them. He wanted to help those "most in need"—"all those young people behind bars." He blamed the war on drugs—a misbegotten crusade that began with the criminalization of opium in the nineteenth century, in San Francisco's Chinatown. He would speak of the illegal stills of his youth in Dutchess County and say wryly, "Prohibition didn't quite work."

Change, he predicted, would be hard won. Mass incarceration had become a national plague. In 2009, his last year in office, 7.3 million Americans—1 in 31 adults—were behind bars, on parole, or on probation. And yet, the climate was shifting. After years of Republican opposition, Albany had repealed the last vestiges of the Rockefeller drug laws, and by 2010, the number of people incarcerated in the state had fallen below 100,000 for the first time since 1987. The city jails were emptying; by 2020, New York City's prison population would drop to below 4,000—the lowest since 1946. He'd been called to testify again, in 2007 before the State Sentencing Commission, and returned to the questions of three decades earlier, when he had chaired it. He again supported "determinate sentencing," but worried about judges who "tended to sentence in part based on their own predilections." He decried the lack of funds for programs providing "drug treatment, educational credits, and vocational skills" to aid the formerly incarcerated in reentering the community.

He would cast the conversation back to "the Harlem leaders," his friends Charlie Rangel, David Dinkins, and most recently, a son of the old "Gang of Four," the former governor David Patterson. Most years, on Martin Luther King Jr. Day, the DA would go up to Harlem, to the Convent Avenue Baptist Church—during the years John F. Kennedy, Jr., was in the office, he'd take him along. "Black leaders have always called for more police," he would say. "Their communities suffer the worst violence." It was a well-worn argument. Yes, "African-Americans wanted more law enforcement," as James Forman, Jr., would write, "but they didn't want *only* law enforcement." Harlem's leaders, and Black officials and activists across the country, also yearned for "jobs, schools, housing—what many termed a 'Marshall Plan for urban America.'" It had never come.

Still, he could look with hope, at least in private, to the emergent generation of new DAs in the boroughs. He'd long supported the move to decriminalize marijuana—coming out in support of its medical use in 2004, a decade before the law was passed. Before retiring, he'd also come to believe in the legalization of cannabis. In New York City, between 1997 and 2003 the NYPD made more than 353,000 arrests for possession of small amounts of marijuana. He considered it a waste of police and prosecutorial resources, but above all, he'd come to see the toll: the "legalized discrimination," as Michelle Alexander would term it in *The New Jim Crow,* that few of those arrested—Blacks and Latinos were five times more likely to be arrested than whites—were ever likely to outgrow.

Still, the new "progressive" thinking had limits. When it came to police reform, there would be no overnight conversion. "Stop and frisk," the NYPD practice of stopping and searching New Yorkers, had grown unchecked, becoming the scourge of communities of color across the city. By 2008, the police were stopping 545,000 people in a single year, 80 percent of them Black and Latino men. And still, he supported the practice until the end. In June 2013, he was called to a press conference at police headquarters to shore up Ray Kelly and Mayor Bloomberg as the city council pushed for two bills, one to create an inspector general to oversee the NYPD, and another to increase opportunities for New Yorkers to sue for racial profiling. "If this legislation is enacted," Morgenthau railed, "it's going to be a major disincentive for police officers to stop people, question them and frisk them. And that's going to be, frankly, a disaster for the city." Two months later the debate turned moot: A federal judge ruled the stops unconstitutional.

| | | |

In November 2016, America elected a new president, Donald J. Trump. Morgenthau had known Trump—"at close range," he would say—for more than forty years.

To those who knew the DA best, the history with Trump made sense. Morgenthau had long kept the real estate clans who controlled acres of Manhattan close: the Rudins, Fishers, Wilpons—Fred Wilpon, for years a principal owner of the Mets, had been a friend since the 1960s. Peter Kalikow, another real estate magnate, and a onetime owner of the *Post,* was a pal, too. The Boss enjoyed wealthy cohorts, but over the decades few called the DA's office, and were called, as often as "the Donald."

"It was a mutual admiration society," Dan Castleman would say, and for decades it centered around PAL, the Police Athletic League, the do-good organization that, since 1914, had organized the summer play of 60,000 city kids. Morgenthau had joined PAL in 1962, not long after becoming U.S. attorney, and had led the cause—secular and civic—ever since.

In 1985, he'd invited Trump onto the board. The association offered the thirty-nine-year-old developer from Jamaica Estates, Queens, what he lacked, and wanted most: a stage at the heart of New York official-dom. Suddenly Trump, second son of an outer-borough developer of red-brick mid-rises, was wearing a tuxedo and mixing with the city's wealthiest executives in media, finance, and real estate—with the photographs appearing in the newspapers the next day. Communiqués from Trump Tower became routine: Across a news clip recounting the DA's latest exploits, Trump would scrawl in a black-Sharpied pat-on-the-shoulder: "BOB—You Are the GREATEST!"—followed by the telltale seismographic signature.

In 1986, Morgenthau again helped Trump build the bridge into Manhattan, brokering Trump's first civic achievement: the renovation of the Wollman Rink in Central Park. The rink had long been a symbol of municipal ineptitude—a sink that swallowed $12 million of city money in six years. Construction had started in 1980, with miles of pipe and a new slab, but leaks in the liquid-Freon system had appeared, followed by a succession of misrepairs. Mayor Koch was facing a political disaster, and asked Morgenthau a favor: Would he be the cutout to Trump? "Ed feared Donald, or at least getting too close to Donald," the DA would recall.

Trump took on not only the main rink, but also its littler sister, the Lasker Rink near East Harlem. "We were especially concerned about the other rink," Morgenthau said. "PAL used it; it was important to the kids." Trump vowed to do the job in six months, for $3 million. He did—in less than four months, for less money. He also made certain that each step, from the pipe-laying to the cement-pouring, was lavishly documented for the press.

"That rink put him on the map," Wayne Barrett, the *Voice* investigative journalist and author, in 1992, of the first biography of Trump, would say. "It was the turning point."

Morgenthau and Trump could never have been considered close; they rarely saw each other in any setting other than awards galas or benefit dinners. From the first, though, when it came to Trump, Morgenthau seemed willing to tolerate his coarse and often reckless views. In May 1989, days after Trump's inflammatory advertisement calling for the death penalty in the jogger case, the DA honored him at the PAL annual fundraising dinner, held at the Plaza Hotel—newly acquired by Trump. And in 1993, when Donald married Marla Maples, the DA was back at the Plaza, among a thousand guests. In the late 1990s, the relationship appeared to grow closer. Trump took to attending the DA's swearing-in ceremonies, and Morgenthau and his family—Lucinda, Josh, and Amy, still a young girl—visited Mar-a-Lago. They flew down during the spring break from school, staying in a cottage on the grounds of the resort.

The relationship had always been transactional, and to the PAL board members who were close to both Morgenthau and Trump, its boundaries were clear. "There was no open season on committing crimes in Manhattan because you wrote a check to PAL," one would say. Morgenthau had no illusions. "Some of these guys are sons of bitches," he told a fellow director. "I know that, but they're my sons of bitches. They stand up. If I need a check or we're going to have to close down the 'Playstreets' [PAL's summer sports and art program], I can call Steve Ross"—the media mogul—"or George Steinbrenner, or Donald."

Trump's aims, too, were plain to see. "Why would Trump want to be close to Giuliani or Bratton or Kelly or Morgenthau?" one PAL board member would ask. "Because he'd like to be able to think he could get somebody to investigate somebody else. Not because he'd get immunity for committing a crime. Donald did not go around worrying about *himself* committing a crime—although he may well have been committing a crime. Because in his worldview, anything he did was legit."

All the while, the contributions continued: The Trump Foundation gave to PAL, and to the DA himself. In his 1985 reelection race, as Morgenthau faced the challenge from the civil rights lawyer C. Vernon Mason, the developer gave $5,000—the campaign's second-largest contribution. In 2005, Trump hosted a fundraiser for the DA in his penthouse at Trump Tower, and the Trumps—Donald and Melania—would donate a total of $20,000 to the campaign. They were newly wed, and Melania newly pregnant. Trump would make a show of leading a tour of the triplex, announcing it was a rarity—allowing guests into the private apartment, even allowing them to wear shoes. In part, Trump agreed to host the fundraiser because a rumor had reached the DA that his sons were raising funds for Leslie Crocker Snyder, Morgenthau's challenger. But Trump's motivation in hosting the Tower fundraiser went beyond embarrassment or fear of upsetting the DA.

"Donald idolized Bob," Lucinda would say. "To him, Bob was the ultimate New Yorker—he was the establishment. Everything he was not."

PAL was the root of the relationship, but Trump would give his biggest check to the other charity Morgenthau chaired, the Museum of Jewish Heritage—"A Living Memorial to the Holocaust," as it called itself—on Manhattan's southern edge. (In 1986, at Mayor Koch's behest, Morgenthau had led the museum's construction, and had chaired it ever since.) Trump gave $100,000, only when the DA complained that his son-in-law, Jared Kushner, a new museum board member and the scion of Kushner Companies, the family real estate company, had failed to make good on a promised donation. "Nasty piece of work," Morgenthau would say of Kushner: "I had to kick him off the board."

||||

The morning after Trump's triumph, Morgenthau sent congratulations. He, too, had been in shock. Within days, the president-elect, as always, offered the effusive black-Sharpie reply:

BOB—
THANKS—
I MISS YOU AND
    NEVER FORGET = YOU
    ARE THE GREATEST!
    BEST WISHES TO
        FAMILY
            DONALD

"He never thought he'd win," Morgenthau would say. "No one did."

In the early days of the Trump presidency, Morgenthau decided to weigh in: He called Trump "on Armenia"—advocating that he declare the mass murder his grandfather had publicized "a genocide." In time, Morgenthau would entertain the idea of bringing his new causes—immigrants, incarcerated youth, veterans—to Trump, as well. Others pressed him to suggest candidates, as he had done in so many previous administrations, for the Supreme Court. "I don't want to call him," he would say, "because I fear he'll just use it. Donald's like that. No one can control him. He'll say, 'Well, I consulted Morgenthau . . .'"

There would be talk during Trump's tenure in the White House of awarding Morgenthau the Presidential Medal of Freedom. Morgenthau caught wind of the lobbying—led by the old guard at the PAL—but during a family consultation at the Vineyard, he vowed to refuse it. In the end, no award would be forthcoming: Trump, for his part, would sour on the man that he, too, called "the Boss."

Each had always seen opportunity in the other: The DA, ever expedient in his drive to fund his favored causes, needed the checks, and the real estate man, ever eager to antagonize a business foe, sought an ally in law enforcement. Trump would come, at least once, to the DA, asking his office to investigate a rival. Morgenthau would listen, but try to keep the benefactor of PAL and the museum at bay. The men who led Morgenthau's investigations division across the decades would be emphatic in their defense, explaining why the office had never launched a full-scale investigation of Trump's business: "Why didn't Morgenthau do anything? Because there was nothing to *do*," said Mike Cherkasky, his investigations chief for six years. The aides, like their former boss, blamed the political process. "You have to raise money to run for DA," said Cherkasky. "You ask people for money, and you can't do anything in return for it. There's no favors, there's no nothing."

And yet the Trump presidency had laid bare a blindness. Morgenthau liked the man, he would say, never heard a racist word, and never had cause to investigate him—or his family. "Donald's been around so long, and he's been such a good friend of PAL—given his time and money," he'd say, as if to explain the shortsightedness, "but we never expected *this*." He could understand the hyperbole and showmanship: Trump had always let his ego rule him. But in all the years that Morgenthau had known him, Trump had never revealed such shamelessness. It had caught Morgenthau by surprise, the racism, the lying, and the brazen insistence on running roughshod over the institutions of justice—and he struggled to understand it. It was more than the serial affronts against decency: Trump had laid siege to democracy. "I was never one who imagined the presidency might change Donald," he would say, "but it surely did."

76. "The Good Life"

2019

"The source of the good life was the land," John Morton Blum, Henry Morgenthau, Jr.'s official biographer, wrote in 1958. And "the purpose of the good life was helping those who needed help. The land and the people were the important things, the things the young man cared about."

Fishkill Farms—278 acres, down from 1,700 at its height before the war, portioned off among the siblings after the father's death—was at last turning a profit. A decade before the DA's retirement, Ray Morris, the farm manager, had declared he was "tired." Ray had started at Fishkill as a boy and never left. His grandfather had come in the farm's first years; his father had served decades as its manager and his mother as the bookkeeper. The Morris family had made a home of the old schoolhouse, a modest clapboard square that still stood across the field from the farm store. When Ray called it quits—"apple farming is dead," he said—Morgenthau saw little choice. He leased out the farm to a succession of local growers, farming families from the Valley, who would keep the orchards alive. Years would pass before the DA, at age eighty-seven, joined his younger son, Josh, recently graduated from Yale, and took it back.

"I worried about the future of the farm," Morgenthau would say. The growers weren't interested in the land. "They only cared about the current year—how much money they could make that season. They weren't planting new trees." Before they ran it to ruin, he said, "we had to give it a try—had to save it."

Josh turned away from painting, his first love, to revive the orchards—

planting new varieties and fruit trees (peaches, plums, cherries). Father and son ran the farm store, too: The old barn, bought long ago from Franklin Roosevelt, Jr., was a relic of FDR Jr.'s failed attempt to raise Thoroughbreds. On one wall, above the artisanal meats and organic jams, a plaque held pride of place: a gift from Governor Roosevelt to Henry Morgenthau, Jr., his conservation commissioner, on the evening of January 30, 1932—FDR's fiftieth birthday. The poem it displayed was a reminder of FDR's fondness for, and fondness for teasing, the man so long at his side:

> When Henry walks amid the fields
> Each tulip adoration yields
> And when he wanders past the trees
> They clap applause with all the leaves
> His agricultural skill and care
> Prevent our fields from becoming bare
> 'Tis proper that all vegetation
> Should praise the boss of conservation

Once again in family hands, Fishkill Farms enjoyed a renaissance. Each fall, the crowds came. In the months before Thanksgiving, the lines of cars snaked for miles along the roads encircling the farm, on pick-your-own weekends.

"The farm always came first," Morgenthau would say. As a toddler, he'd raised hens, sold eggs, milked cows, and, with his brother and sister, picked the apples. At six, he had been taught by his grandfather how to cut chickens' heads off with an axe. At eight, he'd learned to replant trees: "They'd blow a hole with explosives, and let me push the button of the dynamite." As a teen, he'd worked with the Cornell pomologists, learned how to graft, and studied hundreds of apple varieties. During college, when his father considered a new variety, "he'd have me in, discuss what to plant." "I'm going to call it a 'Victory Orchard,'" Henry Jr. said, once the war had come, because "it'll come into full bloom after we win."

Farming had been the constant. "It was always part of my life, even in public office," Morgenthau said. Each morning before arriving at the Courts Building, the DA would call Ray Morris at seven A.M.—"farmers get up early." He felt obliged to his father "to keep something going that he'd devoted his life to." It wasn't just FDR: From the land to the *Amer-*

ican Agriculturist, it was how his father had come to politics. "Without the farm, none of it would've happened."

Even now, as his century neared its end, the farm kept him going. It was a weekend ritual: the drive up and down, timed like a train schedule, no matter the weather, a detective behind the wheel. (Even in retirement, the police escorts would remain.) Yet Morgenthau had felt the opposite pull as well—and he relished the two realms. "City and country"—for many in New York it was a cliché. Not Morgenthau. He had loved to ride horses, fish, skate on the iced-over ponds, and inspect the orchards. Yet he was so much a man of the city—"a landmark," as Sonia Sotomayor would say, "of the history and life of New York City itself."

The city had given him power. From Al Smith to Andrew Cuomo, from La Guardia to de Blasio, he'd seen governors and mayors up close, and witnessed more than one bend the knee. He was no great speaker, nor one to flaunt the trappings of office, but amid the succession of politicians, commissioners, and judges, he had become "the pope" of New York law enforcement. The rule and the reach were without peer. The Morgenthau Army would endure: Whether in Midtown or the Wall Street firms downtown, two generations of lawyers, former assistants at either the U.S. attorney's or the DA's office, had graduated from his school. Those who ruled the corner offices above the avenues, and who formed a kind of tribe, silent and unseen. Whenever an occasion arose, as it did dozens of times each day, he reached for the telephone. Fixer, enforcer, mediator, monitor, lobbyist, advocate, adjudicator, campaigner, patron, or donor—Ida's computer now held them all, 6,719 names, a private universe.

It was, they would say, an elemental force—a key to his power.

Another source was the bloodline. Few could claim a deeper heritage, not to political power, but to the rise of the city itself—the neighborhoods at its northern and southern edges, and their oldest buildings, the first verticals of brick and steel. "It's not a question of muscle or brains," Ed Koch would say. "Only a man with the security of his background could operate the way he has." Only someone of his lineage, the newsmen would echo, could speak out when others kept quiet. "He had a different kind of power," the former crime reporter Nick Pileggi would say, "not power for the sake of power, but to do the kinds of things that he's done, really for the city. It's that simple."

| | | |

When Robert M. Morgenthau breathed his last, ten days shy of his hundredth birthday, a city paused. He had collapsed at home on a Sunday: Lucinda attempted artificial respiration, as Amy, his twenty-eight-year-old daughter who happened to be at his side, performed chest compressions. Together, mother and daughter revived him, restored the breathing. He was taken by ambulance, nine blocks south to Lenox Hill Hospital, but he would never return home. For a time, the doctors spoke of improvement—it was not a heart attack, nor a stroke. Yet the water in his lungs, months of congestion, proved too much to bear.

The governor ordered flags to half-mast, the *Times* obituary (first drafted two decades earlier) filled an entire page, and the president, as the family feared, weighed in. "I was saddened to learn of the recent passing of Bob Morgenthau, a truly great man!" Trump wrote on Twitter. Morgenthau was "a warrior for our Country that he loved so dearly," Trump tweeted—adding minutes later: "Bob Morgenthau, a legend, will be greatly missed!"

On the morning of the funeral, the cathedral synagogue on Fifth Avenue was surrounded by police. Anti-terrorism squad members lined the sidewalks, sharpshooters took to the adjacent roofs, and NYPD vehicles ringed the blocks to the north and south. In the 2,500-seat sanctuary of Temple Emanu-El, one of the world's largest Jewish houses of worship, mourners sat in the rosy light of the Tiffany glass, staring at the glitter of the mosaic arch, marble and onyx that reached more than a hundred feet high. Beneath it, the bimah, the broad stage, was decorated in green, its rear wall blooming with giant apple branches. As speaker after speaker rose, each passed before the tableau's center: a coffin, draped with the Stars and Stripes.

Bobby, the elder son, now sixty-two, would stand at the cantor's pulpit and introduce himself—"I'm Bob Morgenthau . . . really"—to laughter. Before the ceremony, as relatives and close friends gathered in the small side chapel, Bobby had served as host. "Let me try," he said, "to herd our two clans together."

The Morgenthau children knew what he meant. There was the "first family," Jenny, Bobby, Annie, and Barbara, and the second, Josh, Amy, and Lucinda. All told, Morgenthau had left seven children, six grandchildren, and three great-grandchildren. Yet he had a third family: hundreds of men and two women from the U.S. attorney years. And a fourth, as well: the largest, who filled the pews and the sidewalk outside—the thousands from the DA's office, assistant prosecutors, detectives, investigators, secretaries, paralegals. The four families, each a tribe discernible by age, attire, and demeanor, had come together for the first time.

They were all there: de Blasio, the mayor; Vance, the successor; Spitzer, the fallen governor; Sotomayor, the former assistant who had reached the highest court; and near the back, in a corner of the giant temple, Nancy Ryan and Peter Casolaro, the veterans who had helped to set aside the convictions of the Central Park Five. There were the survivors, too: Charlie Rangel and David Dinkins, and nearby, the reigning police commissioner and two predecessors, Ray Kelly and William Bratton. The billionaires in retail and real estate had come as well, and among them sat the DA's bodyguards from his first day in office to his last. The archbishop, who had come to see the former DA bearing birthday greetings weeks earlier, was absent, out of town in midsummer, while a pair of Armenian priests in black vestments sat in a front row, arms folded in repose.

The elders had called the chief rabbi out of retirement. Tall and lean, his hair two shocks of silvery white combed forward, Dr. Ronald Sobel wore a dark suit and no white shawl. He spoke with passion, casting back across the generations to the tale of Moses Morgenthau and the "morning dew." The rabbi's deep voice thundered as he reprised the family tale, "The Morgenthau trilogy," as he called it. He left out the errant Lazarus, the word "faith," and the women entirely—Babette, Settie, Josie, Ellie, Joan, and Martha. ("The women," as Dr. Joan Morgenthau once quipped, "tend to get erased.") It was a spare service, with no music other than an interlude of Mozart, and little pomp—until at the end, when the dark-clad police honor guard slowly shouldered the casket down the center aisle and out into the bright sunlight.

The patriarch, Henry Morgenthau, would have been pleased. The young celebrant of Emerson and Ben Franklin who had helped lead the revolt against Emanu-El, founding the "pewless and dueless" Free Synagogue, had in time returned. No longer America's foremost anti-Zionist, Henry Sr. had also been eulogized in the towering temple: a reading of psalms, the organ prelude to Beethoven's Ninth, and the former mayor, La Guardia, there to see him off. Seventy-three years later, the farewell for his grandson Bob, a lifelong trustee, who had always sat in his grandmother's pew, would be no more overtly religious. There was no kaddish, the prayer for the dead; in two and a half hours, the rabbi spoke a scant few sentences of Hebrew.

"I hope my voice will not break too much with tears as I speak today,"

Justice Sotomayor said. "The Boss" had given her her first job, and helped her every step along the way. "Without Morgenthau," she said, "I would be neither the person nor the justice I am today."

Josh, his son, now thirty-five, spoke of his father's lessons: the importance of farming, and roots. His father had instilled in him "his passion for the land," for planting, canning, making cider. He'd also taught him how to work hard, and peddle: His father had been a master salesman for the farm, hawking chickens at the street markets in Brooklyn, and calling restaurants across the city to take egg orders. Above all, Josh said, his father taught him "to remember where you came from": "The moral imperative" was always "to give back."

Afterward on the avenue outside, many would say the Boss would have enjoyed it. The funeral went just as they had long imagined. But Morgenthau had not envisioned it, and could not. His doctor had warned him throughout the spring, urged him to go to the hospital—to no avail. Bobby Morgenthau, the elder son, understood. When a mourner offered a common lament, "Your father fooled us all: No one thought he'd really die," Bobby said, "I know. *He* didn't believe he would."

East Eighty-sixth Street

I n that final spring on East Eighty-sixth Street, on a Sunday afternoon in April, Bob Morgenthau sat alone on a white sofa crowded not with pillows and blankets but with papers and books.

At ninety-nine, he would still awaken in the middle of the night. It wasn't the machine to ease his breathing that denied him sleep, but his mind, racing ahead. The worries did not cease. Rikers, the Alcatraz of pretrial detention in New York City, was scheduled to close, yet the undocumented inmates faced not a trial, but deportation. In the darkness he was visited, too, by concerns closer to home: Nellie, his third eldest, remained upstate—and had yet in her sixty-eight years to recognize him. He'd gone to see her each year, at times by himself. He'd fought to get her the best care, but what would become of her after he was gone? Amid the swirl of worry, he was besieged by requests without end: A former deputy sought a judgeship; A partner's grandson, a place in law school; the farm needed equipment; Lucinda, driving directions for the back road to Poughkeepsie.

"Strange dreams last night," he said. He'd been visited by the Israeli intelligence officer, the one whose leads on Iran never disappointed. "I dreamt that I was working with him, something so important we had to abandon everything else, and then in a second"—the thin fingers made a half-snap—"it went away." More often, he was visited by nightmares—the most frequent: the night Josh nearly died.

Still, the stamina, decisiveness, and utter absence of regret would endure. For nearly a decade, well into his nineties, Morgenthau went to work each weekday morning at Wachtell Lipton. "This firm does mergers and acquisitions, these are rainmakers!" he would exclaim, making his way slowly through the carpeted corridors—a reminder that old men, like young boys, can deceive, be at once vulnerable and mischievous. In time, he accepted a cane, and then a walker. Yet even as his stoop lowered, it remained clear: Bob Morgenthau would never retire.

In his hundredth year, he no longer walked without assistance. He preferred the police detective—there were three now in the relay—who would offer an arm, but the doctor insisted on a wheelchair. On either wrist, he wore dark plastic bands, devices to measure blood pressure and heart rate, and each week, he would ask the doctor to test his blood, checking the INR levels—to ensure he got the blood thinners right. Still, he remained active, undaunted. He read the four dailies each morning, did a half hour of yoga twice a week, and, on alternate days, for an hour followed the orders of a physical trainer. He did not fear the future; he appeared free of the insecurities that bound nearly all who encountered him each day.

On that spring afternoon, Morgenthau was nearly alone. He sat in a corner of the long sofa, silver-stubbled, red sweater-vest over a purple button-down shirt. The white hair was cottony, combed neatly, the blue eyes pellucid, lit by the radiance of the window. He'd ordered in from the brasserie on the corner: soft-shell crab, white rice, cold spinach, and hard carrots, assembled on a wooden tray. As he spoke, balancing the tray on his knees, he cast back, summoning the people and places who had made him, and whose legacy he kept alive. He remembered the cows and cornfields along the Taconic, and the streetcars on the city's crowded avenues. He spoke, too, of his grandfather's syndicate days, the rise in real estate, and the move to back the New Jersey governor for president. The words carried echoes of Henry Sr.'s books that lined his shelves: on Armenia, antebellum New York, Emerson, and Franklin. Interspersed were volumes from the grandson's childhood library: Henry Sr.'s chronicle, *My Trip Around the World,* inscribed on New Year's 1932. The bookplate read "ROBERT MORRIS MORGENTHAU," above an etching of a black horse, *his* horse, galloping in the wild, and a line from the *Aeneid:* "As dawn dispersed the dewy shadow."

For all the clutter and dark wood, the relics stood out. A ship's clock from the Navy days on a windowsill near the bust of FDR, the New Deal bronze commissioned by his father. And in a far corner, on the bare floor, leaning against the wall: a portrait of his grandfather at eighty. The similarity across the generations had grown strong.

On Eighty-sixth Street, the air outside was chill but bright. As afternoon turned to twilight, the calls on the iPhone kept interrupting.

"Yeah, the legs hurt," he told a doctor.

"So how's the market look?" he asked Bobby.

He was writing a new column, but faced a hurdle: "The target's moving so fast." He feared the new bloodlust, and had trouble keeping pace: the war on immigrants and people of color; the rise of white supremacy. The body politic was "more than divided"—it was diseased. What's my greatest fear? he had asked one recent morning, checking that he had heard the question right. He did not hesitate to answer: "Trump."

He may have slowed, but the fugue continued: The cases still rankled. Shards of fact and memory, they jangled in his mind. He'd won more cases and more battles—legal, municipal, political—than any prosecutor could rightly expect.

And yet, in his final spring, the jogger case threatened to outlast every success. At Morgenthau's hundredth birthday party at the museum downtown, what Justice Sotomayor would later call "an *early* celebration," Cy Vance would praise "the Boss" before a hall of adoring congregants, hundreds of former assistants. Yet Vance, too, felt the weight of the Central Park case anew. There had been a second settlement: The five men who'd lost their youth and seen their sentences set aside had brought another case, filing in the little-known State Court of Claims. In 2016, the lawsuit had ended quietly, with a payment of $3.9 million.

Morgenthau did not shirk blame: The "fuckups" were legion, too many to count—from the night that Trisha Meili was found in the park to the day that Matias Reyes's hat resurfaced. He held his own assistants, and the police, to account, above all for failing to tie the rape of two days earlier to the attack that had nearly cost a woman her life. And he would add, when speaking of the police department's role in the reinvestigation: "They *did* know better, and buried it." Yet at the end, turning the case over in his head so many years hence, he took the responsibility. Whether through negligence, outworn loyalties, or a rush to judgment, justice had been undermined, delayed for far too many years—and he counted himself among the guilty. "The Jogger," said the new DA at Morgenthau's hundredth birthday party, "is the case that will never go away."

Morgenthau had long since disowned Vance; the heir was irredeemable. "Did you see the editorial in the *Post* today?" he asked on that April afternoon at the apartment. " 'He's no Morgenthau,' that's what they said." The tabloid editorial had cut low: "Manhattan DA Cy Vance

Jr. may owe his job to the strong endorsement he got from his illustrious predecessor, but it's been painfully obvious for some time that Vance is no Bob Morgenthau." If once the praise might have raised a smile, the grin now was almost melancholic. Vance had been rash, too attentive to the winds. Morgenthau had always sought to rely, as if by tutelage, on "overnight thinking"—the kind FDR spoke of in his last speech, as he considered a future for Germany: "You know, I've always felt that common sense prevails in the long run—quiet, overnight thinking."

| | | |

After the crab came ice cream, mounds of vanilla drizzled with Dutchess County maple syrup. As he ate in a slow, deliberate attack, he returned to the 1960s, to the Kennedys and Roy Cohn. He thought often of Bobby—and what he could've done had he been given the chance. Morgenthau had seen Cohn reappear in the news—but admitted he'd been taken aback by the late lawyer's connection to the new president.

He returned, too, eyes closed tight to summon the memory, to April 20. For years, when he revisited the night that the *Lansdale* sank, he turned to the present tense: He spoke of the water, the bombers, the shouts in the cold darkness. He had the paddle still, he said. A souvenir of crude aluminum, salvaged from the German bomber crew's raft, it stood in the office, hidden behind the door. What illuminated his mind most now were not the battles, but the wonderment of being twenty-one years old, a boy "turned man overnight," of facing the horror before he could fathom, let alone foretell, its cost.

On the television, a news anchor spoke of Chevron and the Anadarko oil field. "That was my work," he said, no longer afforded time for false modesty. "I did all the legal work, put it together for Panhandle Eastern." Chevron announced an intention to buy the field: "$33 billion," he said, repeating the merger's tally. "Maybe I should've taken the offer"— made by the CEO, periodically, from the 1950s to the 1970s—"and run Panhandle?"

He valued money, and was frugal to a fault, a point both Lucinda and Ida could agree on. He had worn his father's suits to threads, and relished the $12 haircuts from an octogenarian Sicilian on the East Side. He would complain that his wealthy reputation was false—he had not grown up rich. The Settie Lehman Fatman Trust—created under the will of Mayer Lehman's "middle daughter"—was forever a source of frustration: His grandmother on the Lehman side had left his hands tied. "Can't withdraw from it," he'd grumble, "only draw interest." The trust, even twice divided, had grown vast. His share, gained when his mother, Ellie, died in 1949, was $90,000. Now the trust was valued in the millions. The Morgenthau children, Bob, Henry III, and Joan, had in fact been born to wealth: Ellie's father left her nearly a million dollars, and her mother more than doubled it. But the DA had invested well, "extremely so," his son Bobby would say. His assets alone, without tallying the farm, apartment, house on the Vineyard, made him by any measure wealthy.

The talk of oil and pipelines had led him offshore, back to Nixon, greed, and the Swiss bank account—another shard that had not been worn smooth by time. He would not let go of "the Paris thing": the secret meeting with a trusts expert Nixon was purported to have had on his first trip abroad as president, an opportunity to set up a hidden account. Bill Lambert, the *Life* reporter who had chased Cohn, Wolfson, and Fortas, had delivered the tip—"just after he'd been in Paris."

As Morgenthau spoke, the old Oliphant cartoon, the one that once adorned his office, hung on the wall overhead: Morgenthau costumed as Sherlock Holmes, chasing Nixon.

The question of Nixon's off-the-books meeting still bothered him. "Bill was sure of it," he said, with a slight shake of the head. "We'll never know—couldn't prove it."

The polyphony paused, and a stillness filled the room. In a moment, he was plotting again, casting about for his successor's successor—devising a way to the future.

The stillness returned.

"Look," he said, one arm rising to a window. Across the street a steel spine rose against the sky.

"There," he said, the words coming together slowly. "A new building's going up."

Outside on East Eighty-sixth Street, the light had changed. It was early still, but a pre-summer bloom of color shaded the late-afternoon sky. The hands were wraithlike, and purpling black. The exercise equipment sat in the living room, pushed to a corner: weights for the arms, foam roller for the back, wooden step for the legs—all of no use now. The body was going, but the mind could still pierce. The words were spare, the silences long, a quiet free of portent, filled only with waiting.

Morgenthau spoke often of his father and grandfather, but rarely of Lazarus, the great-grandfather he had not known. He knew little of the cigar baron, less of the confidence man. But he was surprised by a recent discovery: a small brown notebook. Its boards were cracked and clasps rusted, but the German hand on its pages remained beautifully intact—the twenty-seven-year-old Lazarus's 1842 diary. "It appeared there," he said, pointing to the disorder of his small desk. "No idea how." He had donated the diary to a center for Jewish history downtown, but he liked to quote it: Lazarus had written of his humble origins for the descendants to come, so "neither pride nor arrogance may gain a foothold in my family."

Lazarus Morgenthau lay in a corner of Salem Fields. The cemetery at Brooklyn's edge was the resting place of Guggenheims and Warburgs, Seligmans and Rothschilds. Amid pink dogwoods and elms, a breeze rising above the subway tracks beyond, the German-Jewish hierarchy of old New York, the nineteenth-century honor guard of Emanu-El, spread across a green slope in towering crypts, edifices of white marble and bronze gates. (Stephen Wise had called the temple "an urban gateway to a suburban cemetery.") Lazarus had joined Babette here. Maximilian, Richard, Siegfried, Ida—a scattering of their children were close by. Max, the eldest son, had arranged for a columbarium: a white-marble cabinet fronted by small bronze doors, no more than three feet off the ground, a holding place for cinerary urns. The headstone inches away, separated by the grass and blue wildflowers, was near-black and squat, a square stone atop a carved plinth. The chiseled letters were worn by wind and age, yet the names and dates remained visible: Lazarus above, Babette below.

Their great-grandson had never visited. The Morgenthaus known to history, his father and grandfather, were outside the city, up along the Taconic Parkway, beneath the stones at Mount Pleasant. It would be his destination, too—about a half-hour drive north, nearly halfway to the farm.

Acknowledgments

Any attempt to tell the story of a family across four generations demands more than time—in this case, a dozen years—but a work of investigative nonfiction of such length also asks, on the part of too many, a leap of faith. I could not have completed this work without the help of hundreds. I am in debt to all those who opened their doors and filing cabinets, scoured attics and cellars, and aided my search of archives and libraries, public and private, and who helped to shape the narrative and make it as complete and accurate as possible.

Not all biographers and historians have the privilege of speaking with those who lived and witnessed so many of the critical turns of the story they hope to tell. The Sources section lists more than 350 people, the majority of whom sat for interviews at length. Still others, including some who deserve it the most, prefer not to be recognized, while many offered guidance, leads, and information, or assisted in the fact-checking. In all, a more accurate count of the number of people I spoke with along the journey would approach 500. I had the good fortune to be schooled by not only a number of the most reticent prosecutors in New York City, but a generation of luminaries among its defense bar. I was honored, as well, to sit for long hours with judges at nearly every station of the judiciary, from the New York County Family Court to the U.S. Supreme Court.

Over the years, a corps of several dozen became frequent interlocutors, tolerating what surely seemed an unending series of "follow-ups," successive calls and emails. Several evolved into a biographer's dream: co-investigators. I would be the lucky recipient of another's discovery: a name resurfacing on a long drive, a box recovered from a flooded basement, a piece of evidence found in an old file. (Just one example: the airline ticket of Abe Fortas, proving a Florida visit to a secret patron, Louis Wolfson—a vital piece in the case that led Fortas to quit the Supreme Court.) For their forbearance, I owe a debt to all those who abided, if not welcomed, my intrusion into their lives.

No one, though, did I speak with more often, and for longer, than the Morgenthaus themselves. Robert M. Morgenthau, beginning in the spring of 2008 until four weeks before his death in 2019, made himself available for hundreds of hours of interrogations. Not once did the former DA block my way, and not once did he ask to read a word. In all, he would grant unfettered access to his papers, unpublished recollections, correspondence, and fabled Rolodexes—all five. The family archive included personal papers, diaries, photographs, and home movies—including long-lost 16mm home movies, shot by the Treasury secretary, of FDR and Churchill at the Morgenthau farm during the war. (Dr. Joan Morgenthau Hirschhorn, the DA's sister, had rescued them from the trash during a home move.) In addition, Robert Morgenthau supported serial requests for personal records and government files, including from the FBI, CIA, and U.S. Navy.

His late wife Lucinda Franks, chronicler of her own love and marriage, was from start to finish a most forgiving and patient source. Lucinda, who died far too early, offered only unflagging encouragement. The DA's daughters, Jenny Morgenthau and Dr. Anne (Morgenthau) Grand, and sons, Robert P. and Joshua, each welcomed with generosity and candor an intruder rooting around their collective past. I am more than grateful, as well, to their spouses: Jenny Morgenthau's late husband, Gene Anderson; Paul Grand; Susan Bryce Moore Morgenthau. Christopher Wadsworth, Jenny's former husband, offered warm, vital memories of his years "on the inside."

Henry Morgenthau III opened his doors widely and often—first in Cambridge, then in Washington, D.C. Henry, the family chronicler, who at 100 would call the DA "my kid brother," shared it all—memories, documents, interviews (raw material for his family memoir, *Mostly Morgenthaus*)—with a candor that at times could shock, an infectious curiosity, and, above all, a belief in the promise of history.

Dr. Joan Morgenthau Hirschhorn, sister of "the boys," endured long interview sessions, and always made herself available to vet sources, living or historical. Her perspective—Joan was in Washington during the war with her parents while Bob and Henry were at sea or in Germany—offered essential context and, often, a vital corrective. Fred Hirschhorn, Jr., Joan's husband of nearly fifty-five years, enriched my early research, recalling his own Our Crowd childhood and memories of roller-skating in the apartment a floor below his neighbor, "Uncle Henry," Henry Morgenthau, Sr. Hirschhorn was among the first to bring to life for me the dual auras—of heroism and hubris—that surrounded the former ambassador on the Upper East Side of Manhattan in the 1930s.

Although it is impossible to thank all those deserving, a partial list is in order. On the Morgenthau family tree: Henry III's children, Sarah, Ben (born "Henry IV," and proud father of Henry V), and Kramer; Joan's daughters, Elizabeth H. Wilson, Joan H. Bright, and Elinor H. Hirschhorn; Margaret Fatman Josten and Werner Josten's children, Peter Josten and Eileen (Josten) Lowe, and Eileen's daughter, Sarah M. Lowe; Ruth Morgenthau's children, George W. Naumburg, Jr., and Ellin London; Robert E. Simon, Jr., founder of Reston, Virginia (the town's name is formed from his initials), who at ninety-six shared vivid recollections; Carol Newborg (granddaughter of Agnes Morgenthau Newborg); John D. Gordan III ("a Lehman cousin of the DA," as he put it, and author of the line—regarding his uncle, the financier Frank Altschul—that reveals Our Crowd's entangled bloodlines: "Uncle Frank's sister was his aunt"); Frederick M. Joseph, Jr. (great-grandson of Mengo Morgenthau); Jessica Mathews (one of Barbara Tuchman's three daughters); and "the English Lehmans," as the DA called them: Lord and Lady Goodhart (Celia and William).

Ida Van Lindt, Robert Morgenthau's executive assistant for the entirety of his tenure as DA, is owed more debts than any mortal can repay. For fifty-two years no one at 100 Centre Street was better informed, and as generations of court reporters and hundreds of assistant DAs learned, no one kept greater order, or more secrets. With intelligence, warmth, and a wonderfully generous spirit, Ida never tired of arcane requests, and never failed to offer even more help.

Early on, I was fortunate to be tutored on all things Henry Morgenthau, Jr., by John Morton Blum in New Haven. Our initial conversation lasted until dark, and continued for years, but from the first time I met him I knew the eminent Yale historian would be a generous guide to the written, and unwritten, record. In time, the crew of enabler-historians grew into a dream team: Kai Bird, Robert Caro, Robert Dallek, Adam Hochschild (whose father was a longtime friend of Henry Morgenthau,

Jr.), David Nasaw, Jean Strouse, and Geoffrey C. Ward (who generously read the Roosevelt chapters and offered essential insights). I am indebted, further, to John Milton Cooper, Jr., and Charles E. Neu for their counsel on all things Wilson, and to Michael Beschloss, whose 2002 work, *The Conquerors,* was an early guide to the rivalries of wartime Washington.

I am blessed, as well, to have had the ear, and in many cases the files, of New York's last generation of great city reporters: Wayne Barrett, Jimmy Breslin, Nicholas Gage, Mike Pearl, Nick Pileggi, and Gay Talese. Whether expert in the annals of the city's courts, crime, or politics, their recollections and writings were invaluable. I must add two reporters, long overlooked but no less intrepid in scooping their cohorts: Norma Abraham (a top court reporter of her day) and Miriam Ottenberg (the first investigative reporter to dig into the Cosa Nostra). I am grateful, too, to Walter Goodman and Paul Hoffman for masterful feats of reporting (their books: *A Percentage of the Take* and *Courthouse*), and among contemporaries, to Ralph Blumenthal, John Eligon, Seymour Hersh, James Kaplan, Jane Mayer (herself a Lehman on the Morgenthau family tree), Daniel Okrent, Tom Powers, William Rashbaum, and Tom Robbins.

So many others helped along the way, offering observations, recollections, or documents. Beyond those listed among the Sources, I owe debts to the following: Meron Medzini (who translated the Morgenthau passages from Ben-Gurion's "War Diaries"); Laura Badger, Marilyn Bauza, Mary de Bourbon, Daniel Farley, Mary Matuszak, Barbara Thompson, Justin Yi (members of the DA's staff, past and present); Douglas Frantz, Larry Gurwin and Peter Truell, and Jonathan Beaty and Sam Gwynne (contemporaneous investigators of BCCI and chroniclers of its demise); Mary Anne Weaver (early investigator of the Abedi–Sheikh Zayed relationship); Elizabeth Lederer and Linda Fairstein (who answered fact-checking queries); Andrea Bernstein, Jesse Eisinger, Daniel Golden, and Maggie Haberman (who generously compared notes on the forty-fifth president and his family).

Hundreds of archives in the United States and abroad hold materials pertaining to the Morgenthaus. I am thankful to all those who helped me to see documents, and visual clues, spanning more than three hundred years:

At the National Archives (NARA), David Ferriero, the former National Archivist and a national treasure—a generous colleague since his years at the New York Public Library. Elizabeth Gray, Tim Nenninger,

Stephen Underhill, and the staff at NARA in College Park, Maryland; New York City; and St. Louis. At the presidential libraries: the FDR Library, Paul Sparrow, former director, and the team of archivists, models of diligence, William Baehr, Christian Belena, Kirsten Strigel Carter, Bob Clark, Virginia Lewick, and Kevin Thomas. At the JFK Library, Michael Desmond and Stephen Plotkin. At the Truman Library, Jim Armistead.

At the New York Public Library, Anthony Marx, and the library staff past and present, above all, Melanie Locay and the custodians of the Frederick Lewis Allen Room, Jay Barksdale, Thomas Lannon, Susan Malsbury, Megan O'Shea, David Smith, and Phil Sutton. At the NYC Parks Department, Steven Rizick. At the Municipal Archives, Ken Cobb and Joseph Van Nostrand. At the Museum of Jewish Heritage—A Living Memorial to the Holocaust, past and present staff, above all, David Marwell, Elissa Schein, and Melissa Martens Yaverbaum. At the FBI, Kirk Cromer and John Fox. And at the Brewster Ladies Library, the guardians of the quiet.

Though I owe a debt to a long list of archivists and librarians, each offered essential pieces of the puzzle: Jennifer M. Cole and Elisa Ho (American Jewish Archives), Susan Woodland (American Jewish Historical Society), Chloe Gerson (Brandeis University), Peter Nelson and Sandy Riley (Amherst College), Richard Pontius (National Center for Jewish Film, Brandeis University), Peter Derrick (Bronx County Historical Society), Thomas A. Wharton (Exeter); Tanya Chebotarev, Thai Jones, Christopher Laico, and Kevin W. Schlottmann (Columbia University), Heather Furnas (Cornell University), Anne D. Lozier (Deerfield Academy), Carol Leadenham, Natalia A. Reshetova (Hoover Archives), James Stimpert (Johns Hopkins University), Deb Weiner (Maryland Jewish Historical Society), Robert Tuggle (Metropolitan Opera), Leena Akhtar (Museum of American Finance); Commander Robert Moss, John Hodges (Naval History and Heritage Command), Janet Linde (New York Stock Exchange), Rebecca Russell (Rice University); Amy Fitch (Rockefeller Archives), Nanci A. Young (Smith College), Joan Adler (Straus Historical Society), Elka Deitsch and Franny Hess (Temple Emanu-El), Jillian Phillips (University of Iowa), Richard Graham and John Wiese (University of Nebraska—Lincoln), William Kevin Cawley (University of Notre Dame), Helen Keil-Losch (U.S. Federal Reserve), Michelle A. King (United States Holocaust Memorial Museum), Taylor Kiland (U.S. Navy Memorial Foundation), Mary Cronin (Wachtell, Lipton, Rosen & Katz), Jennifer Hadley (Wesleyan University), and Claryn

Spies (Yale University). In England: Mark Eccleston, Martin Killeen, and Catherine Martin (University of Birmingham), Ian Strawbridge and Vanessa Smith (National Archives), Clare Kavanaugh (Nuffield College, Oxford University), and the Bodleian Library. In France: Emmanuelle Deleu-Sulmont and Loreline Ribette. In Germany: Alexandra Berend and Claude W. Sui (Reiss-Engelhorn-Museen, Mannheim), Ulrich Nieß and Andreas Schenk (Stadtarchiv, Mannheim), Katrin Nele Jansen (Salomon L. Steinheim-Institut für deutsch-jüdische Geschichte, Universität Duisburg-Essen). In Israel: Sara Palmor (Central Zionist Archives) and the Institute for Contemporary Jewry (Hebrew University). To the staff archivists at the Leo Baeck Institute, Brooklyn Historical Society, Library of Congress, New York Historical Society, Wisconsin Historical Society, and the YIVO Institute.

For access to archives, private papers, and photographs: the Countess of Avon (Clarissa Eden), Thomas S. Crane, Max Kennedy, Herbert Levy, Suzanne Maas, Virginia (Patterson) Montgomery, Donn Neal, Judge Robert P. Patterson, Jr., Peter Soler, Jean Stein, Anna Tendy, and Charles C. Wales. For a variety of assistance—including unearthing the legal records of the 1903 Wagner case, touring Wall Street and the Old Homestead in Fishkill (half of it under tarps, in mid-demolition), and scouring Chinese news sites and William Barclay Parsons's diary of the subway's construction: Richard Buck, Annaline Dinkelmann, Andrew Keith, Max Lewkowicz, Kimberly Lightbody, Robert A. McCaffrey, Jeremy Ribakove, Ann Varney, and Yi Yang.

I cannot imagine a better place to have landed, at near midpoint in my research, than the Leon Levy Center for Biography at the CUNY Graduate Center. I am grateful to all at the Graduate Center, most democratic of city institutions, above all, to its dedicated librarians. My great thanks to the Levy Center's founder Shelby White, former director Gary Giddins, former deputy director Michael Gately, as well as my esteemed colleagues on the center's advisory board.

Thanks are due, as well, to the Hoover Institution at Stanford, where I spent a month in early research, and to my late friend Robert Conquest and his wife Liddie for (among many gifts) a series of evening roundtables on the latest horrors to emerge from the Stalin archives, punctuated by the poet-historian's giggling recitations of Jeff Chaucer's limericks.

My thanks, as well, to my teaching home, the New School, and my wonderful colleagues (past and present) at Eugene Lang College, including Stephanie Browner, Verna de LaMothe, Alex Draifinger, Blake Eskin,

Anjali Khosla, Liesl Schillinger, and Silvia Vega-Llona. And above all, a decade of students, many who are already reporting, editing, and designing a better world.

Editors for advice, commissions, and encouragement along the way: At *The New York Times Magazine,* Hugo Lindgren, Dean Robinson, and the incomparable Alex Star (now executive editor at Farrar, Straus and Giroux). At *Bookforum,* Chris Lehmann and Michael Miller.

For feats of a degree of difficulty that they alone know: Drs. David Blumenthal, Lloyd Feinberg, Jerry Halpern, David Markowitz, and Clifford Salm. Ever available, whether on weekends or lunch hours, they steered me clear of the unseen hurdles.

Only Bob Weil, editor in chief of Liveright, editor of my two previous books at W. W. Norton, knows the depth of my debt to him. Bob's faith and generosity led me to Lynn Nesbit, who has surely been a boon to more writers' lives than any literary agent in the history of American letters. Lynn does not "represent"; she cares deeply about ideas and has devoted her life to bringing them to the page. I am grateful to Lynn for friendship and fortitude, for advice on health and parenting, and for suggesting long ago the idea of a family biography on the Morgenthaus. Life has given me too many blessings to count, but Lynn is one I know and treasure. At Janklow & Nesbit, although so many have worked on my behalf, I must thank in particular Bennett Ashley and Mina Hamedi.

Thanks as well to William Whitworth, guardian angel of nonfiction marathoners, and himself a former New York City reporter, editor at *The New Yorker,* and for two decades, editor in chief of *The Atlantic,* for offering notes on the manuscript and encouragement. I will cherish the hours spent on the phone, as Bill walked me through the pages he'd marked—a tutorial in the sanctity of punctuation and "keeping the traffic moving in the right direction."

He also opened the door to Jack Beatty, as wise and generous a soul as any I've met. With brilliance and gusto, Jack set to work on a massive manuscript, granting me a chance, after years of solo sailing, to begin to make out the distant shore. While all errors and shortcomings remain mine alone, without Jack's guidance from across the ether, I could not have made it to land.

At Random House, I am grateful for the privilege of working with its executive vice president and publisher, Andy Ward. For years, I'd heard writers speak of Andy's work in rhapsodic tones. At once I learned why: I doubt Manhattan holds an editor with less ego, more intelligence, a sharper sense of story, or a bigger heart. Like all great editors, Andy is not only a champion of books, his line-editing is razor sharp and his editorial footwork invisible. Andy challenges a writer not just to write better, but to think harder. Susan Kamil, from the first, believed in the promise of a long tale stretching 153 years across one family; she may well have believed in it even more than I did. Her enthusiasm was infectious, and her death, at sixty-nine, in the summer of 2019, left a chasm in publishing and beyond. I wrote (and rewrote) every page with Susan in mind, and I hope I've not let her down. Thanks, too, to the late Robert Loomis, Tim Bartlett (now at St. Martin's), and all at Random House, especially Kaeli Subberwal and Steve Messina, models of efficiency.

Great thanks, too, are due Tom Hentoff for wise counsel, Sean Lavery for fact-checking, and Crary Pullen for photographic research. To Bruce Vinokour at Creative Artists Agency, I am grateful for a rare set of meticulous notes.

For their impatience and relentless ribbing, great thanks to my brothers, their partners and children, and Jacqueline Jensen for her unending support. Though both of my parents, Gretl and Gerald Meier, died during the early years of research for this book, their memory has indeed become a blessing, and my mother's counsel, exacting to the end, was a catalyst to its completion.

For unflagging encouragement and commiseration, my thanks to friends and colleagues: Amy Baltzell, Catherine Barnett, Kate Boo, Mark Franchetti, Lucy Lehrer, Richard Maloney, Jeffrey A. Mays, John McCarthy, Joe Oliveira, Jonathan Peyser, Julia Rask, Emily Steed, F. Joseph Warin, and Bill Wrubel. And those who went beyond any fair call of friendship, reading swaths of the manuscript: Charlotte Bacon, David Brenner, Bruce Gyory, Robert Jenkins, Nick Viorst, and J. Peder Zane. Your generosity and erudition left me feeling humbled, and blessed.

My forever thanks I reserve for Mia, righteously impatient and loving at every step, and our daughters, Oona and Sasha, who have bloomed far faster than this book—you three give me reason each day not only to chase ghosts and string words together, but to breathe.

Notes

SSW   Stephen Samuel Wise
USHMM   United States Holocaust Memorial Museum

Prologue: One Hogan Place

xix **first transatlantic flight:** On May 8, 1919, three U.S. Navy Curtiss "flying boats" departed from Rockaway, Long Island, New York, bound for Portugal via Newfoundland and the Azores. Only one of the three planes, NC-4, completed the historic journey, arriving in Lisbon on May 27.

PART I | ARRIVAL

1. "Between Profit and Disaster," 1815–1866

3 *Hermann:* Marion Wolfert, *German Immigrants: Lists of Passengers Bound from Bremen to New York,* vol. III (Baltimore: Clearfield, 2009).

4 **Mannheim:** More than two dozen articles in the *Mannheimer Journal* (May 2, 1844, to Jan. 6, 1870) relate the evolution of LM's business, property, and emigration. The earliest notice: 1844 articles report that LM opened a "cloth store" and a "wadding factory" in Ludwigshafen that employed 82 persons (see *Mannheimer Journal,* June 19, 20, 27, and 30, 1844). The *Journal* also published items on the opening of a New York branch, Aug. 2, 1860. Sebastian Parzer, Correspondence.

4 **few dozen were Jews:** The Gleusdorf town register for 1830 indicates 276 residents, including 44 Jews. In 1933, the village had 302 residents, and no Jews. Stefan Rohrbacher, correspondence.

5 **"My dear son!":** Translation and transliteration by Freddy Litten; Rohrbacher correspondence.

5 *Fichtennadel-Brustzucker: Fichtennadel* (more accurately translated as "spruce-needle") *Brustzucker* was a pectoral sugar chest syrup, used in the treatment of coughs, asthma, and chronic catarrh, and sold as "little sticks of bonbon," wrapped in tinfoil and "containing a very little opium." LM's *Fichtennadel-Tabak,* "Pine-Needle Tobacco," is listed in Arnhold James Cooley, *A Cyclopedia of Practical Receipts . . .* (London: J. & A. Churchill, 1880), 723.

6 **His father, Moses:** Moses Morgenthau was born in 1773 and died on Feb. 5, 1834. His father was Gerson HaCohen (c. 1805–1874)—HaCohen, a variant of Cohen, denoting "of the priestly tribe"—who adopted the surname "Her(r)mann." His *matzevah* (tombstone) in the cemetery in the town of Ebern in Bavaria, Germany, gives his *Shem Kodesh* (Hebrew name) as Gershon bar Menke haCohen (Gershon, the son of Menke, a Cohen). Genealogists and archivists have posited how he came by the surname Hermann: Moses Morgenthau, whose parents were poor and died young, orphaning their children at a young age, may have been a half brother of the four Herrmann brothers of Gleusdorf. Two headstones in the Jewish burial ground offer clues to the relations between the families. The first headstone, erected for Moses and Brünhild, was modest, a small stone with a brief epitaph. Decades later (in the 1850s, at the earliest), a second stone, larger and far more elaborate, was placed nearby. The later headstone stands out in the cemetery, and its Hebrew inscription is detailed in describing the miseries of Moses and Brünhild's lives—referencing Brünhild's eye disease, and noting how their children had prospered and made a name for themselves. Scholars believe this second headstone was the work of Moses's half brothers, the Herrmanns. Among the scholars and genealogists who have researched the Morgenthau records in German archives and cemeteries: Elisabeth Böhrer, Thilo Figaj, Karen Franklin, Lars Menk, Sebastian Parzer, Stefan Rohrbacher (Projektgruppe "Jü-

discher Friedhof Ebern," Institut für Jüdische Studien, Heinrich-Heine-Universität Düsseldorf).

7 **"I realized"**: Lazarus Morgenthau, *The Diary of Lazarus Morgenthau, Lebens Geschichte von Lazarus Morgenthau Aus Hürben bei Krumbach Von Ihm Selbst Geschrieben* (Speyer, November 30, 1842), includes Introduction, German and English translation, and a biographical sketch by LM's granddaughter, Louise Heidelberg (New York, 1933), 74.

7 **Brunhilda**: Brünhild (spelling varies, and her name is also listed in some records as "Bräuna") Morgenthau was born Lebrecht, c. 1777, and died on Jan. 30, 1834. Death records of the Jewish community of Freudenberg hold an entry for Brünhild's father, Zacharias Enng, who died on March 8, 1817, at 71, and is listed as a *quiescentirte Juden Schuhllehrer,* a former Jewish teacher. Enng's wife, Bonle, died in Freudenberg on Dec. 3, 1825, at 76. Franklin, Menk, Rohrbacher correspondence.

9 **Rodenstein**: Stadtarchiv Mannheim, Institut für Stadtgeschichte, correspondence, Feb. 2, 2010; Neues allgemeines Deutsches Adels-Lexicon im Verein mit mehreren Historikern, hg. von Ernst Heinrich Knesche, vol. 7 (Leipzig, 1867), 534.

9 **24,000 guilders**: To find a modern approximate equivalent price: The fine weight in silver of the South German guilders in 1850 was 9.545 grams. At 24,000 guilders, this weight would total 229 kg of fine silver. At the 2020 silver price of $53,000/kg, the sale price of the Mannheim house would be equal to $1.2 million.

10 **Friedrich of Baden**: On the occasion of the duke and duchess's wedding, on their return to Mannheim in Sept. 1856, LM organized his entire staff of 200 workers to join the town parade. When the duke visited the Mannheim factory, LM had it adorned with a white flag featuring a green tobacco plant and the golden initials "GM"—for *Gebrüder Morgenthau.* Weeks later, in June 1860, the brothers opened a New York branch. On the grand duke's birthday each year, LM would hold raffles for the staff with cash prizes. Parzer correspondence.

10 **"Your children"**: *Mannheimer Anzeiger.*

10 **"a free citizen"**: Elisabeth Böhrer, Thilo Figaj correspondence.

11 **an evening "illumination"**: *Geschichte der Stadt Mannheim, Mannheim in Vergangenheit und Gegenwart.* See also Sebastian Parzer, *"Der Zigarrenfabrikant Lazarus Morgenthau (1815–1897), in Mannheimer Geschichtsblätter,* Bd. 22, 2011, S. 11–18. Parzer correspondence.

11 **finishing the repairs**: It is unclear from the historical evidence if the "rescue" of the pageant was by one of LM's employees. As described by Max Morgenthau, a fire broke out when LM undertook a rehearsal of the event. A sportsman apparently climbed the walls to put out the flames. Two days later, LM published a notice in the *Mannheimer Anzeiger* (Nov. 12, 1862), wishing to thank the "unknown gymnast" *(unbekannten Turner)* who had saved his house. Parzer correspondence.

11 **"a chance to escape"**: HM Diary, April 26, 1914, HM Papers, LC.

12 **protectionism formed**: The Republican Platform," in *The Campaign of 1860* (Albany, N.Y.: Weed, Parsons & Company, 1860), 16.

12 **"Protection for Home Industry"**: Reinhard H. Lothin, *The First Lincoln Campaign* (P. Smith, 1964), 183.

12 **"in good taste and bad"**: "Central Park: Opening Day," *NYT,* June 3, 1866, 5.

13 **"floating lazarette of pestilence"** "The Horrors of Quarantine," *NYT,* June 3, 1866, 4.

2. At the Edge, 1866–1870

14 **passenger listings**: "Passengers Arrived," *NYT,* June 4, 1866, 8.

14 **$30,000 in cash**: The savings figure: HM3 in Howard Simons, *Jewish Times: Voices of the American Jewish Experience* (Houghton Mifflin, 1988), 40; MM, 39; the extant

evidence indicates that LM sold the Mannheim house at a considerable profit. Notices of the house auction: *Mannheimer Journal,* Dec. 15, 1865, Dec. 23, 1865, Dec. 27, 1865; furnishings for sale, May 8, 1866; the family's farewell notice, May 16, 1866; sales contract, Aug. 13, 1856, with Freiherr von Überbruck-Rodenstein of Bensheim, states a price of 24,000 guilders (gulden) (Leo Baeck Institute, Morgenthau Family Collection). LM appears to have made a down payment of 4,000 guilders and paid the balance in installments, with interest of 4% per year. Installment rates: 400 guilders per ½ year, 800 per year. By 1866, he had paid 4,000 + 8,000 = 12,000 (cf. receipts, LBI). In 1866, LM would have had to settle the balance, 12,000 guilders (plus, perhaps, 4% interest), from the auction price (58,000 guilders). LM also sold his cigar-manufacturing property in Lorsch. In addition, he auctioned all of his household items (*Mannheimer Journal,* May 6, 1866). In 1868, Morgenthau's Mannheim house was bought by the "Bankhaus H. W. Ladenburg & Söhne" for 50,000 guilders. The bank sold it eighteen months later for 51,000 guilders (see *Mannheimer Journal,* July 7, 1868, Jan. 6, 1870). Figaj and Parzer correspondence.

15 **"Mingle a little philanthropy":** Walt Whitman, *Brooklyn Times,* May 1, 1857; in Robert A. M. Stern, Thomas Mellins, and David Fishman, *New York 1880: Architecture and Urbanism in the Gilded Age* (New York: Monacelli Press, 1999), 878.

15 **Theodore Bergen estate:** "The Last of the Old Brooklyn Farms Under the Hammer," *Brooklyn Eagle,* June 11, 1866, 3.

15 **hot and cold running water:** "Houses to Let," *Brooklyn Eagle,* May 12, 1865, 1.

15 **"in a very filthy condition":** Henry Reed Stiles, *A History of Brooklyn, Including the Old Town and Village of Brooklyn . . . ,* vol. 2 (1869), 436.

16 **"has taken root at last":** Strong, *Diary,* 334, 336.

18 **Mary Mack:** Mary Mack: *Brooklyn Eagle,* Aug. 28, 1866, 3; Margaret Roach: "A Case of Cholera," *N.Y. Herald,* July 7, 1867, 8.

18 **Gustave Zittel:** Gustave Zittel and Bertha Morgenthau wed on September 29, 1866.

18 **"wines, liquors, brandies, etc.":** HM Papers, LC.

19 **"splendid counters":** "Sales at Auction," *N.Y. Herald,* July 16, 1867, 1.

19 **"general belief":** ALT, 9.

20 **an outsider:** Cowen, *Memories of an American Jew,* 25.

20 **"mental arithmetic":** ALT, 11.

3. "A Declaration of Independence," 1870–1879

22 **"L. Morgenthau's wholesale depot":** *NYT,* Jan. 23, 1868, 8.

22 **first a tongue-scraper:** *Scientific American,* Oct. 13, 1877, 235; *Scientific American,* Feb. 2, 1878, 75.

23 **popular ensemble:** *Journal of the Mount Sinai Hospital* 9, 929: Mount Sinai Hospital, New York, 1942.

23 **Guest lists were printed:** *NYT,* Dec. 1, 1870, 1; *NYT,* Nov. 30, 1870, 2.

23 **at the Hebrew Waifs' Home:** "Morgenthau, the Philanthropist," *Chicago Tribune,* May 6, 1888, 25.

23 **"the most influential":** "The Jewish Hospital," *Philadelphia Inquirer,* Sept. 15, 1873; Whiteman, 43–44; "Jews' Charity Consecration of the Jewish Hospital Philadelphia—Imposing Ceremony $15,23 Subscribed," *N.Y. Herald,* Sept. 15, 1873, 6.

23 **Mount Neboh Lodge:** *Michigan Freemason* 4, no. 11 (May 1873): 479–80.

24 **"devoted friend of charity":** *The New Era: A Monthly Periodical Devoted to Humanity, Judaism and Literature* 4 (1874): 2.

24 **"Father had the intention":** HM, "Autobiography," HM Papers, LC.

24 **"an ever-constant":** ALT, 13–14.

25 **Colored Home and Hospital:** *NYT* obituary, Feb. 19, 1882, 2.

25 "a beautiful character": ALT, 15.

26 "positively undoubtedly necessary": HM Papers, LC.

26 **Kurzman's two-man firm:** Kurzman had added a partner, George H. Yeaman, the former congressman from Kentucky who had been Lincoln's envoy to Denmark.

26 "Whereas during": HM Papers, LC.

28 "My dearest good Lazarus!": BM to LM, Aug. 7, 1873, HM Papers, LC.

30 **25,000 florins:** LM's advertisements were at least based in fact: Newspaper notices of bond drawings in Berlin and Vienna list the winning numbers featured in his ads, but whether LM in fact sold the bonds as advertised remains uncertain. *Wiener Handelsblatt,* June 3, 1873, 3; *Berliner Börsen-Zeitung,* "Redemptions and Drawings," Aug. 2, 1873, 3. (Correspondence, Freddy Litten.)

31 "one who cannot count three": HM Papers, LC.

31 "No man who lived": ALT, 21–22.

33 "went walking out": HM Diary, Aug. 18, 1874; HM Papers, LC.

33 "were not the easygoing people": ALT, 24.

33 **Chauncey Shaffer:** Legal Obituary, *Albany Law Journal* 49–50 (Jan.–June 1894): 341.

34 **Colonel Henry A. Gildersleeve:** ALT, 25.

34 **O'Toole, Mooney, Fitzgerald:** HM Papers, LC.

34 **made him work all the harder:** ALT, 28.

35 **Henry Behning:** Nancy Groce, *Musical Instrument Makers of New York: A Directory of Eighteenth and Nineteenth-Century Urban Craftsmen* (Pendragon Press, 1991), 11.

35 **bankruptcy:** "Local Business Troubles," *NYT,* April 19, 1878, 8.

36 "I was to do the rowing": ALT, 31.

4. "True Happiness," 1880–1883

38 "Nearly all of Harlem": ALT, 41.

38 **the Freundschaft, or Friendship Society:** "Verein Freundschaft's Home. Informal House Warming of the Elegant New Club Building," *N.Y. Herald,* Jan. 4, 1889, 6.

39 **126th Street:** HM bought and sold a number of properties on 125th and 126th streets during 1880–82. Among his deals: HM purchased four "three-story stone front dwell'gs" on 126th Street for $43,200 (*Real Estate Record,* May 8, 1880, 442); he also arranged the deal for his mother's house, 14 126th Street, a three-story brownstone, bought for $28,500 (*Real Estate Record,* May 7, 1881, 464).

40 **Carrie Rosenfeldt:** 1880 Census: Isaac Rosenfeldt, 62-year-old retired merchant, Bavaria; Carrie Rosenfeldt, 20-year-old daughter at home.

41 **Of her nine children:** JSM was the second-eldest of six sisters. Listed in the 1880 Census: Flora, 8; Bella, 11; Emma, 13; Sophie, 15; Josephine, 17; Charles, 18; Edward, 19; and William, 21, born in Michigan. Also: three servants: Fannie Hirsh, 30, from Bavaria; and Katie Rush, 18, and Mary Marley, 25, both from Ireland.

41 **the large house on Forty-sixth Street:** *Goulding's NYC Directory, May 1, 1877–May 1, 1878:* "Banker, 23 Park Row, h 334 w 46th."

42 **"phenomenal success":** *Chicago's First Half Century, 1833–1883: The City as It Was Fifty Years Ago, and as It Is Today* (Chicago: Inter Ocean Publishing Company, 1883), 94. On Morgenthau Bros: advertisement, *Chicago Tribune,* March 27, 1881, 1. The brothers opened a second store, the Bee Hive, on the same site in 1883, with the Bauland brothers, Jacob and Joseph, as partners: "A New Dry Good Palace," *Chicago Tribune,* Feb. 18, 1883, 10.

42 "To look things plainly": HM Papers, LC.

43 "My own dear Josie": HM Papers, LC.

43 "I am willing": HM Papers, LC.

44 **Charles Weil:** *One of a Thousand: A Series of Biographical Sketches of One Thousand*

Representative Men, Resident in the Commonwealth of Massachusetts, 1888-'89, compiled by John Clark Rand (Boston: First National Publishing Company, 1890), 638–39. See also Albert Ehrenfried, *A Chronicle of Boston Jewry: From the Colonial Settlement to 1900* (privately published by Irving Bernstein, 1963), 624: Charles "Colonel" Weil, 557; Carrie Weil.

45 **"It is hard for me":** HM Papers. #2, 1883–Family, FDRL.

45 **"reading and talking":** HM Papers, LC.

45 **"he ran the risk":** HM Papers, LC.

45 **"Not a single line":** HM to Max Morgenthau, April 12, 1883, FDRL.

46 **"not invite any of the family":** HM to Max Morgenthau, April 12, 1883, FDRL.

47 **"Let us have a serious talk":** HM to Babette, April 16, 1883, HM Papers, LC.

47 **"Papa," he told Josie:** HM to Josie Sykes, May 8, 1883, HM Papers, LC.

47 **"If the saying comes true":** Babette Morgenthau to HM and JSM, May 8, 1883, HM Papers, LC.

47 **"Sincerely regretting":** HM & JS to Babette Morgenthau, May 9, 1883, HM Papers, LC.

48 **"At 11 am. Morgenthal":** HM Papers, LC.

48 **a man in his late thirties:** This unknown figure could have been one Dr. Ephraim Winternitz, an Austrian-born physician. The 1900 Census lists Winternitz, born in 1839, as residing at 218 E. 70th Street. But it also claims he arrived in the U.S. in 1886. The *New York Herald* at the time listed an ad for an elegant six-room, second-floor flat for rent at $34.

49 **the greatest public party:** On the birth of Brooklyn Bridge: Alfred Kazin, *A Walker in the City* (New York: Harcourt, 1979), and "The Brooklyn Bridge," *Harper's Bazaar* 79 (1946): 397, with photographs by Henri Cartier-Bresson; "The Great Bridge," *Chicago Tribune,* May 25, 1883, 1; "The Great Bridge Opens," *N.Y. Herald,* May 25, 1883, 6.

49 **"higher spheres":** Babette Morgenthau to HM & JSM, May 19, 1883, HM Papers, LC.

50 **"the largest caravansary":** "A Virginia Health Resort," *NYT,* Feb. 25, 1882, 5.

50 **"We talk earnestly":** HM to Julius Morgenthau, May 22, 1883, HM Papers, LC.

50 **"It has been twelve days":** JSM to Julius Morgenthau, May 22, 1883, HM Papers, LC.

5. "43, 42, 41," 1884–1892

52 **"Dear Mama!":** HM to BM, March 4, 1884; HM Papers, LC.

53 **twenty grandchildren:** LM and Babette Morgenthau's grandchildren as of May 1884: Bertha and Gustave Zittel's children: Juliet, b. 1867, Carl, b. 1876; Pauline and Edward Simon's: Alfred, b. 1872; Bianca, b. 1873, Carl, b. 1875, d. 1880, Robert, b. 1877; Max and Fannie Morgenthau's: Brunhilde, b. 1873, d. 1874, Adele, b. 1874, James, b. 1875, Alice, b. 1876, Max Jr., b. 1878, Minna, b. 1881, William, b. 1882; Minna and Gustave Heidelberg's: Louise, b. 1877, Max, b. 1878; Ida and William Ehrich's: Jesse, b. 1875, Manfred, b. 1876, William, b. 1878, Elsie, b. 1882, Lilian, b. 1882.

53 **"A Victim of Opium":** "A Victim of Opium," *NYT,* Oct. 24, 1885, p.1.

53 **"I've finally found employment":** Siegfried Morgenthau to Heinrich Morgenthau (HM), Aug. 19, 1875; HM Papers, LC.

55 **"It seemed to me":** ALT, 42.

56 **The second deal:** "Buying Land in Harlem," *NYT,* Feb. 13, 1887, 4.

57 **"sunk to the floor":** "W. J. Ehrich Dead," *NYT,* July 28, 1889, 2.

57 **Ehrich Brothers:** "Preparing to Move," *NYT,* April 23, 1889, 5.

57 **"a model of its kind":** "Ehrich Brothers New Store," *NYT,* Sept. 8, 1889, 9.

58 **On March 18, 1890:** "Grant's New Commission," *NYT,* April 10, 1890, 1.

58 **Rapid Transit Commission:** "Grant's New Commission," *NYT,* April 10, 1890, 1.

58 **Morton-Bliss estate:** "A New Municipal Building," *NYT,* March 28, 1891, 8.

59 Morton was now: "Vice President Morton Sells Valuable Land. One Million for Property on the Upper West Side," *N.Y. Herald,* March 28, 1891.

59 "If Washington and his military": *Real Estate Record and Buyers' Guide* 47, no. 1190 (Jan. 3, 1891) through no. 1215 (June 27, 1891).

59 "the new Washington Bridge": "High-Priced Real Estate," *NYT,* May 27, 1891, 8.

60 Henry had given a "spurt": "Made a Fortune Quickly," *Chicago Tribune,* May 27, 1891, 1.

61 "It was such a joy": HM to Babette Morgenthau, Aug. 2, 1892, HM3 Papers.

61 "Mrs. L. M. Morgenthau": obituary, *NYT,* Aug. 16, 1892, 5; HM3 family tree; MM, 47. A search of the New York State official records yielded no death certificate.

6. "The Temple of Humanity," 1892–1898

63 "The Largest Deal in History": *N.Y. Herald,* Jan. 8, 1895, 6. Also: *The Daily Inter Ocean,* Jan. 13, 1895. On the Siegel-Cooper store: ALT, 54–55.

64 "Unique Idea": "Dowers for Orphan Girls," *NYT,* Nov. 13, 1896, 1. Further news reports of LM's dowry fund: "To Give Dowry to Orphan Girls," *Chicago Tribune,* Nov. 14, 1896, 4; "The Greater New York Orphan Dowry Society," *St. Louis Republic,* Nov. 15, 1896; "A Fund to Provide Dowries," *Springfield Republican,* Nov. 29, 1896; "One of the Newest Ideas," *N.Y. Tribune,* Dec. 19, 1896, 7; "Money Goes with the Girls," *San Francisco Chronicle,* Dec. 19, 1896, 1; "Dot for the Asking: Lazarus Morgenthau's Dowry Association About to Be Incorporated," *Evening Telegram,* Jan. 4, 1897, 6; "To Dower Orphan Brides," *Dallas Morning News* (*N.Y. Sun*), Jan. 24, 1897; "No More Old Maids," *Freeland Tribune* (Pa.) (*N.Y. Journal*), Jan. 25, 1897, 3; "The Orphan Dowry Society," *N.Y. Daily Tribune,* Feb. 9, 1897, 5; "Temple's First Bride," *N.Y. Sun,* Feb. 14, 1897, 8; "Gave Her $100 and a Husband," *Kansas City Star* (*N.Y. Herald*), Feb. 28, 1897, 12; "A Husband and a Dowry," *NYT,* March 15, 1897, 7; "Orphan No. 2 Dowered," *N.Y. Sun,* March 15, 1897, 1; "Temple of Humanity Seized," *N.Y. Sun,* Aug. 22, 1897, 3; "Temple of Humanity Fails," *NYT,* Aug. 22, 1897, 4.

64 *San Francisco Chronicle:* "Money Goes with the Girls," *San Francisco Chronicle,* Dec. 19, 1896, 1.

64 Lazarus envisioned a fund: "Dowers for Orphan Girls," *NYT,* Nov. 13, 1896, 1.

64 "one a Catholic, one a Protestant": "Dowers For Orphan Girlos," *NYT,* Nov. 13, 1896, 1.

65 East Seventy-second off Park Avenue: John J. Tackett correspondence with author.

65 facing the orphan bride: Report on second wedding: "A Husband and a Dowry," *NYT,* March 15, 1897, 7. The second couple were Mary Grieger, described as a "forewoman in Herr Morgenthau's candy factory" (most likely, Mengo's candy factory), and Paul Kroener, "a fresco painter." Some reports claimed LM presided over three, or even four, such weddings. The extant newspaper accounts record only two.

67 "the Clifford cottage": "In the Adirondacks," *Philadelphia Inquirer,* July 11, 1897; HM, Julius (a stamp dealer), and Mengo (a candymaker) had made the "Hebrew Visiting List," a booklet that served as the German Jews' social register: "Hebrew Select Directory and Visiting List," 1896–97, Yale Library.

67 "LM's affairs have reached": HM to JSM, Aug. 14, 1897, HM Papers, FDRL.

67 "pinched her": "Says He Flirted at Eighty-Three," *N.Y. Evening Telegram,* July 15, 1897, 10.

68 A dozen policemen raided: "Lazarus Morgenthau Failed," *St. Louis Republic,* Aug. 21, 1897, 7.

68 The creditors had won: The landlord, who was named, alternately, as Charles Mosser or Nosser, reportedly won a judgment for $262.95, and the furniture dealer for $342.50. "Temple of Humanity Fails," *NYT,* Aug. 22, 1897, 4.

68 **"senility"**: New York City Death Certificate No. 26879, Aug. 31, 1897. Obituaries: "Death of L. Morgenthau," *NYT,* Sept. 1, 1897, 7; "The Crisis At Brown University," *Springfield Republican,* Sept. 2, 1897, 6; "Death of L. Morgenthau," *American Israelite,* Sept. 9, 1897; "Lazarus Morgenthau Dead," *Kansas City Star,* Sept. 2, 1897, 7. Funeral: "Lazarus Morgenthau's Funeral," *NYT,* Sept. 3, 1897, 7.

PART II | ASCENT

7. Among the Plutocrats, 1898–1900

71 **Lots that fetched $200 in 1899:** Moses Rischin, *The Promised City: New York's Jews, 1870–1914* (Cambridge, Mass.: Harvard University Press, 1962), 92.

72 **"Instead of a celebration":** ALT, 57.

72 **he bought two blocks:** "Coming to California to Reside: Huntington Disposing of His Holdings in the East," *San Francisco Call,* Nov. 14, 1897.

72 **forty-four parcels:** The 1898 sale of the Astor properties on the East Side to HM was the subject of great debate. A brief chronology of its evolution reveals how HM adapted to quickly shifting circumstances, and still made a fine profit.

On May 8, the *NYT* reported ("In the Real Estate Field," 10) that HM had just concluded a deal to buy "about 40 lots" for "about $750,000" from William Waldorf Astor. The lots, though, were not empty but "occupied at present by old style tenements and dwellings," and nearly all the ground leases were due to expire within a year. HM had a plan: to raze the tenements and construct "modern apartment houses." The *NYT* termed it a "plan of improvement" that would lead "many German families" from the north of the city to move downtown, closer to their place of work.

On June 9, the *NYT* reported that due to "such general protest among the owners of the properties of William Waldorf Astor just sold to HM, and so many appeals for a chance either to buy the ground or renew their leases, that a new contract has been drawn up." HM would "relinquish his right to take title to all of the properties covered by the original contract, except the block front on the west side of Avenue A, between Seventh and Eighth Streets." Instead, as substitutes "for those which Mr. Astor will retain," HM received a number of new parcels along First Avenue, Avenue A, and Seventh, Sixth and Fifth streets. Above all, the new deal called for "Mr. Morgenthau [to] sell, or in a few instances, lease the lots to the owners of the buildings." ("In the Real Estate Field," *NYT,* June 9, 1898, 10.)

On July 2, the *NYT* reported an East Fourth Street meeting of the local ward taxpayers' association to hear protests concerning the "intention of William Waldorf Astor and John Jacob Astor to increase the rate per front foot of their twenty-year renewals of leases" by more than double, from "$350 to $750 on side streets, and to $1000 for avenue plots." The association moved to form a committee "to remonstrate with W. W. Astor's agents"—Waldorf Astor had moved to England—"and if necessary, to communicate with Mr. Astor in England himself." The brief article concluded with a revelatory sentence: "The tenants are also worked up over Mr. Astor's disposal of many of his holdings to HM, who, they said, has refused to renew leases" ("Leases of Astor Property," July 2, 1898, *NYT,* 7).

By July 18, the deed—covering 41 lots, although "there were in reality 44 parcels"—was recorded. ("In the Real Estate Field," *NYT,* July 19, 1898, 10.) The price HM paid—$676,137—as well as his profit—$284,632—found in "The Immigrant As Landlord: How Frugal Foreigners Succeed to the Estates of the Astors and Other Old Families," *N.Y. Tribune,* Dec. 9, 1900, 11.

72 **"The Immigrant as Landlord":** "The Immigrant as Landlord: How Frugal Foreigners

Succeed to the Estates of the Astors and Other Old Families," *N.Y. Tribune,* Dec. 9, 1900, 11; see also ALT, 56; two years later, in December 1900, Colonel John Jacob Astor also sold property, a series of tenement houses on Fourth and Fifth streets, bounded by First Avenue and Avenue A, for "about $850,000" ("Col. Astor Sells A Block," *NYT,* Dec. 6, 1900, 1).

73 **restoring order, it was said:** "Frederic P. Olcott, Financier, Is Dead," *NYT,* April 16, 1909, 9.

74 **Hugh J. Grant:** Grant's career had been the work of Dick Croker, notorious heir to Tweed. Orphaned young, Grant had come into a sizeable inheritance, and Croker, an Irishman raised in the wilds of pre–Civil War New York, could not miss the opportunity. Croker, who had narrowly missed a conviction on murder charges, had served as county coroner, tax collector, and fire commissioner before at last taking over Tammany. In 1885, Croker had installed Grant as sheriff. But the following year, the scandal had hit. When Croker's daughter Flossie turned two, Grant delivered, it was said, an offering of $25,000 cash in a white envelope. Grant pleaded innocence. He was the girl's godfather, he told the investigators, and Boss Croker was poor. It was a gift, he insisted, and no more than $10,000. The aftermath of the affair proved a testament to the prowess of Tammany. Grant went on to win the mayoralty in 1899, and Croker, for his part, had sunk the money in Harlem real estate. See Gustavus Myers, *The History of Tammany Hall* (Boni & Liveright, 1901), 321, citing *Testimony, NY State Senate Committee on Cities,* vol. 1, 1890, 707–708; "Tammany's Ticket Named," *NYT,* Oct. 11, 1890, 1; "Grant in the Witness Chair," *NYT,* Oct. 20, 1894, 2. For Croker: *Tammany Biographies,* 3rd ed., Revised and Enlarged; *N.Y. Evening Post,* Oct. 1894, 5–6; Lotthrop Stoddard, *Master of Manhattan: The Life of Richard Croker* (Longmans, Green & Co., 1931).

74 **could "sniff" success:** ALT, 59.

74 **a million dollars:** Moses King, *King's Handbook of New York* (Boston: Moses King, 1893), 762.

74 **"rugged honesty":** ALT, 78.

74 **a "closed book":** ALT, 63.

75 **Central Realty:** The history of the birth of HM's trust is a good deal more complex than the story HM sketches in ALT. HM first joined the New York Realty Bond Exchange and Trust Company (later the Central Realty, Bond Exchange and Trust Company; the name was changed in July 1899). In May 1889, the Central Realty & Bond Trust Co. bought the old Real Estate Exchange and Auction Room, a six-story iron building at No. 59–65 Liberty Street, at the time of its dissolution, and soon opened its own offices on its lower floor.

On July 3, 1899, HM's trust bid on the old Custom House, losing only to James Stillman: "In response to said advertisements, the following proposals were received: National City Bank of New York, James Stillman, president, $3,265,000; New York Realty Bond Exchange and Trust Company, Henry Morgenthau, president, $3,075,000; Farmers' Loan and Trust Company, Edwin S. Marston, president, $3,055,000. The proposal of the National City Bank, having been regarded as the most advantageous to the Government, was duly accepted by the Secretary of the Treasury, in writing under date of July 3, 1899.") (Lyman Judson Gage, *Public Depositories, Statement of Secretary Gage* [n.p., 1900], 18.)

On August 25, 1899, the *N.Y. Tribune* reported "New Trust to Open Monday" in new offices "fitted up for it" in the Real Estate Exchange Bldg. On Aug. 28, 1899, the Central Realty, Bond & Trust Company "began business." (Jaffray Peterson, *Sixty-Five Years of Progress and a Record of New York City Banks* [New York: Continental Bank & Trust Company of New York, 1935; reprint, Arno Press, 1980, 97].) Ball & Southack were listed as directors; Grant as vice president and Thorwald Stallknecht as second vice president. (W. Dickerman, *Dickerman's United States Treasury Counterfeit Detector and Bankers' & Merchants' Journal* 16, no. 1 [1899]: 12–13.)

On September 8, 1899, the *New York Sun* ("Real Estate News," 9) reported that another newspaper had printed a rumor that HM had gone to England to buy W. W. Astor's properties. HM told the reporter there was no truth to the rumor; his trip was "only recreation."

HM's trust had bought the building in which it had opened its first offices, the old Real Estate Exchange, for $580,000, and in 1902 sold it to the Building Committee of the Chamber of Commerce for $750,000. The Chamber of Commerce would build new ornate headquarters on the site, and by the end of 1902, HM's trust would reopen its offices in the building. ("The Chamber's New Home," *N.Y. Tribune*, Jan. 9, 1901, 6; "Great Corporations: Growth of Trust Idea," *N.Y. Tribune*, Dec. 31, 1902, 3.)

75 **"They bought me"**: ALT, 63.

75 **"well-known capitalists"**: "More Big Purchases in Washington Heights," *N.Y. Daily Tribune*, Oct. 11, 1900, 12.

8. "A Modest Man," 1896–1903

76 **"three men of fine judgment"**: Gerald White Johnson, *An Honorable Titan: A Biographical Study of Adolph S. Ochs* (New York: Harper & Brothers, 1946), 202.

76 **"The opportunity of your life"**: Elmer Davis, *The History of* The New York Times, *1851–1921* (New York: New York Times, 1921), 178.

77 **"the little boy"**: Iphigene Ochs to Adolph Ochs, Aug. 13, 1896, Ochs Papers, Box 26, NYPL.

78 **"The premises now occupied"**: Letter Park Company (signed Gilbert E. Jones) to Adolph Ochs, Dec. 13, 1897, Ochs Papers, Box 102, NYPL.

78 **"known to nearly every"**: Adolph Ochs to HM, March 18, 1898, Ochs Papers, Box 102, NYPL.

78 **"The sum of $26,913.80"**: R. Delafield to D. E. Seybel and HM, March 24, 1898, Ochs Papers, Box 102, NYPL. More on lease dispute: series of letters from December 1897 to March 1898, including Adolph Ochs to Park Company, Jan. 6, 1898, and Adolph Ochs to HM, Jan. 7, 1898, Ochs Papers, Box 102, NYPL.

78 **United States Realty**: "Big Realty Merger Plans Developed," *NYT*, Aug. 1, 1902, 1. In early 1901, three months after George Fuller's death, Black moved the Fuller Company east. Within weeks, he and HM began talking of an alliance. The Fuller Company would join with HM's Central Realty Bond & Trust Company and New York Realty (itself a recent creation of powerful bankers, including Cornelius Vanderbilt, great-grandson of the original commodore, and the Morgan man Charles Steele). On August 4, 1902, Black and HM incorporated their new mega-trust, to be known as U.S. Realty.

78 **A contagion**: Arthur Stone Dewing, "Corporate Promotions and Reorganizations," *Harvard Economic Studies* 10 (1914): 229. On the rise and fall of the U.S. Realty Company: 227–48.

78 **"What Mr. Morgenthau Says"**: "Big Realty Merger Plans Developed," *NYT*, Aug. 1, 1902, 1.

78 **married the boss's daughter**: Fuller had an elder daughter, Grace, born in 1873, who predeceased her father in 1899. Months after the birth of her son, Grace committed suicide.

78 **he left the company**: "The George A. Fuller Company: The Pioneer Firm in the Building of the Modern 'Sky-Scraper'" and "H. S. Black: President of the George A. Fuller Company & Projector the Great $20,000,000 Building Trust," both in *The Successful American: A Magazine* 3, no. 4 (April 1901): 191–95.

79 "a Napoleon complex": Paul Starrett, *Changing the Skyline: An Autobiography* (New York: McGraw-Hill, 1938), 115–16.

79 **world's most noteworthy buildings:** Mitchell C. Harrison, *Prominent and Progressive Americans: An Encyclopaedia of Contemporaneous Biography,* vol. 1 (New York: New York Tribune, 1902); 38–39.

79 "**Not only has the outward**": "New York, the Unrivalled Business Centre," *Harper's Weekly,* Nov. 15, 1902, 1673–87.

79 "**A Case in Point**": "A Case in Point," *NYT,* Aug. 2, 1902, 8; the *Times* was not alone. The following month, Walter Hines Page's *The World's Work* also saw the creation of the new building trust as part of the essential reforms of the day. "The very conception of making a profit from real estate in this manner is a part of this twentieth century's progressiveness," the magazine wrote. "Up to the present time, the real estate business has . . . been in the partnership stage." "Nearly all real property," it went on, was "owned by private individuals or estates." Rather than a fearful accumulation of power and profit, "the idea of dealing in real estate as so many shares of stock" presaged the arrival of an enlightened market. ("A New Era in Financing Real Estate," *The World's Work* 4, no. 5 [Sept. 1902]: 2486–88.)

80 **On October 30, 1902:** New York Stock Exchange Application, A-2698, cited in Dewing, "Corporate Promotions and Reorganizations," 234.

80 **Hallgarten syndicate:** *The Commercial and Financial Chronicle,* vol. 77, 717 (Sept. 19, 1903); cited in Dewing, 238; "May Lose $6,000,000," *N.Y. Tribune,* Sept. 12, 1903, 16; "No U.S. Realty Reorganizing," *N.Y. Sun,* Sept. 15, 1903, 9.

81 **Electric Illuminated Company board:** "Edison Company Election," *N.Y. Tribune,* Feb. 14, 1900, A2. HM served on the board with Hughey Grant and Nicholas Brady, the 22-year-old son of his partner Anthony Brady, who was fresh out of Yale.

81 **Prince Henry of Prussia:** "Prince Henry to the German Society," *NYT,* March 9, 1902, 1.

81 **Empire City Trotting Club:** "Empire City Meeting Will Offer Good Sport," *Brooklyn Eagle,* Sept. 12, 1902, 7.

81 **the sole Jew:** List of the directors and officers of the Empire City Trotting Club: "Empire City's Meeting," *NYT,* Sept. 14, 1902, 15. These included C.K.G. Billings, who would later visit with HM in Constantinople.

81 **city's biggest taxpayers:** "Personal Taxes in the Borough of Manhattan," *NYT,* July 20, 1902, 28. In 1902, he was levied $40,000 in taxes—an astounding sum, more than a million dollars today.

81 **the celebration reminded:** On the opening of the new N.Y. Stock Exchange: "New Exchange Opened," *N.Y. Tribune,* April 23, 1903, 1; "Stock Exchange's New Building Dedicated," *NYT,* April 23, 1903, 6; John Tauranac, *Elegant New York: The Builders and the Buildings 1885–1915* (New York: Abbeville, 1985), 13. For original text of the Reverend Morgan Dix's benediction, President Keppler's speech, and William Alexander Smith's remarks: New York Stock Exchange (NYSE) Archives.

82 **The guests filled:** "NYSE: Special Committee on Opening Ceremonies, 1902–03," invitation, schedule of events, and photographs, April 22, 1903, NYSE Archives.

82 **the famous men seated:** Among those present: Stillman, Delafield, Levi Morton, Oscar Straus; Belmont (though the latter was not on the invitation list), Lyman Gage, who had just resigned after five years as secretary of the Treasury, Richard McCurdy, president of Mutual Life Insurance Company, and Charles T. Barney of the Knickerbocker Trust.

9. "Let Me Have the Boy," 1903-1911

83 "**social throne**": Mark Sullivan, *Our Times, 1900–1925,* vol. 3, *Pre-War America* (New York: Charles Scribner's Sons, 1930), 544.

83 **"Our good Jews"**: Stephen Birmingham, *"Our Crowd": The German Jewish Families of New York* (New York: Harper & Row, 1967), 258.

83 **Heinrich Conreid**: On Heinrich Conried and his career: Montrose J. Moses, *The Life of Heinrich Conried* (New York: Thomas A. Crowell, 1916), 246; Arthur G. Albrecht, "Das Deutsches Theater in New York," *Staats Zeitung,* April 16, 1905, quoted in Moses, 30.

83 **offered the lease:** "Heinrich Conried, Long Ill, Is Dead," *N.Y. Evening Sun,* April 27, 1909, 9.

84 **"a sort of ghetto"**: Peggy Guggenheim, *Out of This Century: Confessions of an Art Addict* (New York: Universe Books, 1979), 15.

84 **"the best interests of art"**: *Cosima Wagner and Siegfried Wagner v. Heinrich Conried and The Conried Metropolitan Opera Company,* 125 Fed. 798 (SDNY 1903); HM affidavits, dated Oct. 29, 1903 and Nov. 11, 1903; NARA NY.

84 *Rigoletto* **marked Caruso's debut:** "Society, in Superb Array, Ushers in New Opera Season," *N.Y. Herald,* Nov. 24, 1903, 3–4. Conried had not only delivered Caruso, and charged ahead with *Parsifal,* but refurbished the opera house from stage to ceiling. Gutted by fire in the summer of 1892, the Metropolitan had been rebuilt soon thereafter. But Conried ordered a complete renovation. "Everything about the opera was new," a critic wrote in a review of opening night. The new house even featured a smoking room, "frequented by the men." Conried yielded on one point only: the demand of the box-holders in the Golden Horseshoe to keep their lamps burning throughout the performance. He reached a compromise: red shades.

85 **the judge sided with Conried:** "Can Produce 'Parsifal,'" *NYT,* Nov. 25, 1903, 5; "Wagners Cannot Stop Parsifal," *N.Y. Herald,* Nov. 25, 1903, 9; "Parsifal and the Preparations in Society and at the Met Opera House for Its First American Production," *N.Y. Herald,* Dec. 20, 1903, 9; Henry Edward Krehbiel, *More Chapters of Opera,* vol. 1 (New York: Henry Holt, 1908), 331.

85 **Conried thanked one man:** "Praise for Mr. Conried," *NYT,* Dec. 26, 1903, 2.

85 **Ochs needed a new home:** Gerald White Johnson, *An Honorable Titan: A Biographical Study of Adolph S. Ochs* (New York: Harper & Brothers, 1946), 201.

85 **"You don't want to move"**: "Morgenthau, at 90, Optimist on Future," *NYT,* April 26, 1946, 29.

85 **Long Acre:** Elmer Davis, *The History of* The New York Times, *1851–1921* (New York: New York Times, 1921), 323–24.

86 **On January 18, 1904, Iphigene:** Iphigene Ochs and Susan W. Dryfoos, *Iphigene: My Life and* The New York Times: *The Memoirs of Iphigene Ochs Sulzberger* (New York: Times Books, 1987), 49.

86 **"My dear friend"**: Adolph Ochs to HM, Jan. 5, 1904, HM Papers, LC.

86 **$25,000 check:** Johnson, *Honorable Titan,* 203.

87 **Charles Evans Hughes:** On Hughes generally: Robert F. Wessler, *Charles Evans Hughes: Politics and Reform in New York* (Ithaca, N.Y.: Cornell University Press, 1967). On the hearings of the Armstrong Commission, named after the State Senator William W. Armstrong of Rochester: J. Herbert Welch, "Hughes: The Great Modern Inquisitor," *Success,* January 1906, 11–12; Albert Britt, "Hughes, Life Insurance Inquisitor," *Public Opinion* 39, no. 17 (Oct. 21, 1905): 519–20; John L. Heaton, The Story of a Page (New York: Harper & Brothers, 1913), 212–27.

87 **James Hazen Hyde stood:** Among the charges leveled against Hyde, falsely as it turned out, was that he had handed the bill for the famous ball at Sherry's, as well as all his servants and lavish living, to the company. Mark Sullivan, *Our Times, 1900–1925,* vol. 3, *Pre-War America* (New York: Scribner's, 1940), 41–67.

87 **at a cost of $200,000:** On the ball at Sherry's, and James Hazen Hyde generally, see: Patricia Beard, *After the Ball: Gilded Age Secrets, Boardroom Betrayals, and the*

Party That Ignited the Great Wall Street Scandal of 1905 (New York: HarperCollins, 2004).

87 force him from the opera board: Teresa M. Collins, *Otto Kahn: Art, Money, & Modern Time* (Chapel Hill: University of North Carolina Press, 2002), 70; Mary Jane Phillips-Matz, *The Many Lives of Otto Kahn* (New York: Macmillan, 1963), 57; Beard, *After the Ball,* 124; Rose Heylbut and Aimé Gerber, *Backstage at the Opera* (New York: Thomas Y. Crowell, 1937); Eliot Gregory to James Hazen Hyde letter, Jan. 10, 1906, Hyde Papers, NYPL.

87 "prominent and trusted men": ALT, 81.

88 "arouse public opinion": ALT, 82.

88 "campaign contributions, fabulous salaries": Welch, "Hughes," 11.

88 He denounced the men: HM testimony, Dec. 28, 1905: "Testimony Taken Before the Joint Committee of the Senate and Assembly of the State of New York, To Investigate and Examine into the Business and Affairs of Life Insurance Companies Doing Business in the State of New York," vol. 5 (Albany, N.Y.: J. B. Lyon Company, 1906), 4560–67. On HM's role in the scandal and hearings: ALT, 79–84; Burton J. Hendrick, "Ambassador Morgenthau's Story: Introductory Article," *The World's Work,* April 1918, 620–37; "Comment," *Harper's Weekly,* April 1, 1905, 452–55.

88 "barred doors": Welch, "Hughes," 11–12.

88 no longer own stock: Mark J. Roe, "Foundations of Corporate Finance: The 1906 Pacification of the Insurance Industry," *Columbia Law Review* 93, no. 9 (April 1993): 639–84.

89 Robert Simon: Author interview, Robert E. Simon, Jr., 2012. Simon Jr., 98 years old at the time of the interview, was also a real estate pioneer, best known for founding the town of Reston, Virginia—named for his initials. Simon, too, got his start in the business "doing chores" for HM.

89 "all the big plots": ALT, 87.

89 "to pay our stockholders": ALT, 89. On the 1905 merger of Central Realty Bond and Trust with the Lawyers' Title Company: "Big Trust Companies Considering Merger," *NYT,* Feb. 26, 1905, 2; *The Bankers' Magazine* 70 (Jan.–June 1905): 504. The official date of the merger was March 17, 1905: Jaffray Peterson. *Sixty-five Years of Progress and a Record of New York City Banks* (1935; repr., New York: Arno Press, 1980), 97.

89 "on a much larger scale": ALT, 89.

89 The new firm: The Morgenthau Realty Company's office was at 20 Nassau Street. Its five directors were Robert E. Simon, Walter M. Wechsler, Joseph E. Foise, Leonard G. Dorman, and HM. Corporate Records, N.Y. Municipal Archives.

90 "He was crazy": Blum, vol. 1, 5.

90 "Latin, Latin, and more Latin": AFT, 27, FDRL.

91 listless and sleepy: AFT, 27, cut from original manuscript; Gaer, Box 410, FDRL.

91 "Father was as worried": AFT, 26c, FDRL.

91 grew nearly nine inches: Blum, *From the Morgenthau Diaries,* vol. 1, 3, citing EFM in ibid., 55–84.

91 "most severe taskmaster": AFT, 28–29, FDRL.

91 Henry Jr. did miserably: HM2 high school records, 1906 Yearbook, Archives of Phillips Exeter Academy.

92 "goes to work": HM2 to HM, Sept. 20, 1904, FDRL.

92 "Last night": HM2 to HM, Jan. 12, 1905, FDRL.

92 "not do so much": HM2 to HM, March 13, 1905, FDRL.

92 "Now don't forget": HM2 to HM, April 21, 1906, FDRL.

92 "I am sorry": HM2 to HM, Dec. 5, 1906, FDRL.

93 "he would have me leave school": HM2 to HM, May 3, 1906, FDRL.

93 "Ever since I was 10": AFT, 31–32, FDRL.

94   "deeply absorbed": ALT, 129.

95   "People's Rabbi": On SSW: Rischin, *The Promised City;* Melvin I. Urofsky, *A Voice That Spoke for Justice: The Life and Times of Stephen S. Wise* (Albany: State University of New York Press, 1982); Wise's *Challenging Years: The Autobiography of Stephen Wise* (New York: Putnam, 1949); *The Personal Letters of Stephen Wise*, ed. J. W. Polier and J. W. Wise (Boston: Beacon Press, 1956); Geoffrey T. Hellman, "Profile of Stephen S. Wise," *New Yorker,* Nov. 7, 1931, 22–25; William Inglis, "Celebrities at Home," *Harper's Weekly,* Dec. 5, 1908, 13–14.

95   "That my pulpit not be muzzled": "Dr. Wise Surprises Emanu-El Trustees," *NYT,* Jan. 7, 1906, 5.

95   "The Free Synagogue": On the Free Synagogue and HM's role as first president: HM Papers, LC; "Dr. Wise Coming Here," *N.Y. Tribune,* Oct. 19, 1906, 5; "Dr. Wise Here to Establish New Form of Judaism," *N.Y. Tribune,* Oct. 20, 1906, 7; "Dr. Wise's Mission," *N.Y. Tribune,* Oct. 21, 1906, 8; Melvin I. Urofsky, *A Voice That Spoke for Justice: The Life and Times of Stephen S. Wise* (Albany: State University of New York Press, 1982), 59–72.

96   "Mr. Guggenheim's pew": Robert Donald Shapiro, *A Reform Rabbi in the Progressive Era: The Early Career of Stephen S. Wise* (New York: Garland Press, 1988), 237.

96   "not organized simply": "Speech on the First Anniversary of the Free Synagogue," HM Papers, LC.

96   "To start a free synagogue": Voss, *Rabbi and Minister,* 81.

97   "He was tall": Bernays interview, June 29, 1978; HM3 Papers.

97   "I am getting": HM2 to HM, Sept. 7, 1908, FDRL.

97   "You must always": HM to HM2, March 5, 1909; AFT, 43, FDRL.

97   "I do not want": AFT, 39, FDRL.

98   "I was over in Washington": AFT, 40, FDRL.

98   "Keep me in touch": HM2 to HM, Oct. 17, 1909, FDRL.

98   "You know, Papa": HM2 to HM, Oct. 17, 1909, FDRL.

98   "Now, Papa": HM2 to HM, Feb. 16, 1909, FDRL.

98   "I have not mastered": HM2 to HM, Oct. 21, 1910, FDRL.

99   dropped out: HM2's Cornell University transcript reflects that he enrolled for a fourth term, but left the university before completing the coursework in agriculture.

99   "I thought Henry": Geoffrey T. Hellman, "Any Bonds Today?," part 1, *New Yorker,* Jan. 22, 1944, 24–32.

99   struck with typhoid: Joseph Alsop and Robert Kintner, " 'Henny Penny': Farmer at the Treasury," *Saturday Evening Post,* April 1, 1939.

99   The C Ranch: W. N. Pence and his son Leonard managed the ranch, as well as another owned by the Morris Packing Co., the T.O. Ranch, one of the largest American-owned ranches in Mexico. Dorothy Payne, "Nelson Morris and the Chicago Ranch, 1883–1907," Texas Permian Historical Annual VI, no. 1, Dec. 1966 (Permian Historical Society, Odessa, Texas).

99   "Although I have only been": HM2 to HM & JSM, dated Jan. 18, 1910, but it must be 1911, FDRL.

10. Wilson's Call, Spring–Winter 1911

102   "I am *not* a conservative": Wilson to Mary Peck, April 30, 1911, PWW, vol. 22, 598, quoted in John Milton Cooper, Jr., *Woodrow Wilson: A Biography* (New York: Vintage, 2011), 146.

102   "younger generation's hero": ALT, 111; HM–Mengo Morgenthau, Oct. 29, 1876, HM Papers, LC.

102   "heathen Canton": Lawrence Veiller, *Housing Reform*, cited in "Report of the Com-

mittee on Congestion of Population," by Frank G. Goodnow, Columbia University, in *First New York City Conference of Charities and Correction, Proceedings, May 1– December 1910,* vol. 1 (Albany, N.Y.: J. B. Lyons, 1910), 12.

102 **Benjamin C. Marsh:** Benjamin C. Marsh, *Lobbyist for the People: A Record of Fifty Years* (Washington, D.C.: PublicAffairs Press, 1953).

103 **"There is an evil":** HM Speech, May 21, 1909; *U.S. Senate Committee on the District of Columbia, City Planning,* 59, 61 Cong. 2d Session, S. Doc. 422 (1910). The 1909 proceedings are contained in an appendix, 59–105.

103 **"to drift into a disease":** The *NYT* account of HM's speech contains quotes absent from the record of the conference proceedings. "Henry Morgenthau Outlines in Washington a Plan to Obtain Model Homes for the Poor," *NYT,* May 22, 1909, 3.

103 **"a bail brigade":** Rischin, *The Promised City,* 247–48.

103 **He also kicked Marsh:** Marsh, *Lobbyist for the People,* 13. Cited in Richard E. Foglesong, *Planning the Capitalist City: The Colonial Era to the 1920s* (Princeton, N.J.: Princeton University Press, 1986),176.

104 **"I learned a new sound":** "Eye-Witness Tells Story of Disaster," *Standard Union* (Brooklyn), March 26, 1911, 1.

104 **five of the last ten presidential elections:** Cooper, *Wilson,* 140.

104 **"old doctrine":** "Take Politics from Ambush Says Wilson," *NYT,* Feb. 1, 1911, 8.

105 **"I feel as if":** WW speech at the Free Synagogue dinner, April 24, 1911: newspapers printed reports, with slight variation. "Readjustment Going On," *N.Y. Tribune,* April 25, 1911, 7. PWW does not contain a copy of the speech, as delivered. A one-page outline, handwritten and dated April 24, 1911, is in Wilson Papers, PWW, LC, vol. 22, 586.

105 **"Politics and Morals":** "Call Gov. Wilson Man with a Future," *NYT,* April 25, 1911, 3; "High Praise for Wilson at Dinner," *Trenton Times,* April 25, 1911, 3; "Readjustment Going On," *N.Y. Tribune,* April 25, 1911, 7.

105 **"I don't know":** Voss, *Rabbi and Minister,* 122, citing SSW Diary; Variation: Wise, *Challenging Years,* 163; SSW Diary, entries for Feb. 10–11, 1911.

106 **"a narrow racial Jewish protest":** William G. McAdoo, *Crowded Years* (Boston: Houghton Mifflin, 1931), 122.

106 **"not merely affect the rights":** "Rights of the Jews," PWW, vol. 2, 318. Reports of speech: "Demand Break with Russia," *NYT,* Dec. 7, 1911, 1; "Russia Denounced for Discrimination," *N.Y. Tribune,* Dec. 7, 1911, 1.

11. Money Harvest, 1912–1913

108 **$4,000 a month:** J. Kerney, *The Political Education of Woodrow Wilson* (New York: The Century Company, 1926), 155; cited in Arthur S. Link, *Wilson: The Road to the White House,* vol. 1 (Princeton, N.J.: Princeton University Press, 1968), 338.

109 **"Uncle Henry":** ALT, 154.

109 **On June 15:** Link, *Wilson,* 431.

109 **"Some sixty to eighty":** Lewis L. Gould, *Four Hats in the Ring: The 1912 Election and the Birth of Modern American Politics* (Lawrence: University Press of Kansas, 2008), 60.

110 **"We went to Baltimore":** ALT, 146.

110 **The governor telegraphed McCombs:** John Milton Cooper, Jr., *The Warrior and the Priest: Woodrow Wilson and Theodore Roosevelt* (Cambridge, Mass.: Belknap Press of Harvard University Press, 1983), 185, 158.

111 **forty-sixth ballot:** Robert Carl Scott, "William McCombs and the 1912 Democratic Presidential Nomination of Woodrow Wilson," *Arkansas Historical Quarterly* 44, no. 3 (Autumn 1985): 258.

111 **"is the first real estate man"**: "Real Estate Men Organize," *Dallas Morning News,* Sept. 1, 1912, 3.

112 **Wilson named as Henry's deputy**: "Men Who Will Raise Money for Wilson's Campaign," *NYT,* Aug. 18, 1912, 12.

112 **"raise the funds"**: "Wilson's Treasurer Here," *NYT,* Aug. 12, 1912, 3.

113 **"ten cents to $10,000"**: "Democrats Show Campaign Receipts," *NYT,* Sept. 9, 1912, 3.

113 **"Our needs are imperative"**: "More Money Needed for Democratic Campaign," *Daily East Oregonian,* Sept. 30, 1912, 8.

113 **have given more**: According to HM's campaign colleague and friend Josephus Daniels, HM did try to give more money to the campaign. Daniels and HM admired one another, and despite their different backgrounds, got on well. The Southern publisher, it would appear, had no cause to tarnish the reputation of Wilson's finance chairman. But Daniels in his memoirs recounts a curious scene—when, at least in his telling, HM made a dubious proposition. Daniels writes that he was in his office at headquarters one day when HM walked in and handed him "a roll of bills—I think it was about five thousand dollars." "You know our friend Governor Wilson issued a rule that no man should be allowed to make a large campaign contribution," said HM, in Daniels's account. "I have given all they would take, but I know that the committee ought to spend more money than Wilson thinks, and I am not only willing to give more but desirous of doing so. Inasmuch as Wilson will not permit anyone to give more than I have contributed, here is this money. You take it and give it yourself to the campaign fund."

"Of course," Daniels goes on, "I knew that Morgenthau had plenty of money and that he was sincerely interested in the election of Wilson and wanted the committee to have enough money to do larger things than Wilson deemed necessary or the committee had planned." Daniels, in his telling, declined the offer. "I was unwilling to sail under false colors," he writes, "and yet I did not wish to offend him, for I liked him very much. So I said to him laughingly, 'I would like very much to do it but it is impossible.'"

"Why impossible?" Daniels recalls HM replying. "If my creditors in North Carolina should read in the papers that I had contributed five thousand dollars to the campaign fund," Daniels recalls saying, "they would send a telegram here to attach it and the committee would never get the money." "Of course," adds Daniels, HM "saw the point and said no more about it." Daniels, *The Wilson Era: Years of Peace, 1910–1917* (Chapel Hill: University of North Carolina Press, 1944), 83–84.

113 **"a regular old-fashioned political meeting"**: "Garden Crowd Wild for Wilson," *NYT,* Nov. 1, 1912, 1.

114 **"should suffice"**: "91,000 Gave to Wilson Fund," *NYT,* Nov. 16, 1912, 3.

114 **$1,159,446**: "91,000 Gave to Wilson Fund," *NYT,* Nov. 16, 1912, 3; "$1,159,446 Spent to Elect Democrats," *Dallas Morning News,* Dec. 5, 1912, 10.

114 **"if he realized"**: Charles E. Neu, *Colonel House: A Biography of Woodrow Wilson's Silent Partner* (New York: Oxford University Press, 2015), 58.

115 **"in the process"**: ALT, 155.

115 **"Ochs told me"**: AFT, 116, FDRL.

115 **"one of the most"**: "91,000 Gave to Wilson Fund," *NYT,* Nov. 16, 1912, 3.

115 **"Primus"**: House Diaries, vol. 1, May 19, 1913, 227–29; Edward Mandell House Papers, Yale University Library.

116 **an overt anti-Semitism**: On House and the Jews, see House Diary, Oct. 17, 1913; House to Wilson, Oct. 3, 1917; House to Wilson, Nov. 22, 1912 (of Brandeis, House wrote: "There comes to the surface, now and then, one of those curious Hebrew traits of mind that makes one hold something in reserve"). All in House Papers, Yale University.

116 **a Jew in the cabinet:** House to Wilson, Jan. 30, 1913; House Papers.

116 **"I had heard":** House Diary, May 2, 1913, quoted in Morgenthau, *Ambassador Morgenthau's Story,* 2003 ed., 287; House in his diary takes credit for the idea of offering the Turkish posting to HM. He writes that he had earlier, on Dec. 18, 1912, suggested HM for Turkey: "Gov Wilson came at half past one. I talked to him about Morgenthau and suggested him for Turkey. He replied, "There ain't going to be no Turkey," and I said, "then let him go look for it." Edward Mandell House, *The Intimate Papers of Colonel House: Behind the Political Curtain, 1912–1915* (New York: Houghton Mifflin, 1926), 96.

116 **At fifteen minutes past noon:** Tumulty to HM, May 27, 1913, HM Papers, LC.

116 **"the American Jews":** HM to WW, June 12, 1913, HM to House, July 10, 1913, HM Papers, LC; ALT, 159–61.

117 **"Would prominent Methodists":** Draft: June 12, 1913, HM Papers, LC; Final: PWW, vol. 27, 513.

117 **"As far as I have seen":** HM to SSW, no date, either late June or July 1913, HM Papers, LC; Urofsky, *Voice That Spoke,* 113.

118 **"Have reconsidered":** HM to Woodrow Wilson, telegram, n.d., 1913, HM Papers, LC; Woodrow Wilson to HM, telegram, Munich, Aug. 12, 1913, HM Papers, LC; "Morgenthau to Go as Envoy to Turkey," *NYT,* Aug. 13, 1913, 1.

12. "I Want to Be a Farmer," 1912–1914

120 **Carl Schurz Scofield:** On Scofield and the 1913 expedition, see "Account of Morgenthau–Scofield Expedition," FDRL; AFT, 84–104, FDRL. The Department of Agriculture also published a record of the trip: Henry Morgenthau II, Carl S. Scofield, and J. A. Taylor, *Morgenthau Expedition, 1913* (1913); Gaer interview with Scofield, Sept. 23, 1941, Gaer File, MP, FDRL.

121 **"strictly factual":** AFT, 101, FDRL.

121 **"who are not making any money":** HM2 to HM & JSM, April 24, 1913, FDRL.

122 **"the strange feeling":** AFT, 107, FDRL.

122 **Dr. Fritz Regeniter:** Dr. Fritz Regeniter: N.Y., City Directory, 1902; Orange, N.J., City Directory, 1905; 1910 Census. Regeniter died on March 24, 1914.

122 **"For a time":** AFT, 109, FDRL.

122 **bought the farm, for $55,000:** *Poughkeepsie Eagle,* March 27, 1914, 5. Executor: "Pokeepsie, NY," *Evening Enterprise,* April 18, 1914, 2. In time, the story of the sale would evolve: "At 22, He Bought a $55,000 Farm in Dutchess County . . . ," *Time,* Jan. 25, 1943.

122 **sold the $500 lot for $10,000:** "At 22, He Bought a $55,000 Farm," *Time,* Jan. 25, 1943.

123 **"Remember":** ALT, 175.

123 **"Turkey from a diplomatic":** Hotel Astor Farewell Banquet, stenographic transcript, Oct. 30, 1913, HM Papers, LC. The evening was also reported in the newspaper, with varying quotations: "Wish Morgenthau Success at Embassy," *NYT,* Oct. 31, 1913, 7.

124 **"Saw quite some":** HM Diary, Nov. 26, 1913, HM Papers, LC.

124 **Henry and Tim:** Henry Joseph Morgenthau Fox, born May 17, 1907; Mortimer Fox, Jr., born Nov. 28, 1909.

124 **"a moving sea":** ALT, 177.

124 **"At last":** HM Diary, Nov. 27, 1913, HM Papers, LC.

125 **Palazzo Corpi:** The U.S. government had rented the building since 1882. In 1906, the U.S. legation was raised to embassy status. The chancery wing was added in 1910. See Thomas J. Carolan, Jr., "Palazzo Corpi: A National Treasure," *Foreign Service Journal,* November 2002, 26–30.

125 the *Scorpion:* William N. Still, Jr., *American Sea Power in the Old World: The United States Navy in European and Near Eastern Waters, 1865–1917* (Annapolis, MD: Naval Institute Press, 1980), 173–208.

126 "every American interest": ALT, 215.

126 "They were acting": ALT, 206–7.

127 "true mission": ALT, 203.

127 "splendid service": HM Diary, Nov. 2, 1913, HM Papers, LC.

128 "the gospel of Americanism": ALT, 204.

128 "relieved me": ALT, 202.

128 embassy dinner: HM to JSM and Ruth Morgenthau, Dec. 23, 1913, published in ALT, 186–89; "busy trying": Helen Morgenthau Fox to JSM, Dec. 23, 1913, published in ALT, 189–91.

128 "You can't imagine": HM to JSM and Ruth Morgenthau, Dec. 23, 1913; HM Diary, Dec. 22, 1913, HM Papers, LC.

130 After dinner: ALT, 190.

13. "Something Is Brewing," Winter–Spring 1914

131 "Going to all that trouble": ALT, 191.

131 "a dreary exile": ALT, 192–94.

131 "an almost Royal setting": ALT, 192.

132 "There is a feeling here": HM Diary, Jan. 17, 1915, HM Papers, LC.

133 "a small loan from America": HM Diary, Dec. 22, 1913, HM Papers, LC.

133 "consent to assist Turkey": HM Diary, Dec. 23, 1913, HM Papers, LC.

134 "as France was giving money": HM Diary, March 4, 1914, March 5, 1914, HM Papers, LC; AMS, 37–39.

134 "America alone": ALT, 198.

134 Claude Montefiore: SSW even added publicity, authoring an article, "Two Philanthropists of Jewry," in praise of HM and Montefiore, replete with a photograph of all three men. *The Independent,* Dec. 18, 1913, 553.

136 "the best equipped": HM Diary, March 28, 1914, and March 29, 1914, HM Papers, LC.

136 "Has it ever occurred": HM to SSW, March 6, 1914, HM Papers, LC.

136 more than half a million: *Palestine, Report and General Abstracts of the Census of 1922,* compiled by J. B. Barron (Jerusalem: Census Office, 1922), 1914 figures, 3; Gad G. Gilbar, ed., *Ottoman Palestine, 1800–1914,* Studies in Economic and Social History (Leiden: E. J. Brill, 1990), 63; Author correspondence: Professor Eran Kaplan, San Francisco State University.

137 "splendid example": HM to Family, April 11, 1914, HM Papers, LC.

137 "The condition of the people": HM to Family, April 11, 1914, HM Papers, LC.

137 "One feels impressed": HM Diary, April 2, 1914, HM Papers, LC.

137 "The Jews": MM, 131.

138 "to drive out the Arabs": HM Diary, April 12, 1914, HM Papers, LC.

138 "We walked through": HM Diary, March 11, 1914, HM Papers, LC.

139 "There we stood": ALT, 218.

139 "little hopes for adjustment": HM Diary, April 19, 1914, HM Papers, LC.

139 "the most sacred": ALT, 218–19.

14. "Guns of August," Spring–Fall 1914

140 "*seferberlik*": Henry H. Riggs, *Days of Tragedy in Armenia* (Ann Arbor, Mich.: Gomidas Institute, 1997), 3.

140 "Entire empire": RG 59, 867.00/784, NARA.

140 "two strange-looking vessels": AMS, 69–70.

141 "the secrecy of the diplomats": Walter Lippmann, *The Stakes of Diplomacy* (New York: Henry Holt,1915), 5.

141 the British had chased: The British ships: *Indefatigable, Indomitable.*

141 "acting as though": HM Diary, Aug. 15, 1914, HM Papers, LC.

142 "there will be trouble": HM Diary, Aug. 23, 1914, HM Papers, LC.

142 "All our telegrams": HM Diary, Aug. 20, 1914, HM Papers, LC.

142 Capitulations: Under date of Aug. 27 (Sept. 9, 1914), Hollis sent the U.S. Embassy and the State Department a copy of the announcement of the abrogation of the Capitulations; RG 59, 867.00/672; Taner Akçam, *A Shameful Act,* 25–26; Adalian, 165.

143 the kaiser had one goal: HM Diary, Aug. 26, 1914, HM Papers, LC.

143 "remain[ed] neutral": HM Diary, Aug. 27, 1914, HM Papers, LC.

143 "Palestinian Jews": HM to Jacob Schiff, Aug. 28, 1914, HM Papers, LC.

143 "immediate assistance": HM to Jacob Schiff, Aug. 31, 1914, Collection of the American Jewish Committee. The American Jewish Committee, the American Zionist Federation, and Schiff himself contributed funds, establishing the Joint Distribution Committee to provide aid to the Jews in Palestine. Cf. Tuchman, "The Assimilationist Dilemma," 58.

144 8,600 Turkish pounds: HM to Schiff, Sept. 26, 1914, HM Papers, LC. Standard Oil's Constantinople office director, Oscar Gunkel, sought to lend paper money, but HM insisted on gold. Schiff later deposited 11,920 Turkish pounds, or $59,600, into a Standard Oil bank account in New York; Oct. 15, 1914, HM Papers, LC.

144 "Forty thousand Jerusalem Jews": O. Glazebrook to HM, Sept. 24, 1914, HM Papers, LC.

144 "No money entering Palestine": M. Wertheim to HM, Sept. 22, 1914, HM Papers, LC.

145 "from starvation": Tuchman, "The Assimilationist Dilemma," 58. The ambassador's son-in-law, Maurice Wertheim, though, had been careful to distinguish between "the poor" of Jerusalem and the colonists. In his Sept. 22, 1914, cable to HM, he wrote: "Regarding food supply. Colonies not threatened destruction. Colonists personally need little assistance. Their main problem to find new markets. Possibly America for oranges. Will advise later this matter."

145 "Now have my 10th": HM to HM2, Oct. 12, 1914, FDRL.

145 "that they had decided": HM Diary, Oct. 29, 1914, HM Papers, LC.

15. "You Can See and Feel the Hatred," Winter 1914–Spring 1915

147 Ambassador Morgenthau knew: HM Diary, April 27, 1914, HM Papers, LC.

148 "to accompany them": Paul Schwarz to Wangenheim, Dec. 5, 1914, enclosed in Wangenheim to Bethmann-Hollweg, Dec. 30, 1914; published in Wolfgang Gust, ed., *The Armenian Genocide: Evidence from the German Foreign Office Archives, 1914–1916* (New York: Berghahn Books, 2014), 151–52.

148 *Übergriffen:* Wangenheim to Bethmann-Hollweg, Dec. 29, 1914; cited in Uğur Ümit Üngör, *The Making of Modern Turkey* (Oxford: Oxford University Press, 2012), 59.

148 "Your silence to me": HM2 to HM, Aug. 12, 1914, FDRL.

149 "Partly, I suspect": AFT, 174, FDRL.

149 "We owe it": Bryan to President Wilson, Dec. 1, 1914, *Papers Relating to the Foreign Relations of the United States, The Lansing Papers, 1914–1920,* vol. 1; Baker, *Woodrow Wilson: Life and Letters,* vol. 5, 296.

149 On January 15: HM did not cable it to the president, but relied instead on HM2 to deliver it by hand; HM to WW, Jan. 15, 1915, reproduced in AFT, 178–82, FDRL.

149 **"unless Germany succeeded"**: HM to Woodrow Wilson, Jan. 15, 1915, reproduced in AFT, 178–82, FDRL.

150 **Serving as Wilson's eyes**: Charles E. Neu, *Colonel House: A Biography of Woodrow Wilson's Silent Partner* (New York: Oxford University Press, 2015), 135.

150 **"to obtain a protectorate"**: AFT, 185–86, FDRL.

150 **The resulting interview**: "Turks Are Praised by Envoy's Son," *NYT*, March 6, 1915, 2; "Relations Between America and Turkey," published in *Ikvam*, March 30, 1915.

151 **"Our nation"**: Arshavir Shiragian, translated by Sonia Shiragian, *The Legacy: Memoirs of an Armenian Patriot* (Watertown, Mass.: Hairenik Press, 1976), 318.

152 **"battleships, cruisers"**: Winston Churchill, *The World Crisis, 1911–1918,* vol. 2 (New York: Charles Scribner's Sons, 1923), 217.

152 **"reports from certain parts"**: HM to Department of State, Dispatch 614, April 30, 1915, HM Papers, LC; Adalian, 150.

16. "A Campaign of Race Extermination," Spring–Fall 1915

154 **"crimes against humanity"**: In the first draft of the joint note, offered by Russia, the crimes had been "against Christianity and civilization"—but France and Britain feared "offending their own colonial Muslim populations," and won an emendation. Akçam, *A Shameful Act*, 214.

154 **"expressed regret"**: HM to Bryan, June 18, 1915, RG 59 867.4016/70, NARA.

155 **"about five hours' distance"**: Leslie A. Davis to HM, June 30, 1915, RG 59, 867.4016/269, NARA. Davis's 1917 report, along with a collection of his consular reports, and an introduction by Susan K. Blair, are published as *The Slaughterhouse Province, An American Diplomat's Report on the Armenian Genocide, 1915–1917* (New Rochelle, N.Y.: Aristide D. Caratzas, 1989).

155 **"to destroy the Armenian race"**: Leslie A. Davis to HM, June 30, 1915, RG 59, 867.4016/269, NARA.

155 **Wilson dispatched**: PWW, vol. 33, 449.

155 **"Colonel House"**: PWW, vol. 33, 449.

155 **"practically his own"**: Cooper, *Woodrow Wilson*, 295, citing House Diary, June 14, 1915, June 24, 1915.

155 **Henry Riggs**: HM Diary, June 26, 1915, Aug. 9, 1915 (regarding a Riggs report dated July 11, 1915), HM Papers, LC.

155 **"finest citizens"**: Riggs, *Days of Tragedy in Armenia*, 48.

156 **the Reverend Francis H. Leslie**: *The Missionary Herald*, Jan. 1916, vol. 112 (Boston: The Thomas Todd Company, 1917), 18–19; Joseph K. Greene, *Leavening the Levant* (Boston: Pilgrim Press, 1916), 181.

156 **"reign of terror"**: F. H. Leslie report dated June 14, 1915, enclosed in Jackson to HM, June 28, 1915, HM Papers, LC.

156 **"neurasthenia"**: Sean McMeekin, *The Berlin-Baghdad Express: The Ottoman Empire and Germany's Bid for World Power* (London: Penguin, 2010), 257–58.

156 **"These measures"**: HM to Lansing, July 10, 1915, RG 59, 867.4016/74, NARA. See also Gary Bass, *Stay the Hand of Vengeance*, 346.

157 **"Many thousands"**: Davis to HM, July 11, 1915, HM Papers, LC; 11-page report, RG 59, 867.4016/127, NARA.

157 **"From harrowing reports"**: HM to Department of State, July 16, 1915, RG 867.4017/76, NARA, cited in Adalian, 150.

157 **"The Department of State"**: Lansing to HM, July 20, 1915, HM Papers, LC.

157 **"a mob of Turks and Kurds"**: F. H. Leslie report dated Aug. 24, 1915, HM Papers, LC.

157 **Talaat demanded**: HM to Secretary of State, Aug. 20, 1915, HM Papers, LC.

158 **took Reverend Leslie hostage:** Reverend Leslie would be held hostage for nearly two months. (J. B. Jackson to Secretary of State, March 4, 1918, RG 59, 867.4016/373, NARA.) He had seen members of his mission and friends killed—even a local Protestant pastor hanged. (Greene, *Leavening the Levant*, 182.) In late fall, 1915, Leslie was found unconscious on a street, beside the home of a German missionary. (Ibid.) He had swallowed carbolic acid. (*The Missionary Herald*, vol. 112, January 1916, 18–19.) His wife would survive, eventually making it out to Switzerland. So, too, would Elizabeth Louise, the four-month-old baby Reverend Leslie would never see.

158 **"I earnestly beg":** HM to Secretary of State, Aug. 11, 1915, HM Papers, LC.

158 **"Technically, I had no right":** AMS, 218.

159 **For months, Henry:** JSM arrived in New York City on Oct. 14, 1915; "Mrs. Morgenthau Home from Turkey: Ambassador's Wife in Constantinople Heard the Russian Guns," *NYT*, Oct. 15, 1915, 4; HM diaries, LC.

160 **"The United States might be":** John Reed, *New York World* (dateline "Sofia, Sept. 7"), published Sept. 14, 1915; republished as "Armenian Problem" in *The Argus* (Melbourne, Australia), Oct. 22, 1915. See also "Would Send Here 550,000 Armenians: Morgenthau Urges Scheme to Save Them from the Turks—Offers to Raise $1,000,000," *NYT*, Sept. 14, 1915, 2 (republishes *Chicago Daily News* dispatch from Sofia— presumably Reed's); "Presses Armenian Plan: Ambassador Morgenthau Promises $5,000,000 to Send Oppressed Here," *NYT*, Oct. 2, 1915, 11.

161 **"Minister of War":** HM to Secretary of State, Sept. 3, 1915, File No. 867.4016/117, *FRUS Supplement 1915*, 988.

161 **"committee to raise funds":** HM to Lansing, Sept. 3, 1915, FRUS: 1915 Supplement, 988; "Tales of Armenian Horrors Confirmed," *NYT*, Sept. 27, 1915, 5. HM found eager allies among the Christian clergymen: "The Armenians have no one to speak for them," James L. Barton wrote to Dodge, "and it is without question a time when the voice of Christianity should be raised." James L. Barton, *The Story of Near East Relief, 1915–1930* (New York: Macmillan, 1930), 4.

161 **more than $10 million:** Barton, "Ten Million Dollars for Relief," *Missionary Review of the World* 41 (July 1918): 491–96.

161 **"In cruelty and in horror":** "Tell of Horrors Done in Armenia: Report of Eminent Americans Says They Are Unequaled in a Thousand Years, A Policy of Extermination Put in Effect Against a Helpless People," *NYT*, Oct. 4, 1915, 1, 3.

162 **"past when any harm":** Lord Bryce, "The Armenian Massacres," House of Lords, Oct. 6, 1915; Hansards Online, House of Lords Debates (HL Deb), October 6, 1915, vol. 19, cc994-1004, api.parliament.uk/historic-hansard/lords/1915/oct/06/the -armenian-massacres.

162 **commissioned a young Oxford historian:** Arnold Toynbee, *Armenian Atrocities: The Murder of a Nation* (London: Hodder and Stoughton, 1915).

162 **mass meeting:** "Thousands Protest Armenian Murders," *NYT*, Oct. 18, 1915, 3.

162 **He had helped raise:** One of the Rockefeller Foundation's first grants had been to aid the Jews of Palestine. Oscar Straus, Dr. Stanley White, SSW, and Richard Gottheil, Zionists and missionaries, attended a December 14, 1914, meeting at the foundation. *Rockefeller Foundation Annual Report: 1915*, 306–10.

17. "We Are Through with Them," 1915

163 **Dr. John Henry Jowett:** "To Plead for Armenians," *NYT*, Oct. 11, 1915, 4.

163 **"Mass meetings":** Theodore Roosevelt to Samuel Dutton, Nov. 24, 1915, in Theodore Roosevelt, *Fear God and Take Your Own Part* (New York: George H. Doran, 1916), 377. Also: "Roosevelt Heaps Blame on America," *NYT*, Dec. 1, 1915, 4.

164 **it was Talaat:** HM Diary, Aug. 2, 1915, HM Papers, LC. NB: In AMS, the second "he"

in the sentence "He gave me the impression more than before that he is the one that desires to crush the poor Armenians" was changed to "Talaat."

164 **"accomplished more"**: HM Diary, July 18, 1915, HM Papers, LC.

164 **"Why are you so"**: AMS, 333.

164 **"We are through"**: AMS, 390–92.

165 **The ambassador sat**: "Plan der Rache," *Der Spiegel*, No. 51, 1967, 84; "Morgenthau at 90, Optimist on Future," *NYT*, April 26, 1946, 26.

165 **"Nothing will happen"**: Johansson's report was enclosed in HM to Secretary of State, Nov. 9, 1915, RG 59/867.4016/226, NARA. Her original report, in German and an English translation, is found in the HM Papers, LC. Within weeks, a copy of Johansson's report was filed in the German Foreign Office. See Friedrich Schuchardt, Director of the German Christian Charity-Organisation for the Orient, to Rosenberg, Legation Counsellor in the Foreign Office, Nov. 22, 1915, DE/PA-AA/R14089. HM quotes Johansson's report in "The Greatest Horror in History," *Red Cross Magazine* 13 (March 1918): 7–15. Published separately, in Swedish, as *Ett folk i landsflykt: Ett år ur armeniernas historia* (Stockholm: Kvinnliga missions arbetare, 1930).

166 **The nun's statement**: Lansing to Wilson, Jan. 13, 1916, enclosed: HM to Lansing, Nov. 18, 1915, RG 59, 867.00/798.5, NARA.

166 **"a note of loneliness"**: AFT, 198, FDRL.

167 **"I believe nothing short"**: HM to Secretary of State, July 16, 1915, RG 59, 867.4016/76, NARA.

167 **"withholding from"**: Lansing to Philip, Feb. 12, 1916, FRUS: 1916 supplement, 847–48.

167 **"more or less justifiable"**: Lansing to Wilson, Nov. 21, 1916, Lansing Papers, vol. 1, 42–43.

167 **"My modesty"**: AFT, 198, FDRL.

167 **"We will all live"**: HM to EFM, Dec. 27, 1916, HM3 Papers.

168 **"very much complimented"**: Wilson to HM, Dec. 9, 1915, HM Papers, LC.

168 **"I enthusiastically assent"**: HM to Wilson, Jan. 6, 1916, HM Papers, LC.

168 **Six weeks later, on February 22**: News accounts of HM's return to New York: "Morgenthau Not to Take War Post," *N.Y. Tribune*, Feb. 23, 1916, 3; "Honor Morgenthau as World Diplomat," *NYT*, Feb. 23, 1916, 5; "Morgenthau Here, Says U.S. Flag Was a Big Umbrella," *N.Y. World*, Feb. 22, 1916, 3; "Morgenthau Back but Mute on War," *N.Y. Sun*, Feb. 23, 1916, 4; "Morgenthau Reticent," *Washington Post*, Feb. 23, 1916, 3.

168 **"We got up very early"**: HM Diaries, Feb. 23, 1916, HM Papers, LC.

170 **"While I realize"**: Lansing to HM, Feb. 17, 1916, HM Papers, LC.

18. "A Tremendous Asset," 1915

172 **Edith Altschul**: Edith Altschul Lehman was born in San Francisco on August 8, 1889, to Charles and Camilla (Mandlebaum) Altschul. Charles Altschul had been born in London to American parents and educated in Germany, emigrating to San Francisco in 1877. When Edith was eleven, the family moved to New York, where Charles became a partner in Lazard Frères and Company.

173 **"to instill"**: AFT, 23, FDRL.

174 **"Our motto"**: Elinor Fatman, *Vassar Miscellany*, vol. 42, no. 1, Nov. 1, 1912, 47–48.

175 **Beatrice Brinkerhoff**: HM2 to HM, Aug. 12, 1914, FDRL.

176 **"our farm"**: HM2 to HM, May 6, 1914, FDRL.

176 **"I am writing"**: HM2 to HM, May 24, 1914, FDRL.

176 **"only son**: "Experiment in Profitable Farming," *Poughkeepsie Sunday Courier*, June 14, 1914.

177 "that scientific farming": "Starts Cattle Raising in the State of New York," *The Yonkers Herald,* June 18, 1914, 4; AFT, 160a, FDRL.

178 "It is more": HM to HM2, April 11, 1914, FDRL.

178 "for centuries": HM to HM2, April 22, 1914, FDRL.

178 "I have no political ambition": HM to HM2, July 24, 1914, FDRL.

178 "Don't think": HM to HM2, July 24, 1914, FDRL.

179 "My one hope": HM2 to HM, Aug. 12, 1914, FDRL.

179 "God knows": HM2 to HM, undated, 1914, FDRL.

180 "drop in and see": HM2 to HM, undated, 1914, FDRL. The letter was likely written in late November or early December 1914.

180 "more than four months": AFT, 111, FDRL.

181 "He said Billy Phillips": HM2 to HM, undated, 1914, FDRL.

182 John Dugan: FDR to HM2, Dec. 11, 1914, FDRL. On importance of post office appointments and patronage: Davis, *FDR: The Beckoning of Destiny, 1882–1928* (New York: Random House, 1971), 354–55.

182 run for county sheriff: Blum, *From the Morgenthau Diaries,* vol. 1, 12; HM2 to HM, July 20, 1915, FDRL; FDR to HM2, July 22, 1915, FDRL.

183 "You will realize": HM to HM2, Sept. 6, 1915, FDRL.

183 urging Henry Jr.: FDR to HM2, Dec. 11, 1914, and July 22, 1915; AFT, "Part 2: Early Drafts," Box 410, FDRL.

184 "politically innocent": AFT, "Part 2: Early Drafts," Box 410, FDRL.

PART III | WAR

19. Franklin and Henry, 1916–1933

187 wooden ramp: Hazel Rowley, *Franklin and Eleanor: An Extraordinary Marriage* (New York: Farrar, Straus and Giroux, 2010), 180–81.

188 married: "Morgenthau Weds Apr. 17," *NYT,* March 5, 1916, 11, and "Pictures Section," part 4.

188 Dutchess County horse show: "Dutchess County Horse Show Awards," *NYT,* Aug. 31, 1933, 21.

188 Lincoln School: Author interviews: RMM, HM3, JMH, Barney Straus, Mary Arnstein.

189 "We can never go back": Schlesinger, *The Crisis of the Old Order,* 364.

190 banquet at Delmonico's: "Better Times Ahead, Harding Tells Bankers," *N.Y. Tribune,* Jan. 8, 1921, 4.

190 Wilson Foundation: As Wilson and his coterie prepared the soon-to-be-former president for private life, HM continued to be a source of financing. HM's notebooks contain a note, dated Nov. 8, 1920, days after Warren G. Harding's victory, indicating that Dr. Cary T. Grayson, Wilson's physician, sought support from HM as Wilson prepared to leave the White House: "G. told me Wilson lost one eye first year of administration through bursting a blood vessel and that Wilson was sick when he came to White House. Wants 10 to 12 retainers of $1,000 a year from people so as to keep well. I became number 1." MP.

190 "separate peace": Historians of U.S. involvement in the Middle East continue to debate the Morgenthau Mission. Michael Oren called it America's "major debut at Middle East peacemaking" in *Power, Faith & Fantasy: America in the Middle East, 1776 to the Present* (New York: W. W. Norton, 2007), 349. The details are now largely known, but President Wilson's faith in the mission, and the role of Frankfurter, remain subject to debate. Colonel House's diary indicates that he was keenly interested in the Morgenthau plan, only to abandon it once it had failed. Frankfurter is clear on his

own intended role—"I had a nurse's function, to prevent the wilful, but imperious, child from being any more foolish than could possibly be avoided" (*Felix Frankfurter Reminiscences*, 151)—yet how he was enlisted remains unclear. Some have claimed Brandeis deployed Frankfurter as a proxy (Urofsky, *Louis D. Brandeis: A Life* [New York: Schocken, 2009], 847). Yet a June 7, 1917, letter from HM to Wilson indicates that he had to persuade Brandeis to let Frankfurter go. HM wrote Wilson: "My object in wishing to see you was to explain to you the desirability of having Mr. Felix Frankfurter accompany me. When I asked for the appointment Justice Brandeis was somewhat opposed to it. He is now quite reconciled to it but wants an opportunity to discuss the matter with you for a few minutes. He wants you to decide whether this commission is more important than the services that Frankfurter can render in the War Department." See *Trial and Error: The Autobiography of Chaim Weizmann* (New York: Harper & Brothers, 1949), 196–99; *Felix Frankfurter Reminiscences*, recorded in talks with Dr. Harlan B. Phillips (New York: Reynal & Company, 1960), 145–55; William Yale, "Ambassador Morgenthau's Special Mission of 1917," *World Politics* 1 (April 1948): 308–20; F. W. Brecher, "Revisiting Ambassador Morgenthau's Turkish Peace Mission of 1917," *Middle Eastern Studies* 24, no. 3 (July 1988), 357–63; Richard Ned Lebow, "The Morgenthau Peace Mission in 1917," *Jewish Social Studies* 32, no. 4 (October 1970), 267–85.

190 **Schmavonian:** In May 1917, after the break in U.S.-Turkish relations, Schmavonian left Constantinople. By late 1917, he had been transferred to Washington, D.C., where he worked at the State Department as a consultant on Armenian affairs until his death in January 1922.

191 **"great ambition":** On Weizmann's role in the Morgenthau "Secret Mission": cf. Barnet Litvinoff, *Weizmann: Last of the Patriarchs* (New York: Putnam, 1976), 105–108.

191 **"wild goose chase":** Frankfurter, *Felix Frankfurter Reminiscences*, 151. In his memoirs, Frankfurter was so cutting in his recollection of HM that he appeared to have a score to settle. HM, he wrote, had grown accustomed "to have everybody bow and scrape and call him 'Mr. Ambassador' [which] was a kind of scent that thereafter he couldn't live without" (145). And "He wasn't my kind of person, in the sense that his talk was inconsequential and not coherent, but loose and big and rhetorical. You couldn't get hold of anything, but I assumed that was just the froth of the man. I didn't realize that the froth was the man" (146).

191 **offered to sell Palestine:** "Found Turks Eager to Sell Palestine," *NYT*, May 22, 1916, 2.

191 **"fiasco":** House Diary, vol. 5, July 14, 1917, 213; Yale University Library. Colonel House's diary and correspondence for 1917 offer an enlightening commentary on the initial support, progress, and eventual demise of HM's "peace mission." In April, House called on HM for help as a liaison to the American Jewish community: "I asked Morganthau [*sic*] to get the Jews of America, who are foregathering here tomorrow, to send a cable to their kinsmen in Russia asking them to sustain the present government there, and urge them not to make a separate peace with Germany because of the blow such a move would give to democracy throughout the world. He promised to do this" (House Diary, vol. 5, April 14, 1917, 107).

House also recorded how HM "suggested for himself" the "secret peace" mission: "Billy Phillips is over from Washington. We had an extended conference concerning departmental affairs. And this reminds me, I have never told of the mission Henry Morganthau [*sic*] has suggested for himself and upon which he departs this week. His plan is to go to Egypt and try to get an invitation from the Turks to go into Palestine for the ostensible purpose of helping the Jews. The real purpose is to make a separate peace if possible with Turkey, segregating her from her allies, the Central Powers. Morganthau believes he can get an interview with Enver Pasha and, if he can, he believes it will not be difficult to arrange the balance. It is a daring enterprise and one full of danger for Morganthau. I cautioned him about talking for, upon his own confession, a number of people know what he has in mind. In discussing the matter we agreed it would be best to draw Enver out and let the proposal come from him, if possible, so that Morganthau could act as Enver's agent rather than as an agent of the Allies" (House Diary, vol. 5, June 11, 1917, 179).

In June, House wrote to HM that his thoughts go with him on "great work you are undertaking" and that he will "pray for your success." He also wrote that he considered it a mistake to have the two emissaries meet HM en route, as they would never agree (House to HM, June 13, 1917). In the same letter, he wrote HM that "those of us in the 'know' will await news of you with the deepest eagerness and concern."

By July, House noted in his diary: "Polk says Morganthau's trip has turned out to be a fiasco. When Morganthau spoke to me about it in May, I asked him how many people knew of it. He claimed to have told only Houston, Lane, Adolph Miller, Lansing and the President. My advice to Morganthau then was to undo this part before he left. Instead of that, it seems he told a few more, and that it is known to practically every synagogue in New York. He has also undertaken to speak for the United States as to future peace conditions, which is disturbing the President and the State Department. They are undetermined whether to let him go as far as Palestine and bring him home from there, or to bring him home directly from France. I advised the latter" (House Diary, vol. 5, July 14, 1917, 213).

In August, House noted that "Abram I. Elkus came from New York to lunch and to tell of conditions in Turkey. . . . We had a good laugh over Morganthau's peace project. Elkus says Morganthau was even indiscreet enough to write about it to friends in Europe, and that it was well known everywhere that he was bound for Turkey to try to make a separate peace. The remarkable thing about it, as Elkus sees it, was that he intended to make the peace with Enver Pasha, whom Morganthau supposed to be his devoted friend. Elkus says that Enver is nothing more than a German agent and is the last man in Turkey with whom anyone could talk separate peace. Some of the Turkish Cabinet are pro-Ally in their feelings, and would like to get out of the German entanglement" (House Diary, vol. 5, 230).

Finally, in October, House wrote in his diary: "Yesterday we motored to Mount Kisco to be with Mr. and Mrs. Robert Brewster overnight. They have a delightful home. This morning we left there and motored to Mamaroneck to lunch with Frederick Penfield. The other guests were Mr. and Mrs. Abram Elkus and Mr. Bagby, the musical director. I had a talk with Elkus about the possibility of making separate peace with Turkey, and how it could be done. He is eager to undertake it, but since Morganthau's failure, I am skeptical about it and so, I am sure, will be the President. Elkus, however, is more discreet than Morganthau and would not fall into pitfalls" (House Diary, vol. 5, 305).

191 **World's Work:** The first article introducing Ambassador Morgenthau's memoirs appeared in April 1918. Subsequent installments appeared from May 1918 to January 1919.

191 **quit as president:** "Quit Because of Zionism: Morgenthau Explains Resignation as President of Free Synagogue," *NYT*, March 7, 1919, 18; HM's open letter announcing his resignation, March 3, 1919, HM Papers, LC.

191 **peace conference:** HM Papers, LC: Diary for 1919: May 15: "It was strange to wake up overlooking the Rhine—having slept in government palace—such changes in my life from Mannheim in 1866 to Coblenz 1919—and the interim how full historically as I sat listening to American Col. and Majors talking U.S. and eating their oatmeal, eggs and U.S. bacon"; June 27: "Rode with Grayson, Pres. and Miss Buckler—our last ride with Dr. Grayson. He told me of WW [Woodrow Wilson] decision to take Baruch, McCormick, Davis and Lauvert on ship. . . . We all went to Crillon to see Pershing

who was there to see WW. It was a thrilling sight, crowds at the door waiting for W. exit"; "Pershing took us into the living rm and disc'd Harbord matter and also applied for Polish Commission"; "While there, Wilson came in after having talked with newspaper men and Peace Commission and he spoke with Pershing while we were waiting and watching him. I shook hands with Wilson as he departed and we further discussed Dav with Pershing." June 28: "rec'd ticket for grand show of Peace Signing at Versailles, ticket #51; Josie had Terrace ticket; Pershing in seat #49 and Sen. Saulsbury 53; Mrs W Lansing and House sat in front row, Baruch and Hoover and Davis two rows behind us. I spoke to Clemenceau, Lloyd George, and Mr. & Mrs Wilson"; "We all walked up and saw the treaty—like mourners reviewing the corpse there was no excitement or enthusiasm—it was most matter of fact and when over it was like the dismissal of audience after a wedding—all chattering and crowding, no solemnity."

192   **persecution of Jews:** The delegation to Poland was led by HM and lasted July–September 1919. HM's delegation included Lieutenant General Edgar Jadwin, the lawyer Homer G. Johnson (future father of the architect Philip Johnson), and Arthur Lehman Goodhart, EFM's cousin, then a legal scholar at Oxford, as counsel to the mission. JSM in a letter—JSM to HM2, July 4, 1919, on stationery of "The American Commission to Negotiate Peace"—wrote: "Papa and I were discussing this morning the advisability of having you join him in Poland as a special agent, but the fear of being accused of having family around him has prevented him from doing what would have given him more pleasure than anything." In a letter (HM to HM2, Aug. 6, 1919, HM Papers, LC), HM wrote of the Polish trip: "We held regular court sessions, with stenographers, and interpreters, and have unquestionably arrived at the truth. We are so determined to discover all the facts and the full truth that we are offending both contending factions. Both of them wish us to hide some of the truth.... The Jews believe that they have a good reason to feel hurt and they do not want their hurt feeling removed. They consider it an asset. This in turn hurts the pride of the Poles almost beyond remedy, and if no reconciliation is brought about between them it will, in case the Poles fail to establish their republic firmly, eventually lead to their blaming the Jews and visiting their vengeance upon them by killing them by the thousand." Jews across Poland welcomed Morgenthau and the commission. In Warsaw alone, a "wildly cheering" crowd was estimated by the *N.Y. Tribune* to number 35,000.

192   **"misled by [the] Poles":** Schiff to HM, July 3, 1919, HM Papers, LC.

192   **Harbord:** On the Harbord Mission: ALT, 339–47; Jay Winter, ed., *America and the Armenian Genocide of 1915* (New York: Cambridge University Press, 2003), 265; Hoover & HM to Wilson, telegram, July 5, 1919 (PWW, 487); HM to Harbord, June 25, 1919; Harbord to HM, June 25, 1919.

192   **run for Congress:** HM2 to HM & JSM, Jan. 26, 1926, MP.

192   **commission to resettle:** In June 1923, the League of Nations Financial Committee, assisted by Fred Dolbeare of the American Delegation to the Lausanne Conference, tried to devise a plan to fund a relief program for the Greek refugees uprooted by the violence in Smyrna that followed World War I. In September, the League established a settlement commission to help Greek refugees find shelter and work in Greece. HM led the commission from fall 1923 until spring 1924. By 1931, more than 600,000 Greeks were resettled. Of his many post-ambassadorial missions, this assignment is considered one of his most successful, and forms the basis of HM's book *I Was Sent to Athens* (Garden City, N.Y.: Doubleday, Doran, 1929).

193   **"Wilson was sick":** Note dated Nov. 8, 1920, Gaer Papers, MP.

193   **"There is nothing":** HM2 to HM, n.d. (most likely written in late 1921), HM3 Papers.

194   **clambake:** "Barbeque on the Morgenthau Farm," *N.Y. World,* July 16, 1922; "Back on the Farm, Houston Just Raps," *N.Y. Herald,* July 21, 1922; "Houston Opposes

Bonus and Tariff," *N.Y. Herald,* July 21, 1922, all in HM Papers, LC. On the *American Agriculturalist:* Blum, vol. 1, *Years of Crisis,* 11.

194 **$201,000:** HM2 to HM, Feb. 7, 1924, MP.

194 **"Go the limit":** "One of Two of a Kind," *Fortune,* May 1934, 61–138.

194 **The campaigns:** In one 1926 article, the *Agriculturalist* questioned the claims of a rabbit firm promising a $1,000 yield on a $20 investment in "Belgian hares" that were, the paper reported, merely common bunnies. The company sued for libel, and soon offered to settle for $1,000, but HM refused. His lawyer brought a line of witnesses to New York City for the trial, a costly defense, but the publisher was victorious.

194 **"Do you see":** HM2 to HM, March 23, 1924, MP.

20. Henry & Franklin, Elinor & Eleanor, 1922–1928

195 **"I'd never felt":** Earle Looker, *This Man Roosevelt,* 1932, 111–12. Further, on the onset of FDR's illness: Anna Roosevelt, "My Life with FDR: How Polio Helped Father," *The Woman,* July 1949, 53–54. A study by two U.S. doctors has posited—with a number of caveats—that FDR was afflicted not with polio but with Guillain-Barré syndrome: Armond S. Goldman with Daniel A. Goldman, *Prisoners of Time: The Misdiagnosis of FDR's 1921 Paralytic Illness* (Renton, Wash.: EHDP Press, 2017).

196 **"Please write me":** Blum, vol. 1, *Years of Crisis, 1928–1938,* 18.

196 **"And while they were here":** Sara Roosevelt to FDR, July 21, 1918, MP.

196 **"I am anxious":** Joseph P. Lash, *Eleanor and Franklin: The Story of Their Relationship Based on Eleanor Roosevelt's Private Papers* (New York: W. W. Norton, 1971), 135.

196 **"I'd rather":** Cook, *Eleanor Roosevelt,* vol. 2, *The Defining Years, 1933–1938,* 317.

197 **"ELINOR I WANT TO KNOW":** Invitation to FDR's 50th Birthday Luncheon, Jan. 30, 1932, MP.

197 **"We are looking":** FDR to EFM, July 16, 1925, HM3 Papers.

198 **"Have something to say":** Alfred Steinberg, *Mrs. R: The Life of Eleanor Roosevelt* (New York: Putnam, 1958), 136.

199 ***Women's Democratic News:*** The first issue came out in May 1925; Cook, *Eleanor Roosevelt,* vol. 1, *1884–1933,* 331; Eleanor Roosevelt, *This I Remember* (New York: Harper & Brothers, 1949), 31.

199 **Junior Clubs:** "Junior Club Members May Try Contest," *Elmira Star Gazette,* Aug. 20, 1926, 22. EFM helped found the clubs in 1925 and chaired the committee on junior clubs in the state committee.

199 **"Say what you will":** EFM speech draft, n.d., 6 pp., handwritten, HM3 Papers.

200 **"a spiritual transformation":** Frances Perkins, *The Roosevelt I Knew* (New York: Viking Press, 1946), 29.

200 **"I was an awfully mean cuss":** Perkins, 12.

200 **"the years of pain":** Perkins, 29.

200 **"a different person":** Phillips, *Ventures in Diplomacy* (London: J. Murray, 1955), 72.

200 **"A blessing in disguise":** E. Roosevelt, *This I Remember,* 26.

201 **"I am convinced":** *Collier's* Memoranda "FDR and HM Jr.," July 26, 1946, 2, MP.

201 **"He seemed":** Perkins, *Roosevelt I Knew,* 37.

201 **suggested FDR to Smith:** HM to Al Smith, June 13, 1924; HM to JSM, June 13, 1924; HM to JSM and grandchildren, June 27, 1924; HM to FDR, n.d. (most likely June 28, 1924, after FDR's nominating speech of June 26, 1924), HM Papers, LC.

202 **convention in Houston:** ER to FDR, April 27, 1928, FDRL; Cook, *Eleanor Roosevelt,* vol. 1, 372.

202 **"There is quite":** Blum, *From the Morgenthau Diaries,* vol. 1, 13–15.

203 **"spell him":** Freidel, *FDR: The Ordeal* (Boston: Little, Brown, 1954), 254–55.

203 **nearly 7,500 miles:** *Fortune,* May 1934; "The U.S. at War: The $51,000,000,000-a-Year Man," *Time,* Jan. 25, 1943; Hobson file, "Notes on Henry Morgenthau" (March 10, 1934), has 75,000, *Time* Files, New-York Historical Society.

204 **by a side entrance:** Schlesinger, *Crisis of the Old Order,* 384.

204 **calls to a number of sheriffs:** Rosenman, *Working with Roosevelt,* 26.

205 **thinking the worst:** Kenneth S. Davis, *FDR: The New York Years: 1928–1933,* vol. 2 (New York: Random House, 1985), 45–47.

205 **"I felt Gov. Smith's election":** ER to EFM, Nov. 13, no date, #48, FDRL.

205 **"To Henry":** Blum, *From the Morgenthau Diaries,* vol. 1, 34.

21. Albany, 1928–1932

206 **"The Years in Albany":** E. Roosevelt, *This I Remember,* 53.

206 **"brains trust":** John Gunther, *Roosevelt in Retrospect: A Profile in History* (New York: Harper & Brothers, 1950), 268–69.

206 **take on Rosenman:** Author interview: HM3. Schlesinger (*Crisis,* 387) describes FDR's hiring of his counsel, but the extant sources—Rosenman's memoir, *Working with Roosevelt;* his and his widow's oral histories (COHP, 1959 and 1976); his papers, HSTL; and Samuel B. Hand's, *Counsel and Advise: A Political Biography of Samuel I. Rosenman* (New York: Garland, 1979)—elide the question.

206 **Advisory Agricultural Commission:** "Roosevelt Names Farm Study Board," *NYT,* Jan. 7, 1929, 1.

207 **easing taxes:** "Webb-Rice Bills Equalize Taxes," *Catskill Mountain News,* Feb. 8, 1929, 3.

207 **"I am new":** "Recommends Community Reforesting," *Catskill Mountain News,* Feb. 22, 1929, 1.

208 **a local landmark:** *Yearbook of Dutchess County Historical Society,* vols. 44–48 (Poughkeepsie, N.Y.: Dutchess County Historical Society, 1959), 26; 1904 sale: *Real Estate Record and Builders' Guide,* Nov. 11, 1904, 1032; "In the Real Estate Field," *NYT,* Nov. 11, 1904, 14.

208 **leaving an estate:** "Morris Fatman Dies in 73d Year," *NYT,* Sept. 27, 1930, 17. Inheritance: "Morris Fatman Left $3,272,320," *NYT,* April 29, 1933, 13. The estate was valued at $3,879,451 gross, $3,272,320 net—half of which went to his widow, and one-quarter each to his two daughters, EFM and Margaret Josten. His sons-in-law, HM2 and Werner Josten, received $25,000 each.

209 **"to see who would sleep":** Blum, vol. 1, 21; Diary for 1930, MP.

209 **"This is the only day":** Diary for 1930, Oct. 25, 1930, MP.

210 **"some difficulty":** Flynn, *You're the Boss,* 80.

210 **cleaned house:** HM2's own favorite tale featured the "Barber of Binghamton," as he called the case of one Llewellyn Legge, who had reigned for decades as the state's chief fish and game protector. For years, Legge had used a state yacht designated for marine research for his "own private entertainment." He had also won a special appropriation for a European junket. The scheme involved replacing the ruffed grouse—Legge claimed to fear its extinction—with the Hungarian grouse. Legge had gone to Hungary, ostensibly to research how to import the grouse, by way of a string of countries where no grouse lived. HM2 learned more: Legge had moonlighted in the illegal spirits trade, leading expeditions up to the Canadian border and back during Prohibition. As HM2 interviewed him, Legge grew belligerent. He had no notion how many men, trucks, or equipment were under his charge, but felt beyond reproach. HM2 cut him short: "Mr. Legge, you're fired." "He stood up with a sickly grin on his face," HM2 wrote, thinking it "a huge joke." Legge sought "higher-ups" to come to his rescue, but found none.

210   **Dr. George F. Warren:** On Warren's work and life: Bernard Stanton, *George F. Warren, Farm Economist* (Ithaca, N.Y.: Cornell University Press, 2007).

210   **"the waste spaces of today":** Blum, vol. 1, 25.

210   **ruinous lumber companies:** Caro, *Power Broker,* 288.

211   **"the Gas House Gang":** Blum, vol. 1, 26–27; Geoffrey T. Hellman, "Any Bonds Today?," *New Yorker,* Jan. 22 and 29, 1944.

211   **"little less than absurd":** "Roosevelt Policy Ridiculed by Hyde," *NYT,* July 6, 1932, 1.

211   **Elinor and Henry:** Blum, vol. 1, 20.

212   **"It would be":** HM2 to HM, Sept. 2, 1930, MP.

212   **"Uncle Henry rather casually":** Frank C. Walker, *FDR's Quiet Confidant: The Autobiography of Frank C. Walker,* ed. Robert H. Ferrell (Boulder: University Press of Colorado, 1997), 56–63.

212   **$10,000 apiece:** According to contemporaneous correspondence, HM and Walker gave $5,000 in March 1931, and Woodin gave the same amount on April 6, 1931. Frank C. Walker Papers.

212   **Joseph P. Kennedy:** Richard Whalen interview with Arthur Goldsmith, Oct. 12, 1962, Whalen Papers; Richard J. Whalen, *The Founding Father: The Story of Joseph P. Kennedy* (New York: New American Library, 1964), 113; Rose Kennedy, *Times to Remember* (New York: Doubleday, 1974), 195.

213   **"revolution or state socialism":** Blum, vol. 1. 29.

213   **"numb":** "Reports Roosevelt Strong in Mid-West," *NYT,* May 13, 1932, 10.

213   **farm address in Topeka:** September 1932, campaign speech on farm remedies: Schlesinger, *Crisis,* 423–24; Blum, vol. 1, 32; Raymond Moley, *After Seven Years* (New York: Harper & Brothers, 1939), 43.

214   **"No man can cross":** Anne O'Hare McCormick, "The Two Men at the Big Moment," *NYT Magazine,* Nov. 6, 1932.

214   **"I watched the crowds":** Schlesinger, *Crisis,* 429–30.

214   **"Franklin came home":** E. Roosevelt, *This I Remember,* 72.

214   **"I'll get you in":** HM3 interview, Barbara Tuchman, June 1979; HM3 Papers.

215   **"Of course, I'm pleased":** Dorothy Roe, "New First Lady Shuns Honor Till Final Votes Are Received," *Courier-Post* (Camden, N.J.), Nov. 9, 1932, 6. Variant ("New First Lady Is Cautious," *Detroit Free Press,* Nov. 9, 1932, 8): "You're always pleased to have someone you're fond of have what he wants."

22. "The Smell of Revolution Was in the Air," Winter–Spring 1933

216   **"This nation calls":** FDR, inaugural speech, March 4, 1933.

217   **"Seldom in any parliamentary":** Gunther, 278.

218   **"I cannot make this":** FDR to HM2, Dec. 27, 1932, FDRL, in Blum, vol. 1, 31.

218   **"If FDR wants you":** HM to HM2, Feb. 6, 1933, FDRL, in Blum, vol. 1, 31.

218   **"head of an agency":** Blum, vol. 1, 32.

219   **"We could never produce":** Blum, vol. 1, 40.

219   **"Henry Morgenthau's duty":** Henry Wallace, COHP, 1951.

220   **fallen from $6 billion:** David M. Kennedy, *Freedom from Fear: The American People in Depression and War, 1929–1945* (New York: Oxford University Press, 1999), 163.

221   **Judge Charles C. Bradley:** Associated Press, "Iowa Judge Dragged Out of Court by Mortgage Battle," *Washington Post,* April 28, 1933, 1.

221   **"smell of revolution":** "The Morgenthau Diaries V: The Paradox of Poverty and Plenty," *Collier's* 120 (Oct. 25, 1947), 24–86.

221   **"contradictory evidence":** Mary Margaret M'Bride, "Named 'Best Secretary in the New Deal,'" *Arizona Daily Star,* June 5, 1934, 15.

223 **"the biggest agricultural credit agency"**: Geoffrey T. Hellman, "Any Bonds Today?," *New Yorker*, Jan. 22 & 29, 1944.

223 **"gone off gold"**: It was not the first time FDR uttered the words. On March 5, the day after the inauguration, he made the same statement; Professor Warren had heard it, standing beside HM2, in FDR's study that evening. Warren had just flown in—his first time in an airplane—to press his case with Roosevelt. "We are now off the gold standard," FDR declared then, "with a great deal of glee," even if it proved a temporary suspension. Warren diary, March 5, 1933, Cornell Archives.

223 **"Here, Ray"**: Moley, *After Seven Years*, 159.

224 **"This means the end"**: Moley, *After Seven Years*, 160; Feis, *1933: Characters in Crisis*, 129; James Paul Warburg, COHP.

23. "He Could Trust Me Absolutely," Spring–Fall 1933

226 **"break the ice"**: MD, May 9, 1933; FSA Diary, 1933, 17; MP.

227 **friend since childhood**: Welles, at 13, had served as a page boy at "the Roosevelt-Roosevelt wedding." Fred Rodell, "Sumner Welles: Diplomat De Luxe," *American Mercury*, November 1945, 578–85.

227 **joined by four reporters**: White House log, March 19, 1933, FDRL.

227 **four largest wheat growers**: FRUS, 1933, vol. 1, 791–818; MP; On Wheat and London Economic Conference: HM Papers, LC.

228 **"butter-producing cow"**: Frederick E. Murphy. "Bringing the World Together on Wheat," *Review of Reviews*, October 1933, 17–19.

228 **"The whole world"**: "Morgenthau Sails for Wheat Parley," *NYT*, May 3, 1933, 3.

228 **"He was fascinating"**: Barbara Tuchman interview, June 28–29, 1979, HM3 Papers.

228 **"It is strange"**: HM to children, May 21, 1933, HM Papers, LC.

228 **"I am only"**: MD, May 22, 1933, MP.

229 **"status in London"**: MD, May 29, 1933, MP.

229 **"a gesture"**: Barbara Tuchman interview, HM3 Papers.

229 **To make matters worse**: John Brooks, *Once in Golconda* (New York: Harper & Row, 1969; repr., New York: Allworth Press, 1997), 158; Herbert Feis, *1933: Characters in Crisis* (Boston: Little, Brown, 1966), 173, 227.

230 **"quite frank talking"**: MD, June 21, 1933, HM Papers, LC.

230 **"in the near future"**: "Sees Recognition of Russia by U.S.; Russian Commissar Holds Conversations with Morgenthau," *NYT*, June 22, 1933, 2; "Four Nations Agree to Curbs on Wheat," *NYT*, June 23, 1933, 1.

230 **"Hull had absolutely no authority"**: James Paul Warburg, COHP, 929.

231 **"A thrilling experience"**: MD, June 27, 1933–July 3, 1933, MP.

231 **discussion of foreign exchange**: MD, June 29, 1933, and July 1, 1933, MP. Garrett's article: Garet Garrett, "This Thing of Trade," *Saturday Evening Post*, July 1, 1933, 5–7, 54, 57–58.

232 **"The Professor"**: Bernard Stanton, *George F. Warren, Farm Economist* (Ithaca, N.Y.: Cornell University Press, 2007).

232 **"nearly self-taught"**: Author interview: Bernard (Bud) Stanton.

232 **"unknown to the world"**: Brooks, *Once in Golconda;* John Brooks, "Gold Standard on the Booze," *New Yorker*, Sept. 13, 1969.

233 **"my charts"**: MD, June 30, 1933, MP; Feis, *1933: Characters in Crisis*, 220.

234 **scarcely slept**: Feis, *1933: Characters in Crisis*, 223.

234 **"all that we needed to know"**: Moley, *After Seven Years*, 257.

234 **kept his son informed**: FDR had also offered HM a back channel, to write him via his cousin Warren Delano Robbins, a veteran diplomat; MD, May 29, 1933; Alfred B. Rollins, Jr., *Roosevelt and Howe* (New York: Knopf, 1962), 397–98.

235 **"rose to nothing"**: H. G. Wells, *The Shape of Things to Come* (1933; repr., London: Penguin Classics, 2006), 134.

235 **"upwards of $50,000,000"**: "Morgenthau Acts in Soviet Trade," *Washington Post,* Sept. 21, 1933, 1.

235 **"to go ahead and make any loans"**: MD, Sept. 26, 1933.

235 **"Send for Skvirsky"**: MD, Sept. 26, 1933.

235 **Boris Skvirsky**: United Press International, "Plain Mr. Boris E. Skvirsky Speaks," *Cleveland Progress,* May 23, 1933, 1–2.

237 **"Several weeks ago"**: MD, Oct. 18, 1933. See also John Richman, *The United States & The Soviet Union: The Decision to Recognize* (Raleigh, N.C.: Camberleigh & Hall, 1980), 85–93.

239 **"If anybody ever knew"**: Henry Morgenthau, Jr., "The Morgenthau Diaries V—The Paradox of Poverty and Plenty," *Collier's,* Oct. 25, 1947; Blum, vol. 1, 70; Schlesinger, *Coming of the New Deal,* 241.

239 **"a very interesting"**: MD, Nov. 13, 1933.

24. "To Swim with the Tide and Not Sink," Winter–Fall 1934

240 **"his own dictator"**: Rodney Dutcher, "New Purser of the Nation's Ship," *El Paso Herald Post,* Nov. 30, 1933, 7.

240 **"We are delighted"**: Blum, vol. 1, 74.

240 **"a sense of assurance"**: Blum, vol. 1, 74.

240 **"his health failed him"**: "Treasury Headed by Morgenthau, Jr.; Woodin on Leave," *NYT,* Nov. 16, 1933, 1.

241 **"in effect the president"**: "Morgenthau Made Farm Aid Record," *NYT,* Jan. 2, 1934, 9.

241 **"When I was thrown"**: Press conference, June 25, 1935; Blum, vol. 2, 76.

242 **"the most intense"**: Schlesinger, *Coming of the New Deal,* 244–45.

243 **$35 an ounce**: The new price represented a 70 percent leap from the official gold price when FDR became president, yet the rewards were not obvious to all: In October 1933, when gold buying began, the wholesale price index stood at 71.2; by February 1934, it had risen to 73.6. William J. Barber, *Designs Within Disorder: Franklin D. Roosevelt, the Economists, and the Shaping of American Economic Policy, 1933–1945* (New York: Cambridge University Press, 1996), 80.

244 **Herb Gaston**: Blum, vol. 1, 23; Herbert E. Gaston, *The Nonpartisan League* (New York: Harcourt, Brace, 1920). The book's final paragraph reads: "We shall probably, like other peoples, make progress from the ground up and the men who are to lead us must of necessity have their day of being hooted and despised. If we search diligently among the outcasts we may perchance find a real leader who may pass on his great idea or his great spirit before we crucify him or send him to jail to die of disease. We shall not find him in an easy chair or behind a mahogany table. He will be consorting with the riffraff or toiling with the laborer."

245 **"Best Secretary in the New Deal"**: NEA Wire Service, "Best Secretary in the New Deal Is Mother of Five-Year Girl," *Spartanburg (S.C.) Herald-Journal,* June 6, 1934, 2.

246 **In his first days**: "The Cabinet: Morgenthau Week," *Time,* Dec. 4, 1933, 40.

247 **"Gentlemen, you need"**: Geoffrey T. Hellman, "Any Bonds Today?," part 2, *New Yorker,* Jan. 29, 1944.

247 **"any sympathy"**: Ickes, *Secret Diary,* vol. 1, 331 (March 25, 1935).

247 **"He doesn't bite"**: Frederick C. Othman, "Debonair Morgenthau Has Lost Shyness," *Pittsburgh Press,* July 8, 1934.

247 **"grown considerably"**: Farley Diary, May 15, 1935, James A. Farley Papers, LC; Farley Diary entries found in the Arthur M. Schlesinger, Jr., Papers, NYPL.

247 **cover of *Time***: *Time,* Sept. 17, 1934.

25. "We Have Just Begun to Fight," 1932–1934

248   "We would be glad": MD, May 15, 1933.

249   "The place looked": MD, June 11, 1933.

249   "It was just 'The Pres.' ": EFM to HM3 & RMM, May 2, 1934, RMM Papers.

250   Gridiron Widows' Dinner: EFM–ER letters, FDRL; Joseph P. Lash, *Eleanor and Franklin* (New York: W. W. Norton, 1971), 498–99; Cook, vol. 2, 412.

250   "I can't think": ER–EFM, Aug. 19, 1934, FDRL, EFM Papers; Cook, vol. 2, 217.

252   Fourth Liberty Loan: *Annual Report of the Secretary of the Treasury on the State of the Finances for the Fiscal Year Ended June 30, 1934* (Washington, D.C.: GPO, 1935), 9–10; see also Kenneth D. Garbade, *Birth of a Market: The U.S. Treasury Securities Market from the Great War to the Great Depression* (Cambridge, Mass.: MIT Press, 2012), 283–84.

252   "I found him taking a bath": MD, Sept. 6, 1934.

252   "Henry, I give you until midnight": Blum, vol. 1, 231; Schlesinger, *Coming of the New Deal,* 292.

254   "I wish you would": "President Buys First 'Baby' Bond," newsreel, March 4, 1934; "The Sale of 'Baby Bonds' Starts," *Literary Digest,* March 9, 1935, 19; James J. Kimble, *Mobilizing the Home Front: War Bonds and Domestic Propaganda* (College Station: Texas A&M University Press, 2006), 17–20.

255   Elmer Irey: On Irey and his investigations of Huey Long, Dutch Schultz, and others: Blum, vol. 1, 94–98; Elmer Irey with William J. Slocum, *The Tax Dodgers: The Inside Story of the T-Men's War with America's Political and Underworld Hoodlums* (New York: Greenberg, 1948), 93–97. See also Robert G. Folsom, *The Money Trail: How Elmer Irey and His T-Men Brought Down America's Criminal Elite* (Washington, D.C.: Potomac Books, 2010).

255   "If you stayed around here": Schlesinger, *Politics of Upheaval,* 56. The reporter: Frazier Hunt, *One American and His Attempt at Education* (New York: Simon and Schuster, 1938), 389–90.

256   "Red Light Maestri": MD, Nov. 14, 1935.

257   Arthur Flegenheimer: Blum, vol. 1, 110.

257   "the last of the big income tax gangsters": MD, Nov. 1, 1934.

258   "Now I'm not a lawyer": MD, Nov. 28, 1934.

258   "Somebody over here": PD, March 9, 1945.

259   "You can't be too tough": MD, Feb. 20, 1935.

259   "It's just horseshoes": MD, Feb. 20, 1935.

259   "He said only one thing": PD, April 11, 1939.

26. "I Went Over Him and Under Him and Around Him," Fall 1936–Spring 1939

262   "the talk among us": FDR to Colonel Arthur Murray, March 4, 1940, cited in Leonard Baker, *Roosevelt and Pearl Harbor* (New York: Macmillan, 1970), 114.

262   "stolid, stupid": Beschloss, *The Conquerors: Roosevelt, Truman, and the Destruction of Hitler's Germany, 1941–1945* (New York: Simon & Schuster, 2002), 11.

263   "a sort of tingling": HM2 to EFM, Jan. 3, 1916, HM3 Papers.

263   "new world war": "Morgenthau Sees a New World War," *NYT,* May 19, 1919, 1. At times, HM would express hope for Germany's future, but in the interwar years, he remained one of the most vocal prognosticators of a resurgent Germany: "Predicts America Will Lead World," *NYT,* Nov. 28, 1921, 3. In 1927, HM expressed optimism about the future of the German Republic: Hindenburg's "masterful tact," he wrote in a letter to a German newspaper, had "done much to make clear to Americans that

Junkerism and Prussianism no longer rule Germany": "Morgenthau Sees a Greater Germany," *NYT,* March 6, 1927, 24.

264 "very much opposed": John D. Rockefeller III diary, Sept. 5, 1933, Rockefeller Archive Center.

264 "only possible obstacle": FDR to Secretary of State, May 6, 1933. U.S. Department of State, *Peace and War: United States Foreign Policy, 1931–1941,* Publication 1983 (Washington, D.C.: Government Printing Office, 1943), 177.

264 "I think I have averted a war": MD, May 22, 1933.

265 "If the Nazi": MD, Dec. 13, 1934.

266 "If we had ended": Collier's Conferences, "Foreign Relations: the Anti-Axis Treasury Activities," MP.

266 "timorous, conventional": Henry Morgenthau, Jr., "The Morgenthau Diaries III: How FDR Fought the Axis," *Collier's,* Oct. 11, 1947, 20–79.

266 "It was dominated": Collier's Conferences, "Foreign Relations: the Anti-Axis Treasury Activities," MP.

266 "Seldom in recorded history": HM2 speech, "The Road Ahead," Temple University, June 16, 1938 (Philadelphia: Alliance Printing Company, 1938).

267 "for the life of me": MD, Sept. 1, 1948. Blum (vol. 1, 518) has the quote imprecisely as Kennedy's exact words. It's HM2's rendering of FDR's impression.

267 "60–40 chance": MD, Sept. 19, 1938.

268 "He never let anyone": Collier's Conference, July 1946, MP.

268 "common man": Associated Press, "From Tank Corps Private to Assistant Secretary of War Is Woodring's Route," *Lawrence* (Kansas) *Daily Journal,* March 30, 1933, 1.

269 "I went over him": Hellman, "Any Bonds Today?," part 1, *New Yorker,* Jan. 22, 1944, 25.

269 Harold Hochschild: MD, Dec. 4, 1939; Blum, vol. 2, 126–27.

269 "Let us not": MD, Oct. 17, 1938.

271 "Mr. President": Henry Morgenthau, Jr., "The Morgenthau Diaries IV: The Story Behind Lend-Lease," *Collier's,* Oct. 18, 1947, 16–75.

271 "Since I cannot": HM2 to FDR, Dec. 30, 1938; Blum, vol. 2, 69; *Collier's* article, 4th draft, Dec. 2, 1946, includes a line deleted from the published article: MP.

271 The new bomber: Associated Press, "Bomber Pilot Killed in Coast Plane Crash," *NYT,* Jan. 24, 1939, 5. On the Douglas bomber crash and its lead-up: HM2, "The Morgenthau Diaries IV," 16–75; Blum, vol 2, 64–78.

27. "About the Future of Democracy and the World," Fall 1937–Winter 1940

273 Princeton: "Personal Mention," *Poughkeepsie Eagle-News,* Sept. 29, 1937, 4.

273 Morrow Hall: The hall was named after Dwight Morrow, the Morgan partner, Amherst Class of 1895, father of Charles Lindbergh's wife, Anne Morrow Lindbergh. HM2 was pleased: A Lindbergh fan, he had personally coordinated the Treasury hunt for the Lindbergh baby's kidnappers, and at one point asked FDR if he could bring Lindbergh into the government as an advisor on airplanes.

274 Mr. Boyden: John McPhee, *The Headmaster: Frank L. Boyden of Deerfield* (New York: Palgrave Macmillan, 1966).

274 only 5 were Jews: Amherst Class of 1941 members who were Jewish: John Ehrenfeld (who later changed his surname to Edwards), Feingold, Rosen, George Spiegel. Amherst Archives.

274 two Amherst alums: HM2 to William G. Avirett, Nov. 13, 1937; EFM to Richard Ballou, Dec. 7, 1937; MP.

275 "I watched him": William G. Avirett to HM2, Nov. 7, 1937, MP.

275 "resembled a Landon": Richard Ballou to EFM & HM2, Dec. 7, 1937, MP.

275 B's and C's: Amherst coursebook, Fall 1937–Spring 1941, RMM Papers.

276 Karl Loewenstein: Peter Odegard was another influential Amherst professor. Both men later advised HM2 and the federal government.

276 "I learned last week": Loewenstein to HM2, Oct. 17, 1938, MP.

276 He was already: Author interviews: Robert Wiggins, Jack Chester, Chase Morsey.

277 "Bob does his work": Boyden to HM2, April 11, 1934, MP.

278 opened the hearings: "Session Is Closed," *NYT,* Jan. 29, 1939, 1; "President Helped French Air Mission Despite Protests," *NYT,* Feb. 17, 1939, 1; "Publicity Curbed on French Planes," *NYT,* Feb. 16, 1939, 9; "Roosevelt Order for French Study of Plane Revealed," *NYT,* Feb. 18, 1939, 1.

279 "I thought": "President Helped French Air Mission Despite Protests," *NYT,* Feb. 17, 1939, 1.

279 "The airplane deal": "Session Is Closed," *NYT,* Jan. 29, 1939, 1.

279 "the Treasury backyard": U.S. Senate Committee on Military Affairs, Hearings on National Defense, Jan. 27, 1939, MD 173, 255.

279 "Two very simple reasons": FDR press conference, Jan. 27, 1939, FDRL. *Complete Presidential Press Conferences of Franklin D. Roosevelt,* vol. 13, no. 521 (1939), 90.

279 "I want to talk": PD, Jan. 31, 1939, MP.

280 "On account": MD, Feb. 6, 1939.

28. Again, at the Brink, 1939–1940

282 new tax bill: The Revenue Act of 1939: Turner Catledge, "President Plans New Tax Parleys As Profits Levy Appears Doomed," *NYT,* May 17, 1939, 1; Blum, vol. 2, 22–28; MD, May 11, 1939.

283 "been bullying me": MD, May 18, 1939, MP.

284 The Morgenthaus would sail: "Cabinet Member and Wife Off for Europe," *NYT,* Aug. 3, 1939, 16; "Morgenthau to Take Finland His Thanks," *NYT,* Aug. 1, 1939, 16.

284 "study Danish agriculture": "Morgenthau in England," *NYT,* Aug. 8, 1939, 3; "Morgenthau Arrives in Denmark," *NYT,* Aug. 9, 1939, 3; "Morgenthau in Finland," *NYT,* Aug. 21, 1939, 5; "Morgenthau in Finland," *NYT,* Aug. 22, 1939, 11.

284 By August 25: "Americans Abroad Urged to Return," *NYT,* Aug. 25, 1939, 7; "Morgenthau Plans Return," *NYT,* Aug. 25, 1939, 7.

284 "the most seaworthy": MM, 291; "Treasury's Fears on Europe Recede," *NYT,* Aug. 27, 1939, 30.

285 "very nervous": Author interview: JMH.

285 Aboard the U.S. Coast Guard cutter: Blum, vol. 2, 92; "Morgenthau on Way Back on Coast Guard Cutter," *NYT,* Aug. 30, 1939, 4; "Morgenthau Is Flying from Boston to Capitol," *NYT,* Sept. 4, 1939, 6; "Morgenthau Busy After Rush Home," *NYT,* Sept. 5, 1939, 26; "Mrs. Roosevelt Greets a Friend Returning from Europe," *NYT,* Sept. 9, 1939, 8; "Preface to War," *Time,* Sept. 11, 1939.

286 editor of *Collier's:* FDR even signed a three-year contract, dated Jan. 27, 1940; Gunther, *Roosevelt in Retrospect,* 308.

286 "These foreign orders": MD, March 12, 1940, MP.

287 "Have you fired": HM2, "The Morgenthau Diaries IV," *Collier's,* Oct. 18, 1947.

287 "The small countries": Churchill to FDR, May 15, 1940; Churchill, *The Second World War,* vol. 2, *Their Finest Hour* (New York: Houghton Mifflin, 1949), 24; Blum, vol. 2, 149.

288 clandestine campaign: Robert H. Jackson, "The Exchange of Destroyers for Atlantic Bases," in *That Man: An Insider's Portrait of Franklin D. Roosevelt,* ed. John Q. Barrett (Oxford: Oxford University Press, 2003), 82.

288 **Lockheed bought:** "Many Planes Delivered to Canada Here," *Pembina New Era,* Feb. 16, 1940, 25; "Deliver First Shipment of U.S. Planes to Canadian Government at Pembina," *Walhalla Mountaineer,* Jan. 18, 1940, cited in *North Dakota History* (Bismarck: State Historical Society of North Dakota, 1992), 8.

288 **500,000 rifles:** Unpublished memoir, Robert P. Patterson Papers, 27.

289 **"England will be grateful":** "Envoy Flies Here," *NYT,* Nov. 24, 1940, 1.

29. "Not Far from Armageddon," 1940–1941

290 **"in a very good humor":** Blum, vol. 2, 208–209.

290 **"I have been thinking":** The Lend-Lease idea may have begun to form in the president's head months earlier. He had suggested at a defense meeting, according to Stettinius, that "it should not be necessary for the British to take their own funds and have ships built in the U.S., or for us to loan them money for this purpose."

293 **The V-7 program:** July 11, 1940 Consent Form, U.S. Navy documents; RMM Papers.

294 **USS *Wyoming:*** "Anchors Aweigh, My Boys!," *Christian Science Monitor,* July 20, 1940, 9.

294 **"90-day wonders":** Beinecke, *Through Mem'ry's Haze,* 149–50; Author interview: Beinecke.

294 **quit the Colony Club:** Cook, vol. 2, 321.

295 **"Boys should outnumber":** MM, 294.

296 **"informal but not rowdy":** "Party for Joan," *Time,* Jan. 6, 1941; "Joan Morgenthau Bows in the Capital," *NYT,* Dec. 27, 1940, L+17.

296 **"I am sorry":** Herman Klotz to HM3, Oct. 16, 1978, HM3 Papers.

298 **"Appeasers, isolationists":** "Full Debate Urged," *NYT,* Jan. 13, 1941, 1.

298 **"I want to memorize":** MD, Jan. 13, 1941, 347, 158–218.

299 **"statistician and dispenser":** MD, Jan. 14, 1941, 347, 341. In 1947, S. Everett Gleason, sifting through the MD for the two-volume history of the preparation for WWII that he co-authored, alerted HM2 to this Jan. 14, 1941, note. HM2 sent Gleason's notes to EFM: HM2 to EFM, Dec. 11, 1947, HM3 Papers.

299 **"Lacking a formula":** Harold B. Hinton, "No Dollars Left," *NYT,* Jan. 29, 1941, 1.

299 **"Despite your":** Van Wallach, "A Community to Turn To," *Princeton Alumni Weekly,* April 19, 1995, 12–18.

300 **"The Future of American Youth":** ER at Amherst, Feb. 5, 1941: Dorothy King, "First Lady Makes Visit to Amherst," *Springfield Union,* Feb. 6, 1941, 1; Associated Press, "First Lady on War," *N.Y. Sun,* Feb. 6, 1941.

301 **confidential report:** Author was Alfred Wagg; fired by Breckinridge Long. Felix Cohen to RMM, June 5, 1941, RMM Papers. cf: Breitman, *American Refugee Policy,* 136.

302 **sailor suits:** *Sideboy,* the *Prairie State* yearbook, of which RMM was editor in chief; Beinecke, *Through Mem'ry's Haze,* 162.

302 **"Events of the last":** "429 Commissioned in Naval Reserve . . . Son of Morgenthau a Graduate," *NYT,* Sept. 17, 1941, 12.

303 **to fill out a form:** Oct. 21, 1941, U.S. Navy Documents.

304 **"Is it not fine?":** PD, Nov. 22, 1941.

304 **"He really seemed":** PD, Dec. 3, 1941.

304 **"nothing whatsoever":** Gunther, *Roosevelt in Retrospect,* 319.

304 **"Japan is receiving":** H. D. White to HM2, April 4, 1941, MD.

305 **"I should like to know":** FDR to Hull and Welles, Dec. 1, 1941, FDRL.

305 **"screamed as though stabbed":** Michael F. Reilly, as told to William J. Slocum, *Reilly of the White House* (New York: Simon & Schuster, 1947), 4, 6.

306 **"We are freezing":** PD, Dec. 7, 1941; MD, Dec. 7, 1941.

306 **Roosevelt called it:** Claude R. Wickard Papers, FDRL.

307 "It is just unexplainable": PD, Dec. 7, 1941.

307 **ordering blackout curtains:** Merriman Smith, *Thank You, Mr. President: A White House Notebook* (New York: Harper, 1946), 117.

307 **"mardi gras atmosphere":** "Newark, Gay in 'Blackout', Is Far From Totally Dark," Byron Darnton, *NYT*, May 26, 1941, 1.

307 **"sufficiently hardened":** Unpublished memoir, Robert P. Patterson Papers, 127–28.

307 **I.G. Farben's subsidiaries:** Unpublished memoir, Robert P. Patterson Papers, 111.

30. At Sea, Winter 1942–Winter 1943

310 **seventy-nine destroyers:** Theodore Roscoe, *US Destroyer Operations in World War II* (Annapolis, Md.: United States Naval Institute, 1953), 42.

310 **German submarines:** Richard A. Shafter, *Destroyers in Action* (New York: Cornell Maritime Press, 1945), 82.

311 **Task Force 3:** Samuel Eliot Morison, *History of United States Naval Operations in World War*, vol. 1, *The Battle of the Atlantic, September 1939–May 1943* (New York: Little, Brown, 1947), 83. On March 15, 1943, the South Atlantic Fleet was renamed the Fourth Fleet.

311 **"Now, I'm going to ask":** HM2 telcon with Admiral Stark, Nov. 24, 1941, 215–17, MD.

312 **Frank Tuggle:** Enlisted May 1942, CFC (AA). U.S. Navy Documents.

312 **mess attendants:** U.S. Navy Documents; Richard E. Miller, *The Messman Chronicles: African Americans in the US Navy, 1932–1943* (Annapolis, Md.: Naval Institute Press, 2004).

313 **"a dark snub-nosed object":** W. J. Marshall, Commander in Chief, U.S. Atlantic Fleet, Action Report, May 8, 1942, U.S. Navy Documents.

313 **sinking a U-boat:** Richard G. Stone, *Kentucky Fighting Men, 1861–1945* (Lexington: University of Kentucky Press, 1982), 67.

314 **returned to South Carolina:** The *Winslow* only twice returned briefly to the U.S. for repairs: in June 1942 and in October 1943. *Dictionary of American Naval Fighting Ships*, 8 vols. (Washington, D.C.: Government Printing Office, 1959–1981).

315 **In April 1940:** "Mrs. Morgenthau Is Operated On," N.Y. *Daily News*, April 25, 1940, 43.

316 **"has been sick":** Feb. 22, 1943, RMM to HM2, RMM Papers.

317 **"There is no canteen":** Shafter, *Destroyers in Action*, 6.

317 **MOMP:** Samuel Eliot Morison, *History of United States Naval Operations in World War*, vol. 1, 90.

317 **in late 1942:** Morison, *History of United States Naval Operations*, vol. 1, 353.

318 **"Riding herd":** Shafter, *Destroyers in Action*, 4.

319 **new Soviet offensive:** Ralph Parker, "Nazi Armies Flee," *NYT*, Dec. 31, 1943, 1.

320 **third year at Vassar:** Joan Morgenthau entered Vassar with the Class of 1945, but the class "accelerated" their studies due to the war and graduated in December 1944. The class became known as "1945/'44"—"The Class with a Dash."

31. Civilization Fails the Test, Summer 1942–Fall 1943

321 **"Jew Deal":** The August, 15, 1936, edition of *The White Knight* was entitled the "Jew Deal Issue."

321 **"Jewish ancestry":** John Keegan, *The Second World War* (New York: Penguin Books, 1989), 536–38.

321 **"In the dim, distant past":** *The Public Papers and Addresses of Franklin D. Roosevelt*, vol. 4, *The Court Disapproves*, ed. Samuel Rosenman (New York: Random House,

1938), 96–97; FDR to Philip Slomovitz, editor of *The Detroit Jewish Chronicle*, March 7, 1935. Complete text: "I am grateful to you for your interesting letter of March 4th. I have no idea as to the source of the story which you say came from my old friend, Chase Osborn. All I know about the origin of the Roosevelt family in this country is that all branches bearing the name are apparently descended from Claes Martenssen Van Roosevelt, who came from Holland sometime before 1648—even the year is uncertain. Where he came from in Holland I do not know, nor do I know who his parents were. There was a family of the same name on one of the Dutch Islands and some of the same name living in Holland as lately as thirty or forty years ago, but, frankly, I have never had either the time or the inclination to try to establish the line on the other side of the ocean before they came over here, nearly three hundred years ago." Also cited in Geoffrey C. Ward, *A First-Class Temperament: The Emergence of Franklin Roosevelt* (New York: Harper & Row, 1989), 254; Rowley, 229; Grace Tully, *FDR My Boss* (New York: Scribner's, 1949), 101.

321 **Irving Lehman:** Richard Breitman and Allan J. Lichtman, *FDR and the Jews* (Cambridge, Mass.: Belknap Press of Harvard University Press, 2013), 68; cites Lehman to FDR, Sept. 21, 1933, NARA, RG 59, 150.01/2153.

322 **1,241 German émigrés:** "Americans and the Holocaust," USHMM. Correspondence with Rebecca Erbelding, historian and archivist at the USHMM. Since the publication, in 1968, of Arthur D. Morse's *While Six Million Died*, a number of histories of the War Refugee Board have appeared, but no historian has more closely studied the vast archival record than Erbelding. Her *Rescue Board: The Untold Story of America's Efforts to Save the Jews of Europe* (New York: Anchor Books, 2019) stands apart as the most complete and accurate telling of its creation and work—both shortcomings and achievements—as well as offering vivid portraits of its extraordinarily wide-ranging cast of characters.

322 **"has shown amply":** Richard Breitman and Alan M. Kraut, *American Refugee Policy and European Jewry: 1933–1945* (Bloomington: Indiana University Press, 1987), 8.

323 **German colonies:** MD, Jan. 24, 1938; "Refugees, 2nd Draft," 10. HM Papers, FDRL.

323 **an "interfaith" meeting:** "President Confers on Aid to Refugees," *NYT*, April 14, 1918, 16.

323 *Political* **Refugees:** Breitman and Lichtman, *FDR and the Jews,* 106, citing "Confidential Memorandum on WH Conference on Refugees," April 13, 1938, Wise Papers, American Jewish Historical Society (AJHS).

324 **"test of civilization":** Anne O'Hare McCormick, "Europe: The Refugee Question as a Test of Civilization Nation of Free Choice Plight of the Refugee a Way to Rebuke the Reich," *NYT*, July 4, 1938, 12.

324 **"terrible experience":** Golda Meir, *My Life* (New York: Putnam, 1975), 158.

324 **"They gambled":** Peggy Mann, "Prelude to Holocaust," *Washington Post*, April 16, 1978, B1; Peggy Mann, "When the World Passed By on the Other Side," *Manchester Guardian Weekly*, May 7, 1978.

324 **"as is known":** "Concern for Jews Is Held Insincere," *NYT*, Nov. 22, 1938, 4.

325 **At lunch on October 25:** MD, Oct. 25, 1938, 147, 375. Quoted in "Refugees," 2nd draft, 12, MP.

325 **On October 14, 1938:** FDR to Bowman, Oct. 14, 1938, President's Personal File 5575, FDRL.

325 **"Frankly":** Neil Smith, *American Empire: Roosevelt's Geographer and the Prelude to Globalization* (Berkeley: University of California Press, 2003), 295.

326 **more than 30,000:** Martin Gilbert, *Kristallnacht: Prelude to Destruction* (New York: HarperCollins, 2006), 1–3.

326 **"I myself":** Statement, Nov. 15, 1938, FDRL.

326 "nobody is helping him": MD, Nov. 16, 1938.

326 Isaiah Bowman: HM to Bowman, March 17, 1923; Note to File, Isaiah Bowman, Nov. 16, 1938, Bowman Papers, Johns Hopkins.

326 "It is an exciting search": Bowman to FDR, Nov. 21, 1938, Bowman Papers, Johns Hopkins University.

327 the *St. Louis:* Breitman and Lichtman, *FDR and the Jews,* 136.

327 Mussolini: Ickes, *Secret Diary,* vol. 3, 464.

328 Commander E. G. Rose: Transcripts, HM2 conversations with Hull, Welles, Commander Rose, June 5–7, 1939, Holocaust/Refugee Collection, Box 1, FDRL; U.S. Coast Guard Historian site.

329 "A year has passed": PD, June 19, 1939, 124–25. Also: Blum, vol. 3, 208.

32. "War Rumor Inspired by Fear," 1942-1943

331 "Toward the end of 1933": Berger, *The Story of* The New York Times (New York: Simon & Schuster, 1951), 400. See also Tifft and Jones, *The Trust,* 156.

331 "I am a little disturbed": Arthur Hays Sulzberger to HM2, April 27, 1934, MP. See also Leff, *Buried by the* Times, 46–47.

331 "too Jewish": Leff, *Buried by the* Times, 23.

332 "Jewish race": FDR Speech, Oct. 17, 1939.

332 "any anthropologist will": A. H. Sulzberger to HM2, Oct. 18, 1939, MP; Laurel Leff, "A Tragic 'Fight in the Family': *The New York Times,* Reform Judaism and the Holocaust," *American Jewish History* 88, no. 1 (March 2000): 3–51; A. H. Sulzberger lunch with FDR, Dec. 27, 1939: Arthur Hays Sulzberger File, Franklin D. Roosevelt, 1932–1950 Folder, NYT Archives; NYPL.

332 "those of the Jewish faith": Leff, *Buried by the* Times, 47; "A Tragic 'Fight in the Family,'" 26.

332 editorial on the *St. Louis:* Leff, *Buried by the* Times, 44; "Man's Inhumanity," *NYT,* June 9, 1939, 20.

333 "unforgettable three-hours' talk": Leff, *Buried by the* Times, 44–45.

333 "a solution": "Nazis 'Hint' Purge of Jews in Poland," *NYT,* Sept. 13, 1939, 5.

333 "The Poles": April 20, 1940, HM Papers, Box 277, Sulzberger Family, FDRL; Leff, *Buried by the* Times, 61–62.

333 a first story: Untitled UPI report from Stockholm, *NYT,* June 27, 1942, 5.

333 "special gas chambers on wheels": "Allies Are Urged to Execute Nazis," *NYT,* July 2, 1942, 6.

334 Gerhart Riegner: Charles Fenyvesi, "The Man Who Knew the Nazi Secret: The Futile Effort to Stop the 'Final Solution,'" in *The Obligation to Remember: The American Gathering of Jewish Holocaust Survivors, Washington D.C., April 11–14, 1983: An Anthology* (Washington, D.C.: *The Washington Post,* 1983); First: "The Nazi Secret No One Believed," *Washington Post,* Feb. 5, 1983, C1, C4.

334 The Riegners: Gerhart M. Riegner, *Never Despair: Sixty Years in the Service of the Jewish People and the Cause of Human Rights,* trans. from the French by William Sayers (Chicago: Ivan R. Dee, 2006), 18.

334 World Jewish Congress: Richard Breitman and Walter Laqueur, *Breaking the Silence* (New York: Simon & Schuster, 1986), 133.

335 two Swiss intermediaries: Breitman and Laqueur, *Breaking the Silence,* 124.

335 "Was it conceivable?": Riegner, *Never Despair,* 36. See also Clare Nullis, "Gerhart Riegner Dies," *Washington Post,* Dec. 4, 2001, B7.

336 "a giant crematorium": Breitman and Laqueur, *Breaking the Silence,* 146.

336 "earmarks of war rumor": Breitman and Laqueur, *Breaking the Silence,* 148–49.

336 "conservative and equable": SSW to Welles, Sept. 2, 1942, Monty Noam Penkower, *The Jews Were Expendable: Free World Diplomacy and the Holocaust* (Detroit, Mich.: Wayne State University Press, 1988), 67.

336 "Himmler Program": James McDonald, "Himmler Program Kills Polish Jews," *NYT*, Oct. 25, 1942, 10.

336 "stunned into silence": A. M. Sperber, *Murrow: His Life and Times* (New York: Fordham University Press, 1998), 217–18.

339 "One of the things": Interview with John Pehle in Katie Louchheim, ed., *The Making of the New Deal*, 269.

339 Riegner only needed: Riegner, *Never Despair*, 59.

339 "an antiquated home": Robert Bendiner, *The Riddle of the State Department* (New York: Farrar & Rinehart, 1942), 109.

340 "It was Treasury business": Josiah E. DuBois, Jr., *The Devil's Chemists* (Boston: Beacon Press, 1952), 185.

340 Could the United States: DuBois, *Devil's Chemists*, 185.

33. "Courage First," Fall 1943–Winter 1944

341 "Clear the way": "Oil and the Rabbis," *Time*, Oct. 18, 1943, 21. See also "Rabbis Present Plea to Wallace," *NYT*, Oct. 7, 1943, 14.

342 *We Will Never Die*: Judith Tydor Baumel, *The "Bergson Boys" and the Origins of Contemporary Zionist Militancy*, trans. from the Hebrew by Dena Ordan (Syracuse, N.Y.: Syracuse University Press, 2005).

342 "These are the two million": RG-60.1309, film #: 2928, March 9, 1943; USHMM.

342 new Liberator bombers: William D. Hassett, *Off the Record with F.D.R., 1942–1945* (New Brunswick, N.J.: Rutgers University Press, 1958), 185.

343 "HELP Prevent": *NYT*, Nov. 5, 1943, 14.

343 "HOW WELL": *NYT*, Nov. 24, 1943, 13.

343 "May I make": MD, Nov. 23, 1943.

344 "It's like that story": MD, Dec. 6, 1943.

345 "with the difficulties": MD, Winant to Secretary of State, Dec. 15, 1943.

346 "conversations with Treasury": MD, DuBois, "Confidential: Memorandum to File," Dec. 18, 1943.

346 "For Hull by S.W.": MD, Jan. 15, 1944.

347 "While I have not": MD, Cable 460, Harrison to Hull, April 20, 1943.

347 the following evening, a Sunday: MD, Dec. 19, 1943.

348 "was taking his political life": Randolph Paul, undated interview, *Collier's* material, MP.

348 "I've already sent a cable": MD, Dec. 20, 1943, Book 688, part 2, 148–71.

349 At sixty-one, "Breck" Long: Long's correspondence with HM and HM2 is contained in the Breckinridge Long Papers, LC. Long's Diary, also held in the LC, contains numerous references to HM2. Excerpts of the diary were published as *The War Diary of Breckinridge Long: Selections from the Years 1939–1944* (Lincoln: University of Nebraska Press, 1966). Biography of Long: See Breitman and Lichtman, *FDR and the Jews*, 164–65; Arthur Morse, *While Six Million Died* (New York: Random House, 1968), 38–42.

349 "I am surprised": Long Diary, March 20, 1917, LC.

349 "one of the most remarkable": Long to Davies, Sept. 6, 1933, Long Papers, LC; Morse, *While Six Million Died*, 39.

349 "Mein Kampf": Long Diary, Feb. 6, 1938, Long Papers, LC.

349 "My physical": Long Diary, Feb. 15, 1941, Long Papers, LC.

350 "The refugee problem": Long Diary, Aug. 30, 1942, Long Papers, LC; "obstruction-ist": Long Diary, Sept. 24, 1940, Long Papers, LC.

350 "The Jewish organizations": Long Diary, Jan. 11, 1944, Long Papers, LC.

350 "a 4-hour inquisition": Long Diary, Jan. 1, 1944, Long Papers, LC.

350 of the 476,930 aliens: Morse, *While Six Million Died*, 94.

350 "been spreading this stuff": Ironically, the officials Hull sought to blame were Bernard Meltzer and Herbert Feis, who were both Jewish, and who had sought to aid Treasury officials in their quest to activate the State Department. Both would soon leave the State Department. Meltzer, acting chief of Foreign Funds Control, quit to join the U.S. Navy, and later served as a prosecutor at Nuremberg, before becoming a law profes-sor at the University of Chicago. Feis resigned from the State Department in Novem-ber 1943, after serving as economic advisor since 1931. He went on to become a prominent historian, winning the Pulitzer Prize in 1961. DuBois, in a memorandum to the files, Sept. 9, 1943, MD, recorded Meltzer's and Feis's opposition and assistance. DuBois took care to note that Meltzer, contrary to his State Department colleagues' accusations, did not accuse them of anti-Semitism: "Although he was in no position to accuse these men of opposing such proposals because of anti-Semitism, since he could not support such an accusation with concrete evidence (and furthermore because he preferred to be charitable in forming opinions in cases such as this), it was striking that in a case like this such men should be arguing against the proposal on economic warfare grounds."

351 "Your 482-January 21": MD, "Personal Report to the President."

351 "information termites": MD, Jan. 15, 1944.

351 Long himself: MD, Jan. 15, 1944.

351 "We leave it": MD, Dec. 23, 1943; the sentence was not included in the report HM2 handed to FDR.

352 "only one thing to do": MD, Dec. 23, 1943.

352 "He feels this thing": MD, Jan. 10, 1944.

352 "Do you know": MD, Jan. 12, 1944.

353 "In their official capacity": MD, Jan. 13, 1944.

353 "The thing": MD, Jan. 13, 1944.

353 "two Cabinet officers": MD, Jan. 15, 1944.

354 "I don't know": MD, Jan. 15, 1944.

355 "Henry, I would prefer": MD, Pehle Memo, Jan. 16, 1944.

355 "soured on the problem": MD, Pehle Memo, Jan. 16, 1944.

356 "stringing up": PD, Jan. 17, 1944, 1331. HM2 did add the word "proven" in the text as delivered: MD, Jan. 17, 1944.

357 "Let somebody else": Long Diary, Jan. 11, 1944, Jan. 24, 1944, Long Papers, LC.

357 "these lines be bombed": Roswell McClelland, June 24, 1944, Papers of the War Ref-ugee Board (PWRB), Box 66, FDRL; Erbelding, *Rescue Board*, 153–57.

358 "considerable air support": McCloy to Pehle, War Refugee Board, July 4, 1944, War Refugee Board Records, Projects and Documents File; Measures Directed Toward Halting Persecutions; Hungary No. 5, Box 42, FDRL.

34. In the Med: April 20, Winter 1944–Spring 1944

359 USS *Turner:* "Lost Ship Revealed as New Destroyer," *NYT,* Jan. 5, 1944, 1–2.

360 "Howie" Murray: Convoy PQ-16 encountered 108 waves of attacking Luftwaffe bombers, and lost 8 of 25 merchant vessels.

360 "liked to swoop in low": "Disabled Negro Veteran Credits Bob Morgenthau with Sav-ing His Life," *Advance News,* Oct. 21, 1962, 7.

361 "Operation Shingle": Roscoe, *US Destroyer Operations,* 338.

361 thirty-two bombing attacks: Roscoe, *US Destroyer Operations,* 339.

361 to provide cover: Roscoe, *US Destroyer Operations,* 338–42.

361 forcing them to retreat: Fritzel, ed. Peter Soler, unpublished report, a collection of oral histories and recollections by veterans of the USS *Lansdale* (Soler Report).

362 barbershop quartet: "Morgenthau's Shipmates Tell of Heroes at Sea," *Washington Times-Herald,* May 19, 1944.

362 sixteen warships: Twelve destroyer-escorts (6 Coast Guard, 6 Navy), 2 minesweepers (USS *Sustain* and USS *Speed*), and a Dutch light cruiser, *Heemskerck.* They were joined by a British tug (the Texas-built HMS *Vagrant*) and a Coast Guard cutter, the *Taney.*

363 radio transmissions: *Menges* War Diary, *Newell* War Diary, World War II War Diaries, RG 38, NARA; U.S. Navy documents.

363 report from a coastwatcher: Samuel Eliot Morison, *History of United States Naval Operations in World War II,* vol. 10 (New York: Little, Brown, 1956), 268.

364 lit up the waters: Author interviews: Alvin Caplan, Bob Dott, George Fritzel, Marshall Geller, Al Macklin, Ben Montenegro, Raymond Quirion, Edwin Redfern, Sal Rizzo, Roger Sheer, George Sinclair, Peter Soler, Charles Wales. Additional materials: Anne Marie Allison (daughter of Ray Miller) and Soler Report.

364 "Next thing I knew": "Skipper's Quick Thinking Saves Many on Doomed Ship," *Detroit News,* May 26, 1944.

364 a girl from Knoxville: U.S. Navy documents; "Another Naval Hero," *Pittsburgh Courier,* May 20, 1944, 1, with photographs of Marion Porter and his wife, Marie Dawkins Porter.

365 "I am convinced": Secretary of the Navy Frank Knox to Sen. Arthur Capper, Aug. 1, 1940, in Keith Krawczynski, "African American Navy, Marine Corps, Women's Reserves, and Coast Guard Service During World War II," in Steven D. Smith and James A. Zeidler, *A Historic Context for the African American Military Experience,* Cultural Resources Research Center at the U.S. Army Construction Engineering Research Laboratories (USACERL), July 1998, 189.

365 He had put six stewards: James Abbott, C. L. Luster, Willie Hicks, Marion Porter, James Loadholt, Charles W. Mitchell; U.S. Navy Documents.

365 Lieutenant Jim Bever: Lt. James C. Bever: U.S. Navy press release, May 10, 1944.

366 Doug Brewer: Brewer and Van Ness, Soler Report.

367 Bill Neal: William B. Neal, Jr.

368 "Later": Lowell Thomas News, May 10, 1944, 6:45–7:00 p.m.; RMM Papers.

369 Jerry Wroblewski: Anthony J. Wroblewski, RM 2/c, served aboard the *Lansdale,* April 1941 to end.

369 Barclay: Karyes Barclay, Talladega. Service # 2724021.

369 George Haines: U.S. Navy press release: George E. Haines, 24, of Greenwich Conn.; "An Alumnus Advises," *Hotchkiss Magazine,* Fall 2011, 30–32, Remembrance of Bob Johnson, a classmate of Haines, who married Haines's widow; Audrey Haines's son: George Eddison Haines.

370 "While I was taking": Miller, Soler Report.

370 "You could hear": Kevin Lollar, "Navy Veteran Lost Vital Lifebelt in Sunset Attack," *Fort Myers News-Press,* April 20, 1994, 1b.

371 "Swim toward the ship": Soler, Feb. 19, 1994, Soler Report.

371 Max Pecherer could hear: John H. Roberts, Motor Machinist's Mate 2nd Class, Soler Report.

371 Clinton Neuman: U.S. Navy Documents; "Lockport Sailor Declared Dead," *Niagara Falls Gazette,* May 2, 1945, 14; Wroblewski, May 31, 1994, Soler Report.

371 "There are no atheists": Geller, Feb. 2, 1994, Soler Report.

372 **"Put out the light!":** Arthur Green interview, U.S. Coast Guard, June 28, 1944.

372 **The bombers had taken off:** Interrogation Report, May 23, 1944, 6 pp.; "Room Conversation," extracted May 22, 1944.

372 **Men reached across the rails:** U.S. Navy press release, *Newell* War Diary.

373 **"Elinor and I":** PD, April 22, 1944, 1364.

374 **John Cronin:** "Morgenthau's Shipmates Tell of Heroes at Sea," *Washington Times-Herald,* May 19, 1944; John P. Cronin, Seaman 1st Class, # 6117956, buried in the North Africa American Cemetery, Tunis, Tunisia.

374 **five more bodies:** U.S. Navy Documents, Action Report: 235 men rescued by *Newell* and *Menges;* Westhill and Cronin died "just before or just after being rescued."

375 **"bluejackets":** "Lieut. Morgenthau Cited for Heroic Acton as Exec. on USS Lansdale," *Norfolk SeaBag* (U.S. Naval Training Station), Aug. 19, 1944.

375 **the German former POWs:** In the 1990s, the Germans would send cards, on Easter and at Christmas, to the *Lansdale* veterans. "We could not suppress an amused laugh (forgive us)," they wrote, "over the torpedo was meant only for the tanker," but a second one "went under the tanker . . . and hit the Lansdale, forced your crew to take a 'bath.'" "We spent a beautiful day together, after 50 years, thanks to your research and your discovery." "Is a war like that not insane? Only to fulfill the power and idea and wishes of a couple politicians. Let's hope it'll never happen to our countries again." Fedderson spent nearly a year in a camp near Algiers, then two years in a British POW camp in Egypt. Fedderson to Redfern, Dec. 16, 1996, April 7, 1997, Dec. 12, 1997.

35. "And I Mean the German People," Spring 1944

376 *Henry the Morgenthau:* [Wythe Williams], *Washington Broadcast, by the Man at the Microphone* (Garden City, N.Y.: Doubleday, Doran, 1944), 141.

377 **"They paint a picture":** PD, March 7, 1944, 1338.

379 **"Bernstein is a regular little rabbi":** Keynes, Letter to Sir Wilfrid Eady, Oct. 3, 1943, in *Collected Writings of John Maynard Keynes,* vol. 25 (1980), 364; D. E. Moggridge, *Maynard Keynes: An Economist's Biography* (London: Routledge, 1992), 727–28.

380 **with rare dramatic flourish:** HM2, Closing Speech, Bretton Woods Conference, July 22, 1944. *United Nations Monetary and Financial Conference: Bretton Woods, Final Act and Related Documents, New Hampshire, July 1 to July 22, 1944* (Washington, D.C.: U.S. Government Printing Office, 1944).

380 **"I like to think":** U.S. Department of State, *Proceedings and Documents of United Nations Monetary and Financial Conference (Bretton Woods, New Hampshire; July 1–22, 1944),* vol. 1 (Washington, D.C.: GPO, 1948), 1125.

380 **"We are at a crossroads":** U.S. Department of State, *Proceedings and Documents of United Nations Monetary and Financial Conference (Bretton Woods, New Hampshire; July 1–22, 1944),* vol. 2 (Washington, D.C.: GPO, 1948), 1228.

381 **Fred Smith:** In 1947, Smith would write a detailed article based on contemporaneous notes taken during the trip: Fred Smith, "The Rise and Fall of the Morgenthau Plan," *United Nations World* 1 (March 1947): 32–37.

381 **"first with interest":** "Morgenthau's Inside Story: Our Policy on Germany," *N.Y. Post,* Nov. 24, 1947, 2.

383 **"set the spark":** Robert Collins, interview with Fred Smith, Nov. 14, 1953, Time Inc. Records, NYHS.

383 **"As a farmer myself":** "Our Policy Toward Germany," *N.Y. Post,* Nov. 24, 1947, 2.

383 **"It was upsetting":** Author interview: HM3; MM, 358–61.

384 **"This is an opportunity":** MM, 359.

384 **"very attentive":** PD, 1386–88.

385 "war room": MD, 763, 103–105, 111–12, Aug. 17, 1944; PD, Aug. 19, 1944; HM–EFM, Aug. 11, 1944; "Trip to the European Theatre," Aug. 5–17, 1944, bound volume, MP.

36. "Unnatural, Unchristian, and Unnecessary," August 1944

388 "I could not get": HM2, ghostwritten by Arthur M. Schlesinger, Jr., *N.Y. Post,* Nov. 24–29, 1947. 4-part series.

388 "most violent": Stimson and Bundy, *On Active Service,* 566.

388 It had been a short visit: Stimson Diary, Aug. 23, 1944, and Aug. 25, 1944.

389 "gas chambers": MD, Aug. 23, 1944, Book 765, 15.

389 "tires very easily": MD, Aug. 23, 1944.

390 "was shocked for the first time": PD, Aug. 25, 1944.

390 "Your main and immediate": PD, Aug. 25, 1944, 1389–95.

391 "This so-called 'Handbook'": Memorandum by President Roosevelt to Stimson, Aug. 26, 1944, FDRL.

392 the draft: PD: "Suggested Post-Surrender Program for Germany," Sept. 1, 1944; Map dated Sept. 2, 1944.

393 "I wonder": PD, Sept. 2, 1944, 1422–27.

393 "I don't think": MD, Sept. 4, 1944.

393 "The President is entirely agreeable": MD, Sept. 4, 1944, "Disarmament of Germany"; 2 staff meetings: 10:55 A.M., 3:25 P.M.

396 "It was very interesting": Stimson Diary, Sept. 4, 1944.

397 "to prepare how to deal": PD, Sept. 2, 1944, 1422–1427.

397 "Hull has been rather crotchety": Stimson Diary, Sept. 5, 1944.

397 "This is just fighting": MD, Sept. 5, 1944.

397 "All you've got": MD, Sept. 5, 1944.

397 "In all the four years": Stimson Diary, Sept. 5, 1944.

398 "Don't be discouraged": PD, Sept. 7, 1944.

398 "sticks to his guns": Stimson Diary, Sept. 7, 1944.

399 September 9: PD, Sept. 9, 1944; Stimson Diary, Sept. 9, 1944.

399 "breed war, not peace": Stimson and Bundy, *On Active Service,* 574–75.

399 "a question of a soft treatment": PD, Sept. 9, 1944.

400 "I have been much troubled": Stimson Diary, Sept. 11, 1944.

400 *"Childish folly!":* Geoffrey Hodgson, *The Colonel: The Life and Wars of Henry Stimson, 1867–1950* (New York: Knopf, 1990), 18.

401 "more like a reunion": *The Memoirs of General Lord Ismay* (New York: Viking Press, 1960), 373.

401 "such a waste of time": Cook, vol. 3, 514.

401 "how easily": Fred Smith, "The Rise and Fall of the Morgenthau Plan," *UN World,* March 1947.

401 "to cheer us up": Stimson Diary, Sept. 11, 1944.

402 "Say hello": PD, Sept. 13, 1944.

403 "great admirer": Henry Morgenthau, Jr., "Our Policy Toward Germany," *N.Y. Post,* Nov. 24–29, 1947; PD, Sept. 13, 1944, Memo of State Dinner by Harry Dexter White.

403 "dead German": MD, Sept. 19, 1944, 772, at 10 A.M.: 153–55; and again at 3:20: 208–28.

404 "one-man brain trust": MD, 773, Sept. 20, 1944.

405 "were Shylocks": Walter Isaacson and Evan Thomas, *The Wise Men: Six Friends and the World They Made* (New York: Simon & Schuster, 1997), 238.

405 "detested Germans": Colville, *Fringes of Power,* 736.

405 "almost the Prime Minister's": MD, Klotz to HM2, Sept. 14, 1944.

405 "the countries": Memorandum of meeting, Sept. 14, 1944, Cherwell Papers, Nuffield College, Oxford.

406 "so much to ask": Churchill, *The Second World War,* vol. 6, *Triumph and Tragedy* (New York: Houghton Mifflin, 1953), 156.

406 "What do you want": PD, Sept. 15, 1944, 1512.

406 "tears in his eyes": PD, Sept. 15, 1944, 1444.

407 "At a conference": PD, Sept. 15, 1944, 1540–41.

408 "bitter hatred": Eden Notebook, Sept. 15, 1944, AP/20/3/8, Lord Avon Papers, Birmingham University, England; David Dutton, *Anthony Eden: A Life and a Reputation* (London: Arnold, 1997), 171–72.

408 "Morgenthau's interference": PRO, Foreign Office document, J. M. Trontbeck, 15 Nov. 1944 Minutes; Anthony Eden, hand notes on Nov. 19, 1944.

409 "I have yet to meet": Stimson Diary, Sept. 16–17, 1944.

409 "unbelievably good": MD, 772: Sept. 19, 1944, 10 A.M.; 153–63.

410 "whole development": Cordell Hull, The *Memoirs of Cordell Hull,* vol. 2 (New York: Macmillan, 1948), 1614–15; Stimson Diary, Sept. 20, 1944; McCloy Memorandum, Sept. 20, 1944, 6 pp. in Stimson Diary.

410 "a breath of fresh air": MD, 773, Sept. 20, 1944.

37. "For 48 Hours, I Was on the Top of the Heap," Fall 1944

411 "I don't think": Joseph P. Lash, *Eleanor and Franklin: The Story of Their Relationship, Based on Eleanor Roosevelt's Private Papers* (New York: W. W. Norton, 1971), 709.

411 "devoted entirely": PD, Sept. 23, 1944, 1456.

412 "blew up": Drew Pearson, "The Washington Merry-Go-Round," *Washington Post,* Sept. 21, 1944, 9.

412 "the wear and tear": Ickes Diary, Sept. 22, 1944.

412 "always the difficult ones": PD, Sept. 7, 1944, 1430.

413 "taking advantage": Ickes Diary, Sept. 22, 1944, LC.

414 "Throughout the war": Stimson and Bundy, *On Active Service,* 581–82.

414 "For 48 hours": MD, 772, Sept. 19, 1944.

414 "whose qualifications as an expert": Hal Foust, "Dewey Assails FDR Rein on Foreign Policy," *Chicago Tribune,* Oct. 19, 1944, 1.

415 "it hardly matters": Goebbels, *Das Reich*, Oct. 21, 1944, cited in Wallace Carroll, *Persuade or Perish* (New York: Houghton Mifflin, 1948), 324. It was not the first time that the Nazis had seized on the American "Jewish" hunger for revenge: In 1941, a thirty-one-year-old owner of a theater ticket agency in Newark, New Jersey, had called for sterilizing 48 million male Germans. Theodore N. Kaufman's self-published tract, *Germany Must Perish!,* quickly reached Berlin: "This Jew did a real service for the enemy side," Goebbels wrote of Kaufman. "Had he written this book for us, he could not have made it any better," in Peter Longerich, *Goebbels: A Biography,* trans. Alan Bance, Jeremy Noakes, and Lesley Sharpe (New York: Random House, 2015), 491.

415 "was made to order": Albert Speer, *Inside the Third Reich,* trans. Richard and Clara Winston (New York: Simon & Schuster, 1970), 549.

415 "extremely cruel": MP, unsigned memo, Nov. 14, 1944.

415 grueling all-day tour: Ross T. McIntire, "Unconquerable Spirit," *Collier's,* Feb. 2, 1946, 21.

416 "even the pretense": "FDR Urges Action on World Plan," *Brooklyn Eagle,* Oct. 21, 1944, 1; C. P. Trussell, "President Defies Rain, Wind, to Let New York See Him," *NYT,* Oct. 22, 1944, 1.

416 **all but bribed Churchill:** Arthur Krock, "British Ask More on Lease with the Right of Resale," *NYT,* Nov. 3, 1944, 1; MD, Nov. 3, 1944.

417 **At 8:15:** PD, Nov. 4, 1944.

417 **"so clumsy":** "Text of Address by Gov. Dewey at Rally Here," *NYT,* Nov. 5, 1944, 42.

418 **"a cobalt blue":** A. Merriman Smith, *Thank You, Mr. President: A White House Notebook* (New York: Harper, 1946), 158.

419 **"on the day":** MD, Nov. 3, 1944.

38. In the Pacific: "Undivided Attention," Summer 1944–Spring 1945

421 **Richard C. Williams, Jr.:** "R.C. Williams, Pacific Hero, Is Retired As Rear Admiral," *Baltimore Sun,* Nov. 17, 1952, 21.

423 **"speed, maneuverability":** Shafter, *Destroyers in Action,* 5.

423 **"visual communication":** "War Diaries," USS *Bauer,* 65; "Report on Capture of Okinawa Gunto, Phases I & II, 25 March to 11 June 1945," June 12, 1945; U.S. Navy Documents.

424 **assign the messmen:** Among the Black sailors who manned the guns of the *Bauer:* Willie A. Lee, Blackstone, Va.; Ellis E. Winston, Morganville, Ky.; and Charles W. Mitchell, Mobile, Ala. A news photograph of the three men appeared in the *Chicago Bee,* Nov. 4, 1945, 6.

425 **"picket duty":** Robin L. Rielly, *Kamikazes, Corsairs, and Picket Ships: Okinawa, 1945* (Drexel Hill, Pa.: Casemate Publishers, 2010), 5. "The ring was designed to cover the Japanese planes' most likely approaches: each station spaced so that sightings could be passed from one radar picket to another without losing contact, enhancing the fighter direction."

425 **1,465 suicide aircraft:** Rielly, *Kamikazes,* 10, 351–53.

426 **548,000 troops:** Max Kennedy, *Danger's Hour: The Story of the USS* Bunker Hill *and the Kamikaze Pilot Who Crippled Her* (New York: Simon & Schuster, 2009), 198.

426 **At 4:06:** Roy E. Appleman, et al., *The U.S. Army in World War II.* War in the Pacific series. *Okinawa: The Last Battle* (Washington, D.C.: Office of the Chief of Military History, Department of the Army, 1948), 69.

426 **"only a short warning":** "Report on Capture of Okinawa Gunto, Phases I & II, 25 March to 11 June 1945," June 12, 1945, 5.

426 **"hair-trigger gun crews":** Rielly, *Kamikazes,* 10.

427 **355 Japanese planes:** Appleman, *Okinawa,* 69; Max Kennedy, *Danger's Hour,* 201.

428 **"very tired":** HM2 letters to sons, HM3 Papers.

428 **"eyes, gray with fatigue":** Herbert Feis, *1933: Characters in Crisis* (Boston: Little, Brown, 1966), 95.

428 **"the President wouldn't last":** Truman to aides, interviews, 1954, HSTL.

428 **"unconditional surrender":** FDR speech, March 1, 1945.

429 **"I think he must've ad-libbed":** HM2 to RMM and HM3, March 9, 1945, HM3 Papers.

429 **"a bundle of energy":** HM2, "Fate of Reich Turned into a Campaign Issue," *N.Y. Post,* Nov. 27, 1944.

429 **"interim directive":** "Directive to SCAEF Regarding the Military Government of Germany in the Period Immediately Following the Cessation of Organized Resistance (Post-Defeat)," Sept. 22, 1944, FRUS, Yalta, 143–54.

429 **"a clear statement":** "Fate of Reich Turned Into a Campaign Issue," *N.Y. Post,* Nov. 29, 1944.

430 **"I can't tell you":** John D. Hickerson Oral History, 1972, HSTL.

430 **"the best":** MD, Nov. 27, 1944.

431 **"hopelessly incompetent":** Maj. William E. Hurlbert, member of the Jacksonville

(Fla.) police force since 1922, who became the Military Government Officer of Aachen; Sgt. Mack Morriss, "How We Govern Our First Captured German City," *Yank: The Army Weekly,* Dec. 15, 1944, 1–5.

431 "to keep me": MD, 830, 37.

431 "supervise lower-down wages": MD, 804, 13–28.

431 "Let them have soup kitchens!": MD, 830, 35.

432 "It's getting lonesomer": MD, 804, 13–28.

432 "They had whipped something": MD, 832, 40–43.

433 "O.K. F.D.R.": MD, 831, 185–90.

433 "one of the most important": MD, 831, 205–224.

433 " 'pastoral Germany' ": Stimson Diary, March 29, 1945.

434 "You think it has worked out": MD, 832, 40–43.

39. "Henry, I Am with You 100 Percent," April 1945

435 "Then I come back": HM2 to RMM & HM3, March 29, 1945, HM3 Papers.

435 "You are probably not aware": Gertrude Leiner to Morgenthau, n.d., "Vacation—Daytona Beach, Florida," MP; Leiner biographical details: 1940 Census.

436 "similar symptoms": Irving Lehman, at 69, died of a heart ailment in 1945; Author interview: HM3.

436 hysterectomy: HM to FDR, May 25, 1943, MD.

436 "They say she will": PD, 1235.

436 "We do hope": MD, July 28, 1943.

436 On Thanksgiving Day: Hopkins, Nov. 24, 1944, MD, FDRL.

437 and telegraphed Henry: FDR to HM2, telegram, April 9, 1945, FDRL.

437 "You must just rest": ER to EFM, April 5, 1945, FDRL.

438 Why not add more mothers: MD, April 10, 1945, Book 835, 184E–184F.

438 "Why a book": PD, 1498.

438 "The plan": FDR–HM2, March 28, 1945; PD.

439 "organically wrong": Admiral Ross T. McIntire, with George Creel, *White House Physician* (New York: Putnam, 1946), 204.

439 "I had a helluva pain!": Jan K. Herman interview with Dr. Howard G. Bruenn, Historian, Bureau of Medicine and Surgery, Riverdale, N.Y., Jan. 31, 1990.

440 Esperancilla: Irineo Esperancilla, "I Served Four Presidents," as told to Eugene Gonda, *Look,* Oct. 27, 1959.

441 They had sat: Geoffrey C. Ward, ed., *Closest Companion: The Unknown Story of the Intimate Friendship Between Franklin Roosevelt and Margaret Suckley* (New York: Houghton Mifflin, 1995), 414.

441 "He should gain weight": ER to Maud Gray, April 1, 1945; Lash, *A World of Love,* 179.

441 "probably resign": Ward, *Closest Companion,* 412.

442 Henry entered the Little White House: PD, 1499–1503; HM2 to RMM, HM3, April 13, 1945, HM3 Papers.

443 preoccupied with Lucy: HM2 would never divulge the secret about Lucy Mercer Rutherfurd. Arthur M. Schlesinger, Jr., in his memoirs recounts the following exchange: In 1947, Schlesinger asked him, "Who were the ladies?" HM2 named FDR's cousins and Mme. Shoumatoff. Remembering a rumor, Schlesinger also asked, "Was Mrs. Rutherfurd one of the ladies?" "I don't think I have ever said anything with such an immediate impact. The color drained from Morgenthau's face, and he said in a strangled voice something like, 'I told Eleanor she shouldn't try to hide it.' " Schlesinger, *A Life in the 20th Century,* 430.

445 **"gained back"**: McIntire, *White House Physician,* 240–41.

445 **morning mail:** Frances Burns, "Doctor Told F.D. He Would Have OPA Inspect Him and Make Him Slow Down from 65 to 25 Miles An Hour," *Boston Globe,* April 11, 1946, 1, 3.

446 **"a bolt of lightning"**: Smith, *Thank You, Mr. President,* 183.

446 **she'd already called:** Phineas J. Biron, "Strictly Confidential," *Jewish Post,* May 4, 1945, 15.

40. Trouble with Harry, Spring 1945

447 **"had lost his sponsor"**: Blum, vol. 3, 420.

447 **"I want every one"**: PD, April 12, 1945, 1547.

447 **"Mr. Truman"**: PD, April 14, 1945, 1548.

449 **"readjusting is not"**: ER to EFM, April 16, 1945; Lash, *A World of Love,* 186.

451 **"Some of my own sons"**: ER, "My Day," May 9, 1945.

452 **"and Churchill, Stalin and I"**: PD, May 4, 1945, 1579.

452 **"I'm not going"**: MD, May 29, 1945, 850, 45–46.

452 **"I realize you don't"**: PD, May 2, 4, 9, 1945, 1580–81.

452 **He taped the president:** PD, May 10, 1945, 10:09 A.M., 1599.

453 **"plan for rehabilitation"**: *Off the Record: The Private Papers of Harry S. Truman,* ed. Robert H. Farrell (Columbia: University of Missouri Press, 1997), 25.

453 **"This is a big day"**: MD, May 10, 1945, 846:18.

41. In the Pacific: "A Quiet Station," Spring–Summer 1945

454 *O'Bannon:* The medical officer, Lt. Malcolm M. Dunham of Raritan, N.J., was a veteran of Guadalcanal, where he had treated scores of the wounded, and told a fellow officer that being on the *San Francisco* after the battle "was like walking through a death chamber." John F. Wukovits, *Tin Can Titans: The Heroic Men and Ships of World War II's Most Decorated Navy Destroyer Squadron* (Boston: Da Capo, 2017), 66–67.

455 **largest raid yet:** U.S. Navy Documents, May 1, 1945 report, Commanding Officer to Commander, Amphibious Force, Pacific Fleet, "Observations made during air attack 29 April 1945," 77; "Report on Capture of Okinawa Gunto, Phases I & II, 25 March to 11 June 1945," June 12, 1945, 2.

455 **Overhead, the lookouts:** DM26 War Diaries, U.S. Navy press release, Aug. 3, 1945.

455 **the Lilly:** DM26, Action Reports, "Enclosure B, Secret ltr.," May 1, 1945, "Observations made during air attack 29 April, 1945", 77–79; DM26, War Diary, 29 April 1945, U.S. Navy Documents; U.S. Navy press release, August 3, 1945, "USS Harry F. Bauer Fights Off Kamikaze Attack," 3 pp.; "U.S. Minelayer Beat Off Four Suicide Plane Attacks," *N.Y. Herald Tribune,* Aug. 4, 1945, 2.

456 **picket station #5:** U.S. Navy Documents, File No.: DM26/A16-3/ajs, "Observations made during air attack 11 May 1945," 81–93.

456 **ten men:** Rielly, *Kamikazes,* 267.

457 **"bounced off"**: Map by J. F. Orren, Radioman 3rd Class; correspondence with Alex Weinberg.

457 **None of the *Bauer*'s crew:** USS *Harry F. Bauer* (DM26), Serial 006, "Report of Capture of Okinawa Gunto, Phases I and II, 25 March to 11 June 1945, 12 June 1945," 38.

457 **"flycatcher patrol"**: Rielly, *Kamikazes,* 289; latitude 26-03.9 N, longitude 127-50.5 E.

457 **At dawn on June 6:** Action Report, War Diaries, Ship Logs, June 6, 1945, U.S. Navy Documents.

458 **Three threads:** Richard J. O'Keefe, "Death Lurks Underfoot: Ship Held Unexploded Jap Bomb 17 Days After Battle," *Philadelphia Inquirer,* June 30, 1945.

42. Big Man Falling, Spring–Summer 1945

460 "My motives": MD, 848, 207–208.

461 "to see my son": PD, 1601.

461 **Emboldened, on June 13:** PD, 1659–60.

462 "We must get over fear": "Mrs. Roosevelt Accepts Medal, Then Speaks Out Against Fear," *Poughkeepsie Journal,* June 15, 1945, 1.

462 "how lonesome": PD, 1650–52.

463 "to make a little speech": PD, 1666–68.

464 "my able and conniving": Truman Diary, July 7, 1945, HSTL.

464 "we were pretty near ready": Stimson Diary, July 3, 1945.

464 "encroaching on his ground": Stimson Diary, July 4, 1945.

465 "Look, Mr. President": PD, 1673–74.

467 "I just thought": MD, July 5, 1945, 862: 53–55.

467 "My dear sons": HM2 to RMM and HM3, July 16, 1945, MP.

467 "I'm not going": MD, July 6, 1945, 862: 119–20.

467 "broke their long friendship": Samuel Irving Rosenman, with Dorothy Reuben Rosenman, *Presidential Style: Some Giants and a Pygmy in the White House* (New York: Harper & Row, 1976), 449.

468 "not very complimentary": PD, 1666.

469 "Morgenthau didn't know": Martin Weil, *A Pretty Good Club: The Founding Fathers of the U.S. Foreign Service* (New York: W. W. Norton, 1978), 224.

469 "block head": Truman to Jonathan Daniels, Feb. 26, 1950, in *Off The Record: The Private Papers of Harry S. Truman,* ed. Robert H. Ferrell (Columbia: University of Missouri Press, 1997), 174.

43. Home Is the Sailor, Fall 1945–Winter 1946

472 **September 2, 1945:** U.S. Navy Documents: War Diary, September 2,1945.

472 **On September 24:** "USS Laws Back from 20 Months Fight in the Pacific," *Seattle Times,* Oct. 14, 1945.

473 "After my father": Author interview: JMH.

474 **at a B'nai B'rith gala:** "To Honor Morgenthau," *NYT,* Oct. 26, 1945, 17; "Morgenthau Asks Aid for Homeless," *NYT,* Nov. 8, 1945, 3.

475 "released to inactive duty": Nov. 26, 1945; RMM FBI File.

476 **birthday interviews:** "Morgenthau, at 90, Optimist on Future," *NYT,* April 26, 1946, 23; "Good Cheer at 90," *NYT,* April 27, 1946, 16.

476 **a half-page portrait:** S. J. Woolf, "Morgenthau, 80, Sees Democracy Safe," *NYT,* April 26, 1936, SM5.

477 **On a Monday night in November:** On HM's final days and funeral: "Elder Morgenthau Urges Finish Fight," *NYT,* April 25, 1943, 14; "Nazi Fate Forecast by Morgenthau Sr.," *NYT,* Jan. 9, 1944, 29; "Morgenthau Sr. Sees Post-War Prosperity," *NYT,* April 26, 1944, 14; "Observing His Eighty-Eighth Birthday," *NYT,* April 27, 1944, 27; "Morgenthau Sr., 89, Sees Lasting Peace," *NYT,* April 25, 1945, 25; "Henry Morgenthau Is 89," *NYT,* April 27, 1945, 17; "Morgenthau, at 90, Optimist on Future," *NYT,* April 26, 1946, 23; "Topics of the *Times,*" *NYT,* April 27, 1946, 16; S. J. Woolf, "How to Live to 90—and Make It Worth While," *NYT,* April 28, 1946, SM20; "H. Morgenthau Sr. Dies in Home at 90," *NYT,* Nov. 26, 1946, 18; Editorial, "Henry Morgenthau Sr.," *NYT,* Nov. 26, 1946, 27; "Bearers Named for Morgenthau: Hull,

Einstein, Baruch Among Notables Listed—Messages from Truman, O'Dwyer," *NYT,* Nov. 27, 1946, 25; "Final Tribute Paid H. Morgenthau, Sr.," *NYT,* Nov. 28, 1946, 27; "Morgenthau Estate Left to 4 Children," *NYT,* Dec. 15, 1946, 26.

PART IV | THE SOVEREIGN DISTRICT

44. After the Fall, 1945–1948

483 **"When President Roosevelt":** HM2 to Henrietta Klotz, Aug. 5, 1945, 11 pp., HM3 Papers.

484 **Roosevelt Memorial Library:** April 12, 1947, Frank C. Walker Papers.

485 **"a workable source":** Allan Nevins to HM2, June 28, 1946, FDRL; Emile Despres to HM2, Jan. 30, 1946, April 25, 1946; author correspondence. The Nevins project was aborted. Instead, Nevins in 1948 established Columbia's Oral History Program, and opened the Morgenthau papers to his graduate students. One result: Allan Seymour Everest, *Morgenthau, the New Deal and Silver: A Story of Pressure Politics* (New York: Columbia University Press, 1950).

485 **"candid and honest":** Harold Faber, "Morgenthau Diary Gives 'Inside' Data," *NYT,* Dec. 31, 1946, 1; Snyder: Sidney Shalett, "Return 'Diary' to Treasury,' Snyder Asks Morgenthau," *NYT,* Jan. 27, 1947, 1.

485 **"Never had such a man":** "After Pepys," *Time,* Jan. 13, 1947, 27.

485 **"scrapbook":** Feb. 13, 1947, HM2 press release, 4 pp., Frank C. Walker Papers.

485 **"photostats":** Associated Press, "Morgenthau Answers Snyder," *NYT,* Jan. 27, 1947, 21; "Morgenthau Is Defended," *NYT,* Jan. 29, 1947, 22.

487 **Whittaker Chambers:** On September 2, 1939, the day after Hitler invaded Poland, Chambers had met with Adolph Berle, a State Department official. (Chambers had led a Soviet spy network in Washington in the 1930s that he called the "Ware Group," defecting in 1938.) During the meeting, Berle took notes; while the "Berle Notes" (evidence in the Hiss case, 1949–1950) include the names of Alger Hiss and minor officials in the Treasury and other agencies, Harry Dexter White's was not among them. Nor did White's name appear in two FBI interviews with Chambers. Not until 1945, after Yalta, is Chambers recorded having spoken of White: "Harry White of the Treasury was described as a member at large but rather timid," State Department investigator Ray Murphy wrote in an interview dated March 20, 1945. Chambers stated as well that White had "put on as assistants in the Treasury" men who were Party members. Chambers repeated the allegations in HUAC testimony in 1948 and in his 1952 memoir, *Witness.* On each occasion, he clarified that White was not a member of the Ware Group or the Party. Years would pass before Chambers gave the FBI any information on White (FBI documents, Nichols to Tolson, June 3, 1955, HM3 Papers); double life: While the scope and details of White's cooperation with the Soviet secret services remains in dispute among historians, of the more than three hundred individuals he did hire or recommend for government positions, several low- to mid-level Treasury bureaucrats were alleged to have participated in a Soviet spy ring: Solomon Adler, Frank Coe, Harold Glasser, Sonia Gold, William (Ludwig) Ullman, and, briefly, Nathan Gregory Silvermaster, considered the ringleader of the "Silvermaster Group." Of these six (named by Elizabeth Bentley and/or Chambers), none was prosecuted on espionage charges. Coe moved to China, where Adler joined him; Ullman and Silvermaster settled on the New Jersey shore, becoming local real estate barons.

488 **four sheets:** The notes Chambers attributed to White skated across a disparate array of topics, but offered a shorthand panorama of Treasury policy: "Jan. 10, 38. Taylor tried to press the Secretary (indirectly through Feis to Hull to Sec.) to hurriedly accept an offer from Hungary of settlement of her 2 million dollar debt to U.S. Govt. . . . Re-

ported yesterday through [indecipherable] Jap. banking connection (unknown but supposed to be important) that J. will not declare war on China for sometime at least. Sec. reading Red Star Over China and is quite interested . . . About a month ago, the Pres. asked Sec. M. to secretly place as many obstacles in the path of imports from Japan as possible under existing regulations . . . State Dept. believes British moves toward Italy and Germany will reduce substantially European fear of war in the near future. If Japan repeats another incident like the Panay incident Treasury machinery is all ready to embargo Japanese imports into U.S. & freeze her dollar resources. This was done at the Pres. wishes. It remains unknown outside of Treasury. Bullitt just cabled to Sec. (copy not available) comment by Herriot, Blum, Reynaud to him. Herriot says that if he were premier he would quickly strengthen ties to U.S.S.R. & reassure Czech. that France will at once come to her military aid if Germany enters Czech . . ."; James Reston, " 'Pumpkin Papers' Enter White Case," *NYT*, Nov. 11, 1953, 18; Whittaker Chambers, "The Herring and the Thing," *Look*, Nov. 29, 1953, 14–18; Alan Weinstein, *Perjury* (New York: Random House, 1978), 212–13; R. Bruce Craig, *Treasonable Doubt: The Harry Dexter White Spy Case* (Lawrence: University Press of Kansas, 2004), 48, 299–300. The FBI confirmed the handwriting as White's on Dec. 6, 1948. His motives: *Witness*, 431.

488 **Ten days later:** C. P. Trussell, "Currie and White Deny Under Oath They Aided Spies," *NYT*, Aug. 14, 1948, 1.

489 **"He put HUAC":** Craig, *Treasonable Doubt*, 6.

489 **"I believe":** "An American Creed," *New Republic*, Aug. 23, 1948, 7.

489 **heart attack:** United Press International, "Harry Dexter White, Accused in Spy Inquiry, Dies at 56," *Washington Post*, Aug. 18, 1948, 1.

489 **"White never did anything":** HM2 Oral History, with Joseph Wall, May 29, 1957, "Herbert H. Lehman Project," COHP.

489 **"I was shocked":** HM2 to Anne White, Aug. 18, 1948; "Two Treasury Chiefs Gave White Praise," *NYT*, Nov. 12, 1953, 20.

45. "No Sense of Proportion," 1946–1949

491 **Meyer Weisgal:** Klotz interview, Sept. 19, 1978, HM3 Papers; Recording of HM2 fundraising for Israel on behalf of the United Jewish Appeal on the program "VE Day Plus 350," April 23, 1946, NBC News Archives.

491 **United Jewish Appeal (UJA):** "Morgenthau Gets Jewish Fund Post," *NYT*, Jan. 3, 1947, 44.

492 **$170 million:** "United Jewish Appeal Sets Goal of $170,000,000 on Eve of Drive," *NYT*, Feb. 23, 1947, 1.

492 **revival:** HM2 announced nearly two dozen gifts, each more than $20,000—including $1 million from the heirs of Julius Rosenwald, the Sears, Roebuck magnate. Marc Lee Raphael, *A History of the United Jewish Appeal, 1939–1982*, Brown Judaic Studies, No. 34 (Scholars Press, 1982), 29.

493 **"Jesus Christ":** Wallace diary, July 30, 1946, quoted in *The Price of Vision: The Diary of Henry A. Wallace, 1942–1946*, ed. John Morton Blum (New York: Houghton Mifflin, 1973), 607.

493 **cursory meeting:** "Truman Hopeful on Admitting DP's," *NYT*, Jan. 12, 1948, 2; "145,000 DP's Aided; Morgenthau Lists Assistance Given Since Nazi Defeat," *NYT*, May 9, 1948, 5; "Morgenthau Cheered by Talk with Truman," *NYT*, July 8, 1948, 2.

494 **" 'We appear' ":** Truman to Eisenhower, Sept. 29, 1945, Truman Papers, HSTL.

494 **"Had ten minutes":** President Harry S. Truman's 1947 Diary Book, 1947 Diary and Manual of the Real Estate Board of New York, Inc. The page was marked "6:00 P.M. Monday July 21, 1947," and only discovered decades later; HSTL, President's Secretary's Files, Diaries Files, 1947–1953.

494 **"no sense of proportion"**: Ibid. Truman wrote more: "Henry brought a thousand Jews to New York on a supposedly temporary basis"—the refugees who were housed after the war behind barbed wire in the upstate hinterland of Oswego—"and they stayed." The Oswego case was a rare exception, but Truman blamed it for the rightward tilt in the 1946 elections—the Republicans had gained 55 seats, and the majority in Congress. "When the country went backward," he wrote, "and Republican in the election of 1946, this incident loomed large on the DP program."

495 **"I fear"**: Truman to ER, August 23, 1947, HSTL.

495 **"When they get on top"**: Truman to Jonathan Daniels, unsent Feb. 26, 1950, in *Off the Record: The Private Papers of Harry S. Truman,* ed. Robert H. Ferrell (Columbia: University of Missouri Press, 1997), 174.

495 **Goldie Meyerson**: Golda Meir, *My Life* (New York: Putnam, 1975); Menachem Meir, *My Mother Golda Meir: A Son's Evocation of Life with Golda Meir* (Westminster, Md.: Arbor House, 1983), 115–16; "Palestine Jews to Fight On, Leader Says," *Los Angeles Times,* Feb. 25, 1948, 5; Sam Pope Brewer, "Mrs. Myerson Due on Zionist Mission," *NYT,* Jan. 23, 1948, 13; Full-page advertisement in *NYT,* March 16, 1948, 56; Lucy Freeman, "Zion Envoy Urges Cash Aid at Once," *NYT,* Jan. 25, 1948, 11.

496 **yet they listened**: Meir, *My Life,* 214.

496 **"They fought"**: *NYT,* full-page advertisement: "After Seven Hours . . . ," March 16, 1948, 56.

496 **relief and resettlement**: HM2, UJA Papers, Box 5, FDRL.

496 **"tears began to roll"**: Henry Montor, Jeff Hodes interview, Oct. 14, 1975, Institute of Contemporary Jewry, the Hebrew University. Further on the Meyerson/Meir UJA fundraising trip in 1948: Montor, Menahem Kaufman interview, April 15, 1975; Harry Beale (June 27, 1975); Ralph Wechsler (March 28, 1976); Sam Feingold (March 19, 1976); Joe Mazer, William Mazer, Gottlieb Hammer, Mathilda Braelove (March 2, 1975), Institute of Contemporary Jewry, the Hebrew University.

497 **Henry was in Israel**: En route HM2 stopped to see Mrs. Roosevelt in Paris, where the General Assembly was convening; she was leading the drafting of the U.N. Declaration on Human Rights, but had grown exasperated. Ben-Gurion had invited her to Israel, but she declined. She must remain, she said, "an impartial observer." Eleanor proposed, instead, HM2 should take her eldest grandson, Curtis "Buzzie" Boettiger. Buzzie would assist the UJA party, helping Nathan Straus, Jr., who was recovering from retina surgery, with his bags, but be free to explore on his own. They flew from Paris in a secondhand DC-4. It was the first, and only, airplane of the new Israeli airlines, El Al. HM2, Buzzie, and Straus, owner of the WMCA radio station in New York and Macy's, sat in club chairs, without seatbelts, as the engines' din muffled the sounds of the chickens and goats behind them. In Haifa, the pilot executed a lights-out landing on a rough clearing. Author interview: Curtis Roosevelt, Nov. 13, 2014; Curtis Roosevelt, *Eyewitness in Israel: 1948* (Amazon e-book). Arab refugees: McDonald to ER, Oct. 29, 1948, in C. Roosevelt, *Eyewitness.*

497 **On his first trip**: "Morgenthau to Israel," *NYT,* Oct. 13, 1948, 2; "Jewish Colonies Man 'Burma Road,'" *NYT,* Oct. 25, 1948, 7; "Morgenthau Under Fire," *NYT,* Oct. 25, 1948, 3; "Mrs. Roosevelt Grandson Is at Front in Negeb: Curtis Boettiger, 19, Flies In with Morgenthau . . . ," *N.Y. Herald Tribune,* Oct. 21, 1948, 12; "Simchat Torah Celebrated Joyously in Israel; Ben Gurion, Morgenthau Dance in Street," Jewish Telegraphic Agency (JTA), Oct. 26, 1948; "Henry Morgenthau Returns from Israel," newsreel, Nov. 2, 1948.

497 **saved his life**: "How a U.S. Ambassador Saved a Future Prime Minister," *Canadian Jewish Review,* Nov. 26, 1948, 6; letter, Ben-Gurion and Ben-Zvi to Justice Brandeis, Aug. 31, 1916; Tom Segev, *A State at Any Cost: The Life of David Ben-Gurion* (New York: Farrar, Straus and Giroux, 2019), 129.

498 **"naïve, decent"**: Ben Gurion, *The War of Independence—Ben Gurion's Diary* (Tel Aviv: Ministry of Defense, 1982), Oct. 21, 1948, 757.

499 **ruins of an Arab village**: Prior to the war, the Arab village Khirbet Beit Far was home to several hundred people, shepherds and farmers and their families. Its original name, Tal-Boqer (*boqer* is Hebrew for "morning"), gave way to the more euphonic Tal Shahar, Dew of Dawn; Benny Morris, *The Birth of the Palestinian Refugee Problem Revisited* (Cambridge: Cambridge University Press, 2004), 376, 380; Morris correspondence.

499 **not only thrombosis**: EFM postmortem, New York Hospital, Dr. David P. Barr, Feb. 18, 1950, HM3 Papers; "Mrs. Henry Morgenthau Jr. Dies," *N.Y. Herald Tribune*, Sept. 22, 1949, 22.

499 **"Fluid in the abdomen"**: EFM suffered from Budd-Chiari syndrome, a rare disorder characterized by the occlusion of the veins of the liver. At the time of her mother's death, JMH was a fellow at New York Hospital; when the doctors revealed the autopsy report to the medical students, she made sure to attend.

500 **"She would have wanted"**: "Mrs. Roosevelt Praises Mrs. Morgenthau at Rites," *N.Y. Daily News*, Sept. 24, 49, 6; "Morgenthau Rites Held at Emanu-El," *NYT*, Sept. 24, 1949, 13.

46. "A Little Righteous Indignation," 1948–1952

501 **"such a quiet time"**: Author interviews: Louise Ransom, Jack Chester, Nicholas Katzenbach, Bayless Manning, Fred Nathan, Louis Oberdorfer, Robert Sweet; Navasky Papers, JFKL: Interviews with Lovell, Logue, Pittman; RMM FBI file.

502 **"always happily concluded"**: *Yale Reporter*, 1946 Supplement, 86.

503 **Byron White**: On White: Raymond G. Carey, "Byron R. White, Deputy U.S. Attorney General," *American Oxonian*, April 1961, 61–65.

504 **46th in a class of 80**: Fellow Yale Law students: Katzenbach, Burke Marshall, Oberdorfer, and two brothers from Oyster Bay: George Lindsay, Jr. (BA, Yale, '41) and John Vliet Lindsay, who joined RMM in the Law School Forum.

505 **Bob Patterson**: Robert P. Patterson, *Arming the Nation for War: Mobilization, Supply, and the American War Effort in World War II*, ed. Brian Waddell, foreword by RMM (Knoxville: University of Tennessee Press, 2014); Manfred Jonas, "Union Worthies, No. 21: Robert Porter Patterson," Union College, 1966, 5–14; RMM Speeches: 2007, 2012; Thomas J. Watson with Peter Petre, *Father, Son & Co: My Life at IBM and Beyond* (New York: Bantam Books, 1991), 233.

506 **"would never do more"**: Patterson, *Arming the Nation*, 89.

506 **"When I look"**: Patterson, *Arming the Nation*, 72.

507 **eight formidable partners**: Belknap had clerked for Oliver Wendell Holmes and, like Webb, had served with Patterson on the *Harvard Law Review*.

508 **most prominent lawyers**: Edwin Weisl of Simpson Thacher represented Lehman Brothers, the bankers. "Twentieth Century Fox Nearing Settlement," *Box Office*, June 12, 1948, 29; $4,281,000: "Decision Reserved on N.T. Settlement," *Box Office*, Aug. 4, 1948, 1.

508 **"Mr. Pollack"**: Ann Davis and Randall Smith, "Judge Pollack's Investor Lectures," *Wall Street Journal*, July 3, 2003, C1.

509 **"an example"**: "Lawyers Criticize Congress Inquiry," *NYT*, Sept. 30, 1948, 15.

509 **Dorothy Kenyon**: "Miss Kenyon Cites Patriotic Record to Refute Charges; Replies to Senator M'Carthy," *NYT*, March 15, 1950, 1.

509 **"Communist sympathizers"**: "Ex-Army Men Hit as 'Red' Backers," *NYT*, July 10, 1947, 13.

511 **Flight 6780**: "Plane Falls in Elizabeth," *NYT*, Jan. 23, 1952, 1; Henrietta: photograph and caption, *The Lock Haven* (Pa.) *Express*, Jan. 24, 1952, 9; "29 Die as Airliner Hits

2 Houses in Elizabeth, Ex-War Chief Patterson Among 23 Plane Victims," *Newark Star-Ledger,* Jan. 23, 1952, 1; wrists broken: Post by one of Reid's daughters on the Arlington Cemetery website, arlingtoncemetery.net/robertpo.htm.

511 **"public-spirited citizen":** Patterson, *Arming the Nation,* xvi.

47. "This Thing He Married," 1950–1955

512 **In October 1950:** Photograph # 611110, USHMM; Robert Capa, dir. "The Journey," USA, 1951, 22 min.; "Morgenthau—Trip to Israel," 9 mins., Brandeis Film Archive.

513 **rumors:** The archives of Soviet foreign intelligence, according to notes taken in the 1990s by Alexander Vassiliev, even contain a reference to the love child of a secret relationship; Allen Weinstein and Alexander Vassiliev, *The Haunted Wood: Soviet Espionage in America—the Stalin Era* (New York: Random House, 1999), 166. The report in question, dated June 23, 1945, is contained in Vassiliev's "White Notebook #3," and is recorded as having been sent from Iskhak Akhmerov (codenamed "Albert"), then the KGB *resident* in Washington, D.C. It reads in part, regarding Klotz: "She is an attractive, very intelligent, liberal-minded, but not very well-educated woman. She is married and has a 14 year-old daughter, whose real father—is the boss. This is, of course, a highly confidential, private matter." In interviews with the author, HM2's children called the report unfounded, as did Klotz's daughter, Elinor Walden. The Vassiliev notebooks can be found online (thanks to the historian John Earl Haynes) at the website of the Woodrow Wilson International Center for Scholars: https://digitalarchive.wilsoncenter.org/collection/86/vassiliev-notebooks. The report regarding Morgenthau (codenamed "Nabob") and Klotz ("Mora") is found on p. 22 of the Russian original and English translation.

513 **"Morgenthau to Wed":** Associated Press, "Morgenthau Takes Bride," Nov. 22, 1951; "Morgenthau to Wed Mrs. Hirsch This Week," *NYT,* Nov. 20, 1951, 47.

515 **He called FBI headquarters:** G. A. Nease to Hoover, Jan. 21, 1952: HM2 called, "would like to know definite evidence"; D. M. Ladd to Hoover, Jan. 24, 1955; Nichols to Tolson, June 1, 1955; Belmont to L.V. Boardman, June 2, 1955; Nichols to Tolson, June 3, 1955: "Although we interviewed Chambers in 1942, 1943, and 1945, he gave us no information on White until 1948"; Nichols to Tolson, June 7, 1955: anonymous call; Nichols to Tolson, July 6, 1955, re MD, FBI file, HM3 Papers. On the morning of Jan. 24, 1952, the FBI director was "busy." HM2 met with Mickey Ladd, an assistant director. He explained that this was not his first time trying to get to the facts. Not only had he consulted Tom Clark, Truman's first attorney general, but he had spoken with his successor, J. Howard McGrath. McGrath had read him, HM2 said, a memo that sounded like a condensation of Elizabeth Bentley's book. Ladd told HM2 that although he could not show him the documents, the FBI possessed evidence of White's guilt: the four pages in White's handwriting, summaries of department documents scrawled out on yellow-lined paper and dated January 10, 1938, which Chambers had turned over. Truman, too, Ladd said, had known of the allegations. "Information concerning Harry Dexter White," he said, "had been furnished to the White House on November 8, 1945, and on numerous occasions subsequent thereto." Before leaving, HM2 asked for a favor: He was worried about any bad apples among the relief corps he was running now. Could the FBI check "the names of employees" with UJA, to see if any were Communists? Out of the question, Ladd replied. The FBI was not in the business of vetting for private entities. HM2 did not give up. A special squad in the New York Police Department, he said, had once done such vetting for him, but a new man had taken charge and forbidden it. Perhaps the Bureau could recommend a retired agent? Someone in New York who could take over the job now? Again, the answer was no.

515 **"covert operation":** Curt Gentry, *J. Edgar Hoover*, 389.
515 **Now two Senate investigators:** "Morgenthau Due to Discuss Diary," *NYT*, Oct. 27, 1955, 15.
516 **"His attitude":** Nichols to Tolson, June 1, 1955, FBI file, HM3 Papers.
516 **"very happy note":** Newsreel, HM2 Testifies on Capitol Hill, Oct. 29, 1955.
517 **a photograph of the meeting:** C. P. Trussell, "Senators to Get Morgenthau Text," *NYT*, Oct. 29, 1955, 1.
518 **"consult closely":** Schlesinger to HM2, Dec. 28, 1953, Schlesinger Papers, NYPL.
518 **"a professor":** Blum–Schlesinger, May 6, 1954, Schlesinger Papers, NYPL.
519 **started with the sisters:** Alma Morgenthau divorced the banking scion Maurice Wertheim early, and had been remarried since the 1930s to Paul Weiner, a German-born architect, eight years her junior. She had followed her days of singing in New York and Europe to become a patron of the arts—founding the Cos Cob Press and publishing the music scores of modern American composers; she was Aaron Copland's first major American publisher. That winter one of her daughters, Barbara Wertheim Tuchman, a physician's wife and herself a mother of three girls, was at work on a first book of history. Alma, though, had died, at 66, after a long illness, on Christmas Day two years earlier. Helen Fox had cultivated her own world, become a well-known author of gardening books. Ruth, youngest of HM and JSM's daughters, had recently divorced her second husband, a businessman she had married within a year of her first divorce. Yet each of HM2's sisters, whether out of jealousy or disappointment, faced her own troubles. "My aunts," JMH would say, "were always fighting—two were always against one, and that wasn't always the same two. They were constantly warring with each other."
520 **"Henry Sr. and Henry Jr.":** Author interview: Blum.
520 **"any of the Jew boys":** Author interview: Blum; MM, 435; Stimson Diaries: An entry for July 4, 1945, regarding a phone conversation with Jimmy Byrnes, does state: "He incidentally told me that Henry Morgenthau was on the prowl and was going to turn up in Germany 'just on the chance that he might be needed.' Apparently, he had done this on his own. Byrnes and I laughed over it together." But a search of the diaries did not yield the Truman quote, as relayed by Blum.

48. "To Hell with It," 1959–1961

523 **Lochland:** Archibald MacLeish, the poet who had worked at the War Department during the war and become Librarian of Congress, had a sister who lived near the school. Ishbel MacLeish Campbell had long supported Lochland, and been the one who led the Morgenthaus there.
526 **American Veterans Committee:** Navasky interview with Dick Lovell, JFKL.
527 **"could not":** Clayton Knowles, "Kennedy Sets Up Citizen Unit Here," *NYT*, Aug. 20, 1960, 1.
527 **Citizens for Kennedy, he said:** Knowles, "Kennedy Sets Up Citizen Unit Here," 1.
528 **"my son Jack":** Anna Peterson, "Story of 'My Son Jack' Is Told by Kennedy's Mother in Bronx," *NYT*, Sept. 20, 1960, 35.
529 **On December 16:** Associated Press, "Bob Kennedy, Dillon Tapped; Final Cabinet Member May Be Named Today," *Toledo Blade*, Dec. 16, 1960, 1.
530 **"To hell":** "Recollections," RMM Papers.

49. "You Should Have Known Me When I Was Somebody," 1952–1967

532 **"any money":** "Morgenthau Ready to Give Up His Diary," *Los Angeles Times*, Jan. 28, 1947, 1.

50. Bobby and Bob, 1961–1964

539 **"the scene":** Milton S. Gould, *The Witness Who Spoke with God, and Other Tales from the Courthouse* (New York: Viking, 1979), 109.

539 **"The Mother Court":** Sonia Sotomayor, *My Beloved World* (New York: Knopf, 2013), 293.

539 **sworn in:** "Robert Morgenthau Made U.S. Attorney," *N.Y. Herald Tribune*, April 19, 1961, 12.

542 **"Morgenthau loved that":** Author interview: John Adams.

542 **Black prosecutors:** In 1967, when women comprised less than 5 percent of law school graduating classes, RMM also hired the first woman to serve as an attorney in the SDNY: Patricia Hynes, a Fordham Law alumna, who would later head the New York Bar Association.

543 *primus inter pares:* Stanley Penn, "Unlikely Crusader: Prosecutor Morgenthau Makes Mark in Fight Against Business Crime," *Wall Street Journal*, Nov. 29, 1968, 1.

51. "Our Thing," 1957–1963

545 **"The fellows":** RMM interview with Jean Stein, JFKL.

545 **"an inn of court":** Gould, *The Witness Who Spoke with God*, 131.

546 **"Very tactfully":** "Attorney General's Visit to New York City," redacted memo, C. A. (Courtney) Evans–Mr. (Alan) Belmont; 2 pp., June 15, 1961; FBI file, RMM Papers.

547 **Albert Anastasia:** "Anastasia Slain in a Hotel Here. Led Murder, Inc.," *NYT*, Oct. 26, 1957.

547 **"Is there any":** *Hearings Before the Select Committee on Improper Activities in the Labor or Management Field*, 85th Congress, Part 17 (Washington, D.C.: Government Printing Office, 1957), 6744.

548 **"hoodlums and racketeers":** RFK Statement, "Before the Subcommittee No. 5 of the House Committee on the Judiciary, in Support of Legislation to Curb Organized Crime," May 17, 1961.

548 **"baloney":** Ronald Kessler, *The Bureau: The Secret History of the FBI* (New York: St. Martin's, 2003), 113; Gentry, *J. Edgar Hoover*, 327.

548 **two feet:** Valachi File, FBI, FOIA.

549 **Saupp:** Valachi file, FBI, FOIA; Peter Maas, *The Valachi Papers* (New York: HarperCollins, 2003), 8; "Check-Thief Suspect Held," *Pittsburgh Post-Gazette*, March 1, 1957, 14.

549 **"some construction work":** Maas, *Valachi Papers*, 7.

550 **He would only talk:** Peter Maas, "Mafia: The Inside Story," *Saturday Evening Post*, Aug. 10, 1963, 19–25; RMM Recollections.

551 **"in the base of his skull":** Maas, *Valachi Papers*, 48–49; Valachi File, FBI, FOIA.

554 **" 'Causa Nostra' ":** Valachi File, SAC, NY–Director, FBI, Sept. 14, 1962, FBI, FOIA; Further, Flynn recorded an additional misunderstanding of an Italian phrase: "Concerning the various 'mobs' in the NY area, the subject then readily stated they were really 'families' or '*avugads*' "—perhaps a Bronx corruption of *avvocato*, Italian for "attorney"—"within the framework of 'Causa Nostra.' "

554 **"La Causa Nostra":** "FBI, La Causa Nostra, New York Office," Jan. 16, 1963, FBI, FOIA.

555 *The Real Thing:* Joseph Valachi Personal Papers, JFKL; Author interviews: William Geoghegan, Jack Rosenthal, Joe Mohbat.

555 **Miriam Ottenberg:** Miriam Ottenberg (*Washington Star* staff writer), "Ex-Mob Member Reveals Secret Society Ruling Nation's Crime," *St. Louis Post-Dispatch*, Aug. 4,

1963, 1; drafts in Ottenberg Papers, Wisconsin Historical Society; Maas: "Mafia: The Inside Story."

555 **"He must be crazy"**: Valachi File, FBI, FOIA.

555 **"conservatively speaking"**: RFK, "Statement to the Permanent Subcommittee on Investigations of the Senate Government Operations Committee," Sept. 25, 1963, Dept. of Justice.

52. "A Lehman Candidate," 1962

557 **Carlyle Hotel**: "Wagner & Kennedy Discuss New Haven and Urban Problems," *NYT,* Jan. 20, 1962, 2.

557 **"Wagner and Kennedy"**: Author interviews: Lou Harris.

558 **"Democrats Consider"**: Warren Weaver, Jr., "Democrats Consider Robert Morgenthau," *NYT,* Aug. 16, 1962, 1.

558 **"not a Bobby Kennedy move"**: Reich interview, Cary Reich Papers, 20 pp., n.d., Rockefeller Archive Center.

560 **"Right here"**: Leo Egan, "Morgenthau Bid Gains Momentum," *NYT,* Aug. 30, 1962, 25.

561 **cursed and yelled**: Philip J. Bigger, *Negotiator: The Life and Career of James B. Donovan* (Bethlehem, Pa.: Lehigh University Press, 2006), 120.

561 **"BOB AND FRANK"**: Luther F. Bliven, "Bob and Frank Slug It Out," *Syracuse Post-Standard,* Sept. 16, 1962, 1; Woodie Fitchette, "Democrats Nearly Riot at Convention," *Evening Press* (Binghamton, N.Y.), Sept. 18, 1962, 1.

561 **At 8:02 in the evening**: JFK Personal Papers, 962: KP138–KP144, JFKL.

562 **"Race for Governor"**: "Race for Governor," September 30, 1962, 11–11:30 P.M. Host: Allyn Edwards, Producer: Metropolitan Broadcasting TV over WNEW-TV, New York City; Brandeis University Library; Morse Communications Research Center Collection.

563 **"absolutely incredible"**: Robert D. Novak, *The Agony of the GOP, 1964* (New York: Macmillan, 1965), 81.

563 **"appeal to the youngsters"**: Bruce Biossat, "Rocky Expected to Win in N.Y.," Newspaper Enterprise Association (NEA), *Ames* (Iowa) *Daily News,* Nov. 1, 1962, 4.

564 **Hank Walter**: Author interview: Henry Walter.

564 **Pat Moynihan**: Daniel Patrick Moynihan Oral History interview, JFK #1, May 3, 1972, JFKL.

566 **"Mrs. Morgenthau Gives Interview"**: Katherine Harrington, "Mrs. Morgenthau Gives Interview in Her Charming Home in Riverdale," *Albany Knickerbocker,* Oct. 7, 1962, 8.

566 **"I'm terribly sorry"**: Ray Herman, "Mrs. Morgenthau Charms Listeners," *Buffalo Courier Express,* Oct. 12, 1962.

566 **read her husband's words**: Associated Press, "Mrs. Morgenthau, Rocky Campaign in Buffalo," *Democrat and Chronicle* (Rochester, N.Y.), Oct. 12, 1962, 2; James T. Lawless, "Wife Delivered Message: GOP Played Politics with Aides' Pay Hike, Morgenthau Charges," *Civil Service Leader,* Oct. 16, 1962, 1, 10.

567 **"unleashed"**: Ray Herman, "Mrs. Morgenthau Charms Listeners," *Buffalo Courier Express,* Oct. 12, 1962.

567 **"Fellow citizens"**: Oct. 11, 1962, JFKWHA-136-003, JFKL.

568 **"A candidate"**: Associated Press, "Morgenthau Gets Boost from JFK," *Democrat and Chronicle* (Rochester, N.Y.), Oct. 13, 1962, 3.

569 **"Jeszcze Polska"**: Joseph A. Loftus, "Kennedy Affirms Links to Poland," *NYT,* Oct. 14, 1962, 19.

570 **"well calculated"**: Gore Vidal, "The Best Man, 1968," *Esquire,* May 13, 2008.

570 **November 4:** Robert T. Gray, "Face-to-Face Exchange Climaxes NY Battle," Associated Press, Nov. 5, 1962; Associated Press, "White-Hot Exchange of Words Marks Rocky-Morgenthau," Nov. 5, 1962; Clayton Knowles, "Morgenthau Opens Drive; Hits Rockefeller's Record," *NYT,* Sept. 6, 1962, 1.

570 **"I'm going to move":** Associated Press, "Rockefeller, Morgenthau Nearly Meet at Luncheon," Nov. 1, 1962.

571 **"They were very":** Reich interview, Cary Reich Papers, 20 pp., n.d., Rockefeller Archive Center.

53. "White Whale," 1962–1964

573 **"a great white mountain":** HM3, "Mrs. Roosevelt—the Last Visit," HM3 Papers.

576 **"an instinctive hatred":** Liman interview, Navasky Papers, JFKL.

576 **"I saw":** William O. Douglas to Felix Frankfurter (Dec. 8, 1933), Douglas Papers, LC.

578 **Albert Cohn:** There was even a family tie: Governor Lehman, RMM's great-uncle, had named Al Cohn to the Appellate Division, and the governor, along with his brother, Chief Judge Irving Lehman, had loyally come to his rescue more than once.

578 **"A little kingmaker":** Keith Wheeler and William Lambert, "Roy Cohn: Is He a Liar Under Oath?," *Life,* Oct. 4, 1963, 24–30, 99–102.

579 **Alexander Guterma:** Wheeler and Lambert, "Roy Cohn," 24–30, 99–102.

584 **"Biggest crowd":** Milton Lewis, "Back on the Attack—Roy Cohn," *N.Y. Herald Tribune,* Sept. 6, 1963.

584 **"caught up":** Wheeler and Lambert, "Roy Cohn."

585 **"an official vendetta":** Edward Ranzal, "Roy Cohn Indicted by US as Perjurer in Stock Case," *NYT,* Sept. 5, 1963, 1; Norma Abrams and Henry Lee, "A Victim of Plot, Cohn Insists as He Loudly Pleads Not Guilty," N.Y. *Daily News,* Sept. 4, 1963, 4.

585 **"wanted to try":** Wheeler and Lambert, "Roy Cohn."

585 **The U.S. attorney was retaliating:** United Press International, "Cohn Calls Self Vengeance Target," *Detroit Free Press,* Sept. 6, 1963, 12B.

587 **"But Roy insisted":** Ken Auletta, *Hard Feelings: Reporting on the Pols, the Press, the People and the City* (New York: Random House, 1980), 109.

587 **"I've got to dismiss":** Author interview: Gerald Walpin; Cohn FBI File.

588 **"good progress":** Associated Press, "Father of Juror Dies, Declare Mistrial in Cohn's Trial," *Indiana Gazette,* April 20, 1964; Homer Bigart, "Cohn Mistrial Is Declared," *NYT,* April 20, 1964, 1.

588 **"I thank God":** "Jury Acquits Roy Cohn in Perjury Case," *Chicago Tribune,* June 17, 1964, 3.

589 **"700 persons":** Stanley Penn, "Unlikely Crusader: Prosecutor Morgenthau Makes Mark in Fight Against Business Crime," *Wall Street Journal,* Nov. 29, 1968, 1.

589 *"Nouveau riche parvenu":* Cohn to Navasky, Dec. 10, 1968, Navasky Papers, JFKL.

589 **"A man is not immune":** William Lambert, "The Hotshot One-Man Roy Cohn Lobby," *Life,* Sept. 5, 1969, 26–32.

54. After Dallas, 1964

590 **thirty-eighth birthday:** Author interview: Ramsey Clark; Evan Thomas, *Robert Kennedy: His Life* (New York: Simon & Schuster, 2002), 275.

590 **"melancholic":** Author interview: Ramsey Clark.

591 **"It was a good meeting":** Bill Davidson, "A Profile in Family Courage," *Saturday Evening Post,* Dec. 14, 1963, 32b–d.

591 **cuff links:** Author interviews: Ramsey Clark, William Geoghegan, Herbert (Jack) Miller, Jack Rosenthal.

592 **clam chowder:** On Hickory Hill events: William Manchester interview with RMM, June 1, 1964, handwritten notes and typewritten version, Wesleyan University Archives; Davidson, "A Profile in Family Courage," 32b–d; James A. Wechsler, "RFK's Ordeal," *N.Y. Post,* Dec. 3, 1963, 34; Jean Stein interviews with RMM, Nov. 21, 1969, April 20, 1970, Stein Papers, JFKL.

593 **Christmas party:** Peter Maas, "What Will RFK Do Next?," *Saturday Evening Post,* March 28, 1964, 17–21.

594 **"cater to":** Charles Grutzner, "Mafia Steps Up Infiltration and Looting of Businesses," *NYT,* Feb. 14, 1965, 1.

596 **Lucchese pleaded the Fifth:** Edward Ranzal, "Robert Kennedy Briefed on Mafia by Morgenthau," *NYT,* Feb. 14, 1964, 1.

597 **"how difficult it was":** Jean Stein interviews with RMM, Stein Papers, JFKL.

597 **The two saw each other often:** Thomas, *Robert Kennedy: His Life,* 283.

55. The Junkman, 1966–1968

599 *U.S. v. Simon:* The defendants were Carl Simon and Robert Kaiser, partners in the Lybrand firm, and a senior accountant, Melvin Fishman, SDNY report, 1967–69; RMM Recollections. Judge Henry J. Friendly, Court of Appeals, the Second Circuit's opinion: "The footnote in the annual report disclosed just enough to arguably comply with the accounting rules but left out information crucial to understanding what had truly happened." "The jury," Judge Friendly wrote, "could reasonably have wondered how accountants who were really seeking to tell the truth could have constructed a footnote so well designed to conceal the shocking facts."

600 **"accepted accounting principles":** *U.S. v. Simon* was "a thin case," Morgenthau would concede, "but I prosecuted them because they were guilty. . . . We pressed for jail sentences not out of sadism, but because we believed that the defendants should experience prison, even if only for 10 days," to give warning to an industry "shot through with self-delusion." In the end, no one went to jail, the biggest fine levied was $7,000, and in one of his first acts as president, Richard Nixon pardoned the convicted; David M. Dorsen, *Henry Friendly, Greatest Judge of His Era* (Cambridge, Mass.: Belknap Press of Harvard University Press, 2012), 239.

600 **"In our complex society":** *U.S. v. Benjamin,* 328 F.2d 854 (1964), 863; cf. Dorsen, *Henry Friendly,* 236–39.

600 **"most spectacular corporate raider":** Leslie Gould, *The Manipulators* (New York: D. McKay & Co., 1966), 1; Leslie Gould, "Wolfson, 'Til Now, Had Charmed Life," *Orlando Sentinel,* Sept. 25, 1966, 8B; William Lambert, "Fortas of the Supreme Court: A Question of Ethics," *Life,* May 9, 1969, 32–37; William Lambert, "The End of the Fortas Affair," *Life,* May 23, 1969, 38–39.

601 **"Wolfson had immunity":** Wechsler interview, Navasky Papers, JFKL.

602 **"worth far more":** Robert Sobel, *Dangerous Dreamers: The Financial Innovators from Charles Merrill to Michael Milken* (New York: John Wiley & Sons, 1993), 14.

602 **"ingesting":** Arthur Liman, *Lawyer: A Life of Counsel and Controversy* (New York: PublicAffairs, 1998), 86.

602 **a $25,000 bribe:** Two engineers were involved: David R. Knapp worked for the federal Maritime Commission, and Fred Weber for Wolfson's Florida Pipe and Supply Company; Frederick C. Othman, "Once Upon a Time, 2 Fellows. . . . ," *The Republic* (Columbus, Ind.), June 27, 1947.

602 **"It came by accident":** Author interview: Stuart Allen.

603 **two front-page cases:** On Wolfson investigation and trials, author interviews: Michael Armstrong, Justin Feldman, Paul Grand, William Haddad, Nicholas Katzenbach, Robert Morvillo, Jack Rosenthal.

603 **"not peanuts":** Gould, "Wolfson, 'Til Now, Had Charmed Life," 30.
603 **During the investigation:** Richard Henry, "Four Plead Guilty in Parking-Meter Bribe," N.Y. *Daily News,* Nov. 11, 1964, 2.

56. "Joe Bananas," 1964–1985

609 **"JOE BANANAS":** Tom Robbins, "Joe Bananas, You Don't Find 'Em Alive Anymore," N.Y. *Daily News,* Nov. 21, 1999, 31.
611 **"Bill was raised":** Author interview: Gay Talese.
612 **bullets flew:** Charles Grutzner, "Gun Fight Leaves Police Puzzled," *NYT,* Feb. 1, 1966, 36.
612 **delivered the most wanted man:** Author interviews: Albert J. Krieger, Gay Talese.
613 **"It was as if the government":** Gay Talese, *Honor Thy Father* (New York: Harper Perennial, 2009), 168; on Bonanno's reappearance: *Honor Thy Father,* 166–180; Edward Ranzal, "Bonanno Gives Himself Up After 19 Months in Hiding," *NYT,* May 18, 1966, 1.

57. Amid Darkness, "Sunlight," 1967–1970

618 **Bill Barry:** Author interviews with Barry: July 16, 2008, April 21, 2009.
619 **In the studio:** Jean Stein interviews with RMM, Nov. 21, 1969, April 20, 1970, JFKL.
619 **"what happened":** Jean Stein interviews with RMM, Nov. 21, 1969, April 20, 1970, Stein Papers, JFKL.
622 **"490 million gallons":** Associated Press, "Drought Lessons Hold in East," March 31, 1967; American Water Works Association, *Percolation and Runoff* 59, no. 4 (April 1967): 38.
623 **"always had a suntan":** Walter Goodman, *A Percentage of the Take* (New York: Farrar, Straus and Giroux, 1971), 12.
624 **Mario Brod:** An NYU law graduate, Brod had served in U.S. military intelligence in Sicily during WWII, and briefly afterward for the U.S. Treasury in Rome. Itkin met Brod in 1962, when Itkin rented space in a Madison Avenue office shared with several other lawyers. Two Morgenthau AUSAs interviewed Brod and learned that he worked for the CIA, but not the extent of the history: James Angleton himself had recruited Brod for the OSS in Italy in 1944, and relied on him as a top source on organized crime in New York. When Morgenthau threatened to subpoena Brod as a grand jury witness, the CIA objected. The CIA's general counsel, Lawrence Houston, wrote to the Agency director, Richard Helms, after a meeting with Morgenthau: "We, of course, do not want to expose" Brod.
625 **"I wouldn't do that":** Goodman, *A Percentage of the Take,* 214.
625 **"I tried":** Warren Moscow, *The Last of the Big-Time Bosses* (New York: Stein and Day, 1971), 214.
626 **"promised a nasty":** Peter Maas, "Nixon v. the City's Top Crimefighter," *New York,* June 30, 1969, 24–27.
628 **a round-trip ticket:** Author interview: Stuart Allen; FBI, FOIA, Fortas File, 625 pp.; Robert Shogan, *A Question of Judgment: The Fortas Case and the Struggle for the Supreme Court* (Indianapolis: Bobbs-Merrill, 1972), 210; Lambert, "Fortas of the Supreme Court," 32–37; Lambert, "The End of the Fortas Affair," 38–39; John P. MacKenzie, "Fortas Letters Seized," *Washington Post,* May 17, 1969, 1; Martin Waldron, "Wolfson Recalls Hiring of Fortas," *NYT,* March 4, 1970, 17; Bob Woodward, "Fortas Tie to Wolfson Is Detailed," *Washington Post,* Jan. 23, 1977, 1.
631 **"hit as a shock":** Author interview: Ramsey Clark.
631 **"integrated housing":** Shogan, *A Question of Judgment,* 218.

631 **"I paid":** Ramsey Clark Oral History, Interview 5, June 3, 1969, by Harri Baker, LBJ Library.

632 **"as close as anybody":** Stanley Penn, "Wolfson's World: Industrialist, Facing a Year in Jail Friday, Turns Cold Shoulder Toward Wall Street," *Wall Street Journal*, April 22, 1969, 40.

632 **Bill Moyers:** Author interview: Walter Slocombe; Slocombe Memorandum.

632 **"Wolfson not only confirmed":** Lambert, "The End of the Fortas Affair," 38–39.

58. "Sinewy Fingers," 1969

638 **In January 1969:** Edward Ranzal, "Cohn Is Indicted in Bribery Case," *NYT*, Jan. 18, 1969, 1.

638 **"they are more like hunters":** Lesley Oelsner, "Cohn Bids Judge Give Up His Case," *NYT*, Sept. 23, 1969, 36.

638 **although one inmate:** The inmate, Milton "Mannie" Pollack, met with Morgenthau assistants from 1966 to 1968. Affidavits by Charles Stillman and Peter Fleming; Navasky Papers, JFKL.

639 **after only three hours:** Cohn Oral History, JFKL.

640 **"a whole bouquet":** In his last months as U.S. attorney, RMM expanded his jurisdiction to Capitol Hill, prosecuting two associates (Nathan Voloshen and Martin Sweig) of the Speaker of the House, John W. McCormack, for influence-peddling and perjury. Asked to explain the extent of the goings-on in his own office, the Speaker said, "I am not an inquiring fellow."

640 **"sinewy fingers":** Jack Anderson, "Anderson Merry-Go-Round," *Sacramento Bee*, Jan. 7, 1970, 19.

640 **"unprepossessing pink brick":** "Hidden Key Biscayne . . . ," *Cincinnati Enquirer*, Nov. 28, 1970, 10a.

640 **$515,850:** Jim Malone, "Nixon Has $400,000 Worth of Dade Island," *Miami Herald*, Oct. 10, 1968, 1.

642 **"We even find":** RMM "Remarks" (23 pp.), National Industrial Conference Board, June 26, 1969; Robert E. Dallos, "Morgenthau Deplores Attitudes on Crime," *Los Angeles Times*, June 27, 1969, 27.

642 **House Banking Committee:** Neil Sheehan, "More Americans Cheating with Swiss Bank Accounts," *NYT*, Nov. 30, 1969, 1, and "Crooked Deals in Swiss Accounts Aided by Inaction of Banks," *NYT*, Dec. 1, 1969, 42; "Morgenthau Statement Before House Banking & Currency Committee," RMM Papers. Further on RMM and Swiss banking: Ovid Demaris, *Dirty Business: The Corporate-Political Money-Power Game* (New York: Harper's Magazine Press, 1974); Leslie Waller, *The Swiss Bank Connection* (New York: Signet, 1972); Nicholas Faith, *Safety in Numbers: The Mysterious World of Swiss Banking* (New York: Viking, 1982).

643 **Five days later:** Maurice Carroll, "Mayor Comes Out for Morgenthau: Asks Nixon Administration to Retain U.S. Attorney," *NYT*, Aug. 20, 1969, 33.

PART V | THE BOSS

59. "A Job That I Know," 1970–1974

649 **"a basically nonexistent job":** Martin Tolchin, "Morgenthau Joins Lindsay's Cabinet as Deputy Mayor," *NYT*, Jan. 6, 1970, 1.

649 **"I ran 8 years ago":** Thomas Poster, "Morgy Runs for Governor on Anti-Boss Note," N.Y. *Daily News*, March 27, 1970, 3; Dorothy Schiff Papers, NYPL.

650 **"I told him"**: May 13, 1970, 5 pp., Dorothy Schiff Papers, NYPL.

652 **Bill Matheson**: A Southerner, five years younger, Matheson was a fellow Navy man, who had married well, twice, and lived in elegance at 10 Gracie Square. As a boy, he'd been raised by a great-aunt: his father served as a minister in a small town in Georgia and when his mother died could not take care of him. Morgenthau had been at Patterson Belknap two years when Matheson arrived in 1950.

655 **October 5**: "Mrs. Martha Morgenthau Dies; Wife of Former U.S. Attorney," *NYT,* Oct. 6, 1972, 46.

656 **"granite qualities"**: Barbara Thacher, "For MPM," RMM Papers.

657 **"dirty doings"**: Paul Hoffman, "Is It Time for Hogan to Step Down?," *New York,* Jan. 3, 1972, 56–60.

658 **"stop and frisk"**: Author correspondence: Joshua A. Segal.

659 **"Quite possibly"**: "Playboy Panel on Homosexuality," *Playboy,* April 1971; James W. Maddock and Deborah L. Dickman, editors, *Human Sexuality: A Resource Book,* book 3 (Minneapolis: The Medical School, University of Minnesota, 1972), 155.

659 **"assertive in ways"**: "New District Attorney," *NYT,* Feb. 6, 1974, 35.

659 **"no Democrat"**: Judith Michaelson, "In for Hogan," *N.Y. Post,* Feb. 9, 1974, 22.

659 **he published the first**: Nat Hentoff, "The Idealistic (Sic) Prosecutor," *Village Voice,* Feb. 14, 21 & 28, 1974; Laurie Johnston, "Idealistic Prosecutor," *NYT,* Feb. 4, 1974, 40.

659 **dispatching an inspector**: Author interviews: Nat Hentoff, Nicholas Scoppetta; cf. Martin Garbus, *Ready for the Defense* (New York: Farrar, Straus and Giroux, 1971).

660 **"was it all true?"**: Author interview: Nat Hentoff; David L. Lewis, *The Pleasures of Being Out of Step . . .* (New York: CUNY Journalism Press, 2013).

660 **"Dear Dolly"**: RMM to Dorothy Schiff, March 18, 1974, Schiff Papers, NYPL; "Morgenthau's Candidacy," *N.Y. Post,* March 17, 1974, 26.

661 **"one of the most powerful"**: Judy Klemesrud, "Young, Small, Bright and Powerful—A Key to the City's Future," *NYT,* Jan. 15, 1976, L39.

661 **Mid-Manhattan Democratic Club**: Steven R. Weisman, "Cohn in Dispute with an Old Foe," *NYT,* May 21, 1974, 48.

661 **death penalty**: Frank Lynn, "Morgenthau in District Attorney Race," *NYT,* May 21, 1974, 48.

662 **illegal wiretaps**: R. W. Apple, "Kuh Points to Morgenthau and a Bugging," *NYT,* Oct. 26, 1974, 14; "Kuh Asks Morgenthau to Open 20-Year-Old Wiretapping File," *NYT,* Oct. 28, 1974, 26; Tom Goldstein, "Political Race for Nonpolitical DA," *NYT,* Sept. 7, 1974, 61, RMM Papers.

662 **"a great similarity"**: Tom Buckley, "Manhattan DA Race Bears Imprint of Past," *NYT,* June 4, 1974, 39.

663 **"I took Morgenthau"**: Koch oral history, COHP.

60. Riot, 1975-1978

664 **"Is he a good scrounger?"**: "Morgenthau Office, After 2 Years, Still Is in the Throes of Transition," *NYT,* Feb. 6, 1977, 1.

665 **"a 45-year addiction"**: Nick Pileggi, "The Men Around Beame: That Old Hack Magic," *New York,* March 25, 1974, 35.

669 **"Why on earth"**: Author interview: Jack Chester.

672 **"It was so sudden"**: "White Youths Attack Black in Washington Sq.," *NYT,* Sept. 9, 1976, 43.

672 **kicked a pregnant woman**: Wayne Mulrenan, an Irish boy from Staten Island, friend of many assaulted, saw worse: the boy swinging a baseball bat into the woman's preg-

nant belly. Washington Square riot (WSR) (*The People of the State of New York v. Michael Andriani, Rocco Areena, Carlos Boutureira, Edward Burns, Joseph Chiapetti, Michael Doyle, Robert McLamb, Anthony Paolini, Andre Sanchez*), Case # 4707, 7 cu. ft.: Transcripts of Trial, Grand Jury proceedings, DA notes, and memoranda; Trial transcript, 4116, 4156.

672 "Bonecrusher": WSR trial transcript, 4055.

672 "I was scared": John L. Mitchell, "He Felt He Would Die," *N.Y. Post,* Sept. 10, 1976, 3.

672 "like a watermelon": "Police Arrest 10 Youths in Attack in Park That Injured 13 Persons," *NYT,* Sept. 11, 1976, 11.

672 "about one hundred": Paul Hoffman, *Courthouse* (New York: Hawthorn Books, 1979), 90–91.

673 his mother: Mota was Alminda Heredia's only child; Correspondence with Heredia; Author interview: Juan Sierra.

673 "very clean guy": Author interview: Natividad Montilla, March 14, 2021.

674 "Any six-shooters": Grand Jury proceedings, 1365, 1383.

675 "long-standing feud": Mitchell, "He Felt He Would Die," 3.

675 nine young men: At least three others would be arrested, but not indicted: Otto Thompson, Harry Bushwick, Michael Stewart.

675 "Don't blame our youths!!!": Jared Kopel and William T. Slattery, "Rally for Youths Accused in Riot," *N.Y. Post,* Sept. 11, 1976, 15.

677 "no immediate plans": Jared Kopel, "Park Death: No Murder Rap Now," *N.Y. Post,* Sept. 14, 1976, 12.

677 "tended to quell": Kopel, "Park Death: No Murder Rap Now," 12.

678 "We'll be back": WSR trial transcript, 4074.

678 "smashed someone": WSR trial transcript, 4131–32.

680 "designed to drive Blacks": Mike Pearl, "Ten Indicted in Fatal Washington Sq. Riot," *N.Y. Post,* Dec. 15, 1976, 3; United Press International, "DA Claims Riot Was Planned to Rout Blacks from City Park," Dec. 16, 1976.

681 "the primary purpose": "The Future of Sentencing in New York: Recommendations for Reform" (New York: New York State Commission on Sentencing Reform, Jan. 30, 2009), 15.

681 "in the throes": "Morgenthau Office, After 2 Years, Still Is in the Throes of Transition," *NYT,* Feb. 6, 1977, 1.

61. City on Edge, 1977

683 "Where's Kennedy Airport?": "Vignettes from a Night in the Dark," AP, Morning News (Wilmington, Delaware), July 15, 1977, 8; also quoted in Jonathan Mahler, *Ladies and Gentlemen, the Bronx Is Burning: 1977, Baseball, Politics, and the Battle for the Soul of the City* (New York: Farrar, Straus and Giroux, 2005), 186.

683 1,037 fires: Martin Gottlieb and James Glanz, "The Blackouts of '65 and '77 Became Defining Moments in the City's History," *NYT,* Aug. 15, 2003, A22.

684 Every cell: Timothy Crouse, "How 'Proximity to a Salami' Became a Crime: The Criminal Justice System Copes with Largest Mass Arrests in N.Y. History," *Village Voice,* Aug. 15, 1977, 1, 19, 20, 21.

685 Torres did not pause: Crouse, "How 'Proximity to a Salami' Became a Crime."

686 "Working by candlelight": Richard B. Lowe III, Memorandum, July 22, 1977, RMM Papers.

686 "deeply disturbing week": "The Added Danger of a Savage Week," *NYT,* Aug. 5, 1977, 16.

687 **56 of 229 were women:** Hoffman, *Courthouse,* 16; Barbara Lyne, "The Women of One Hogan Place," *Manhattan Lawyer,* March 1990, 24–26.

688 **to handle juvenile offenders:** "Morgenthau Sets Up Unit to Prosecute Youth," *NYT,* Oct. 25, 1977, 41.

688 **"You can't try cases":** Hoffman, *Courthouse,* 16.

688 **"vocational school":** "Morgenthau Office, After 2 Years, Still Is in the Throes of Transition," 1.

688 **Morgenthau had begun to date:** Jane Howard Papers, Columbia University.

689 **"hateful town":** Lucinda Franks, *My Father's Secret War* (New York: Miramax, 2007), 55.

690 **"identifying":** Lucinda Franks, *Timeless: Love, Morgenthau and Me* (New York: Farrar, Straus and Giroux, 2014), 15.

690 **five-part series:** Gregory Gordon and Ronald E. Cohen, *Down to the Wire: UPI's Fight for Survival* (New York: McGraw-Hill, 1990), 28; United Press International, "The Story of Diana Oughton: The Making of a Terrorist," Sept. 14–18, 1971; Tom Powers later published the Oughton story as a book, *Diana: The Making of a Terrorist* (New York: Houghton Mifflin, 1971); author interview: Tom Powers.

690 **the draft dodgers:** Lucinda Franks, *Waiting Out a War: The Exile of Private John Picciano* (New York: Coward, McCann and Geoghegan, 1974).

691 **Schlesinger townhouse:** "Reunion at Arthur's," *New York,* July 26, 1976, 30.

692 **"He knew the names":** Franks, *Timeless,* 61.

692 **"He's quite handsome":** Lucinda Franks letter, June 19, 1976; Franks, *Timeless,* 43–44.

62. "The Color of His Skin," 1978

697 **"None of you":** Hoffman, *Courthouse,* 62.

698 **"the judges have a pool":** Hoffman, *Courthouse,* 72.

699 **"to dissuade elements":** Hoffman, *Courthouse,* 75.

699 **"less than 12 feet":** WSR trial transcript, 4060.

700 **Charles Febee:** Andriani and Doyle Respondent Supplemental Brief 31379.

700 **"I started running":** Hoffman, *Courthouse,* 91.

701 **Murray Kempton:** Murray Kempton covered the trial and sentencing for the *N.Y. Post:* "The Night 'Law and Order' Invaded Washington Square," Feb. 23, 1978, 25; "Justice Is Done, but . . . ," March 16, 1978, 13; "Five Young Men Who Weren't Sorry," May 13, 1978, 7.

702 **"Reception parties":** Mike Pearl and James Norman, "6 Park Rioters Under Guard," *N.Y. Post,* March 16, 1978, 13.

63. "Failure After Failure," 1983–1989

705 **"forbidden territory":** Franks, *Timeless,* 115–16.

705 **"You will want":** Franks, *Timeless,* 115–16.

706 **"I am a pig'":** Franks, *Timeless,* 214.

708 **390 murders in 1960:** Nicholas Pileggi, "Open City," *New York,* Jan. 19, 1981, 20–26.

708 **After two rounds:** On Jan. 1, 1985, Goetz was arrested in Concord, N.H., and charged with four counts of attempted murder and one count of unlawful possession of a weapon. On Jan. 3, 1985, RMM arraigned Goetz on the attempted murder charges, and instructed his assistants to present the case to the grand jury, expecting it to follow suit. Instead, on Jan. 25, 1985, the grand jury returned a one-count indictment, charg-

ing Goetz with illegal weapons possession. On March 27, 1985, a second grand jury, after eight days of testimony, issued an indictment on thirteen felony counts, including four counts of attempted murder, four counts of assault, one count of reckless endangerment, and one count of possessing a weapon with the intent of using it. In June 1987, Goetz was acquitted on all but the weapons charge. On Oct. 19, 1987, he was sentenced to six months in jail, but the sentence was overturned on appeal in June 1988. On Jan. 13, 1989, Goetz was re-sentenced to a $5,000 fine and one year in jail. On Sept. 20, 1989, after serving eight months in jail, he was released. In 1996, Goetz would file for bankruptcy, after being ordered to pay $43 million in damages to one of the four youths he shot. The verdict resulted from a civil lawsuit brought by Darrell Cabey, who had been left paralyzed and with brain damage. Another of Goetz's victims, James Ramseur, died in 2011, on the twenty-seventh anniversary of the shooting. At forty-five, after serving twenty-five years for the rape of a pregnant woman, Ramseur was found dead of an apparent drug overdose at the Paradise Motor Inn in the Bronx. In 2013, at sixty-five, Goetz, who had made an unsuccessful bid for mayor in 2001, was arrested for selling $30 worth of marijuana to an undercover policewoman in Union Square.

712 **more than a billion dollars:** Subcommittee on Oversight and Investigations, Committee on Education and the Workforce, U.S. Congress, "Hearing on the Teamsters Investigation," April 29, 1998, Cherkasky Testimony, 81.

712 **Ron Goldstock:** In 1968, as a law student, Goldstock had been a summer intern during Morgenthau's tenure as U.S. attorney.

713 **name for himself:** In the spring of 1983, Goldstock led a landmark undercover operation, overseeing the team that planted a bug in the dashboard of the Jaguar XJ-6 used by Morgenthau's old nemesis, Antonio "Tony Ducks" Corallo. The captured conversations between Corallo and his associates were rare and valuable evidence—and the news traveled fast throughout the law-enforcement circles of New York. Goldstock and Giuliani soon cut a deal: The Jaguar tapes would be lent to Giuliani for use in the "Commission Case," centerpiece of Giuliani's war against the Mafia. Morgenthau was furious. "When Goldstock goes to Rudy," a Morgenthau assistant would say, "the Boss goes livid. It was a sea change."

714 **unseen, and illegal, confederacy:** James B. Jacobs, with Coleen Friel and Robert Radick, *Gotham Unbound: How New York City Was Liberated from the Grip of Organized Crime* (New York: New York University Press, 1999), 23.

716 **top Democrats:** Manfred (Fred) Ohrenstein, a onetime New York state senator, who years later would sit on the boards of the Museum of Jewish Heritage, the city's memorial to the Holocaust, alongside its chairman, RMM.

717 **"Lock-Kee Transportation":** Trial transcript, *State of N.Y. v. Thomas Gambino, Joseph Gambino et al.,* 11859/90 & 11858/90; Ralph Blumenthal has "Lok-Kee" in "When the Mob Delivered the Goods," *NYT Magazine,* July 26, 1992.

718 **"That's right":** Trial transcript; Blumenthal, "When the Mob," 178.

720 **1,500-square-foot shop:** Trial transcript; Author interview: Ronnie Rivera.

722 **"Hear me out":** Blumenthal, "When the Mob," 178.

722 **"Maybe my guys":** Trial transcript; edited versions: Stone Phillips, *Dateline NBC,* July 7, 1992; Geraldo Rivera, "The New Godfathers" (Tribune Entertainment, two-hour live primetime broadcast from Palermo, Sicily), Jan. 20, 1993; Ronald Sullivan, "Prosecution Provides Glimpse of Gambino Tactics," *NYT,* Feb. 9, 1992, 48.

64. "To Change an Industry," 1989–1991

728 **"as if measuring":** Author interview: Arthur Friedman.

728 **"You can't manufacture":** Jacobs, *Gotham Unbound,* 135.

65. "A New Endgame," 1992–2015

735 **"We knew we had them"**: Gay Jervey, "Waltzing with the Wise Guys," *American Lawyer,* May 1992, 84–91.

735 **"What if running through"**: Jervey, "Waltzing," 84–91.

739 **"adrenaline rush"**: Peter Elkind, *Client 9: The Rise and Fall of Eliot Spitzer* (New York: Portfolio/Penguin, 2010), 23.

740 **"For the first time"**: Selwyn Raab, "Curb on Mob Aids Garment Makers," *NYT,* June 12, 1995, A1; Arthur Friedman, "McGuire: The Trucks Are Rolling," *Women's Wear Daily,* March 7, 1995: 8.

66. "The Bank of Crooks and Criminals International," 1992–2019

743 **BCCI:** Description of the July 29, 1992, indictment: Larry Gurwin and Peter Truell, *False Profits: The Inside Story of BCCI, the World's Most Corrupt Financial Empire* (New York: Houghton Mifflin, 1992), xiii–xvii; Douglas Frantz and David McKean, *Friends in High Places: The Rise and Fall of Clark Clifford* (New York: St. Martin's Press, 1995), 380–81. A number of book-length journalistic accounts appeared in the wake of the BCCI collapse, and a host of investigative journalists went to extraordinary lengths to expose the myriad offshoots of the bank scandal. Truell and Gurwin were among the first to report on BCCI's rapid rise: Gurwin in *Institutional Investor* as early as 1979, and Truell for *The Economist* in 1981. Others I have relied on, and cite here, include James Ring Adams and Douglas Frantz, *A Full Service Bank: How BCCI Stole Billions Around the World* (New York: Pocket Books, 1992); Jonathan Beaty and S. C. Gwynne, *The Outlaw Bank: A Wild Ride into the Secret Heart of BCCI* (New York: Random House, 1993).

746 **"In Morgenthau, you had"**: "The Bank of Crooks and Criminals," *Frontline,* Rory O'Connor, producer, GlobalVision, April 21, 1992.

748 **"rent-a-sheikh"**: Gurwin and Truell, *False Profits,* 320.

748 **"It was simple enough"**: Author interviews and correspondence: Robert Mazur. The C-Chase operation was first reported by a Tampa investigative reporter: Bentley Orrick, "A Man Called Musella," *Tampa Tribune,* Aug. 13, 1989, 1. The most comprehensive account of the operation, based in large part on the transcripts of his undercover recordings, is Robert Mazur's memoir, *The Infiltrator: My Secret Life Inside the Dirty Banks Behind Pablo Escobar's Medellin Cartel* (New York: Little, Brown, 2009).

750 **man who had built:** Mohammed Asghar Khan, a former air marshal and political figure, was known as "the father of Pakistan's air force." He founded the Tehrik-i-Istiqlal party in 1970; Mazur, *Infiltrator,* 121.

750 **latest laundering products:** Mazur, *Infiltrator,* 87.

752 **"My sense was"**: Author interview: Mazur; *Infiltrator,* 110–12.

756 **"with skepticism"**: Michael Cherkasky to Senator Kerry, Nov. 21, 1991, S. Hrg. 102–350, Part 3, 771; "Kerry Report": *The BCCI Affair A Report to the Committee on Foreign Relations, United States Senate,* by Senator John Kerry and Senator Hank Brown, December 1992, 102d Congress, 2d Session Senate, Print, 102–40.

67. "Either . . . Stupid or Venal," 1989–1992

757 **"punching my arm"**: Franks, *My Father's Secret War,* 157.

759 **"You can't do"**: Adams and Frantz, *A Full Service Bank,* 61.

760 **"hand-knotted carpet"**: Najam Sethi, "BCCI Founder: 'These Things Happen,'" *Wall Street Journal,* July 29, 1991, A10.

763 **"too incredible"**: Beaty and Gwynne, *The Outlaw Bank,* 59–60.

764 "Bill feels BCCI": Beaty and Gwynne, *The Outlaw Bank,* 103.

764 "Bill hasn't committed": Gurwin and Truell, *False Profits,* 301.

764 "If the Fed": Paul Houston, "Ex-Defense Chief Denies Lying over Bank Sale," *Los Angeles Times,* March 17, 1991.

764 "seeming stupid or venal": Neil A. Lewis, "Washington at Work; Clark Clifford, Symbol of the Permanent Capital, Is Faced with a Dilemma," *NYT,* April 5, 1991, 14.

765 "Jesus Christ": Frantz and McKean, *Friends in High Places,* 360.

765 "one of our most flexible fronts": Gurwin and Truell, *False Profits,* 302.

765 "stock transactions": Jim McGee and Sharon Walsh, "Foreign Bank Financed Stock Deal," *Washington Post,* May 5, 1991, A1.

766 **Douglas P. Mulholland:** Mulholland had come to Treasury from the CIA in 1982 at the suggestion of the then-director William Casey. In 1987, he left the federal government to join George H. W. Bush's presidential campaign, and later served in the State Department. On the CIA analytic reports regarding BCCI: Kerry Report; Frantz and McKean, *Friends in High Places,* 322; Beaty and Gwynne, *The Outlaw Bank,* 326–27; Gurwin and Truell, *False Profits,* 382, 429.

767 **Hatch would come to regret:** U.S. Senate speech, Feb. 22, 1990. Hatch also admitted to having called Swaleh Naqvi, the BCCI president, on March 22, 1990, in an attempt to get a loan for a friend, Monzer Hourani, a businessman of Lebanese ancestry based in Houston, Texas, and a fellow Mormon; Dean Baquet with Jeff Gerth, "Lawmaker's Defense of BCCI Went Beyond Speech in Senate," *NYT,* Aug. 26, 1992, 1.

767 **The Senate leadership:** *Frontline,* April 21, 1992; Martin Tolchin, "Washington at Work: Senator Who Hunted Bank Scandal Is Watching Doubters Take His Path," *NYT,* July 29, 1991, 10.

767 "I have heard": Hearing, Subcommittee on Consumer and Regulatory Affairs, of the Committee of Banking, Housing and Urban Affairs, U.S. Senate, S. 1019, May 23, 1991, 47–167; Kerry Report, 219.

769 **off-the-record interviews:** On battle with Mueller: Robert S. Bennett, *In the Ring: The Trials of a Washington Lawyer* (New York: Three Rivers Press, 2008), 165–66; Frantz and McKean, *Friends in High Places,* 379; William Safire, "BCCI: Justice Delayed," *NYT,* July 25, 1991, 21.

769 "Nobody has ever": Jim McGee, "No BCCI 'Foot-dragging' Says Top Justice Official," *Washington Post,* July 25, 1991, A1.

769 "maybe 20 to 25 percent": Dean Baquet, "New York Lodges Criminal Charges Against Big Bank," *NYT,* July 30, 1991, 1.

770 **Rahman said:** Rahman testimony, Aug. 8, 1991, Kerry Report.

771 **more than $200 million:** Kerry Report, 254; Gurwin and Truell, *False Profits,* 427.

771 "maverick prosecutor's office": Gurwin and Truell, *False Profits,* 401.

68. "Only Good People," 1992

773 was "going to take a hit": Author interview: Robert B. Fiske, Jr.

774 "We've done": Frantz and McKean, *Friends in High Places,* 337.

774 "It is narrower": Frantz and McKean, *Friends in High Places,* 379.

774 offered to cooperate: Author interview: John Moscow.

775 "practically everything": Frantz and McKean, *Friends in High Places,* 381.

775 He would have trouble: Michael Beschloss, "Clifford Speaks," *New Yorker,* September 6, 1993, 44–51.

775 its civil suit: The Federal Reserve Board's summary of charges ran 141 pages, its 350 numbered paragraphs detailing the distance between the paper trail and Clifford's and Altman's sworn representations before the banking body. The Fed also announced a

$200 million fine of BCCI, and an intention to bar the alleged front men for life from banking in the United States.

775 **"I guess I should":** *Frontline,* April 21, 1992.

775 **"We'd had four years":** Clifford interview 1994, Frantz and McKean, *Friends in High Places,* 335.

776 **"possible plea bargains":** Sharon Walsh, "Clifford Trial Postponed by N.Y. Judge; Former Defense Secretary Granted Time for Surgery," *Washington Post,* March 3, 1993, F01.

777 **"While I have discussed":** Sharon Walsh, "U.S. to Broaden Charges Against Clifford, Altman: Long Awareness of BCCI's Plans Alleged," *Washington Post,* March 10, 1993, F1; Author interview: Gustave Newman.

779 **$550 million:** Author interviews: Eric Lewis, Brian Smouha. "All told the sale was nearly $1 billion, with its debt," said Smouha, the Touche Ross partner who led the liquidation.

780 **some $8.5 billion:** Asa Fitch, "BCCI Creditors Head to Saudi for One Last Collection," *Wall Street Journal,* Nov. 19, 2013.

780 **Naqvi served five years:** Adil Ahmad, "Swaleh Naqvi Interview Transcript," April 14, 2015.

781 **He lived out his last days:** Sethi, "BCCI Founder: 'These Things Happen,'" A10.

781 **The two Pakistani bankers:** Kerry Hearings, Part 6, July 30, 1992, Kerry Report.

781 **A Florida banker:** David Paul of CenTrust Bank; Author interviews: Jack Blum; Beaty and Gwynne, *The Outlaw Bank,* 185.

781 **"Only good people":** Gurwin and Truell, *False Profits,* 434.

69. The Jogger, 1989

782 **Joe Walsh:** Author interview: Joseph Walsh.

783 **"First thing I saw":** CPJ Trial Transcript, *People v. McCray, Salaam & Santana,* Walsh Testimony, 4347–93.

783 **"how she was tied":** Author interview: Joseph Walsh.

783 **"a ligature":** "Affirmation in Response to Motion to Vacate Judgement of Conviction," Indictment No. 4762/89, *The People of the State of New York v. Kharey Wise, Kevin Richardson, Antron McCray, Yusef Salaam, and Raymond Santana* ("Ryan Affirmation"), 4.

783 **At 2:11:** CPJ Trial Transcript, *People v. McCray, Salaam & Santana,* Dr. Estelle Paris Testimony, 4488.

784 **"severe brain damage":** Stuart Marques, "Park Marauders Call It: WILDING," N.Y. *Daily News,* April 22, 1989.

784 **"Most people":** Timothy Sullivan, *Unequal Verdicts: The Central Park Jogger Trials* (New York: Simon & Schuster, 1992), 130.

784 **"Nightmare in Central Park":** "Nightmare in Central Park," N.Y. *Post,* April 21, 1989, 1.

784 **"Central Park Horror":** "Wolf Pack's Prey," N.Y. *Daily News,* April 21, 1989, 1.

784 **"Rape Suspect's Jailhouse Boast":** Patrick Clark and Ruth Landa, "Rape Suspect's Jailhouse Boast: 'She Wasn't Nothing,'" N.Y. *Daily News,* April 23, 1989.

784 **"'It Was Fun'":** Mike Pearl, Sonia Reyes, Karen Phillips, "Rape Suspect: 'It Was Fun,'" N.Y. *Post,* April 23, 1989.

784 **"New Yorkers learned":** Murray Weiss, Charles M. Sennott, Andrea Peyser, "Wilding— the Newest Term for Terror in City That Lives in Fear," N.Y. *Post,* April 22, 1989, 2–3.

785 **"that chilled and titillated":** J. Anthony Lukas, "Wilding—as American as Tom Sawyer," *NYT,* May 28, 1989, E15.

785 "'Lord of the Flies' rape": Sam Roberts, "The Region: When Crimes Become Symbols," *NYT,* May 7, 1989, A1.

785 "They were coming": Pete Hamill, "A Savage Disease Called New York," *N.Y. Post,* April 23, 1989, 4, 32.

785 an old *Lansdale* shipmate: Pat Mascati, RMM Diaries.

788 "If someone walked": Katherine Bouton, "Linda Fairstein v. Rape," *NYT Magazine,* Feb. 25, 1990, 21, 58–60.

788 "He just went places": Author interview: Linda Fairstein.

790 "Whitey": Michael Stone, "What Really Happened in Central Park," *New York,* Aug. 14, 1989.

790 "It sounded like a bullet": Gene Mustain and Stuart Marques, "3 Faced Pack," N.Y. *Daily News,* April 22, 1989, 4.

791 **Robert Garner:** Lizette Alvarez, "Park Case Witnesses: Their Night of Terror," N.Y. *Daily News,* June 28, 1990; Trial transcript; Ryan Affirmation.

791 "a dozen or more": CPJ Trial Transcript, *People v. McCray, Salaam & Santana,* Loughlin Testimony, 3770.

791 "What are you looking at?": "Transcript of Trial: *People v. McCray, Salaam & Santana,*" 3766–3873; "Transcript of Trial: *People v. Wise and Richardson,*" 9202–9288; "Transcript Re Grand Jury Testimony of John Loughlin (undated)," NYCLD_013209.

793 "headlights everywhere": Author interview: Eric Reynolds.

793 more than three dozen: Ryan Affirmation, 3.

70. "A Brilliant Job," 1989–2002

795 "brilliant job": Author interview: Linda Fairstein.

795 "laughing and telling jokes": "Teens Tell of Brutal Rape of Jogger in Central Park," *Newsday,* April 23, 1989, 33.

796 **"Pack Ignored Her Cries":** "Investigators on Park Rampage: Pack Ignored Her Cries, Called It Fun," *Newsday,* April 23, 1989, 1.

796 She started smoking again: Timothy Sullivan, *Unequal Verdicts,* 225.

796 protection order: Susan Helen Anderson, "Chronicle," *NYT,* Aug. 22, 1990.

796 "a vivid, incriminating picture": Katherine Bouton, "Linda Fairstein v. Rape," 60.

796 "whistling, screaming": Nov. 13, 1989, Suppression Hearing Testimony of ADA L. Fairstein, NYCLD_015201-015204; cf.: CPJ Trial Transcript, *People v. McCray, Salaam & Santana,* 8004–8095; *People v. Wise and Richardson,* 10602–10720.

798 "a large tree": Nov. 13, 1989 Suppression Hearing Testimony of ADA L. Fairstein, NYCLD_015201–0152103.

798 forensic ties: The 2002 DA's report on the reinvestigation described the forensics— blood, semen, hair—in detail and concluded that "ultimately, there proved to be no physical or forensic evidence recovered at the scene or from the person or effects of the victim which connected the defendants to the attack on the jogger"; Ryan Affirmation, 16.

798 DNA: Harlan Levy, *And the Blood Cried Out* (New York: Basic Books, 1996), 59–85; "Sex Crimes Unit," Producer, Lisa Jackson, HBO, 2011.

798 "This most composed woman": Levy, *And the Blood Cried Out,* 59.

798 confessions: Regarding the statements (four videotaped and, in the case of Yusef Salaam, one written) of the five defendants and how they varied, ascribing different actions to different individuals, the chart produced during the DA's reinvestigation is revelatory: "Chart Re Statements of Teenagers in the Park Relating to the Sexual Assault of Patricia Meili (undated)" (NYCLD_028482).

799 "We was walking": CPJ Trial Transcript, *People v. McCray, Salaam & Santana,* Salaam Testimony, 7674.

800 **a solid metal bar:** Timothy Sullivan, *Unequal Verdicts,* 312; Sarah Burns, *The Central Park Five,* 6.

800 **"I don't have a pipe":** CPJ Trial Transcript, *People v. McCray, Salaam & Santana,* Salaam Testimony, 7698.

800 **"And did you hit her?":** Ronald Sullivan, "Taped Confession Played at Jogger Trial," *NYT,* July 19, 1990, B3.

801 **in both instances voted to convict:** Ronald Sullivan, "Jogger Trial Jury Relied on Physical Evidence, Not Tapes," *NYT,* Dec. 13, 1990, B1.

801 **Four defendants:** Ryan Affirmation, 10–11: "On August 18, 1990, after ten days of deliberations, the jury convicted each defendant of one count of Assault in the First Degree and Rape in the First Degree for the attack on the Central Park jogger; Robbery in the First Degree and three assault charges for the attack on John Loughlin; Assault in the Second Degree for the attack on David Lewis; and Riot in the First Degree." "Since each was under 16, the court, on September 11, 1990, set aside all their convictions except those for First Degree Robbery and Rape, and then sentenced each of them, as juveniles, to consecutive prison terms of from three and one-third to ten years on each count. This resulted in an aggregate term of from five to ten years pursuant to Penal Law Section 70.30(1)(d)."

"Kevin Richardson and Kharey Wise were tried jointly, also before Judge Galligan, from October 22, 1990, to December 11, 1990. The jury deliberated for eleven days. Richardson was found guilty of each count of the indictment. Wise was convicted of Assault in the First Degree and Sexual Abuse in the First Degree with respect to the attack on the Central Park jogger, and of Riot in the First Degree. He was acquitted of the remaining charges. Because of Richardson's age, Justice Galligan set aside all of Richardson's convictions except for those for Attempted Murder in the Second Degree and First Degree Robbery, Rape, and Sodomy. The court sentenced Richardson, as a juvenile, to consecutive prison terms of from three and one-third to ten years on each count, resulting in an aggregate term of from five to ten years. Wise was sentenced to terms of imprisonment of five to fifteen years for Assault in the First Degree, two and one-third to seven years for Sexual Abuse in the First Degree, and one to three years for Riot. The sentences were imposed concurrently, for an aggregate term of five to fifteen years." In all, when prosecutors counted those who had plea-bargained, the night of havoc and violence resulted in the convictions of ten young men.

802 **"Justice has been done":** John J. Goldman, "3 Found Guilty in Central Park Jogger Attacks," *Los Angeles Times,* Aug. 19, 1990.

803 **timeline:** Timothy Sullivan, *Unequal Verdicts,* 231; CPJ trial transcripts; "Timeline of Events in Central Park and the Discovery of Patricia Meili (4-19-1989 through 4-20-1989), NYCLD_028534.

803 **electronic ankle bracelet:** Celestine Bohlen, "New York Will Try House Arrest for Some Prisoners," *NYT,* Sept. 29, 1988, B1.

803 **seven thousand cells:** Edward A. Gargan, "Cuomo Planning 7,000 New Cells For State Prisons," *NYT,* Jan. 21, 1983, B1.

804 **"just didn't seem right":** Author interview: Todd Clark.

805 **Reyes's childhood:** Author interview: Dr. N. G. Berrill.

806 **"to impress girls":** Michael Daly, "He's an Ice Man Who Confessed," N.Y. *Daily News,* Oct. 20, 2002, 8. Citing Dr. N. G. Berrill, 1991, Medical Report.

806 **"I kept on stabbing":** "New Suspect in Central Park Gang Rape," *Primetime Live,* Sept. 26, 2002.

807 **Elizabeth Reynolds:** "Reynolds" is a pseudonym, used for privacy concerns.

807 **final day of February:** Vern Fonda's first interview: Jan. 17, 2002. Fonda call to Elizabeth Lederer, Feb. 28, 2002, NYCLD_027081.

809 **ADAs Ryan, Casolaro, Lederer:** Vern Fonda has "present": Ryan, Lederer, McCabe, Mooney, Casolaro, "unit members"; NYCLD_027081.

810 **"I just had":** Kevin Flynn, Jim Dwyer, "A Crime Revisited: Prosecutors in a Reversal," *NYT*, Dec. 6, 2002, B4; NYCLD_012013, Interview of Matias Reyes by Nancy Ryan, May 23, 2002; NYCLD_029508, Interview of Matias Reyes by Nancy Ryan, May 30, 2002.

811 **"She makes the turn":** "New Suspect in Central Park Gang Rape," *Primetime Live,* Sept. 26, 2002.

812 **"with blood on him":** NYCLD_033583, DD5 Report Re Interview of Det. Charles Freitag, by Det. William Hicks (11-4-2002).

71. "One Good Thing," 2002–2003

814 **police task force:** At least one high-ranking member of the NYPD task force on the reinvestigation of the jogger case would come to a dissenting conclusion: Joseph Reznick would testify, after reviewing all available evidence in 2002, that "all this led me to believe that the plaintiffs in this case [the 'Central Park 5'] did not commit this rape." "Deposition Transcript Joseph Reznick, October 22, 2013," NYCLD_065731.

814 **"Manhattan prosecutors":** William Rashbaum, "Convicted Killer and Rapist Says He Attacked Central Park Jogger," *NYT,* June 12, 2002, B2.

815 **August 30:** Alice McQuillian, "Jogger Case Confession," N.Y. *Daily News,* Sept. 4, 2002, 5; Susan Saulny, "3 Seek to Overturn Verdicts in '89 Rape of Park Jogger," *NYT,* Sept. 5, 2002, B4.

815 **Only one:** Raymond Santana had been released in April 1997 for his conviction in the jogger case, but he had pled guilty in a new case, for narcotics, in 1999. In December 2002, he, too, was released.

816 **"don't necessarily trust us":** NYCLD tapes, Ryan & Reyes, undated.

817 **a ring:** "Photograph Re Victim of Matias Reyes," NYCLD_029845.

818 **"I wanted to say a prayer":** "Handwritten Statement, by Victim of Matias Reyes," NYC CPJ, NYCLD_029678; Jackie Herbach: *Connie Chung Tonight,* CNN, Dec. 12, 2002; Ryan Affirmation, 28.

820 **"CLOSED":** NYC CPJ, NYCLD_069871.

821 **"Likely U-Turn":** Jim Dwyer, "Likely U-Turn by Prosecutors in Jogger Case," *NYT,* Oct. 12, 2002, A1.

821 **"opened the door":** "Justice for Sexual Assault Victims: Using DNA Evidence to Combat Crime," Hearing Before the Subcommittee on Crime and Drugs of the Committee on the Judiciary, U.S. Senate, One Hundred Seventh Congress, Second Session, May 14, 2002.

822 **"the French Connection crew":** Author interview: Linda Fairstein.

823 **"28 Not in the News":** Don Terry, "A Week of Rapes: The Jogger and 28 Not in the News," *NYT,* May 29, 1989, 25.

824 **"every prison":** Author interview: Robert Mooney.

826 **"a very Merry Christmas":** "Central Park Justice," *PBS NewsHour,* Dec. 24, 2002.

827 **blunt letters:** RMM to Raymond W. Kelly, Dec. 23, 2002, RMM Papers.

827 **red baseball cap:** On the hat found in NYPD storage and related evidence, including the "rape kit" from the April 17, 1989, attack: Melissa Mourges to RMM, December 10, 2002, NYCLD_028294; Chris Prevost to Nancy Ryan, "Voucher #D480425," April 2, 2004; Chris Prevost to James Kindler, chief assistant DA, "Search for Property," May 27, 2003, NYCLD_028209; Prevost to Nancy Ryan, "Property Search (April 17, 1989 Rape in Central Park)," August 21, 2002; "Photographs Re Physical Evidence Relating to the April 17, 1989 Rape in CP, by the NYPD," NYCLD_007353.

72. "No Guile," 2003-2014

829   "the most racist prosecution": Simone Weichselbaum, "Still Haunted by 'Wolf Pack' Label, Men Wrongly Convicted in Central Park Jogger Case Speak," N.Y. *Daily News,* April 12, 2009.

831   a name but no photograph: Another misstep: Barney Barros, the man who interrupted the April 17 rape, was a freelance artist. Right away, he had created a sketch of the rapist for the police, a sketch that Detective Rivera never saw.

831   "It's that weird nose": Author interview: Irma Rivera.

834   "so many contradictions": Timothy Sullivan, *Unequal Verdicts,* 314.

834   "You weren't there": Timothy Sullivan, *Unequal Verdicts,* 314-15.

835   his hands: Author interview: Jermaine Robinson. At a 1989 hearing, Robinson pled guilty to "robbery in the first degree." When asked by Judge Thomas Galligan, "Did you use or threaten the use of a dangerous instrument?," Robinson answered: "Yes, sir." *People of the State of New York v. Jermaine Robinson,* Indictment #4762-89, October 5, 1989, NYCLD_062055.

836   "felt so good": Tara Parker-Pope, "Central Park Jogger Still Running 20 Years Later," *NYT,* April 20, 2009.

73. "The Price of Liberty," 1995-2009

838   New York Court of Appeals: *People v. Smith,* 63 N.Y.2d 41.

839   "Things have changed": Robert Kolker, "Happy 85th Birthday, Bob Morgenthau," *New York,* July 16, 2004.

842   Stephen Flatow: Stephen Flatow, father of the young woman murdered in the Gaza bombing more than a decade earlier, had already received a share of Tehran's money. Of the Iranian millions frozen since the days of the shah in U.S. government accounts, the Flatows would receive $25 million. For years, the U.S. government would claim that Flatow and other families of terror victims were excluded from receiving any share of the $400 million in Iranian funds, which had sat frozen for more than twenty years in a Pentagon account, proceeds from an aircraft sale to the shah. In 2001, President Clinton relented, instructing an aide to negotiate with Flatow, Terry Anderson, and the rest of the former Beirut hostages and their families. Jack Lew, an Orthodox Jew, then serving as director of the Office of Management and Budget, led closed-door negotiations, in cooperation with Stuart Eizenstat, deputy secretary of the Treasury, and Senators Connie Mack (R-Fla.) and Frank Lautenberg (D-N.J.) on behalf of the victims' families. The government would divide $400 million among the victims' families. "Out of this whirlpool," Flatow said, "we got a settlement." Alisa's father was relieved: the fight was over, but he no longer believed his government. Whether under the Clinton, Bush, or Obama administration, the State Department had blocked him from suing Iran. Fear of further alienating Iran, Flatow reckoned, was more important than an American killed by terrorism. He could see the calculus, but refused to believe it. "Why wouldn't they," he wondered, "let me send the government of Iran a message?"

843   Alisa's organs: Melissa Radler, "Alisa's Smile," *Jerusalem Post,* April 4, 2003, 15.

843   "We don't know": Mike Kelly, *The Bus on Jaffa Road* (Guildford, Conn.: Lyons Press, 2014), 130.

844   $247.5 million: Author interview and correspondence: Stephen Flatow. The trial consisted of a "proof hearing," two days of testimony, March 2-3, 1998. U.S. District Court Judge Royce Lamberth arrived at the monetary award by adding the amount ($25 million) the Flatows' attorneys requested in compensatory damages, based in

part on pain and suffering, Alisa Flatow's potential support for the family, and loss of comfort, and then trebling the amount (to $75 million), offered in expert testimony as an estimate of the annual total Iran spends to support terrorism.

844 **"I think Alisa":** James Dao, "Judgment for Terrorism Is $248 Million," *NYT,* March 12, 1998, 5.

844 **opened the floodgates:** Author interview: Steven Perles. By 2006, the list of those seeking justice had grown long: Among the plaintiffs were the families of those killed in the Beirut bombings of 1983—the attack on the U.S. Marine barracks that killed 299 and the bombing of the U.S. Embassy six months earlier that killed 63—as well as the Americans once held hostage in Lebanon.

845 **begun to acquire assets:** Author interview: George Ennis.

845 **"It was like a Mafia operation":** Author interview: Abbas Milani.

845 **Manoucher Shafie:** Alan S. Oser, "Leasing Pahlavi Building," *NYT,* Dec. 19, 1979, D18; Kathleen Teltsch, "New Course Set for Shah's U.S. Foundation," *NYT,* Nov. 15, 1979, A17.

847 **a former Alavi president:** On February 18, 2004, Hanif Partnership ("Hanif"), a New York partnership, filed a lawsuit against Assa Corp., Assa Co. Ltd., and the Alavi Foundation in the Supreme Court of the State of New York, for breach of contract and tortious interference with contract; *USA v. All Right, Title, and Interest of Assa Corporation, Assa Company Limited, Bank Melli Bank, and the Alavi Foundation in 650 Fifth Avenue Company . . . ,* filed Nov. 12, 2009, Verified Amended Complaint, 08 Civ. 10934 (RJH), 51.

847 **a representative of Bank Melli:** Verified Amended Complaint, 53.

74. " 'Judas' Morgy," 2009

858 **"Summer 2003":** Verified Amended Complaint, 61–62.

859 **new trial:** The Second Circuit decision in 2019 remanded the case for new proceedings, however, as of early 2022, no trial date had been set.

860 **Mossad:** Author interview: Israeli intelligence officer. The Israelis had directed Morgenthau's attention to China and to Thailand. On December 12, 2009, when the Thai police seized an Ilyushin Il-76 jet in Bangkok, the DA knew the reason. The cargo plane had flown in from North Korea, laden with arms and matériel. ("North Korean Plane Carrying Smuggled Arms Seized in Thailand," *Guardian,* Dec. 13, 2009.) Despite the Iranian denials, Morgenthau would tell the press that the shipment was bound for Tehran.

863 **The *Post* headlined the turn:** Laura Italiano and Maggie Haberman, " 'Judas' Morgy Backs Cy over Aide," *N.Y. Post,* March 4, 2009.

75. "On the Outside," 2011–2018

868 **"Everyone has dropped the ball":** James Freeman, "The World's District Attorney," *Wall Street Journal,* Dec. 26, 2009.

869 **"look with favor":** David B. Byrne, Jr., to RMM, June 12, 2017, RMM Papers.

872 **"John Doe indictments":** Correspondence with Martha Bashford, Lisa Friel (unit chiefs, Sex Crimes Unit); Barbara Ross, Alice McQuillian, and Dave Goldiner, "Indictment by DNA Genetics Get Unknown Man Charged as E. Side Rapist," *N.Y. Daily News,* March 16, 2000.

873 **The city jails were emptying:** See Judith A. Greene and Vincent Schiraldi, "Better by Half: The New York City Story of Winning Large-Scale Decarceration While Increasing Public Safety," *Federal Sentencing Reporter* 29 (October 2016): 22–38.

874 **well-worn argument:** Michael Javen Fortner, *Black Silent Majority: The Rockefeller*

Drug Laws and the Politics of Punishment (Cambridge, Mass.: Harvard University Press, 2015).

874 **"more law enforcement"**: James Forman, Jr., *Locking Up Our Own: Crime and Punishment in Black America* (New York: Farrar, Straus and Giroux, 2017), 12–13; see also Lee A. Daniels, "Black Crime, Black Victims," *NYT Magazine,* May 16, 1982, sec. 6, 38.

874 **353,000 arrests**: Harry G. Levine and Deborah Peterson Small, *Marijuana Arrest Crusade: Racial Bias and Police Policy in New York City, 1997–2007* (New York: New York Civil Liberties Union, 2008), 4.

874 **"legalized discrimination"**: Michelle Alexander, *The New Jim Crow: Mass Incarceration in the Age of Colorblindness* (New York: The Free Press, 2012), 7.

875 **Wollman Rink**: Peter Blauner, "Ice Capades: Donald Trump Takes On the Wollman Rink," *New York,* June 23, 1986.

876 **"That rink"**: James Tyson, "City Opens Central Park Rink After Developer Rescues Renovation," Associated Press, Oct. 31, 1986.

877 **Trump hosted a fundraiser**: Aug. 29, 2005, RMM diaries.

879 **his family**: Months after Morgenthau's retirement, in early 2010, the new DA, Cyrus Vance, Jr., did open an investigation into the Trump SoHo, a forty-three-story hotel and condominium project in downtown Manhattan. The investigation centered on complaints about the Trump Organization's hyperinflated reports of sales and lasted two years before Vance dropped it. On both sides of the probe, the ties to Morgenthau ran deep: his son-in-law, Paul Grand, was on the defense team. (Grand was also a former partner of the new DA; Vance had spent four years at the same law firm in Manhattan.) Joining Vance on the defense was Gary Naftalis, another veteran of Morgenthau's U.S. attorney's office. After a civil lawsuit was settled in 2011, Grand and Naftalis argued against the criminal investigation. Their task, by extension, was to safeguard all others involved: the Trump children, the Trump Organization, and Donald Trump. At the DA's, Adam Kaufmann oversaw the investigation and "believed in it"—until Vance, convinced there was no viable criminal case, "overruled" his assistants and closed the case on August 3, 2012. (See Andrea Bernstein, Jesse Eisinger, Justin Elliott, and Ilya Marritz, "How Ivanka Trump and Donald Trump, Jr., Avoided a Criminal Indictment," *New Yorker,* Oct. 4, 2017. The story, a collaboration, was published in conjunction with ProPublica and WNYC.) As of 2017, the Trump SoHo had become the "Dominick," and only 128 of the 391 units in the building were sold.

76. "The Good Life," 2019

880 **"The source of the good life"**: Blum, vol. 1, 1.

Epilogue: East Eighty-sixth Street

887 **Nellie**: Elinor Gates Morgenthau died, at age sixty-nine, on September 20, 2020, at a community home of the New York Office for People with Developmental Disabilities, near Rome, New York, where she had lived for many years. She is buried in the family plot at the cemetery in Valhalla, New York.

Sources

INTERVIEWS AND CORRESPONDENCE

Parts I and II:

On the Morgenthaus in the 19th-century German states: Ralph Bloch, Elisabeth Böhrer, David Brenner, Thilo Figaj, Karen Franklin, Freddy Litten, Lars Menk, Sebastian Parzer, Stefan Rohrbacher. **The rise of New York City:** Christopher Gray, Clifton Hood, Ken Jackson, Barry Lewis, Moses Rischin, David M. Scobey, Rebecca Read Shanor, John Gordon Steele, John Tauranac. **Woodrow Wilson:** John Milton Cooper, Jr., Charles E. Neu, Norman Saul. **Turkey and the Armenians:** Taner Akçam, Rouben Adalian, Harry C. Keshian, Carolyn Mugar, Ara Sarafian, Maria Småberg, Uğur Ümit Üngör.

Part III:

Morgenthau friends and associates, 1920s–1940s: Mary Arnstein, Delia Heming Cantor, Mary Draper Janney, Justin N. Feldman, Barney Straus, Sr. **RMM at Amherst College:** Jack Chester, Chase Morsey, Jr., Bob Wiggins. **Roosevelt years:** John R. Boettiger, Blanche Wiesen Cook, John C. Culver, John Hyde, Curtis Roosevelt, Eleanor (Roosevelt) Seagraves, Robert A. Slayton, Anthony Smith, Bernard Stanton, Elinor (Klotz) Walden, Geoffrey C. Ward. **U.S. Naval history:** Glenn Knoblock, David W. McComb, Richard E. Miller, Robin L. Rielly, Commander E. Andrew Wilde, Jr. **On RMM's wartime service, fellow USN veterans:** William S. Beinecke, Alvin Caplan, Robert Dott, David Cisneros Garcia, George Fritzel, Marshall Geller, Al Macklin, Ben Montenegro, Guy N. Perenich, Raymond Quirion, Edwin Redfern, Sal Rizzo, Roger Sheer, George Sinclair, Peter Soler, Francis D. Tuggle, Alex Weinberg, Charles C. Wales. **Relatives of USN and Coast Guard veterans:** Anne Marie Allison, Carolyn Bartholme, Cameron Beck, James M. Loadholt, Jr.

The Holocaust and the War Refugee Board: Richard Breitman, Rebecca Erbelding, Henry Feingold, Laurel Leff, Gregory Wallance. **Europe during WWII and aftermath:** Elinor Balka, Benjamin Ferencz, Sophie (Taub) and Samuel Kahn. **Harry D. White:** Svetlana Chervonnaya, R. Bruce Craig. **Palestine under the British Mandate:** Elinor Burkett, Eran Kaplan, Meron Medzini, Benny Morris, and Itamar Radai.

Parts IV and V:

RMM at Yale Law: Bayless Manning, Frederic S. Nathan, Louise B. Ransom. **RFK as attorney general and RMM's investigations and cases:** Bill Barry, John J. Cassidy, Ramsey Clark, William Geoghegan, Ronald L. Goldfarb, Nicholas deB. Katzenbach, Anthony Lewis, Herbert J. Miller, Jr., Joe Mohbat, Victor Navasky, Jack Rosenthal, John Seigenthaler, Ted Sorensen. **Vietnam War resistance and civil liberties:** Taylor Branch, Barry L. Johnson, Alan Levine, Vincent McGee, Jr., Aryeh Neier, Roger Neville Williams. **Abe Fortas:** Stuart Allen, Scott Armstrong, John Griffiths, Daniel P. Levitt, H. David Rosenbloom, Walter Slocombe, Bob Woodward.

On **New York politics and criminal justice, 1960–2009:** George Arzt, John Catsimatidis, David C. Condliffe, John V. Connorton, Jr., Irene Cornell, Lee A. Daniels, David N. Dinkins, Betsy Gotbaum, Victor Gotbaum, Rudy Giuliani, Ronald Goldstock, Judah Gribetz, Bruce Gyory, Bill Haddad, Lou Harris, Nat Hentoff, Woody Klein, Ed Koch, Albert J. Krieger, Michael Kuh, Leonard Levitt, John LoCicero, C. Vernon Mason, Chief Terence Monahan, Charles O'Byrne, Richard Ravitch, Nicholas Scoppetta, Lucy Kostelanetz Schrader, Josh Segal, Frank Selvaggi, Donna Shalala, Marty Steadman, William vanden Heuvel, Hank Walter, Fred Wilpon, Sidney Zion. **At the FBI, retired special agents:** Bill Barry, James P. Flynn, Richard X. McCarthy, William Vericker.

Part V:

Members of the Manhattan DA's office (DANY) and the U.S. attorney's office in the Southern District of New York (SDNY), including alumni of either office, many of whom, as the tradition holds, went on to join the defense bar.

At the DA's office, 1974–2022: Walter M. Arsenault, Patricia Bailey, Steven P. Barry, Martha Bashford, Laura Billings, Ben Brafman, Bridget Brennan, Lanny Breuer, Austin V. Campriello, Owen B. Carragher, Jr., Peter Casolaro, Daniel J. Castleman, Michael Cherkasky, Katharine T. Cobb, Daniel Connolly, Jessica de Grazia, Michael Dougherty, Carey Dunne, Linda Fairstein, Leroy Frazer, John Fried, Lisa Friel, Richard Girgenti, Kevin Hynes, Beth D. Jacob, Beth Karas, Adam Kaufmann, James M. Kindler, Peter Kougasian, John "Artie" McConnell, Robert McGovern, Matthew Menchel, Melissa Mourges, John W. Moscow, Matt Murphy, Leonard Newman, Maureen O'Connor, Richard T. Preiss, Luke Rettler, Tom Shiels, Marc Frazier Scholl, Eric Seidel, Calvin Solomon, Eliot Spitzer, Robert K. Tanenbaum, Sheila Tendy, Ida Van Lindt, Cyrus Vance, Jr., Harold Wilson, Aaron T. Wolfson.

Veterans of the U.S. attorney's office (SDNY): Elkan Abramowitz, John R. Adams, Eugene R. Anderson, Michael Armstrong, Bob Arum, Thomas H. Baer, John R. Bartels, Jr., Tom Cahill, David Dorsen, John Doyle, Michael S. Fawer, Peter Fleming, Paul Galvani, Marty Gold, Paul Grand, Patricia Hynes, Howard Jacobs, Stephen E. Kaufman, Andrew M. Lawler, Robert McGuire, Andrew J. Maloney, Robert Morvillo, Gary Naftalis, Bernie Nussbaum, Paul L. Perito, Charles Rangel, John R. Robinson, Paul K. Rooney, Arthur I. Rosett, Charles A. Stillman, Victor Temkin, Frank Thomas, Frank Tuerkheimer, Gerald Walpin, Peter Zimroth.

The judges: Howard Baer, Jr., Mark Dwyer, Hugh Humphreys, Sterling Johnson Jr., Barbara S. Jones, John F. Keenan, James Kindler, Peter K. Leisure, Pierre Leval, Edward J. McLaughlin, Roslynn R. Mauskopf, Louis F. Oberdorfer, Robert P. Patterson, Jr., Leonard P. Rienzi, Abraham Sofaer, Sonia Sotomayor, Helen Sturm, Joan Sudolnik, Robert W. Sweet.

On the DA's investigations and prosecutions, among those not acknowledged elsewhere: **Investigators and detectives:** John Capers, Richard Condon, Peter Fiorillo, Osceola (Ozzie) Louis Fletcher, Dave Garcia, John Girdusky, Jennifer Mackovjak, James Rodriguez.

The "Washington Square Riot": Michele Andriani, Elizabeth Botros, Stephen F. Durnin, Ernest Hammer, Alminda Heredia, George Kosefas, Howard Meyer, Natividad Montilla, Christopher Pukit, Juan Sierra, Nancy Trichter, Clark Whelton. **The Gambino garment center case:** Ralph Blumenthal, Harry Bridgwood, Anthony Carro, Arthur Friedman, Nicholas

Gravante, James Jacobs, Sergio Lalli, Franz Leichter, Joel Machlis, Robert Mass, Ronnie Rivera, Glenn von Nostitz, Michael Rosen, Andy Rosenzweig, Gerald Shargel, Dan Wiese.

On BCCI, the DANY investigation, trial, and aftermath: Adil Ahmad, Kazim Alam, Jonathan Beaty, Robert Bennett, Akbar Bilgrami, Jack Blum, Alberto Calvo, Ali Chishti, Robert B. Fiske, Jr., Douglas Frantz, Larry Gurwin, S.C. Gwynne, Eric Lewis, Robert Mazur, Gustave Newman, Elyn Rahman, Masihur Rahman, Omar Quraishi, Najam Sethi, Brian Smouha, Peter Truell, Mary Anne Weaver.

The Central Park jogger case: Melvin Beldock, N. G. Berrill, Todd Clark, Karen Dippold, Jane H. Fisher-Byrialsen, Vernon N. Fonda, Brandon Garrett, Ray Kelly, Dr. Robert Kurtz, James Lansing, Harlan Levy, C. Vernon Mason, Trisha Meili, Robert Mooney, John O'Sullivan, Roger Parrino, Eric Reynolds, Irma Rivera-Duffy, Jermaine Robinson, Aaron Rosenthal, Barry Scheck, Michael Sheehan, Tim Sullivan, Michael Vigna, Joseph Walsh.

The Alavi Foundation investigation and Iranian banking cases: Eitan Arusy, Patrick Clawson, Rachel Ehrenfeld, Stephen Flatow, Abbas Milani, Liam O'Murchu, Steven R. Perles, Kesari Ruza, Daniel S. Ruzumna, Liviu Vogel. **At the FBI:** George J. Ennis, Jr., Martin Feely, Marc Van Driessche.

The Morgenthau family members: Eugene R. Anderson, Anne Morgenthau Grand, Paul Grand, Peter Josten, Ellin (Naumburg) London, Eileen (Josten) Lowe, Sarah Lowe, Henry M. Morgenthau III, Joan Morgenthau Hirschhorn, Jenny Morgenthau, Joshua Morgenthau, Linda Franks Morgenthau, Robert M. Morgenthau, Robert P. Morgenthau, Susan Bryce Moore Morgenthau, George W. Naumburg, Michelle Naumburg, Robert E. Simon, Jr., Christopher D. Wadsworth.

ELECTRONIC RESOURCES

America's Historical Newspapers (U.S. newspapers, 1690–1922, online database; NYPL)
Chronicling America (LC)
Fold3 (NARA military records, including "WWII War Diaries"; online database)
Frontline Diplomacy: The Foreign Affairs Oral History Collection of the Association for Diplomatic Studies and Training (LC)
Eleanor Roosevelt's "My Day" columns, 1932–1965 (Eleanor Roosevelt Papers Project, George Washington University)
Proquest Historical Newspapers
JSTOR
Vassiliev Notebooks (Wilson Center, Washington, D.C.)

PRIVATE COLLECTIONS

John Gordan III Papers

A. L. Goodhart correspondence from Poland, 1919

Robert P. Patterson Papers

Unpublished memoir, c. 1945–1947

GOVERNMENT ARCHIVES

National Archives (NARA)

Record Groups 56, 59
NARA War Diaries
SDNY Records

Franklin D. Roosevelt Library (FDRL)

John R. Boettiger Papers
Anna Roosevelt Halsted Papers
William Hassett Diary and Papers
Harry Hopkins Papers
Joseph P. Lash Papers
Henry Morgenthau, Jr., Papers and Diaries
Henry Morgenthau, Sr., Papers
Samuel Rosenman Papers
Sumner Welles Papers
Oral Histories: Rexford G. Tugwell (Interview with Henry A. Wallace)

Lyndon B. Johnson Library

Drew Pearson Papers

Harry S. Truman Library

Dean Acheson Papers
Bernard Bernstein Papers
Harry Truman Papers
Oral Histories: Bernard Bernstein (July 23, 1975); Jonathan Daniels (Oct. 4, 1963); Josiah
   DuBois (June 29, 1973); Samuel Rosenman (Oct. 15, 1968, April 23, 1969)

John F. Kennedy Library

Ernest Hemingway Personal Papers
Joseph P. Kennedy Personal Papers
Victor S. Navasky Personal Papers
Arthur M. Schlesinger, Jr., Personal Papers
Jean Stein Personal Papers
Oral Histories: W. Walton Butterworth; Roy Cohn; Justin M. Feldman; RFK; Herbert J.
   Miller; Daniel P. Moynihan

National Archives, UK

Foreign Office Records (1916–1949)
Treasury Office Records
War Office Records

State Archive of Economics of the Russian Federation

Records pertaining to Bretton Woods Conference

FOIA MATERIALS

CIA, FBI, IRS
U.S. Navy
U.S. State Department

U.S. Department of Defense
U.S. Department of Justice

PUBLIC ARCHIVES

Library of Congress (Manuscript Division)

Joseph and Stewart Alsop Papers
Courtney Letts de Espil Papers
Felix Frankfurter Diaries and Papers
Arthur J. Goldberg Papers
Cordell Hull Papers
Harold L. Ickes Papers
William D. Leahy Papers
Breckinridge Long Diary and Papers
Henry Morgenthau Papers
Robert Morgenthau Collection, Veterans History Project
Edith Bolling Galt Wilson Papers

New York City Municipal Archives

District Attorney Closed Case Files
District Attorney Indictment Records
Mayoral Papers: Lindsay, Beame, Koch, Dinkins, Giuliani

New York County Clerk's Office

Old Records Division, Case Files

New York Public Library (Archives and Manuscripts)

James H. Hyde Papers
Levi Morton Papers
New York Times Company Records: Adolph S. Ochs Papers
New York Times Company Records: Arthur Hays Sulzberger Papers
Dorothy Schiff Papers
Arthur M. Schlesinger, Jr., Papers
Nathan Straus Papers
Lillian Wald Papers

PRIVATE ARCHIVES

Archives of American Art (Smithsonian)

S. J. Woolf Papers, 1835–1986

American Jewish Archives

Kaufmann Kohler Papers
Adolph S. Ochs Papers
Jacob H. Schiff Papers

Felix M. Warburg Papers
Stephen S. Wise Papers

Amherst College

Graduates' Quarterly; Alumni News; Biographical Record; Yearbooks
Karl Loewenstein Papers
John McCloy Diary and Papers

Leo Baeck Institute

Morgenthau Family Collection, 1938–1968

Bodleian Library, University of Oxford

Papers of Arthur Lehman Goodhart

Birmingham University, England (Cadbury Research Library)

Lord Avon Papers

Brandeis University (Robert D. Farber University Archives and Special Collections)

Stephen S. Wise Collection

Central Zionist Archives (Jerusalem)

Peter Bergson File

Columbia University

Charles R. Crane Papers
Jane Howard Papers
William G. Lambert Papers
Herbert H. Lehman Papers
Robert M. Morgenthau Papers
William Barclay Parsons Diary, 4 vols., 1900–1904

Columbia University Oral History Project (COHP)

David Norman Dinkins, 2014
Justin N. Feldman, 1968
Edward S. Greenbaum, 1965
Burton J. Hendricks, 1949
Edward I. Koch, 1975–1976
Mary Lasker, 1965, 1982
Herbert H. Lehman, 1959
Henry Morgenthau, Jr., 1957
Frances Perkins, 1951–1955
Henry Stimson, 1949

Henry Agard Wallace, 1951, 1953
James Paul Warburg, 1952

Cornell University

Alumni Records
Edward Roe Eastman Papers
George F. Warren Papers

Deerfield Academy

Alumni Records; Yearbooks

Denver Public Library

Abby S. Hagerman Comstock Shafroth Papers

Phillips Exeter

Alumni Records; Yearbooks

Georgetown University

Cornelius Van H. Engert Papers

Harvard University

Louise E. Kirstein Papers
William Phillips Papers
Belle Mayer Zeck Papers

The Hebrew University (Institute for Contemporary Jewry, Jerusalem)

Oral Histories: Harry Beale (June 27, 1975); Mathilda Braelove, Leon Gerber, Joe Mazer, William Mazer (March 2, 1975); Sam Feingold (March 19, 1976); Henry Montor (Oct. 14, 1975); Ralph Wechsler (March 28, 1976)

Hoover Institution Archives

William J. Marshall Papers
Raymond Moley Papers
Richard J. Whalen Papers

Johns Hopkins University

Isaiah Bowman Papers

New-York Historical Society

Time Inc. Records

New York Stock Exchange Archives

Historical Records; Art Collection

Nuffield College (University of Oxford)

Frederick Alexander Lindemann (Lord Cherwell) Papers

Princeton University

Bernard Baruch Papers
Edward S. Greenbaum Papers
Arthur Krock Papers
Jacob Viner Papers
Harry Dexter White Papers

Rice University (Woodson Research Center, Fondren Library)

Panhandle Eastern Corp. Historical Records
PEPL History Project transcripts: Robert Morgenthau, March 16, 1956

Rockefeller Archive Center

Cary Reich Papers
John D. Rockefeller III Diary

Smith College (Sophia Smith Collection)

Agnes Morgenthau Newborg Papers

UCLA

Hearst Metrotone News Collection, 1933–1949

United States Holocaust Memorial Museum

Henry Morgenthau III Papers
Personal Papers, Documents, Photographs
Interviews: Edward Bernays; Edward Bernstein (Jan. 27, 1979); John Morton Blum (May 15, 1984); Josiah DuBois (Feb. 26, 1981); Henrietta Stein Klotz (Sept. 19, 1978); John McCloy (Oct. 8, 1986); Iphigene Ochs; John Pehle (Jan. 29, 1979); Sylvia Porter; Gerhart Riegner (June 1994); Barbara Tuchman (1979)

University of Iowa

Henry Agard Wallace Papers

University of Notre Dame

Frank C. Walker Papers

University of Wisconsin (Wisconsin Historical Society)

Miriam Ottenberg Papers

Wellesley College

Margaret Clapp Papers

Wesleyan University

William Manchester Papers

Yale University

Irving Fisher Papers
Burton Hendricks Papers
Edward Mandell House Papers
The New York Hebrew Select Directory and Visiting List (New York: Select Publishing Co., 1896)
Henry Lewis Stimson Diaries

YIVO Institute for Jewish Research

Records and Art, Morgenthau Polish Mission, 1919

PUBLISHED SOURCES

American Architect and Building News
Architectural Record
Brooklyn Eagle
New York Evening Post
New York Herald
New York Sun
New York Times
New York Tribune
New York World
Poughkeepsie Sunday Courier
Real Estate Record and Builders' Guide

U.S. Congressional Reports

Bank of Credit and Commerce International (BCCI) Investigation: Hearing Before the Committee on Banking, Finance, and Urban Affairs. U.S. House of Representatives, 102nd Congress, 1st session. Parts 1–3, 1991, 1992.

The BCCI Affair: A Report to the Committee on Foreign Relations. U.S. Senate, 102nd Congress, 2nd session. (Penultimate draft, December 1992.)

Foreign Bank Secrecy and Bank Records. Hearings, 91st Cong., 1st and 2nd sessions, on H.R. 15073. House Committee on Banking and Currency. U.S. Government Printing Office, 1970.

Legal and Economic Impact of Foreign Banking Procedures on the United States. Hearing, 90th Cong., 2nd session, Dec. 9, 1968. United States Congress. House Committee on Banking and Currency, 1968.

Documentaries, Film and Television

"The Bank of Crooks and Criminals." Rory O'Connor, producer. *Frontline.* 60 mins, broadcast, April 21, 1992.

"The Bank That Didn't Add Up." Gerard Baker, producer. Panorama/BBC Films. 42 mins., broadcast, Nov. 18, 1991.

Laurence Jarvik, director. *Who Shall Live and Who Shall Die,* 90 mins., 1982.

Books and Articles

Abraamian, G. A., and T. G. Sevan-Khachatrian, eds. *Russkie istochniki o genotside armyan v Osmonskoi imperii 1915–1916. Sbornik dokumentov i materialov.* Vol 1. [Russian sources on the Armenian genocide in the Ottoman Empire, 1915–16: Collection of documents and materials]. Yerevan: "Areresum"-Ani, 1995.

Acheson, Dean. *Among Friends: Personal Letters of Dean Acheson.* Edited by David S. McLellan and David C. Acheson. New York: Dodd, Mead & Company, 1980.

———. *Present at the Creation: My Years at the State Department.* New York: W. W. Norton, 1987.

Acheson, Dean, and Harry S. Truman. *Affection and Trust: The Personal Correspondence of Harry S. Truman and Dean Acheson, 1953–1971.* New York: Knopf, 2010.

Adalian, Rouben Paul, comp. and ed. *Guide to the Armenian Genocide in the U.S. Archives, 1915–1918.* Alexandria, Va.: Chadwyck-Healey, 1994.

———. "American Diplomatic Correspondence in the Age of Mass Murder: Documents of the Armenian Genocide in the U.S. Archives." In *America and the Armenian Genocide,* edited by J. M. Winter. Cambridge: Cambridge University Press, 2003.

Adams, James Ring, and Douglas Frantz. *A Full Service Bank: How BCCI Stole Billions Around the World.* New York: Pocket Books, 1992.

Akçam, Taner. *A Shameful Act: The Armenian Genocide and the Question of Turkish Responsibility.* New York: Metropolitan Books, 2007.

Alexiou, Alice Sparberg. *The Flatiron: The New York Landmark and the Incomparable City That Arose with It.* New York: St. Martin's, 2010.

Ali, Tariq. *A Banker for All Seasons.* London: Seagull, 2007.

Allen, Frederick L. *Since Yesterday: The 1930's in America, September 3, 1929, to September 3, 1939.* New York: Harper & Row, 1940.

Alsop, Joseph, and Robert Kintner. "The Great World Money Play." *Saturday Evening Post,* April 8, 1939, 16–86.

———. "Henny Penny: Farmer at the Treasury." *Saturday Evening Post,* April 1, 1939, 98–103.

———. "The Secret Finale." *Saturday Evening Post,* April 5, 1939, 25–102.

Alter, Jonathan. *The Defining Moment: FDR's Hundred Days and the Triumph of Hope.* New York: Simon & Schuster, 2006.

Ambrose, Stephen. *Eisenhower: Soldier, General of the Army, President-Elect.* New York: Simon & Schuster, 1983.

Andrews, Lewis M. *Tempest, Fire and Foe: Destroyer Escorts in World War II and the Men Who Manned Them.* Victoria, B.C.: Trafford Publishing, 2004.

Appleman, Roy E., et al. *Okinawa: The Last Battle.* The U.S. Army in World War II: The War in the Pacific series. Washington D.C.: Center of Military History, U.S. Army, 2005. First published in 1948.

Armstrong, Michael. *They Wished They Were Honest: The Knapp Commission and New York City Police Corruption.* New York: Columbia University Press, 2012.

Auletta, Ken. "Don't Mess with Roy Cohn." *Esquire*, Dec. 5, 1978.

———. *Hard Feelings: Reporting on the Pols, the Press, the People and the City.* New York: Random House, 1980.

———. *The Streets Were Paved in Gold: The Decline of New York, An American Tragedy.* New York: Random House, 1979.

Baker, Ray Stannard. "The Trust's New Tool—The Labor Boss." *McClure's*, November 1903, 30–43.

———. *Woodrow Wilson, Life and Letters: 1890–1910, Princeton.* 8 vols. New York: Doubleday, Page & Co., 1927.

Balakian, Peter. *The Burning Tigris: The Armenian Genocide and America's Response.* New York: HarperCollins, 2003.

Barber, William. *Designs Within Disorder: Franklin D. Roosevelt, the Economists, and the Shaping of American Economic Policy, 1933–1945.* Cambridge: Cambridge University Press, 1996.

Barrett, Wayne, and Jack Newfield. *City for Sale: Ed Koch and the Betrayal of New York.* New York: Harper & Row, 1988.

Barton, James L. "Ten Million Dollars for Relief: A Brief Account of the Work of the American Committee for Armenian and Syrian Relief." *Missionary Review of the World* 41 (July 1918): 491–96.

Bass, Gary. *Freedom's Battle: The Origins of Humanitarian Intervention.* New York: Alfred A. Knopf, 2008.

———. *Stay the Hand of Vengeance: The Politics of War Crimes Tribunals.* Princeton, N.J.: Princeton University Press, 2000.

Batiuk, V. I. *The Sources of the Cold War: The Soviet-American Relations in 1945–1950.* Moscow: RNF—The Russian Research Fund. In Russian, published as *Istoki "holodnoi voiny": Sovetsko-Amerikanskie otnoshenija v 1945–1950 gg.* Moscow: RNF—Rossiiskii nauchnyi fond.

Beard, Patricia. *After the Ball: Gilded Age Secrets, Boardroom Betrayals, and the Party That Ignited the Great Wall Street Scandal of 1905.* New York: HarperCollins, 2003.

Beaty, Jonathan, and S. C. Gwynne. *The Outlaw Bank: A Wild Ride into the Secret Heart of BCCI.* New York: Random House, 1993.

Beinecke, William S., with Geoffrey M. Kabaservice. *Through Mem'ry's Haze: A Personal Memoir.* New York: Prospect Hill Press, 2000.

Beisner, Robert L. *Dean Acheson: A Life in the Cold War.* Oxford: Oxford University Press, 2006.

Ben-Gurion, David. *War Diary: The War of Independence, 1948–1949.* Edited by Gershon Rivlin and Elhanan Orren. Tel Aviv: Ministry of Defense, 1982. (Published in Hebrew as *Yoman ha-milhamah: Milhemet ha-atzma'ut tashah–tashat.*)

Ben-Veniste, Richard. *The Emperor's New Clothes: Exposing the Truth from Watergate to 9/11.* New York: Thomas Dunne/St. Martin's, 2009.

Berg, A. Scott. *Wilson.* New York: Putnam, 2013.

Berger, Meyer. *The Story of* The New York Times: *The First 100 Years, 1851–1951.* New York: Simon & Schuster, 1951.

Berlin, Isaiah. *Isaiah Berlin.* Vol. 1, *Letters, 1928–1946.* Edited by Henry Hardy. Cambridge: Cambridge University Press, 2004.

Beschloss, Michael. *The Conquerors: Roosevelt, Truman, and the Destruction of Hitler's Germany, 1941–1945.* New York: Simon & Schuster, 2002.

———. *Kennedy and Roosevelt: The Uneasy Alliance.* New York: W. W. Norton, 1980.

Bird, Kai. *The Chairman: John J. McCloy, The Making of the American Establishment.* New York: Simon & Schuster, 1992.

Blum, John Morton. *From the Morgenthau Diaries*. 3 vols.: vol. 1, *Years of Crisis, 1928–1938*; vol. 2, *Years of Urgency, 1938–1941*; vol. 3, *Years of War, 1941–1945*. Boston: Houghton Mifflin, 1959–67. Revised and condensed version issued in a one-volume edition in 1970 as *Roosevelt and Morgenthau*.

———. *A Life with History*. Lawrence: University Press of Kansas, 2004.

Blumenthal, Ralph. "When the Mob Delivered the Goods." *New York Times Magazine*, July 26, 1992.

Bocage, Leo J. "The Public Career of Charles R. Crane." Ph.D. diss., Fordham University, 1962.

Boettiger, John R. *A Love in Shadow*. New York: W. W. Norton, 1978.

Bonanno, Joseph, with Sergio Lalli. *A Man of Honor: The Autobiography of Joseph Bonanno*. New York: Simon & Schuster, 1983.

Bowers, Robert E. "American Diplomacy, the 1933 Wheat Conference, and Recognition of the Soviet Union." *Agricultural History* 40, no. 1 (January 1966): 39–52.

Brands, H. W. *Traitor to His Class: The Privileged Life and Radical Presidency of Franklin Delano Roosevelt*. New York: Doubleday, 2008.

Breitman, Richard. *Official Secrets: What the Nazis Planned, What the British and Americans Knew*. New York: Hill & Wang, 1998.

Breitman, Richard, and Alan M. Kraut. *American Refugee Policy and European Jewry, 1933–1945*. Bloomington: Indiana University Press, 1987.

Breitman, Richard, and Walter Laqueur. *Breaking the Silence*. New York: Simon & Schuster, 1986.

Breitman, Richard, and Allan J. Lichtman. *FDR and the Jews*. Cambridge, Mass.: Harvard University Press, 2013.

Breitman, Richard, Barbara McDonald Stewart, and Severin Hochberg, eds. *Advocate for the Doomed: The Diaries and Papers of James G. McDonald, 1932–1935*. Bloomington: Indiana University Press, 2007.

———, eds. *Refugees and Rescue: The Diaries and Papers of James G. McDonald, 1935–1945*. Bloomington: Indiana University Press, 2009.

Breslin, Jimmy. *Damon Runyon: A Life*. New York: Laurel, 1992.

Brill, Steve. "Fighting Crime in a Crumbling System." *American Lawyer*, July & August 1989.

Broesamle, John J. *William Gibbs McAdoo: A Passion for Change, 1863–1917*. Port Washington, N.Y.: Kennikat Press, 1973.

Brooks, John. "Gold Standard on the Booze." *The New Yorker*, Sept. 13, 1969, 107.

———. *Once in Golconda: A True Story of Wall Street, 1920–38*. New York: Allworth Press, 1997. First published in 1969.

Brown, John Crawford. "Early Days of the Department Stores." In *Valentine's Manual of Old New York, No. 5*, edited by Henry Collins Brown. New York: Chauncey Holt Company, 1921.

Brown, John H. "The Disappearing Russian Embassy Archives, 1922–1939." *Prologue: The Journal of the National Archives* 14 (Spring 1982): 5–13.

Burns, Sarah. *The Central Park Five: A Chronicle of a City Wilding*. New York: Knopf, 2011.

Butow, R. J. C. "Pearl Harbor Jitters: Defending the White House Against Attack." *Prologue* 23 (Winter 1991).

Butturff Dow, Dorothy. *Eleanor Roosevelt, An Eager Spirit: The Letters of Dorothy Dow, 1933–1945*. Edited by Ruth K. McClure. New York: W. W. Norton, 1984.

Caro, Robert. *The Powerbroker: Robert Moses and the Fall of New York*. New York: Vintage, 1974.

Castaneda, Christopher J., and Clarance M. Smith. *Gas Pipelines and the Emergence of America's Regulatory State: A History of Panhandle Eastern Corporation, 1928–1993*. New York: Cambridge University Press, 1996.

Chambers, William Nesbitt. *Yoljuluk: Random Thoughts on a Life in Imperial Turkey*. London: Simpkin Marshall, 1928.

Churchill, Winston. *The Second World War*. 6 vols.: *The Gathering Storm; Their Finest Hour; The Grand Alliance; The Hinge of Fate; Closing the Ring; Triumph and Tragedy*. Boston: Houghton Mifflin Harcourt, 1948.

Cohan, William D. *The Last Tycoons: The Secret History of Lazard Frères & Co*. New York: Doubleday, 2007.

Cohen, Adam. *Nothing to Fear: FDR's Inner Circle and the Hundred Days That Created Modern America*. New York: Penguin Press, 2009.

Cohen, Naomi Wiener. *Jacob H. Schiff: A Study in American Jewish Leadership*. Hanover, N.H.: Brandeis University Press, 1999.

Cohn, Roy M. *A Fool for a Client: My Struggle Against the Power of a Public Prosecutor*. New York: Hawthorn Books, 1971.

Cohn, Roy M., and Sidney Zion. *The Autobiography of Roy Cohn*. Secaucus, N.J.: Lyle Stuart, 1988.

Collins, Theresa May. *Otto Kahn: Art, Money, & Modern Times*. Chapel Hill: University of North Carolina Press, 2002.

Colville, John. *The Fringes of Power: 10 Downing Street Diaries: 1939–1955*. New York: W. W. Norton, 1985.

Condit, Carl W., and Sarah Bradford Landau. *Rise of the New York Skyscraper: 1885–1913*. New Haven, Conn.: Yale University Press, 1999.

Conway, Ed. *The Summit: The Biggest Battle of the Second World War, Fought Behind Closed Doors*. London: Little, Brown, 2014.

Cook, Blanche Wiesen. *Eleanor Roosevelt: A Biography*. Vol. 1, *1884–1933*. New York: Viking, 1992.

———. *Eleanor Roosevelt: A Biography*. Vol. 2, *The Defining Years, 1933–1938*. New York: Viking, 1999.

———. *Eleanor Roosevelt: A Biography*. Vol. 3, *The War Years and After, 1939–1962*. New York: Viking, 2016.

Cooper, John Milton, Jr. "A Friend in Power?: Woodrow Wilson and Armenia." In *America and the Armenian Genocide*, edited by J. M. Winter. Cambridge: Cambridge University Press, 2003.

———. *The Warrior and the Priest: Woodrow Wilson and Theodore Roosevelt*. Cambridge, Mass.: Belknap Press of Harvard University Press, 1983.

———. *Woodrow Wilson: A Biography*. New York: Knopf, 2009.

Costello, John. *The Pacific War, 1941–1945*. New York: Harper Perennial, 1981.

Cowen, Philip. *Memories of an American Jew*. New York: International Press, 1932.

Craig, R. Bruce. *Treasonable Doubt: The Harry Dexter White Spy Case*. Lawrence: University Press of Kansas, 2004.

Culver, John C., and John Hyde. *American Dreamer: The Life and Times of Henry A. Wallace*. New York: W. W. Norton, 2001.

Cunningham, Barry, and Mike Pearl. *Mr. District Attorney: The Story of Frank Hogan*. New York: Mason/Charter, 1977.

Dallek, Robert. *Franklin D. Roosevelt and American Foreign Policy, 1932–1945*. New York: Oxford University Press, 1995.

Daniels, Jonathan. *White House Witness: 1942–1945*. New York: Doubleday, 1975.

Daniels, Josephus. *The Cabinet Diaries of Josephus Daniels, 1913–1921*. Edited by E. David Cronon. Lincoln: University of Nebraska Press, 1963.

———. *The Wilson Era. Years of Peace*. Chapel Hill: University of North Carolina Press, 1944.

Davidowicz, Lucy. "American Jews and the Holocaust." *New York Times Magazine*, April 18, 1982.

Davidson, Bill. "A Profile in Family Courage." *Saturday Evening Post*, Dec. 14, 1963, 32–36.

Davis, Kenneth S. *FDR: The Beckoning of Destiny, 1882–1928.* New York: Putnam, 1972.

———. *FDR: The New York Years, 1928–1933.* New York: Random House, 1985.

———. *FDR: The New Deal Years, 1934–1937.* New York: Random House, 1986.

———. *FDR: Into the Storm, 1937–1940.* New York: Random House, 1993.

———. *FDR: The War President, 1940–43.* New York: Random House, 2000.

Davis, Leslie A., and Susan K. Blair, eds. *The Slaughterhouse Province: An American Diplomat's Report on the Armenian Genocide, 1915–1917.* New Rochelle, N.Y.: A.D. Caratzas, 1989.

Derrick, Peter. *Tunneling to the Future: The Story of the Great Subway Expansion That Saved New York.* New York: New York University Press, 2001.

DuBois, Josiah E., Jr., with Edward Johnson. *The Devil's Chemists: 24 Conspirators of the International Farben Cartel Who Manufacture Wars.* Boston: Beacon Press, 1952.

Ehrenfried, Albert. *A Chronicle of Boston Jewry: From the Colonial Settlement to 1900.* Privately published by Irving Bernstein, 1963.

Eiler, Keith. *Mobilizing America: Robert P. Patterson and the War Effort.* Ithaca, N.Y.: Cornell University Press, 1997.

Elkus, Abram. *The Memoirs of Abram Elkus: Lawyer, Ambassador, Statesman.* Princeton, N.J.: Gomidas Institute, 2004.

Erbelding, Rebecca. *Rescue Board: The Untold Story of America's Efforts to Save the Jews of Europe.* New York: Doubleday, 2018.

Faber, Doris. *Printer's Devil to Publisher: Adolph S. Ochs of* The New York Times. New York: Messner, 1963.

Faith, Nicholas. *Safety in Numbers: The Mysterious World of Swiss Banking.* London: Hamish Hamilton, 1982.

Feingold, Henry L. *Bearing Witness: How America and Its Jews Responded to the Holocaust.* Syracuse, N.Y.: Syracuse University Press, 1995.

———. *The Politics of Rescue: The Roosevelt Administration and the Holocaust, 1938–1945.* New Brunswick, N.J.: Rutgers University Press, 1970.

Feis, Herbert. *1933: Characters in Crisis.* Boston: Little, Brown, 1966.

Fenyvesi, Charles. "The Nazi Secret No One Believed; Remembering the Man Who Knew." *Washington Post*, Feb. 5, 1983.

Flynn, Edward J. *You're the Boss.* Westport, Conn.: Greenwood Press, 1975. First published in 1947 by Viking Press.

Frankfurter, Felix. *Felix Frankfurter Reminiscences.* Recorded in talks with Dr. Harlan B. Phillips. New York: Reynal & Company, 1960.

Franks, Lucinda. *My Father's Secret War.* New York: Miramax, 2007.

———. *Timeless: Love, Morgenthau and Me.* New York: Farrar, Straus and Giroux, 2014.

———. *Waiting Out a War: The Exile of Private John Picciano.* New York: Coward, McCann & Geoghegan, 1974.

Freidel, Frank Burt. *Franklin D. Roosevelt: Launching the New Deal.* Boston: Little, Brown, 1973. 3 vols.: *FDR: The Triumph* (1956); *FDR: The Ordeal* (1954).

Gage, Nicholas. *The Mafia Is Not an Equal Opportunity Employer.* Foreword by Robert M. Morgenthau. New York: McGraw-Hill, 1971.

Gentry, Curt. *J. Edgar Hoover: The Man and His Secrets.* New York: W. W. Norton, 1991.

Glanz, Rudolf. "The Rise of the Jewish Club in America." *Jewish Social Studies* 31, no. 2 (April 1969): 82–99.

Goldfarb, Ronald L. *Perfect Villains, Imperfect Heroes: Robert F. Kennedy's War Against Organized Crime.* New York: Random House, 1995.

Goldstock, Ronald, Martin Marcus, Thomas D. Thacher II, and James B. Jacobs. *Corruption and Racketeering in the New York City Construction Industry: The Final Report of*

New York State Organized Crime Task Force. New York: New York University Press, 1991.

Goodhart, Arthur Lehman. *Poland and the Minority Peoples*. London: G. Allen & Unwin, 1920.

Goodman, Walter. *A Percentage of the Take*. New York: Farrar, Straus and Giroux, 1971.

Goodwin, Doris Kearns. *No Ordinary Time: Franklin and Eleanor Roosevelt; The Home Front in World War II*. New York: Simon & Schuster, 1994.

Gould, Leslie. *The Manipulators*. New York: D. McKay & Co., 1966.

Greenbaum, Edward Samuel. *A Lawyer's Job, in Court, in the Army, in the Office*. New York: Harcourt, Brace & World, 1967.

Gurwin, Larry, and Peter Truell. *False Profits: The Inside Story of BCCI, the World's Most Corrupt Financial Empire*. New York: Houghton Mifflin, 1992.

Haight, John McVickar. *American Aid to France, 1938–1940*. New York: Atheneum, 1970.

Harriott, Frank. "Three Who Saw FDR Die." *Negro Digest,* May 1951, 17–27.

Hassett, William D. *Off the Record with F.D.R., 1942–1945*. New York: Enigma, 2016. First published by Rutgers University Press, 1958.

Hellman, Geoffrey T. "Any Bonds Today?" *The New Yorker,* Jan. 22 & 29, 1944.

———. *Mrs. de Peyster's Parties and Other Lively Studies from the New Yorker*. New York: Macmillan, 1963.

Hentoff, Nat. "The Idealistic (Sic) Prosecutor." *Village Voice,* Feb. 14, 21 & 28, 1974.

Heylbut, Rose, and Aimé Gerber. *Backstage at the Opera*. New York: Thomas Y. Crowell, 1937.

Hodgson, Geoffrey. *The Colonel: The Life and Wars of Henry Stimson, 1867–1950*. New York: Knopf, 1990.

Hoffman, Paul. *Courthouse*. New York: Hawthorn Books, 1979.

Hood, Clifton. *722 Miles: The Building of the Subways and How They Transformed New York*. Baltimore: Johns Hopkins University Press, 1995.

Ickes, Harold L. *The Secret Diary of Harold L. Ickes*. Vols. 1–3. New York: Da Capo Press, 1974.

Irey, Elmer, with William J. Slocum. *The Tax Dodgers: The Inside Story of the T-Men's War with America's Political and Underworld Hoodlums*. New York: Greenberg, 1948.

Jacobs, James B., with Coleen Friel and Robert Radick. *Gotham Unbound: How New York City Was Liberated from the Grip of Organized Crime*. New York: New York University Press, 1999.

Jennings, John Henry. "A History of the New Theatre, New York, 1909–1911." Ph.D. diss., Stanford University, 1952.

Jervey, Gay. "Waltzing with the Wise Guys." *American Lawyer,* May 1992.

Johnson, Gerald White. *An Honorable Titan: A Biographical Study of Adolph S. Ochs*. New York: Harper & Brothers, 1946.

Kalman, Laura. *Abe Fortas: A Biography*. New Haven, Conn.: Yale University Press, 1990.

Katzenbach, Nicholas deB. *Some of It Was Fun: Working with LBJ and RFK*. New York: W. W. Norton, 2008.

Kaufman, Menahem, and Mira Levine. *Guide to America–Holy Land Studies, 1620–1948*. Vol. 4, *Resource Material in British, Israeli and Turkish Repositories*. New York: Praeger, 1984.

Kennedy, David M. *Freedom from Fear: The American People in Depression and War, 1929–1945*. New York: Oxford University Press, 1999.

Kennedy, Joseph P. *Hostage to Fortune: The Letters of Joseph P. Kennedy*. Edited by Amanda Smith. New York: Viking, 2001.

Kennedy, Maxwell Taylor. *Danger's Hour: The Story of the USS* Bunker Hill *and the Kamikaze Pilot Who Crippled Her*. New York: Simon & Schuster, 2009.

Kennedy, Rose. *Times to Remember.* New York: Doubleday, 1974.

Kerney, James. *The Political Education of Woodrow Wilson.* New York: The Century Co., 1926.

Kessner, Thomas. *Capital City: New York City and the Men Behind America's Rise to Economic Dominance, 1860–1900.* New York: Simon & Schuster, 2003.

Keynes, John Maynard. *The Collected Writings of John Maynard Keynes.* Edited by Elizabeth Johnson and Donald Moggridge. Cambridge: Cambridge University Press, 1980.

Kochan, Nick, and Bob Whittington. *Bankrupt: The BCCI Fraud.* London: Victor Gollancz, 1991.

Lambert, William. "The End of the Fortas Affair." *Life,* May 23, 1969, 38–39.

———. "Fortas of the Supreme Court: A Question of Ethics." *Life,* May 9, 1969, 32–37.

———. "The Hotshot One-Man Roy Cohn Lobby." *Life,* Sept. 5, 1969, 25–31.

———. "The Murky Men from the Speaker's Office." *Life,* Oct. 27, 1969, 52–58.

Lambert, William, and Sandy Smith. "Special Report: The Mob." *Life,* Jan. 26, 1968, 54A.

Lambert, William, and Keith Wheeler. "Roy Cohn: Is He a Liar Under Oath?" *Life,* Oct. 4, 1963, 24–30, 99–102.

Lash, Joseph P. *Eleanor and Franklin: The Story of Their Relationship, Based on Eleanor Roosevelt's Private Papers.* New York: W. W. Norton, 1971.

———. *From the Diaries of Felix Frankfurter.* New York: W. W. Norton, 1975.

———. *Love, Eleanor: Eleanor Roosevelt and Her Friends.* New York: Doubleday, 1982.

———. *A World of Love: Eleanor Roosevelt and Her Friends, 1943–62.* New York: Doubleday, 1984.

Leff, Laurel. *Buried by the Times: The Holocaust and America's Most Important Newspaper.* New York: Cambridge University Press, 2005.

———. "A Tragic 'Fight in the Family': *The New York Times,* Reform Judaism and the Holocaust." *American Jewish History* 88, no. 1 (March 2000): 3–51.

Lelyveld, Joseph. *His Final Battle: The Last Months of Franklin Roosevelt.* New York: Alfred A. Knopf, 2016.

Lepsius, Johannes. *Deutschland und Armenien: Sammlung Diplomatischer Aktenstücke.* Potsdam: Der Tempelverlag, 1919.

Liaquat, Ahamed. *Lords of Finance: The Bankers Who Broke the World.* New York: Penguin Press, 2009.

Lichtman, Robert M. "Goldberg and Hoover: How Two Disparate Washington Insiders Resolved a McCarthy-Era Problem to Mutual (and the Nation's) Advantage." *American Communist History* 10, no. 3 (December 2011): 205.

Liman, Arthur L. *Lawyer: A Life of Counsel and Controversy.* New York: PublicAffairs, 1998.

Lindley, Ernest. *The Roosevelt Revolution: First Phase.* New York: Viking Press, 1934.

Link, Arthur S., ed. *Papers of Woodrow Wilson.* 69 vols. Princeton, N.J.: Princeton University Press, 1966–1994.

Lockwood, Charles. *Manhattan Moves Uptown: An Illustrated History.* Boston: Houghton Mifflin, 1976.

Logan, Andy. "Court Games." *The New Yorker,* March 18, 1974, 110.

———. "Lawyers, Guns, and Money." *The New Yorker,* April 28, 1986, 100.

Long, Breckinridge. *The War Diary of Breckinridge Long: Selections from the Years 1939–1944.* Lincoln: University of Nebraska Press, 1966.

Louchheim, Katie, ed. *The Making of the New Deal: The Insiders Speak.* Cambridge, Mass.: Harvard University Press, 1983.

Lyne, Barbara. "The Women of One Hogan Place." *Manhattan Lawyer* 3, no. 15 (March 1990): 24–26.

Maas, Peter. "The Killer Who Told on the Mob." *Saturday Evening Post,* Nov. 23, 1963, 21–2.

———. "Mafia: The Inside Story." *Saturday Evening Post,* Aug. 10, 1963, 19–25.

———. *The Valachi Papers.* New York: HarperCollins, 2003.

Mallmann, Klaus-Michael, and Martin Cuppers. *Halbmond und Hakenkreuz: Das "Dritte Reich," die Araber und Palästina.* Darmstadt: Wissenschaftliche Buchgesellschaft, 2006.

———. *Nazi Palestine: The Plans for the Extermination of the Jews in Palestine.* New York: Enigma, 2010.

Masters, Brooke A. *Spoiling for a Fight: The Rise of Eliot Spitzer.* New York: Times Books, 2006.

Mazur, Robert. *The Infiltrator.* New York: Little, Brown, 2009.

McAdoo, William G. *Crowded Years.* New York: Houghton Mifflin, 1931.

McIntire, Ross T., with George Creel. *White House Physician.* New York: Putnam, 1946.

———. "Unconquerable Spirit." *Collier's,* Feb. 2, 1946, 21.

McPhee, John. *The Headmaster: Frank L. Boyden, of Deerfield.* New York: Farrar, Straus and Giroux, 1966.

Meacham, Jon. *Franklin and Winston: An Intimate Portrait of an Epic Friendship.* New York: Random House, 2003.

Medoff, Rafael. *Blowing the Whistle on Genocide: Josiah E. DuBois and the Struggle for a U.S. Response to the Holocaust.* West Lafayette, Ind.: Purdue University Press, 2009.

Meili, Trisha. *I Am the Central Park Jogger.* New York: Scribner, 2003.

Meir, Menachem. *My Mother Golda Meir: A Son's Evocation of Life with Golda Meir.* Arbor House, 1983.

Mooney, James. *Dictionary of American Fighting Ships.* Washington, D.C.: Department of the Navy, 1991.

Morgenthau, Henry. *Ambassador Morgenthau's Story.* With a foreword by Robert Jay Lifton, an introduction by Roger W. Smith, and an epilogue by Henry Morgenthau III. Detroit: Wayne State University Press, 2003. First published by Doubleday, Page and Company, 1918.

———. *My Trip Around the World.* New York: privately published, 1928.

Morgenthau, Henry, with French Strother. *All in a Lifetime.* New York: Doubleday, Page, 1922.

———. *I Was Sent to Athens.* New York: Doubleday, Page and Company, 1929.

Morgenthau, Henry, II. "American Tractor Expedition to France." *Oregon Countryman* 10, no. 1 (June 1917): 161–62.

———. *Germany Is Our Problem: A Plan for Germany.* New York: Harper & Brothers, 1945.

———. "The Morgenthau Diaries." *Collier's,* Sept. 27, 1947, 11–82.

———. "The Morgenthau Diaries II: The Struggle for a Program." *Collier's,* Oct. 4, 1947, 20–21, 45–49.

———. "The Morgenthau Diaries III: How FDR Fought the Axis." *Collier's,* Oct 11, 1947, 20–79.

———. "The Morgenthau Diaries IV: The Story Behind Lend-Lease." *Collier's,* Oct. 18, 1947, 16–75.

———. "The Morgenthau Diaries V: The Paradox of Poverty and Plenty." *Collier's,* Oct. 25, 1947, 24–86.

———. "The Morgenthau Diaries VI: The Refugee Run-Around." *Collier's,* Nov. 1, 1947, 22–65.

———. "Our Policy Toward Germany." Four-part series, ghostwritten by Arthur M. Schlesinger, Jr. *New York Post,* Nov. 24–29, 1947.

Morgenthau, Henry, II, Carl S. Scofield, and J. A. Taylor. *Morgenthau Expedition,* 1913. Privately published, 1913.

Morgenthau, Henry, III. *Mostly Morgenthaus: A Family History.* Foreword by Arthur M. Schlesinger, Jr. New York: Ticknor & Fields, 1991.

Morgenthau, Lazarus. *The Diary of Lazarus Morgenthau.* New York: Privately published, 1933. First published: Speyer, Nov. 30, 1842.

Morison, Samuel Eliot. *History of United States Naval Operations in World War II.* 15 vols. Boston: Little, Brown, 1947–1962.

Morse, Arthur. *While Six Million Died.* New York: Random House, 1968. First published by Overlook Press in 1967.

Moscow, Warren. *The Last of the Big-Time Bosses: The Life and Times of Carmine De Sapio and the Rise and Fall of Tammany Hall.* New York: Stein and Day, 1971.

Moses, Montrose J. *The Life of Heinrich Conried.* New York: Thomas A. Crowell, 1916.

Nasaw, David. *The Patriarch: The Remarkable Life and Turbulent Times of Joseph P. Kennedy.* New York: Penguin, 2012.

"Natural Gas." *Fortune* 22, no. 2 (August 1940): 56–61, 96–100.

"Natural Gas—Whoosh!" *Fortune* 40, no. 114 (December 1949): 199.

Navasky, Victor. *Kennedy Justice.* New York: Atheneum, 1971.

Neu, Charles E. *Colonel House: A Biography of Woodrow Wilson's Silent Partner.* New York: Oxford University Press, 2015.

———. "Wilson and His Foreign Policy Advisers." In *Artists of Power: Theodore Roosevelt, Woodrow Wilson, and Their Enduring Impact on U.S. Foreign Policy,* edited by Charles E. Neu and William N. Tilchin. Westport, Conn.: Praeger Security International, 2006.

———. "Woodrow Wilson and Colonel House: The Early Years, 1911–1915." In *The Wilson Era: Essays in Honor of Arthur S. Link,* edited by Charles E. Neu and John Milton Cooper, Jr. Arlington Heights, Ill.: Harlan Davidson, 1991.

Nevins, Allan. *Herbert H. Lehman and His Era.* New York: Charles Scribner's Sons, 1963.

Nihon Senbotsu Gakusei Kinen-Kai (Japan Memorial Society for the Students Killed in the War—Wadatsumi Society). *Listen to the Voices from the Sea (Sinpan Kike Wadatsumi no Koe).* Translated by Midori Yamanouchi and Joseph L. Quinn, S.J. Scranton, Pa.: University of Scranton Press, 2005.

Ochs, Iphigene, and Susan W. Dryfoos. *Iphigene: My Life and* The New York Times: *The Memoirs of Iphigene Ochs Sulzberger.* New York: Times Books, 1987.

Okrent, Daniel. *Great Fortune: The Epic of Rockefeller Center.* New York: Viking, 2003.

"One of Two of a Kind." *Fortune,* May 1934, 60–64.

Oren, Michael. *Power, Faith and Fantasy.* New York: W. W. Norton, 2007.

Parkin, Robert Sinclair. *Blood on the Sea: American Destroyers Lost in World War II.* New York: Da Capo Press, 2001.

Pears, Edwin. *Forty Years in Constantinople: The Recollections of Sir Edwin Pears, 1873–1915.* London: H. Jenkins, 1916.

Phillips, Williams. *Ventures in Diplomacy.* Boston: Beacon Press, 1953.

Power, Samantha. *"A Problem from Hell": America and the Age of Genocide.* New York: Harper Perennial, 2003.

Powers, Thomas. *Diana: The Making of a Terrorist.* New York: Bantam Books, 1971.

Raab, Selwyn. *Five Families.* New York: Thomas Dunne, 2005.

Raphael, Marc Lee. *A History of the United Jewish Appeal, 1939–1982.* Brown Judaic Studies 34. Chico, CA: Scholars Press, 1982.

Rapoport, Louis. *Shake Heaven & Earth: Peter Bergson and the Struggle to Rescue the Jews of Europe.* Jerusalem: Gefen Publishing House, 1999.

Real Estate Record Association. *A History of Real Estate, Building and Architecture in New York City During the Last Quarter of a Century.* New York: Arno Press, 1967. Reprint of the 1898 edition.

Reilly, Michael F., as told to William J. Slocum. *Reilly of the White House.* New York: Simon & Schuster, 1947.

Reppetto, Thomas. *American Mafia: A History of Its Rise to Power.* New York: Henry Holt, 2004.

———. *Bringing Down the Mob: The War Against the American Mafia.* New York: Henry Holt, 2006.

Richman, John. *The United States & the Soviet Union: The Decision to Recognize.* Raleigh, N.C.: Camberleigh & Hall, 1980.

Riegner, Gerhart M. *Never Despair: Sixty Years in the Service of the Jewish People and the Cause of Human Rights.* Translated from the French by William Sayers. Chicago: Ivan R. Dee, 2006.

Rielly, Robin L. *Kamikazes, Corsairs, and Picket Ships: Okinawa, 1945.* Drexel Hill, Pa.: Casemate Publishers, 2010.

Rischin, Moses. *The Promised City: New York's Jews, 1870–1914.* Cambridge, Mass.: Harvard University Press, 1962.

Rockefeller, David. *Memoirs.* New York: Random House, 2002.

Rollins, Alfred B., Jr. *Roosevelt and Howe.* New Brunswick, N.J.: Transaction Publishers, 2002. First published by Alfred A. Knopf, 1962.

Roosevelt, Eleanor. *The Autobiography of Eleanor Roosevelt.* New York: Da Capo Press, 1992.

Roscoe, Theodore. *United States Destroyer Operations in World War II.* Annapolis, Md.: United States Naval Institute, 1953.

Rosenman, Samuel. *Presidential Style: Some Giants and a Pygmy in the White House.* New York: Harper & Row, 1976.

———. *Working with Roosevelt.* New York: Harper, 1952.

Rovere, Richard H. "Father Hogan's Place." *The New Yorker,* Aug. 16, 1947, 36.

Russell, Lindsay. "Charles E. Hughes, the Pilot of the Insurance Investigation." *The Green Bag* 17 (1905): 633–37.

Sachs, Emanie N. *Red Damask: A Story of Nature and Nurture.* New York: Harper & Brothers, 1927.

Saul, Norman. *The Life and Times of Charles R. Crane, 1858–1939: American Businessman, Philanthropist, and a Founder of Russian Studies in America.* Lanham, Md.: Lexington Books, 2012.

Schanberg, Sydney H. "A Journey Through the Tangled Case of the Central Park Jogger." *Village Voice,* Nov. 20, 2002.

Schlesinger, Arthur M., Jr. *The Coming of the New Deal, 1933–1935.* Vol. 2 of *The Age of Roosevelt.* Boston: Houghton Mifflin, 1958.

———. *The Crisis of the Old Order.* Vol. 1 of *The Age of Roosevelt.* Boston: Houghton Mifflin, 1957.

———. *Journals: 1952–2000.* New York: Penguin Press, 2003.

———. *A Life in the 20th Century: Innocent Beginnings, 1917–1930.* New York: Houghton Mifflin, 2000.

———. *The Politics of Upheaval.* Vol. 3 of *The Age of Roosevelt.* Boston: Houghton Mifflin, 1960.

———. *Robert F. Kennedy and His Times.* Boston: Houghton Mifflin, 1978.

———. "The Roosevelt Family." *Life,* April 7, 1947, 112–29.

Scobey, David M. *Empire City: The Making and Meaning of the New York City Landscape.* Philadelphia: Temple University Press, 2002.

Sevostiyanov, Grigory N., ed. *Moscow–Washington: Policy and Diplomacy of the Kremlin, 1921–1941: A Collection of Documents.* 3 vols. Moscow: Nauka, 2009. Published in Russian as Москва-Вашингтон: политика и дипломатия Кремля, 1921–1941: сборник документов в трех томах; *Moskva-Vashington: politika i diplomatiia Kremlia, 1921–1941: sbornik dokumentov v trekh tomakh.*

Shafter, Richard A. *Destroyers in Action*. New York: Cornell Maritime Press, 1945.

Sherwood, Robert. *Roosevelt and Hopkins: An Intimate History*. New York: Harper, 1950.

Shogan, Robert. *A Question of Judgment: The Fortas Case and the Struggle for the Supreme Court*. Indianapolis: Bobbs-Merrill, 1972.

Simons, Howard. *Jewish Times: Voices of the American Jewish Experience*. Boston: Houghton Mifflin, 1988.

Simpson, Christopher. *The Splendid Blond Beast: Money, Law and Genocide in the Twentieth Century*. New York: Grove Press, 1993.

Smith, Jean Edward. *FDR*. New York: Random House, 2007.

Smith, Neil. *American Empire: Roosevelt's Geographer and the Prelude to Globalization*. Berkeley: University of California Press, 2003.

Sorensen, Ted. *Counselor: A Life at the Edge of History*. New York: HarperCollins, 2008.

Spector, Ronald H. *At War at Sea: Sailors and Naval Combat in the Twentieth Century*. New York: Viking, 2001.

Stanton, Bernard. *George F. Warren, Farm Economist*. Ithaca, N.Y.: Cornell University Press, 2007.

Starrett, Paul. *Changing the Skyline: An Autobiography*. New York: McGraw-Hill, 1938.

Stimson, Henry L., and McGeorge Bundy. *On Active Service in Peace and War*. New York: Octagon Books, 1971.

Stokes, I. N. Phelps. *Iconography of Manhattan, 1498–1909: Compiled from Original Sources and Illustrated by Photo-Intaglio Reproductions of Important Maps, Plans, Views, and Documents in Public and Private Collections*. 6 vols. New York: Robert H. Dodd, 1915–1928. (Online via Columbia University Libraries Digital Collections.)

Stone, Michael. *Gangbusters: How a Street-Tough, Elite Homicide Unit Took Down New York's Most Notorious Gang*. New York: Doubleday, 2000.

Stone, Richard G. *Kentucky Fighting Men, 1861–1945*. Lexington: University Press of Kentucky, 1982.

Strong, George Templeton. *The Diary of George Templeton Strong*. Edited by Allan Nevins and Milton Halsey Thomas. Abridged by Thomas J. Pressly. Seattle: University of Washington Press, 1988.

Sullivan, Timothy. *Unequal Verdicts: The Central Park Jogger Trials*. New York: Simon & Schuster, 1992.

Swiaczny, Frank. *Die Juden in der Pfalz und in Nordbaden im 19. Jahrhundert und ihre wirtschaftlichen Aktivitäten in der Tabakbranche: Zur historischen Sozialgeographie einer Minderheit*. Mannheim: Institut für Landeskunde und Regionalforschung der Universität Mannheim, 1996.

Talese, Gay. *Honor Thy Father*. New York: HarperCollins, 2009.

Tauranac, John. *Elegant New York: The Builders and the Buildings, 1885–1915*. New York: Abbeville, 1985.

Thomas, Evan. *Robert Kennedy: His Life*. New York: Simon & Schuster, 2000.

———. *The Man to See: Edward Bennett Williams, Ultimate Insider; Legendary Trial Lawyer*. New York: Simon & Schuster, 1991.

Tifft, Susan E., and Alex S. Jones. *The Trust: The Private and Powerful Family Behind* The New York Times. Boston: Little, Brown, 1999.

Traub, James. "The D.A.'s Dilemma." *The New Yorker*, July 28, 1997, 26–35.

Truman, Harry S. *Off the Record: The Private Papers of Harry S. Truman*. Edited by Robert H. Ferrell. New York: Harper & Row, 1980.

Tuchman, Barbara. "The Assimilationist Dilemma: Ambassador Morgenthau's Story." *Commentary* 63, no. 5 (May 1977): 58–62.

Urofsky, Melvin I. *Louis D. Brandeis: A Life*. New York: Pantheon, 2009.

———. *A Voice That Spoke for Justice: The Life and Times of Stephen S. Wise*. Albany: State University of New York Press, 1982.

Vanden Heuvel, William, and Milton Gwirtzman. *On His Own: Robert F. Kennedy, 1964–1968*. Garden City, N.Y.: Doubleday, 1970.

Vidal, Gore. "Homage to Daniel Shays." *New York Review of Books*, Aug. 10, 1972.

Von Hoffman, Nicholas. *Citizen Cohn*. New York: Doubleday, 1988.

Voss, Carl Hermann. *Rabbi and Minister: The Friendship of Stephen S. Wise and John Haynes Holmes*. New York: World Publishing Company, 1964.

Wallance, Gregory. *America's Soul in the Balance: The Holocaust, FDR's State Department, and the Moral Disgrace of an American Aristocracy*. Austin, Tex.: Greenleaf Book Group, 2013.

———. *Papa's Game*. New York: Rawson, Wade, 1981.

Waller, Leslie. *The Swiss Bank Connection*. New York: New American Library, 1972.

Warburg, James Paul. *The Long Road Home: The Autobiography of a Maverick*. New York: Doubleday, 1964.

———. *The Money Muddle*. New York: Knopf, 1934.

Ward, Geoffrey C. *Closest Companion: The Unknown Story of the Intimate Friendship Between Franklin Roosevelt and Margaret Suckley*. New York: Houghton Mifflin, 1995.

———. *A First-Class Temperament: The Emergence of Franklin Roosevelt*. New York: Harper & Row, 1989.

Wecter, Dixon. *The Saga of American Society: A Record of Social Aspiration, 1607–1937*. New York: Charles Scribner & Sons, 1937.

Weil, Martin. *A Pretty Good Club: The Founding Fathers of the U.S. Foreign Service*. New York: W. W. Norton, 1978.

Wells, Rollo. *Report of the Treasurer, the Democratic National Committee, Receipts and Disbursements Prior to Nov. 30, 1912*. St. Louis, 1913.

Whalen, Richard J. *The Founding Father: The Story of Joseph P. Kennedy*. Washington, D.C.: Regnery, 1993. First published by New American Library, 1964.

Whelton, Clark. "What Price Peace in the Park?" *Village Voice*, Sept. 27, 1976, 16–17.

[Williams, Wythe]. *Washington Broadcast, by the Man at the Microphone*. Garden City, N.Y.: Doubleday, Doran, 1944.

Winter-Berger, Robert. *The Washington Pay-off: An Insider's View of Corruption in Government*. Secaucus, N.J.: Lyle Stuart, 1972.

Wise, Stephen S. *Challenging Years: The Autobiography of Stephen Wise*. New York: Putnam, 1949.

———. *The Personal Letters of Stephen Wise*. Edited by Justine Wise Polier and James Waterman Wise. Boston: Beacon Press, 1956.

Woodward, Bob, and Scott Armstrong. *The Brethren: Inside the Supreme Court*. New York: Simon & Schuster, 1979.

Woolf, S. J. *Here Am I*. New York: Random House, 1941.

Wyman, David S. *The Abandonment of the Jews: America and the Holocaust, 1941–1945*. New York: Pantheon, 1984.

———, ed. *America and the Holocaust: A Thirteen-Volume Set Documenting the Acclaimed Book* The Abandonment of the Jews. New York: Garland, 1989–1990.

Illustration Credits

PAGE 8, TOP: Henry Sr. with American officers in Poland: United States Holocaust Memorial Museum Archives, Washington, D.C.

PAGE 8, BOTTOM: Henry Sr. at an orphanage in Athens: Bain News Service/Library of Congress

PAGE 9, TOP: Wilson Democrats: Franklin D. Roosevelt Library

PAGE 9, BOTTOM: Henry III, Henry Jr., Henry Sr., and Robert: United States Holocaust Memorial Museum Archives, Washington, D.C.

PAGE 10, TOP: Henry Jr. with Elinor Fatman, wedding portrait: courtesy of Robert Morgenthau

PAGE 10, BOTTOM: Lehman family: courtesy of Robert Morgenthau

PAGE 11, TOP: Henry Jr. with his sisters: United States Holocaust Memorial Museum Archives, Washington, D.C.

PAGE 11, BOTTOM: Henry Jr. at Gallipoli: United States Holocaust Memorial Museum Archives, Washington, D.C.

PAGE 12, TOP: Henry Jr. with FDR: Franklin D. Roosevelt Library

PAGE 12, BOTTOM: Henry Jr. and FDR picnicking: Franklin D. Roosevelt Library

PAGE 13, TOP: Henry Jr. and FDR in car with inscription: Franklin D. Roosevelt Library

PAGE 13, BOTTOM: Henry Jr. sworn in as commissioner of conservation: United States Holocaust Memorial Museum Archives, Washington, D.C.

PAGE 14, TOP: New Dealers at the White House: Harris & Ewing/Library of Congress

PAGE 14, BOTTOM: FDR buying bonds from Henry Jr.: United States Holocaust Memorial Museum Archives, Washington, D.C.

PAGE 15, TOP: Elinor Morgenthau at the Chrysler tank plant: United States Holocaust Memorial Museum Archives, Washington, D.C.

PAGE 15, MIDDLE: Elinor Morgenthau talking with Henry Jr.: United States Holocaust Memorial Museum Archives, Washington, D.C.

PAGE 15, BOTTOM: Elinor Morgenthau and Eleanor Roosevelt horseback riding: United States Holocaust Memorial Museum Archives, Washington, D.C.

PAGE 16, TOP: Henry Jr. with his daughter Joan on the farm: United States Holocaust Memorial Museum Archives, Washington, D.C.

PAGE 16, BOTTOM: Joan and Henry Jr. at the White House: Franklin D. Roosevelt Library

INSERT 2

PAGE 1, TOP: Henry Jr. with reporters and Henrietta Klotz: Harris & Ewing/Library of Congress

PAGE 1, MIDDLE: Henry Jr. with Ronald Reagan: United States Holocaust Memorial Museum Archives, Washington, D.C.

PAGE 1, BOTTOM: Henry Jr. filming ruins in France: courtesy of Andrew Meier

PAGE 2, TOP LEFT: Political supporters and onlookers surrounding FDR: Bettmann/Getty Images

PAGE 2, TOP RIGHT: FDR with Henry Jr. in car: Bettmann/Getty Images

PAGE 2, MIDDLE: Henry Jr. and John Maynard Keynes: Alfred Eisenstaedt/The *LIFE* Picture Collection/Shutterstock

PAGE 2, BOTTOM: Henry Jr. with Harry Truman: courtesy of Andrew Meier

PAGE 3, TOP: Morgenthau family on horseback: United States Holocaust Memorial Museum Archives, Washington, D.C.

PAGE 3, MIDDLE: Henry Jr. at his farm: CSU Archives/Everett Collection/Alamy

PAGE 3, BOTTOM: Henry Jr. and his second wife, Marcelle Hirsch Morgenthau: courtesy of Andrew Meier

PAGE 4, TOP: Henry Jr. photographs immigrants in Tal Shahar while Robert Capa films: United States Holocaust Memorial Museum Archives, Washington, D.C.

PAGE 4, BOTTOM: Henry Jr. and Mrs. Klotz with Golda Meir and Eliezer Kaplan: United States Holocaust Memorial Museum Archives, Washington, D.C.

PAGE 5, TOP: Photomaton picture of Henry Jr. and Robert: United States Holocaust Memorial Museum Archives, Washington, D.C.

PAGE 5, MIDDLE: Robert in Navy uniform, Rio de Janeiro, 1942: courtesy of Robert Morgenthau

PAGE 5, BOTTOM: Robert and Martha Pattridge Morgenthau on their wedding day: courtesy of Robert Morgenthau

PAGE 6, TOP: Coast Guardsmen scrape oil from a Navy seaman's body: Arthur Green, courtesy of U.S. Coast Guard

PAGE 6, MIDDLE: Robert checks members of his crew: Arthur Green, courtesy of U.S. Coast Guard

PAGE 6, BOTTOM: Funeral for Navy seamen killed on the USS *Lansdale:* courtesy of Robert Morgenthau

PAGE 7: Robert with family: courtesy of Robert Morgenthau

PAGE 8, TOP: Robert with Robert F. Kennedy: AP/Shutterstock

PAGE 8, MIDDLE: Robert in RFK's office: courtesy of Robert Morgenthau

PAGE 8, BOTTOM: Robert in car with John F. Kennedy: Eddie Hauser/*The New York Times*/Redux

PAGE 9, TOP: U.S. attorney's office, Southern District of New York: courtesy of Robert Morgenthau

PAGE 9, MIDDLE: campaign comic: Political Comics Collection, University of Nebraska—Lincoln Libraries

PAGE 9, BOTTOM: Robert campaigning for governor: Grey Villet/The *LIFE* Picture Collection/Shutterstock

PAGE 10, TOP: Roy M. Cohn: Bettmann/Getty Images

PAGE 10, MIDDLE: Joseph Bonanno with his attorney: Hal Mathewson/NY *Daily News* Archive via Getty Images

PAGE 10, BOTTOM: Carmine De Sapio: Bettmann/Getty Images

PAGE 11, TOP: Robert sworn in as DA: Meyer Liebowitz/*The New York Times*/Redux

PAGE 11, BOTTOM: Robert holding his son Joshua, with his wife Lucinda Franks: courtesy of Robert Morgenthau

PAGE 12: DA "Trial Bureau 50" including Sonia Sotomayor: District Attorney's office, New York County

PAGE 13, TOP: *Daily News* front page: NY *Daily News* Archive via Getty Images

PAGE 13, BOTTOM: Lawyers and defendants in the Central Park Jogger case: Jim Estrin/*The New York Times*/Redux

PAGE 14, TOP: Clark Clifford and Robert Altman: Mark Reinstein/MediaPunch/Alamy

PAGE 14, MIDDLE: Joseph Gambino and Thomas Gambino: Thomas Monaster/NY *Daily News* Archive via Getty Images

PAGE 14, BOTTOM: Robert with seized cocaine: Kevin Larkin/AP/Shutterstock

PAGE 15, TOP: Robert with Ed Koch: Jim Estrin/*The New York Times*/Redux

PAGE 15, MIDDLE: Robert jumping rope: Dith Pran/*The New York Times*/Redux

PAGE 15, BOTTOM: Robert announces organized crime indictments: Bryan Smith/Zuma Press/Alamy

PAGE 16: Robert with Lucinda Franks: Katherine Taylor/*The New York Times*/Redux

Index

Page numbers of photographs appear in italics.

About the Author

ANDREW MEIER is the author of *Black Earth: A Journey Through Russia After the Fall* and *The Lost Spy: An American in Stalin's Secret Service*. Both books were named to a number of "Books of the Year" lists, and *Black Earth* was widely hailed as one of the best books on Russia to appear since the end of the USSR. His work has been recognized with fellowships from the Cullman Center for Scholars and Writers at the New York Public Library, as well as from the Leon Levy Center for Biography, the National Endowment for the Humanities, the Woodrow Wilson International Center for Scholars, and the Alicia Patterson Foundation. A former Moscow correspondent for *Time*, he has contributed to *The New York Times Magazine*, among numerous other publications. A graduate of Wesleyan and Oxford, he lives in Brooklyn, New York, with his wife and their two daughters.

andrewmeier.com

About the Type

This book was set in Sabon, a typeface designed by the well-known German typographer Jan Tschichold (1902–74). Sabon's design is based upon the original letterforms of sixteenth-century French type designer Claude Garamond and was created specifically to be used for three sources: foundry type for hand composition, Linotype, and Monotype. Tschichold named his typeface for the famous Frankfurt typefounder Jacques Sabon (c. 1520–80).